C·R·E·A·T·I·N·G
A HEALTHY
HOUSEHOLD

C·R·E·A·T·I·N·G
A HEALTHY
HOUSEHOLD

the ultimate guide
for healthier, safer, less-toxic living

by Lynn Marie Bower

The Healthy House Institute

613.5
Bower

Published by:
The Healthy House Institute
430 N. Sewell Road
Bloomington, IN 47408
www.hhinst.com

Printed on recycled paper with soy-based ink.

DISCLAIMER: The information in this book should not be considered medical advice. Sensitive, allergic, or asthmatic individuals should always consult with a physician before making any changes in their home environment

Publisher's Cataloging-in-Publication Data.
Bower, Lynn Marie
Creating a Healthy Household: the ultimate guide for healthier, safer, less-toxic living.
Includes Bibliographical references, resource listing, index.
1. Consumer product safety—popular works. 2. Housing and Health.
   3. Indoor air pollution—Health aspects.
 I. Bower, Lynn Marie. II. Title.
TH4813.B69   2000
693'.8

Library of Congress Catalog Card Number: 99-96306
ISBN 0-9637156-7-4 $23.95 Softcover

For John
With love and gratitude.

AVAILABLE FROM THE HEALTHY HOUSE INSTITUTE

The Healthy House:
  How to buy one, how to build one, how to cure a sick one

Creating a Healthy Household:
  the ultimate guide for healthier, safer, less-toxic living

The Healthy House Answer Book:
  Answers to the 133 most commonly asked questions

Understanding Ventilation:
  How to design, select, and install residential ventilation systems

Healthy House Building for the New Millennium:
  A design and construction guide

Your House, Your Health:
  A non-toxic building guide (VHS video)

The Healthy House:
  Designing, building and furnishing a non-toxic home
  (13-episode VHS video series)

ACKNOWLEDGMENTS

I'd like to thank my husband, John, and all those who offered ideas, information, inspiration, and other help, as well as Valerie Long and Bob Baird for copy editing early incarnations of this book. And a very special thank you to the Reference Librarians at the Monroe County Public Library for all their assistance.

CONTENTS AT A GLANCE

TABLE OF CONTENTS

Table of Contents

Table of Contents

PART 3: TEXTILES

CHAPTER 7: HEALTHIER FIBERS & STUFFINGS

Table of Contents

Men's Clothing _____ 211

Table of Contents

Table of Contents

Table of Contents

Table of Contents

Table of Contents

PART 5: LIFESTYLE 437

Table of Contents

Table of Contents

Table of Contents

CHAPTER 25: IMPROVING YOUR WATER _____ 597

Table of Contents

Part 1
THE BASICS

INTRODUCTION

Today, over 50 millions Americans have allergies and 14 million have asthma. In fact, the asthma rate doubled between 1980 to 1994 and asthma is now the most common childhood disease according to the **American Academy of Allergy, Asthma and Immunology**. In addition, a 1995 study by the California Department of Health Services found that nearly 16% of 4,000 randomly chosen men and women reported that they were "unusually sensitive" to chemicals in typical household products. And 6.3% of those surveyed said they had already been diagnosed with Multiple Chemical Sensitivity (MCS) by a physician.

Unfortunately, these conditions are no longer as unusual as they were not so long ago. Instead, they've become rather commonplace. In fact, they are so common that you probably know of one or more people, in your close circle of friends and relatives, with at least one of them. Perhaps it is you, yourself, who have allergies, asthma, or MCS. But why are these conditions becoming more widespread?

While genetics and stress play an important role (as they do in most medical conditions), something else seems to be a contributing factor—unhealthy indoor environments. We know that outdoor air quality has steadily improved but, unfortunately, indoor air quality has steadily declined. Interestingly, back in 1989, a Massachusetts Special Legislative Commission report concluded that "Indoor air pollution is a growing problem in the United States and accounts for up to 50% of all illness."

At first, this may sound simply unbelievable. How could our indoor environments be making so many people sick? Actually, the answer lies in two significant housing trends. First, there is an ever-greater reliance on synthetic and petrochemically derived ingredients in the building materials, furnishings, cleaning products, and personal-care items we commonly use indoors. Second, most homes are being made tighter to increase energy efficiency, yet many of them don't have a mechanical ventilation system that's specifically designed to bring in fresh air.

As a result of these two trends, a majority of Americans live with stale indoor air that is saturated with harmful chemical emissions from carpeting, cabinets, cosmetics, laundry products, and clothing. Consequently, many of us breathe dangerous levels of formalde-hyde, and hundreds of other chemical gases, daily. Of course, dust mite feces, pollen, com-bustion by-products, mold spores, radon, and animal dander are also routinely a part of this noxious mix. Some people are able to live in this polluted air with no apparent ill effects. But growing numbers of us cannot.

Unfortunately, most Americans are still not aware of the potential hazards within their own home environment. While they may not have asthma, allergies, or MCS, they may have other life-draining health complaints such as chronic sinus irritation, sore throat, tired-ness, mild depression, or insomnia. Often these symptoms are attributed to viruses, aging, hormones, or tension. Sometimes these factors really do contribute to these maladies. How-ever, it's now believed that many of these everyday symptoms are actually the result of breathing polluted indoor air. Even life-threatening conditions, such certain birth defects and even some cancers, have been linked to living in unhealthy houses.

The good news, however, is that you can choose to be at less risk. And, if you already have allergies, asthma, or MCS, you can choose to lessen the factors that may be contribut-ing to your condition. In other words, you can decide to live a healthier lifestyle that goes beyond just eating better food, taking nutritional supplements, and exercising—you can choose to have a healthy, less-toxic, less-allergenic household.

That's what this book is all about. It will be your complete guide to learning about sources of dangerous indoor contamination, and it will offer suggestions for healthier alter-natives. In fact, *Creating a Healthy Household* offers hundreds and hundreds of suggestions and sources for healthier products, techniques, and services. You'll find information on unscented and natural personal-care items, healthful housekeeping procedures, natural-fi-ber clothing, safer pest-control measures (including dust-mite reduction), nontoxic interior decorating, as well as discussions of electromagnetic fields, air and water filtration, and much, much more. There is a special emphasis on information for those with allergies, asthma, and MCS—on topics ranging from bedding to pets.

Creating a Healthy Household explores so many subjects simply because they all impact your home and your health. The truth is, everything you bring into your house, every activity you perform indoors, and all that is on your body, affects your home's indoor air quality. Admittedly, this can sound rather intimidating. Some of you may feel that changing your present unhealthy household into a healthy one is just too big a job. However, this book will help you learn where to order, and how to sample, test, and experiment with new products and living patterns. Actually, this isn't difficult to do. It just requires a certain degree of desire and commitment. Obviously, you are already well on your way—or else you wouldn't be reading this right now.

Some of you may also fear changing from a familiar (but unhealthy) lifestyle, to some-thing new, because you may be labeled odd. Using alternative products may cause some neighbors and family members to question you about your new changes, while they con-tinue to live like "everyone else does." However, instead of feeling different or even eccen-tric, you should view your healthy modifications as signs of maturity, individuality, and good common sense. You may even inspire others to follow your example.

However, at the same time, you should have realistic expectations about the transition towards your new, healthier lifestyle. You need to know, from the beginning, that you'll occasionally get frustrated along the way. Also, you should anticipate that you may need to discard some of your early choices, and you may have to make some imperfect compro-mises. Yet, for the most part, you'll likely experience very satisfying results. Best of all, your efforts will ultimately provide you with better control over your health and that of your family. In fact, by choosing a less-toxic lifestyle, you'll very likely enjoy many years of better health ahead.

Of course very few, if any, readers will (or could) follow all the suggestions and advice contained in the following chapters. As human beings we all tend to be, and in fact need to be, selective. Also, you should know that you don't have to make all the desired changes at once. For many people, transforming how they live is a gradual process. Those with chemical sensitivities may want to start by switching to healthier personal care-items and laundry products. On the other hand, those with allergies and asthma will probably want to begin with home decorating and cleaning. But, wherever you start, as time and finances allow, you should expand into other areas. If you continue to make changes—even small ones—over time you'll eventually have a healthy household sooner than you ever imagined.

It's hoped that *Creating a Healthy Household* will enable you to transform your unhealthy interior environment into one that brings you both pleasure and good health. I know, from personal experience, how a typical modern lifestyle can make people sick. You see, I'm just one of thousands of individuals who was made seriously ill by their home. I became ill two decades ago during a major home restoration/remodeling project. My husband and I used common construction materials. We finished the interior with typical carpets, fabrics, furniture, and paints. We also wore typical clothing and cleaned using widely advertised products. Like many renovated houses, ours was newly insulated and caulked—and it had no planned ventilation system.

As a result of this very average life and home, I acquired Multiple Chemical Sensitivity (MCS), which resulted in respiratory problems, joint and muscle pain, gastrointestinal distress, ringing in the ears, and a host of other symptoms—some more debilitating than others. My hair became brittle, I got acne, and I became hypersensitive to synthetic fragrances, printing ink, and common cleaning products. Eventually, building a healthy house, and creating a healthy household inside it, helped me significantly—although optimum health has never completely returned. I'm telling you this because I am far from an isolated case. I am aware that thousands of others have similar stories to tell. Maybe your home results in allergy, maybe asthma, maybe MCS, or maybe low-level depression or a chronic sore throat.

Sadly, you too could be ill because of your present lifestyle—especially if it's like the typical lifestyle most people are currently living. However, you do have the power to change your home environment. You can make your home less toxic and less allergenic. And you can regain some measure of well-being and sense of control over your life again. Remember, every choice you make can bring you one step closer toward better health. Here's to better choices and the creation of your own healthy household.

Lynn Marie Bower

HOW TO USE THIS BOOK

Creating a Healthy Household is written as a reference book, in easy-to-understand language. As a reference work, background facts, developmental history, production-method explanations, operational descriptions, and product listings are given under many topic headings. All this information is included so you can make more informed decisions as you create your new healthier household. If you want to find specific product suggestions immediately, the introductory background material can be skipped for now. It can always be returned to at a later time, to give you a better understanding of why some products are inherently healthier than others.

As you read through this book, you may find that some of the information is repeated under different chapter headings. This is because each section is designed to be fairly complete in itself. After all, because of it's size and scope, it's unlikely that many people will read the book straight through. So, if you have a question about a particular topic, you should be able to look it up and get a satisfactorily answer within that section of the book. There are no sidebar stories, or case examples, because they can sometimes be missed. However, where appropriate, in certain sections, I have included suggestions for additional information that can be found elsewhere in the book. Product manufacturers and/or dealers names, as well as certain agencies and organizations, are shown in **bold type** throughout the text. Their addresses, telephone numbers, and internet websites are listed in the *Resource Listings* section toward the end of the book.

As a very brief summary, *Part 1: The Basics* explores allergies, asthma, and chemical sensitivity as well as provides basic information on choosing and buying healthier products. *Part 2: Cleaning* covers cosmetics and toiletries, laundry procedures and products, as well as products and techniques for various household cleaning jobs. *Part 3: Textiles* delves into natural fibers and stuffings, specific clothing suggestions, and bedding and towels. *Part 4: Your House* addresses remodeling materials, products, and procedures. Also covered are making a safe refuge within your home, cars and garages, fire protection, and pest control. Stationery, reading, hobbies, exercise equipment, telephones, electronics, and appliances are all found in *Part 5: Lifestyle*, as well as cookware, paper goods, and household storage. Finally, *Part 6: Air, Water, and EMFs* considers common air and water pollutants, testing, and filters, as well as electromagnetic fields, EMF hot spots, and reduction methods. *Part 7: Resources* contains the listing of companies and organizations found in **bold type** in the text, a listing of books mentioned in the text, and a complete index. It should be mentioned that, before you start searching for specific suggestions, make sure you have first read *Chapter 2: Getting Started*. The basic information provided in this chapter should help you in making personal decisions throughout the rest of the book.

It needs be made clear that what I have written should be considered *suggestions*. I am not in a position to make *recommendations* based on rigid laboratory testing or research science. The Healthy House Institute's purpose is to disseminate information on what appear to be healthier alternative product choices and procedures. Therefore, the selection of products and materials in this book was based on one or more factors. For example, I reviewed manufacturer's material safety data sheets (MSDSs) and product literature. I also spoke with technical-service individuals, consumer-affairs specialists, and dealers. Plus, I've listed a number of alternative catalogs that have a reputation for offering high-quality, healthy items. These have been routinely mentioned by various agencies, researchers, and organizations, and they are often mentioned in health-oriented periodicals, fact sheets, and books. And, finally, I have relied on the testimonials of asthmatic, allergic, and chemically sensitive individuals who have successfully used certain items and techniques.

All this was compiled and presented in this book so that, in the end, *Creating a Healthy Household* would empower you to feel more confident in the options *you choose* for your home and lifestyle. I wish you the best of luck, and the best of health, as you begin the process of creating your own healthy household.

CHAPTER 1: YOUR HOUSEHOLD & YOUR HEALTH

Now that you're seriously considering creating a healthy household, this chapter will supply more information about the correlation between the healthfulness of your indoor environment and your personal health. It'll also provide you with names of physician's associations, support groups, as well as helpful organizations, government agencies, and more.

Modern Lifestyle Consequences

Is our modern American lifestyle so bad that we really need to change it? Yes, at least some of it certainly is. Admittedly, this is, in some ways, unfortunate. After all, most consumer products are designed to be convenient to use, to make our housekeeping jobs easier, to provide comfort and pleasure. However, another side of the equation is rarely considered—even by people who are committed to recycling, saving whales, and preserving rain forests. That's the impact our modern way of living has on our own health.

Sadly, "better" and "more convenient" products, that are made of synthetic materials and petroleum-based chemicals, often create very harmful indoor surroundings. In fact, indoor home environments are commonly five to ten times more polluted than the outdoor environment—even if you live in a major city. As a result, most houses and apartments have the potential to negatively affect the health of the people living there.

In the *Introduction*, I mentioned several health problems that have been associated with poor indoor air. These included sore throats, insomnia, headaches, and mild depression, among others. Here are some specific examples of typically used products, and their suspected health outcomes. New synthetic carpeting can give off *xylene*, *ethylbenzene*, and *methacrylic acid*. In fact, chemicals from carpeting have been shown to cause neurological impairment, and even death, in laboratory mice. *Formaldehyde*, which is given off by everything from particle-board closet shelving, permanent-press clothing, some types of paper, and certain personal-care items, can irritate the mucous membranes and eyes. Formaldehyde can also sometimes cause menstrual irregularities, provoke asthma, and depress the central-nervous system. Some synthetic scents in personal-care items, paper goods, laundry products, and cleaning supplies are *neurotoxic* (capable of damaging the nervous system including the brain and spinal cord). And *combustion gases* (including *carbon monoxide*) given off by wood stoves have been shown to cause a dramatic increase breathing problems in children.

And chemical-laden air isn't the only problem within our homes. There's also evidence that *chlorinated* drinking water increases the likelihood of bladder cancer. Plus, a Scandinavian study found that there was "strong epidemiological evidence for an association between asthma and wall-to-wall carpeting." After all, carpets commonly harbor tens of millions of potentially allergenic microorganisms, especially dust mites, within each square foot, and dust mites are commonly bothersome to people with allergies. In fact, as many as eighty percent of asthmatics react to dust-mite skin-provocation tests. Other symptoms of dust-mite exposure include sneezing, irritated eyes, nighttime coughing, and runny, blocked, or itchy nasal passages. Sadly, the list of products, materials, devices, and practices commonly used in houses and apartments, and their accompanying adverse health effects, could go on and on.

Because most homes don't have chlorine-removing water filters, hard-surfaced floors—let alone adequate ventilation—most of us are subjected to indoor contaminants and allergens on a continuous basis. Every minute of every day, year after year, we expose ourselves to these potentially health-damaging influences. The lack of adequate ventilation is usually not often understood, not often considered and, therefore, not often addressed. Yet, as far back as December 1988, a Congressional Research Service report to Congress, entitled *Indoor Air Pollution: Cause for Concern?*, concluded that "...*No* one is immune to the effects of indoor air pollution." Incidentally, it should be mentioned that even in houses where there *is* adequate ventilation, if the outdoor air is contaminated, the indoor air will be, too—unless the incoming air is properly filtered. Like a growing number of experts and concerned consumers, I firmly believe we should end the complacency of how most of us presently live. It's time to make our home environments healthier.

With so many stresses and problems already existing everywhere, I know many people simply don't want to hear that their own homes could be making them sick. I realize that many people would prefer to think that, at least inside their house, they're safe from the worries of the world. Well, it would be nice if the dangers of pollution were all "out there"—at abandoned oil refineries, mismanaged landfills, and polluted rivers and streams. However the sad truth is, there are likely many dangers inside your house right now of which you should become aware. Seemingly innocuous grease-cutting cleaners, foam-filled lounge chairs, stain-resistant cut-pile floor coverings, and wrinkle-free clothes could be jeopardizing your health, and the health of your family, at this very moment. This is neither fiction nor exaggeration—it's just reality.

The next sections will focus on three significant conditions often associated with unhealthy households. Because it may be the least familiar to you, the first will be Multiple Chemical Sensitivity (MCS). Then there will be a discussion of both allergies and asthma, two far more common, better understood and, therefore, much more medically accepted conditions. However, you should remember that many people living in unhealthy houses experience adverse health affects that do not fit into one of these three, specific conditions.

Multiple Chemical Sensitivity (MCS)

Since World War II, increasing numbers of people have become ill with a host of baffling symptoms. For example, joint pain, mental confusion, digestive complaints, and skin rashes may be reported by a single individual, while others report their own set of seemingly unrelated problems. To make diagnoses difficult, the common tests that are frequently used to determine the nature of many medical conditions are often unable to provide any sure indication of what these people have, or why they have it.

Because of this, much of the medical community has dismissed those unfortunate enough to have such mysterious complaints, labeling them hypochondriacs, neurotics, menopausal, temporarily suffering an unusual manifestation of stress, or just plain flaky. *However, this does not mean it is not a real medical condition.* It simply means that it has *not yet* been validated by the mainstream medical establishment. After all, in the not-too-distant-past, common conditions such as premenstrual syndrome (PMS), post-partum depression, impotence, epilepsy, and depression weren't believed to have a physical cause.

At the same time, it should be noted that patients complaining of several simultaneous symptoms were first described decades ago in a 1962 ground-breaking book, *Human Ecology and Susceptibility to the Chemical Environment,* by Theron G. Randolph, M.D. This physician did not arbitrarily dismiss his patients' complaints as delusional. Instead, he believed that the varied effects were due to one general cause—the effect of exposure to low levels of chemicals in the home, at the workplace, and in food. Randolph termed the condition *Ecological Illness.* A growing number of other health professionals have since agreed with Randolph's assessment.

Since the publication of Randolph's first book, Ecological Illness has been called by a number of other names—Twentieth Century Disease, Total Allergy Syndrome, Chemical Allergies, Chemical Sensitivity, and Chemical Hypersensitivity. Currently, the most widely accepted term is *Multiple Chemical Sensitivity,* or *MCS.*

By the way, it's suspected that at least some cases of Chronic Fatigue Syndrome (severe and persistent tiredness), Fibromyalgia Syndrome (chronic muscle and joint pain with fatigue), and Sick Building Syndrome (various symptoms temporarily exhibited by certain persons when inside a particular building) may be forms of MCS—or at least related somehow. Interestingly, a recent book, *Chemical Exposures: Low Levels and High Stakes,* by well-respected occupational medicine researchers Claudia S. Miller and Nicholas A. Ashford, provides compelling evidence for an entirely "new theory of disease." Termed TILT (toxic induced loss of tolerance), they contend it may actually be the originator of a number of the above medical conditions, as well as others.

The Nature of MCS

Now, let's focus in on Multiple Chemical Sensitivity (MCS). What exactly is it? Despite the many reported symptoms, MCS is generally considered (by at least some experts) to be a single condition: one that results from chemical injury. Unfortunately, to explain how toxic chemicals could so variously affect certain individuals, the specific physiological/biochemical theories are generally written in complex medical language, which can be difficult for most of us to comprehend.

However, to put it very simply, our bodies frankly haven't had enough time to evolve into lifeforms that are able to successfully coexist with the tens of thousands of chemicals with which we now surround ourselves—compounds which never existed before in human history. We know that trees in Germany's Black Forest have turned brown and sickly from acid rain, that great numbers of fish in the Great Lakes have tumors, and that certain bird species now lay thin-shelled eggs that break before chicks ever hatch. All these are fellow lifeforms that are unable to thrive within polluted environments. Why do we think humans are exempt?

Many of you may be wondering, "Why do some people get MCS, or some other serious condition, while others seem to be doing okay?" The answer is, *we are never all equally susceptible.* A particular individual's MCS susceptibility is due to a number of factors including age (the very young and the very old have less-functional immune systems), other previous or presently existing medical conditions (those with allergies or bacterial, viral, or fungal illnesses have already-compromised immune systems), poor nutrition, stress, work exposure (those employed in petrochemical industries, those involved with pesticides, or those who work in sick buildings), genetic make-up (some individuals just have stronger constitutions than others), your home's proximity to toxic-waste sites—and just plain luck. One person might acquire MCS as the result of a one-time toxic event, while others may acquire it as the result of an accumulation of small exposures over several years.

Often, persons with MCS report initially becoming ill after they moved into a new house, mobile home, or apartment. Those living in older buildings, might report a feeling of sickness following the installation of new kitchen cabinets or living-room carpeting. MCS has also been associated with painting a master bedroom, newly-applied termite treatments— or with any other major or minor chemical exposure in the home, at work, or at school.

Some who have MCS have noted that, at first, it seemed they simply had the flu. However, unlike the flu, the achiness, tiredness, and general malaise did not go away within the expected week or two—and their former sense of well-being never returned. Instead, the sense of being "under the weather" lingered, then progressed into a variety of new symptoms.

Whatever the ultimate cause, an affected individual may soon find that he or she now feels sick around perfume, typical cleaning products, cigarettes, gas heat, vinyl, new clothing, etc. In many cases of MCS, the number of intolerable substances tends to increase, while at the same time, the level of exposure capable of producing symptoms decreases. This effect is known as *increased sensitivity* or *hypersensitivity.* Some individuals also find that they've acquired food allergies or an intolerance to electromagnetic fields (EMFs) (See *Electromagnetic Sensitivity* on page 645). In severe cases of MCS, a great many synthetic materials, or even natural items, will provoke a multitude of symptoms if inhaled or ingested.

You should be aware that each individual with MCS has his or her own set of unique symptoms—each symptom having its own degree of severity and duration. These particular symptoms can manifest themselves physically, psychologically, or both. This shouldn't be seen as odd or remarkable—many petrochemicals are actually neurotoxic and affect the brain. Interestingly, some MCS complaints mimic already-established medical conditions such as arthritis. Actually, MCS symptoms have been associated with virtually every organ, body system, or mind function. The following is a limited list of some reported symptoms:

> Nausea, headache, hives, insomnia, depression, anxiety, gastrointestinal problems, urinary tract inflammation, menstrual irregularities, sinus inflammation, respiratory distress, heartbeat irregularities, mental confusion, chemical hypersensitivity, loss of coordination, memory impairment, joint pain, tremors, muscle aches, blurred vision, sensitivity to light, ringing in the ears, changes in normal perspiration, and anaphylactic shock.

MCS Treatment

The ability to recognize and treatment of MCS varies enormously from doctor to doctor. The following will acquaint you with common medical responses.

Mainstream Response to MCS

Today, several million people in the United States have symptoms both severe and persistent enough to be called Multiple Chemical Sensitivity (MCS). This illness is increasingly being recognized by state and federal authorities as a legitimate medical condition. For example, MCS has been included in the U.S. Social Security Administration's Social Security Income Benefit guidelines (see *Social Security Income Benefits* on page 55).

However, despite the growing numbers who are affected, some government recognition, and books such as those by pioneer Theron Randolph, M.D. and researchers Nicholas Ashford and Claudia Miller, some physicians remain unfamiliar with MCS; others simply dismiss it as not being a "real" medical condition. Actually, the lack of positive help MCS patients commonly receive from doctors, while discouraging, is understandable. After all, it was probably never studied (at least seriously) in medical school, nor treated during medical training, nor written much about in medical journals, nor spoken about at conferences, nor discussed openly with colleagues. And pharmaceutical salesmen don't offer physicians samples of drugs or devices to treat MCS.

It should also be recognized that much of the medical community tends to be relatively traditional or conservative. This may be surprising to many, but it's the reality in most of the medical world. And it isn't just out of fear of malpractice lawsuits. Accepted medical knowledge, as with most other fields, often changes though slow evolution—not rapid revolution. It's not uncommon for decades to pass between the time new information, procedures, drugs, and practices are first proposed and the time they're routinely implemented by local family physicians. Doctors with busy schedules can read, absorb, and change only so much. It's not too surprising, then, that highly touted drugs or surgical techniques promising dramatic results with straight-forward, easy-to-understand illnesses, are far more likely to generate interest, than MCS with all its vagaries and uncertainties.

At the same time, it also appears that some physicians and major medical associations are simply adamantly opposed to the concept that everyday chemical exposures can cause negative reactions—in spite of increasing evidence to the contrary. These doctors believe there isn't enough proof (double-blind studies, convincing medical tests, etc.) to show that MCS is anything but a dramatic fear of chemicals in any form. In fact, some of them believe there never will be proof. With physicians holding this narrow viewpoint, it is quite unlikely that they will be open to changing their minds. Remember, there are headstrong people in every profession. The medical community is no different.

Physicians Who Recognize and Treat MCS

Fortunately, for individuals with Multiple Chemical Sensitivity who seek medical help for their condition, there are physicians who are not only familiar with MCS but also offer treatment programs. For example, some occupational-medicine practitioners are beginning to diagnose chemical-injury illnesses resulting from exposures in the workplace. However, these doctors may not use the term Multiple Chemical Sensitivity.

Those physicians who are members of the **American Academy of Otolaryngic Allergy (AAOA)** recognize and treat MCS. The AAOA is made up of doctors who are ear, nose, and throat allergy specialists. In addition, there are specialized physicians who have actually dedicated their practices to treating MCS. These are *clinical ecologists* or *environmental medicine specialists,* and most belong to the **American Academy of Environmental Medicine (AAEM)**. Interestingly, many AAEM members became interested in MCS after they themselves, a family member, or a friend came down with the condition.

What does MCS therapy entail? Actually, the therapy prescribed varies with each doctor and each patient. However, it often includes strategies to strengthen the immune system, desensitizing drops or shots to counteract (or *neutralize*) specific exposures and symptoms, intracutanious allergy testing (suspected allergens are placed into the skin), antioxidant supplements (vitamin C, etc.), and detoxification regimes to reduce the levels of accumulated toxins in the body. Most individuals find that avoiding synthetic chemicals, and other symptom-provoking substances, is also necessary. In fact, for many people with MCS, living a less-toxic lifestyle often makes a real and dramatic difference in the quality of their lives.

To find a physician member of the AAOA in your area, you can call or write to them. They also offer a member list on their website. To locate a physician who is a member of the AAEM, you can write or call for a list of all their members in your geographic area. Finally, the **MCSurvivors** website has physician-referral information.

More Information on MCS

A number of excellent sources are available for more in-depth information on MCS. A good introductory article is "Multiple Chemical Sensitivity" by Betty Hileman which appeared in *Chemical and Engineering News* (July 22, 1991, Vol. 69 (29), pp. 26–42). If your local library doesn't have it, you'll need to contact the **American Chemical Society** to see how you can get a copy.

Long time, highly recommended books on MCS include *An Alternative Approach to Allergies* by Theron G. Randolph, M.D. and Ralph W. Moss, Ph.D. and *Coping with your Allergies* by Natalie Golos and Frances Golos Golbitz. As was mentioned earlier, a newer book, *Chemical Exposures: Low Levels and High Stakes,* by Nicholas A. Ashford and Claudia S. Miller contains a great deal of detailed and very technical information.

More consumer-friendly, are books by Doris Rapp, M.D. One of her best known is *Is This your Child?* This soft-cover book provides specific clues to determine if your child has MCS. Sherry Roger, M.D. has written extensively on the subject. Her *Tired or Toxic: A Blueprint for Health* is a favorite of many with MCS. It offers a biochemical explanation of chemical hypersensitivity and yeast infections, and methods to promote health.

Other books on MCS you may like to read are *Healthy Living in a Toxic World: Simple Ways to Protect Yourself & Your Family from Hidden Health Risks* by Cynthia E. Fincher, Ph.D. which covers possible chemical-injury causes, their symptoms, and avoidance measures. Of course, there are also many other fine books on the subject. Check for them in the catalogs available from **N.E.E.D.S., E.L. Foust Co., Inc., Karen's Natural Products**, and **TerrEssentials**, among others.

You'll also want to check internet booksellers such as **Amazon.com, Borders.com**, and **Barnesandnoble.com**. Interestingly, **Medsite.com** is the internet's largest medical/health search engine. They also offer the **Medbookstore.com** website that sells primarily technical medical books. Of course, you shouldn't forget your local library and area bookstores.

There are now a number of MCS-related periodicals. For information on these, see *Helpful Organizations* on page 52. Another helpful publication is **Healthy Environment Information & Referral Service** which publishes the *Clean Living Resource Directory*. Included are nearly 60 categories of addresses and phone numbers for healthy products, informational sources, and health facilities. It's said that it is updated every six months.

Allergies and Asthma

Allergies have probably been around as long as people have been around, and it's well established that genetics plays a role in who will likely get them. But, in the last two decades, the numbers of people with allergies has been mysteriously growing. Some researchers believe that up to 30% of the population now exhibit allergic symptoms, and many of these people have become allergic to substances found in their household environment. Problematic substances include dust mites (more specifically, dead dust-mite body parts, and fecal pellets), animal dander (skin flakes), cat saliva, scents and perfumes, pollen (brought in from the outdoors or from indoor flowering plants), mold, dust, and cockroaches.

As it turns out, most people with asthma also have allergies. In fact, many of the substances that trigger allergic symptoms can also trigger asthmatic attacks. Sadly, the incidence of allergies and asthma has doubled in the last twenty years. Unbelievably, there are now apparently 17 million Americans with asthma (of whom 5 million are children). And there is an annual death toll of 5,500. Furthermore, the U.S. Centers for Disease Control has reported that, during the past 13 years, the number of children with asthma has doubled. And, according to the American College of Emergency Physicians, asthma now causes 9 million lost works days each year.

The question no one has yet been able to answer is, "Why the relatively sudden increases in the incidences of these often debilitating conditions?" Perhaps likely contributors are the unhealthy households so many Americans live in. Homes are getting bigger, and more elaborate, with more and more amenities containing man-made wood products and synthetically derived materials. And, as was mentioned earlier, they are being routinely cleaned and "freshened" with new and "improved" chemically-laden scented products. As a result, our homes are actually becoming more and more polluted. This noxious situation is often combined with the fact that houses are also being built tighter to reduce energy costs—but with no planned ventilation system to exchange the stale contaminated air for incoming fresh air.

Are our immune systems (especially of developing and growing children) being overloaded? Perhaps. It's not too surprising, then, that the **American Lung Association** has sponsored a number of "Health Houses" around the country. Many of these model homes highlight the use of less-toxic, less allergenic products, as well as good ventilation.

Does it make health-sense to routinely use wall-to-wall carpet, which can be home to thousands of dust mites and other microorganisms, pollen, mold, dirt, and debris. It couldn't possibly promote good health. With some statistics showing that 80% of asthmatics are allergic to just one common resident of carpet—dust mites—could we, as a society, have exchanged our health for plush flooring?

In the end, it may be time for you to reassess what makes for a desirable, comfortable, healthy household. Then, you should search for choices beyond what builders, decorators, magazines, friends, or even relatives, say or do—and decide for yourself. If you already have allergies or asthma, this could result in a significant improvement in your condition.

The Nature of Allergies

Let's begin with a brief discussion of what allergies actually are. The word *allergy* is derived from the Greek and literally means abnormal response. Not surprisingly then, allergies are defined as adverse reactions to substances that should normally be harmless. Interestingly, these reactions never occur with the first exposure.

An allergic reaction occurs when a person's immune system, (which provides normal defenses against dangerous foreign substances) "determines" for some reason that a particular, ordinarily benign substance is now a harmful invader. When this happens, the formerly innocuous substance becomes an *allergen*, and the immune system starts a defensive attack against it. This is what's ultimately experienced by the individual as an allergic reaction.

One of the most common ways the immune system of an allergic person reacts (apparently there are different mechanisms), is by creating *antibody* molecules known as *immunoglobulin E*, or *IgE*. These IgE molecules seek out and combine with the allergen molecules, then they bind to certain specialized cells called *mast cells* and *basophils*. It's this binding process that causes the release of *histamines* (and other compounds). And, it's the presence of histamines that then affects blood vessels and mucous membranes. Histamines cause them to dilate, swell, congest, and begin to leak, which leads to typical allergic symptoms: runny nose, swollen and itchy eyes, and sneezing, etc. By the way, *allergic rhinitis* is a term referring to allergic nasal lining inflammation, *allergic conjunctivitis* refers to allergic eye inflammation, and *allergic dermatitis* is used to describe allergic skin reactions.

Unfortunately, long-term allergic symptoms, especially allergic rhinitis, can lead to *sinusitis* (inflammation of the sinuses), fluid retention in the ears, ear aches, nasal *polyps* (small growths), general fatigue, and the worsening of an asthmatic condition. Those people who are unfortunate enough to allergically react to many substances (often an inherited condition) are known as *atopic*. It should be pointed out that household allergens generally come into contact with individuals through their eyes, nose, throat, or lungs. However, some people also react through skin contact or ingestion.

Allergy Treatment

When a person goes to a physician for allergy treatment, the first thing usually done is to take a thorough patient history (including family illnesses and symptoms experienced around suspected substances). Then *skin provocation testing* (also known as patch testing) is done by placing a small amount of various substances under the skin. A red whorl around the site indicates a positive (allergic) response. However, these can sometimes be false positives.

After the physician has made up a list of allergens (allergy provoking substances), several approaches, alone or in some combination, are then used. Suggested treatments might include avoidance, desensitization shots (injections with a tiny amount of allergenic substance to "teach" the immune system not to react to these particular compounds), and symptom-relieving medications. Currently, three types of such medications are typically prescribed. These are *antihistamines* (to counter histamine release), *anti-inflammatory agents* such as *cortiocosteroids* (to control immune/stress reactions), and *decongestants* (to relieve congestion, but for a limited time only).

It should be noted that, with the discovery in 1988 of the structure of the IgE receptors on mast cells, a totally different type of treatment began to be developed. Now, in initial clinical testing, *IgE inhibitors* may be able to block any allergic reaction from any allergen.

The Nature of Asthma

Some researchers believe that asthma is probably a group of diseases that all create an inflammation of the *bronchi* (air passages into the lungs) and spasms in the muscles surrounding them. Asthmatics typically have inflamed bronchi, even when they're not in the midst of an attack. When they are having an attack, they typically feel short of breath, a constriction in their chest, and begin wheezing. Other common symptoms are fatigue and coughing. In a worse-case scenario, death results.

What actually happens in the body of someone with asthma? As was noted earlier, it seems most people with asthma are allergic. In fact, it's speculated that most attacks are probably started by allergic reactions. Most of the time, it's inhaled allergens that are the source of trouble, such as mold spores, dust-mite body parts and feces, pollen, and animal *dander* (skin flakes). In addition to these, inhaled chemical irritants may trigger attacks. It should be noted that the ingestion of allergic foods, stress, infections, and physical exercise can become triggering events, as well.

When an asthmatic experiences one of his (or her) triggers, an enzyme present in their lungs releases a certain *blood-protein peptide*. This peptide then strongly stimulates the squeezing of their bronchial muscles, causing restricted breathing. Interestingly, a person undergoing an asthma attack usually finds it easier to inhale than to exhale. This imbalance of breath can over inflate the lungs which further limits their ability to function properly. To add to all this, an overproduction of the their mucous membranes may also occur.

Research has revealed that asthma is far more frequent in children than in adults. And, the severity of the attacks are worse in younger people than older ones. A special category of asthmatics are those with *intrinsic asthma*. In this condition the attacks become less common and less severe. However, the individual apparently recovers less well between attacks. Therefore, in time, their airways may become chronically restricted.

Asthma Treatment

Asthma patients typically have similar treatments to control their allergies as other allergic people. (See *Allergy Treatment* on page 50.) In addition, certain anti-asthma drugs may be injected or taken orally. However, today, the most common treatment is the prescribed use of inhaled aerosol *corticosteroids* which can counter inflammation and swelling. *Bronchodilators* (drugs able to open the smaller, air passages in the lungs) may be given in metered doses. In some cases, oxygen may also be prescribed, as well as exercises to promote relaxation and breathing.

Physicians Who Treat Allergies and Asthma

Because allergies and asthma are "well-established," physiologically explainable conditions, those who suspect they have allergies and/or asthma should have no trouble finding help and treatment from the medical community. While family-practice physicians may treat them, they'll often refer you to a specialist.

As it turns out, physicians specializing in allergy and asthma treatment often belong to the **American Academy of Allergy, Asthma, and Immunology (AAAAI)** or the **American College of Allergy, Asthma, and Immunology (ACAAI)**. By contacting either of these professional organizations, they'll send you a listing of members in your area.

Also, the **American Academy of Otolaryngic Allergy (AAOA)**, whose members specialize in ear, sinus, and throat allergies, may be helpful. You can locate a physician belonging to this group by logging on to their website or by calling them directly.

More Information on Allergies and Asthma

There is a great deal of information on allergies and asthma that can be helpful to you. For example, the **American Academy of Allergy, Asthma and Immunology** and the **Ameri-**

can College of Allergy, Asthma and Immunology both have brochures that you can request by mail. Also, the **National Institute of Allergy and Infectious Diseases (NIAID)** at the National Institutes of Health has a free informational packet you can request by mail or download from their website.

In addition, there are national patient support groups such as **Asthma and Allergy Network, Mothers of Asthmatic, Inc. (AAN/MA)** and **Asthma and Allergy Foundation of America (AAFA)** that have a number of fact sheets and brochures available. With membership, you'll receive their newsletters, too.

Some helpful books you may want to read are *The Best Guide to Allergy* by N.D. Schultz M.D., A.V. Giannini, M.D., and T.T. Chang M.D. which offers allergy and asthma treatment methods you can do yourself, and explanations of physician-conducted testing and treatment options. *How to Outsmart Your Allergies* by Art Ulene, M.D. is a book created in conjunction with the **Asthma and Allergy Foundation of America**. It provides medical causes for allergies, and how you can go about determining your own particular allergens.

In addition, *Taming Asthma and Allergy by Controlling Your Environment: A Guide for Patients* by Robert A. Wood, M.D. has both medical information along with "environmental control measures" you can do in your own home. Finally, *Taking Charge of Asthma: A Lifetime Strategy* by B.B. Wray M.D. is also written to aid you in making your home environment more asthmatic-friendly. A resource listing is included.

As you might expect, there are also many other books in local libraries and bookstores on both allergies and asthma. You'll also want to look at what's currently available at on-line bookstores such as **Amazon.com, Barnesandnoble.com**, and **Borders.com**. Also, one of the largest medical search engines on the internet is **Medsite.com**. They have their own bookstore, **Medbookstore.com**, which handles mostly highly technical books.

Helpful Organizations and Websites

This section includes some helpful non-physician-based organizations. Some focus on the needs of those with MCS, others are devoted to those with allergies or asthma, while others are dedicated to helping the general population.

Obviously, there are more groups out there than are listed here, but this should provide you with some good starting points. You'll find that most of the groups included here have their own websites. Furthermore, website-only groups are listed, too. All are listed in alphabetical order.

The **Asthma and Allergy Network, Mothers of Asthmatic, Inc.** is a tax-exempt organization that was founded "to help all people with allergies and asthma." Membership (in any size donation) includes a subscription to *The MA Report*, a monthly newsletter. First-year members receive booklets and 13 fact sheets. The organization's catalog offers a variety of pertinent books and videos, as well as asthmatic breathing aids. Members receive a 10% discount on most items. A listing of physician members can be found on their web site. The organization also does research activities such as surveys and focal groups.

The **Asthma and Allergy Foundation of America (AAFA)** is a non-profit, national, patient-advocacy organization. It is involved with public education, research support, and it also has a national network of local chapters and support groups. In addition, the AAFA has a catalog of helpful allergy- and asthma-related books for both adults and children, CDs, videos, booklets, and AAFA Information Fact Sheets on topics relating to allergy and asthma.

With dues, you receive the bimonthly *Advance* newsletter. A 10% discount on AAFA catalog orders also comes with membership.

The **American Environmental Health Foundation (AEHF)** is a non-profit organization founded to promote research and education into Chemical Sensitivity and Environmental Medicine. It sponsors conferences, and has an extensive catalog with products, books, and reprints of articles dealing with MCS. There's a 10% discount to members on most catalog items.

The **American Lung Association (ALA)** is a non-profit, national organization whose mission is to "prevent lung disease and promote lung health." Free brochures on allergies, asthma and other lung-related issues are available. Local chapters often publish their own newsletters. The ALA has sponsored the construction of a number of "Health Houses" around the country that are built to promote good respiratory health, through the use of less-toxic or less allergenic materials, as well as good ventilation. Because each house is different, specific goals, products and techniques are varied.

American PIE (Public Information on the Environment) is a non-profit organization "offering free assistance to people having environmental questions and concerns." You may contact them on their toll-free telephone line. Membership includes the quarterly newsletter, *American PIE*.

The **Bio-Integral Resource Center (BIRC)** is a non-profit organization "dedicated to providing practical least-toxic methods for pest management." It publishes technical bulletins and two journals (*IPM Practitioner* for professionals, and *Common Sense Pest Control Quarterly* for consumers or non-professionals). With membership, comes the journal-of-choice and free consulting for pest-control answers.

The **Chemical Injury Information Network (CIIN)** is a national organization providing information to those who are ill due to chemical injury. There is no set membership fee, but donations are accepted which will entitle you to receive *Our Toxic Times*, a monthly newsletter. Also available is a *CIIN Environmental Directory*, the *CIIN Buying Guide*, and *CIIN Legal Packets* on a large variety of topics including Social Security, fair housing practices, etc., all at low cost.

The **Chronic Fatigue Immune Dysfunction Syndrome Association (CFIDSA)** is a national non-profit organization that provides information about CFIDS to the public, and to those already having this condition. It also supports research, and does advocacy work. Membership includes the quarterly publication *The CFIDS Chronicle*.

Eco-Home Network is a Los Angeles-based non-profit organization promoting environmentally sound, energy efficient, economical, urban housing in southern California. The group offers tours, programs, books, and informational packets. With membership, you receive the quarterly journal *Elocution*.

The **Electrical Sensitivity Network (ESN)** is a non-profit national support and advocacy organization for those with Electrical Sensitivity (ES). Membership is $20 annually and includes a bimonthly newsletter, *Electrical Sensitivity News*.

eMD.com is a website offering information and products to help those with allergies and asthma create healthier lifestyles. They also have a question-and-answer forum.

The **Fibromyalgia Network (FN)** is a national, for-profit organization promoting self-help and advocacy for those with fibromyalgia. The FN keeps a data base of support-group leaders and physicians who treat the condition. You can request to receive by mail a free listing for your area. Income from subscriptions to the quarterly *The Fibromyalgia Network Newsletter* goes toward publishing and advocacy work.

The **Human Ecology Action League (HEAL)** is a non-profit, national, information and support organization for those with MCS. It produces many helpful directories, fact sheets, resource lists, reading lists, on a wide range of topics, which are available at low cost. With membership, you receive the quarterly newsletter, *The Human Ecologist*. Local HEAL chapters are also found throughout the U.S. You can locate the nearest chapter by contacting the national organization.

The **Labor Institute, NYC** is a non-profit education and research organization in New York City. It provides worker-oriented training programs and materials to unions and groups nationwide. The seven-person staff all belong to the Oil, Chemical, and Atomic Workers Union Local 8-149. An excellent booklet, *Multiple Chemical Sensitivities at Work: A Training Workbook for Working People* has good information about MCS, symptoms, and reasonable accommodation for MCS in the workplace. While it's now out of print, copies may be able to be found at COSH (Committees on Safety and Health) organizations at various local unions in the US. (COSH groups are non-profit, membership groups, funded by governmental and private grants, to provide advocacy for worker health on the job.)

MCS Referral & Resources is a national non-profit professional outreach organization offering "patient support and public advocacy devoted to the diagnosis, treatment, accommodation and prevention of Multiple Chemical Sensitivity Disorders" for professionals (both doctors and lawyers) and patients. The group offers referrals, collects and disseminates MCS information (on medicine, law, and policy), and participates in advocacy projects. It accepts no funding from chemical or insurance companies.

MCS Resources has a website focusing on housing issues pertaining to persons with MCS. It also has a Safer Travel Directory and links to other sites.

MCSurvivors has a website offering MCS-related articles and books. It also offers a bulletin board, physician referral information, and links to other sites.

National Center for Environmental Health Strategies (NCEHS) works to urge Federal and state legislatures and agencies to seriously consider the dangers of chemical pollutants. It also documents the experiences of those already made ill. Much of this effort is put forth by NCEHS's founder and president, Mary Lamielle. From time to time, the group publishes the *Delicate Balance* listing the latest information on governmental developments, programs, benefits, and studies of interest to those with Multiple Chemical Sensitivities (MCS) and other chemical injuries.

The **National Foundation for the Chemically Hypersensitive (NFCH)** is a non-profit, volunteer organization founded by Fred Nelson devoted to promoting research, education of the general public, referrals (physician and lawyer), and information on housing, social security, and other issues for those with chemical hypersensitivity. It also complies case histories.

The **Practical Allergy Research Foundation (PARF)** was founded by Doris Rapp, M.D. The foundation's catalog offers books and audio and video tapes about allergic and chemically sensitive children as well as other topics. With membership, you receive the *Allergy Insights Newsletter*.

The **Rachel Carson Council, Inc.** is a non-profit organization devoted to safer environments (outdoors and indoors)—especially through the elimination of dangerous pesticides. Membership includes the periodic newsletter, *Rachel Carson Council News*.

The **T & Y Beacon of Hope Foundation** (for the chemically injured) is under the umbrella of the non-profit National Heritage Foundation. It's dedicated to educating the public about the dangers that toxic chemicals have on human health and the environment;

assisting and supporting those already chemically injured and, particularly, the creation of safe-housing communities. Donations of money, office equipment, and land to reach their goals are welcomed.

The **Washington Toxics Coalition** is a non-profit organization "dedicated to preventing pollution in industry, agriculture, and the home." Membership includes the quarterly *Alternatives* newsletter. Many helpful fact sheets are available, as well as a Toxic Hotline telephone number (to answer questions not covered in their publications).

Other Assistance

The next sections will cover assistance that's available that may help you with certain important home or lifestyle issues.

Agency Assistance in General

A Federal agency whose mission is to provide information on all other government programs at the federal, state, and local levels for the disabled (including those with chemical injuries, severe asthma, etc.) is the **Clearing House on Disability Information** at the Office of Special Education and Rehabilitative Services. From them, you can request a free manual entitled *Pocket Guide to Federal Help for Individuals with Disabilities*. It covers Federal programs, education, employment, financial assistance, medical assistance, civil rights, housing, tax benefits, social-security benefits, and transportation. Also, if you have children who are ill, the federally funded, **National Information Center for Children and Youth with Disabilities**, can provide you with an resource-listing guide for your state.

In addition, don't forget to also look under "Government-Federal," "Government-State," and "Government-Local" as well as "Social Services" in your classified telephone directory. If an agency's name sounds as if it might have something to offer, call them. They just might be able to help you directly, or refer you to more appropriate public or private agencies.

Federal Income Taxes

It may be possible to list, as valid medical-expense deductions, certain home-remodeling expenses, or items purchased specifically for health reasons. However, these will generally require a written physician's letter or prescription stipulating that such alterations or special purchases are, in fact, medically necessary. All of the bills for such items must be carefully documented. This is generally a one-time deduction. (Note that, tax laws are constantly undergoing change.)

For more information, you'll need to request *IRS Publication #502: Medical and Dental Expenses* from the **U.S. Internal Revenue Service** (IRS). It can be obtained by calling their toll-free IRS Forms and Publications telephone number. For answers to specific tax questions, you'll need to call the toll-free IRS General Information telephone number.

Social Security Income (SSI) Benefits

It may be possible for you to acquire Social Security Income (SSI) benefits if you are disabled by Multiply Chemical Sensitivity (MCS), severe allergies, or asthma and, as a result, are unable to work. If you qualify, this program will issue you a monthly income check. As it turns out, recipients of SSI are usually eligible for Medicaid as well as food stamps. However, acceptance into the SSI program is often far from automatic. And, with the goal of lowering the numbers of those receiving government assistance, getting SSI benefits is certainly not becoming any easier.

You'll find that when you apply for SSI, your household income, and the monetary worth of your accumulated assets (usually not including your home or car), must be below a maximum established total limit. You must also be able to provide compelling medical documentation for your disability. In other words, you must have convincing evidence that your condition is long-term and that you're sufficiently physically and/or mentally compromised to prevent being employed. Whether you're condition can be controlled adequately by medication or not may also come into play.

Yet, even with your physician's statement, you may still initially be turned down for SSI program acceptance. This is especially true if you happen to have a controversial condition such as MCS. However, the Social Security Administration does provide a series of appeal procedures to present further evidence and testimony on your behalf, if you've been rejected. If you're eventually successful, your benefits will then be granted. For more specific information on SSI, write the **Social Security Administration** at the U.S. Department of Health And Human Services. You may also want to get information about how to apply for SSI at your local Social Security office.

To better help you acquire SSI benefits, it's a very good idea to speak with others who have already gone through the process and have qualified. Therefore, if you belong to a local health-related support group, bring this up at one of their meetings or in the group's newsletter. In addition, your personal physician or health-care provider may offer the names of other patients who have received SSI with whom you could speak.

You should also be aware that the **Chemical Injury Information Network (CIIN)** has a low-cost *CIIN Legal Packet* that contains information on how to acquire SSI benefits. Also, the **Human Ecology Action League (HEAL)** has helpful fact sheets that are reasonably priced. In the end, you may have to hire a lawyer who specializes in this field. If you don't get a personal recommendations from someone, you can check your classified telephone directory or contact your city or state bar association to find an attorney that specializes in this field.

Housing

Housing is one area where many people need some form of assistance. Following are several sources of helpful information.

Fair-Housing Laws

If you have Multiple Chemical Sensitivity (MCS), you'll be interested in knowing that the **U.S. Department of Housing and Urban Development (HUD)** has issued a policy statement recognizing MCS as a disability. For more information on this, you may want to contact them directly. Or you may also contact the **National Center for Environmental Health Strategies (NCEHS)**.

To better understand what housing rights disabled individuals are due, you may want to read *What Does Fair Housing Mean to People With Disabilities* by the Judge David Brazelon Center for Mental Health Law.

Mortgages for Healthy Housing

A new, small, mortgage company is now in business whose focus is to provide "financing to the chemically injured for appropriate housing." In this case, the chemically injured are defined as those with "multiple chemical sensitivities (MCS), chronic fatigue syndrome, fibromyalgia, chemically induced asthma, chemically induced lupus, chemically induced pophyria and autoimmunity."

The founder of the **National Home Mortgage Company (NHMC)**, Fred Nelson, says in the company literature that the NHMC will "very closely supervise, monitor, and consult with those performing the new building construction or older building modernization. We will also provide safety inspections for existing homes." All this is to provide ecologically clean living environments, while at the same time offering "the most attractive rates and terms." For more information, you'll need to contact them directly.

Personal Home Consultants

To locate personal consultants who deal with various less-toxic issues in the home, including house construction, remodeling, contaminant problem solving, safer pest-control methods, lifestyle issues. interior decorating, and more, you'll want to see *Helpful Consultants* on page 65.

Lifestyle Adjustment

Often those who are severely affected by chemical injury, asthma, or allergies, find that creating a new, healthy lifestyle can be very difficult. In these cases, a local Center for Independent Living can sometimes be very helpful.

The first Center for Independent Living (CIL) opened its doors in 1972 in Berkeley, California. Its purpose was to focus on helping disabled individuals function more effectively as independent persons in society. The success of this initial program eventually led to the passage of the 1978 Title VII of the Federal Rehabilitation Act, which provided funding to establish CILs across America. Now there are over 350 such centers all across the United States.

Each CIL has some disabled persons on its advisory board and staff to better understand the needs of physically and mentally challenged persons. Each center provides a variety of services, which generally include maintaining files on accessible housing, employment opportunities, and also appropriate social activities, etc. In addition, training courses are usually offered in order to help those with disabilities gain independent living skills. Peer (people with the same disability) counseling is also available for many types of disabilities. Furthermore, some local centers are able to create individual living plans for their disabled clients. These are outlines of specific goals for achieving effective and satisfying life routines and activities.

You should be aware that the extent to which any specific disability is served by a particular local CIL will vary greatly. However, even if you're disabled by Multiple Chemical Sensitivity (MCS), the personnel at some of these centers may be able help you create a less-toxic home and lifestyle. If you're interested in working with a local CIL, look in your classified telephone directory under "Social Services" or similar headings. You may also want to contact **Independent Living Research Utilization (ILRU)** in order to purchase a CIL directory.

Lessons

Today, the number of individuals who have Multiple Chemical Sensitivity (MCS) is still relatively small—that is, when compared to many other "conventional" medical conditions. However, their ranks appear to be steadily growing. And, it's important to know that many with MCS are convinced that an unhealthy home environment was a major (if not *the*) factor that caused them to become chemically injured in the first place.

On the other hand, the number of people with allergies and asthma (always somewhat greater than those with MCS) is increasing at a very alarming rate. While these individuals may not be certain exactly why this has happened to them, it's likely that, again, an unhealthy home environment played a role. If not a direct cause, it can certainly aggravate any existing health problems.

Because MCS, severe allergies, and asthma all have symptoms that can be debilitating and long-term, it's wise to take measures to prevent you and your family from acquiring any of them. Unfortunately, you can't remove all the possible risk factors. For example, when we're young our immune systems aren't yet fully developed, most of us will have declining immune systems as we age, and we can't change our basic genetic make-up. At the same time, some of us may not realize it if our homes are situated near buried toxic-waste sites. Obviously, we have little control over these and other factors. *Yet, it's generally within our own homes where we encounter the worst air quality—precisely where we typically spend most of our time. Certainly, we all can do something to make our interior environments healthier places to breathe, and to live.*

As I mentioned in the *Introduction*, some experts have concluded that perhaps one-half of all illness is caused by indoor air pollution. Feeling tired or having a headache, muscle ache, anxiety, or insomnia are so commonplace these days that we often say, "That's life." However that doesn't have to be the case because, if these symptoms are the direct result of polluted indoor home environments, that's something that can be changed.

Therefore, if you decide to create a healthy household, you'll likely reduce your chance of acquiring a serious condition (or making it worse) such as MCS, allergies, or asthma—but you'll also very likely increase your chances of just feeling better in general. Shouldn't this be incentive enough to start creating your very own healthier household? I personally hope so.

CHAPTER 2: GETTING STARTED

This is the chapter that gets you started on your way toward creating your own healthy household. It will cover healthy definitions, general testing information, and suggestions on where to find healthier products.

What is Safe or Healthy?

Of course, to create a healthier indoor environment, you'll need to choose healthier items to put in it. However, there are different ways to define the word *healthy*—and manufacturers and advertisers often project a healthy image by whatever convoluted means possible. After all, right now, *healthy* sells.

Some products may very well have real, positive health benefits—but in reference to "hot-button" issues such as landfills, the ozone layer, endangered species, fur-bearing animals, or old-growth forests. While such products may be healthy for Mother Earth in some respect, they may or may not be the healthiest choices for the interior of your house or apartment. Planetary health is certainly extremely important, but in this book, I'll stress buying and using products that are, above all, designed to be healthy for you personally.

Healthy Definitions

Following are some terms that are often applied to *healthy* household products. You should consider them carefully because some of the meanings are not going to be as clear as you first thought. Other healthy definitions will appear elsewhere in the following chapters.

All-Cotton

All-cotton refers to stuffing or fabric consisting of 100%-cotton fibers. However, this term doesn't always mean such items are all-natural or nontoxic. Because of conventional

American farming practices, cotton production uses tremendous quantities of pesticides, herbicides, and other toxic agricultural chemicals. Inevitably, some residues from these compounds get on cotton fibers.

In addition to chemical contamination acquired through cultivation, wrinkle-resisting chemicals (which can be *formaldehyde-based resins*), synthetic dyes, stain-resistant treatments, and other compounds are often added to cotton fibers during the milling process. As a result, all-cotton fabric can be, in many cases, very chemically laden (see also *Cotton* on page 178). And, be careful about purchasing items labeled "made with organic cotton." They might not be *100%* organic cotton.

All-Natural

All-natural means "derived solely from materials or substances in their native state." These products are neither synthetically nor artificially created. Many natural products are quite benign, but some are not. Lead, ammonia, radon, and asbestos are natural products and they're potentially quite dangerous. Turpentine, which is made from pine trees, and mint oil, are both natural as well. However, both can be very bothersome to sensitive or allergic persons.

Biodegradable

Biodegradable is defined as "the ability of natural biological decay processes to break down complex compounds into simple molecules." This is truly an asset for any product to have—especially if it's to be composted. However, at the present time, most potentially biodegradable trash is buried in landfills, and because of the manner in which landfills are constructed, virtually nothing in them can ever biodegrade. The tight compaction of alternating layers of trash and clay in typical landfills generally won't permit the breakdown of materials—even when they have the innate capacity to do so under normal circumstances.

Interestingly, in a surprising reversal of popular trends, some products are now actually said to be healthy for the environment because they will not biodegrade. Non-biodegradability is promoted as a positive feature because it helps prevent *leachate* (seepage) from leaving landfill sites and contaminating water supplies.

Hypoallergenic

Hypoallergenic means that a product is less likely to cause allergic reactions than other typical products. You should understand, however, that such labeling is not a guarantee against *all* allergic reactions that could result from a hypoallergenic product's use. In fact, in most cases, only the most common types of allergy-provoking substances are removed. In addition, other ingredients in certain hypoallergenic formulations may include petroleum-derived substances, even perhaps formaldehyde, that may not be innately healthful.

Made From Recycled Materials

Made from recycled materials is a phrase often used when all or part of an item is made from a previously manufactured material or product. Corrugated cardboard boxes, some papers, and many glass bottles often have labels stating they're made from recycled material. This is highly commendable. However, the percentage of recycled material that is used may be quite low. Sadly, at this time, only a limited number of items are created of 100% *post-consumer material*. Some of the products labeled "made from recycled materials" have actually been manufactured from scrap material left over from factory production. Using material swept up from the factory floor rather than throwing it away makes good environmental sense, but calling it "recycled" can be misleading.

Nontoxic

Nontoxic is defined as not being harmful at concentrations normally used. However, most people believe that it means a substance is innately harmless—and this just isn't so. In fact, according to the U.S. Federal Hazardous Substances Act, a substance can legitimately be called "nontoxic" if it does not cause acute (sudden-onset) health effects. By this narrow, legal definition, some products that cause long-term problems such as cancer or birth defects, or are slow-acting or accumulating poisons, can be called "nontoxic."

No Preservatives or Biocides

No preservatives refers to the fact that nothing has been added to a product in order to prevent or slow the decay process. *No biocides* means nothing has been added to kill microorganisms. Many preservatives and biocides commonly used are bothersome to sensitive people, so they routinely avoid all of them, as do many other individuals wanting to live an eco-conscious, chemical-free life.

However some preservatives, such as vitamin C, are generally considered both safe and naturally derived. Small amounts of such relatively harmless preservatives are often appropriate in products that otherwise would have very short shelf-lives. This is especially true for foods, in order to prevent possible food poisonings. Also keep in mind that, if you use a product such as biocide-free wallpaper paste or bathtub caulking, you risk unwanted fungal or bacterial growth. Therefore, some products using less-toxic biocides can be better choices than biocide-free versions.

No Volatile Organic Compounds (VOCs)

No *volatile organic compounds (VOCs)* means that a product does not contain a class of chemicals made up of certain hydrocarbons which are able to rapidly evaporate (see also *Volatile Organic Compounds* on page 526). VOCs are often found in solvents, paints, caulking materials, household cleaning products, etc. They can be harmful and some are extremely dangerous. However, the natural VOCs released by onions, oranges, and baking bread are considered reasonably safe.

Recyclable

Recyclable means an item is able to be reused in its present state or form, or is able to be broken down and reformulated into another manufactured product. This is seen almost universally as a positive attribute. Yet, many companies are not fully utilizing the recyclable items that municipal sanitation departments are amassing through recycling projects and, even today, many communities don't yet have mandated recycling programs. Therefore, many potentially recyclable materials continue to be buried in landfills, shipped to and dumped in Third World countries, or incinerated. Although being recyclable is obviously an ideal, too much of the material that is called "recyclable" is currently not being recycled because of cost factors, technological limitations, and/or lack of interest.

Unscented

Unscented would seem to indicate that a product contains no natural or synthetically derived fragrance. However, some manufacturers use this term or *scent-free* when the scent has been altered so it can't be smelled. In some cases—especially with detergents—certain major companies use an additional *masking fragrance* to cover up or counter the odor of the original fragrance. Obviously, this type of labeling can be somewhat confusing, if not misleading. Unfortunately, for some chemically sensitive persons, the presence of the original scent and the masking fragrances will have an adverse effect. This is because, for them, it's the chemical composition of the scents that's bothersome—not the odors themselves.

Problems of Personal Tolerance

Obviously, the above *healthy* definition list above isn't complete. However, it's long enough to show you that word meanings and manufacturers' advertising can be misleading. As a result, unless you are very cautious, you can easily buy products you really wouldn't want. If you knew all the facts, you might have made different choices. Therefore, it's important to read catalog descriptions, product literature, and labels carefully—and skeptically—in order to make informed purchasing decisions. Remember, the first criteria for anyone buying any product should be how it will affect your personal well-being and that of your family.

For healthy individuals, choosing items based on a thorough reading of product literature may be all that is necessary to create their healthy household. This generally works well for most people with mild allergies and asthma, too. However, it should be noted that, if you are already highly allergic, or chemically hypersensitive, reading labels may not be enough. That's because labels may not have all ingredients listed and certainly not their percentages.

Because we are each unique biological beings, we each have our own set of personal tolerance levels. For those with Multiple Chemical Sensitivity (MCS), or severe allergies, the degree of tolerability is often very low to a wide range of synthetic and/or natural products. *Therefore, you must keep in mind that what one person finds healthy may be entirely inappropriate for someone else.*

If you already know you have tolerability problems, you'll need to follow some special precautions when choosing healthier household products. First, you'll want to consult with your physician or other health-care professional in order to create a list of what he (or she) suggests you must avoid in order to prevent a bad reaction—and also what you can probably buy and safely use. For example, you should find out if there are certain natural herbs that you should stay away from, or whether there are particular animal proteins that could be dangerous to you. Plus, you should determine whether you'll be able to tolerate some products containing man-made chemicals if they have minimal odor, and so on. With this information, you can better choose products that'll most likely be suitable for you. However, for some hypersensitive individuals, it'll still be essential to test products for their own personal tolerability.

Testing

For those of you who are very allergic or chemically hypersensitive, it's extremely important to test all products you have never used before. *Of course, if you have a history of having negative reactions to substances, make sure to consult your physician prior to testing any untried product at home. For those with asthma, or for those who typically experience severe reactions, testing at home should NOT be done, period. In such cases, you should only test products under your doctor's direct supervision.*

By the way, except for those that don't fit the "do not" categories above, testing can be a good practice for almost anyone trying new items. After all, no one can absolutely rely on the recommendations of others that a particular product will be safe for them. Only by testing will you know for certain if you'll experience a negative reaction. And, because testing is relatively easy to do, it won't take up much time or be too complicated to master.

Actually, simple at-home tolerance testing can be done in a number of ways, depending on the product. (There are specific guidelines for testing adhesives, lubricants, etc. in *Chapter 9: Home Workshop*.) The process usually involves a brief initial exposure to a new product to determine if there are any immediate undesirable symptoms. For example, a bottle of a previously untried dish soap can be opened and lightly sniffed to determine if the odor is obviously troublesome or not. If there's concern about possible skin reactions, a small amount of the dish soap can be placed on the inside of your lower arm to see if contact dermatitis erupts. For latent effects, your hands can be washed with the dish soap and the product not used again for four to seven days. As it turns out, most delayed reactions—if they're going to occur—will become evident within that time period. To further test a product's tolerability, you can place a sample on your bedside table overnight. A good night's sleep generally indicates good tolerance. A restless night often means intolerance.

Of course, testing can provide information besides tolerability. It can be used to compare the effectiveness and cost of similar products. By the way, you can save money while testing by purchasing sample-size packages or the smallest sizes available. When testing, you'll want to make a written chart, on which you can write the testing date, place of purchase, brand name, size, cost, and your observations and comments. Of course, both tolerability testing and effectiveness testing can be done at the same time. In the end, the best products will be those that produce no negative reactions—and that perform their job well. Price is also an important consideration, but it should always be considered secondary to personal tolerability.

Buying in Quantity

Once you have found an item that seems to suit your needs, you should consider buying it in quantity if you plan to use it regularly. As you probably know, some products come in a variety of package sizes. This is especially true for certain cleaning products that might be manufactured in sizes ranging from a few ounces to a gallon or more. Commonly, the price per ounce when buying a gallon is cheaper than when buying in smaller amounts. By the way, if you order products through the mail, keep in mind that shipping costs will tend to be lower with one large order than with several, separate small orders. Minimum shipping fees can quickly add up.

Another important reason to buy in large amounts is that manufacturers sometimes change product formulations, create new packaging, or "improve" items in ways you may find intolerable. Companies also occasionally drop certain products from their lines. You should be aware, too, that many firms making less-toxic or all-natural products are relatively small and, as with many small enterprises, it's not uncommon for them to go out of business. If any of these events should happen, a once-relied-upon, acceptable product may no longer be available when you need to reorder. Therefore, purchase in bulk when an item is currently acceptable and you have a place to properly store it. But don't buy too much. After all, products do have a shelf life, so they won't last forever.

Storage Concerns

If you buy in bulk, it's important that the products be stored correctly. Do you have the necessary space? Will the temperature, light, and humidity be acceptable? Will you forget what you've stored?

As a general rule, do not buy more of an item than you'll actually use within a year. If there's an expiration date, do not purchase more than you'll be able to use before that date. Otherwise, all your good intentions may sour, rot, come out of solution or, in a myriad other ways, become useless and expensive garbage.

To determine the best conditions and length of storage time for a particular product, you'll want to check the label, contact the dealer, or consult the manufacturer directly. To remember what you have purchased, you might want to keep a storage list with the brand names and date of purchase, then not buy any replacement items until you've first checked the list.

Finally, remember to rotate your stock. When you purchase any new products, put them on the back of the shelf so that the oldest products will end up being the easiest to retrieve and, therefore, the first used.

Finding Healthier Products

Where do you go to find sources of safer, less-toxic, less allergenic, more-natural, alternative-living products? For local suppliers, you can check the classified section of your phone directory for health-food stores and co-op groceries. Also, you can ask people you know who are already living a healthier lifestyle that seems compatible to the one you're hoping to live. Often, they'll be more than willing to share their personal experiences. In addition, your physician or health-care professional may offer some suggestions.

By the way, even discount stores can yield some healthy products—if you know what to look for. Actually, finding local sources of healthier products is getting easier all the time. Fortunately, there's a business trend today to target the expanding, environmentally aware market. However, be careful that the particular definition of healthy used by others to describe a product will be one that is both applicable and acceptable to you. (See *Healthy Definitions* on page 59.)

Helpful Books, Resource Guides, and Catalogs

Furthermore, besides this particular book, there are now a number of books and magazines available on healthier lifestyles that contain mail-order and/or homemade sources for alternative products. For example, *Clean & Green,* by Annie Berthold-Bond, contains 485 suggestions (recipes and product suppliers) for cleaning your home and yourself. Anita Guyton's *The Natural Beauty Book: Cruelty Free Cosmetics to Make at Home* contains over 180 pages of homemade formulas for nontoxic face creams, shampoos, and other cosmetics.

Another helpful book is *The Safe Shopper's Bible* by David Steinman. Several books published by **The Healthy House Institute**, including *The Healthy House, Healthy House Building for the New Millennium,* and *Understanding Ventilation,* all by John Bower, offer extensive information on healthier construction and remodeling materials and suppliers.

It should also be mentioned that a number of resource guides are also available. For example, the **Chemical Injury Information Network (CIIN)** has produced a *CIIN Buying Guide* with over 50 categories of merchandise. And **Healthy Environment Information & Referral Service** publishes a *Clean Living Resource Directory* with nearly 60 categories. Furthermore, the **Human Ecology Action League (HEAL)** and the **Washington Toxic Coalition** offer fact sheets on a variety of subjects, some including product listings. Then, too, several organizations, such as the **American Environmental Health Foundation, Asthma and Allergy Foundation of America**, and **Asthma and Allergy Network, Mothers of Asthmatic, Inc.** have created their own catalogs from which anyone can buy healthier products.

You should also be aware of a growing number of mail-order companies and internet sites that focus primarily on serving chemically sensitive and allergic people. Then, too, certain mail-order firms targeting the eco-conscious consumer market have good selections of earth-friendly *and* people-friendly products. There are even quite a few catalogs geared to a more diversified customer-base that also offer a number of healthy product choices. Many of these catalogs and internet sites are listed in this book.

Helpful Consultants

If you need personal assistance, consultants may be able to supply you with alternative ideas along with manufacturer and dealer addresses and phone numbers. This very small sampling is listed by alphabetical order. Other consultants may be found in the low-cost *CIIN Environmental Directory* from **Chemical Injury Information Network (CIIN)** or by contacting **Human Ecology Action League (HEAL)**.

American PIE is a non-profit organization "offering free assistance to people having environmental questions and concerns" on their toll-free telephone line.

The Bio-Integral Resource Center (BIRC) is a "non-profit organization dedicated to providing practical least-toxic methods for pest management." Membership allows you to call for specific pest-control answers.

Environmental Education and Health Services, Inc. is Mary Oetzel's consulting company. She specializes in offering both telephone and on-site consultations to solve building-related problems for those with MCS. She also deals with schools.

CRG Designs for Living is owned by Cedar Rose Guelberth. She is a professional building consultant who also offers a large selection of natural products in her catalog.

Healthy Homes Consulting is the name of Robin Barrett's Canadian consulting firm. He offers consulting concerning "indoor air quality problems and cost effective solutions."

Interior Elements is the name of Margie McNally's company. She is an accredited, professional designer/environmental consultant who specializes in "creating healthy indoor environments."

David Kibbey is a professional consultant. He is a certified baubiologist (healthy building expert) who consults on many building-related issues.

Kitchens & Baths by Don Johnson is a father/son team of certified kitchen designers. They also market special kitchen cabinetry for the chemically sensitive.

Nigra Enterprises is headed by Jim Nigra. He is both a consultant and dealer. He offers information and products aimed at improving your home's air and water.

Safe Schools is the name of Irene Wilkenfeld's consulting firm. She is a professional "safe building consultant" with an emphasis on schools. She's particularly interested in using less toxic materials and products.

The **Washington Toxics Coalition** is a non-profit organization "dedicated to preventing pollution in industry, agriculture, and the home." A Toxic Hotline telephone number (to answer questions not covered in their publications) is available.

Cost

You need to understand that it's not unusual for natural or less-toxic products to cost more than their less-healthy, but more commonly available, counterparts. This is because the ingredients used in alternative items are often of a higher grade or quality, and they may be more difficult to obtain and/or process. Then, too, small manufacturers have a much lower volume of production than large corporations which produce popular, name-brand items. In addition, alternative product catalogs, which are generally small in scale, can only buy relatively small quantities at wholesale prices compared to large local retailers selling products to the general public. Sadly, in a few cases, it should also be added that some companies charge more for healthier products because they believe that people wanting such items will be willing to pay extra to get them.

On the other hand, some healthy products actually cost less than typical store-bought brands. This is especially true for simple, homemade alternatives. For example, inexpensive baking soda can be used as a scouring powder instead of a prepackaged cleanser. Also, a solution of hydrogen peroxide and water can be substituted for conventional bottled mouthwash. (Many of these low-cost alternatives will be covered in the chapters that follow.)

However, as a rule, you should expect healthy products to cost more. Of course, if their use results in better health and fewer visits to your doctor or other health-care professional, then the extra expenditure will have been well worth it.

Making Choices

The remainder of this book deals with specific information on how you can create a healthy household. It should be noted that improving indoor air quality will be a top concern. This is because, as previously noted, some synthetically derived fragrances are neurotoxic, and odors given off by many new carpets, cleaners, man-made wood products, and paints have the potential to be carcinogenic or mutagenic. Even scents derived from natural and nontoxic sources can be intrusive and bothersome to certain allergic, asthmatic, or chemically sensitive people. Therefore, you'll find that suggested products and practices are often unscented, odor-free, or have only a minimal odor.

However, while improving indoor air is a major focus, other heath issues such as water quality, electromagnetic fields, "naturalness," and issues related to planetary health are also discussed and taken into account. It's hoped that, after you read through the information offered in the following chapters, you'll be better equipped to choose what's truly appropriate for you and your family or household. Remember, what's offered are only suggestions—the ultimate decisions are yours. With that in mind, let's begin.

Part 2
CLEANING

CHAPTER 3: BASIC INGREDIENTS

It's important to choose your personal-care and cleaning items (and the ways you use them) *very* carefully. The truth is, these products (and how they're used) have the potential to either create healthy or unhealthy effects for you, your family, and your home.

Why? Well, for example, many toiletries and cleaners come in direct contact with your skin, and all give off their own particular odors. You not only inhale them, but they become absorbed into your clothing, bedding, furnishings, and walls. A particular formula, when applied to the body or handled, may be benign, cause minor rashes, or induce severe reactions. The health effects will be determined by the product's specific ingredients, the duration of exposure, and your personal tolerability.

To help you make better—and healthier—choices, this chapter will begin with a short section on natural versus synthetic products, then there will be a much more extensive look at scents and fragrances. Following, will be sections on understanding soaps and detergents, and some information on current government regulations. Because proper cleaning is often essential to controlling conventional allergies and allergens, this chapter ends with a section on allergen reduction. However, all of this is intended only as a brief introduction to the subject. Therefore, notes are provided on where to find more comprehensive coverage on reducing specific types of allergens.

While this chapter is meant to cover the important, basic, health-related information pertinent to each of the three chapters which follow it, there will be additional information pertaining to the specific ingredients in personal-care items, laundering necessities, and household cleaning products included within those separate chapters.

Natural vs. Synthetic Products

Should you only choose "all-natural" products? It might seem like the right thing to do. But as discussed in the last chapter (see page 60), all-natural doesn't necessarily mean benign or non-toxic. At the same time, synthetic or man-made does not automatically mean non-biodegradable or dangerous. The truth is, there are rarely any absolutes in life. Ammonia which is often considered a natural ingredient is found in some "all-natural," "green," or "earth-friendly" cleaning products. Yet, for even those who are not chemically sensitive, highly allergic, or asthmatic, ammonia-containing products can be unpleasant to breathe and even dangerous if improperly used. Nylon pot scrubbers are, of course, a synthetic product, but they're affordable, durable, odorless, and skin reactions to them are rare. Which product is better?

You should also keep in mind, that many "synthetic" ingredients used by numerous manufacturers of alternative products are not derived from petroleum, but instead are made from vegetable sources—such as coconut or corn oils. It's not uncommon for these companies to label their formulas as "all-natural." Other products with "all-natural" on their labels utilize only minerals and botanicals that are chemically unaltered. They claim they're the only real "all-natural" product lines. How natural must something be to really be natural? That's a decision you must ultimately make.

The truth is, there are many factors to consider when deciding to use *any* all-natural, all-synthetic, or combination product. However, the first thing to think about should be that product's direct health consequences to you and your family. All other factors should be secondary. There will be more on this important and highly charged topic of natural vs. synthetic ingredients in the other chapters throughout *Section: 2.*

Scented vs. Unscented Products

The odors given off by personal-care preparations and home cleaning products can arise from several sources within each item. For example, some products have a particular smell because of the basic ingredients used in them: "Almondy" is the predominate smell of almond-oil skin lotion while "citrusy" describes the odor of citrus-solvent cleaners. However, most products today also contain very concentrated natural and/or synthetic scents. These fragrances usually have absolutely nothing to do with product effectiveness. Rather, their purpose is to create an intentionally conspicuous atmosphere, or ambiance, surrounding their use.

What Are Scents?

Scents are often defined as aromatic compounds obtained from plants and other substances. Generally, their unifying characteristic is their capacity to be readily noticed, to linger, and to spread. Scents in concentrated forms (such as *essential oils*), as well as perfumes, magnify these traits.

Many experts believe that scents were aromatic substances that were originally connected with sacred ritual ceremonies. However, in time they became popular for secular and personal uses. Surprisingly, far from being an ancient phenomenon, what we now know as perfume (essential oils and other ingredients diluted in alcohol) did not make its appearance until fourteenth-century Hungary. Soon afterward, perfume quickly became popular among the nobility and well-to-do. This may have been partially due to the lifestyle common in that era—one in which bathing was generally infrequent. Perfume may have provided a more appealing atmosphere than unwashed human bodies.

Eventually, the use of perfume and perfumed products expanded to the middle classes. By the end of the nineteenth century, fragrances were a part of many women's feminine wardrobe along with fine clothing and jewelry. Fragrance use has since expanded dramatically—especially since the creation of cheap, artificial scents. Scents (either naturally derived or synthetic) are now added to nearly all manufactured cosmetics, toiletries, and cleaning products.

Natural Essential Oils and Perfumes

Until relatively recently, virtually all perfumes and scented products used naturally derived *essential oils*. The adjective *essential* refers to the medieval alchemist's belief that these extracts were the very essence of certain plants. Since that time, chemists have scientifically analyzed essential oils. They're actually complex organic compounds—mostly mixtures of particular hydrocarbons known as *terpenes*.

To extract essential oils, steam distillation is commonly used. In this procedure, volatile compounds evaporate from plant materials (leaves, flowers, bark, seeds, roots, or wood) in the presence of hot vapor and then condense in water. Further processing removes this water, leaving a highly concentrated essential oil. Today, there are approximately two hundred commercially produced essential oils. Three very popular ones are orange blossom, jasmine, and rose.

The perfumes of the past, and the natural ones of today, not only contain essential oils but also other ingredients derived from nature. These may include some resins (plant solids or semisolids that don't readily evaporate) and animal substances such as civet (cat scent), musk (deer scent), castor (beaver scent), and ambergris (sperm-whale intestinal secretions). Other possible ingredients are balsams, which are fragrant fluids from certain tree species. Perfumes also usually have fixatives which help bind all these components together and equalize their evaporation rates. By the way, some fixatives are the same previously mentioned fragrant plant resins and animal ingredients; it isn't unusual for a substance to serve dual purposes within a perfume's formula.

Once a satisfactory blend of essential oils, resins, and animal substances is achieved, it's then diluted with alcohol, chilled, filtered, and aged. Perfume has the highest concentration of non-alcohol ingredients, while cologne has a lower concentration. The lowest concentration of non-alcohol ingredients is in toilet water.

Synthetic Scents and Perfumes

Today, natural scents are generally being replaced by synthetic ones. These man-made counterfeits are used in everything from pine-tree car deodorizers and kitchen garbage bags, to the most exquisite designer perfumes. No longer associated with special ritual, religion, wealth, or even sexual seduction, cheap synthetic scents, and products using them, are now virtually omnipresent.

For the most part, synthetic scents have existed for only about a hundred years. However, since the first ones were created, a synthetic fragrance (and flavor) industry has developed and expanded rapidly. The reason is simple—the cost savings of producing synthetics, compared to finding, growing, gathering, and processing naturally aromatic ingredients into essential oils is enormous. A pound of natural ingredients (tuber rose for example) can cost as much as four thousand times more than a pound of a synthetic version.

Today, with gas chromatography and mass spectroscopy, scientists can map out the chemical structures of almost any natural ingredient. With this information, they're then able to create close copies by manipulating simple organic-molecule building blocks. These *builder molecules* are often originally derived from petroleum. Once a prototype for a synthetic essence has been achieved, it can be duplicated on a commercial basis.

Although some natural aromas (such as coffee) cannot yet be synthesized, other natural fragrances continue to be analyzed and simulated. Two popular laboratory creations are synthetic wild cherry (benzaldehyde) and synthetic rose (B-phenylethyl alcohol). These two fragrances have relatively simple formulations, but many synthetic scents contain hundreds of individual components. Interestingly, some of the newer scents no longer attempt to mimic natural ones. Instead, they convey such intangibles as *fresh* and *clean*.

Even if you just consider women's fine bottled perfumes, it's likely that many of them contain at least some synthetic scents—no matter what the price tag. In fact, they may also contain synthetic fixatives and other man-made additives such as methyl ethyl ketone, formaldehyde, etc. These synthetic components are often considered, by the fragrance industry, to be safe, but a number of them have already been shown to have negative health effects. Unfortunately, the truth is, many modern scent and perfume ingredients have had only minimal toxicity testing—or none at all. Interestingly, it's precisely because of this concern that The Environmental Health Network of California recently filed a petition with the U.S. FDA (Federal Food and Drug Administration) to have one popular perfume, Calvin Klein's Eternity, declared "mislabeled." The group is asking for a printed warning on the product stating that the ingredients used in its formulation have not been adequately tested. (Note: At this time, the outcome of this petition has not been decided.)

Problems with Scents

Anymore, the majority of Americans accept fragrances, scents, incense, potpourri, etc. as a part of daily life. In fact, a growing number of people feel that scents are not only pleasurable, but beneficial. Popular therapies now focus on applying certain aromatic oils to the body or heating particular fragrant oils so they'll evaporate into the room air to be inhaled. "Aroma therapy" has become big business. Yet, there is another side to fragrances and scents that needs to be seriously considered. That is, while most people are not aware of any ill effects, *any* natural or synthetic odor has the capacity to be unpleasant or irritating—at least to some people. A survey taken not long ago in North Carolina found that 4% of the population admitted that perfumes and other scented products "made them feel sick."

Certain fragrances, aromas, and perfumes can actually provoke allergic or asthmatic responses. In fact, the U.S. Food and Drug Administration (FDA) has reported that perfume-provoked respiratory symptoms are experienced by 72% of all asthmatics. And a great many people with MCS (Multiple Chemical Sensitivity, see *Multiple Chemical Sensitivity* on page 45) also report that they, too, experience negative reactions when they inhale scents and perfumes. But that's still not the full extent of the possible ill effects from being exposed to fragrances.

In "Patient Education: Scents Make No Sense" in the Fall 1991 issue of *The Environmental Physician*, author Irene Ruth Wilkenfeld wrote that in 1989 The National Institute of Occupational Safety and Health (NIOSH) recognized 884 of 2,983 substances (both naturally and synthetically derived) used in the fragrance industry as toxic. Some of these ingredients actually act as *neurotoxins*—that is, they're capable of harming the central nervous system. For example, linalool (a clear fragrant terpene alcohol compound obtained from several types of essential oils) has been reported to cause ataxic gait (an abnormal stride due to loss of muscle coordination in the extremities) and depression. Methyl ethyl ketone (a colorless, flammable solvent that's commonly synthesized) has the capacity to induce stupor and unconsciousness. Cyclohexanol (a clear flammable synthesized solvent with a peppermint-like odor) can inhibit motor activity and instigate spasms, and generally depresses the central nervous system. And on and on. **Anderson Laboratories, Inc.** (an independent research company), decided to perform some testing in order to determine what effects, if any, four colognes and one toilet water made with these types of ingredients would produce in mice inhaling them. Sadly, the results consistently showed that the mice experienced irritation of the eyes, nose, throat, and lungs and that there was decreased air flow in their lungs as in asthmatic attacks. The research also revealed that a number of the mice had neurotoxic symptoms such as loss of balance and abnormal gait. Worse, some of the mice tested actually died. These results were eventually published in a peer-review scientific journal. (Note: Copies of this article, as well as a video of the mouse/fragrance test, can be purchased from **Anderson Laboratories, Inc.**)

While the majority of people have not been obviously or severely impacted from being exposed to perfume and fragrance ingredients, it is also probably true that increasing numbers of people are being affected by them—at least to some lesser degree. In any case, many of the compounds used in scents and perfumes don't appear to be innately safe or healthy for humans.

As fragrances and scented products have become more popular (it has been estimated that the average consumer now uses about twenty scented personal-care items each day), the interiors of our homes have been absorbing more of these potentially bothersome (and/or illness provoking) odors. Unfortunately, fragrances which are inherently designed to quickly spread are often extremely difficult to remove from skin, hair, walls, floors, and furnishings. It's no wonder then that the term *ineluctable* has been applied to the use of scents. This big word conveys the simple idea that fragrances are now virtually impossible to evade—at least totally. By the way, many people don't realize that some of the various scent ingredients can actually chemically interact with each other—creating new, totally unplanned synthetic compounds. No one can even guess what health effects these compounds could ultimately induce.

Interestingly, negative sensory and aesthetic consequences are seldom, if ever, discussed as problems associated with perfumes and scents—but from all indications they should be. Because fragrances can be found nearly everywhere all the time, many people are unable to perceive that a background of perfume and scent odors is even present. Surrounded and saturated by no-longer-discernible odors, some individuals (usually women, but increasingly men) feel they must apply large amounts of bottled perfume to their bodies in order to know they even have it on. The resulting wafting odor is often unpleasantly strong to those people who have been trying to avoid scents, or at least minimize their exposure to them. By the way, the intensity of their perfumes would probably be unpleasantly strong to those same perfume wearers if they, too, were trying to avoid using or being around scented products for a few weeks and re-acquired their normal sense of smell.

Also, from an aesthetic standpoint, being constantly in the presence (consciously or unconsciously) of scents could tend to diminish some of life's special moments. For example, being in the presence of a magnificent blooming lavender bush or at the edge of a pounding ocean could be sensed just as "nice" smells amid the ever-present daily barrage of other "nice" smells—from hand lotion, eye shadow, bath beads, shampoo, deodorant, fabric softener, dishwasher detergent, window cleaner, and toilet tissue. As a result, real-world events can be lost or at least watered down by the banal and contrived olfactory experiences of everyday life.

Perhaps not surprisingly, there are individuals who have decided they'd like to avoid the many scents to which others have grown accustomed. This decision is often reached when they find their own personal health has been (and usually continues to be) seriously affected by fragrances. Unfortunately, it requires real determination to limit scent and perfume exposure—especially in situations outside your own home. The truth is, you probably will have very little control over what products are used in public buildings, public transportation, other dwellings, or on other people. Even within your own residence, if you decide to create a scent-free environment, it'll take a great deal of resolve and personal commitment. However, it can be done—and using unscented personal-care and cleaning products is key to doing this. Therefore, before buying, making, or using any personal-care preparation or cleaning product, seriously consider the probable odor consequences.

Scent-Free and Hypoallergenic Products

Today, people who find scents and perfumes bothersome or intolerable often try name-brand toiletries and cleaning products labeled *scent-free* or *fragrance-free*. Usually such items have formulas similar to the standard varieties, but they contain no scent additives. However, many name-brand, sent-free laundry products are exactly the same as regular formula products with the addition of a *masking fragrance* to counter the odor of the original scent. For many individuals, these types of low-odor products are quite acceptable alternatives.

In addition, complete product lines of specially created *hypoallergenic* cosmetic and personal-care items are available. In most cases, however, only the most commonly allergenic substances are left out of these formulations—ingredients such as fragrances and/or lanolin. Unfortunately, sometimes other ingredients remain that many people would consider undesirable. For example, until very recently, at least one hypoallergenic shampoo was still made with formaldehyde. By the way, both scent-free versions of conventional products, as well as those labeled hypoallergenic, often contain many synthetic compounds.

Products Developed for the Chemically Sensitive

There are a number of smaller alternative companies that originally developed their product lines with chemically-sensitive and/or highly allergic individuals in mind. Some of these make only toiletries, others only household cleaning products, while some manufacturer both personal-care and cleaning products. As it turns out, most of the company philosophies, and resulting formula choices, fall into two major categories.

The first of these are lines stressing minimal odor and non-reaction provoking ingredients. As a rule, these manufacturers include some simple synthetic ingredients such as very-low-odor surfactants. In many cases, these have been vegetable-derived. Some products lines making both toiletries and cleaning items in this group include Granny's Old Fashioned Products (**Granny's Old Fashioned Products**), and Safe Choice (**AFM**). Although EnviroRite (**BioForce Enviro-Tech, Inc.**) does not disclose the nature of its ingredients, the company's line likely best fits into this first category. Allens Naturally (**Allens Naturally**) has only cleaning products and Simple (**Smith & Nephew Consumer Products, Ltd.**) just toiletries.

Lifetime Solutions' (**Lifetime Solutions, Ltd.**) biodegradable, non-toxic, non-caustic products also fit into this first group—but with a twist. Ingredients such as amino acids, vegetable-based acids, nonionic surfactants, and others "are blended at specific time intervals, temperatures, and sequences." This is done until they lose their former individual properties and characteristics and become what's known as *colloidal micelles*. These extremely minute molecular structures remain in suspension and have the capacity to attract and break up oil molecules. Once fragmented, the oil can be much more easily rinsed away.

Product lines in the second group focus on the absolute "all-naturalness" of their ingredients as key to minimizing reactions. Many of these firms utilize citrus extracts as base ingredients, so there's usually a mild, but detectable, citrus odor surrounding their use. Some brands making both personal-care and cleaning products of this kind include Nature Clean (**Frank T. Ross & Sons, Ltd.**) and LifeKind (**LifeKind Products**).

Virtually all the product lines in this entire section are not only less-toxic and safer than most their conventional counterparts, they also contain no dyes, artificial preservatives, or artificial fragrances. Most are very low odor. In fact the majority have no added scents of any kind. Still, it is cautioned that all sensitive persons test *every* prospective product before using it. (See *Testing* on page 62). And, it is important to note here that while product lines in this section are a boon to hypersensitive people, they can be ideal choices for everyone.

Another warning should be added here. A few cleaning products, especially name-brand hand dish washing detergents now say "Sensitive Formula" or words to that effect on them. One company spokesman of such a product said this *does not* mean that their liquid dish detergent was formulated for highly allergic or chemically sensitive people. Rather, it means that the normally added dyes have been eliminated and milder surfactants have been used. (See *Soaps V. Detergents* on page 75 for a discussion). In other words, these are simply standard, perfumed products that are less likely to cause dry or irritated skin.

Soaps Vs. Detergents

What exactly is soap? What is detergent? Many home cleaning products are classified as either soaps or detergents. Interestingly, many people really don't know what these everyday words mean. However, it's a good idea to take the time to learn, so you can understand their basic similarities and differences. That way, you can better judge what types of products will meet your personal cleaning preferences.

Soaps

Soaps have a long history. They've been used to clean for thousands of years—at least in certain parts of the world. However, it wasn't until the ancient Greek era and then the Roman age that soap making techniques were better understood and the product became somewhat more consistent. Later, during the Middle Ages, a number of towns in Spain, England, and France became well known as important soap-making centers. Yet, producing soap still remained a relatively slow and difficult process that usually yielded soaps of low or varying quality.

It was not until the 1800s that soap and soap-making changed much. At that time, with the emergence of modern chemistry and the industrial revolution, exact formulas, processes, and machinery were finally developed. As a result, soap manufacturing finally began to take place on a large scale. That trend continued, so that today in the U.S. there are literally hundreds of different types and brands of soap available. Despite other alternatives in the marketplace, soap remains the most popular skin-cleaning product. However, since the development of detergents, soaps are no longer commonly used for washing hair, dishes, laundry, or general housework.

By definition, soaps consist of natural animal fats and/or plant oils combined with some form of lye, usually *sodium hydroxide* (NaOH$_3$, which is a white, water-soluble, solid, caustic compound sometimes known as *caustic soda*). Soap comes in bars, liquids, flakes, and granular forms. Unfortunately, soaps used in *hard water* (water with a high calcium and magnesium content) create a scum known as *soap curd*. Soap curd is an insoluble, white, solid matter formed when the dissolved calcium and magnesium react with the fats and oils making up the soap. Soap curd reduces the effectiveness of any soap to clean well and, at the same time, creates a scum on sinks, tubs, etc. that can be difficult to remove.

Soaps are able to clean because they contain natural *surfactants* (__surf__ace __act__ing compounds). Surfactants are necessary because they counter the effects of normally occurring *surface tension* in wash water. In water droplets that do not contain surfactants, the water molecules are much more attracted to each other than they are to the surrounding air molecules. This causes the droplets to pull in (or tense) on themselves, creating comparatively large, rubbery-surfaced spheres.

However, water containing surfactants behaves quite differently. This is because all surfactant molecules have one end which attracts water molecules (a *hydrophilic polar end*) and an opposite end that doesn't (a *hydrophobic non-polar end*). Therefore, the presence of these "strangely" behaving surfactant molecules alters the usual attraction patterns in water droplets, which would otherwise cause them to pull tightly inward. The lowered surface tension results in relatively small water droplets having surfaces that are less rubbery. These smaller droplets can more easily form very thin sheets of water, as in soap bubbles, therefore more suds are possible. Smaller droplets are also better able to penetrate and lift up dirt particles as well as keep them in suspension. Finally, smaller droplets permit more thorough rinsing. All of these factors contribute to better cleaning.

Detergents

Because the fats and oils in soaps create problems with soap scum, detergents were developed. This actually occurred fairly recently, during the 1930s, when very simple *unbuilt detergents* were first created. These early granular products consisted simply of one or more naturally derived surfactant compounds. Although they did reduce the water's surface tension and didn't form as much scum, they didn't clean as effectively as was expected. As a result, after World War II the first modern *built detergents* were created and marketed. Generally, these detergent formulas contained synthetically derived surfactants originating ultimately from crude oil and additional builder ingredients. These included substances such as phosphates, carbonates, silicates, amines, zeolites, sodium EDTA, and sodium sulfates. (Minute quantities of metals such as cadmium, lead, mercury, and arsenic were also frequently present as contaminants.) These builder compounds further controlled the minerals in hard water, increased the alkalinity, and enhanced the surfactants' capacity to lower the water's surface tension. Eventually, other ingredients were added to certain detergent formulas, including compounds to prevent dirt particles that are suspended in the water from redepositing themselves, *oil emulsifiers* (compounds able to stabilize oil in water), *opti-*

cal brighteners (compounds able to give cleaned items the appearance of being whiter), bleaching agents, suds-controlling compounds, perfumes, and dyes.

Despite their cleaning advantages, over the years detergents have had certain problems. For example, virtually all the early detergents used surfactants that couldn't biodegrade easily. Because of this, huge quantities of foamy suds began forming and accumulating in American sewers and waterways in the 1950s and early 1960s. Another major concern has been with certain phosphate-containing ingredients. As it turns out, when these phosphate compounds dissolve in water they release phosphorus. When the phosphorus reaches lakes and streams, it acts as a fertilizer, causing algae and other aquatic plants to proliferate much too rapidly. The resulting overgrowth, or *blooms*, can create unbalanced ecosystems in which algae and plants clog the surface of the water.

Fortunately, since 1965, all laundry detergents in the U.S. are now voluntarily made to be biodegradable. Also, the amount of phosphate content has been either lowered or eliminated. (Certain states and localities have completely banned all phosphate containing detergents.) To compensate for the cleaning effectiveness that has been lost through phosphate reduction or removal, a number of other ingredients (such as the optical brighteners mentioned earlier) are now commonly added.

Today, you can buy detergents in granular, gel, and liquid forms. Although most detergents contain totally synthetic formulas, a few are being made with naturally derived compounds. Because of their effectiveness, detergents are now used for most cleaning jobs. That is, except for washing skin—although there are some detergents designed to do that as well.

Should You Use Soap or Detergent?

Both soaps and detergents contain surfactants that are able to lower wash water's surface tension. Therefore, both have the capacity to lift soil and suspend it in the water in order to clean. However, detergents have been specially designed to have these qualities enhanced— and to minimize soap scum. On the other hand, soaps tend to be made of mostly natural ingredients, while detergents generally are not. Also, soaps usually have simple formulas while most detergents contain a more complex variety of ingredients.

Of course, whether to use a soap or detergent is ultimately your own personal decision. However, for sensitive or highly allergic individuals, using any of the typically available soap and detergent brands may prove too bothersome. For such people, alternative unscented products with basic formulations in either category are often far more tolerable.

Government Regulations

Many Americans believe cleaning product manufacturers—and especially cosmetics and toiletries companies—have volumes of strict regulations they must follow. It's also commonly believed that their ingredients, products, and production lines are continually being monitored by government agencies. Unfortunately, these assumptions are wrong. In reality, the laws protecting citizens from potentially dangerous cleaning and personal-care products remain absent, minimal, or rarely enforced.

For many centuries, there were no laws whatsoever concerning cleaning products, cosmetics and toiletries. Finally, the public demanded some type of restrictions be placed on cosmetics at least. And so, in this country, government regulation began with the passage of the 1938 U.S. Federal Food, Drug, and Cosmetic Act. Its purpose was to stop mislabeling and product adulteration (the addition of dangerous or impure substances). A number of regulations have since followed. Now, clear, accurate labeling of all cosmetic ingredients (*except* flavorings, fragrances, and colors) is required. Also, laws forbid the use of known cancer-causing ingredients and the inclusion of some particular dangerous substances in certain products. For example, compounds containing mercury can no longer be used in skin preparations.

Despite these federal regulations, ingredients that some researchers and consumers consider potentially harmful still remain in some cosmetics. This is due to several factors, a major one being that cosmetic manufacturers are not required to register their company, products, ingredients, or adverse reactions with the Food and Drug Administration. Instead, experts on an industry-created Cosmetics Ingredient Review Board determine product safety. Even if the Board decides to take some action, company compliance is only voluntary. Even in situations where regulations require the Food and Drug Administration itself to get involved, cosmetic-industry surveillance is still very limited because of budgetary and personnel limitations. Therefore, in many respects, government supervision and enforcement is only superficial at best.

Actually, for many personal-care items, as well as certain ingredients in otherwise regulated products, there are few or no government requirements or restrictions at this time. As it turns out, many toiletries, such as soap, are not legally classified as cosmetics, and, therefore, are completely unregulated. The same is true for most personal and home cleaning products. Also, as previously noted, fragrance, dye, and flavoring ingredients, even in a legally classified cosmetic preparation, are exempt from product-labeling regulations. Unfortunately, this is particularly distressing because the single word "fragrance" on a product label can mean that hundreds of individual chemical components have been added—but exactly what they are, no consumer will ever know. Keep in mind, too, some product ingredients can remain unknown to the public because they're legally defined as *proprietary trade secrets*.

Reducing Conventional Household Allergens

With the dramatic increase in allergies and asthma, there's a growing population of people concerned with reducing allergens in their homes. Typically, those with conventional household allergies and/or asthma find their symptoms are commonly triggered by exposure to scents, pollen, pet dander, mold, cockroaches, and dust mites (or more accurately dust-mite body parts and feces). In most cases, using appropriate cleaning products and techniques, as well as personal care products, will go a long way toward increasing the well-being of not only the allergic or asthmatic member of the family, but also the entire household

First, by only choosing unscented products, reactions to fragrances can be greatly minimized (see *Scents Vs. Unscented Products* on page 70). Not bringing in flowers and filtering the air coming into a home can greatly reduce indoor pollen counts. (See *Pollen* on page 536 for more on reduction methods and appropriate filters.)

Pets can be kept outdoors and/or washed and groomed regularly to reduce dander problems (see *Household Pets* on page 468). Mold can be countered by fixing water leaks and controlling humid indoor conditions with proper ventilation and dehumidifiers. (See also

Chapter 22: Indoor Air Quality on page 521) And, the proper clean up of existing mold cultures should greatly reduce allergenic problems (see *Mold* on page 534). It's usually possible to rid your home of cockroaches, by thorough cleaning and the use of less-toxic insecticides (see *Cockroaches* on page 408).

However, dust mites are more complicated. Some common cleaning methods can make dust-mite reactions less frequent, such as laundering bedding. However, vacuuming your home can actually increase the amount of airborne dust-mite allergens. That is, unless an alternative vacuum cleaner is used (see *Vacuuming* on page 144). Then, too, washing your carpet to extract dust mites can have the reverse effect by increasing their populations. That is, unless a water soluble borate solution is used (see *Rug and Carpet Shampooing and Wet Extraction Cleaning* on page 158). The truth is, to deal with dust mites effectively, you'll need to follow an on-going comprehensive approach. For this, you'll need to read *Dust Mites* on page 410. Dust mites will also be covered in specific sections of some of the chapters that follow.

CHAPTER 4: PERSONAL CARE

Ideally, personal-care products should be readily available (either easy-to-find in local stores or through mail-order suppliers, or easy-to-make at home), convenient-to-use, effective, affordable, odor-free, nontoxic, biodegradable, organic, and simple in formulation. It would also be nice if they contained no endangered plant or animal by-products, were not tested on animals, contained no preservatives, had an inherently long shelf-life, and were packaged in recycled, natural materials that could, in turn, be recyclable. That is a long wish list. While there are a few such products, in most cases, compromises have to be made.

However, with the increasing variety of alternative products now being manufactured, and with the knowledge of how to create homemade ones, it's possible for even sensitive and highly allergic individuals to satisfactorily meet most of their personal-care needs. By the way, you'll want to check local pharmacies and health-food stores from time to time to see what acceptable choices they have in stock. After all, new products that may be suitable for you are coming out every day. Also, your local bookstore and library should have several books with natural, do-it-yourself recipes for personal-care products.

It's important to give yourself the freedom to experiment with preparations that are new to you. However, be sure to test any new product first, whether manufactured or home-made. This step is absolutely critical for sensitive or allergic individuals. (Remember, many personal-care formulas, especially homemade ones, contain food substances.) For those who are asthmatic, or who have experienced severe reactions in the past, such testing should only be done under the supervision of a physician or another health-care professional (see *Testing* on page 62).

At the end of this chapter there are listings of the most necessary personal-care items with some specific product suggestions. These suggestions (not recommendations) are likely to be tolerable even for very sensitive and allergic persons and they tend to have minimal odor. A number of all-natural preparations that happen to contain essential oils or aromatic base-ingredients are also included as alternative choices. However, as has been pointed out, this book stresses healthfulness to the individual and indoor air quality. Therefore, while other characteristics were taken into account, mild, unscented or low-odor, simple-formula, natural or synthetic products were given priority.

What are Cosmetics and Toiletries?

Cosmetics and toiletries are preparations that soothe, alter, or enhance the face, skin, and hair. They generally fall into several commonly recognized classifications. These include powders (minute granular materials which adhere to skin and absorb moisture), emulsions (oil particles dispersed in water such as creams and lotions), lipsticks (semisoft compounds made of oils, waxes, and pigments), eye make-up (often similar to lipstick or powder), and miscellaneous products (depilatories, deodorants, hair preparations, etc.).

Cosmetics have a long history, traceable to prehistoric rituals. Later, like scents, they became commonly used simply for personal pleasure. By the 1700s (sometimes known as the Age of Artifice), upper-class European men and women routinely whitened their faces, drew blue vein lines on their skin, and wore other forms of make-up. The Victorian Era ushered in a period of austerity in cosmetic and toiletry use. However, by the end of the nineteenth century the use of personal-care items, particularly cosmetics worn by women, greatly increased. This was due to several factors, including the beginnings of large-scale manufacturing and advertising, combined with a growing middle-class. Today, cosmetic and toiletry production and use continues to rise, especially since the creation of inexpensive synthetic ingredients. Men are also using more personal-care preparations and cosmetics, though not nearly to the same degree as women. Another trend is the use of make-up and toiletry items by girls at ever-earlier ages.

Early Natural and Synthetic Ingredients

During most of human history, the ingredients in personal-care products and cosmetics were derived from minerals, plants, and animals. Although they originated naturally, not all these products were safe. For example, lead dust was used for thousands of years for a white face powder. Later, early chemists brought other dangerous ingredients into the public's hands—red mercuric sulfide (lip colorant), sulfuric acid (hair bleach), and sublimate of mercury (wart and freckle lightener) to name just three. Surprisingly, these toxic products were often extremely popular, despite the risk of poisoning and disfiguring. Fortunately, most of the early hazardous preparations are now outlawed. However, surprisingly, a few highly noxious ingredients are still allowed limited use in certain applications (see *Government Regulations* on page 77).

Typical Modern Ingredients

Some of the ingredients used in today's personal-care preparations remain natural. Most of these are considered quite safe, but some do cause health problems. For example, talc (the natural mineral hydrous magnesium silicate) can cause lung problems if inhaled over time (talcosis). Other natural ingredients, such as certain plant oils, can produce skin and mucous-membrane irritation or pose other health risks.

While a few manufacturers use natural substances exclusively, the majority of today's cosmetics and toiletries contain synthetically derived ingredients. In many cases, these ultimately originate from petroleum or coal tar. A few of the more common synthetic-ingredient categories are dyes, flavoring agents, base components, preservatives, and scents. Many of the synthetic compounds in use have unpronounceable polysyllabic names combined with hyphenated numbers. However, while an intimidating name sometimes coincides with the potential for negative side effects, this is not always the case. As has been discussed earlier, *healthy* isn't a word with a simple, clear-cut definition, nor is it an effect or condition that's universally agreed upon and understood (see *Healthy Definitions* on page 59).

Of course, many natural ingredients have desirable properties—and they definitely have an aura of goodness about them. After all, some individuals choose to use only naturally derived products for very valid ecological, philosophical, medical, or spiritual reasons. But not every synthetic ingredient is bad; in fact, they vary considerably from one to another. Like natural ingredients, each synthetic ingredient has its own appearance, consistency, odor, effect on the environment, and toxicity. The known possible negative effects of synthetic personal-care substances range from none at all, to mild skin irritation, to chromosomal damage—and yes—even to cancer.

Of course, the precise heath effects of any ingredient (natural or synthetic) on a particular individual will depend on many factors. Some of these include the chemical make-up of the substance, the quantity used, the duration of use, and the susceptibility of the person using it. For example, the synthetic colorant FD&C Blue No. 1 can cause allergic reactions in some people while others seem to be unaffected. However, this same dye has been shown to be carcinogenic in animals when they're intentionally exposed to relatively large amounts over time. How will this same product affect you? No one can predict for sure.

At the same time, it should be kept in mind that many recently created synthetic ingredients have been used by the consuming public for only a few short years. As a result, there hasn't been enough time to establish a true history of what negative outcomes could conceivably occur. Thus, while it *appears* certain synthetic substances have not caused any health problems so far, the long-term effects are often relatively unknown. Because cosmetic and toiletry regulations are minimal, nonexistent, or poorly enforced, each of us must educate ourself to determine what to use and what to avoid. One source of more in-depth information is *The Consumer's Dictionary of Cosmetic Ingredients* by Ruth Winter. This and similar books should be available in your local library, or from your favorite bookseller.

Alternative Cosmetics and Toiletries

In many cases, sensitive and highly allergic individuals are best able to tolerate low-odor, mild, undyed, synthetic or natural-formula personal-care products better than all-natural formulations containing aromatic essential oils. However, remember that no expert can really say what is best for you, especially if you are allergic or sensitive. That is only gauged by your own personal research, testing, and experience. Below are some types of alternative personal-care items you may want to consider. (See also *Products Developed for the Chemically Sensitive* on page 74 and *Scent-Free and Hypoallergenic Products* on page 74.)

Items Created for the Chemically-Sensitive

There are alternative product lines that were first developed especially for the highly allergic and/or chemically sensitive population. Some companies focused on the "all-naturalness" of their products and made sure they had no added scents. Other manufacturers chose to use simple synthetic ingredients—stressing extremely low odor and mildness. No matter which approach was used, virtually all of these products were formulated without dyes, preservatives, or petrochemical derivatives that were likely to be bothersome.

Scent-Free and Hypoallergenic Products

As was mentioned in *Chapter 3: Basic Ingredients*, name-brand products labeled *un-scented*, *scent-free*, or *fragrance-free* usually have formulas similar to their regular counterparts—with the exception of added scents. On the other hand, some large cosmetic and toiletry companies have lines specifically marketed as *hypoallergenic*. As a rule, only the most common allergy-provoking substances (fragrance and/or lanolin, for example) are missing. Such products have been acceptable choices for many people, even some sensitive people. However, these products often have many synthetic ingredients, dyes, and preservatives that others find objectionable.

All-Natural Products

A few companies now produce skin and hair-care preparations that are *all-natural*. For a large segment of the population who are seeking alternative, eco-friendly products, these can be the best choice. Unfortunately, it seems that the term all-natural is rather loosely defined. Therefore, some products labeled as having all-natural ingredients may actually contain components considered synthetic by some companies. Two such ambiguously classified ingredients are sodium lauryl (an emulsifier) and methyl paraben (a preservative).

Another potential concern with many all-natural products is that they often contain essential oils or other highly aromatic ingredients. This may be a problem for certain allergic or sensitive individuals, or for those who have simply decided to avoid fragrances.

A few books are now out there dealing specifically with all-natural cosmetics and toiletries. *Natural Organic Hair and Skin Care* by Aubrey Hampton is one of them. Its 400-plus pages not only covers ingredients, but has skin care and hair care guides. Among other sources, it may be purchased from **Aubrey Organics**.

Homemade Preparations

Instead of purchasing ready-made body-care preparations, you can create them yourself at home from scratch. Because you select the ingredients yourself, you will have complete knowledge and control over what will be applied to your skin or hair. If you want, you can use only organic ingredients.

Remember, of course, that making homemade products will require you to first obtain the necessary vegetables, fruits, grains, clays, etc. It'll also be necessary for you to take the time to cut, mash, mix, or do whatever else is necessary for proper preparation. Also, you should keep in mind that your homemade products could have very short shelf-lives; in many cases they could become quickly contaminated by mold and bacteria. Therefore, without preservatives, certain homemade preparations may need to be stored in a refrigerator and used chilled, or heated on a warm stove each time they are used. And they will need to be thrown out regularly as they go bad, and new batches will need to be made to replace them as needed.

If you decide to make your own skin and hair-care preparations, it's undoubtedly easiest to use already established formulas and methods. One book you may find helpful is *The Natural Beauty Book: Cruelty Free Cosmetics to Make at Home* by Anita Guyton. Around for many years, this British guide provides a wide variety of natural cosmetic recipes. Of course, there are other books, especially on soap making. So, check your local library, or your favorite bookseller, if you are interested in creating your own toiletry products.

Personal-Care Product Suggestions

Following are suggestions for a variety of specific personal-care products that are healthier than most of the commonly available, off-the-shelf preparations that are in stores. Most of the following have been found suitable for allergic or chemically sensitive people. However, no personal care product is universally tolerable for all people, so you must decide for yourself—based on the discussion in the first half of this chapter—which criteria to use in selecting items for your own personal use.

Astringents

Most astringents sold in stores are alcohol-based and some come with an added perfume. All of these should probably be avoided, not only because of the odor (which many sensitive and certain allergic persons would find bothersome), but also because of their drying effect on skin.

A few all-natural lines using essential oils, herbs, and botanicals offer astringents. For example, Aubrey Organics Herbal Astringent is made with a witch-hazel base and herbal extracts. Order it directly from **Aubrey Organics** or from **Natural Lifestyle**. Ecco Bella Purifying Toner (**E.B. Botanicals, Inc.**) is made with apple-cider vinegar and witch hazel. You can buy it form the company or from **Internatural**. Aloe & Green Tea (**Kiss My Face**) is available from the manufacturer, or from **Frontier Natural Products, N.E.E.D.S.**, and **Tucson Cooperative Warehouse**.

A good alcohol-free low-odor astringent can be made simply with equal amounts of hot water and apple-cider vinegar. Other homemade options include cold chamomile tea, fresh lemon juice in cool water, strained cucumber juice, and strained tomato pulp. If you plan to use tomato pulp, you'll want to leave it on your skin a few minutes. Then, you can rinse it off with tepid water. Generally, refrigerating any of your natural preparations will allow them to keep for a few days.

Baby Care

A low-odor liquid Castile soap perfect for many infants is Dr. Bronner's Baby Supermild Unscented Castile Soap Liquid (**Dr. Bronner's**). Although commonly found in health-food stores, if you choose, you can order it directly from the company, or from **Tucson Cooperative Warehouse, Karen's Natural Products**, and **Frontier Natural Products**.

If you want to use a bar soap on your baby that is especially formulated for infants, try Babykins Face and Body Soap. This is a fragrance-free Castile bar made with olive oil, cocoa butter, and aloe vera. A mail-order source is **TerrEssentials**. Dr. Bronner's Magic Baby Supermild Unscented Soapbar (**Dr. Bronner's**) is a bar form of their liquid baby Castile soap. Buy it at health-food stores or order it directly from the company. Dr. Bronner products are also sold by **Tucson Cooperative Warehouse, Karen's Natural Products,** and **Frontier Natural Products.**

There is a tearless shampoo formula that can be appropriate called Gently Yours (**Granny's Old Fashioned Products**). All Granny's Old Fashioned Products are formulated without scents, dyes, or phosphates. This line can sometimes be found in health-food stores. Mail-order sources include **The Living Source, N.E.E.D.S., Bio Designs, Allergy Relief Shop, Inc., American Environmental Health Foundation,** and **Health One Co.** By the way, the **Coastline Products** catalog offers Granny's shampoos under its own label: Coastline Old Fashioned. Also, for your infant's hair, a beech wood-handle, goat-hair bristle Baby Hair Brush can be purchased from **Natural Baby.**

Most parents want the convenience of boxed baby wipes. However, most brand-name baby wipes are made with alcohol. Tushies Baby Wipes (**RMED International, Inc.**) are alcohol-free. They contain aloe and a naturally-derived "light scent." Check your local alternative grocery or health-food store or order from the manufacturer. Seventh Generation Baby Wipes (**Seventh Generation**) are very similar and are also commonly found at alternative retailers. In addition, they can be mail-ordered from **Harmony, Tucson Cooperative Warehouse,** and ordered on-line from GreenMarketplace.com.

For a baby lotion, you may find some of the options listed under *Moisturizers* below suitable. One homemade baby oil you can try is a combination of wheat germ oil, apricot oil, and vitamin E oil. (Remember: If you have any questions about the appropriateness of certain natural oils or manufactured products, always check with your pediatrician or family physician first.) Aubrey Organics Natural Baby & Kids Body Lotion (**Aubrey Organics**), which is made with herbs, aloe and almond oil, is another choice you might make. You can order it from the company or **EcoBaby Organics.** A soothing salve formulated especially for infants is Heaven's Essence Chinese Herbal Healing Salve available from **TerrEssentials.** It's a natural botanical preparation for diaper rash with no added fragrance.

If you choose to use a powder on your baby, use it sparingly. Powders can easily become airborne and can enter the respiratory system causing irritation. It should also be noted that talcum powder (which many name-brand powders contain) is made of purified ground talc, a powdered magnesium silicate. There's concern that this may be implicated in the lung disease talcosis.

Another note of caution: Although baking soda can be a good choice as a powder for adults, you'll want to avoid using it as a powder applied directly on your baby's skin. As better alternatives, many parents have found that corn starch or arrowroot powder work well, or a combination of the two. Another choice is to use rice starch. Arrowroot powder and rice starch are often sold in bulk at health-food stores, but they will be costlier and hardier to find than corn starch. Then, too, there are manufactured products you might opt for. One is Mountain Rose Baby's Body Powder Unscented which is made with fine white clay, arrowroot, and herbs. It can be purchased from **Simmons Natural Bodycare.** Another talc-free, no-fragrance-added choice is Heaven's Essence Chinese Herbal Baby Powder handled by **TerrEssentials.**

Bath Soaks

Womenkind offers organic rice bran and cotton sacks to put it in. Simply fill a sack and place it in your tub to provide a soothing bathsoak. They're available from **Natural Lifestyle.** Unscented Dead Sea Mineral Bath Salts are an interesting option. Purchase them from

TerrEssentials. Mineral Salts Unscented from **Karen's Natural Products** is also a Dead-Sea salt preparation. Usually, such products contain naturally occurring minerals such as chloride, bromide, sulfate, sodium, potassium, magnesium, calcium, and lithium.

By dissolving 1/2 cup of baking soda in a tub of tepid water, you can create a soothing bath that will neutralize perspiration odors. You might also want to try pouring 1/2 gallon of milk in a tub of tepid bath water, followed by a shower to rinse, to help nourish your skin.

Aromatic botanical-ingredient soaks are available from **Kiss My Face**, **Frontier Natural Products**, **N.E.E.D.S.**, and **Tucson Cooperative Warehouse**.

Blackhead Therapy

If you have acne or severe blackheads, it would be best for you to consult a physician. However, for milder conditions you may want to try a number of simple solutions. For example, a mixture made of equal parts of baking soda and water can be gently rubbed on the face to loosen blackheads. Also, fresh lemon juice can help remove blackheads, and at the same time, lighten the presence of any that remain. Another option is to boil 2 teaspoons of rosemary in a pint of distilled water. You can then carefully place your face in the steam to open the pores.

Combs, Brushes, and Scrubbers

Combs made of metal, bone, or wood are excellent all-natural choices, often both attractive and long-lasting. The same goes for boar-bristle brushes with hardwood handles. To purchase natural combs and brushes for your hair, check catalogs such as **Simmons Natural Bodycare**, **Allergy Relief Shop, Inc.**, **The Body Shop**, **Natural Lifestyle**, **Vermont Country Store Apothecary**, **Fuller Brush Co.**, **Caswell-Massey Co., Ltd.**, **Inner Balance**, **TerrEssentials**, and **Janice Corporation**. Also, **Frontier Natural Products** has hardwood-handle brushes with either natural or nylon bristles for adults and children. Widu wood-handle, wood-bristle combs and brushes can be purchased from **Karen's Natural Products**.

For your face, beechwood-handled, natural-bristle complexion brushes are offered in the **TerrEssentials** catalog. **Karen's Natural Products** has natural-cellulose facial sponges.

Vermont Country Store Apothecary sells hardwood-handle, natural-bristle body/bath brushes, as does **Natural Lifestyle**, **Frontier Natural Products**, **Simmons Natural Bodycare**, and the **Tom's of Maine** catalog. In addition, **Karen's Natural Products** offers wood-handled, vegetable-fiber bath brushes.

After you've purchased natural brushes, you'll occasionally need to wash them—gently so they aren't damaged. You'll find that using a mild shampoo works well to clean away dirt and body oil without harming the brush fibers. Afterwards, you should rinse the brushes with warm, clear water, shake out the excess water, shape any soft fibers with your fingers, then air-dry.

For scrubbing, natural *loofa* scrubbers work well. They're made of the interior of certain dried fibrous tropical gourds. Other good natural scrubbers, that are commonly available, are made from woven grasses such as sisal. To find natural scrubbers, you'll first want to see what your local health-food store handles. If you prefer mail-order, **Simmons Natural Bodycare** offers loofa scrubbers and *ayates* (Mexican natural-fiber washcloths). Loofas with wooden handles, loofa mitts, wooden-handled sisal bath brushes, and other natural scrubbers are available through **Frontier Natural Products**. Loofa and sea sponges (*porifera*) are offered in the **Tom's of Maine** catalog as well as **Karen's Natural Products**. You can order sisal scrubbers and natural Flax Exfoliating Bricks from **The Body Shop**.

See *Dental Care* next for toothbrushes, *Make-Up* on page 97 for cosmetic brushes, and *Shaving Needs* on page 102 for shaving brushes.

Dental Care

Fluoride has been a mainstay in most toothpastes in America for decades. Today, it's usually at the concentration of 4,000 ppm (parts per million) of fluoride. While the American Dental Association (ADA) still recommends fluoride as an aid to reduce tooth decay, there are vocal critics who feel it is a harmful additive. In any case, you should be aware of relatively new warnings now required on fluoride-containing toothpastes. They read: "Children 2-6 years: Use only a pea-sized amount...(and) minimize swallowing...Under 2 years: Ask your dentist or physician." "Warning: Keep out of the reach of children under 6 years of age. In case of accidental ingestion, seek professional assistance or contact a Poison Control Center immediately." Fluoride, it seems, is potentially toxic and definitely controversial. So, seriously consider if you do, or do not, want fluoridated dental products. (For more on fluoride see *Fluoride* on page 588.)

A more benign dentifrice is baking soda (sodium bicarbonate). It has been used successfully for many years as a toothpowder. So has table salt. Both of these are low-cost, effective, and safe choices you may want to try—as long as you're not on a low-sodium diet. In addition, baking soda can be mixed with 3% dilution hydrogen peroxide (the concentration usually sold in pharmacies) to be used as a good tooth whitener. For those who want added minty freshness, **Allergy Relief Shop, Inc.** offers Salt'N'Soda toothpowder made with salt, sodium bicarbonate and peppermint oil.

You might already be aware that a number of alternative dental products are now being manufactured. Peelu Tooth Fiber (**Peelu USA**) is one. It's a tooth powder derived from *salvadora perisia* shrub fiber. In the Mideast and Asia, where the plant grows, it's been used to clean teeth for centuries. Peelu is a beige, slightly gritty product that's normally marketed with a natural mint (peppermint or spearmint) oil as a flavoring agent. It is also made without flavoring as "mint-free." If you don't care for tooth powders, Peelu Toothpaste (**Peelu USA**) is an option. Beside peelu, it contains sorbitol (derived from mountain ash berry juice) and tea tree oil, among other ingredients. Peelu Toothpaste comes in peppermint, spearmint, cinnamon, or mint-free. Peelu products can be ordered directly from the company or from **Frontier Natural Products** and **Karen's Natural Products**.

Of course, there are several other all-natural toothpastes you might want to try. A popular one is Tom's of Maine Natural Toothpaste (**Tom's of Maine**) which is available with or without fluoride in several natural flavors. This particular brand is commonly sold in heath-food stores, but it can also be ordered from the company's own catalog, or from **Frontier Natural Products, American Environmental Health Foundation, Tucson Cooperative Warehouse**, and **N.E.E.D.S.**

Logona Toothpaste (**Logona USA, Inc.**) is another all-natural toothpaste with no added fluoride. Purchase it directly from the company or suppliers such as **Internatural**. You should also be aware that **Janice Corporation** and **Natural Lifestyle** catalogs handle several other alternative toothpastes as does **Allergy Relief Shop, Inc.** and **Karen's Natural Products**.

Janice Corporation offers natural-bristle toothbrushes with wood handles. Other sources for wood-handle, natural-bristle toothbrushes include **Allergy Relief Shop, Inc., Caswell-**

Massey Co., Ltd., and **Karen's Natural Products** who also sells a children's version. Natural-bristle toothbrushes with plastic handles are sold in **Tom's of Maine** and **Simmons Natural Bodycare** catalogs. Fuchs natural boar-bristle toothbrushes for both adults and children are sold by **Frontier Natural Products**. Natural bristle tooth brushes can also be purchased from **American Environmental Health Foundation**. Ekotek hard cellulose-handled toothbrushes with replaceable nylon-bristle heads can be found in the **Simmons Natural Bodycare** catalog.

Most dental floss today is made of nylon. Fortunately, this is a material which is generally well-tolerated by many sensitive persons. This is especially true for unwaxed and unflavored types. One national brand, Butler Fine-Thickness Shred-Resistant Floss (**John O. Butler Co.**) is available unwaxed and unflavored in disposable plastic packages. In addition, the company offers a small, plastic, barrel-shaped refillable dispenser. Two-hundred yard refills come on styrofoam spools. John O. Butler products can be ordered directly form the company or bought (or ordered) at many local pharmacies. If you do prefer waxed, one interesting possibility is Desert Essence Tea Tree Dental Floss made with natural wax and tea tree oil which is available from **Karen's Natural Products**. (See *First Aid* on page 94 for information on tea tree oil.)

As a rule, the majority of typical mouthwashes are primarily artificially dyed and flavored alcohol solutions. However, Tom's of Maine Natural Baking Soda Mouthwash Alcohol-Free (**Tom's of Maine**) comes in natural peppermint and ginger/mint flavors. You can order from the company or from **Frontier Natural Products, Tucson Cooperative Warehouse, N.E.E.D.S.**, or **American Environmental Health Foundation**. You'll also want to check your local health-food stores to see if it's available there. An all-natural, inexpensive, unflavored mouthwash is simply a solution of water with a pinch of dissolved table salt. One teaspoon of baking soda added to a half glass of water will also help neutralize mouth odors. If you're on a low-sodium diet, you might prefer to gargle using equal parts of 3% dilution hydrogen peroxide and water.

Deodorants

Many of the deodorants and antiperspirants on the market are scented or they contain potentially bothersome ingredients—and they're usually expensive, too. Fortunately, there are better alternatives. For example, baking soda makes a good, low-cost, natural deodorant powder. However, it has a tendency to leave a white ring on dark clothing. Cornstarch can be substituted—but it can be messy, too.

Instead, you may want to try one of the unscented, hypoallergenic deodorants or antiperspirants. These are sold in pump, cream, or roll-on forms under nationally distributed brand names in many drugstores. However, you should be aware that hypoallergenic deodorants and antiperspirants usually contain a variety of synthetic ingredients, and in most cases, aluminum as well. As you may already know, aluminum deposits found in the brain have been associated with Alzheimer's disease. Until more is understood about the connection of aluminum to this disorder, it might be wise to avoid personal-care products containing this ingredient.

If you're seeking an alternative deodorant that is effective, non-marking, natural, unscented, and aluminum-free, a good choice is Crystal Body Deodorant (formerly Le Crystal Naturel) (**French Transit Ltd.**). In its original form, it's a fist-sized chunk of alum mineral salts. Crystal Body Deodorant is now also sold in smooth, solid push-up, liquid roll-on, and a liquid spray. You can order all varieties directly from the company or some types (usually the chunk form) from mail-order sources including **Janice Corporation**, **Harmony**, and **Karen's Natural Products**. Since this brand was originally marketed, other similar products are commonly seen. For example, Fragrance-Free Liquid Rock (**Kiss My Face**), a roll-on, is one. You can purchases this particular brand from the company or from **Tucson Cooperative Warehouse**, **N.E.E.D.S.**, and **Frontier Natural Products**. Lifekind Unscented Crystallite (**Lifekind Products**) is a liquid, mineral-salt and water solution in a pump spray. Order it directly from the company catalog.

All these all-alum mineral products act as deodorants, but not antiperspirants. They work by inhibiting bacterial growth on the skin rather than stopping wetness. Interestingly, it's the by-products of bacterial metabolism which are the source of body odor—not the perspiration itself. By the way, **Chock's**, **Vermont Country Store Apothecary**, **N.E.E.D.S.**, **Bio Designs**, **Allergy Relief Shop, Inc.**, **Simmons Natural Bodycare**, and **American Environmental Health Foundation** are all catalog sources for crystal deodorant products. They're also now commonly available at health-food stores.

Another all-natural, aluminum-free choice is Le Stick French Clay. This product is compressed baking soda, clay, chlorophyll and a few other ingredients. **Vermont Country Store Apothecary** sells it and you'll want to check your local health-food stores to see if they handle it, too. Fragrance-Free Enzyme Stick (**Kiss My Face**) is made with clay, baking soda, and natural enzymes. Order from the company or from suppliers such as **Tucson Cooperative Warehouse**, **Frontier Natural Products**, **American Environmental Health Foundation**, and **N.E.E.D.S.**

There are also quite a few natural, herbal/botanical deodorants on the market. One popular brand is Tom's of Maine Natural Deodorant Unscented Roll-on (**Tom's of Maine**). It's a combination of aloe, lichen, and coriander and is commonly sold at health-food stores. The same brand has unscented deodorant sticks, too. These products are available from the company's catalog, **Frontier Natural Products**, and **N.E.E.D.S.** In addition, **Aubrey Organics** makes several all-natural deodorants (most are naturally fragrant). They can be bought from the company or from **N.E.E.D.S.**

Diapers

If you are going to be diapering, seriously consider purchasing *Diaper Change: The Complete Diapering Book and Resource Guide* by Theresa Rodriguez Farrisi. You'll find this book especially helpful if you are going to be using non-disposable diapers. It covers everything you'll need to know as well as buying sources. Purchase it at your favorite bookstore or from **EcoBaby Organics**.

Today, the biggest concern most people have with diapers is whether to use washable cotton or disposable paper. This is indeed a major decision when you realize the average baby requires well over 5,000 diaper changes annually until he or she is toilet trained. Obviously, paper disposable types are convenient, but they can have major drawbacks. Most disposable diapers are made with a plastic exterior layer, an absorbent padding layer treated with super-moisture-absorbent chemicals, and finally an inner liner. Sodium polyacrylate (an acrylic-acid polymer salt) is one of the more commonly used moisture-absorbing compounds. It's tiny granules can sometimes be shaken out of new disposable diapers that have been treated with it. The reason sodium polyacrylate is used is because it turns into a gel when it comes in contact with moisture—so liquid is less likely to leak out of the diaper. Unfortunately, acrylic acid polymer salt can apparently trigger allergic reactions, and it can be lethal to cats. Hopefully, your pets won't be eating disposable diapers in your home. But, the inner liner on a diaper might tear, causing direct skin contact with a possibly irritating substance. Then, too, most disposables have synthetic dyes added and they may contain dioxin as a by-product from the bleaching of paper pulp.

On an environmental scale, it has been estimated that 10,000 tons of disposable diapers are put into the trash daily—adding vast quantities of untreated human waste to landfills. So, from a number of view points, disposables are becoming less desirable to use these days.

Of course the big drawback with washable diapers is the mess and clean-up required. If a diaper service is available in your area, this will greatly lessen these problems. But even if there isn't, once a workable routine is established, it should become less overwhelming. And, you'll have the peace of mind of knowing that your baby is exposed only to naturally soft, untreated (or organic) 100%-cotton diapers that have been washed in mild, unscented laundry products (see *Laundering Diapers* on page 121).

Now, if you decide to buy washable diapers, there are increasing numbers of choices available to you. Simple, organic 100%-cotton diapers are sold by **EcoBaby Organics**, **Karen's Natural Products**, **Decent Exposures**, and **Natural Selections**. Untreated 100%-cotton baby and adult diapers, as well as diaper fabric by the yard can be purchased from **B. Coole Designs**. Green-cotton baby diapers are available from **Natural Baby** and **Karen's Natural Products**. All-cotton diapers are sold by **Gohn Bros.**

Kushies is interesting diaper option. They're an "all-in-one" diaper made of 8 layers of 100%-cotton flannel with a nylon-coated vinyl layer, and concealed elastic. Kushie products are sold by **EcoBaby Organics** who has a very extensive collection of natural diaper options. Other cotton all-in-one diapers are sold by **Natural Baby**.

If you prefer disposable baby diapers, you might try alternative brands such as Tender Care Diapers (**RMED International, Inc.**) and Tushies Diapers (**RMED International, Inc.**). Both of these are perfume-free, and they have no gel or other artificial moisture-absorbing agents. The Tushie Diaper is especially nice, being a very thick blend of cotton and paper pulp with a soft cover layer. Both types are often found at health-food stores, alternative groceries, and diaper services. They can be ordered from the manufacturer if you can't find them locally. Something you might also consider is joining the company's The Tushies Club and get automatic scheduled deliveries of diapers, wipes, and other baby-care products directly from **RMED International, Inc.** Besides the convenience, members get diapers at a discount.

Dusting Powder

Breathing dust of any kind can be damaging to the respiratory system, so dusting powder is often not recommended. This is especially true of talcum powder which is simply a purified powdered magnesium silicate. This substance may be implicated in the lung disease, talcosis.

If you're an adult and really want to use a dusting powder, try using a light sprinkling of baking soda. Corn and rice starches as well as arrowroot are other dusting powder possibilities you might want to use. Finely, ground zeolite can work, too. Dasun All Natural Zeolite Pro Powder (**Dasun Co.**), is a very fine, unscented product which you can purchase from the company.

If you still insist on using talcum powder, one you might use is Simple Pure Fine Talc (**Smith & Nephew Consumer Products, Ltd.**). This is an unscented version which can be ordered from **N.E.E.D.S.** and **American Environmental Health Foundation**.

Eye Care

For puffiness around the eyes, you might want to try the following procedure. Lie down and place cold cucumber slices on your closed eye lids for approximately 15 minutes. By the way, cooled, steeped tea bags will also help. Green Goddess Bright Eyes Tea Bags (**Burt's Bees, Inc.**) is an herbal version of this. You can order it directly from the company and may also find it at local health-food stores.

To temporarily tighten the skin around your eyes and to minimize lines and wrinkles, simply apply a small amount of egg white. Another approach is to lightly dab a tiny amount of olive oil under the eye area to provide gentle moisturizing. Note: Be sure to take special care to keep all preparations out of your eyes.

Eye Zone cream (**Smith & Nephew Consumer Products, Ltd.**) is an especially gentle product that is formulated for the delicate skin around the eye. You can purchase it from **N.E.E.D.S.** and **American Environmental Health Foundation**. Another product you might try is Immediately Visible Eye Renewal Gel Cream (**Rachel Perry, Inc.**) which has a natural, unscented formula. You can order it directly from the manufacturer or from **Frontier Natural Products**.

Facial Masks

All-natural homemade facial masks are easy to make. A simple one is made with a raw egg white, or the egg white can be mixed with a drop or two of olive oil. (The egg white can be whipped if desired.) After applying it to your skin, leave the mask on for around 30 minutes, then rinse it off with warm water.

Another toning mask you might try is uncooked rolled oats combined with enough honey to make the mixture sticky. After you've mixed it, pat the concoction on your face and leave it on for 20–30 minutes. (Lying down is best during this time.) Then, you'll want to rinse it off with warm water. This mask is admittedly a bit messy, but it can be very beneficial to your skin.

Of course, there are "ready-made" masks available too. Simple Deep Cleansing Mask (**Smith & Nephew Consumer Products, Ltd.**) is a product you may want to try. Made of natural clay, you can buy it from **N.E.E.D.S.**, **Allergy Relief Shop, Inc.**, and **American Environmental Health Foundation**. A mask made of Fuller's earth (a special dried clay) is offered by **Bio Designs**. Several all-natural herbal/botanical personal care product lines make aromatic facial masks. **Aubrey Organics** is one. Their products can be ordered directly from the company or from **N.E.E.D.S.**

Facial Scrubs

Baking soda sprinkled on a washcloth works well as an inexpensive, all-natural facial scrub. Another option is to mix a little oat flour and water in the palm of your hand and apply the mixture to your face with a gentle scrubbing action. After applying a facial scrub, you'll want to rinse it off with tepid water.

A fragrant all-natural Exfoliating Face Wash (**Kiss My Face**) can be ordered from the maker or from **Tucson Cooperative Warehouse, Frontier Natural Products**, as well as **N.E.E.D.S.** Another choice is Apricot Scrubble (**Jason Natural Cosmetics**) containing herbs, aloe vera, and apricot kernels. Order from the manufacturer or from **International**.

Feminine Hygiene

Some women simply can't tolerate most of the nationally distributed brands of menstrual pads and tampons. One major reason for this is that commonly available feminine napkins and tampons have likely been treated with chemicals to increase absorbency and to mask menstrual odors. Even if a woman purchases unscented pads, these can still be odorous and, thus, bothersome because they often absorb fragrances from the boxes of scented pads that sat adjacent to them on store shelves.

Truly unscented paper-based mini, maxi, and panty-shield pads are also being manufactured. One line that's been around for a while is **Seventh Generation** which can be mail-ordered from **Harmony, Tucson Cooperative Warehouse**, and on-line from GreenMarketplace.com. These paper products are bleached with hydrogen peroxide. As a result, they're dioxin-free. (Dioxin is a toxic, carcinogenic chemical commonly found in minute quantities in paper goods bleached with chlorine.) NatraCare pads are also dioxin-free and sold by **Bio Designs** and **Allergy Relief Shop, Inc.**

If even these alternative paper-based pads prove to be too irritating or otherwise unacceptable, washable 100%-cotton-cloth feminine napkins are available that you can launder and reuse. You can obtain Harmony Moon 100%-organic washable cotton pads in light to medium and medium to heavy from **Natural Lifestyle**. Glads washable organic 100%-cotton pads and waterproof tote bag are sold by **Allergy Relief Shop, Inc.** In addition, cotton washable menstrual pads are handled by TerrEssentials, **Simmons Natural Bodycare, Decent Exposures**, and **Frontier Natural Products**. **Frontier Natural Products** also sells Jade & Pearl washable menstrual sea sponges.

For those who prefer tampons, **Organic Essentials** makes organic-cotton tampons. They're available at some health-food stores and by mail from **Natural Lifestyle, Simmons Natural Bodycare**, and **Tucson Cooperative Warehouse**. Organic cotton tampons are handled, in addition, by TerrEssentials, **Karen's Natural Products**, healthyhome.com and **American Environmental Health Foundation**. NatraCare organic 100%-cotton tampons are handled by **Bio Designs, Harmony** and **Allergy Relief Shop, Inc.**

By the way, if you're caught without your all-cotton tampons, in an emergency you may be able to get by with Tampax Tampons (**Proctor & Gamble**). These are constructed of a combination of cotton and rayon, though probably not as additive-free as the alternative brands mentioned above. However, this brand is available at most pharmacies and grocery stores.

If you're looking for them, 100%-cotton-knit menstrual sanitary panties are available from **Vermont Country Store Apothecary**. These have a protective plastic liner sandwiched between the cotton fabric in the crotch.

For women who choose to douche, it's wise, of course, to use only a naturally mild solution. One you might try is a very weak dilution of apple cider vinegar and tepid water. Or, you might even use warm water by itself, although the acetic acid in the apple cider vinegar will create a healthy, slightly acidic condition. A botanical douche preparation that may be an option is Earth Harvest Herbal Douche Concentrate made with yarro, peppermint, and comfrey root in an apple cider vinegar base. It can be ordered from **Karen's Natural Products**. (Note: Before using *any* douching solution, check with your physician for his or her recommendations concerning safe ingredients suitable for you.)

First Aid

An excellent antiseptic for minor cuts and scrapes is simply a 3% solution of hydrogen peroxide (the type commonly available at drugstores). Besides having germicidal properties, it is low-cost, colorless, and virtually odorous. Another possibility is pure tea-tree oil (also called melaleuca tree oil). Used as an effective, natural topical antiseptic in Australia for years, it's now commonly sold in health-food stores. One brand is Thursday Plantation (**Nature's Plus**), though there are several others. Tea tree oil can be mail-ordered from **Bio Designs**.

Aqueous Zephiran Chloride (**Sanofi Pharmaceuticals**) is often tolerated by sensitive individuals as a topical antiseptic—despite it's mild medicinal odor. Aqueous Zephiran Chloride is actually the brand name for a benzalkonium chloride solution. Previously sold as a concentrate, it's now in a diluted form which can be specially ordered for you by your local pharmacist. Handy benzalkonium chloride towelettes (100 to a box) are sold by **American Environmental Health Foundation**.

Another often-tolerable first-aid preparation is aloe vera. This is actually the juice from the leaves of the water-aloe plant, a succulent member of the lily family. It's available in bottles and creams at most health-food stores. Aloe vera has the ability to soothe many minor burns and skin irritations. Another simple first-aid solution is a paste made from three parts baking soda and one part water. It can be applied to poison ivy outbreaks and insect bites to help relieve itching. You'll want to allow the paste to dry, then later gently wash it off with warm water. (Note, if redness, irritation, or swelling persists or increases after a few days using any remedy, you should always consult your personal physician.)

Unfortunately, plastic bandage strips are often bothersome to sensitive individuals and to some allergic persons. However, many find that cloth bandage strips or sterilized cotton gauze held in place with first-aid tape are better tolerated. These items are available in most drugstores. By the way, you may want to simply use sterile cotton cloth that has been torn into strips. These can be tied around small wounds on fingers or limbs in place of tape.

Foot Care

A number of foot preparations are available or that can be made that are generally well-tolerated by most sensitive and allergic individuals. For example, your feet can be soaked for 10–20 minutes in a solution consisting of nothing more than 4 tablespoons of baking soda in a quart of warm water. This acts as a skin soother and at the same time neutralizes foot odors and softens calluses. Of course a small amount of Epsom salts (magnesium sulfate crystals) dissolved in tepid water is an old standby. However, while perfumed or dyed Epsom salts can be found at most drugstores, far fewer will carry it without these extra ingredients. Fortunately, an Unscented Dead Sea Salts foot soak from **Karen's Natural Products** is an unadulterated product consisting of just natural mineral salts.

After soaking your feet, you may also want to safely remove calluses or toughened skin by gently rubbing your feet with a pumice stone. (Pumice is actually a frothy-appearing, hard, volcanic glass.) These stones can be ordered from **Karen's Natural Products** and

Simmons Natural Bodycare. Afterwards, you can rub in a few drops of olive oil or other well-tolerated vegetable oil to soften the skin.

To help absorb foot perspiration and odor, you can lightly dust your soles with baking soda or Dasun's All-Natural Zeolite Pro Powder (**Dasun Co.**). Zeolite is a natural mineral that adsorbs many types of odors. You can order it from the company.

Another option to help control foot odor is to apply an unscented alum-mineral product such as Crystal Foot Deodorant Spray (**French Transit Ltd.**) or Crystal Body Deodorant Stone (**French Transit Ltd.**). To use a stone type, first wet the crystal. Then rub it across the soles of your feet. **Karen's Natural Products, Janice Corporation, Harmony,** and **Frontier Natural Products** are a few of many catalog sources for crystal deodorants. (Note: See also *Deodorants* on page 89 for other suppliers.) They're also commonly available at health-food stores.

Hair Colorants

The safety of conventional hair coloring products has been a source of debate and concern for years. One study will conclude that cancer-provoking ingredients are indeed present, while another study reports just the opposite. One thing is for certain, most conventional hair colorings (especially the permanent types) are odorous and have at least some ingredients that most sensitive, allergic, and all-natural-ingredient proponents will want to avoid. For example, some popular colorants may have hormones in them. To get an inexpensive, 16 page fact sheet *Hormones in your Hair?*, contact the **Washington Toxics Coalition.**

There are three basic categories of alternative hair colorants—herb-based rinses, semi-permanent henna-based colorings, and permanent vegetable/herbal-based colorings.

One brand of color rinse you might try is Paul Pender's Color Me Naturally. It contains no ammonia or peroxide, and is gone in about three hair washings. This product comes in six colors and can ordered from dealers including **Internatural** and **N.E.E.D.S.**

Henna is used for semi-permanent hair colors. It is simply the powdered leaves from henna shrubs native to the Mid-East. Henna has been used as a reddish hair and skin colorant for thousands of years. These days however, a wide range of natural henna colors are available including brunette and blonde shades. Henna has the advantage of washing out very slowly, so there is a less noticeable distinction between the dyed and undyed hair growing out. It can also thicken and soften hair. All this is possible because henna only coats the surface of hair shafts.

When dying with henna, wear waterproof household gloves, or the resinous henna tannic acid present will dye fingers and nails (see *Waterproof Household Gloves Suggestions* on page 137). Also use distilled water and avoid having the solution come in contact with metal bowls or spoons because of possible chemical reactions. You'll also want to make sure that your hair is very clean and has no chemical residues (hair spray, conditioners, permanent chemicals) so that you achieve the correct color. The common auburn shade is sold both prepackaged and in bulk at some health-food stores. Light Mountain has henna in shades from black to blond. This brand is sold in some heath-food stores and pharmacies. It can be mail-ordered from **Frontier Natural Products** and **Internatural.**

The other alternative hair colorant option is to use permanent vegetable/herb-based hair colorants. These products penetrate the hair shaft. Unfortunately, they tend to contain natural fragrances. One that's been around for some time is Vita Wave hair color (**Vita Wave Products**). It contains vegetable dyes and has no harsh chemicals. The colors available range from Bright

Red to Medium Brown to Golden Blond. Vita Wave hair colors are sold directly by the company and through **N.E.E.D.S.**, **Natural Lifestyle**, **Karen's Natural Products**, and **Allergy Relief Shop, Inc.** Logona Pure Vegetable Hair Color (**Logona USA, Inc.**) comes in 10 shades. You can mail-order it from the manufacturer, **TerrEssentials**, **Karen's Natural Products**, and **Internatural**. Another alternative brand is Naturcolor (**Herbaceuticals**) which is herbal-based and contains a tiny amount of peroxide. It, too, comes in a wide color range. It's sold at some health-food stores. However, if you can't find it locally, you can order it from the company. Note: The suggestions for coloring with henna apply to using vegetable/herb-based products (or any hair coloring product) as well.

Hair Conditioners

Many conventional hair conditioners contain scents or other ingredients that can be bothersome to some allergic or sensitive persons.

One you might try is the organic conditioner made by **Frank T. Ross & Sons Ltd.** which has milk enzymes, wheat germ, hemp, and vitamin-E oils. Order it from the company or from its dealers.

All-natural conditioners made with naturally fragrant ingredients are available too. **Aubrey Organics** (available from the company and from N.E.E.D.S.) and **Kiss My Face** (also directly available from the company and from **Tucson Cooperative Warehouse**, **N.E.E.D.S.**, and **Frontier Natural Products**) are just two you might consider. Check with your local health-food stores for other ready-made products.

You can also make your own excellent hair conditioner at home. One simple deep conditioner consists of a small amount of a tolerable brand of mayonnaise (or your own homemade mayonnaise) that you rub into your hair. After 20 minutes or so, rinse it off using warm water.

An egg yolk beaten with a few drops of tolerated oil works well as a hair conditioner. Again, you'll want to rub the preparation into your hair and leave it on for about 20 minutes before rinsing with warm water.

Hair Sprays

Often, one very intolerable product for those with sensitivities or allergies is hair spray. This is of little wonder when you consider that many conventional products contain lacquer and/or alcohol, plus a host of synthetic ingredients including synthetic scents. If you are unable to tolerate typically available hair sprays, you may be able to tolerate some of the hypoallergenic brands available in certain drugstores.

Fresh Botanical Hair spray (**Jason Natural Cosmetics**) contains yucca, nettle, lavender, and sage. It's an alcohol-free formula. You can mail-order it from the company or from **Internatural**. Honeybee Gardens is another alcohol-free spray sold on-line at **GreenMarketplace.com**. Vita Wave Natural Hair Spray is a water soluble hair spray which can be ordered from **N.E.E.D.S.**, **Allergy Relief Shop, Inc.**, and **Bio Designs**. Magick Fragrance-Free Hair Spray contains alcohol. This can be purchased from **Simmons Natural Bodycare**.

Incidentally, a simple, odorless homemade hair spray can be made using 1/4 teaspoon powdered gelatin dissolved in 1/3 cup of very hot water. Pour a small amount of the solution into a spray bottle and make sure to use it before the gelatin cools. If any is remaining, refrigerate it. You should be aware that this cooled hair spray solution must be reheated before it can be reused. Those with food allergies should know that, although gelatin can be derived from certain plants (such as agar from some seaweeds), it's most commonly an animal by-product, usually from cattle.

For those who are not bothered by citrus products, you can put one roughly chopped, unpeeled lemon in a saucepan, add 2 cups water, or enough to cover the lemon, and boil the mixture down to 1 cup. Then, cool the solution and strain it through cheesecloth. Finally, pour the mixture into a spray bottle. (You may need to thin it down with additional water before using.) This homemade hair spray will keep for several days if you store it in the refrigerator.

Hair-Setting Solutions

Many of the hair-setting products available—like most cosmetics and toiletries—contain scents. A simple low-odor homemade recipe is 2 tablespoons of flaxseed dissolved in 1 cup warm water (You'll need to strain the solution before using). Another homemade formula to use is a solution consisting of 2 tablespoons of superfine white sugar dissolved in $1/2$ cup warm water, which you apply to your hair while the solution is still warm.

Make-Up

Several make-up lines sold nationally in department and drugstores are marketed as being hypoallergenic. As has been discussed, such products are generally free of the harshest irritants most allergic people find a problem. However, they usually contain a number of synthetic or natural ingredients that could still provoke a negative reaction in a smaller percentage of the population. Yet, even for some sensitive and highly allergic people, certain hypoallergenic cosmetics are acceptable.

Others must use not only very-low-odor products, but also ones containing all-natural ingredients. Fortunately, a few companies offer totally natural, unscented products. For instance, an unscented undyed cosmetic rice powder can be ordered from **Vermont Country Store Apothecary**. Then there's Indian Earth Original (**Indian Earth Cosmetics**) made of only one ingredient—a natural, deep reddish/orange unrefined powdered clay. It comes packaged in small earthenware pots with cork lids. Indian Earth Original can be used as an eye shadow, cheek blush, and lip color. A tiny amount goes a very long way, so it lasts a long time. This product can be found at some local retail cosmetic counters or you can order it directly from the company. Another source for clay-based blushes in ceramic pots is **Well & Good**. As a note of caution, some firms making simple natural make-up products such as clay blushers often also make other products which are scented or contain synthetic ingredients. This includes Indian Earth Cosmetics. Therefore, you'll want to make sure you read the ingredient list of each cosmetic you intend to buy—no matter who manufactures it.

These days, many consumers want all-natural make-up. However, many of these products have noticeable natural scents from essential oils. These aromatic oils are either an integral part of the cosmetic formula or are added for aesthetic reasons. So, sensitive and allergic people should be aware that they could be a problem for them. One cosmetic line that is unscented, has no synthetic preservatives, and is all-natural, with which you may want become familiar is Ida Grae Cosmetics. This line can be purchased from **Karen's Natural Products**. BWC (Beauty Without Cruelty) products use no added fragrances, petrochemicals, animal products, or mineral oils and are available from **Inner Balance**. Ecco Bella (**E.B. Botanicals, Inc.**) is an all-natural cosmetic line with no added scents. You can buy these particular products from the maker or from dealers such as **International** and **Frontier Natural Products**. One all-natural cosmetic line that a number of sensitive persons use is Paul Penders which can be bought from **Natural Lifestyle**, **TerrEssentials**, **International**, **Karen's Natural Products**, **Tucson Cooperative Warehouse**, and **N.E.E.D.S.**

One well-known cosmetic line is Aubrey Organics (**Aubrey Organics**). This company takes special pride in making sure all their ingredients are truly natural. Products include lip color, blushes, and Make-up Powders. Order from the company or from dealers such as **N.E.E.D.S.** and **Karen's Natural Products**. (It should be noted that both of these dealers have a good selection of other natural cosmetics, too.) Logona Cosmetics' products (**Logona USA, Inc.**) contain no synthetic preservatives or petrochemical derivatives but do have added natural scent. These are sold directly by the manufacturer and **International**, among others.

An excellent lip gloss you might want to try is Nanak's Lip Smoothee, Unscented (**Golden Temple Natural Products**). Its ingredients are natural oils (almond, safflower, vitamin E, and apricot), aloe, natural sunscreen, and beeswax. This product works well alone, or as a gloss over an application of natural powdered clay such as Indian Earth Original. Actually, this particular combination makes a very good substitute for conventional lipsticks. By the way, Nanak's Lip Smoothee is also a good moisturizer—to prevent or treat chapped lips. You can often purchase this product at local heath-food stores or order it from **Frontier Natural Products**. Other often-tolerable clear glosses are available from **Indian Earth Cosmetics**. In addition, just using a small amount of petroleum jelly on your lips often works well as a gloss. Despite being a petroleum-based product, petroleum jelly tends to be tolerable for a number of sensitive individuals. An all-natural mint lip preparation that may work for you is Burt's Bees Lip Balm (**Burt's Bees, Inc.**) Made with coconut oil, beeswax, vitamin E, peppermint, comfrey root, and rosemary; it can be ordered from the company or purchased at some health-food outlets.

Of course, many women will want to use other brands, types, and colors of make-up. Several catalogs, including **International**, **Frontier Natural Products**, and **N.E.E.D.S** sell a good variety of alternative cosmetics you may want to try. For new products available locally, you'll want to remember to check the cosmetic counters of nearby health-food stores, department stores, and pharmacies from time to time.

For applying make-up, use pure, natural cotton balls (see *Swabs* on page 107), sea sponges, or natural-fiber brushes. Never reuse cotton balls, and wash your complexion sea sponges and brushes regularly with a gentle shampoo, then rinse, and air dry. It is important to keep your cosmetic tools clean to prevent skin irritation or infection. One nice wood-handled, natural-bristle make-up brush that has the added advantage of being self-standing is available from **Logona USA, Inc.** Fine Ida Grae natural cosmetic brushes are sold by **Karen's Natural Products**.

Moisturizers

A moisturizing product which seems to have no detectable odor is Moisture Guard (**Granny's Old Fashioned Products**). Like most products offered by this company, it's inexpensive, has a simple formula, and is available packaged in a variety of sizes. Granny's line is often sold in health-food stores and is also handled by several catalogs including **The Living Source**, **Allergy Relief Shop, Inc.**, **Health One Co.**, **American Environmental Health Foun-**

dation, **Bio Designs**, and **N.E.E.D.S.** Packaged under their own label, **Coastline Products** also handles Granny's lotion.

In addition, **Coastline Products**, **American Environmental Health Foundation**, and **N.E.E.D.S.** are dealers for Simple (**Smith & Nephew Consumer Products, Ltd.**) unscented lotions and moisturizers. This product line has been used by many sensitive and allergic persons for years. Logona Free (**Logona USA Inc.**) offers a number of moisturizing products free of synthetic preservatives, colorants, petrochemical derivatives, herbal extracts, essential oils, as well as natural and synthetic fragrances. These can be ordered directly from the company.

A different kind of product you might opt for is Lifekind Unscented Lotion with MSM (**Lifekind Products**). It contains methysufonylmethane which is described as "a natural healing sulfur compound." This soothing product can be ordered from the company's catalog. Another soothing product is Simmons Cocoa Butter Creme (**Simmons Natural Bodycare**) formulated with cocoa butter, almond oil, aloe vera, vitamin E and no fragrance. Order it from the company catalog.

There are now dozens of popular national brands of conventional-formula moisturizers that also come in unscented, hypoallergenic forms. These lotions may moisturize effectively but generally contain many synthetic chemicals, some of which could be bothersome to certain individuals. However, one such product you may want to consider is Oil of Olay Beauty Fluid for Sensitive Skin, which is sold at most drug, discount, and department stores. This perfume-free version of Oil of Olay not only effectively moisturizes, it is also absorbed quickly into the skin and is *non-commodious* (won't clog your pores). Other possibilities are Neutrogena Hand Cream Fragrance-Free and Neutrogena Body Oil Fragrance-Free (**Neutrogena Corp.**). This brand is commonly found in department stores and drugstores. Neutrogena products can be also be purchased on-line from **Drugstore.com** and **Planetrx.com**.

Another product you might try is a moisturizer produced by a small hypoallergenic-cosmetic company. Ar-Ex Unscented Chap Cream (**Ar-Ex, Ltd.**) has a thicker formulation and comes packaged in a plastic tube. It's sold in a few pharmacies and may be ordered directly from the company.

Annmarie hypoallergenic fragrance-free moisturizer and other skin care products are available from **Well & Good**.

All-natural botanical-based moisturizers are an option others prefer. Some under the Aubrey Organics label are good choices, though most will be naturally fragrant because of the ingredients used. They can be ordered from the company (**Aubrey Organics**) or from **Natural Lifestyle**. Another brand is Kiss My Face, sold directly by the manufacturer or by **Tucson Cooperative Warehouse**, **N.E.E.D.S.**, and **Frontier Natural Products**. TerrEssential Moisture Cream Fragrance-Free (**TerrEssentials**) is a rich moisturizer made with shea-toulou and vitamin E.

Jason (**Jason Natural Cosmetics**) has a variety of moisturizers made with botanicals. One interesting product is Beta-Gold Re-Hydrating Freshner which is a spray made without alcohol and fragrance. Order from the manufacturer or **Internatural**.

Of course, some pure natural oils such as lanolin, apricot, virgin olive oil, or jojoba can be used as moisturizing fluids. Probably the best time to use these oils (or any type of moisturizer for that matter) is immediately after showering or bathing. This is because a small amount of oil applied at that time helps retain the water that was just absorbed by your skin. Unfortunately, a drawback to natural oils is that they tend to be greasy. As a result, they could contribute to clogging your skin pores (some believe this is not true for virgin olive oil) or staining your clothes, so use them sparingly. **Common Sense Products** offers lanolin, jojoba oil, and cocoa butter. These can also be purchased from **Karen's Natural Products**. **Janice Corporation** has Janice jojoba Oil. **Frontier Natural Products** has its Frontier cosmetic oils that include lanolin, cocoa butter, shea butter, and castor oil. Natural oils are also available at **Bio Designs** and most local health-food stores.

Nail Care

Frontier Natural Products has hardwood-handled nail brushes. Pirarucu fish scale nail files, and wood-handled vegetable-fiber nail brushes can be ordered from **Karen's Natural Products**, which also carries a vitamin-E stick for shiny, healthy nails. Hemp Hand Protector made with ingredients such as hemp seed oil, lanolin, and glycerin can also be very beneficial to the nails and cuticles. It can be ordered from **The Body Shop**.

Powdered natural-clay colorants can be used as nail color. However, they require a clear, hard coating so the color does not rub off easily. Indian Earth Original (**Indian Earth Cosmetics**) can be ordered from the company. Another brand is available from **Well & Good**.

Nursing Pads

Organic-cotton nursing pads can be mail-ordered from **EcoBaby Organics**. All-cotton nursing pads are sold by **Decent Exposures** and **Natural Baby**.

Permanents

Most at-home and salon permanents contain potentially harmful chemicals. These ingredients are designed to alter the molecular structure of your hair shafts. Fortunately, a far less toxic product is available: Vita Wave permanent (**Vita Wave Products Co.**), which will give bounce and curl to your hair. However, it should be noted that it does contain some fragrance. Catalog sources for Vita Wave include **N.E.E.D.S.**, **Natural Lifestyle**, **Allergy Relief Shop, Inc.**, and **Karen's Natural Products**. It can also be mail-ordered directly from the manufacturer.

To avoid the use of permanents all together, you might consider a hairstyle that can work attractively with your hair's own innate texture and curling ability. To find an appropriate style, look in hairstyle booklets, guides, magazines, and books—or consult with a professional hair stylist.

Shampoos and Rinses

Many sensitive persons have trouble finding a tolerable shampoo, as do some allergic individuals. This can be a serious concern because hair will retain the odor of whatever you put on it for some time. (Note: For very mild shampoo options, consider those listed under *Baby Care* on page 85.) Fortunately, some individuals have found that all-natural, unscented Castile soaps can often work well as shampoos. Dr. Erlander's Jubilee Castile Soap (**Erlander's Natural Products**) is one of several liquid shampoos you may wish to try. It can be purchased directly from the company. (For other Castile-soap brands, see *Soaps* on page 103.) By the way, any liquid or bar Castile soap works especially well for fine or thinning hair. With coarse or thick hair, Castile soap oils can sometimes build up. A cleansing rinse of apple-cider vinegar or lemon juice mixed with water should help solve this, but these rinses will leave their characteristic smells on your hair. If you are bothered by these odors or have allergies to apples or lemons, it may be best to avoid them.

Of course, there are usually a number of all-natural shampoos available at most local health-food stores, drugstores, and cosmetic departments. Although some contain sea kelp, vitamins, or proteins, which have minimal odor, the majority of these shampoos are made with herbs, spices, essential oils, and sometime additional added natural scents. Aubrey Organics is a brand that has several shampoos and rinses that fit this classification. They're sold by **Aubrey Organics, N.E.E.D.S.**, and **Natural Lifestyle**. Tom's of Maine has coconut-oil-based shampoos in honeysuckle or aloe and almond. These products are handled in many health-food stores and can be ordered from the **Tom's of Maine** catalog, **Frontier Natural Products**, and **N.E.E.D.S.** Still another option is Herbal Shampoo (**Frank T. Ross & Sons Ltd.**) which contains balm mint, mistletoe, and chamomile. Order from the company or from its dealers. **Kiss My Face** offers a number of naturally fragrant, all-natural shampoos and rinses. Purchase them directly from the manufacturer or from suppliers such as **Frontier Natural Products, N.E.E.D.S.**, and **Tucson Cooperative Warehouse**. TerrEssentials Island-Rain Fragrance-Free Hair Cleansing Bar (**TerrEssentials**) has botanical extracts, and vegetable oil in a solid bar form. You might have to experiment with these all-natural types of shampoos to see if one or more will be appropriate for you.

There are also a few unscented alternative shampoos available that contain few ingredients other than a mild synthetic *surfactant* (natural or synthetic) and water (see *Soaps versus Detergents* on page 75 for more on surfactants). Certain brands of these have proven to be particularly tolerable for most sensitive and allergic people. One that lathers well, despite its inexpensive price, is Rich & Radiant (**Granny's Old Fashioned Products**). All Granny's products are formulated without scents, preservatives, dyes, or phosphates. This line is commonly available in health-food stores. Mail-order sources include **N.E.E.D.S., The Living Source, American Environmental Health Foundation, Bio Designs, Allergy Relief Shop, Inc.**, and **Health One Co.** By the way, the **Coastline Products** catalog offers Granny's shampoos and conditioners under the name Coastline Old Fashioned. In addition, this catalog offers a very good assortment of other undyed, unscented shampoos and conditioners including Simple (**Smith & Nephew Consumer Products, Ltd.**). Small samples for some of their products are available. It should be noted that **N.E.E.D.S.** also handles Simple products as does **American Environmental Health Foundation** and **Allergy Relief Shop, Inc.**

Still another shampoo you might consider is SafeChoice Shampoo (formerly Satin Touch) (**AFM**). This is another unscented, synthetic-surfactant shampoo option. If you're interested in purchasing it, it's handled by **N.E.E.D.S., The Living Source, healthyhome.com, Simmons Natural Bodycare, American Environmental Health Foundation**, and **Allergy Relief Shop, Inc.** EnviroRite Hair & Body (**BioForce Enviro-Tech, Inc.**) is also undyed and unscented. It can be mail-ordered from the company. AllerSpa Shampoo, sold by **Inner Balance**, has no fragrances or dyes and is low odor. Logona Free Shampoo & Shower Gel (**Logona USA, Inc.**) is free from many of the often-problematic ingredients. For example, it's free of synthetic preservatives, colorants, petrochemical derivatives, herbal extracts, essential oils, and both natural and synthetic scents. You can order it directly from the company. A number of unscented shampoos that may work for you can be found in the **Simmons Natural Bodycare** catalog.

One product that's not labeled "shampoo" you may find quite acceptable as a shampoo anyway is GNLD Green (**Golden Neo-Life Diamite**). This mild sea-kelp containing personal cleaner has often been recommended for sensitive individuals, although it does have added dye and a mild fragrance. **American Environmental Health Foundation, Inc.** is a mail-order source.

Of course, other unscented shampoos can be found among hypoallergenic cosmetic lines in drug and department stores. Although perfumes may not have been added to these products, they can contain other ingredients that most sensitive persons, and some highly allergic may find bothersome. Only by testing will you know whether certain hypoallergenic shampoos will be acceptable for you (see *Testing* on page 62).

You can also create your own shampoo at home. One old-fashioned hair cleaning method is to simply rub a beaten egg vigorously into your hair and scalp. (The egg can also be combined with one to two cups of cool water.) A final rinse with a dilute lemon juice and water solution is suggested. For dry shampooing, you can vigorously rub 1/2 cup cornmeal or oat flour into your hair and scalp, then brush it out. You'll probably find that doing this outdoors makes clean-up afterwards much easier.

Unfortunately, an increasing problem for children these days is head lice. Many anti-lice shampoos contain harsh chemical compounds. One gentle all-natural product you may want to use is Lifekind Lice Out (**Lifekind Products**). It's formulated with lemon grass, citronella, almond, apricot, safflower, and vitamin-E oils, as well as citrus extracts and aloe-vera gel. It can be ordered from the company's catalog.

Shaving Needs

To avoid shaving-cream intolerance, you might consider using only an electric shaver. However, if you just don't like using an electric shaver, other options are available that may be acceptable.

For those who want all-natural ingredients, Fragrance-Free Natural Moisture Shave (**Kiss My Face**) may be a good choice. It's a creamy foam made with aloe, golden seal, and olive oil packaged in a pump container. It can be mail-ordered directly from the manufacturer or from **Tucson Cooperative Warehouse**, **N.E.E.D.S.**, and **Frontier Natural Products**. Another unscented product you might use is Simple Shaving Cream (**Smith & Nephew Consumer Products, Ltd.**) available from **N.E.E.D.S.**, **Allergy Relief Shop, Inc.**, and **Coastline Products**.

Tom's of Maine Natural Shaving Cream (**Tom's of Maine**) may be acceptable for those able to handle odors. It's available only in mint or honeysuckle formulas. Generally, Tom's Shaving Cream is handled by local health-food stores. You can also order it from the company catalog, or from **N.E.E.D.S.** and **Frontier Natural Products**. **Aubrey Organics** has a herb and ginseng shaving cream. That product can be purchased from the company or from **N.E.E.D.S.**

Simmons Unscented Aloe Shaving Soap (**Simmons Natural Bodycare**) is formulated with aloe vera and vitamin E. A thick lather for shaving can be created also with Unscented Pearlized Sink and Shower Soap for Hands, Face, and Body offered by **Coastline Products**. Or you can use any other tolerable, natural unscented bar or liquid soap. Another possibility is to dissolve 4 tablespoons of baking soda in 1 pint hot water and apply.

Fortunately, natural badger-hair shaving brushes are still available. Mail-order sources include **Simmons Natural Bodycare**, **Caswell-Massey Co., Ltd.**, **Vermont Country Store**

Apothecary, Vermont Country Store Voice of the Mountains, and Allergy Relief Shop, Inc. After each use you'll need to rinse the brush thoroughly. Then, if possible, allow it to hang-dry by placing the handle in a shaving-brush stand. This will greatly prolong the life of your brush's bristles. Stoneware shaving mugs are sold by Vermont Country Store Apothecary, Simmons Natural Bodycare, and Caswell-Massey Co., Ltd.

Many women would prefer to have a hair-removal method that's longer lasting than shaving. Many department and discount stores carry electric plucking tools. Some are able to pull-out a swath of hair at once. Others are designed to remove one hair at a time. In either case, by removing the entire hair from its root, the hair-growing follicles should remain hair-free for several weeks. While this is definitely a plus, don't expect plucking (either by mechanical means or radio-wave-frequency energy) to be a permanent solution. While many manufacturers suggest that hairs treated with their particular equipment will grow in finer, or eventually not at all, it's unlikely that most women will achieve such results.

Waxing has been popular for some time now. However, the uncomfortable nature of having warm liquid wax put on your skin (hopefully not hot enough to burn) and having it pulled off when it's set, is not something many look forward to. A lot of women have found they've had to go to salons to have it done correctly rather than doing it at home—making waxing both costly and inconvenient as well. In addition, there's some concern raised from time to time about the possible reuse of wax which may have been contaminated by previous customers.

As a result of these problems, sugaring has caught on. In this method, manufacturers use natural sugar boiled until it's achieved a somewhat soft, sticky consistency when cooled. Other ingredients are usually added to the sugar base—perhaps honey, herbs, and scents. Sugaring products don't need to be heated, but are applied at room temperature to the skin with a spatula-like tool. A cloth is then pressed on and rapidly pulled off taking most of the sugar and hair imbedded in it. Any sugar left on the legs can simply be washed off with water. Because of the ease of application, sugaring is often done at home very successfully. A product in this category with which you may want to experiment is MOOM. It's sold at some drugstores and pharmacies and through Harmony.

Shower Caps

Most shower caps are made of vinyl or other types of plastic and, so, are often bothersome to sensitive persons. One solution is a double-layer, 100%-cotton shower cap available from Janice Corporation.

Soaps

A number of soaps are marketed today that many chemically sensitive and allergic people often find tolerable. (Note: See *Baby Care* on page 85 for other very gentle options). One of the most common is Castile soap. Castile soap was originally made from olive oil in Castile Spain. Today, Castile soaps are made everywhere, and the definition has been expanded to include natural soaps made with a combination of vegetable oils. You'll find that Castile soaps are sold in two basic forms: liquid and bar.

Liquid Castile soaps are usually sold in health-food stores and through alternative health catalogs. Often, these liquid formulas have almond, mint, or other natural scents added. A Canadian firm (Frank T. Ross & Sons Ltd.), is especially aware of the needs of chemically sensitive people and makes a very pure, unscented Castile Liquid Soap. It can be ordered from the company or from it's dealers. Dr. Erlander's Jubilee Castile Soap (**Erlander's Natural Products**) is an excellent olive-oil, unscented, liquid, Castile soap that you can order directly from the company.

Unlike liquid Castile soaps, Castile bar soaps are often made of olive oil with the addition of palm or coconut oils whose solid fats permit hardening. Other vegetable oils may be included as well. One Castile bar soap that is particularly good is Simmons Special Unscented Soap (**Simmons Natural Bodycare**) available from the company and **Bio Designs**. It's an olive/palm/coconut oil bar with 200 I.U. of vitamin E. This soap contains no perfume, deodorant, coloring, animal fat, or synthetic additives of any kind. Dr. Erlander's Jubilee Castile Bar Soap (**Erlander's Natural Products**), which can be mail-ordered from the company, is a bar version of their liquid Castile soap.

Dr. Hunter's Castile Soap is another good unscented, undyed choice made and sold by **Caswell-Massey Co., Ltd.** as is Tom's of Maine Natural Moisturizing Soap. This Tom's of Maine product is made with jojoba oil, olive oil, and vitamin E and can be bought through the **Tom's of Maine** catalog, **N.E.E.D.S.**, **Frontier Natural Products**, and at many local health-food stores.

An all-natural "glycerin/creme" soap (more on glycerin later in this section) made with palm and coconut oils, and no dyes or scents, is Sappo Hill Natural (**Sappo Hill Soapworks**). It is sold without a wrapper in some health-food stores, directly from the maker (if local suppliers aren't available), **Frontier Natural Products**, **Health One Co.**, and **Tucson Cooperative Warehouse**. Lifekind Castile Unscented (**Lifekind Products**) can be a good choice for many. It is made with olive, palm, coconut, almond, and apricot oils. You can order it directly from the company's catalog. Face & Body Bar Soap (**Frank T. Ross & Sons Ltd.**) contains vitamins A and E as well as horse chestnut. You can purchase it from the company or from its dealers.

Other sources for gentle bar soaps are **Vermont Country Store Apothecary** which sells an unscented coconut-oil Castile soap, **Janice Corporation** which handles Bocobelli Pure Castile and others, and **Coastline** which sells a very good selection of undyed, unscented soaps including Simple (**Smith & Nephew Consumer Products, Ltd.**). It should be noted that this imported British Simple soap is also sold by **Janice Corporation**, **Allergy Relief Shop, Inc.**, **American Environmental Health Foundation**, and **N.E.E.D.S.**

Very aromatic Castile soap with herbs, essential oils, and other botanicals have now become relatively common. They're sold in many department stores, alternative groceries, drugstores, and health-food stores. One possible option in this category that some sensitive and scent-allergic people might be able to tolerate is Fruit of Her Hands Unscented (**Priorities**). Although this bar soap has an innate aroma, at least it will not have added scents or fragrances. Order it directly from **Priorities**.

Perhaps a better choice (from an scent-free standpoint) are Castile soaps just containing added whole grains. Simmons Pure Unscented Oatmeal Soap (**Simmons Natural Bodycare**) is one worth trying. It can be ordered directly from the company's catalog. Another good choice is **Sappo Hill Soapwork's** Natural Oatmeal. Sappo Hill soaps (which are usually sold unwrapped) can be bought in some health-food stores, ordered directly from the company (only if you can't find it locally), or from **Tucson Cooperative Warehouse**, **Health One Co.**, and **Frontier Natural Products**. You may also want to try the simple oatmeal/Castile soap handled by **Vermont Country Store Apothecary** or Caswell-Massey Oatmeal Soap (**Caswell-Massey Co., Ltd.**). Instead of oats, rice bran is used by some soap makers. Unscented rice bran containing soaps by Ki Essentials (Handcrafted or French Milled) are sold by **Natural Lifestyle**.

Other soaps you may want to try are those made primarily of unscented glycerin. Glycerin (also known as glycerol) is a sweet, syrupy substance specially derived from certain fats and oils. While glycerin soap is available in liquid form, more commonly it's sold as translucent orange-brown bars. Although mild, glycerin bar soaps have a major drawback: They tend to dissolve quickly. Thus, after using a bar, be sure to set it in a soap dish and allow it to air-dry. Otherwise, the bar will turn into gooey glop. Another concern is that some of the liquid and bar varieties of glycerin soap tend to be relatively expensive.

One very popular unscented glycerin soap is Neutrogena Original Formula, sold in Liquid Fragrance-Free and Bar Soap Fragrance-Free versions (**Neutrogena Corp.**). A newer offering from the same manufacturer is Neutrogena Dry Skin Formula Bar Soap Fragrance Free. Neutorgena products can be purchased at many local pharmacies and department stores and on-line from **Planetrx.com** and also **Drugstore.com**. Tom's of Maine Natural Glycerin Soap Unscented (**Tom's of Maine**) may also be a good choice. Buy it directly from the company or from suppliers such as local health-food stories and **Tucson Cooperative Warehouse** and **Frontier Natural Products**. Logona Free Glycerin Soap (**Logona USA, Inc.**) makes a very pure round glycerin bar. Order it directly from the manufacturer.

An interesting combination are rice/glycerin soaps. Ki Essentials unscented, undyed liquid and bar varieties are handled by **Natural Lifestyle**. TerrEssentials Unscented Glycerin Soap and TerrEssentials Unscented Glycerin Soap with Oatmeal can be ordered from **TerrEssentials**.

Anymore, you'll find that most local health-food stores carry a large selection of alternative soaps—far more than can be mentioned here. If you want to experiment with several types, that many sensitive and scent-allergic people have already found to be acceptable, you might consider ordering the Soap Sampler from **Janice Corporation**, which contains several different brands of alternative bar soaps. Although they don't have a Soap Sampler, you'll want to check the **Allergy Relief Shop, Inc.** catalog for a good selection as well.

Still another approach is buying custom-made soaps from **C. Dalton, Inc.** Every order is specifically created for each customer. So, unscented Castile and glycerin bar soaps are options, as well as those containing essential oils, herbs, or other requested natural ingredients. Check the company's website for further information about what choices from which you can choose. If you want to experiment making your own soap, many books are currently available on the subject. One good one is *The Natural Soap Book* by Susan Miller Cavtich. Check your library and favorite bookstores for availability.

By the way, because alternative soaps are often costly, you might want to try this conservation tip when using flat bars of the same brand. When an old bar is nearly used up, you simply wet both it and the new replacement bar with water. Then rub them together back to back to create a small amount of lather, press the two bars firmly together, and set them aside until they're dry. This will bond both the bars together creating a single slightly-larger one—so you won't have any wasted slivers. You can also use a soap chip compressor to create one large round bar out of several left-over soap slivers. Order this clever device from **TerrEssentials**.

Today, besides soap, other options are available to wash your skin. One alternative is SafeChoice Head and Body Shampoo (**AFM**). This product can also be used as liquid hand cleaner. Sources to buy it are **N.E.E.D.S.**, **Allergy Relief Shop, Inc.**, and **The Living Source**. Another choice might be LifeTime Solutions Hand Cleaner (**LifeTime Solutions**). This is an unscented, undyed liquid is a unique *colloidal-micelle* solution. GNLD Green (**Golden Neo-Life Diamite**), a mild kelp-containing cleaner, has been recommended for sensitive individuals. This is despite having dye and a mild fragrance. **American Environmental Health Foundation, Inc.** is one mail-order source.

For those of you with extremely dry skin who can't use any "store bought" soaps or cleaners, try applying just a small amount of virgin olive oil to your skin. Then, gently remove the oil with cotton balls or gauze (see *Swabs* on page 107). Then, rinse your skin with clear water and pat it dry. You may want to follow this procedure occasionally with a facial scrub. An unusual body cleaning solution is to use Lava Erde Hair and Body Cleanser which has no soap, fragrance, or surfactants. It cleans by absorbing dirt and excess skin oil with natural clays. This product can be purchased from **TerrEssentials**.

For especially ground-in grime, sprinkle baking soda on a wash cloth and gently rub soiled skin. Scrubbing with Bon Ami Cleaning Bar (**Faultless Starch/Bon Ami Co.**), which contains unscented soap and ground feldspar, also works well. It's handled by some health-food stores and grocery stores, or it can be mail-ordered from the company's own catalog, the **Agelong Catalog**. Natural soaps with cornmeal as the abrasive agent, sometimes known as "gardeners' soaps," can be another option. One version is Farmer's Friend Soap (**Burt's Bees, Inc.**). However, this brand is quite fragrant with lavender oil, rosemary, eucalyptus and other aromatic ingredients. It can be ordered directly from the company and is sometimes found in health-food stores.

For more on understanding soaps, see also *Soaps vs. Detergents* on page 75.

Sunscreens

Sunscreens have the ability to help protect your skin from cancer-causing rays from the sun. However, you may not know that skin that has been repeatedly treated with sunscreen solutions apparently produces lower quantities of vitamin D—an essential vitamin needed by the human body. There is also the concern that people using sunscreens may overestimate the protective capacities of these products and, therefore, unknowingly overexpose themselves to sunlight. For these and other reasons, one of the best defenses against ultraviolet (UV) solar radiation is to simply limit the amount of time you spend in the sun. Above all, the most important times to avoid direct sunlight are between 11 AM and 2 PM. When you are outdoors, a good way to avoid sun rays is to wear a large brimmed hat and other protective clothing. But, be aware, most clothing will not completely block UV rays.

If you feel you must use a sunscreen, choose one that will do the job effectively. Sunscreens are rated according to their Sun Protection Factor (SPF). The higher the SPF number, the greater the protection, because each number represents how many times longer a person can be safely exposed to UV rays. So, an SPF of 6 means that a person can remain in the sun six times longer without burning than if he or she had not applied the product, while an SPF of 40 means they can remain out 40 times as long. But, that's under what sunscreen researchers consider ideal conditions. That means there's no sweating, swimming, or moisture applied to the skin, or any other loss of protection. Unfortunately, when you're in the sun, it's pretty difficult to not perspire. So, ideal conditions can be difficult to achieve or maintain. Of course, there are some SPF products designed to be worn when swimming. However, most people probably overestimate the protection provided by all types of sunscreen applications.

These days, ratings of 2 to 30 are common for sunscreens, though some products have much higher ratings. You should be aware that, until recently, the term "sun block" was often applied to many higher-rated SPF products. However, Federal regulations no longer permit this term (or the word "waterproof") on SPF product labels. This is to clear up the public's misunderstanding of the actual capabilities of these preparations. After all, no SPF skin product can truly "block" UV rays, nor be totally unaffected by water.

Most people who choose to use a sunscreen should pick one with *at least* SPF 10 or above—especially if you have fairer skin. Most conventional sunscreens are made with para-aminobenzoic acid (PABA), a B-vitamin analog, as their active ingredient—although other substances can also block UV rays. Currently though, PABA is the only sunscreen absorber that *can* be derived from natural sources which the FDA (U.S. Federal Food and Drug Administration) will validate. Unfortunately, some people do not tolerate PABA well, especially if it's not of a high food-grade quality. So, some manufacturers are using other sun screening ingredients instead, such as sesame seed oil. (An application of just sesame-seed oil to the skin can reputedly screen out some 30% of the sun's UV rays.)

One low-odor, skin-protecting line you might consider is from **Lily of the Desert**. None of their sunscreen products contain PABA, scents, or dyes. They're nongreasy, water-resistant, and come in SPF 16 or a very high SPF 40. **Lily of the Desert** items are available in some drug- and health-food stores. You can also order from the company or from **Frontier Natural Products**. **Coastline Products** carries Mountain Ocean Sun Screen and Mountain Ocean Lip Trip, both unscented and undyed with SPF ratings of 15. Still another good choice is Simmons SPF Sunscreen (**Simmons Natural Bodycare**) formulated for sensitive skin with no PABA, mineral oil, or fragrance. Instead, it has natural sun screening ingredients as well as vitamins A, D, and E. Order it from the company's catalog.

Vermont Country Store Apothecary offers a "hypoallergenic" oat protein sunscreen with an SPF of 30. Then there's Mustela of Paris, a fragrance-free, non-chemical hypoallergenic product available from **Harmony, Tucson Cooperative Warehouse**, and on-line from **GreenMarketplace.com**. Sunscreen is also sold by **Perfectly Safe**. You may also want to try the unscented, major hypoallergenic brands of sunscreens found in some pharmacies, or organic SPF products sold in some alternative grocery and health-food stores.

Though they have an innate natural odor (type and intensity depending on the ingredients), some prefer botanically based products. Ecozone Outdoor Skin Protector is made with sesame oil, cedar wood oil, and other ingredients. It can be ordered from **Natural Animal Health Products, Inc.**

Other all-natural sunscreen products are made and sold by **Aubrey Organics**. This company uses food-grade PABA in a vegetable-based glycerin, as well as herbs. Their line is also carried by **American Environmental Health Foundation**, as well as **Natural Lifestyle**.

Swabs

Organic Essentials makes 100%-organic cotton balls, cosmetic rounds, and stick swabs. They are sold through some health-food stores and can be mail-ordered from **Natural Lifestyle, Harmony**, and **Simmons Natural Bodycare**. Organic-cotton balls, rounds and swabs are also sold by **American Environmental Health Foundation** and **Allergy Relief Shop, Inc.** An internet source for organic cotton balls and swabs is **healthyhome.com**.

CHAPTER 5: LAUNDERING

Because clothing is continually in direct contact with your skin, it's important to use laundry products that will properly clean the clothes and still be a healthy choice for you. Of course, this is of primary importance for sensitive and allergic people who often find that typical laundry products can make their garments unwearable. To help these people and others, this chapter will offer suggestions for alternative laundry products and methods. As always, choose those that best suit your own particular needs. It should be noted that more information on laundering specific types of fibers and stuffings are found in *Chapter 7: Healthier Fibers & Stuffings*.

Laundry Basics

When you're ready to wash your clothes and other washable household fabric items, certain laundry basics are worth keeping in mind. First, try using the least amount of soap or detergent necessary to do the job. This will make rinsing more effective and will save you money. Thorough rinsing is necessary so that cleaning-product residues don't remain on fabric fibers. This gummy residue can act as a glue, attracting dirt particles, and it can abrade the fibers as well. It's also a good idea to wash each load on the shortest and gentlest cycle of your washing machine that still offers effective cleaning. By doing this, you subject your machine washables to the least amount of wear and tear from the rotating agitator.

Of course, it's always best to sort your laundry items carefully to create loads that are similar in color, fiber, and fabric weight. You can use 100%-cotton laundry bags for this. One source is **Janice Corporation**. Making your own out of pillow cases is a possibility too. A 100%-cotton canvas laundry bag with its own foldable chromed-steel holder is available from **Kitchen & Home** and **Harmony**.

A more elaborate, and perhaps more efficient set up is to use a *laundry sorter*. Most consist of metal racks holding two or more removable, canvas laundry bags. A chromed tubular-steel version with 100%-cotton canvas bags can be ordered from **Hold Everything** and **Harmony**. A two-level version with three 100%-cotton canvas bags and an upper rack is sold by **Kitchen & Home**.

Furthermore, it's often wise to use the lowest water levels at the coolest temperature settings that will still permit effective washing, in order to minimize problems with color fading and fabric shrinkage, and to save on energy costs. Of course, hot water is required to kill dust mites.

One final note, periodically check the hot and cold water supply hoses to your washer. These can fail as the rubber fatigues over time from the constant water pressure inside them. Sometimes you can spot an "aneurysm" before the hose actually breaks. This will appear as a bulging area. Even if you don't spot a bulge, it's a good idea to replace these hoses at least every three years so you don't risk having gallons of water spill out onto your floor. When you replace them, consider using stainless-steel-mesh reinforced washer hoses. The outer metal mesh will not only make bursting far less likely but will help to seal in any new rubber odors. These types of washer hoses are sold in many hardware and building centers. They can be mail-ordered from **Improvements**.

Fabric Care Guide

A new fabric-care guide system has been developed by **The Soap and Detergent Association** and the Federal Trade Commission (FTC) to aid consumers. It involves the use of simple universal symbols on clothing and fabric labels. There are six basic pictographs (machine wash, bleach, tumble dry, dry, iron, dry clean). An X through a symbol means "do not." Dots represent temperature—the more dots, the hotter the water, dryer setting, or iron temperature which can be safely used. Bars represent the added degree of gentle treatment required. So if a machine wash symbol is combined with one bar, the permanent press cycle would be indicated. Two bars would mean the delicate/gentle cycle.

With the permission of **The Soap and Detergent Association**, these symbols and explanations are reprinted here. By becoming familiar with the coded messages, you'll be able to know, before purchasing a product, whether you'll be able to care for a particular item at home or not. Plus, it will take the guesswork out of how to best do it.

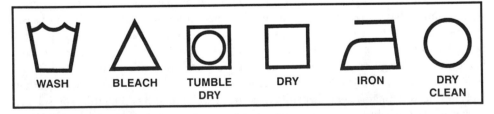

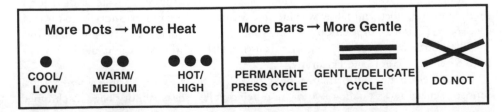

Your Guide to Fabric Care Symbols

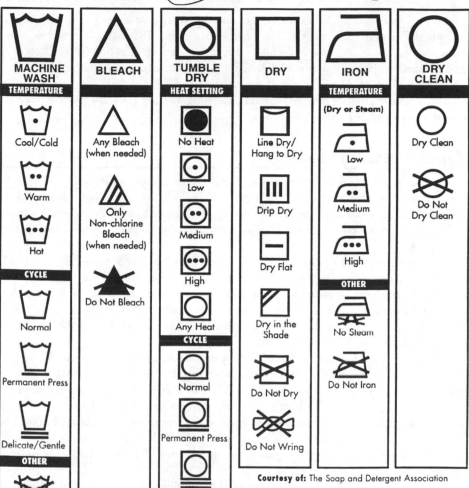

MACHINE WASH	BLEACH	TUMBLE DRY	DRY	IRON	DRY CLEAN
TEMPERATURE		**HEAT SETTING**		**TEMPERATURE**	
Cool/Cold	Any Bleach (when needed)	No Heat	Line Dry/ Hang to Dry	(Dry or Steam) Low	Dry Clean
Warm	Only Non-chlorine Bleach (when needed)	Low	Drip Dry	Medium	Do Not Dry Clean
Hot	Do Not Bleach	Medium	Dry Flat	High	
CYCLE		High	Dry in the Shade	**OTHER**	
Normal		Any Heat	Do Not Dry	No Steam	
Permanent Press		**CYCLE** Normal	Do Not Wring	Do Not Iron	
Delicate/Gentle		Permanent Press			
OTHER		Delicate/Gentle			
Do Not Wash		**OTHER**			
Hand Wash		Do Not Tumble Dry			

Courtesy of: The Soap and Detergent Association

Laundry Products

If you're a person who chooses to purchase and wear only washable, all-natural-fiber clothing and other household fabric items, you'll probably want to take special care in selecting all of your laundry products. As everyone knows who has been in a supermarket, there are dozens of laundry products currently available. However, it's wise to consciously decide what qualities and ingredients touted by these products are truly desirable or essential for you and your family—rather than simply purchasing what's on sale, what's been recently advertised on TV by a celebrity, what your mother uses, or even what you've used in the past.

Some factors you might want take into account when you choose a laundry product include the naturalness of the formula, whether or not it's biodegradable, whether it contains *phosphates* (which release phosphorus that can cause ecological problems in waterways and streams), whether the product is liquid or powder, and of course, whether it works well and is cost effective. However, for many sensitive and scent-allergic individuals, and all those interested in minimizing indoor odors, knowing whether a laundry product is scented or not will also likely be a top priority.

Typical Laundry Products

As has been mentioned, many sensitive and highly allergic individuals find that, for them, typical laundry products are intolerable. This shouldn't be too surprising when you consider that most conventional laundry detergents contain bleaches, enzymes, whiteners, softeners, and many other potentially bothersome ingredients, as well as synthetic dyes and fragrances.

However, it's not just people with MCS (Multiple Chemical Sensitivity) or those who experience acute allergic reactions who have found typical laundry products unacceptable. The ingredients in most modern laundry products often account for tolerability problems in a certain segment of the general public outside these two groups. Often, for these people, it's the synthetic dyes and fragrances that cause them to experience—for the first time— skin irritation or respiratory symptoms.

Yet, even if the added scents used in laundry products are naturally derived, they can still be intolerable, or just plain unwelcome for some sensitive persons. So, if you plan to use scented laundry products, remember that a fabric's fibers will tend to absorb ever-greater amounts of "citrus lemon," "pleasantly herbal," or "outdoors fresh." These scents can be difficult to remove if you ever decide you don't want them in your clothes any longer. Even with extended airings outdoors or washing in unscented alternative products, certain fragrance-saturated items may never again be completely free of those scented, laundry-product odors.

In order to reach the sizable market of those individuals who are opposed to using scented laundry products for whatever reason, some major manufacturers are now marketing versions of their popular scented detergents as "scent-free." In a number of cases, these are not simply the same products made *without* scents as most people suspect. Instead, they're often products made with the original scents *plus* added *masking fragrances.* Synthetic masking fragrances are added because they're capable of countering or masking the odors of the original scents. As a result, a "scent-free" product becomes a complex chemical mishmash.

Therefore, in a strange twist of chemistry, as well as popular definition, some unscented products actually contain *more* synthetic fragrances than the scented products—the original frangrance *and* the masking fragrance. For those individuals who find that the odor of these scents is simply undesirable, masking fragrances may make a popular name-brand laundry product acceptable to them. However, for others who react to synthetic fragrances because of their chemical make-up, supposedly "scent-free" laundry products with masking fragrances can be bad options.

Alternative Laundry Products

Fortunately, for those people who want to use laundry products that have uncomplicated formulas without a lot of extra additives, a growing number of alternative products are now available. The following sections will discuss some of them you might want to try.

Laundry Disks

Over the last several years, *laundry disks*, balls, and other special configurations have been introduced as an almost miraculous way to clean your clothes with no, or very little, added cleaning product required. Some of these are made of ceramic, others are plastic. Some have magnets, others have a static electrical charge, some release electrons. There are those that are solid, some that are mesh-like, and others are hollow containing a fluid or some other substance. They sound interesting, but do they work?

At least one brand using a plastic sphere filled with a blue liquid had many satisfied customers. Thousands of this relatively expensive product were sold before it was discovered that the amazing blue fluid was simply water with an attractive blue dye added for visual effect. Eventually, this company was forced by regulators to quit marketing its ineffective, but highly lucrative, item.

However, there are still many other types of laundry disks in the marketplace. They, too, often have ardent followings. Do they work any better? At this point, only you can be the true judge of that, but the research isn't promising.

It's been speculated that laundry disk manufacturers using minerals such as zeolite and borax are attempting to produce the same ion-exchange water softening ability created by conventional (salt-using) water conditioning units (see *Typical Water Softeners* on page 613). Furthermore, those using ceramic magnets may be attempting to align calcium ions so they're unable to bond to soap. This would alleviate soap scum. Calcium ion alignment is a common approach to water softening utilized by alternative (non-salt) equipment (see *Alternative Water Softeners* on page 615). Some disks employ both approaches at the same time.

Unfortunately, the laundry-disk critics say that trying to recreate water softening technology in simple laundry disks is an unlikely possibility. They hypothesize that drastically cutting back on the use of laundry cleaners, as suggested by many laundry-disk manufacturers, is the real key. You see, clothes will typically get just as clean if you only use half (or even less) of the amount of cleaner suggested on many product labels. So, whether you use the laundry disks or not, the clothes will be clean anyway.

If you'd like to experiment with laundry disks, most alternative groceries and health-food stores sell them. You can also mail-order them from **Harmony**, **Bio Designs**, **Allergy Relief Shop, Inc.**, and **Real Goods**. You may find they work just fine for you. If not, choose those with a money-back guarantee.

Powdered Alternative Laundry Products

Many powdered alternative laundry products are very simple compounds that can be purchased in bulk at very low prices. If you decide to go ahead and buy in bulk, be aware that wholesalers usually deal in very large quantities (see *Buying in Bulk* on page 63). Therefore, one bag purchased from a chemical-supply company could weigh 50–100 lbs.

If you decide to purchase that much of a compound, be sure you have a proper storage container on hand so it can be kept dry and not spill out (see *Metal Containers* on page

514). To find a chemical-supply company near you, you'll want to check in your classified telephone directory.

Sodium Hexametaphosphate

For some time now, unscented *sodium hexametaphosphate* (*SHMP* or sometimes, *SHP*) has been recommended as an alternative laundry cleaning product for sensitive and allergic persons. SHMP is actually a powdered natural sodium-phosphate compound which is soluble in water.

Once, SHMP was commonly used as a water-softening agent to enable soaps and detergents to suds easier. However, because of its phosphate content, its use has diminished. As it turns out, phosphates were found to disrupt normal water ecology and cause overabundant algae growth in streams downstream from sewage treatment plants. Because of this, phosphate laundry products have become illegal in some states and local jurisdictions. SHMP laundry products would fall under such regulations.

However, if phosphates haven't been banned in your state or locale, you might try SHMP. Suggested use is about 1/4 cup per wash load. Five pound bags are sold by **Bio Designs**. It also can be mail-ordered from **Nigra Enterprises**. For large amounts, consider purchasing it in bulk from a nearby chemical-supply house.

Washing Soda

Another natural alternative to conventional laundry detergent is old-fashioned *washing soda*. Also known as *sal soda*, it's actually a form of sodium carbonate. For your washing machine, 1/4 cup per load is often suggested.

Arm & Hammer Washing Soda (**Arm & Hammer**) is one brand of pure washing soda often sold in both conventional and alternative grocery stores. Unfortunately, because it's an highly absorbent powder, it often picks up the scents of the fragranced cleaning products shelved near it.

Another unscented washing soda under the name Dr. Erlander's Jubilee Washing Compound (**Erlander's Natural Products**) can be mail-ordered directly from the company. This washing soda is far less likely to have picked up fragrances from other products.

It should also be mentioned that local chemical-supply companies often handle washing soda. If so, it is often sold under its chemical name, sodium sesquicarbonate, in 50- or perhaps 100-pound bags. FMC Sesqui is one brand that is available in bulk.

Baking Soda

A few extremely sensitive and allergic persons have used as little as 1/2 cup of baking soda (sodium bicarbonate) in their washing machine—without any other laundry product—to clean their clothes and other fabric washables. This may work well for you, too, and it's certainly a very mild substance.

Of course, there's usually no problem finding baking soda in your local grocery store. Arm & Hammer Baking Soda (**Arm & Hammer**) and cheaper generic store brands are widely available. But if you plan to use large quantities, you might consider purchasing it in bulk from a chemical-supply company to save money. This means a large bag in at least a 50-pound quantity.

For additional uses for baking soda, you'll want to look through the book, *Baking soda: Over 500 Fabulous, Fun and Frugal Uses You've Probably Never Thought Of* by Vicki Lansky. Check your local library or your favorite bookstore to see if it's obtainable.

Borax

Borax is basically hydrated sodium borate, a mined, water-soluble mineral. It's been used as a laundry soap or as a detergent supplement for many, many years. One reason for this is that it can help soften the wash water so that soaps and detergents will clean better. However, another big advantage to using borax in your washing machine is that it helps remove odors from your laundry. Interestingly, some sensitive and highly allergic individuals use unscented borax as a substitute for conventional laundry detergents; in other words, they use it just by itself. If you plan to do this, 1/4 cup per load generally works effectively, although you might choose to use more (perhaps up to 1/2 cup). Note: Borax has a mild bleaching action, so be careful with darker colors.

Of course, 20 Mule Team Borax (**20 Mule Team Borax**) is often available in grocery stores. Although it's unscented, its absorbent nature means it will take on the odors of its fragranced shelf-mates. If you don't care to use laundry products containing fragrance (even inadvertently acquired fragrances), you can buy unscented borax in bulk from most local chemical-supply companies in 50-100 pound bags.

Zeolite

Zeolite is the name of a family of naturally occurring minerals that have the capacity to *adsorb* many common odors. In other words, some molecules making up an odor will ionically adhere to the surface of zeolite molecules because they have opposite, and therefore naturally attracting, charges.

In powdered form, zeolite is a common ingredient in conventional laundry detergent. However, a number of sensitive and scent-allergic people buy zeolite powder in it's pure form to remove odors from their clothes. If you'd like to try it, start with just one or two level tablespoons per load. (Wearing a protective dust mask may be necessary for some when using this product.) Dasun Zeolite Powder (**Dasun Co.**) in two pound containers is sold by the company and by **Bio Designs.** Two and ten pound containers of natural zeolite can be ordered from **healthyhome.com.** Also check with your local chemical supply companies which often have it available in much larger bulk bags. However, because so little zeolite is used with each load, it may be preferable to buy it in the more convenient smaller packages.

Other Alternative Powdered Products

Actually, a number of alternative powdered laundry products are now being manufactured. In this section, some of them are discussed. Others can be found in alternative product catalogs, as well as in health-food and alternative grocery stores. If you're particularly sensitive or have a history of allergies, experiment with several brands before using any with a full load of wash. A bonus with alternative powders is their concentrated formulas. So, although some may cost more than conventional brands up front, they should last a long time before needing to be repurchased.

One alternative laundry powder you might like to try is Allens Naturally Ultra Concentrated Powder Laundry Detergent (**Allens Naturally**), which can be ordered directly from the manufacturer, **N.E.E.D.S., Health One Co., Allergy Relief Shop, Inc., Tucson Cooperative Warehouse, Coastline Products,** and **Janice Corporation.** It's also sometimes sold in alternative grocery and health-food stores. This particular product is biodegradable, undyed, and perfume-free. Just 3 tablespoons per load is all that's needed.

Nature Clean Laundry Powder (**Frank T. Ross & Sons Ltd.**) can be an excellent option. It contains no dyes or perfumes, EDTA, phosphates, or bleaches. Cleaning agents derived from corn are used. You can order it from the company or from **American Environmental Health Foundation**.

Another good product is Ecover Concentrated Laundry Powder (**Ecover**). It's available through dealers such as **Karen's Natural Products** and **Tucson Cooperative Warehouse**. It's also sometimes sold in alternative grocery stores. This particular powder is an all-natural, biodegradable detergent that's both enzyme- and phosphate-free. It contains no perfume but it does have a natural citrate which gives it a mild citrus smell. A special measuring scoop is included to enable you to use the right amount.

Many have found Seventh Generation Natural Concentrated Laundry Detergent (**Seventh Generation**) acceptable. A white powder with enzymes, it has no chlorine, optical brighteners, dyes, or artificial fragrances. However, it does have a mild natural citrus odor. A brand new offering is Seventh Generation Free & Clear Natural Concentrated Laundry Detergent (**Seventh Generation**). This is the same product without added scent. Use the handy scoop provided for the correct amount in each wash load. Seventh Generation products can be purchased through **Harmony**, **Tucson Cooperative Warehouse**, **GreenMarketplace.com**, and at many local alternative groceries.

Bi-O-Kleen laundry powder is a phosphate-, chlorine-, and synthetic-fragrance-free product made with grapefruit seed and orange-peel extract. This citrus-based cleaner has the addition of Bac-Out. This is an active bacterial culture capable of producing enzymes which break down organic stains and odors. It's sold through **Real Goods** and **EcoBaby Organics**. One more choice is Bio Shield Compact Laundry Soap (**Eco Design Co.**), a concentrated vegetable-based soap product with no artificial scents. It can be purchased from manufacturer.

Earth Friendly Ecos All-Natural Concentrated Laundry Powder (**Earth Friendly Products**) uses naturally-derived surfactants. Unlike their liquid version, this product is unscented. Check with **Priorities** and **Real Goods** for availability, as well as local alternative grocery stores.

A good unscented soap-based option is Auro Awalan Laundry Powder Soap. This laundry cleaner is sold by **Sinan Company**.

Liquid Alternative Laundry Products

Some individuals prefer liquid laundry products over powder types. Liquids tend to dissolve completely, while powders may not. (Undissolved powders can leave white streaks on clothing or hardened lumps in the washing machine's soap/detergent dispenser.) The following sections offer some liquid product suggestions you might try.

White Vinegar

Some very sensitive and allergic persons simply use white, distilled vinegar without any other products in their washing machines to clean their clothes and household fabric washables. Using vinegar in your washer has several advantages. It's natural, nontoxic, biodegradable, relatively inexpensive, and can help remove many odors. It can also help fabrics retain their original color. Interestingly, most of the distilled vinegar available in grocery stores is actually made of fermented grain (alcohol) that has undergone a distillation process to produce purified acetic acid. This acid is then diluted with water. Therefore, full-strength kitchen-use white vinegar is only 3–6% acetic acid and the rest is water.

To use white vinegar, try ½–2 cups in your washing machine per load, depending on the size of your load. (You should probably experiment with a range of dilutions to see what works best for you.) It should be noted that certain individuals may find vinegar odors unpleasant or bothersome. If you do, you might want to open a nearby window or activate a ventilation fan. Fortunately, vinegar odors in wet items will virtually disappear after they're hung outside to dry or they're dried in the automatic dryer. However, you should be very cautious about soaking items overnight in your washing machine using vinegar; it can cause some metal parts to rust or corrode.

If you plan to use white vinegar regularly in your washing machine, it's a good idea to buy gallon-size jugs of a generic store brand. That way, you'll save a lot of money, compared to buying several small bottles.

Other Alternative Liquid Products

There are a number of manufactured liquid alternative laundry products you may want to try. Following is a selection of some of them. You'll likely find others in alternative product catalogs and in local alternative groceries. Remember: If you're sensitive or allergic, you'll likely have to try several brands until you find one that works well for you. And, never use a previously untried product with a full wash load. Bothersome ingredients may be difficult to remove from fabric fibers later.

One product many with sensitivities and allergies have used successfully is Power Plus/ Laundry Concentrate (**Granny's Old Fashioned Products**). It's sold through dealers such as **N.E.E.D.S., Allergy Relief Shop, Inc., Bio Designs, Health One Co., American Environmental Health Foundation**, and **The Living Source**. This product contains naturally derived surfactants and is undyed, biodegradable, and very affordable. The manufacturer recommends you use just 1 tablespoon per wash load. This same product under the Coastline Old Fashioned label is offered by **Coastline Products**.

Nature Clean Laundry Liquid (**Frank T. Ross & Sons Ltd.**) is a very good option as well. It's contains corn-based ingredients without optical brighteners and enzymes, dyes, or perfumes. You can order it from the company and from **American Environmental Health Foundation**. EnviroRite Laundry Detergent (**BioForce Enviro-Tech Inc.**) has been used by many sensitive and allergic people. This undyed, unscented product can be ordered from the manufacturer or from **Allergy Control Products, Inc.**

LifeTime Solutions Laundry Concentrate (**LifeTime Solutions**) is a clear, near-odorless liquid detergent with a unique *colloidal-micelle* formulation. You can order it directly from LifeTime Solutions. Lifekind Laundry Liquid (**Lifekind Products**) is a concentrate with no added scents, but it does contain natural softeners and non-chlorine bleach. Made with citrus extracts, it has an innate mild citrus smell. It can be bought from **Lifekind Products**.

You might also want to try Seventh Generation Natural Ultra Laundry Detergent (**Seventh Generation**). This product contains natural coconut-oil surfactants (compounds that lower the water surface tension) and citrus oils. It has no added artificially-derived fragrance, is undyed, and is biodegradable. You'll find that Seventh Generation Natural Liquid has a mild citrusy odor. Something new is Seventh Generation Free & Clear Natural Ultra Laundry Detergent (**Seventh Generation**) which has the same formulation but no added citrus scent. Both products are sold through the **Harmony**, and **Tucson Cooperative Warehouse** catalogs, on line from **GreenMarketplace.com**, and in many alternative grocery stores.

Earth Friendly Ecos Liquid All-Natural Laundry Detergent (**Earth Friendly Products**) is another ultra-concentrated product. It's formula includes natural surfactants and botanical oils, giving it a fragrant quality. You can order it from **Priorities** and **Real Goods**. Well & Good Laundry Liquid (**Well & Good**) is a concentrated product which uses just 1 oz. per load. It is made with "natural plant-based cleaning agents" and has a natural citrus scent.

Bi-O-Kleen Laundry Liquid has oxygen bleach and Bac-Out. This is an active bacterial culture that digests organic stains and odors through enzymatic action. Bi-O-Kleen has no dyes or synthetic scents. This citrus-extract cleaner can be bought from **EcoBaby Organics**.

Ecover Liquid Laundry Wash (**Ecover**) is sold by Ecover dealers including **Tucson Cooperative Warehouse**, **Karen's Natural Products** and some alternative grocery stores. This detergent is natural, biodegradable, and undyed. It also contains natural perfume in the form of essential oils.

Liquid soaps are gentle washing options that some prefer. Auro Awalan Laundry Soap is an unscented "natural chemistry" liquid sold by **Sinan Company**. The ingredients in Bio Shield Liquid Laundry Soap (**Eco Design Co.**) include vegetable-based soap, ethanol, citrates, and essential oils which provide a natural fragrance. This product can be purchased from the manufacturer.

Alternative Bleaches

Most natural soaps, washing compounds, and alternative-formula detergents—and of course vinegar and baking soda—don't contain additives such as optical brighteners (compounds that make fabrics appear brighter), enzymes, and bleaches, all of which are found in typical laundry products. As a result, after using alternative products for awhile, you may find that your clothes don't look as bright as they did before. Therefore, you might decide you need something extra in your wash. For a number of people, bleach is that something extra. If you do decide to use a bleach, seriously consider using an oxygen-type bleaching agent rather than chlorine.

Hydrogen Peroxide

Hydrogen peroxide, like chlorine, is unstable and reactive. But, hydrogen peroxide has virtually no odor and is much safer to handle. To use the common generic liquid hydrogen peroxide (the 3% dilution sold in drugstores), fill your washer with water first and then pour in $1/3$–$1/2$ cup of the hydrogen peroxide. After that, you can add your washables and run the wash cycle through as usual.

Other Alternative Bleaching Products

One popular alternative bleach is Ecover Non-Chlorine Bleach (**Ecover**). This is simply a concentrated hydrogen-peroxide-and-water product. It is available through Ecover dealers, including **Tucson Cooperative Warehouse** and **Karen's Natural Products**. It's also sometimes sold in alternative grocery stores.

Another bleaching product you might try is Seventh Generation Free & Clear Natural Concentrated Non-Chlorine Bleach (**Seventh Generation**). This is a biodegradable liquid that uses an oxygen-based compound as the active bleaching agent. It has the added bonus of containing no dyes or scents. To use it, the manufacturer suggests you try 2 oz. per load. Seventh Generation products are available from **Harmony**, **Tucson Cooperative Warehouse**, **GreenMarketplace.com**, and sometimes at local alternative grocery stores.

Nature Clean Non-Chlorine Bleach (**Frank T. Ross & Sons Ltd.**) is an unscented, liquid, hydrogen-peroxide/water solution. It can be ordered through the manufacturer. **American**

Environmental Health Foundation also handles it. Another powdered unscented alternative product is Lifekind Non-Chlorine Oxygen Bleach (**Lifekind Products**). This laundry aid can be purchased from the company.

EnviroRite Powdered Power Whitener & Deodorizer (**BioForce Enviro-Tech Inc.**) is a laundry aid you might consider. It's ingredient list contains no dyes or added fragrance, but has a *proprietary* (trade secret) deodorizing agent to freshen wash loads. You can order it directly from the company.

Bio Shield Bleach (**Eco Design Co.**) is a fragrance-free powdered sodium percarbonate product which can be ordered from manufacturer. You also may be interested to know that **Real Goods** offers Bi-O-Kleen Oxygen Bleach Plus. This is a granular product without dyes or added scents that's boron-free. **EcoBaby Organics** handles the liquid version, Bi-O-Kleen Liquid Oxygen Bleach.

Oxi-Clean is an unscented, undyed hydrogen-peroxide alkaline powder. It can be ordered from **Harriet Carter Gifts, Harmony,** and **Real Goods.** It's now possible to find it in some grocery stores as well.

Although they're not considered by most people as bleaches, sodium hexametaphosphate (see *Sodium Hexametaphosphate* on page 114) and borax (see *Borax* on page 115) do have a mild bleaching effect on fabrics. However, for the most effective alternative bleaching, you'll probably want to use one of the alternative bleaching products discussed above.

Stain-Removal Products

Typical stain-removal products for fabric usually contain certain ingredients that can be very bothersome to sensitive individuals, and to some allergic people as well— namely synthetic solvents or perhaps synthetic colorants and fragrances. Therefore, these individuals sometimes have difficulty locating products to remove spots and stains from clothing items. Fortunately, there are now a number of alternative products that work fairly well and that should be less bothersome.

For a prespotter on laundry day, SafeChoice Super Clean (**AFM**) used in a 1-to-1 dilution with water often works well. (For certain stubborn stains, you might even use it full-strength.) Super Clean is an unscented, undyed, synthetic, multi-purpose liquid cleaner that's especially effective on many grease and oil stains. You can purchase this product through AFM dealers such as **N.E.E.D.S.** and **The Living Source.** To use Super Clean, dab the solution onto the spot, rub it into the cloth, and then let it sit a few minutes before putting the item into the washing machine for laundering.

A popular alternative stain-removing product is White Wizard All Purpose Cleaner & Spot Remover (**L.B. Roe Corp.**). This is a white, jelly-like product sold in 10 oz. plastic tubs. The company also makes White Wizard Odorless Household Cleaner which can be used as a prewash. These products can be ordered from the company and they can be found in some local grocery and hardware stores. The original tub version can also be mail-ordered from **Solutions, Harmony,** and **Real Goods.** Both White Wizard cleaners are nontoxic and have no odor, but are strong enough in many instances to remove blood, ink, and grease stains from a range of fabrics.

By the way, **Real Goods** also sells Ossengal, another stain remover. This is an organic, odorless, chemical-free, white soap-like stick. Because of it's handy shape, it's easy to use.

Soil Away (**Granny's Old Fashioned Products**) is an unscented, biodegradable, stain and soil remover that has been specially formulated to remove ink, blood, crayon and many other stains. Granny's products, including this one, can be mail-ordered from **N.E.E.D.S. The Living Source, Health One Co., Allergy Relief Shop, Inc., Bio Designs,** and **American Environmental Health Foundation.** The same product under the Coastline Old Fashioned label is sold by **Coastline Products.**

LifeTime Solutions Laundry Pre-Spot (**LifeTime Solutions**) is a one-of-a kind liquid organic-based, *colloidal-micelle* solution. Having no dyes or scents, it can be a good choice for many allergic and sensitive people. It can be ordered directly from the company.

Lifekind Laundry Prespotter (**Lifekind Products**) also has no dyes or added scents. With a natural formula including citrus extracts, it has a fresh citrus smell. Lifekind Products can be ordered directly from the company's catalog. Another choice is EnviroRite Laundry Pre-Treat (**BioForce Enviro-Tech Inc.**). This product has no dyes or fragrances and can be purchased through the company as well as **Allergy Control Products, Inc.**

Ecover Stain Remover (**Ecover**) is a vegetable, soap, and sugar-based surfactant product that includes glycerin, natural acids, and natural salts. It contains no perfumes. It's often sold in local alternative groceries and can be mail-ordered from **Tucson Cooperative Warehouse.**

Bi-O-Kleen Bac-Out Waste & Odor Digester contains active bacterial cultures which produce enzymes capable of digesting organic stains and odors. This product has no added scents or dyes. It can be purchased from **EcoBaby Organics.**

Earth Friendly Stain & Odor Remover (**Earth Friendly Products**) is made with natural enzymes and lemon oil. Check with **Real Goods** and **Priorities** for this lemony fragrant cleaner, and also local alternative groceries.

To remove rust stains from fabrics, you might try moistening the affected areas with water and sprinkling them with enough Bar Keepers Friend (**Servaas Laboratories, Inc.**) to make a paste. Then let this set for 5–10 minutes. After that, rinse the fabric thoroughly with clear water. (Note: Always test on an inconspicuous area on the fabric first, and keep in mind that dark colors may lighten.) In addition, to remove an orangish coloring from items that have been repeatedly washed in water having a high iron content, add 3–4 tablespoons of Bar Keeper's Friend to your washer for each 2 gallons of water. Then simply run the load through as usual. This product is an unscented, undyed, fine powder that's commonly sold in grocery and hardware stores. Because the active ingredient is oxalic acid, which is toxic, Bar Keepers Friend should definitely be stored in a place where it's inaccessible to children and pets.

For other alternative stain-removal remedies, read *Clean and Green* and *Better Basics for the Home*, both by Annie Berthold-Bond. Important note: No matter what stain-removal product or homemade recipe you decide upon, it's always best to first carefully test it on an inconspicuous spot to see whether the fabric's color will fade or the fibers will in some way be damaged from using the product.

Fabric Softeners

Many sensitive and allergic persons are bothered by typical fabric softeners because they can leave intolerable residues on fabric fibers. What do typical fabric softeners contain? Liquid types of fabric softeners contain water, synthetic surfactants (compounds able to lower the water surface tension), emulsifiers (compounds able to suspend oil molecules in water), and synthetic fragrance. Almost all fabric softener dryer sheets are sections of non-woven rayon saturated with surfactants and synthetic perfume. (Note: If you can find a truly unscented sheet version, you may want to experiment with them.) What fabric softeners actually do is make cloth fibers more porous to water. It's been said that they act as moisturizers for fabric.

If you find typical fabric softeners bothersome, you might try using 1/4 cup white vinegar or 1/4 cup baking soda, which you can add to the wash water of each load. While neither of these will be quite as effective as typical fabric softeners, they can help make your clothes feel less scratchy and stiff.

An alternative fabric softer you might try is Allens Naturally Anti-Static Fabric Softener (**Allens Naturally**). It can be ordered directly from the company or from **N.E.E.D.S., Janice Corporation, Tucson Cooperative Warehouse, Coastline Products, Health One Co.**, and **Allergy Relief Shop, Inc.** It can also be bought in some alternative grocery stores. This particular product uses soy-bean derived ingredients, is unscented, alcohol-free, and biodegradable.

One more alternative fabric softener worth considering is Ecover Fabric Softener (**Ecover**). This is a biodegradable liquid formulated with coconut surfactants and "cationic surfactants based on vegetable fatty acids" with a natural scent added. All you need is one capful per load in the final rinse water. This product is available from dealers such as **Tucson Cooperative Warehouse** and **Karen's Natural Products**, and is sometimes sold in alternative groceries as well.

An unscented, undyed product is Nature Clean Fabric Softener (**Frank T. Ross & Sons Ltd.**) which is formulated with jojoba oil. You can order it from the manufacturer and from **American Environmental Health Foundation**.

Seventh Generation Natural Ultra Fabric Softener (**Seventh Generation**) is another option. A canola oil-containing product, it has no dyes or water-repelling compounds. However, it does have a natural scent added. You can buy it from **Harmony, Tucson Cooperative Warehouse, GreenMarketplace.com**, and most local alternative groceries. You may also want to try Bio Shield Softener (**Eco Design Co.**) containing powdered zeolite with a mild natural citrusy scent. It can be ordered from manufacturer.

Fabric Fluffer is a simple way to fluff up towels, diapers, etc. This product adds no softening liquid to the rinse water or a chemical-coated sheet to the dryer. Instead, it consists of two solid, synthetic-composition rings which you place in the dryer with the load to be dried. Of course, sensitive people will want to determine whether they could release any potentially bothersome odors that could be absorbed into their clothes and bedding by using them first on perhaps a load of wet cotton rags. Fabric Fluffers can purchased from **EcoBaby Organics** and **Harmony**.

An interesting way to cope with static electricity building up on clothes in your dryer is to use X-Static Hand Maid. At first glance, this product appears to be an odd pair of work gloves. However they're manufactured with silver, a very electrically conductive substance that, apparently, has the ability to dissipate static charges as they form. One source for X-Static Hand Maid is **Harmony**.

Laundering Diapers

There are a number of ways to deal with cleaning diapers. One approach you might try is to rinse a diaper soaked only in urine in a sink. Then, quickly wash it out using a mild, unscented dish soap such as Safe Suds (**Ar-Ex, Ltd.**). Safe Suds can be ordered directly from company. (For other choices see *Hand Dishwashing Products* on page 166.) Then, place the diaper in a diaper pail that holds only urine-soaked diapers and clean the sink.

For diapers with stools on them, shake the loose waste into the toilet and flush. Then, leave the diaper in the toilet bowl to soak for a time, but don't forget about it! It only needs to soak long enough to loosen the stool matter that remains on the cloth. Later, agitate the diaper in the toilet water to remove more of the remaining stool and flush. Agitate the diaper again and flush. At this point, wring the diaper out and place it in the diaper pail reserved for stool-soiled diapers. By having the stool-soiled diapers separated in their own diaper pail, they'll be presorted and ready for any additional laundry treatment that the urine-only diapers may not require.

By the way, it's been suggested that diaper pails should have a small amount of tolerable detergent, laundry soap, baking soda, or borax mixed with water in their bottoms. Another possibility is to use Bi-O-Kleen Bac-Out Waste & Odor Digester and water. This product contains no dyes or added fragrance, but contains active bacterial cultures that produce natural enzymes which digest organic stains and smells. You can purchase it through **EcoBaby Organics**. A good selection of other unscented enzyme-based products are sold by **Dasun Co.** Using any of these options will help neutralize unpleasant odors between wash loads. To further minimize odors, you'll need to wash all the diapers in both pails as often as you can. Hopefully, that would be at least every few days, but obviously that's an ideal and not always possible. Plus, you'll want to routinely clean both diaper pails. If you can, set them outside in the sun to freshen from time to time.

When you're ready to launder the dirty diapers, place them in the washer and immediately run the final spin cycle. This will help rid the diapers of any contaminated soaking water. Then, start the washer using hot water and a tolerable detergent or laundry soap. As soon as the washer has filled and has had enough time to dissolve and thoroughly disperse the cleaning agent, turn the washer off and let the diapers have a long soak. Setting a timer that comes with a neck cord, or a watch with a timer alarm, and keeping it with you will remind you when to start the washer again. (Note: From time to time you may want to add an oxygenated bleach to whiten diapers that have become dingy looking.) After soaking, run the load through at least one, or better two, rinse cycle(s) to make sure all the fabric fibers are free of cleaning product residues. Finally, a second (or third) rinse using $1/4$ to $1/2$ cup of white vinegar added to it will lower the pH of the diapers. The slightly acidic condition this creates will help discourage bacterial growth. When the final spin cycle is complete, the diapers should be ready for drying.

An excellent book on diaper care is *Diaper Changes: The Complete Diapering Book and Resource Guide* by Theresa Rodriquez Farrisi. To find a copy, check your local library and favorite bookstores. It should be noted here that although borax is often recommended for diapers and other baby clothes, there are those who feel that borax is just not gentle enough for infants and may cause skin rashes or other reactions. For more on this viewpoint, check the **B. Coole Designs** website.

Laundering for Allergic People

Those who have conventional allergies to dust, dust mites, and other household allergens will want to make sure to clean their clothes and bedding frequently, using gentle, low-odor products. This means, of course, they'll need to purchase items which are not only easily washable and dryable, but also sturdy enough to withstand repeated launderings. In particular, how to care for bedding is a big concern. The following are some suggestions you may wish to follow.

For sheets and pillows, it's best to wash them weekly. Pillows (unless the manufacturer's tags state otherwise) need only a short agitation cycle of about two minutes on a gentle cycle using warm water. However, you'll want to use a full rinse cycle to make sure all the laundry detergent has been completely removed. Then place them in the dryer. (Again, that is unless the manufacturer's tags state otherwise.) It should be mentioned that if you use pillow protectors to seal out dust mites, the pillows themselves might only need to be washed every 3 months.

Blankets, comforters, quilts, and mattress pads will need laundering at least every 3 months. However, for those who experience severe allergic reactions to dust mites, this can be done more frequently. Again, if you use allergen-impermeable protectors on the comforters and quilts, they won't need laundering as often. All these items should be washed with gentle cycles using warm water, then dried in the dryer.

Electric blankets require special care. Only wash them for a short time, perhaps for only 2 or 3 minutes. Then, place in a dryer, but only if the manufacturer's tags specifically recommend this. Otherwise, dry over two clothes lines. Don't take your electric blanket in to be dry cleaned. This isn't just because of the problem of bothersome dry cleaning odors your blanket would absorb, but also because the cleaning solvents could damage wiring inside the blanket.

By the way, don't forget to launder washable area rugs and curtains regularly, too. Too often, these are overlooked. For good, information on common allergens and suggested cleaning procedures and schedules, write to **The Soap and Detergent Association** for their 8$1/2$" x 11", 35-page booklet entitled *Clean and Healthy Strategies for Today's Homes: Allergies and Asthma Reference Manual.* An abridged, 14-page version called *Clean and Healthy Strategies for Today's Homes: Managing Allergies and Asthma* can be directly downloaded from their website.

It should be mentioned here that Allerwash, sold by **Inner Balance** is an "anti-allergen laundry liquid" designed to remove and neutralize dust mite allergens from bedding and other items. However, it's a scented product. If you want to avoid scents and perfumes, this product may not be the best choice for you.

Removing Odors from New Clothing

Unfortunately for some allergic and most sensitive people, brand-new garments, even if they're made of untreated 100%-cotton, can release strong odors that will require special cleaning techniques to remove them. Otherwise, even after one or more normal washings, the innate bothersome odors can still make the clothes unwearable.

Why is this so? Many new-clothing odors are due to the presence of chemicals that have been applied to the fibers. This may have occurred during the plant's cultivation, or later during milling and manufacturing. For example, a non-water-soluble form of formaldehyde has become a common chemical treatment applied to some 100%-cotton items. Undergoing this process provides permanent wrinkle-resisting qualities. Realistically, non-water-soluble formaldehyde odors can be difficult if not impossible to significantly remove. The best advice is to avoid buying items with wrinkle-resisting treatments in the first place.

While the use of formaldehyde as a wrinkle-resisting compound is fairly well known, fewer people are aware that other items may have similar chemicals in them. That's because some dyes and *sizings* also use bothersome chemical compounds. What is sizing? Sizing is nothing more than a temporary, stiffening glaze. Its purpose is to help retain the original shape of an item, so its appearance remains attractive to potential purchasers. Unlike the formaldehyde chemicals used to create wrinkle resistance, the chemicals used in sizing are usually water soluble. Therefore, they're generally designed to wash out in about three to four washings. (Of course, chemically sensitive people may find it'll require more than that for them.)

Unfortunately, it should also be noted that even undyed organic-cotton fabric can be bothersome—just because of cotton's strong, natural, grainy smell. This is probably the result of crushed cotton seeds releasing their natural resins and oils into the surrounding cotton fibers during ginning.

Furthermore, any item—no matter what it's made of—can (and usually does) absorb a variety of ambient odors. These may include perfumes, air fresheners, pesticides, combustion gases, or tobacco odors picked up at manufacturing plants, warehouses, transport vehicles, or at retail outlets.

If you find new clothing odors objectionable, some sensitive people have found that adding $1/2$–1 cup of powdered milk per wash load will help remove these smells. Also, borax (about $1/3$–$1/2$ cup per load) will often help. However, be careful when using borax with dark fabrics because of its mild bleaching effect. In addition, baking soda can help make your new clothes more tolerable. In this case, you might try using $1/2$–1 cup per load. Many sensitive people find that in order to sufficiently remove the odors using one of these natural powders, they often have to repeat the wash cycle over and over again—perhaps as many as ten times—depending on how sensitive they are.

One product that some people have found particularly effective at removing new clothing odors is zeolite. Dasun Zeolite Powder, in a two-pound container, can be ordered from **Bio Designs** or **Dasun Co.** Two- and ten-pound containers of natural zeolite can be ordered from **healthyhome.com**. Powdered zeolite can also often be purchased from local chemical supply companies in bulk (50 or 100 pound bags) at lower cost. To use this simple mineral powder, add two level tablespoons to the washer and agitate to dissolve the granules completely. (Note: Some people may want to wear a dust mask when using this product.) After that, add a new garment and soak it for several hours. Then run it through a complete wash/rinse/spin cycle. Of course, you can repeat the entire regimen from the beginning if you find it necessary.

Another simple odor reducer is white vinegar. Vinegar has the added benefit of helping fabric retain its color—something that the powders mentioned above can't do. To use white vinegar, pour 1-2 cups into the washer—the exact amount depends on the load size. By the way, a number of sensitive individuals find that if they alternately wash with vinegar and then baking soda, their new clothes seem to become tolerable sooner.

Yet another possibility to remove unwanted odors in new clothing is to use about $1/8$–$1/4$ cup SafeChoice Super Clean (**AFM**) for each wash load. This unscented, undyed, biodegradable, synthetic, liquid detergent is sold by most AFM dealers including **N.E.E.D.S.**, **American Environmental Health Foundation**, and **The Living Source**. However, be aware that Super Clean can bleach some colors slightly.

It should be mentioned that it's not uncommon for some sensitive individuals to want to soak their problem clothing overnight in the washing machine in order to reduce unwanted odors. If you're using baking soda, that may be fine. However, soaking overnight with vinegar, products containing bleach (regular or alternative bleaches), or other fairly reactive compounds can be potentially corrosive to the washer's interior metal parts. Therefore, rust formation could easily form on steel that is sometimes exposed along the edges of porcelainized or painted surfaces. This rust could discolor fabrics. To soak clothing for more than a few hours, use a plastic bucket or some other type of container incapable of reacting. Then, remove the clothing, place it in the washer, and then add the liquid contents of the bucket to the load. At that point, you can run a complete wash cycle through.

It should be pointed out that, no matter what you use to remove new clothing odors, extended airing may also be necessary. However, be sure to hang your clothing outdoors only in dry, uncontaminated surroundings. Some individuals have actually had to air certain items daily for a week or more. In fact, airing for months is not that uncommon for those persons who are extremely sensitive.

Machine Washing Delicates

Your more delicate items can be successfully machine washed—if you follow some guidelines. First, turn garments inside out unless there's some compelling reason not to. By having them inside out, any wear from rubbing against the agitator and tub walls won't occur on the good side of your clothes. Place small, extremely delicate, or items with cords, straps, or ribbons in delicate wash bags. One source for these is **Janice Corporation**.

The third thing you need to remember is to use only the cool or cold water setting, unless the manufacturer's label says otherwise. Fourthly, choose your washer's most gentle cycle. That is, unless the manufacturer's label indicates that a more rigorous one is suitable.

Finally use a very gentle cleaning product—and as little as you can. Ecover Delicate Wash (**Ecover**) is one soap-based possibility. However, it does contain natural perfume. You can order it from **Karen's Natural Products** and **Tucson Cooperative Warehouse** as well as find it at some alternative groceries. Actually, most of the manufactured alternative liquid laundry products that have been mentioned previously will work. (See *Other Alternative Liquid Products* on page 117.) Refrain from using dishwashing liquids. Unless you take great care to use only use a very minute amount, they can easily create far too many suds. Powders, because of their granular nature, usually aren't as gentle as liquids, however, soap flakes can be.

Hand-Laundering

Washable knits, delicate fabrics, woolens, and embellished articles should generally be hand-laundered only. Ideally, for this job, you want to choose a mild, unscented cleaning product. Of course, this is especially important for very sensitive and scent-allergic persons.

For hand-laundering, alternative hand-washing dish detergents often work very well. One you might try is Safe Suds (**Ar-Ex, Ltd.**). Safe Suds is a mild, unscented, undyed, biodegradable, synthetic detergent that can be ordered directly from the manufacturer or purchased through a local pharmacy. An advantage to this particular product is that it is pH balanced. That means it does not create an acidic or alkaline condition for your clothes. (For other possible dishwashing products, see *Hand Dishwashing Products* on page 166).

Some wool items can also be washed with gentle soap-based products. Soap is less likely to remove wool's natural lanolin oils than detergents, so it's probably the better way to go. Auro Awalan Laundry Soap, an unscented liquid, from **Sinan Company** is one you might choose. Other soaps include Dr. Erlander's Jubilee Liquid Castile Soap (**Erlander's Natural Products**) which can be ordered directly from the company, and Dr. Bronner's Baby Supermild Unscented Castile Soap Liquid (**Dr. Bronner's**), which is available from the company, **Tucson Cooperative Warehouse**, **Frontier Natural Products** and many local health-food stores.

To use Safe Suds or a liquid soap for hand-laundering, simply add a small amount to a sink or basin which is half-filled with water. (Cooler water will minimize shrinkage and maximize color retention.) Then, swish the water to create suds. Next, place your garment in the basin and gently squeeze the sudsy water through the fibers. (Another option is to simply allow the item to soak for a few minutes.) Then, rinse the garment several times in cool, clear water. After that, remove the item and *gently* squeeze out the water. It is important not to wring, especially rayon whose fibers become much weaker in water.

You may also want to lay the item on a large, clean towel and roll it up to absorb any excess water. Finally, the garment can be hung to dry or laid flat on a clean, dry towel, or special sweater drying rack (see *Flat Drying* on page 127).

For more on safe procedures for hand-laundering, you'll want to check out *Chapter 7: Healthier Fibers & Stuffings*. A helpful book is *Better Basics for the Home* by Annie Berthold-Bond. It's found at many libraries and bookstores.

Drying Your Laundry

Most people automatically think of drying their clothes in a dryer but, surprisingly, there are more options than that. Of course, you'll want to choose the method most appropriate for each particular article.

Air-Drying

The two main methods of air-drying are hang-drying and flat-drying. Each has a number of possible approaches and methods. Some of these will be discussed below.

Keep in mind that air drying a large number of items indoors can often result in excessive indoor humidity as the moisture evaporates from the clothes into the air. When the humidity indoors gets too high, mold growth is a real possibility. So, be very careful about air drying too many items indoors, especially in the winter when the moisture can condense on window frames and other cool surfaces.

Hang-Drying

Hanging clothes and other washable items outdoors to dry is not only an inexpensive way to dry them, but it also can give them a renewed freshness. This is because the air blowing through fabric fibers helps lift out odors, while at the same time the ultraviolet rays from the sun will act as a mild bleach and disinfectant.

However, if you plan to dry your items outside, be alert for the presence of unwanted outdoor odors, especially if you're chemically sensitive. This is because smoke from burning leaves, barbecues, and fireplaces as well as traffic exhaust can quickly become absorbed by fabric fibers. You should also be alert to days with a high pollen count if you're an allergic person, and not hang your clothing outside on those days either. In addition, everyone should make certain that his or her clothesline and clothespins are clean and in good repair so they won't soil or damage hanging items.

Handy single-line retractable (up to usually 40 ft. long) clotheslines are commonly found in hardware stores. By mail-order, you can buy them from **Vermont Country Store Voice of the Mountains, Lillian Vernon,** and **Improvements.** Although commonly used outdoors, they can be used in some locations indoors, too. Large collapsible outdoor *umbrella dyers* with multiple rows of concentric lines are sold by **Real Goods** and **Harmony.**

For drying small hand washables indoors, you might want to purchase a solid-wood, folding, drying rack. These are made with a number of dowel rods in alternating positions so that many of your small items can be dried at the same time. Such racks are often sold in hardware stores. You can also buy them from the **Vermont Country Store Voice of the Mountains** and **Harmony.**

Also, certain damp clothing items can be hung to dry using heavy *anodized aluminum* hangers. (Anodized aluminum has a protective coating.) Such hangers won't rust or bend out of shape. These may be purchased at some department stores, and they can be mail-ordered from **Colonial Garden Kitchens.**

A handy piece of equipment for drying hangable items is a collapsible metal rack. Some have castors, some do not. Some are tubular chromed steel, others are painted metal. Many of these can be temporarily placed in the tub, in your utility room, or outdoors on a flat surface. By mail order, you can buy them from **Improvements.** A more elaborate version is sold by **Get Organized.**

For drying slacks, you might try using special *pants stretchers.* Slacks dried on these metal-frame devices usually don't have to be ironed—a real plus. Once popular, then rare, pants stretchers are now becoming available again. A mail-order source is **Vermont Country Store Voice of the Mountains.**

Flat-Drying

A number of washable items in your home, including most sweaters, are best dried by flat-drying. Of course, a very common way to do this is to lay your damp sweater, or other item, on a thick 100%-cotton terry towel that's completely colorfast. This is fine, but sweater drying racks have real advantages over using towels.

Sweater racks usually consist of a collapsible metal frame and a stretched mesh fabric. The rack lifts the sweater up off the floor while the mesh allows the air to pass under and through the garment. This hastens drying while lessening the chance for mustiness to develop. You can buy sweater drying racks in some local department and discount stores. They can also be mail-ordered from **Vermont Country Store Voice of the Mountains** and **Get Organized.**

Whenever you need to flat-dry an item, it's often a good idea to use a pattern as a layout guide, to make sure it'll retain its prewashed size and shape. To make a drying pattern, before washing simply lay the dry clothing item on a piece of heavy, plain, undyed paper. Then, draw a line around the garment with a pencil. Next, remove the item, cut the paper along the drawn line, and label the pattern as to the garment for which it was created. After your garment has been washed and placed on the drying towel or rack, you can then place the pattern on top of it and shape the clothing to match the pattern. Finally, you'll want to remove the pattern, allow it to dry, and save it for reuse. Instead of paper patterns, some people make fabric patterns, which are not as easily damaged by moisture or repeated use.

Machine-Drying

Of course, most of your washable items can be put in an automatic clothes dryer to dry them. Certainly, automatic dryers are quick and convenient. However, if your dryer operates on natural gas or propane, there are some concerns of which you should be aware.

Some sensitive individuals using gas dryers have reported that they can't tolerate items dried in them. Apparently their clothes absorb natural gas odors or, more likely, the by-products of combustion. (Unfortunately, modifying a gas dryer so that absolutely no combustion by-products reach what's being dried inside is impossible.) It must be pointed out that sensitive persons can be affected by extremely minute quantities of pollutants. Therefore, if you are a very sensitive person, it is generally best to only use an electric dryer (see *Clothes Dryers* on page 500).

Sometimes, dyers don't seem to dry efficiently. This can be because lint has built up in the outdoor vent, restricting the air flow. Dryer vent cleaning brushes can often be used safely and easily clean them. One purchasing source is **Improvements.** A dryer vent can also be cleaned by a company that specializes in cleaning furnace ducts.

If you're sensitive or highly allergic, it would be wise to not use any typical fabric-softener sheets in your automatic dryer. Sometimes their synthetic fragrances and other potentially bothersome ingredients can make your dryer intolerable for some time. A better choice might be to use Fabric Fluffer to fluff towels and diapers. This product is made of two solid, synthetic-composition rings which you place in the dryer with the load to be dried. (Experiment first before using them on a load of clothes to make sure the rings don't transfer any synthetic odors to the clothes.) Fabric Fluffers can purchased from **EcoBaby Organics** and **Harmony.**

Ironing

It's doubtful if many people like to iron. However, if it has to be done, you might as well do it in the most healthful manner possible. This section offers some suggestions for doing just that.

Electric Irons

In bygone days, irons were made of heavy, cast iron with ground and polished bases and handles attached on top. These irons had to be repeatedly heated over a fire or hot stove after releasing their absorbed heat. Therefore, people often owned two of them to use alternately. Today, electric irons heat themselves, and many create their own steam. Note: Steam irons should only have distilled water used in them so that their small steam vent openings don't become clogged with hard-water buildup (see *Distilled Water* on page 637).

Many irons now available in the U.S. are made with nonstick *sole plates* (the flat ironing surfaces). In some cases, this is achieved by applying or bonding certain synthetic chemical compounds to the metal's surface (see *Nonstick Coatings* on page 502). While permitting a smoother, gliding ironing action, some of these synthetic nonstick surfaces could have the potential to outgas synthetic odors when they're heated. This can be bothersome to some sensitive persons. In addition, some of these coatings are not exceptionally durable, although most are much more scratch-resistant than they were a few years ago.

A healthier nonstick iron is one with a stainless-steel sole plate. Stainless-steel is inherently non-sticking, so there's no need for synthetic chemical compounds. However, because synthetic, nonstick irons are now more durable (as well as cheaper) new irons with stainless-steel sole plates can be somewhat difficult to find. Fortunately though, they're still manufactured. Several Rowenta models (**Rowenta**) have stainless-steel sole plates. Manufactured in Europe, they can be purchased at many Target Stores, Jo-Ann Fabrics & Crafts Stores, other discount and department stores, and fabric shops. If you prefer mail order, check Hold **Everything**. In addition, **Service Merchandise** handles Rowenta irons in both their local outlets and catalog. Proctor-Silex Model 14420 (**Hamilton Beach/Proctor-Silex, Inc.**) has a stainless-steel sole plate and it can be found in some discount and department stores.

By the way, you can sometimes find used stainless-steel irons in second hand stores or at garage sales. If you do find one, check to see if its cord and plug are damaged and then plug the iron in to see if it heats properly. Remember, you might not be able to return used merchandise. Note: Some very sensitive and allergic individuals will have to carefully clean and air outdoors a recently purchased used iron to remove any absorbed perfume, tobacco, and laundry-product odors, etc. Unfortunately, in some cases, the odors will be difficult to remove, and the iron will remain intolerable.

An alternative to a stainless-steel iron is one with a polished-aluminum sole plate. One manufacturer of these is Black & Decker. They can be purchased at some discount and department stores. **Service Merchandise** offers them both in their stores and catalog. Keep in mind though, some persons may find such irons have a tendency to "drag" on certain fabrics, especially if the sole plate has any built-up residue on it. Therefore, it's important to keep a polished-aluminum sole plate as clean as possible.

Ironing-Board Pads and Covers

For sensitive individuals in particular, ironing pads and covers should be washable, untreated, 100%-cotton. Teflon-coated, or other similar ironing-board covers, and those containing flame-retardant compounds can be bothersome. Despite their real and obvious advantages of easier ironing and fire prevention, the chemicals used in them can be released into the air by your heated iron. If you'd like to buy untreated, undyed 100%-cotton ironing-board covers, they can be ordered from **Janice Corporation**.

For ironing-board padding, you might try using a folded, untreated, 100%-cotton, flannel blanket. Ready-made, untreated, cotton, ironing-board pads are sold by **Janice Corporation**. Ironing-board cover fasteners to hold your cover and pad securely in place are handled by **Vermont Country Store Voice of the Mountains.**

Spray Starches

Most of the typical spray starches sold in grocery stores contain a variety of substances, including corn starch, silicone, propellants, and sometimes *proprietary ingredients* (compounds that are company secrets) such as corrosion inhibitors. Some products might also contain scents. These spray starches are designed to not only give your soft, limp fabrics firmness, but they're also formulated to allow your iron to glide across them more easily.

If you want to avoid typical spray starches, you can make a simple homemade version by dissolving 2 teaspoons of cornstarch in 1 cup of water. Then, pour the mixture into a spray bottle and spray the solution on your clothes as needed while ironing.

Because cornstarch can sometimes leave a noticeable whiteness on dark fabrics, you might want to spray dark items using cold black tea instead of the cornstarch/water mixture. (However, refrain from spraying black tea on light-colored items.) Of course, if you use tea bags to make the tea, no tea-leaf particles will get on your clothes. If you use regular black tea, you can effectively strain it by pouring it through a coffee filter.

Making Ironing Tolerable

Many sensitive persons find that ironing is something that—quite literally—makes them sick. This is because some clothing that seems odor-free at room temperature can emit bothersome odors when it's warmed by an iron. The high heat actually causes the release of perfume and other odors that had been deeply embedded in the fabric fibers.

Therefore, if you are a sensitive individual, it's important for you to iron with good ventilation. Simply opening the windows in the room where you are ironing can often help. However, operating a window fan will work even better. You might also want to wear an activated-charcoal-filled mask (see *Personal Facial Air Filters* on page 569).

Steaming

Sometimes using steam is a good option for dewrinkling your clothes. Simply hanging up an item on a hanger in the bathroom during and immediately after taking a hot shower is an easy method to do this.

Of course, hand-held portable home garment steamers can be also used. Some require a small amount of salt to be added and most suggest using distilled water rather than tap water. You may be able to find these at local department and discount stores. A large professional canister model on casters is sold by **Hold Everything**.

Dry Cleaning

Most dry-cleaning chemicals are often intolerable to virtually all chemically sensitive people and to some allergic and asthmatic people. Actually, the term *dry-cleaning* is a bit of a misnomer. The process is called *dry* only because water isn't used. Instead, a liquid petroleum-based solvent is the primary cleaning solution. (Sometimes special soaps and detergents are used along with the solvent.)

Professional dry cleaning has been around for about a century and a half. It began in France when kerosene and turpentine were used to cut grease stains and clean clothes. Since that time, carbon tetrachloride, benzene, benzol, naphtha, and even gasoline have been used as dry-cleaning solvents. However, the dangers of fire and explosion from these fluids were so great that less-combustible *chlorinated hydrocarbon solvents* began to replace them during the 1930s. One of those, *perchloroethylene (perc)* is the most common dry-cleaning solvent used today.

Interestingly, perc was first created to be a metal degreaser, not a garment cleaner. And, although it certainly is less dangerous and explosive than gasoline-like solvents, it is not a benign cleaning agent by any means. In fact, the **EPA (Environmental Protection Agency)** has classified it as a hazardous air contaminant. Other agencies have labeled it a likely carcinogen. Over the years, researchers working in animal studies have reported a host of adverse symptoms in test subjects exposed to perc—in nervous systems, kidneys, livers, generative organs, and other body tissues.

Obviously, humans working directly with perc are likely to be the most adversely affected by this potentially dangerous solvent. However, when dry-cleaned clothing is brought home, solvent residues will likely remain on the fabric fibers. In many cases, these will emit solvent odors which can be dangerous to breathe, even for the healthiest of individuals. Therefore, if you have a garment that's just been dry cleaned, be sure to remove it from it's protective plastic bag and hang it outdoors as soon as you can. You'll need to air it out *at least* several hours, or until most of the characteristic dry-cleaning odor has dissipated. (Note: Some very sensitive people may always sense the presence of dry-cleaning chemicals, no matter how long a garment has aired.)

You should be aware that, as a service to their customers, some dry cleaners routinely add mothproofing chemicals to all wool items. To avoid these potentially bothersome chemicals, you'll want to specify clearly that you don't want your wool items treated against moths.

Recently, home dry-cleaning products (usually scented ones) have become available. However, these products are rarely tolerated well by sensitive individuals. Furthermore, it seems their capacity to clean satisfactorily is still rather debatable. When confronted, manufacturers have stated their products are only designed to remove some small stains, or to "freshen" a tie or blouse. However, many customers expect these products to replace professional dry-cleaning—as the advertising may seem to imply. The truth is, in most cases, they can't and won't.

Specialized Wet Cleaning

In the last few years, a number of professional cleaning companies (many of them already established dry cleaners) began offering what has been termed *specialized wet cleaning*. First developed over a half century ago, this is not a single cleaning method. Instead, it encompasses a whole variety of alternative cleaning procedures, each developed especially for a specific type of item (or fiber) that is normally dry cleaned.

Specialized wet cleaners use water and water-based cleaners. They utilize machine washers, hand washing, or steam coupled with air drying, machine drying, and/or pressing to achieve results comparable to cleaning with conventional dry-cleaning solvents. Surveys have revealed the cost is comparable, too.

It's been recently estimated that 100 to 200 firms currently offer specialized wet-cleaning services around the U.S. Therefore, if you need to have a dry-clean-only item professionally cleaned, check with your local cleaners to see if its an option. (A note of caution: Products used in these procedures, especially if scented, may not be tolerable for some sensitive or allergic people.)

Lint Removal

There are a number of methods to remove lint from your clothes. The most common today is a replaceable sticky paper (often in a tube shape) mounted in a plastic handle. These are sold in most discount stores. For many, this is a satisfactory solution.

Another option is to use a brass fiber brush. Brass fibers usually do not damage woven items, although they can be difficult, if not impossible, to use on some knits. They have the advantage of not needing replaceable parts or refills. All they require is periodic hand cleaning. Once commonplace, brass fiber lint brushes are not easily found. One mail-order source is **Vermont Country Store Voice of the Mountains.**

To remove balls and nubs that form on sweaters, *sweater rocks* or *stones* can be used. These are chunks of hard, stiff, very porous material which are often of volcanic origin. Although they're simple natural tools, when they're used, they can give off unpleasant sulfurous odors as tiny bits of their surface layer break off. Supposedly, this odor will quickly dissipate. However, most sensitive people would probably prefer another option. If you would like to try a sweater rock, look in the **Vermont Country Store Voice of the Mountains** catalog.

A less aromatic sweater ball remover is called a *sweater shaver*. This is usually a small hand-held plastic tool with a large flat, circular metal head. Generally, they run on batteries. Sweater shavers are easy to use and very effective. Many discount stores carry them. Sometimes they're sold in the **Harriet Carter Gifts** catalog, among others.

CHAPTER 6: HOUSE CLEANING

A major way to keep your household healthy is to keep it clean. Fortunately, quite a few products are now available to use, and by using them, you'll definitely help create better indoor air for you and your family. This chapter provides basic information to help you make more knowledgeable house cleaning decisions. It also gives specific suggestions for both healthier cleaning products as well as healthier cleaning techniques.

Cleaning Products

As everyone knows, grocery aisles are filled with a huge variety of cleaning products. Nearly all claim to work better, act faster, and smell fresher than all the others, including previous versions of the same product. A portion of these products are now also labeled "safer to the environment." Generally, such cleaning products claim to be "green," "Earth-friendly," or "eco-friendly" because they're biodegradable, are concentrated (requiring smaller plastic packages), have refills available, have packages made of recycled material, or have packages capable of being recycled. Surprisingly, the ability of the products to directly affect human health isn't usually an "eco-consideration." As a result, only a few national brands offer items that are unscented or simply formulated. Even fewer are all-natural.

In reality, most typical modern cleaners are made with complex formulas comprised of synthetic ingredients, artificial colors, and artificial fragrances (see *Problems with Scents* on page 72). Some products also contain powerful solvents and/or strong disinfectants. Therefore, many common cleaning products have label warnings for their proper use and storage, as well as suggestions for antidotes. Unfortunately, most consumers buy and use these products without much forethought, assuming that if they're on the shelves, they *must* be safe. Therefore, printed warnings are often ignored or briefly scanned because it's thought they contain somewhat overprotective advice. The reality is, the warnings contain good, important advice.

In America, where over ninety percent of all poisonings occur at home, the leading cause of reported cases is from cleaning products. Generally, these poisonings are distinct, singular, acute events. Commonly, they involve the swallowing of some type of cleaner by a toddler. However, how children (as well as adults) fair from exposure to such products over a period of years, when they're used as intended, is far less clearly understood. Interestingly, some individuals who have acquired MCS (Multiple Chemical Sensitivity) believe that typical cleaning products were a contributing factor, sometimes a major factor, to their acquiring the illness in the first place (see *Multiple Chemical Sensitivity* on page 45). Yet, no matter how they initially got the condition, many people with MCS eventually become unable to tolerate most typically available cleaners.

Alternative Cleaning Products

Fortunately, a growing number of alternative cleaning products are becoming available. Many of these have formulas that most sensitive and allergic people can tolerate.

Even major manufacturers and retailers are aware of the environmentally conscious "green market" and they want to tap into it as much as they can. Therefore, consumers wanting less-toxic or more natural products shouldn't be lulled into complacency by product labels that simply proclaim they're "eco-safe." Often this type of term is not legally regulated. Anyway, "environmentally friendly" claims may simply be based on the packaging—not the contents itself.

The truth is, it will usually take some effort on your part to determine if an alternative product is really healthier for you to use. Of course, a complete and thorough reading of a product's label is a good first step. By doing this, you can eliminate certain prospective cleaners simply by reading the fine print. Unfortunately, labels may not reveal everything you'd like to know. For example, the word *nontoxic* doesn't legally mean the product has no hazardous ingredients or is safe if ingested (see *Healthy Definitions* on page 59). Also, some toxic substances legally don't have to be listed as ingredients, if they're in small-enough quantities, or *proprietary* (a trade secret).

As a result, many people who are interested in finding truly safer cleaning products often end up bypassing conventional retail stores. After all, there are now a number of outlets that are more likely to offer acceptable, healthier alternatives. Some even specialize in them. These include health-food shops, food co-ops, alternative grocery stores, alternative catalogs, as well as on-line alternative shopping web sites.

Homemade Alternative Cleaning Products

Often, you don't need to buy prepackaged alternative cleaning products. Some of the simple, common, natural ingredients you probably already have on hand can often clean surprisingly well. One excellent example is baking soda. Baking soda and water can cleanse and deodorize everything from clothing to bathtubs. (*Baking Soda: Over 500 Fabulous, Fun and Frugal Uses You've Probably Never Though Of* by Vicki Lansky is a book filled with baking soda cleaning methods and tips.) Also, white vinegar with water can clean hard-surfaced floors, remove calcium buildup, and make windows sparkle.

Combining two or more household substances can accomplish still other cleaning jobs, such as mixing salt and lemon juice to clean brass. However, it's probably best not to create your own multi-ingredient cleaning products, unless you're using time-tested, well-researched recipes. After all, there's the possibility you could inadvertently create something harmful—both to what you're cleaning as well as to you. For additional suggestions, read *Clean and Green* and *Better Basics for the Home*, both by Annie Berthold-Bond. Another good book is *Clean Your House Safely & Effectively Without Harmful Chemicals* by Randy Dunford. All these books contain many homemade cleaning-solution formulas that are relatively easy to make, generally effective, inexpensive, and above all, safe. Other similar books should be available at your local library or bookstore.

Some Suggested Alternative Cleaning Products

You may want to become familiar with several brands of safer cleaning products. These are ones that have been well tolerated by many sensitive and allergic individuals. While there are certainly many other very good options on the market, these particular products are excellent to start with in your personal quest for developing a healthy household. Remember, test *any* new product for personal tolerability before using it, especially if you're a sensitive or allergic person (see *Testing* on page 62).

Note that cleaning-product suggestions for specific cleaning tasks are listed under their appropriate headings in the other sections of this chapter, such as *Household Cleaning, Kitchen Cleaning,* and *Bathroom Cleaning.*

Alternative Product Line Suggestions

One alternative line of cleaning products you'll probably want to become acquainted with is Allens Naturally (**Allens Naturally**). This brand is sold in many alternative groceries and health-food stores, and can be ordered directly from the company. It's also available from **Janice Corporation, Health One Co., Allergy Relief Shop, Inc., Tucson Cooperative Warehouse,** and **Coastline Products.** The house-cleaning line includes a glass cleaner, a household cleaner, an automatic-dishwasher detergent, and a dish washing liquid. All the various cleaners are biodegradable, concentrated, contain no dyes or perfumes, and they're very economical.

AFM SafeChoice (**AFM**) has been making low odor alternative products for some time now. Their home-cleaning product family includes a concentrated all-purpose cleaner, a glass cleaner, a mold cleaner, and a carpet cleaner. These are sold through **The Living Source, N.E.E.D.S., Allergy Relief Shop, Inc., Priorities,** healthyhome.com and **American Environmental Health Foundation.**

In addition, **Granny's Old-Fashioned Products** manufactures highly concentrated, biodegradable, dye-free, perfume-free, inexpensive cleaners. These include laundry products, carpet cleaners, and dish washing liquids. Most of Granny's cleaners come in a range of package sizes. You can purchase these products through catalogs such as **N.E.E.D.S., Allergy Relief Shop, Inc., Health One Co.,** and **The Living Source.** The same formulations under the Coastline Old Fashioned label are sold by **Coastline Products.**

Nature Clean (**Frank T. Ross & Sons Ltd.**) is Canada's oldest brand of natural cleaning products. (They can be easily purchased by those outside Canada as well.) Formulated without perfumes or dyes, they can be ideal choices for sensitive and scent-allergic people. Nature Clean items include an all-purpose cleaner, toilet bowl cleaner, bathroom cleaners, a dishwashing liquid, and a dishwasher powder. These all can be ordered from the company.

A unique offering is LifeTime Solutions (**LifeTime Solutions**) which utilize *colloidal micelles*. No dyes, or scents are used in the all-liquid line that has all-purpose, bath, carpet, and glass cleaners, a degreaser, and a wood polish. These can be purchased from **LifeTime Solutions**.

Lifekind Products (**Lifekind Products**) has a whole family of undyed, no-added-scent organic cleaning products using citrus extracts. These consist of an all-purpose cleaner, dishwasher powder, glass cleaner, and disinfectant spray, and a stain and odor eliminator. These can all be ordered from the manufacturer.

Only undyed, unscented formulas are used by EnviroRite (**BioForce Enviro-Tech Inc.**). Products offered by this company include cleaners for general purpose, mold, bath, and carpets. They also have a carpet stain remover and a dishwashing liquid. EnviroRite products can be ordered from the company. Some EnviroRite cleaners are available from **eMD.com** and **Allergy Control Products, Inc.**

Another fine alternative cleaning product line is Seventh Generation Natural (**Seventh Generation**). These products include toilet, dish, and all-purpose household cleaners. All of these are biodegradable, dye-free, phosphate-free, and synthetic perfume-free. Their dishwashing liquid, and their dishwasher detergent have no added scent at all. Seventh Generation products can be ordered through **Harmony, Tucson Cooperative Warehouse**, and **GreenMarketplace.com**. Some alternative groceries and health-food stores carry them as well.

Ecover (**Ecover**) natural-detergent cleaners use coconut-oil-derived *surfactants*. Ecover products are biodegradable and contain no phosphates, chlorine, enzymes, or synthetic perfumes. However, you should be aware that certain of their cleaners do contain aromatic essential oils and, therefore, will have a fragrant scent (see *Natural Essential Oils and Perfumes* on page 71 as well as *Problems with Scents* on page 72). Their line includes several household cleaners, a toilet cleaner, a dishwasher powder, a rinse agent, and a hand dishwashing liquid. They're sold through some alternative retail outlets and by mail order from **Tucson Cooperative Warehouse, Karen's Natural Products**, and **Simmons Natural Bodycare**.

White Wizard (**L.B. Roe Corp.**) has a all-purpose cleaner and spot remover gel, a household cleaner, and an upholstery cleaner. All of these are virtually odorless, non-toxic, and bio-degradable. The complete line is sold directly by the company. The original gel cleaner is sold in many alternative food stores and catalogs. (See *Gel and Cream Multi-Purpose Products* on page 139 for sources.)

Still other fine alternative product lines include hypoallergenic Earth-Rite sold by **Natural Lifestyle** and **N.E.E.D.S.**, and Earth Friendly Products/Ecos (**Earth Friendly**) whose products (all-purpose cleaner, window cleaner, stain remover, polish, dish soap, and dishwasher detergent) use plant-based ingredients including some essential oils. This line is sold in many alternative food stores, as well as through **Real Goods** and **Priorities**. Also, Natural Chemistry, made with natural cleaning agents and enzymes with no added scents, is handled by **Befit Enterprises Ltd., Karen's Natural Products** and **Allergy Relief Shop, Inc.**

All-natural lines whose products are imported from Germany include the Livos brand, which are handled by **Natural Home by Natürlich** and **Karen's Natural Products**; and Auro Awalan, which is handled by **Sinan Company**. Some items offered are naturally fragrant due to essential oils being included in their formulation—especially in the Livos line. However, items such as the bathroom cleaner, dishwasher powder, and laundry soap from Auro Awalan are neither scented nor have citrus-based formulas. Another multi-product, German formulation line you may wish to try is Bio Shield. These products, are made and sold by an American company, **Eco Design Co.** Bio Shield natural cleaners are made without dyes, phosphates, or synthetic perfumes. The line includes dish soap, floor cleaner, toilet cleaner, and dishwasher rinse agent. Most of their products have a natural citrusy smell.

Of course, even as extensive as this section is, it is not a complete listing. You'll undoubtedly find many other fine product choices available in different catalogs and local outlets.

Waterproof Household Glove Suggestions

Before this chapter goes any further into specific house-cleaning products and methods, a short discussion of waterproof household gloves is in order. Women in particular commonly use these gloves to protect their hands and nails when doing a range of chores. Up until recently, just buying "rubber gloves" at any grocery, hardware, discount, or drug store would have been an easy solution for most of them. However, in the last decade or so, there's been an increasing population of latex-sensitive people. Many with this condition have acquired it in settings where they were routinely required to wear latex gloves, as in a hospital or dental clinic, to prevent the spread of communicable diseases. Unfortunately, in certain cases, these gloves were of poor quality with the result that some experienced constant exposure to potentially reactive latex proteins. Thereafter, a percentage of those exposed acquired the symptoms of a latex allergy which can range from mild to life-threatening. Of course, another segment of the population that's had trouble with conventional latex gloves is the chemically sensitive.

One solution for those in both categories can be to use vinyl household gloves. Nyplex Gloves (**Magla Products**) are made of a vinyl compound that's been tolerable to many latex-sensitive people. Unhappily, some chemically sensitive people may find that vinyl is as much a problem for them as was latex. For those individuals, they'll have to experiment to determine which type of glove material works best for them. Wearing very thin 100%-cotton gloves as liners may make either type more tolerable, although it will not reduce the vinyl or latex odors. (Thin liner gloves are often sold in pharmacies.) Nyplex gloves are sometime sold in local grocery stores and pharmacies and they may also carry similar products. By mail-order, you can acquire Nyplex Gloves from the **Vermont Country Store Apothecary**.

Multi-Purpose Cleaner Suggestions

Multi-purpose products can make shopping, storage, and cleaning easier because just one cleaner can do so many jobs. Here are some suggestions for products to try.

Liquid All-Purpose Products

One very useful cleaner is SafeChoice Super Clean (**AFM**) sold by **N.E.E.D.S.**, **The Living Source**, **Bio Designs**, **Priorities**, **Allergy Relief Shop, Inc.**, **healthyhome.com**, and **American Environmental Health Foundation**. This is a concentrated, synthetic, liquid cleaner containing no dyes, perfumes, or phosphates. It's also non-caustic, non-acidic, and biodegradable. Super Clean is designed to be diluted with water into various concentrations in order to do specific cleaning tasks, including degreasing.

Allens Naturally Heavy-Duty All Purpose Cleaner (**Allens Naturally**) is another good option. It's also highly concentrated and contains no dyes or scents. This product has the addition of borax as a cleaning/deodorizing agent. This cleaner can be bought at many local alternative food stores as well as from the manufacturer, **Allergy Relief Shop, Inc.**, **Health One Co.**, **Tucson Cooperative Warehouse**, **Janice Corporation**, and **Coastline Products**.

Frank T. Ross & Sons Ltd. has created Nature Clean All Purpose Cleaner. This product is made with coconut derivatives and contains no dyes or fragrances. It can be ordered from the company as well as from **American Environmental Health Foundation**.

LifeTime Solutions Multi-Purpose Cleaner (**LifeTime Solutions**) is undyed and unscented with a unique blend of *colloidal micelles*. Both cleaners can be ordered from the manufacturer.

EnviroRite Multi-Purpose Cleaner with Deodorizer (**BioForce Enviro-Tech Inc.**) is an unscented, undyed product with a trade-secret deodorizer to freshen. This cleaner, which you may want to try, is available from the company as well as from **eMD.com** and **Allergy Control Products, Inc.**

Seventh Generation Natural All-Purpose Cleaner (**Seventh Generation**) is biodegradable, phosphate-free and very gentle. However, it does have an added citrus scent. This cleaner can be purchased from **Harmony**, **Tucson Cooperative Warehouse**, and **GreenMarketplace.com**.

Another multi-use liquid you might like is E-Z Maid Dish & Multi-Purpose Liquid (**Granny's Old Fashioned Products**). This has a very mild, unscented formula. Interestingly, the company suggests that you can add powdered borax and 3%-dilution hydrogen peroxide (the type sold in pharmacies) to create a disinfecting cleanser. E-Z Maid is sold by **N.E.E.D.S.**, **Allergy Relief Shop, Inc.**, **Health One Co.**, **healthyhome.com**, and **The Living Source**. The same product under the Coastline Old Fashioned label is offered by **Coastline Products**.

Safe-Suds (**Ar-Ex, Ltd.**) is a concentrated (dilute it with three parts of water), mild, synthetic detergent containing no lanolin, perfumes, fillers, water softeners, or bleaches. It's biodegradable and non-alkaline. It can be used for washing dishes by hand and a variety of household cleaning chores. Safe-Suds can be ordered from the manufacturer. Of course, other alternative dish cleaning liquids can often be similarly used (see *Hand Dishwashing Products* on page 166).

Crystal (Simple Green) All-Purpose Cleaner/Degreaser (**Sunshine Makers, Inc.**) is a synthetic, highly concentrated cleaner with no petroleum distillates, dyes, or scents. A detailed dilution chart is available from the company. (Note: When using Crystal Simple Green full strength, spot test on an inconspicuous place first.) You can call the manufacturer for a dealer near you.

Natural Chemistry All-Purpose Cleaner is unscented and contains natural cleaning agents and enzymes. You can acquire it from **Befit Enterprises Ltd.** and **Karen's Natural Products**. Ecover All-Purpose Cleaner (**Ecover**) has no dyes or phosphates. This is a coconut-based surfactant solution with natural perfume. It's handled by **Karen's Natural Products** and **Tucson Cooperative Warehouse**.

Heavenly Horsetail All-Purpose Cleaner (**Jedmon Products**) is a soap-based product made with sodium laurel sulfate, extract of horsetail and other natural herbs, olive oil, and lemon juice The manufacturer offers it directly to customers or you can order from **Karen's Natural Products**. A highly concentrated plant-soap solution is Auro Awalan Cleaning Solution sold by **Sinan Company**.

Today there are several highly concentrated, natural, citrus-solvent cleaners you might find acceptable. You should be aware however, that *undiluted*, such products could possibly have "moderate to high acute toxicity or causes skin or eye irritation" and perhaps have a chronic toxicity (long-term effects) as suggested in **Washington Toxics Coalition**'s *Buy Smart, Buy Safe: A Consumer Guide to Less-Toxic Products* by Phillip Dickey. Fortunately, the same publication noted that at a 50:1 dilution (a common concentration for many cleaning purposes), citrus-solvents were only "slightly to moderately toxic or irritating to the skin" and generally safe to use. However, even at low concentrations, citrus-concentrate products will still have a natural citrusy odor that certain sensitive or allergic individuals may find bothersome. One well known highly concentrated citrus-solvent cleaner is Citra-Solv Cleaner & Degreaser Concentrate (**Shadow Lake, Inc.**) which is sold in some local groceries and retail outlets. In addition, it is available through mail order from **Harmony, Frontier Natural Products, Real Goods,** and **Simmons Natural Bodycare.**

Pre-diluted, multi-purpose citrus-solvent cleaning products have become very popular. Although these are much healthier to use than concentrates, they will, of course, all have a citrus odor to some extent. Today, these types of cleaners are sold in most alternative food stores. De-Solv-It Citrus Powdered All-Purpose Cleaner Concentrate (**Orange-Sol Household Products, Inc.**) in a spray bottle is one you can order directly from the company and from **Agelong Catalog**. Another similar product is Citra-Solv Multi-Purpose Cleaner & Degreaser (**Shadow Lake, Inc.**) in a sprayer. This can be purchased from **Frontier Natural Products.** One more is Earth Friendly Orange Plus (**Earth Friendly Products**) that's commonly sold in alternative food stores. **Real Goods** may be a mail order source. Furthermore, a number of brands are offered by **Vermont Country Store Voice of the Mountains.**

Livos Trena Neutral Cleaner is a concentrated, neutral, liquid soap made with a type of citrus oil and ethanol, and has a mild (it's considered by the manufacturer to be low odor) citrusy smell. Trena can be used for cleaning wood, linoleum, tile, and, stone surfaces. It can be ordered from **Natural Home by Natürlich** and **Karen's Natural Products**

Lifekind All-Purpose Cleaner (**Lifekind Products**) is an undyed, unscented organic detergent made with citrus extracts. This fine product can be ordered from the company.

Aubrey Organics Natural All-Purpose Cleaner (**Aubrey Organics**) is a fragrant, all-natural, formulation. It may not be appropriate for those trying to avoid scents. It can be ordered from the company or from **Natural Lifestyle.**

Powdered Multi-Purpose Products

Two products that most sensitive (and allergic) persons find they can tolerate well are Bon Ami Cleaning Powder and Bon Ami Cleaning Cake (**Faultless Starch/Bon Ami Co.**). Both are unscented, undyed soaps combined with finely powdered mineral feldspar. They can be used to clean everything from pots to window glass. These Bon Ami products are sold at some groceries and through **Erlander's Natural Products** and Bon Ami's **Agelong Catalog. Bio Designs** sells just the cleaning powder, **Simmons Natural Bodycare** just the cleaning cake.

Bon-Ami also offers Bon Ami Polishing Cleanser (**Faultless Starch/Bon Ami Co.**) which does not contain soap. Instead, it's an unscented, undyed powdered biodegradable detergent product—with the addition of sodium carbonate as a water softener, oxygen bleach, and ground feldspar and calcite as mild abrasives. This item is found in most food stores and can be ordered from **Agelong Catalog.**

Gel and Cream Multi-Purpose Products

White Wizard Stain Remover and All-Purpose Cleaner (**L.B. Roe Corp.**) is an odorless, undyed white jelly-like cleaner that can remove stains from a variety of surfaces. This cleaner is available from the manufacturer, and from **Harmony, Vermont Country Store Voice of the Mountains, Solutions, Real Goods,** and the **Agelong Catalog.**

Ecover (**Ecover**) Cream Scrub is an undyed cleaner created with colloidal clay, chalk, glycerin soap and coconut-based surfactants. Natural perfume has been added, however. You can purchase it from **Karen's Natural Products** and **Tucson Cooperative Warehouse.**

Household Cleaning

The following sections offer suggestions for specific healthier cleaning products and practices for the most common household jobs. While many possible alternative cleaners are now available, only a few are mentioned below. For the most part, these are ones that have worked most successfully for sensitive and allergic individuals. They're generally effective and affordable, and many are of the undyed and unscented variety.

As you'll also notice, a number of products are listed a variety of headings because of their ability to do a number of household jobs very well. The truth is, only a few products are really necessary to safely clean your entire home.

Household Cleaning for Allergic and Asthmatic People

Because dust, dust mites, pollen, mold, and scents are common *allergens* (substances people react to), keeping the household clean with safe, unscented products is essential for those with conventional allergies and asthma. If at all possible, those who experience serious symptoms to dust, dust mites, pollen, and mold should find someone else to do their cleaning for them. If someone is found who can vacuum or dust, the allergic or asthmatic person should not enter the newly cleaned area for at least 30 minutes. If they find that they must do these chores themselves, they should wear a protective dust mask (see *Personal Protective Gear* on page 264.) In addition, liquid spray cleaners should only be misted directly into cleaning cloths rather onto the surfaces that are to be cleaned. This is to minimize the amount of potentially irritating aerosol droplets in the air hat could be inhaled.

To help eliminate dust-mite feces and dead mite body parts from carpeting and upholstery, these items should be vacuumed often (live dust mites cling so tightly to fibers that they can't be vacuumed up). This means at least once a week. If it's pollen season outside, or if there's an indoor pet, it may be wise to vacuum daily. Small washable area rugs and curtains should be laundered regularly, too. Furthermore, mattresses without dust-mite-proof protectors should be vacuumed *thoroughly* twice a month on both sides (at least two minutes per side) to help reduce dust-mite populations. For more on dust mites and methods and products to control them, see *Dust Mites* on page 410. See also, *Laundering for Allergic People* on page 122 and *Allergies, Bedding, and Bedrooms* on page 223.

Dusting

As most homemakers know, dusting can seem to be an endless job. However, certain dusting methods are more effective than others. One product that, when applied to wood, acts as a dust repellent is LifeTime Wood & Leather Protector (**LifeTime Solutions**). This is a clear, unscented unique *colloidal-micelle/*silicon solution that you can order from the manufacturer.

One old-time method is using a feather duster. The oil in the feathers causes dust to cling to the duster. If you'd like to try one, an ostrich feather duster made by **Fuller Brush Co.** can be purchased through the company, its dealers, and **Vermont Country Store Voice of the Mountains**. **Williams-Sonoma** is another source for ostrich dusters.

An alternative approach would be to dust using a lightly dampened, untreated, washable, 100%-cotton flannel cloth. You can easily make your own from fabric scraps. If you prefer, all-cotton household cleaning cloths are manufactured by **Fuller Brush Co.** They can be bought directly from the company or its dealers. Keep in mind that if you use a cotton cloth, make sure to re-dampen it as necessary while you're dusting. If the cloth becomes too dry, the dust will not cling effectively. It will just be swept off surfaces to resettle on them again a few minutes later.

For dusting hard-surface floors, washable, 100%-cotton-cord floor mops lightly misted with water often work very well. They are sometimes still sold at hardware and grocery stores. Popular Fuller Brush Floor Dusters (**Fuller Brush Co.**), made of untreated handwashable, 100%-cotton cording, can be ordered from Fuller Brush and their dealers. (Note: A treated version is also offered that's supposed to grab dust more easily.)

Another good dusting approach is to use a natural-wool duster. Interestingly, dust particles initially cling to the wool because of static electricity. Then, the wool's natural *lanolin* (sheep-skin oils) helps the dust to more securely adhere to the wool fibers—until you shake the duster out. You might be able to find wool dusters locally. Lambs wool dusters are made by **Fuller Brush Co.** and can be bought from the company and its dealers. They are also available from **Vermont Country Store Voice of the Mountains** which, in addition, handles wool mops. Furthermore, **Janice Corporation** and **Allergy Relief Shop, Inc.** sell lambswool dusters as does **Williams-Sonoma**.

Relative newcomers to dusting products are synthetic dusters that rely on their own innate static-electric charge to attract and hold dust particles. Some of these dusters are in the form of stiff fiber "star bursts" on wands while others are in soft, pliable sheets. Of the sheet type, some are washable and reusable, others are designed to be used briefly and thrown away. A few manufacturers offer a floor mop which can be wrapped with a dust sheet. As a rule, these statically charged synthetic dusters have not been chemically treated and they do not need any substance (water or cleaning/dusting agent) applied to them to perform to their maximum ability. The drawback that they do have is that they're manufactured out of synthetic, rather than natural, materials, which some people may find objectionable.

If you're interested in synthetic dusters, Rainbow Duster star-burst-type duster on a wand, and Dust Bunny washable sheets are both handled by **Allerx**. Washable Miracle Cloths are positively charged, polyester/poyamide microfiber cloths are sold by **Solutions** and **Taylor Gifts**. These can be used damp or dry. **E.L. Foust Co., Inc.** offers Quik Towels. These have the same fiber content and static charge. They're designed to be used damp.

Befit Enterprises Ltd. sells OKO-clean washable dust mitts and cloths made of a microfiber fabric. It's suggested that they're best used when slightly moistened. A similar Dust Grabber dusting cloth is sold by **Allergy Clean Environments**. Euroclean Dust Magnets (**Euroclean**) are a line of synthetic cloths and mitts, plus floor sweeping mops with aluminum handles and disposable, electrostatically charged sheets. Finally, a number of micro-fiber dusting products are now sold in conventional grocery stores.

Remember, if you have allergies to dust or to dust mites you should wear a mask when dusting (see *Personal Protective Gear* on page 264). If your allergies are severe, have someone else dust for you if possible, and don't enter a newly dusted area for thirty minutes.

For more on what actually makes up dust, see *Dust* on page 540. Also, for information on dusting lamps and bulbs, see *Floor and Table Lamps* on page 361.

Polishing

Polishing is defined as bringing a luster to any material, usually by rubbing or buffing. It's generally one of those jobs few people seem to look forward to—not only because of the elbow grease required, but also because many typical polishes are extremely odorous and, thus, can't be used by sensitive or asthmatic individuals.

The following sections offer a few safe and effective polishing suggestions you might want to try. For other specific polishing needs, check *Clean & Green* and *Better Basics for the Home,* both by Annie Berthold-Bond and *Clean Your House Safely & Effectively Without Harmful Chemicals* by Randy Dunford.

For polishing linoleum see *Linoleum* on page 310, and for polishing shoes see *Leather* on page 187.

Polishing Metals

Polishing brass or copper can be accomplished using a simple solution made of equal parts of fresh lemon juice and table salt. White vinegar can be substituted for the lemon juice. When you're ready to polish, be sure to use a sponge or soft cotton cloth to prevent scratching. Fuller Brush all-cotton household cloths (**Fuller Brush Co.**) can be used for this and are available from the company and its dealers.

Bar Keepers Friend (**Servaas Laboratories, Inc.**) also works well on copper and brass, as well as on stainless steel. It's commonly sold in grocery stores and in some hardware stores. To use it, just sprinkle a small amount of the powder on a wet soft cotton cloth or sponge. Then, gently rub the cloth across the metal. Once clean, rinse any residue off the metal with clear water and towel dry.

In addition, both Bon Ami Polishing Cleaner with a detergent-based formula and Bon Ami Cleaning Powder with a soap-based formula (**Faultless Starch/Bon Ami Co.**), do good jobs cleaning chrome and stainless steel. They can be found in some local grocery stores and hardware stores. You can also order them from the company's **Agelong Catalog.** Bon Ami Cleaning Powder is handled as well by **Erlander's Natural Products** and **Bio Designs.** To use either one, you'll want to follow the same directions as for Bar Keepers Friend cited above. Be sure to test these powdered products first on a small inconspicuous area before using them on highly lustrous surfaces.

One very effective metal polishing product you might want to try is Maas Polishing Cream (**Maas Polishing Systems, Inc.**) sometimes available in local grocery stores. If not, you can order it from the company. Maas is a European-developed white cream which comes packaged in tubes. It works quickly on most metals to create a brilliant sheen. Unlike most other manufactured cream-type polishes, Maas is both low-odor and nonflammable. To use it, just dab a small amount of the cream onto a soft cotton flannel. Then gently rub the metal surface. Finish up by lightly buffing with another clean cotton flannel cloth.

Polishing Woods

For polishing woods, you might try using a solution containing equal parts of lemon juice and a rancid-resistant vegetable oil such as virgin olive oil. (Some suggest using almond oil instead of olive oil.) To use this type of polish, just dab a soft cotton flannel cloth into the mixture and rub the wood's surface in the direction of the grain. It should be noted that, as a rule, oil-based products should only be applied to woods originally oil finished rather than to those having a hard varnish-like clear coating. That is, unless the product label says otherwise.

Most alternative oil polishes are quite fragrant because of the addition of one or more citrus oils. Earth Friendly Furniture Polish (**Earth Friendly Products**) is an olive-oil-based liquid with an orange-oil scent sold by **Priorities**. Livos Dryaden Polish is an oil product made with linseed, strand, and orange-peel oils plus drying agents. It can be purchased from **Karen's Natural Products**, **Natural Home by Natürlich**, and **Building for Health Materials Center**. BioShield Wood & Furniture Polish (**Eco Design Co.**) has vinegar, ethanol, and orange peel oil. You can order this polish from the manufacturer.

A product safe for wooden salad bowls, children's toys, etc. is Non-toxic Preserve which is a combination of nut oils to polish and preserve. It is handled by **Priorities**. In addition, **Harmony** has an unscented, non-toxic nut-oil mixture for "woodenware."

Block Brothers WoodCare Polish and Block Brothers Block Oil have formulas made with paraffin oils, lemon oil, and vitamin E. They're sold by **Simmons Natural Bodycare**.

A polish which would be a good choice for woods with hard, clear-coated finishes is LifeTime Solutions Wood & Leather Protector (**LifeTime Solutions**). This is an unscented, undyed liquid with a unique *colloidal-micelle*/silicon formula. You can order this polish directly from the company.

Some people prefer waxes to liquid polishes. Livos Furniture Waxes are made with natural ingredients in Germany and sold in this country by **Building for Health Materials Center, Natural Home by Natürlich**, and **Karen's Natural Products**. Another German formulation is the Bio Shield Furniture Wax (**Eco Design Co.**) This product contains beeswax, linseed oil, orange peel oil among others. You can order it directly from the maker. (Note: Other types of waxes can be found under *Wax Finishes* on page 279.)

Scratches can mar the appearance of the best furniture pieces. Fortunately, most can be easily concealed on medium- or dark-wood pieces by rubbing the nicked areas with a piece of walnut or pecan nut meat. Then, buff the area lightly with a soft cotton flannel cloth. On light unstained woods, you might try using a cotton swab dipped in a tiny amount of virgin olive oil. Then, carefully apply the oil just to scratches and lightly buff the area with a soft cotton flannel cloth.

If you do not have soft rags at home to use for these chores, Fuller Brush 100%-cotton household cloths (**Fuller Brush Co.**) may be an answer. They're available from the manufacturer and its dealers.

Sweeping

For routine sweeping jobs, hardwood-handled *broomcorn-bristle* brooms have done a good job for centuries. Broomcorn is actually a particular type of sorghum plant specially cultivated for producing stiff bristles. However, because it's a natural material, it's important to keep broomcorn-bristle brooms dry to prevent rot or mildew. Broomcorn, or other natural-bristle brooms, are still usually available at grocery, discount, and hardware stores. A good variety of broomcorn bristle brooms can be found in the **Shaker Shops West** catalog.

Another fairly effective sweeping method is to use a lightweight carpet sweeper. These require no electricity, yet they can pick up surface dust and some loose dirt and debris as well. Carpet sweepers are designed to work on low-nap carpets and rugs, and on smooth surfaces such as wood, linoleum, and tile floors. One you may wish to try is the Fuller Brush Electrostatic Carpet Sweeper (**Fuller Brush Co.**). This particular model has a metal case, a replaceable boar-bristle brush, and can fold flat for easy storage. It's available from the manufacturer and its dealers.

A very popular sweeper is the Bissell Carpet Sweeper, sold in many local discount and department stores. Mail-order suppliers include **Vermont Country Store Voice of the Mountains**, **Real Goods**, and **Service Merchandise**.

An alternative approach to using a bristle-brush sweeper is to try the Hoky Carpet Sweeper by Oreck. The Hoky utilizes rotating rubberized spiral blades, which are said to provide superior pickup action compared to bristles. However, if rubber odors are bothersome to you, these machines may not be appropriate. Hoky sweepers can be found in some local department and discount stores, or mail-ordered from **Silvo Home**, and **Solutions**.

The **Williams-Sonoma** catalog also sells carpet sweepers. Check with other stores in your area for additional sources.

Vacuuming

Vacuuming can be an excellent and healthy method to remove dust and debris from your floors, walls, and furniture. That is, if the vacuum is powerful enough *and* properly filtered or vented to the outdoors. Most vacuums currently being used don't have very efficient filters and, as a result, aren't very healthy.

Of course, vacuum cleaners have been around for some time now. The first one was actually invented in the mid-nineteenth century. On early models, a suction was created by manually operating fans or bellows while pushing the unit back and forth. Not surprisingly, users found that this was complicated, tiring, and inefficient. It wasn't until small, reliable, electric motors became available sometime after the turn of the century that vacuum cleaners became more commonly used in homes. Unfortunately, many portable electric vacuums haven't advanced all that much since that time. This section explains how vacuum cleaners work, and suggests some healthier vacuum cleaner brands. For information on reducing dust mites in your carpet

How Vacuum Cleaners Work

Many people vacuum one or more days a week. But, how many of them actually understand how these familiar machines work? Some vacuums contain rotating brushes or beating agitators which first loosen the surface dirt on the floor. At the same time, a high-speed fan whirls inside the motor's housing to create a powerful suctioning action. As the air is pulled into the vacuum, it brings along with it the loosened debris, which is deposited into a paper or cloth filter bag, or sometimes into a special self-contained receptacle. The air then flows through the bag or receptacle and quickly back into the room—supposedly leaving the dirt behind. By the way, while one or two swaths across the same section of carpet is how most people use their vacuum, it actually takes a minimum of six to eight swaths for most vacuums to pull up at least some of the debris embedded deep down in the carpet fibers.

Unfortunately, even if a lot of the debris does get sucked in, many traditional portable vacuum cleaners are ineffective in separating the dirt from the air that returns to the room. As a result, a fairly large percentage of particulate matter is often blown back into the air of the area you've just cleaned. (The precise percentage depends on the vacuum model, as well as how full the collection bag or permanent receptacle is.)

It should be noted that particulate matter is made up not only of soil grains, but also lint, human and pet hair, human and pet *dander* (skin flakes), mold spores, pollen grains, and dust mite fragments and feces, among other unpleasant contaminants. If you operate an inefficient vacuum, you'll end up breathing this "delightful" concoction continually as it passes through the filter into the room. It should not be surprising to learn that many susceptible persons find that vacuuming actually provokes allergic and asthmatic symptoms rather than preventing them. (See *Dust Mites* on page 410 for information on ridding your home of dust mites, including in your carpets.) Therefore, it's not surprising that some health experts suggest that those with respiratory allergies and asthma not vacuum themselves, if at all possible. Even if someone else does the vacuuming for them, it has been recommended that they not enter the just-cleaned area for at least thirty minutes. Finally, if someone with allergies and asthma has to do the job for themselves, it is further advised that they wear a dust mask. (See *Personal Protection Gear* on page 264.)

It should also be mentioned that traditional vacuums (as described above) use a simple *straight line* airstream though a cloth or paper debris-collection bag. As the bag fills and the interior surfaces get coated with dust, the airflow through the bag becomes increasingly blocked. With use, a vacuum with this design will lose more and more of its suctioning capacity. Therefore, it's best to only allow the bag to get half full. Whenever you change it, you'll find that bag replacement is usually a messy, dusty job. So, wearing a dust mask and doing the job outdoors are essential precautions for everyone, even if they're in good health.

As an improvement, a number of vacuum models now employ *cyclonic* technology in which a whirlwind airstream is formed. The powerful centrifugal force that is created *precipitates* (throws out) the particulate matter against the walls of a collection bin. The debris then falls to the bottom of the bin. As a further advance, some vacuum manufacturers design their products to create two cyclones. The first precipitates the heavier particulates, the second one, spinning at an even faster speed, precipitates the lighter ones. As in single-cyclonic designs, all the debris falls to the bottom of the reusable collection bin. When the collection bin is full on a cyclonic vacuum, it's simply removed and dumped out. Of course emptying such a receptacle means you no longer have to buy replacement bags, but you'll still have to take care to not inhale dust particles when pouring out the receptacle's accumulated contents. Again, doing this outdoors with a dust mask on are good ideas. Cyclone vacuums don't lose their suctioning ability as they fill with debris.

Besides differences in suctioning strategy, everyone knows that conventional portable vacuums also come in two basic configurations—upright and canister. Uprights have the vacuum motor and powerhead connected together and they are pushed and pulled (unless they're self-propelled) across surfaces. For some, this is convenient, for others, not. As a rule, uprights are difficult to maneuver under beds and furniture. Most models require the user to attach a hose for uses where the unit can't lie flat enough to go under certain objects such as a bed or sofa, and for uses such as vacuuming furniture, cushions, stairs, or draperies. (A few models do have built-in hoses from just a few feet to up to 7 feet long, depending on the manufacturer.)

Canister vacuums are designed with a motor/receptacle unit on casters with a long hose attached. Many come with a power head attachment on the end of the hose for added agitating/suctioning. The long hoses of canister models can go places uprights can't, but they do require the user to lift or drag the canister unit around the house. Again, some find this advantageous, others do not. Which type is better, is ultimately a personal decision. However, what is most important in selecting a unit is its healthfulness.

More Efficient Replacement Bags

The healthiest vacuum should be one that not only is convenient to use and has good suction, but above all, one that prevents the debris it draws in from escaping back into the room.

If you don't care to—or can't at the moment—replace your present conventional portable vacuum cleaner, you might consider buying more efficient vacuum cleaner replacement bags for the model you currently own. Such bags are designed to more effectively trap and retain small particles than standard vacuum bags.

More efficient filtering bags are available at some local vacuum-cleaner shops and other outlets where vacuum cleaners are sold. By mail order, multiple-layer MicroClean replacement bags treated with Bactrastat (to inhibit microbial growth in the bags themselves) can be bought from **Gazoontite, Priorities,** and **Allergy Control Products, Inc.** Enddust microfilter vacuum bags made with filter paper exteriors and electrostatically charged media on their interiors are sold by **Allergy Clean Environments.** Note that more efficient replacement vacuum bags may still not be effective enough for those with severe allergies.

Alternative Portable Vacuum Cleaners

If you want to better ensure that your home's air is not recontaminated with dust and allergens after vacuuming, you'll want to purchase a portable vacuum cleaner with an effective filtration system, or install a whole-house vacuum cleaner with an outdoor exhaust. (More on whole-house vacuum cleaners later in this chapter.)

Primarily because of the dramatic increase in conventional household allergies, alternative portable vacuum models are now more commonly available. The following sections will introduce you to some of their features.

HEPA-Filtered Vacuum Cleaners

There are now quite a few vacuums in the marketplace that use *HEPA* filters. HEPA is an acronym for <u>H</u>igh <u>E</u>fficiency <u>P</u>articulate <u>A</u>rresting (sometimes the <u>A</u> stands for <u>A</u>ccumulator or <u>A</u>ir). HEPA filters are generally made of a specially constructed synthetic material such as fiberglass. The spaces within this filtering fabric are so tiny that most minute particles can't pass through it.

In many of the HEPA-equipped consumer vacuum cleaners, almost all the particles larger than 0.3 microns are trapped. Therefore, bacteria (0.3–30 microns) and pollen (10–100 microns) are usually stopped. Interestingly, certain specialized commercial-grade HEPA filters are even more efficient. Some are even able to filter out the infinitesimally small particles making up tobacco smoke. It's no wonder then that HEPA-equipped vacuums are used by professional asbestos and lead-paint removal contractors who must thoroughly and safely remove hazardous material. Note that when comparing filter efficiencies, several different efficiency tests can be used (see also *HEPA & ULPA Filters* on page 553).

Until rather recently, most home-model HEPA-filtered vacuums were manufactured by small companies, many of them European, that catered to highly allergic clientele. However, with the dramatic increase in household allergies, coupled with an economy in which buyers are willing to pay more for the "best," the traditional American vacuum manufacturers have been offering HEPA and HEPA-like filters on particular models. Some vacuum manufacturers using HEPA filtration state that their products have "certified HEPAs." In most of these cases, independent certification laboratories have examined and tested the filters and given them their seal of approval. If you are uncertain what "certified HEPA" means on a vacuum you're interested in, ask the company representative to supply specific information on the certification, including who has done the certifying.

Miele (**Miele, Inc.**) offers several Advance Emission Guard canister vacuums in their 300/400 series which have, as an option, a HEPA filter. All are made of ABS plastic, the same type of plastic used in making football helmets. They come equipped with a double-layer bag, plus the Super Air Clean filter, which is an *electrostatic* type that uses an electrical charge to attract particles (see *Electrostatic and Electret Filters* on page 554). Another option is the Active Air Clean filter which contains activated charcoal. A Miele Allergy Control model with 3-stage filtration that includes a HEPA, as well as activated charcoal, is sold by **Allergy Control Products, Inc.** Certain Miele models are also handled by **eMD.com**, **The Allergy Store**, **healthyhome.com**, and **Williams-Sonoma**. Call the company for local dealers and other mail-order outlets.

Euroclean uses multiple filtration on their vacuums. The Euroclean Hip Vac is a 6.4 pound unit with optional HEPA filter. This hip mounted vacuum has Velcro straps and a complete aluminum-shaft tool kit. The Euroclean Allervac has four-stage filtration with HEPA filter. This is a canister model with an aluminum tool wand. Euroclean DU 135 is the upright version. Selected models can be ordered from **Well & Good** and **Harmony**.

There are also vacuums under the Nilfisk brand (**Nilfisk-Advance America, Inc.**). This company has been in the forefront manufacturing HEPA vacuums for industry as well as for consumers. Most models come equipped with 4-stage filtration, including *cyclonic* action (see *How Vacuum Cleaners Work* on page 144) and a HEPA. An optional ultra-efficient *ULPA* (ultra low penetration air) filter is available with 99.999% efficiency which captures particulates down to a very minute 0.12 microns. Nilfisk vacuums are sold by **E.L. Foust**. A Nilfisk Backback HEPA model weighing only 9.9 pounds and a professional-grade canister model are both sold by **Gazoontite**. The Nilfisk GD 90C ULPA canister model is available from **Allergy Clean Environments**. A Nilfisk ULPA model is also handled by **Priorities**.

Fantom vacuums (**Fantom Technologies**) come in canister or upright models with HEPA filtration on the exhaust. All Fantom vacuums use *dual cyclonic* technology. There are no bags and no loss of power as the collection bin fills. Widely sold in the U.S. through infomercials on TV, these vacuums can also be purchased from the company. Selected models can be ordered from **Service Merchandise**, the **J.C. Penny Catalog** and **Allerx**.

Dirt Devil Vision Gold is an upright vacuum with a 3-stage filtration system which includes a HEPA. These are sold in some department and discount stores. They can be mail ordered from **Taylor Gifts**.

The Eureka Sanitaire Heavy Duty upright vacuum (**Eureka Co.**) is a true HEPA vacuum with poycarbonate construction and metal tool wand. Eurekas are sold through vacuum, discount, and department stores. Some models are available in the **J.C. Penny Catalog**.

It should be mentioned that HEPA-like is actually a rather vague term. Companies using this label are suggesting that, although their vacuums don't use a real HEPA filter, the filtering strategies they do use produce similar results. It may be that this is the case, but it's probably a good idea to get more information on the actual filtration system that is used, any independent efficiency ratings, and information that may be supplied in consumer product magazines. In reality, if you are primarily trying to capture conventional allergens, such as mold and pollen, HEPA vacuums are probably more efficient than you need, so a HEPA-like vacuum may work just fine for you. However, if you are interested in capturing as many tiny particles as possible, you will most likely want to opt for a true HEPA vacuum.

Creating a Healthy Household

If you're interested in a consumer-quality, portable, HEPA-like vacuum, several merit your consideration. Vita-Vac (**Vita-Mix Corp.**) is a metal-canister unit sold directly by the company. Dealers such as **N.E.E.D.S.** also handle it. Vit-a-Vac has a 4-stage filtering system. The first is a hygienically sealed bag that inhibits fungal growth. Next is a 14-layer cellulose bag filter that's designed to remove visible dust. Then there's an activated-charcoal filter to adsorb odors (see *Adsorption Filters* on page 551). Finally, there's a "HEPA-type" filter that's said to be 99% efficient in eliminating particles that are larger than 0.3 microns in size.

Hoover makes the WindTunnel model with a six-stage microfiltration system. The Allergen Filtration model is said to capture "almost 100%" of pollen. It has the added feature of having a light sensor to indicate when the area you're vacuuming is clean. Hoover vacuums are sold in most department and discount stores and independent vacuum stores. They can be mail-ordered from **Service Merchandise** and the **J.C. Penny Catalog**.

Some Eureka Boss vacuum models (**Eureka Co.**) have "micron filtration" and "Dirt Alert" sensing. These are sold in many vacuum cleaner, department, and discount stores. Certain models are available from **Service Merchandise** and the **J.C. Penny Catalog**.

The Oreck Upright Hypoallergenic Vacuum, which weighs just 8 pounds, can be had with a canister unit too. The company claims that it's able to trap 99.75% of common allergens. The inner double-layer filter bag is treated to kill bacteria while the outer layer is "the equivalent of 30 layers of filtering material." One mail-order source is **Silvo Home** and the **J.C. Penny Catalog** is another.

Befit Enterprises Ltd. and **Priorities** offer the Windsor Sensation. This upright portable vacuum has a "micro-fine" filter which claims to remove particles down to 0.3 microns.

Miele, Inc. has many models of portable canister vacuums. Even without the HEPA-filter option, these vacuums are superior to most conventional vacuums because of their double-layer bags, electrostatic filters, optional charcoal filters, and their sealed systems which prevent leaking air and dust. Upright models have 6-stage filtration, as well as sealed systems. To purchase one of these vacuums, contact the company for a mail-order source or local dealer.

Some negative points about buying a HEPA or HEPA-like vacuum should be considered. First, all of these units are going to be more costly than conventional models—some are, in fact, quite expensive. Many of the smaller manufactures also won't have dealers in your hometown, so if repairs become necessary, you may have to ship your machine to a far-away repair center. You also should remember that the bags and filtering materials will have to be replaced periodically. Another important consideration, particularly if you're a sensitive person, is that HEPA filters can often outgas minor odors from the resins and other synthetic materials making up the filtering fabrics. These odors can be bothersome to certain susceptible individuals.

Water-Filtered Vacuum Cleaners

An unusual alternative portable vacuum approach is water filtering. Rainbow SE (**Rexair, Inc.**) is one brand that uses this method. (To locate a nearby dealer, call the manufacturer.) The Rainbow SE works by creating a powerful air flow that pulls dirt and debris into a water reservoir. Ideally, most of the dirt is left in the water as the air bubbles its way though. The unit has a small HEPA Neutralizer which is said to be "a micro-filtration system able to remove non-wettable material and microscopic particulates." Incidentally, Rainbow SE vacuums have an optional extraction-carpet-cleaning head available. Another brand is the Thermax

AF sold by **Allergy Relief Shop, Inc.** This water-filter vacuum cleaner is also able to be converted to an extraction carpet cleaner.

Unfortunately, it seems, water-filter-equipped vacuums may not work particularly well on certain types of particulates. This includes dust-mite parts and feces as well as bacteria which remain suspended inside tiny air bubbles in the water, then are exhausted. That's why some of these vacuum cleaners come with additional built-in filter technology.

Furthermore, there's some concern that water-reservoir units could become potential havens for mold and mildew growth, and that the motors could get rusty or musty smelling in time. At any rate, these vacuums are somewhat cumbersome to maneuver, they must have their dirty water dumped out after use, and they tend to be relatively expensive to purchase.

Central Vacuum Cleaners

Many persons find that, for them, the easiest and most efficient home vacuums are *central vacuum systems.* Central vacuum systems have large, permanently mounted canisters with a motor attached. These are usually placed near or on an exterior wall in a utility room or basement. Most of these units are vented to the outdoors, although some models are designed to vent indoors. Of the two, the exterior-venting types are considered much healthier. With outdoor-venting, the air that's pulled into the vacuum is sent outdoors (*not* back into the living space) after it passes through the filter. This eliminates any concerns over particulates getting past the collection container.

No matter which model you purchase, all central vacuums require special tubing to be permanently installed within the walls of the house. Special vacuum hose inlets, which are connected to these tubes, are located strategically in various places on the home's walls. The tubes and inlets are typically installed while a house is being built, but there are also ways to install them in an existing house.

To operate a central vacuum, you simply plug the hose (usually 20-30' long) into one of the inlets. Plugging in the hose automatically turns on the vacuum motor. A variety of cleaning attachments are available, including an agitating power head. With only the hose to maneuver, many people find these vacuums can be easier to use than portable models.

There are two different strategies currently used by central-vacuum manufacturers. The first uses direct *straight line* suction though a cloth or paper dust-collection bag. As with portable vacuums using this approach, the more the bag fills up and the walls of the bag's sides gets coated with particulate matter, the more the vacuum loses suction. With *cyclonic* technology on the other hand, a whirlwind airstream is formed which causes the heavier particles to *precipitate* (be blown out) to the sides of a permanent collection bin and then fall to the bottom of a canister unit while the lighter weight particles continue directly through the unit to the outdoors. Although the vacuum won't lose suction as the receptacle fills, some dust will inevitably fall onto motor bearings. This may damage them in time. So, as a further improvement, a few central vacuum manufacturers have opted for cyclonic action combined with special internal filters to trap the wayward dust. Unfortunately, these filters must be periodically removed and cleaned. Other companies have designed special self-cleaning filters, where the air flow itself continually cleans off the filtering surfaces.

If you're interested in having a central vacuum, there are a number of lines in the marketplace. One brand to consider is Beam (**Beam Industries**). Beam has several models with cyclonic technology and self-cleaning filters. None use filtering bags. One model, the Serenity, is designed for ultra-quiet operation. An interesting option from Beam is the Vac-

Pan. This is a built-in, toe-operated rocker portal. You sweep debris over to the portal with a broom, then push the rocker panel open with your toe. Immediately, the vacuum turns on and suctions in the debris. Then, you just rock the portal with your toe to close it again. Vac-Pans can be very handy in kitchens where quick sweeping/vacuuming jobs are common. Other companies with several models each to check out are Broan (**Broan Mfg. Co., Inc.**) and **Nutone**. To purchase any these central vacuum cleaners, contact the companies for their nearest dealers. And, don't forget to look in your local phone book for other brands and retailers.

Be aware that there are a few drawbacks to owning a central vacuum unit. First, central vacuums are rather expensive to buy and to have installed. Because they require built-in piping, they also can be difficult to incorporate into some existing homes, although manufacturers generally have a number of tips in their product literature. Then, too, some people don't want to maneuver a 30' hose around their house, no matter how lightweight it is. Also, it's important that sticks, Christmas-tree needles, toothpicks, etc., don't get sucked into the vacuum's piping within the walls. If such items should become lodged, they could trap debris and could begin to clog the pipe. Finally, as with many vacuums, the brands that use a collection bag must have it replaced periodically for maximum suctioning efficiency. For models without a bag, the receptacle must be emptied. However, because central vacuum's generally have large bags or receptacles, this needs to be done far less often than with portable vacuums, sometimes only once a year.

Coping with Vacuum Hose Odors

Whether you decide on a conventional vacuum cleaner, an alternative portable model, or a central system, some sensitive individuals find the vacuum hose very bothersome. This is likely due to the odors given off by the vinyl or other plastic materials, of which the hoses are made. To rectify this situation, you can try washing your hose with diluted ($1^1/_2$–2 cups in 1 gallon water) SafeChoice Super Clean (**AFM**) and then rinsing. This product is sold by most AFM dealers including **N.E.E.D.S., Priorities, Bio Designs, Allergy Relief Shop, Inc., healthyhome.com, American Environmental Health Foundation**, and **The Living Source**, It's likely you'll have to wash a vacuum's hose several times. You might even need to increase the concentration of Super Clean to water, if necessary.

Sometimes hanging an odorous hose outdoors for several weeks in dry uncontaminated surroundings will make it more tolerable. If you can't hang it outside, you might suspend it in a room that's seldom used, but well-ventilated. If the hose remains too odorous, even after cleaning and airing, you should consider using untreated 100%-cotton barrier cloth to make a long tube that can be used as a hose cover. Barrier cloth is a special tightly woven cotton that often seals in many odors. An untreated type is available from **Janice Corp.** and you can get organic barrier cloth from **Sleeptek Limited** (in Canada) and from **N.E.E.D.S.** or **Furnature** (in the U.S.). When the cover has been sewn together, simply pull the vacuum hose through the cloth tube. The ends can be held in place using strings or rubber bands. Of course you'll, no doubt, want to remove the cover from time to time to wash it using a tolerable laundry product.

Cleaning Hard-Surfaced Flooring

Sometimes various hard-surfaced flooring materials require their own particular cleaners and care products. Generally, however, all hard-surface floors can be cleaned with the same equipment. For example, to pick up dust and dirt, 100%-cotton dust mops lightly misted with water, or dry all-wool dust mops work well on all hard floors. Simple carpet sweepers are another good choice for light pick-ups. For vacuuming, a soft brush attachment is a good option, for all types of vacuum cleaners.

For washing hard-surface floors, ideally you should choose floor-cleaning equipment that will be kind to your floors, the environment—and you. Two examples of safer floor-washing tools are the Fuller Brush cellulose sponge mop and the Fuller Brush 100%-cotton-string wet mop (**Fuller Brush Co.**). They can be purchased from Fuller Brush and most of their dealers, or by mail-order from **Vermont Country Store Voice of the Mountains**. Of course, similar products are sold in many local hardware, grocery, and discount stores.

Ceramic Tile and Vinyl Floors

Ceramic tile and vinyl floors are relatively easy to care for. Here are some healthier cleaning options.

Washing Ceramic Tile and Vinyl Floors

Ceramic tile and vinyl flooring can be safely washed using a mop with a simple dilute solution of 1 cup white vinegar in 2 gallons of water. No rinsing is necessary with this solution.

One-eighth cup of liquid soap mixed in 2 gallons of water can also be used to wash ceramic and vinyl floors. A pure, unscented Castile soap, such as Dr. Erlander's Jubilee Liquid Castile Soap (**Erlander's Natural Products**) is one you could use. This product can be ordered directly from the company. Dr. Bronner's Baby Supermild Unscented Castile Soap Liquid (**Dr. Bronner's**) is another unscented Castile product. It's often sold by local health-food stores and can be ordered from the company. You can also mail-order it from **Tucson Cooperative Warehouse** and **Frontier Natural Products**. With either product, you'll need to rinse the floor thoroughly after cleaning.

Livos Trena Neutral Cleaner is a neutral, soap-based cleaner made with a type of citrus oil. Dilute $1/4$ cup in $2^1/2$ gallons of warm water to use. Trena can be purchased from **Natural Home by Natürlich** and **Karen's Natural Products**. Heavenly Horsetail All-Purpose Cleaner (**Jedmon Products**), which is sold by **Karen's Natural Products**, is a liquid-soap cleaner with fragrant herbs. **Eco Design Co.** makes and sells Bio Shield Soap Cleaner for floors. It's a vegetable-based soap/glycerin/essential-oils product. Ecover Floor Soap (**Ecover**) is a naturally perfumed vegetable-oil soap. It's sold by **Karen's Natural Products** and **Tucson Cooperative Warehouse**. Auro Awalan Cleaning Solution is a highly concentrated plant-soap liquid sold by **Sinan Company**. You'll want to follow package directions on all these cleaners for best performance and make sure to rinse them off thoroughly.

Safe-Suds (**Ar-Ex, Ltd.**) is yet another type of product that can be used to wash ceramic or vinyl floors. It's a concentrated, unscented, liquid, synthetic detergent that can be bought at some local pharmacies or ordered directly from the manufacturer. To use it, mix 1 teaspoon in 2 gallons of water and then mop. You'll find that rinsing is necessary.

SafeChoice Super Clean (**AFM**), which is available from **N.E.E.D.S.**, **American Environmental Health Foundation**, **Bio Designs**, **healthyhome.com**, **Priorities**, **Allergy Relief Shop, Inc.**, and **The Living Source**, is also a good unscented liquid detergent option. To use this product, mix 1 cup of it in 1 gallon of water and mop, then rinse. Still another alternative for washing your ceramic or vinyl floors is Citra-Solv Cleaner & Degreaser Concentrate (**Shadow Lake, Inc.**). This product is sold in many health-food stores and by mail order through **Real Goods, Harmony, Frontier Natural Products,** and **Simmons Natural Bodycare,** among others. To use it, dilute it at a ratio of 1 oz. to 2 cups water, or even a weaker solution. After mopping, rinse the floor with clear water. As you might expect, Citra-Solv has a natural citrusy odor. (For more information on concentrated citrus cleaners, see *Liquid All-Purpose Products* on page 137.)

As a final note remember that other very good alternative cleaners for washing ceramic and vinyl floors are undoubtedly available from other catalogs and local alternative grocery stores.

Cleaning Oily Grout Stains

To remove oil and grease stains from unsealed ceramic tile grout joints, use *fuller's earth*. Simply mix the fuller's earth with water to create a paste. Then, apply the gray, wet, plaster-like paste to the stain and leave it overnight. The next day you can either wash it off, or you can brush it off with a stiff brush or broom, then vacuum up the dusty residue. Be aware, though, that this entire procedure might have to be repeated in order to remove some stubborn stains.

Fuller's earth is a type of powdered, natural clay. However, it does have a somewhat earthy pungent odor when wet. Fuller's earth can be purchased or special ordered through some drugstores and hardware stores. It can be mail ordered from **Bio Designs.**

Filling Small Nicks in Glazed Ceramic Tile

If you drop a sharp or heavy object on a glazed ceramic floor tile, the tile may chip. When this happens, the tile's surface color will be missing and the base clay itself (often off-white) will show through. To repair these little nicks, simply fill them using a crayon that closely matches the color of the glazed tile. Surprisingly, the wax in the crayon creates a filler that is usually fairly durable. Note: Sealants or other products that impart a shiny-finish probably won't adhere to a waxy crayon. However, most glazed ceramic-tile floors don't require such sealants or finishes.

Linoleum Floors

Linoleum is a product made from linseed oil, and a variety of other naturally derived materials. Today, vinyl has replaced real linoleum in popularity, but linoleum is making a comeback. If you have a natural linoleum floor, it's important to care for it properly to ensure it has a long, attractive life. The following sections will tell you how to do just that.

Washing Linoleum Floors

Linoleum floors can usually be washed safely with 1/8 cup Dr. Erlander's Jubilee Liquid Castile Soap (**Erlander's Natural Products**) mixed in 2 gallons of water. To use it, mop with the solution and then rinse. Dr. Erlander's products can be ordered directly from the company. As an alternative soap, you can use Dr. Bronner's Baby Supermild Unscented Castile Soap Liquid (**Dr. Bronner's**). You can buy it from the company, some local alternative food stores, **Tucson Cooperative Warehouse** and **Frontier Natural Products.**

You also might want to try Heavenly Horsetail All-Purpose Cleaner (**Jedmon Products**). This liquid, herbal, soap-based product is available at some local health-food stores and **Karen's Natural Products.** Or try Bio Shield Soap Cleaner (**Eco Design Co.**) for floors (it contains vegetable-based soap/glycerin/essential oils) which you can order from the manufacturer. Another similar product is Ecover Floor Soap (**Ecover**) which is simply a naturally perfumed vegetable-based soap. This product is handled by **Karen's Natural Products** and **Tucson Cooperative Warehouse**. Another option is Auro Awalan Cleaning Solution. This is a highly concentrated, plant-soap liquid sold by **Sinan Company**. Follow the label directions for proper usage. (Note: These particular product's natural herbal or essential-oil odors may prove to be too bothersome for some sensitive and allergic persons.)

Livos Trena Neutral Cleaner is a soap-based solution made with a type of citrus oil. To use it, dilute 1/4 cup in 2 1/2 gallons of warm water. Trena can be purchased from **Natural Home by Natürlich** and **Karen's Natural Products**. If you wash your linoleum floors with a soap cleaner, they'll need to be rinsed.

You might also try Citra-Solv Cleaner & Degreaser Concentrate (**Shadow Lake, Inc.**). This extremely concentrated cleaner is often available in local health-food stores and can be mail-ordered from **Real Goods, Harmony, Frontier Natural Products**, and **Simmons Natural Bodycare**. For general cleaning, use a dilution at a ratio of 1 oz. (or less) to 2 cups of water. To remove heel marks, use a much more concentrated solution. If you choose to use Citra-Solv on your floors, it's a good idea to rinse afterwards with clear water. Remember, this product has a citrusy odor. (For more information on concentrated citrus cleaners, see *Liquid All-Purpose Products* on page 137.)

A manufactured product that may be appropriate is Auro Awalan Wax Cleaner, a cleaner for waxed surfaces. It can be ordered from **Sinan Company**. In addition, a number of natural-formula wood/linoleum cleaners are available from **Real Goods**.

Linoleum Polishes, Wax Removers, & Other Products

An easy, homemade linoleum polish is simply 6 tablespoons of cornstarch dissolved in 1 cup water. Apply with a soft cotton flannel cloth in a sweeping, buffing motion. Those with corn allergies should probably avoid using this.

To remove wax build-up, you can use a heavy concentration of *washing soda* and water. Apply the solution with a sponge or sponge mop, allow it to dry, then rinse with clear water. If you choose to do this, an unscented washing soda is probably best, if you're sensitive or highly allergic. Dr. Erlander's Jubilee Washing Compound (**Erlander's Natural Products**) is one scent-free washing-soda brand which can be ordered directly from the company. Arm & Hammer Super Washing Soda is also unscented and has the advantage of being available in most grocery stores. However, this product often absorbs the scents of fragranced laundry products shelved nearby, so it can be bothersome to some sensitive and scent-allergic people. You can also obtain washing soda in bulk quantities (50-100# bags) from a local chemical supply company.

Another wax-removing option is to use Citra-Solv Cleaner & Degreaser Concentrate (**Shadow Lake, Inc.**) This product is often available in local health-food stores. It can also be ordered from **Real Goods, Harmony, Frontier Natural Products**, and **Simmons Natural Bodycare**, among others. To use it, mix 1 cup with 10 cups water. You'll need to scrub the floor using a floor brush, then rinse with water. If the wax doesn't come off easily, try a stronger concentration. (For more information on concentrated citrus cleaners, see *Liquid All-Purpose Products* on page 137.)

Bio Shield Floor Milk (**Eco Design Co.**) is formulated with carnuba wax and coconut soap for "protective maintenance." You can order it from the manufacturer. Several wood/linoleum protection products are handled by **Real Goods**. You might also talk with your linoleum dealer for his or her suggestions for linoleum care. Remember that natural, unsealed linoleum can be negatively affected by water. Therefore, you'll want to make certain your linoleum's surface is effectively protected. If you're an allergic or sensitive person, make sure the products you use are tolerable to you (see *Testing* on page 62).

Cork Floors

Cork floors can be cleaned in a similar way to linoleum flooring. (See *Linoleum* on page 310.) However, You'll want to make sure to apply only a minimal amount of water when washing and rinsing. Otherwise, cork floors can deteriorate.

Solid-Wood Floors

An option for cleaning wood floors is to use unscented, liquid Castile soap. Dr. Erlander's Jubilee Liquid Castile Soap (**Erlander's Natural Products**) is one such product. It may be ordered directly from the company. Dr. Bronner's Baby Supermild Unscented Castile Soap Liquid (**Dr. Bronner's**) is a comparable soap product. It's often sold by local health-food stores and can be ordered from the company, **Tucson Cooperative Warehouse**, and **Frontier Natural Products**. To use either of these, pour 1/8 cup liquid Castile soap plus 1/2 cup white vinegar into 2 gallons of water. After washing, rinse your floors with clear water.

Another liquid natural-soap product you might try is Heavenly Horsetail All-Purpose Cleaner (**Jedmon Products**). Note: this product contains herbs that may make it bothersome to some sensitive or highly allergic individuals. Heavenly Horsetail is sold in some health-food stores and by **Karen's Natural Products**, and by the company. Bio Shield Soap Floor Cleaner (**Eco Design Co.**), is a vegetable-based soap/glycerin/essential-oils floor cleaning product you can order from the manufacturer. Yet another choice is Auro Awalan Cleaning Solution. This is a highly concentrated plant-soap liquid handled by **Sinan Company**.

Tucson Cooperative Warehouse and **Karen's Natural Products** handle Ecover Floor Soap (**Ecover**). This biodegradable, vegetable-oil-based soap contains essential oils of rosemary, eucalyptus, and citronella that are aromatic and can linger. So it can be bothersome to certain sensitive and allergic individuals (see *Problems with Scents* on page 72). Use 1 capful in 1 gallon of water, wash the floor, then rinse.

Livos Trena Neutral Cleaner is a neutral, soap-based cleaner made with citrus oil. Dilute 1/4 cup in 2 1/2 gallons of warm water to use. Trena can be ordered from **Karen's Natural Products** and **Natural Home by Natürlich**. This product, too, will need to be rinsed off.

Some people may want to try using a mild, unscented dish detergent with water, followed by rinsing. However, using detergents may not be as good for your wood floors as soap products which contain oils and/or fats.

Note: Avoid using too much water on your wood floors. Even if they're sealed, small breaks or cracks in the hard protective surface will permit water to become absorbed by the wood. Excess moisture can easily cause damage, such as discoloration or warping. Therefore, always wring sponges or mops thoroughly before using them on wood floors.

If your wood floor has a wax finish, you might use Bio Shield Floor Milk (**Eco Design Co.**) to maintain its appearance. It contains carnuba wax and coconut-oil soap. This can be ordered from the maker. For floor waxes, see *Waxe Finishes* on page 279.)

Cleaning Rugs and Carpets

Rugs and carpets require special care to keep them clean and looking good. Ideally, only tolerable, less-toxic, lower-odor products should be used, especially if you're a sensitive or highly allergic person.

Removing Rug and Carpet Dust

If small, 100%-cotton rugs have only surface dust on them, it can be removed by vigorously shaking the rugs outdoors. Of course, you'll want to hold your breath or wear a dust mask (see *Personal Protective Gear* on page 264) when you do this so as not to inhale the airborne dust particles. Another easy method of removing dust is to put small cotton rugs in the clothes dryer for about fifteen minutes. Using the "heat" rather than the "air" setting will help tighten the yarns that may have stretched out of shape in *dhurrie* rugs (flat, heavy, woven, cotton rugs). (Note: If you're allergic to dust mites, it's best to wash them instead with hot water.)

A very old rug cleaning method that can remove deeply imbedded dust and debris is to beat your rugs while they hang securely on an outdoor line. Unfortunately, finding a rug-beating tool can be a problem. However, heavy, looped-wire, wood-handled beaters might be found in local antique shops. If you can't find a real rug beater, you might try using an old tennis racket or broom instead. If you use a racket, make sure that there are no protruding knots in the string, or other rough areas, that could snag the rug's fibers. Because beating a rug can take some time, it's a good idea to wear a protective dust mask (see *Personal Protective Gear* on page 264).

Of course, large rugs and carpets that can't be removed should be vacuumed regularly, ideally with a specially filtered portable vacuum or a central vacuum system that's vented to the outdoors. Vacuuming can reduce the accumulated dirt that is abrasive to your carpet's fibers, and will minimize dust mite and flea problems.

Removing Rug and Carpet Odors

Of course, pure, dry baking soda can be sprinkled on rugs and carpets to absorb (soak up) odors. Another choice is to use powdered *zeolite*. Zeolite is a mineral that, like activated carbon, can adsorb odors. (Odor molecules adhere to zeolite's surface due to natural electrostatic charges.) To use either material, sprinkle it over the surface of your carpet, give it some time to adsorb, then vacuum thoroughly. It is probably a good idea to wear a dust mask when doing this. (See *Personal Protective Gear* on page 264.) EcoFresh Deodorizing Powder is a zeolite product. You can order it from **TerrEssentials**. Dasun All Natural Zeolite Powder (**Dasun Co.**) is in a 2 pound shaker container and is handled by **Bio Designs**. It can also be ordered directly from the company. Note: Two pounds of zeolite is enough for about 200 square feet of area. Both a 2 pound shaker container as well as a 10 pound bucket of powered, natural zeolite are carried by healthyhome.com.

Nature's Key Odor Eliminator is a specially formulated, unscented, active-enzyme product. It can be ordered from **Dasun Co.**

To remove both stains and odors, look for appropriate products in *Removing Rug and Carpet Stains* next.

Removing Rug and Carpet Stains

Most people who use rugs and carpeting invariably have to deal with stains that get on them. While there are a number of highly-odorous, solvent-type, carpet stain removers on the market, these can be very bothersome, especially to sensitive persons. Fortunately, there are some less noxious alternatives. Actually, many small spots can be safely removed using a club-soda solution, which often works well with small, fresh stains. Simply pour a small amount of the club soda on the affected area. Then, blot the dampness away using a clean sponge or a clean 100%-cotton towel. You might find you'll have to repeat the procedure, if necessary.

For removing greasy stains from carpet, try using 1 oz. Citra-Solv Cleaner and Degreaser Concentrate (**Shadow Lake, Inc.**) dissolved in 2 cups of water. Citra-Solv is a heavy-duty cleaner that's often available at local heath-food stores. It can also be ordered from **Real Goods, Frontier Natural Products, Harmony,** and **Simmons Natural Bodycare.** Apply the solution to the stain with a clean sponge and then alternately brush and blot the area with a clean damp cotton cloth. Finish up by rinsing with clear water and blotting. Note that this cleaner is citrus-based, so it does have a citrusy odor. (For more information on concentrated citrus cleaners, see *Liquid All-Purpose Products* on page 137.)

Another product you might use to remove carpet stains is White Wizard Spot Remover and All-Purpose Cleaner (**L.B. Roe Corp.**). This is an odorless, nontoxic, eco-friendly product in a paste-like consistency. The manufacturer claims the product can get out many grease, blood, ink, and other stains. It's sold in 10 oz. plastic tubs in some local grocery and hardware stores. It's also available by mail order from the maker, **Vermont Country Store Voice of the Mountains, Agelong Catalog, Solutions, Real Goods,** and **Harmony.** To use it, carefully follow package directions.

Then, too, EnviroRite Carpet & Upholstery Spot Lift Stain Remover (**BioForce Enviro-Tech Inc.**) can be a good option. It's an undyed, unscented liquid which can ordered directly from the company.

Removing pet odors from carpets can be difficult. You can try Lifekind Pet Stain Remover (**Lifekind Products**). This is an undyed, unscented cleaner formulated with citrus extracts. It can be purchased from the company. Pet-Clean Pet-Stain Cleaner & Odor Neutralizer (**Orange-Sol Household Products, Inc.**) is an orange-solvent based cleaner in a spray bottle. You can buy it from the manufacturer.

Another approach for pet stains and odors is to use enzymes created by active bacterial cultures. These literally digest organic materials such as the residues pets can leave behind. One Earth Stain and Odor Remover (**Eight-In-One Pet Products**) uses no synthetic solvents or artificial colors. It has biologically active enzymes and an added natural scent. You'll need to call the company to find a local outlet. Pet Odor Eliminator (**Unique Marketing**) is a concentrated version with an added natural scent. It is also made with active bacterial-culture enzymes. To use it, mix 1 part in 8 parts water. It can be ordered directly from the maker if it's not available locally. Natural Chemistry Smell & Stain Remover uses active enzymes with no added scent. It's sold by **Allergy Relief Shop, Inc.** Two products that can be purchased from **Dasun Co.** are a non-staining, unscented enzyme-based spray called The B.O.S.S., and Nature's Key Spot and Stain Remover & Presoak (unscented). Earth Friendly Stain & Odor Remover (**Earth Friendly Products**) is one more enzyme cleaner. This one, which has a natural lemon scent added, is often found in alternative food stores.

For additional ideas, check *Clean & Green* and *Better Basics for the Home*, both by Annie Berthold-Bond and *Clean Your House Safely & Effectively Without Harmful Chemicals* by Randy Dunford for more specific stain-removal suggestions. It's important to note that whatever you use to clean your carpet, it's wise to test it first to make sure it won't bleach or damage the carpet fibers, and that it'll be tolerable to you.

Thorough Cleaning of Rugs and Carpets

Of course, from time to time, your rugs and carpets will have to be thoroughly cleaned—not just vacuumed or spot cleaned. This section discusses some methods that can be used to accomplish this. As you'll see, in some cases, the problems associated with cleaning carpets both thoroughly and safely can be great. In fact, one medical condition, *Kawasaki Syndrome*, has been linked to newly cleaned carpets. It seems that in some instances, 16 to 25 days after a carpet's been cleaned, the condition manifests itself in certain children. The symptoms are systemic and generally include a high fever. That's one of the major reasons why hard-surface flooring options are often suggested for ideal healthy houses.

It should be pointed out that it is erroneous to think that sprinkling baking soda or zeolite on a carpet, and then vacuuming it, will actually clean the carpet. This simply is not true. All they can do is absorb some of the carpet odors without adding any additional ones. Note that any baking soda or zeolite that isn't completely vacuumed up will tend to accumulate in your carpet.

Simple Rug Washing

Many small 100%-cotton rugs can be safely laundered in your washing machine, then dried in an automatic dryer or hung on a line. This is the best approach for thorough cleaning, especially for those allergic to dust mites. However, you should realize that, in many cases, there will be some shrinkage, especially after the initial washing and drying.

Surprisingly, some wool Oriental rugs made with waterproof dyes can actually be laid flat outdoors and gently scrubbed with mild soap and water (see *Soaps* on page 75 for suggestions). To do this, first place a rug on a clean concrete driveway or sidewalk. Using a soft brush dipped in a solution of warm water and soapy lather, scrub the rug in the direction of the nap. Afterward, the lathered rugs should be thoroughly rinsed with clear water simply by using a hose. Next, use a clean, smooth dowel rod and repeatedly push it across the rug going in the direction of the nap. This will act like a squeegee, and should be repeated until the excess liquid water is removed. This will take some time. Then, place the rug on a dry, clean, flat surface (outdoors in the sun) to dry, making sure that the top surface is up. Leave the rug there until it is completely dry. (Note: You can place folded flannel blankets underneath the wet rug to absorb more of the water and remove them after a few hours.) This do-it-yourself washing method should *only* be undertaken after talking with the dealer from whom you bought the rug. For more on hand washing Oriental rugs, check *The Practical Guide of Oriental Rugs* by George Griffin Lewis or *Handwoven Carpets, Oriental and European* by A.F. Kendrick & C.E.C. Tattersall, as well as other traditional Oriental rug books that may be at your local library.

If you don't want to wash your rugs yourself, or the type of rugs you have shouldn't be hand washed at home, consult with your Oriental-rug dealer to see if he or she can suggest a professional rug-cleaning company that will use less-toxic cleaning products. Some rug dealers offer such a service themselves, and will pick up your rugs, clean them in their shop, then return them to your home. Some rugs will have "dry clean" only labels, or your dealer may recommend dry cleaning. However, you may not need to have that done—if specialized solvent-free wet cleaning is available in your area. (See *Dry Cleaning* on page 130 and *Specialized Wet Cleaning* on page 131 for more information.)

Solvent Cleaning Rugs and Carpets

Some manufacturers recommend that their natural-fiber rugs be dry-cleaned only. As it turns out, dry-cleaning uses petroleum-derived solvents rather than water as the cleaning fluid. For certain rugs, this may be necessary in order to prevent the dyes from running, or the fibers from deteriorating. When you bring your rugs to a dry-cleaning establishment, ask that no added scents, deodorizers, or moth-preventive chemicals be used on your rugs. This is especially important for all sensitive and many allergic persons. Once your newly cleaned rugs are home, it's a very good idea to air them outdoors in shaded, dry, uncontaminated surroundings until the chemical odors have dissipated.

If you can't (or don't care to) take your large rugs to a dry-cleaner, there are now companies that use milder dry-cleaning solutions to clean them right in your house. (This method is also used on wall-to-wall carpeting.) The companies that do this promote the fact that they don't use water, and, thus, their cleaning methods won't promote the growth of micro-organisms.

With home dry-cleaning, solvents are first sprayed directly onto the rugs or carpeting. They then enter the fibers causing the dirt to be pushed toward the surface. Next, the freed dirt has to be removed. To do this, some companies use a second solution containing *ionizers*. These provide charged ions that attach themselves to the dirt particles. The solution also usually contains *optical brighteners* (to make the newly cleaned carpets appear brighter-looking) and perhaps deodorizers and other additives as well.

After an ionizing solution has been applied, a special machine is used that has a whirling nylon pad that is able to pick up the dirt particles *electrostatically*. The pad is oppositely charged from the ionized dirt particles, so the opposite charges to attract. The pads are repeatedly rinsed or replaced until they no longer get dirty—meaning they aren't able to pick up any more dirt particles, and the rug or carpet is considered clean.

Note that solvent-based rug/carpet cleaning solutions nearly always contain scents, either natural or synthetic. These scents may linger for a long time after the cleaning is done. Also, the solvents can be bothersome to a large proportion of both allergic and sensitive persons. If you absolutely must have this type of cleaning done in your home, it's wise to have good ventilation, and to be out of the house while the actual cleaning is taking place. In fact, if you're very sensitive, you may have to stay elsewhere for some time until the odors are tolerable.

Using powdered, solvent cleaners rather than wet, solvent sprays is another in-home dry-cleaning approach for cleaning your rugs and carpets. With this method, rugs and carpets are often first lightly dampened with water. Then, the powdered solvent is sprinkled on them. In some cases, this material is composed of cellulose (a natural material derived from plants) saturated with solvents, detergents, and other additives. After it's been applied, it remains there for a predetermined length of time to absorb the dirt.

Next, using some type of extraction equipment or a very powerful vacuum, the powdered solvent is removed. However, in reality it's impossible to remove all of it, so some will remain imbedded in your rugs or carpets. As you routinely vacuum though, more and more of the powdered solvent will eventually come out. Fortunately, these powders are designed to be nonabrasive to carpet fibers. Note that the same concerns and prudent measures suggested earlier in connection with the wet-solvent cleaners apply to the powdered solvent cleaners as well.

Rug & Carpet Shampooing & Wet-Extraction Cleaning

Many people avoid solvent rug cleaners altogether because of the odors they generate and, thus, opt for rug and carpet cleaning methods that use water. However, it should be noted that using a water solution can result in damp fibers, backing, and padding, which could easily accelerate bacterial, mold, and dust mite growth. (For a water soluble borate compound added to carpet cleaning solutions formulated to kill dust mites, see *Dust Mites*

6: House Cleaning

on page 410). You can compound the problem with inadequate ventilation, which will result in extremely high indoor humidity that can magnify these problems exponentially.

A worse-case scenario of this occurred not long ago in New Orleans. The Earl K. Young Library had it's carpets wet cleaned, turned off the climate control equipment, and closed up the library. Upon returning, the entire library was covered with mold, including the book collection. The lesson: *Never* completely close up a room that's just had it's carpet wet cleaned.

As you probably know, water-solution rug and carpet cleaning can be done using either a rotating head shampoo machine or an application/extraction machine. This type of cleaning device is commonly called a *steam cleaner*. True steam cleaners do exist, such as the AmeriVap Systems Vapormax. This particular canister unit uses low pressure and high temperature to spew sanitizing steam which is then extracted. You can purchase a Vapormax from **Bio Designs**. Another version is the Steam Mop offered by **Harmony**. This upright model uses sterilizing steam to clean hard-surfaced floors. However, the vast majority of application/extraction machines, even some with the misleading word "steam" in their name, use liquid water—not steam. They work by providing both a spraying action and a suctioning action that occur simultaneously. If you have your home professionally cleaned using a water solution, it's likely that this type of equipment will be used—unless the company specifies that they use true steam.

Application/extraction machines remove a great deal of the detergent and moisture they put in the carpet, but simple shampooing machines don't. This is important because any remaining detergent can leave a gummy coating on the carpet fibers that will act as a glue that will attract dirt particles in the future. So, rugs or carpets that have been recently cleaned with a shampoo machine may be loaded with detergent residues and may have to be cleaned again rather quickly. In addition, shampoo machines can leave excess moisture in your carpet that will require more time to evaporate. If the moisture and detergent remain on the carpet for an extended time, it could potentially damage certain carpet fibers and backing materials, and it can greatly encourage microbial growth. Another distinct advantage to extraction machines over shampooing machines is that their vacuuming effect is able to pull up deeply imbedded dirt—not just surface dirt.

No matter which type of machine you choose, you should be aware that typical carpet shampoos generally contain a complex mixture of synthetic ingredients, including colorants and fragrances. Therefore, these products are often not very well tolerated by most sensitive and certain allergic people. Fortunately, there are now several alternative rug and carpet cleaning products that have more simple formulas. Some are even unscented.

One of these you might want to try is SafeChoice Carpet Shampoo (AFM). It's sold by most AFM dealers including **N.E.E.D.S.**, healthyhome.com, **Building for Health Materials Center**, **Priorities**, **Allergy Relief Shop, Inc.**, **American Environmental Health Foundation**, and **The Living Source**. It can also be bought from **Gazoontite**. This product is an unscented, water-based, synthetic emulsion, designed to be low-odor. It can be used in shampooing machines or application/extraction machines. Be sure to follow the package directions carefully to get the best results.

Another alternative carpet shampoo is Karpet Kleen (**Granny's Old Fashioned Products**). This can be purchased from dealers such as **N.E.E.D.S.**, **Bio Designs**, **Allergy Relief Shop, Inc.**, **Health One Co.**, and **The Living Source**. Karpet Kleen contains no dyes, fragrances, phosphates, or preservatives. It's recommended for use in an application/extraction-type carpet cleaning machine. The company suggests adding $1/2$ cup each of borax and vinegar to the solution to neutralize pet odors and to add freshening power. By the way, the same version under the Coastline Old Fashioned label is sold by **Coastline Products**.

LifeTime Solutions Carpet Clean (**LifeTime Solutions**) can be a very good choice for your floors. This is an undyed, unscented cleaner with a unique formula using *colloidal micelles*. You can order it directly from the company.

EnviroRite Carpet & Upholstery Cleaner (**BioForce Enviro-Tech Inc.**) can be a fine cleaning product for many sensitive people. Like all the products in this line, it's unscented and undyed. It can be ordered from the manufacturer.

Natürlich Carpet Shampoo is a citrus-based cleaner that leaves no soapy residue. It has a low pH and is safe for wool, cotton, and synthetic rugs. Because it is citrus-based, it will have an innate mild citrus odor. You can purchase it from **Natural Home by Natürlich**.

Important note: if you choose an unscented carpet shampoo, be sure to consider the condition of the cleaning equipment in which you plan to use it. After all, rented units will have absorbed odors from perhaps hundreds of cleanings with typical carpet-cleaning solutions containing perfumes, natural lemon scents, disinfectants, deodorizers, etc. Therefore, it may be wise to own your machine if at all possible, especially if you're a sensitive or highly allergic person. Carpet-cleaning machines are sold in most department stores, vacuum shops, and discount stores.

Cleaning Windows

Most common window cleaners are quite odorous. This is because many contain ammonia, perfumes, alcohol, or other aromatic ingredients. Generally, they can't be safely used by most sensitive and asthmatic persons, or by some with allergies. However, there are more tolerable window-cleaning solutions available.

For example, a very weak dilution of SafeChoice Super Clean (**AFM**) in water works quite well to clean windows. It can be purchased from most AFM dealers, including **N.E.E.D.S., Priorities, Bio Designs, American Environmental Health Foundation, Allergy Relief Shop, Inc., healthyhome.com,** and **The Living Source**. You need to use only 5 drops from an eye dropper of this unscented, synthetic liquid in a spray bottle filled with 16 ounces of water. Then, you simply shake the bottle well, spray the window, and clean it using tolerable paper towels. Another alternative window-cleaning option is to use Bon Ami Cleaning Powder or Bon Ami Cleaning Cake (**Faultless Starch/Bon Ami Co.**). Both are available in some local grocery stores and can be mail-ordered from **Erlander's Natural Products** and the company's **Agelong Catalog**. The cleaning powder is sold by **Bio Designs**, the cleaning cake by **Simmons Natural Bodycare**. To use them, sprinkle a small amount of the white unscented powder on a wet sponge, or gently rub a wet sponge across the cleaning cake. Then, apply a thin even coating to the dirty windows. Finally, buff away the film before it dries, using a clean, dry, soft non-linty cotton cloth.

A truly excellent window cleaner is LifeTime Solutions Sparkling Glass (**LifeTime Solutions**). This is a clear, unscented liquid with a one-of-a kind *colloidal-micelle* formula. You can buy it directly from the manufacturer.

Nature Clean Window & Glass Cleaner (**Frank T. Ross & Sons Ltd.**), has no dyes or scents and is made with ingredients such as witch hazel and grain alcohol. You can order this product directly from the manufacturer and **American Environmental Health Foundation**.

One more option is Lifekind Glass & Shiny Surface Cleaner (**Lifekind Products**) which has no dyes or added scents. This product contains citrus extract and can be purchased from the manufacturer. From the EnviroRite line comes EnviroRite Clearly Clean Glass & Plexi Cleaner (**BioForce Enviro-Tech Inc.**). The formula for this cleaner uses no dyes or scents, and can be ordered from the company.

Allens Naturally Non-Toxic Glass & Surface Cleaner (**Allens Naturally**) is biodegradable, and contains no scents or dyes. This cleaner can be purchased at many local alternative food stores, from the company, and from **Janice Corporation, Allergy Relief Shop, Inc., Health One Co., Tucson Cooperative Warehouse,** and **Coastline Products.**

You might also try SafeChoice Glass Cleaner (**AFM**). This is an unscented and undyed, biodegradable synthetic product which is handled by **N.E.E.D.S., The Living Source, Allergy Relief Shop, Inc., Priorities, healthyhome.com,** and **American Environmental Health Foundation.**

Another product that may be suitable for you is Seventh Generation Natural Glass Cleaner (**Seventh Generation**). It uses no dyes, phosphates, or synthetic scents. However, it does contain citrus scents. It can be ordered from **Harmony, Tucson Cooperative Warehouse,** and on-line from **GreenMarketplace.com.**

Befit Enterprises Ltd., Allergy Relief Shop, Inc., and **Karen's Natural Products** handle Natural Chemistry Glass Cleaner. This product has a formula made with naturally derived cleaning agents, enzymes, and citric acid with no added scent.

Eco Design Co. makes and sells Bio Shield Vinegar Cleaner. It's made with vinegar, citric acid and sugar-based cleaning agents. It can also be used for the surfaces of refrigerators and appliances.

Earth Friendly Window Kleen (**Earth Friendly Products**) uses vinegar, plant-based surfactants and has no added scents. This cleaner is sometimes sold in local alternative food stores and it can be ordered from **Harmony** and **Priorities.** Check also with **Real Goods,** to see if they currently handle it.

Of course, a homemade cleaner is a white vinegar and water solution. It's nontoxic, all-natural, inexpensive, and effective. However, certain sensitive persons might find the vinegar odor somewhat bothersome. To use vinegar on your windows, mix 1/4 cup with 1 quart of water and pour it into a spray bottle. Another option is to use 1 tablespoon of fresh, strained lemon juice poured into a 1-quart spray bottle. After filling the sprayer with water, shake thoroughly. With either solution, mist the glass lightly and clean it off with tolerable paper towels or non-linty cotton cloth.

Non-linty cotton cloth such as flannel is a good choice for window washing. You can either use your own fabric scraps or cloths with bound edges. Fuller Brush 100%-cotton household cloths (**Fuller Brush Co.**) will also work well. They can be ordered from the company and its dealers.

Another window cleaning option is to use a household squeegee. They're sold by **Allergy Control Products, Inc.** and **Fuller Brush Co.** A household squeegee with an extendible handle can be ordered from **Williams-Sonoma.** They're also often sold in hardware stores.

Cleaning Walls

In most cases you usually don't have to clean your home's painted interior walls very often. But when you do, you'll want to choose less-toxic, low-odor products to do the job, especially if you're very sensitive or asthmatic or have certain allergies.

Most painted walls can be safely washed with a solution of SafeChoice Super Clean (**AFM**) and water. This unscented liquid cleaner can be ordered from AFM dealers including **N.E.E.D.S., Bio Designs, Allergy Relief Shop, Inc., healthyhome.com, American Environmental Health Foundation, Priorities,** and **The Living Source.** To clean your walls, mix 1 cup Super Clean in 1 gallon of water. Then dip a sponge or soft cotton cloth into the solution, lightly wring it, and very gently scrub the walls. Finish by rinsing with clear water.

You might also try Citra-Solv Cleaner & Degreaser Concentrate (**Shadow Lake, Inc.**) to clean your painted walls. This highly concentrated product is sold in some local health-food stores or it can be ordered from **Real Goods, Frontier Natural Products, Harmony,** and **Simmons Natural Bodycare.** To use Citra-Solv, mix 1 cup in 1 gallon of water. Then apply and rinse as with the Super Clean/water solution. Note that this cleaner has a citrusy odor. (For more information on citrus cleaners see *Liquid All-Purpose Products* on page 137.)

Another option is to use TSP (trisodium phosphate) and water in a very weak solution. TSP is a crystalline material that can be used as a powerful, unscented cleaner. At least one brand of TSP—Red Devil TSP/90 Heavy Duty Cleaner (**Red Devil, Inc.**)—has a modified trisodium phosphate formula that is phosphate-free. It's usually sold in paint and hardware stores. To use Red Devil TSP, mix 2 teaspoons of it in 1 gallon of warm water. Then, dip your sponge in the solution and wring it nearly dry. Next, you can gently scrub the walls starting from the wall bottom up to avoid creating streaks. You'll find that cleaning just a small area at a time usually works best. In most cases, rinsing isn't necessary. By the way, whenever you use TSP, wearing waterproof household gloves is a good idea to prevent any skin irritation. (See *Waterproof Household Gloves Suggestions* on page 137.)

Before using any cleaning solution on your walls, it's best to test a small inconspicuous spot first, perhaps in a closet. That way you ensure that your painted surfaces won't be harmed before you proceed any further. (For greasy walls, see *Cleaning Greasy Problems* on page 165.)

Kitchen Cleaning

Your kitchen requires several cleanups practically every day. Ideally, you'll choose products for this job that are effective, low-odor, and well-tolerated by you. This means avoiding most of the typical kitchen cleaning products available in your local grocery store. Fortunately, the sections below offer some safer kitchen cleaning product alternatives.

Sponges and Brushes

Bright, synthetically dyed *cellulose* (a natural material derived from plants) sponges are sold in nearly every grocery store. However, you should be aware that most cellulose sponges are now modified to have anti-microbial properties. Such sponges are designed to prevent the sour odor (mostly from bacterial contamination) that many sponges develop. O-Cel-O (**3M Home and Commercial Care Div.**), one of the more popular sponge brands, states that their "StayFresh process...is protection...permanently bound within the sponge" and that it should last for hundreds of uses. However, exactly what this StayFresh process is, is not explained.

Generally, there are two basic approaches that manufacturers use to achieve microbial control. The first is to add an antibacterial substance (a bacterial poison) capable of continually leaching out of the sponge fibers onto the surface until the substance is used up. The second method is to permanently bond an inert substance to the sponge fibers in order to create a physically inhospitable environment for microbes live on. Unfortunately, finding out what a company uses can often be difficult.

However, if a product has "Aegis" on its label, you will know for certain that minute silicon particles were used. Aegis (**Aegis Environments**) is a "microbe shield technology" invented by Dow Corning Corporation. It uses "organosilicon agents" that are permanently bonded in place. What this means is that extremely minute, sharp-edged, silicon particles are used to puncture the living cells of microbes—killing them without using an active poisoning agent. It would seem to be that this type of antimicrobial approach, which doesn't use a antibiotic solution, is a better choice for very sensitive people.

Information on some types of antimicrobial techniques and agents is available from the **National Antimicrobial Information Network (NAIN)**. This is a free service staffed by university specialists, and is sponsored by the **EPA (Environmental Protection Agency)**. However, if a particular agent or method has not been officially registered as antimicrobial, they will not have much data to share with you.

If you want to use sponges, but don't want dyed or "antimicrobially-altered" cellulose sponges, you might try undyed cellulose sponges sold by **Karen's Natural Products**, and **Harmony**. This latter company in particular, offers a good selection of sizes. You might also opt for the natural sea sponges (*porifera*) sold in the **Tom's of Maine** and **Karen's Natural Products** catalogs. However, you should know that these alternative sponges can be rather expensive, especially the sea sponges.

Fuller Brush kitchen sponges (**Fuller Brush Co.**) are dyed cellulose sponges with a synthetic scrubber on one side. Currently, these are untreated items. They can be purchased from the company and its dealers. Untreated pop-up cellulose sponges are available from **Williams-Sonoma**.

No matter what type of sponges you choose, it's a good idea to rinse them out thoroughly after each use, then wring them out, allowing them to dry. In addition, you might occasionally boil your cellulose sponges in water a few minutes to freshen them. A baking soda-and-water solution can also be used. After soaking, you'll need to rinse the sponges completely with clean water. Two other very simple ways to clean your cellulose sponges are to wash them in your automatic dishwasher (on the top rack, secured in place) or your clothes washer.

If you like to use brushes in your kitchen, natural-bristle, wood-handle, vegetable brushes are available from **Karen's Natural Products** and **Simmons Natural Bodycare**. Check your local health-food stores for others. After you use your natural-fiber brushes, they should be completely dry before being stored. In addition, you should clean the brush heads routinely. However, it's probably best to test before soaking any brushes in a cleaning solution to see if the natural bristles are affected. Although it is unlikely the bristles could be damaged, it could occur. To test, simply place a similar old brush or a few bristles from a new one in the solution and see what happens.

Scouring

Many typical cleansers and scouring products contain chlorine bleach and synthetic colorants and dyes, all of which can bother many sensitive, asthmatic, and allergic persons. However, a number of alternative products are readily available and are quite safe to use.

Probably the most benign of all cleansers is baking soda sprinkled on a sponge or soft cloth. It can be used to gently scour pots, pans, countertops, and stove tops. Also, the family of mild, unscented Bon Ami products (**Faultless Starch/Bon Ami Co.**) work well. Bon Ami Cleaning Powder is very tolerable to most very sensitive persons. It consists only of powdered soap and finely ground feldspar (a natural mineral). Bon Ami Cleaning Cake has the same formula, but in a compressed bar form. In addition, Bon Ami Polishing Cleanser is an unscented, undyed powder with a biodegradable detergent. Other ingredients are feldspar and calcite as mild abrasives, sodium carbonate as a water softener, and an oxygen bleach. Bon Ami products, especially the cleanser, are available in some local grocery and hardware stores. They can also be ordered from the company's **Agelong Catalog**. The cleaning cake and powder are both sold by **Erlander's Natural Products**. Just the powder is sold by **Bio Designs**. Just the cake is sold by **Simmons Natural Bodycare**.

Nature Clean Tub & Tile Cleanser (**Frank T. Ross & Sons Ltd.**) is formulated with baking soda and calcium carbonate. It has no chlorine, fragrances, or dyes. You can purchase it from **American Environmental Health Foundation** as well as from the company.

A choice you might not have thought of is E-Z Maid Dish & Multi-Purpose Liquid (**Granny's Old Fashioned Products**). This is a very mild, unscented product that the company suggests can have a small amount of powdered borax and 3%-dilution hydrogen peroxide (the type sold in pharmacies) added to create a mild disinfecting cleanser. E-Z Maid is sold by **N.E.E.D.S.**, **Allergy Relief Shop, Inc.**, **Health One Co.**, and **The Living Source**. The same product under the Coastline Old Fashioned label is sold by **Coastline Products**.

An unusual choice is to use a pumice stone to clean mineral deposits and stains in sinks. Supposedly, this natural volcanic material is softer than porcelain or china. However, to be sure it will not harm your sink, you'll want to test it in an inconspicuous spot first. Pumice stones are sold by **Simmons Natural Bodycare**.

Unfortunately, most brand-name soap pads usually contain detergents, fragrances, and dyes that can be bothersome to many sensitive and certain allergic individuals. For these people, stainless-steel pads without soap or detergent can be a better choice. These types of pads can be used over and over again with your own tolerable soap, cleanser, or detergent— and the pads will never rust. Fuller Brush Stainless-steel Sponges (**Fuller Brush Co.**) is one brand you might try. They're sold by Fuller Brush Company and their dealers. Another source for stainless-steel pads is **Simmons Natural Bodycare**. Also, bronze scouring pads are available under the Chore Boy name in many grocery stores. Copper pads and those made of 100% nylon are other good options. Usually, a variety of metal and nylon scouring pads made without soap or detergent are handled by local grocery and hardware stores.

Rust and Calcium Removal

If your tap water has high levels of iron and calcium minerals, it can cause your sink, faucet, and glasses to become discolored or crusty-looking. Unfortunately, removing rust and calcium build-up can be a difficult job, but some products can effectively remove it.

For removing rust stains (and calcium), Bar Keeper's Friend (**Servaas Laboratories, Inc.**) is often very effective. This product is a finely powdered, unscented cleanser containing *oxalic acid* as its active ingredient. In this concentration and form, the oxalic acid is relatively safe. In fact, it's considered safe enough to use in your automatic dishwasher to clean rust stains and lime scale that have built up there. However, any oxalic-acid-containing product, because it's poisonous, should always be stored safely away from children and pets. Bar Keeper's Friend is often sold in grocery stores. Another similar product is Zud, which is sold in some grocery and hardware stores.

To remove *lime scale* (the crusty, white, hard-water buildup made mostly of calcium compounds), you might try full-strength white vinegar. The encrusted object or area should be soaked with the vinegar for 5–30 minutes. (Exactly how long will depend on how thick the scale is.) Then, you can clean the scale off with a non-abrasive scrubber.

For stubborn calcium deposits and rust spots, try CLR (**Jelmar**). This clear, almost-odorless fluid is basically a phosphoric and glycolic acid combination. While these particular products are usually nonpoisonous, they can cause inflammation. Therefore, wearing waterproof household gloves is a good idea when using CLR (see *Waterproof Household Gloves Suggestions* on page 137). Also, be sure it's stored so that children and pets can't obtain access. When using CLR, carefully follow the label instructions. This product is sold by many drug, grocery, and hardware stores. You can also order it from the company.

Cleaning Greasy Problems

Of course, a number of pine-solvent and petroleum-derived solvent cleaners can be found on grocery-store shelves. While most of them are very effective at cleaning grease, the solvents and other ingredients (dyes, fragrances, etc.) are often intolerable for sensitive, asthmatic, and allergic persons. Below are some alternative products that such people might want to try. It's suggested that, when using degreasing products, you wear gloves to protect your hands. (See *Waterproof Household Gloves Suggestions* on page 137.)

For greasy areas on painted walls or finished cabinet doors, a solution of diluted Safe Suds (**Ar-Ex Ltd.**) often works well. This concentrated, unscented, undyed detergent is sometimes available at local pharmacies. It can also be ordered directly from the company. To use it, try squeezing about 2 tablespoons into a gallon of warm water. (You'll probably want to experiment with the concentration.) Then, dip a sponge or cotton cloth into the solution and wring it out. Scrub the greasy areas and then rinse them. While Safe Suds isn't as heavy-duty as some other products, it's very mild and gentle to use.

One very good product for removing grease is SafeChoice Super Clean (**AFM**) which can be mail-ordered from many catalogs including **N.E.E.D.S.**, **American Environmental Health Foundation**, **Allergy Relief Shop, Inc.**, **Bio Designs**, **Priorities**, **healthyhome.com**, and **The Living Source**. To use this particular heavy-duty, unscented, undyed, synthetic liquid, use about 1 cup in 1 gallon of warm water. (You may need to increase the concentration up to perhaps 2 cups in 1 gallon water if the area is particularly greasy.) Then proceed as with the Safe Suds solution. Some greasy objects can be soaked in the solution for 15 minutes, then scrubbed and rinsed.

LifeTime Solutions Heavy Duty Cleaner & Degreaser (**LifeTime Solutions**) is an unscented, undyed unique *colloidal-micelle* solution that's quite effective. This item can be ordered from the manufacturer.

Yet another grease-cutting product you might try is a concentrated citrus solvent cleaner that has been properly diluted in water. One such cleaner is Citra-Solv Cleaner & Degreaser Concentrate (**Shadow Lake, Inc.**), which is available at some local retail outlets such as grocery and hardware stores. Citra-Solv can also be mail-ordered from **Real Goods**, **Harmony**, **Frontier Natural Products**, and **Simmons Natural Bodycare**. To use it, mix 1 oz. in 2 cups of water and proceed as with the Safe Suds mentioned above. If the grease isn't totally removed, try using the product at nearly full-strength. You can also soak certain greasy objects, then scrub and rinse them. Note that, this product is citrus-based and has a citrusy odor. Concentrated, this product can be potentially harmful. Therefore, very sensitive persons and those allergic to citrus should take special care. (For more information on concentrated citrus cleaners and other citrus-cleaner brands, see *Liquid All-Purpose Products* on page 137.)

Yet another grease-cutting alternative is TSP (trisodium phosphate). TSP is a white crystalline substance that acts as a powerful, unscented cleaner. It is often tolerable for even sensitive persons. One phosphate-free brand is Red Devil TSP/90 Heavy Duty Cleaner (**Red Devil, Inc.**), commonly sold in paint and hardware stores. To use TSP to remove grease, try using 2 level tablespoons dissolved in 1 gallon of warm water. As with the other cleaners, follow the directions given with Safe Suds above.

Of course, other catalogs and alternative grocery stores offer other less-toxic, low-odor cleaners you might try as well. But no matter which product you choose, it's important that when cleaning grease from painted walls or finished cabinets, that you test a small inconspicuous area first with the solution of your choice. This is to find out for sure if damage could result from its use, before applying it over a large area. For cleaning greasy stains from grout, see *Washing Ceramic Tile and Vinyl Floors* on page 151.

Disinfecting Countertops and Sinks

Many of the products listed under *Alternative Bleaches* on page 118 can be used as countertop disinfectants. This is especially true of the liquids. Another choice is Lifekind Disinfectant Spray & Wipe (**Lifekind Products**). This particular product is undyed and unscented. You can order it directly from the company.

An interesting option is to uses E-Z Maid Dish & Multi-Purpose Liquid (**Granny's Old Fashioned Products**). This is a very mild, unscented product that the company suggests can have a small amount of powdered borax and 3%-dilution hydrogen peroxide (the type sold in pharmacies) added to create a disinfecting cleanser. E-Z Maid is sold by **N.E.E.D.S.**, **Allergy Relief Shop, Inc.**, **Health One Co.**, and **The Living Source**. The same product under the Coastline Old Fashioned label is offered by **Coastline Products**.

By the way, many disinfectants are unable to successfully do their job instantaneously. Some require from 1/2 minute up to 10 minutes of surface contact time in order to effectively kill mold and bacteria. So, make sure that you take your time, especially when a disinfecting job is important.

Washing Dishes

As with most types of cleaning products, commonly available dish soaps and automatic-dishwasher compounds usually contain fillers, colorants, and fragrances—among other potentially bothersome ingredients. No wonder many sensitive, asthmatic, and allergic people find they just can't use them.

The following two sections suggest a few of the alternative dishwashing products now on the market that tend to be better tolerated. Some of these are made with all-natural ingredients, while others are unscented, synthetic detergents. Of course, you'll want to choose the products that best suit your own personal needs.

Hand Dishwashing Products

One synthetic product that's both mild and effective for hand-washing your dishes is Safe-Suds (**Ar-Ex, Ltd.**), which is available at some pharmacies or can be ordered directly from the manufacturer. This concentrated liquid is biodegradable and non-alkaline. It contains no enzymes, phosphates, fillers, perfumes, or dyes. Because it's so concentrated, one bottle will last three times as long as a conventional dishwashing liquid.

Then, too, you might consider Seventh Generation Natural Free & Clear Dish Liquid (**Seventh Generation**). This has a naturally derived formula with no dyes or scents. It's sold in many alternative food stores, through **Harmony**, **Tucson Cooperative Warehouse**, and on-line from **GreenMarketplace.com**.

Another excellent dishwashing liquid you may want to try is Allens Naturally Dishwashing Liquid (**Allens Naturally**). This product is sometimes sold in alternative grocery stores and can be easily ordered from the company, **Janice Corporation**, **Tucson Cooperative Warehouse**, **Allergy Relief Shop, Inc.**, **Health One Co.**, and **Coastline Products**. It contains no dyes, harsh chemicals, or scents.

Many sensitive people use E-Z Maid Dish & Multipurpose Liquid (**Granny's Old Fashioned Products**). This inexpensive, gentle, undyed, unscented dishwashing liquid is sold by **N.E.E.D.S.**, **Allergy Relief Shop, Inc.**, **Health One Co.**, **The Living Source** and others.

Earth-Rite Dishwashing Liquid is hypoallergenic and is both dye- and perfume-free. It can be ordered from **Natural Lifestyle** and **N.E.E.D.S.** Nature Clean Dishwashing Liquid (**Frank T. Ross & Sons Ltd.**) is a dye- and scent-free formula made with corn derivatives. This liquid cleaner is offered by **American Environmental Health Foundation** and can be ordered from the company.

Another product a number of sensitive and allergic persons have used is EnviroRite Kitchen Sink Dishwashing Liquid (**BioForce Enviro-Tech Inc.**). If you'd like to use it, you can order it from the company.

Ecover Dishwashing Liquid (**Ecover**) is a natural, vegetable-based cleaning detergent with no enzymes or synthetic perfumes. Ecover products are sold through dealers such as **Tucson Cooperative Warehouse** and **Simmons Handicrafts**.

Earth Friendly Ecos Dishmate is a concentrated natural cleaner with coconut-oil-based surfactants and essential oils, including that of almond. If a fragrant dish cleaner is tolerable for you, you can order it from **Priorities** and **Real Goods**.

Eco Design Co. makes and sells Bio Shield Dishwash Soap, a concentrated product with a vegetable-based cleaning agent. It contains no perfumes or dyes.

Many sensitive people have trouble tolerating typical vinyl-over-wire dish draining racks and the vinyl or latex drainer trays beneath them. A better choice are those made of stainless or chromed steel. Stainless-steel dish drainers can be purchased from **Williams-Sonoma** and **Hold Everything**. Stainless-steel dish-drainer-and-tray sets can be ordered from **Natural Lifestyle**. A chromed-steel dish drainer is sold through **Harmony**.

Automatic Dishwasher Products

Sodium Hexametaphosphate (SHMP or sometimes, SHP), a simple phosphate powder, can be a good, low-cost, odorless automatic dishwasher cleaner. While probably not quite as effective as products packaged specifically for dishwashers, it still does an admirable job. Naturally, those who don't want to use phosphates because of their environmental consequences, will want to choose another product. If you do want to try SHMP, you can purchase it in bulk at nearby chemical supply houses or in smaller quantities from **Bio Designs** and **Nigra Enterprises**. (Note: To store bulk SHMP, see *Metal Containers* on page 514.)

One alternative powdered dishwashing detergent most sensitive and scent-allergic people can handle well is Allens Naturally Automatic Dishwasher Detergent (**Allens Naturally**).

This is a highly-concentrated, unscented product that's sometimes found in alternative grocery stores. It can also be mail-ordered from the company, **Tucson Cooperative Warehouse**, **Janice Corporation**, **Health One Co.**, **Allergy Relief Shop, Inc.**, and **Coastline Products**.

Another brand you might consider is Seventh Generation Natural Automatic Dishwasher Detergent (**Seventh Generation**). This detergent is free of phosphates, chlorine, and scents, and can be ordered directly from the **Harmony** and **Tucson Cooperative Warehouse** catalogs or on-line from **GreenMarketplace.com**. It can also often found on alternative grocery store shelves. (Note: Seventh Generation Natural Automatic Dishwasher Gel has a green-apple scent added.)

Lifekind Automatic Dishwasher Powder (**Lifekind Products**) is an unscented, undyed cleaner made with citrus extracts. This product can be bought from the company. Then, too, there's Nature Clean Dishwasher Powder (**Frank T. Ross & Sons Ltd.**) which is dye-, scent-, and phosphate-free and is made with washing soda and an oxygen-based bleach. You can order it from **American Environmental Health Foundation** or the manufacturer.

Eco Design Co. makes and sells Bio Shield Dishwasher Concentrate. This has no chlorine or phosphates, dyes, or synthetic fragrances and is made with sodium percarbonate. **Tucson Cooperative Warehouse** handles Ecover Dishwasher Tablets (**Ecover**) and Ecover Automatic Dishwashing Powder (**Ecover**) made with citrates and sodium carbonate.

Auro Awalan Dishwasher Powder contains no phosphates, chlorine, or scents. It's so concentrated that only 1-2 teaspoons are required per load. However, you must have soft water to use this product effectively. The Auro Awalan line is sold by **Sinan Company**.

Earth Friendly Wave Automatic Dishwasher Powder (**Earth Friendly Products**) is created with natural enzyme cleaning agents and has an added natural lemon scent. Sold in many alternative food stores, you can call the company for a mail-order source or a nearby dealer if your local grocery doesn't carry it.

On a side note, to help eliminate lime scale (calcium buildup) and/or iron stains inside your automatic dishwasher, fill the machine's dispenser from time to time with 1 heaping tablespoon of Bar Keeper's Friend (**Servaas Laboratories, Inc.**). Then, run the dishwasher empty with no dishes through a normal cycle. This unscented powdered product contains oxalic acid as it's active ingredient. Because of this, make sure this product is stored so children and pets can't obtain ready access to it. It is usually available at local grocery stores.

Finding a tolerable rinse agent for your dishwasher can be difficult. Bio Shield Clear Rinse (**Eco Design Co.**) dishwasher rinse agent, which is formulated with citric acid and ethanol, may be a solution. This is an undyed product without synthetic fragrance. You can purchase it from the manufacturer. Another choice is Ecover Rinse Aid (**Ecover**) whose formula includes sugar-fermented alcohol, citric acid, "sugar-based non-ionic surfactants," and fatty acid. This product does not contain added scent. It can be ordered from **Tucson Cooperative Warehouse**.

Cleaning Drains

A number of alternative drain cleaners are now available. One of these, Dispoz-all Liquid Drain Cleaner, is described as a nontoxic product that contains no lye (an extremely caustic and dangerous substance). Instead, it works by bacterial enzymatic action. This product is sold by **Vermont Country Store Voice of the Mountains**. A similar product, Drain Care, is handled by **Allergy Relief Shop, Inc.** Nature's Key Drain Opener and Nature's Key Plumbing Cleaner are two enzyme-based versions offered by **Dasun Co.** Earth Friendly Earth

Enzymes (Earth Friendly Products) is yet one more unscented drain cleaner. It's often sold in alternative food stores.

A simple homemade drain-cleaning solution, which works best if the drain isn't completely blocked, is to pour $1/2$ cup of baking soda down the drain, followed by $1/2$ cup of white vinegar. After letting it work for five minutes, pour 2 quarts of boiling water into the drain. If you do this as a preventive measure every few months, you'll probably never develop severe clogs.

Cleaning Ovens and Stovetops

Practically everybody knows how odorous and harmful many typical oven cleaners are. Some are among the most dangerous kitchen products currently available. Fortunately, the following sections discuss some safer alternatives.

Conventional Ovens

Let's face it, a full-scale oven-cleaning job is unpleasant no matter what you use. Therefore, preventive measures are a good idea to minimize the necessity for doing it at all. For example, if your oven's owner's manual allows it, place a sheet of heavy-duty aluminum foil on the bottom of your oven to capture any spills. Also, to prevent burned-on splatters from building up on your oven's interior walls, scrub them occasionally with baking soda, using it as a mild scouring powder. To do this, just sprinkle some baking soda on a wet sponge or cotton dish cloth and go over the walls. Afterwards, rinse them thoroughly.

Some concentrated all-purpose cleaners can be used to clean ovens as well. (See, *Multi-Purpose Cleaner Suggestions* on page 137.) One is Crystal (Simple Green) All-Purpose Cleaner/Degreaser (**Sunshine Makers, Inc.**). To find this product, you'll need to contact the company for a nearby dealer. Another option is SafeChoice Super Clean (**AFM**). AFM products are sold by **N.E.E.D.S., Allergy Relief Shop, Inc., Bio Designs, The Living Source, Priorities, healthyhome.com,** and **American Environmental Health Foundation.** Both brands are synthetic concentrates made without dyes, scents or petroleum distillates. For ovens, apply full strength, allow time to penetrate greasy buildup, scrub, and then rinse. Of course, you'll want to wear waterproof household gloves when you do this (see, *Waterproof Household Gloves Suggestions* on page 137).

Self-Cleaning Ovens

Naturally, cleaning a self-cleaning oven is different than cleaning a conventional oven. While it doesn't require manual labor, you'll need to follow the proper procedure as laid out in your oven's owner's manual for the best results.

Generally however, the first step is to remove all the oven racks. If they're left in the oven during the cleaning cycle, the high heat will likely discolor their chrome finish. Therefore, you'll want to clean the racks separately in the sink. After the racks have been removed, you can activate the cleaning cycle.

However, you should realize that it's very important to have good ventilation when the cleaning cycle is in operation—as well as afterwards while it's cooling off. After all, the incineration of greasy substances can be very odorous. It can be a good idea to close off your kitchen from the rest of the house, if possible. Before actually activating the cleaning cycle, you'll want to open a kitchen window and put the range-hood fan on high. (Note: Range hoods that aren't vented to the outdoors are virtually useless.)

Glass-Top Stoves

For cleaning your glass stovetop, you might try Bon Ami Cleaning Powder or Bon Ami Polishing Cleanser (**Faultless Starch/Bon Ami Co.**) as gentle, non-scratching scouring products. Both are available in some grocery stores and can be ordered from the company's **Agelong Catalog**. In addition, the cleaning powder is sold by **Erlander's Natural Products** and **Bio Designs**.

To use either one, simply sprinkle the powder on a wet sponge or soft wet cotton cloth, then gently rub across the glass. After that, rinse the stovetop. For stubborn spots, make a paste of the powder and water, then, leave the damp mixture on the affected areas for at least five minutes (you may find you need to leave it on longer). When the burned-on drips are softened, gently scrub them off and then rinse the glass top. As an alternative, try baking soda. For the very worst burned-on spots, try scraping them off carefully using a single-edged razor blade.

Bathroom Cleaning

Bathroom cleaning is another one of those humbling, repetitive household jobs that no one seems to look forward to doing. But, by using less-toxic, low-odor products, the job is at least a healthier one.

Mold and Mildew

As most people know, mold and mildew are not only unsightly, they also can provoke allergic and asthmatic attacks in susceptible persons. Unfortunately, mold and mildew can be a common problem in bathrooms.

Mold and Mildew Prevention

A logical method for minimizing mold growth in your bath area is to squeegee the shower walls after you've taken your shower. Standard squeegees are often available at local auto-supply and janitorial-supply outlets. However, many will probably be fairly large and unattractive.

Fortunately, squeegees designed specifically for use in bathrooms are often available in bath stores and bath departments. Bathroom squeegees tend to be small and generally made with molded plastic handles. Interestingly, some of these squeegees have a built-in hook so they can be hung over your shower head when not in use. A more utilitarian household squeegee is made and sold by **Fuller Brush Co.** Others are handled by **Allergy Control Products, Inc.** and **Williams-Sonoma.** Of course, if you don't want to squeegee, you can simply sponge off the shower walls, although it'll probably take longer.

In addition, another very effective anti-mold strategy is to have good ventilation in your bathroom. After all, mold and mildew thrive in moist surroundings. Therefore, anything you can do to lower the relative humidity of the bathroom's air is a good idea—and ventilation is an important way to do that. If your bathroom doesn't have a window or you simply don't want to open it, you might consider installing a bathroom exhaust fan. Once it's installed, you'll have to remember to use it regularly unless it comes on automatically in conjunction with the room's light. Another option is to have the ventilation fan wired to a *dehumidistat.* This is a special device that can measure and monitor the air's relative humidity. It can be set to automatically turn on the ventilation fan when the humidity reaches a predetermined level. (For more on relative humidity, dehumidistats, and ventilating fans, see *High Relative Humidity* on page 530.)

An important note: Don't try to lower the relative humidity in a bathroom with zeolite, calcium chloride, or small plug-in drying dome units in bathrooms. While they can sometimes work well in closets, they are *not* designed to effectively cope with the consistently moist air in bathrooms.

SafeChoice X-158 Surface Stabilizer (AFM) can be applied as a preventative treatment to surfaces. The manufacturer says it will inhibit fungal growth from one to six months. You'll need to check the label for application specifics. This AFM product can be purchased from **N.E.E.D.S., Allergy Relief Shop, Inc., healthyhome.com, The Living Source, Building for Health Materials Center, Gazoontite, Priorities,** and **American Environmental Health Foundation.**

Solving Mold and Mildew Problems

If, despite your best efforts, mold or mildew becomes a problem in your bathroom, some less-toxic solutions are available for combating it other than the typical mildew-removal spray products sold in grocery stores. For example, hydrogen peroxide (H_2O_2 is one highly effective mold killer. (Note: This is the 3% dilution sold in pharmacies for use as an antiseptic.) To use this clear, odorless liquid, simply pour the hydrogen peroxide into a spray bottle and thoroughly spritz the affected areas: the bathroom fixtures, tile, and/or grout. Wearing protective eye wear is probably a good idea whenever you do this (see *Personal Protective Gear* on page 137). Because hydrogen peroxide is a bleaching agent, avoid spraying it on shower curtains made of colored fabric. By the way, you can use alternative laundry bleaches made with hydrogen peroxide, too (see *Alternative Bleaches* on page 118).

Another mold-killing option is full-strength white vinegar. Just apply it to the moldy areas, either with a sponge or a sprayer. Then leave it there a few minutes and rinse it off. (Some very sensitive persons might find the vinegar odor bothersome.)

Yet another natural alternative is a solution of unscented borax and water which can be used to sponge the affected areas. Try 1 tablespoon in 2 cups warm water. If that doesn't remedy the situation, experiment with other dilutions. Afterwards, be sure to rinse. It should also be mentioned that borax has a mild bleaching effect. The 20 Mule Team brand of borax (**20 Mule Team Borax**) is widely sold in food stores. This product may smell of fragrances picked up from scented laundry products shelved near by. Bulk borax, from local chemical supply houses, is often a better choice for sensitive and highly allergic people.

Another natural fungicide is pure tea tree oil. Try using it in a ratio of 2 teaspoons to 2 cups water and apply to the affected areas. Tea tree oil for mold killing can be purchased at most health-food stores and from **Bio Designs.**

In addition, some individuals have used antiseptic solutions, such as Aqueous Zephiran Chloride (**Sanofi Pharmaceuticals**) to deal with their mold and mildew problems. This particular product is a diluted *benzalkonium-chloride*/water solution. Aqueous Zephiran Chloride is available in your drugstore, although you may have to special order it. Suggested use is to simply apply the solution directly to the mold or mildew problem area. Rinsing it off is probably a good idea. It should be pointed out that products such as Zephiran are relatively expensive and they tend to have a mild, somewhat medicinal odor. Yet, many sensitive persons have found that they tolerate this product very well.

An unscented, undyed spray cleaner you can use to thwart mold is EnviroRite Mold, Mildew & Bacteria Detergent & Disinfectant Spray (**BioForce Enviro-Tech Inc.**). You can order it from the company or from **Allergy Control Products, Inc.**

To clean up mildew and mold and remove their stains, try SafeChoice Safety Clean (**AFM**). These are low-odor, non-toxic products sold by AFM dealers such as **The Living Source**, **Allergy Relief Shop, Inc.**, **Priorities**, **Building for Health Materials Center**, **healthyhome.com**, **American Environmental Health Foundation**, and **N.E.E.D.S.** In addition, you can purchase it from **Gazoontite**.

For cleaning mold from air-conditioners, see *Mold* on page 534. Note: Very sensitive persons, or those with mold allergies, should never do mold and mildew cleanup work themselves. One last piece of information to keep in mind is that many disinfecting cleaners require any where from $1/2$ minute up to 10 minutes of surface contact time to kill mold effectively. So don't rush. Any live mold could quickly multiply, if conditions are right.

Cleaning Sinks, Tubs, and Tile

Ideally, for cleaning your bathroom's sink, tub, and ceramic tile, you'll want to use products that can do the job, yet are tolerable to you. Three such products you might try are baking soda, Bon Ami Cleaning Powder (**Faultless Starch/Bon Ami Co.**), which is unscented soap and ground feldspar, and Bon Ami Polishing Cleanser (**Faultless Starch/Bon Ami Co.**) made with unscented biodegradable detergent, oxygen bleach, sodium carbonate as a water softener, and ground calcite and feldspar as mild abrasives. Another option is Nature Clean Tub & Tile Cleanser (**Frank T. Ross & Sons Ltd.**). This is an undyed, unscented chlorine-free cleanser made with sodium bicarbonate (baking soda) and calcium carbonate.

To use any of them, simply sprinkle the powder onto your sponge or soft cotton cloth and scrub. Because these products can leave white streaks behind as they dry, be sure to rinse thoroughly. Bon Ami products are sold in some grocery and hardware stores, and can be ordered from the manufacturer's **Agelong Catalog**. The cleaning powder is also sold by **Erlander's Natural Products** and **Bio Designs**. Nature Clean products can be purchased from the company and from **American Environmental Health Foundation**.

LifeTime Solutions Bath & Tile Cleaner (**LifeTime Solutions**) is a unique liquid alternative that has no dyes or scents. What makes it different is that it's formulated with *colloidal micelles*. This cleaner can be ordered directly from the company.

EnviroRite Tub & Tile Cleaner (**BioForce Enviro-Tech Inc.**) also has no dyes or scents. It can be bought from the company or from **eMD.com** and **Allergy Control Products, Inc.** Auro Awalan Bathroom Cleaner is a "natural chemistry cleaning product" with no added scent sold by **Sinan Company**.

Important note: If you have an acrylic or fiberglass tub, be sure to first carefully test the cleaning product you plan to use on a small, inconspicuous spot to make sure it won't bleach it (if your tub is colored) or leave abrasive marks. (For suggestions on removing calcium scale or rust stains, see *Rust and Calcium Removal* on page 164.)

Cleaning Toilets

Nature Clean Toilet Bowl Cleaner (**Frank T. Ross & Sons Ltd.**) is made with citrus solvents and grain alcohol. This product will have a mild citrusy odor. Nature Clean products can be ordered directly from the company and from the **American Environmental Health Foundation**.

Bio Shield Toilet Bowl Cleaner uses no phosphates, petroleum derivatives, bleaches, dyes, or synthetic fragrances. It's formulated with citric acid, ethanol, and sugar-based cleaning agents. **Eco Design Co.** is one source.

Seventh Generation Natural Toilet Bowl Cleaner (**Seventh Generation**) uses enzymes as its active ingredients. As a result, it'll take several hours to work, if not overnight. This cleaner has "natural mixed scents" and is sold by **Harmony**, **Tucson Cooperative Warehouse**, and **GreenMarketplace.com**.

Ecover Toilet Cleaner (**Ecover**) is available from dealers such as **Tucson Cooperative Warehouse**, and is made with citric and lactic acid, vinegar-and-sugar-based surfactants, and natural perfumes.

If you're a sensitive person, or are allergic to scents, and need to clean the toilet quickly, and you also don't want to be exposed to any added odors, you might try 1/8 cup of full-strength SafeChoice Super Clean (**AFM**), which is sold by AFM distributors such as **N.E.E.D.S.**, **The Living Source**, **Priorities**, **Allergy Relief Shop, Inc.**, **Bio Designs**, **healthyhome.com**, and **American Environmental Health Foundation**. To use this liquid synthetic cleaner, just pour a small amount around the inside of the bowl and scrub thoroughly with a toilet brush. Then, flush to rinse the bowl. It should be noted that this product doesn't claim to be sanitizing or *germicidal* (the ability to kill microorganisms). However, as noted in **Washington Toxics Coalition**'s *Buy Smart, Buy Safe: A Consumer Guide to Less-Toxic Products* by Phillip Dickey, in most cases toilet bowl cleaners "don't need disinfecting properties" because after their first use, toilet bowls are immediately exposed to germs again. Instead, the author concludes, what is most important is simply "to clean the toilets often."

Another option is using powdered, unscented borax to clean your toilet. A real plus for borax is that it has some germicidal properties and can act as a natural deodorizer. To use borax, just sprinkle a small amount (1/8 cup or less) around the interior of the toilet bowl. Then, scrub *at once* with a toilet brush and flush to rinse. Important note: If borax powder is allowed to sit for even a few moments, it'll form a hard crystalline crust. This is not only difficult to remove, but once it breaks free, this crust could possibly lead to a clogged toilet drain. By the way, powdered borax can be used along with SafeChoice Super Clean. To use it this way, pour the SafeChoice Super Clean in the toilet first, then the borax. Twenty Mule Team Borax (**20 Mule Team Borax**) is readily available in boxes in most grocery stores. However, it commonly acquires the fragrances of its scented shelf mates. Bulk borax, which is less likely to have taken on scented odors, can be purchased at chemical-supply companies in 50- or 100-pound bags. To find a chemical-supply company near you, check your local classified phone directory. To store bulk borax, see *Metal Containers* on page 514.

If your toilet bowl's interior has rust stains, sprinkle Bar Keeper's Friend (**Servaas Laboratories, Inc.**) inside it. Then, let sit for a few minutes. After that, scrub the bowl with a toilet brush, then flush to rinse. Bar Keeper's Friend is a white, unscented, powdered cleaner containing *oxalic acid*. Therefore, this isn't a nontoxic product, although it's relatively safe in this particular form and concentration. However, you'll want to store it so that children and pets can't get access to it. Bar Keeper's Friend is sold through many local grocery stores. A similar product is Zud, which is also sold in some grocery and hardware stores.

Toilet stones, pumice stone on a handles, can remove stubborn mineral stains from toilets. Supposedly, the hard pumice is not hard enough to remove or scratch the vitreous china glaze of the toilet itself. You can purchase one from **Vermont Country Store Voice of the Mountains**. A toilet stone by Etna Products Co., with a 7" wood handle, is sold by **Harriet Carter Gifts**.

A product that will help keep stains from building up in toilets is ChemFree Toilet Cleaner (**Impex Systems Group, Inc.**). This item is a small, plastic cartridge filled with natural "hydro mineral magnets," that aid in reducing staining, and a disinfectant-treated fibrous material called Bact-O-Bane, capable of killing mold and bacteria. To use ChemFree effectively, you'll first need to thoroughly clean the toilet tank. Then, simply place the cartridge in the bottom of the tank. If your water is not chlorinated by your utility or you have a whole-house water filter that removes chlorine, your tank will probably require two cartridges. The manufacturer states they should remain effective for five years. ChemFree cartridges can be ordered from the company and from **Improvements**.

Cleaning Mirrors

(See *Cleaning Windows* on page 160.)

Part 3
TEXTILES

CHAPTER 7: HEALTHIER FIBERS & STUFFINGS

This chapter will discuss all the various options available for healthy fibers. It will cover both natural fibers such as cotton, wool, silk, linen, ramie, jute, and hemp as well as some of the healthier synthetic fibers. Plus, it will discuss leather and fur, and various options for stuffing, such as cotton, wool, buckwheat hulls, kapok, syriaca clusters, Hypodown, feathers, down, and natural latex. And, finally, it will wrap up with a few specific textile-related concerns, such as shrinkage, dry cleaning, and dyes.

Natural Fibers

Many people have learned that untreated natural-fiber fabric offers a number of benefits over petroleum-derived synthetic alternatives. For example, natural-fiber garments "breathe," thus allowing the wearer's perspiration to readily evaporate. While a few synthetics have been specially engineered for "breathability," most have not. Natural fibers are also biodegradable and made from renewable resources. In addition, the appearance and feel of natural-fibers is usually more visually and tactually pleasing than their synthetic counterparts.

Very importantly, untreated natural-fiber cloth can't outgas low-level, potentially bothersome odors that have been associated with some synthetic fibers. Finally, some sensitive people have noticed that odors from tobacco smoke and perfume are easier to remove from natural-fibers than from synthetic ones—either by laundering or airing.

Natural Plant Fibers

Natural plant fibers include cotton, ramie, linen, jute, and hemp. These, in particular, are used to create the majority of the natural-fiber yarns and fabrics currently available. To help you become more knowledgeable about them, the sections below provide background information on cultivation, milling, fiber traits, etc. The most complete descriptions are for cotton—the most popular fabric—and hemp. In the last few years, hemp has taken on a symbolic status for less-toxic, more earth-friendly living. However, the public at large still knows very little about how it's grown, where it's grown, or the fiber's characteristics.

Cotton

Although cotton is, by far, the most popular natural fiber today, few of us realize how many steps (and possible chemical treatments) are involved between planting cotton seeds and purchasing a finished cotton garment. Unfortunately, many of these steps can make some cotton garments intolerable for chemically sensitive persons.

Cotton Cultivation

Because cotton is so widely used, it has been called the "universal fiber." Cotton is popular for several reasons: It is widely cultivated, processing and milling are relatively easy, and the cotton fibers themselves are soft, fairly strong, and they can be manipulated in a variety of ways. Unlike most other natural fibers—which have rather limited uses—cotton fibers can be woven, knit, made into lace, tufted (chenille is an example of tufting), and formed into nonwoven fabrics with chemical resins. Cotton also takes dyes, soil-resistance, fire-retardance, and other chemical treatments well. Finally, most cotton items are easy-to-clean.

Cotton is a subtropical plant of the mallow family. It has been cultivated for thousands of years in Egypt, Asia, and South America. Today, it's grown in warm climates around the world, wherever its soil and moisture needs can be met. While wild cotton is a perennial, as a cultivated crop it's planted annually. As cotton plants mature, they eventually grow three to six feet tall. The cotton fibers appear as soft, fluffy "hair" (*lint*) surrounding cotton seeds within the pods (*bolls*). Each fiber is a long, cylindrical single cell.

There are three main commercial cotton species, each with a number of varieties. Of all the cotton types grown, the finest, such as Egyptian and Pima, produce the longest, strongest, and silkiest fibers. By the way, all cotton varieties, besides having longish cotton fibers, have very short, stout fibers known as *linters*. Linters are considered the very lowest quality of cotton. However, they're commonly used as stuffing in upholstery and mattresses, as well as raw material in cotton-content papers.

Between the planting of cotton seeds and finished fabric, many steps abound. First, the seeds are planted in the spring. During the growing season, large amounts of fertilizer and pesticide are usually applied to the fields. The pesticides are targeted against boll weevils and pink boll worms. Unfortunately, because weevils are so persistent, newer and deadlier chemicals continue to be used against them. Incidentally, some once-popular pesticides are no longer used because of health concerns associated with them, or because weevils have become resistant to them. Actually, the pink boll worm only became a serious pest when potent anti-weevil pesticides killed the insects that naturally kept pink boll worm numbers in check. Because of the potential for serious negative health effects with most chemical pesticides, synthetic pheromones that mimic female sex-attractant chemicals are beginning to be used in some areas as an alternative pest-control method. However, chemical attack remains the most popular approach.

When the cotton plants are mature, their bolls burst open. After the cotton fibers air-dry, they are ready for harvesting. In the U.S. (and in other countries harvesting cotton mechanically) it's common practice to spray chemical defoliants on the plants before the picking equipment goes into the fields. Defoliants cause the leaves to wither and fall off, leaving only the bolls on the stems. Herbicides or flame jets may then also be used to kill surrounding weeds. Once the cotton fibers are finally harvested, they're dried further. Then they're cleaned of debris and seeds by gins. The last pre-milling step is to compress the cotton into bales.

Typical Cotton-Mill Processing

At the mills, cotton bales are transformed into rolls of flat batting (*laps*). Carding machines then align the fibers within these laps. As a result, the cotton takes on the appearance of rope-like strands, known as *slivers*. To produce *combed cotton*, the slivers go on to mechanical combers to further straighten and align the fibers. Finally, the slivers are sent to spinner machines to be transformed into yarn or thread.

In cotton-cloth manufacturing, yarns or threads are woven by mechanical looms. The fabric produced is termed *raw*, *gray cloth*, or *greige* at this stage. The cloth then may undergo quite a few treatments before it's considered done. For example, it may be *kier boiled*—to further clean it and remove any natural plant waxes. The cloth may also be bleached (usually with chlorine) to whiten it. In addition, it may be *mercerized* (a process using a caustic soda solution) to add luster, strength, and dyeability.

After these treatments, the fabric is then generally *tentered* (stretched into proper proportions) and sheared to remove any surface nubs. At this point, most cotton cloth is dyed by a process called *piece dyeing*—the simplest and cheapest method of dyeing. (By the way, *yarn dyed* means that the cotton threads or yarn is dyed just prior to weaving. When the dyeing occurs still earlier—when the cotton consists of raw fibers—it would be termed *stock dyed*.) Today, the majority of dyes are made of synthetically derived ingredients.

However, dyes are not the only synthetic chemicals that are applied to cotton cloth. In fact, most of the fabric now produced undergoes a series of additional treatments. These are designed to add wrinkle-resistance, soil-resistance, flame-resistance, mildew-resistance, rot-resistance, and/or water-repellence. The chemicals used for these often include formaldehyde and other potentially bothersome compounds.

Alternative Cotton and Cotton Processing

Not surprisingly, some consumers are demanding cotton clothing made with fewer chemicals—or no chemicals at all. To cater to this market, some specialty growers are now raising *certified organic cotton*. Certification is usually made by state agencies enforcing strict regulations in order for crops to be legally classified as organic. Unfortunately, it seems, certain mills and manufacturers say that their items are "made with organic cotton," but this is sometimes done in an attempt to mislead. Some "organic" cotton is uncertified, or it may consist of a tiny percentage of truly organic cotton with the rest being conventionally grown cotton. So, as a wary consumer, you should be aware of these possible deceptions. If you would like to receive a list of manufacturers who use Texas Organic Cotton Marketing Co-Operative cotton fabrics, contact **Cotton Plus, Ltd.**

Interestingly, a few growers are producing organically grown cotton with naturally occurring pastel shades of color. One popular brand name of such cotton is Foxfibre. These natural colors make otherwise bland cotton more visually exciting.

A relatively new trend in the cotton industry is the manufacture of *green cotton*. In this case, *green* doesn't refer to the color of the cotton, or mean the cotton has been organically raised. Instead, green cotton is commonly defined as cotton fabric that has gone through processing and manufacturing without chemical treatments. Therefore, green cotton items are unbleached, undyed, and have no added formaldehyde. However, they were made with cotton that was chemically treated during cultivation.

You should also be aware that some cotton fabric is described as *unbleached*. This is cotton in its natural beige color. Cotton labeled unbleached may or may not have undergone other chemical treatments. On the other hand, *non-permanent-press cotton* simply indicates that no wrinkle-resisting treatments were applied. (A formaldehyde-resin application, sometimes called a *resin treatment*, is often used for wrinkle-resistance.)

Cotton Articles

Of all the natural fibers, cotton is undoubtedly the most affordable and easiest to find in clothing. A real plus is that most 100%-cotton garments can be machine- or hand-washed as well as machine- or line-dried. However, not all clothing made of 100% cotton can be laundered safely at home. Some specialty cotton items may come with a label recommending "dry-clean only." This is most likely to be true for lined items, tailored pieces, or garments with embellishments. (See *Is Dry Cleaning A Problem?* on page 196.)

If you plan to wash your cotton clothing at home, remember to be careful. Cotton has the capacity to shrink—sometimes it can shrink a great deal. To minimize shrinkage, follow the care-instructions on labels explicitly (see also *How Much Shrinkage Should be Expected?* on page 195).

By the way, for those people who want washable, untreated-cotton garments but just don't like ironing, consider buying textured cottons. Deva cloth is one such fabric. It has a permanent pebble-like surface. Deva cloth, as well as other textured fabrics, are sold by **Deva Lifewear**—both as yardage and in finished clothing. Other minimal-care cotton options include gauze, voile, and seersucker fabrics. In addition, most cotton corduroys, knits (jersey and interlock, for example), and flannels can be easily smoothed by hand while they're still warm from the dryer.

Linen

Linen cloth has a coarse, somewhat lustrous, nubby texture that is visually very appealing. Linen is a sturdier, cooler fabric than cotton, and it is relatively resistant to damage from sunlight—making it popular for both warm -weather clothing as well as curtains and drapes. Linen also tends to soil less easily than cotton. It's main drawback is that, if untreated, linen cloth wrinkles easily.

Linen fabric has been used since ancient times. In fact, in medieval Europe linen was the most commonly used plant-derived fiber. However, newer methods of increasing production were few and far between as compared to cotton. So, when the cotton gin was invented, the manufacture of cotton products soared, and that of linen products plummeted.

The actual linen fibers come from the stems of fiber-flax plants. (There are also oil-flax plants that produce linseed oil.) Flax was originally cultivated around the Mediterranean Sea and in southern Asia. Today, it's grown around the world in temperate climates. Linen from Belgium is now considered to be among the finest linen cloth available.

In the fields, flax plants grow from one to four feet tall. The mature plants are eventually harvested after their stems have yellowed. Traditionally, the cut stalks are allowed to *ret*—a planned decomposing process in which the stems are immersed in a watery solution that causes woody tissues and plant gums to rot. Afterwards, the flax fibers can be pulled apart from most of the decayed by-products. Then comes *scutching*, a scraping procedure which removes any remaining woody portions of the plant. Next, the flax fibers are combed, cleaned, and readied for spinning. The final steps are dyeing and weaving.

As was mentioned earlier, linen was once used extensively for clothing, but it has also been used for upholstery, draperies, tablecloths, and bedding (hence, the still-popular terms *table linens* and *bed linens*). However, actual linen fabric is no longer commonly used in the manufacture of any of these items. In fact, linen is now generally considered a luxury fiber.

However, it must be said that linen is being used more frequently than in the last several decades. Still, most 100%-linen items today are expensive suits, dresses, and luxury bedding items. Yet there are also some more affordable linen items out there—especially in fabric blends, such as linen/cotton.

To ensure that you clean your linen items correctly, make sure to read cleaning instructions on labels carefully. Unfortunately, you'll often find that while some linen articles may be safely laundered at home, manufacturers may recommend dry cleaning. Because of the health risks associated with the petroleum solvents used in conventional dry cleaning, professional specialized wet-cleaning is a better choice. (See also *Is Dry Cleaning A Problem?* on page 196.)

If you do decide to launder "washable" linen items at home, only wash colored fabrics in cool water. (Naturals and whites can be washed in warm water.) While this book never recommends using chlorine bleach, it's especially important not to use it on linen because it will cause a yellow discoloration.

Ramie

Ramie is a soft, lustrous, light to medium-weight fiber that somewhat resembles linen. Ramie fibers are relatively strong, but lack elasticity. Therefore, ramie cloth can wear or abrade fairly easily.

Ramie fibers come from the inner stems of certain perennial Asian plants in the nettle family. These plants are bushy and fairly tall—up to six feet high. The plants are cultivated mostly in semitropical areas of the Far East, although some are now grown in the southern U.S. When they're mature, ramie stalks are either cut and stripped of their fibers by hand, or machine-harvested and stripped. No matter how they're separated from the bark, the fibers are next cleaned and readied for spinning. At this point, ramie fibers are sometimes called *China grass*. Dyeing usually follows—and ramie takes dye very well. Finally, the fibers are ready for weaving.

One-hundred-percent ramie fabric (also known as *grass cloth*) isn't commonly made anymore. Instead, today, ramie is usually blended with cotton or other fibers. When you do find a ramie item, its price range is generally between that of cotton and linen. Many items made entirely, or partially, of ramie can be hand-washed, though certainly not all. Often, ramie articles need to be dried flat. This is especially true for knit items. To be sure, you'll need to read the manufacturer's tags carefully. Interestingly, ramie shrinks very little.

Jute

Jute is one of the lowest-cost natural fibers. Surprisingly, after cotton, it's the most-used plant fiber in the world. Unfortunately, it's also one of the weakest and tends to fall apart if exposed to prolonged moisture. Jute is actually a name that is applied to two tall annual plants of the Asiatic linden family. Almost all jute is grown in hot and humid areas of India and Bangladesh. Because its cultivation has not yet been mechanized, intense hand labor is usually required.

Jute plants grow to a height of 2–12 feet. After the mature plants have been cut, they're soaked in running water for several days to rot the outer-bark and loosen the inner jute fibers—a type of *retting* process (see *Linen* on page 180). Afterwards, the stems are dried. Then comes *scutching* (hand-kneading and crushing that frees the fibers). Interestingly, a tremendous number of long fibers can be removed from just a single stalk. Next, the fibers are ready for spinning—and possibly bleaching and dyeing. However, jute usually does not take bleach or dye particularly well. (When jute is dyed, the colors may be somewhat harsh-looking.) Finally comes weaving.

The finer grades of jute are similar to linen in appearance. They're sometimes used in wearing apparel, including fine suits. Lesser grades might be used in shoes, handbags, tote bags, and carpet backing. Relatively recently, area rugs made of jute have been marketed. Burlap is a type of cheap, coarsely woven jute fabric. To clean any jute item successfully, you must follow the manufacturer's directions closely.

Hemp

Recently, a growing number of hemp-fiber articles (besides the old standby, hemp rope) have become available in the U.S. Some international-aid groups have been encouraging hemp cultivation in poor countries to replace coca-plant production. This is understandable when you realize that hemp is a low-maintenance crop (requires no weeding, or chemicals), it can be grown in most climates, and it is harvestable in just 100 days. Hemp is currently grown in China, England, France, Holland, Hungry, and Russia.

It should be noted that "hemp" is a generic term that is often applied to a group of unrelated plants. The only common trait these various plants have is that fibers are derived from their stalks. However, there is a *true* hemp plant, *Cannabis sativa L.*, or simply cannabis. And today, it's the one from which hemp fibers are likely to have originated.

Hemp Cultivation

Interestingly, the U.S. Department of Agriculture has called hemp the "oldest cultivated fiber plant," having been grown for 10 millennia. In 4500 BC, the Chinese grew hemp for rope and fishnets, and later paper and *hempen cloth*. Eventually, hemp cultivation spread to the Mid-East and then to Europe by 400 BC. In the 1500's, knowledge of Oriental hemp paper and cloth was applied to make hemp canvas, which was used by oil painters. In fact, the very word "canvas" is derived from cannabis.

In the New World, hemp was commonly grown and used. In fact, the first draft of the Declaration of Independence were apparently written on hemp paper. Unfortunately, since 1937 when the U.S. Marijuana Tax Act was passed (to stop hemp from being grown for drug use), industrial hemp production plummeted due to many layers of red tape. By the way, hemp that is grown for fiber typically contains 1%, or less, of the hallucinogenic compound *delta-9 tetrahydrocannabinol* (or *THC*), while the THC content of hemp raised for drug is 3-15%.

Hemp grows well in cultivation with little or no chemical help to a height of 6-16 feet in a short amount of time (70-110 days). A real plus for hemp farmers is that natural herbicides from the hemp itself renders the soil nearly weed-free for the next crop. Because chemical fertilizers or pesticides aren't often needed, much of hemp grown is considered *organic hemp*.

Traditionally, in cultivation, mature hemp plants were cut and left on the ground to *ret*. (This is a rotting process of the unwanted plant materials.) Usually only 25% of the stalks, the *basts* (long fibers in the outer stalks) remained usable, the remaining *hurds* (short inner stalks) were burned in the fields. Separating was time consuming and the disposable of the hurds represented a tremendous loss of revenue. However, around the time of World War I the invention of *decortticating machines* allowed for a way to quickly and easily separate hemp fibers from hurds. At the same time, these hurds were found to be valuable for making hemp paper. So, production of industrial hemp increased dramatically in the U.S. That is until 1937, when the Marijuana Tax Act was passed.

Hemp Processing

It should be further explained that once hemp fibers are loosened and freed from the woody debris (whether by hand or by machine), they are then combed. This further cleans and aligns the individual fibers. At this point, the hemp fibers are ready to be spun into thread or yarn. The final steps involve dyeing and weaving.

Hemp Articles

True hemp articles can be woven with a soft, linen-like feel, or through increasingly coarser grades that end in a rough canvas. Hemp has the unique quality of being naturally mildew resistant—so it's perfect for socks and active sportswear. Hemp is also abrasion-resistant because it's one of Nature's strongest vegetable fibers. Hemp is more lustrous and a better absorber than cotton. In addition, hemp fabric can protect the skin from UV radiation better than most other natural fibers.

Because garment-grade hemp production has been so low, prices have tended to be relatively high, but costs have recently begun to drop significantly. Today, sweaters, jeans, t-shirts, and socks are the most common garments found, although you can find a whole range of clothing articles from time to time. In addition, hemp bedding items are also starting to be manufactured.

For proper cleaning instructions for your hemp articles, you'll need to read the information provided on manufacturers' tags. However, most hemp-made articles can be cleaned in a manner similar to that of cotton. To get listings of both hemp informational and product resources, contact HEMPTECH.

Natural Animal Fibers

Of course, besides natural plant fibers, there are also important fibers derived from animals. These include silk and several varieties of wool.

Silk

Silk is perhaps one of the world's most luxurious fabrics. It has always been prized for its naturally opulent look and feel, as well as its ability to take dyes. No other natural fiber can be dyed as well as silk. However, despite its lightweight and fragile appearance, silk is extremely strong—as strong as synthetic nylon. Woven silk also "breathes." In fact, it's the coolest fabric to wear in hot climates. Yet, woven silk also has tremendous insulating properties; it's sometimes used in thermal underwear and thermal liners for gloves, etc. In addition, silk can absorb up to 30% of its weight in moisture and still not feel damp to the touch. If all that were not enough, silk is naturally heat-resistant—it'll burn only when a flame comes directly in contact with it.

The following sections will explain how this remarkable fiber is derived and ultimately woven into garments.

Sericulture and Silk Processing

Silk comes from the unraveling of cocoons spun by domesticated silk-moth caterpillars, also known as silk worms (*Bombyx mori*). Silk-moth cultivation (*sericulture*) began thousands of years ago in China. At that time, the source of silk, and how it was produced, were closely guarded state secrets. Revealing this information was punishable by death. Eventually, however, Byzantine emissaries learned the truth and smuggled silkworm eggs out of China. As a result, sericulture eventually spread to other countries.

In sericulture, silk moths are confined in order to lay harvestable eggs. The eggs then hatch into hungry caterpillars. After eating mulberry leaves (their only food) for about five weeks, the caterpillars crawl into specially built frames to spin their cocoons. Interestingly, each caterpillar produces not one, but two slender filaments at once. These are almost immediately bonded together to become a single filament by a sticky secretion known as *sericin*. The sericin also is responsible for gluing the cocoon together as it's being created by the silk worm.

Once the cocoons are completely spun, they're subjected to high heat that kills the insects inside without damaging the cocoons. The cocoons are then removed from the frames and bathed in hot water. This dissolves the sericin so that the cocoons can be unreeled.

Each cocoon produces a single filament from eight-hundred to twelve-hundred yards long. However, because it's so delicate and fine, several cocoons are unreeled at the same time and combined to create a single, stronger thread. The small amount of sericin remaining on the individual filaments holds this larger, united thread permanently together. At this point, the reeled silk thread is known as *raw silk*.

Other procedures may follow, such as *throwing* (in which several larger threads are twisted together), a *weight treatment* (in which oil or some other substance is added to the threads, although this is no longer commonly done), dyeing, and/or steaming (to add luster). Finally, the processed silk is ready for weaving or knitting.

Silk Articles

Because of its sheen, softness, strength, and other properties, silk was, until fairly recently, popularly used despite its relatively high cost. However, after World War II, less-expensive rayon, nylon, polyester, and other synthetic substitutes nearly replaced silk in all its previous uses. However, in recent decades, silk production has increased enormously—and prices have come down substantially. Today, as a result, silk items are not only more commonly seen, but they also tend to be much more affordable. So, silk underwear, ties, hosiery, blouses, shirts, suits, sheets, etc. are now offered by a wide range of stores and mail-order catalogs.

Many people shy away from purchasing silk items because they're unfamiliar with, and somewhat afraid of, cleaning them. Actually, some silk articles can be safely cared for at home. For example, certain unlined, sand-washed, raw, or noile silks are hand-washable. A few such pieces may sometimes even be laundered in the washing machine on a short, gentle cycle. After laundering, most washable silk items should be laid flat. However, to be safe, unless manufacturers' tags say otherwise, all silk items should probably be considered dry-clean-only items. Otherwise, they could shrink or lose their shape.

Sadly, dry cleaning, a petroleum-solvent process, can pose health problems to sensitive people as well as the public at large. Of course, a specialized wet-cleaning service can be used as an alternative—if available in your area. (See *Is Dry Cleaning a Problem?* on page 196.)

Wool

Wool is, by far, the most widely used animal fiber—and it always has been. As you, no doubt, already know, wool has many excellent properties. For example, it can be easily spun into yarn, or formed into matted felt. Of great importance is wool's tremendous ability to insulate. In fact, even when it's wet (and wool can absorb a lot of moisture), it still provides warmth to the person wearing it. Wool is also naturally attractive and it takes dyes well. In addition, wool is naturally fire-resistant and *resilient* (it retains its bounce or loft).

To help you learn more about this natural fiber, this section will provide information on different aspects of wool and wool production.

Typical Wool Production

Wool is often defined as the curly fleece of sheep and lambs. Interestingly, it has been estimated there are about 450 different domesticated wool-bearing sheep breeds. Each of these produces wool with its own particular characteristics. By the way, the term wool also refers to the fleece of alpacas, llamas, Kashmir goats (*cashmere*), angora goats (*mohair*), camels, etc.

It took herders centuries of selective breeding to produce the types of coats seen on domesticated sheep today—those with mostly wool and very little hair. Actually, wool is made of the same substance as hair—*keratin*—but wool fibers are constructed much differently. Hair is composed of aligned, adjacent cells. The cells that make up wool filaments, on the other hand, are crimped and overlapped. Because wool's cells are shingle-like, they're able to enmesh with one another or mat (*felting*). In addition, because the filaments are crimped, they're naturally elastic. It should also be noted that raw sheep's wool is waterproof. This is due to the lanolin or *sheep grease* which is secreted by certain sweat glands in the sheep's skin and absorbed by the wool fibers themselves.

Unfortunately, domesticated sheep are often subjected to certain chemical treatments to minimize insect infestations. These treatments, known as *sheep dips*, generally involve leading the animals through tanks or pits filled with special solutions. Then, in early spring, just before the winter coats are shed naturally, the fleeces are removed. While some wool is still removed by shearing, increasing numbers of ranchers are now using a hormone injection which allows the entire coat to be peeled off. After the fleece has been removed, the raw wool is graded. The best wool has the slenderest and longest filaments, the whitest color, and the thickest density. *Merino wool* is considered one of the finer grades. The lowest grade is *carpet wool* which often contains a fair quantity of hair fibers.

Typical Wool-Mill Processing

At mills, raw wool is cleaned and possibly combed (to align the wool fibers). It's then commonly spun into thread or yarn, or made into felt. However, processing may also include bleaching, dyeing, insect-resistant chemicals, or other treatments.

There are two major types of wool thread and yarn. *Worsted wool* thread consists of only combed, long fibers that have been spun together. It is generally of very fine quality that might be woven into smooth fabrics for suits or even hosiery. On the other hand, *woolen processed* yarn uses no special combing. It is spun with long and short fibers, or simply just short fibers. The resulting yarn is coarser than worsted-wool thread. It's often used to make blankets or bulkier, tweedy fabrics. By the way, if the wool is to be felted, it's soaked in a soapy water solution, rolled, and then pressed. Wool felt is commonly used to make hats.

Alternative Wools and Wool Processing

While most sheep fleeces are white, some wool-bearing animals are purposely bred for their gray, brown, tan, black, or mottled coats. Such wool is naturally colored and undergoes no bleaching or dyeing treatments. Icelandic sheep's wool items, as well as some Central- and South-American llama-wool articles, are often created with naturally colored wool.

There are also a few specialty sheep raisers who don't subject their animals, or the sheared wool, to synthetic chemicals. Wool of this type is often termed *organic wool*. When wool is said to be *untreated*, it generally means it has not been bleached, dyed, or undergone moth-proofing treatments. In addition, some untreated wool may not have gone through a sheep-dipping treatment. However, at this time, there are no clearly accepted standards (legal, or otherwise) for either organic or untreated wool, so what these terms exactly mean can be unclear.

Wool Articles

Today, 100%-wool clothing is generally fairly expensive and relatively uncommon—that is, compared to before World War II. Today, wool is commonly blended with less costly natural and/or synthetic fibers. Because many types of wool can cause skin irritation, garments such as wool or wool-blend skirts and pants are usually lined with another less irritating fabric.

Incidentally, *virgin wool* refers to wool that has never been used in a previous manufacturing process. On the other hand, the term *shoddy* applies to reused wool—wool that was previously spun, knitted, or felted. Shoddy wool is sometimes added by manufacturers to increase fabric strength, especially in knits.

As you probably know, most wool items require special care—to both clean and store. This is because of wool's tremendous capacity to shrink, as well as its appeal to destructive clothing moths (see *How Much Shrinkage should be Expected?* on page 195, and *Clothing Moths* on page 406). While some wool items can be hand-washed and dried flat at home, most have manufacturers' tags recommending that they be dry-cleaned.

If you wash your unlined wool items at home, use a liquid, soap-based product such as Auro Awalan Laundry Soap, which is an unscented liquid from **Sinan Co**. You may also choose a very gentle dish soap (see *Hand Dishwashing Products* on page 166 for product suggestions.) Soap, unlike detergent, is much less likely to strip wool of it's natural lanolin. Once the wool item has been cleaned, lay it out flat to dry. (For more information, see *Hand-Laundering* on page 125.)

You should be aware that there are some garments made of *boiled wool* that can be washed at home, even in a washing machine, without ever shrinking them. (Note: Some boiled wool items do have "dry clean only" tags.) This is possible because of the unique manner in which such articles are made. You see, to create boiled wool clothing, items are purposely produced significantly oversized. Then they're boiled in water to shrink them to their final, correct proportions. The resulting clothing is sturdy, dense, and virtually incapable of further shrinkage. However, boiled wool, like other types of wool, still needs to be protected from clothing moths.

Still, most people feel they must take their woolens to the dry cleaners to be cleaned. Unfortunately, this will mean that dry-cleaning-solvent odors will cling to the newly cleaned items. To avoid this, check first to see if a professional wet-cleaning service is available in your area as an alternative. (See *Is Dry Cleaning a Problem?* on page 196.)

You need to know, too, that any type of professional cleaning company might add a moth-preventing treatment to your wool items as a free service. Therefore, if you don't want a moth-prevention treatment on your woolens, you'll want to clearly specify this when you take them to be cleaned.

Leather and Fur

Leather and fur are two natural, animal materials used in clothing—but they're not considered fibers. Despite increasing concerns for animal rights, they still remain popular.

Leather

Leather is a natural material which typically undergoes many chemical treatments to process it, and later maintain it. Not surprisingly, leather, especially new leather, can be bothersome to chemically sensitive people.

Leather Types

By definition, leather is the tanned skin of any animal. Some popular leather choices include cow, calf, pig, sheep, lamb, goat (kidskin), snake, lizard, alligator, deer, and eel. When you purchase leather, there are several terms with which you'll want to become familiar to better help you know exactly what you are buying. First, you should know that some thin leathers are used intact; these are said to be *unsplit*. However, thick hides, such as those from cattle, often have several layers cut or *split* from them. *Full-grain* refers to leather that has the natural skin texture (*grain*), whether from an unsplit or split hide. *Top-grain* is the uppermost layer of a split hide. Top-grain is considered the best grade of split leather because it's the only one that is full-grain. *Genuine leather* simply means that it's not a synthetic product or a composite-leather material. Often, leather that is stamped "genuine leather" is from a split hide, but it's not top-grain.

On the other hand, *bonded-leather* is a composite leather material; it's actually made of finely shredded leather scraps held together with glue. Bonded-leather can often be stiff and it is generally less durable than genuine leather. Products made of bonded-leather are usually inexpensive, but they can be very odorous because of the adhesives used to make them. Therefore, as a rule, bonded-leather should be avoided by sensitive people.

Leather Processing

Leather can be *tanned* in a number of ways. Tanning is defined as any treatment that transforms animal skins or hides into a pliable, long-lasting product. Occasionally, deerskin and other game hides, are tanned using animal brains or other natural animal substances. A few leathers are also tanned using natural oils. Once a common natural tanning method, oak-bark solutions (containing active *plant tannins*) are still sometimes used. However, most of today's commercial tanning processes use synthetic chemical solutions.

As you may well know, the surface of leather can be textured into a variety of distinctive forms. One favorite process to do this is with *embossing*, a relatively inexpensive stamping procedure. Embossing is often done on lower-cost leather to mimic higher-priced or endangered-animal leathers. To create *suede*, the inner sides of hides (sides that don't have grain) are mechanically rubbed or brushed to produce a velvety feel.

Colors (often synthetic) are routinely added to leather. This can be accomplished through *surface-dyeing* (when only the topside of a piece of leather receives dye), hand painting, or *vat-dyeing*. In vat-dyeing, whole hides are soaked in dye-filled tanks. Because the color completely saturates the leather, nicks, scratches, and wear are less noticeable on items dyed in this way.

Leather Articles

As was mentioned earlier, new leather articles are often intolerable for sensitive individuals. This is likely due to a combination of factors: the natural odor of the leather itself, and the processing chemicals used in tanning, texturing, or coloring. However, many new genuine-leather items will lose most of their odor over time. Unfortunately, it isn't unusual for it to take up to two years of airing before some new leather items are tolerable for certain very chemically sensitive individuals. Many times, finding a suitable location for this extended aging process can be difficult. Therefore, it's wise to choose leather items carefully, and well in advance of when they'll actually be needed.

In caring for your leather goods, additional problems with intolerance can arise. One major reason for this is that leather clothing must usually be professionally cleaned using special leather-cleaning treatments performed by your dry cleaner. (See *Is Dry Cleaning a Problem?* on page 196.) Unfortunately, the odors from the cleaning solutions (commonly these are solvents and other synthetic compounds) are absorbed by the leather. In any case, airing your newly cleaned leather items outdoors will help to dissipate these bothersome odors somewhat. If your have a specialized wet-cleaning service in your area, you may be able to have your leather items cleaned without the use of petroleum-solvent compounds. (See *Specialized Wet Cleaning* on page 131.) In either case, as a rule, professional leather cleaning can be costly.

Of course, you can generally care for your leather footwear at home. Wood-handle/horse-hair-bristle shoe brushes you are sold by **Fuller Brush Co.** and **E.T. Wright**. There is one product most sensitive people can use on many types of leather items (not suedes) including leather upholstery. That is LifeTime Wood and Leather Protector (**LifeTime Solutions**), which can be ordered directly from the company. This is a clear, unscented, non-toxic, biodegradable *colloidal micelle* solution. It can both restore and polish leather goods.

Most of the readily available colored shoe polishes, as well as waterproofing products, are made with strong-smelling—often very objectionable—petroleum-based ingredients. Therefore, it's a good idea to have a less sensitive person polish or waterproof your shoes or boots with these products for you outdoors. Once your footwear has been treated, let them air outside in a sheltered location until the odors are no longer noticeable.

So, should you buy leather? Despite initial intolerability, leather can still be a good choice for many people—if it doesn't conflict with your personal philosophy, and if the leather items can be easily maintained and cleaned using tolerable products. After all, leather articles, including shoes, belts, wallets, handbags, clothing, and upholstered seating are naturally derived, long-lasting, and attractive to look at and touch.

Fur

Fur is soft, attractive, warm, and luxurious. However, there are a variety of negatives associated with it that usually make it less than ideal, especially for sensitive and allergic persons.

Fur Types and Processing

The garment industry defines fur as any hairy animal pelt resistant to shedding. Of course, fur is an ancient material; in fact, it was probably humankind's first clothing. Interestingly, it wasn't until the Middle Ages that fur was considered prestigious or special. About that time, laws were invoked to restrict commoners from wearing fur, and so it became reserved for nobility and the well-to-do. Today, fur still has those upper-class connotations linked to it.

These days, most furs are obtained from captive animals raised on farms, although a number of fur-bearing species are still trapped or hunted in the wild. The most popular types of fur are probably mink, rabbit, fox, squirrel, coyote, raccoon, beaver, lynx, seal, and sable. For temperate and polar-region species, a thick winter coat is known as *prime fur*. Pelts taken at other times of the year from such animals are considered *unprime*.

After a fur-bearing animal is killed, it's skinned. This *raw fur* is sent to *dressing processors*. There the pelts are *dressed* (cleaned and tanned) using a variety of chemical solutions. Afterwards, some furs are left in their natural hue while others are bleached and/or dyed. In some cases, natural dyes are used, but often the dyes are synthetically derived. The actual dyeing process may involve complete immersion (for total coloring), stenciling (to create a pattern), or *tipping*. (*Tipped-fur* has only the very ends of the fur hairs dyed.) After dyeing, furs are ready for shipment to *furriers* (fur article-makers) to be made into garments or, in some cases, area rugs.

Fur Garments and Accessories

Although fur apparel is both soft and warm, it's usually expensive to purchase, store, and clean. In addition, fur can be quite odorous when new. This can be due to several factors: the innate smell of the fur itself, the dressing chemicals, the dyes, and/or the added insect-resisting treatments. Such odors can actually remain in the fur hairs for long periods of time, despite lengthy airings outdoors. Unfortunately, when furs are worn, they can easily absorb other odors such as perfume and tobacco. In addition, professionally cleaned and/or stored furs will likely absorb more bothersome odors. All these accumulated odors can be very difficult to remove. Furthermore, some fur items may begin to shed after only a few years of use. Because of odor and shedding problems, fur items are usually not suggested for sensitive or allergic persons.

It should also be mentioned that growing numbers of people today object to the production, sale, or wearing of fur. Such individuals believe, for personal and/or philosophical reasons, that killing any animal simply for its fur is distasteful, cruel—even immoral. In fact, wearing fur can sometimes subject the wearer to verbal abuse, or worse, by outspoken, anti-fur advocates.

Natural Stuffings

Although many individuals consider natural fibers important in their clothing (as well as their furnishings), they often forget about batting, padding, and loose-fill material. Unlike most synthetic counterparts, natural stuffing allows moisture to evaporate, and because it's made from renewable resources, it's biodegradable. One drawback, however, is that natural stuffing can sometimes be a haven for dust mites.

Cotton Stuffing

Cotton is a fine stuffing material, it is relatively inexpensive and washable, and it has fairly good loft. However, it has largely been replaced by polyester, which is even cheaper and stays fluffier over time. Unfortunately, most of the cotton stuffing and batting still available in fabric and craft stores has been bleached and chemically treated. This type of cotton batting is sold by **Gohn Bros.**, **Janice Corporation**, and **Home-Sew**. Organic, unbleached cotton batting is available from **Janice Corporation**, **Gohn Bros.**, **The Natural Alternative**, **Furnature**, and **Heart of Vermont**.

Buckwheat Hulls

An unusual type of filling, at least to Westerners, is buckwheat hulls. However, buckwheat hulls have been used in the Far East for pillows for some time. Because of it's characteristics, it's good to use for pillows here too.

Buckwheat hulls have the advantage of conforming to your head, thus providing good support. They also provide a cooler night's sleep because the hulls dissipate heat and absorb moisture. Drawbacks include the fact that the hulls create a muffled crunchy noise when you move, and they can't be easily cleaned. However, because they're relatively cheap, most people can affordably change the filling material when necessary. A more important problem is that the hulls can be dusty, and so create airborne irritants that bother some asthmatic and allergic people.

Some health-food stores sell buckwheat hulls in bulk. You can also order some from **Caudill Seed Co., Inc.**, **The Natural Alternative**, and **Furnature**.

Kapok

Kapok is the white, silky material surrounding the seeds of the large deciduous kapok tree (silk-cotton tree). At harvest time, each tree produces nearly 100 pounds of fiber. Originally native to Asia, kapok is now cultivated throughout the tropics. Once it was commonly used as a stuffing material, but it has now generally been replaced by synthetic alternatives.

Kapok fibers resemble those of cotton, but unlike cotton, kapok fibers can't be spun. But they are naturally fluffy, buoyant, and waterproof. As a result, kapok is still used in some flotation equipment such as life preservers. Pillows and other items stuffed with kapok are now rare but are still occasionally available. You can purchase kapok stuffing from **The Natural Alternative**.

Syriaca Clusters and Hypodown

Syriaca clusters are the floss of silky-seeded milkweed plants. The name is derived from the particular species, *Aslcepais Asclepiadaceae syriaca*. Milkweeds are widely dispersed, common, perennial shrubs—all of which have a creamy white sap. Generally, they're considered nuisance plants. However, in a few places, such as on some farms around Ogallala, Nebraska, syriaca clusters have become a cash crop. There, milkweed seeds are sown in rows and harvested in the Fall using corn planting equipment. The syriaca clusters make up about 20% of the harvestable plant material.

Surprisingly, despite being quite robust when they pop up on their own one at a time, when they're grown in *monocultures* (fields planted with one plant species), they tend to be less hardy. And, because they're a broad-leaf "weed" themselves, typical herbicides can't be used. So, they remain a somewhat special, limited commodity.

In recent times, the floss of milkweeds has largely been ignored. However, for a time in the 1700's, French weavers were using it to create a silk-like cloth. Two centuries later during World War II, wild syriaca clusters were picked to make marine lifesaving vests. Then in 1987, the **Ogallala Down Co.** was formed which began marketing syriaca clusters as a natural stuffing material that was, apparently, inherently hypoallergenic. It can be used alone, with wool, or with goose down. When combined with goose down, it goes by the name Hypodown.

"Hypodown" (hypo-allergenic down) was named not just because the clusters are non-allergenic, but also because they have the capacity to "stabilize" the components in goose down to which people tend to react. This is apparently possible because the hollow cellulose tubes of the syriaca shafts naturally "trap and suppress goose down allergens." It should be mentioned here that, for most people, the allergens associated with down are not due to the down itself, but rather to what's on it, such as dust mites and bird *dander* (skin flakes). Another plus for Hypodown, over plain goose down, is that it's apparently both sturdier and warmer.

Like down, Hypodown is rated in different grades. The highest grade (over 700) is a combination of syriaca clusters and Baltic white goose down. You can purchase syriaca cluster filling, as well as various grades of Hypodown, from **Ogallala Down Co.** (See also *Feathers and Down* on page 191.)

Wool Stuffing

Wool stuffing is also an excellent insulating material. Unlike cotton, wool retains heat even when it's wet because it's able to maintain it's loft. It is also slow to catch fire. Therefore, it's often used in the manufacture of all-natural mattresses, where Federal law mandates the use of fire-resisting materials.

While wool stuffing is now less likely to be used in garments, it is increasingly being used in both bedding items (such as comforters and futons), and in furniture. If you'd like to purchase pure wool stuffing, it's sold by **Heart of Vermont**, **Furnature**, and **The Natural Alternative**.

Feathers and Down

Although they both have many uses, feathers are less valuable than down. This is because down lacks the *barbicels* (minute hooks) that lock other feather types into stiff, definable shapes. As a result, down is extremely soft and fluffy. It actually has a free-form, three-dimensional configuration that can trap large volumes of air. This trapped air gives down its remarkable capacity to insulate. Different varieties are rated by their *fill power*. This is calculated by compressing and then releasing one ounce of a particular down sample and calculating how big a volume of space it fills in cubic inches. The higher the number, the better the quality. So, a 700 down bedding item would be superior to one with a 300 rating.

Besides bedding, feathers and down are still used as stuffing in some coats, and in furniture. White Peking ducks and white domestic geese are the two main sources of feathers and down. Baltic white geese provide one of the highest grades. However, feather and down products can be derived from other poultry, too.

In the U.S., most feathers and down are actually by-products of poultry packing plants. In such plants, slaughtered birds undergo a series of processing steps leading to a dip in hot resinous wax. This wax is allowed to cool and harden so it, along with the wax-embedded feathers, can to be pulled off together. The feathers are then washed to clean and sterilize them, and to remove any natural oils. Drying under high heat further sterilizes the feathers by killing any remaining microbes. The feathers and down are then separated, sorted, and bagged. By the way, some clothing (or bedding or furniture) manufacturers may later add mildew-resistant or insect-resistant chemical treatments to the feathers or down.

Unfortunately, there are many people with allergies and asthma who react to feathers or down. This can be due to intolerability with the actual feather/down proteins or, more commonly, to bird *dander* (skin flakes) in the filling material, or to a reaction to dust mites living on the material. So, some companies selling down and feathers give it a special deep cleaning to render their products as dust- and dust-mite-free as possible. However, one company, the **Ogallala Down Co.** has found that by combining *Syriaca clusters* (milkweed floss) with down, the allergens remain naturally suppressed. This combination filling is called Hypodown and can be purchased from the company. (See *Syriaca Clusters and Hypodown* on page 190.)

Certain feather and down items can be safely laundered in the washing machine, if set on a gentle cycle. That is, unless the manufacturers' tags recommend dry cleaning (see *Is Dry Cleaning A Problem*? on page 196), and the items are small enough to fit in your machine. Because the oils that naturally make feathers and down waterproof have been removed during processing, they will absorb a considerable amount of water when they become wet. Therefore, it's extremely important to dry all feather and down items thoroughly. It's important to note that it's possible for outer fabric coverings to feel dry, while the feather or down stuffing inside is still slightly damp. Unfortunately, if an item isn't completely dry, it could lead to fungal or microbial growth. (This is especially true if the feathers or down are untreated.) Therefore, an extra cycle through your clothes dryer may be necessary for complete drying. Incidentally, a clean, washable, tennis shoe placed in the clothes dryer with a down-stuffed item will help fluff the down. Another option is to use Fabric Fluffers. These are synthetic rings sold by **EcoBaby Organics** and **Harmony**. (Because of their synthetic composition, experiment with them first if you're chemically sensitive.)

Natural Latex (Rubber)

Natural latex is extracted by tapping trees, most commonly hybrids of the Brazilian Para. Natural latex is a *polymer,* that is, a substance whose chemical structure is made of very long molecular strands with few cross links. This is what makes latex incredibly flexible.

First used by Native Americans for game balls and religious rites, since the time of the Spanish conquistadors, Europeans have also utilized natural latex. First, they kept portions of it as oddities. Later, they found more practical applications. Interestingly, in the late 1700s, the well-known English scientist, Joseph Priestly, discovered that latex could "rub out" pencil marks. Hence, *rubber* thereafter became the popular name for latex.

Natural rubber is never used as is. Instead, it requires other substances, processes, and additives to make it stable in both heat and cold. One method originally devised by Charles Goodyear in the 1830s, is *vulcanization*, a process using an acid treatment, which is still common in manufacturing.

Some people, especially those with dust and dust-mite allergies, prefer natural latex stuffing to other natural materials. It retains its shape, supports well, and it doesn't easily support microbes. In addition, it is less dusty than many other natural fillings. However, those who have acquired latex allergies should choose another material. Also, there is some concern that latex foam can sometimes become moldy in humid weather. Natural latex batts (97% latex, 3% binders) in a few larger sizes can be ordered from **Furnature.**

As a final note, it should be mentioned that sometimes, natural latex is mixed with synthetic latex. This is done, according to some sources, because synthetic latex is more *resilient* (returns to its original shape) than natural latex. If this is a concern for you, check the manufacturer or supplier of a latex-filled item first before purchasing.

Acceptable Synthetic Fibers

In the not-too-distant past, all clothing was made from natural fibers and stuffing, leather, and/or fur. Today, many garments are manufactured with synthetic fibers and stuffing that have been derived from petroleum, natural gas, or coal. These man-made materials are easy to care for and usually less expensive than their natural counterparts. However, they have a number of drawbacks that many consumers routinely fail to consider. While it may be understood that the majority of synthetic fibers are made of non-biodegradable, non-renewable resources, there are other concerns of which you may not be fully aware.

One such problem is that synthetic clothing generally doesn't "breathe" (that is, moisture doesn't readily evaporate), so wearers can become unnecessarily hot and sticky. Also, some synthetic fabrics and stuffing emit low levels of potentially bothersome odors. In addition, sensitive persons have found that certain synthetic fibers seem to retain perfume, tobacco, and other odors, despite repeated cleaning and airing.

Nylon

While many synthetic fibers are bothersome to chemically sensitive individuals, nylon is often an exception. Nylon was actually the first truly synthetic fiber ever produced. In 1935, during an experiment at E.I. DuPont De Nemours and Co., a long, glossy fiber was accidentally created. The material was a *polymer* (a compound created from many small molecules). When the specific molecular composition of the fiber was determined, it was trademarked as Nylon—an arbitrary name that included the *-on* suffix so as to be reminiscent of the man-made fiber rayon. One of the earliest uses for Nylon was as a silk substitute. Eventually, Nylon became the generic term *nylon* (with a lower case n) after several different nylon types were developed.

Nylon fibers are extremely tough and resilient. It may be because of this that they give off very little synthetic chemical odor. Some sensitive individuals have also reported that nylon seems to retain fewer fragrance and tobacco odors after cleaning than other synthetic fibers. Nylon fabric is also easy to care for—washing either by hand or in a machine. Some nylon garments can even be dried in the dryer, though most must be line-dried. However, nylon does have some drawbacks. For example, nylon does not "breathe," and it is not biodegradable.

Today, 100% nylon is often used to make hosiery, lingerie, coats, sportswear, and linings. It's also the fabric of some ties, dresses, blouses, and skirts. In addition, nylon is used as the covering material on many boots and athletic shoes. Unfortunately though, most outerwear and shoe manufacturers have begun to routinely add water-repelling chemicals to their nylon products. For example, in the case of nylon winter boots, the boots may have a vinyl, urethane, silicone, or other type of synthetic resin coating. Some of these chemical treatments may make otherwise tolerable nylon clothing intolerable for chemically sensitive people. Therefore, you'll want to read manufacturers' tags carefully before purchasing any

193

nylon item to see if it's water-repellent or not. By the way, many fabric blends contain a portion of nylon. Nylon is included to add either sheen or strength, or both.

Rayon

Another man-made fiber that is often well-tolerated by sensitive people is rayon. Rayon has a relatively long history. At the 1889 Paris Exposition, inventor Count Hilaire de Chardonnet first revealed his *Chardonnet silk* to the public, later known as rayon. By the way, "rayon" is a coined word with no particular meaning other than an intended allusion to the sun for some reason. At any rate, rayon was originally created as an silk substitute.

Strictly speaking, rayon isn't a synthetic fiber. It's actually reworked *cellulose*, the same natural material that makes up the cell walls of plants. To make rayon, very short cellulose fibers are transformed through special processes into long silky strands. Unlike a true synthetic material, the cellulose isn't altered at the molecular level into a new substance; it merely changes its physical shape.

During the manufacturing process, wood pulp, or other plant material, is bleached. Then it's mixed with certain chemical solutions that break down the tough cellulose making up the plant cell walls. (The particular chemicals used will determine the type of rayon being produced.) The cellulose/chemical solution is next filtered, aged, and eventually mixed with a coagulating liquid to cause it to solidify. Finally, rayon threads are extruded by *spinnerets* (devices with tiny holes through which the congealing solution is forced). The hardened threads are then ready for dyeing and weaving.

Rayon is often well-tolerated by many sensitive individuals. Like many natural fibers, it can "breathe" and is biodegradable. Some items made of rayon can be machine- or hand-washed—especially those in rayon challis. But be careful: rayon fibers apparently lose much of their strength when wet. Therefore, take care not to wring rayon items tightly or to stretch them. To dry, washable rayon clothing is usually laid flat or hung up. Many rayon garments, however, are labeled "dry-clean only," so you should check manufacturers' labels carefully. As has been mentioned before, if possible, avoid dry cleaning because of the petroleum-based solvents that are used. If possible, if a specialized wet-cleaning service is in your area, that can be used instead. (See *Is Dry Cleaning a Problem* on page 196.)

Rayon has traditionally been used for blouses, dresses, and lingerie because of it's lightweight, lustrous feel, and its excellent dyeing capacity. For many years though, rayon products were often considered to be of poor quality. However, today's better technology has created modern rayons that better retain their shape, have improved appearance, and can be cleaned more satisfactorily. As a result, rayon is becoming more widely used again.

Tencel

Tencel (generically, it's called lyocell), like rayon, is a man-made fiber created from cellulose. The name is trademarked by the inventor, Acordis Fibers, and was probably derived from a combination of tensile (able to undergo tension, is able to be stretched) and cellulose. The name is appropriate, because this fiber is stronger even than cotton, when either dry or wet. Rayon, on the other hand, looses much of its strength when damp.

Not surprisingly, Tencel is made in a manner that is not a great deal different than rayon. However, Tencel's manufacturing process was specifically designed to be as earth-friendly as possible. It's made by mixing wood pulp (from managed tree farms) and amine oxide (a non-toxic solvent). The amine oxide dissolves the wood pulp and leaves it in solution. The next phase is filtering, in which any wood pulp impurities are removed, then a *spinning extrusion process* begins. This is done by forcing the solution through minute holes to produce continuous filaments which harden.

The filaments are then washed to remove the amine oxide solution, dried, crimped, and finally cut into usable staple fibers. Meanwhile, the diluted amine oxide is purified, heated to remove the water, and is used again. Thus, unlike rayon production, no chemical reactions are required, so no polluting by-products are formed.

Tencel fibers have a soft, smooth texture. Because it's a relatively new product, there are still not many manufacturers using it yet. However, some dresses and blouses and other drapey-like clothing articles made of Tencel are available. It's usually suggested that Tencel items be washed in cold water only, either by hand or on a gentle washing cycle. Of course, for best results, check labels for specific care instructions.

Specific Textile Concerns

Natural fiber textiles have many pluses. However, there are some special considerations to keep in mind. The following sections will discuss some of these.

How Natural are Some Natural-Fiber Textiles?

It's important to point out that just because a fiber or stuffing is naturally derived *does not* mean it is free from chemical treatments; sometimes a lot of chemicals have been used. This fact is sometimes overlooked. Many natural-fiber crops, such as cotton, are commonly grown using huge amounts of fertilizers, herbicides, and pesticides. During manufacturing, bleaches, synthetic dyes, and sizings, as well as wrinkle-resisting, soil-resisting, insect-resisting, mildew-resisting, water-repelling, or flame-resistant or fire-retardant treatments, among others, using formaldehyde or other petrochemicals may have been applied.

Therefore, know what you're buying, especially if you are very sensitive. Some of these chemical treatments are difficult—even impossible—to remove. As a result, people who are extremely chemically sensitive or highly allergic are strongly advised to only purchase natural-fiber garments that have undergone as few chemical treatments as possible; ideally, they should have had none. So, with this in mind, a "pecking order" would be: textiles made with "organic" fabric, followed by those made with "green" fabric (a term usually applied only to cotton), followed by "untreated" fabrics, then finally, "regular," commercial-grade fabrics.

How Much Shrinkage Should be Expected?

A common concern with natural-fiber textiles is shrinkage when it's washed. While ramie is an exception, most natural fibers will shrink during laundering. Of these, cotton and wool are probably the two fibers of most concern, because they make up the majority of the natural-fiber textiles, and are often cared for at home.

Cotton Shrinkage

Most washable cotton textiles can be successfully laundered at home, if proper care is exercised. For example, certain items should be hand-washed rather than put in a washing machine. As a rule, these would include cotton-knit sweaters, delicately woven items, and embellished pieces. After washing, these should usually be dried flat. (See *Hand Laundering* on page 125.) Of course, most manufacturers' labels should provide helpful information.

If cotton items are machine washable, make sure to choose an appropriate water temperature to wash them. As a rule, the cooler the temperature, the less shrinkage, and the better the color retention. However, cleaning can be less effective in cool or cold water. After machine washing, some cotton clothing should be line-dried or dried flat. Sturdier items usually hold up well when dried in a warm or hot dryer.

Commonly, with machine washing and drying, cotton clothing can shrink 3–15%, unless it was preshrunk during the manufacturing process. However, how much a particular cotton garment actually shrinks depends on whether it's knit or woven, the looseness of the knit or weave, the type and size of the thread or yarn used, and the temperatures of both washing and drying. Therefore, for cotton items that are untreated and not preshrunk, it's often a good idea to buy one size larger to account for any shrinkage. For items such as thermal knits and muslin slips, buying two sizes larger is suggested.

Wool Shrinkage

Wool textiles have a well-earned reputation for tremendous shrinkage. This is because the crimped fibers have the ability to tightly contract. And once they have contracted, they're usually permanently in this state. If wool items are not made of washable boiled-wool (see *Wool* on page 185) and you want to clean them at home, you must usually gently handwash them in cool water, then dry them flat (see *Hand Laundering* on page 125).

Is Dry Cleaning a Problem?

Dry cleaning can cause problems. It's expensive and often inconvenient. But far worse, dry cleaning saturates your articles with solvent odors—odors that, even after extensive airing, may not entirely dissipate. This can be a problem for many sensitive persons.

Why is this so? When you drop an item off, it's first sorted by color, fabric, and weight; then placed in a solvent-filled rotating cleaning drum. (After a time, the excess fluid is spun out and hot air evaporates any remaining liquid fluid. (Note: Certain items, such as leather and fur, have their own specialized cleaning processes.) Unfortunately, not all the solvent (which is most likely a *chlorinated hydrocarbon* called *perchloroethylene* or *perc*) evaporates away. Some residues remain on fabric fibers.

Another, often unexpected problem is the fact that many dry cleaners routinely apply mothproofing treatments to your woolens, even if you didn't request them. This free courtesy service can be avoided if you instruct your dry cleaner of your wishes when you bring your items in.

A much more comprehensive explanation of dry cleaning is found in *Dry Cleaning* on page 130. Also, it should be mentioned that specialized wet-cleaning services can usually be used instead of dry cleaning. For more information on that, read *Specialized Wet Cleaning* on page 131.

Why is 100%-Cotton Denim Often Intolerable?

Although most of the denim used in jeans, vests, jackets, coats, tote bags, etc. is untreated, 100%-cotton (which means it's all-cotton fabric which has not undergone wrinkle-resisting, waterproofing, treatments, etc.), it's often intolerable, when new, for many sensitive people. Generally, the reason is the dye. While blue denim can be colored with natural indigo or synthetic indigo dyes, it seems the real problem isn't the source of the dye but the fact that such large quantities of it are absorbed by the cotton fibers.

As it turns out, many traditional dark-blue denim items are dyed using a process known as *range-dyeing*. In range-dyeing, the cotton yarns, which are used to weave the denim, first go through a soaking in an indigo dye bath. Then, they're air-dried. This particular dyeing method allows the deep-blue tint to gradually fade through repeated launderings. However, if you choose blue denim items that are labeled as being already faded, pre-washed, silicone-washed, stone-washed, acid-washed, or bleached, then a great deal of the indigo dye will have been removed at the mill. Therefore, such denim pieces are often tolerable, even when first purchased.

Are Acceptable Textiles Hard to Find?

Many sensitive people believe it's extremely difficult to find tolerable textiles. Actually, it's becoming easier all the time. This is because natural fibers have become more popular with the general public in recent years. Therefore, more can be found in local stores to meet this demand. This is particularly true for 100%-cotton and 100%-silk items.

You can also find some acceptable textiles made from a variety of natural fibers in popular mail-order catalogs such as **L.L. Bean**, **Eddie Bauer**, and **Lands' End, Inc.** However, the best selections are usually found in specialty, natural-fiber catalogs such as **Deva Lifewear**, **Under the Canopy**, **EcoBaby Organics**, **B. Coole Designs**, **HempWorks** and **WinterSilks**, to name a few. (See also the specific listings in the next two chapters.)

In addition, you can often find textiles made of natural-fibers at secondhand shops and garage sales. However, for sensitive and scent-allergic individuals, buying at these places often must be avoided. That's because most used textiles have accumulated, over months or years, a great deal of perfume, fragrances from laundry products, and/or tobacco odors (see *Problems with Scents* on page 72). Very often, these contaminating odors will cause tolerance problems. While repeated laundering and airing may help, it often doesn't help enough for sensitive people.

Unfortunately, many new, untreated, natural-fiber textiles can also be intolerable, at least initially. This is likely due to all the chemicals typically added during milling. However, even organic-fiber pieces can sometimes have a strong grainy odor some people find bothersome. This is likely the result of cotton-seed oils and resins that have been absorbed by the cotton fibers. In addition, *any* new textile can be intolerable because of the perfume and/or tobacco odors picked up between the time it left the mill and when it was purchased. Fortunately, in many, if not most, cases, the minor odors clinging to new, untreated, washable, natural-fiber items can be removed through airing and special laundering procedures (see *Removing Odors from New Clothing* on page 123).

By the way, if you go to the effort and expense to find and buy items made of natural-fibers, make sure you care for them properly. This includes only laundering of washable items with tolerable cleaning products. Unscented brands are best for most sensitive and scent-allergic individuals. (See *Testing* on page 62.) Also, make sure your closets, drawers, and other storage areas are free from dust, mildew, and potentially contaminating odors (see *Closets* on page 511). Finally, store your natural-fiber items in such a way that there will be no damage from clothing moths (see *Clothing Moths* on page 406).

Are Low-Impact Dyes Important?

In the last few years, the term *low-impact dye* has been used, usually in regards to textiles that have otherwise been subjected to minimal treatment. What does it mean? While there doesn't seem to be an "official" definition, it usually means that the yarn, thread, or cloth have had a less-toxic dye applied through a "more natural process."

To make sense of this you need to know what a dye is. A dye is simply a colorant, usually meant to be permanent. It's used in a diluted form in a liquid solution. Natural dyes are derived mostly from plant materials and a few animal substances. Common ones that have been used for centuries are henna (red), turmeric (yellow), and indigo (purple/blue). However, by the end of World War I, German scientists developed a series of synthetic alternatives from *aniline* (a compound derived from benzene) and coal tar. These were cheap to produce and easy to use. The synthetic dye industry has since boomed, and today it's been estimated that 2,000 specific synthesized chemical compounds are available. In fact, virtually all dyes used in manufacturing are synthetic except for a natural black dye used on nylon.

But that's not the end of the story. Dyes alone often do not get absorbed well or remain long on most fibers. In fact, the majority of natural dyes won't enter and adhere to the center of fibers composed of cellulose. That includes cotton, of course. So, *mordents* are used. These are fixative compounds that combine with the dye and cause it to adhere more securely to fibers. Alum was, and is, commonly used by home weavers and dyers. Chromium salts are the mordents of choice for industrial dying processes.

It should also be mentioned that heat is commonly required for dyeing too. In fact, modern mills often use both heat and pressure, and if they're dyeing certain synthetics, such as polyester, very high temperatures (and perhaps pressures) may be utilized.

So, "low-impact dying" usually refer to yarn, thread, or fabric that has been processed with less-toxic synthetic dyes and less-toxic mordents. It may, or may not, also mean that, any heat and pressure generated, and/or fluids (such as water) that were utilized, were used in an "earth friendly" manner. Therefore, while this term remains somewhat vague, it's likely a plus for sensitive people, and those concerned with the ecology of the environment. Unfortunately, most manufacturers don't disclose what dye or mordant they use.

A type of low-impact dye you can use at home are is handled by **B. Coole Designs**. Called Procion Dyes, these are synthetic, and said to be more colorfast and "safer" than many of the natural dyes being used for natural fibers. By the way, these particular dyes can be used in cold water and require soda ash as the fixative. Note: Items dyed with Procion Dyes should not be washed in vinegar.

CHAPTER 8: CLOTHING

This chapter contains listings of sources for a wide variety of healthy clothing options for both men and women, and also children and infants. Plus it offers some suggestions for custom-made clothing.

Most of the clothing suggestions given in this chapter are ones that have proven satisfactory for a number of chemically sensitive persons. While they may represent the segment of the population most interested in healthier garments, individuals with asthma, allergies, and other immune conditions should also choose healthy clothing so as not to further compromise their health. For your convenience, you'll find the various types of clothing listed alphabetically.

By the way, "untreated," when used to describe cotton fabric, means that, at the very least, no formaldehyde resin treatments were used to minimize wrinkling. Because "untreated" doesn't have a strict legal definition, it may also mean that other common treatments (such a dyes, bleaches, etc.) have been eliminated. (See *How Natural are Some Natural Fiber Textiles* on page 195.)

Important note: Unless otherwise stated, you should assume that clothing items have been made with commercial-grade fabric and stuffing, which may or not have had various chemical treatments, including flame retardants on certain children's items. If you're concerned, ask a company representative before ordering to supply you with the information you desire.

Women's Clothing

Obtaining attractive *and* tolerable garments can be easier than you think, as long as you know where to look. Here's an alphabetical listing of basic clothing items, with several sources of where to purchase them, to help get you started in creating a healthy wardrobe. These suggestions are generally items that many sensitive individuals can tolerate.

Accessories

Ideally, you should probably choose metal, natural fabric, or leather belts (but not bonded leather). There are some belt choices, however, you'll not find locally. **Deva Lifewear** offers a variety of attractive untreated natural-cotton sashes and cummerbunds from time to time. Hemp belts are marketed by **Tomorrow's World** and **HempWorks**.

Casual, 100%-cotton canvas and leather belts are sometimes available by mail order from **L.L. Bean, Inc.** (Catalog for Women), **Deerskin Trading Post**, and **Lands' End, Inc.** Other styles of leather belts are handled by the **JC Penney Catalog**. Of course, most department stores will have a greater selection of leather belts—including dressier styles.

Elegant 100%-cotton and 100%-linen women's handkerchiefs are often sold in upscale clothing stores. A catalog that happens to sell ladies' cotton handkerchiefs is **Gohn Bros.** Of course as another option, you can simply purchase men's 100%-cotton hankies, which are very affordable and readily available. (See *Handkerchiefs* under *Men's Clothing* on page 212.)

Cotton canvas and denim bags and totes are sometimes found locally. For ethnically inspired all-cotton bags, check **Marketplace: Handwork of India** and **Karen's Natural Products**. Undyed and unsized cotton totes can be bought from **Dharma Trading Co.**

Hemp purses, wallets, and totes are available from **Tomorrow's World**. From **Janice Corporation**, you can order an all-cotton quilted eyeglass case.

Leather purses and wallets are handled by most department and shoe stores as well as the **JC Penney Catalog** and **Deerskin Trading Post**. Attractive leather purses are also offered by **J. Jill**. (Note: For scarves, see *Hats, Gloves, and Scarves* on page 204.)

Aprons and Smocks

Cobbler's aprons and other apron styles that are all-cotton and made without dyes and sizings are offered by **Dharma Trading Co.**

A full-length cotton-canvas chef's apron in several colors can be ordered from **Janice Corporation**. All-cotton "half-aprons" can be ordered from **Vermont Country Store Voice of the Mountains**. All-cotton duck aprons and smocks can also be found in many kitchen specialty departments and shops. In addition, kitchen/cooking catalogs handle them from time to time.

Tip: All-cotton, untreated white twill laboratory coats can make for great kitchen cover-ups because your clothes are completely protected from neck to knee as well as down to your wrists. These particular items shrink tremendously if you wash them in hot water and dry them in a hot dryer. Therefore, you'll need to purchase two to three sizes larger than your normal size. Fashion Seal style # 416 is one that can usually be ordered through a local uniform-supply store.

Brassieres

Untreated natural-fiber bras "breathe." Because heat and moisture isn't trapped, they're more comfortable for all women.

Cotton Bras

Remember: All cotton bras may shrink to some degree, unless they're labeled otherwise. Therefore, you'll want to select your size accordingly.

Organic-cotton brassieres are offered by **Deva Lifewear, Tomorrow's World, Well & Good, Under The Canopy**, and **Harmony**. It should also be mentioned that a number of organic-cotton bras are available from **Natural Selections**. However, because they have no mail-order catalog, you'll need to check their website. For even more possibilities, you'll want to call the company directly.

A unique bra source is **Decent Exposures**, a very small company run by and for women. They sew custom-made (organic or dyed) 90%-cotton/10%-Lycra bras to fit *any* cup or figure type. Green-cotton bras in a number of styles can be purchased from **Under The Canopy** and **Harmony**.

Interestingly, large brassiere companies usually manufacture a few 100%-cotton bras (generally, despite being labeled "all-cotton," they usually have a small amount of Lycra added), even though most of their lines are all-synthetic-fabric bras. You'll need to check your local department stores for these cotton models, some of which are tagged "sport bras," "soft cups," or "leisure/sleep bras." Catalogs offering cotton bras include **Janice Corporation, Karen's Natural Products**, and **Deva Lifewear**. Other sources include **Garnet Hill** and **Vermont Country Store Voice of the Mountains**. A few cotton bras can be ordered from the **JC Penney Catalog** and **Lady Grace**. In addition, **Back to Basics** has a good selection on their website with many available in larger plus sizes.

Bras of Other Fibers

Silk bras are perhaps the ultimate in softness, but their high cost is often a drawback. To find them locally, you'll need to check lingerie stores and women's foundations in fine department stores. Fortunately, the **WinterSilks** catalog offers washable, all-silk brassieres, many of which are affordably priced.

Coats

Acceptable coats that are attractive, tolerable, and easy to care for—especially winter ones—are not easy to find. Therefore, if you own one, it's extremely important to take good care of it so it won't need to be replaced until absolutely necessary. (Note: See *Custom-Made Clothes* on page 222 for other coat options.)

Cotton Coats

By mail order, unlined, medium-weight, 100%-cotton jackets and coats are occasionally available from **Deva Lifewear**. These will likely have had no formaldehyde-resin treatments to prevent wrinkling.

A few casual denim jackets are sometimes offered by the **JC Penney Catalog**. All-cotton, machine-washable-and-dryable "field jackets" and full-length dusters are carried by **L.L. Bean** (Catalog for women). Locally, many department stores handle 100%-cotton denim jackets, dusters, and coats. These all-cotton choices are usually not only generally tolerable, but machine washable and dryable as well.

Wool Coats

Of course, wool coats are an old favorite, but most of them are tagged, "dry clean only" (see *Is Dry Cleaning A Problem?* on page 196) and require proper storage to prevent moth damage. You should be aware that some new wool items are pretreated with mothproofing chemicals, so be sure to check the garment's labels.

Genopalette makes and markets shawls of naturally colored wool from "ecologically raised sheep" and **Casco Bay Wool Works** uses virgin wool and mohair to create full-length buttoned capes. Full-length wool capes are also sold by **B. Coole Designs**. In addition, unusual ethnic-style, full-length coats and capes are sometimes offered by **Daily Planet**.

Generally, most fine apparel shops and department stores offer at least some 100%-wool coats. Dressy wool coats by mail-order can be purchased from **Norm Thompson** and **J. Jill**. A number of wool coats are also sold by the **JC Penney Catalog**. Wool/alpaca coats are offered by **J. Jill** and **Peruvian Connection**.

Leather Coats

Leather coats can be good choices—if the odor of the new leather isn't overly objectionable. Often, airing a new leather coat will reduce this initial odor problem. However, completely removing the odor may take months or years if you are extremely sensitive. You should also be aware that some leather outerwear could have been treated with waterproofing chemicals, which can be bothersome to certain individuals. So, you'll need to read all labels and catalog descriptions carefully.

To find a leather coat, check at local leather shops and department stores. By mail order, **Deerskin Trading Post** offers a good selection of coats made from a variety of leather types including deer, pig, and calf. Other sources are the **JC Penney Catalog** and **Eddie Bauer**.

Coats of Other Fibers

Silk casual jackets have become popular. Therefore, you may be able to find them in local stores. A hemp jacket is handled by **Under The Canopy**.

Nylon coats filled with down have often proven acceptable for many chemically sensitive people. However, you'll want to check first to see if the coat is labeled as water-resistant. If so, it may have been treated with chemicals that could become bothersome, if you're a sensitive person. Generally, nylon coats are available in local sports, clothing, and department stores. Also, you'll want to check the **L.L. Bean** (Catalog for Women), **Eddie Bauer**, **Sierra Trading Post**, and **Lands' End, Inc.** catalogs for what they're currently offering.

Dresses, Blouses, Skirts, Pants, Etc.

Natural-fiber clothing for women is probably not as difficult to purchase as it was a few years ago. However, making sure that items have not been treated with potentially bothersome chemicals is essential for sensitive people.

Cotton Dresses, Blouses, Skirts, Pants

Tomorrow's World, Fisher Henney Naturals, and **Under The Canopy**, as well as **Harmony** sell women's wear (dresses, tops, skirts, slacks, etc.) made of organically raised cotton fabric. A few organic-cotton tops are sold by **Karen's Natural Products** and **Back to Basics** (check on their website). Furthermore, organic-cotton T-shirts can be ordered from **Tucson Cooperative Warehouse** and organic-cotton jeans from **Karen's Natural Products**. Organic-cotton women's wear is also available from **Natural Selections**, but they have no mail order catalog. Some items are listed on their website, but for the best selection, you'll need to call the company.

B. Coole Designs also designs and sews most of what they sell from "PFD" (prepared for dyeing), unbleached, non-chemically treated (no sizing, for example), 100%-cotton.

This company's clothing is colored with less-toxic, "low-impact" dyes in colors of your choice. Other undyed, no-sizing items are sold by **Dharma Trading Co.**

Then there are catalogs who specialize in mostly natural-fiber clothing—much of it in all-cotton, and cotton/linen, and cotton/ramie. These include **Orvis, Garnet Hill,** and **California Style.** Another similar type of catalog is **Tweeds.** An interesting option are items made of Peruvian cotton, which are available from the **Peruvian Connection.**

If you're after particularly easy-to-care-for clothing, **Deva Lifewear** designs and produces much of their line themselves from fabrics that are preshrunk and require little or no ironing. Deva items usually have no wrinkle-resisting treatments. **Tiburon** only sells items that are preshrunk and machine washable. They offer all-cotton, cotton/Lycra, and cotton/nylon fashionable clothing including skirts, tops, pants, and suits. Then, too, **National Wholesale Co.** and **Tilly Endurables** carry a good variety of easy-care, crinkled-cotton items from which to choose.

Catalogs devoted to clothing inspired by third-world ethnic appearance, such as **Marketplace: Handwork of India** and **Daily Planet,** offer unusual, natural-fiber garments, many of which are all-cotton. However, with this type of clothing you'll need to be cautious. Some items may not have been made using colorfast dyes. Therefore, it's essential to read descriptions and garment labels carefully, then wash such clothing pieces correctly to avoid color bleeding or running.

You'll find that mail-order companies such as **L.L. Bean** (Catalog for Women), **Lands' End, Inc., Eddie Bauer,** and **JC Penney Catalog** have casual all-cotton lines that are both attractive and comfortable. Other mail-order outlets for all-cotton women's clothes are **Chadwick's of Boston, Appleseed, Draper's & Damons, Hanna Anderson, Vermont Country Store Voice of the Mountains, Well & Good, J. Jill,** and **Norm Thompson.** Still more are the several **Orvis** catalogs (Mays Pond, Orvis, Mary Orvis Marbury), **Early Winters, Paula's Hat Box and More, Blair, Smith & Hawken, Lerner New York,** and **Newport News.** Finally, don't forget to look in local women's shops, departments, and stores.

Wool Dresses, Blouses, Skirts, Pants

All-wool items can often be found in local department stores and specialty clothing shops. However, they will require special measures to both properly clean and store them (see *Wool* on page 185).

Some wool and wool/nylon women's items are offered in-season by **Chadwick's of Boston, Norm Thompson, Orvis, Blair,** and **Hanna Anderson.**

A small selection of wool clothing is marketed by **Lands' End, Inc.** A few wool blazers are carried by **L.L. Bean** (Catalog for Women) and wool and cashmere dresses are handled by **J. Jill.** Wool and cashmere jackets are sometimes sold by **Lands' End, Inc.** Clothing woven of all-Peruvian wool and alpaca can always be ordered from **Peruvian Connection.**

Silk Dresses, Blouses, Skirts, Pants

Silk clothing is now sold in a range of stores, the biggest selection often in fine-quality, upscale shops. A good selection of undyed silk items can be ordered from **Dharma Trading Co.** This includes skirts, tops, dresses, and shorts. Ethnically inspired silk items are sold by **Daily Planet** and sometimes by **Deva Lifewear.**

An excellent mail-order source for silk items is **WinterSilks** which sells washable-silk dresses, blouses, pants, jackets, and more. A nice variety is also offered by the several **Orvis** catalogs (Mays Pond, Orvis, Mary Orvis Marbury), as well as the **Tweeds** catalog.

Of course, other companies handle silk women's clothing, too. They include **Norm Thompson**, **Blair**, **Paula's Hat Box and More**, **Under The Canopy**, **Tilly Endurables**, and **Chadwick's of Boston**.

Rayon and Tencel Dresses, Blouses, Skirts, Pants

Undyed rayon dresses and tops can be bought from **Dharma Trading Co.** All-rayon garments are also generally available in most local retail outlets. Unusually beautiful ethnic-influenced rayon garments are sold by **Daily Planet** and **Deva Lifewear**.

Paula's Hat Box and More handles some rayon items as does **Blair**, **California Style**, **Appleseed**, and **Chadwick's of Boston**.

Tencel, which is a new rayon-type fiber, will be seen more and more in women's clothing. For now, a number of Tencel garments are available from **Under The Canopy**, **Orvis** (May's Pond catalog), and also **Well & Good**. There are some cotton/Tencel blend jumpers, skirts, pants, tops and jackets are carried by **L.L. Bean** (Catalog for Women).

Dresses, Blouses, Skirts, Pants, of Other Fibers

A good selection of linen tops, skirts, and dresses can be obtained from **J. Jill** and **Tweeds**. A few linen items are handled by **Paula's Hat Box and More**, **Orvis** (Mays Pond and Mary Orvis Marbury catalogs), and **Norm Thompson**.

A number of hemp outfits are available from **Harmony**, **HempWorks**, **Under The Canopy**, and **Well & Good**. **Tomorrow's World** has hemp blue jeans. Nice hemp/cotton casual clothing can be ordered from **Early Winters**,

Leather skirts, dresses, pants, blazers, and vests are sold through the **Deerskin Trading Post** catalog. Also, you'll want to check your area department stores and specialty shops for other selections.

Hats, Gloves, and Scarves

This section will help you find the added outdoor protection you need.

Warm-Weather Items

Undyed-cotton hats are available from **Dharma Trading Co.** Unusual cotton hats are sold by **B. Coole Designs** and attractive ethnic looking ones can be ordered from **Marketplace: Handwork of India**. From **Tomorrow's World** and **HempWorks**, you can purchase all-hemp hats.

Warm-weather hats of cotton and natural fibers such as straw and palm are often found in local stores. By mail-order, a good variety of all types of hats is available from **Paula's Hat Box and More**. Other sources for warm-weather hats include **Vermont Country Store Apothecary** and **Vermont Country Store Voice of the Mountains**.

Scarves of 100% silk, cotton, rayon, or nylon are good choices and are widely available in many local stores. All-cotton scarves in five sizes are sold by mail-order from **B. Coole Designs**. **Dharma Trading Co.** has both cotton and silk scarves available with no dyes or sizing added.

Cool-Weather Items

The vast majority of winter-wear accessories are now probably made of acrylic. However, winter scarves, hats and mittens of cotton can be ordered from **Janice Corporation**. An unusual "muff hat" (a combination hood and muffler) of cotton fleece is sold by **B. Coole Designs**. If you're interest in silk glove liners, they're handled by **WinterSilks**. They also handle silk unisex *balaclavas* (a knitted hood-like covering for head, face and neck).

Wool items can be good choices because they can provide insulation despite getting wet. However, your wool items will need to be properly cleaned and stored. One interesting wool-item source is **Genopalette**. This small company makes and markets attractive scarves made of naturally colored wool from "ecologically raised sheep."

Dressy wool hats are offered by **Norm Thompson** and **Paula's Hat Box and More**. If you'd like all-wool caps, scarves, and gloves, they are sometimes sold by **Sierra Trading Post** and **Vermont Country Store Apothecary**. Some area stores should also carry these in season.

Hats made of leather and fur are sold by **Deerskin Trading Post**. This same company also sells leather gloves. Other leather items are usually available locally.

(Note: Also check out *Custom-Made Clothes* on page 222 for a few additional options.)

Larger-Sized Clothing

A number catalogs under the other headings offer some larger-sized women's clothing. Although not a larger-size-only catalog, items generously sized are sold by **Deva Lifewear** in easy-care, naturally textured fabrics. **B. Coole Designs** offers some larger-sized garments, too, such as cotton/spandex bras and leggings of 93% cotton/7% Lycra up to 5X. **Decent Exposures** can custom-make cotton bras in any size, even with organic cotton. Also, all-cotton chafe shields are sold by **Janice Corporation**. These companies are not likely to have items treated with formaldehyde resins to reduce wrinkling.

One of the best specialty catalogs for stylish larger-sized women's clothing is probably **Silhouettes**. This company has some (certainly not all) items in natural fibers. This includes all-cotton pants, tops, dresses, and sweaters, as well as washable-silk blouses and tops. They also have wool/nylon and leather coats, all proportioned to properly fit.

Junonia is an excellent larger-sizes catalog that has a special interest in offering active-wear clothing. In that line, they have many 100%-cotton tops, pants, and yoga wear (pants, tops) from which to choose. Also offered are organic-cotton sweatwear pieces and nylon/Lycra swimsuits. **Junonia** also handles Danskin cotton/Lycra sport bra/tops and leggings. But there's more. This company has 100%-cotton nightgowns, pajamas, robes, t-shirts, and panties, as well as 100% silk thermal wear. Especially nice are their 65%-Tencel/35%-cotton separates collection. Finally, they offer stylish all-cotton pant sets, cardigans, vests, and denim items including coats.

It should also be mentioned that the **JC Penney Catalog** usually offers its own larger-sized women's specialty catalog. Finally, local stores should offer some natural-fiber alternatives that are acceptable.

Leotards, Exercise Clothes, and Bathing Suits

Untreated leotards of 97%-cotton and 3%-Lycra are sold by **B. Coole Designs**. One-hundred-percent-cotton leotards may be available in your local sports shops and department stores. You'll also want to also check the **Back to Basics** catalog.

You'll find that **Yoga Zone** has 100%-cotton, cotton/Lycra, and organic-cotton yoga/work-out clothes. **Inner Balance** sells 90%-organic cotton/10%-Lycra yoga/workout wear including shorts, tops and "unitards."

Organic-cotton, or dyed cotton, bra tops, tank tops, and panty bottoms that can be worn while swimming are sold by **Decent Exposures**. Undyed 90%-cotton and 10%-Lycra (sewn with cotton thread) bathing suits in one- and two-piece styles can be obtained from **Dharma Trading Co.**

Maternity and Nursing-Mother Clothing

When you're expecting, **Garnet Hill** offers some all-cotton. maternity clothing for you. Organic-cotton maternity/nursing gowns are sold by **Earthlings**. This same company also sells 95%-cotton/5%-Lycra pants and tops for expectant mothers.

All-cotton clothing designed for nursing mothers, including dresses, casual wear, slacks, sleepwear, and undergarments, are available from **Motherwear** and **Garnet Hill**. Also, the JC Penney Catalog, **Gohn Bros.**, and **Natural Baby** have cotton nursing bras. Of course in addition, you'll want to check your local department stores and maternity shops.

Panties

Panties of 100%-natural fibers "breathe." Therefore, they may help prevent the emergence of yeast infections.

Cotton Panties

Organic-cotton or dyed-cotton panties with latex-free neoprene elastic are made and sold by **Decent Exposures**. Other organic "undies" can be ordered from **Well & Good**, **Tomorrow's World**, **Janice Corporation**, **Deva Lifewear**, **Harmony**, **Karen's Natural Products**, and **Natural Lifestyle**.

If you prefer green-cotton panties, they can be ordered from **Karen's Natural Products**. From **Harmony**, you can purchase green cotton/Lycra panties.

Sources for "regular" commercial-grade, cotton-fabric panties include local department and discount stores, **Deva Lifewear**, **Lady Grace**, **Garnet Hill**, **National Wholesale Co.**, **Vermont Country Store Apothecary**, and **Vermont Country Store Voice of the Mountains**. Others sources are **Gohn Bros.**, the JC Penney Catalog, and **Back to Basics** (check their website). It should also be noted that a very good selection (including Calida and Calvin Klein) is offered by **Chock's**.

Note: For cotton menstrual briefs with absorbent linings and moistureproof barriers, see *Feminine Hygiene* on page 93.

Panties of Other Fibers

All-silk panties are available from **Janice Corporation** and **WinterSilks** and in some finer stores.

As stated above, nylon panties, even those with inner cotton crotch linings, are not recommended because nylon can't "breathe."

Shoes and Boots

If you're a chemically sensitive person, you should realize that most new shoes and boots, no matter of what they're made, will often require an extended airing period. This will help dissipate the often bothersome "new" odors.

Shoes

Of course, some footwear choices are better than others. An example is shoes made of cotton canvas. But some footwear is also made of fairly tolerable leather. Then, too, untreated nylon shoes are usually low-odor items. However, nylon footwear doesn't "breathe," so there can be a buildup of perspiration.

Unusual footwear include hemp shoes, sold by **Tomorrow's World**, and cotton Mary Janes (embroidered or plain black) from **Deva Lifewear**.

There are many local outlets for "typical" women's shoes. By mail order, **JC Penney Catalog**, **L.L. Bean** (Catalog for Women), and **Deerskin Trading Post** catalogs offer a fairly good selection. Still other catalogs that handle some women's shoes include **Under The Canopy** and **J. Jill**.

A larger selection of leather shoes in a wide range of sizes is offered by shoe specialty catalogs such as **Maryland Square**, **B.A. Mason**, **Stuart McGuire**, and **Wissota Trader**.

Boots

While leather boots are readily available, they may require waterproofing treatments. These treatments commonly contain highly odorous compounds and generally must be reapplied every so often. Untreated nylon is a good boot choice, but many nylon boots are now chemically waterproofed during the manufacturing process. Certain of these applications may be bothersome to some chemically sensitive individuals.

If you need boots, especially for damp or winter conditions, you might be more tolerant of all-rubber or all-vinyl boots that are inherently waterproof. However these, too, can pose tolerance problems because vinyl and rubber odors can be bothersome to some people. Then, too, those with latex allergies must avoid items manufactured with latex rubber.

As you can see, finding tolerable boots can be a real problem. As a result, when not being worn, boots are best stored in an enclosed porch or "mud room." In this way they are separated from the actual living space, but are still within easy reach.

Of course, as with shoes, there are local stores nearby that handle boots. By mail order, you'll want to check **Wissota Trader**, **Maryland Square**, **B.A. Mason**, **Sierra Trading Post**, **L.L. Bean** (Catalog for Women), and **Deerskin Trading Post**. Sheepskin boots are sold by **Aussie Connection**.

Sleepwear

Natural-fiber sleepwear items can be found in many local stores. However, you'll want to check to see if they've been treated with fire-retardant chemicals, which can be bothersome to some individuals.

Nightgowns and Pajamas

If you're seeking organic nightgowns, they're handled by **Well & Good** and **Heart of Vermont**. **Fisher Henney Naturals** has organic-cotton nightgowns, and pajamas, too. Organic-cotton sleepwear is also sold by **Natural Selections**, but they have no mail order catalog. Some items are listed on their website, but for more information, call the company.

Deva Lifewear and **Janice Corporation** carry untreated, all-cotton sleepwear. **Harmony**, **Tweeds**, and **Under The Canopy** sell pajamas and gowns made of 100%-green-cotton. **Fisher Henney Naturals** handles a variety of green-cotton nightgowns and pajamas.

Cotton, rayon, and nylon sleepwear are popular items in department, clothing, and even discount stores. By mail order, 100%-cotton gowns and pjs are sold by **Orvis**, **National Wholesale Co.**, **JC Penney Catalog**, **Garnet Hill**, **Lands' End, Inc.**, and **Hanna Anderson.**

Specialty bedding catalogs that also sell a few all-cotton women's items are **The Company Store**, **Chambers**, and **Cuddledown of Maine**. Nightgowns woven from all-Peruvian cotton are sold by **Peruvian Connection**. A few ethnically-inspired cotton nightshirts are handled by **Marketplace: Handwork of India**

All-silk sleepwear is sold by **California Style**, **Tweeds**, and **WinterSilks**. You'll want to visit fine women's shops and departments for other options.

Bathrobes and Slippers

Heart of Vermont sells a 100%-organic-cotton terrycloth robe as does **Fisher Henney Naturals**. Green-cotton robes are available from **Karen's Natural Products**, **Harmony**, and **Under The Canopy**. **Deva Lifewear** usually has mid-weight robes and caftans in naturally textured fabrics. Deva items usually have no wrinkle-resisting treatments. An untreated-cotton robe is sold by **Tomorrow's World** and both untreated-cotton flannel and cotton terrycloth robes can be ordered from **Janice Corporation.**

All-cotton bathrobes are available in most stores locally, and from **Orvis**, **Lands' End, Inc.**, **Hanna Anderson**, **Vermont Country Store Voice of the Mountains**, **Cuddledown of Maine**, **The Company Store**, **JC Penney Catalog**, and **Garnet Hill.**

Beautiful silk robes are handled by **WinterSilks**. Locally, you may be able to find silk items in lingerie, department, and fine clothing stores.

All-cotton and sheepskin slippers can be purchased from **Janice Corporation**. And **Vermont Country Store Voice of the Mountains** handles women's slippers in either 100%-cotton-terry or wool-slipper-sock (with leather soles) styles. Washable-sheepskin slippers are sold by **Aussie Connection**. Several leather and sheepskin slipper selections are sold by **Deerskin Trading Post.**

Slips and Camisoles

Organic-cotton slips and camisoles can be bought from **Tucson Cooperative Warehouse**. Both organic-cotton and "regular" cotton slips and camisoles are sold by **Back to Basics** (use their website for greater selection). All-cotton ones can be purchased from **Deva Lifewear**, **Vermont Country Store Voice of the Mountains**, **Janice Corporation**, and **Chock's.**

Slips made from silk are available from some fine local department stores or from **Deva Lifewear** and **Janice Corporation**. Other very attractive silk camisoles and slips are handled by **Tweeds** and **WinterSilks**. Nylon, and even silk slips, are likely to be found locally, too.

Socks and Hosiery

Besides all-cotton, there is an increasing variety of silk, wool, and hemp socks and hosiery now available.

Socks

Natural-fiber socks "breathe" so they're usually very comfortable to wear. If you need socks for hiking or cold weather, you might consider wearing wool socks. Wool can absorb a large percentage of its weight in moisture and still provide insulating warmth. Hemp is both breathable and has natural antifungal qualities. This makes it a good choice for athletic socks.

It should be noted that many natural-fiber socks (especially cotton) have a tiny percentage of an elastizer, such as Lycra, added. Wool socks sometimes have nylon added to increase durability.

Organic-cotton socks can be ordered from a number of sources. These include **American Environmental Health Foundation, Tucson Cooperative Warehouse, LifeKind Products, Under The Canopy, Natural Lifestyle,** and **Tomorrow's World.** Organic cotton socks with 10-15% natural rubber added are sold by **Dharma Trading Co.**

Socks of 80% organic cotton, 18.7% green cotton, and 1.3% natural rubber are handled by **Harmony** and **Karen's Natural Products** has green-cotton socks.

Of course, most department stores, sport shops, and women's clothing stores will carry at least some cotton socks. By mail order, a good selection of all-cotton socks are handled by **Chock's.** Other sources include **Janice Corporation, National Wholesale Co., Vermont Country Store Voice of the Mountains,** and **Vermont Country Store Apothecary.**

Hemp socks are harder to find. However, you can get socks of 77% organic cotton, 20% hemp, and 3% Lycra from **Harmony.** Cotton/hemp fiber socks are also sold by **Tucson Cooperative Warehouse** and **Tomorrow's World.**

Women's socks of wool/nylon/spandex are handled by **Vermont Country Store Voice of the Mountains.** From **Janice Corporation** and **WinterSilks** you can order silk socks.

Hosiery, Tights, and Leggings

Breathable cotton stockings and panty hose are available from **Vermont Country Store Voice of the Mountains.** Silk hosiery is often sold in fine local department stores. By mail-order, you can get silk pantyhose from **Janice Corporation,** which also sells cotton garter belts.

Organic-cotton tights are handled by both **Janice Corporation** and **Natural Lifestyle.** And organic cotton/Lycra tights by **Under The Canopy.** In addition, tights in several colors of 75% cotton, 20% Supplex, 5% Lycra are sold by **Deva Lifewear.**

Organic-cotton leggings are handled by **American Environmental Health Foundation** and cotton leggings by **Decent Exposures.** Leggings of 70% cotton and 30% nylon in a number of colors are what **Karen's Natural Products** offers, while **B. Coole Designs** has leggings of 93% cotton and 7% Lycra.

Sweaters

There's nothing as comfortable as natural-fiber sweaters. Here are some shopping sources for you.

Cotton Sweaters

A source for organic-cotton sweaters is **Under The Canopy.** Cotton sweaters, sometimes a few organic ones, are available from **Karen's Natural Products.**

Sweaters created from all-Peruvian cotton can be obtained from **Peruvian Connection.** Other special sweaters are sometimes found in the **French Creek Sheep & Wool Co.** and **Deva Lifewear** catalogs. Sweaters guaranteed to be preshrunk and machine washable of 100%-cotton, are carried by **Tiburon.**

Of course, all-cotton sweaters, or a blend of cotton/ramie, are sold in most department stores and a number of "conventional" catalogs. You'll want to check, therefore, **L.L. Bean** (Catalog for Women), **Eddie Bauer**, **Lands' End, Inc.**, **Norm Thompson**, and the several **Orvis** catalogs (Orvis, Mary Orvis Marbury, Mays Pond). Others that usually offer some are **Lerner New York**, **Newport News**, **California Style**, **Hanna Anderson**, **J. Jill**, and **Garnet Hill**. Still more are **Chadwick's of Boston**, **Early Winters**, **Blair**, and **Appleseed**.

Wool Sweaters

For those wanting unbleached, undyed, pure-wool sweaters, they can be ordered from **Under The Canopy**. A few special wool sweaters are offered by **French Creek Sheep & Wool Co.** while beautiful sweaters made of Peruvian wool and alpaca are sold by **Peruvian Connection**

Other women's catalog sources for wool sweaters include **Hanna Anderson**, **Orvis**, and **Norm Thompson**. From **L.L. Bean** (Catalog for Women) you can order washable lambswool and wool/viscose blend sweaters. **Eddie Bauer** has both all-wool and wool/alpaca blend sweaters. Both wool and cashmere sweaters can be obtained from **J. Jill** and **Chadwick's of Boston**. Of course, wool sweaters are also often sold in season in local outlets.

Sweaters of Other Fibers

Silk and silk-blend (silk/cotton, silk/wool, silk/cashmere) sweaters are regularly handled by **WinterSilks**. Silk and silk-blend sweaters are also offered by **Tweeds**.

For linen and linen-blend knit items, you'll want to check from time to time **Paula's Hat Box and More**, the several **Orvis** catalogs (Orvis, Mary Orvis Marbury, Mays Pond), and **Norm Thompson**.

Sweatwear

Much of the sweatwear that's marketed is made, either partially or entirely, of synthetic materials. Fortunately, it's sometimes possible to find 100%-cotton sweat shirts, pants, etc. locally.

Organic-cotton sweatwear by mail order is sold by **Janice Corporation**, **Well & Good**, **Karen's Natural Products**, and **American Environmental Health Foundation**. You can get larger sizes only from **Junonia**. In addition, **Natural Selections** has some organic-cotton sweat clothes, but they have no mail order catalog. Some items are listed on their website, but for the best information, you can call the company.

A source for ready-for-dying, all-cotton sweatwear is **Dharma Trading Co.** All-cotton French terry sweatshirts and pants can be purchased from **Harmony**,

Hemp is just now being used to make sweatwear. This makes good sense because it's both breathable and has antifungal qualities. Cotton/hemp sweatwear for women can be purchased from **J. Jill**.

Thermal Underwear

Finding women's all-natural-fiber thermal underwear locally can sometimes be difficult. Fortunately, all-cotton long johns and tops are handled by mail-order companies such as **Chock's**, **Gohn Bros.**, **Lady Grace**, the **JC Penney Catalog**, **Janice Corporation**, and **National Wholesale Co.**

All-silk women's thermal underwear, in several styles, are available from **WinterSilks**. These are light in weight, very durable, and they have excellent insulating properties. (See *Custom Made Clothes* on page 222 for other options.)

Men's Clothing

As it turns out, natural (and tolerable synthetic) clothing choices for men are more limited than the choices available for women. However, there are a number of sources for acceptable items that should meet most of your needs.

Bathing Trunks and Exercise Clothes

Cotton or nylon bathing trunks are common in local stores. You can also sometimes buy cotton trunks (often with nylon liners) from catalogs such as **Lands' End, Inc.**, **Eddie Bauer**, and **L.L. Bean** (Catalog for Men). Hemp bathing trunks are sold by **Tomorrow's World**.

All-cotton yoga/work-out clothing is sold by **Yoga Zone**. These items appear to be very comfortable.

Belts, Braces, and Wallets

Cotton canvas belts, in several colors, are usually sold in army/navy surplus stores. So check locally for these. For something different, a company called **HempWorks** markets hemp belts for men.

Locally, most men's clothing stores and department stores should carry a good selection of leather belts. (Avoid bonded leather.) Mail-order companies, such as **JC Penney Catalog**, **Lands' End, Inc.**, **L.L. Bean** (Catalog for Men), and **Eddie Bauer** often handle a variety, too. So does the **Deerskin Trading Post**.

Dressier styles of leather belts are sold by **Huntington Clothiers & Shirtmakers** and **Paul Fredrick Menstyle**. This last company also sells leather braces.

Hemp wallets can be ordered from **Tomorrow's World**. Nylon wallets can be a good choice, too. Look for them in sporting-goods, discount, and department stores.

Men's leather wallets are sold in most men's shops, and department and discount stores. A mail-order source for wallets made from a variety of leathers is **Deerskin Trading Post**.

Coats

Finding tolerable outerwear (especially for cold weather) can often be extremely difficult for sensitive people. Therefore, if you have a coat or jacket that is acceptable, try to keep it in as good a shape as possible for as long as you can. However, there are a few sources where you may be able to buy an acceptable replacement coat. (Note: See *Custom-Made Clothes* on page 222 for other options.)

Cotton Coats

Deva Lifewear occasionally offers a few unlined, washable, medium-weight, 100%-cotton jackets with no added stain or water-repelling treatments. (Deva Lifewear items usually have no wrinkle-resisting treatments.)

Casual, all-cotton denim coats are sold in most men's-wear departments. They can be a good choice. By mail order, simple Amish-style, untreated, all-cotton work jackets can be purchased from **Gohn Bros.** Also, **Daily Planet** offers uniquely styled full-length unisex coats in all-cotton from time to time.

Wool Coats

If you want a 100%-wool coat, these can be few and far between, except for expensive overcoats which are often chemically mothproofed. These should be available in most men's shops and department stores. Used, boiled-wool European military jackets are sometimes handled by local army-navy surplus stores. These are often washable and may not have been mothproofed—however, mothproofing information may not be available on used clothing.

Wool coats are not often encountered in catalogs for men. However, check from time to time. **Daily Planet** occasionally offers unusual full-length unisex coats in all-wool.

Leather Coats

If it's not too bothersome, a new leather coat can sometimes be a good choice, that is, after it has aired for an extended period of time. This could be months or years, depending on the coat and how sensitive you are.

To find leather coats and jackets, you'll want to look in local department stores, men's clothing stores, and leather shops. By mail order, **Deerskin Trading Post** sells a number of styles made from several types of leather. Other good sources are the **JC Penney Catalog** and **Eddie Bauer.**

Coats of Other Fibers

If you're seeking something a little more unusual, a hemp jacket is handled by **Under The Canopy.**

Unlined, lightweight, nylon jackets—and those that are cotton-lined—are often available in local stores. These can make ideal jackets for sensitive persons, unless the nylon has been treated with potentially bothersome water-repelling chemicals. So, be sure to read the tags and labels to see if the coat is water-resistant before purchasing.

By the way, untreated nylon jackets filled with down are good choices for wintertime. Although rare, they are offered from time to time. You'll want to check **Lands' End, Inc.**, **Eddie Bauer**, and **L.L. Bean** (Catalog for Men) to see what they currently handle. Also, **Sierra Trading Post** offers overstocks, close-outs and seconds, so their prices are discounted.

Handkerchiefs

Untreated, 100%-cotton handkerchiefs are sold through most local men's departments and clothing stores. They can also be ordered from **Vermont Country Store Voice of the Mountains** and **Gohn Bros.**

Linen handkerchiefs and silk pocket handkerchiefs might be available at fine men's clothing stores. Or you can get them from **Vermont Country Store Voice of the Mountains.**

Hats, Gloves, and Winter Scarves

The following section will suggest a variety of items made of healthier fibers to help protect you outdoors.

Warm-Weather Items

Undyed, cotton hats are available from **Dharma Trading Co.**, and from **HempWorks** you can buy hats made of hemp.

Warm-weather hats of 100%-cotton and natural fibers, such as palm and straw, should be available in local stores. However, you can also get them from **Vermont Country Store Apothecary**, **Vermont Country Store Voice of the Mountains**, and **Gohn Bros.**

Cool-Weather Items

Most winter accessories these days seem to be made of synthetic fibers such as acrylic, but natural fibers are still around. Woolen items are great because they'll keep you warm even if they get wet. Of course, wool gloves, etc. require proper cleaning and storage.

All-cotton winter scarves can be purchased from **Janice Corporation** and **Genopalette** makes and sells scarves of naturally colored wool from "ecologically raised sheep." Wool caps, scarves, and gloves are sometimes sold by **Sierra Trading Post** and **Vermont Country Store Voice of the Mountains**.

Silk *balaclavas* (a knitted hood-like covering for face, head, and neck and silk glove liners are sold by **WinterSilks**. A number of leather and leather/fur hats and gloves can be ordered from **Deerskin Trading Post**.

(Note: See *Custom-Made Clothes* on page 222 for other options.)

Shoes and Boots

Usually, new footwear (especially if made of leather) needs to be aired for a period of time before it can be worn, particularly for chemically sensitive people.

Shoes

One of the better shoe materials from an outgassing standpoint is untreated, 100%-cotton canvas. Also, untreated nylon is often relatively low at emitting potentially bothersome odors. But then, nylon can't "breathe." Therefore, nylon shoes (particularly unvented nylon shoes) can lead to foot perspiration and odor problems. Very unusual items are shoes made of hemp sold by **Tomorrow's World**. Hemp not only "breathes," but is naturally antifungal.

Of course, leather shoes are in virtually every local shoe store. Catalogs with men's shoes include **Huntington Clothiers & Shirtmakers**, **L.L. Bean** (Catalog for Men), and **JC Penney Catalog**. Shoes and moccasins in a variety of styles are handled by **Deerskin Trading Post**. Sheepskin moccasins are sold by **French Creek Sheep & Wool Co.**

The best mail-order selections can be found in shoe specialty catalogs. For leather casual and dress shoes in sizes up to 20 and widths ranging from AAA through EEE, check **Stuart McGuire**, **Knapp Shoes**, **B.A. Mason**, and **E.T. Wright**. Other catalogs with a broad range of styles and sizes include **Maryland Square** and **Wissota Trader**.

For slippers, see *Sleepwear*, on page 215.

Boots

Unfortunately, finding acceptable boots is even more challenging than finding acceptable shoes. While damp- or winter-condition leather boots are commonly available, they generally need repeated waterproofing treatments, which can make them intolerable. On the other hand, vinyl and rubber boots are inherently waterproof, but they have their own odors which can be bothersome to certain people. Nylon boots, which were once made from untreated material and, therefore, were quite tolerable, are now generally coated with a synthetic substance to make them waterproof.

In the end, it seems that the best solution is to just buy boots made of the materials that seem to pose the least problems to you. Then, keep them stored in an enclosed porch or mud room away from the living space, if at all possible, or in a sealed container.

As is well known, men's boots are sold in many men's shoe stores. They're also offered by mail from **Wissota Trader, B.A. Mason, Executive Shoes, Knapp Shoes, Stuart McGuire, Maryland Square, L.L. Bean** (Catalog for Men), and **Deerskin Trading Post**. Another source is **Sierra Trading Post**. Sheepskin boots are sold by **Aussie Connection**.

(Note: See *Custom-Made Clothes* on page 222 for other options.)

Slacks, Shirts, Etc.

Natural-fiber garments for men are becoming a little more available in the last few years. Here are some sources for them.

Cotton Slacks and Shirts

Organic-cotton tops, shirts, and slacks can be purchased from **Tomorrow's World**, and organic-cotton tops and shirts from **Under The Canopy**. The **Karen's Natural Products** catalog has organic jeans and tops. Some organic-cotton menswear is also available from **Natural Selections**. However, this company doesn't print a mail-order catalog. Some items are listed on their website, but for the most information, simply call them.

Some "PFD" (prepared for dying) articles in untreated cotton are sold by **B. Coole Designs** and they will dye them with a "low-impact dye" of your choice. Other PFD tops made with cotton thread are sold by **Dharma Trading Co.**

You might also check **Tilly Endurables** and **Deva Lifewear** for casual slacks, shirts, and tops made with naturally textured cottons. (Deva items usually have no wrinkle-resisting treatments.) Untreated all-cotton shirts and slacks can be found in a number of department stores and men's wear shops although, lately, wrinkle-free versions have begun replacing them. By mail order, **Norm Thompson, Eddie Bauer, Lands' End, Inc.**, JC Penney Catalog, and **L.L. Bean** (Catalog for Men) all offer a good variety of 100%-cotton men's clothing. Another source is **Smith & Hawken**. A few all-cotton shirts are handled by **Gohn Bros.**

A good variety of fine 100%-cotton casual tops as well as shirts (some made of Egyptian cotton) can be purchased from **Paul Frederick's Menstyle**. In addition, good quality cotton shirts and tops are also sold by **Orvis**. All-cotton (including some of Egyptian cotton) shirts, tops, and slacks are offered **Huntington Clothiers & Shirtmakers** which, interestingly, will also custom make shirts for the perfect fit.

Wool Slacks and Shirts

Generally, 100%-wool clothing can be found in fine men's stores. However, some of it may have been chemically mothproofed. Reading the garment tags and labels may give you this information.

If you're wanting wool pants, tops, and sweaters, they can be ordered from **Norm Thompson** and **Huntington Clothiers & Shirtmakers**. In addition, **Under The Canopy** has wool overshirts. **Paul Fredrick Menstyle** has fine lambs-wool tops and cashmere vests.

Slacks and Shirts of Other Fibers

Silk shirts are now becoming far more popular—and affordable. Often, your local department stores, men's clothing shops, and even some discount stores will be handling them.

By mail order, silk shirts are sold by **Huntington Clothiers & Shirtmakers** and **Tilly Endurables**. Some silk and linen items can be ordered from **Orvis**. **WinterSilks** not only handles a good selection of washable-silk shirts, they also offer silk slacks and shorts.

Hemp is just starting to be used as a fabric fiber. For a selection of all-hemp tops and pants, check the **Under The Canopy** and **HempWorks** catalogs. In **Tomorrow's World** you'll find hemp blue jeans. Cotton/hemp items are offered by **Early Winters**.

Sleepwear

It's important for chemically sensitive persons to check for the addition of chemical treatments such as fire-retarding or wrinkle-resisting compounds before purchasing any sleepwear item.

Pajamas and Nightshirts

An organic-cotton nightshirt can be purchased from the **Karen's Natural Products** catalog. Other organic nightshirts in two different lengths are sold by **Heart of Vermont**.

Of course, all-cotton sleepwear can be found in a variety of stores and catalogs. By mail order, **Janice Corporation**, **Chock's**, and the **Vermont Country Store Voice of the Mountains** carries a number of 100%-cotton pajamas and nightshirts. All-cotton pajamas are sold by the **JC Penney Catalog** and **Lands' End, Inc.**

Silk sleepwear is generally offered by a few better local department stores. If you wish, you can order silk pajamas and nightshirts from **WinterSilks** and **Chock's**.

Bathrobes and Slippers

Well made, 100%-organic-cotton robes are handled by both **Under The Canopy** and **Heart of Vermont**. Green-cotton terry robes are handled by **Karen's Natural Products** and green-cotton fleece robes by **Harmony**.

An untreated-cotton robe can be bought from **Tomorrow's World**. Untreated-cotton terry and flannel bathrobes are sold by **Janice Corporation**. **Deva Lifewear** often has medium-weight, naturally textured robes and caftans. (Deva items usually have no wrinkle-resisting treatments.)

You should be able to find a variety of all-cotton bathrobes locally. However, if you'd like to mail-order them, they're available from **Chock's**, **JC Penney Catalog**, **Lands' End, Inc.**, **Vermont Country Store Voice of the Mountains**, and **Huntington Clothiers & Shirtmakers**. They're also sometimes offered by **L.L. Bean** (Catalog for Men).

Cotton terry-cloth slippers are sold in a number of local men's stores. All-cotton, as well as wool-and-leather slipper socks, can be purchased by mail order from **Vermont Country Store Voice of the Mountains**. Washable sheepskin slippers are sold by **Aussie Connection**. Sheepskin and leather slippers are sold by **Deerskin Trading Post**.

Socks

Men's socks need to "breathe." Therefore, make sure to purchase natural fiber socks for better comfort and to reduce foot infections such as athlete's foot.

Cotton Socks

If you're seeking organic-cotton socks, they can be purchased from **LifeKind Products**, **Natural Lifestyle**, **American Environmental Health Foundation**, and **Tomorrow's World**. They're also sold by **Under The Canopy**. Organic-cotton socks with 10-15%-natural rubber added are handled by **Dharma Trading Co.**

From **Harmony**, you can get socks made of 80% organic cotton, 18.7% green cotton, 1.3% natural rubber. Untreated-cotton socks are sold by **Karen's Natural Products**.

All-cotton sport socks are sold in many stores. Men's departments and specialty stores also usually carry a few cotton dress socks. An excellent selection of 100%-cotton men's socks are handled by **Chock's**, **Janice Corporation** and **Vermont Country Store Voice of the Mountains**.

Cotton/nylon/spandex dress socks can be ordered from **E.T. Wright** and cotton/nylon socks from **Huntington Clothiers & Shirtmakers**. Cotton/nylon dress socks are marketed by **Paul Fredrick Menstyle**.

Wool Socks

Socks of wool with nylon can be purchased from **Vermont Country Store Voice of the Mountains**. Wool/nylon/spandex dress sock are offered by **E.T. Wright** and wool/nylon ones from both **Huntington Clothiers & Shirtmakers** and **Paul Fredrick Menstyle**.

Socks of Other Fibers

Silk socks are sometimes found in finer men's shops and departments. They can also be ordered from **WinterSilks** and **Janice Corporation**.

A newer fiber being used for socks is hemp. Hemp is both "breathable" and has natural antifungal qualities. Socks of 77% organic cotton, 20% hemp, and 3% Lycra are available in the **Harmony** catalog. Hemp/cotton socks can be purchased from **Tucson Cooperative Warehouse** and **Tomorrow's World**.

Sport Jackets and Suits

Sport jackets and suits made of 100%-cotton, cotton/linen blends, and/or all-wool are sometimes sold at local men's departments. A good selection is also offered by **Huntington Clothiers & Shirtmakers**. This particular company even has a cashmere sports coat in their fine collection.

In addition, all-cotton or all-wool suits and sport jackets are sometimes available through **Norm Thompson**, **JC Penney Catalog**, **L.L. Bean** (Catalog for Men), **Eddie Bauer**, and **Lands' End, Inc.** catalogs. Fine lambs wool sports coats are sold by **Paul Fredrick Menstyle**.

You should be aware that virtually all the garments in this category will be labeled "dry-clean." (See *Is Dry Cleaning A Problem?* on page 196.) However, **Deva Lifewear** sometimes offers 100%-cotton, medium-weight, unstructured, washable sport jackets in a variety of colors. Deva items usually have had no wrinkle-resisting treatments.

Orvis sells not only cotton-corduroy and linen-fabric sports jackets, but a washable, cotton-canvas sports jacket, too.

Some fine men's stores also occasionally handle suits and jackets made of rayon/natural-fiber blends or perhaps all-silk versions. Through mail order, you can purchase silk sports jackets from **WinterSilks**, and a nice hemp/cotton sports jacket can be ordered from **Tomorrow's World**.

Of course, local leather shops often feature sport jackets made from various leathers. The **Deerskin Trading Post** catalog offers several leather sport jackets and vests.

Sweaters

The best sweaters are usually those of all-natural fibers. Here are some buying sources for them besides your local men's stores.

Cotton Sweaters

Sweaters knit from Peruvian cotton are offered by **Peruvian Connection**. All-cotton sweaters guaranteed to be preshrunk and machine washable are sold by **Tiburon**.

In addition, 100%-cotton or cotton/ramie-blend sweaters are often handled by **French Creek Sheep & Wool Co., Orvis, Eddie Bauer, Lands' End, Inc.**, and **L.L. Bean** (Catalog for Men). And some cotton men's sweaters are also sometimes available from the **Deva Lifewear** catalog.

Wool Sweaters

Unbleached, undyed pure-wool sweaters are handled by **Under The Canopy**, and **French Creek Sheep & Wool Co.** has some all-wool sweaters. Attractive wool and alpaca sweaters can be purchased from **Peruvian Connection**. **Huntington Clothiers & Shirtmakers** offers a few wool and cashmere sweaters, as does **Lands' End, Inc.**

Sweaters of Other Fibers

WinterSilks sells men's silk and silk-blend (silk/cotton, silk/wool, silk/cashmere) sweaters. Other sweaters of knitted silk are sometimes found in local fine men's shops and departments. Hemp sweaters are just beginning to be available. Some local outlets may have them already.

Sweatwear

All-synthetic or synthetic-cotton-blend sweatwear is, by far, the most commonly encountered. Fortunately, **American Environmental Health Foundation, Janice Corporation**, and **Karen's Natural Products** sell organic-cotton sweat clothes. Also, an all-cotton hooded sweatshirt can be purchased from **Tomorrow's World**. **Natural Selections**, too, has organic sweat pieces. However, they have no mail order catalog. Some items are listed on their website, but for the most complete information, call the company directly.

Undyed, all-cotton sweatwear is available from **Dharma Trading Co.** All-cotton, French-terry sweatwear pieces are sold by **Harmony**.

Ties

Ties in 100% cotton, rayon, and silk are widely available. **L.L. Bean** (Catalog for Men) and **Eddie Bauer** are two mail-order sources that offer these items from time to time. For something unusual, **Tomorrow's World** sells hemp ties.

An excellent selection of 100%-silk ties is sold by **Huntington Clothiers & Shirtmakers** and **Paul Fredrick Menstyle**. Others are sold by **Lands' End, Inc.** While the **JC Penney Catalog** sells silk ties, they're usually treated with Teflon for stain resistance.

Thermal Underwear

Finding men's all-natural-fiber thermal underwear locally is usually not too difficult. But, there are mail-order sources, if you prefer. All-cotton long johns and tops are sold by **Chock's, Gohn Bros., JC Penney Catalog**, and **Janice Corporation**. All-silk versions are offered by **WinterSilks**. (Note: See *Custom-Made Clothes* on page 222 for other options.)

Underwear

Natural-fiber underwear is breathable, so it's more comfortable. Fortunately for men, finding all-natural-fiber underwear is easy to do.

Cotton Underwear

Organic-cotton T-shirts can be ordered from **American Environmental Health Foundation** and **Tucson Cooperative Warehouse**. Another source is **Dharma Trading Co.** All-cotton boxers (some in organic cotton) are sold by **Janice Corporation**. Organic-cotton men's underwear, including shirts and briefs, are sold by **Karen's Natural Products, Natural Lifestyle**, and **Tomorrow's World**.

T-shirts and undershorts of 100%-cotton are very popular, and so they're always found in local department and clothing stores. Mail-order sources include **Lands' End, Inc., Vermont Country Store Apothecary, Vermont Country Store Voice of the Mountains**, and **JC Penney Catalog**. Several brands, including Calida and Bill Blass, are sold by **Chock's**.

A few companies are now starting to offer men's underwear made with hemp. Hemp fibers "breathe" and hemp has natural antifungal qualities. You'll want to check the **HempWorks** catalog for the current availability of T-shirts made with hemp.

Underwear of Other Fibers

Silk underwear is sold in upscale men's departments locally. By mail order, you can buy silk boxers and briefs from **WinterSilks**.

Work Clothes

It's getting difficult to find all-natural fiber work clothes anymore. Some that may suit your needs are in the Skillers line from **Duluth Trading Co.** These clothes are constructed of 100%-cotton-duck and include work pants, shorts, and jackets designed with tool holsters and extra pockets.

Children's Clothing

Warm weather clothes for children are commonly made of cotton. However, finding natural-fiber colder-season items is often difficult.

Coats

A few organic 100%-cotton coats for very young girls are available from **Xanomi**. And, a few 100%-cotton jackets for boy's are offered by **Gohn Bros.** Also, **Sierra Trading Post** sometimes has nylon-and-down coats for children at close-out prices. (Note: See *Custom-Made Clothes* on page 222 for other options.)

Hats, Mittens, Scarves

Some interesting all-cotton hats for children are handled by **B. Coole Designs**. Boy's Amish straw hats can be ordered from **Gohn Bros.**

For cool weather, an untreated, cotton-fleece "muff hat" for children, which is a combination of hood and muffler, is sold by **B. Coole Designs**.

Play, School, and Dress Clothing

Finding appropriate untreated clothing is usually possible locally, especially all-cotton items. Here are some other sources.

Boy's Wear

Organic-cotton clothes for young boys, are sold by **EcoBaby Organics**. Some organic boy's clothes (especially in warm season catalogs) are sold by **Patagonia**. Organic-cotton boy's clothes (up to age 7) can also be ordered from **Natural Selections**. However, they don't have a mail order catalog. So you'll need to check their website, and for even more styles, call the company directly.

Some "PFD" (prepared for dying) untreated-cotton clothes are sold by **B. Coole Designs**, and they will dye the clothes to a color of your choice. Boy's clothes made of all-cotton (including the thread) with no dyes or sizing added are available from **Dharma Trading Co.**

Boy's cotton clothes are sold by **JC Penney Catalog** and a few 100%-cotton shirts by **Gohn Bros.** All-cotton young boys clothing can be ordered from **Garnet Hill**, **Perfectly Safe**, and **Hanna Anderson**.

Girl's Wear

A few organic-cotton dresses, jumpers, blouses, and pants are handled by the **Xanomi** catalog. All-cotton clothing for girls is offered in the **JC Penney Catalog**. In addition, all-cotton young girls clothes is available from the **Perfectly Safe**, **Garnet Hill**, and **Hanna Anderson** catalogs.

Styles for very young girls in organic cotton can be purchased from **EcoBaby Organics**. Also, a variety of organic-cotton clothes (up to age 7) is offered by **Natural Selections**. However, because they have no mail-order catalog, check their website, and for even more offerings, call the company. **Patagonia** generally offers some organic-cotton girl's clothing in their warm-season catalogs.

Some "PFD" (prepared for dying) untreated-cotton clothes are offered by **B. Coole Designs**, and they will dye the clothes to a color of your choice. Clothes for girls made of all-cotton (including the thread) with no dyes or sizing added are available from **Dharma Trading Co.** In addition, this same company has undyed bathing suits of 90% cotton and 10% Lycra in one and two-piece styles.

All-cotton clothing for girls is offered by the **JC Penney Catalog**. One-hundred percent cotton young girls clothes can also be purchased from **Perfectly Safe**, **Garnet Hill**, and **Hanna Anderson**.

Sleepwear

Nice organic-cotton nightgowns for very young girls can be found in the **Xanomi** catalog. A green-cotton robe for children can be ordered from **Karen's Natural Products**. Check for gowns, pajamas, and robes of all-cotton in **EcoBaby Organics** and **Natural Selections** which may offer them from time to time.

Socks and Tights

Organic-cotton socks for youngsters are handled by **EcoBaby Organics**. And **Dharma Trading Co.** has organic-cotton socks with 10-15% natural rubber added.

Of course, cotton has always been popular for children's socks, so local stores should have them. If you don't want to purchase them nearby, you can order them from **Chock's**. A source for girl's cotton tights is **Vermont Country Store Voice of the Mountains**.

Shoes and Boots

Local department and shoe stores have children's shoes and boots. The advantages of using these sources rather than mail order is that their selection is usually better and there's often someone there who can help determine proper fit. In addition, some very attractive sheepskin moccasins for children are available from **French Creek Sheep & Wool Co.**

Thermal Underwear

Sometime it's hard to find children's natural-fiber thermal underwear. However, 100%-cotton thermal tops and bottoms for children are handled by **Chock's** and **Gohn Bros.**

(Note: See *Custom-Made Clothes* on page 222 for other options.)

Underwear

If you're looking for 100%-cotton boy's and girl underwear locally, it's usually not difficult to find. However if you prefer, you can mail order it from **Chock's**.

Winter Gloves, Hats, and Scarves

See *Custom-Made Clothes* on page 222 for some options.

Baby Clothing

It's usually fairly easy to locate 100%-cotton clothes for infants in local stores—unless you're interested in green or organic items.

Bibs

One-hundred-percent-organic-cotton baby's bibs are sold by **Karen's Natural Products**. Both organic-cotton bibs, as well as burp pads, are sold by **EcoBaby Organics**. Plus, **Decent**

Exposures handles all-cotton burp cloths. In addition, all-cotton bibs can be ordered from the **Chock's** catalog.

Daywear

Some all-organic-cotton baby items are handled by **Earthlings**, **EcoBaby Organics**, **Well & Good**, **LifeKind Products**, **Xanomi**, and on-line from **GreenMarketplace.com**. Others are sold by **Natural Selections**. Because this company has no mail-order catalog, you'll need to check their website. For even more styles that are currently available, you can call the company. Many all-cotton clothing items, including some organic ones, are sold by **Natural Baby.**

Both green-cotton and organic-cotton baby clothes are sold by **Under The Canopy** and **Karen's Natural Products.** Baby clothes of untreated PFD (prepared for dying) cotton are sold by **B. Coole Designs.** For a good selection of 100%-cotton (including the thread) baby clothes with no dyes or sizings added, order from the **Dharma Trading Co.** catalog.

One-hundred-percent-regular-cotton baby clothing is sold by **Perfectly Safe**, **Garnet Hill**, and **Hanna Anderson**, and it should also be available in most local stores that handle clothes for babies.

Diapers

(Note: for all types of diapers, see *Diapers* on page 90.)

Diaper Wraps, Swim Diapers, and Underwear

Both cotton and wool diaper wraps can be purchased from **EcoBaby Organics** and **Natural Baby.** This last company sells all-cotton diaper covers, too. **Karen's Natural Products** is another source for cotton diaper wraps.

All-cotton baby swim diapers with waterproof nylon linings are great for water playtime. They're sold by **One Step Ahead.**

100%-cotton underthings for babies are "musts." You can order Gerber Onesies one-piece (top and bottom attached) and Carter T-shirts from **Chock's.**

Footwear

Organic-cotton socks for babies can be obtained from **EcoBaby Organics** and **Karen's Natural Products.**

Organic-cotton booties are available from **Xanomi.** Washable sheepskin booties are offered by **Aussie Connection.**

Sleepwear

Some 100%-cotton sleepwear for babies may have been treated with fire retardants. If that's something that is of concern to you, always make sure to read the item's manufacturer's tag in the store before purchasing or ask before placing an order.

Organic-cotton baby sleepwear is handled by **Xanomi.** Sleepwear in untreated "PFD" (prepared for dying) cotton is sold by **B. Coole Designs.**

Check also **Karen's Natural Products**, **Tomorrow's World**, **Natural Baby**, **Earthlings**, **EcoBaby Organics**, **Well & Good**, **LifeKind Products**, and **Under The Canopy** for their current sleepwear selection.

A source for 100%-cotton infant sleepers is **Garnet Hill**, and **Chock's** sells 100%-cotton layette gowns, and Jamakins (one-piece, top-and-bottom pajamas).

Hats

Organic-cotton baby caps are handled by **Xanomi** and **Decent Exposures**. Some un-treated, 100%-cotton baby hats "PFD" (prepared for dying) are sold by **B. Coole Designs**.

Custom-Made Clothes

You don't always have to search catalogs or local stores to find natural-fiber or acceptable synthetic clothing. You can create much of what you need right in your home. Even if you can't tolerate sewing machine odors, consider buying the patterns, materials, and notions and having a friend, family member, or professional seamstress do the actual work. However, remember to choose a person who doesn't smoke or use perfume, and who won't be working in an area where others do. Otherwise, your custom-made clothing could absorb these odors and end up being too bothersome for you to wear.

While you likely already know of the name-brand patterns that have been sold in fabric stores for years, there's a new one with which you should become familiar: **Green Pepper**. Unlike others, this small company has a tremendous variety of outwear patterns available such as ski-style coats, polar boots, and gloves for men, women, and children. They also have thermal underwear patterns for the whole family.

The company sells the patterns directly to consumers, or through retailers such as Jo Ann's Fabrics and Crafts. Plus, if you contact them, they will have all the materials, as well as zippers and other findings, in stock, and the individual items are also sold separately. Because much of the fabric is waterproofed nylon, you can purchase your own fabric else-where, if you prefer. However, the findings, which can be hard to locate, are something you may wish to get from them.

In addition, if you call their *non*-toll-free phone number (the toll-free line is for an automatic ordering system only), you can talk with someone who can help you select what you need and who will answer any sewing questions you might have that could come up when using their patterns.

For a thorough discussion of sewing at home, see *Sewing* on page 456.

CHAPTER 9: LINENS

In creating an ideal healthy household, linens should be as toxic-free as possible. This chapter will cover all aspects of bedding, from mattresses to bedspreads to dust ruffles. It will also cover towels and kitchen linens.

Bedding

The most healthy items in your house should include sheets and bedding, which are in direct contact with you from 6–9 hours daily. These should promote both good sleep and good health. Every aspect of bedding is covered in the following chapter, except for bed frames and headboards. You'll find them under *Solid Wood Furniture* on page 331 and *Metal Furniture* on page 333.

Bedding Concerns

The two sections under this heading cover allergies and bedding, and common chemical treatments on new bedding.

Allergies, Bedding, and Bedrooms

For most of the people with conventional allergies related to bedding, the reactions are often not to the fabrics and stuffings, but to dust mites, dust-mite feces, and/or to scents from laundry products that cling to the fibers. Therefore, some very good advice is to buy linens, sheets, pillows, mattress covers, and pads which you can remove and wash frequently in an unscented cleaning product. This means washing sheets, blankets, and pads weekly, and barrier-cloth-protected pillows, comforters, and quilts every three months. The barrier-cloth protectors themselves should be cleaned every few weeks. (See also *Laundering for Allergic People* on page 122.) In addition, you'll want to replace your pillows yearly.

For dust-mite control, it's often suggested that bedding be sprayed every six months with tannic acid *neutralizing* solutions. However, there is the possibility that it may leave visible stains on certain bedding fabrics. A bigger concern, according to some experts, is that tannic acid solutions are ineffective for mattresses, which are far too thick for the sprays to penetrate. (For more complete information on dust-mite neutralizers and other treatments, read *Dust Mites* on page 410.) Another approach that has been recommended is to vacuum both mattress sides thoroughly (at least two minutes per side) twice a month. This can work to help reduce dust-mite populations, but it's obviously time consuming and sometimes difficult to do.

It's commonly believed that the best approach for bedding-related allergy control is to use a variety of synthetic items, such as vinyl mattress and pillow protectors to seal dust mites out of new bedding and to seal dust mites into old bedding. Yet, it seems that untreated 100%-cotton *barrier cloth* will work just as effectively. (Note: Barrier cloth uses relatively thick yarns which are very tightly woven together. It was originally developed for use in surgery and medicine.) By opting for this natural-fiber alternative, there will be no *outgassing* (emitting) of potentially bothersome chemicals, such as vinyl chloride—chemicals which could actually compromise *anyone's* immune system, sick or not. Sources for barrier-cloth protectors are listed in various places later in this chapter.

So, to avoid odors given off by synthetic fabrics and protectors, in this chapter *only* all-natural bedding items are recommended, and those with the fewest treatments are considered the best. These are usually not only good choices for those with allergies, but they're also excellent options for those with asthma and chemical sensitivities—as well as for the public-at-large.

Yet, there are still individuals who want synthetic "allergy bedding," and it must be admitted that such items can often handle frequent washings. So, companies offering these types of items are listed here. Most are specialty "allergy catalogs." These include **Allerx, Gazoontite, Bio Designs, Inner Balance,** and **InteliHealth Healthy Home**, as well as **Allergy Relief Shop, Inc.** From **The Allergy Store eMD.com,** and **Allergy Control Products, Inc.,** you can also get allergy bedding items—including crib-size ones. Other good sources to check are **Priorities, Allergy Clean Environments** (which handles an interesting disposable pillow protector, too), and **healthyhome.com**. General merchandise catalogs that have allergy bedding selections include **Vermont Country Store Voice of the Mountains, Coming Home, Harmony,** and **JC Penney Catalog**. In addition, AllerCare (**S.C. Johnson & Son, Inc.**) synthetic pillow protectors are now stocked on local grocery-store and pharmacy shelves. AllerCare mattress protectors can be ordered from the manufacturer.

Often, people want to use some type of air treatment device in their bedroom to alleviate their symptoms. If you do, choose a piece of equipment that can really do the job, such as a HEPA air filter. Negative ionizers, which many people put in their bedrooms, have not been proven to be of much value. Ozone machines, which add an extremely reactive pollutant to the air, should not be used. This is especially true for people experiencing respiratory problems (For more on air treatment, see *Chapter 23: Improving Your Indoor Air*.)

Also, it's important to have a room decorated in such a manner as not to promote dust-mite populations. This means smooth, hard-surfaced floors, furniture, metal blinds or washable curtains, and washable rugs—and you should clean all of them regularly. If you vacuum, use a vacuum that won't blow the debris it has just picked up back into the room. (See *Household Cleaning for Allergic and Asthmatic People* on page 140 *Alternative Portable Vacuum Cleaners* on page 146, and *Central Vacuum Cleaners* on page 149.)

You should also keep the relative humidity in your bedroom below 35-45%. At lower humiditys, dust mites and other microbial life will not reproduce and thrive as well as in more humid conditions. (See *High Relative Humidity* on page 530.)

Common Bedding Treatments

Most bedding that is made and sold in the U.S. has had several chemical treatments applied. Usually crops such as cotton and flax have had numerous chemicals applied to them in the fields. Sheep, too, usually have had chemicals applied to them to reduce vermin in their wool.

Then there are treatments applied in milling and manufacturing. The most common one is bleaching. In this procedure, yarns or fabrics are subjected to a *blanching solution* (such as chlorine) to remove the innate off-white color of cotton and other natural fibers. Very little chlorine compounds should remain by the time the items reach consumers. However, for those who are acutely sensitive to chlorine, it may still be enough to pose a problem. Then, too, for those concerned with the environment, chlorine bleaching can produce *dioxins* (extremely toxic, chlorinated teratogens) as by-products. To avoid chlorine bleaches in the items you buy, choose only those that state "bleached with hydrogen peroxide" or some other oxygen bleach, or buy those that are unbleached.

Another common treatment is dyeing. Dyes and the *mordents* (fixatives) that are used may, or may not, have bothersome chemicals in them, but this information is almost never provided to consumers. If you're concerned, items with labels that state "low-impact dyes were used" may be a better choice. Even better, use undyed items or those with naturally-hued fibers.

Commonly a *sizing* agent has been applied. This is a temporary glazing solution to give the item a "crisp" look when new. In the past, these glazes were not particularly a problem. However, some sizings are now chemical compounds that are designed to wash out after three or four launderings. Obviously, this can be bothersome to sensitive people, and for them it will likely take more than just a few launderings. However, even for them, this type of sizing should be able to be removed eventually.

Many times, one of the nastiest treatments is for wrinkle-resistance. In this case, a resinous solution, often a formaldehyde-containing one, is used. This is designed to keep the fibers somewhat stiff, so that a smooth surface is achieved without ironing. Unlike sizing, this treatment is meant to last the life of the items to which it's applied. So, it can be much more difficult, if not impossible, to remove entirely.

Another treatment is the addition of *fire* or *flame retardants*. These are compounds that will reduce the innate flammability of fibers and stuffings. Federal law in the U.S. requires that these compounds be applied to mattresses and to certain other children's bedding items. The specific chemical is usually not stated. It could be a boron compound, or something entirely different. To avoid any type of fire-retarding chemical, choose alternative mattresses manufactured from inherently flame-resistant materials, such as wool. It is also possible to have a cotton mattress made without flame retardants. However, you will need to provide the manufacturer with a physician's note or prescription stating that you cannot tolerate these chemical treatments.

Still, another treatment you may come across is for stain resistance. This is commonly a synthetic glaze that make fibers less penetrable. Stain-resisting treatments are a feature of some conventional mattresses, and they may be applied to other items as well. To avoid them, buy an alternative mattress using *green* or organic materials.

In the end, the best advice on avoiding bedding treatments is to buy organic items whenever possible. That way, all chemical treatments, from the field through packaging, will have been avoided. The next best option is to buy green items. By the way, this doesn't mean the color, but rather that no chemicals were added after milling. (Some chemicals could have been used earlier during cultivation.) Finally, the third best choice are items that have had no permanent wrinkle-resisting treatments, although other treatments have been used. Sometimes, items that have no formaldehyde-based wrinkle-resistant treatment are described or labeled as "untreated." This term is usually used for sheets and other fabric items, such as mattress protectors. However, the word "untreated" can have other meanings in different contexts, such as referring to a mattress without fire-retardants. To add further confusion, some manufacturers and dealers use "untreated" to mean the same as green when referring to cotton. Obviously, buyer beware. If uncertain, make sure you inquire before purchasing.

It should be mentioned that, sometimes, by simply modifying the suggestions listed under *Removing New Clothing Odors* on page 123, you can make certain bedding items tolerable, even if some treatments were used on them. However, this is not usually true for formaldehyde-based wrinkle-resisting treatments.

Specific Bedding Suggestions

Fortunately, natural-fiber mattresses, sheets, pillow cases, blankets, quilts, comforters, and bedspreads are becoming more readily available. Some are made of untreated, or even organic, materials. In the following sections most of the product suggestions have been used successfully by sensitive and allergic individuals.

Note: Sizes twin through king are mentioned in all the bedding listings below. In addition, an attempt has been made to always specify when crib-sizes are available. While some companies also handle California King, bunk, cot, long twin, and other "unusually sized" items, they aren't listed here, so as not to be too overwhelming or confusing. However, if you need something in an unusual size, please contact an individual supplier for availability. If you still can't find what you need, there's a section on custom-made bedding on page 254.

By the way, when "untreated" is used in conjunction with cotton fabric (not stuffing), it means that, at the very least, no formaldehyde-resin treatments for wrinkle resistance were used. Because this term does not have a specific, legal definition, it may be that other common treatments such as bleaching, dying, sizing, etc., were also omitted. (See *Common Bedding Treatments* on page 225.)

Important note: Unless otherwise stated, it is best to never assume what treatments might have been used. After all, bedding items may or may not have been made with commercial-grade cotton ticking that has been treated with formaldehyde resins against wrinkling. Wool stuffings may or may not have been treated for moth prevention, and feathers and down may or may not have had chemical treatments against mildew or pests. Cotton stuffings may, or may not, have had chemical treatments, including fire resistance (this is only Federally required on mattresses and a few other items). If you're concerned, ask a company representative before ordering for the information you desire.

Mattresses

At one time, mattresses were little more than large cloth sacks filled with straw, wool, cotton, or rags. The forerunners of modern box springs were simply wood frames strung with a grid of ropes. By comparison, many of today's mattresses and box springs are engineering marvels.

Conventional Mattress and Waterbed Concerns

Most manufacturers of mattresses commonly use specialized coils and patented support systems, combined with a variety of synthetic foams, battings, and covering materials. *Fire-retardants* are added to meet Federal regulations for flammability, and stain-resistant chemicals are routinely applied to tickings. (See *Common Bedding Treatments* on page 225.) All these have the potential to *outgas* (emit) a range of chemicals into the air; air that will be inhaled by those laying on them and hoping for a good and healthy night's rest.

Because of their own interest and concern about the materials and treatments commonly used in mattress manufacturing, **Anderson Laboratories, Inc.** (an independent research laboratory) decided to test five crib mattresses. They found that they all released toxic compounds into the air. "These chemical mixtures caused toxic effects on the eyes, nose, throat, and lungs and caused asthma-like decreases in airflow velocity" into and out of the lungs of their test subjects (mice). (Booklets and copies of their published research covering the toxic mattress findings can be purchased from **Anderson Laboratories, Inc.**) It's not surprising that many humans, especially sensitive ones, simply can't tolerate conventional mattresses.

Of course, one of the more recent mattress innovations is the water bed. However, these are only occasionally better tolerated. A water bed is basically a large vinyl bag, usually supported by a particleboard or plywood frame. The vinyl, the formaldehyde-based glue, and the natural pine aroma (composed of *terpenes*, which are naturally occurring pine-tree compounds related to turpentine) in the frames can outgas low-levels of bothersome odors that can be offensive. If the waterbed has a built-in electric heater to comfortably warm the bed, it can actually increase the outgassing rates.

Alternative Mattress Considerations

Fortunately, an increasing variety of all-natural bedding alternatives exist, some of which are available without fire-retarding or stain-resisting chemicals. As you might expect, these alternative mattresses can be relatively expensive. This is due to higher material costs, low production, and factory-to-home freight charges. Therefore, if you purchase a special mattress, it's wise to protect your investment. If at all possible, use washable natural-fiber mattress covers or protectors. (see *Encasing your Mattress* on page 230). Protectors made of cotton *barrier cloth* (barrier cloth is a special, extremely tight woven fabric made with relatively thick yarns) are especially good. They're the best natural-fiber choice to keep out odors, dust, and dust mites.

By the way, you can lengthen your mattress's life considerably by flipping it over and rotating it occasionally. To help you, **Taylor Gifts** has nylon webbing "mattress-turner straps" that can make this job easier. A good schedule is to flip the mattress over on the first of January, May, and September; and rotate it head to foot on the first of March, July, and November. Thumb tacking a small card with this schedule in your linen closet is a good way to be reminded to do this.

Alternative Mattress Buying Sources

There are now a plethora of alternative mattresses out there from which to choose. This is a far cry from just a few years ago when the selection was extremely limited.

Cotton Mattresses

Some of the most popular alternative mattresses are constructed with metal innersprings and stuffed with cotton. You should be aware, however, that most new cotton mattresses, especially organic cotton mattresses, have an innate odor that can be fairly strong. This is primarily caused by the natural grainy smell of the cotton itself. Apparently, a few cotton seeds become crushed during processing. As a result, their oils and resins become absorbed into the surrounding fibers. Generally, this smell will dissipate after a few weeks or a few months and finally become almost unnoticeable to even very sensitive individuals.

However, for those who find the "raw" cotton odor bothersome, consider using an all-cotton *barrier-cloth* mattress protector to help seal it in. For mattress protectors, see *Mattress Protectors* on page 230.)

Note: All mattresses are required to have fire-retarding treatments to meet U.S. federal regulations (see *Common Bedding Treatments* on page 225). If you feel that these would be bothersome to you, some suppliers listed below can omit them from the bedding they make for you— if your physician provides a prescription stating they can't be used for health reasons.

Sleeptek Oasis bedding (**Sleeptek Limited**) will make, in any size, organic-cotton mattresses and foundation box springs. These box springs are especially nice because they're made with unfinished hardwoods and no glues. Also available are non-innerspring mattresses. If you reside in Canada, you can order directly from the manufacturer. If you live in the U.S., they're available through **N.E.E.D.S.** and **Furnature**.

The Natural Bedroom line (**Crown City Mattress**) includes cotton mattresses and cotton mattress/box spring sets in a range of sizes from crib up. You have your choice of commercial-cotton, green-cotton, organic-cotton, or hemp tickings. Your options in cotton stuffings are commercial grade, green, and organic. Also offered, are 3" non-innerspring versions with unbleached-cotton ticking. These all can all be ordered directly from the manufacturer or from its dealers, one being **Building for Health Materials Center**.

Another good alternative mattress source is **Janice Corporation**. They have all-organic-cotton mattresses and box springs in all sizes. You can order them with either 100%-organic cotton, or organic-cotton ticking over commercial-cotton stuffing. Mattresses and box springs are also offered by **Bio Designs**. These can be ordered in twin through king sizes, as well as crib. They also sell unpainted, metal bed frames with casters in twin/full and queen/king sizes. **Palmer Bedding Co.** makes and sells 100%-organic-cotton mattresses and box springs in twin through king sizes. They'll also make custom sizes. Their box springs, by the way, can be made with either poplar or oak.

From **Well & Good**, you can order mattresses and mattress/box-spring sets with 100%-unbleached-cotton ticking and organic-cotton stuffing in twin through king sizes. Jubilee innerspring mattresses and box springs (**Erlander's Natural Products**) have organic-cotton batting and prewashed (in unscented washing soda) cotton ticking. Available in twin through king size, convertible sofa, roll-away, and custom sizes, these can be ordered through the company's catalog. **Allergy Relief Shop, Inc.** has mattresses and box springs of 100%-prewashed-cotton ticking over untreated-cotton stuffing (no fire-retardants added). These are offered in twin through king sizes.

Cuddledown of Maine has "formaldehyde-free" cotton mattress and box springs in a range of sizes. **Garnet Hill** sells 100%-cotton mattresses and box springs in popular sizes, including crib. These are made with commercial cotton. Both these companies generally use fire retardants on all mattresses.

Wool and Wool & Cotton Mattresses

Interestingly, no physician's prescription is usually necessary if you purchase a wool or wool-blend mattress. The reason is because wool is inherently fire-resistant. The mattresses below, generally use inner springs.

From **Well & Good**, you can get 100%-unbleached-cotton ticking over organic-wool mattresses. Sets of mattress and box springs can also be ordered. All these come in twin through king sizes. **Tomorrow's World** has baby mattresses made of 80% organic cotton and 10% wool (for fire retardancy).

Lifekind Bedding (**LifeKind Products**) mattresses and box springs are made with Pure Grow Wool cores with organic-cotton batting surrounding them. (Pure Grow Wool is defined as wool sheared from clean sheep who were undipped, untreated, free-ranging animals.) The ticking used is organic cotton. You can order sizes from twin to king from the company catalog. Similar mattress and box spring sets can be purchased from **EcoBaby Organics** (crib size available, too), **Heart of Vermont**, and **Bio Designs**. This last company also offers unpainted, castored, metal bed frames in twin/full and queen/king sizes.

A number of options are offered by **Crown City Mattress**. Their Natural Bedroom line includes 6"-thick mattresses and box springs (crib through king) stuffed with Pure Grow Wool, wrapped in organic-cotton batting. Ticking choices are organic cotton or hemp. A 6"-thick 100%-Pure-Grow-Wool mattress with organic-cotton ticking is another option. Three-inch-thick, all-wool, and wool/cotton mattresses, with unbleached-cotton covers are also available. All these items can be ordered directly from the maker, or its dealers such as **Building for Health Materials Center**.

Mattresses of Other Materials

The Sleeptek Oasis label (**Sleeptek Limited**) has natural-rubber latex mattresses with organic-cotton, quilted ticking. The quilted ticking uses pure, untreated (no moth-proofing) wool as a stuffing. These mattresses come in all sizes. In Canada, they can be ordered directly from the manufacturer. In the U.S., order through their distributors: **Furnature** and **N.E.E.D.S.**

You can special order hemp mattresses from **Bio Designs** in several sizes. A three-inch thick, all-hemp mattress is made and sold by **Crown City Mattress**. This mattress can also be ordered from their dealers such as **Building for Health Materials Center**.

(See also *System Mattresses* following.)

System Mattresses

System mattresses are relatively new entries into the bedding market in the United States. As the name implies, instead of buying a simple mattress (and perhaps a box spring) and placing it on a separate metal or wooden bed frame, these mattress systems are usually made up of several separate, but integral, layers, including a special bed frame.

The Natura bedding system, offered by both **Natural Home by Natürlich** and **Harmony**, has for its first layer a maple mattress frame with optional legs. Then you can chooses a "wood slat mattress" with optional adjustable positions for the next layer. This wood slat mattress is made with untreated cotton-canvas duck fabric, and canvas-covered natural-rubber, latex-foam side cushions. The next layer is a support mattress, also made of natural-rubber latex-foam covered with untreated cotton-canvas duck cloth. The final, top layer is a pad constructed of untreated (non-mothproofed) wool, covered with untreated duck canvas. This mattress system is available in a range of sizes.

The extensive Natural Bedroom line from **Crown City Mattress** has a wood "foundation" with cotton padding in twin and king sizes, and a "slat bottom frame" in twin and queen sizes. For the mattress layer, they offer 3" thick hemp mattresses, as well as several 3" latex mattresses. These have a core of either 60% synthetic latex/40% natural latex or 100% natural latex. Tickings can be unbleached-cotton fabric or organic-cotton quilted material (wool stuffing is used in quilting). This company also offers a 6"-thick mattress of organic cotton/Pure Grow Wool that is covered with organic-cotton, a 3" all-hemp mattress, a 3" wool mattress with an unbleached muslin cover, and 3"-thick organic-cotton, wool-filled mattress, among others. You can order any of these from the maker or its dealers, one of which is **Building for Health Materials Center**.

Encasing Your Mattress

Mattress covers and protectors will help protect your mattresses from soiling. Today, most covers are made of synthetic fibers such as polyester. Fortunately though, washable, 100%-cotton, untreated mattress covers and protectors are available from a few sources. Protectors are generally made of a denser, more impervious material than covers.

Mattress Covers

Organic-cotton mattress and box spring covers are sold by **Janice Corporation** in a full range of sizes that includes crib. You can also get wide, untreated fabrics and long zippers to make your own covers.

Untreated-muslin cotton covers for both mattresses and box springs in a wide size range (including crib) are also sold by **Janice Corporation**. The Natural Bedroom line includes unbleached-muslin, 3"-thick mattress covers for 3" mattresses in twin through king. They can be ordered from **Crown City Mattress** and it's dealers, such as **Building for Health Materials Center**.

All-cotton mattress covers, in a complete range of sizes (including crib), can be purchased from **Garnet Hill**. Box-spring covers of 100%-cotton in twin through king sizes can be ordered from **Chambers**. Stretch cotton terry covers for mattress (twin through king sizes, plus crib) and for box springs (twin through king sizes), and be ordered from **Priorities**. (All these in this last group probably use regular, commercial cotton that may or not have been treated for wrinkle-resistance. Ask the representative before ordering if he or she can supply you with this information, if you're concerned.)

Mattress Protectors

Cotton *barrier-cloth* mattress protectors are difficult to find but important for many allergic and sensitive people to ensure a good night's sleep. It should be mentioned again, because it's so important, that barrier cloth is an extremely tight-woven, 100%-cotton fabric made with relatively thick yarns. It was originally developed for medical use. However, the tight weave has since been found to be a reasonably good odor barrier, and it is used for that reason by many sensitive people. By completely encasing a mattress and box springs in cotton barrier cloth, most of the unwanted bedding odors are prevented from escaping into the room. This can often make some beds tolerable, even if they're made of synthetic battings, foams, and ticking, or if they have a strong natural odor from new, organically raised cotton. The main drawback to cotton barrier-cloth mattress covers is their relatively high cost. However, if they can make an otherwise intolerable bed tolerable, they're well worth the expense.

For those allergic to dust mites and their feces, cotton barrier cloth mattress protectors have an added benefit. They can help prevent dust mites from populating a new mattress. Dust mites require moisture and skin flakes to live, and what better place than bedding. By the way, cotton barrier-cloth protectors can also seal in dust mites in older bedding, making an otherwise unacceptably allergenic mattress usable.

If the cotton-barrier cloth mattress protectors are untreated (no formaldehyde resin added to reduce wrinkling), or better yet, made of organic cotton, they won't be *outgassing* (emitting) any chemicals. This is not the case with vinyl or other synthetic materials, or even with treated commercial cotton fabrics.

Sleeptek Oasis organic-cotton barrier-cloth mattress protectors (in any size) are made by **Sleeptek Limited**. If you're Canadian, you can order directly from them. If you live in the U.S., you can order them from **Furnature** or **N.E.E.D.S.** In addition, organic-cotton barrier-cloth mattress protectors in twin through king sizes, can also be purchased from **EcoBaby Organics**, and **Heart of Vermont**, in crib through king sizes.

Untreated-cotton barrier-cloth mattress protectors are sold by **Janice Corporation**. These are available in a range of sizes, including crib size. You can also purchase the barrier-cloth fabric and long zippers from them to make your own mattress protectors.

All-cotton barrier cloth mattress and box spring protectors are also sold by **Bio Designs**. These come in twin through king, as well as crib.

Mattress Pads

Mattress pads are now made in a variety of styles and fabrics. Here are some all-natural fiber and stuffing options.

Cotton Pads

Sleeptek Oasis organic-cotton "overlays," as well as organic-cotton barrier-cloth mattress pads (in any size you request) are available from the manufacturer, **Sleeptek Limited** of Canada. If you live in the U.S., you'll want to order through an American distributor, such as **N.E.E.D.S.** or **Furnature**. Organic-cotton mattress pads are also available from **LifeKind Products**, **Heart of Vermont**, and **Natural Selections** in a range of sizes, including crib. In addition, 100%-organic-cotton mattress pads in twin through king sizes are sold by **EcoBaby Organics**.

Untreated (no formaldehyde resin treatment), 100%-cotton quilted mattress pads (fitted and flat) in a range of sizes (including crib), can be ordered from **Janice Corporation**. Another source for untreated-cotton mattress pads is **Building for Health Materials Center**, which has them in twin through king sizes.

All-cotton chenille pads, in twin through king sizes, can be found in the **Harmony** catalog. All-cotton mattress pads in a range of sizes are handled by **Allergy Relief Shop, Inc.**, **The Vermont Country Store Voice of the Mountains**, **Garnet Hill**, **Eddie Bauer** (Home catalog), **Linensource**, and **The Company Store**. The **Chambers** catalog has nice cotton-chenille pads in twin through king sizes. (The items in this final group are probably made with commercial cotton.)

Tip: Two or three all-cotton flannel blankets can be substituted for a mattress pad.

Wool and Wool & Cotton Pads

Besides cotton, wool/cotton fill, all-wool, and shearling-fleece mattress pads are available. They, too, can be healthy choices, especially if they haven't been treated with mothproofing chemicals. You'll need to check the manufacturers' tags carefully for this information—and for proper cleaning procedures.

All-wool pads in many sizes, described as "chemically free," are available from the **Harmony** catalog.

Washable all-wool mattress pads, in twin up to king size, can be ordered from **Coming Home**. From **Natural Baby**, you can order 100%-wool mattress pads in twin and crib sizes. **The Company Store** and **The Vermont Country Store Voice of the Mountains** and **Cuddledown of Maine** have wool-fleece mattress pads in a full range of sizes. (Those in this group are likely made with commercial wool that may have been moth-proofed, or they may have other treatments.)

Sleeptek Oasis wool "overlays" with organic-cotton ticking can be created for you in any size by **Sleeptek Limited**. If you live in Canada, you can order from them directly. If you live in the U.S., you can get their products through **Furnature** and **N.E.E.D.S.** Nice mattress pads made with organic-wool with organic-cotton ticking are sold by **EcoBaby Organics**. These come in sizes twin through king.

Mattress pads with pure wool filling and untreated-cotton ticking are sold by **Janice Corporation**. Described by the company as quilted "pillow top" mattress pads, they come in a range of sizes. Other similar ones are handled by **Harmony**. In addition, **Crown City Mattress** (and its dealers, such as **Building for Health Materials Center**), have The Natural Bedroom line of mattresses pads in all sizes, including crib, covered with unbleached-cotton and stuffed with Pure Grow Wool. (Pure Grow Wool is from sheep which haven't been treated or dipped). Then, too, **Natural Home by Natürlich** sells Natura pads made with untreated wool filling (no moth-proofing compounds added) that are covered with untreated, 100%-cotton. Most sizes are available.

Wool mattress pads with cotton covers in twin through king are offered by **Tomorrow's World** and **Garnet Hill**.

Down Pads

Both the **Cuddledown of Maine** and the **Chambers** catalogs have mattress pads made of goose down that's been quilted with a 100%-cotton cover fabric. These are available in a full range of sizes.

Moisture-Controlling Pads

Waterproof pads can be helpful where simple incontinence, illness, or age (the young or the old) means that mattresses need extra protection. For this reason, **Vermont Country Store Apothecary** and **Vermont Country Store Voice of the Mountains** offer pads in a number of sizes made of natural gum rubber, covered in layers of heavy cotton flannel. Flannel-covered rubber sheeting is sold by **Janice Corporation**. Snug'n Dry versions, in crib, youth, and twin sizes, are available from **Chock's**.

If you prefer not to use rubber, try wool moisture-controlling pads. Wool pads are very absorbent and will not feel clammy to the skin when wet. They're often actually described as being "waterproof." Unless the manufacturer's tag says otherwise, to clean them, you simply rinse them in warm water and allow them to air dry. Merino wool pads, in twin through king sizes (plus crib and "baby" sizes), are available from **LifeKind Products**. Similar ones in the same sizes can be ordered from **EcoBaby Organics**. All-wool pads in twin, queen, crib, and "puddle size" are available from **Natural Baby**. Finally, all-wool "Puddle Pads" can be purchased from **Tomorrow's World**.

Crib and Cradle Bumpers

Crown City Mattress makes organic-cotton bumper pads, as well as covers for them. You can order them from the manufacturer or its dealers. One is Building for Health Materials Center.

Lifekind crib bumpers (LifeKind Products) are 100%-organic cotton. They can be ordered from the company's catalog. EcoBaby Organics sells both organic-cotton crib and cradle bumpers.

Featherbeds and Mattress Toppers

Featherbeds are similar to comforters in construction. They are usually *baffle-quilted* (quilted in sections to hold fillings in place) and packed with a stuffing material. The difference is, featherbeds are designed to go under the sleeper; comforters go over the sleeper. *Mattress toppers* are several-inch-thick versions of mattress pads. Both featherbeds and mattress toppers can make any mattress much more cushiony and plusher feeling.

Featherbeds with all-feather filling and cotton ticking are fairly difficult to find. However, they're available in twin up to king sizes from Coming Home.

Feather-and-down featherbeds with green-cotton ticking in many sizes are offered by Harmony.

Cotton-covered, feather-and-down-filled featherbeds in a range of sizes are sold by Vermont Country Store Voice of the Mountains, The Company Store, Garnet Hill, Cuddledown of Maine, and JC Penney Catalog. another source for feather-and-down featherbeds with cotton ticking is Eddie Bauer (Home catalog).

Unusual, two-layer featherbeds with cotton-ticking are available from Chambers. The lower level is a blend of feathers and down while the top layer is all down. These come in a range of sizes.

All-organic-cotton mattress toppers are sold by EcoBaby Organics and Heart of Vermont. You can get them in sizes from twin through king. Heart of Vermont also offers a crib size.

Lifekind Bedding Wool Toppers (LifeKind Products) are all-organic, with organic-cotton ticking and organic-wool stuffing. These 3"-thick toppers are made in sizes twin through king. You can simply order from the company's catalog. In addition, from Natural Selections, you can get organic-cotton-covered, organic-wool-stuffed "top mattresses." These come in many sizes, including a crib size. Similar ones are also offered in the Heart of Vermont catalog.

Crown City Mattress makes unbleached cotton-covered/Pure-Grow-Wool-filled "mattress toppers" in a full range of sizes that includes crib. These untreated-wool items (no chemicals added to wool) are 3" thick. You can order directly from them or their dealers, such as Building for Health Materials Center.

Several-inch-thick synthetic-latex/natural-latex mattress toppers are another option. These can be purchased in twin through king sizes from healthyhome.com. Of course, these are not for those with latex allergies.

Encasing Your Featherbed

If possible, you'll want to encase your featherbed to keep it clean longer. Here are some buying sources for you. While both covers and protectors can be used to encase a featherbed, protectors are designed to be more impervious, but they are also usually somewhat more expensive.

Featherbed Covers

Sleeptek Oasis (**Sleeptek Limited**) can create for you organic-cotton featherbed covers in any size you request. You can order directly from the company if you're in Canada. In the U.S., you can order them through **N.E.E.D.S.** and **Furnature**.

You can also get wide untreated fabric and long metal zippers to make your own featherbed covers from **Janice Corporation**.

Crown City Mattress makes The Natural Bedroom line of unbleached-cotton covers for 3"-thick mattress toppers in a range of sizes. They can be ordered from them or their dealers, including **Building for Health Materials Center**.

All-cotton featherbed covers in twin through king can be purchased from **Chambers**. (These are likely commercial-grade materials.)

Featherbed Protectors

Sleeptek Oasis (**Sleeptek Limited**) will sew for you organic-cotton, barrier-cloth featherbed protectors in any size. You can order from the manufacturer if you reside in Canada. If you live in the U.S., you can order from **N.E.E.D.S.** and **Furnature**. By the way, you can also get organic-cotton barrier cloth from them.

You can also purchase from **Janice Corporation** wide, untreated-cotton, barrier cloth fabric and long metal zippers to make your own cover.

Futons

For an increasing number of people, especially college students living off-campus, futons can make good sense. After all, they're far more portable and affordable than conventional mattresses. And, on the right frame, they can be used for seating by day.

Futon Considerations

Futons (also known as *shikibutons*) are thin, cotton-covered mattresses stuffed with cotton batting. They're the traditional bedding in Japan where relatively thin futons are unrolled directly onto the floor for sleeping. In the West, futons are generally placed on wooden frames. Some of these frames are specially designed to convert into sofas (see *Solid Wood Furniture* on page 331).

It should be pointed out that futons can be somewhat cumbersome. The thin, traditional Japanese futons are lightweight and easily rolled up, but the 4"-to-8"-thick Western models are fairly weighty. Most are simply too bulky to wash at home. Therefore, it's important for you to air your futon frequently outdoors in uncontaminated air. It's also highly suggested that you use removable 100%-cotton futon covers or protectors, which can be taken off and laundered regularly. (See *Encasing your Futon* on page 235.)

Cotton Futons

Note: all-cotton futons that are not treated with fire-retardant chemicals will require a doctor's prescription before purchase. Wool, which is natural fire retarding, will not.

Sleeptek Oasis (**Sleeptek Limited**) 100%-organic-cotton futons are made and sold by the maker in Canada. These come in all sizes. In the U.S., you can get them from **Furnature** and **N.E.E.D.S.** Also, organic-cotton futons, in both 3" and 5" thicknesses and in five sizes, can be purchased from **Bio Designs**. A wonderful source for all-organic futons is **Heart of Vermont**. They offer them in 3", 4", 6", and 8" thicknesses, in crib through king sizes. Then, too, **Bio Designs** offers organic-cotton futons in most sizes.

Karen's Natural Products is a dealer for Bright Future futons. These are made with untreated, prewashed, cotton ticking and organic-cotton stuffing. They are available in crib through king sizes.

Green cotton futons in twin and crib sizes are handled by Natural Baby. All-cotton futons with no fire-retarding chemicals and prewashed cotton ticking in two- and four-inch thickness are sold by Allergy Relief Shop, Inc. These come in either twin or full sizes.

Wool and Wool & Cotton Futons

Untreated-wool (wool from free ranging sheep that have had no chemical treatments) futons with organic-cotton covers are made and sold by Heart of Vermont. These come in 3", 4", 6", and 8" thicknesses, in crib through king sizes.

Sleeptek Limited has Sleeptek Oasis 2"-thick organic-cotton/wool futons in any size with organic-cotton ticking. If you're a Canadian, order directly from the manufacturer. In the U.S., order from N.E.E.D.S. or Furnature. The $4^{1}/_{2}$" futons from LifeKind Products have an organic wool core wrapped in organic cotton. The tickings are organic cotton. These, in crib through king sizes, are offered in the company's catalog. Similar ones, in twin to king, can be ordered from EcoBaby Organics. "Futon mattresses," stuffed with 80% organic-cotton and 20% wool (for natural fire-retardancy) in 3" and 6" thicknesses, and in a range of sizes, are sold by Tomorrow's World.

Other Futon Materials

Three- and six-inch-thick futons covered and stuffed with hemp are sold by Tomorrow's World. These come in sizes twin through king.

Encasing Your Futon

Covers and protectors for your futons are a great idea. Generally, the companies that sell futons also handle covers that fit them. In most cases, futon covers and protectors, no matter where you get them, are 100% cotton. Protectors are typically made of a denser fabric than covers, so they tend to make a better barrier to odors and dust mites.

Futon Covers

Sleeptek Oasis (Sleeptek Limited) makes organic-cotton futon covers in any size. Order directly from the company if you're in Canada. In the U.S., order through N.E.E.D.S. and Furnature.

Attractive organic-cotton futon covers, to fit futons of various thicknesses, can be made for you by Heart of Vermont. They also sell wide organic-cotton fabric.

From Janice Corporation, you can order wide, untreated fabric and long metal zippers to make your own. They may also make covers for you.

Karen's Natural Products sells Bright Future prewashed cotton futon covers to fit sizes twin through king, plus crib. Tomorrow's World sells "natural cotton" futon/mattress covers (for 3" and 6" futons) in twin to king.

Futon Protectors

Sleeptek Oasis (Sleeptek Limited) will create for you organic-cotton, barrier-cloth futon protectors in the sizes you need. You can order from the manufacturer, if you're in Canada. If you live in the U.S., order through N.E.E.D.S. and Furnature. They are also sources for organic-cotton barrier cloth by the yard.

From **Janice Corporation**, you can buy wide untreated-cotton, barrier-cloth fabric and long metal zippers to make your own futon protector. This company may also make the protectors for you.

Pillows

Because your head is in direct contact with your pillow for 6-9 hours, it's really wise to choose a pillow that's naturally low in toxicity to help you get healthful, restful sleep. Natural stuffings and tickings are often the best choices.

Tip: To freshen your natural pillows, hang them outdoors in uncontaminated air or place them in your clothes dryer (not buckwheat hulls) for at least 15 minutes. To keep the ticking on your pillows cleaner, use removable, washable pillow covers and protectors. (See *Pillow Protectors* below.)

Cotton Pillows

You should be aware that organic-cotton pillows generally have a strong, grainy smell when first purchased. This smell is from oils and resins originating from crushed cotton seeds. Despite having a natural botanical origin, it can be bothersome to some sensitive people.

Hanging your new cotton pillows outside to air in dry, uncontaminated surroundings (no car exhaust, wood smoke, high pollen counts, etc.) for several days will greatly help to dissipate the natural odor. Another approach is to place the pillows (no more than two at a time) in your clothes dryer on high heat for about thirty minutes. You can keep repeating the drying cycle until the pillows become tolerable. Yet another option is to use pillow protectors made of *barrier cloth* (a special tightly woven cotton made with relatively thick yarns) over your pillows to help seal in odors. (See *Pillow Protectors* on page 239.)

Sleeptek Oasis 100%-organic-cotton pillows (**Sleeptek Limited**), can be ordered in any size. If you're Canadian, order directly from the company. In the U.S., purchase them though **Furnature** and **N.E.E.D.S.** Other all-organic-cotton pillows in many sizes (including crib and travel) are sold by **Natural Selections**. **Heart of Vermont** sells not only all-organic pillows in many sizes, including crib, they sell the batting and ticking kits for standard size pillows to make your own.

Pillows stuffed with 100%-organic-cotton in three sizes can be purchased from **Janice Corporation**. They're also available from **Tomorrow's World**. In addition, you can opt for The Natural Bedroom organic-cotton pillows made by **Crown City Mattress**. They come in standard, queen, king, and travel, and can be ordered from the manufacturer and dealers, including **Building for Health Materials Center**.

Green-cotton ticking is used on the organic-cotton-filled pillows from **Harmony**. These come in two sizes: standard and travel. **Karen's Natural Products** handles standard-size, Bright Future pillows. These are made with organic stuffing and prewashed cotton ticking.

The all-cotton pillows sold by **KB Cotton Pillows, Inc.** have cotton ticking sewn with cotton thread that's been prewashed in baking soda. These come in a range of sizes including travel. The manufacturer notes that these can be washed on a cool cycle and air dried (in the sun, if possible). Other sources for KB Pillows include **Karen's Natural Products, N.E.E.D.S., American Environmental Health Foundation**, and **Priorities**.

A source for Jubilee untreated cotton pillows in three size with prewashed cotton covers (in unscented washing soda) is **Erlander's Natural Products**. These come in three sizes. Cotton pillows with prewashed ticking in many sizes, including European square and baby, can be ordered from **Bio Designs** and **Allergy Relief Shop, Inc.** Furthermore, all-cotton pillows in several sizes are also sold by **Janice Corporation**.

Vermont Country Store Voice of the Mountains is a source for all-cotton pillows in sizes that include "travel." **The Company Store** sells 100%-cotton pillows in standard, queen, king and in a 26"-square European size.

Wool and Wool & Cotton Pillows

Although not as common as cotton-filled pillows, there are also pillows stuffed with wool, and they can be a healthy choices, too.

Sleeptek Oasis (**Sleeptek Limited**) has organic-cotton-covered, wool-filled pillows are available in all sizes. Order directly from the company if you're Canadian. In the U.S., order though **Furnature** and **N.E.E.D.S.** In addition, The Natural Bedroom cotton-ticking-covered, Pure-Grow-Wool-filled pillows are made and sold by **Crown City Mattress**. These come in a very large selection of sizes, including European square and neck. The wool used is a special type that's not been subjected to chemical treatments. These pillows can also be purchased from their dealers, including **Building for Health Materials Center**. And, **Heart of Vermont** offers similar wool pillows with organic-cotton coverings in many sizes, including crib. They also sell wool batting and organic-cotton ticking kits for standard-size pillows—so you can make your own.

Wool-filled pillows with untreated-cotton ticking in three sizes are offered in the **Janice Corporation** catalog. Two sizes, standard and queen, are sold by **Natural Home by Natürlich**. **Real Goods** also has wool pillows covered with 100%-cotton ticking.

Natural Baby offers wool-stuffed pillows in standard and child sizes, with cotton ticking. (Commercial materials are likely used that may or may not have had treatments.) Standard-size wool pillows with hemp-fabric ticking are handled by **Tomorrow's World**.

All-organic pillows, made with all-wool stuffing, or with a wool core and cotton batting surrounding it, are available from **Natural Selections**. These are available in a large range of sizes that includes crib and travel. Similar ones are sold by **EcoBaby Organics**. Theirs come in standard, child, and crib sizes.

Feathers, Feathers & Down, and Down Pillows

For many people natural feather or down-filled pillows can make good pillow choices. However, sometimes these materials are chemically treated to prevent mold or insect damage. These treatments could be intolerable for some sensitive persons, so you'll want to check the manufacturer's labels carefully before purchasing them.

It's a good idea for individuals with dust-mite or bird-dander allergies, who want down and feather pillows, to get those described as "deep washed," or those using other similar terms. This means that a special added cleaning process has been done to remove most surface debris, making them less allergenic. Hypodown, which is apparently innately hypoallergenic, is another option to consider. (See *Syriaca Clusters* on page 190.) Also, make sure to use pillow protectors—especially ones of untreated-, green-, or organic-cotton *barrier cloth*. This type of tightly woven fabric, made with relatively thick yarns, will help to seal out dust and dust mites from contaminating new pillows. They can also be easily removed, laundered regularly, and replaced.

Your should be able to find that local department stores will have feather, feather-and-down, or down pillows. However, if you want to order them by mail, there are several sources available.

Chambers is a source for all-feather-filled pillows with cotton ticking. These pillows come in two sizes, standard and king.

The **JC Penney Catalog**, **L.L. Bean** (Furnishings Catalog), **Coming Home**, and **Garnet Hill** sell feather/down pillows covered with cotton ticking in three sizes. So does **Cuddledown of Maine** and **The Company Store** which, in addition, carries a 26"-square European size. Other sources for feather and down pillows with all-cotton ticking are **Chambers** and **Eddie Bauer** (Home catalog).

Green-cotton ticking covers over goose-down pillows in standard size are offered by **Harmony**.

Chambers sells down pillows with cotton covering fabric in two sizes. **Garnet Hill** and **Linensource** handles cotton-covered, down-filled pillows in several sizes as does **Eddie Bauer** (Home catalog), and **Coming Home**. The **Vermont Country Store Voice of the Mountains** also have these, plus a travel size. On the other hand, **The Company Store** has three common sizes, plus an European square size.

Syriaca Clusters and Hypodown Pillows

Syriaca clusters are a fancy name for mikweed floss. Because of their innate hollow structure, they apparently have the ability to trap many types of allergens found in goose down.

Green-cotton covered, goose-down-and-syriaca-cluster-filled pillows (in standard, queen, and kings sizes) are sold by **Under The Canopy**.

Ogallala Down Company makes Hypodown (mix of syriaca clusters and goose down) pillows with "regular" cotton ticking or unbleached cotton. The last, are called Harvester line pillows. All are available in three popular sizes in several grades. If you can't find the ones you want locally, you can order directly from the manufacturer. Hypodown pillows, with cotton-covering fabric, are also handled by **Priorities**. They're offered in three sizes.

Buckwheat Hull Pillows

Odd-shaped (by American standards), traditional Japanese pillows stuffed with buckwheat hulls are now being seen more frequently. Buckwheat-hull pillows with organic-cotton ticking in standard and neck styles are sold by **Natural Selections**. Organically grown buckwheat-hull pillows with cotton tickings in a 9" x 15" size can be ordered from **Karen's Natural Products**.

Harmony has green-cotton ticking on it's buckwheat-hull pillows. Two sizes are offered, standard and neck. From **Well & Good**, you can get standard-sized buckwheat pillows with unbleached cotton-jersey ticking. Another source for buckwheat pillows with all-cotton covers is **Natural Lifestyle**.

A very unusual pillow is one made with wool, buckwheat, and organic-cotton filling, and covered with organic-cotton ticking . This item is sold by **Harmony** in a 17" x 12" size.

Kapok Pillows

Erlander's Natural Products will make for you their Jubilee brand kapok pillows with prewashed (in unscented washing soda) covers. The sizes they offer include standard, queen, king, baby, and neck. For more on kapok, see *Kapok* on page 190.

Natural-Rubber Latex Pillows

Latex pillows are sometimes suggested particularly for those with dust mite allergies. Apparently, dust mites can't thrive as well in this type of material. However, it has been said that latex foam can become moldy in humid conditions. Another potential problem is that latex odors can be bothersome to some chemically sensitive people. Then, too, those with latex allergies should choose another type of pillow.

However, if you prefer natural-rubber latex pillows, Sleeptek Oasis (**Sleeptek Limited**) has them with an organic-cotton ticking. They can be ordered directly from the manufacturer in any size. If you're Canadian, simply order directly from them. In the U.S., you can get these pillows though **Furnature** and **N.E.E.D.S**.

Pillows made of a combination of natural and synthetic latex are handled by **healthyhome.com**. These come in standard, queen, king, and travel sizes with removable polyester/cotton ticking. This ticking, of course, can be replaced by an all-cotton ticking that you can easily make yourself.

Encasing Your Pillows

In addition to pillow cases, it's also a good idea to purchase pillow protectors. While the pillow ticking itself is usually permanently sewn shut around the stuffing, pillow protectors are commonly zippered. In actual use, they're placed around the pillow with the pillow case going over them. Pillow protectors should be removed and washed regularly, but that doesn't have to be done nearly as often as for the pillow cases, which should be washed weekly.

If you are not overly sensitive or allergic, a lower-cost zippered cover between the pillow's ticking and the slipcase can be an acceptable alternative to a higher-priced protectors. However, protectors are designed to be more impervious to odors and dust mites. So, for very sensitive people, zippered protectors are recommended for pillows because you will be breathing very close to them all night long.

Pillow Covers

Zippered pillow covers, fabricated of organic cotton, in three sizes, are available from **Janice Corporation**. A Canadian firm, **Sleeptek Limited**, custom makes many types of alternative bedding items. If you live in Canada, you can contact them to create Sleeptek Oasis organic-cotton pillow covers in any size you need. If you live in the U.S., you can order them through their distributors: **N.E.E.D.S** or **Furnature**. Other organic-cotton pillow covers, in standard and king, are sold by **American Environmental Health Foundation**.

Green-cotton pillow covers, in three sizes, are sold by **Heart of Vermont**. Standard and child-pillow sizes can also be obtained from **Natural Baby**. A source for untreated, cotton-muslin pillow covers, is **Janice Corporation**. These come in standard, queen, and king. **Janice Corporation** also sells wide, untreated fabric and long zippers, to make your own.

The Natural Bedroom unbleached-cotton-muslin pillow covers come in a huge variety of sizes, including neck roll. They're made and sold by **Crown City Mattress**. Their dealers, such as **Building for Health Materials Center**, can also get them for you.

All-cotton pillow covers, in a variety of sizes, are sold by **Erlander's Natural Products**, **Vermont Country Store Voice of the Mountains**, and **Linensource**. These are probably made with standard materials which may or may not have been treated.

Very unusual flannel pillow covers made with 80% green cotton and 20% linen are available from **Harmony**. These come in several sizes.

Pillow Protectors

Barrier-cloth (tightly woven, thick-yarned cotton) pillow protectors help keep ticking especially clean. They also help keep bothersome pillow odors sealed in, and they help keep dust mites and dust out of the pillow itself. **Sleeptek Limited**, custom makes alternative bedding under their own name. If you live in Canada, you can order directly from them. If you live in the U.S., you can order through **N.E.E.D.S** and **Furnature**. You can also purchase organic barrier cloth by the yard.

Janice Corporation is a supplier of untreated, cotton-barrier-cloth pillow protectors in standard, queen, and king sizes. This same company also sells untreated, cotton barrier cloth by the yard and metal zippers, so you can create your own protectors.

All-cotton, barrier-cloth pillow protectors in various sizes, including infant, can be ordered from **Bio Designs**. Check to see if these are of treated cloth before buying, if that's important to you.

Body Pillows

Body pillows are exactly what they sound like—long, large pillows your whole body can rest on. Some people with physical ailments, as well as pregnant women, use them to adjust their legs and weight for a more comfortable night's sleep.

Organic, all-cotton body pillows are sold by **Heart of Vermont**. And **Crown City Mattress** has a Natural Bedroom brand, 20" x 60" body pillow stuffed with Pure Grow Wool (a special wool that has not been subjected to any chemical treatments) and covered with cotton-muslin ticking and a matching cover. They can also be ordered from it's dealers, which include **Building for Health Materials Center**.

All-cotton, fabric-covered, feather-and-down body pillows can be purchased from **The Company Store** and **Cuddledown of Maine**. These are likely made with commercial-grade materials that may or may not have been treated.

Kapok-filled body pillows with unbleached-cotton covers are sold by **Tomorrow's World**.

Encasing Your Body Pillow

It's important to encase all your pillows, even body pillows. This is especially true for allergic people who should also use protectors as an extra means of controlling allergens.

Body Pillow Covers

Heart of Vermont sell an organic-cotton cover to fit the body pillow it handles. A Canadian firm, **Sleeptek Limited**, custom makes many types of alternative bedding items. If you live in Canada, you can contact them to create a Sleeptek Oasis organic-cotton body pillow cover in any size. If you live in the U.S., you can order through their distributors, **N.E.E.D.S** and **Furnature**.

A source for wide, untreated fabric and long metal zippers, so you can make your own body-pillow covers, is **Janice Corporation**. They may also make covers for you.

All-cotton, body-pillow covers in a range of sizes are sold by **Cuddledown of Maine**. These are likely made with commercial-grade materials that may or may not have been treated in some way.

Body Pillow Protectors

A cotton *barrier-cloth* (tightly woven, thick-yarned cotton fabric) protector will help keep your body pillow cleaner and will provide protection from dust mites. You can get organic-cotton, barrier-cloth protectors custom made for you by **Sleeptek Limited** with the Sleeptek Oasis label. If you live in Canada, you can order directly from them. If you reside in the U.S., you can order through **N.E.E.D.S** or **Furnature**. You can also purchase organic-cotton, barrier cloth by the yard to make your own. For making your own protectors, a supplier of untreated-cotton barrier cloth and long metal zippers is **Janice Corporation**. They may also make protectors for you.

Sheets and Pillowcases

There are more sheet options than ever before. To say the least, it can get somewhat confusing. Here are some descriptions and buying suggestions.

Types of Sheeting

The descriptions below are for a variety of natural-fiber sheeting fabrics that you may come across in stores and catalogs.

Cotton Jersey Knit Sheets

The newest sheeting material is *jersey knit*. This is a fabric that is soft with a inherent *elasticity* (give). It's basically no more than a type of T-shirt material. Jersey knit sheets are often affordable. They're big drawback is that they can snag much easier than woven fabrics.

Cotton Flannel Sheets

Flannel sheeting is loosely woven fabric made with thicker, fluffier threads than other sheeting materials. The result is a fairly lightweight fabric that has good insulating properties. Flannel sheets are often fairly inexpensive, but are usually only available in cooler months.

Cotton Muslin Sheets

Even less costlier are *muslin* sheets. Muslin is woven of still thicker, coarser, cotton yarns, with at least 128 threads per square inch. Although not as soft and smooth as percale, muslin is extremely durable and much more affordable.

Cotton Percale Sheets

Combed-percale refers to the better cotton sheeting fabric available. The finest-quality combed-percale sheets have a thread count of at least 200 per square inch and the threads used are the best available—thin and strong. This kind of thread, and the very tight weaving, results in lightweight sheets with a smooth, soft texture. With at least 180 threads per square inch, *muslin* is slightly coarser, so it's less expensive and not quite as luxurious.

Luxury Cotton Sheets

Recently there has been a trend toward prestige cotton sheets. These often use high grade cottons, such as Egyptian cotton, which has longer fibers. This allows for a finer textured thread to be woven. In particular, Egyptian cotton comes in several grades, with Giza 75 as the very best.

Besides the type of cotton, prestige level sheeting usually has a very high thread count, often 250 threads per square inch and up. Sometimes, the type of weaving used is also of premiere quality. For example, cotton *damask* sheeting is now seen in a number of stores and catalogs. This is a durable, and reversible, but extravagant, sheeting material, that has a figure-pattern woven into the design. It's sometimes termed *Jacquard weaving*. Often, you'll find that luxury cotton sheets have been imported from Europe. They have not been treated for wrinkle resistance, although other treatments are common—such as bleaching, dying, sizing, etc. (See *Common Bedding Treatments* on page 225.)

Linen Sheets

Linen sheets are very rare and very expensive. It has a beautiful natural sheen and is slightly coarse. It makes excellent sheets because its stronger and cooler than cotton. Because of this, if you do find linen sheets, it's usually during warmer seasons.

Silk Sheets

Another luxury sheeting fabric is *washable silk*. Silk fabric is exceptionally durable and has the ability to feel cool in summer and warm in winter. It also can absorb body moisture without feeling clammy itself.

Sheet and Pillowcase Buying Sources

It should be mentioned that it's not unusual for specialty bedding catalogs to offer free (or at very low cost) samples of fabrics used in the sheets they sell. Simply contact the company to request them.

Tip: To get the most wear for your money, you might consider purchasing only flat sheets, rather than sets with both flat and fitted sheets. Flat sheets can be used in either the top or bottom bed-making position. By rotating them, your sheets will be less likely to acquire the typical wear patterns that often occur in the centers of fitted sheets, which are always used in the bottom position. Also, the corners of flat sheets are less likely to rip than those of fitted sheets whose seams must be continually stretched.

Cotton Jersey Knit Sheet Sources

T-shirt-soft sheets of cotton jersey knit are becoming a popular choice these days. Organic-cotton, jersey-knit sheets and pillow cases, in twin through king sizes, can be ordered from **EcoBaby Organics** and **Fisher Henney Naturals**. Both organic-cotton and untreated-cotton jersey-knit sheet sets, can be found in the **Harmony** catalog. Untreated, jersey-knit sheets and pillowcases, in a range of sizes, are also available from **Janice Corporation**, and **Heart of Vermont** has untreated all-cotton jersey-knit sheets and pillowcases to fit cribs, as well as twin through king-size beds. They also make custom sheets to order.

All-cotton, jersey-knit pillow cases and sheets in twin through king sizes are handled by **Domestications**, **The Company Store**, **Cuddledown of Maine**, **Real Goods**, and **Coming Home**. Other sources include **Eddie Bauer** (Home catalog), **L.L. Bean** (Furnishings Catalog), and the **JC Penney Catalog**. In addition, **Garnet Hill** has them in those sizes, plus a crib size.

One Step Ahead has crib-size and bassinet-size jersey sheets and **Karen's Natural Products**, **Chock's**, and **Natural Baby** has just the crib size.

Cotton Flannel Sheet Sources

Another healthy cotton-sheet option to consider is flannel. Just be aware that when choosing them, matching pillowcases are sometimes offered, sometimes not.

Organic-cotton flannel sheets and pillow cases for twin through king sizes, as well as cradle and crib, can be ordered from **EcoBaby Organics**. Foxfibre Colorganic (organic cotton with innate natural coloring) flannel sheets and pillowcases can be purchased from **Heart of Vermont**. These are offered in twin through king, plus crib sizes. You can also order custom sizes, if you need them.

Green-cotton flannel sheet and pillowcase sets in a range of sizes are sold by **Harmony**. Full, queen, and king sizes are sold by **Under The Canopy**.

Untreated flannel sheet/pillowcase sets in a range of sizes are offered by **Janice Corporation**. Also, from **Well & Good**, you can get untreated flannel sheets in twin through king, and pillowcases in standard and king.

Cotton-flannel sheets in twin through king are sold by **Erlander's Natural Products**, **Vermont Country Store Voice of the Mountains** and JC Penney Catalog. Cotton-flannel sheets and matching pillow cases in twin through king are handled by **L.L. Bean** (Furnishings Catalog) and **Eddie Bauer** (Home catalog). Cotton-flannel sheets and pillow cases, in twin through king sizes plus crib, can be ordered from **Garnet Hill**. From **One Step Ahead**, you can get flannel crib and bassinet sheets. Flannel sheets are commonly available during the fall and winter seasons in department stores.

Unusual, 80%-green-cotton, 20%-linen sheet sets in all sizes, are sold by **Harmony**.

Cotton Percale and Muslin Sheet Sources

Wonderful organic-cotton sheets and pillowcases in many sizes are sold by **Janice Corporation, Building for Health Materials Center, Harmony**, and **Under The Canopy**. Other sources include **Coming Home, healthyhome.com, Real Goods**, and **Well & Good**. Organic-cotton sheets and pillow cases in many sizes, including crib, can be purchased from **Natural Selections** and **LifeKind Products**. (Lifekinds' are usually quite affordable.)

Organic-cotton chambray sheets to fit cribs, cradles, and grown-up beds (twin through king) are sold by **EcoBaby Organics**. Organic-cotton crib sheets can also be ordered from **Tomorrow's World**. Then, too, **Crown City Mattress** has The Natural Bedroom line of organic-cotton crib sheets and pillowcases.

Green-cotton sheet sets for twin through queen, plus fitted crib sheets, as well as standard pillowcases, are sold by **Karen's Natural Products**.

Untreated, unbleached, 230-count (threads per square inch) cotton sheets and pillow cases in a range of sizes are handled by **Natural Home by Natürlich**. Untreated, natural-color cotton 200-count sheets and pillowcases in twin through king sizes, are sold by **Allergy Relief Shop, Inc.** From **Harmony** and **Priorities**, you can get untreated-cotton sheets too, in sizes twin through king.

Erlander's Natural Products handles Wamsutta untreated white sheets and pillowcases in several sizes, as does **The Vermont Country Store Voice of the Mountains**. And **Janice Corporation** sells both untreated, white Wamsutta sheets and pillowcases, as well as Martex untreated, natural-grown, natural-color cotton, sheet/pillowcase sets. You should also know that you can purchase from **Janice Corporation**, untreated fabric wide enough to make your sheets. They also sell the elastic you'll need for fitted sheets.

There are several specialty bedding catalogs which sell cotton-percale sheets and pillowcases, which, according to company representatives, haven't been specially treated for wrinkle-resistance. However, these same representatives want buyers to know that, despite this, these sheets have probably undergone other treatments, such as bleaching, dying, and sizing. (See, *Common Bedding Treatments* on page 225.) **The Company Store, Chambers, Eddie Bauer** (Home catalog), and **Cuddledown of Maine** have such "untreated" sheets and pillowcases for twin through king-size beds. So does **Garnet Hill**, which, in addition, offers them in crib size. **One Step Ahead** has both crib- and bassinet-sized cotton sheets.

A source for cotton sheets (and pillow cases) in twin through king that may or may not have wrinkle-resisting treatments include **Linensource**. This company's spokesperson said that "treatments would vary with the manufacturer." Unfortunately, their order takers do not have access to this particular information.

Regular, commercial-grade, treated-cotton sheets and pillowcases can usually be purchased locally. Two mail-order sources that offer a good selection in most sizes, (sometimes baby, too) include **JC Penney Catalog** and **L.L. Bean** (Furnishings Catalog). From **Gohn Bros.** you can get crib sheets.

Luxury Cotton Sheet Sources

A number of bedding specialty catalogs now have luxury-cotton sheets and pillow cases. These high-thread-count (per square inch) items are often made of Egyptian cotton. (For more information, see *Luxury Cotton Sheets* on page 241.)

Lifekind organic-cotton damask sheet sets (**LifeKind Products**) are special. These beautiful bedding items are available in twin through king, as well as crib sizes. Order directly from the company's catalog. Similar sheets and pillow cases in popular sizes are handled by **Harmony.**

Green, Egyptian-cotton sheets, as well as pillowcases, in several sizes, can be ordered from **Harmony.** Untreated, 100% Egyptian-cotton sheet sets in twin through king are handled by **Bio Designs.**

Garnet Hill, Chambers, Cuddledown of Maine, and **The Company Store** have many kinds of premium quality sheets in twin through king, plus pillowcases. These particular companies have noted that while these items have probably undergone various treatments during milling and manufacturing, they've not undergone any wrinkle-resisting treatments.

Barrier Cloth Sheet Sources

Sleeptek Oasis (**Sleeptek Limited**) has organic-cotton barrier cloth by the yard. If you're Canadian, you can order Sleeptek Oasis products from the manufacturer. If you're living in the U.S., order from **N.E.E.D.S.** and **Furnature.** With the correct yardage, you can make your own sheets.

Untreated, 100%-cotton *barrier-cloth* fitted sheets in a full range of sizes including crib, plus a 120" x 90" flat sheet, can be ordered from **Janice Corporation.** (Barrier cloth uses relatively thick yarns that are tightly woven to seal in mattress odors and seal out dust and microorganisms.) By the way, you can also buy untreated-cotton barrier cloth by the yard from **Janice Corporation** to make your own sheets.

Silk Sheet Sources

Silk sheeting is, of course, a true luxury. You can sometimes find it sold locally in a few very fine stores. Mail-order sources for washable-silk sheets and pillowcases in a range of sizes include **Cuddledown of Maine, Well & Good,** and **Janice Corporation.** All-silk pillowcases in standard and king are sold by **Chambers.**

Linen Sheet Sources

Linen sheets are just as rare as silk ones, so their cost can be extremely high. Check fine linen shops and department stores locally. Mail-order sources for 100%-linen sheets and pillowcases in twin through king are **Chambers** and **Cuddledown of Maine.**

Blankets

Ideally, your blankets should be comfortable, but also tolerable and easy to care for. Individuals with dust-mite allergies, in particular, will definitely want blankets to be washable and dryable at home.

Because many blankets can be expensive, choose them carefully and store them properly when not in use. However, refrain from placing them in cedar chests, especially if you are a sensitive person. Cedar chests can transfer potentially bothersome cedar odors into your blankets. Surprisingly, this odor apparently has little or no effect at deterring clothing moths. (See *Clothing Moths* on page 406.)

Acrylic and Electric-Blanket Concerns

Acrylic blankets are soft, machine-washable, and machine-dryable. They're also inexpensive and clothing moths won't damage them. It's not surprising then that they've almost replaced natural-fiber blankets. However, blankets made of acrylic do have serious drawbacks—they can often lose their attractive initial appearance after only a few launderings, and worse, they have the potential to emit minor synthetic chemical odors from the acrylic fibers themselves. Of course, these blankets are also made from nonrenewable resources, and they not biodegradable.

Electric blankets, which tend to be made of acrylic, are popular in very cold climates. However, they have an additional problem related to their embedded wiring. In older electric blankets, this wiring can produce unacceptably strong electromagnetic fields (EMFs) that can have negative health effects (see *Chapter 27: Dealing With Electromagnetic Fields*). Fortunately, newer electric blankets are wired in special patterns designed to counter most—but not all—of these electromagnetic fields.

However, even with reduced EMFs, warming up an acrylic blanket has the potential to increase the outgassing rate of odors originating from the acrylic fibers. Also, many electric blankets require special handling to clean them, so cleaning may not be done regularly. (Note: Dry cleaning may damage wiring in some blankets.) Because of the negative health issues associated with acrylic and electric blankets, you are strongly urged to use natural-fiber alternatives.

Cotton Blankets

Several types of 100%-cotton blankets are available today. Below are several categories.

Cotton Flannel Blankets

Thick, 100%-cotton flannel blankets are bedding options you might consider. Hospitals often use such blankets for their patients because they're relatively inexpensive, lightweight, comfortable, and they're machine-washable and dryable. It should be mentioned, as a note of caution, that fire-retardant chemicals may have been applied to certain flannel blankets to meet hospital requirements. These treatments could be bothersome to sensitive people

Fortunately, however, because flannel blankets have become more popular lately, ones manufactured strictly for home use are much more likely to be the ones you'll come across in the marketplace these days. Therefore, fire-retarding treatments are probably less likely to have been applied to them. Yet, it's still is a good idea, when buying flannel blankets, to read the manufacturer's tags and literature carefully.

Mail-order companies handling untreated, unbleached, flannel blankets in several sizes include **Janice Corporation** and **Priorities**. **B. Coole Designs** handles unbleached, lightweight flannels in a full size.

Vermont Country Store Voice of the Mountains, Coming Home, and **Cuddledown of Maine** all handle cotton-flannel blankets in a range of sizes. **Erlander's Natural Products**

carries a twin size. From **Coming Home** and **L.L. Bean** (Furnishings Catalog), you can order flannel baby blankets, and from **Karen's Natural Products**, you can get 36" x 50" flannel blankets.

Thermal, Woven, and Chenille Cotton Blankets

Natural-fiber thermal, woven, and chenille blankets can also be good choices, with thermals being among the most common. Thermal all-cotton blankets are woven in a specially designed open-weave pattern that is designed to trap air. Trapped air in these blankets functions as an effective insulation. Most thermal-cotton blankets are machine-washable, and many are machine-dryable, though some suggest line-drying only. One unfortunate characteristic of thermal blankets is their tendency to stretch out of shape.

Green-cotton thermal blankets are sold through **Harmony** in twin through king sizes. Unbleached, 100%-cotton thermals are sometimes available from **B. Coole Designs**.

Catalog sources for all-cotton thermal blankets (in a range of sizes) include **Erlander's Natural Products**, **Allergy Relief Shop, Inc.**, **American Environmental Health Foundation**, and **Janice Corporation**. Other places to get them include **Coming Home**, **Cuddledown of Maine**, and **The Company Store**. Still more sources are **JC Penney Catalog**, and **L.L. Bean** (Furnishings Catalog). **Gohn Bros.** sells them in full and queen sizes only. Of course, they're often sold in local department stores, and in many discount stores too.

In addition, there are other attractive types of cotton blankets to consider. A beautiful, organic-cotton, knit blanket in a 54" x 63" size is carried by **Fisher Henney Naturals**. From **Under The Canopy**, you can get several types of organic- and green-cotton woven blankets in queen and king sizes. Unbleached, undyed cotton blankets in twin, queen, and king sizes can be purchased from **Well & Good**. And **Harmony** has natural-ecru and green-cotton blankets with a color-grown hue, in several sizes. Particularly attractive are their chenille blankets.

Finely woven cotton blankets in twin through king sizes are sold by **Heart of Vermont**. In twin and full sizes, you can get them from **American Environmental Health Foundation**. All-cotton woven blankets in limited sizes are sold by **B. Coole Designs**.

Attractive, woven (some chenille), 100%-cotton blankets in twin through king size can be ordered from **Chambers**, **Garnet Hill**, **Cuddledown of Maine**, and **Linensource**. Other sources are **Coming Home**, and **Eddie Bauer** (Home catalog). **Chock's** carries crib sizes.

An usual cotton/linen blend blanket in three sizes can be ordered from **Chambers**.

Cotton Baby and Receiving and Blankets

Both all-organic-cotton baby-sized, and receiving, blankets are handled by **Karen's Natural Products**. Also, organic-cotton baby blankets are sold by **Harmony**, **Tomorrow's World**, **Earthlings**, **LifeKind Products**, and **Well & Good**. Sleeptek Oasis (**Sleeptek Limited**) organic-cotton receiving blankets are sold by the maker in Canada and by their distributors, **N.E.E.D.S.** and **Furnature** in the U.S. Attractive, color-grown, organic-cotton receiving blankets can be found in the **Xanomi** catalog.

EcoBaby Organics sells organic-cotton receiving blankets and "regular" commercial-grade cotton baby blankets. **B. Coole Designs** handles unbleached light-weight flannels in crib and receiving sizes.

All-cotton baby blankets are available from **Decent Exposures**, **One Step Ahead**, and **The Company Store**. In addition, **One Step Ahead** and **Chock's** have all-cotton receiving blankets. **Natural Baby** carries several cotton crib and receiving blankets. One that's particularly interesting is a crib size blanket that is constructed of silk with a cotton-flannel backing layer.

Wool and Wool-Blend Blankets

All-wool blankets have always been popular. This isn't surprising; wool blankets are warm, comfortable, attractive, and long-lasting.

Wool Blanket Considerations

Today, wool blankets are still relatively easy to find, but they've become quite expensive. Popular styles now available include trader stripes (blankets like these were originally exchanged for furs at frontier trading posts), plaids, and solid colors. However, there are two major drawbacks to wool blankets. First of all, they need to be protected from moth damage and, second, they are often tagged "dry-clean only."

Some manufacturers attempt to prevent moth damage by chemically treating their blankets with moth-repellent chemicals. Unfortunately, this "helpful" treatment may prove intolerable to sensitive individuals, so you'll want to check the manufacturers' tag or catalog description, or ask a company representative, before purchasing *any* new wool blanket to determine if mothproofing treatments have been applied. Then make an informed decision. Tip: For effective, non-toxic, moth-damage prevention, the key is proper storage. Items must be clean and stored in well-sealed containers or bags.

If your wool blanket's care label says, "dry clean only," ask your professional cleaner if they offer a specialty wet-cleaning alternative procedure that won't use solvents. Also, take care to request that he or she not add mothproofing chemicals. (Some dry cleaners routinely mothproof wool items as a service to their customers.) If you have no choice but to have your blankets dry-cleaned with solvents, as soon as you bring them home, air them outdoors in uncontaminated surroundings to eliminate as much of the residual solvent odor as possible (For more, see *Is Dry Cleaning A Problem?* on page 196).

Wool and Wool-Blend Blanket Buying Sources

It's generally not too difficult to find wool blankets locally; most major department stores handle them. However, if you prefer mail-ordering them, **Heart of Vermont** has undyed, non-mothproofed woolen blankets in three size.

Note: For all the blankets listed below, check before ordering to see if moth proofing compounds have been added. **Harmony** sells a number of wool blankets in several sizes and styles. In **The Company Store, Garnet Hill, Chambers,** and **The Vermont Country Store Voice of the Mountains** catalogs, you can find a number of wool blanket styles in sizes twin through king, some of which are washable. The **JC Penney Catalog** and **Eddie Bauer** (Home catalog) are other sources for wool blankets in a range of sizes.

Wool trader-stripe blankets, and other styles, are sold by **L.L. Bean** (Furnishings Catalog) in several sizes. They also sell 95%-wool/5%-silk blankets. **Gohn Bros.** has wool trader-stripe blankets in full and king sizes. **Casco Bay Wool Works** has wool/nylon blankets.

Of course, more luxurious wool blankets are another option. From **Harmony**, you can get a 60%-cashmere, 40%-wool blanket in full, queen, and king sizes. These are said to have no chemicals added to them, except a small amount of low impact dye. From **Coming Home**, you can order washable-wool and merino-wool blankets in twin through king sizes.

Long-hair-alpaca blankets in twin, full/queen, and baby size can be ordered from **Peruvian Connection**. Wool/alpaca as well as cashmere/angora/wool blankets in twin, full/queen, and king are sold by **Chambers**. Luxurious cashmere blankets can be bought from **Cuddledown of Maine**. These come in two sizes—full/queen and king.

Down Blankets

Down-filled, cotton-covered quilted blankets in a range of sizes are sold by **Vermont Country Store Voice of the Mountains** and **Cuddledown of Maine**.

Comforters

Comforters have really become popular in the last few years. They're not only insulating, they don't require a bedspread over them to make your bed look "finished." Just be sure you understand what you're getting when you purchase one.

Comforter Considerations

Comforters made of natural fibers and natural stuffing make for good, healthy alternatives to blankets for most people. Comforters are lightweight, attractive, and warm. They are available in different grades, weights, and *baffle styles* (quilt patterns) Although nearly all bedding departments and shops will have synthetic-fabric, polyester-filled versions, natural-fiber comforters are again becoming more popular. So, you may be able to find them as well, particularly feather and down comforters.

By the way, sometimes you'll see comforters called *duvets*. This can be confusing because various companies use "duvet" to mean either a standard comforter, a special light-weight comforter, or a comforter cover. Still others refer to duvets as a set that includes a comforter cover, shams, and a bed skirt. So, be careful when ordering.

To properly clean your natural-fiber-and-stuffing comforters, be sure to follow the care or instruction tags that came with them. If possible, when buying them, choose comforters that are washable, so you won't have to be exposed to dry-cleaning-solvent odors whenever they need to be cleaned. To help minimize the frequency for cleaning, consider using washable untreated-cotton comforter covers or protectors. (See *Encasing your Comforter* on page 250.) To freshen your comforters between cleanings, hang them outdoors in uncontaminated air.

If, in time, you need your down comforter reconditioned or repaired, you may be able to find a company locally to do this for you. If not, you can have **Cuddledown of Maine** do the work, either with their materials, or yours.

Cotton Comforters

All-organic, 100%-cotton Sleeptek Oasis comforters in any size you want, are made by **Sleeptek Limited**. If you're Canadian, order directly from them. If you live in the U.S., you can order from **Furnature** and **N.E.E.D.S.** Comforters in several sizes, including crib, made entirely of organic cotton, are offered by **Heart of Vermont**. Organic-cotton crib comforters can be purchased from **EcoBaby Organics**. **Harmony** handles cotton comforters with green-cotton covers in three sizes. Untreated-cotton ticking is used on the 100%-cotton-filled comforters (in three sizes) that are sold by **Janice Corporation**. One-hundred-percent "natural-cotton" comforters in a range of sizes are sold by **Tomorrow's World**.

Wool and Wool & Cotton Comforters

All-organic, cotton-covered Sleeptek Oasis comforters that are filled with wool or cotton and wool, in any size you want, are created by **Sleeptek Limited**. If you're Canadian, order directly from them. If you live in the U.S., you can purchase them from **Furnature** and **N.E.E.D.S.** Comforters with organic-cotton ticking and organic-wool filling in twin through king sizes, are available from **EcoBaby Organics**. Similar ones, made for crib to king-sized beds, are available from **Natural Selections**.

Comforters filled with untreated-wool and covered with untreated-cotton ticking, in a full range of sizes including crib, are available from **Natural Home by Natürlich**.

The Natural Bedroom comforters (**Crown City Mattress**) are made with Pure Grow Wool (a special type of untreated wool) with unbleached-cotton ticking in sizes twin through king, plus crib. They're sold by the manufacturer and its dealers such as **Building for Health Materials Center**.

Comforters made of organic-cotton ticking with chemical-free wool, as well as green-cotton ticking with standard wool, are two choices sold by **Harmony**. These comforters come in three sizes. **Heart of Vermont** sells organic-cotton ticking with chemical-free, wool-filled comforters in several sizes including crib.

Merino wool comforters, with untreated all-cotton covers, can be purchased from **Janice Corporation**. These are sold in twin, full/queen, and king sizes. From **Natural Baby**, you can get a 36" x 42" wool comforter with unbleached-cotton-muslin ticking. Wool-filled, cotton-covered, crib-size comforters are sold by **Tomorrow's World**

Feather & Down Comforters

Of all the choices available, comforters filled with pure down are generally considered some of the warmest. They're also usually the most expensive. However, it is possible that feathers and down may have been treated with chemicals to discourage insect or microbial infestations (see *Feathers and Down* page 191). This can become a problem for some sensitive individuals.

Those with dust-mite allergies or allergies to dander, will want to get down and feather products that have been described as "deep washed," or similar terms, which is an intensive cleaning process which removes dust. Another suggestion is to use a comforter protector, especially if you can get one of untreated cotton *barrier cloth*. This tightly woven, thick-yarned fabric will guard against dust-mite infiltration, and it can be easily removed, laundered, and replaced. By the way, Hypodown, which is apparently innately hypoallergenic, is another option to consider.

Comforters with green-cotton ticking and goose-down filling are offered by **Harmony** in several sizes. Goose-down comforters with untreated-cotton ticking, in three sizes, are sold by **Janice Corporation**.

Goose down comforters with cotton ticking in several sizes, can be ordered from **Garnet Hill**, **Cuddledown of Maine**, **Eddie Bauer** (Home catalog), **L.L. Bean** (Furnishings Catalog), and **Linensource**. Light weight "duvets," as well as heavier comforters, are sold by **Chambers** in three sizes.

Duck-down comforters (twin through king size and crib sizes), with cotton ticking, are available from **Cuddledown of Maine**. All-cotton ticking, or a silk/cotton-blend ticking, are options for the covering fabric on the goose-down comforters from **The Company Store**. These are available in twin through king sizes.

Syriaca Cluster and Hypodown Comforters

Syriaca clusters are mikweed floss. These apparently have the ability to trap many allergens found in goose down. (See *Syriaca Clusters and Hypodown* on page 190.)

Green-cotton ticking is used with goose-down-and-syriaca-cluster-filled comforters sold by **Under The Canopy**. They're offered in one size: queen/king.

Ogallala Hypodown comforters (**Ogallala Down Co.**) are ticked with 100%-cotton fabric and stuffed with a combination of white goose down and syriaca clusters. Twin, queen, and king sizes are offered in several quality grades and weights. Especially nice is their Harvester line, which is covered with unbleached cotton ticking. You can order these directly from the company, if you're unable to find what you want locally.

The Harvester line with unbleached ticking is also available from **Bio Designs** in twin through king sizes. Other sources for various types of Ogallala Hypodown comforters in several sizes are **Comfort House** and **Priorities**.

Silk Comforters

All-silk (ticking and stuffing) makes for a luxurious comforter. They're extremely light weight, but have great insulating properties. All-silk comforters in a range of sizes are sold by **Janice Corporation**. All-silk duvets in three sizes are handled by **Chambers**. Note: Silk comforters are usually not washable.

Encasing your Comforter

All-natural comforters can be expensive. To help protect your investment, you should encase them in washable, 100%-cotton comforter covers or protectors. These are designed to be easily removed for regular launderings, so you don't need to clean the comforters themselves as often. Barrier-cloth protectors, in particular, will guard against dust and dust-mite contamination.

Comforter Covers

Very attractive organic-cotton comforter covers in damask cotton are sold by **Harmony**. These come three sizes, plus shams. From **Heart of Vermont**, you can get organic-cotton comforter covers for twin, full/queen, king, and crib beds. These come in your choice of two fabrics: chambray or flannel. From **EcoBaby Organics**, you can order organic-cotton comforter covers to fit twin to king-size comforters. These are also sold by **Natural Selections** who, in addition, offers a crib size.

Sleeptek Oasis comforter covers of organic-cotton fabric, are manufactured by **Sleeptek Limited**. They can be made in any size you request. If you live in Canada, order directly from them. If you live in the U.S., order from **N.E.E.D.S** or **Furnature**.

Lifekind organic-cotton comforter covers and shams (**LifeKind Products**) are offered in a full range of sizes that includes crib. These come in either percale or an attractive damask fabric. Order directly from the company's catalog. Organic, 100%-cotton comforter covers in twin through king (plus shams) are offered by **Under The Canopy** and **Coming Home**.

Untreated, naturally colored cotton comforter covers in 3 sizes, plus shams, are sold by **Allergy Relief Shop, Inc.** and **Harmony**.

The Natural Bedroom comforter covers (duvets) (**Crown City Mattress**) come in several fabrics (organic cotton is one choice) in a range of sizes, including crib. Also available are matching shams. These all can be ordered directly from the maker, or its dealers. One is **Building for Health Materials Center**.

Green-cotton comforter covers in full/queen and king, plus standard shams are handled by **Under The Canopy**. And **Natural Home by Natürlich** sells unbleached, untreated, cotton comforter covers in sizes from twin to king. Custom-made, untreated-cotton comforter covers may be available from **Janice Corporation**. By the way, you can also purchase untreated, wide cotton fabric and long metal zippers from them to make your own cover.

All-cotton comforter covers in twin, or full/queen can be ordered from **Garnet Hill**. From **Linensource** and **Cuddledown of Maine**, you can get 100%-cotton comforter covers in twin through king size. All-cotton covers in several sizes, and matching shams, can be ordered from **L.L. Bean** (Furnishings Catalog), **Coming Home**, and **Chambers**, and all-cotton crib comforters can be ordered from **The Company Store**.

From **Natural Baby**, you can get a colorful flannel comforter cover to fit their 36" x 42" comforters. Cotton stretch-terry comforter covers, in sizes to fit most comforters, are handled by **Priorities**. Unusual, ethnic-inspired cotton comforter covers, in twin and queen sizes, are handled by **Marketplace: Handwork of India**.

A beautiful, 100%-linen comforter cover, offered in a range of sizes, is sold by **Cuddledown of Maine** and **Crate & Barrel**. Also available, are matching shams in several sizes. Eighty-percent-green-cotton/20%-linen-flannel comforter covers in several sizes, can be ordered from **Harmony**. Comforter covers in three different sizes, and shams, all made of a linen/cotton blend, can be ordered from **Well & Good**.

For a luxurious look, all-silk comforter covers in twin through king sizes (with matching shams in standard, king, and European square), can be bought from **Cuddledown of Maine**.

Comforter Protectors

Sleeptek Oasis organic-cotton, barrier-cloth comforter covers, in any size you need, can made by made for you by **Sleeptek Limited**. If you're Canadian, you can order directly from them. In the U.S., you can order from **N.E.E.D.S** or **Furnature**. You can also purchase organic-cotton barrier cloth by the yard from each of these companies.

Janice Corporation sells untreated-cotton barrier cloth and long metal zippers, so you can make your own comforter covers. They may also make them for you.

Comforter Storage Bags

Heart of Vermont has untreated, 100%-cotton comforter storage bags in two sizes. All-cotton comforter storage bags, in a range of sizes, are sold by **Cuddledown of Maine**.

Quilts

Few bedding items are more appealing than a beautiful quilt. However, there are some things you need to keep in mind.

Quilt Considerations

The quilts produced in recent decades are often made with polyester/cotton coverings, although a few are still made with all-cotton coverings. Many of these new quilt coverings have been chemically treated for wrinkle-resistance and/or stain-resistance. Many of the quilts on the market, no matter what the coverings are made of, are filled with polyester, rather than cotton, batting. This is because polyester batting is apparently better at resisting balling, bunching, and flattening, and it's usually less expensive than cotton batting.

Therefore, unless you commission someone to make a quilt for you, or you make it yourself, it can be difficult to find a new quilt made of untreated 100% cotton—both inside and out.

Another approach to acquiring an all-cotton quilt is to buy an older (pre-1960) quilt. Unfortunately, older quilts may be contaminated with perfume, tobacco, mildew, or scents from air fresheners and detergents. They also may retain odors from previous owners' soaps and shampoos. If you are a sensitive person, any or all of these odors can be very bothersome. However, if a quilt isn't heavily saturated, airing it outdoors in the shade can often help. Of course, be sure the air is fresh and clean. Note: it's important not to expose valuable antique quilts to the sun; exposure to ultraviolet light could damage dyes or fibers.

Tip: If you're allergic to dust mites, you may want to encase your quilts. (See *Quilt Covers & Protectors* on page 252.)

Quilt Buying Sources

Untreated cotton fabric is used to cover the quilts available from **Janice Corporation**. These are, actually, thinner versions of their comforters and they come in three sizes. You also have your choice of goose down, wool, or cotton filling.

All-cotton quilts, in crib through queen sizes, can be ordered from **Karen's Natural Products**. Cotton quilts (usually with matching shams available), in twin through king sizes, can be bought from **Coming Home**, **JC Penney Catalog**, and **Eddie Bauer** (Home catalog). Other sources are **Linensource**, **Chambers**, **L.L. Bean** (Furnishings Catalog), and **Crate & Barrel**. Other sources that sell crib sizes, are **Garnet Hill**, **Cuddledown of Maine**, and **The Company Store**.

Quilt Covers and Protectors

Despite covering their attractive designs, it's often a good idea to protect your quilts with cases. By using ones of cotton barrier cloth, you'll not only reduce the need for washing, but seal-in any odors, and seal-out dust and dust mites.

Quilt Covers

Sleeptek Oasis organic-cotton quilt covers in any size can made for you by **Sleeptek Limited**. In the U.S., you can order through **N.E.E.D.S** and **Furnature**. If you're Canadian, you can order directly from the manufacturer.

You can buy from **Janice Corporation** wide, untreated, cotton fabric and long metal zippers to make your own quilt cover. Custom-made, untreated-cotton quilt covers may be available from them as well.

Quilt Protectors

You can order Sleeptek Oasis' (**Sleeptek Limited**) custom-made, organic-cotton, barrier-cloth quilt covers in any size. If you reside in Canada, order directly from the company. If you live in the U.S., order through **N.E.E.D.S** or **Furnature**. You can also get organic-cotton barrier cloth by the yard.

Untreated-cotton barrier cloth is sold by **Janice Corporation**, which also sells the appropriate length metal zippers you'll need if you want to make your own. It may be that they'll also make the ones you need for you.

Coverlets and Matelasses

All-cotton coverlets, including *matelasses* (coverlets with a double-woven knit), have become more popular lately. Generally, a bedskirt or ruffle is used with them.

Under The Canopy sells both organic- and green-cotton coverlets in queen and king sizes. Coverlets, made with green-cotton yarns, and dyed with low-impact dyes, are sold by **Harmony**. These come in a range of sizes with shams available.

Cuddledown of Maine has all-cotton, woven coverlets in traditional patterns is . These come in several sizes. Coming Home has a good collection of matelasses and shams in twin through king sizes as does Eddie Bauer (Home catalog).

Bed skirts and Dust Ruffles

Bedskirts of organic cotton to fit beds twin through king size are available from Coming Home. The Natural Bedroom crib skirts (Crown City Mattress) are made of an attractive, organic-cotton fabric. They can be ordered directly from the manufacturer, or its dealers such as Building for Health Materials Center. In addition, Under The Canopy has organic-cotton dust ruffles in queen and king sizes.

All-cotton bedskirts in many sizes can be purchased from Garnet Hill, Chambers, and Cuddledown of Maine. Another source is Coming Home.

Linen bedskirts in a range of sizes are handled by Cuddledown of Maine. From Linensource you can get 100%-linen bedskirts in twin through king sizes, and matching shams, in standard, king, and European square (26" x 26").

Bedspreads

Of course, bedspreads are old standbys for bed toppings. But, don't buy one just for its good looks—it must be healthy for you, too.

Bedspread Considerations

Bedspreads these days seem to becoming more and more elaborate. As with most modern bedding, they are often made almost exclusively of chemically treated synthetic materials. Some are washable, but others require dry cleaning. Unfortunately, dry cleaning is often intolerable to sensitive individuals (see *Is Dry Cleaning a Problem?* on page 196). Although they are relatively few and far between, 100%-natural-fiber bedspreads are still possible to find.

From a health standpoint, washable, untreated, all-cotton construction is an ideal choice for bedspreads. Corduroy, cording, woven plaid, print, and tufted chenille are a just a few of the 100%-cotton bedspread styles currently available. Of these, corduroy and cording spreads are particularly tough and durable. Prints and woven spreads, which come in so many colors and styles, can be pleasing to a wide range of personal preferences. Depending on the pattern, tufted-chenille spreads can appeal to traditional, colonial, or contemporary tastes.

To find washable, 100%-cotton bedspreads, especially in tufted chenille, you should check your local department stores. If you'd like woven, hand-printed, or batik styles at a reasonable cost, these can sometimes be found in import shops.

Tip: Between washings you can occasionally tumble your bedspreads in a warm or hot dryer for about fifteen minutes. This will help to remove light surface dust.

Bedspread Buying Sources

You can get custom-made bedspreads in your choice of two styles from Homespun Fabrics & Draperies. These are made in a range of sizes from any of their formaldehyde-free, 10'-wide, attractively textured fabrics. If you prefer, you can buy the fabric and/or patterns from them and create your own spreads.

In its catalog, The Vermont Country Store Voice of the Mountains offers a good selection of washable, 100%-cotton bedspreads in a full range of sizes. Included are seersuckers, traditional woven-chenille looks, and rip cords.

A number of all-cotton bedspreads, to fit beds twin through king sizes, are available from the **Coming Home** catalog. More limited selections are offered by **Janice Corporation**, the **JC Penney Catalog**, **L.L. Bean** (Furnishings Catalog), **Gohn Bros.**, as well as **Linensource**.

Custom-Made Bedding

Most of the alternative mattress makers are, in reality, custom-bed manufacturers. So, it's often possible to get mattresses of unusual size created for you by them. One company, in particular, **Sleeptek Limited**, advertises that it'll make all types of custom bedding items. These are fabricated with the organic materials under their Sleeptek Oasis label. If you are in Canada, you can contact the company directly, if in the U.S., you'll need to talk to one of their distributors—**Furnature** or **N.E.E.D.S.**

Heart of Vermont will make organic-cotton, custom-sized sheets to order, and they sell organic-cotton and chemical-free wool batting by the yard. **Palmer Bedding Co.** and **Erlander's Natural Products** say that they can make custom-sized, natural-fiber-and-stuffing beds.

You can have some custom bedding items, such as quilt covers, made with untreated-cotton fabric or untreated barrier cloth by **Janice Corporation**. These will have no formaldehyde resins added to reduce wrinkling. This company also sells wide, untreated fabric and long zippers, too. It's also likely that other alternative mattress and bedding companies can do custom work for you. (For other alternative bedding manufacturers, see *Alternative Mattress Buying Sources* on page 227.)

Another possibility is to check with local mattress and futon manufacturers. They, too, may be able to make certain items for you out of the fabrics and stuffings you request. However, you may have to supply them with some of the raw materials, if they don't already have sources for organic, or otherwise less common, materials.

Furthermore, a few bedding specialty catalogs geared toward the general public offer custom-work using either their materials or yours. This is especially true for comforters, pads, etc., but it can sometimes include a broader range of products as well. Catalog companies that do this type of custom work include **The Company Store** and **Cuddledown of Maine**.

Note: Companies that ordinarily don't deal with chemically-sensitive clients may have workers who use perfume, scented products, and who may possibly smoke. So, what they make for you could easily pick up these odors.

Toweling

Natural-fiber towels are soft, absorbent, biodegradable, and, thank goodness, still readily available in stores and catalogs.

Important note: Unless otherwise stated, you should assume that toweling items made with commercial-grade cotton and cotton stuffings (in pot holders and oven mitts) may, or may not, have had chemical treatments such as bleaching, dying, etc. With kitchen items, such as pot holders and oven mitts, this may include fire retarding treatments, even though this isn't required by law. If you're concerned, ask a company representative before ordering to supply you with the information you desire.

Bath Towels

All-cotton bath towels remain popular, despite the introduction of less-expensive synthetic-blend towels.

Bath-Towel Considerations

While all-cotton towels are relatively easy to find in local department and discount stores, you should know that not all of them are created equal. Generally, the most expensive towels are made from high-grade cottons such as *Pima* and *Egyptian*. (High-grade cottons have very soft, long fibers.) Less-expensive towels commonly use lower-grade cottons. This results in toweling with a stiffer, scratchier feel.

Another consideration when buying towels is their texture. Bath towels now come in *terry* (complete loops) or *velour-style* (cropped loops). Many people find looped, terry towels are more absorbent, but they're relatively easy to snag. On the other hand, velour towels tends to be less absorbent, but they retain their appearance longer. No matter which type you choose, the more loops per square inch (the thicker the loop density), the better the quality of the toweling. By the way, you'll also want to check a towel's *underweave* (the yarns woven between the looped rows). A firm, tightly woven underweave usually indicates an item with more durability.

Of course, color is also important when you buy towels. Sensitive people who find dyes bothersome, however, should only purchase natural, ecru, or white towels; these have very little or no added dye in them. Another plus for light-colored towels is they result in minimal color-bleeding problems when washed. Unfortunately, white or off-white towels can look gray as they age, especially if they're washed in hard water. Darker towels have the advantage that stains are far less noticeable on them. Overall, darker towels look better over time than most light-colored towels.

Bath-Towel Buying Sources

Bath towels made of 100%-organic-cotton are sold by **Building for Health Materials Center, Tomorrow's World,** and **Natural Selections.** Other sources include LifeKind Products, **Karen's Natural Products, Heart of Vermont, Fisher Henney Naturals,** and **Harmony.** Organic-cotton hand towels and face cloths are sold by **Janice Corporation.**

Green-cotton towels are sold by **Karen's Natural Products, Priorities** and sometimes **Janice Corporation.** Unbleached, all-cotton bath towels are handled by **American Environmental Health Foundation.**

"Regular" commercial cotton bath towels should be readily available in your local department stores, discount stores, and bath shops. Of course, **JC Penney Catalog,** always offers a good variety. Other catalogs that handle some include **L.L. Bean** (Furnishings Catalog), **Coming Home, Chambers,** and **Cuddledown of Maine.** In addition, other catalogs to check out are **Eddie Bauer** (Home catalog), **The Company Store, Domestications,** and **Vermont Country Store** (Voice of the Mountains catalog).

Baby Towels

From **EcoBaby Organics,** you can order untreated-cotton or organic-cotton baby wash cloths. They also handle organic-cotton hooded baby towels, as does **Chock's.** In addition, **Decent Exposures** sells 100%-cotton baby wash cloths.

Guest and Hand Towels

Organic-cotton hand towels are sold by **Janice Corporation**. Also, check for hand towel sizes in *Bath towels*, above.

Chambers has attractive linen hand towels.

Kitchen Towels

In the kitchen, 100%-cotton dish towels are highly suggested over towels made of synthetic blends.

Cotton Kitchen Towels

Kitchen towels made of cotton are both natural and extremely absorbent and, from an environmental standpoint, they are often preferred over paper towels. Fortunately, all-cotton dish towels are still commonly available at most local department and discount stores, although some have had "antimicrobial technology" added to them. Usually, this isn't explained, so unless you are comfortable with this, use towels without this added "bonus."

By mail-order, **LifeKind Products** offers honeycomb weave kitchen towels that are organic cotton.

Also, **Karen's Natural Products** and **Janice Corporation** handle all-cotton kitchen towels. Other mail-order sources include **The Company Store**, **Coming Home**, and **Vermont Country Store Voice of the Mountains**.

Linen Kitchen Towels

All-linen kitchen towels are an attractive alternative to cotton. They can be ordered from **Vermont Country Store Voice of the Mountains** and **Janice Corporation**. In addition, check local fine department and kitchen stores,

Pot Holders and Oven Mitts

Locating all-cotton pot holders was once easy to do. Now, it's becoming far more difficult. Synthetic fabrics and stuffings, nonstick coatings, and fire-retardant treatments are very common today.

Organic-cotton pot holders can be found in the **Janice Corporation** catalog. All-cotton pot holders can also be found in the **Karen's Natural Products** catalog.

Ethnic-inspired all-cotton pot holders can be ordered from **Marketplace: Handwork of India**. More conventional styles, and oven mitts, are sold by **Coming Home**.

Tablecloths, Placemats, and Napkins

Washable, natural-fiber table linens can add warmth to any home, without adding synthetic-fiber odors. Even better, from a health point of view, are natural-fiber table linens without any stain or wrinkle-resistant chemical treatments. Sometimes your local department stores and kitchen shops will handle a few types. Of course, you can always make your own table linens.

9: Linens

Important note: Unless otherwise stated, assume table linens have been made with commercial-grade cotton and cotton stuffing (in certain placemats) which may or not have had chemical treatments. If you're concerned, ask the representative before ordering to supply you with the information you desire.

Organic-cotton table napkins can be ordered from **LifeKind Products.** The **Vermont Country Store Voice of the Mountains** regularly offers tablecloths, placemats, and napkins made of 100%-cotton fabric. Other sources include **Coming Home, Crate & Barrel,** and **The Company Store.** A few all-cotton placemats and napkins are handled by **Sur La Table.** All-cotton woven placemats are found in the **Shaker Shops West** catalog.

Tablecloths, placemats, and napkins are also occasionally available in specialty kitchen catalogs such as **Williams-Sonoma.** And **Marketplace: Handwork of India** has unusual cotton table cloths, placemats, and napkins with an ethnic-look.

Tomorrow's World has washable hemp tablecloths and hemp-cotton-blend placemats and napkins.

Part 4
YOUR HOUSE

CHAPTER 10: THE HOME WORKSHOP

This chapter will discusse your home workshop—its proper location, the storage of materials, and your own personal protection. It also covers the various types of materials and products that are often encountered in projects that homeowners (and renters) might take on themselves. Even if you don't consider yourself to be a do-it-yourself type, you will likely find some of the information in this chapter helpful. After all, sooner or later, you will probably need to do some painting or caulking, or you may want to update some cabinetry or a floor covering.

This chapter also discusses some useful testing procedures, for individuals who are chemically sensitive, so they can determine which construction and remodeling products will be the best tolerated. *Chapter 11: Home Remodeling*, will cover information on specific remodeling projects.

Locations for Your Home Workshop

Ideally, a home workshop should be located in its own separate structure. Another good choice would be in a portion of an insulated, detached garage where the temperature, and perhaps the humidity, can be regulated. Yet, in reality, most home workshops are going to be located in basements, utility rooms, and in attached garages.

Unfortunately, in these locations a home workshop can pose a potential dangers to the rest of the house, and to those who occupy it. After all, a number of the products and materials typically found in home workshops have the capacity to cause skin irritation, to be toxic, to easily catch on fire—or even to explode. And some materials are also quite odorous and many are very hazardous to breathe. A few really noxious products may have all of these undesirable qualities. Therefore, if your home workshop is located *anywhere* within your house, or in an attached garage, the potential for indoor-air contamination (and other potentially dangerous problems) can be quite high.

Safe Home-Workshop Basics

The following sections offer some general guidelines to help make your home workshop a safer and healthier environment.

Proper Product Storage and Disposal

There are several basic safety measures for any home workshop that are worth considering. One of these is to always read product labels carefully. Among other things, this will give you a manufacturer's recommendation for the correct storage conditions for a particular product. As it turns out, most paints, clear finishes, adhesives, caulkings, etc. should be stored within a certain temperature range. Keeping products within this suggested range guarantees longer product life and, in some cases, it will also reduce the potential for leaks or even explosions.

Other important aspects of proper storage are good organization and security. To meet these needs, metal storage cabinets with doors are often ideal. As an added bonus, items stored in cabinets are less likely to contaminate the room air with their odors. Of course, cabinets with locking doors (or ones designed to accept a padlock) are best if there are small children around the house. By the way, it's often a good idea to have at least two metal storage cabinets in your home workshop—one to hold odorous paints, caulkings, adhesives, stains, and finishes, and a separate one to hold sandpaper, tools, and personal protective gear.

You'll find that metal cabinets are sold at many office-supply stores. If you can't find them locally, the large office supply catalog, **Reliable Corp.**, offers several, including those made by **Edsal Manufacturing Co., Inc.** and **Lee Metal Products**, in a limited number of standard office colors. Those offered are available in either desk or full sizes, in industrial or office grades, and with features such as locks, wardrobe racks, and adjustable shelves. (See also *Household Storage* on page 511.)

Having heavy-duty open shelving systems can also he helpful in your home workshop. Often, local building centers and hardware stores will have a good selection. **Inter-Metro Industries Corp.** manufacturers a particularly attractive, heavy-duty, chrome-plated, wire shelving. To find a local dealer, call the company.

Another home workshop storage basic is to keep only what you really think you'll actually use again. In other words, rid your shop of old paints and other compounds that were used for a one-time project, or containers that only have a small quantity of material left in them. Although it may seem thrifty to hold on to everything, in many cases, extended age can cause a product to degrade or deteriorate markedly. Some materials can become contaminated with mold or bacteria, or actually change in chemical composition. Then too, liquid or masticducts that have been stored for too long may simply dry up or come out of suspension.

When you are ready to dispose of unneeded paints, etc., be sure to call your local board of heath or sanitation department. They often have established, proper, disposal procedures to follow with certain products—especially ones considered "household hazardous waste." Many communities have drop-off locations where such products can be left. By the way, if you have a considerable amount of paint in one color that's still in good condition, you might consider donating it to a local charity. Under no curcumstances, should these products be poured down a drain.

Proper Working Conditions

Proper working conditions are essential for a safe and healthy home workshop. One of the most important of these conditions is good ventilation. Therefore, when you use paint, glue, mastic, etc., open the room's windows and exterior doors (if possible) and consider using a window fan, or a permanently installed fan, and blow any odors outdoors (for more on ventilation fans, see *High Humidity* on page 530).

A sturdy work bench is essential, too. Butcher-block tops on heavy-duty legs can take a lot of abuse. **Balley Block Co.** and **Michigan Maple Block Co.** make good maple, butcher-block tops, however they're bonded with urea-formaldehyde glue and pressure. Call the companies for a nearby dealer. It must be said though, if you can find a good workbench made without formaldehyde, it would be a healthier choice. If you require a smooth, easy-to-clean work surface, **Inter-Metro Industries Corp.** makes "clean tables" of 14-gauge stainless steel with 34"-wide tops and 5' or longer lengths. You'll need to call the company for a nearby dealer.

Of course, proper protective gear is essential for personal safety. Your chemical respirator mask, rubber gloves, neoprene gloves, ear protectors, shop coats, safety glasses, and goggles should be handy, in good condition, and always used when appropriate to do so (see *Personal Protective Gear* on page 264). You'll also want to wear and use a tool carrier that is healthful as well as durable. **Duluth Trading Co.** has Skillers 100%-cotton-duck tool vests, jackets, and pants with extra pockets and holsters. They also have Skillers tool bags, as well as bib- or waist-style tool aprons made from the same duck fabric.

Then, too, it goes without saying that every home workshop should have a multi-purpose fire extinguisher that is in good working order and easily accessible (see *Portable Fire Extinguishers* on page 388). In addition, it's also a good idea to have a small metal canister with a tight-fitting metal lid, or a small garbage can with a lid, for oily or solvent-containing rags, paper, or other flammable materials. It's also important to have an operating smoke detector (see *Smoke Detectors* on page 386). Note: Place the smoke detector so it isn't directly over a location where a great deal of dust will be generated, because the airborne dust could affect the sensitivity. Also, gently dust or vacuum the detector regularly. Make sure, too, that you change the batteries at least once a year and test the unit weekly.

Keeping your workshop clean is another safety essential. That way, particulate debris will not accumulate and recirculate into the air. To clean thoroughly, it's advisable to use a powerful vacuum that can pick up dirt, grit, and sawdust easily. Another shop basic involves proper lighting. This means having a good overhead light source as well as a swing-arm lamp, flashlight, and/or electric lanterns for close-up work.

One more safety measure is to keep all your cutting tools sharp. It may seem safer to use dull tools, but in practice, sharp tools slip less and cause fewer accidents. Finally, you'll want to have an easily accessible, well-stocked first-aid kit. Your local drugstore should have a ready-made kit in its own storage box, or they can order one for you. Or you can make up a kit yourself. Check your first-air kit from time to time to see that the expiration dates on antiseptic ointments and other medications have not passed. By the way, an intercom in your shop will permit you to make an easy and immediate call for help to other family members if necessary. You may want a telephone as well to be able to make a 911 call quickly.

Important note: Do as much of your shop-type work as possible in a properly outfitted workshop—or perhaps outdoors. Unless absolutely necessary, it's best to avoid doing any project—especially if it is odorous, potentially dangerous, or just plain messy—within the living space of your home. Of course, certain repairs or remodeling will require that some work be done at a specific site, such as in the kitchen. However, if you must work somewhere besides your shop, continue to follow as many safety precautions as is possible. Above all, be sure to have adequate ventilation and wear appropriate protective gear.

Personal Protective Gear

If you plan to do your own home projects, it's essential to own, correctly maintain, properly store, and *actually use* good-quality personal protective gear. Good intentions are not enough. Despite the awkwardness some safety equipment adds to working (*i.e.* breathing through a mask or using rubber gloves), proper protection is essential to ensure your physical health. And another thing, you must choose equipment actually designed for the job you're expecting it to do. For example, a thin, inexpensive, disposable, paper dust mask might be adequate protection if you only plan to sand one piece of wood for a few minutes—but it simply can't possibly shield you from dangerous solvent odors if you plan to use an oil-based stain.

Therefore, before doing any project, analyze what face, eye, ear, hand, respiratory, etc., protection you'll need. Then, be certain you have the necessary equipment on hand—and that it's in good working order. Under no circumstances should you begin work on a project if you won't be sufficiently protected.

Fortunately, finding protective gear is not difficult. Usually, your local hardware store will have a fairly good selection on hand. This will likely include eye protectors (goggles, face masks, safety glasses), different types of ear protectors, and carious kinds of gloves. And most stores will be willing to order a specific item if it is not in stock. In addition, you might like to know about two large national companies that carry an extensive inventory of personal protective equipment. These are **W.W. Grainger, Inc.** and **Orr Safety Corporation**, both of which have local outlets and mail-order catalogs. For additional ideas, see also *Personal Facial Air Filters* on page 569.

By the way, **E.L. Foust Co., Inc.** offers several types of disposable dust masks capable of trapping most larger dust particles including the 3M High Efficiency Particulate Mask (**3M Construction & Home Improvement Products Div.**). The company also handles 3M Disposable Dust/Mist Respirators (**3M Construction & Home Improvement Products Div.**), which have a thin, activated-charcoal layer in them. These particular masks are designed to provide protection from not only many types of particulates but also minor airborne chemical exposures as well. In addition, **eMD.com**, **Allerx**, **N.E.E.D.S.**, **Allergy Clean Environments**, and **Nigra Enterprises** handle 3M Dust Masks. It should also be mentioned that **Befit Enterprises Ltd.** offers Respro Anti-pollution Masks made of *neoprene* (a special type of rubber that's particularly oil and chemical resistant) with your choice of a particulate-trapping filter or an activated charcoal filter.) Being constructed of latex, these masks are not for those with latex allergies.

For chemically sensitive people, wearing a 100%-cotton face mask containing an activated-charcoal insert can be very helpful. The activated charcoal can adsorb a great deal of the bothersome odors before they reach the wearer's nasal passages. There are several mail-order sources for all-cotton filtering masks, including **Allerx**, **Allergy Relief Shop, Inc.**, and **Bio Designs**. From **American Environmental Health Foundation** you can get masks of either untreated 100%-cotton or silk, with your choice of activated-coconut-shell charcoal, activated-lignite charcoal, or activated-bituminous-charcoal inserts. (Different types of charcoal are offered because sensitive people sometimes react negatively to one form, but not another.) All the masks by these companies are washable and refill inserts are available.

If you plan to work with an odorous material such as a paint or adhesive for more than a few minutes, you'll want to use a good quality, cartridge-type respirator, rather than a disposable mask, because it will contain a more generous amount of activated carbon. These can be purchased locally at paint, hardware, or building-supply stores, or by mail order from **W.W. Grainger, Inc.** or **Orr Safety Corporation**. Be sure to get one tailored to the job. For example, some are designed for pesticides, others work best with VOCs, and some are suited to capture particulates.

Home-Workshop Materials and Products

It's important to choose safer materials and products for your workshop projects in order to reduce air-quality problems and other potential risks. Therefore, the following sections will discuss typical materials and products, testing procedures, and it will suggest specific less-toxic brands you might want to use in your next project.

Typical Home-Workshop Materials and Products

Unfortunately, some of the typical products and materials used in home workshops are potentially harmful. Many contain petroleum-based solvents and/or other harmful volatile organic compounds (VOCs) that are can be dangerous to breathe. In some instances, inhalation of certain VOCs can cause respiratory inflammation or even central-nervous-system damage (see also *Volatile Organic Compounds* on page 526). Then, too, some typical products are very flammable, and others have the potential to cause skin irritation. Plus, unfortunately, a number of them are toxic.

You might think that by using only water-based products you'd avoid all such problems. However, as it turns out, most water-based latex paints contain some VOCs. In addition, many contain other very odorous ingredients.

Although health problems with paints, finishes, and other coatings are somewhat familiar to many people, less is known about the risks posed by certain types of wood, wood products, and drywall compounds. In reality, some wood species release natural compounds that can be irritating to the skin and/or respiratory system. While it's more common to be affected by newly cut wood, some sensitive individuals find oak, for example, bothersome for several months. In addition, many types of man-made wood products release relatively high levels of formaldehyde (see *Formaldehyde* on page 527). Typical drywall compounds generally contain fungicide, antifreeze, adhesive, and other additives that can make walls intolerable for months for some chemically sensitive people.

As hard as it is to believe, the truth is that nearly all of the typical building products and materials used today have at least some health risk associated with them. Yet these products are often relatively inexpensive, easy to work with, and readily available at most local lumberyards and hardware stores. But there is little, if any, government regulation covering many of them. Unfortunately, their use has become "standard practice."

But there are healthier, alternative products and materials available. For example, instead of using ubiquitous oak which has odorous natural *tannin* compounds, you could substitute a less irritating solid wood that's currently not as popular, but nevertheless very attractive—such as maple, birch, or tulip poplar—if you happen to find oak irritating. And you could use solid boards of these same woods in place of formaldehyde-containing, man-made wood products.

You can also purchase drywall compound with few chemical additives. Unlike typical brands, it is usually well-tolerated by sensitive people—even when wet. In addition, there are a number of less-noxious paints, finishes, adhesives, and glues.

Note: For more in-depth information on potentially problematic products, and healthier alternatives, than is supplied here, you'll want to also read *The Healthy House* by John Bower. This comprehensive book can be ordered directly from **The Healthy House Institute** or your favorite bookseller. Another good, but more limited source of information, is a 16-page fact sheet titled *Paints, Solvents, and Wood Preservatives* that you can order from the **Washington Toxics Coalition**.

Materials and Products

Ultimately, it's up to you whether to use healthier alternative materials and products. Because very few governmental regulations currently cover most building products, the typical unhealthy types will, no doubt, continue to be the norm for many years. As a result, they'll be the products most often stocked by local hardware stores, lumber yards, and build-ing-supply centers. They'll also be what most builders and contractors will be familiar with and will want to automatically use. If you want healthier materials to be used for your home projects, it'll be up to you to take the initiative in finding and buying them. The following pages should help you a great deal in this regard.

It should be noted that nearly all of the liquid alternative products are water-based rather than oil- or solvent-based. Formaldehyde, VOCs, and other potentially bothersome or harmful ingredients are usually minimized, or completely omitted. Many liquid alterna-tive products are formulated to have less odor when applied and/or when completely dry. In addition, many such products contain fewer preservatives. Thus, their shelf life may be shorter. Alternative wood products are manufactured without the use of formaldehyde glues.

As you might expect, these alternative products and materials can sometimes be more costly than typical brands—but not always. Higher prices can be due to smaller production runs or sometimes because the ingredients or materials are of higher quality. You'll find, too, that some alternative items require you to learn new methods of application. For example, an alternative ceramic-tile grout can require a special curing procedure.

Because alternative-product manufacturers and distributors tend to be small, and the number of dealers carrying these items is somewhat limited, you'll often need to special-order many of them. However, this isn't difficult. Fortunately, there are a number of fine mail-order sources now available. One in particular, **Building for Health Materials Center**, carries a large and varied inventory. For suggestions for a specific type of material, look it up in the index for the appropriate page location.

Testing Home-Workshop Products and Materials

Although alternative products and materials are safer than their typical counterparts, some items may still be bothersome to you personally. After all, each of us is biologically unique, so we all tolerate different things to different degrees. With products and materials used in home-improvement projects (furniture, cabinets, walls, floors, etc.), testing is particularly important inasmuch as these projects are often large in size and relatively permanent. The expense, time, and stress to redo such a project can be great. Therefore, testing is crucial, especially for sensitive individuals.

You should be aware that different types of products will require slightly different testing procedures. However, these are simply variations of the basic testing procedure described in the beginning of this book (see *Testing* on page 62). Of course, it should be stated that testing can reveal more than personal tolerance. It can also help you determine how a clear finish will look, what a paint will look like when dry, whether a certain glue will adhere well, etc. Remember though, it's important to do your testing sufficiently ahead of the time—before you actually need to use a particular product or material in your project. That way, there will be no last-minute panic or work delays, if you find you must use something else.

If you test more than one product at a time, it's a good idea to keep the information about your testing in written form, such as in a chart. It's also a good idea to record product prices for a cost comparison. When finished with your tests, you may want to keep the samples and written test results for later use. However, you should know that companies tend to change their products' formulas periodically. Therefore, the data from a older test might not be valid in the future. As a result, you should always prepare a new test sample using currently available products.

Important Testing Considerations

Important: Sniff testing should be done with low toxicity products only after they've had time to cure. If you're very chemically sensitive, do not sniff test any product without your physician's permission and/or supervision. For those with asthma, sniff testing may not be a good approach at any time. Sniff testing may actually irritate respiratory systems and trigger an asthmatic attack. If fact, even if you're healthy, or if you have any concern about testing products, consult with your physician for his or her opinion.

If you're an allergic individual, make sure to get specific ingredient information. If you are known to react to latex, milk, or citrus, for example, you can avoid these ingredients in the products you choose. For anyone interested in specific information about a product, contact the manufacturer for a *Material Safety Data Sheet (MSDS)*. An MSDS is required by federal regulations and should be available to you. It will list a variety of ingredients, safety precautions, and health effects. Admittedly, MSDSs can be written in scientific terms, they can sometimes be a bit overwhelming and confusing, and certain ingredients do not have to be included—such as *proprietary ingredients* (trade secrets), or certain "inert ingredients," etc. So, they can be somewhat misleading. Yet, they can provide helpful information in your buying decisions.

Testing Paints and Finishes

For sensitive people, before purchasing a large quantity of a paint or other finish, it's best to test several brands first to determine how odorous they will be when wet, what their finished sheen will be, how well they cover, and their true finished color. (Make sure to read *Important Testing Considerations* above before proceeding.) You'll also want to test for any residual odor once they're dry to determine how long (if ever) it takes for the product to become tolerable to you personally. Of course, this is especially important for chemically sensitive individuals. When a sample is completely dry, you might also want to test for how washable or scrubbable it is.

After weighing all the information from your testing, you can then confidently choose the best paint or finish for the job you need to do. And, you'll also have a good idea of how long it will take after it's been applied before it will be tolerable for you. However, you must keep in mind that walls cover large areas, and most testing samples are very small in comparison. Therefore, an entire room may require a longer time period to air out than a sample to be no longer bothersome.

To test a paint or clear finish, all you need do is coat a piece of aluminum foil with a prospective product and label it as to its brand name, color and/or sheen, and date of application. Then on a piece of paper, record how the finish smelled when fresh. Then set the sample aside in a dry, uncontaminated place for *at least* several days. After that, you can *very lightly* sniff the coated surface once every few days (or weeks) until you can no longer detect any smell. Once odor-free, you'll want to place the test-sample near your pillow. If you're able to sleep normally, the sample is probably tolerable. Of course, you'll need to record the date of tolerability on the sample and on your chart. Finally, you can write down information on how well the finish covered, how the sheen looked, how scrubbable it was, etc.

Testing Adhesives

To test alternative water-based glues and other adhesive compounds, purchase the smallest sizes they come in—and make sure to read *Important Testing Considerations* on page 267 first. With each product, apply a small amount on a separate piece of aluminum foil, each of which has been identified by brand name and application date. On a sheet of paper, record how much each product cost and its particular odor when wet. Then, set the samples aside in a dry, uncontaminated area to cure.

The next day, very lightly sniff the samples and repeat this every few days or so, until you can no longer detect an odor with one or more of them. At that point, record the date on the foil and on your chart. If you want to be even more sure that a particular product won't be bothersome to you, lay an odorless sample by the head of your bed. If you are able to sleep well through the night, it often means you're going to be able to tolerate that product. As a rule, a small amount of glue often isn't a significant concern. For example, there wouldn't be very much glue used in a furniture project, so it may not be a significant concern compared to the amount of glue used to adhere all the floor tile in a large room.

While this testing procedure will determine your personal tolerability, it can't be used determine how well a certain product will do its job of adhering. To do that, you'll need to apply the glue or adhesive to a scrap or small section of what you intend to glue, then let it dry. After it has had a chance to cure, you can examine your test sample for proper adherence. Again, record your results. Although this test won't give you long-term guarantees, it will give you a general idea of whether the product is suitable for the job or not.

Testing Lubricants

In most home situations, lubricants are used very sparingly. However, if they happen to be very odorous, they can be bothersome or intolerable to chemically sensitive persons for a very long period of time. Of course, you should realize to begin with, that many petroleum-based lubricants have an odor no matter how long they've been exposed to the air. For example, sewing-machine oil can have a long-term odor. However, there are other types of lubricants that you might find worth sampling.

If you want to test a lubricant, you can try the following procedure, but be sure to read *Important Testing Considerations* on page 267 before proceeding. First, purchase one or more brands and apply a small amount of each (typically less than a drop) to its own separate sheet of aluminum foil. On the foil, and also on a separate piece of paper, record the date, brand, and cost. Then, lightly sniff each sample and note the odor. You can later lightly sniff the samples over several days. If a sample seems to have little or no odor, record the date on the foil and your chart. An odorless sample should be placed near your bed's headboard. A good night's sleep often indicates that you're tolerating the product reasonably well.

Keep in mind that you generally don't need to apply very much of a lubricant to do the job. In fact, using less of the product will mean less chance of it running and discoloring or damaging something. So, always use as little as possible.

The best way to find out if a product will do a good job of lubricating is to actually use it on something. For example, if you want to find out how well it will work on your kitchen cabinets, apply it to a single hinge. After determining how well that seems to work, you can then decide if you want to go ahead and use it on all the other hinges. It might be a good idea to keep the records of your testing for tolerability and effectiveness permanently, because lubricant formulas rarely change. Therefore, what you learned could very well be useful in the future.

Testing Woods

To test your personal tolerance for a specific wood species, it's best to get small pieces of several different types of wood. Of course, make sure to read *Important Testing Considerations* on page 267 first. Then write the name of the species on each sample and very lightly sniff to determine its odor. Record the results on a separate sheet of paper. Next, sand all sides of each sample. Vacuum off the dust and lightly sniff again and record your observations. The odor will likely be much stronger.

Next, completely coat the sanded sample with the tolerable paint or finish you plan to eventually use on the wood (see *Testing Paints and Finishes* on page 267). After waiting for the finish to become tolerable (your previous testing should give you an estimated date), lightly sniff the coated wood and record your findings. Then, put a second coat on all surfaces of the sample, so that it ends up getting two coats of finish. Again, wait for the finish to become tolerable, test-sniff, and record your results. This information should give you at least a basic understanding of a particular wood species' initial odor, its odor after being sanded, its odor after one coat of a tolerable finish, and its odor after two coats. Next, take the sample that seems most acceptable and place it near your pillow. If you're able to sleep well, it's likely that you'll tolerate that particular wood and finish combination.

While this testing should prove to be of great help, some variables are worth keeping in mind. For example, a small sample is not going to be nearly as potent as 150 square feet of newly laid hardwood floor. Plus, in some cases—such as with a hardwood floor—the bottom surface usually won't be coated with a finish. So, it isn't unusual for such a large finished project to have more of an odor than you anticipated. Fortunately, however, with age, most wood surfaces lose a great deal of their initial innate odor. Of course, additional coats of finish could be applied to help seal in a persistently bothersome wood odor if necessary.

Important note: For testing alternative particleboard or construction-grade plywood for use in interior applications, you can follow similar testing procedures to that just described with solid wood. However, these types of items will often have a strong piney smell (arising from natural *terpene* compounds) for some time, and construction-grade plywood will be *outgassing* (emitting) formaldehyde, as well. Therefore, use extreme caution if you are very chemically sensitive.

Suggestions for Alternative Materials and Products

In the following sections, you'll find suggestions for some specific alternative home-workshop materials and products to consider using for your next project. Most are somewhat healthier that the products typically available in paint, hardware, or building-supply stores. For more in-depth information about healthier construction and remodeling materials (as well as hundreds of additional suppliers of healthier products) see *The Healthy House* by John Bower. It can be ordered directly from **The Healthy House Institute** or your favorite bookseller.

Paints

In most cases, paints have quite complex formulas made up of many different compounds. As you probably already know, there are many types and brands of paint currently available. However, only some of the more popular alternatives will actually be mentioned here by brand name, with sources where they can be obtained. These particular paints are generally less bothersome, or they have potentially less harmful ingredients, or they are designed to be nearly odorless when dry. It should be mentioned that some of these "safer" alternative paints only come in a limited number of off-white or pastel colors, although other brands have recently added more colors to their lines. You can certainly have colorants added to a light-colored or white paint, but colorants often contain a small amount of *VOCs* (volatile organic compounds), depending on their composition. So, ask ahead of time, if you're concerned.

Whenever you paint, be sure to follow the recommended application directions on the label *exactly*. This is especially important for chemically sensitive people because, for example, if not enough drying time is allowed between coats, it may take longer for the paint to become tolerable. See *Wall Paint* on page 295 for suggested application procedures.

Oil-Based Vs. Water-Based Paints

Before choosing any paint, you may want to know more about the two basic types: oil- and water-based. Actually, both types have *pigments* (natural or synthetically derived colorants), *binders* (compounds that hold or bind all the ingredients together), and *vehicles* (the liquid base). Of course, there are usually a number of other minor ingredients in paints as well.

In fact, depending on the particular type and brand of paint, it could also contain anti-freeze, *anti-skinning agents* (to prevent a film from forming on the paint's surface in an unopened can), *anti-settling agents* (to keep the ingredients in suspension), *biocides* (to prevent the paint from going bad in the can), *catalysts* (compounds that hasten chemical reactions without being altered themselves), curing agents, defoamers, *dispersing agents* (compounds that cause the ingredients to disperse uniformly throughout the paint), dryers, *emulsifying agents* (compounds that permit minute droplets of one liquid to remain suspended in another), *extenders* (compounds that increase volume or bulk), *fillers* (compounds that simply add solid particles), fire retardants, fungicides, preservatives, surfactants (compounds that reduce surface tension), thickeners, *thixotropic agents* (compounds that permit a gel to adhere to a vertical surface without running), and many other possible ingredients.

However, it's the vehicle that's primarily responsible for the difference between oil- and water-based paints. (Note: Oil-based paints were once made using natural oils such as linseed oil and soybean oil. However, today conventional oil paints are generally made with synthetic *alkyd resins,* but the term "oil-based" is still popularly used for them.) Because the oils (or alkyd resins) are very thick, they're combined with solvents to thin them down. Not surprisingly then, it's this oil/solvent vehicle in oil-based paints (or the water vehicle in water-based paints) that greatly determines a paint's odor, it's flammability, the cleanup requirements, it's scrubbabilty—and the paint's potential negative health effects. Because significantly more solvents are used in oil-based paints, they release more dangerous *volatile organic compounds (VOCs)* into the air than water-based paints (see *Volatile Organic Compounds* on page 526).

It's also interesting to know that the oil/solvent (or alkyd-resin/solvent) vehicles in oil-based paints don't dry through evaporation. Instead, they cure through a *chemical oxidation reaction process.* Once oil paints have cured, they're very durable. On the other hand, paints using water as their vehicle dry primarily through evaporation. Unfortunately, water-based paints are often less durable (sometimes, quite a bit less) than their oil-based counterparts. However, the shinier the *sheen,* generally the more washable a water-based paint is. (See *Wall Paint* on page 295 for a broader discussion of paint sheen.)

Taking into account all the pluses and minuses, it shouldn't be surprising that water-based products (paints, as well clear finishes, stains, etc.) are often recommended by most, though not all, health-conscious people, over counterparts containing high levels of solvents. That's why you'll find that many of the alternative paints, clear finishes, and stains in the sections below are water-based. (Important note: Even alternative water-based products still require some time after they've been applied to become tolerable for most chemically-sensitive individuals.)

Latex Paint Considerations

For several decades now, the most common type of indoor house paint used in America has probably been water-based latex. *Latex* is a natural or synthetic rubber product used as a paint binder. Most brands of latex paint can provide good coverage, but as a rule, they aren't as scrubbable as, say, oil-based paints. Overall, latex-binder paints have been popular for their low cost, their ease of application, and their easy cleanup.

Despite their pluses, it appears that latex paints may be becoming a thing of the past. This may be because certain paint formulators feel that other binders produce better paints—or are simply less costly. Another impetus may be the dramatic increase and concern over latex allergies. (These allergies have often been a consequence of the AIDs epidemic, which requires the daily use of latex gloves in medical and dental settings, some of which have been of poor quality.) Whatever the reason or reasons, formulations using natural latex binders are being replaced, in many cases, with *thermoplastic acrylic-resin binders.*

So, in reality, "true latex" paints are not all that common. Despite this, the term "latex paint" in modern usage has generically come to mean *any* water-based paint—whether it contains latex or not. So, if you're allergic to latex rubber, there are probably far more "latex-paint" options available than you may have first suspected.

National-Brand Alternative Lines

Although most national-brand, water-based interior paints contain far smaller quantities of harmful *volatile organic compounds* (VOCs) than oil-based paints, there are still some VOCs in their formulas. Typical water-based paints also have ingredients such as preservatives and other additives that may be bothersome for certain sensitive individuals. However, some major paint manufacturers have developed their own alternative paint lines that many sensitive people are finding to be quite acceptable. While these paints still usually have preservatives, they now have only very a tiny quantity of VOCs—or none at all.

Using a major paint company's low- or zero-VOC paint line has many advantages. The most obvious one is convenience, for you can often find them locally. Therefore, you don't have to place an order for your paint, pay to have it shipped, or wait for its arrival. And, if you run short, you can simply go to local retailer and get more of what you need. Another consideration is cost. Because these companies have much higher production runs, the cost of their products can often be less than for specially made paints. Finally, if you hire someone to do the painting for you, he or she will likely be familiar with the brand of paint, if not the particular line, you've chosen. As a rule, contractors prefer working with materials and products they've used before. That way, they know what to expect of the paint (coverage, ease of application, etc.) and can better estimate a completion time, and their costs.

One of these national-brand alternative lines you might try is Glidden ProMaster Series (ICI Paints) latex-binder paints. These paints contain no VOCs and are low in odor. ProMaster paints include MP 7610 flat, MP 9310 eggshell, and MP 7810 semi-gloss. These all come in standard white. Although you can have a colorant added, the colorant will have a small amount of VOCs in its formula—however, it's usually not much. Glidden ProMaster paints should be available at your local Glidden stores and dealers. (Note: These may not be a good choice for latex-allergic persons.)

Another national-brand alternative line you should consider is ICI. The ICI Lifemaster 2000 (ICI Paints) paints have an acrylic binder, no VOCs, and are low in odor. The LM 9200 flat, LM 9300 eggshell, and 9300 semi-gloss all come in white and many popular colors with custom colors available. The Lifemaster 2000 line can be purchased at ICI stores and dealers nationwide. By the way, other national and regional companies have also begun making low or zero-VOC paints, such as Benjamin Moore and Sherwin Williams. So, check your favorite paint store to see if they, too, have something in stock.

It should be said that despite all the pluses associated with national-brand alternative lines, they're still not what some discriminating individuals want to use. So, those who require, or simply desire, interior paints created to be more inherently tolerable and/or made of natural ingredients, will need to consider paints listed in the sections that follow. Above all, don't do what some sensitive people have done: stir a pound of baking soda into each gallon of paint. Although this may reduce bothersome paint odors somewhat, it does have major drawbacks. For example, the added baking soda can affect the paint's durability, texture, or color. In fact, this procedure should only be attempted (if ever) with very light colors. At any rate, no paint manufacturer recommends adding baking soda to their products. So, if the paint surface ends up unsatisfactory in any way, they'll take no responsibility.

Alternative Synthetic-Formula Paints

While the alternative lines from major paint companies may meet the needs of most people very satisfactorily, they aren't for everyone. Fortunately, there are a number of smaller companies that have chosen to make and market interior paints to meet the expectations of an even more discerning public.

Some of these manufacturers have developed synthetic-formula paints that were originally created for the chemically sensitive. While each company in this group has its own unique formulations, it must be said that these paints are somewhat similar to the paints mentioned in the *National-Brand Alternative Lines* section above. Importantly, however, what they have done is gone one step further by creating paints that are even lower in odor.

10: Home Workshop

Yet, you should understand that each of these small paint manufacturers has its own definition of "very low odor." Therefore, some paints have formulations that generate minimal odors during application and drying, such as certain low- or zero-VOC paints. But other paints don't achieve their "very low odor" status until they've become thoroughly dried. So, try to understand exactly what "very low odor" means for the particular paint brand you're thinking about buying. If you need to contact the manufacturer for more information, do so. (Note: Virtually all wall paints will have at least some odor when wet, even very-low-odor brands.)

It should also be mentioned that many alternative synthetic paints have low- or zero-*biocide* formulas as well. This is a real departure form national brands that simply add biocides to all their paints. Keep in mind that paints without (or with minimal quantities of) ingredients designed to kill mold, bacteria, etc. should not be stored for a very long period of time. That's because they can go bad in the can. In addition, they should probably not be used in damp areas such as bathrooms.

One very good, very-low-odor alternative paint you might want to try is Microsol (**Best Paint Co., Inc.**). Microsol latex-binder paints come in 2000 (semi-gloss), 2120 (satin low gloss), 2020 (flat), and 2030 (low sheen). Also available are a PVA 50 Primer/Sealer (latex binder), Best Floor Paint (acrylic binder), and Best Moisture Guard (acrylic binder). All these paints can be ordered directly from the manufacturer. These paints have "superior scrubbabilty," "give off no VOCs," and are "non-toxic." They also have a 15-year warrantee for performance and appearance from date of purchase. Best paints are often well tolerated by chemically sensitive people, but they may not be suitable for those with latex allergies.

Enviro-Safe Paint (**Chem-Safe Products Co.**), which uses 100% acrylic resin as a binder, is another brand particularly well tolerated by chemically sensitive persons. These paints have no VOCs or toxic preservatives. A flat, satin, and semi-gloss are available in a range of popular colors, with custom colors optional. Also in the Enviro-Safe line is a primer paint. You can order Enviro-Safe Paint directly from the manufacturer.

Murco Wall Products, Inc. has also created paints that many chemically sensitive people have used. Murco Great Flat Wall Paint GF-1000 (with a synthetic latex binder) and Murco High Gloss Latex Enamel LE 1000 (with a combination latex/acrylic binder) have been created without slow-releasing compounds and so they will release no airborne fungicides. (The fungicides apparently remain permanently bound up in the dried paint.) The shelf life of Murco paints is controlled by the pH and "in-can preservatives" only. Murco latex paints come in 9 stock colors plus light tint bases. All can be ordered from the maker. (Note: These may not be a good choice for those with latex allergies.)

Acro Paint (**Miller Paint Co.**), which is available directly from the manufacturer, is a line of solvent-free, low-VOC, water-based interior paints. Miller adds no biocides to any of their paints. The only biocides present are those in the bulk ingredients the company purchases from its suppliers. Acro #6450 LB Flat and Acro # 2850 LB semi-gloss have acrylic binders, while #1450 LB Satin uses a vinyl/acrylic binder. All Acrco paints come in white and a range of soft pastels.

Another low-odor brand of alternative paint you may be interested in using is AFM Safecoat Zero-VOC Paint (**AFM**). Safecoat is a water-based product described by its manufacturer as being made with a "multi-polymer system, including acrylic." It comes in white but can be specially ordered in a number of soft pastel shades. This company also has developed low-odor, water-based primers (Primer Undercoat, Transitional Primer, Wallboard HPV, MetalCoat Metal Primer), several enamel formulations including a Cabinet & Trim Enamel, and a paint for concrete surfaces (CemBond Masonry Paint) All these can be obtained from AFM dealers including **Bio Designs, Building for Health Materials Center, N.E.E.D.S., healthyhome.com, Allergy Clean Environments, Allergy Relief Shop, Inc., The Living Source,** and **American Environmental Health Foundation**.

A few water-based alternative acrylic paints have actually been specially designed as sealants (see also *Acrylic Finishes and Sealants* on page 277). One of these is Crystal Shield (**Pace Chem Industries, Inc.**). You can order it from the company or from dealers such as **Karen's Natural Products**. However, this finish can remain bothersome to sensitive persons for several weeks after it's been applied (some sensitive individuals find this is the case for up to two months). However, when completely dried, it is quite inert.

Alternative Natural-Formula Paints

Interestingly, various forms of milk paint and *casein* (a milk-protein derivative) paint have been used for hundreds of years. That's because they're fairly durable. Today, powered casein paints have become popular as natural-ingredient wall paints.

There are many persons who consider powdered casein paints to be the best ecological choice. However, there are drawbacks to consider. First, because most are in a powdered form, they require the extra step of adding water and thorough mixing. Because they generally contain no *biocides* to inhibit mold growth, they can't be stored as a liquid for very long, or used in damp areas. In addition, casein paint might be intolerable for someone with milk allergies because walls painted with casein paints can have a faint milky odor for some time.

If you're interested in using an alternative powdered casein paint, Old Fashioned Milk Paint (**Old Fashioned Milk Paint Co.**) is one you might try. It comes with no preservatives in 16 colors. The company also makes Extra-Bond (a water-borne acrylic) that can be mixed into the paint to make it adhere better to nonporous, or previously painted, surfaces and Clear Coat (a waterborne acrylic) top coat to make it more durable. All these products can be ordered directly from the company or from **Shaker Shops West**.

Another powdered casein paint is Bioshield Casein "Milk" Paint #10 (**Eco Design Co.**), which can be ordered directly from the company and from **Building for Health Materials Center**. This is an original German formulation manufactured in the U.S. While it only comes in white, Bioshield pigments are available to add color. From **French Creek Sheep & Wool Co.**, you can purchase Real Milk Paint. This powdered product comes packaged to make one quart. Eleven colors are offered.

Auro Plant Chemistry makes a powdered casein wall paint called Auro #751 Powder Chalk Casein Wall Paint as well as a liquid Auro #361 Casein Wall Paint. As with most Auro liquid paints, #361 contains essential oils and plant terpenes and uses borax and other borate compounds as natural preservatives. Both come in standard white, but you can probably add Auro color pigments. Auro products are available from **Sinan Co.** and **Karen's Natural Products**. Still another powdered milk paint in six colors is sold by **Bio Designs**.

Besides powdered casein paints, the other all-natural paints that are available are alternative German-formulation liquid paints. These were developed as a consequence of the influential "natural house" movement known as *Baubiologie* (a German word meaning building biology). It should be said that some of the ingredients have changed over the years. However, a few have used (or still use) turpentine (derived from softwood trees such as pine) and citrus solvents (derived from oranges, citrons, etc.)—substances implicated in a condition known as *painter's rash*. Therefore, in certain cases, some of the bothersome natural ingredients have been replaced by less-bothersome petroleum-derived compounds. It should be mentioned that these German-formulation alternative liquid paints often have a strong natural odor when wet, although they do air out in time. Also, be aware that some brands are low- or zero-biocide, which may make them inappropriate for use in high humidity areas of your home. So, check with your dealer for specific ingredients before purchasing.

One well-known liquid German formulation is Bioshield Solvent Free Wall Paint #18 (**Eco Design Co.**). This is a zero-VOC, water-based paint made of natural oils and waxes. Ingredients include chalk, talcum, carnuba wax, and linseed oil, among others. It has a "linseed aroma" according to the manufacturer. The standard color is white, but you can add Bioshield Pigments if desired. If you'd like to try this paint, you can order it from Eco Design Co. or from the **Building for Health Materials Center**.

A popular line of imported German paints is Livos, which can be purchased from the North American distributor (**Livos Phytochemistry, Inc.**) as well dealers such as **Natural Home by Natürlich**, **Karen's Natural Products**, and the **Building for Health Materials Center**. Livos Albion is a water-based flat wall paint containing hemp oil (by the way, hemp oil is naturally anti-fungal agent), and orange-peel oil, among other natural ingredients. They also have two oil-based products. Livos Cantos is a satin-finish paint containing linseed oil, orange-peel oil, *citron oil* (oil from a type of citrus fruit), *ethanol* (alcohol), and other natural compounds, while Livos Vindo is a high-gloss version made with castor oil, linseed oil, pine oil, and citron oil, among others. Be aware that these oil-based products are going to be particularly odorous, especially when fresh. Overall, because of the oils and solvents used in any oil-based paints, it's highly suggested that readers review *Oil-Based Vs. Water-Based Paints* on page 270 before purchasing. Also, individuals with citrus allergies may want to avoid Livos paints because of the orange and citron oils used.

It should be mentioned, that another alternative, imported, German paint line you may come across is Auro Plant Chemistry. Auro #332 Professional Wall Paint, Auro #301 Wall Paint Primer and Auro #321 Emulsion Wall Paint are all white, water-based paints with natural oils and resins. Most formulations contain water, kalkspat, dammar, linseed-stand oil, citrus terpenes, rosemary oil, eucalyptus terpenes, and plant alcohol. Boric acid and other borate compounds are added as natural preservatives. Not surprisingly, these paints are said to have "a pleasant fragrance" when applied. Auro #330 Natural Color Concentrate (earth pigments in natural binders) can be purchased to add color. All these are sold by **Sinan Co.** and **Karen's Natural Products**.

Homemade Paints

If you're the adventurous type, you may want to make your own paint. However, you'll certainly want to experiment, test, and sample ahead of time to get a good indication of what you've created. Directions to make paint as well as the raw materials to do so are sold by **Building for Health Materials Center**. Ingredients offered are dry casein powder, mica, powdered clays, earth pigments, chalk, and borax. Also sold are natural oils, plant resins, essential oils, and more.

Remember, you'll not get any product-specific specifications, guarantees, or warranties when you make your own paint. If your paint has no preservatives, it will have a very short shelf life. If it has no fungicides, it may not be appropriate for damp areas.

Clear Finishes

Alternative clear finishes come in a variety of formulas. Most of are water-based (see *Oil-Based Vs. Water-Based Paints* on page 270). Some are designed to be applied to raw wood while some are for use on other types of surfaces. Naturally, it's important to choose the finish most suitable, durable, and tolerable for the job.

As has been stressed throughout this book, sensitive people should test any product first before using it. (Read *Important Testing Considerations* on page 267 for exceptions.) This is especially a good idea if you plan to use a clear finish on a large area, such as a floor. (See also *Testing Paints and Finishes* on page 267. You may also want to check out *Solid-Wood Floors* on page 308 and *Ceramic Tile Floors* on page 314, as well as *Unfinished and Kit Furniture* on page 335, for suggestions on actually applying clear finishes.)

Water-Based Polyurethane

Polyurethane finishes use *polyurethane resin* as a binder. However, because this particular resin is expensive, its often mixed with other synthetic binders such as acrylic resins. In most cases, polyurethane finishes are clear (some have stains or solid pigments added) and they work well at protecting wood surfaces.

However, you should be aware that there are both oil- and water-based polyurethane clear finishes. Of the two, the oil-based types should be avoided. This is because their solvents are very strong-smelling and potentially harmful when the finish is being applied and while it's curing. While oil-based polyurethanes are admittedly very durable finishes, some very chemically-sensitive persons have found that, even many months after application—long after they should have been cured—they're still bothersome.

Fortunately, the relatively new water-based polyurethane finishes can be used instead of the oil-based versions. These products tend to dry quickly and generally have little or no residual odor after less than a week. As a result, many very chemically sensitive individuals find that water-based polyurethane finishes are quite tolerable. Other advantages to using these particular products include the fact that they're commonly stocked in local stores, and they are lower in cost than many other types of alternative, clear finishes. Their big drawback is their wearablity. Some brands warn that they're "not for use in heavy traffic areas." Therefore, before purchasing any water-based polyurethane product, read labels carefully to know what you're getting *before* you apply it. You should also consider what *sheen* (light reflectablity) you want. Most brands are made with either a satin or gloss finish, and some have other sheens available.

There are several national brands of clear, water-based polyurethane you might want to try. Olympic Water Based Polyurethane (**PPG Architectural Finishes, Inc.**) is one that can be used as a wood-floor finish, but only for light-traffic floors. Aqua Zar Water Based Polyurethane (**United Gilsonite Laboratories**) is another product. Aqua Zar should not be used for high-traffic areas. These brands, and similar ones, may be carried by your local building center or hardware store. It's likely that most brands will work successfully for you. It should be added that Hydroline Wood Floor Finish and Street Shoe (both by **Basic Coatings, Inc.**) are professional water-based finishes requiring a separate additional catalyst ingredient. If you are having your floors done, it might be one you'd like your contractor to use. It will be more durable than some of the non-catalyzed finishes.

An alternative product that may work for you is AFM Safecoat Polyureseal BP (**AFM**). This BP product is said to have "exceptional durability and abrasion resistance" for residential wood floors and is even recommended for "high-use gyms and warehouses." It contains no acrylic or formaldehyde and has a very low VOC content. You can obtain it from AFM dealers including **N.E.E.D.S., Bio Designs, Building for Health Materials Center, Allergy Relief Shop, Inc., American Environmental Health Foundation**, and **The Living Source**.

Acrylic Finishes and Sealants

Clear acrylic finishes create a hard, durable, low-odor coating primarily on woods. Yet, when they're wet and during their drying period, some formulations are somewhat more odorous than the water-based polyurethane finishes. This is true despite their being water-based products. Chemically sensitive individuals often report that some clear acrylic finishes take up to two months before they are tolerable to them. After that, they often become nearly odorless.

One you might try is AFM Safecoat Acrylacq (**AFM**). This is a lower-odor, clear, acrylic finish for furniture. (Also available is AFM Safecoat Lock-In Sanding Sealer which is formulated to raise wood grain for sanding prior to applying a finish coating.) To seal unglazed, porous clay tiles, concrete, and stone, you might try AFM SafeCoat Paver Seal .003 (which is a presealer) or AFM Safecoat MexeSeal.

In addition, **AFM** manufactures AFM Safecoat Hard Seal which is said to "form a continuous membrane when applied properly" which "is particularly effective at sealing in pollution or outgassing of toxic chemical compounds from surfaces." It's specifically recommended "for use as a sealer for vinyl, porous tile, concrete, plastic, and unfinished (*e.g.* plywood) cabinetry." Furthermore, it's said to leave a glossy finish after several coats have built up. The company notes, however, to "always test for adhesion prior to use" and not to use it where there will be "heavy moisture." Besides Hard Seal, you could opt for AFM Safecoat Safe Seal. This clear acrylic-formula finish was created primarily to seal in the formaldehyde *outgassing* (emissions) from particleboard and plywood. (Note: Many sensitive people find that such sealers help, but not enough to make a bothersome material tolerable. In other words, sealants tend to be imperfect.) AFM Safecoat Safe Seal is also said to add water repellence to concrete and other porous surfaces, but will not add sheen. All AFM finishes can be ordered from **The Living Source, N.E.E.D.S., healthyhome.com, Building for Health Materials Center, Bio Designs, Allergy Relief Shop, Inc.,** and **American Environmental Health Foundation.**

In addition, you might want to try using either Crystal Aire or the more durable floor finish, Crystal Shield, both of which are manufactured by **Pace Chem Industries, Inc.** These products have been especially created, not only as clear finishes, but also as *sealants*. In fact, four coats of Crystal Aire are said to reduce formaldehyde emissions from typical particleboard by up to 92%. Although this is commendable, the remaining 8% is still too bothersome to many sensitive people. Once completely dry, Pace Chem products are quite inert. If you want to buy them, they can be ordered directly from the company or from dealers such as **Karen's Natural Products.**

Shellac and Shellac Sealants

Shellac is an ancient finish, being first developed in the Far East. It uses purified *lac resin* (a secretion deposited on tree branches by female lac insects) as its binding agent. Lac—and therefore, shellac—varies in color from pale, translucent yellow to dark orange, depending on the variety of tree the lac insects live on. As it turns out, shellac produces a fairly tough finish that is commonly used to coat wood. However, white discolorations can manifest themselves rather quickly if water gets on a shellacked surface.

It's important to understand that shellac is neither a water-based, nor an oil-based, product. Instead, it uses alcohol as its vehicle. Therefore, *denatured alcohol* is necessary for cleaning up. (Denatured alcohol is a common thinner made simply of alcohol altered in such a manner as to make it undrinkable.) In fact, because of the alcohol content in shellac, it's quite flammable. It's also extremely odorous when wet. Fortunately, the alcohol evaporates very quickly, and when the finish is completely dry, shellacked items are often tolerable to many sensitive individuals. However, some people have noted that, sometimes, a noticeable, and bothersome, "shellacky" odor will persist.

Most people consider shellac to be a completely pure and natural finish. However, most brands today contain a few additives—sometimes synthetic ones. When you're ready to purchase shellac. You'll find that there are usually several conventional shellac brands to choose from in your local building center, hardware, or paint store. A popular brand is Bull's Eye Shellac (**Wm. Zinsser & Co.**) A source for pure shellac, as well as other natural resins (dammar crystals, sandarac, congo copal, etc.), is the **Building for Health Materials Center**. German Auro #211 and #213 Clear Shellacs can be purchased from **Sinan Co.** and **Karen's Natural Products**.

Some paint and finish manufacturers use shellac in their sealant products. For example, **Wm. Zinsser & Co.** markets B-I-N Primer Sealer. This is a fast drying white sealing paint, made primarily of shellac. It's commonly used by professional paint contractors to cover up water stains on walls. It can be purchased at most hardware stores, paint stores, and building centers. (Note: Some report that the "shellacky" odor persists after it has dried.)

Livos Masking Shellac is a German-import formulation which can be ordered from the North American distributor (**Livos Phytochemistry, Inc.**), as well as dealers such as **Karen's Natural Products**, **Natural Home by Natürlich** and the **Building for Health Materials Center**. It's described as being able to mask and seal toxic chemicals and emissions from conventional products used to manufacture cabinetry by up to 98%. For most people, this may be sufficient. However, very sensitive people may find that the emissions that permeate through the shellac are still problematic. Then, too, there may also remain a mild "shellacky" odor.

Note: It's important to test more than one brand of shellac (if possible) to see how they look, and how well you tolerate them (see *Important Testing Considerations* on page 267 and *Testing Paints and Finishes* on page 267).

Penetrating-Oil Finishes

Some individuals may want to try a natural *penetrating-oil finish* on their wood items. A penetrating-oil finish doesn't leave a thin, hard coating on wood surfaces, but instead it penetrates down for some distance into a piece and saturates the very fibers of the wood itself. Therefore, if the wood's surface ever becomes scratched or abraded, you can simply apply more oil to the damaged area and it will blend in without the need for stripping and refinishing.

However, there is a downside. Many of the oils used as wood finishes are fairly odorous when applied. And, they can remain quite odorous for a considerable amount of time afterwards as well. In fact, their smells could continue to be bothersome for up to several months—or longer. Of course, this depends on the specific oil, wood, and your personal tolerance but, in general, oil finishes are not well tolerated by chemically-sensitive people.

Two of the more popular natural penetrating oils are *tung oil* (derived from the nuts of tung-oil trees) and *linseed oil* (derived from flax seeds). Of these, tung oil is not recommended. This is because it's been implicated in suppressing immune system functions, as well as reactivating chronic Epstein-Barr virus infections. However, there are certainly other oils available.

Livos makes several penetrating oils which are offered by their North American distributor (**Livos Phytochemistry, Inc.**) and their dealers such as **Karen's Natural Products, Natural Home by Natürlich** and the **Building for Health Materials Center**. One, Livos Ardvos (formulated with linseed oil, orange-peel oil, and others), is said to be good for furniture, floors, and butcher blocks. Similar oil finishes are made under the Bio Shield Natural Choice Collection label (**Eco Design Co.**). They include Bio Shield Hardwood Penetrating Oil Seal #8 (linseed oil, citrus terpenes, essential oils, etc.), as well as other linseed-oil-based products such as Hard Oil #9, Natural Resin Floor Finish #4, Herbal Oil Finish, and Hardwood Floor Finish & Sealer #6. These can all be ordered from the manufacturer or from the **Building for Health Materials Center**. (Note: Oil finishes using orange oils are not recommended for citrus-allergic people.) Auro Plant Chemistry, too, produces comparable products such as Auro #121 Natural Resin Oil Primer and #126 Natural Resin Oil Sealer. Auro products can be purchased from **Sinan Co.** and **Karen's Natural Products**.

Of all the oils, probably the most commonly used one is linseed. Linseed oil, which is naturally anti-bacterial, is available in two varieties: *raw* and *boiled*. While raw linseed oil will not dry properly when applied to wood, boiled linseed oil will. In the past, many manufacturers simply heated raw linseed oil to give it drying properties but, today, most "boiled" linseed oil has not been heat-processed at all. Instead, manufacturers add toxic heavy-metal additives, such as lead acetate or cobalt manganese, to aid in drying. Fortunately, there are two types of boiled linseed oil still being made without these types of additives. Varnish Oil (nontoxic, 100% linseed oil) and Original Wood Finish (nontoxic linseed oil and beeswax). Both are available by mail order from **Garrett Wade Co.**

Auro #143 Linseed Oil is offered by **Sinan Co.** and **Karen's Natural Products**. In addition, natural linseed oil is handled by **Building for Health Materials Center** which also has a tremendous variety of other natural oils including walnut, poppy, sunflower, lavender, etc.

One final note, if you find you need to use a penetrating oil finish on salad bowls or kitchen-knife handles, consider using *virgin olive oil*. Olive oil is not only nontoxic, it's also resistant to becoming rancid. Also, Non-toxic Preserve is a combination of nut oils said to polish and preserve wooden salad bowls, children's toys, etc. One mail-order source is **Priorities**. Contacting **Building for Health Materials Center** to see what they have that's appropriate is a good idea, too.

Wax Finishes

Waxes such as *carnuba wax* (derived from the plant waxes found on certain palm leaves) and *beeswax* (derived from honeycombs) are sometimes used to create clear, natural finishes on wood. Like penetrating oils, waxes provide protection that can be easily repaired if a scratched area should develop. This is because they penetrate and saturate wood rather than form a thin brittle layer that lies on the surface. For some people, natural waxes can be good wood-finishing choices.

However, it's important to know that many natural waxes are somewhat hard in consistency. Therefore, these pure waxes are heated or mixed with denatured alcohol, turpentine, or another volatile solvent to make them more workable. Of course, solvents could make a wax application intolerable to many chemically sensitive individuals. However, it should be noted that, once the added solvent has completely evaporated, the finish could be quite acceptable for these very same people. Of more concern are packaged wax formulations which may have paint thinners or similar solvents added, as well as other odorous ingredients such as oils and resins. Therefore, make sure to check the ingredients of any wax product before purchasing it, if such ingredients could be a problem for you. Remember: Testing is important, especially if you're chemically sensitive (see *Important Testing Considerations* on page 267 and *Testing Paints and Finishes* on page 267).

A long-time, popular wax choice is beeswax. But it should mentioned that beeswax tends to have a somewhat flowery odor. Although some people may find this attractive, others may find it bothersome. You can generally purchase pure beeswax from local bee-keepers. To find a beekeeper, check your local classified telephone directory. Livos beeswax is sold by the North American distributor (**Livos Phytochemistry, Inc.**) and dealers including **Karen's Natural Products, Building for Health Materials Center**, and **Natural Home by Natürlich**. Auro #181 Liquid Beeswax Finish can be obtained from **Sinan Co.** and **Karen's Natural Products.**

Carnuba wax (a tree wax) is also popular for finishing wood. Often, you'll be able to find carnuba wax in your local hardware store. One popular brand that has a turpentine-like odor is Trewax. However, a pure carnuba wax is handled by the **Building for Health Materials Center**. In addition, **Natural Home by Natürlich** has it's own Natürlich Carnuba Wax which contains a liquid carnuba wax and 2% acrylic. Other natural-formula waxes you can order from the same company are manufactured by Livos, such as Livos Hydro Wax (a water/wax product). Livos Waxes, are also available from the North American distributor (**Livos Phytochemistry, Inc.**) and dealers including **Karen's Natural Products** and the **Building for Health Materials Center**.

Other wax products are manufactured and sold by **Eco Design Co.** For example, Bio Shield Floor Wax Impregnation #30 (linseed oil, tung oil, carnuba wax, orange peel oil, essential oil, and other ingredients) is one for use in high traffic areas. Also available is a Bioshield Floor & Furniture Hardwax #32 (beeswax, linseed oil, orange oil, essential oils, carnuba wax, etc.) designed to be used after a penetrating oil primer/sealer. By the way, another source for Bio Shield products is **Building for Health Materials Center.**

Lastly, the Auro Plant Chemistry line includes Auro #173 Larch Resin Furniture Wax (larchwood resin and beeswax) and Auro #171 Floor and Furniture Plant Wax (an ointment of beeswax and plant waxes). If you're interested, these can be ordered from **Sinan Co.** and **Karen's Natural Products.**

Water Glass

Water glass is a term applied to certain water-soluble *sodium silicate compounds*. Interestingly, these compounds have a similar chemical composition to ordinary window glass. As it turns out, water-glass solutions used as finishes are transparent and virtually odor-free. This is also true when they're wet. Not surprisingly, these are commonly very tolerable products for sensitive individuals.

Water glass was once a popular product. However, since World War II, synthetic sealants have nearly replaced it. But water glass is still sometimes used as an effective grout and concrete sealer. As it turns out, when water glass comes into contact with the calcium (and certain other substances) in these materials, a chemical reaction takes place. The result is the creation of a hard, clear, crystalline surface that's very durable. Water glass can also be used to protect your ceramic-tile grout joints by applying it carefully to the dry grout joints—not the tile—with a small artist's paint brush.

It should be noted that water glass should not be applied to a concrete floor—if you ever plan to apply ceramic tile to it later. This is because the sealed surface would be nonporous. As a result, it would prevent the adhesion of the ceramic-tile mortar. Another consideration to keep in mind is not to use too much water glass when you're applying it. A little goes a long way, and applying too much could result in a film that might peel off.

Three types of water glass is manufactured by **AFM**. AFM Penetrating Water Stop has a thin formula to allow it to soak in easily, while AFM Water Shield has a thicker formula to better create a surface coating. Also available is AFM Safecoat Grout Sealer. This product contains not only water glass but acrylic, and other synthetic polymer resins, to make it adhere better to grout. All these are sold by most AFM dealers including **N.E.E.D.S.**, **The Living Source**, **Bio Designs**, **Allergy Relief Shop, Inc.**, **Building for Health Materials Center**, and **American Environmental Health Foundation**. Another brand, The Natural Paint Company Water Glass, is sold by **Building for Health Materials Center**.

Stains

Many woods look interesting and attractive just as they are. And by leaving them natural, you'll avoid using at least one potentially bothersome product—wood stain. However, if you decide you really want to use a stain anyway, following is some basic information about stains that you may find useful.

Wood stains are generally available in either oil-based or water-based formulas. Oil-based types often produce richer, deeper tones than their water-based counterparts. Unfortunately, they're also usually somewhat more odorous. They also require paint thinner or turpentine for cleanup (see *Oil-Based Vs. Water-Based Paints* on page 270).

While water-based stains generally don't appear as rich-looking, they do have other distinct advantages. For example, they contain fewer *VOCs* (volatile organic compounds) and they don't need noxious solvents for cleanup. As a result, although water-based stains are not odor-free, they're less bothersome than their oil-based counterparts.

If you want to use a water-based stain, it's best to test several brands for appearance and personal tolerance. Of course, tolerance testing is always essential for chemically sensitive persons. By the way, it is best to stain a sample piece of wood, as well as apply two coats of clear finish, then test for tolerability (see *Important Testing Considerations* on page 267 and *Testing Paints and Finishes* on page 267). This is important because the clear finish will often seal in any minor odors from the stain. But you won't know for sure until you've actually tested the sample.

Local paint stores often stock typical water-based stains. However, water-based stains can also be purchased by mail order. One of these is AFM Safecoat Duro Stain (**AFM**). This particular brand was originally target-marketed to chemically sensitive people and is very low in odor. These stains contain no coal tar, aniline dyes, waxes, or aromatic solvents. Duro Stain is available from AFM dealers including **N.E.E.D.S.**, **The Living Source**, **Allergy Relief Shop, Inc.**, **Building for Health Materials Center**, healthyhome.com, and **American Environmental Health Foundation**.

In addition, some of the German-formula natural paint companies also make alternative stains you might want to try. The #630 Auro Water Based Interior Natural Stains are made with water, earthen and mineral pigments, linseed oil, tung-stand oil, safflower-stand oil, rosemary oil, eucalyptus terpenes, liquid ammonia, plant alcohol, etc. with borax and other borate compounds added as natural preservatives. These are sold by **Sinan Co.** and **Karen's Natural Products**. Livos stains are attractive, but oil-based. They're available from their North American distributor (**Livos Phytochemistry, Inc.**) and dealers including **Natural Home by Natürlich** and **Building for Health Materials Center**. Under the Bioshield (**Eco Design Co.**) label is Resin & Oil Stain Finish #3. This is an oil-based finish/stain combination which can be ordered from the manufacturer or **Building for Health Materials Center.**

Paint Strippers

Virtually all paint strippers in the past were *extremely* noxious products. This is because they were solvent-based and contained powerful, dangerous chemicals (such as methylene chloride) that were harmful if inhaled or came in contact with your skin. Many were also flammable.

While many of the old nasty strippers are still around, there are now a few water-based paint strippers available. The active stripping agent is usually an *organic ester* (a certain class of carbon compounds). These can dissolve most paints just like the solvent-based strippers, but they tend to require more time to do so. And, it must be admitted, sometimes they aren't always as effective.

By the way, wood that's been stripped with a water-based product generally requires an application of a *neutralizing solution*. This is necessary to counter the caustic action of the organic esters. However, this can be easily done by simply sponging on a vinegar-and-water solution. For the correct dilution, follow the label directions for the product you're using.

To find a water-based stripper, check your local paint store, hardware store, or building center. One popular brand usually stocked is Safest Stripper Paint and Varnish Remover (**3M Construction & Home Improvement Products Div.**). This product uses dimethyl esters as its active ingredients. Another brand you might find locally is Strypeeze (**Savogran**), a biodegradable stripper with "no harmful fumes." It is recommended that a TSP (trisodium phosphate) solution be used for cleaning it off. Ready-Strip is a lower-odor, nonflammable, biodegradable, water-clean-up product sold by **healthyhome.com**. Interestingly, it changes color when it's done it's job so you know when to remove it.

A German all-natural import is Auro #461 Paint Stripper. This product has a different type of formulation than some of the other alternatives. It's made with water, potash lye, wheat meal, linseed potash soap, citrus terpenes, eucalyptus terpenes, liquid ammonia, plant alcohol, and beeswax (ammonia soap). Boric acid and other borate compounds are added as natural preservatives. It's likely that the ammonia, as well as some of the other ingredients, will make this an odorous product to use. If you'd like to purchase it, you'll find that it's carried by **Sinan Co.** and **Karen's Natural Products.**

(For more on how to use paint strippers, see *Antique Furniture* on page 339.)

Adhesives

In the sections that follow, all types of adhesive products are discussed—everything from tapes to caulkings. Some of these products are quite benign. However, others will require, at a minimum, good ventilation. As always, it's important to carefully read and follow the label directions for the best results. For most people it's wise to test a prospective adhesive first for both tolerance and effectiveness before using it on a large project (see *Important Testing Considerations* on page 267 *Testing Adhesives* on page 268).

(Note: For information on safe application procedures for certain types of adhesives, see the appropriate sections in *Chapter 11: Home Remodeling.*)

Tapes

Clear plastic tapes are probably the most common household adhesive product. Although tapes are often made of petrochemically derived transparent film coated on one side with glue, they're usually relatively low in odor. Although clear plastic tapes are extremely popular, if you'd prefer a more natural material, cellophane tapes are still available.

Cellophane tapes are made from a transparent film derived from plant cellulose (see *Cellophane Goods* on page 510). Although it's a natural material and virtually odorless, cellophane (and, therefore, cellophane tape) has the drawback of yellowing and degrading with age. As you probably already know, both plastic and cellophane tapes are sold in many drugstores, discount stores, and office-supply stores.

In situations calling for a wider, stronger tape, *aluminum-foil duct tape* can be a good choice. However, you should realize that this type of duct tape isn't the same as fabric-backed duct tape, which is made of a heavy woven fabric with glue on one side and a plastic coating on the other. With time, many low-cost fabric-backed duct tapes tend to lose their ability to adhere and so become unstuck relatively quickly. In addition, fabric-backed duct tape often has an odor that sensitive individuals find bothersome.

On the other hand, aluminum-foil duct tape is generally of higher quality and more costly. It's made of a very thin strip of heavy-duty aluminum foil with glue on one side. Aluminum-foil duct tapes are generally lower in odor because the metal surface seals in most of the adhesive odors from the sticky side. However, although aluminum-foil duct tape usually adheres better than fabric-backed duct tape, it may still eventually loosen.

Aluminum-foil duct tape is not difficult to find. It's often available in local hardware stores and is generally handled by most heating/cooling equipment suppliers. One brand that has proven to be especially tolerable for many sensitive individuals is Polyken aluminum-foil tape. It's sold by mail order by **American Environmental Health Foundation** in both 2" and 3" widths and by **E.L Foust Co., Inc.**

Incidentally, an alternative to aluminum-foil tape is stainless-steel tape. Both are made in a similar manner. However, some aluminum-sensitive persons prefer this more inert material. Though difficult to find, stainless-steel tape can sometimes be located in hardware stores, building centers, and furnace-supply shops.

Glues

For gluing paper, inexpensive, common *mucilage glue* can work quite well. True mucilage glue is made of gummy plant secretions. However, this term is now also applied to a range of similar, simple liquid glues. Generally, mucilage glues are safe to use (many are labeled "nontoxic") and they don't have much of an odor. One you might try is Elmer's Mucilage (**Elmer's Products, Inc.**), which is labeled as nontoxic. It, and other similar brands, are sold in drugstores, office-supply stores, and some discount stores. Other glues from **Elmer's Products, Inc.** that your family may want to use include Elmer's Sno-Drift (a washable, nontoxic, white paste) and Elmer's Glue Sticks and Glue Gels (nontoxic, handy-to-use formulas.).

Of course, *white household glue*, such as the nontoxic Elmer's Glue-All (**Elmer's Products, Inc.**) and Weldwood Hobby 'N Craft Glue (**Dap, Inc.**), is an very popular, low-odor product. White glues are chiefly soluble-synthetic-resin-and-water solutions, or more specifically, *polyvinyl acetate (PVA) emulsions*. In other words, water is their vehicle and PVA is their binding agent. As they dry, the water evaporates, leaving a thin, semi-brittle, plastic film.

White glues are designed primarily for gluing paper, cardboard and wood. However, because they're so readily available and convenient to use, many people use them for jobs for which they were never intended. Unfortunately, white glues aren't waterproof. No matter how long they've been dried, they can become liquefied if they ever become wet. Therefore, white glues shouldn't be used for anything that will be outdoors, or exposed to moisture indoors. If you'd like to purchase a white glue, it will be available at most local grocery stores, pharmacies, office-supply stores, and discount stores.

Another fairly common household glue is *yellow carpenter's glue*. This type of glue is often very similar to white glue in composition. However, it can contain extra additives that permit better adhesion to woods. Two brands of yellow carpenter glue are Elmer's Carpenter Wood Glue for Interior Use (**Elmer's Products, Inc.**) and Weld-Wood Carpenter's Glue (**Dap, Inc.**). The Weldwood product is described as having an aliphatic resin base.

For many years, all yellow carpenter's glues were water-soluble. However, some brands are now available in waterproof formulations as well. One of these is Elmer's Carpenter Wood Glue for Exterior Use (**Elmer's Products, Inc.**). (Note: In some cases, waterproof glues may be more odorous than non-waterproof types.) If you'd like to purchase a carpenters glue, they're generally found in lumberyards, building centers, and hardware stores.

An entirely different type of wood glue is *casein glue*. Casein glues use a milk by-product as their main adhesive component. One you might try is Auro #789 Powder Casein Wood Glue. It is recommended for furniture and interior wood construction, but not floors. To use this Auro glue, mix it with water, apply to the wood surfaces, and clamp overnight. Auro products are available from **Sinan Co.** and **Karen's Natural Products**.

If you need a glue for jewelry or other unusual items, often an *epoxy glue* works well. In fact, epoxy will work on virtually any material: metal, ceramic, wood, and even fabric. Generally, this type of glue comes packaged with two tubes: one containing a *catalyst agent*, the other containing an *epoxy resin*. To use epoxy glue, it's necessary to mix equal amounts from these two tubes together. The combination of the two compounds produces the chemical reaction that results in an extremely strong, durable, and waterproof bond. Unfortunately, most epoxy glues have a strong odor due to their chemical ingredients. If you must use an epoxy glue, make sure to have plenty of ventilation. If you're a chemically sensitive or asthmatic person, someone else may have to do the gluing for you, and you'll also need to set the newly epoxied item aside a few days until all the odor has dissipated.

In some situations, you may need to use a *contact cement* in your home. Contact cement is a synthetic adhesive. To use it, both surfaces to be joined are coated with adhesive, the glue is allowed to dry, then the surfaces are brought into contact with each other, creating a permanent bond.

In homes, contact cement is commonly used to attach a hard, plastic laminate (Formica is one popular brand) to a man-made wood product (such as particleboard) in order to create a countertop (see *High Pressure Plastic Laminates* on page 323). Unfortunately, most typical contact cements have a very strong odor. However, fairly recently, much less odorous, and much less hazardous, water-based versions have been developed. Whether these adhere as well as conventional contact cements, is still debatable however. One of these you might want to try is Weldwood Non-Flammable Contact Cement (**Dap, Inc.**) This particular brand is polychlororoprene based. Call the manufacturer for a dealer in your area or check your local hardware stores and building centers for it, and similar brands.

Wallpaper Pastes

When you're wallpapering, you can use one of the wheat, or other vegetable-starch, wallpaper pastes that are often still available at many local wallpaper stores. However, you should be aware that some of these products may contain fungicides, that act as mold inhibitors, or biocides to deter insects, bacteria, and mold. Unfortunately, some of these chemical fungicides and biocides can be odorous or otherwise bothersome to certain people.

One wallpaper paste you might try is Auro #389 Natural Wallpaper Adhesive which can be ordered from **Sinan Co.** and **Karen's Natural Products.** It's an all-natural German formulation in a dry powder form that you mix with water. The only ingredient is methyl cellulose. By the way, the company recommends it be used for "light-to-medium paper-based wall coverings." While you may conclude that this is simply because it doesn't have enough "holding power" for heavier coverings, there is another, often overlooked, reason behind this. Vinyl or foil types of wallpaper, unlike light-to-medium weight paper, are non-porous so they can't "breathe." Even very thick papers have slowed air penetration, compared to thinner papers. As a result, the wet wallpaper paste underneath these materials stays wet longer, so it can be an ideal environment for fungal growth.

Of course, some people may want to make their own wallpaper paste by simply mixing wheat starch and water. If you do this, however, it's a good idea to add one tablespoon of boric acid powder to each quart of paste (this also can be added to any prepackaged all-natural wallpaper paste). Boric acid has innate mold- and insect-inhibiting qualities, yet it doesn't seem to bother most sensitive people.

You'll find you can usually purchase boric acid at your local drugstore. Although it's considered much safer than many petrochemical pesticides, you should realize it's not a totally nontoxic substance. Therefore, children or pets should not have access to boric-acid powder or any wallpaper paste containing it.

Drywall Compounds

Many people assume that drywall compounds are simple all-natural, completely harmless substances. Actually, this is not the case. Although drywall compounds are made primarily of gypsum with some mica, talc, limestone, and clay, they also contain vinyl adhesives, fungicide preservatives, and often antifreeze. In addition, up until 1977, some drywall compounds also contained asbestos. (It should be noted that typical drywall compounds are usually marketed as thick, gray, mud-like pastes in plastic tubs.)

Unfortunately, because of their many ingredients, most typical modern drywall compounds tend to have relatively strong odors, especially when wet. As a result, some sensitive individuals have been bothered for months (or years) by walls coated with typical drywall compounds.

Fortunately, an alternative drywall compound is now available—Murco Hypo M100 (**Murco Wall Products, Inc.**). This is a powdered, "all-purpose joint cement and texture compound with inert fillers and natural binders, no preservatives or slow releasing compounds." It has no fungicides, formaldehyde, or petroleum-derived solvents. Therefore, this particular product is extremely well-tolerated by even the most sensitive individuals. In fact, it's almost odor-free even when wet! Murco Hypo M100 can also be used for minor spackling jobs.

Unlike typical drywall compounds, Murco M100 is packaged in bags as a dry powder that must be mixed with water just prior to use. Because it's fungicide-free, once mixed, it should not be stored for more than a day. Important note: this particular product should not be used on walls that will have an alcohol-based paint or sealant applied directly over the drywall joint compound. This is because, in some cases, the ingredients in the Murco Hypo M100 have chemically reacted with the alcohol, resulting in a deterioration of the joint compound. This could lead to cracking and crazing. If you'd like to purchase Murco

Hypo M100, it can be ordered directly from the company and from **Building for Health Materials Center.**

Thinset Ceramic-Tile Mortars

Thinset mortars—also known as dry-set mortars—are cement-like adhesives used to adhere ceramic tile to a base material. Unfortunately, some typical thinset mortars are very odorous because of various additives. The precise ingredients are usually considered trade secrets by manufacturers, so it's impossible to say exactly what they are, but they likely include fungicides (to retard mold growth) and a variety of other substances to prevent cracking and crumbling. At any rate, the odor from these ingredients is strongest when the thinset mortar is wet. Fortunately, in many cases, if your thinset has only a mild odor, once the thinset has dried, the ceramic tile and the grout in the joints will likely successfully seal in any residual odors.

By the way, it should be noted that you can sometimes "guesstimate" fairly well how odorous a thinset mortar will ultimately be. This can be done simply by judging the odor you perceive when you open a bag of the dry, powdered thinset product. However, an even better indication is to get a small sample and mix it with water. If you detect a strong "chemical-type" odor, don't use it. If it has only a mild odor, there's a good chance it will be acceptable when used in your home. (Important note: This sniffing procedure should be tried *only* by healthy people, and even then, they should take only a very light sniff.)

Important note: If you're a chemically sensitive person and plan to use any thinset mortar, it's extremely important to test it more thoroughly. (See *Important Testing Considerations* on page 267.) To do this, first purchase a large, odor-free patio block. On its backside, write down the date and the brand of thinset you plan to test (as well as the type of grout and tile). Then, simply apply a layer of thinset mortar to the topside of the patio block. Next, adhere some of the same ceramic tile you plan to use in your upcoming home project. When the thinset mortar is dry, you can then apply the grout to the joints, making sure that none of the thinset mortar is left uncovered around the edges. (If the grout requires damp-curing, you'll need to mist the tile/grout surface and cover it with plastic sheeting. For more on this, see *Ceramic Tile Installation* on page 315.) After the grout has cured, you can then very lightly sniff the surface of the sample block. (This procedure, as with all sniff tests, is not recommended for asthmatics.) If there's an odor, wait a week and lightly sniff it again. Repeat this until no odor is detected, then you can put the sample block next to your bed. If you sleep well through the night, it usually means you can easily tolerate the thinset, the grout, and the tile. Finally, you'll need to make a note on the backside of the patio block as to how long it took to become tolerable.

C-Cure is one manufacturer of thinset ceramic-tile mortar that has often worked well for adhering tile to a variety of surfaces with minimal odor. One product in particular, Multi-Cure 905, has often proven to be quite acceptable, although there are others in their line with even fewer additives. While these may be more tolerable to some people than Multi-Cure 905, they can't always be used on as many different surfaces. You may purchase C-Cure thinsets in many local ceramic-tile stores. If you have trouble finding them, call the company for its nearest dealer.

Important note: Multi-Cure is made in several factories across the U.S. As a result, formulations will vary from one part of the country to another depending on which supplier provided which ingredients. Actually, this is true with many thinset manufacturers—a product sold in one part of the U.S. may have a very low odor, while the same brand sold in another area may have a strong chemical odor. Therefore, one particular brand isn't always recommended for sensitive people. Instead, it is better to see if the locally available brand has a strong chemical odor. If it does, choose a different brand.

By the way, the grout that goes between the tiles doesn't need as many additives as the thinset, to do its job well. So, a nontoxic grout can be made with simply water, sand, and Portland cement. Because it doesn't have any extra additives, this grout must be damp cured. Complete instructions for mixing, applying, and curing home-made grout are covered in *Healthy House Building for the New Millennium* by John Bower. The book can be ordered from **The Healthy House Institute** or through your favorite bookseller.

Caulkings

Typically, caulkings are very odorous, especially while being applied. Unfortunately, the odor can sometimes linger for a long time afterwards. This shouldn't be too surprising when you realize that most modern caulking products contain a variety of synthetic, petroleum-derived ingredients. As a result, a caulking could release acetone, methyl ethyl ketone, methyl porpionate, and a variety of other noxious substances into the air, depending on the exact type and brand.

One-hundred-percent *silicone* caulkings are often suggested for sensitive individuals. Silicone is actually a synthetic product consisting of alternating oxygen and silicon atoms. This particular molecular combination results in a material that's both rubbery and very stable. As a result, silicone caulkings are resistant to high temperatures and water. Although most 100%-silicone caulkings are quite strong-smelling when first applied, once they're dry they are often quite inert. However, the main reason they've been recommended to sensitive persons for some time now is that they're quite durable, so they don't have to be replaced for many years. One serious drawback to 100%-silicone caulkings is that, as a rule, they can't be painted. Fortunately, some brands are now made in white, brown, and a few other basic colors besides clear. If you're interested in purchasing 100%-silicone caulking, it's usually sold in most local hardware stores and building centers.

Most silicone caulkings contain acetic acid, which aids in curing. "Neutral-cure" silicone caulkings don't use acetic acid, so they are a little less odorous, but they can be more difficult to find. Some people recommend using *aquarium-grade silicone* caulkings. These caulkings are usually FDA approved, but they generally contain acetic acid. To buy aquarium caulking, check with local pet centers and tropical-fish shops.

In situations where it's desirable to paint the caulking, you might try a "latex" caulking. Originally, these were made with natural or synthetic rubber (along with other ingredients). However, some caulkings that are called "latex" today use entirely different formulations, because the word "latex" has now become a generic term for any water-based caulking.

A real advantage to "latex" caulkings is that, unlike silicone caulkings, drips and smears can be easily cleaned up with water—that is, if they haven't had a chance to dry yet. But one real disadvantage to latex caulkings is that they're not nearly as durable as their 100%-silicone counterparts. You should also be aware that "latex" caulkings are not odor free. They definitely have an odor when they're being applied, which could persist for a few days or a few weeks. Then, too, those with real latex in them are obviously not suitable for latex-allergic people. If you're interested in using a "latex" caulking, virtually all hardware stores and building centers stock them.

One type of siliconized acrylic caulk that you might try is Elmer's Squeez 'N Caulk (**Elmer's Products, Inc.**). This product is sold in clear, white, and almond colors. It is water-

and mildew-resistant and nontoxic. For your convenience, it comes in a handy, squeezable plastic bottle.

A caulk with an especially effective mildew-resistant formula that you may want to try is Dap Kwik Seal Tub & Tile Adhesive Caulk (**Dap, Inc.**). This "nontoxic," paintable, latex-polymer product is useful for persistently wet locales where mold can quickly grow. Of course, some people would prefer to use products in their homes that contained no fungicides. However, around bathtubs and sinks, the problems arising from inevitable mildew and mold colonization are likely far worse than any that could arise from the antifungal chemicals. Fortunately, you should know that despite containing fungicide additives, Kwik Seal often becomes nearly odor-free within a week or two, and it is widely tolerated by chemically sensitive people. This brand of caulking is sold in many local hardware stores and building centers. However, if you have trouble finding it, contact the manufacturer for its nearest dealer.

One paintable "latex" caulking often tolerated by chemically sensitive people is Phenoseal Vinyl Adhesive Caulk (**Gloucester Co., Inc.**). This particular brand contains no latex, but is instead a type of polyvinyl-acetate emulsion similar to that of common white glues such as Elmer's Glue-All. This caulking is flexible, non-toxic, water- and mildew-resistant, and non-flammable. Like other "latex" caulks, Phenoseal only requires water for cleanup of wet drips or smears. It does have an odor that can be noticeable for a period of time after it's been applied. However, some people feel that this type of caulk is more tolerable for chemically sensitive individuals than other caulking products. If you can't find Phenoseal locally, you can order directly from the manufacturer or from the **Building for Health Materials Center, healthyhome.com**, and **American Environmental Health Foundation**.

Another alternative caulk is AFM Safecoat Caulking Compound (**AFM**). This water-clean-up, acrylic-formulation is handled by the **Building for Health Materials Center, N.E.E.D.S., The Living Source, Bio Designs, Allergy Relief Shop, Inc.**, and **American Environmental Health Foundation**. This product is sold in quart and gallon cans, so you must purchase a pastry bag to apply it.

Note: Because of the odors and ingredients in most caulkings, it's best to following certain precautions when using them. Above all, have plenty of ventilation when you're applying them. Also, it's a good idea to wear a chemical respirator mask (see *Personal Protective Gear* on page 264). It should be stressed that the actual time that will be required for any caulking product to become odorless will depend on the brand, the amount used, the temperature, the relative humidity, and your individual tolerability.

Construction Adhesives

In certain situations where nails or screws aren't appropriate or aren't strong enough alone, construction adhesives are usually used. These come in tubes for use in a caulking gun, or in plastic tubs to be applied with a notched trowel. The caulking gun types are usually used for walls and the tub types as *mastics* for flooring. When using any of these products, use as small an amount as you can, yet enough to do the job.

It should be said right off that, if construction adhesives can be avoided, don't use them. For example, if you're installing a wall mirror in the bathroom, ask your supplier if mirror clips will be sufficient to hold it securely in place. Often times, clips will be adequate. If you're installing vinyl sheet flooring, it may be that the quarter-round molding around the perimeter of the room will hold the flooring in place just fine. However, it must be said that some jobs simply need an adhesive, such as installing some bathtub surrounds. In those situations, choose only water-based products. There should be a number of brands available in local hardware and building centers.

One lower-odor, water-based adhesive you can use for adhering a wide range of flooring (and countertop) materials is AFM Safecoat 3 in 1 Adhesive (**AFM**). The manufacturer says this mastic will adhere ceramic-tile, vinyl, carpet, slate, parquet, and other materials to subfloors. You can order this from AFM dealers such as **N.E.E.D.S.**, **Bio Designs**, **Allergy Relief Shop, Inc.**, **Building for Health Materials Center**, **American Environmental Health Foundation**, **healthyhome.com**, and **The Living Source**.

There are now a number of companies who offer a complete line of zero- or low-VOC adhesives and mastics that you might be able to find locally. They include the Chapco line (**Chicago Adhesive Products Co.**), **Franklin International**, and **W.F. Taylor Co., Inc.** They typically have solvent-free general-purpose adhesives, flooring mastics, carpet adhesives, etc. The Solvent Free Titebond Construction Adhesive by **Franklin International** airs our particularly quickly and has been used by a number of chemically sensitive people. If you can't locate any of these products locally, you can call the companies for a nearby supplier.

A German all-natural-formula-type of mastic is Bio Shield Natural Cork Adhesive #16. It's designed to be used on cork, jute-backed carpet, and linoleum tile. It contains natural latex, plant oils, and plant resins. This is made and sold by **Eco Design Co.** It can also be purchased from **Building for Health Materials Center**.

Another German formulation is Auro #380 Natural All-Purpose Floor Adhesive. This is made with "organic binders in a watery dispersion." Ingredients include citrus terpenes and rosemary oil, and it's recommended for use of cork, linoleum, carpeting and parquet. Said to have "a pleasant odor during and after application," #380 is sold by **Sinan Co.** and **Karen's Natural Products**.

(Note: Remember that construction adhesives having latex as an ingredient should never be handled by latex-allergic people.)

Lubricants

Many typical lubricating products are quite odorous. This is usually because they're petroleum-based. Therefore, they're almost universally bothersome or even intolerable to chemically sensitive individuals for months or even years. Fortunately, however, certain lubricants are now available that have very little odor. These can often be used satisfactorily in a number of situations—but certainly not in all.

Some simple low-odor lubricating options to use on your cabinet and door hinges include petroleum jelly, pharmaceutical-grade mineral oil, or natural plant oils such as jojoba. However, although all of these products can lubricate, they can also leave behind greasy stains. In addition, some of them, in time, will become gummy, and some natural plant oils can eventually become rancid or attract mold or bacteria. However, if you'd like to try one of these options, they're not difficult to find. Petroleum jelly and pharmacy-grade mineral oil are available at drugstores. Jojoba and other plant oils are usually sold in health-food stores, and in some cosmetic departments, or they can be mail-ordered from catalogs offering them listed under *Moisturizers* on page 98.

As another option, household *graphite* lubricating products often work well to lubricate hinges and latches. Graphite lubricants are actually composed of slippery, fine carbon particles. Generally, pure-graphite lubricants have only nominal odor and never become gummy or rancid. Unfortunately, graphite's big drawback is that it often leaves sooty black dust and smears around where it was applied. If you're interested in purchasing a graphite lubricant, check your local hardware store for the brand it carries. Look for a pure product, one that doesn't contain added oil.

One lubricating product that's very good at stopping metal-to-metal squeaks, and at the same time is often well-tolerated by sensitive individuals, is E-Z-1 Synthetic Lubricant (E-Z-1). This product, which comes in a plastic 3.5 oz. bottle with a spray tube attachment, is nearly odorless, non-aerosol, non-flammable, can't conduct electricity, and contains no solvents. It's apparently able to actually penetrate a certain amount of corrosion to loosen rusted nuts and can lubricate, not only metals, but even woods. The maker says it dissolves tar and asphalt, too. To top it off, E-Z-1 is biodegradable. You might find this product in local hardware stores. If not, it can be mail-ordered from **E.L. Foust Co., Inc.** and **Allergy Relief Shop, Inc.**

For machinery, clocks, or any other mechanical devices that require periodic lubrication, it is often wise to use only the type of lubricant recommended by the manufacturer. Unfortunately, in most cases, this means you'll have to use an odorous petroleum-based product. However, if you substitute another kind of lubricant and it doesn't do its job well, it could result in damage as well as voiding of any product warranties or guarantees. Of course, you can place newly lubricated equipment outdoors in dry, uncontaminated surroundings, or indoors in an infrequently used room with good ventilation until they become more tolerable.

In cases where the lubricated item remains bothersome (as with a sewing machine), you might consider using a fan situated so that it blows across the machine and away from your face. This should help dispel the oily smells. In many cases, people tend to use far more lubricant than is necessary. So, only apply a very small amount. It will not only be less odorous, but less messy as well. As a final note: if at all possible, purchase items that don't require lubrication.

Foil Barriers

Many times, chemically sensitive people find they need large aluminum-foil sheets to block certain objectionable odors in their homes. This is often done as a temporary solution, but it can also be semipermanent. Rather than taping together several 12"-wide strips of heavy-duty household aluminum foil, you can use *builder's foil.* This is a fairly durable product that's often sold as a *reflective insulation/vapor barrier.* It's actually a "sandwich" consisting of brown Kraft paper with a thin layer of aluminum applied one or both sides. Builder's foil often comes in 36"-wide rolls.

One brand you might want to use is Dennyfoil Reflective Foil Insulation (**Denny Sales Corp.**). Their 36"-wide product comes with either foil on one side or on both sides, and in a solid-foil type or a "breather" version which is lightly perforated. You can call the company for local dealers. By mail-order, you can get Dennyfoil from the **Building for Health Materials Center** and **E.L. Foust Co., Inc.** It should be noted that while **E.L. Foust Co., Inc.** only stocks Dennyfoil #245 (the non-perforated type with foil on both sides) in 500 sq. ft. rolls, if you order in quantity, they'll get other types for you as well. Of course, you may want to check with local lumberyards and building centers to see what brands of reflective-foil insulation products are carried there.

FSF KShield is another type of reflective foil insulation. This product has a nylon core material with laminated foil on both sides. The result is a very strong foil. This product is available in two widths (25" or 48") in two roll sizes (500 sq. ft. or 1000 sq. ft.) from **American Environmental Health Foundation.**

Still two other options are manufactured and sold by **Advanced Foil Systems, Inc.** These are the non-perforated Aluma-Foil made with a heavy Kraft paper core and aluminum on both sides as well as the non-perforated Aluma-Foil Plus made with a fiberglass *scrim* (mesh fabric) covered with foil on both sides.

Another type of foil product that you might want to use in some applications is *aluminized sheathing*. This is a much more substantial material than builder's foil. It's constructed of an ⅛"-thick, gray, cardboard core with an aluminum-foil layer on each side. This foil-faced sheathing generally comes in 4' x 8' sheets. One brand is Thermo Ply (**Simplex Building Products**). Check your local building center to see if they handle these types of products, or call Simplex for their nearest dealer.

(Note: These foil-faced products tend to be more popular in warm, sunny climates.) By the way, to adhere builder's foil, or to seal the seams between sheets, simply use aluminum-foil duct tape (see *Tapes* on page 282).

Wood

Of course, many home projects require wood construction. However, there are some basic guidelines for storing and using wood that are always good to know and follow. First, all wood should be stored in a dry area. This will minimize warping and possible mildew growth. Also, when you sand or saw wood, it's always wise to wear a cartridge-type respirator mask rather than a simple, inexpensive disposable dust mask (see *Personal Protective Gear* on page 264). This is because newly cut wood can release natural, but irritating, compounds as well sawdust. And sawdust is considered carcinogenic.

(Note: For more suggestions and precautions for using wood, see the appropriate sections in *Chapter 11: Home Remodeling*.)

Man-Made Wood Products

In an ideal healthy home interior, there would probably be no man-made wood products. This means no plywood, no particleboard, and no sheets of wall paneling. Admittedly, these materials have real advantages associated with them—they're relatively cheap, often made of wood that would otherwise be wasted (inferior logs, mill scraps, sawdust etc.), they resist warping, and in some cases they are stronger than solid wood.

However, typical man-made wood products have health-related drawbacks, especially for sensitive people. For example, they're nearly always made of softwoods (primarily pine or fir) that can release strong-smelling natural *terpenes* when they're freshly cut or sanded. These compounds can be irritating and bothersome to breathe for some people. Even worse, man-made wood products are generally held together with formaldehyde-based glues. Unfortunately, formaldehyde can cause a wide variety of health problems from nasal irritation and respiratory problems, to menstrual irregularities and cancer.

Sadly, formaldehyde will likely be emitted from man-made wood products for many years. This is because the formaldehyde glues used can have a *half-life* of 3–5 years. In other words, in three to five years after the cabinets are first made, only half of the formaldehyde that was originally in them will have been released into the air. In the next three to five years, half of the remaining formaldehyde will be emitted. And so on. Therefore, many things made with man-made wood products can be ongoing, long-term problems.

However, you should be aware that there are actually two basic types of formaldehyde-based glues that are used in the wood-products industry. *Phenol-formaldehyde (PF)* glues are generally used in products designed for use outdoors and in construction-grade plywood.

As it turns, out PF glues only emit about 10% as much formaldehyde as the other popular formaldehyde-based glue, *urea-formaldehyde (UF)* glue. UF glues are often used for indoor construction and are common in cabinet-grade plywood. Obviously, if you must use a man-made wood product containing a formaldehyde glue, you'll want to choose one that's held together with PF glue rather than UF glue.

You should also know that, although typical plywood (of any type) is definitely a source of formaldehyde, typical particleboard is a far worse emitter. That's because much more glue is required to make particleboard than to make other man-made wood products. Unfortunately, the glue that's usually used in particle board is the UF type. Because particle board is cheaper than plywood (after all, it's only composed of tiny wood scraps and glue), builders often use it for subfloors, and it is widely used in cabinet construction as well. As a result, typical UF particleboard is often a major source of formaldehyde in new homes.

Fortunately, there are alternative particleboard products now available that can be substituted for typical particleboard products, and sometimes typical plywood products as well. Three of these are manufactured by **Sierra Pine Limited**. Medex is their formaldehyde-free particleboard for moisture-area applications, such as in countertops and bathroom cabinets. Medite II is their formaldehyde-free version for non-moisture uses, such as in kitchen cabinets, and Medite FR is similar again, but with added *flame retardants*. While these particular particleboard products are made with a non-formaldehyde glue, the softwood *terpenes* released from them could still make them intolerable for certain chemically sensitive individuals. Therefore, you'll want to test these products for personal tolerance before you purchase a large quantity (see *Important Testing Considerations* on page 267 and *Testing Woods* on page 269). In the end, you might find that a better choice would be to use a tolerable solid wood whenever you can. By the way, it should be noted that none of these alternative particle board products are recommended for structural uses. If you'd like to purchase **Sierra Pine Limited** alternative particleboards, contact the company for its nearest dealer.

Solid Wood

As a rule, solid wood is often preferable to man-made wood products from an aesthetic as well as a health standpoint. After all, solid wood has an innate beauty that is pleasing to look at and to touch. And being solid, it's not constructed with formaldehyde glues, or any other type of glue for that matter. (Of course, sometimes individual narrow boards are glued together to create a wide panel, but this is often done with a less-toxic carpenter's glue.)

However, there are certain drawbacks to solid wood you should keep in mind. First, as compared to man-made wood products, solid wood can be relatively expensive. Although you can purchase *construction-grade wood* (which is a more economical grade of solid wood), the boards in this category often have large knots, actual knot holes, or other deformities. Also, you should know that most solid wood is somewhat susceptible to warping and this often creates problems of wasted, unusable lumber.

Of course, another drawback to solid wood is that it's sold as individual boards—not in large 4' x 8' sheets. Therefore, solid-wood boards can't be used to cover large areas quickly. As a result, using solid wood can mean an increase in both material and labor costs. Also, solid wood can significantly expand or shrink due to changing temperature and humidity conditions. So, people who plan on using solid wood must account for this in their project's design and construction.

If you choose to use solid wood, it's wise to become familiar with the two basic categories: *softwoods* and *hardwoods*. Softwoods are *conifers*, or cone-bearing trees, having needles or scale like leaves. Hardwoods are defined as broad-leafed trees. Confusingly, the terms hardwood and softwood don't always describe the firmness or density of a particular wood. As it turns out, certain hardwoods may actually be softer than many softwoods. For example, balsa wood is botanically classified as a hardwood. However, as a general rule, most softwoods are softer than most hardwoods.

Common softwood lumber (pine or fir boards) is generally cheaper, comes in more standardized sizes, and is more readily available than hardwood lumber. Therefore, virtually all major construction projects use softwood lumber. Unfortunately, pine and fir can emit strong, and sometimes irritating, natural *terpene* odors when newly cut or sanded. These odors can be very bothersome to certain sensitive individuals. Interestingly, some people have reported that, when choosing between pine and fir lumber, fir seemed to be better tolerated. Unfortunately, finding out whether the softwood lumber you're about to purchase is actually pine or fir can be difficult. In reality, in most cases anyway, the differences are relatively minor.

Generally, if a softwood—whether pine, spruce, hemlock, or fir, etc.—is used for framing a house, its odors may not pose a problem because the wood is enclosed inside wall cavities. If *foil-backed drywall* is used to cover the framing and the house is tightly constructed, the odors will be prevented from entering the living space. However, you shouldn't automatically specify foil-backed drywall for your next room addition. That's because, in some climates (such as in Florida) doing so could result in hidden condensation problems, and mold growth or rot. For more detailed information on this important topic, see *The Healthy House* by John Bower. It can be ordered from **The Healthy House Institute,** or your favorite book seller.

If you're bothered by terpene odors, any softwood lumber that you use within the living space (such as in cabinets, furniture, and tongue-and-groove paneling, etc.) will be of more concern. Fortunately, in time, any emissions from the wood will naturally diminish. But if you want to immediately reduce the terpene odors, you can always apply a sealant finish over any exposed softwood surfaces (see *Acrylic Finishes and Sealants* on page 277). However, bear in mind that sealants won't give you 100% protection, and they are often very odorous in their own right.

One softwood that's often well-tolerated by sensitive individuals in particular is redwood. Although redwood is a softwood, it emits fewer irritating odors than other softwood species. This may be because redwood's terpenes are water-soluble, so within a relatively short time after it has been cut or sanded, its odor diminishes greatly. One well known plus for redwood is that it resists termite damage and rot. If you use it outdoors, for patio furniture for example, it'll weather naturally so no protective finish is required, although you might choose to use one anyway if you don't like the weathered, dull-gray color.

In fact, from a health standpoint, redwood is a superior choice for any outdoor project when compared to the more popular *salt-treated* softwood lumber. Few people realize that this benign-sounding descriptive phrase—"salt treated"—doesn't mean table salt (sodium chloride) but, instead, it refers a toxic copper-chromium-arsenic salt. During its manufacture, salt-treated lumber has had these noxious salts driven deeply into it under pressure. Therefore, this type of wood is also known as *pressure-treated* lumber. Obviously, redwood is a far safer material for you and your family to be around.

Yet, for some projects indoors, you probably won't want to use redwood. This is because it's fairly soft, making it susceptible to dings, scratches, and nicks. In addition, there are some environmental concerns related to cutting down redwood trees. However, redwood is still commonly used indoors in saunas (see *Choosing Tolerable Sauna Materials and Equipment* on page 463).

If you're bothered by softwood terpene odors, it's often best to use hardwoods for those projects that will be kept indoors. Although hardwood lumber costs more than softwood lumber, it's generally far more attractive and durable. So, in the end, you'll have made a good investment in both appearance and quality, as well as your own better health. Hardwood lumber is ideal for use in flooring, furniture, wall treatments, cabinets, etc.

However, be aware that certain hardwood species are naturally less odorous than others. Some of these low-odor hardwood species include apple, aspen, basswood, beech, birch, elm, gum, maple, pecan, sycamore, and tulip poplar, among others. Though not always easy to find, these woods are often suggested for some sensitive persons to use instead of the more popular red oak, white oak, and walnut, which have much stronger natural odors. Of course, the emissions from all woods will decrease in time, and you can always coat them with a sealant as was described with softwoods earlier.

Tulip poplar is one hardwood with which you might want to especially become familiar. The lumber from this species presents an interesting variegated pattern of tones that's rather similar to pine. Although it's somewhat greenish when newly cut, the wood changes to an attractive tan as it ages giving it a butternut-look. Tulip poplar is also quite affordable, often fairly easy to find (this will vary in different parts of the country, of course), and it's very easy to work with. Therefore, it can be an excellent wood for many projects. However, it is one of the softer hardwood species.

Important note: It's always a good idea to test a wood species for personal tolerance before you use it for a home project, especially if you're a sensitive person (see *Important Testing Considerations* on page 267 and *Testing Woods* on page 269).

CHAPTER 11: HOME REMODELING

The following sections will help you through common household remodeling projects. If you require more in-depth information, you'll want to read *The Healthy House* by John Bower. You can order this book directly from **The Healthy House Institute** or from your favorite bookseller.

Walls and Ceilings

In your house, you are surrounded by, and continually exposed to, hundreds of square feet of walls and ceilings. Because this represents a considerable surface area, it should be covered and decorated with materials that are as inert as possible.

Wall Paint

Paints have been used since prehistoric times. For thousands of years, paint ingredients were natural substances. Many of the ingredients were fairly benign, but others, such as lead, were poisonous. As chemistry developed and, later as the use of petrochemical solvents and other compounds began to be used, paints continued to become potential sources of illness. Today, most typical paints can contain scores of ingredients including *volatile organic compounds (VOCs)* and *synthetic biocides* (see also *Paints* on page 270).

Therefore, of all the interior decorating decisions you'll have to make, few will be as important as the wall paint you choose. You must keep in mind that once the paint is on the walls, it can't be easily removed, and putting another layer on top of it could result in even more bothersome odors. You should be aware that all paints—even alternative synthetic brands with low or zero VOCs, or alternative natural ingredient brands—will have a fairly strong odor when first applied. Then, too, you should keep in mind that the painting process itself can be expensive, disruptive, and labor-intensive. Therefore, before you decide to go ahead and paint, ask yourself if it is really necessary. You may decide that merely a thorough cleaning is all that's really needed.

If you decide to clean your walls rather than repaint them, consider using *trisodium-phosphate (TSP)*. One popular brand of TSP with no phosphates (which can damage waterways and ecosystems) is Red Devil TSP-90 Heavy Duty Cleaner (**Red Devil, Inc.**) which is sold in many hardware and paint stores, as well as building centers. If you're unfamiliar with TSP, it's a white or clear crystalline powder that can be used as a powerful, unscented cleaning product. TSP cleaners usually do a very good job of removing dirt, grease, and grime from painted surfaces. To prevent skin irritation, it's best to wear waterproof gloves. (See *Waterproof Household Glove Suggestions* on page 137.) For directions on cleaning walls with TSP, see *Cleaning Walls* on page 161.

Testing for Lead

Surprising to many people, the existing paint on your walls and woodwork could contain lead—and you don't have to live in a deteriorating tenement house to have valid lead-paint concerns. The truth is, lead was still used as a paint ingredient up until the mid-1970s. Fortunately, though, if the paint is intact and not deteriorating, it may not be hazardous. However, if it's peeling, or if you plan to scrape or sand it, you must first make sure your wall paint is indeed lead-free.

LeadCheck Swabs (**HybriVet Systems, Inc.**) can be used for a quick and simple lead test, and you can use them easily yourself. These are sold in many hardware and building centers, and can be ordered from the company, and from **American Environmental Health Foundation** and **Allergy Relief Shop, Inc.** If you find that the lead test is positive, you should contact your local board of health for suggestions and regulations how to proceed. *Never* sand or scrape lead-containing paint yourself—especially without taking any proper precautions. Lead particles that are ingested or inhaled can cause mental retardation in children and serious illness in adults (see *Lead* on page 538).

For additional information on lead, call the EPA's **National Lead Information Center.** They offer printed material about lead poisoning and preventive measures you can take. Also included is a list of state and local agencies that can provide further help. In addition, you can get a low-cost fact sheet, *Managing Lead in Older Homes*, from **Washington Toxics Coalition.** They have a "Toxic Hotline Phone Number," but it's only for information not already covered in their publications.

Choosing the Right Paint

Many people, especially chemically sensitive individuals, ask "What paint should I buy that will be safe for me and my family?" As it turns out, there are a growing number of alternative healthier brands from which you can choose. (See, *Paints* on page 270.) Because of personal tolerances, personal preferences (for example, all-natural ingredients or synthetic types, bright colors or neutral ones), as well as the particular requirements of the room (scrubbable walls for kitchens and moisture-resistant ones for bathrooms) there is no single correct paint for all people, for all jobs.

For very sensitive people, it's really best to purchase small containers of several different brands and test each one for personal tolerance (see *Important Testing Considerations* on page 267 and *Testing Paints & Finishes* on page 267). In fact, chemically sensitive people should probably *never* do any painting without first testing the product. Besides determining tolerability, testing helps you judge a paint's appearance (color and sheen), coverage, and scrubbabilty. Because test samples should air out for a period of time, testing should be started well in advance of any painting project. Sensitive people, in particular, should not expect to test a paint today and use it tomorrow. Testing takes time, sometimes several weeks, and if it's done early and thoroughly, the entire painting process should go much more smoothly.

While it's impossible to actually recommend a specific paint, in general, most sensitive people seem to tolerate one or more of the alternative low-odor water-based paints currently on the market. These paints usually cover well, and they don't require turpentine, alcohol, or paint thinner for cleanup. As a rule, alternative water-based paints contain fewer additives than their typical mainstream counterparts.

Of course, whenever you choose a paint, color is an important consideration. If you pick a neutral color, such as white, almond, ecru, or pearl gray, you're more likely to be able to live with it for a long time. Unusual or intense colors, though exciting at first, can quickly grow tiresome. This may lead you to repaint after only two or three years. Another plus for neutral colors is that they provide the most decorating options, and they're always in style. In addition, neutral tones can be used as ceiling paints. This eliminates the need to buy separate wall and ceiling paints, while at the same time hastening the actual painting process. Using all neutral colors will also result in a room that appears more spacious. By the way, some alternative water-based paints *only* come in neutral colors.

Still another paint consideration is its sheen. Products are often sold in *gloss, semigloss*, and/or *flat* formulas. Flat paint minimizes the appearance of any flaws or imperfections on walls. However, flat paints are usually not as durable or scrubbable as gloss paints. Gloss paint works well on doors and trim. However on walls, its reflective qualities are often considered somewhat unattractive. As a compromise, many people find that semigloss paint works fine on both walls and woodwork. A flat paint often works out well on a ceiling. Note that, for kitchens and bathrooms, semigloss or gloss are good choices because they are better able to resist moisture and are easier to clean than flat paint.

You should be aware that many alternative paints must be ordered through the mail. The exceptions being alternative lines from major paint companies. For these, either look in your classified phone directory for a local dealer or contact the manufacturer directly to inquire about an outlet near you. Whether ordering or buying from an area store, when you're ready to begin a painting project, be sure to initially purchase enough paint so you won't run out while actually painting a room. (Of course, this is especially important in the case of mail-ordering. After all, reordering can mean a delay while you wait for additional paint to arrive. This can be costly in terms of both labor and time, especially if the paint must be come some distance.) Ordering enough is also important because there's always the possibility that your new cans of paint could come from a different batch, perhaps resulting in a slight color variation. If that happens, your new paint may not match what's already been used, and you'll have to repaint everything or live with a somewhat two-tone look.

Because all paint has an odor when first applied, you may have to make special arrangements during and after painting. Unfortunately, it isn't unusual for chemically sensitive people to find fresh paint odors unacceptable for up to several weeks—occasionally even several months. Ideally, to help quicken the time for your newly painted walls to become tolerable, you should paint only during those months when you can have the windows open for long periods of time. In addition, you'll find that using window fans is often helpful. If you are extremely sensitive or asthmatic, you may actually need to find temporary accommodations elsewhere until the paint loses it's new smell.

The Painting Process

Before they're painted, your home's walls should be in good condition. This will guarantee a more attractive, long-lasting finish. If the walls are dirty, you can clean them with a solution of *TSP (trisodium phosphate)* in water, then rinse them. (For more information how to clean walls with TSP, see *Cleaning Walls* on page 161.)

After the walls have been cleaned, fill all the nail holes and imperfections with a low-odor product such as Murco Hypo M100 All-Purpose Joint Cement & Texture Compound (**Murco Wall Products, Inc.**). Murco is packaged as a dry powder in 25-pound bags. Even though you may only need a small amount for patching, it's relatively inexpensive and can be stored indefinitely, if it's kept dry. To purchase Murco drywall compound, simply order it directly from the manufacturer or from **Building for Health Materials Center**.

When you're ready to begin painting, remove as much of your furniture from the room as possible. Then protect what you can't take out, as well as the floors, with drop cloths. Washable, 100%-cotton-canvas drop cloths are probably the best type. While old bed sheets are often used, they generally aren't thick enough to prevent paint from penetrating through them. Of course, plastic drop cloths are readily available in stores. They're inexpensive and can be thrown away after painting, but they can release minor, but bothersome, odors when new. However in reality, they probably won't be as bothersome as the fresh paint itself.

It's important to make sure there's plenty of ventilation whenever the painting is in progress—and until after all of the odors have dissipated. It's also a good idea for the person actually doing the painting to wear a cartridge-type respirator mask. These masks can usually be found in local hardware and building-supply stores. Other protective measures would include wearing a long-sleeved shirt and a hat (to prevent paint from dripping onto the body). If you plan to paint overhead, protective eye wear is highly recommended (see also *Personal Protective Gear* on page 264).

As a rule, chemically sensitive or asthmatic individuals should never actually apply the paint themselves, but have someone else do the work for them.

Wallpaper

In Europe during the late 1400s, strips of decorative paper were first glued on the walls of a few homes. By the mid-1700s, the use of wallpaper became more commonplace. At that time, many types of wallpaper were available, and nearly all were made by hand with block-printed designs. By 1850, most wallpapers consisted of continuous paper rolls rather than separate strips and the patterns were then printed by printing presses. Today, most wallpapers are still manufactured in basically the same way. Because of the wide array of designs, surface textures, etc., wallpaper is a more popular wall treatment than ever. Despite the fact that it's relatively inexpensive and a quick way to give any room a new look, wallpaper is not often suggested for use in healthy households. Here's why:

Wallpaper Types

Truly healthy wallpapers are extremely difficult to find. This is because most of the wallpapers manufactured today are either all-vinyl sheeting or vinyl-coated paper sheeting. Unfortunately, vinyl wallpapers have the potential to outgas synthetic chemical odors which may bother sensitive people. Even if they're first unrolled in an uncontaminated garage to air a few weeks, the remaining vinyl odors can often still be a problem.

On the other hand, old-fashioned paper wallpapers don't give off vinyl odors, but they can smell like printing ink, they're often attacked by microorganisms, and they can't easily be washed. Natural-fiber coverings, such as jute or grass, are sometimes available. However, they might have been treated with potentially harmful chemical biocides to prevent insect or mold damage. Like paper wallpaper, these coverings are difficult to clean. Natural-fiber fabrics can be glued directly to walls, but they're also virtually impossible to care for except for an occasional gentle vacuuming. If your interested, **Homespun Fabrics and Draperies** has its Homespun 10-foot-wide, 100%-cotton fabrics you can use on your walls. These are naturally textured and have no formaldehyde or other chemicals added to them. By the way, they're also offered by **Building for Health Materials Center** which also carries sisal and cork wall coverings.

Of all the varieties of wall coverings available, foil papers seem to be one of the better choices. Their aluminum foil surfaces are inert and they can often seal in odors originating from the paper backing, or the paste, and even the walls themselves. Foil papers are also generally washable. However, wallpaper pastes may not dry quickly underneath foil papers, which could lead to hidden mold or mildew problems. You may have difficulty finding outlets that handle aluminum-foil-faced/paper-backed wallpapers, however. In fact, they've virtually disappeared in recent decades.

You should be aware that the adhesives used to attach wallpapers or wall coverings can pose additional problems. For example, starch-based pastes can provide appealing food for mold, mildew, and other microorganisms. Not surprisingly, some adhesives contain chemical *biocides* (literally, life-killing compounds) to curb these problems. Yet, these "helpful" chemicals themselves can be intolerable for some sensitive people. Other wall treatment adhesives designed to glue heavy coverings are sometimes made of strong-smelling synthetic compounds.

An option to covering an entire wall with wallpaper is to use only decorative *border strips*. These narrow bands (often only 2" to 6" in width) minimize all the problems associated with wallpapering simply because they cover much less area. Border strips are now being manufactured in a wide variety of patterns and colors. Although only a few inches wide, they can add new visual interest to any room by providing an attractive band of color. Border strips are generally used on walls just below the ceiling, but you might consider other possibilities. For example, they can be used around window and door frames, or to surround a room at chair-rail height.

The Wallpapering Process

If you decide to go ahead and use wallpaper, make certain the old, painted wall surfaces are properly prepared. First, a thorough cleaning is usually necessary to remove surface grease that could prevent good adhesion. One excellent cleaning product to use is a solution of *TSP (trisodium phosphate)* and water. (For directions on washing walls with TSP, see *Cleaning Walls* on page 161.)

Next, fill any nail holes or other wall imperfections with a low-odor spackling compound. Many sensitive people find that Murco Hypo All-Purpose Joint Cement & Texture Compound (**Murco Wall Products, Inc.**) works well for this job. Murco is sold in powdered form and is mixed with water just before being used. Murco can be ordered directly from the manufacturer or from the **Building for Health Materials Center**.

Some wallpaper manufacturers next recommend an application of *sizing* to the walls. Sizing is generally a starchy glue product that creates better adhesion. However, some of these materials may contain biocides that could be bothersome to sensitive individuals. So, read the label before applying, if you're concerned about this.

To adhere your wallpaper you could use Auro #389 Natural Wallpaper Adhesive. This all-natural, German-import product can be purchased from **Sinan Co.** and **Karen's Natural Products.** Or you could make your own natural paste. In those situations where mold and mildew growth could be a concern, you might want to add 1 tablespoon of boric acid powder to each quart of wallpaper paste. Boric acid is an effective mineral biocide that is generally less of a problem for sensitive individuals than are synthetic biocides. (See also *Wallpaper Pastes* page 284.) Note that, wallpapers with prepasted backings may possibly contain potentially bothersome ingredients, including synthetic chemical fungicides and glue compounds.

Stripping Wallpaper

At some point, wallpapers usually need to be removed. As anyone who's done this can say, it can be a horrible, time-consuming, and messy job—that is, if the paper was not especially designed to be "easily strippable." Scraping off old wallpaper can create irritating and harmful dust, and it can damage the walls. Steam equipment is popular, but the heat and moisture can activate dormant mold spores or cause the release of *biocides* (micro-organism killers) into the air. Very old wallpapers sometimes actually contained arsenic compounds to inhibit mold growth. Because of all these potential health concerns, wearing a cartridge-type respirator mask, rubber gloves, protective eye wear, and having plenty of ventilation when tackling this chore is essential. (See *Personal Protective Gear* on page 264.) This is definitely *not* a job for sensitive or asthmatic persons.

Stenciling

An interesting, and usually much healthier, alternative to wallpaper is *stenciling*. Actually, stenciling has been used to decorate walls for thousands of years. In the last few years, it's gained renewed popularity because it's such a simple and fun way to make a large plain surface more exciting.

In stenciling, paint is lightly dabbed over a cutout pattern (today, they're usually made of clear plastic) to form a uniform surface design. Bands of stenciled patterns can be used around windows and doors, just below the ceiling line, or surrounding a room at chair-rail height. In some cases, a repeating pattern used all over the surface of a wall can create a visual statement similar to that of wallpaper. Actually, with stenciling you are only limited by your imagination.

Stenciling equipment such as plastic patterns, brushes, sponges, special texturizing tools, and instruction books can usually be purchased at wallpaper outlets or at craft stores. Your local library and favorite bookstore may have appropriate books. You can also mail-order how-to stenciling books from **Eco Design Co.** Of course, chemically sensitive people should only use paints that have been tested first for personal tolerance. (See *Important Testing Considerations* on page 267, *Testing Paints & Finishes* on page 267, and *Paints* on page 270.)

Whenever you use paints, it's a good idea to wear proper protective gear including eye protection and a cartridge-type respirator mask, and to have plenty of ventilation. If you are asthmatic or very sensitive, you'll probably need to have someone else do the work for you. In fact, you may need to be out of the house entirely while it's being done if the area being painted can't be sealed off sufficiently from the rest of the house.

Marbleizing and Visual Texturizing

Beside stenciling, there are other creative wall treatments including *marbleizing* (using paint in such a way as to imitate the color and veining of natural marble) and *visual texturizing* (using paint to give the illusion of wood or to create free-form designs). All these are often surprisingly easy to do. As with stenciling, there are books on creating marble and wood looks available in local craft stores (they will have any special tools, too), libraries, and most bookstores. You can also mail-order marbleizing and "creative paint finishing" books from **Eco Design Co.**

One interesting and very easy method to create visual texturizing is to use Wall Magic (**Wagner Spray Tech Corp.**). This is a one- or two-headed roller, with patterned rollers. (With two rollers, you can use two different colors at the same time.) You can quickly make marbled and other imaginative looks. To purchase, check your local paint stores, hardware stores, and building centers. You can also order it directly from the company. By the way, you may find similar products are now available from other manufacturers.

Note: The precautionary information necessary for marbleizing and visual texturizing is the same as it is for stenciling. (See *Stenciling* above.)

Wood Paneling

Wood paneling can give a room an entirely new look, while at the same time covering damaged walls. However, for anyone wanting a healthy house, it's wise to avoid man-made wood paneling. Although it is relatively cheap and easy to install, virtually all types of man-made paneling are constructed with *urea-formaldehyde (UF)* glue. Unfortunately, UF glue emits high levels of harmful formaldehyde—much more than from the *phenol-formaldehyde (PF)* glue, which is commonly used in construction-grade products. (See *Formaldehyde* on page 527 as well as *Man-Made Wood Products* on page 291.) In addition, man-made paneling is often created, all or in part, from softwoods. Softwoods can give off strong natural *terpene* odors that can be bothersome to some sensitive people (see *Solid Wood* on page 292).

A healthier alternative to man-made paneling is traditional, solid hardwood, tongue-and-groove boards. (Again, softwoods such as pine are sometimes not tolerable for sensitive people because of terpene odors.) Solid hardwood paneling has always been associated with the dining halls, dens, libraries, and other rooms of the well-to-do. As a result, most people today don't even consider using solid hardwood paneling because they just assume it's going to cost too much. However, it can be affordable, if you choose the right wood.

For example, tulip poplar is actually a relatively inexpensive hardwood species. It's also attractive and easy to work with (see *Solid Wood* on page 292). To further reduce your costs, you can install the solid-wood paneling on just one wall, rather than on all four. Odds are, this will still provide the atmosphere you had in mind. Another less-costly wall-paneling option is to use *wainscoting*. Typically, wainscoting is paneling that's applied to only the lower third of walls. It can be an excellent decorating choice for dens, family rooms, and dining areas. Simply applying *chair-rail molding* is even less expensive, and yet it can still dress up a room. Chair-rail molding is typically a 2–3" wide strip of decoratively cut and shaped solid wood. It's usually mounted horizontally, one-third of the way up the walls.

To find solid hardwood paneling and molding, check nearby lumberyards to see what they stock or can order for you. Also, there may be mills in your part of the country that can supply material made from locally grown wood. To find one, look in your classified telephone directory. You might also check with an Industrial Education teacher at a local high school, if woodworking is still offered as a course.

When you're ready for installation, try to avoid using construction adhesives whenever possible. Instead, use only nails or screws. Construction adhesives can contain potentially harmful ingredients and they're nearly always very odorous. However, there are a few less-toxic water-based products that are now starting to appear on the market that you may want to try—if an adhesive must be used. (See *Construction Adhesives* on page 288.)

Wood stains can sometimes be bothersome to sensitive people. To avoid the problem, simply leave the wood its natural color. To protect paneling or molding, it should be coated with a tolerable clear finish. Whoever does this work should wear proper protective gear and have plenty of ventilation. As with painting, this type of work should generally not be done by chemically sensitive or asthmatic individuals themselves.

Tip: To minimize construction odors indoors, cut, stain, and finish your solid-wood trim or paneling outdoors or in a garage. If the prefinished wood is allowed to air out ahead of time, it may be inert enough to be installed inside without requiring a sensitive person to leave the premises.

Floors

Your choice of flooring is extremely important because it covers a large surface area, costs you a great deal of money, and (maybe surprisingly) has the potential to greatly affect your well-being. Health considerations regarding flooring are very real, not something for only a few sensitive adults to think about, but for everyone to have concern over. This is particularly true in regards to children. After all, children generally play for hours directly on the floor, so they are often much closer to it than adults.

Carpeting

Most people are still not aware that carpeting, in particular, can pose health dangers. When you're deciding what to put on your floors, you should remember that you don't have to put down carpeting just because everyone else does—there *are* other flooring options. The following sections will discuss typical carpet and it's problems, and offer a few healthier carpeting choices—if you still feel that's what you want.

Carpet Developments

Carpeting is defined as any heavy fabric that's permanently attached to a floor. Its use goes back thousands of years to the Orient. In the West, it periodically goes in and out of favor. Today, carpeting is fashionable. In fact, since World War II, wall-to-wall carpeting has become the norm in virtually all U.S. homes.

At one time, only natural dyes were used to color the yarns that made up carpeting. However, as early as the 1880s, synthetic *aniline dyes* started replacing the natural coloring agents (aniline is a toxic oily liquid derived from *nitrobenzene*).

Up until the 1950s, the carpet yarns themselves were still made almost exclusively of natural-fibers, such as cotton or wool. Then in the late 1950s, a revolution occurred in carpet manufacturing. New equipment became available that could *tuft* yarn into a backing material (a tuft is a loop of yarn fastened at its base). At about the same time, a new process was invented that allowed thin nylon yarns to take on a bulky quality called *loft*. These developments meant that new synthetic carpets could be produced much more quickly, and sell for much less money, than their traditionally made counterparts of the past.

Today, 97% of all machine-made carpets consist of synthetic fibers, and about 90% of these are tufted. Generally, the tufts are held in place with a synthetic latex or latex-like compound. In addition, stain- and wear-resistant treatments are commonly applied to the fibers. Backings on modern carpets are either natural jute or man-made materials. Sometimes, the entire backing receives an additional vinyl coating or a layer of foam-cushioning. Carpets without a layer of foam attached to the back must generally have some other form of padding underneath in order to minimize carpet wear, and provide comfort underfoot. Often, a synthetic foam material is used, although other types of padding are available.

Typical Carpet and Padding Concerns

With all the synthetic components in new carpeting, it's not surprising that carpet often outgasses a hundred (or more) different chemical compounds into the air, including xylene, ethylbenzene, and methacrylic acid. Unfortunately, a number of these chemicals are known to be toxic. Interestingly, experiments performed at an independent laboratory (**Anderson Laboratories, Inc.**) have found that laboratory mice that breathe air first blown across certain carpet samples suffered severe neurological symptoms as a result of their exposures. So severely were some of these mice affected, that some of them died. Some of the carpet samples that became *rodenticides* (mouse killers) were from brand-new synthetic carpeting—but others were taken from carpets as much as eight years old. On the October 29, 1992, broadcasts of the "CBS Evening News with Dan Rather" and the same network's "Street Stories," these findings were reported. However, despite this publicity, little has been done to truly resolve the problem of toxic carpets, and the popular media seems to have lost interest in the issue altogether.

It should be noted that since the initial Anderson Laboratories' report was publicized, the carpet industry decided to duplicate the experiments in the hopes coming up with more positive results. However this turned out not to be the case; their results were exactly the same. Interestingly, not long after this, the carpet industry changed the experiment. The air they now started using had a much higher relative humidity than previously. This time, the results were different, the mice didn't die at such alarming rates. At this point, they announced that Anderson's results could not be duplicated—the fact that the test was different seems to have been "overlooked."

Interestingly, not long after this, despite the carpet industry's strong dismissals and denials of any carpet toxicity, the Carpet and Rug Institute began a new Green Labeling program. Carpeting with this seal was said to be especially safe with no unsafe toxic emissions. Yet, Anderson Laboratories performed their standard carpet/mouse tests on a number of Green Labeled carpets, and some of these samples caused the same problems in test mice as some of carpeting without the label. However, the Carpet and Rug Institute continues to insist that their products, particularly the Green Labeled ones, are completely safe. They say that years of installation in millions of homes proves this. So in the end, ultimately you must decide for yourself what to believe—and what to use. By the way, you can purchase booklets, video tapes, and copies of Anderson's published carpet research from **Anderson Laboratories, Inc.** You can also have carpet samples sent to them for testing.

Because of suspected problems with synthetic carpets, some people believe that if they opt for carpeting made of all-natural yarns, it should be inherently safer and therefore shouldn't cause them any health problems. Unfortunately, even carpets made with 100% wool or 100% cotton can sometimes be intolerable for sensitive and allergic people. This is because of the chemicals used during the yarn and carpet milling processes (wool may also have been treated with additional mothproofing chemicals), and because of the odors that can be given off by many carpet glues, backings, and paddings. In addition, all carpeting, whether all-natural or not, acts as a highly effective allergen reservoir. In fact, vast quantities of dirt particles and pollen grains, as well as tens of millions of microorganisms (mold spores, dust mites, and other microbes) are actually present in *each* square foot of carpet. (Note: The Carpet and Rug Institute alleges that carpeting is better than easy-to-clean hard-surface flooring for allergic people because it traps all the dust mites and debris in its fibers, making the allergens less likely to become airborne when someone is walking across the floor. In other words, they are suggesting that carpeting acts like a filter to trap allergens. But, they don't go to the next logical step and suggest that your carpet be replaced as often as your furnace filter.)

Another problem with carpeting is that it eventually wears out as the integrity of the surface yarns breaks down. When that occurs, the fibers making up these yarns become house dust. If they happen to be synthetic fibers and they come into contact with a hot surface (such as a furnace or baseboard heater), tiny amounts of *phosgene* (also known as chloroformyl chloride, a deadly nerve gas), or *hydrogen cyanide* (used in gas chambers) can be produced. Even though only very minute quantities would be formed, *no* amount of these gases can be said to be good to breathe.

Sadly, many individuals with Multiple Chemical Sensitivity (MCS) have attributed the onset of their illness to newly laid carpet. Apparently, there is also "strong epidemiological evidence" in Scandinavia associating wall-to-wall-carpeting and asthma. Quite frankly, wall-to-wall carpeting is simply *not* a healthy flooring. Other available options, such as wood or ceramic-tile floors, are long-lasting and usually pose minimal health risks. Although they can cost more to buy and to install than carpeting, the added expenses can be justified. Wood and tile usually last a very long time, in fact, they're often considered permanent. However, carpeting needs to be replaced about every eight years or so. Therefore, over a floor's lifetime, carpeting has a higher per-year-of-use cost than wood or tile floors. You should also keep in mind that if a new carpet causes you or a family member to have chronically ill health, you should factor in the costs of medical bills. Admittedly, this sounds a bit overly dramatic, but is new wall-to-wall carpeting really worth the risk? For even more information on carpet-related health issues, read *Toxic Carpet III* by Glenn Beebe. To get a copy, contact the **Toxic Carpet Information Exchange**.

Healthier Carpet and Padding

Despite learning about all the negatives associated with carpeting, some people still want it on their floors anyway. For those individuals, a few carpet choices tend to be healthier than others. Be aware though, that despite outgassing fewer chemical compounds, these carpets still have the potential to become reservoirs for dirt, pollen, and literally millions of microorganisms.

Healthier Carpet Suggestions

One of the healthier options is to buy carpet made from 100%-wool yarn. Fine local carpet stores may have some. However, an excellent mail-order source is **Natural Home by Natürlich** which offers Nature's Cinna carpeting. This is an undyed, non-mothproofed wool carpet with no pesticides or glue. Also available from this same company is New Zealand Wool Carpeting described as having no formaldehyde, stain-repellents, or flame retardants. It's constructed with natural-rubber latex to adhere the wool tufts to a jute backing. While this New Zealand Wool Carpeting has been moth-proofed, apparently the moth-proofing agent has "no off-gassing characteristics" (won't cause emissions). In addition, **Natural Home by Natürlich** sells woven grass matting made with sisal or sea grasses. These particular flooring options come with natural-latex rubber backings.

Another good carpet source is the **Building for Health Materials Center**. They handle 100% wool carpets that are untreated. They also carry sisal carpeting.

Carousel Carpet Mills manufacturers many types of mothproofed wool carpeting. They also make all-cotton carpeting. However, these natural-fiber, low-production-run floorings are quite expensive. To find a dealer near you that carries them, contact the maker. It should be mentioned too, that a few upscale local stores will likely handle other brands of wool, cotton, and other natural-fiber carpeting as well.

You should be aware that unrolling any new carpeting where it can air for several weeks will help diminish, but probably not eliminate, many of its bothersome odors. Ideally, it's best to choose a place that's dry, uncontaminated by unwanted odors, and has good ventilation. After the carpet installation job, some people have applied a special coating designed to help seal in any remaining odors. **AFM** makes two such products, AFM Safechoice Carpet Seal and Safechoice Lock-Out. Both are water-soluble sodium siliconates. Carpet Seal should be applied first. If you require added sealing ability, apply Lock-Out afterwards. (Lock-Out will also help repel dirt.) Both are sold by AFM dealers such as **N.E.E.D.S.**, **Building for Health Materials Center, American Environmental Health Foundation, Bio Designs, Allergy Relief Shop**, and **The Living Source**. Unfortunately, the reported results from using odor-stopping carpet coatings are somewhat mixed. This is likely due to several factors: the amount of outgassing from a particular carpet, the degree of sensitivity of the person(s) bothered by the carpet, and the fact that sealants tend to be imperfect.

If you feel you must glue your carpeting down, choose a low-odor water-based product. One is AFM Safecoat 3 in 1 Adhesive (**AFM**). This synthetic mastic is sold through dealers including **N.E.E.D.S., Bio Designs, Allergy Relief Shop, Inc.,** healthyhome.com, **Building for Health Materials Center, American Environmental Health Foundation**, and **The Living Source**.

An all-natural, German-formula product with natural latex, plant oils, and resins is Bio Shield Natural Cork Adhesive #16, made and sold by **Eco Design Co.** This product is recommended for jute-backed carpets. By the way, it's also handled by **Building for Health Materials Center**. (Note: Of course, those who are allergic to latex should not handle products containing latex.) Another German-formulation is Auro #380 Natural All-Purpose Floor Adhesive made of "organic binders in watery dispersion." It's described as having "a pleasant odor during and after application." This is sold by **Sinan Co.** and **Karen's Natural Products**. It should be emphasized that these all-natural products may be less tolerable to some chemically sensitive people than certain water-based synthetic products, which are often available locally.

Healthier Padding Suggestions

Ideally, the padding under your carpet should be as nontoxic and odor-free as the carpet itself. Some sensitive people assume that natural jute padding would be a healthy choice. Unfortunately, some jute padding can contain potentially bothersome binding agents made from synthetic resins, or biocides. However, in its favor, all-jute products are naturally fire-resistant.

Natural Home by Natürlich recommends using 100%-wool felt as carpet padding. They handle a type made with no pesticides or glue. You can order this directly from them. Another padding option is 100%-nylon padding, which has been tolerable for some sensitive people. Some treated wool as well as nylon carpet padding may be available from local carpet suppliers.

Composite Floors

Originally, wood floors were made with relatively thick, solid-wood planks. However, today, composite-flooring products are more commonly used in both new construction and remodeling.

Composite Flooring Types

Two basic types of *composite flooring* (multiple-layer laminated products) exist. The first uses all wood. With these, a thin, attractive, hardwood top layer is glued to a less-costly, solid softwood (*i.e.* pine), or more commonly, to a plywood or other man-made wood-product base. Composite all-wood flooring often comes both prestained and prefinished. Prefinished types generally have surface coatings of clear solvent-based or water-based polyurethane. (See *Water-Based Polyurethane* on page 276.)

The second type of composite flooring uses *a high-pressure plastic laminate* (like the material used on countertops, Formica being one particular brand name) glued to some type of man-made wood product. (For information on high-pressure laminates, see *High Pressure Plastic Laminates* on page 323.) Often termed *laminate flooring*, and despite being a relative new-comer to the marketplace, its already become extremely popular, replacing both solid-wood, ceramic tile, and vinyl flooring in many instances. There are several reasons for this. One is that its hard surface makes it less subject to certain forms of minor damage (stains, cuts, etc.) than wood, linoleum, or vinyl. Another is that it can give the warmth of a wood-like appearance (a few look like stone) to places where wood flooring has not been commonly used, such as kitchens and recreation rooms. But probably the biggest reason is that its cheaper than real wood to buy and much cheaper to install. And this applies not just to plastic-laminate versions, but to all-wood composite products as well. In fact, it's been reported that composite flooring is up to three times faster to install than solid wood flooring. This is possible because all that's required is simply applying glue (sometimes stapling is suggested) to the tongue and groove joints; there's no nailing to the actual structure of the house. The result is a floor that actually "floats" on top of the flooring surface beneath it.

Composite Flooring Concerns

Unfortunately, there are several drawbacks to using composite products for flooring. First, some people complain that "floating floors" have a hollow sound when walking on them. Also, with all-wood composite floors, the thin top hardwood layer can't be sanded or refinished in the future. As far as the longevity of high-pressure laminate types go, manufacturer's do give product guarantees, some for a fairly long time. However, because these flooring materials are new, they haven't acquired much of a track record yet. Another concern with plastic-laminate flooring is that, in many people's eyes, it just doesn't look like real wood. In fact, it appears to some to be downright disturbing— especially when the same wood-grain pattern is repeated over and over again. Finally, there's the concern that some types of plastic-laminate flooring are being installed in areas where they shouldn't be, such as such as in bathrooms. This is because the man-made wood layers can deteriorate when moisture penetrates between the seams.

From a health standpoint, the major minus for all types of composite flooring is the potential for *outgassing* (emitting) of bothersome compounds. This is especially true for products fabricated with man-made wood layers beneath their top "presentation surface." Commonly, these man-made wood layers are manufactured with nasty formaldehyde glues. Then, too, *all* composite flooring products use glues, often formaldehyde containing ones, to bond the separate layers together.

Something else to think about, as far as outgassing goes, is the adhesive products that all composite floorings generally require for their installation. Fortunately, some manufacturers (not all) suggest a simple household white glue or a yellow carpenter's glue will work. One more outgassing problem could arise from the woods used in the composite flooring's fabrication. Potentially irritating *tannins* from oaks (commonly used as a top layer in the real-wood products), and/or *terpenes* from pine layers, could be released. Finally, the stains and clear coatings used to finish the surfaces of real-wood composite-flooring products could easily be a problem unless low-odor, water-based, non-formaldehyde-containing products were used.

While, admittedly, the potential outgassing sources lie beneath a hard, top layer in high-pressure laminate flooring, formaldehyde (or other VOCs) could still escape through the seams and from around the perimeter of the floor. In all-wood versions, it could rise up through the top hardwood layer as well.

Composite Flooring Sources

If you're interested in an all-wood composite product, a good one seems to be PermaGrain FineWood made by **PermaGrain Products, Inc.** It's offered as either prefinished or unfinished "engineered wood planks with formaldehyde-free plywood with a top layer of hardwood." Hardwoods available are red oak, white maple, ash, beech, and cherry. PermaGrain FineWood can be simply stapled together, avoiding installation glues completely.

If you still want a hard, high-pressure, plastic-laminate composite floor, all the big names in vinyl flooring now make these, too. This includes Bruce, Armstrong, and Mannington, among others. However, one of the most popular was one of the first to come on the market: Pergo (**Perstorp Flooring, Inc.**) which is imported from Sweden. Pergo is made with a top layer consisting of a heat-compressed paper impregnated with *melamine resins* (liquid, hard, clear plastics). Under that, is a heat-compressed, softwood chipboard made with urea-formaldehyde glue (which has the potential to outgas a great deal of formaldehyde). Pergo comes in several grades. Warranties are from 10 to 20 years, depending on which grade purchased. The company recommends that you use water-based carpenter's glue for installation. If you're interested, you'll need to call the company for a local distributor.

One brand of high-pressure, plastic-laminate flooring that can be safely used in bathrooms and other moist areas is Formica Flooring (**Formica Corp.**). This is possible because Formica Flooring's man-made wood core is impregnated with extra melamine resin to make it much more water-resistant than most products Therefore, the company is able to give it's product a 15 year wear *and* water-damage guarantee. You can contact the manufacturer for their nearest dealer.

Solid-Wood Floors

Solid-wood flooring is an attractive, healthful option that has been available for years. So ancient is the use of wood flooring that it was probably one of the first permanent flooring materials to replace earthen floors. Today, solid-wood floors are still being installed in homes. In fact, it has gained in popularity as the economy has improved. Yet, it's still less commonly used than composite products, carpet, or vinyl.

Solid-Wood Flooring Options

While initially more expensive to purchase, solid-wood flooring is extremely long-lasting. In fact, if the surface should ever become badly marred or damaged, it can simply be sanded and refinished. Another plus is that solid-wood floors usually don't require potentially bothersome adhesives; they can often be simply nailed down.

Today, solid hardwood flooring comes either unfinished or prefinished. If you purchase it unfinished, you can use the tolerable finishes of *your* choice. The wood itself is available as long tongue-and-groove strips and planks, or as *parquet squares* (short strips or blocks of wood, glued or back-wired into decorative patterns). While parquet is attractive, if glues are used to hold it together, it can be bothersome to sensitive persons. Then, too, if the parquet flooring must be glued down rather than nailed, that's another potential problem. Furthermore on a different note, parquet patterns often become tiring to look at over time.

You should be aware that solid-wood flooring (strips or planks) comes in several grades. *Clear grades* have no imperfections and a uniform color. On the other hand, *#2 or #3 grades* have more color variation and occasional knots, and they are much more affordable. In addition, the wider and longer the strips, the more expensive they'll be.

Ideally, if you are very sensitive, you'll want to choose a low-odor *hardwood* species for your floor, such as maple, birch, or beech. Admittedly, these can sometimes be difficult to find. However, they have far less odor than the more commonly used red or white oak which can release natural *tannins*. (see *Important Testing Considerations* on page 267 and *Testing Woods* on page 269). *Softwoods*, such as yellow pine, can be less expensive choices. However, their naturally occurring *pine-terpene* odors could be intolerable to some sensitive persons. Of course, softwood flooring is often an acceptable and less-costly flooring material for people who aren't particularly sensitive. Sometimes, solid hardwood (or softwood) flooring is available through local lumberyards, building centers, and flooring specialty stores. Also, in a few parts of the country, local woodworking mills can supply flooring made from locally grown timber. (To find such a mill, check your classified telephone directory under Woodworking, Wood Mills, Lumber, or Flooring Manufacturers. Local interior designers and architects may possibly know of a local source, as well.)

If you'd like prefinished solid-wood flooring, you may want to consider 2¹/₂" or 3" wide tongue-and-groove hardwood flooring milled by **PermaGrain Products, Inc.** The species available include red oak, white maple, ash, cherry, and beech. The finish is a product called PennThane. This is a zero-VOC (volatile organic compound) liquid that's cured with ultraviolet (UV) light. Nothing evaporates; rather the finish simply changes state from a liquid to a solid. You can call the company for a dealer near you. Also available from the company are solid-wood 12" x 12" parquet and "one dimensional" tiles in cherry, red oak, white maple, or ash. The company recommends that tiles should be adhered using their P-68 solvent-free urethane mastic. Local flooring installers will likely have other brands of solid-wood flooring available.

Solid-Wood Flooring Installation

To install solid-wood flooring, you'll want to have a clean, smooth, wooden subfloor. (If you have a concrete floor, special installation procedures and materials are necessary.) Professional installers nearly always then roll out asphalt-impregnated felt paper as an underlayment. It's often done "to prevent creaking." However, this is usually not necessary and certainly chemically sensitive people should not use it anywhere in their home's interior. If you feel you absolutely must use something for an underlayment, cork underlayment is available from **Building for Health Materials Center**. Yet, you should be aware that cork can often be odorous, too. (See *Cork Flooring* on page 311.) Those who are concerned about formaldehyde *outgassing* (releasing) from particleboard or plywood subfloors, can use a builder's foil (an aluminized-Kraft paper) to seal in the odors. (See *Foil Barriers* on page 290.) In other cases, you may not need any type of underlayment at all.

The tongue and groove planks of your solid-wood flooring can then be installed starting at one wall and proceeding across the room. The first two or three rows will require nails placed directly through the top surface. (This is because the floor-nailing tool can't be used effectively near a wall.) These nails should be *set* with a nail-setter tool so that the nail heads are slightly below the wood surface. Then the holes should be filled in with a low-odor wood filler compound. (As an alternative, you can mix carpenter's glue with sawdust, but this can have a somewhat dark appearance on light floors.) After the first couple of rows, after placing a new plank's groove around the tongue of the previous plank, you pound it gently into place with a rubber mallet. Then, nail through the tongue using a floor-nailer tool (which you can rent) into the subfloor. (You can also rent a chop saw to cut the flooring to length.) Make sure your joints are tight and even; including the butt joints where ends of planks meet. Tip: Try laying out a sampling of several planks first to see if the variations in natural color, length, and grain are attractive together before actually installing the floor.

If you have used a prefinished solid-wood flooring, at this point, your installation is virtually done. All that's required is to install the baseboard molding around the perimeter of the room. Keep in mind though that, while some prefinished wood flooring can be tolerable for even chemically sensitive individuals—especially if water-based finishes were used on them—it's always best to test a sample of the flooring first, before installing anything. (See *Important Testing Considerations* on page 267 and *Testing Woods* on page 269.)

In some situations, it's better buy unfinished solid-wood flooring, and apply a tolerable finish, *after* the flooring has been installed. If that's your choice, once the planks have been laid, the next step is sanding and finishing them. For do-it-yourselfers, sanding is usually done with rental equipment. If you hire someone to do this, they will likely have their own equipment. In either case, sanding can be dusty, so it is important to seal off the room to be sanded very carefully so you don't contaminate the rest of the house with sawdust.

Once the floor has been properly sanded, it is time for staining and finishing. Unfortunately, the typical stains and clear finishes often used on solid wood floors can pose problems. Some products have inherently odorous formulas. Then, too, some woods, such as maple and pine, don't stain particularly well anyway. In any case, you may want to seriously consider omitting stain and letting the natural beauty of the wood show through. Remember, if you decide not to stain, you've already eliminated one potentially bothersome product. (If you choose to stain, see *Stains* on page 281.)

Next, comes the finishing. Because the clear protective finish is exposed directly to the living space, it must be chosen with care. Ideally, it should be durable and low-odor. Water-based polyurethane floor finishes usually work very well for many people, especially those who are sensitive. These finishes tend to lose most of their odor within a week or so. Unfortunately, some are not quite as durable as their solvent counterparts. (See *Water-Based Polyurethane* on page 276.) Before purchasing, check product labels. Some may state, "not for use in high traffic areas." Know what you're getting ahead of time. (Other types of floor finishes including waxes are discussed under *Clear Finishes* on page 275.)

Important: Whenever any sanding, staining, or finishing is being done, the person doing the work should wear a cartridge-type respirator mask and eye protection, and have good ventilation (see *Personal Protective Gear* on page 264). Obviously, this isn't a project for an asthmatic or chemically sensitive individual to do themselves. In fact, he or she may need to make arrangements to live elsewhere during the finishing process—and for several days, or even several weeks afterwards—until the outgassing of stains and finishes has dissipated.

Linoleum

At one time, *linoleum* was the most popular kitchen flooring and countertop material. Traditionally, it was made with oxidized linseed oil, ground cork or wood flour, and *rosin* (a type of resin formed from the distillation of oil of turpentine) or other plant resins. This mixture was then pressed onto a burlap or felt backing under high heat and pressure. Generally, it was available in rolls or square tiles.

Linoleum had many good qualities. Besides being all-natural, it was *resilient* (able to return to its original shape after being compressed), dimensionally stable at varying temperatures and humidities, fairly easy to clean, resistant to burning, and less expensive to buy and install than ceramic tile. Another interesting plus is that linoleum has natural antibacterial characteristics thanks to it's main ingredient, linseed oil. However, by the 1960s, linoleum began to be rapidly replaced by vinyl. This was primarily because vinyl flooring was available in brighter patterns, was more moisture resistant, and required less maintenance.

Modern Linoleum

Surprising to many people, natural linoleum is still available today, most often in rolls. It's gained renewed, but limited, popularity primarily because it continues to have an all-natural ingredient list. Modern linoleum is still made of linseed oil, pine resins, powdered wood, and jute backing. Sometimes termed *battleship linoleum* (because of the drab, gray-colored material used for art projects and industrial applications over the years), linoleum flooring is now available in a variety of solid colors and marbleized patterns. These colors are not just surface treatments; they extend through the entire thickness of the material.

If you're considering linoleum for your floor, you should be aware that it's often not tolerated very well by sensitive persons, despite being an all-natural product. That's because linoleum has a rather strong, innate odor that can be bothersome, and it is more susceptible to water damage than vinyl. Forbo Artoleum and Marmoleum types of linoleum, in many color and visual textures, are distributed by **Forbo Industries** and sold by **Building for Health Materials Center**. Another good source for natural linoleum is **Natural Home by Natürlich**.

Linoleum Flooring Installation

In most installations, linoleum is glued directly to the subfloor. Some mastics and adhesives manufactured for this job are made of petrochemicals, which can be extremely odorous. So, be careful to choose water-based products. And certainly, no one with latex allergies should handle products with latex ingredients.

One alternative that should work is AFM Safecoat 3 in 1 Adhesive (AFM). This is a lower-odor, water-based synthetic mastic that can be ordered from N.E.E.D.S., Bio Designs, Allergy Relief Shop, Inc., Building for Health Materials Center, American Environmental Health Foundation, healthyhome.com, and The Living Source. For other low-odor adhesive possibilities, see *Adhesives* on page 282.

There are also German all-natural formulations that will likely have more odor. Therefore, these products may prove too bothersome for some sensitive individuals (see *Important Testing Considerations* on page 267 and *Testing Adhesives* on page 268). Bio Shield Natural Cork Adhesive #16 (Eco Design Co.) is made with natural latex, plant oils, and plant resins. This mastic can be ordered from Eco Design Co. or from Building for Health Materials Center. Auro #380 Floor Adhesive uses "organic binders in a watery dispersion." Auro products are available from Sinan Co. and Karen's Natural Products. You'll also want to check with Natural Home by Natürlich to see what they're currently handling.

Local hardware stores and building supply outlets will likely contain water-based adhesives that often have less odor than some of the products made with natural ingredients just mentioned. No matter what type of adhesive is used, make sure there's plenty of ventilation when applying it. It is also a good idea for whoever is doing the actual installation work to wear a cartridge-type respiratory mask (see *Personal Protective Gear* on page 264.) as a precaution, as well as have good general ventilation. It should be stressed that type of work isn't recommended for sensitive persons to do themselves. (Note: Natural Home by Natürlich recommends that only professional installers lay your linoleum.)

By the way, it's often possible to install linoleum without *any* adhesives—as long as the linoleum is wide enough to be installed without seams. To do this, first remove the room's baseboard molding. Then cut the linoleum to fit closely up to the walls. Finally, replace the molding; if it rests firmly on top of the linoleum, it will hold it in place. If you do this, you may need to install a threshold at doorways to hold the linoleum down.

Once laid, the linoleum's surface must be sealed to protect it against moisture and scuffing. A sealant coating may also help reduce the natural odor of the linoleum, but it will add its own characteristic odor which can sometimes be a problem in itself.

To purchase a sealant, check with your linoleum supplier. Chemically sensitive people should test both the linoleum and the sealer prior to installing an entire floor (see *Important Testing Considerations* on page 267 and *Testing Finishes* on page 267.) It's often a good idea to test a piece of linoleum with the finish already applied.

Cork Flooring

Like linoleum, cork flooring was more popular in the past than it is today. Yet, it still can provide an attractive all-natural floor. Cork is not wood, but the bark of the cork-oak tree, *Quercus suber*. This is an evergreen tree that originated around the Mediterranean Sea. Today, it's still being cultivated in Spain and Portugal where it's sometimes planted between olive groves and vineyards. Other cork-producing areas are in India and in the western U.S.

After about 20 years, a cork oak tree is first ready to be harvested. This is done by stripping-off the external bark. This does not kill the tree. In fact, in about ten years time, the tree will have grown a new bark covering that will also be ready for harvesting. Surprisingly, the cork quality seems to improve with each harvesting.

Modern Cork Flooring

Modern cork flooring has actually changed very little over the years. (It's been made for over a century.) By the way, strict laws, particularly in Portugal, are enforced to make sure cork oaks are not needlessly cut down or damaged.

Once harvested, the cork bark sections are cleaned, boiled, and have their outermost layer (a very rough material) removed. Then bottle stoppers are stamped out. What remains of the sections are then ground, mixed with some type of *binder* (either natural proteins or resins, or a natural or synthetic glue) which will allow it to keep it's shape. Then the material is rolled, baked, and cut into lengths to create smaller rolls (for wall applications), or it can be molded into blocks, baked, and sliced into tiles for flooring. Newer cork-flooring variations include a tongue-and-grooved product fabricated of a top cork layer glued over a man-made "pressboard" backing, and a vinyl-cork-hybrid tile.

Real cork flooring has a number of pluses. It's a natural material that comes from a sustainable resource. Because the bark cells are hollow, airtight, yet flexible 14-sided structures, cork floors act as good insulators against cold and noise. Cork flooring is usually long lasting, naturally resists moisture and rot, and also has the ability to be stained like wood. It should also be pointed out that cork floors are *resilient.* (able to regain their original shape after being compressed). So, they are comfortable to walk on. Finally, cork flooring is easy to clean by vacuuming, sweeping, or washing (use only a minimal amount of water.)

However, there are negatives associated with cork floors. One of the most important is that, these days, cork flooring is quite expensive. Then, too, it will require the added work of applying a sealer and protective finish (polyurethane or wax) unless already prefinished, and the periodic reapplication of wax to maintain it (if wax was originally used). Another concern is that cork flooring can acquire permanent accidental stains. And while the cork bark is inherently waterproof, cork isn't a good choice for places where it could come into contact with water, such as bathrooms, where moisture could eventually enter in the cracks between the tiles.

Far worse than these minuses however, are the potential *outgassing* problems. Some binders are fairly noxious. In fact, *urea-formaldehyde (UF)* glue is used by some companies. Of course, if a mastic is required to adhere the tiles, that could be a potential problem as well. Conventional installers often use a solvent-based polyurethane-type product for this. Then, too, top finishes (polyurethanes or waxes) could be odorous too. Although alternative products, some of which are water-based, are listed in the *Cork Flooring Installation* section below, if you're sensitive, it may be wise to seriously reconsider your decision to use cork for your floors. If you'd like to try cork flooring, **Natural Home by Natürlich** handles Portuguese natural cork tiles pre-finished with carnuba wax. These come in a 12" x 12" size. Cork tiles are also sold by **Eco Design Co.** and **Building for Health Materials Center.**

Cork Flooring Installation

A cork-tile installation will require a *mastic* (a type of construction adhesive). If at all possible, choose one that's water-based and low in odor. Of course, those products containing latex should never be handled by those with latex allergies.

An alternative synthetic mastic that may work is AFM Safecoat 3 in 1 Adhesive (AFM), which was especially formulated to be a lower-odor product. You can be order it from **N.E.E.D.S., Bio Designs, Allergy Relief Shop, Inc., healthyhome.com, Building for Health Materials Center**, and **The Living Source.** There are also water-based, "German natural-formula" products you can use for adhering cork flooring. One is Bio Shield Natural Cork Adhesive #16 (**Eco Design Co.**) made with natural latex, plaint oils, and resins. It's sold by the manufacturer and it's dealers, including **Building for Health Materials Center**. One more similar product is Auro #380 Natural All-Purpose Floor Adhesive from **Sinan Co.** and **Karen's Natural Products**. Finally, several natural cork adhesives are handled by **Natural Home by Natürlich**, and other low-odor adhesives can be found under *Adhesives* on page 282. (Note: Wearing a cartridge-type respirator mask (see *Personal Protective Gear* on page 264) is important as well as good general ventilation.

After the tiles have been laid, wait for the mastic to properly set. Then, if your tiles aren't prefinished, use a water-based polyurethane finish. If you choose a wax instead, use a natural-ingredient one, hopefully without odorous solvents. If your tiles come already coated with a carnuba wax finish, apply two or three additional coats to provide sufficient protection. **Natural Home by Natürlich** has their own Natürlich brand you might try. This is a liquid carnuba with 2% acrylic resin. Order directly from the company. Again, wearing a respirator mask and opening a window are recommended.

Vinyl Flooring

Vinyl flooring has become commonplace in kitchens, bathrooms, utility rooms, and recreation rooms since the early 1960s. Vinyl virtually replaced linoleum as a flooring material because it is fairly low in cost, attractive, simple to install, easy to care for, and available in many styles and patterns. (Most of the vinyl flooring now being made doesn't need sealants, protecting compounds, or special sheen products.) Just recently however, high-pressure laminate composite products have made considerable inroads in vinyl flooring sales.

Vinyl Flooring Types

Vinyl flooring is available in both sheet goods and individual tiles through local flooring stores and building-supply centers. Unlike linoleum, vinyl is made primarily of a synthetically derived resin, usually *thermoplastic polyvinyl chloride (PVC)*. However, pure PVC is actually a very stiff material, so it must be combined with noxious *plasticizing compounds* to make it soft and supple. As a result, a certain *resiliency* (the ability to return to its original form after being compressed) is evident in vinyl flooring which not only gives you a surface that's less likely to marred by dents, but one that provides some give and comfort when walked upon.

Although the ingredients making up vinyl flooring can certainly *outgas* (emit) potentially bothersome chemical odors, these often cause fewer problems than those given off by carpeting. (Carpet can release one hundred or more different compounds.) With vinyl floors, you also get the advantage of having a relatively impenetrable, smooth surface—one that's water-resistant, unable to harbor millions of dust mites, pollen grains, and mold spores, and one that's easy to sweep and wash clean.

Several grades of vinyl flooring are available in stores. All are basically fabricated with a clear top layer over a layer with a printed, embossed, or inlaid pattern. Sometimes, there's also a plain bottom layer or backing. While there certainly can be other differences, as a rule there's one thing of which you can be certain; the more expensive a vinyl floor is, the greater the thickness and quality of its clear top coating.

Of the various vinyl flooring options on the market, it's probably wise to choose harder vinyl products, at least from a health standpoint. This is because fewer plasticizing chemicals are required in their production. Self-sticking tiles should also be considered. This is because they eliminate the need for additional mastic compounds that are required to adhere other vinyl-flooring products in place.

Vinyl Flooring Installation

If you decide to use vinyl sheet flooring, your exposure to its outgassing can be reduced by first unrolling it in an unpolluted place. This can be outdoors, on a porch, in an empty garage, or anywhere that's dry and uncontaminated by objectionable odors. Generally, new vinyl flooring will need to air for *at least* several days. Some sensitive persons find it necessary to leave it unrolled for several weeks. Once the flooring has lost its "new" odor, it can then be brought indoors and installed.

While most vinyl flooring is held in place with adhesives, it is possible to completely avoid them. In many cases the flooring can be held in place with just the baseboard molding that surrounds the perimeter of the room (see *Linoleum Flooring Installation* on page 310). However, adhesives are sometimes necessary. They definitely are needed where two sheets of vinyl flooring abut each other. Actually, at these junctures the two edges are often *seam-welded* together. This is accomplished using a special synthetic compound that dissolves the edges of each vinyl sheet. After the liquefied vinyl has cured, the seam becomes invisible. Seam-welding is generally accompanied by a several-inch-wide band of adhesive under each side of the seam.

In other installations (very large rooms, multiple connecting areas, etc.), adhesives are used more extensively. But whenever they're necessary, they should always be water-based mastics and adhesives rather than solvent-based types. This is because the water-based versions are usually less toxic and less odorous. A number of water-based products are probably available through your local flooring supplier or a local building supply store. One you may want to try AFM Safecoat 3 in 1 Adhesive (AFM) carried by **N.E.E.D.S., Bio Designs, Allergy Relief Shop, Inc., Building for Health Materials Center,** healthyhome.com, **American Environmental Health Foundation,** and **The Living Source.** Other low-odor adhesives can be found under *Adhesives* on page 282. Of course, the use of adhesives, mastics, or synthetic welding fluids always requires plenty of ventilation and the use of a cartridge-type respirator mask (see *Personal Protective Gear* on page 264). Sensitive and asthmatic individuals should probably not to do this type of installation themselves.

Ceramic Tile

Ceramic tile is made of baked natural clays, sometimes with a glass-like glaze on the surface. It's actually one of the world's oldest flooring materials. Although it's been out of favor for awhile, it's now being used more and more. This is good news, because ceramic tile can be one of the healthiest of flooring choices.

Choosing Ceramic Tile

Ceramic tile has usually been thought of as a flooring for bathrooms and kitchens, but it can provide a natural, durable, easy-to-maintain floor for any room in the house. As a result, some "healthy homes" are now being built with ceramic-tile floors throughout. With tiles available in a wide variety of sizes, shapes, colors, and surface textures, these floors can be very attractive. While it's easier to lay ceramic tile directly on a concrete slab, it can be installed over other surfaces, so it's use is not limited by the type of subfloor your house has.

Many people assume that ceramic tile is out of their price range. However, there are generally less-expensive (some downright cheap) tile lines sold through building-supply centers. Sometimes, *seconds* (tiles with minor surface imperfections) are available at a surprisingly low cost directly from the manufacturers. (These can be purchased through their local company stores.) In addition, if homeowners do the installation work themselves, labor costs are virtually eliminated. Installing ceramic tile only requires a few tools for cutting and shaping, and you can get these at most tile shops and building centers. Tile cutters can also usually be rented at local rental shops. Note: Be sure to wear protective eye wear whenever you cut tiles.

When you're ready to pick out your ceramic tile, you'll find that there are two basic types: unglazed and glazed. Unglazed tiles, and *Mexican pavers* (sun-baked tiles) are all-clay. As a result, their top surfaces must be coated with a protective sealer or finish after being installed. Otherwise, they'll absorb moisture readily and become easily soiled.

Glazed tiles have a *vitreous* (glass-like) top layer which requires no sealing. Glazed tiles are naturally water-resistant, they permanently retain their hard, colored surface, and they need no additional sealers. Although they cost more than unglazed tiles, they're the better, healthier choice. To find glazed tiles, you'll want to check your local building centers, flooring centers, tile shops, and bathroom/kitchen outlets. Glazed-tile manufacturers include **Summitville Tiles, Inc.** and **Daltile Corp.** (Interestingly, Daltile also handles marble, granite, and slate, which can make for attractive floors as well.)

Generally, glazed tiles are odorless. However, in rare cases, some tiles may have absorbed natural-gas odors from the gas-fired baking kilns, or other odors from manufacturing and warehousing procedures. Therefore, it's important for chemically sensitive people to test the tile for personal tolerance. To do this, first lightly sniff a sample tile. If it seems okay, place it on a table near your pillow. If you sleep well, you'll likely be able to tolerate it once it's on your floors. However, be aware that the sample tiles given to customers are sometimes stored in an office or closet where they could have become contaminated by tobacco smoke or perfume. If at all possible, always request a sample from an unopened box in the warehouse.

Ceramic-Tile Installation

Today, ceramic tiles are most commonly adhered directly to the subfloor (usually plywood or concrete) or to a *cement board* that is installed over a plywood subfloor. Cement board is a sheet product made of Portland cement, fillers, and additives commonly in a $1/2$" thickness, although other thicknesses are available. Once installed, it will give you an ideal, tile-ready, smooth and level surface. Cement board is usually installed by bedding it in a product known as *thinset mortar* (also termed *dry set mortar*) and then screwing it down to the subfloor. Then the seams are taped with fiberglass mesh tape. Finally, the seams are coated with thinset mortar. Cement board is sold in most building centers and tile stores. Two brand that some people feel are less odorous than others are Wonderboard (**Custom Building Products**) and Durock (**USG Corp.**). If you'd like to find a local supplier, call the companies. By the way, once the tile and grout are over cement board, any minor odors that it may have are generally sealed in. So, cement board rarely poses a tolerability problem.

A thinset mortar or *mastic* can be used to adhere the tile to the cement board (or directly to a concrete subfloor). Of the two materials, mastics are usually more odorous. Most thinset mortars consist primarily of Portland cement (which is relatively inert) and some synthetic additive compounds (which can be odorous). Actually, a few thinset mortars have a very strong odor when wet, and the odor can linger for extended periods of time, even after the tiles have been installed. However, there are also thinset products that are relatively odor-free and tolerable even for sensitive people.

It is generally possible to use a thinset from your local tile or building-supply store. Simply get a small sample, mix it with water, and see if it has a strong chemical odor. Most thinsets have a mild odor, so if you get a sample with a strong chemical odor, don't use it. Of course, sniff testing should not be done by individuals with serious chemical sensitivities or asthma. For more on testing information, product brand names, and other sources, you'll need to read *Thinset Ceramic-Tile Mortars*, on page 286.

The grout used to fill the spaces between the tiles is another cement-based product you'll need to test. (Do the same testing procedure as with thinset mortars above.) Actually, most locally available grouts consist simply of Portland cement, sand, and a few minor synthetic additives. As with thinset mortars, the additives can sometimes be odorous.

In addition, you might like to know that you can make your own additive-free grout. The recipe is Portland cement, clean dry sand, and water. The proportions depend on the width of the grout joint—for joints less than 1/8" wide mix 1 part cement with 1 part sand; for joints up to 1/2" wide use 1 part cement to 2 parts sand; for joints over 1/2" use 1 part cement to 3 parts sand. To create colored grout, you can add natural, *mineral pigments* to the basic recipe. These powdered-rock colorants are often used by brick masons, so they're usually available wherever mortar is sold. They can also be ordered from **Building for Health Materials Center.**

Because there are no synthetic additives, this simple homemade sand/Portland-cement/water grout will require *damp-curing*. With damp-curing, a freshly grouted ceramic-tile floor is covered with plastic sheeting (plastic drop cloths) for three days to prevent rapid drying. (Rapid drying can cause the grout to become weak and crumbly.) After that, the plastic is removed and the tiles are scrubbed cleaned. Incidentally, the entire installation procedure for ceramic tile following this process is covered in text and photographs in *Healthy House Building for the New Millennium* by John Bower. This book can be ordered directly from **The Healthy House Institute** or your favorite bookseller.

To prevent stains, the cured grout joints can be sealed by carefully brushing them with a product called *water glass*. Water glass is a clear, odorless sodium-silicate solution. Chemically, it's very similar to window glass, but in a liquid form. When water glass is applied to grout, it chemically reacts with the calcium in the grout, forming a hard, transparent crystalline surface.

Three types of water glass solutions are manufactured by **AFM.** Two are "pure" products: AFM Penetrating Water Stop and AFM Water Shield. Water Shield has a thicker formula to coat a surface, while the Penetrating Water Stop has a thinner consistency that allows it to soak in. AFM Safecoat Grout Sealer is made with water glass, but also synthetic resins to make it adhere more permanently to grouts. (This particular product may have an odor when applied.) All these available from **The Living Source, Bio Designs, Allergy Relief Shop, Inc., Building for Health Materials Center, American Environmental Health Foundation,** and **N.E.E.D.S.** (For other product choices, see *Water Glass* on page 280.)

Cabinetry

Permanently installed cabinets are a relatively recent phenomenon. In kitchens, prior to the 20th century, supplies and utensils were generally stored in freestanding units (tables, bins, cabinets, etc.), or on wall shelves and hooks. Cabinets surrounding bathroom sinks didn't really become popular until the late 1950s and early 1960s. When the first permanently installed cabinets were used in either of these locations, they were custom-built and made entirely of solid wood. Later, companies began manufacturing more-affordable wood or metal *stock units* (readily available separate cabinets that could be combined to create the look of a custom-cabinet job).

Today's cabinets come in a variety of styles with all types of special features, such as sliding trays, vegetable bins, etc. While a few are still made entirely of metal, the majority are made of a combination of wood products (man-made, veneer, and solid softwood or hardwood). Some cabinets are also made using a combination of wood products and plastic laminates. Unfortunately, many people don't realize that most new cabinets now being installed, except for all-metal cabinets and expensive solid-wood custom-made cabinets, can pose serious health dangers. This section explores some of these potential problems and offers several healthier cabinet alternatives.

Typical Modern Cabinets

As just noted, virtually all of the kitchen and bath cabinets installed in homes today are made with at least some man-made wood products. While very expensive upscale cabinets of cherry (or some other prestigious wood) may have solid-wood doors and drawer fronts, the drawer sides and bottoms, the cabinet shelves and backs, and often the end panels are going to be made of plywood or particleboard. While some of these components may have a fancy wood veneer surface, they are still often made with less expensive man-made wood products (see *Man-Made Wood Products* on page 291). While man-made materials are more stable (they shrink and expand less when the temperature and humidity fluctuates), and are cheaper than solid wood, they can pose real health risks. Here's why:

Cabinet-grade plywood and particleboard is made primarily of thin layers or bits of wood, such as pine, held together with glue. The pine can give off fairly strong natural *terpene* odors. These are actually gaseous hydrocarbon compounds that can be irritating to your mucous membranes. Not surprisingly, some individuals (especially chemically sensitive ones) find these airborne terpenes bothersome. (People who are not highly sensitive may only be bothered by terpene odors at higher concentrations, such as would be released by turpentine.)

A bigger concern with man-made wood products involves the glues used to construct them—especially the *urea-formaldehyde (UF) resins*. UF glues can emit high levels of formaldehyde for years. To make matters worse, the clear finishes commonly applied to cabinets are made from urea-formaldehyde resins. As a result, kitchen and bath cabinets are often major sources of formaldehyde pollution in homes. This is a serious situation that can lead to the development of a number of unhealthy symptoms. For example, formaldehyde can cause sinus and respiratory irritation, menstrual irregularities, and an acquired hypersensitivity to many other substances (see *Formaldehyde* on page 527).

It's been suggested that you can reduce the emissions released from your cabinets by simply coating all the surfaces with a sealant (see *Acrylic Finishes and Sealants* on page 277). However, even applying four coats will not be able to seal in all the bothersome gases completely. While they'll be greatly reduced, the remaining emission levels are often still intolerable, especially for sensitive individuals. Then too, sealants are often very odorous in their own right. In fact, they could take several months to lose their odor after being applied.

As an alternative to sealants, some people have tried stapling heavy-duty, household aluminum foil inside their cabinets. Generally, this won't form a perfect seal either. In most cases, the emissions will still be noticeable. Also, in time, the heavy-duty foil will likely tear. However, if you want to try this approach, *builder's foil* (aluminum on one or both sides of Kraft paper) is a more durable choice. Two mail-order sources for the Dennyfoil brand are the **Building for Health Materials Center** and **E.L Foust Co., Inc**. (For other foil options as well as tapes, see *Tapes* on page 282 and *Foil Barriers* on page 290.)

As you can see, making problematic new cabinets tolerable is often difficult—even impossible in many cases. Time may be a better cure, though it'll probably take several years before the emissions are significantly reduced. However, eventually the terpene and formaldehyde levels given off will decrease as the cabinets age. Obviously, the ideal approach would be to install healthier cabinets to begin with.

New Alternative Cabinets

In any home-construction or remodeling project requiring new cabinetry, it's best to choose cabinets that won't compromise your own health or that of your family. In the following sections, some less-toxic cabinet suggestions are offered.

Alternative Solid-Wood Cabinets

Solid-wood cabinets can be a healthy choice—if the woods, glues, and finishes are carefully chosen. Such cabinets are attractive and long-lasting, but you should realize that they'll likely be quite expensive. This is not only because solid wood costs more than man-made wood products, but also because solid-wood cabinets will probably need to be custom-built. (Note: Some commercially made cabinets are advertised as being "made from solid wood" when, in fact, they contain plywood. If you ask about this discrepancy, the suppliers will usually claim that, by their definition, plywood *is* solid wood. However, no matter how they define *solid wood*, if plywood was used to construct the cabinets, they will likely contain formaldehyde glues—glues it's best to avoid if at all possible.)

To help locate a capable woodworker locally to make you *real* solid-wood cabinets, you can check in the classified sections of your phone book under Cabinetmakers, Woodworking, etc. Another good idea is to ask at local lumberyards handling hardwoods, industrial/vocational education departments at local schools or colleges, and interior decorating shops for any suggestions or recommendations they may have. When you do find a prospective woodworker, ask him (or her) for photographs of cabinetry already done for clients and ask if you can examine any work-in-progress currently in their shop. You'll also want to find out if the craftsperson is willing to use finishes that are tolerable to you, but which may be unfamiliar to them. Furthermore, you should request written estimates of the total project cost and how long the project will take for its completion. In addition, it's important to find out whether there could be smokers in the workshop whose tobacco smoke could permeate and contaminate your cabinets. This may be unlikely simply due to the danger of fire, but it's best to ask ahead of time anyway. After you have all this information, you can then make a well-informed decision whether you want to go ahead or not.

The next step is to decide on the type of wood to be used in your cabinets. Some people may want to use a softwood such as pine. It's certainly a low-cost choice and it's easy to find in local lumberyards. This is a viable option for many people; however, new pine gives off relatively strong natural terpene odors that can be too bothersome to some sensitive people.

11: Home Remodeling

Ideally, a hardwood species that naturally has little odor should be chosen instead. Some low-odor hardwoods you might consider are maple, birch, and tulip poplar (see also *Solid Wood* on page 292). Tulip poplar is often a good choice; it's fairly inexpensive and should fit in most budgets. Tulip poplar is also easy to work with and has an informal, yet attractive, appearance.

"What can we use for drawer bottoms?" is a question often asked by people wanting all solid-wood cabinets. Actually, a simple solution is to use *galvanized sheet metal.* Sheets of galvanized steel will provide a washable, sturdy surface, eliminating the need for plywood or other man-made wood products that are normally used. By the way, galvanized sheet metal is simply thin, zinc-coated steel (zinc coating is a finishing treatment to prevent rusting). You may have seen furnace ducts made of it. Sheets of this material can be purchased and custom-cut at most sheet-metal shops. (To find one, look in your classified telephone directory under "Sheet Metal Fabricators" or similar headings, or contact a local furnace company to see if they can do the work for you. If they can't, they may know where you can have it done.) A 24-gauge thickness will generally provide cabinet drawers bottoms with adequate support, but for extra-wide drawers, it's better to use a slightly thicker material.

By the way, new galvanized metal may have a thin surface coating of oil on it. This is sometimes picked up during the manufacturing process as the metal passes though rollers and other machinery. Fortunately, this oil coating can often be easily washed off by using a solution of *trisodium phosphate (TSP)* and water. TSP is a white or clear crystalline powder that can be used as a powerful, unscented cleaner that even many chemically sensitive persons tolerate well. You can purchase TSP at most local hardware stores and paint/wallpaper shops. One phosphate-free brand is Red Devil TSP-90 Heavy Duty Cleaner (**Red Devil, Inc.**). To use it, dissolve 2 level tablespoons of TSP in 1 gallon of warm water. Then, dip your sponge into the solution, wring it, and thoroughly wipe the metal. Finish up the process by rinsing with clear water. It should be mentioned that wearing waterproof gloves to prevent skin inflammation is a good idea. (See *Waterproof Household Glove Suggestions* on page 137.)

Another factor to consider with solid-wood cabinets is stain. In reality, stain is often unnecessary. Without any stain, a wood's natural beauty (color and grain) will clearly show through. At the same time, a possible source of intolerance (the stain itself) is eliminated. Another point to decide on is what glue to use. Often, a low-order carpenter's glue or a white glue makes a good choice. Finally, you'll need to choose a tolerable and durable clear finish. (For information on all these, see the appropriate sections in *Chapter 10: Home Workshop.*)

Remember, your new cabinets will likely have a "new" odor immediately after being made, no matter what materials, glues, and finishes you have chosen. This odor can actually persist for some time. Therefore, if possible, store your new cabinets in a dry, uncontaminated area for several weeks before their final installation. If you're a chemically sensitive individual, it's best not to put them in your kitchen or bathroom until they're completely odor-free.

One source for custom-made, solid-wood cabinets is **Charles R. Bailey Cabinetmakers.** They will build and ship anywhere their Second Life Furniture cabinetry which is made "especially for the chemically sensitive." They enjoy speaking with you to plan and build exactly what you want. In fact, you pick the design, hardwood, and finish. Second Life cabinets are "made of solid American hardwoods throughout." Each finished piece is signed by the maker.

Alternative Particleboard Cabinets

Medite II (for non-moisture areas such as kitchen cabinets) and Medex (for moisture areas such as countertops and bathroom cabinets) (**Sierra Pine Limited**) are two particleboard products that can be used instead of solid wood when constructing new cabinetry for your home. Unlike typical particleboards, these are not made with formaldehyde-based glues. While Medite II and Medex cost more than other particleboards, they're much less expensive than using solid hardwood. Also, the skill required to work with them is much less than with solid wood. Therefore, labor costs should be lower. If you want to purchase **Sierra Pine Limited** products, you can call the manufacturer for a dealer in your area.

However, you should be aware that despite using healthier glues, these alternative particleboards are often still too bothersome for many sensitive people. This is usually because they release natural hydrocarbon *terpenes* from the softwoods of which they're made. Softwoods also often contain a tiny amount of naturally occurring formaldehyde. Completely coating all the alternative particleboard's exposed surfaces with up to four coats of a sealant will help reduce these odors, but it will not completely eliminate them. Also, it's important to keep in mind that sealants are often very odorous in their own right.

To make alternative-particleboard cabinets more tolerable as well as attractive, all the surfaces can be covered with a *high-pressure plastic laminate*. (For more on laminates, see *High-Pressure Plastic Laminates* on page 323.) High-pressure plastic laminates are thin, very dense sheets which will not only seal in much of the odor being released from the wood underneath, but will also give your cabinets a sleek, modern "European" look. Remember though, some minor leakage of terpenes and/or formaldehyde may still occur where seams meet, or where holes have been drilled for shelf supports.

If you choose to use high-pressure plastic laminate over particle board, consider using a water-based contact cement as an adhesive. Weldwood Non-Flammable Contact Cement (**Dap, Inc.**) is a less-toxic brand. It is often available at local hardware stores and building centers. Whenever laminating is being done, having plenty of ventilation and wearing a cartridge-type respirator mask as preventive safety measures are a good idea (see also *Personal Protective Gear* on page 264).

One source of manufactured particleboard-containing cabinets that may work for you is The Natural Collection (**Neil Kelly Cabinets**). These are made with sustainable or recycled wood and environmentally friendly finishes (water-based, natural oils, low VOC paints). Standard interiors are made of "laminated wheatboard." However, Medite II (medium-density fiberboard made without formaldehyde glues) is offered as an alternative option. Order directly from the maker.

Alternative-Plywood Cabinets

Cabinet-grade, furniture-grade, and hardwood plywoods are generally not suggested for the same reasons typical particleboards aren't recommended. That is, they all release relatively high levels of formaldehyde from the *urea-formaldehyde (UF)* glues. However, if you really want to use plywood, you might consider choosing a construction-grade product.

Construction-grade plywood (either interior or exterior grade) is usually made of much-less-attractive fir or pine, but its layers are held together using a water-resistant *phenol-formaldehyde (PF)* glue. These products all have an American Plywood Association (APA) grade stamp. A PF glue emits much lower quantities of formaldehyde than the non-water-resistant urea-formaldehyde (UF) glue. To make construction-grade plywood even more tolerable, you might consider the various options discussed above for alternative-particle-board cabinets.

Metal Cabinets

Today, metal is an often overlooked, but excellent choice, for cabinets. Metal cabinetry can be attractive, low-odor, easy to clean, and very durable. However, many people continue to think of metal cabinets as the drab, white, cheap-looking products that were sold in the 1950s. But metal cabinets are now available that are much better looking with many more features than those earlier cabinets.

Kitchens & Baths by Don Johnson is a certified kitchen designer/dealer offering Healthy Green Steel custom metal cabinetry especially created for the chemically sensitive. Many baked-on colorful finishes are offered with attractive hardwood door and drawer fronts optional. If you like, you can even choose to have all-stainless-steel cabinets made for you. These are low production, top of the line products and so are relatively expensive. However, they can be well worth the cost, if low odor is important to you.

Another choice is St. Charles Cabinets (**St. Charles Mfg. Co.**). Formerly an all-purpose cabinet manufacturer, the company now primarily markets to medical suppliers. However, some of their metal cabinets are appropriate for homes. These have welded steel cases with a plain or textured finish, adjustable shelves, and fluorescent recessed fixtures in the upper cabinets. The cabinets come in a range of painted colors. You can order these directly from the company or ask for a dealer in your area. These cabinets are somewhat pricey, but can be good choices.

Metal cabinetry is also offered by **Ampco**. Their Ampco low-cost kitchen cabinets come with a powder-coating, baked-on finish in white or almond. No asphaltic material is used for sound insulation—just corrugated cardboard inside the doors. To locate a nearby dealer, you can contact the company. You can also special order these through both Ace Hardware and Tru-Value Hardware stores. (They may not realize that they have them available, but these steel cabinets can be found in their franchise's special-order literature.)

Arctic Metal Products Corp. makes low-cost metal cabinets, too—in kitchen, bathroom, and medicine-cabinet styles. Like the Ampco brand, these are powder-coat finished. Again, no asphaltic compounds are used for sound deadening; just cardboard insulating material in the doors. All this cabinetry comes in white, with some styles available in other colors as well. You'll need to contact the manufacturer for a local dealer. (May be available in only certain areas of the country.)

Another option are Dwyer Compact Kitchen Units (**Dwyer Products Corp.**). These are complete mini-work centers available in stainless steel or four standard colors, with custom colors optional. Countertops for these units can be porcelainized steel, Corian, or stainless steel. Call the manufacturer for a local dealer.

Updating of Old Cabinets

Maybe you've decided to keep your old wood cabinets, rather than installing new ones. Actually, giving sturdy old cabinets a new appearance, rather than replacing them, has real advantages. For one, the formaldehyde glue used in the manufactured man-made wood materials utilized in most cabinets has a *half-life* of 3 to 5 years. This means that after every 3 to 5 years, half the formaldehyde remaining in the cabinets will have dissipated. Because of this, older cabinets are much less potent formaldehyde emitters than typical new cabinets. Another reason for choosing to update your cabinets is that it's nearly always cheaper to redo existing cabinets than to purchase new ones.

Painting Older Cabinets

Painting your old cabinets with a tolerable, durable finish may be all that's needed to update them satisfactorily (see *Paints* on page 270). Of course, it's important to test several brands of paint first (see *Important Testing Considerations* on page 267 and *Testing Paints & Finishes* on page 267). Besides the new paint itself, buying and installing attractive replacement hardware will easily, and affordably, add to the new look.

Before beginning to paint your old cabinets, you'll need to properly prepare them. This will ensure a more-attractive and longer-lasting finish. The first essential step is a thorough cleaning to remove any acquired grime, cooking grease, and perhaps layers of built-up wax. To clean cabinets, one method is to go over all the surfaces with a strong concentration of *TSP (trisodium phosphate)* and water. TSP is a white or clear crystalline powder that's used as an unscented, heavy-duty cleaning powder. It's usually sold at paint, hardware, and wallpaper stores. One popular brand is Red Devil TSP-90 Heavy Duty Cleaner (**Red Devil, Inc.**), which is phosphate-free. To use TSP, dissolve 2 level tablespoons in 1 gallon of warm water. Dip a sponge into the solution and wring it, then wipe just a small section of your cabinets at a time. If the cabinets are particularly dirty, you may need to go over them a second time, then rinse with clear water. By the way, you should wear waterproof gloves to prevent any possible skin irritation. (See *Waterproof Household Glove Suggestions* on page 137.)

Besides washing, you should lightly sand the old cabinets. Fresh paint often adheres to sanded surfaces better. However, if you're cabinets already have a painted finish, you'll want to test it for lead. You can get a simple test kit at many local hardware stores and building centers. LeadCheck (**HybriVet Systems, Inc.**) uses a swab that changes color if lead is present. If you can't find it in your area you can mail order this product from the manufacturer, **American Environmental Health Foundation** or **Allergy Relief Shop, Inc.** If there's lead, DO NOT SAND. In fact, if lead-painted cabinets have peeling or chalking paint, it is probably best not to save them. You may want to call your local board of health and ask them what you should do next. A low-cost brochure that may help is, *Managing Lead in Older Homes*, from **Washington Toxics Coalition**. You can also call them on their "Toxic Hotline" phone number, but only for information not available in their publications.

If you do sand, you'll want to wear a good-quality dust mask, such as a cartridge-type respirator (see *Personal Protective Gear* on page 264). When you're finished sanding, thoroughly vacuum all surfaces of the cabinets with a soft dusting attachment. At this point, you're ready to paint, using an appropriate brand you've already pretested.

There's one additional matter of which you should be aware: Some old cabinetry may have been polished with a silicone-containing product. If so, in some cases, new paint may not stick to the cabinets properly. If you know silicone polish was used, don't attempt the whole paint job until you try to paint an inconspicuous spot first to see how it adheres. It may work just fine. If not, the silicone will need to be removed from the cabinetry surfaces prior to painting.

Unfortunately, this can sometimes be a difficult task because many silicone products are designed to be waterproof. So, it may not come off using typical wax-removal techniques. If it doesn't, it may be necessary to thoroughly sand the cabinets or even use a paint stripper. If you find that you'll have to strip the cabinets, a less-toxic water-based stripper is a better choice than a traditional solvent-based product. Fortunately, water-based strippers are now usually available at local hardware, building-supply, and paint stores. One popular brand commonly handled is Safest Stripper Paint and Varnish Remover (**3M Construction & Home Improvement Products Div.**). This stripper uses dimethyl esters as its active ingredients. However, when using any type of stripper (either water-based or solvent-based), it's best to wear protective gear such as safety goggles, heavy *neoprene* gloves (neoprene is a special type of oil- and chemical-resistant synthetic latex), and a cartridge-type respirator mask, and have plenty of ventilation. (See *Personal Protective Gear* on page 264.)

You should keep in mind that painting your cabinets will be not only disruptive, but also odorous. Therefore, ideally, you should only do this type of work in those seasons when you can have the windows open. Using a window fan blowing outdoors from the room where the painting is taking place is also a good idea. Of course, if you're a chemically sensitive person or an asthmatic this isn't a job for you to do personally.

Older Cabinet Facelifts

While painting all the surfaces of your old cabinets is one option for updating them, there are others. One is to paint only the fronts of the cabinets' frames, then install new replacement solid-hardwood doors and drawer fronts. Naturally, these new door and drawer fronts will need to be coated with a durable, yet tolerable, finish. Remember, whenever you're doing any painting or coating, you need plenty of ventilation and appropriate protective gear. It should be much easier to find a woodworker or cabinetmaker to create solid-wood drawers and door fronts than to create a complete set of cabinetry of solid wood.

Another approach to modernizing your older, outdated kitchen cabinets is to use new solid-wood doors and drawer fronts, but instead of painting the existing cabinet frames, you can have hard, *high-pressure plastic laminate* applied to them. Of course, this type of project will require someone who is skilled at working with plastic laminates. To find such a person, you can ask for recommendations at local kitchen cabinet shops and building-supply centers. You can also check in the classified section of your telephone book under "Countertops" or "Kitchen Cabinets," or "Remodeling Contractors."

No matter who does the laminating work, a nontoxic water-based contact cement such as Weldwood Non-Flammable Contact Cement (**Dap, Inc.**) is a better choice to use rather than a noxious solvent-based brand. This particular product, as well as similar ones, are now often available at hardware stores and building centers. Having good ventilation during the laminating process, and wearing appropriate protective gear, including a cartridge-type respirator mask, is still highly advised. By the way, the plastic laminate should only be applied to the cabinet surfaces after the cabinets have first been cleaned in order to ensure good adhesion. (See the recommendations for cleaning and preparation work under *Painting Older Cabinets* on page 322.)

Countertops

Since the 1950s, almost all cabinet tops have been made of hard plastic laminates. That is, until the last decade or so. Now there are a surprising number of countertop options. This section will cover several of the more common types now being used.

High-Pressure Plastic Laminates

Hard, $1/16$"-thick *high-pressure plastic laminate* is still probably the most popular countertop surface in the U.S. today. This isn't surprising; this material inexpensive, waterproof, attractive, and relatively easy to install. Laminated countertops are also a cinch to keep clean and disinfect, and they require no added oils or finishes. Plastic laminate countertops are so common that they can be readily purchased at nearly all building centers and cabinet shops. One of the more familiar brands is Formica (**Formica Corp.**), but there are a number of others. Despite being plastic products, high-pressure plastic laminates are so hard and dense, that they tend to release relatively few synthetic odors. Therefore, the laminate itself is often tolerable for most sensitive people.

What exactly are plastic laminates? Plastic laminates are actually made of several layers of Kraft paper bonded together with plastic resins under heat and very high pressure. The topmost layer of resin-impregnated paper is colored or patterned. This gives the laminate sheet its particular appearance. Modern plastic laminates now come in a wide variety of designs, colors, textures, sheens, and grades. However, they're all subject to scorching and chipping to some degree.

Unfortunately, plastic laminate sheets are much too thin ($^1/_{16}$") and brittle to serve as countertops as they are; they must have a supporting surface beneath them. Therefore, plastic laminates are always permanently glued to thick, smooth, stable, solid, *substrates* (base materials). Generally, particleboard is used for this. Sadly, from a health standpoint, most particleboard gives off high levels of formaldehyde from *urea-formaldehyde (UF)* glues. Particleboard will also outgas potentially bothersome softwood *terpene* odors. However, alternative particleboards made without formaldehyde, or construction-grade plywoods, which use a less problematic *phenol-formaldehyde glue (PF)*, can be substituted. (Note, these still will emit terpenes.) Some people are tempted to use plastic laminates over solid wood, but this generally doesn't work very well because solid wood can warp and change dimensions too much as the humidity fluctuates with the seasons.

While it's usual practice to only apply plastic laminate to the top and front edge of the substrate, you might seriously consider covering *all* the sides—top, bottom, and each of the four edges. This encasement approach is especially important for chemically sensitive individuals. If this is done, most of the formaldehyde, as well as the natural pine terpene odors are sealed in.

If you choose not to apply plastic laminate to all sides, you may want to coat the exposed plywood or particleboard surfaces with a sealant (see *Acrylic Finishes and Sealants* on page 277.) You should be aware, though, that sealants can't totally seal in formaldehyde emissions—even with four coats—and they can be very odorous in their own right. Another option would be to glue or staple heavy-duty aluminum foil to the exposed plywood or particleboard base material. However, this isn't completely effective either, and the foil will likely tear. *Builder's foil* (Kraft-paper with aluminum on one or both sides) is stronger and more durable. Aluminum tape is a good choice for keeping the builder's foil in place. (See *Tapes* on page 282 and also *Foil Barriers* on page 290.)

For gluing plastic laminate to a substrate, a water-based, low-toxicity contact cement can be a good option. Weldwood Non-Flammable Contact Cement (**Dap, Inc.**) is one such product, and it's often available at local hardware stores and building centers. During the actual laminating process, there should be good ventilation and, of course, appropriate protective gear should always be worn. (See *Personal Protective Gear* on page 264.)

Butcher-Block Countertops

Another countertop option is a wood *butcher block*, which is becoming more popular. Most butcher block countertops consist of narrow maple or oak strips held together with glue. Originally, butcher-block surfaces were only made of *end grain* wood (cut across the width of the trunk) because it's more durable than wood cut parallel with the grain. Real butcher blocks had to withstand the abuse of cleavers and knives without chipping or splitting. However, today's butcher-block countertops usually don't receive this kind of daily assault. Therefore, many aren't made with end-grain work surfaces. Incidentally, if you have the choice, it's best to choose maple over oak for your new butcher-block countertops, if you are a very sensitive person. This is because oak contains natural, strong-smelling *tannin compounds,* which can be irritating to the mucous membranes of susceptible people.

Unfortunately, the glues and surface-sealing treatments used in the manufacturing of certain butcher-block countertops can also be a problem for some sensitive people. Another point to consider is that although they're extremely attractive when new, many butcher-block counters eventually get stained by foods, especially if no sealant or clear finish was used on them, and scorched by hot pans. However, minor stains and scorch marks can often be removed with light sanding.

One maker of maple, red oak, and white oak butcher block countertops to seriously consider is **Block Tops**. These are made with a polyvinyl glue (similar to Elmer's Glue-All). They come prefinished, with your choice of a mineral oil, or their own "Salad Bowl Oil." If you're interested, you'll need to contact the company for a dealer near you. (Currently, there are dealers only in the Western U.S.)

John Boos & Company produces maple or red oak "thermo-bonded" butcher-block countertops. These apparently come finished in your choice of either "Varnique" semi-gloss *catalyzed lacquer* (a potent urea-formaldehyde finish) or a penetrating Mystery Oil (primarily a blend of linseed and mineral oils). Mineral oil is suggested for touch-ups. You can contact the company for a local supplier.

Two manufacturers that make identical butcher block countertops are **Balley Block Co.** and **Michigan Maple Block Co.** These are maple countertops using a "Wood Welded" electronic bonding process requiring pressure and *urea-formaldehyde* glue. Unfortunately, this is a nastier type of glue capable of *outgassing* (emitting) a great deal of formaldehyde. These particular butcher-block countertops come standard with Dura Kryl 102 acrylic finish. However a "Good Stuff" finish (a mixture of oils and a urethane gel) is an option, as is a completely unfinished product. They say in their literature that tung oil is a good oil for completely coating unfinished tops or for touch up (You should know that tung oil has been implicated in suppressing immune-system functions as well as reactivating chronic Epstein-Barr-virus infections.) They also suggest vegetable oil or mineral oil for touching up cutting surfaces. Call for a dealer near you if you're interested.

It's important for chemically sensitive individuals interested in having butcher-block countertops to request samples to be tested for personal tolerance (see *Testing Woods* on page 269). Sniff testing should only be done by persons with asthma or severe sensitivities after an initial airing out period. However, be aware that testing will only give you a general indication because the sample you receive may be relatively old. As a result, it may have already aired out, or it may have been stored in an office or warehouse near smokers or persons wearing perfume. You should keep in mind, too, that samples are generally quite small compared to the total square footage of installed countertops.

Corian-Type Countertops

After high-pressure plastic laminate, some of the most popular countertops are solid, mineral/polymer countertops. Originally, available only in white, they now come in a number of colors and visual textures. The first to be developed was Corian (**DuPont Corian (E. I. duPont de Nemours and Company)**). Corian has been successfully used by a number of sensitive individuals.

Corian is a specific, patented formulation made up of marble dust and a synthetic resin. Despite the synthetic content, Corian seems to have only a slight odor, perhaps because it's so hard and dense. One very positive feature of Corian is that, if you get the solid 3/4"-thick type, in many installations it won't require a plywood or particleboard *substrate* (base material) for support. This eliminates formaldehyde glue and softwood terpene problems that are usually associated with these man-made wood products. However, because the typical thickness is 1/2", the options available to you in a 3/4" thickness could be limited to a few standard colors, although other colors might be able to be special ordered. By the way, Corian also comes in 1/4" thickness for "wet walls" such as for bathroom showers.

On the plus side, Corian is relatively stain-resistant and, even if it acquires some minor discolorations (or scratches), these can often be sanded out. Of course, this must be done very carefully. (Remember to follow any manufacturer's guidelines.) To purchase Corian, check with your local kitchen/bath cabinet dealers. If necessary, you can call the company for a dealer near you.

You should be aware that there are several other Corian-like products that are also being commonly used. These come in two forms: a solid material or a laminated version with a thin attractive top layer over an underlying man-made wood layer. While the laminated types are less expensive, they could theoretically pose more of an intolerance problem. However, if the mineral/polymer material completely encases the man-made material, much of the formaldehyde and softwood terpene odors coming from the core material should be sealed in. (Note: Edges and seams may leave the man-made wood slightly exposed in some installations.) It should also be noted that the different manufacturers use a different polymer in their formulations, so if you don't tolerate one particular brand, you may be able to tolerate another.

Ceramic-Tile Countertops

One of the oldest countertop materials, ceramic tile, can still be an attractive option for today's kitchens and bathrooms. Ceramic tile is beautiful, natural, durable, and generally well-tolerated by even very chemically sensitive people. However, it's best to only choose glazed, kiln-fired ceramic tiles. This type of tile has a *vitreous* (hard glass-like) surface which doesn't require any sealing treatment. These days, ceramic tiles are available in a variety of sizes, patterns, colors, and shapes to give your countertops an attractive and personal touch. (See *Choosing Ceramic Tile* on page 314.)

However, it should be stated that there could be a few potential problems with ceramic-tile countertops. One is with the *substrate* (base material) used beneath the tiles themselves. Commonly, ceramic tile is adhered to a construction-grade plywood substrate using a *thinset* (also called dry-set) mortar or a mastic. Unfortunately, some of these products can be bothersome to sensitive individuals. For such people, testing is essential. (See *Important Testing Considerations* on page 267 and also *Thinset Ceramic Tile Mortars* on page 286.)

Another concern is with the substrate material itself. Construction-grade plywood emits formaldehyde from *phenol-formaldehyde (PF)* glue and natural hydrocarbon *terpenes* from the softwoods that can be bothersome to some sensitive people. Often, a healthier substrate option is to use two layers of 1/2" *cement board* (a cementitious product sold in sheets). Unfortunately, even this material is sometimes fairly odorous. However, some sensitive persons find they can tolerate cement board better than construction-grade plywood. Cement board is available through some building centers and lumberyards, and through ceramic-tile suppliers. There are several different brands on the market, including Wonderboard (**Custom Building Products**) and Durock (**USG Corp.**). You can call these companies for their nearest dealers.

To help block any objectionable emissions from either a plywood or cement-board substrate, you could coat the exposed underside surfaces with a sealant. Four coats will often seal in most odors, but all sealants are imperfect. Cement board can often be sealed successfully by coating the exposed surfaces with a layer of thinset mortar. Another option would be to cover any exposed plywood or cement-board surfaces with an aluminum-foil product.

Yet another common worry with ceramic-tile countertops is the grout. Many prepackaged grouts contain chemical additives which can be bothersome to some sensitive people. However, a simple grout with no additives can be made by mixing clean dry sand, water, and Portland cement (see *Ceramic Tile Installation* on page 315). To add color, you can use a small amount of natural mineral pigments. These can usually be bought locally wherever mortar is sold. They can also be mail-ordered from **Building for Health Materials Center**. Because it's additive-free, home-made grout without additives must be *damp-cured*. This means that the newly grouted tile countertop will have to be covered with plastic sheeting (plastic drop cloths) for three days. This is done to prevent rapid drying and allow the grout to become strong and durable. After the plastic is taken off, the tiles are scrubbed to remove any grout film. (For compete information on tile installation, see *Healthy House Building for the New Millennium* by John Bower, which can be ordered from **The Healthy House Institute** or your favorite bookseller.)

Many people are also afraid that stains and mold growth will get on the grout lines. Actually, you can greatly minimize these problems by laying the ceramic tiles very close together. In addition, after installation, the grout itself can be sealed by carefully brushing it with *water glass* (sodium silicate). Water glass is a colorless, odorless liquid that is chemically similar to window glass. When it's applied to grout, it chemically reacts with the calcium in the grout to form an impermeable crystalline structure in the surface.

Several types of water glass are manufactured by **AFM**. One, AFM Safecoat Grout Sealer, contains not only water glass, but acrylics and other polymer resins to make it adhere more permanently to grout. (Note: Because of the added synthetic resins, this sealer may have an odor when newly applied.) Two other products from **AFM** are more "pure." AFM Safecoat Penetrating Water Stop has a thin consistency to sink in, while AFM Safecoat Water Shield is thicker to create a surface coating. Sources for all these are **The Living Source, Bio Designs, Allergy Relief Shop, Inc., Building for Health Materials Center, American Environmental Health Foundation**, and **N.E.E.D.S.** (See also *Water Glass* on page 280.)

Stainless-Steel Countertops

One of the healthiest countertop choices is *stainless steel*. It's been used in commercial kitchens for years but it's just now being used a little more commonly in residential applications. It's hoped that it will become even more widely used as people realize its sleek modern appearance is, indeed, appropriate in their own home kitchen.

What exactly is stainless steel? Stainless steel is defined as any steel alloy that has at least a 12% chromium content. Chromium gives steel tremendous rust and corrosion resistance. Nickel, molybdenum, or other elements may also be used in certain stainless-steel alloys. Currently, the most popular stainless steel is called 18-8. This grade contains 18% chromium, 8% nickel, and 0.15% carbon. This particular alloy of stainless steel is generally used in flatware, cooking utensils, plumbing fixtures, and it works very well for kitchen countertops.

One drawback to stainless-steel countertops is that they're often relatively expensive. First, the stainless-steel sheets themselves can be quite pricey, and then you have to add in the cost of having them custom-made into countertops by skilled fabricators. Yet, stainless steel's advantages are considerable. Stainless steel is virtually indestructible and it won't support microbial growth. It's also stain-resistant, scorch-resistant, and not subject to cracking or peeling. In other words, stainless-steel countertops should last forever and, therefore, will never have to be replaced. If your stainless-steel countertops are of a fairly simple design, the cost can be comparable to Corian-type countertops—and sometimes less.

Because stainless-steel countertops are almost always custom-made, you can have finished countertops manufactured with many special features. For example, you can choose to have extra-tall backsplashes, or none at all, and perhaps a seamless integral sink. Though they're more expensive than using a "drop-in" sink, integrated sinks offer a clean, streamlined look. This is because all the separate components of a stainless-steel countertop and the sink(s) are welded together and the weld seams are ground and polished so they become invisible. Therefore, an integrated countertop/sink eliminates the seams found when a typical drop-in sink is used—seams which could eventually become traps for food particles or microbial growth.

It should be pointed out that when you're having your stainless-steel countertops made, you can specify that they be fabricated using a particular *gauge* (thickness). It's best for chemically sensitive people to choose a gauge that's relatively heavy because with thin stainless steel, a plywood or particleboard *substrate* (support base) is required. This man-made wood material can release formaldehyde from formaldehyde-based glues and softwood *terpene* odors. (For more on man-made wood substrates, see *High-Pressure Plastic Laminate* on page 323.) To eliminate the substrate altogether, stainless steel with at least a 14-gauge thickness will have to be used. Stainless-steel countertops of that thickness will probably only need a few solid-wood braces underneath for sufficient support. If you are a very sensitive individual, consider using a hardwood for the braces rather than pine, to avoid any terpene odors.

To find a company in your area that can fabricate stainless-steel countertops, you can check your telephone classified section under "Commercial Kitchen Suppliers." If none are listed there, ask at local restaurants and other commercial kitchens to find out where their countertops were made. When you find a fabricator, make certain that his work will be of sufficient quality to be used in a home kitchen. Also you'll want to get a total cost estimate which will include materials, labor, shipping, etc., as well as an expected date your countertops should be completed. You should be aware, however, that some fabricators do not actually install countertops. In that case, you'll have to make arrangements with someone else to install them. Remember to be extremely careful when giving countertop measurements to your stainless-steel fabricator. Any mistakes can mean expensive countertops that don't fit. Stainless-steel countertops can't be easily modified once fabricated, so accurate measurements are mandatory.

CHAPTER 12: HOME DECORATING

Ever since prehistoric men and women lived in caves, humans have felt compelled to adorn their homes with paint and other materials, as well as objects, to add comfort and a sense of their own individuality. However, most of the wall and window treatments, paints and stains, furniture and floor coverings used today, while often attractive, can actually be sources of air pollution, discomfort, and illness. This is because many of the materials now used to make decorating and furnishing materials are man-made creations that can *outgas* (emit) potentially harmful chemical odors.

At the same time, certain home components, such as carpeting, soft furnishings, and elaborate window dressings, are made to be difficult, if not impossible, to clean thoroughly on a regular basis. So, they become havens for dust, and microorganisms such as dust mites.

As you begin to create your own healthy household, remember that, while color and style are important, your primary decorating consideration should always be the potential health effects of what you put in your home. No matter what the current fashion dictates, your well-being and that of your family should always come first. Therefore, choosing truly cleanable, less-toxic, low-odor materials is extremely important.

If you you need professional help with your home decorating, some interior designers are now becoming aware of how homes and furnishings can lead to ill health, so you may find a local person knowledgeable about healthy decorating. Some interior-design companies, such as **Interior Elements**, are including health considerations in all their projects. Margie McNally, who owns this particular company, is an accredited, professional designer/environmental consultant who specializes in "creating healthy indoor environments."

Decorating for Allergic People

It's especially important for people allergic to dust mites to choose items that can be easily and thoroughly cleaned. Window treatments should be simple. Good choices are metal or wood blinds or 100%-cotton or linen curtains that can be regularly washed. For rugs, good choices are, washable, 100%-cotton ones you can care for yourself at home.

Furniture should also be "easy-clean." Solid-wood or metal pieces are probably the best for seating. Soft furniture items covered in leather can be wiped clean, so they can be good choices too. If you prefer fabric upholstery, choose items with removable, washable, all-cotton slip-covers. Toss pillows should also have removable and washable covers, and afghans or throws should be designed to take repeated launderings.

For accent pieces, avoid small knick-knacks that are dust collectors and are time consuming to clean properly. It may be best to give your lovely, but potentially problematic items, to friends or relatives. If you don't want to part with them, and you can afford it, and have the space, consider purchasing a glass-fronted curio cabinet to display them. Better yet, a custom-made cabinet could be built of solid wood, without plywood or particleboard panels. It should also be noted that frames on art work and mirrors should be simple and unadorned, so they can be dusted quickly.

Those bothered by pollen, should not bring cut flowers indoors. Nor should they have flowering plants growing within a home's living space. For those allergic to mold, it's probably best to eliminate live potted plants because their soil can be a prime place for fungal growth. In addition, the shower curtains should be replaced with free-draining, frameless glass doors to minimize places where mold and mildew could grow. If that's impossible, use washable cotton or hemp duck-fabric for a shower curtain and launder it weekly.

Above all, use common sense and have patience. As you go through the following sections, think about how the items suggested could affect you. Then buy accordingly. It is possible for you to make a comfortable and attractive home despite the limitations allergies and asthma can sometimes impose, but it *will* take time and forethought. Eventually though, you will have rooms that anyone, allergic or not, will find appealing.

Furniture

Furniture originated out of simple utilitarian necessity. However, with time, the decorative aspects became more and more prominent. As designs and construction techniques improved and evolved, professional furniture making became an occupation—sometimes an art. For centuries, skilled craftsmen and their assistants made individual pieces by hand.

However, during the 1800s, factories began mass-producing furniture. As the prices went down, the quality sometimes did, too. With the proliferation of cheap man-made materials after World War II, most furniture began being made with at least some synthetic components. Today, the use of man-made materials is greater than ever. Unfortunately some of the furniture now sold isn't particularly well-made, aesthetically pleasing, or long-lasting. Actually, a great deal of the furniture made in the last four or five decades is throwaway furniture. Completely hand-crafted pieces using solid woods along with natural fabrics and stuffing are now quite rare, and often very expensive. Fortunately, there are a few furniture-making companies that do produce affordable furniture using *real* materials.

Typical Modern Manufactured Furniture

Today, furniture is often constructed with some solid wood (often a softwood such as pine, or an inexpensive hardwood), as well as some composite man-made materials (hardboard, particleboard, or plywood). In factories, furniture parts are machine-cut and sanded, then quickly assembled with mechanical nailers, screw guns, staplers, and quick-drying glues. Some pieces may also have hardwood *veneers* (very thin layers of solid wood) and/or plastic laminates, permanently attached to them with the use of synthetic adhesives. The use of sprayed-on synthetic stains and finishes is routine on most exposed-wood parts.

Soft pieces (sofas, etc.) are usually upholstered with synthetic stuffings, tapes, and fabrics. Frequently, upholstery materials are chemically treated to repel dirt and stains. Interestingly, furniture sold in California may now have to meet mandated flame-retardant standards—meaning the addition of borate compounds or synthetic fire-retardant chemicals. These standards are now being expanded to furniture made elsewhere as well.

Therefore, it's not surprising that most new furniture releases many potentially harmful chemicals, including formaldehyde. Man-made wood products, finishes, stains, glues, tapes, stuffing, fabrics, and special treatments all emit a variety of compounds that can pollute a home's indoor air. As a result, typical new furniture is often intolerable for most sensitive individuals.

Acceptable New Manufactured Furniture

Fortunately, healthier furniture selections do exist. The following sections offer some alternatives for you to consider.

Solid-Wood Furniture

Solid-wood furniture can be a healthy furnishing choice and, luckily, there are still a fair number companies and individuals making it. The styles now available range from traditional, country-look, and Shaker, to modern contemporary. The most commonly used woods are probably still pine and oak. Unfortunately, for some very sensitive individuals, both of these woods can be a problem because of the natural terpenes in softwoods and the tannins in oak. These natural compounds can be both odorous and irritating. If you can find it, furniture made with solid maple, beech, birch, or cherry is usually more tolerable for sensitive people. A more difficult problem to overcome is the fact that items with drawers, large panels, or backings will likely have plywood used in their construction, no matter how much they cost. That is, unless you have special custom pieces made for you. Therefore, sensitive persons will have to be alert and decide what is appropriate for their needs, then buy accordingly.

You may be able to find some appealing solid-wood furniture at your local furniture stores. However, if you can't, there are a number of mail-order sources. For example, **Shaker Workshops** offers hand- finished Shaker-style benches, bookcases, stools, platform beds, end tables, rockers, and dining-room tables and chairs constructed of solid maple and cherry. **Shaker Shops West** sells similar hand-finished furniture. Their line includes cherry, walnut, and maple (some pine, too) items such as stools, benches, shelves, tables, chairs, rockers, and standing cupboards.

Classic American reproductions of tables, beds, chairs, and benches in hand-finished pine, maple, and other woods can be purchased from **Cohasset Colonials**. In addition, **Bartley Collection** (which includes many reproduction pieces) offers hand-finished beds, chairs, benches, and tables in solid cherry, maple, walnut, and mahogany. Their dressers, chests, and wardrobes are built of a combination of solid wood with some *hardwood veneered plywood* (plywood with a thin top layer of desirable hardwood) being used, too.

This End Up sells solid-pine dining tables, chairs, benches, and beds. From **Yield House**, you can get hand-finished all-pine beds, stools, chairs, rockers, racks, shelves, and tables. Solid pine combined with plywood is used on their storage cabinets, desks, entertainment centers, and armoires. Solid-pine accent tables and stools can be purchased from **French Creek Sheep & Wool Co.** These come in your choice of several milk-paint finishes. (For more on milk paints, see *Alternative Natural Formula Paints* on page 274.)

In addition, birch chairs and tables, oak tables and oak-with-oak-veneered-plywood lawyers bookcases (glass fronted) are available. Solid-maple with maple-veneered plywood are used in the 2-, 3-, or 4-tier lawyers bookcases handled by **Ballard Designs**. They also have chairs and stools with mahogany frames and rush seats, and solid-wood racks and shelves. **Smith & Hawken** carries solid-ash dining tables and matching chairs. These tables have beautiful solid, quarried "greystone" tops.

L.L. Bean (Furnishings Catalog) sells solid-ash Mission-style tables, beds (twin through king), convertible bed/couch futon frames, and bookshelves. Other items they carry include beech dining chairs with rush seats, maple stools, and hardwood shelving. You can also order an attractive oak/rattan rocker. Solid-wood beds and chairs (pine and hardwoods) are sold by **Pottery Barn**. Beechwood director chairs with 100%-cotton-canvas seating, as well as solid-wood benches, dining tables, dining chairs, and shelving racks are all sold by **Home Decorators Collection**. This company also carries oak mission-style end tables that are particularly nice. From the **Crate & Barrel**, you can order solid-wood beds, side tables, shelves, dining tables and matching chairs, stools, and benches. These come in different woods.

Solid-wood kitchen carts, racks, dinettes, stools, and rockers (made from several types of wood) are carried by the **JC Penny Catalog**. From **Get Organized**, you can order solid-wood corner shelves and wine racks. They also have solid-pine bookcases and a very nice solid-beech, portable, folding, eating/work counter with matching stools. This is an ideal unit for very small spaces. Then, too, **Kitchen & Home** has beechwood-and-rush dining chairs and stools, as well as solid-pine dining tables. **Colonial Gardens Kitchen** is a source for oak baker's racks and magazine racks. On the other hand, the **Service Merchandise** catalog not only carries solid hardwood baker's racks, but stools, kitchen-island units, carts, tables, and dining tables made from different wood species.

Heart of Vermont makes and sells solid-red-oak or solid-ash (finished or unfinished) futon beds, couch frames, and convertible bed/couch frames. (For futons to put on them, see *Futons* on page 234.) **Garnet Hill** has solid-pine beds in twin through king sizes. Solid-cherry-and-maple beds in twin through king sizes are sold by **Cuddledown of Maine**. Other solid-wood beds (in various species) are sold by **Linensource**, **Coming Home**, **Eddie Bauer** (Home catalog), and **Chambers**.

Natural Baby carries solid-wood high chairs and pine toddler's bedroom furniture (bed, storage bench, night stand) that's finished with a non-toxic, water-based finish. However the crossboards under the beds are plywood. **EcoBaby Organics** handles Pacific-Coast-Maple baby and children's furniture. This line includes cribs, child-size beds, and other bedroom pieces finished with beeswax and tung oil.

Of special note is **Pompanoosuc Mills**, which has a complete solid-hardwood furniture line in a number of species including oak, birch, maple, cherry, and walnut. The company also has dining-room sets, benches, living-room seating options, desks, coffee tables, and bedroom suites in several styles. Also offered are kitchen work tables, bookcases, and storage units. Most importantly, this company welcomes sensitive clients. In fact, its catalog specifically states that the company "offers special materials, stains, and finishes for chemically sensitive individuals."

(For more solid-wood furniture options, see *Unfinished and Kit Furniture* on page 335, *Custom-Made Furniture* on page 337, and *Patio Furniture* on page 334.)

Metal Furniture

Metal furniture can be an excellent healthy choice for your home's interior. Often, manufacturers combine metal with glass, both of which are generally inert. More popular then ever, brass, wrought iron, painted steel, stainless steel, and chromed pieces are easy to find at most local furniture stores, bedroom shops, and import stores. You can also buy metal desks, bookcases, and chairs at many office-supply stores. These particular pieces often work very well in your den or home office.

A number of companies offer metal furniture through the mail. One of the best is **This End Up**. They have metal-based, glass-topped dining tables, end tables, coffee tables, and bookcases. They also have metal-wire shelves and racks. **Get Organized** carries metal baker's racks and metal-tiered carts. **Ballard Designs** also handles metal baker's racks as does **Colonial Gardens Kitchen**. The **Home Decorators Collection** has decorative steel storage racks and **Hold Everything** offers some metal (chrome or stainless) racks. Metal racks and stools are handled by **Kitchen & Home**. A good-looking metal/glass dining table set with metal/wicker chairs is sold by **Crate & Barrel**. The **JC Penny Catalog** offers all-metal as well as metal-and-wood racks for your storage needs. **Get Organized** has powder-coated steel CD holders and TV stands. From **Service Merchandise**, you can order metal-and-glass desks and book shelves.

Utilitarian looking steel TV/video storage units and bookcases with water-based, baked-enamel finishes are made by **Lee Metal Products**. You can call the company for a nearby dealer. Similarly styled shelving and mobile computer-workstation cabinets with doors are manufactured by **Edsal Manufacturing Co., Inc.** These items have baked-enamel finishes on steel. Again, you'll need to contact the company for a local supplier. (Note: Some **Lee Metal Products** and **Edsal Manufacturing Co., Inc.** items are offered in the **Reliable Corp.** catalog.) Heavy, yet good-looking, chromed-steel shelving is manufactured by **Inter-Metro Industries Corp.** They also make all-stainless-steel tables with heavy 14-gauge tops. These "clean tables" are 34" wide and they come in 5' and longer lengths, through dealers only.

For years, beds have been made of various kinds of metal. While brass beds have consistently been popular, new wrought-iron beds have come to the forefront in the last few years. **Crate & Barrel** sells attractive metal beds in a full range of sizes, as well as chairs. **Brass Bed Shoppe** handles brass beds, headboards, and daybeds in all sizes. But, besides brass, they also have a good variety in painted and hand-forged steel ones as well. The **Garnet Hill** catalog has beds in twin through king made of wrought iron, aluminum and iron. Then, too, **Pottery Barn**, **Cuddledown of Maine**, **Coming Home**, **Eddie Bauer** (Home catalog), **Ballard Designs**, **L.L. Bean** (Furnishings Catalog), and **Linensource** all handle several metal-bed styles in a range of sizes.

Unusual items you might be interested in are the butterfly chairs that are available from **Harmony**. These have a black steel frame with a powder-coated finish. Stretched across the frames are quilted green-cotton seating fabric. Unfortunately, the stuffing they use is synthetic Polyfil. These come in two styles with ottomans available. Similar chairs and ottomans are sold by **Solutions**. Their covers are made of prewashed 100%-cotton, but they are also stuffed with polyester padding.

Note: Metal furniture that has been painted or lacquered (brass items are often coated with a clear lacquer) will often require some time to air out for sensitive people. This can be done in uncontaminated surroundings before being brought indoors. If possible, choose only products with a baked-on finish because they usually require less airing.

(For other metal furniture, see *Patio Furniture* on page 334.)

Wicker Furniture

Many people assume that wicker and reed furniture, which is made of natural grasses, would be a good choice in a less-toxic home. These pieces do have certain pluses, such as being appropriate for most rooms and often being relatively inexpensive. However, there can be some problems with this kind of furniture. Particular parts, for example, shelves or seat bottoms, are often made of plywood or other man-made wood products. These materials can emit formaldehyde from the glues, as well as softwood terpene odors, that can be bothersome to some sensitive people. Also, it's possible that mold or mildew may have contaminated some reed or wicker pieces. This is understandable if you realize that, in most cases, these materials are damp when they're woven. (To make sure a piece you're interested in has not been contaminated by fungus, you'll need to check the bottom and back for telltale dark fungal discolorations.) Finally, another concern is that some wicker and reed pieces are rather difficult to thoroughly clean.

If you're interested in this type of furniture, you'll want go to wicker shops, import stores, and furniture stores to see what's available locally. If you'd prefer to order through the mail, **Pottery Barn** handles some very attractive wicker pieces including, of course, chairs. The **JC Penny Catalog** has useful metal-and-wicker racks while **Get Organized** offers wicker/metal storage baskets, an entertainment center and an unusual, 3-tiered folding screen. Metal-and-wicker chairs and stools are sold by **Crate & Barrel**. Finally, **EcoBaby Organics** handles very nice natural-palm-fiber baby baskets and bassinets. The liners are 100%-cotton (some are organic cotton).

Patio Furniture

One classification of metal furnishings you may not have considered for the interior of your home is patio furniture. Actually, this furniture can often be suitable for most rooms in your house. It will give your rooms an unexpected "fresh" look, or a casual country look, depending on how you decorate. However, to make sure patio furniture is healthy, you'll need to replace any vinyl and synthetic-foam seat cushions with washable, removable, natural-fabric-covered cushions filled with natural-fiber batting. You can either make them yourself or have an upholsterer do it for you. (See *Chapter 7: Healthier Fibers & Stuffings* as well as *Sewing* on page 456.)

As you well know, you can purchase metal patio furniture locally in patio shops, as well as in many furniture, department, and discount stores. However, good-looking metal pieces are often available in garden catalogs, too. **Crate & Barrel** carries all-metal patio furniture including chairs, tables, and benches. **Carolina Patio Warehouse** has good-looking tables and chairs in wrought and cast aluminum as well as wrought iron. (Note: The paint on metal patio furniture may need time to air sufficiently before bringing it into the house, if you're a sensitive person.)

Wood patio furniture has become more popular again. So, local outlets for patio furniture should have some styles available from which you can choose. Again, you may also want to check garden and patio catalogs such as **Smith & Hawken**. This particular company has many styles of unfinished, solid-teak furniture. Pieces include benches, chaise lounges, side tables, coffee tables, dining tables, and dining chairs. **Carolina Patio Warehouse** has solid-teak chairs, benches and chaise lounges. These have no oils or finishes added. **Capers Reef** makes and sells a line (chairs and tables) of Southern-cypress patio furniture. These, too, have no oils or finishes added. If you desire, you don't have to add anything to them. That way, you can avoid any problematic finishes. (Note: Pieces without any finish will often absorb accidental stains more easily.) In the **Adirondack Design** catalog you'll find unfinished redwood chairs, love seats, benches, and chaise lounges. As you would expect, these are in the Adirondack style, which has a large, sturdy cottage-look.

There are other catalog sources for solid-wood patio furniture that carry it only in season. **Design Toscano** handles solid-teak patio furniture (bench, chairs, end tables, and coffee tables). **Harmony** carries all-birch patio furniture that includes tables, chairs, and rockers. These are coated with a clear, water-resistant, water-based finish. **Crate & Barrel** has a solid-wood line of tables, chairs, and benches.

Ceramic and Plaster Furniture

Ceramic or plaster seats, pedestals, and end tables can be exciting home additions. This is because they're commonly made in unusual shapes such as elephants, columns, or even winged lions. However, there can be other advantages to owning ceramic and plaster items. For example, they tend to be virtually odorless and they're also easy-to-clean, especially the ceramic ones. If you place glass tops on appropriate designs, you can have attractive tables (or shelving for the available brackets). Make sure to get heavy glass, at least $1/4$" thick. (Some people use glass as thick as $1/2$".) Thin glass can break much too easily, but keep in mind, the thicker the glass the more it will cost. Your local glass stores should be able to cut if for you in any size and shape including ovals and rounds.

Locally, import shops and furniture stores may handle a few plaster or ceramic furniture items. Garden and decorator catalogs often carry them, too. In the **Design Toscano** main catalog, you can find classic pedestal columns. And, in the **Design Toscano** Columns & Pedestal catalog, you'll come across a few decorative columns and bases in plaster and concrete. (Most are now created with synthetic plastic resins.) **Ballard Designs** offers quite a few plaster pieces such as columns, pedestals, wall brackets, and table bases.

Unfinished and Kit Furniture

Unfinished furniture is another furnishing option you might seriously consider. Not surprisingly, unfinished furniture often costs much less than comparable finished pieces. These days, there are a number of stores and catalogs offering it, and recently the styles offered have become more varied and elaborate.

You'll find that virtually all unfinished furniture consists of "hard" pieces, such as benches, rockers, cabinets, etc. In some cases, the furniture is completely assembled and all you have to do is apply paint, or stain (if desired) and clear finish. This gives you complete control of the finishing products actually used on your furniture, a real plus for sensitive individuals.

Another do-it-yourself option is *kit furniture*. While most unfinished furniture comes assembled, kit furniture doesn't. Therefore, this furniture is often termed *knockdown* or *KD furniture*, meaning it comes to you in separate pieces. However, most kit furniture can be easily put together using a few screws, clamps, and a tolerable carpenter's glue. One popular brand is Elmer's Carpenter's Wood Glue for Interior Use (**Elmer's Products, Inc.**). It's sold at many hardware stores and building-supply centers. Once a kit furniture is assembled, it should be lightly sanded, vacuumed, and then stained and finished with tolerable products.

The quality, materials, style, and cost of both unfinished and kit furniture varies enormously. However, you'll want to avoid, especially if you are sensitive, very cheap pieces made with tempered hardboard, plywood, particleboard, or solid softwoods such as pine. While pieces constructed with these materials are readily available and inexpensive, they'll most likely give off bothersome formaldehyde from the glues, and softwood terpene odors. Also, it's often wise for sensitive people to avoid solid-oak kit furniture—unless you've personally tested oak and found it tolerable for you. This is because new oak tends to release natural tannin compounds, which some people can find irritating. (See *Important Testing Considerations* on page 267 and *Testing Woods* on page 269.) Fortunately, some companies offer fine-quality unfinished and kit furniture in more-tolerable hardwoods. Some even handle museum-quality reproductions.

Union City Chair manufactures unfinished solid-oak and solid-maple chairs, stools, rockers, benches, dining tables, side tables, and swivel office chairs. **Whittier Wood Products** makes unfinished, solid-wood (maple, alder, and birch) chairs, stools, dining tables, end tables and bookcases (their bookcases use plywood). Look for these brands at local unfinished-furniture stores, or call the companies for their nearest dealers. Of course, other fine company lines should be available in local unfinished furniture stores as well.

Surprisingly, the **JC Penny Catalog** carries a large section of unfinished pine furniture. (Plywood may be used for drawers and backs on certain items.) Included are pieces suitable for about every room in your home. **Yield House** offers many all-pine (tables, chairs, rockers, beds, shelves, racks) and pine-with-plywood items (armoires, desks, dressers, storage cabinets, entertainment centers). They also have hardwood with hardwood-veneered-plywood lawyer's bookcases. From **Workshop Showcase**, you can order red-oak or white-pine end tables, coffee tables, and writing tables. As expected, however, the drawers are constructed with plywood. **Heart of Vermont** offers contemporary, unfinished, red-oak, or ash, convertible, futon/couch frames and beds.

Mail-order kit furniture is available, too. **Cohasset Colonials** has kits of classic American pieces in maple (dining tables, chairs, accent tables, beds) and pine beds, too. These come with the glue and stains included. **Bartley Collection** offer reproduction kits for beds, chairs, tables, and more. Woods used are solid cherry, maple, walnut, or mahogany. Some pieces use *hardwood veneered plywood* (plywood with a thin top layer of desirable hardwood).

Shaker-style furniture kits are also available from **Shaker Shops West**. This company's line includes cherry, walnut, and maple chairs, stools, rockers, tables, and more. (A few items are solid-pine). As their name implies, **Shaker Workshops** offers similar furniture. Their pieces (beds, end tables, dining tables, rockers, and chairs) come in solid-maple or solid-cherry.

Great care should be taken when you finish your unfinished or assembled kit furniture pieces, so they'll not only have a professional look, but also be healthy, too. With any kit or unfinished furniture item, first lightly sand it. Then thoroughly vacuum it using a soft dusting attachment. Next, apply the finish. Of course, you'll only want to use personally tested, tolerable brands. As an alternative, consider not using a stain. That way, the natural beauty of the wood shows through and you don't have to worry whether the stain will be tolerable or not. (See *Important Testing Considerations* on page 267, *Testing Paints & Finishes* on page 267, *Clear Finishes* on page 275, and *Stains* on page 281.)

It's important to remember that whenever you are coating a piece of furniture with any type of finish, you need to have adequate ventilation and wear a cartridge-type respirator mask. (See *Personal Protective Gear* on page 264.) This work may not be appropriate for many sensitive or asthmatic persons to do themselves. When you're done, let the furniture air out in dry, uncontaminated surroundings. This could be outdoors, or indoors in an unused room that is well-ventilated—until the piece becomes tolerable.

(Note: For unfinished patio furniture, see *Patio Furniture* on page 334.)

Customized Catalog Furniture

A number of decorating and bedding catalogs now offer simple traditional-style sofas, love seats, and side chairs (sometimes sleeper sofas and ottomans, too) that can be acceptable options for some people. At the very least, they're certainly much better than many soft furniture options you usually find. Most use hardwood frames and cotton-duck canvas or muslin "under upholstery" along with removable and washable "outer upholstery." Many use synthetic paddings and stuffings. However, some companies offer natural-fiber fabric and stuffing options, too. So, despite being relative large companies offering furniture to the general population, you're getting essentially custom pieces. However, for those who want even more control, and/or organic materials, this type of furniture may not meet their needs. For them, they'll want to see *Custom-Made Soft Furniture* below.

Pottery Barn offers sofas upholstered in 100%-cotton-twill, with removable 100%-cotton slip covers. There are several stuffing options as well as slip-cover fabric choices. The items offered by **Coming Home** are much the same, however the slipcovers are prewashed cotton twill. **Cuddledown of Maine** has similar items. These are made with a mix of synthetic padding with feather/goose-down stuffing. You can choose slip covers in untreated-cotton-denim or linen. The versions sold by **Ballard Designs** come with down-blend cushions (down/feathers/cotton) with 100%-cotton muslin under upholstery and washable, untreated, 100%-cotton slipcovers. Or, you can send in your own fabric for the slipcovers and they'll make them for you out of that.

Upholstered sofas, love seats, and chairs made with hardwood frames, synthetic padding and stuffing, and covered with 100%-cotton and cotton/linen fabrics are sold by **Crate & Barrel**. According to a company representative, natural padding and stuffing options are available, but only through their local stores. It should be mentioned that these particular items don't have removable slipcovers.

Custom-Made Furniture

Despite the fact that most furniture is mass-produced and mass-marketed, you can still purchase custom-made furniture. However, the cost of such pieces can sometimes be high. For example, there are artist/cabinetmakers whose finished work sells for thousands of dollars, but there can also be local cabinet shops and upholsters who may make items for you with less artistic flair, but at more affordable prices. No matter who makes your furniture, you'll want to make sure they use tolerable materials and products you have specified.

Custom-Made Hard Furniture

Many people are worried that they have to come up with their own designs for hard furniture, but that isn't necessarily so. You can create your own designs if you like, or you can purchase published plans and patterns. Furniture plans are offered for sale in wood-working magazines and also in how-to books that are usually available at lumberyards. Of course, many furniture-makers will draw designs and plans specifically for your project. However, the more work he (or she) does on your job, including designing, the more your furniture will ultimately cost.

When it comes time to choose a hardwood species, it's often best to pick one that's naturally low in odor (maple, tulip poplar, beech, or birch), if you're a sensitive person. While softwoods such as white or yellow pine are less expensive, the natural terpenes they give off could be bothersome. It should also be noted that oak, although a very popular furniture hardwood, can release natural tannin compounds. These, too, may be irritating for long periods of time to susceptible persons. Naturally, it's important that only tolerable glues and finishes be used. (See *Important Testing Considerations* on page 267, *Testing Woods* on page 269, *Testing Adhesives* on page 268, and *Testing Paints & Finishes* on page 267.) If webbing is required for your custom seating pieces, 100%-cotton webbing (also known as *chair tape*) can be purchased from **Shaker Workshops** and **Shaker Shops West** in a variety of colors. Most types come in two widths, $5/8$" and 1". Cotton webbing can be woven to make very attractive, and comfortable, back and seat supports.

If you decide to actually build your custom hard furniture yourself, you'll want to work in as safe a manner as possible. This means having plenty of ventilation and wearing neces-sary protective gear. (See *Personal Protective Gear* on page 264.) However, no matter who makes your custom furniture, sensitive individuals should be aware that it'll likely be intol-erable for some time, primarily due to the recently applied finishes. Therefore, ideally, you should put the new furniture outside to air, or place it in a little-used room that can be well-ventilated—until it is odor-free. Whatever place you choose, it should be dry and free of contaminating odors.

To find a capable local furniture-maker, you can check your classified phone directory under Cabinet Makers, etc. You can also ask for suggestions at local interior-decorator stu-dios and lumberyards handling hardwoods, or you might ask a woodworking teacher at a local school or vocational college. (For more on finding the right woodworker, see *Alterna-tive Solid Wood Cabinets* on page 318.)

One mail-order firm you may want to contact to make custom hard furniture is **Charles R. Bailey Cabinetmakers**. This firm makes Second Life Furniture pieces, including tables, chairs, beds, cribs, dressers, end tables, and bookcases, especially for the chemically sensi-tive. You, as their customer, have the option of choosing the design, hardwood species, and finish. In addition, **Pompanoosuc Mills** welcomes sensitive clients and will sometimes make items especially for you—if they're not too dissimilar to what they normally build.

Custom-Made Soft Furniture

An interior-decorating company that will make custom upholstered pieces using or-ganic materials is **Furnature**. They will custom-make for you soft upholstered pieces in a variety of styles using organic-cotton fabrics and your choice of stuffings, including organic cotton, organic wool, and natural-rubber latex. It should be mentioned that this company particularly prides itself on its organic-cotton stuffing which has very low natural odor because of the special care taken to eliminate the cotton seed from the raw cotton. (It's the oils and resins from crushed seeds that is said to give organic cotton its typical somewhat strong, grainy smell.) The frames for their pieces are kiln-dried rock maple, which also has very little odor. The support is provided by steel banding, organic-cotton duck cloth, and steel springs covered with organic-cotton batting. All styles are permanently covered with organic-cotton barrier cloth. This helps seal in any odors that are present as well as helps seal out dust mites. The "top" upholstery is made from removable, washable organic fabric in your choice of many designs. This company has a special chemical tolerance test and information sheet for chemically sensitive clients to fill out when ordering to insure that none of the materials used will pose a potential tolerability problem. Be aware that it'll take 12 to 14 weeks to make a special piece for you, plus shipping time. (Note: This company can do other types of custom work, too.)

An excellent source for custom-made upholstered goods is **The Natural Alternative**. This one-woman company has a real commitment to using only high-quality materials such as kiln-dried maple frames, steel springs, cotton upholstery tapes, as well as jute, coir, and camel-hair specialty paddings. She particularly prides herself on her selection and use of organic fabrics and stuffings. For example, for fillings, you have your choice of organic cotton, organic wool, or kapok fillings. Her upholstery fabrics include attractive organic cottons in natural and color-grown hues as well as blends of organic natural fibers. Many of these have woven, textural patterns. All the furniture pieces she makes are actually multi-layer upholstered. On the items themselves are two permanent layers. These are an under layer of organic-cotton sheeting with a top layer of heavy organic-cotton canvas. (She may soon be offering organic-cotton barrier cloth, too.) Over these, go the form-fitting, removable-and-washable slip covers. For more information you can call the company for a free brochure. Better yet, check out the "Interactive Website" that will show you what your custom pieces will look like. With a deposit, you can request that an on-loan Furniture Design Kit be sent to you. With this, as a prospective buyer, you can see first hand actual samples of all the finishes and stuffings, as well as upholstery fabrics. When you place an order, you'll need to wait 12 to 16 weeks (plus shipping time) to receive your furniture. By the way, The Natural Alternative can also make custom slipcovers for your existing furniture, too. (See *Making Used Furniture Tolerable* on page 340.)

If you decide to have a local upholstery shop make something for you, you'll probably have to provide your own fabric and stuffing, especially if you want organic-cotton fabrics and stuffing and/or untreated wool batting. Organic-cotton upholstery fabric can be purchased from **Furnature** and **The Natural Alternative**. You can also order untreated Homespun all-cotton upholstery/drapery fabric (**Homespun Fabrics and Draperies**) from the company and from **Building for Health Materials Center**. This last catalog also has a good selection of upholstery fabrics in untreated-cotton or hemp. For sources of natural stuffings, you'll want to see *Natural Stuffings* on page 189. Make sure that your local upholstery shop does not smell like tobacco smoke, perfume, or other strong and bothersome odors. Otherwise, your custom pieces may end up intolerable for you.

Antique Furniture

Antique furniture is often made of solid wood, or a combination of solid and *veneered wood* (a thin layer of a valuable hardwood glued over a lesser quality wood base). Usually, the glues used in antique pieces are natural, as well as the fabrics and battings; that is, unless the furniture has been redone at some point using synthetic materials.

Antique pieces can lend warmth and charm to your home, but they can have drawbacks. Unfortunately, perfume, tobacco, and musty odors are fairly common in old pieces. Anther possible problem is mold or mildew contamination, either in the past or ongoing. Therefore, you should check all antique furniture for personal tolerance before placing it in your house. If you can detect only mild odor problems, it may be that airing the furniture outdoors for a time will make it acceptable. Make sure to choose a location that is both dry and uncontaminated with other odors.

However, sometimes objectionable odors will have permeated the wood of your antique furniture. If that's happened, you may have to strip the finish off, sand the piece, and then refinish it before the furniture will become tolerable for you. (Note: Refinishing a piece of antique furniture may negatively affect its value.) If you decide to do furniture stripping yourself, you'll want to do it outdoors if at all possible. If you have to do it indoors, you must have very good ventilation. Using a water-based, less-toxic stripping product, such as Safest Stripper Paint and Varnish Remover (**3M Construction & Home Improvement Products Division**) whose active ingredients are dimethyl esters, is suggested over using typical solvent-based brands. Water-based strippers should be available at your local paint and hardware stores (see *Paint Strippers* on page 282). Whenever stripping a paint or finish, be sure to wear protective eye wear, rubber or neoprene gloves, and a cartridge-type respirator mask. (See *Personal Protective Gear* on page 264.) Even with these precautions, stripping furniture generally isn't a job for an asthmatic or chemically sensitive person to do themselves.

After the antique piece has been stripped, you'll need to lightly sand and vacuum it. Then, if necessary, you can stain the furniture using a tolerable water-based product. Finally, you'll want to coat the piece with a pretested, tolerable, clear finish. When you're all done, it's usually best to place the refinished antique furniture outdoors, or perhaps in a well-ventilated room, until the newly applied finishes are no longer bothersome. As always, the place you choose for airing should be dry and free of contaminating odors.

By the way, if you have a piece of antique furniture that has absorbed very strong perfume or tobacco odors over the years, here is a suggestion that has worked for some chemically sensitive people. Take the piece to a commercial furniture stripper and have them remove the old finish with their powerful, toxic, stripping chemicals. This will often remove any accumulated odors as well. However, the piece will then need to be aired out (in an uncontaminated area) until it loses the odor of the chemical stripper. At that point it can be coated with a tolerable, low-odor finish.

If antique furniture must be reupholstered, good choices for replacement materials are natural-fiber fabrics and stuffing (see *Custom-Made Soft Furniture* on page 338 for fabric sources, *Natural Stuffing* on page 189, and *Sewing* on page 456). You can also supplement natural batting with metal springs for items requiring firmer support. It should be noted that any cloth used as a covering fabric should be laundered to remove any intolerable new-fabric odors before the actual upholstery work is done. This is particularly important for chemically sensitive people (see *Removing Odors from New Clothing* on page 123).

One very important cautionary note for sensitive individuals who want to have furniture upholstered is this: Be sure that whoever does the work does not smoke, wear perfume, or work in an area where others do. Otherwise, your newly reupholstered pieces could pick up these odors and be intolerable to you. While airing could help dissipate these odors, there is, of course, no guarantee this would be absolutely successful.

Making Used Furniture Tolerable

Sometimes individuals own bothersome furniture they don't want to—or simply can't afford to—replace at the moment. For example, a person may own a sofa covered and stuffed in odorous synthetic materials, but it's only a few years old, and he (or she) can't afford to buy a new one made of healthier materials. What do you do? Some sensitive people choose not to have a sofa, rather than one that could pose health problems for them. However, for those who are less sensitive and want to try a less-drastic approach, there are options. For example, the sofa could be put outdoors to air for several days (or weeks) in dry, uncontaminated surroundings, for example, on a covered patio. This might cause enough chemical, perfume, and/or tobacco odors to be released so that the sofa becomes tolerable enough to be placed back indoors. However, if airing doesn't help enough, the sofa could be draped or covered with *barrier-cloth* yardage. Barrier cloth is an undyed, densely woven, untreated, 100%-cotton fabric that can help block many odors. It has the advantage for dust-mite allergic people of sealing out the dust mite allergens already present in the furniture's upholstery. Mail-order sources for organic-cotton barrier cloth include **Sleeptek Limited** (in Canada) and **N.E.E.D.S.** or **Furnature** (in the U.S.) **Janice Corporation** has untreated barrier cloth. Unfortunately, from an aesthetic viewpoint, barrier cloth isn't very attractive. However, it can be dyed (for less-toxic dyes, see *Finding Acceptable Dyes* on page 457).

If you decide to refinish or reupholster a contemporary piece of furniture, most of the section about antique pieces will apply to it as well (see *Antique Furniture* above). If you have the choice, you'll want to have at least the seats made with *removable* cushions stuffed with natural stuffing and covered in washable all-natural-fiber fabrics. (Non-removable cushioning is more difficult to clean.) This means you may have to purchase the materials necessary yourself and give them to the person who will actually do the work. (See *Custom-Made Soft Furniture* on page 338 for material sources.) All upholstery fabrics should be washed before using, to remove "new" odors. (See *Removing Odors from New Clothing* on page 123.) Obviously, this is most important for chemically sensitive people.

An even better choice is to have removable slipcovers made by a local interior-decorating company or upholstery shop. Cushions should each have their own covering as well as a covering for the frame. If you can't find anyone locally, **The Natural Alternative** will custom make washable, organic-cotton or organic-fiber-blend removable slip covers for you. However, you'll need to send your sofa or chair to the company for the exact fit. In addition, untreated-cotton slipcovers can be ordered from **Building for Health Materials Center.**

Ready-made, natural-fiber slipcovers are sometimes available in local department stores, upholstery shops, and interior-design studios. These will have a less-accurate fit, but are usually designed with ties or other means to give the slip-cover a more "form-fitting" look. Generally, they come in a limited number of sizes. From **Harmony,** you can get green-cotton slipcovers with ties for sofas, love seats, and chairs. **Pottery Barn** sells 100%-cotton "loose fit" slip covers with ties that are particularly attractive. Sofa slipcovers of 100%-cotton duck are offered by **Coming Home** and **Solutions. Linensource** has 100%-cotton slip covers for chairs, love seats, sofas, and pillows. **Crate & Barrel** has all-cotton or all-linen slipcovers for dining chairs (parson's chairs) as does **Ballard Designs.**

Less form fitting options are throws especially designed to cover a sofa or side chair. These are usually large sections of fabric than are sometimes fringed around the edges. A throw is literally thrown over a furniture piece and then neatly tucked in around the arms and cushions. All-cotton furniture throws in three sizes (sofa, long sofa, and chair) are available from **Vermont Country Store** (Voice of the Mountains catalog). Another option is from **Homespun Fabrics and Draperies.** From them, you can purchase untreated, 10'-wide cotton fabrics in attractively woven textures that won't wrinkle easily. Another plus, it that these fabrics have had no formaldehyde or other chemicals added to them. Directions to make furniture throws are found in their catalog. By the way, you can also get Homespun fabrics from **Building for Health Materials Center**.

Floor Rugs

Rugs have been used for centuries to provide comfort and beauty to homes. In nomadic cultures, rugs were particularly popular because they could easily be rolled up and moved, then unrolled in a new location to provide instant protection from the bare earth. Various cultures developed their own rug-making techniques and most of these are still used today, at least to some extent in some places.

However, many of the area rugs available in the U.S. today are manufactured *tufted* rugs. In tufting, small clusters of yarn are attached to a backing material and then held in place using a latex compound. An additional vinyl-cushioning layer is then often applied to the rug backs. Other rugs that can be purchased are made by needle-punching, hooking, or braiding. Woven rugs are also popular, usually being made by machines in Europe, and sometimes on hand looms in Asia.

Overwhelmingly, most of the rugs sold today are created with synthetic fibers, such as nylon or polypropylene (see also *Carpeting* on page 302), and nearly all rely on synthetic dyes for coloring. In addition, many rugs have chemical stain-resistant treatments. Despite their obvious similarities to wall-to-wall carpeting, rugs have one major advantage—they can be removed for thorough cleaning, not only to better remove dirt, but also to minimize a buildup of dust mites and other microorganisms.

Unfortunately, many chemically sensitive people find new, non-machine-washable, synthetic rugs intolerable. However, some of these individuals have found that if they repeatedly clean a bothersome rug with low-odor alternative cleaning products (see *Rug and Carpet Shampooing & Wet-Extraction Cleaning* on page 158) and air it outdoors in dry, uncontaminated surroundings, their rug is far less of a problem for them. Of course, the ideal solution is to purchase only untreated natural-fiber rugs that can be machine-laundered and machine-dried. This is especially important for those with dust mite allergies who should thoroughly wash the rugs in their homes regularly.

Cotton Rugs

Despite their sometimes higher cost, untreated natural-fiber area and accent rugs can add a great deal of warmth and appeal to any room. They're especially attractive when laid over hardwood or ceramic tile floors. Many natural-fiber rugs are machine-made, but handmade imports are also readily available.

All-cotton rugs come in a variety of styles and sizes. Popular types include chenille, *dhurrie* (flat, woven, non-pile rugs), and rag. Ideally, you'll want to choose machine-washable, all-cotton rugs. That way, you won't require the services of either a professional rug cleaner or a dry cleaner who might use odorous cleaning solutions. And, as has previously been mentioned, regular machine washing is important for dust-mite control. Remember though, if you plan to wash your rugs at home, carefully follow any manufacturer's recommendations listed on their tags or labels. Also, make sure to only use tolerable laundry products. You should be aware, too, that in many cases there will be some shrinkage of your rugs after their first laundering.

To find 100%-cotton rugs locally, check department stores, discount houses, and import shops. **Home Decorators Collection** offers all-cotton dhurrie and other styles of all-cotton area rugs, and smaller all-cotton throw rugs. Cotton chenille and dhurrie rugs are sold by **The Company Store**. **Coming Home, Natural Home by Natürlich**, and **Crate and Barrel** offer a few choices in all-cotton rugs as well. **Carousel Carpet Mills** manufactures a few all-cotton rugs. You'll need to call the company for a local dealer. A limited selection of 100%-cotton throw rugs is offered by **Janice Corporation, Pottery Barn, Linensource**, and **Vermont Country Store** (Voice of the Mountains catalog). Green-cotton bath rugs can be purchased from **Priorities**.

Wool Rugs

Wool is another good natural-fiber rug option. Most wool rugs are not only beautiful and long-wearing, but some are also considered investments. Of course, rugs of this caliber are higher in cost. Yet they are generally durable enough to last for several generations, and are often one-of-a-kind handmade works of art. Many of these are made with hand-spun yarns and natural vegetable dyes. This is especially true of fine Oriental and *rya* rugs (Scandinavian hand-loomed shaggy rugs).

However, other more-affordable wool rugs are also available. Although they may not be of interest to investors, they'll still provide an attractive, natural floor covering without breaking your budget. Included in this group are lesser-quality Oriental-style rugs, reproductions of Native-American rugs, as well as braided, hooked, and contemporary designer look rugs. Usually these are machine-made, mass-produced products using synthetic dyes.

Unfortunately, many wool rugs are treated with mothproofing chemicals that are often bothersome to chemically sensitive persons. Sometimes the manufacturer's labels will provide this information. However, if a wholesaler or dealer has moth-treated a rug, this information will probably not be known by the manufacturer of the rug. Airing bothersome rugs outdoors can help reduce these treatment odors, but in some cases it may not eliminate them.

It's not difficult to find wool rugs in the marketplace. Fine-quality wool rugs are usually sold in upscale department stores, decorator studios, and specialty rug shops. Because the cost of "real" Oriental rugs can be high, you may want to read some books on the subject or talk with several reputable dealers before actually purchasing one. (Most libraries offer a number of such books.) One word of warning: Never buy an expensive Oriental rug from a transient dealer who rents store space for only a few weeks and then leaves the area. Often their rug prices are high, despite claims of unloading bankrupt dealers' inventories. Even if you get a good price, you may not be able to contact the seller if a problem arises at a later date.

If you are after a lower-cost wool rug, a number of styles are usually available at local import shops, as well as at moderately priced department stores and some carpet stores. One place you may not have thought of looking into is in larger building-supply centers. Many of these stores now have rugs departments with fairly large selections. One catalog source for good-looking wool rugs is **Home Decorators Collection**, which offers Oriental-styles and others. They also handle wool/jute rugs. **Peerless Imported Rugs** sells many affordable wool rugs in a variety of sizes and styles as does **Ballard Designs**. One manufacturer of many varieties of wool area rugs is **Carousel Carpet Mills**. To buy them however, you'll need to call the company for a local dealer.

Very nice 100%-wool hooked rugs with cotton backing are offered by **Cuddledown of Maine**. Similar rugs are sold by **L.L. Bean** (Furnishings Catalog) which sells wool dhurrie and braided rugs, too. In addition, **JC Penny Catalog** handles a few styles of wool rugs as does **Coming Home**. Uniquely designed wool rugs are carried by **Linensource** and **Pompanoosuc Mills**. In the **Kitchen & Home** catalog, you'll find a selection of hand-tufted wool rugs, hand-hooked rugs with cotton backings, and several Oriental-style rugs. Other suppliers of wool rugs include **The Company Store** and **Garnet Hills**. A few wool-cotton-blend rugs are sold by **Crate & Barrel**.

If you're seeking custom rugs with a carpeting-look, **Natural Home by Natürlich** can cut to size and edge-bind their Nature's Cinna carpet. This fine flooring product is made of non-mothproofed wool. Other all-wool area rugs are handled, too.

Interesting wool-rug alternatives are *wool shearling rugs* (sheepskins). Besides being cozy and provocative, these rugs can often be fairly inexpensive. Sometimes they're even washable, but always read the catalog descriptions and/or manufacturers' tags carefully first. **French Creek Sheep & Wool Company** is one catalog source for washable sheepskin rugs. Another is **Deerskin Trading Post** which has a 28" x 40" sheepskin rug. Very nice lambskin rugs are sold by **Natural Baby** and **Aussie Connection**. By the way, sheepskin rugs can often be found in local leather or craft shops.

Proper care is essential for your wool rugs. They should be vacuumed regularly—or beaten on a line outdoors—to remove the particulate matter that can damage the wool yarns. (Note: When rug beating, always wear a dust mask to prevent inhalation of the airborne debris. For sources for dust masks see *Personal Protective Gear* on page 264.) Of course, this isn't a job for dust-mite-allergic or asthmatic people. Now, to avoid solvent odors, you'll want to have your wool rugs professionally cleaned by carpet-cleaning firms or sent to dry cleaners only when absolutely necessary. Although you may not be aware of this, some wool Oriental rugs can actually be hand-washed outdoors with a garden hose (see *Simple Rug Washing* on page 157).

Other Natural-Fiber Rugs

Sometimes, natural-fiber rugs are made of sisal, jute, *coir* (coconut-husk fiber), or hemp. These can be attractive, but in some cases difficult to clean. Therefore, you'll want to talk with your rug dealer and read the manufacturers' tags carefully before cleaning any with a water or solvent solution. You should also know that most of these rugs, especially jute, should not be placed where they'll receive direct sunlight. Sunlight can cause jute to deteriorate fairly quickly.

If you're interested in having an alternative natural-fiber rug, check your nearby import stores to see what's available locally. By mail order, you can purchase attractive sisal and coco-fiber rugs from **Peerless Imported Rugs**. Also, the **Natural Home by Natürlich.** catalog offers several area rugs made of natural-fibers from which to choose. These are actually rugs custom cut and edge-bound to the sizes you need, and they can be made of sisal, seagrass, and other grass matting. **Building for Health Materials Center** has large sisal area rugs. From **Home Decorators Collection**, you can choose from sisal, coir, and wool/jute rugs. Jute/wool rugs are also sold by **Kitchen & Home**. All-jute area and/or throw rugs can be purchased from **The Company Store, Cuddledown of Maine**, and **Linensource**. Rugs of jute/coir and all-sisal are sold by **Crate & Barrel**. Jute and jute/coir rugs can also be found in the **Ballard Designs** catalog.

Rug Grips

Unfortunately, natural-fiber rugs without latex or vinyl backings may slip on slick, smooth flooring surfaces. To solve this common, but potentially dangerous, problem, manufacturers have created a variety of latex or vinyl rug-gripping products to securely hold rugs to the floor. Some of these rug grippers may be available in your local import stores, department stores, and rug shops.

By mail order, **Home Decorators Collection** sells a rug-gripping underlayment to fit under most sizes of rugs. Washable rubberized "underlay mats" in several sizes are sold by both **Crate & Barrel** and **Cuddledown of Maine**. In addition, rug grips coated with PVC (polyvinyl chloride) in 3' x 5', 5' x 8', and 9' x 12' sizes are handled by **Kitchen & Home**. (Note: Rug-grip pads or mats that are too large can usually be cut down to size.) Latex-covered rug grip stripping is available from **Harriet Carter Gifts**.

Unfortunately, these products are often intolerable for chemically sensitive people. Therefore, they may have to air them outside in a sheltered, uncontaminated area for days or weeks until their odors have dissipated somewhat. Experimenting with several different types of rug gripping products and brands may also be necessary. Of course, latex-allergic people will want to avoid all rug-gripping products manufactured with latex

Window Treatments

Originally, windows (derived from *wind eyes*) were just open holes in walls. They let in light and air, and in some cases allowed smoke to leave. As architecture advanced, windows also became important from an aesthetic standpoint. In time, complex window-pane designs as well as elaborate interior-decorating treatments became fairly common, at least in the residences of the upper-class. Today, more people than ever have window treatments that are more decorative than functional. However, for certain windows, privacy and energy savings are still very important considerations.

Unfortunately, most modern interior window treatments have real problems that few people seem to recognize. For example, many decorative treatments can't be easily dusted or thoroughly cleaned. Also, the fabrics used to make typical curtains and draperies are usually synthetic. These can release bothersome chemical odors from the compounds making up the fabric fibers. Then, too, most fabrics, especially certain natural-fiber fabrics, will break down over time from having been exposed to ultraviolet (UV) radiation from the sun. Unfortunately, deteriorating fabric creates loose bits of fiber that become airborne dust. It also means that nearly all fabric curtains and draperies must periodically be replaced.

The good news is that there are more practical and healthier choices for interior window treatments than many of the typical ones now being used. Ideally, a healthy window treatment should be attractive, functional, made of all-natural materials, be easy to maintain, and not be subject to rapid deterioration by ultraviolet rays from sunlight. This section will discuss some of the better window treatment options to consider for your home.

Metal Blinds

From a health standpoint, metal blinds are an excellent window-treatment choice, and they're usually tolerable for chemically sensitive individuals. Generally, metal blinds are made of either aluminum or steel, colored with baked-on enamel paints. (Some companies don't use a baking process.) Because they're metal, they hold-up well even in strong sunlight. Another advantage is that all-metal blinds are adjustable—by raising or lowering the blinds and altering the angle of the slats, they can easily adapt to different natural lighting needs and conditions.

Today's metal blinds can be purchased in a wide selection of colors and slat widths. In addition, you can buy them in either horizontal or vertical slat designs. Vertical mini-blinds look more like draperies, and they don't collect dust easily. Recently though, vinyl, acrylic, and other synthetic materials have been more commonly used for vertical blinds. So metal ones may be much more difficult to find. Horizontal metal blinds tend to be less expensive than verticals and are usually available with more options. For example, some horizontal blinds can be purchased with a special privacy feature that allows them to be closed much more tightly than standard blinds.

Metal blinds can be purchased either ready-made or custom-made. Ready-made blinds are usually sold in only a few standard sizes and colors, but you can get them right away and they're very economical. To find them locally, check department stores, building centers, and discount stores. A source for ready-made 1"-steel mini-blinds, with baked-enamel finishes, in a variety of colors, is the **JC Penny Catalog**. (Window Authority specialty catalog). From the large **JC Penny Catalog**, you can get painted steel or aluminum versions. On the other hand, custom-made blinds are manufactured to fit a specific window, so they must be specially ordered. Of course, their price is higher than for standard ready-made blinds, but you can get them in the exact color, size, and style you want.

While your local department stores and drapery shops should be able to order custom-made metal blinds, there are a number of discount mail-order companies that sell custom metal blinds directly to the public at very affordable prices. You can often find their advertisements in remodeling and decorating magazines. One such company is **Baron's Window Coverings**. They offer 1" aluminum mini-blinds custom made to your specific sizes in a range of colors. In addition, **National Blind & Wallpaper** has a very large selection of colors from which it can make your mini-blinds. This company also has a number of special options available including Lightstopper Blinds (specially designed blinds that are able to block more of the incoming light) and an Auto-Vue remote control system able to operate your blinds from a distance. The Auto-Vue system can even be set up with a light sensor to open or close the blinds when a preset light level is reached outdoors. In addition, a more "upscale" catalog, **Smith & Noble**, can custom make 1" aluminum mini-blinds in a range of colors as well.

One of the advantages to metal blinds is that they're easy to maintain. Of course, this is an especially important plus for those concerned about dust mites. You see, metal blinds can be simply swept free of dust by using your vacuum cleaner's soft dusting attachment on both sides. Special mini-blind vacuum attachments are also available. You can check local vacuum dealers for their availability. Or, you could use a Blind-Brite Tool (**Orange-Sol Household Products, Inc.**). This hand-held plastic tool is designed with 6 washable, removable, untreated, wool-covered fingers whose small size works well to dust blinds. You can order it directly from the manufacturer. Of course, occasionally you may want to wash your metal mini-blinds. To do so, use a soft sponge or cloth that has been dipped in a tolerable dishwashing detergent and water solution. Next, wring out the sponge and gently go over the slats. Then, rinse the slats using the sponge and clear water. To prevent spotting gently dry the slats using a soft towel.

Chemically sensitive individuals should be aware that the new paint on their metal blinds could outgas bothersome odors, particularly if the finish hasn't been baked-on. However, in any case, washing the blinds (as described above) and then hanging them outdoors, or in a well-ventilated unused room, will usually dramatically decrease these odors after a few days or weeks. Be sure the place you choose for airing is uncontaminated by other potentially polluting odors.

Wood, Reed, and Bamboo Blinds

Wood, reed, and bamboo blinds are all-natural, attractive choices for window treatments. Depending on the material, and whether or not it's been split, the slats could be less than 1/4" wide (sometimes known as *matchstick*) up to 1" wide. These types of blinds can be rolled up or down, but there's no way to adjust the angle of the slats. To purchase wood, reed, or bamboo blinds, check your local department stores, drapery shops, and import stores. Usually they're sold as uncoated (natural), stained, or painted, in a few standard sizes. All are usually inexpensive or moderately priced. More expensive custom sizes may be available at some department stores and drapery shops.

A mail-order source for 2"-hardwood blinds in natural, white, and other looks is the **JC Penny Catalog** (Window Authority specialty catalog). From **Smith & Noble** you can custom order basswood blinds, and bamboo blinds can be purchased from **Building for Health Materials Center**.

You should be aware that any new wood, reed, or bamboo blind that has been stained or painted may need to air for some time before it becomes tolerable, if you're a sensitive person. To do this, simply hang the blinds outdoors where precipitation and contaminating odors can't reach them—or in a well-ventilated, unused room—until they lose their odor.

There are still other concerns with wood, reed, and bamboo blinds you might want to consider before purchasing them. First, natural materials will eventually deteriorate from exposure to ultraviolet radiation from the sun, so they'll probably have to be replaced at some point. Fortunately, this could be many years from when you first hang them. Another possible concern is how you maintain natural blinds. Actually, you can remove most dust by using a vacuum cleaner's soft dusting attachment. Of course, if you do need to wash them, it's best to read the manufacturers' tags first for their recommended cleaning instructions. However, simply sponging the blinds with clear water often works well. Make certain they're able to dry quickly, to prevent mold or mildew growth.

Roman Shades

Roman shades often make an interesting window treatment. They're a special type of blind made to fold up into continuous uniform horizontal layers when raised. If you decide on Roman shades, consider buying those made with untreated, natural-fiber fabric. Linen is an especially good choice because it doesn't deteriorate from sunlight exposure. By the way, some shades are now also offered in natural grass and reed materials.

However, you should be aware of certain drawbacks with Roman shades. First of all, shades of this type can sometimes be difficult to clean. While you can gently vacuum any Roman shade with a dusting attachment, certain shades can't be washed. Also, most of the fabrics used (except linen) will eventually break down due to exposure to the ultraviolet rays from the sun.

To purchase Roman shades, first check local department stores and drapery shops. These retail outlets can usually custom-make them for you. By mail-order, from **Smith & Noble**, you can purchase custom-made Roman shades out of your choice of batuk, kyoto, rattan, and bamboo, or pleated-fabric shades of silk or linen. **This End Up** can custom make Roman-style shades from fabrics that includes untreated all-cotton and all-linen.

If you decide to made them yourself, you can use a **Green Pepper** Roman Shade pattern. You can get these at some fabric centers such as JoAnn's Fabrics and Crafts, or you can call on the company's automatic toll-free phone number and order directly from them. By the way, if you call their non-toll-free phone number, someone there will answer your sewing questions concerning their patterns. **Homespun Fabrics and Draperies** offers formaldehyde-free, 10'-wide cotton fabrics in several woven textures. Due to their unique weaves, these materials need no ironing. This company can custom create your Roman shades for you, or you can buy their fabric and make your own. Directions for Roman shades are in several of the window treatment books listed for sale in their catalog. By the way, you can also get Homespun custom, untreated, all-cotton window treatments and fabrics by mail order through **Building for Health Materials Center**. (For healthier sewing information, see *Sewing* on page 456.)

Roller Shades

Fabric rollers as window treatments have been around for decades. They're simply rods equipped with a metal spring that have a length of fabric attached to them. Today, fabric rollers are generally inexpensive and made with synthetic materials such as vinyl. However, custom drapery departments and shops can often make fabric rollers in any materials and dimensions you choose. You should also be aware that **Smith & Noble** can make roller shades in your choice of 100%-cotton or 100%-linen fabrics. It may be that **This End Up** can also make them for you.

It should also be mentioned that **Homespun Fabrics and Draperies** offers untreated (no formaldehyde), 10'-wide cotton drapery fabrics. These have attractive woven textures that makes ironing them unnecessary. This company also custom makes many types of window treatments and offers how-to books so you can make them yourself. You can also get Homespun fabrics and custom-made shades through **Building for Health Materials Center**.

Unfortunately, fabric rollers will eventually deteriorate when exposed to the sun's ultraviolet radiation, that is, unless you choose linen. Also, because most fabric rollers can't be laundered, you'll want to occasionally take them down and thoroughly vacuum them. To do this, lay them on a clean, smooth surface and completely unroll them. Then very carefully vacuum one side at a time using a soft dusting attachment. You may find you'll need someone to hold the fabric down securely while you're vacuuming.

Curtains and Draperies

Washable, untreated, 100%-natural-fiber curtains can usually provide a softer appearance for your windows than blinds, shades, or rollers. Sometimes all-cotton curtains are available in ready-made sizes, styles, and colors at local department stores and drapery shops. Another popular window-treatment option is lined draperies. Linings help protect the decorative room-facing fabric from damaging sun exposure. Generally, lined draperies are much heavier than curtains and provide more privacy, but they can be fairly expensive. This is because most lined draperies are custom-made, requiring the labor and skill of a professional seamstress to construct them, and they require two layers of fabric.

Unfortunately, many lined draperies must be dry-cleaned in order to better maintain their shape. (Special wet cleaning methods may sometimes be an option.) Not only can this be expensive, but it means your draperies will acquire harmful solvent odors. (See *Is Dry Cleaning a Problem?* on page 196.) If professional cleaning must be done, hang the newly dry-cleaned draperies outdoors so the solvent odors can dissipate before rehanging them. (Note: Some chemically sensitive people may find that, despite their best airing efforts, enough solvent odors remain to make their draperies permanently intolerable for them.) Between cleanings, it's best to regularly vacuum both sides of your lined draperies using a soft dusting attachment. For those particularly concerned about dust-mite control, vacuuming should be very thorough.

There are a number of mail-order sources for all-cotton curtains. But before ordering, please check to see if the style you're interested in can be laundered at home or not. **Pottery Barn** has some 100%-cotton curtains in several simple styles, as does **Crate & Barrel**. While it has many different styles, the **Country Curtains** catalog sells only a very few untreated, all-natural-fiber curtains. Unusual ethnic-inspired all-cotton curtains are carried by **Marketplace: Handwork of India**. Attractive curtains of 100%-cotton or 100%-linen are sold by **Garnet Hill**. All-cotton curtains and unlined, full-length draperies in natural color, or denim, are sold by **JC Penny Catalog** (Window Authority specialty catalog). These are listed as being washable. In addition, washable, unlined, 100%-cotton draperies are handled by **Coming Home**.

Of course, natural-fabric curtains and draperies can also be custom-made. Local department stores, upholstery shops, and drapery specialty shops should be able to provide this service for you. By mail, **Smith & Noble** offers custom-made drapery panels in linen, hemp, and all-cotton fabric. Then, too, **This End Up** will custom make curtains and draperies from their selection of over 300 fabrics, some of which are untreated linens and cottons. Of special note is that **Homespun Fabrics and Draperies** offers untreated, 10'-wide cotton fabric in several textures that is specially woven so as to not require ironing. A nice feature of these fabrics is that they've had no formaldehyde or other chemicals added to them. This company will custom make your curtains and draperies, or you can buy their fabrics and make your own. To help you, they handle a number of books in their catalog on making draperies, curtains, and other window treatments. You can also get Homespun custom, untreated, all-cotton curtains and fabrics by mail order from **Building for Health Materials Center**.

For hanging your curtains or draperies, **Country Curtains** and **This End Up** has a good variety of metal and wood rods and metal tie backs. **JC Penny Catalog** (Window Authority specialty catalog) carries wood and metal curtain rods. Finally, **Pottery Barn** has attractive metal curtain rods, as does **Coming Home**.

Swags

A popular window treatment is using a *swag*. A swag is defined as a valance, or "festoon." In home decoration, it's commonly a swath of decoratively folded or gathered curtain fabric suspended over a window. A few years ago when the "country look" reached it's peak, many swag treatments became quite complicated and, in some cases, just plain odd. Sometimes twigs, artificial flowers, and even bird's nests were combined with the fabric to be draped around windows. Fortunately, the zeal for such swag arrangements has waned. Today, simple "scarf looks" are considered more fashionable. From a health standpoint, in an ideal household, swags should be made of washable, untreated, 100%-natural-fiber fabric, and be designed so that they can be easily taken down and laundered.

During the country-look swag fad, special swag hardware became available so that nearly anyone could create attractive swags themselves. Some were metal units with baked-on, enamel-coated, finishes that you could pull your fabric through easily (and remove it easily, too). However, these have become much more difficult to find. While a few local department stores and drapery shops sell these do-it-yourself supplies, the hardware is often made of plastic. Sometimes plastic pieces can easily bend or break, and in some cases they can emit minor odors that certain sensitive persons may find bothersome.

A healthy "do-able" swag option is to install either a large metal rod or wooden dowel across your window top, then, simply artistically drape fabric over it. Another option is to have large drapery hooks, rings, or corbels mounted on the upper sides of the window fame. To make use of these, first lay your fabric on a clean floor and gather it into large soft pleats. Then, carefully lift it up and insert one end over (or into) the hardware. Then pull to even out the fabric length. Finally comb the pleats with your fingers. By the way, besides draping, you can braid (use two or three fabric lengths) or create rosettes. To hold the rosettes in place, simply use brass cup hooks which can easily be screwed into the wood frame. All these, of course, are versions of the scarf look (especially if lightweight fabrics are used) mentioned earlier. (For possible fabric choices, see *Sewing* on page 456.) If done neatly, this method can make for very stylish windows.

Scarf valances in washable, 100%-cotton fabric in your choice of denim or natural colors are sold in the **JC Penny Catalog** (Window Authority specialty catalog). **Homespun Fabrics and Draperies** sells untreated, 10'-wide cotton fabrics in several textures. These formaldehyde-free materials have a special woven texture that doesn't require ironing. The company can custom make valances for you, or you can buy the fabric and how-to-books from them and do it yourself. You can get Homespun custom, untreated, all-cotton valances and fabrics by mail order from **Building for Health Materials Center** as well. For decorative wood and metal rods and tie-backs, see *Curtains and Draperies* on page 348.

Shutters

Wood shutters can provide an all-natural, homey, window treatment that can also give you a great deal of privacy. Unfortunately, wood shutters are commonly made of softwood pine. When new, many softwoods can give off *terpene* odors that can be irritating to certain sensitive persons

Actually, a number of wood-shutter styles are available, including those with adjustable slats and fabric inserts. Generally, however, only certain standard sizes are offered, and these are often sold prefinished, with either a paint, or a stain with a clear finish. However, they are also often available in an unfinished, natural state. Chemically sensitive individuals should be aware that any stain or paint can be intolerable for some time when it's fresh. If you personally find a stain or paint bothersome on your new shutters, place them outside in an area protected from the weather and polluting odors, or put them in a well-ventilated, unused room until they become tolerable.

Of course, if you decide you'd like to paint, stain, or apply a clear finish to the wood shutters yourself, you'll want to use only tolerable products (see the appropriate sections in

Chapter 10: Home Workshop). It's also important that this work be done only with good ventilation while wearing a cartridge-type respirator mask and other appropriate protective gear. (See *Personal Protective Gear* on page 264.) After the finish has been applied, the shutters will need to air in a dry, uncontaminated area until they become odor-free. Note: the actual finishing shouldn't be done by very sensitive persons or those with asthma.

For wood shutters designed to have fabric-panel inserts, it's best to choose untreated, washable, natural-fiber fabrics. After purchasing the cloth, launder it first before cutting it to size. That way, the fabric will be both preshrunk—and tolerable.

As a rule, wood shutters are relatively easy to maintain. They can be easily vacuumed regularly with a soft dusting attachment. Those shutters with fabric panels can have the fabric occasionally removed and washed in a tolerable laundry product.

To purchase wood shutters, check your local department stores, drapery shops, building centers, or unfinished-furniture stores. If you would prefer mail order, **Smith & Noble** has custom sizes of basswood shutters in several styles (solid panel, louvered panel, and grass-reed paneled).

Decorative Glass

Decorative glass can be used to create beautiful and unexpected window treatments. *Stained glass* (generally, glass colored with metallic oxides fused through the entire depth of the glass), *enameled glass* (glass that's been permanently surface-decorated using baked-on translucent or opaque glazes), and *beveled glass* (thick glass with angled edges) can be used by craftspeople or artists to meet your specific window needs. To find such a skilled glass worker, check your telephone directory's classified section under Stained Glass or Windows. Of course, when you find a prospective artisan, you'll want to see examples of his (or her) work before you agree to a commission, and make sure to get price and time estimates. You should be aware ahead of time that any one-of-a-kind creation will likely be expensive. As a rule, the larger and more complicated the design, and the more renowned the reputation of the glass worker, the higher the finished price will be. In addition, the cost will also depend on the types of glass actually used.

If you can't afford an entire custom-made window, you might consider just hanging a small *roundel* (circular disk) or rectangular decorative glass panel. Many museum shops, art fairs, and catalogs sell these at reasonable prices. Another option is to simply buy a single sheet of colored glass, or an antique panel of stained glass, and frame it with metal or wood. Once framed, you can securely hang it by a chain in front of the window glass. Not only can this provide your room with interest, it can increase your privacy as well. To find sheets of colored or stained glass, you'll want to check at local glass stores and craft shops. Note that, these stores are often also able to cut the glass sheets to size for you.

Another relatively inexpensive option is to actually replace the clear glass in your window with a single sheet of opalescent or textured glass. Of course, this will involve some installation work using window putty. Unfortunately, these putties may prove bothersome to some sensitive individuals. Therefore, testing beforehand is important. (See *Testing* on page 62.) However, most newly applied putty is not a significant problem because it is used primarily on the exterior side of the window.

Some stained, enameled, or beveled-glass panels, and roundels, are held together with brass or copper foil or *cames* (grooved metal ribbons) and non-lead solder. However, a great many decorative glass items are created with lead came and lead solder. Unfortunately, lead is a toxic heavy metal. It can cause a variety of negative health effects if swallowed or inhaled. Yet it needs to be said that lead came and solder that's already in place is very unlikely to cause problems for adults because it doesn't outgas anything. However, if children handle it or put their mouths on it, the lead would be harmful to them. If you are concerned about this, you should only buy decorative-glass pieces held together with copper or brass, using lead-free solder.

Shower Curtains and Doors

An ideal shower curtain or shower door should protect your bathroom from water damage, and not be a cause of potential health problems for you and your family. While most people don't consider the potential negative health consequences when they buy a shower curtain or door, it's something that is wise to take into account.

Tub & Shower Curtains

For several decades now, shower curtains have become more decorative and elaborate. Some now consist of several layers of lace and fabric panels. However, virtually all shower curtains have an inner layer of waterproof vinyl. Unfortunately, vinyl can pose certain problems. New vinyl can outgas chemical odors (*i.e.* vinyl chloride) that can be bothersome, especially for chemically sensitive people. While not usually a health concern, older vinyl can easily crack and tear.

A relatively recent innovation in shower curtains is a treatment that enables them to be advertised as "unable to support mold growth." It's likely that such curtains have been treated with chemical fungicides to resist mildew contamination. While resisting fungus is an admirable trait, a shower curtain's relatively large surface area could expose you and your family to a considerable amount of potentially intolerable compounds. Of course, certain sensitive persons would be more susceptible to these negative effects than others.

A healthier shower-curtain choice would be one made of untreated, 100%-natural fibers. These are generally made of a heavy, plain-weave fabric that can be regularly machine-washed and dried. Cotton-duck and barrier-cloth shower curtains are available from **Janice Corporation**. Two sizes of Atlantic Earthworks 100%-cotton-duck shower curtains are sold by **French Creek Sheep & Wool Company**. These come in white (bleached with hydrogen peroxide) or natural color (unbleached). Two sizes of Clothcrafter untreated, 100%-cotton shower curtains are carried by **Simmons Natural Bodycare** with similar ones available from **Allergy Relief Shop, Inc.** In addition, **American Environmental Health Foundation** offers all-cotton shower curtains in your choice of white or unbleached. **Tomorrow's World** handles both 100%-cotton-duck or all-hemp shower curtains. You may not realize this, but hemp is probably superior to cotton in this application because it's naturally mildew resistant. **Real Goods** is another source for hemp shower curtains.

It should also be noted that **Coming Home** and **Eddie Bauer** (Home catalog) have all-cotton shower curtains, too. However, these are supposed to be used only with waterproof liners. By the way, if you like color in your bathroom, you can easily dye plain, natural-fiber shower curtains. **B. Coole Designs** offers a wide selection of less-toxic dyes you might use.

To remain mildew free, a natural-fiber shower curtain must be able to dry quickly after a shower. This is only possible in a bathroom that has an adequately sized ventilation fan.

Tub & Shower Doors

A very good alternative to shower curtains is glass shower doors. These are attractive, inert, and permanent. An ideal style is one that has glass doors with polished edges rather than glass panels set into metal frames. You should also look for a free-draining lower track rather than a water-blocking lipped track. Without conventional frames and lower tracking, water can drain away quickly, so there are fewer places for mold to grow.

There are a number of manufacturers now that make these particular types of products. For example, **Sterling Plumbing Group, Inc.** manufactures its Sterling PRO Line bathtub and shower doors. Then, too, **Alumax Bath Enclosures** offers Alumax Series 1040 bathtub doors and Alumax Series 1038 shower doors. While Alumax is a national brand, it is not sold in the Midwest. However, similar products under the Basco label (**Basco Co.**) are available exclusively in the Midwest. Other brands that offer free-draining, frameless tub and shower doors include **Duschqueen, Inc.** and **Work Right**. To purchase any of these products, call the individual companies for the location of a nearby dealer. Quite likely, your local building centers and plumbing-supply stores will handle at least one of these brands, or very similar ones.

Keep in mind that new glass shower doors will require some installation work. This obviously will add to their expense if you can't do the work yourself. Also, shower-door installation always requires caulking, which generally has a fairly strong odor when newly applied. One brand of caulking you may want to try for this is Dap Kwik Seal Tub & Tile Adhesive Caulk (**Dap, Inc.**). While this product does contain a mildew preventive, it's often well tolerated by chemically sensitive individuals within a relatively short period of time. Unfortunately, if a caulk doesn't contain any fungicides, it can become contaminated with mold or mildew very quickly, so it'll need to be replaced over and over again. That means, repeated exposures to odorous, newly applied compounds.

Of course, no matter what type of caulk you use, it's best to apply it with good ventilation and while wearing a cartridge-type respirator mask. (See *Personal Protective Gear* on page 264.) As might be expected, this isn't a job for sensitive persons, or those with asthma, to tackle themselves.

Lighting

Good lighting is important for both safety and aesthetics. Sunlight from windows and skylights can provide a certain amount of light, but it may not be enough, or, for privacy reasons, you may not be able to fully take advantage of it. Of course, at night, windows and skylights offer no help in illuminating your home's interior, so artificial lighting is necessary, either from electric lamps or from flames.

Most people don't think of the health ramifications of the lamps and fixtures they use daily in their homes, except perhaps whether the light given off is bright enough to do an intended job. However, when you buy bulbs and tubes, you may want to consider the light spectrum they emit, and also their energy efficiency and life expectancy. When you buy lighting fixtures and decorative lamps, you might also consider how easy they'll be to clean, and what materials were used in their construction. Still another consideration is the amount of heat they emit. Ultimately, everything you put in your home has a potential effect on your well-being—even what you choose for lighting.

Some Artificial Light Basics

The first artificial illumination was undoubtedly campfires and torches of dried grasses or wood. Eventually, stone lamps were developed, containing liquefied fat or oil and a wick. These were followed by the creation of candles made of beeswax or hardened animal fat. Lamps (later using kerosene with glass chimneys) and candles remained the major interior illumination sources until gas lighting began being used in cities and towns in the 1800s. With the invention of electric lighting in the late 19th century, lighting with gas became passé. Today, except for emergencies, in places where the occupants choose not to use electricity, and when a special mood is sought using flames, virtually all artificial lighting in American homes is with electric bulbs and fluorescent tubes.

Many people want to know, "How much artificial light do I need in my home?" Actually, over the years, lighting engineers have changed the recommended lighting requirements from time to time. As a rule though, in most situations there needs to be overall *general illumination* sufficient enough to see clearly when there's no other sources of light. Extra *task lighting* is required over kitchen countertops or in reading areas, for example. Remember, it's usually best to err on the side of having too much light than not having enough for safety's sake, and yet *glare* (harsh, piercing light coming directly from a lighting source) and *reflected glare* (glare that has bounced off objects) can sometimes pose safety problems.

If you want to be absolutely certain of the ideal lighting requirements for your home (locations for certain illumination, types of fixtures needed, etc.), you should contact a professional lighting engineer. (Check in the phone directory under Lighting.) While, his (or her) services are very desirable, they could also be fairly costly. As an alternative, local lighting stores may have lighting consultants who will come to your home at a reasonable cost. These people usually don't have an engineering background, but are familiar with typical home-lighting needs and popular lighting trends. However, you should keep in mind that consultants who are connected with lighting stores may tend to suggest more fixtures, and costlier ones, than you may truly need. Remember, nearly every fixture permanently mounted into ceilings or walls will require installation by an electrician, and every bulb or tube that is turned on means a higher utility bill. Therefore, it's important to combine suggestions from others with your own common sense.

Whenever you buy a bulb or tube for a fixture or lamp, be sure to get the correct wattage. For example, some fixtures come with a label stating, "Don't use a bulb over 60 watts." These warnings are issued because bulbs of greater-than-recommended wattage could create too much heat for the fixture to operate safely. Therefore, always check to see if a fixture or decorative lamp has a recommended wattage label. Also, when replacing a bulb or tube, be certain that the electricity to the fixture or decorative lamp is turned off in order to prevent accidental electrocution.

Bulbs and Tubes (Lamps)

The two major categories of lamps are: incandescent bulbs and fluorescent tubes. In the lighting industry the word *lamp* refers to both types. Admittedly, this can be confusing inasmuch as most people think of a lamp as a base unit with a shade that sits on a table or the floor. However in this section, the word lamp will follow the industry standard and apply to both incandescent bulbs and fluorescent tubes.

Typical Lamps

For decades, both incandescent bulbs and fluorescent tubes have been commonly used in homes. Each type has its advantages and drawbacks. The following sections will discuss some of these.

Typical Incandescent Lamps

The oldest type of electric lamp is the incandescent bulb, the first practical one having been created in 1879 by Thomas Edison. With the construction of electric-generating stations, incandescent lamps soon became commonplace. Today, they remain the most popular kind of lamp used in American homes.

By definition, an *incandescent lamp* is a clear, or frosted, glass bulb having a looped filament and a metal screw base. Inside the bulb, the air (with its relatively high level of oxygen) has been removed so that combustion can't occur. Generally, an inert gas (from a combustion standpoint) such as nitrogen, or a mixture of inert gases, is then pumped in at about a third of the normal atmospheric pressure. These inert gases are added to slow down the filament's *sublimation* (a change of state from a solid directly to a gas). Sublimation results in the black discoloration seen in older bulbs. When too much of a filament has sublimated, the bulb will burn out. Because of the inevitable process of sublimation, typical incandescent lamps generally don't last as long as typical fluorescent lamps.

In many incandescent bulbs, the looped filaments are made of *tungsten*, a rare metallic element. When an incandescent bulb is turned on, the electric current enters through the metal screw base and flows into the tungsten filament. The filament temperature rises rapidly, up to several thousand degrees Fahrenheit. This causes the tungsten to glow. In reality, several forms of radiation are emitted. These include visible light, some ultraviolet rays, and a great deal of infrared radiation (heat). In fact, a large percentage of the electricity used by typical incandescent bulbs goes, not to producing light, but to generating unwanted heat.

Traditionally, incandescent bulbs have been chosen over other lamp types for most residential applications: table and floor lamps as well as bedroom, hall, and bath ceiling fixtures. This is because incandescent bulbs can be manufactured at low cost, in virtually any size or shape to fit nearly all types and sizes of fixtures. Also, their yellowish-white glow is considered by many to be warm and friendly.

Typical Fluorescent Lamps

The other relatively common type of lamp used in homes is the fluorescent tube. Actually, fluorescent tubes are a much more recent invention, having been first shown to the public in 1933. However, by the 1950s they had nearly replaced incandescent lamps in public institutions, offices, and commercial buildings. They also began to be used more frequently for certain residential applications.

By definition, a fluorescent lamp is a glass tube with an interior phosphor coating and a special gas (usually a combination of argon and mercury) filling the interior. The ends of the tube are sealed with metal caps having one or two prongs. When a fluorescent tube is turned on, the electricity passes from one end of the tube to the other. As the electricity travels through the gas-filled interior, ultraviolet radiation is created. It's actually the ultraviolet rays that cause the phosphor coating on the tube walls to glow, creating visible light— usually a white or bluish-white light. Because of the blue/white color, some people feel typical fluorescent lamps make a room look cold.

As mentioned previously, fluorescent lamps have been the lighting choice for decades for nonresidential uses. This is because they've been commonly manufactured as very long tubes (4'–8') that emit a great deal of light, produce little heat, and use less electricity than incandescent bulbs. However, they do have their drawbacks. For example, until recently fluorescent lamps have been limited in shape to long narrow tubes. (Sometimes the tube is formed into a circle.) They also require *ballasts* (transformers) in their fixtures to convert 110-volt electricity into the much higher voltage needed to cause the phosphor coating to glow. Unfortunately, at one time, highly-toxic *polychlorinated biphenyls (PCBs)* were used in some of these ballasts. Even though the ballasts created today no longer contain PCBs, older ballasts filled with PCBs still exist in some fluorescent fixtures, and these have the potential to leak this poisonous liquid as they wear out.

Another problem with typical fluorescent lamps is that they create potentially problematic electromagnetic fields (EMFs) (see *Chapter 26: Electromagnetic Fields*). In some cases, these fields can actually be fairly strong. In addition, typical fluorescent fixtures emit low levels of X-rays. Finally, some fluorescent lamps tend to produce a rapidly flickering light that goes on an off 60 times a second—a light which some people find disturbing.

Lamp Innovations

In recent years, a number of lamp manufacturers have devised variations on typical incandescent bulbs and fluorescent tubes to overcome their limitations.

Incandescent Lamp Innovations

Incandescent lamps are now available that are designed for longer life or to emit a full spectrum that mimics natural-light.

Long-Life Bulbs

One interesting innovation that began a decade or so ago was the use of special *diodes* that were attached to the tips of the metal screw bases of certain incandescent bulbs. Diodes are tiny electronic devices that only permit electric current to pass through them in one direction. Home electric lines carry *alternating current (AC)* in which the flow of electricity repeatedly switches directions 60 times a second. Because a diode-equipped bulb uses only electricity flowing in one direction, it is only on half the time. This creates a continuous on/off light pattern, but it's so rapid that most people can't perceive it, so they just see continuous light. By having the bulb on only half the time, the bulb's life expectancy can be greatly extended. Bulbs with this particular adaptation are now not as commonly encountered as they once were.

Other developments to make bulbs last longer are the use of solid-brass screw bases, supports for the tungsten filament, and the use of krypton gas to slow down the sublimation rate. It seems that krypton causes tungsten atoms to "bounce back" onto the filament. These days, most bulbs with "long life" on their labels use at least one of these approaches.

There are a number of sources for long-life bulbs these days including local lighting stores and building centers. Watt-Saver bulbs (**Duro-Test Lighting**) that use krypton are rated for 9,000 hours of use. You can order them directly from the manufacturer. From **Karen's Natural Products**, you can buy EcoWorks long-lasting bulbs in several wattages. These have brass bases and reinforced filaments. They're said to last three times as long as typical bulbs. **SilvoHome** and **Harmony** offer 20,000-hour incandescent bulbs in several styles. The variety sold by **Improvements** have a lifetime guarantee.

Halogen Bulbs

One major development was the introduction of *halogen bulbs*. Originally invented by General Electric in 1957, these are a bulb inside a bulb. The innermost bulb, filled with bromine and iodine under pressure, contains a tungsten filament. These *halogen gases* (a class of elements of which bromine and iodine belong) cause the tungsten molecules that are normally lost through sublimation to simply redeposit themselves on the filament. At the same time, the tungsten is able to burn more intensely. Surrounding this inner pressurized bulb is an outer protective bulb.

Halogen bulbs burn intensely, giving off a whiter light than typical incandescent bulbs, so there are more *lumens* (a measurement for the flow of light) per watt. These bulbs are also longer lasting—usually being rated for 2,000 to 3,000 hours of use. Another plus is their ability to create a more focused light source.

However, there are problems with halogen bulbs. A major one is the tremendous amount of heat that they produce. In fact, an amazing 90% of the energy created by halogen bulbs is in the form of infrared radiation (heat). As a result, some bulb temperatures reach as much as 1230° F. Therefore, halogen bulbs must be used *only* in fixtures designed for them.

By the way, not long ago halogen *torchiers* (floor lamps with reflector bowls and no shades designed to cast light upwards) became a hot news item. Apparently, people were placing them too near fabric curtains, which caught on fire. This is not surprising when you realize that these lamps operate at temperatures high enough to instantly cause paper and most fabrics to ignite. Now, newly manufactured halogen torchiers have protective grills above their reflector pans to help prevent accidental fires. However, it's still a good idea to keep any halogen torchier *at least* several feet from any curtain or drapery. As a precaution, it may be a good idea, if you have a pet or small child that might accidentally knock a halogen torchier over, to remove it from your home and find another lighting option.

Another problem is the risk of the bulbs exploding. A warning in a GE Lighting catalog notes that, halogen lamps which are "constructed of a glass bulb with a pressurized internal filament tube that operates at high temperatures could unexpectedly shatter. Should the outer bulb break, particles of extremely hot glass could be discharged into the fixture enclosure and/or surrounding environment, thereby creating a risk of personal injury or fire." Not a pleasant thought, but apparently this is a fairly uncommon scenario.

If you're interested in halogen bulbs, again, make absolutely sure your fixtures are designed for them. Halogen bulbs should be available at most lighting stores. It should be mentioned that **GE Lighting** has created improved Halogen-IR bulbs. These have an inner reflective film which causes much of the infrared heat to reflect back onto the filament. The result is a cooler bulb that's 40% more efficient. These products should be able to be purchased, or special ordered, locally.

Color-Corrected (Full Spectrum) Bulbs

An incandescent innovation is the *color-corrected bulb*. Lamps of this type are designed to closely mimic the spectrum of natural sunlight, rather than the yellowish glow of typical incandescent bulbs. Some people feel that humans derive a health benefit by being exposed to light indoors that is similar to sunlight, but this health benefit has not held up to current research. However, full-spectrum lamps can make colors seem more natural indoors.

One of the original brands of color-corrected incandescent bulbs is Chromalux (**Lumiram Electric Corp.**) which was developed in Finland. They achieve a more natural light using *neodymium*-tinted glass. (Neodymium is a rare, rosy/violet-colored earth element.) Chromalux bulbs now come in a broad range of styles and wattages. Dealers selling the complete line of Chromalux clear and frosted bulbs (including floods) include **Building for Health Materials Center**, and **Karen's Natural Products**. **Tomorrow's World** handles the frosted types in 60W, 100W, and 150W, as well as a frosted 3-way (50W, 100W, 150W) and a 75W flood version. Other sources for Chromalux bulbs are **Bio Designs** and **Allergy Relief Shop, Inc.**

Furthermore, **BioLight Systems** makes and sells bioLightbulbs. These, too, are full-spectrum bulbs using neodymium and are rated for 3,500 hours of life. Frosted, standard, and flood-style bulbs in various wattages are available. Seventh Generation Full-Spectrum Bulbs (**Seventh Generation**) in 60, 75, and 100 watt sizes can be purchased from **Harmony** and **GreenMarketplace.com**. Full-spectrum bulbs are also handled by **Real Goods**, **Inner Balance**, and **healthyhome.com**.

Full-spectrum bulbs are also carried by **Natural Lifestyle**. These 20,000-hour versions come in standard or flood styles in 75W, 100W, and 150W.

Fluorescent Lamp Innovations

As with incandescent lamps, fluorescent lamps with improved design features are now available.

Warm-White Fluorescents

One popular innovation is the *warm-white* fluorescent tube that emits less light from the blue and green portions of the visible light spectrum. As a result, the light from warm-white fluorescent lamps appears less harsh than the light given off by typical fluorescent lamps. (Note: There are now actually a whole range of specific warmer appearing fluorescent lamps available.) To purchase warm-white fluorescent lamps locally, check lighting centers and hardware stores. By mail order, you can purchase bioLightubes (**BioLight Systems**). These are described as "broad-spectrum" fluorescent tubes, and they come in a range of wattages and configurations. BioLight products are also handled by **N.E.E.D.S.**

Full-Spectrum Fluorescents

Another development is the *full-spectrum* fluorescent tube, which gives off light that more closely duplicates the spectrum of natural sunlight. Some believe that there are positive health benefits from using full-spectrum lighting instead of conventional indoor lighting. For example, a number of years ago bright full-spectrum lights were found to be useful in treating *Seasonal Affective Disorder (SAD)*. SAD is a form of depression that reoccurs every winter. It affects certain susceptible individuals because, for them, the decreased amount of sunlight during the shorter winter days triggers a biochemical imbalance in their bodies. While the original researchers worked with full-spectrum lamps, subsequent research has revealed that individuals with SAD will generally improve if they sit in front of any type of bright light—full-spectrum or not—for a few hours each day during the winter.

By the way, there are a number mail-order companies offering special SAD fluorescent-lamp units. **BioLight Systems** makes and sells the Ott Winter Bright 2001 bioLight System portable light box which has a brightness of 10,000 *lux* (a lux is a standard unit of illumination) using conventional fluorescents. This attractive, white, baked-enamel finished, metal light box is EMF (electromagnetic field) shielded and has an electronic ballast. These are also sold by **Inner Balance**, **Harmony** and **N.E.E.D.S.** From **N.E.E.D.S.**, you can also get a Sun-A-Lux portable combination fluorescent light box. This unit comes with three settings (full-spectrum light, bright 10,000 lux non-full-spectrum light, and a combination of both). It has shielded cathodes (to stop X-rays) and has an electronic ballast (to minimize EMFs). **Lumiram Electric Corp.** makes Aurora portable light systems. This achieves 10,000 lux using full-spectrum tubes. You'll need to contact the company for suppliers. Full-spectrum light boxes are also sold by **Allergy Relief Shop, Inc.**

If you're interested in having full-spectrum fluorescents tubes, Vita-Lite full-spectrum fluorescent tubes (**Duro-Test Lighting**) are available in sizes ranging from 15" to 96". They can be ordered directly from the company. Vita-Life full-spectrum lighting is handled by **Nigra Enterprises**, and in some health-food stores. **Healthyhome.com** handles Lumichrome brand fluorescent tubes. Sun-A-Light full-spectrum tubes are handled **Bio Designs.**

Lumichrome full-spectrum tubes (**Lumiram Electric Corp.**) are another option. Contact the company for suppliers. Furthermore, **BioLight Systems** manufactures and sells full-spectrum Ott bioLightube fluorescent tubes with shielded *cathodes*. (Cathodes are the metal ends of the tubes where electricity enters and leaves the lamps.) These shields are designed to block X-rays. A wide range of wattages, tube lengths, and shapes are offered. IBioLightubes are not only electronically ballasted, but they are especially designed to minimize buzzing and flickering. You can also get them from **N.E.E.D.S.** and **Befit Enterprises Ltd.** (For full-spectrum compact fluorescents, see *Compact Fluorescents* below.)

Yet other retail sources for full-spectrum tubes are **Real Goods** and **Inner Balance**, and a good selection is offered in the **Harmony** catalog.

Compact Fluorescents

One very popular fluorescent-lamp innovation is the *compact fluorescent (CF)*. These fluorescent lamps have smaller-diameter tubes (in a variety of shapes, some quite complex), built-in *ballasts* (transformers), and screw bases. Therefore, compact-fluorescent lamps can be used in many of the same fixtures, and decorative table lamps, as incandescent bulbs. While they're more expensive to purchase, they're very long-lasting and quite energy-efficient, so that, over time, they can save you a considerable amount of money. One minus has been that some are just too large to fit in fixtures and table lamps that were originally designed for smaller incandescent bulbs. Fortunately, smaller CFs are now more commonly available.

It should be noted that the built-in ballasts used in CF lamps come in two types: magnetic and electronic. The electronic ballasts cost a little more but they don't cause the light to flicker as much, and they give off lower-intensity electromagnetic fields (EMFs) (see *Chapter 26: Electromagnetic Fields*).

To find compact fluorescent lamps, you'll want to check your local hardware stores, building-supply outlets, and lighting centers. Also, your electric-power utility may offer them at discounted prices. By mail order, you can purchase several types from **Real Goods**. A few brands can also be purchased from **Tomorrow's World** and **NRG Savers**. It should be noted that Spiralux (**Duro-Test Lighting**) is one of the smallest types currently available. As the name implies, the tube is twisted into a spiral shape. Spiralux compact fluorescents be ordered directly from the company.

Recently, full-spectrum compact fluorescents have become available. **Duro-Test Lighting** manufactures and sells Vita-Lite compact fluorescents. Like the regular Spiralux, these also come in a twisted configuration. Sun-A-Light compact fluorescents with electronic ballasts are handled by **N.E.E.D.S.** and **Bio Designs.** Finally, full-spectrum compact fluorescents are to be found in the **Befit Enterprises Ltd.** and **Harmony** catalogs.

Another option is the Ott bioBulb (**Ott bioLight Systems Inc.**) "broad-spectrum" compact fluorescent, which is sold by the company and through dealers such as **Tomorrow's World**, **healthyhome.com**, and **N.E.E.D.S.** Though not a true "full-spectrum" product, these are described as being "almost full-spectrum" and have qualities similar to daylight. A company representative said that by having the tubes emit broad-spectrum rather than full-spectrum light, they produce a brighter light.

LED Lamps

One of the newest lamp innovations is the *LED (light emitting diode) lamp*, also called *diode array bulb*. These are a unique approach to lighting. It should be explained that a diode is a special type of electronic device. It has two electrical terminals which allow current to run through it in only one direction. Diodes manufactured from certain materials can give off visible light. Thus, they're called light-emitting diodes or LEDs. Gallium arsenide phosphide (GaAsP), for example, produces the red, green, or yellow light commonly seen in alarm clocks. In a diode array bulb, multiple LEDs are arranged within a single bulb.

LED-array lamps with this design use $7/10$ of a watt to produce the same brightness as a typical 10W incandescent bulb. They're also considered much more efficient than even compact fluorescents. Amazingly, LED-array lamps are rated to last 100,000 hours (about 20 years). Currently, it seems, only 10W bulbs are marketed which can fit into standard incandescent fixtures.

At this time, there has been little written about LED-array lamps and their availability is still quite limited. Right now their initial cost is extremely high—about $100 a bulb. Therefore, they might be best used in spots that are difficult to reach, so that once installed, the bulbs won't have to be replaced for perhaps two decades. One source for LED-array lamps is **Real Goods.**

Choosing the Right Lamp

Because of all the varieties available, it's important to know what you really want before purchasing a lamp for a specific application. Some considerations to keep in mind are the fixture's recommended lamp wattage, the desired brightness, the type of socket the fixture has, the size of the bulb compared to the size of the fixture, the lamp's energy efficiency, the amount of heat given off, the type of light spectrum emitted by the lamp, the lamp's initial cost, the lamp's lifetime operating cost, and whether the lamp has a flickering quality, or gives off a steady uniform light.

Admittedly, it can be confusing to compare different types of bulbs and tubes in order to figure out the best lighting option. Often, personnel working at your local electrical supply companies and lighting centers can be helpful.

Fixtures and Decorative Lamps

The following sections will discuss the different mounting devices available for bulbs and tubes or, in other words, fixtures and decorative lamps.

Ceiling and Wall Fixtures

Ceiling and wall fixtures can be attractive lighting additions to your home. However, ideally, you might want to avoid those made of plastic, especially if you are a sensitive person. Plastic fixtures can emit unpleasant "plasticky" odors when they're hot, which some people find bothersome. Also, you might want to avoid fixtures with open-bowl shades, if possible. The open bowls tend to become dust and insect accumulators. While intricate chandeliers may be attractive, you should keep in mind that they'll probably be very difficult to clean. This is particularly true for most crystal/glass chandeliers.

It's not difficult to find healthfully designed ceiling and wall fixtures. Most department stores, lighting stores, and building centers now carry good selections. You can also mail-order fixtures as well. For example, metal-and-glass ceiling fixtures (including stained-glass ones) are often available from **Home Decorators Collection, Ballard Designs**, and the JC Penny Catalog.

Floor and Table Lamps

It's best to choose lamps that are innately healthy. From an air-quality standpoint, floor and table lamps having metal, wood, glass, or ceramic bases with glass shades are ideal. Shades that are made of natural fabric or paper can be good second choices, but generally these can't be washed. If possible, avoid lampshades made of synthetic fabrics or plastics, especially if you are a sensitive person. The heat generated by hot bulbs can cause these shades to release potentially intolerable odors.

Of course, heat is a problem for halogen *torchiers*. These open-topped floor lamps can produce strong light for reading but often with tremendous amounts of heat. (See *Halogen Bulbs* on page 357.) While newer models of halogen torchiers have grills above them to keep out curtain fabric, they should still be kept some distance from decorative fabric window treatments. Halogen torchiers are sold in many department stores and discount stores.

It should be fairly easy to find non-halogen types of floor and table lamps at local furniture stores and lighting centers. Some very good selections (from a health standpoint) can also be mail-ordered. For example, **Pottery Barn** sells several attractive metal table and floor lamps with *vellum* (parchment) shades. You should be aware that **Home Decorators Collection** sells both attractive metal floor and table lamps. Their lamps with metal bases and stained-glass shades are particularly good looking. Some of these are made with copper foil (instead of lead) *came* (a grooved metal ribbon designed to hold sections of glass). For those of you who don't want to have lead items in your home, they're an excellent alternative. Stained-glass-and-metal lamps are also carried by **Design Toscano**.

Table and floor lamps with metal bases are in the **This End Up** catalog. These come with either linen or paper shades. **The Company Store** carries quite a few metal-based lamps. Some have paper shades and others glass. Several metal-and-glass lamps are carried by **Real Goods, Crate & Barrel, Ballard Designs**, and JC Penny Catalog.

Pompanoosuc Mills offers hardwood Mission-style lamps in table and floor models. Interestingly, the shades of these lamps are a combination of a wood framework with paper inserts. **L.L. Bean** (Furnishings Catalog) sells its own version of Mission-style lighting, also in both table and floor models. These lamps have linen shades. They also have a variety of metal floor and table lamps with linen, parchment, or stained-glass shades. Combination wood-and-metal table lamps with paper shades can be found in the **Linensource** catalog. **Shaker Workshops** handles cherry-wood table lamps with linen shades. Sleek-looking, white, Ott-Lite task lamps in desk and floor models use full-spectrum fluorescents. They're offered by **Befit Enterprises Ltd.** and **BioLight Systems**. The desk model is handled by healthyhome.com.

One option is making your own lamp shades. Some craft stores offer wire frames that you can cover with any type of fabric you want, such as organically raised cotton.

You should remember that floor and table lamps need to be routinely cleaned. Lamp bases can be regularly dusted with a soft, all-cotton flannel cloth. It's also best to remove any glass shades from time to time and wash them with a tolerable dish detergent. On the other hand, fabric shades can be occasionally removed and carefully vacuumed using a soft dusting attachment. Of course, you'll want to be especially gentle when you vacuum paper shades because they can be easily damaged.

It's also important to occasionally dust the tops of the light bulbs used in open-shade lamps. This is necessary, especially for some chemically sensitive individuals, because accumulated dust particles on the bulbs can burn and give off odors when the bulbs are on for a while and become hot. In order to safely dust bulbs, you'll first need to unplug your lamps. Then, you can go over the bulbs using a dry, soft, 100%-cotton flannel cloth. If you can tolerate a static-charged synthetic microfiber dusting cloth that can be used dry, that will work even better. (See also *Dusting* on page 140.) You shouldn't use a dampened cloth or a vacuum attachment for dusting light bulbs because of the possibility of breaking the bulb and causing electrocution.

Flames

Ideally, it's wise to avoid burning kerosene, vegetable oil, bottled gas, Sterno (a trademarked brand of canned, flammable, hydrocarbon jelly), alcohol, and other fuels for lighting indoors. This is especially true for chemically sensitive individuals, and those with asthma or other breathing problems. This advice also applies to all types of candles, even those made of natural materials such as beeswax, or animal-and-vegetable *tallow* (hard fat). In addition, you should avoid fireplaces and wood stoves, except those with well-sealed glass doors, outside-air supplies, and sealed combustion chambers.

The reason for avoiding these items is that they can give off polluting combustion gases, and smoke, when they're lit. Both smoke and combustion gases can cause serious negative health effects, including respiratory inflammation. (See *Combustion Gases* on page 524 and *Smoke* on page 540.) Another potentially serious problem involves the fragrances that are now added to many candles and kerosene. These scents may add an aroma, but they do not improve air quality. Instead, they simply add to the problems already inherent in burning any candle or kerosene indoors. Interestingly, recent research has shown that potentially dangerous volatile organic compounds (VOCs) are given off by at least some burning scented candles. In various tests, acetone, benzene, and xylene, were all given off. Of course, this is along with the carbon dioxide and soot particles. One of the reasons scented candles can be problematic is the fact that some of the fragrances used are not designed to burn cleanly. In addition, many candle wicks contain lead, which is released into the air as they burn.

Home Decorating Accessories

Accent pieces can give your home personality, but it's probably best to pick only those that are nontoxic and natural. Of course, this is especially important if you are a chemically sensitive person. Also, you should probably put more thought into choosing each accent piece than a superficial reason such as picking "a color that would go with the carpeting." After all, you don't have to fill each empty nook and space of an entire room or house all at once. Instead, you may want to try acquiring only very special things, items that are truly meaningful to you and your family. These special pieces would be added to your home slowly, perhaps over many years. Whatever you decide to do, keep in mind that too many "little extras" can create a confusing and cluttered appearance, and they can become hard-to-clean dust accumulators. Individuals with dust-mite allergies will especially want items that can be thoroughly cleaned.

Collectibles and Accent Pieces

What could possibly be an attractive, healthy, low-outgassing collectible? Well, good choices include ceramic figurines, plates, porcelain dolls, bronzes, pewter items, tin ware, crystal, shells, and rocks and minerals, to name a just a few. To find items for a special collection, you might check museum shops, galleries, and art or craft fairs, as well as shell-and-rock shops, among other places. By the way, a good suggestion for your small-item collection would be a solid-wood display unit with glass doors, which you might purchase, or have specially built (see *Custom-Made Furniture* on page 337). These can be used to show off your small, delicate pieces to their best advantage. They're available as freestanding units, hanging wall cabinets, or glass-topped tables. In such a display case, your collectibles will be protected from airborne dust.

Other healthful home accents include wooden pieces (carvings, etc.) and baskets. Oval, cherry, Shaker-style boxes are available from **Shaker Workshops**. Similar ones in both cherry and walnut are sold by **Shaker Shops West**. Both companies have nice selections of wooden Shaker baskets and hardwood bowls. Unfinished wooden boxes that you can decorate yourself can be ordered from **Home Sew**, while finished, ethnic-look handmade boxes can be purchased from **Marketplace: Handwork of India**.

Wicker baskets are always very popular. Most import shops should have a good selection. Other outlets, such as department and discount stores, should also have some. A few are sold by **Crate & Barrel**. Very nice ones are found in the **Shaker Shops West** and **Shaker Workshops** catalogs. Rush and bamboo accessories are found in the **Ballard Design** catalog. Check these items carefully before purchasing to see if there are any indications of mold, such as dark spots or stains.

Glass and ceramic items can make beautiful and inert decorating additions. Of course, these can be found in many local stores and finer pieces can be purchased at artist studios and galleries. Two catalogs that often handle glass vases are **Pottery Barn** and **Crate & Barrel**. **Crate & Barrel** also carries decorative ceramic ware such as pots and bowls. Stoneware pitchers and bowls are available from **Shaker Shops West**. A few European-style stone-and-plaster statues and other *objects d'art* are sold by **Design Toscano.**

Then, too, special accent furnishing pieces of metal can add visual interest to your home's interior, and local furniture stores generally offer a variety of these. Metal wall sculptures, CD racks, and a very large selection of metal wastebaskets appropriate for dens, bedrooms, and libraries are available by mail order from the **Home Decorators Collection**. Sometimes, they also handle brass hall trees and umbrella stands, as does **Service Merchandise**. Tinware boxes, small baskets, and waste-paper baskets are found in the **Shaker Shops West** catalog. Metal bowls and art objects are usually sold by **Crate & Barrel**. Metal statuary and urns are found in the **Design Toscano** catalog.

In addition, you might consider buying metal picture frames. These are available in a range of colors and styles that are attractive, inert, and easy to clean. (Note: Certain lacquered or painted metal frames may require an airing period in uncontaminated surroundings before they become tolerable for some chemically sensitive people.) **Graphik Dimensions Ltd.** is one popular mail-order source for metal picture frames. They have a tremendous selection and sell mats and matting equipment (cutters, etc.) as well.

Throws and Toss Pillows

To give your home a cozy feel, you can add natural-fiber afghans, quilts, hangings, and pillows. These are not only charming, but also practical. **Under the Canopy** has washable, green-cotton throws while **Deva Lifewear** has untreated, undyed, 100%-cotton afghans. Ethnic-inspired lap throws are found in the **Marketplace: Handwork of India** catalog. A number of outlets offer wool throws. For example, **Genopalette** makes and sells throws of naturally colored virgin wool sheared from "ecologically raised sheep." The wool has been "gently washed before spinning and is hand-woven." Virgin-wool throws are also sold by **Cosco Bay Wool Works**. Wool/cashmere throws can be purchased from **Linensource**. An unusual option are long-hair alpaca throws. You can buy these from **Peruvian Connection**.

Decorative toss pillows made with natural-fiber fabrics and natural stuffings, in several styles, can be found in the **Crate & Barrel** and **The Company Store** catalogs. The variety offered by **Cuddledown of Maine** have feather/down stuffings. **Marketplace: Handwork of India** sells ethnic-look toss-pillow covers made of all-cotton.In addition, **Deva Lifewear** has interesting toss-pillow covers made in both silk and cotton.

Of special note are the large 14" x 14" cotton-stuffed toss pillows from **Janice Corporation**. You can get these with *barrier-cloth* (a special tightly woven cotton cloth) ticking and removable barrier-cloth protectors. (Other options are also available.) Obviously, these are wonderful for those with dust-mite allergies because the barrier cloth can seal out dust mites. You can get custom-made toss pillows in 11 different sizes, with your choice of 4 stuffings, from **The Natural Alternative**. They can make removable covers for you. This company prides itself in its use of high quality materials, including organic stuffings and fabrics.

Of course, you might make your own afghans and pillows (see *Knitting and Crocheting* on page 458 and *Sewing* on page 456). **Cuddledown of Maine** has toss-pillow forms in a variety of shapes and sizes, including rounds, squares, and rectangles. All have Egyptian-cotton ticking with your choice of goose down, duck down, or feather/down stuffings.

House Plants

Live plants inside your home can provide a sense of unity with nature. Many people also believe that their house plants will clean their home of air pollution. Actually, some early studies by the National Aeronautics and Space Administration (NASA) did indicate that some living plants could provide reduced formaldehyde levels. In their initial research, NASA scientists placed plants inside a sealed chamber, injected a certain amount of formaldehyde into the chamber, then measured the concentration of formaldehyde after a certain amount of time had passed. After a while, the formaldehyde had, in fact, disappeared. What appeared to have happened was the plants metabolized the formaldehyde and used it as food. Later, it was determined that it was actually bacteria on the plant's roots that did the formaldehyde metabolizing, not the plant's themselves.

At any rate, NASA's early findings have since been challenged. More-thorough research at Ball State University, and at other laboratories, has concluded that house plants (or the root bacteria) simply can't substantially reduce formaldehyde or other contaminant levels found in indoor air. (Note: Plants can reduce carbon dioxide (CO_2) levels, but CO_2 is not considered an air contaminant.) In these more recent tests, plants were again placed in sealed chambers, but with a *continuously* outgassing source of formaldehyde, such as particleboard. (Houses often contain particleboard and other continuously outgassing sources of formaldehyde, so these new experiments were designed to mimic a real-world situation.) The results were disappointing. There was only a slight lowering of formaldehyde levels— no really significant reductions. So, in a real-world situation, where there's a continuously outgassing source of formaldehyde, plants (or their accompanying bacteria) can slowly metabolize some of it, but not as quickly as additional formaldehyde released.

Interestingly, if you have very many plants in your home, this can lead to a higher indoor relative humidity (from the ongoing watering), and formaldehyde outgasses at a faster rate as the air's moisture content goes up. So, you may actually *increase* formaldehyde levels inadvertently. In the end, it must be concluded that, while house plants will create a certain amount of oxygen, they simply aren't effective air filters.

Even though they aren't going to substantially improve the air in your home, you'll probably still like to have a few live house plants around. If so, you might consider choosing either cacti or *succulents* (plants with thick waxy leaves). Cacti and succulents require only occasional watering and misting, and little in the line of routine maintenance. Without the need for a great deal of water, these plants rarely become contaminated with mold or mildew—a real plus for mold-allergic people. Having lower water requirements also tends to lessen the chances of insect infestations and plant diseases. Finally, fertilizer applications with cacti and succulents are usually kept to a minimum.

With any live plant, it's always best to choose containers with drainage pans to prevent over-watering and rot. Usually, flower shops, craft galleries, and import stores sell many attractive and appropriate plant pots. For displaying your plants, **Ballard Designs** offers unusual plaster and ceramic plant-pot pedestals. A few plaster and concrete plant pedestals are available from **Design Toscano** (Columns & Pedestal catalog). You'll also want to check **Home Decorators Collection** and **This End Up** for other attractive plant stands. While not carried all the time, theses two catalogs do handle them from time to time.

Accessories for Special Rooms

Most "task rooms" require their own types of accessories. Below are a few sources.

Kitchen Accessories

Home Decorators Collection has a good selection of metal kitchen waste cans including step-on ones. Some of these come in stainless steel. Stainless-steel and chromed-steel kitchen racks are sold by **Hold Everything**. Other similar items should be available in local kitchen specialty shops and department stores.

Bathroom Accessories

Inert and attractive ceramic bathroom-sink accessories have been popular for some time. You can order a few styles from **Hold Everything**. Both ceramic and glass bathroom sink items are available from **Chambers**.

A collection of "homey" wicker bathroom items are found in the **Coming Home** catalog. Very nice metal bathroom wastebaskets are available by mail order from the **Home**

Decorators Collection. Other bathroom accessories should be offered in most bath sections in local department stores and discount stores. Other good places to look are in import shops.

Home-Office Accessories

A good variety of metal wastebaskets that can be used in your home office can be found in the **Home Decorators Collection** catalog. **Staples, Inc.** has steel-mesh desk accessories such as trays, letter holders, and waste cans. These come in black or chrome finish. Similar items are found in the **Reliable Corp.** catalog. From **Colonial Gardens Kitchen**, you can order oak magazine and letter racks. Furthermore, **L.L. Bean** (Furnishings Catalog) carries rattan/wire desk items. For additional healthful home office accessories, check your local office-supply stores, discount stores, and import shops.

CHAPTER 13: THE SAFE HAVEN

A number of very sensitive individuals find they require a *safe haven* within their own home. This chapter discusses what a safe haven is and how you can go about making one.

Why Create a Safe Haven?

Some people with severe Multiple Chemical Sensitivity (MCS) symptoms find it very beneficial to create a single room within their house that is ultra-safe for them. This special place is commonly termed a *safe haven*, a refuge, or an oasis. A safe haven is simply an uncontaminated and healthy retreat with better air quality than the rest of the home. With appropriate modifications to reduce dust mites, a safe haven can be created for highly-allergic individuals, too. For these people, see also *Allergies, Bedding, and Bedrooms* on page 223, *Dust Mites* on page 410, and *Decorating for Allergic People* on page 329.

Of course, the actual reason why it's necessary to create a safe haven varies with each individual, and the specific circumstances. For example, a person might just be too ill to convert his or her entire home into a healthy house. In other situations, unaffected family members may decide they're just not willing or able to give up their familiar (but toxic or bothersome) lifestyle in the rest of the home that they all share. In still other cases, a lack of money, energy, or time might allow only a small portion of a home's living space to undergo an immediate health-oriented transformation.

Whatever the reason, a safe haven can often result in beneficial effects, not only for the ill person, but also the entire family. Having a personal sanctuary for an ill person generally lessens physical *and* emotional stresses both for that person, as well as for other family members who must cope with the sick person. Although making a safe haven can be time-consuming, it can be an extremely positive step toward giving the ill person a sense of control over his (or her) own life and, at the same time, it can help to restore harmony within the family as a whole.

Making the Safe Haven

If you're ill with severe sensitivities, your physician or other personal health-care professional may prescribe or recommend a specific procedure for you to follow to create a safe haven. Of course, your health-care provider's suggestions should take precedence when there is a conflict in the suggestions below. However, if you have no idea how to make a safe haven, the procedure given here is one you might find very helpful. Even so, you'll want to first share it with your physician for his or her approval or disapproval, as well as to see if he or she has any suggestions for modifications, before you start. (Note, in many cases sensitive people may be too ill to actually create a safe haven themselves, so it may need to be created for them by someone else.)

Choosing the Best Location

The first step is to decide *where* to create your safe haven. As a rule, it should be the room where you'll spend the most time. In the majority of situations, that's a bedroom. To create a safe-haven bedroom, choose the one bedroom in the house that's already the least bothersome to you—that is, if that room can actually meet your needs. In other words, your proposed safe haven should ideally be a room that has as few obvious health problems as possible and is, at the same time, large enough so it doesn't feel confining. It should be relatively near the bathroom, or better yet, have its own bathroom, as well as its own closet space. Other desirable features are a room with a good source of fresh, uncontaminated outdoor air, one that's fairly quiet, and one that doesn't have any trauma associated with it. This last quality may seem somewhat odd. But if being in a particular room evokes strong memories of an intensely unhappy event, it's doubtful you'll ever feel well in that room—no matter how physically healthful it is.

Removal of Potential Problems

Once you've selected the room, remove all the furniture, clothing, wall decorations, curtains, and area rugs that are in it. If there's carpeting, you should probably remove it as well. Naturally, this is especially important if the carpet is new, moldy, musty smelling, or is in some other way known to be bothersome. However, you should know that removing the carpeting could be a major undertaking, especially if it has been glued down. Carpet glue is not only extremely difficult to remove from the floor, but exposing it could also create new intolerance problems with which you'll have to deal. Therefore, it's often a good idea to do some simple investigative work before attempting to remove any carpet. One way to do this is to pull back a corner of the carpeting in an inconspicuous place, such as in the closet, to see how it's attached and what's under it.

Even if you find that the carpeting is attached to the floor with tacks or tack strips, you'll still have to take into account what is under it. If it turns out that solid, finished hardwood floors are beneath the carpet, you're in luck, because the odds are you'll immediately have a fairly attractive and tolerable floor. If concrete is beneath the carpeting, you'll still probably have an acceptable floor. (Because bare concrete is rarely very attractive, you might consider covering it with ceramic tile. See *Ceramic Tile* on page 314.) If you remove the carpeting and find a particleboard or plywood subfloor, the subfloor could end up being even more of a problem than the carpeting.

If for some reason you're stuck with an intolerable carpet, subfloor, or some other type of less-than-perfect flooring, don't despair. Often, you can still make the room safe by covering the floor with 4' x 8' sheets of aluminum-foil-faced cardboard sheathing. One brand you might choose is Thermo-Ply (**Simplex Building Products**). You can call the company for nearby dealers. The seams between the sheathing sheets (and the joint around the perimeter of the room, where the sheets meet the wall) can be taped with aluminum-foil duct tape. Polyken aluminum-foil tape is often considered a particularly tolerable brand. You can order this product from **American Environmental Health Foundation** and **E.L. Foust Co., Inc.**, if you can't find it locally. Doing this procedure should effectively block most of the odors released by an objectionable floor. Keep in mind that aluminum foil-faced sheathing should not be considered a permanent floor covering. While it can last for several months, or more, the foil will likely eventually wear through due to foot traffic. Admittedly, an aluminum-foil floor can look odd, but for someone who's health is severely compromised, it can be a relatively inexpensive way to get an inert floor.

Thorough Cleaning

The next step in creating the safe haven is to consider washing all of the painted wall and ceiling surfaces. This will not only help remove any surface grease and dirt, but will also help lessen the odors of tobacco smoke, fragrances, etc. that they have absorbed. To wash the walls, use an unscented, tolerable product. One that's often acceptable is TSP (trisodium phosphate). TSP is a white, crystalline powder that can be used as a powerful, unscented cleaner. A popular brand found in most paint and hardware stores is Red Devil TSP/90 Heavy Duty Cleaner (**Red Devil, Inc.**), which has a modified formula that's phosphate-free. To use this product, mix 2 teaspoons into 1 gallon of warm water. Then, dip your sponge in the solution and wring it nearly dry. Next, gently scrub the walls starting from the wall bottom up. This will help minimize streaking. You'll find that cleaning only a small area at a time works best. In most cases, rinsing TSP isn't necessary. However, in a safe haven, it may be a good idea.

By the way, whenever you use TSP, wearing waterproof household gloves is a good idea to prevent any skin irritation. (See *Waterproof Household Gloves Suggestions* on page 137.) It should be mentioned that, before using any cleaning solution on your walls, you should test a small inconspicuous spot first, perhaps in a closet. That way you ensure that your painted surfaces won't be harmed if you proceed any further. Other low-odor wall-cleaning solution options are found in *Cleaning Walls* on page 161. Once the walls (and ceiling) are completed, make sure the floor is also clean. For that, you'll want read the appropriate sections also in *Chapter 6: House Cleaning*.

Appropriate Modifications

If you suspect you have electromagnetic sensitivities, it's best to shut off the electricity to your safe haven at night, if at all possible (see *Lowering EMF Risks in Homes* on page 652). If the room has registers for a forced-air furnace or air conditioner, they may be a source of mold, dust, minute amounts of combustion gases, or other substances to which you could react. So, temporarily tape the registers shut with aluminum-foil tape. Sealing the registers will also prevent contaminated air from the rest of the house from getting into the safe haven. If you find the room is too hot in the summer, either find a tolerable window air conditioner or use a portable fan. If the room is too cold in the winter, find a tolerable portable electric space heater or wear heavier clothing and cover yourself with more blankets at night.

If your house is fairly tightly constructed, you will likely have to periodically open the windows in the safe haven to air it out, or you might consider installing a ventilating fan just for that room.

Maintenance

Naturally, once you've created your new safe haven, you should keep it as pristine as possible. This means using only unscented personal care products (see *Chapter 4: Personal Care*). Also, it would be wise to use only tolerable natural-fiber clothing, especially for nightclothes (see *Chapter 8: Clothing*). In addition, all your laundry should be washed in tolerable, unscented products (see *Alternative Laundry Products* on page 113). Of course, your room should contain only natural, untreated, tolerable bedding (see *Chapter 9: Linens*).

Moving into the Safe Haven

After emptying out and cleaning the safe haven, it's time to move in. This can be a slow process inasmuch as it involves moving in one item at a time, testing the room's tolerability with that item in it, then moving another item in, and so on. At this point, if you have known food intolerances, it's especially important that you only eat non-reactive foods for a while. Also, if you know that you have other allergies or sensitivities, everything should be done to minimize triggering them. That way, if a negative reaction occurs when you move into the room, it can easily be limited to something in the room itself—and not to some other exposure. This is the only way to determine if the safe haven will actually be a healthy environment for you.

The First Night

The first night you actually use the room, you may want to try sleeping with your tolerable bedding directly on the floor. This is especially important if you believe you might have trouble tolerating the bed (with its possible perfumey or musty odors, dust mites, or bothersome frame, headboard, mattresses, or box spring, etc.). You might use several untreated 100%-cotton or 100%-wool blankets placed on top of one another to form a thin mattress. You might also consider using a tolerable futon. Another option is using an exposed-metal box spring as a bed foundation, and placing a number of blankets on top of it. Still another approach is to sleep on a tolerable 100%-cotton canvas cot.

Assessing Your Safe Haven

The next morning, you should question yourself about how well you slept and how you generally feel. You may actually feel better. If not, you may want to wait a few days before changing anything. This is because you might still be reacting to some previous exposure that occurred before you moved into the room. After 4–7 days have passed, an improvement in your well-being should have occurred.

Possible Additional Modifications

If you still don't feel better, you might try using different bedding or nightclothes, etc. If you don't notice any improvement, there are still other measure to try.

Further Air Quality Improvements

Perhaps your safe haven requires further improvement in air quality before it will be acceptable for you. To do that you could bring additional fresh outdoor air into the room with a window fan. You might also operate a tolerable portable air filter in the room. If you opt for the later, you should pick the simplest piece of equipment capable of doing the job you need done. Don't get a unit with six different filtering strategies when a unit with one strategy will suffice. That's because, while air cleaning/purifying devices will remove pollutants from the air, they can also add a small amount of something that wasn't there before.

You see, many filters use synthetic materials as *media* (the actual substance or material used to trap pollutants). For example, popular HEPA (high efficiency particulate arresting) filters often use tightly woven fiberglass fabric that's held together with a synthetic resin. Other units can add reactive ozone to the air. Of course, this obviously includes ozone generating machines (which are not recommended), but to a lesser degree also ionizers and electrostatic precipitators. Even UV (ultra-violet radiation) purifiers create a small amount of ozone as they react with contaminants. Then, too, odors from motors, housings, and even electrical wiring and cords could be intolerable for certain people.

If you're chemically sensitive and decide to try a filter, one that primarily removes *gaseous contaminants* (such as formaldehyde) may be all you need. You should only get a unit with a HEPA, or other *particulate* (minute particles) filter if you feel that *particulates* in the air are probably what's bothering you (such as dust mites or mold spores). However, hopefully by now, your safe haven shouldn't have these problems anyway. At any rate, whatever approach you choose, make sure to pick a filter designed with chemically sensitive people in mind. These units will likely have a metal housing with a motor that is not mounted in the filtered air stream. (This is to prevent any problematic motor odors from being blown into the room.) Therefore, companies with air-filtering equipment to seriously consider include **E.L. Foust Co., Inc., Allermed, Aireox Research Corp.**, and **Austin Air**. For more help on indoor air equipment, you'll need to read *Choosing the Right Air Improvement Equipment* on page 559. In fact, all of *Chapter 23: Improving Your Indoor Air*, will provide you with valuable information, descriptions of various models from these particular manufacturers, and buying sources.

Further Room Modifications

If filtering the air still doesn't bring much improvement, you could tape (with aluminum-foil duct tape) reflective insulating builder's foil on all the walls and even the ceiling. Unperforated Dennyfoil #245, which has an aluminum-foil facing on each side of a Kraft paper center, may be available locally. Mail-order sources include **E.L. Foust Co., Inc.** and **Building for Health Materials Center**. Once you have aluminum foil on the walls and ceiling, there should be nothing from the existing walls being released into the room. An all aluminum room can look odd but, again, it can be a small price to pay to obtain a safe haven that will help you regain your health.

If you haven't already put 4' x 8' sheets of aluminum foil-faced cardboard sheathing on the floors, you might go ahead and cover them with this material, too. If this doesn't help, you may need to wash the aluminum surfaces with a TSP/water solution and then rinse with water as suggested for the room's walls. This is because some foil-faced materials have a very slight oil film on them from the manufacturing process, a film that the TSP should be able to remove.

Once you start feeling better, you can start making some changes that will make the room look more attractive. But the first step is to make the room tolerable, by whatever means necessary. After all, your health is worth it.

Creating Another Safe Haven

If there's still no improvement, another room in the house could be tried as a safe haven. In some cases, one particular room, or even an entire home, may have been unknowingly contaminated with a pesticide or some other substance that causes continual reactions. Therefore, moving out of the room (or perhaps moving out of the house) may be the best solution. It's possible that the overall air quality in the house is simply too bothersome to allow the creation of a safe haven. In that case, you might ask a friend or relative if you can make a safe haven room in his or her home.

The Successful Safe Haven

Fortunately, most sensitive (or allergic) individuals end up feeling somewhat better after a few days in a safe haven. If you do, you should only introduce new items into your sanctuary gradually. Don't move all your old furniture and belongings in at once. Instead, introduce just one item at a time so you can properly test the room for personal tolerance with that item in it (see *Testing* on page 62). If an item seems tolerable, wait at least four days before bringing something else into the room. Granted, this can take a considerable amount of time, but it is the best way to determine if everything in your safe haven will be tolerable to you.

By the way, if you introduce an item and it causes a tolerance problem, you can store that item somewhere until you feel stronger and then try it again later. Sensitivities change, and you may find you will be able to tolerate it in a few months. However, if the item provoked a very strong negative reaction, it might be best to replace it with something less bothersome. This testing procedure will need to be repeated with all your old belongings as well as with any new ones you wish to bring inside your safe haven. In time, at least one room in your house should become a safe, comfortable, and healthy retreat for you. This will give you a place to build up your strength and improve your health.

CHAPTER 14: GARAGES & AUTOMOBILES

Garages are often forgotten places in terms of health. However, they really shouldn't be. As everyone knows, many of today's garages are directly attached to the house. And they generally have entry doors that open directly into a home's living space. Some houses also have bedrooms that are located directly above an attached garage. Unfortunately, an attached garage can mean health problems if automobile exhaust gases or gasoline odors (among others) migrate from the garage, through tiny openings in the walls, around an unsealed entry door, or even around light fixtures in the garage ceiling, and then enter the living space (see *Combustion Gases* on page 524). An automobile's combustion gases can also get into the living space through leaky heating/cooling ductwork that is located in a garage.

The truth is, the majority of attached garages have not been designed or built to prevent garage-generated pollutants from passing indoors. And this is true no matter what the age of the house, or how much it cost. In fact, if there is an entry door between the living quarters and the garage, a certain amount of garage air will enter the house whenever that door is opened.

Therefore, some experts believe that healthy houses should have detached, rather than attached, garages. Of course, with proper sealing techniques, it is possible to isolate the garage from the house, but this is rarely done (for more on sealing techniques, you may want to read *The Healthy House* and *Healthy House Building For the New Millennium* by John Bower, which can be ordered from **The Healthy House Institute** or your favorite bookseller.

If you live in a home with an attached garage, there are several positive steps you can take to minimize any potential air-quality problems. These are covered in the following sections. By the way, some of this information can also be applied to detached garages, so that they can become safer and healthier spaces as well. Other sections discuss the environment inside an automobile itself.

Garage Organization and Safety

One simple way to make your garage safer and healthier is to keep it both clean and well-organized. Doing this will lessen the accumulation of dust and debris, and therefore, potential pest habitats. It'll also lower your risk of tripping accidents. The first step in doing this is to simply discard (or sell, or give away) all the "stuff" you don't really need, or will likely never use again. Remember, however, you'll want to dispose of properly any items considered "household hazardous waste" such as pesticides and solvent-based products. To learn what procedures to follow, contact your local sanitation department or board of health.

Another good thing is to replace gasoline-powered yard equipment with manual or electric models, if at all possible. A piece of powerful equipment that runs on gasoline can be extremely odorous. Plus, it will require cans of gasoline (and oil) to be in your garage to operate it. The clothing worn by people who use these types of machines can quickly become saturated with combustion gases, which may be difficult or even impossible to remove. Naturally, the individual operating the equipment will have inhaled these dangerous pollutants, and their hair and skin will have absorbed their unpleasant odors just as their clothes did. If you decide to replace your gasoline-powered equipment, manual and electric alternatives should be available locally. Mail-order sources for manual lawn mowers are **Vermont Country Store** (Voice of the Mountains catalog), **Harmony**, and **Solutions**.

To conveniently store items you intend to keep, consider buying metal cabinets with doors. These cabinets work well at holding tools, hoses, sprinklers, car-cleaning products, etc. You'll find that these are available at most office-supply stores. If you can't find them locally, a number of cabinets made by **Edsal Manufacturing Co., Inc.** and **Lee Metal Products** can be ordered from **Reliable Corp.** (a large office supply catalog). One line that's especially nice is the Flammable Liquid Cabinets from **Edsal Manufacturing Co., Inc.** These would likely be very handy to store many types of flammable liquids often found in garages. To find a local supplier for these particular units, you'll need to call the company. Note: Metal storage cabinets with locking mechanisms, or ones that are designed to accept a padlock, are excellent choices if children are around your home.

In addition, heavy-duty, metal-mesh shelving units designed for mounting on walls can also provide good, solid storage sites. Sometimes these are handled by local hardware stores and building centers. Also check larger office-supply stores. **Inter-Metro Industries Corp.** makes very attractive heavy-duty chromed wire shelving. These are free-standing units. To locate a dealer, contact the company. Then, too, you might consider using sturdy wall-mounted metal brackets to hang your rakes and other long-handled tools. Again, many neighborhood hardware stores and building centers sell them. Another good place to look is in garden-supply centers. (For more storage ideas, see *Household Storage* on page 511).

Finally, for proper fire safety, you'll want to make sure your garage is equipped with a multipurpose fire extinguisher (see *Portable Fire Extinguishers* on page 388). You'll want to keep this in a prominent place. And from time to time you'll need to remember to check your extinguisher's gauge to see if it's properly charged.

Controlling Odors within Garages

Most garages contain a variety of products and devices that can generate polluting odors. However, of all the potential airborne contaminants, gasoline and oil odors, and combustion gases, are perhaps the most dangerous. These odors are not just unpleasant smelling; they're also toxic. In addition, evaporated gasoline can explode if concentrations become high enough. As was mentioned earlier, houses with attached garages will likely have these pollutants entering their living quarters fairly regularly.

Fortunately, you can help lessen these air-pollution problems by following some simple precautions. One is to only fill gasoline-powered machinery outside your garage. Also, start all motorcycles, chain saws, trimmers, and lawn mowers outdoors. In addition, after using any combustion-driven item, shut it off and let it cool outdoors, and only then bring it inside your garage.

Another precaution you might consider is to place vehicular mats under parked cars, trucks, and motorcycles that are stored inside your garage. These can capture oil and other fluid drips from leaking transmissions, cooling systems, brake lines, etc. before they become absorbed into your concrete garage floor. Such mats may be available at auto-supply stores, or you might simply use a piece of heavy cardboard. Of course, whatever you use will need to be replaced or cleaned from time to time. If you want to use a concrete sealer on your garage floor, Safecoat Penetrating WaterStop (a thin solution) or Water Shield (a thicker, surface coating) (both made by **AFM**) are ones you might use. These can be purchased from AFM dealers such as **American Environmental Health Foundation**, **N.E.E.D.S.**, **Bio Designs**, **Allergy Relief Shop, Inc.**, **Building for Health Materials Center**, and **The Living Source**. AFM also makes a lower odor Safecoat Dyno-Seal Driveway/Asphalt Sealer.

If oil or other fluid stains do end up on your garage floor, you might try sprinkling unscented, clay, cat-box litter on them. The litter material should be left on the floor long enough to have a chance to absorb the liquid, then swept up, and disposed of properly. If you want to purchase simple, unscented, clay cat litter, it can still sometimes be purchased at local pet-supply stores. However, it must be admitted that it's become a rather rare item with the advent of "improved" scoopable, scented products.

Some oily or greasy stains may be removed with low-odor, concentrated cleaners. One such synthetic cleaner to try is AFM SafeCoat Super Clean which you can purchase from **N.E.E.D.S.**, **American Environmental Health Foundation**, **Allergy Relief Shop, Inc.**, **Bio Designs**, **Priorities**, **healthyhome.com**, and **The Living Source**. To use it, mix it with an equal part of water. You can then sponge on or spray the greasy area, allow the solution to work for a time, agitate it with a sponge, and then rinse it off with clear water. Of course, wearing waterproof household gloves is a good idea. For other safer, low-odor degreasing options you'll want to read *Cleaning Greasy Problems* on page 165.

To help minimize auto exhaust odors inside your garage, you might want to follow this procedure. After pulling your car into the garage, turn off the ignition and leave the garage door open for 15–30 minutes. If this isn't possible, you should consider installing in your garage an exhaust ventilation fan with its own crank timer. These timers are designed so they can be manually set to shut off the fan after a preset time. After you pull your car into the garage and shut the door, simply activate the timer for 30–45 minutes and the exhaust fan will air out the garage, then shut itself off. Crank timers themselves are generally relatively inexpensive to purchase and install. If you're interested, **Broan Mfg. Co., Inc.** and **Nutone** are two ventilation-fan timer manufacturers. However, there are many others. Usually, several brands can be found in local **W.W. Grainger, Inc.** stores and catalogs.

If you have a forced-air furnace or air conditioner in the garage, make sure all the ducts are properly sealed. Otherwise, garage odors can be pulled into the leaky ducts and blown into the living space. Good information on proper duct sealing, and problems caused by leaky ducts, can be found in *Understanding Ventilation* and *The Healthy House*. Both books are by John Bower. You can order these from **The Healthy House Institute** or your favorite bookseller.

Finally, make sure all entry doors leading directly into your home's living quarters are kept shut except when they're actually being used to enter or leave your house or garage. Also, it's important that the door be properly weather-stripped. The doors that often do the best job of sealing have magnetic weather-stripping, like a refrigerator. If your door is not well sealed, you'll need to check local building-supply outlets for simple weather-stripping kits. They'll also have, or can order for you, magnetic-sealing doors if you feel that it's best to replace your exiting door.

The Car

If you're like many Americans, the interior of your automobile is a place where you spend a lot of time. So, it should be as healthy as possible. The following sections suggest some ways to lessen any problems that could arise.

Car Care

Most typical car-care products are odorous and/or potentially harmful. Fortunately, there are healthier alternatives.

Typical Car-Cleaning Products

Many typical products used to clean car interiors and exteriors have formulas containing dangerous petrochemical solvents. These volatile organic compounds (VOCs) can cause a range of negative health effects if inhaled (see *Volatile Organic Compounds* on page 526). Not surprisingly, a great many car-care products are labeled "hazardous" and have a list of warnings on them. If you find you simply must use one of these products, apply it to your car while it is outside the garage and while wearing a chemical respirator mask (see *Personal Protective Gear* on page 264).

Unfortunately, one particularly bothersome solution, that's often hard to avoid, is windshield-washing fluid. So, if at all possible, don't dispense this cleaning fluid when your car's windows or air vents are open. When you do use the cleaning fluid, wait until it has completely evaporated or been washed off by rain or snow before allowing the exterior air to come inside again through the vents. Of course, if you live in a year-around warm climate, where freezing isn't a problem, you could substitute plain water, a water/vinegar solution, or one of the tolerable, unscented window cleaners listed under *Cleaning Windows* on page 160. Keep in mind though that the makers of these products did not market them for this particular purpose. Therefore, any problems that arise from using them in your car's windshield fluid dispenser might not be covered by the manufacturer's warranty. Then, too, if you plan to travel to where the temperatures drop below freezing, you'll have to remember to drain the dispenser and fill it with a standard, anti-freeze containing product.

Alternative Car-Cleaning Products

You might be surprised to learn that baking soda and water can harmlessly and effectively perform a number of car-cleaning jobs. For example, a sponge or soft cotton cloth saturated with a solution of 4 tablespoons of baking soda dissolved in 1 quart warm water can clean your car's chrome trim and mirrors. When done, rinse them with clear water. By the way, you can use this same solution (and procedure) to clean your car's vinyl upholstery, wiper blades, and floor mats. For additional uses for baking soda, you'll want to look through the book, *Baking soda: Over 500 Fabulous, Fun and Frugal Uses You've Probably Never Thought Of* by Vicki Lansky. Check your local library or favorite bookstore to see if it's obtainable.

Other products to try are BonAmi Cleaning Power and Bon Ami Cleaning Cakes (**Faultless Starch/Bon Ami Co.**) Both of these are simply unscented, undyed soaps combined with finely powdered mineral feldspar. They can be used to clean your vehicle's window glass, mirrors, white-sidewall tires, and chrome. Bon Ami products are sold at some groceries and through **Erlander's Natural Products** and Bon Ami's own **Agelong Catalog**. The **Bio Designs** catalog sells just the cleaning powder and **Simmons Natural Bodycare** just handles the cleaning cake.

To wash your car, you may want to use Crystal All-Purpose Cleaner/Degreaser (**Sunshine Makers, Inc.**). This is a synthetic, highly-concentrated cleaner with no petroleum distillates. It's also undyed and unscented. The company suggests mixing it in a concentration of 30 parts water to 1 part Crystal Cleaner for a good car-washing solution. To buy Crystal Cleaner, you'll need to call for the company for a distributor in your area. If there is none, you can order directly from manufacturer. By the way, a detailed dilution chart is available upon request. From the **Agelong Catalog**, you can purchase a high-pressure water wand that often requires no detergent at all to clean. While useful for driveways, upper-story window cleaning, and other jobs, it's also said to effectively wash cars. Called the Pro Jet 2000 Cleaning System, it's said to be "five times more powerful than other hose-attached sprayers." This tool is especially designed to create a high speed, rotating (up to 1500 revolutions per minute) water stream that apparently can remove most dirt. However, it does come with a soap cup if you want to add your favorite liquid detergent.

For the inside of your vehicle, try White Wizard Stain Remover and All-Purpose Cleaner (**L.B. Roe Corp.**). This is an odorless, undyed, white jelly-like cleaner able to remove stains from a variety of surfaces, including many types of car upholstery and carpeting. This product can be ordered from the manufacturer and from **Harmony**, **Vermont Country Store** (Voice of the Mountains catalog), **Solutions**, **Real Goods**, and the **Agelong Catalog**. Also of interest is White Wizard Upholstery Cleaner, an odorless, nontoxic, undyed spray. To use it, simply spritz it on and wipe the surface with a clean cotton terry-cloth towel. This spray can be ordered directly from the maker, **L.B. Roe Corp.**

Of course, these days a few manufacturers now make alternative products especially for automobiles. Some of these might be handled by auto-supply stores in your area. If they are, they're most likely labeled as "earth-friendly," "eco-friendly," or "green" items. (You'll have to read the product labels carefully to see if they're going to be healthy-for-people products, as well as healthy for the planet.) Planet-friendly products you may come across include certain car-wash concentrates, upholstery cleaners, and protective finishes. However, one alternative company, **LifeTime Solutions**, makes and sells a number of alternative products created with people's health as their number one priority. Generally, even very chemically sensitive people can use them without experiencing problems. The manufacturer uses unique blends containing *colloidal micelles*. Products you may want to try in their line include Car & Boat Shine, Wood & Leather Protector (which can be used on leather upholstery), Tire & Vinyl, Sparkling Glass, Heavy Duty Cleaner & Degreaser, and an especially interesting one, Bugs Away (able to remove most insects and tar splats from cars).

(Note: For other cleaning products and procedures that may be applicable to your car, you'll want to see the appropriate sections in *Chapter 6: House Cleaning*.)

Rustproofing

As everyone knows, car-rustproofing treatments are done to help prevent corrosion of the steel parts making up an automobile. Although many cars are now routinely rustproofed as part of the manufacturing process, some car owners still feel that additional treatment is necessary. Of course, this is especially true for those who live in coastal areas and in locations where road salt is commonly used. No matter who performs the rustproofing, if your car is properly treated, it will likely look good for years, and you'll be more likely to keep it longer. Being able to keep your car longer is very important for many sensitive individuals. This is because it sometimes can take up to three years for some sensitive persons to become comfortable with the synthetic interior of a new car. Unfortunately, after three years, many non-rustproofed cars begin to show rust, so trading them in at this time is common.

While the procedure should make your car last longer, there's also a downside to rustproofing. This is because nearly all rustproofing compounds are thick, greasy or waxy, petroleum-based coatings. Not surprisingly, these gummy chemicals release very strong odors. As a result, a newly treated car will end up being surrounded by these odors for several weeks or more. You should also be aware that some rustproofing companies recoat vehicles annually, rather than merely perform a simple visual inspection on them. Therefore, coping with persistent rustproofing odors could become a yearly event.

Something you might want to consider is having the rustproofing done during the hottest time of the year. That way the very warm air can help dissipate the rustproofing odors as quickly as possible. While the odors will end up being more intense than if the treatment was done during colder weather, they'll generally linger for a much shorter period of time. (Note, some chemically sensitive persons actually prefer the odors to be less intense and longer lasting, so this is a definitely a case of personal preference.)

After any rustproofing has been performed, keep your car parked outdoors rather than inside your garage for a while, if at all possible. This is for two reasons: 1) so your car can air out faster outside, and 2) so you won't fill you garage with noxious chemical odors. In addition, provide good ventilation within the car while this airing-out process is going on. It should be mentioned that a car air filter may help lessen somewhat any rustproofing odors that seep into the interior (see *Car Interior Air Filters* on page 379).

Car-Interior Odor Concerns

Car interiors are often unhealthy environments for a variety of reasons. In the sections below, common pollution sources are discussed as well as things that can be done to help improve the air within your car.

New Car Interior Concerns

New car interiors can outgas a considerable amount of synthetic chemicals, primarily from their stain-proofed synthetic carpets and upholstery. Other sources of airborne pollution are the vinyls, foams, and plastics used in dashboards and door and ceiling panels. To help speed up the release of these gases, you might want to consider buying your new car only in a hot-weather month. That way, you may be able to let the car "bake" in the sun with the doors and windows open for an extended period of time.

To help reduce the outgassing from the carpeting, you may want to use one or two "sodium siliconate" products manufactured by **AFM**. The first is AFM SafeChoice Carpet Seal which should be applied right after carpeting has been washed. It's said to create an "odor-free membrane" that seals in carpet odors for up to one year. The second product is AFM SafeChoice Lock Out. This not only provides additional sealing of odors but is described as a dirt repeller as well. Both of these are handled by AFM dealers including **American Environmental Health Foundation, N.E.E.D.S., Bio Designs, Allergy Relief Shop, Inc., Building for Health Materials Center**, and **The Living Source**.

However, you should be aware that carpet sealants can't seal in 100% of the chemicals released by carpeting. Therefore, some chemically sensitive individuals have found that, while carpet sealants help, they simply aren't effective enough. As a result, as a final solution, they've ended up removing all the offending carpeting. However, before you do this, really think this out because it's a rather drastic solution. Once done, your car will lose much of it's resale value. And the carpet or padding will likely be glued in place anyway, making removal difficult.

Sensitive individuals often deliberate whether to purchase a car with cloth, vinyl, or leather upholstery. As it turns out, many sensitive persons have found that leather interiors are fairly tolerable to them. Yet for a few, leather interiors are much too odorous. The truth is, there is no simple answer. In the end, each person must ultimately choose the car upholstery material that seems to suit him (or her) best. Of course, sitting in cars with different types of upholstery should help you reach a decision. However, in actuality, most chemically sensitive individuals will find any new car upholstery to be problematic, whether leather, vinyl, or fabric. Unhappily, for them it may take several weeks, months, or in a few cases, years, before a new car interior is no longer bothersome.

However, there are a few measures you can take to make your car's upholstery more acceptable to you. For example, you could drape cotton barrier cloth over the seats. This is a special type of cotton fabric that's very densely woven so that many odors are unable to pass through it. Mail-order sources for organic cotton barrier cloth include **Sleeptek Limited** (in Canada) and **N.E.E.D.S.** or **Furnature** (in the U.S.). **Janice Corporation** has untreated barrier cloth. Though it can be very expensive and time-consuming, some sensitive people have completely reupholstered the interior of their car with less-toxic materials. For information on safer upholster fabrics, see *Custom-Made Soft Furniture* on page 338.

Less dramatic options are natural-sheepskin bucket-seat covers, seat-belt covers, and steering-wheel covers, sold by **Aussie Connection**. These are described as washable. Also said to be washable are lambskin rugs from **The Right Start**. As a nice service, the company will provide you with written instructions showing you how to fit the lambskin into a baby's or young child's safety car seat. Then, too, the **French Creek Sheep & Wool Company** offers sheepskin car-seat covers in natural as well as in several colors. These are available in standard sizes or custom ones. In addition, the company has steering-wheel covers, too. Finally, from the **Deerskin Trading Post**, you can purchase sheepskin seat covers in three styles (low bucket, high bucket, and sport-utility vehicle), as well as seat-belt covers, and steering-wheel covers.

Car Interior Air Filters and Ionizers

Many chemically sensitive individuals are inclined to use an air filter or ionizer in their car. However, it's important to realize that these devices can only reduce the airborne pollutants found within the car's interior—they cannot totally eliminate them.

Car Interior Air Filters

Several air filters are available for cars that were designed initially for chemically sensitive people. These units operate on 12 volts by plugging into the dashboard's cigarette lighter. Some models also come with special adapters which allow them to operate on standard 110-volt house current. Although it's probably not a good idea to use an adapter on a continuous basis, having one on your car filter could be useful for a stay overnight in a motel room or at a friend's house. Be aware that while these filters come with their own "standard" media, you can often specify that another type of activated charcoal, zeolite, or an activated-charcoal mixture be used instead.

One popular car-interior filter is the #160-A Auto Air Purifier (**E.L. Foust Co., Inc.**). This unit is a chromed-metal, cylindrical canister that comes with a metal "cradle" to hold it. The canister contains a mix of about three pounds of 60% activated-coconut-shell charcoal and 40% PuraPel (activated alumina impregnated with potassium permanganate) which together are effective at removing many types of chemical odors. (See *Adsorption Filters* on page 551.). In addition, there's also a FilterDown layer inside. This synthetic fabric is said to be able to trap particles down to 0.5 microns. If you prefer not to use a synthetic material, an untreated cotton fabric can be used instead. However, this will not be as efficient a filtering medium. By the way, an AC adapter is available. The #160-A Auto Air Purifier can be ordered directly from the company. One last note of interest is that E.L. Foust offers a "filter exchange service" so you don't have to change the media yourself. When you're ready, a newly filled canister can be sent directly to you. Then you simply send the canister you've been using back to them.

Another very good air filter to consider is the Autoaire II (**Allermed**). This is a rectangular, 10" x 10" x 9" metal unit with two side vents, that take in air, with a third vent on top, where cleaned air emerges. Because of it's stable shape, you can place this filter easily on a car's seat as well as on the floor. Interestingly, each intake vent has its own "filtering packet." Within a "beverage board" cardboard frame, are multiple layers with non-woven polyester sides. In between is a granular mixture of coconut-shell activated-charcoal and *potassium permanganate* (to trap formaldehyde), as well as two layers of coconut-shell activated-charcoal-impregnated non-woven polyester fiber fabric, and two layers of "high-efficiency synthetic media, 90%-95% efficient." Autoaire II is designed to remove exhaust odors, and pollen, dust, smoke, and other types of particles, too. You can order the Autoaire II from the manufacturer or from dealers such as **Building for Health Materials Center**.

Still another fine activated-charcoal filtering device is the Aireox Car Air Purifier (**Aireox Research Corp.**). This is a good-looking, all-metal, cylindrical unit using $2^1/2$ pounds of a coconut-shell-derived activated charcoal and Purafil (activated alumina impregnated with potassium permanganate) mixture. An AC-adapter option is available. It can be ordered directly from the company or from distributors including **N.E.E.D.S.**

Allerx offers yet another option—the Allergy Traveler. This 10" x 7" x 7" plastic unit has both "high-efficiency filters" and activated charcoal. An optional 110-volt AC adapter is available.

And the Allergy Traveler has a metal housing with an activated-charcoal mesh filter as well as a "post particulate filter." It plugs into your car's cigarette lighter and also has a 110-volt AC adapter. You can order it from **Ozark Water Service and Environmental Services**.

Besides these types of filters, smaller plastic models designed for the "public-at-large" are now being made. You can sometimes find these at auto-supply stores. One such unit is the

Amaircare Auto Air Filter. This small, plastic device (8" diameter x 3" high) has a 3-stage filtration system inside it. The first filter is a polyester fabric impregnated with activated charcoal to trap larger particles, the second is an *electret* material (a static-charged media), and the third filter is polyester fabric impregnated with zeolite. Interestingly, the Amaircare has a strap which allows it to hang on the back of a front seat. It plugs into the cigarette lighter. The unit itself, and filter refills, are sold by **Befit Enterprises Ltd.** The **Gazoontite** catalog also sells Amaircare car filters.

Although portable car filters are helpful, they can't eliminate all your car's interior odors, let alone all the smog and combustion gases that enter the car from the outdoors. Therefore, when you're in heavy traffic, it's often a good idea to close your car's exterior air vents and windows. However, you must not keep them closed all the time. After all, you'll need to regularly replenish your supply of oxygen and remove any excess moisture and carbon dioxide that has built up.

Car Interior Negative-Ion Generators

A number of people are now purchasing *negative-ion generators* (also known as ionizers) for their cars. These are designed to reduce the levels of interior airborne pollution. As a rule, negative-ion generators designed for automobiles plug directly into the cigarette lighter.

All negative-ion generators, including home models, operate by producing large quantities of negatively charged electrons that attach themselves to dust, mold spores, and many minute particles. These ionized particulates then leave the air and cling to the dashboard or ceiling, etc. When these substances become attached to your car's interior surfaces, you won't be able to inhale them.

This sound good, but there are problems with negative ionizers. First, it'll be necessary to clean the surfaces inside your car more frequently to remove the buildup of contaminants. Another consideration to keep in mind is that some of these contaminants will eventually lose their charge and become airborne again. Because of these concerns, some ionizers come with filters that are able to trap the particles within the unit itself. Still another drawback is that these units produce a certain amount of highly reactive ozone. This gas is a potentially dangerous pollutant in it's own right. Finally, there is some debate over the very effectiveness of ionizers, especially with certain types of particulates. (For a more thorough explanation of how ionizers work, see *Negative-Ion Generators* on page 558.)

Sometimes you can find negative-ion generators at local auto-supply stores that are designed to sit on the dashboard or the car's seat. However, these generally have plastic housings. In addition, there are mail-order sources for car ionizers. For example, the N-3 Car Ionizer is an extremely simple, tiny unit that somewhat resembles in appearance an old-fashioned vacuum tube. It's made to plug directly into the dashboard lighter, so it has no cord. This ionizer is available from **Real Goods**. Two other sources for similar ionizing units are **Gazoontite** which carries the Auto Ionizer and **BreatheFree.com** which offers the Whistler. The Zestron Automobile Model negative-ion generator is a more powerful unit. This particular device is sold through **Befit Enterprises Ltd.** which handles other car-ionizer brands as well.

Allergies and Driving

Those with conventional allergies can take some measures to make their time in their car more enjoyable. With allergies to pollen, if you're able to, choose days to drive when pollen counts are low (local TV weathermen often report pollen counts during the pollen season). All during growing seasons, keep your car's windows and fresh air vent closed as much as possible. Of course, you must still allow fresh air to enter periodically. By the way, wearing a dust mask can be helpful, too. (See *Personal Protective Gear* on page 264.)

To control dust-mite allergens, vacuum the car thoroughly and often. Choosing vinyl upholstery over cloth is best. (Leather would be a good second choice.) Vinyl can be wiped clean repeatedly with no damage. If you have cloth upholstery, you can cover the seats with yardage of untreated cotton barrier cloth. This will help seal out dust mites from new upholstery and seal in dust mites in old upholstery. Of course, you'll need to remove the cloth and wash it regularly in hot water. Sources for organic cotton barrier cloth include **Sleeptek Limited** (in Canada) and **N.E.E.D.S.** or **Furnature** (in the U.S.). **Janice Corporation** has untreated barrier cloth.

If pet dander is an allergenic problem for you, the best defense is never to travel with your dogs or cats. If you must take a pet to the veterinarian, use a small traveling crate specially made to hold pets. These are sold, or can be ordered, at most local pet-supply stores. If you have a sport-utility vehicle or station wagon, put the pet's travel crate in the back section away from the seats. Covering the crate with cotton cloth will help confine any airborne fur, saliva, etc. By the way, in this situation it's probably not best to use barrier cloth because it could restrict the pet's air flow too much. (See *Pet Carriers* on page 466.)

An obvious solution would seem to be a car air filter. If you decide to get one, make sure it's able to remove particulates (airborne particles such as pollen, dust, etc.) effectively. Many units are just too small, have weak fans, or are only designed to remove gases. So, be careful what you purchase. (See *Car Interior Air Filters* on page 379.) Ionizers can also work to remove some particulate matter from the air, but are probably much less capable than a good quality air filter. Then, too, ionizers have apparently not been proven effective with dust-mite allergens. Of course, as mentioned earlier, ionizers have other problems associated with them.

To cope with food allergies, you should, of course, bring your own beverages and snacks when traveling. Having a small cooler that's handy is a good idea. It can keep all your food items together in one place, as well as keep them at a cool temperature. Having a stocked cooler will also lessen the temptation to stop at a convenience store and succumbing to eating something that could cause problems later.

While admittedly challenging, traveling in your car can not only be possible, but even enjoyable, despite your allergies. What's needed most is proper planning and then following through using the best methods available to limit exposures to potential allergy-triggering substances.

CHAPTER 15: FIRE PROTECTION

Since the human race discovered fire, people have been afraid of uncontrolled blazes. Virtually all of us still are—and with good reason. Fire can quickly destroy our belongings and wreck our lives. Statistics reveal that home fires are the leading cause of accidental home deaths and that each year over 400,000 homes are damaged or destroyed by fire. Therefore, it's vital that every household be equipped with appropriate smoke detectors, fire extinguishers, and fire ladders that are handy and in good working order. So, in this chapter, these devices are explained, and buying sources are listed, as well as suggestions on escape plans, and more.

What is Fire?

To best know how to combat a fire, it's a very good idea to understand exactly what fire is. By simple definition, fire is a form of combustion that occurs when a material is ignited in the presence of oxygen, producing light, heat, and flames. Oxygen is required both to initially ignite the fire as well as to sustain it—even though the oxygen doesn't burn itself. On a molecular level, fires are actually rapidly occurring molecular chain reactions. Without oxygen, the molecular reaction stops. Therefore, depriving a fire of its chief oxygen source—air (which contains about 21% oxygen)—is one of the most basic fire-fighting approaches.

Another basic fire-fighting method is to introduce *fire-retardant chemicals*. Fire-retardant chemicals are designed to stop the fire's chain reaction by "mopping up" the extremely reactive *free radicals* (unstable atoms or molecules with unpaired electrons) that perpetuate an on-going fire. You see, in a fire, reactive free radicals grab electrons from stable molecules, making these donor molecules themselves into reactive free radicals, and so on. However, if fire-retardant chemicals "mop up" the free radicals, the chain reaction stops and the fire goes out.

While the explanation of what fire is may sound somewhat "dry" and benign, everyone knows the potential destruction that fires can bring about. Every year thousands of in-home fires burn furnishings, the structures themselves, and the occupants. However, fires also produce extremely dangerous but invisible *combustion gases*, as well as visible smoke. In many cases, the smoke and combustion gases, from even an extremely small, short-lived fire, can quickly spread throughout an entire house and become absorbed into virtually everything. Unfortunately, if you want to remove smoky odors from your belongs, it can be very difficult. Sometimes, however, *ozone* (O_3, a very reactive unstable form of oxygen) produced by ozone-generating machines is sometimes helpful in eliminating smoky smells (see *Ozone Generators* on page 557). Because of the inherent dangers of breathing ozone, this procedure should only be done by a professional, and while the house in unoccupied.

While the damage from smoke (and combustion gases) to a home's interior can be bad, the potential effects on the occupants from exposure to these airborne substances can be even worse. Interestingly, although it's dangerous to breathe the smoke and gases created by burning natural materials, it's far more devastating to inhale the extremely toxic substances produced by many synthetic materials as they burn. For example, certain man-made plastics, when they're burning, can create the extremely toxic gas *phosgene*, which has been used as a chemical warfare agent. It should be little wonder that the results of inhaling smoke and combustion gases from an in-home fire can include respiratory distress, severe lung damage, suffocation, and/or poisoning. Not surprisingly, far more people are harmed and killed by these combustion by-products than by burning.

Home Fire Preparedness

Remember: When it comes to home fires, you should be well-informed and prepared. While there is much information supplied on the topic in this section, also check with your local fire department. They'll likely have a number of excellent free booklets and fact sheets available on preventing and dealing with home fires.

Basic Fire-Safety Tips

Following are a number of safety tips that can help reduce the risk of fire in your home. Remember, prevention is the number one way to avoid a home fire.

Take all the clothes out of the dryer after the cycle stops. Keep appliances and power tools unplugged when not in use, and if you see or smell smoke near an appliance, unplug it immediately. Never trust a heat-producing device (such as an iron or automatic coffee pot) to turn itself off, especially if it has an internal clock or timer. Don't leave a stove or burner unattended, and don't wear loose-fitting clothes while cooking because they can catch fire more easily. Don't plug too many items into the same electrical outlet or circuit, and routinely check wires and cords for damage. Don't run an electrical cord under a carpet or rug because it could wear and short out. Leave plenty of space around heaters, fans, water heaters, and furnaces, and never store flammable materials nearby. In fact, you should always store combustible materials (including stacks of newspapers, or cans of gasoline) in a cool, well ventilated place, away from heat sources. Have your wood stove, furnace, water heater, and chimney inspected, cleaned, and maintained by a professional once a year. Finally, keep matches and lighters away from where children can get to them.

Escape Plans

Everyone should have a definite escape plan in case of a home fire. In actuality, there should be two plans for each occupied bedroom. One plan should be the "best route" with a second plan as an alternative back-up should the first escape path not be usable. In any case, all plans should eventually lead to a "safe meeting zone" where family members are to go once they're outside the house. This congregating area should be far enough away so that dangerous smoke, falling debris, or fiery splinters are unlikely to be a problem. A landmark such as a swing set or a mailbox are often easy spots to remember, and find, at such times. Once the routes have been determined, your family should go over these together regularly. Physically going through them is best. Using blindfolds from time to time can make everyone prepared to follow their route successfully, even during the low visibility conditions present during many home fires.

Importantly, while you're escaping, you should stay close to the floor. This is to avoid the most intense heat and the most noxious gases. Whenever a door is reached, it should touched to see how warm it is. If it seems warmer than it normally should be, open it very, very slowly. If the fire is on the other side, be ready to shut it immediately. If the door is hot, don't even attempt to open it.

It's significant to know that experts now believe you should not first call the fire department, or even 911. Neither should you get any possessions or pets. Admittedly, this is difficult to do. After all, these actions can seem, not only appropriate, but even obvious, automatic responses. Yet, research has shown that even partial seconds count in home-fire survival. Therefore, in most cases, when you see serious flames, get out! Of course, some minor fires can, and should, be put out quickly by yourself—for example a small grease fire in a pan can be stopped by putting a lid on the pan.

Escape Ladders

Something that too few homes have are collapsible fire ladders. This is unfortunate, especially for homes with bedrooms above the first floor. By having them, the possibilities of having safe, usable escape routes increases enormously and, therefore, your chances of survival as well.

Generally, home-fire ladders are made with metal rungs and heavy synthetic rope holding them together, and some means of quickly, but securely, holding the ladder to the interior side of the window sill. Often, this is done with metal brackets or hooks that are simply laid over the sill.

It's been suggested that *each* bedroom above the first floor have its own escape ladder. It should be stored under the bed so its out-of-the-way, yet handy. If you have an upper level that is used for living space, but not for bedrooms, having at least one on fire ladder on that floor is also a good idea.

When you purchase a fire ladder, make sure that it'll be long enough. Fire ladders do come in different lengths and it makes no sense to get one too short because you, or a family member, could become injured jumping from a last rung that's six or eight feet off the ground. You should also check to see what the ladder's weight limit is. Some fire ladders could break if a person climbing down is too heavy. Once you purchase your ladders, its probably a good idea for every family member (except those who are too ill, too disabled, too young, or too old to use one) to practice climbing down it. (Note: Absolutely DO NOT take needless risks! The point is to increase family safety, not cause potential harm.) By practicing in this way, there will be less panic if the time should come when a ladder is actually needed in an emergency.

To practice using an escape ladder, attach it to a *first* floor window have everyone try climbing out and stepping down to the ground until they're comfortable (or at least familiar) with the procedure. Having someone right outside the window during this practice time is an excellent idea, not only as a helpful coach, but as a "spotter" to prevent someone from slipping or falling. By the way, you must remember that having too many people on the ladder at one time could overload it and lead to equipment failure.

Because you shouldn't put your family at risk needlessly, you probably shouldn't practice escaping from a second-story (or higher) window. If everyone understands the procedure by climbing out of a first-floor window, they should be able to do the same from an upper story in an emergency. However, you could certainly include a practice drill involving pulling the ladder out from under the bed and *installing* it in an upper window.

To purchase a collapsible ladder locally, check at your building supply centers and hardware stores. Brands you might find are Kidde Fire Escape Ladder in 15' and 25' lengths (**Kidde Safety**). If you can't find them, your local fire department may know of a store that carries them. Of course, if you prefer, you can mail order escape ladders. **Improvements** carries both two- and three-story, lightweight, sturdy fire-escape ladders that are able to hold up to 1,000 pounds. These are made to fold compactly. From **One Step Ahead**, you can also get two- and three-story lightweight, sturdy fire-escape ladders that fold compactly. However, their rating is for 600 pounds.

Smoke Detectors

Smoke detectors are important. Even in homes where there are no combustion appliances, no tobacco smoking, and no burning candles or fireplaces, the threat of smoke from unplanned and unsuspected fires still exists. Fires that get started from lighting, electrical shorts, or when objects are too near electric stovetops, hot water tanks, and heating units can—and do—occur. Because smoke (and fire) are so dangerous, it's best to continually monitor your home for its presence with smoke detectors. Actually, in a great many locales, their installation is required by law. This is understandable because, after all, homes with working smoke detectors can reduce fatalities by up to 90%. When smoke is present and detected, these units will sound off loudly. (Some do other things as well.)

Many experts now believe that smoke detectors should be installed on each floor, including the basement, and outside bedrooms (in the hallway). A good location is on the ceiling, away from any air ducts or vents.

Be aware that there are two basic types of smoke detectors. Perhaps the most common variety is the *ionization unit*. These smoke detectors continually release *ions* (an ion is an atom or group of atoms with an electric charge) from an internal *radioactive component*. (Most ionizing smoke detectors use an isotope of americium, a decay product of plutonium 241.) If smoke is present, the smoke particles will attach themselves to these ions. When this occurs, it reduces the electric flow inside the detector which, in turn, sets off the alarm. The other type of smoke detector is the *photoelectric* or *optical unit*. These generate a tiny light beam. If smoke is present, the beam is either blocked or scattered, causing a change in the electric flow which triggers the alarm. It's believed that ionizing smoke detectors are better at detecting fast-flaming fires, while photoelectric models are generally better at detecting slow, smoldering fires, which is how most fires start. So, a photoelectric model can often detect a fire in the earlier stages.

Although the amount of radioactivity released during "normal operation" by ionization-type smoke detectors is tiny, there is some concern that during a fire, if the plastic housing becomes damaged, it could end up dispersing americium. In any case, it's probably a good idea to avoid having any radioactive sources in your home whenever possible anyway. Unfortunately, most smoke detectors available at local hardware stores are generally the radioactive type. However it's becoming easier to also find stores who stock nonionizing, photoelectric smoke detectors as well. Brands of nonionizing photoelectric models include **Kidde Safety** (they make a variety of detectors, some with Hush Buttons to silence nuisance alarms) and **BRK Brands, Inc.** (this company also makes several models). By mail order, you can obtain an EcoWork nonionizing, photoelectric smoke detector from **Karen's Natural Products**. This unit is apparently not set off by cooking smoke or high humidity. **Building for Health Materials Center** handles the BRK brand as well.

If you have smoke detectors in your home, be sure to keep them in proper working condition. For example, gently and carefully vacuum the exterior of photoelectric smoke detectors occasionally to remove any dust. You also should test all your smoke detectors weekly to see if the alarm is working properly. (Most units have a "test" button to press.) You can use your finger, or if the unit is mounted too high, you can use a broom handle.

It should be mentioned that some smoke detectors run by batteries, while others are designed to be wired into your home's electrical circuitry. (Some units will operate both ways.) If smoke detectors are required by law in your locale, the regulations often require that they be connected to the house's electric wiring. In units that use batteries, the batteries should be replaced twice a year.

New models of smoke detectors have now come out that have additional features you may want. For situations where bathroom steam or kitchen cooking causes a typical alarm to go off, you can now choose one designed to work in those situations. In addition, some smoke detectors come with lights that activate to help guide you during a fire, while others combine two or more monitoring systems. For example, some units are both smoke detectors and carbon-monoxide detectors. Some use both photoelectric and ionizing smoke detection monitoring systems. Still others combine all these features. One, Kidde Nighthawk Combination (**Kidde Safety**) has both smoke and fire detectors, a carbon-monoxide detector and a voice that announces when necessary, "fire," "carbon monoxide," or "low battery!" Of course, the more features, the costlier the detector.

Home Fire-Fighting Strategies

At the moment they start, many types of *very small* fires can often be extinguished quickly by smothering. This is simple oxygen deprivation. In practice, a pot lid can often quickly put out a grease fire in a pan. Also, a boot or shoe can effectively stifle an escaped fireplace ember that has landed on the carpet. Or a throw rug can smother a small fire.

Of course, many people believe water is the best and simplest means to put out a fire. However, water has its limitations. With some types of fire, it can actually make a bad situation worse. For instance, water should never be used on grease fires because it can cause dangerous splattering. Also, water should never be used to douse fires involving electric wires or appliances because the risk of electrocution is far too high.

Baking soda is another substance often considered an easy, universal fire stopper. In fact, baking soda has been used for fighting home fires for decades. Baking soda works fairly effectively on grease fires as well as on electrical fires, but it's not very effective on burning plastic, paper, fabric, or wood. If you plan to rely on a full box of baking soda for fire fighting, it's necessary to actually have at least one full large box (or better yet, several) conveniently on hand specifically for that purpose. So, don't accidentally use it for something else, or it won't be there when you need it to put out a fire.

In-Home Sprinkler Systems

A fire-fighting technology that has been used successfully for decades in institutions and commercial buildings involves sprinkler systems. Now, they're starting to be installed in homes—usually in new, more expensive homes. However, they can make good sense (and cents) for more modestly priced houses, too. Research has shown that buildings with sprinkler systems experience very little damage as compared to structures without them. In fact, most end up with only very minor interior burn and smoke damage and, of course, water damage from the activated sprinklers. Another plus is that a sprinkler system is always ready whether you're home or not, awake or asleep, or have forgotten to put new batteries in your smoke detector. Generally, homes with professionally installed sprinkler systems pay less for fire insurance.

Home sprinkling systems use very basic technology that has really changed very little over the years. Professional contractors place plumbing lines through the ceilings and connect them to the building's main water line. At intervals, heat-sensing sprinkler heads are attached to the water lines. Then, the system is filled with water. (The lines are always filled with water.) Whenever the air near the sensor-sprinkling head reaches about 150°F, a low-melting point material starts to liquefy, allowing the sprinkler to immediately spray water. (By the way, a 150°F temperature is often reached near the ceiling in only a matter of seconds after a fire has been ignited.) It's the sensor-sprinkler's quickness of action, right in the vicinity of the fire, that makes home sprinklers so incredibly effective.

Once a fire has been put out, the company that installed your system will have to come back and replace any sensor-sprinkler heads that have been activated. The newest models have automatic shut-off valves, and some systems will automatically transmit an alarm to the local fire station.

If you're interested in having a sprinkler system in your home, a recent estimate concluded that it would probably cost between $1.00 and $1.50 per square foot for a home under construction, and double that for an existing home. Usually, most local companies that install systems in commercial buildings can also do residences. To find one, look in your telephone classified directory. In addition, someone at your local fire station may know of a nearby company that can do the work.

Portable Fire Extinguishers

For effective fire fighting, peace of mind, and sometimes to meet legal requirements, or to lower your insurance premiums, it's important to have portable fire extinguishers handy and available for quick use throughout your home. Quick use is imperative because these portable devices work best on very confined, small fires. They aren't intended for much more than that. Many experts believe that, ideally, you should have a portable fire extinguisher placed in your kitchen, your garage, and your home workshop, as well as have one in the central portion of your house. It's also suggested that, if your home has several levels, you should have at least one extinguisher on each floor.

It's extremely important to have the right kind of fire extinguisher in a particular area. An extinguisher should be designed to cope with the specific types of fires likely to occur in the locations they serve. After you've purchased and conveniently located all your fire extinguishers, it's important to make sure that you and all your family members know how to actually operate them. It's vital to read the label directions thoroughly before a fire occurs. However, you SHOULD NOT test-spray an extinguisher. You only need to understand how to use it.

Commonly, modern portable fire extinguishers consist of a canister filled with an *extinguishing agent*, a pressure-producing device, and a nozzle or hose for dispersal. To work properly, many extinguishers must have adequate internal pressure. Therefore, you'll want to check all your fire-extinguishers' pressure gauges at least once a year. If you find the pressures inadequate, call your local fire department for advice on where to get your fire extinguishers recharged. Sometimes, the fire department itself will recharge an extinguisher for free, or at a minimal cost, as a public service.

Fire Type Classifications

Although virtually all home fires are rapid molecular chain reactions requiring oxygen, there are certain differences too, based on exactly what material is being burned. However, research has shown that there are only three basic in-home fire classifications. Research has also determined which particular fire-fighting strategies work best against each of these three fire types.

The three fire classifications are known as *Type A*, *Type B*, and *Type C*. Type A fires involve the burning of common combustible materials such as wood, paper, fabric, many plastics, and rubber. They are typically extinguished by the heat-absorbing effect of water (or water-based liquids) or by smothering the fire with a dry chemical. Type B fires are burning flammable fluids including gasoline, oil, kitchen grease, tar, oil-based paints, and also natural gas. These fires are usually extinguished with dry chemicals, carbon dioxide, foam, or a liquefied gas (also known as halon). Type C fires involve burning electrical equipment such as wiring, electronic devices, and electric appliances. Type C fires must be extinguished with something that won't conduct electricity (in order to avoid an electrocution hazard) such as a dry chemical, carbon dioxide, or halon. (There is also a *Type D* fire, that involves burning metals, but this is unlikely in a home.)

It should be noted that fire extinguishers capable of handling the A and B classifications are also rated for the size of fire they can adequately handle. In other words, a extinguisher designated 2A has double the fire-extinguishing capacity of a 1A model. When a fire extinguisher is labeled for Type C fires, it simply means the *extinguishing agent* won't conduct electricity. There are no numerical prefixes used to rate Type C extinguishers. Often, fire-prevention specialists advise that your kitchen fire extinguisher be a BC type, while the others in your home be multipurpose ABC units. Of course, buying an extinguisher with a higher AB numerical prefix (such as 2A40BC) has more fire-fighting capacity than one with a lower numerical prefix (such as 1A10BC).

Fire Extinguisher Types

The first truly modern portable extinguishers were *soda-acid extinguishers*. These were designed with a sodium-bicarbonate-and-water solution in a container mounted under another container containing sulfuric acid. When the extinguisher was turned upside down, the contents of the two containers mix and formed carbon-dioxide gas. This pressurized gas then forced a liquid out through the hose to extinguish the fire.

Today, soda-acid extinguishers are still found in some older buildings. However, for the most part, they've been gradually replaced by other types of extinguishers. The following sections will discuss the kinds that are now commonly available for home use.

Water Extinguishers

Water is still the most commonly used extinguishing agent—but only for Type A fires. It cools the burning material and smothers the fire by depriving it of oxygen. Simple ways to use water in the home are with a bucket or a garden hose.

Ammonium Phosphate (Dry Chemical)

Ammonium-phosphate dry-chemical fire extinguishers are generally called *multipurpose extinguishers*. They have ABC ratings, and therefore will work against all home fire classifications. (Numerical prefixes, if present, depend on the particular model.

With these extinguishers, *monammonium phosphate* is the extinguishing agent. When it's dispersed, it's a fine powder. Therefore, you should keep the dispersal spray away from your face to avoid inhaling these dusty chemicals. Because this fine chemical powder can be broadly distributed, cleanup can sometimes be tedious after spraying it. A dry-chemical ammonium phosphate extinguisher will put out an electrical fire but it will most likely ruin any electronic equipment with which it comes in contact.

Sodium Bicarbonate

Sodium bicarbonate fire extinguishers simply use baking-soda powder as their *extinguishing agent*. These units are rated BC for grease, oil, and electrical fires. (Numerical prefixes, if present, depend on the model.) Sodium bicarbonate extinguishers create no odor, and clean up problems are minimal. As stated earlier, baking soda doesn't work against Type A fires, that is wood, paper, fabric, or plastic fires.

Carbon Dioxide

Carbon dioxide fire extinguishers are also rated for Type B and Type C fires. When carbon-dioxide units are activated, they release extremely cold, snow-like carbon dioxide particles. These smother the fire and then immediately vaporize. Carbon dioxide extinguishers pose no odor or cleanup problems. However, because they are not recommended for Type A fires, their effectiveness is limited.

Halon

Halon fire extinguishers Are designed to extinguish Type B and Type C fires. They have been used in computer rooms and on airplanes because, unlike multipurpose dry-chemical extinguishers, halon does not damage electronics and it leaves no residue. Obviously, this is quite a plus. However, these extinguishers contain *liquefied halocarbon gases* (carbon compounds containing chlorine or fluorine, etc.), which have been shown to damage the Earth's protective ozone layer. As a result, since 1994, halon fire extinguishers have no longer been allowed to be sold to the general public. However, those purchased before the ban, can be still be used. So, if you have one in your home that's in working order, and its use will not conflict with your eco-philosophy, it can still be a usable, home fire-fighting tool.

Home Fire Extinguisher Suggestions

For your kitchen, the sodium bicarbonate fire extinguisher, First Alert Kitchen KFE2S5 (**BRK Brands, Inc.**), has been highly recommended in several consumer magazines. These units come in white canisters with a convenient mounting bracket. Kidde Kitchen (**Kidde Safety**) also comes in a white decorator container and contains sodium bicarbonate. These brands are often available at local hardware and discount stores. If you're unable to locate them, call the companies for the nearest dealer.

An interesting option for your kitchen is the Pyrocap B-250 (**Pyrocap International Corp.**) extinguisher. This unit has a stainless-steel case. It's filled with one liter of a nontoxic liquid able to control grease and cooking-oil fires. It's said to "convert burning oil into soap," so it's obviously easy to clean up after it's been dispensed. You can order this extinguisher directly from the manufacturer.

For other areas in your home and garage, dry-chemical ammonium-phosphate extinguishers having ABC ratings are probably the best choice. First Alert Multi-Purpose FE1A10G (**BRK Brands, Inc.**) has been cited as a particularly good unit. This model is rated at 1A10BC. A similar extinguisher is the Kidde Full Home (**Kidde Safety**). Both of these are generally sold in hardware and discount stores. If necessary, call the manufacturers for their nearest dealers. While chemically sensitive people might be bothered by the powder dispensed by these extinguishers, combustion by-products, smoke, and a fire itself would be of much greater concern.

An extinguisher whose agent is likely to be more tolerable, but less able to handle all types of home fires is the Fire Cap. This extinguisher is described as using a nontoxic, biodegradable fire suppressant agent for A or B fires but not C fires. Therefore, it could be used against common paper, wood, and fabric fires as well as against grease and oil fires. However, it could not be used to for electrical fires. The Fire Cap is handled by **Allergy Relief Shop, Inc.**

CHAPTER 16: UNDERSTANDING PEST CONTROL

One of the biggest concerns in many households is pest control. No matter whether you're rich or poor, no one wants pests in their home. Therefore, this chapter will offer a basic understanding of the preventive steps everyone can take to lessen the chances that pests will ever become a problem. It'll also explain how, even if you don't want them, having a few certain types of "pests" may not be such a terrible situation after all.

Simple Pest-Preventive Measures

Unfortunately, some pests are not only unsightly, but also destructive, allergenic, or disease carrying. And, of course, virtually no one willingly chooses them as house mates. Yet, perhaps unknowingly, many homes almost seem to put out pest "welcome mats."

If you don't want pests sharing your home, the first line of defense is to do everything possible not to attract them. This means there should be no conveniently accessible foods in your house that pests would find appetizing. Therefore, all your tables, countertops, and floors should be kept free of crumbs and spilled liquids. Also, all your food should be stored in tightly sealed containers inside closed cabinets. Furthermore, to deter clothing moths (that can devour wool and other fabrics) store your clean, natural-fiber clothing in tightly sealed bags, etc. So as not to readily invite termites, you should keep dead shrubs and woody debris away from your house foundation.

You should also keep in mind that your home should not have appealing habitats for pests to live and nest in. Therefore, clean all the excess clutter from your home and thoroughly dust, clean, and vacuum frequently. One very important thing to do is to be sure to eliminate any moisture problems in your home. This is because many household pests are extremely fond of taking up residence in damp environments. Therefore, be sure to fix any leaky pipes, wet basements, damp crawl spaces, and overly humid rooms. (For information on high humidity and ventilation fans, see *High Humidity* on page 530.)

Finally, your house should be as completely sealed from the outside as is practicable. This will make it extremely difficult, if not impossible, for most species to enter in the first place. To do this, make sure any cracks in the foundations, walls, and attic spaces are sealed (see *Caulkings* on page 287). Also check to see that all the exterior doors close completely when shut. If they don't, you'll need to add weather-stripping, or perhaps perform some repairs. In addition, you'll want to check that your window screens are in good condition and repair, or replace, them if necessary.

Coping with Pests

If, despite your best efforts, pests still take up residence inside your home, the next step is deciding whether you can tolerate their presence. Actually, some creatures are classified as "pests" even though they may be quite beneficial. This is certainly true for some small, non-dangerous spiders. Other pests such as silverfish, which admittedly look rather disgusting, are apparently harmless. At their worst, silverfish usually only eat some paper or glue.

However, while a nonpoisonous spider or a few silverfish may be acceptable, if large populations develop, you may decide they all have to go. After all, a swarm of anything in your home is usually not a tolerable situation. However, if you're not allergic to something like dust mites, large numbers of these microscopic creatures would unlikely cause any problems, or even be visible. (Actually, researchers only discovered they even existed about thirty years ago.) On the other hand, pests such as rats, wouldn't be welcome even if only one found its way into your home. When pests must be removed from residences, they're usually either killed or taken outside. Using techniques (or chemical compounds) to stop the reproduction or maturation of the next generation is a third option. For the most part, this approach isn't widely used, although such methods are now available for combating certain pests.

In most pest-control situations, *extermination* is the management method chosen. This means that something deadly to the pest is employed. This may not be as ominous to human and planetary health as it first sounds. For example, it may simply involve recruiting the pest's natural biological enemy—such as obtaining a cat to control mice. Unless you have cat-related allergies, this extermination method would be benign to both you and the environment. Another safe approach would be to use sticky fly paper whose non-toxic glue permanently traps bothersome flying insects. Unfortunately, though, many extermination methods involve the utilization of potentially dangerous, but legal, synthetic organic chemicals, such as the termiticide Dursban.

Typical Pesticides

Chemical pesticides derived from nature have been popular for centuries against many types of household pests. However, in more recent times, scores of petroleum-derived substances that are toxic to pests have been introduced. Unfortunately, it was not until after their introduction, and widespread use, that the effects of many of these newer pesticides on human beings was more completely understood.

Early Pesticides

These days, most Americans commonly use chemical applications to solve their household pest problems. Actually, this is not a new concept. In the first century AD, the ancient Greeks had already recognized that *arsenic* (a toxic mineral element) would exterminate many pest populations. In the Orient, the Chinese were also using arsenic compounds as well as various natural-oil extracts. By the 1700s in Europe, both tobacco juice (whose nicotine is poisonous) and *pyrethrum* (chrysanthemum flower heads) were found to be effective pesticides.

Because of great advancements in chemistry, the 1800s saw the introduction of pesticides created from copper oxide and a combination of copper and arsenic salts. Later, during the 1930s, pesticides based on *inorganic heavy metals*, such as lead and mercury, were developed. However, these heavy-metal compounds were usually not used around homes, instead they were used on crops growing in the fields. In any case, because they accumulated in the soil and were only effective at levels that were found to be toxic to non-pest species, they have since been virtually abandoned.

Modern Organic Pesticides

The so-called modern pesticide era began with the creation of *synthetic organic pesticides* that eventually replaced the overtly toxic heavy-metal pesticides. However, it's now known that they, too, have potentially serious negative health consequences.

Modern Organic Pesticide Types

Many modern pesticides are known as *organic pesticides*. In this case, "organic" doesn't mean pure, natural, and untainted as it does with organic food. As applied to pesticides, the word organic means that these compounds contain carbon atoms (generally occurring in chains), and it's these carbon atoms that happen to be the basis of the molecules making up all living organisms. (Actually, organic pesticides also contain hydrogen and may include other elements such as oxygen, sulfur, phosphorus, chlorine, bromine, or nitrogen). Most organic pesticides are man-made compounds derived from petroleum, which itself ultimately originated from microscopic aquatic organisms that lived millions of years ago.

Surprising to many people, organic pesticides first began to be used in 1920s. However, it was not until 1939 that organic pesticides became popular. That was when the organic compound *DDT (dichlorodiphenyltrichloroethane)*, (which had first been synthesized back in 1874) was observed to kill most pests while seemingly not harming humans or the environment. Soon, DDT was sprayed on almost everything, and everyone, with a pest problem—or a potential one. It became known as an inexpensive "chemical wonder." Its success inspired the creation of other *organochlorine pesticides* (organic pesticide compounds containing chlorine)—primarily between 1940 and 1970.

Other organic pesticides, classified as *organophosphate* types (organic pesticide compounds containing phosphate), were introduced after World War II. Interestingly, many of these formulations were based on Nazi research.

Modern Organic Pesticides' Toxic Consequences

The effects on humans, and other non-pest populations, of being exposed to some of the older, more natural, but still toxic, pesticide compounds (such as arsenic and heavy-metal-based compounds) soon became apparent—and fairly well known. However, this was not true with many of the synthetic organochlorine pesticides. Unfortunately, they've now been found to have toxic side effects that, for years, were unsuspected by most people. It was Rachel Carson's book *Silent Spring*, originally published in 1962, that helped arouse public concern over the possible environmental consequences (to birds, etc.) of these supposedly "safe" pesticides.

Unfortunately, using synthetic, organic chemicals to eliminate pests has not only harmed nature, but has had a human toll, something that has also become evident. Symptoms vary as to dose, chemical composition, type, length of exposure, and the individual. Certain organochlorine pesticides have been associated with the onset of *chloracne* (a severe, and often chronic, type of acne due to chlorine exposure), lowered sperm counts, *peripheral neuropathy* (nerve damage in the limbs, feet, or hands), and some forms of cancer. New research now indicates some organic-chemical pesticides may actually mimic natural estrogen compounds. It's speculated that such estrogen-like action may lead to hormonal disturbances, which in turn could lead to a variety of abnormal conditions. (This could account for the lowered sperm counts, by the way.) Despite more product warnings and governmental regulations, occupational physicians continue to see patients who have become ill on the job due to the toxicity of these modern pesticides.

Although most pesticide-poisoning cases are, in fact, linked to actually working in pesticide-producing chemical plants, or to using agricultural pesticides on crops, that's not the full extent of the problem. Some pesticide-toxicity cases have turned up in homeowners, and their families, after their houses were treated for termites, or other common pests. Most of these situations are probably the result of pesticide applications that were incompetently done. However, in at least some cases, illnesses have occurred despite "correct" usage. Interestingly, a number of individuals with Multiple Chemical Sensitivity (MCS) firmly believe that they first acquired their condition as a result of a specific organic pesticide application that either occurred at their home or at their workplace.

Despite having some knowledge that synthetic organic pesticides can be harmful, it seems most Americans still routinely turn to them to solve their household-pest predicaments. It's easy to understand why. Consumer-oriented "bug hotels," "insect bombs," rodent pellets, and anti-flying-insect aerosol cans are conveniently sold in colorful, handy-sized packages in nearly all hardware, grocery, and discount stores. These products require little physical effort, or money, to quickly kill many problem creatures. And for widespread or serious pest problems, most people still contract pest-management companies to spray, inject, or fumigate their homes with synthetic organic pesticides.

By the way, if you'd like to determine if typical pesticides are present in your home, you can purchase a SpotCheck test kit for surfaces. These are sold by **Befit Enterprises Ltd.** Home test kits for water-soluble pesticide in the air, water, and soil are available from **American Environmental Health Foundation**. If you have any air-quality specialists in your geographic area, they may be able to do more thorough testing. To find one, look in your classified telephone directory or ask your local board of health for suggestions.

Alternative Pest-Control Measures

If you want to use safer, less-toxic pest-control alternatives, there are quite a few available. In the following sections, you'll be introduced to a number of them.

Neutralizing Allergenic Properties of Pests

In some situations, where the main concern about a pest's presence is the allergic reactions it causes, the use of simple *allergen neutralizers* can be used. This is most commonly done against microscopic dust mites. What an allergen neutralizer does is to *inactivate* offending allergenic properties. In reality, what this means is that an active agent (commonly a tannic-acid/water solution which can be derived from black tea) is used to alter the structure of certain proteins making up both dust-mite body parts and dust-mite feces. Once these proteins have been changed, the allergic person's immune system no longer recognizes them as "dust-mite" proteins, proteins that it's already determined are "the alien enemy," and so ignores them. Therefore, the dust-mite *antibodies* (specialized molecules that, in allergies, bind themselves to allergens) remain dormant and no *histamines* (highly unstable, reactive compounds released to destroy them) are released. Thus, the dust-mite allergic person won't experience the typical dust-mite-allergy symptoms that histamines can cause, such as inflammation, swelling, etc. in the respiratory system. (For a more comprehensive description of allergies and allergic responses, see *Allergies and Asthma* on page 49.)

For some allergic people, the use of allergen neutralizers is all they feel is necessary to combat the dust mites in their homes. However, these products must be sprayed over carpets and upholstery every 60 days (they don't seem particularly effective on thick mattresses). Then, too, tannic acid sprays have the potential to stain light-colored fabrics and fibers. It's not surprising that many people with dust-mite allergens try multiple approaches, for example by regular and thorough home cleaning, as well as using some type of allergen neutralizers. (For more on tannic-acid neutralizers, see *Dust Mites* on page 410.)

Alternative Pesticides and Capture Methods in General

Although most people still prefer the quick, sure effectiveness of synthetic, organic pesticides, growing numbers of people prefer to use less-toxic means. As a result, pesticides derived from natural plant extracts are again becoming more available. These include chrysanthemum-derived *pyrethrum* (powdered chrysanthemum flower heads) and *pyrethrin* (a liquid extract from chrysanthemum-flower heads), as well as a variety of tobacco-based products whose active ingredients are *nicotine compounds,* and *d-Limonene* (derived from orange peels). Such plant compounds, while usually biodegradable (*i.e.* pyrethrin is rapidly broken down by ultraviolet radiation—in other words, by exposure to sunlight) and are much less toxic to humans than synthetic organic pesticides. However, they are, after all, active substances and should not be used indiscriminately.

Take pyrethrin for example. Pyrethrin works as a natural pesticide, apparently because it can chemically break down a specific enzyme (acetyl cholinesterase) present in animals (Note: Here the term "animal" represents the broad class of living things). Acetyl cholinestrase's job is to counter, or "turn off" acetyl choline, a nerve stimulant. However, after pyrethrin has destroyed the acetyl cholinesterase, nerves no longer have the means to turn off, ever. The pest dies as a result. Not surprisingly, pyrethrin (and other plant-derived pesticides) could affect pets and humans, at least to some degree. Nicotine, is another type of nervous-system agent. In this case, the nicotine has the ultimate effect of causing paralysis. This compound (which can be absorbed through the skin) has long been known to cause respiratory failure and paralysis in humans. So powerful is nicotine that it seems only two or three drops of it, in a purified form, placed in the mouth of an adult human, will quickly prove to be fatal.

Fortunately, pure concentrations are rarely encountered, but it's clear that nicotine should be used wisely. Finally, the compound d-Limonene is a natural solvent capable of destroying the waxy coatings of insect respiratory systems. For humans, it can be a skin irritant.

In addition, relatively safe powders such as *boric acid, diatomaceous earth* or *DE* (a fine silica powder made up of the cell walls of microscopic algae), and even *talc* are regaining some popularity as more-natural pesticides. Again, these are much safer than most synthetic organic pesticides, but they should also be used with care. Boric acid acts as a type of *digestive poison* (a lethal substance that must be ingested to work). It can also sometimes act as a *contact poison* (a lethal substance that acts on, or is able to penetrate through the outer surfaces, to work). However, according to the **National Pesticide Telecommunications Network (NPTN)**, which is an **EPA (Environmental Protection Agency)** sponsored service, researchers are unsure exactly how boric acid and other boron-containing pesticides actually work. Naturally, such a powder should not be used in a manner, or stored, where children or pets could ingest it. Diatomaceous earth, is a *desiccant*, or drying agent. It kills by literally drying up body moisture. This substance is not something you want to inhale (especially if you have asthma), even though it would take much more to dry up a large animal, like a pet or human, than a tiny insect. DE could still be quite irritating and has the potential to cause *silicosis*, a lung disease. Heat-treated diatomaceous earth increases the chances of acquiring this condition, so if you decide to use DE, make certain it's not heat treated. Talc is used to block the *spiracles* (body pores used by insects for respiration) of ants, so they suffocate. In humans, breathing enough talc and cause *talcosis*, a lung disease.

In certain circumstances, high heat or electric shock are being utilized as pest eliminators. Also, a wider range of trapping products are now being marketed, and homemade trapping methods are being devised and used. These include snap traps, live-capture traps, special sticky-substance traps, *pheromone* traps (traps that have compounds in them that mimic natural attractant chemicals to capture mature adults, usually males), and even lights over water. All these particular approaches generally target specific pests. They can be placed and removed at any time, and, best of all, they have little capacity to inadvertently create human or environmental side effects.

Alternative Pest Deterrents in General

Using *pest deterrents*—which are meant to discourage the presence of pests, but are not designed to kill or capture them—is another less-toxic approach to dealing with household pests. As you might suspect, these are nearly always less toxic than using synthetic organic pesticides. Therefore, *oil of pennyroyal* (extract from a mint-family plant) and *eucalyptus oil* (oil from eucalyptus trees) are regaining favor. With these particular oils (and similar ones), it's their rather intense natural odor that tends to act as an effective pest repellent in certain situations. (Of course, they aren't uniformly effective against all pests.) Unfortunately, some humans, especially many sensitive individuals, also find their odor repelling, as well as persistent.

Another method of deterring pests is using *physical barriers*. Of course, screening and netting are obvious examples of how simple nontoxic mesh fabrics can easily bar mosquito, spider, and other insect entry. However, there are also less-well-known barrier approaches. For example, it's been shown that having a layer of 12-grit sand surrounding your home's foundation can act as a fairly effective obstacle to subterranean termites. (For specifics, see *Subterranean Termite Alternative-Control Methods* on page 431.)

Other types of pest deterrents include *ultrasonic units,* which have been promoted to ward off a wide variety of household pest species. Ultrasonic units are said to work because the ultra-high-pitched whine they emit is almost unbearable to most pest species but isn't heard by humans (or cats and dogs). Ultrasonic units vary in size from small battery-operated pendants to fairly large, freestanding, plug-in models. The very small pet pendants are marketed primarily as flea deterrents, and the similar-sized models for people as mosquito deterrents. However, research has established that ultrasonic pest controls are not effective against fleas, rodents, bats, etc. In fact, the Federal Trade Commission has even stated that they are ineffective.

Implementing Household Pest-Control Measures

Knowing when and how to use alternative pest control measures is imperative, if you are to safely and effectively solve a pest problem. Sometimes, though, there are roadblocks which you'll encounter in your attempts at using them. You may even find you have to use a more toxic procedure. In any case, it's best to be as well-informed, and as well-prepared, as possible.

Alternative Pest-Control Information Sources

If you have decided you want to use less-toxic pest-control measures in your household, it's important to have alternative home pest-management information on hand. That way, you'll know what to do immediately if a particular pest shows up. While this book can act as a good basic source for the most common pests, and the most common less-toxic solutions, you may also want to have more thorough literature on hand (or know where you can get it quickly), to consult when necessary.

Some examples of good alternative pest-control publications are the low-cost, well-researched, multiple-page, household-pest fact sheets available from the **Washington Toxics Coalition**. From the **National Pesticide Telecommunications Network (NPTN)**, you can order low-cost **EPA (Environmental Protection Agency)** booklets. An excellent, small, inexpensive paperback to consider owning is *Least Toxic Home Pest Control* by Dan Stein. Your favorite bookseller may have it. If not, you can order it from the **Washington Toxics Coalition**. One of the most complete low-toxicity pest manuals is the voluminous 715-page hardback, *Common-Sense Pest Control* by William Olkowski, Sheila Daar, and Helga Olkowski. You may be able to find it in your local library's reference collection.

By the way, a book you may want to have in your home collection that was written by a physician is *Designer Poisons: How to Protect Your Home From Toxic Pesticides* by Marion Moses MD. The author, by the way, belongs to The Pesticide Education Center. Again, you should be able to get a copy through your library or favorite bookseller.

For even more written information, you might want to contact your county extension agent, who sometimes has free informational materials on less-toxic pest control. Finally, you'll definitely want to check your local libraries and bookstore to see what appropriate books they currently have.

If you find you need personal, one-on-one help, you may want to call the **Washington Toxics Coalition**. This group is a "non-profit organization dedicated to preventing pollution in industry, agriculture, and the home." It offers a "Toxic Hotline" telephone service, but only to answer questions not already covered in their publications. By the way, if you join them, you'll receive their quarterly newsletter, *Alternatives*. Another excellent source of information is the **Bio-Integral Resource Center** (**BIRC**). This organization (of which the authors of *Common-Sense Pest Control* are an integral part) offers less-toxic pest-control consultations to its members. It describes itself as a "non-profit organization dedicated to providing practical least-toxic methods for pest management." Annual membership includes your choice of quarterly newsletters: *IPM Practitioner* (for professionals) and *Common Sense Pest Control Quarterly* (for consumers and non-professionals). Membership also allows you to call them for specific pest-control answers.

In addition, you may want to call the **National Pesticide Telecommunications Network** (**NPTN**) Hotline. This is a free, **EPA** (**Environmental Protection Agency**) sponsored service that can answer many of your questions. It's staffed by pesticide specialists with access to a wide range of information. By the way, at the same location is the **National Antimicrobial Information Network** (**NAIN**). Finally, you'll want to check your classified phone directory to see if there's a less-toxic pest-control company nearby. Someone there may be knowledgeable, and be able to quickly perform the alternative pest control work you desire.

Obstacles to Using Alternative Pest Control

Unfortunately, at this point, it must be noted that sometimes you come up against obstacles that make it difficult to use the safer pest-control alternatives you'd like to, especially against termites. For example, some banks, mortgage institutions, and insurance companies will *only* authorize the use of the familiar types of chemical termiticides. After all, these business people want to make sure that your home will continue to be in good shape; they have a real economic stake in it. Therefore, understandably, they tend to want to use the "tried and true" means that seem to have worked well to protect other homes they've mortgaged, insured, etc. in the past.

To get around this problem, you can use literature provided by the books and organizations listed above to thoroughly and technically, make your case. If that doesn't work, you may have to spend some time finding another mortgage lender and/or insurer that'll agree with your less-toxic approach.

Another obstacle you may come across is that the safe, effective, alternative control measures you want to use haven't yet been legally classified as "registered pesticides" in your state. They may, in fact, be effective and less toxic, but unless they are registered, a pest control professional may not want to, or legally be able to, use them. Finally, in some cases, it may be most effective to spot-treat with a toxic synthetic organic pesticide to successfully eliminate a particular infestation.

All this is not meant to discourage you from trying to use less-toxic alternative pest-control measures, but rather to let you know of the possible problems you may encounter. The good new is, if you're determined to use less-toxic means to control your household pests, in most cases you'll be able to do so with very satisfactory results.

When Typical Pesticides Must be Used

Now, in those (hopefully rare) situations where you have little choice but to use typical pesticides, don't feel you've lost control of the situation. Instead, take it upon yourself to actively make sure that only a very reputable, licensed, highly-trained professional does the job. That means you'll want to talk with the pesticide company management, see their certification, and request that someone who has successfully done the work for several years perform your job, too. You'll also want to know of any written guarantees, warranties, and bonding that covers the success or failure related to eliminating the pests, and also how damages to your home or to your family because of misapplication, negligence, etc. would be covered.

By the way, it's a good idea to inquire at your local better business bureau to see if any complaints have been registered against the particular company your interested in using. (Note: Sometimes, you may not get specific reasons for the complaints. However, it's often good to know if others were dissatisfied *for any reason* when it comes to using a firm that utilizes potentially dangerous pesticides in or around your home.).

When you decide on a company, make sure that you emphasize that you want as little pesticide as necessary used—to do the job effectively—and no more. Then, too, no one should be in the home when the treatment is being employed. This is especially important for chemically sensitive or asthmatic persons who, by practicing prudent avoidance, may want to stay away for several additional days or weeks.

So, in the end, have toxic pesticides applied only "with your eyes wide open," knowing you did everything you could to make it as safe for your family and home as you could. After that, don't think negatively. In other words, don't let your apprehension be the cause for stress and other health problems that the pesticide itself may not have played any direct role in causing. It is possible that the pesticide, if applied correctly and sparingly, will not cause harm to anyone except the pests it was meant to harm. Then, the next time a minor situation comes up, you may be able use less-toxic methods.

CHAPTER 17: CONTROLLING SPECIFIC PESTS

This chapter will offer some specific alternative methods for controlling specific types pests. Most of the information concerns pests you're likely to encounter indoors. The very last section, however, covers alternative personal pest protection you may want to try outdoors.

Important Note: Read all product labels and literature carefully before using a pest-control product, or having it used, in your home, and follow all the instructions exactly. Store all products so that children and pets will not have access to them. Wear appropriate protective gear including dust masks, waterproof gloves, respirators, etc. (See *Personal Protective Gear* on page 264 and *Waterproof Household Glove Suggestions* on page 137.) Very sensitive, highly allergic, or asthmatic individuals should be especially prudent.

Simple Alternative Pesticide Sprays

Often it's convenient to have a simple spray on hand that you can use against a variety of common household pests. Of course grocery stores and hardware stores are well stocked with synthetic petroleum-derived products and, for many years, these were about the only options available. Fortunately, a few simple, natural-ingredient sprays are now being marketed that are usually much safer for you and your family. Yet, these will not be as easy to find as "standard" insect-killing products.

If you do decide to use an alternative insecticide, there are some things to keep in mind. First, even though they pose less danger, it's important not to use any product designed to kill indiscriminately. Also, these are sprays that, as a rule, should be spritzed only onto surfaces—not into the air. Finally, remember to read their package directions carefully and to store them securely away from children and pets.

If you're interested in purchasing an alternative pest spray, one to consider is Concern Multi-Purpose Insect Killer (**Necessary Organics**) This is a pyrethrin (derived from chrysanthemum flowers) product that kills by acting on pests' nervous systems. Look for the Concern line at your local alternative grocery store, or contact the manufacturer for the nearest dealer.

Another product you may want to have on hand is Orange Guard Pest Control which contains d-Limonene (derived from orange rinds). Orange Guard apparently kills by destroying the waxy coating on insect respiratory systems. A plus for this product is that it's said to be safe enough to use "even in the pantry." Be aware that, as you might suspect, Orange Guard has an "orangey odor" that could be bothersome to citrus-allergic people. To find it, look in area alternative grocery stores. By mail order, you can get it through **Real Goods**. By the way, a similar-type product is Concern Citrus Home Pest Control (**Necessary Organics**). This is a water-based product also containing d-Limonene. The manufacturer says that d-Limonene "breaks down the *keratin* coating" (the outer waxy coating) as well as "disrupts the ability of insects to find their nests again." As with the Concern pyrethrin product mentioned earlier, you may find it at local alternative grocery stores. If not, you can call the company for a nearby outlet that handles it.

Victor Flying Insect (**Woodstream Corp.**) can also be a good choice. It uses sodium lauryl sulfate (a common ingredient in shampoos) "to clog insect spiracles," and mint oil to "over excite the nervous system." This biodegrade insecticide apparently kills in seconds and will remain active for up to four weeks. By the way, this aerosol has a less-toxic carbon-dioxide propellant and, like all Victor-Poison-Free products, has Green Cross Certification from Scientific Certification Systems to be "poison-free, thus eliminating accidental poisonings." Again, check local alternative grocery stores, or call the company for the nearest buying source.

For other alternative multi-species pest-killing sprays, check local alternative groceries and plant nurseries. (Note: Asthmatics should probably not use these products themselves.)

Controlling Specific Household Pests

The following sections will cover less-toxic treatment suggestions for some of the most common household pests. The pest-control options mentioned are, for the most part, ones that sensitive individuals have often found both effective and tolerable. However, keep in mind that these are only suggestions—not absolute recommendations that you must rigidly follow. Every pest situation is unique. Therefore, it is you yourself who must ultimately determine the extent of your particular pest problem, what solutions you feel would be acceptable and, in some cases, finding out what regulations and restrictions will apply to your situation. Remember, killing anything is serious business. Therefore, you'll always want to proceed carefully and with forethought regarding your own personal program for household pest management.

Carpenter Ants

Carpenter ants can sometimes cause extensive damage to the wood in homes. To combat this pesky insect, this section will explain a little about their lifestyle, and some ways of eliminating their infestations.

Carpenter Ant Traits

The term carpenter ant is actually a generic name for several large ($^1/_4$–$^1/_2$" long) ant species, which are found in many areas of the U.S. Although their color varies with the species, solid black is probably the most common. As it turns out, most of these ants like living in or near wood.

Interestingly, if a carpenter-ant colony decides that the wood they want to live in happens to be your home, you might hear them moving around within your walls. More likely though, you'll find some fine wood dust on your floors, which they have pushed out of their tunnels and nests. It seems that most people assume that the carpenter ants are eating their house. Actually, unlike termites, they can't digest wood. They only tunnel into the wood to meet their housing needs. Their preferred diet is sweet substances such as nectar.

As a rule, carpenter ants are especially attracted to damp wood. This may be because it's simply easier to bore through than dry wood. However, they will go ahead and dig their way into dry wood if they find they need to. Carpenter-ant infestations often spread through the creation of new *daughter* or *satellite nests*. Therefore, the original source of the *daughter nests* in your home probably came from a *mother nest* outside. It's likely the ants entered your house through a crack in an outside wall.

Suggested Carpenter-Ant Control Measures

Before killing the ants inside your home, there are other measures to take so you're less likely to have a reinfestation. One is to follow the ants back to where they enter and leave your home, because the nest could be outside the home's structure. From there, you can then follow them back to their place of origin, usually in dead wood that isn't too far away. Because they tend to be active at night, locating an outdoor nest can be rather challenging. If you are able to find it you'll need to destroy it using one of the products described below, or by pouring boiling water on it. You'll also want to find and repair all cracks and separations in your home's foundation—not just the ant's single entry point. This will help prevent any future carpenter-ant problems because there will no longer be an easy way through which they can pass in and out.

To rid your home of carpenter ants, you'll first need to locate their nest. You may be able to do this by listening for them as they scurry around (a stethoscope can help), or by seeing wood-dust piles. If you can get to the nest, some of the products below can be used. If the nest is hidden inside walls, you will most likely need to hire a pest-control professional.

Using Pyrethrin Against Carpenter Ants

If you have access to the nest, you can use a pyrethrin (a chrysanthemum flower head extract) spray such as Concern Multi-Purpose Insect Killer (**Necessary Organics**) on each nest. To find a local dealer, you'll need to contact the manufacturer.

If you want a professional do the job for you, consider having them use Tri-Die (**Whitmer Micro-Gen Research Laboratories, Inc.**) Tri-Die is a powdered-pyrethrin aerosol, whose ingredient list does include some petroleum-derived solvents and propellants. It comes in a handy metal spray can with its own special injection attachment. (Note: Tri-Die is not sold directly to consumers and must only be applied by pest control professionals.)

It should be added that if you have adequate access, you may be able to use a simple, pure pyrethrum powder. In doing this, perhaps a bulb-applicator might be helpful. You might be able to get one at an area hardware store or local pest control company. EcoZone

Roach, Ant, Flea, Silverfish Insect Powder (**Natural Animal Health Products, Inc.**) is one product you might try for this. This 100%-pyrethrum product is sometimes sold in alternative grocery stores. You can also order it from the manufacturer and from **Bio Designs**. By the way, wearing a dust mask is important when applying it. (See *Personal Protective Gear* on page 264.)

Using Boric Acid Against Carpenter Ants

If you have adequate access to the nest, you could perhaps use a bulb-sprayer (available at hardware stores and pest-control firms) to apply a boric-acid powder (a boron compound). A popular one is Roach Prufe (**Copper Brite, Inc.**). Roach Prufe has "an electrostatic charge that makes it cling to insects" as well as a small amount of added dye. This, and other boric-acid preparations, can be applied (so that children and pets won't get into it) to carpenter-ant trails as well as to the "mother nest" outdoors. Keep in mind that whenever you apply boric-acid powder, you should wear a protective dust mask to prevent inhaling it. (See *Personal Protective Gear* on page 264.) If you're interested in trying Roach-Prufe, it's usually sold in hardware stores. You can also order it from **American Environmental Health Foundation**.

A boron-based compound in solution that is sprayed into the infested wall can also be a good tactic. Usually, this will require a professional to do the work for you. One good product they could use is Tim-bor (**U.S. Borax, Inc.**). This is a fine, white powder that will require mixing with water. A simpler method is to spray Perma-Dust Pressurized Boric Acid Dust (**Whitmer Micro-Gen Research Laboratories, Inc.**) into an infested wall cavity. This particular aerosol product comes with its own special injection attachment. Perma-Dust's drawbacks are that it contains some petroleum-derived solvents and propellants. A borate product that consumers can use themselves is Termite Prufe (**Copper Brite Inc.**) which contains disodium octaborate tetrahydrate. This comes as a dry powder that must be mixed with water. The manufacturer says it can be brushed on, injected, or sprayed (a garden sprayer often works well). They also note that this formulation "does not penetrate the skin or cause irritation." You may be able to find Termite Prufe at local hardware stores (Ace Hardware stores should carry it, or they can order it for you) and building-supply centers. If you can't locate it, call the company for the nearest dealer or you can mail-order it from **American Environmental Health Foundation**.

Other Alternative Products Against Carpenter Ants

A product you may want to try on an occasional carpenter-ant problem is Victor Poison-Free Ant (**Woodstream Corp.**). This is a mint-oil and sodium-lauryl-sulfate solution in an aerosol container using carbon dioxide as the propellant. It kills quickly and will last up to four weeks. You can spray this product inside your walls if a nest is hidden. To buy this Victor product, check area alternative grocery stores, or call the company for the nearest dealer. Obviously, this will have a minty odor.

Asthmatics should not be using this or any other aerosol product themselves.

Clothing Moths

As most people already know, damage to natural-fiber items can be extensive if proper preventative steps are not taken against clothing moths. Fortunately, there are simple, safe approaches that will usually deter them.

Clothing Moth Traits

The term *Clothing moth* is applied to several small moth pest species. Of these, perhaps the most common is the *webbing clothing moth*. The adults of this particular variety are a pale golden color with red head hairs. It's not commonly known, but it's the clothing moth's larvae—not the winged adults—that do the damage to your clothing. And the $1/2$"-long cream-colored larvae have the ability to eat *all* natural fibers, not just wool. However, despite their capacity to bite off and digest these various fibers, the moth larvae would rather eat the oils and food particles found on them.

By the way, in addition to the information below, you may want to purchase the low-cost 16-page fact sheet, *Clothes Moths—Prevention and Control*, available from the **Washington Toxics Coalition.**

Wool and Clothing Moths

Why is moth damage generally associated with wool? Actually, for a several reasons. One is that wool contains the natural oil lanolin (sometimes called sheep grease). Lanolin is an appealing larval food—a food the other natural fibers lack. As it turns out, when the larvae attempt to eat the tasty lanolin, the wool fibers get devoured, too. In addition, wool items are usually cleaned less often than their machine-washable counterparts such as items made of cotton or ramie. As a result, human body oils and food crumbs tend to accumulate on wool clothing more than on other fibers. Body oils and food crumbs are very appealing to the larvae, so as they attempt to feast on these, the wool fibers get eaten, too. Finally, wool and moth damage are linked together because wool clothing and blankets are often stored in closed drawers or chests for months at a time. This creates the ideal conditions for adult female moths to lay their eggs: dark, undisturbed places on or near potential food sources. Once the clothing-moth larvae hatch, their nest (your wool items with the oils and crumbs) becomes both a serving platter as well as dinner.

Safely Preventing Clothing Moth Damage

To counter any potential clothing-moth damage, be sure to clean your natural-fiber items before you store them. Then immediately after they've been cleaned, place them into tightly sealed bags, containers, or storage units. This is, of course, especially important with your wool items.

However, if for some reason, you're unable to clean and quickly store your natural-fiber items in sealed containers as an alternative you can tumble them in your clothes dryer for about 15 minutes approximately once a month. You could also simply vigorously shake them out. Either of these methods can be effective deterrents because clothing-moth eggs are not firmly attached to the fabric fibers they're residing on. Thus, they usually fall off rather easily. In addition, high heat in a clothes dryer will apparently kill moth eggs, live larvae, and any adults as well. However, high heat might shrink or tighten some natural fibers even if they're dry, so a low-heat setting may be better for certain items.

A product you may want to use to protect your woolens is The Clothes Moth Alert (**Verdant Brands**). This is a small cardboard carton that uses *pheromone* lures to capture the moths. (Pheromones are substances emitted by creatures that elicit certain responses. Many are sex attractants.) Apparently, there are no poisons or pesticides used. The Clothes Moth Alert may be found in local hardware stores, discount stores, or alternative groceries. If you can't find them, contact the manufacturer for a local dealer.

Concerns About Using Certain Clothing Moth Deterrents

Many people believe they can avoid clothing-moth damage by simply storing a special deterrent substance along with their stored items. This would seem to be an easy solution. Unfortunately, neither cedar wood, cedar oil, nor potpourri will kill, or effectively repel, clothing moths. Worse, using *mothballs* (which are commonly made from *pardichlorobenzene (PDCB)*, *naphthalene*, or *camphor*) can be potentially dangerous to both humans and the environment.

Of course, all these popular anti-clothing-moth measures give off strong odors. After all, their intent is to be extremely unpleasant for moths to be around. However, what's often not seriously considered is how tenaciously the fibers of your clothing, and other stored items, will absorb and hold onto these very same smells, especially from chemical mothballs. This could make your belongings quite bothersome and perhaps even intolerable to you, particularly if you're a sensitive person. Unfortunately, even repeated cleanings and airings can't always remove all these odors.

Cockroaches

Most everyone abhors cockroaches. To combat them, here are some less-toxic methods you can use.

Cockroach Traits

Cockroaches are flat, long-legged insects that vary in size. However, many are about $1/2$" long. Although there are a number of species, only a few varieties typically become household pests. These make nests in your home, scavenge for food, and leave their feces behind.

While there are several varieties in the U.S. (including several new immigrant species in certain locales) the most common variety of indoor cockroach in the U.S. is still the brown German cockroach. Fortunately, cockroaches aren't a continuous problem in most houses. (Exceptions may be some houses in warm or hot climates, poorly kept homes, and certain multiple-dwelling buildings.) However, a large percentage of American homes will likely become infested at one time or another for various lengths of time. Because it's been estimated that a single pair of cockroaches has the potential to produce 500,000 offspring within one year, it's understandable why this can happen.

If possible, cockroaches are pests you should try to completely eradicate from your home. Besides being unsightly and destructive to food supplies, there is growing suspicion in the medical community that cockroaches are probably linked to the onset of some human illnesses. Recent research has also suggested that allergies to cockroaches, and their feces, may be far more common than previously thought.

Using Boric Acid Against Cockroaches

Once they've gotten in your home, cockroaches often find your kitchen particularly appealing. The food, the convenient dark places to nest and hide, and moisture from perhaps under-sink pipes or water lying in automatic defrost refrigerator drip pans (among other damp places), make for ideal cockroach conditions.

To rid your kitchen of cockroaches using less-toxic means, try putting boric-acid powder in a small insecticide bulb dispenser. You may be able to buy one of these at a local hardware store or at a pest-control company. Once you've filled the bulb, you simply squeeze it to blow the powder into crevices along the baseboard molding, or under cabinets. It's especially important to do this behind the stove and refrigerator.

Boric acid is a white crystalline substance. It's commonly derived from borax. You can use the pharmacy-grade boric-acid powder (which is primarily sold to be mixed with water to make a mild antiseptic) available at some drugstores, or a lesser-grade dyed boric-acid powder packaged as a pesticide. One popular brand of boric-acid pesticide you might already be familiar with is Roach-Prufe (**Copper Brite, Inc.**). Interestingly, this product has "an electrostatic charge that makes it cling to insects" as well as a tiny amount of added dye. It's often available in hardware stores, although you can call the manufacturer to find the nearest dealer if you're having trouble locating it. You can also order it from **American Environmental Health Foundation**. Important note: Whenever you apply boric-acid powder, you should wear a protective dust mask to prevent inhaling it. (See *Personal Protective Gear* on page 264.)

If you plan to use boric acid against cockroaches, be aware that it will not instantly solve your cockroach problems; it will take a certain amount of time to become effective. This is because the boric-acid powder must first be tracked back to the cockroach nest on the legs and bodies of some of the insects. From these carrier roaches, it will eventually end up getting on nearly all the other roaches in the nest. Then, as they begin to preen, they'll ingest the powder. Because it's toxic to their systems, they'll finally die.

As it turns out, boric-acid powder lasts almost indefinitely, so reapplications are generally unnecessary. When you are confident that the infestation is over, you can leave the powder in the crevices where it will act as a preventive. However, if you prefer to clean it up, you can vacuum the crevices using an appropriate attachment while wearing a protective dust mask. You could then thoroughly wash baseboard areas with clear water and a sponge while wearing waterproof gloves. (See *Household Waterproof Glove Suggestions* on page 137.)

By the way, if you prefer that a professional to do the work for you, it's suggested that they use Perma-Dust Boric Acid (**Whitmer Micro-Gen Research Laboratories, Inc.**). This product is 99% boric acid with no added dyes.

Important note: Although boric-acid powder is much safer than typical petrochemical insecticides, it is certainly not a totally harmless substance. Therefore, don't let children and pets get access to it.

Using Sticky Roach Traps Against Cockroaches

An alternative to using boric-acid powder against cockroaches is to use *sticky roach traps*. These are usually just small cardboard boxes, or sometimes metal containers, with an entrance hole and a gluey substance inside, along with a roach-appealing bait. (Note, some sticky roach traps may have a pesticide within them as well.) Once the roaches go inside, they usually become permanently stuck. If you'd like to use this approach, you can try placing three or four traps in each problem area in your home. As they fill up, they should be replaced.

You should be aware that sticky roach traps will not have any effect on the insect nests themselves. Therefore, these traps are more of a reduction measure than an elimination method. The Victor Poison-Free Roach Magnet (**Woodstream Corp.**) sticky roach trap is one brand that's apparently both safe and effective. It's a *pheromone* trap that uses compounds that mimic natural attractants to lure cockroaches in, and sticky glue to hold them. In addition, the entry has a slippery silicone-coated edge so any "unstuck" roaches find it nearly impossible to escape. Victor Poison-Free Roach Magnets are available at some local hardware and alternative grocery stores, or you can call the company for a nearby dealer. Cockroach traps by mail order are available from **Solutions**.

Plaster of Paris Against Cockroaches

A very old but effective method to kill cockroaches is with *plaster of Paris*. Plaster of Paris is a heavy, white, gypsum-containing powder and, as most people know, when it's mixed with water a heat-producing chemical reaction occurs that results in the formation of a very hard material. You can get plaster of Paris at most local hardware stores.

Here's one way to use plaster of Paris for cockroach control. Mix it in a bowl with an equal amount of white flour. Then pour a small amount into some plastic or metal jar lids (or other flat containers). Then place the lids under the sink, behind the refrigerator, etc. Be careful not to place any plastic where it could get too hot, melt, or catch fire.

Once in place, the cockroaches will find the flour and eat the plaster of Paris along with it. Then, the reaction will begin as soon as it comes into contact with the insects' body fluids. Soon, there will be dead cockroaches with hardened plaster of Paris in their stomachs. Any live roaches that get back to their nest will have the deadly mixture on their legs and bodies, and it will get passed onto other roaches.

When the infestation is over, remove the lids and clean up any powder that has spilled. Also, this mixture should not be placed where children or pets could have access to it.

Other Methods to Control Cockroaches

Some people believe that *ultrasonic emitters* are a good method to repel, and therefore rid your home of, cockroaches. However, it seems that there is no evidence that these units have any value against most pests. Built of plastic, and broadcasting a high-pitched whine (beyond human-hearing range), they're generally plugged into outlets, though some use batteries. If you'd like to experiment, **Improvements** and **Harmony** handles them. You can also often find them in hardware stores and building centers.

An usual approach to cockroach control is electrocution. The Zapper sends out a weak electrical charge that's apparently just strong enough to kill cockroaches. This small, flying-saucer look-alike can be ordered from **Bio-Designs**.

Dust Mites

Those with conventional household allergies commonly react to dust mites—or more accurately—to dust-mite body parts and especially to their feces. In fact, some researchers have found that most individuals in the allergic population react to dust mites. Common reactions include sneezing, itching eyes, night coughs, and itchy, runny, or blocked nasal passages. Dust mites can also cause *atopic dermatitis* (eczema), a chronic inflammatory skin condition often found in families with histories of allergies. Furthermore, roughly 80% of asthmatics react to dust-mite skin-provocation testing. Fortunately, for the 70% of the population without allergies, the presence of dust mites in their homes generally causes no health problems. And since they are microscopic, they're not even noticed.

This section, however, is written for those households where controlling dust-mite allergens is essential. It includes a variety of methods for reducing mite populations and controlling their allergens. Other information that you may want to use can be found in the Winter 1999 *Commonsense Pest Control Quarterly*. This back issue, which was devoted entirely to dust-mite control, can be purchased from the **Bio-Integral Resource Center**.

In the end, you must make the decision which methods will be most helpful and applicable in your own home. First, however, it's a good idea to have an understanding of dust mites themselves.

Dust Mite Traits

Dust mites are tiny (less than $4/100$" long) *arachnids* (creatures related to spiders and scorpions) which live off human skin flakes. So unnoticeable are they, that they were only discovered to exist about thirty years ago. In the article, "How to Control Dust Mites" that appeared in the Spring '99 *Human Ecologist,* author Preston Strugis noted that there are actually several household dust-mite subspecies. As with most mites, they begin as eggs, go through a series of life stages including larval and nymph, and after more molts ultimately reach adulthood after about six weeks. One particular subspecies, *Dermatophagoides farinae,* is able to go through a "resting phase" which itself may last weeks or months. When adulthood is reached in any species, each fertilized female is able to lay about four-dozen eggs. Then, this cycle repeats in a new generation.

Dust mites eat human skin flakes, something we all shed all the time. So, dust mites live and breed in places where human skin flakes accumulate—naturally, that includes homes. One estimate is that 90% of all houses have dust mites living in them. (Note: If you want to know for sure if your house has them, and at what level of infestation, Aclotest dust-mite detection kits, that you can use yourself, are sold by **Allergy Clean Environments**.)

Favorable locales for dust mites include bedding, carpeting, and soft furnishings. Surprisingly, your bed likely contains around 10,000 dust mites. Having a higher indoor humidity will tend to increase, not only dust-mite populations, but also their production of feces. Therefore you should avoid humidifiers. To control existing moisture, try increasing the *ventilation rate* (the amount of air exchange into and out of a structure) in your home. This means installing and using a range-hood fan, bathroom fans, utility-room fans, and other devices, to expel moisture from your home. If necessary, also use a dehumidifier. (For more specific information on controlling high humidity, see *High Humidity* on page 530.)

By the way, you should be aware that live dust mites rarely cause allergic reactions. That's because they're relatively heavy and do not become airborne easily. Then, too, dust mites on carpets and fabrics cling so tenaciously to fibers, they can't even be vacuumed up. However, dead dust-mite body parts, and dust-mite feces, are unattached, extremely light in weight, and they can become airborne easily, where they are inhaled. These, especially the feces, are what cause most of the negative reactions in susceptible individuals.

Because people will always shed dead skin flakes, these creatures are going to be present in most homes. Therefore, control means significantly reducing their numbers, not eliminating them. One way to control them is to replace soft, difficult-to-clean items with hard, easy-to-clean ones wherever possible. This could mean having vinyl, ceramic, or hardwood floors installed instead of carpet, and hard-surfaced seating, instead of soft upholstered furniture. (See also *Decorating for Allergic People* on page 329.)

Using protective encasements on mattress and pillows can also be critical. These can stop dust mites from infesting new items and seal-in dust mites in old ones. Replacing pillows twice a year is another very positive step. Of course, washing your bedding as well as rugs, curtains, etc. regularly, is also essential. (See also *Allergies , Bedding, and Bedrooms* on page 223.)

Another control option includes applying substances that can kill dust mites in carpeting and upholstery. Plus, proper air filtration can help reduce the quantity of dead dust-mite body parts and feces in the air. In addition, there are methods to neutralize the dust mite's allergenic properties, so even if their body parts and feces are present, they're unable to provoke allergic reactions.

Obviously, dealing effectively with dust mites requires comprehensive management using, perhaps, a variety of approaches. Unlike ridding your home of sugar ants or flies, which may infest your kitchen periodically, and are usually quickly eliminated, dust-mite control typically requires an on-going, rigorous effort throughout your home. Admittedly, this can seem daunting. However, by making the necessary changes in decor, cleaning procedures, lifestyle, etc., many dust-mite allergic people are able to live quite comfortably in their houses.

Using Borate Compounds Against Dust Mites

Perhaps one of the safest and most effective means of controlling dust mites in carpeting, and in some soft upholstery, is to use borate-containing substances. These kill by acting as digestive poisons.

One borate product you may want to try is Ecology Works Dust Mite Control (**Ecology Works**). Developed in conjunction with researchers at the University of California and Wright State University, it is formulated with disodium octaborate, an **EPA (Environmental Protection Agency)** approved dust-mite killer. (This powdered substance is related to borax and boric acid that have been used to kill cockroaches for years.) In this product, both acidic and alkaline powdered borate compounds are present; the combination results in a neutral pH. Highly soluble, Dust Mite Control is usually used in a cleaning solution in an extraction-type carpet-cleaner. (See *Rug & Carpet Shampooing & Wet-Extraction Cleaning* on page 158.)

To use Dust Mite Control, the manufacturer suggests mixing 1 cup in 1 gallon of carpet-cleaning water/detergent solution. Wearing waterproof household gloves is a good idea when doing this. (See *Household Waterproof Glove Suggestions* on page 137.) Then, clean your carpeting as usual. In the process, the Dust Mite Control's borate compounds are forced deep into the carpet fibers where they bond with them, so much so it seems they can't be removed even by normal vacuuming. Meanwhile, the deep cleaning itself removes any existing dust-mite body parts and feces. After cleaning, the residual borate compound saturates any food (skin flakes) left in the carpet to kill any remaining dust mites before they can re-infest the freshly the cleaned environment.

It should be noted that, initially, the moisture put into the carpet from the cleaning will actually cause any surviving dust mites to quickly multiply. However, after a couple of weeks, they should start dying off. By eight weeks, they the mite population should be tremendously reduced. By the way, **Ecology Works** guarantees one treatment to be effective for six months.

If you're interested in using Dust Mite Control, you'll find that a 2.6-pound package will treat 1300 sq. feet of carpet. If you hire a professional cleaning service to clean your carpets, they can apply it with a pump sprayer. Dust Mite Control can be ordered from **Allergy Clean Environments** and the manufacturer. A similar product, with the name of Acarosan, is available from **eMD.com** and **Allerx**.

Incidentally, Dust Mite Control was suggested by the **Bio-Integral Resource Center** in their Winter 1999 *Commonsense Pest Control Quarterly* issue. (This organization's mission is to use less-toxic pest-control measures.) Also, when Dust Mite control was reviewed by the California Environmental Protection Agency, the "toxicity registered so low as to have an insignificant exposure risk associated with application." However while this, and most other borate-containing products, are generally much safer than typical pesticides, you should still store any unmixed powder in such a way that children and pets can't get into it.

Using Diatomaceous Earth Against Dust Mites

For carpets, it's been suggested by some that a very light application of *diatomaceous earth,* or *DE,* can be helpful in killing live dust mites. This is possible because DE is a *desiccant* (a drying agent), able to literally dry up and destroy the outer waxy coating on a dust mite's body. One manufacturer's representative suggested that to use diatomaceous earth, you simply pour a tiny amount out onto the carpet, dip a broom into it, and then work it across the room brushing it in and moving the pile as you go. As little as 5 ounces should do as much as 1,000 square feet. (Supposedly, it's safe to walk on immediately after treatment.) After 48 hours, the desiccating effect will have done its work, so you should then vacuum. It's absolutely essential to remember that treated rooms must be vacuumed *thoroughly* to remove, not only any remaining diatomaceous earth, but all the dead mites. Otherwise, dust-mite body parts will still be present to become airborne, thus creating a greater problem for the dust-mite sufferer than before the diatomaceous earth was applied.

Sources for diatomaceous earth include Natural Animal Diatom Dust Insect Powder (**Natural Animal Health Products, Inc.**). This can be purchased from the company or from their dealers which include **TerrEssentials, Priorities, Karen's Natural Products, Allergy Relief Shop, Inc.**, and **Simmons Natural Bodycare**. (Note: Not all dealers stock it.) Concern Diatomaceous Earth is handled by **Frontier Natural Products**. Still other sources for diatomaceous earth are **American Environmental Health Foundation** and **Bio Designs**. This last mail-order company has it in both one- and five-pound bags.

It should be noted that there are important concerns to address with diatomaceous earth. First, when applying it you must wear an effective dust mask so you don't inhale any of it. (See *Personal Protective Gear* on page 264.) This substance is a silicon-containing dust that can be irritating, and has the possibility of causing *silicosis,* a lung disease. Furthermore, don't use heat-treated diatomaceous earth which apparently could increase your chances of getting silicosis. Finally, it should be noted that there's a rather strong opposing view to using diatomaceous earth for dust-mite control. These individuals believe that, since this product is applied as a dry desiccating powder that can become airborne, it is not the best choice for asthmatics, or those with respiratory problems, even if a "healthy" person does the application for them. Finally, make sure to store DE where no children or pets can get into it.

Using Benzyl Benzoate Against Dust Mites

Benzyl benzonate has been used in veterinarian and human medicine as a topical mite-control preparation for years. It was even used on U.S. military troops. However, in these applications, it was used as a mite repellent, not as a mite-killing agent.

Though not currently on the market, AllerCare Dust Mite Carpet Powder and AllerCare Dust Mite Allergen Spray for Carpet and Upholstery (**S.C. Johnson & Son, Inc.**), both used benzyl benzonate as their active ingredient. They also had the addition of a synthetic scent. (A company representative said that the perfume helped mask the odor of the benzyl benzonate.)

Unfortunately, some consumers reported having asthma attacks and other respiratory problems after using these products. As a result, in January 2000, after the urging of the

EPA, the manufacturer issued a complete recall, and removed both from production—even though the negative effects supposedly only affected a small percentage of people.

Incidentally, the manufacturer suggested that the problem was due to consumers reacting to the level of fragrance in the products—something many sensitive people have trouble tolerating. (See *Problems with Scents* on page 72.) In addition, as reported in the Winter 1999 *Commonsense Pest Control Quarterly*, benzyl benzonate doesn't appear to be terribly effective in killing dust mites in carpeting. And it is even less so on mattresses. Because it has usually been used as a mite repellent, in reality, it may simply work best in that mode, and not as potent dust-mite killer.

In very high concentrations benzyl benzonate could cause convulsions and loss of limb control, according to the **National Pesticide Telecommunications Network (NPTN)**, an **EPA (Environmental Protection Agency)** sponsored program.

While these products are not available as this book goes to press, they may be reintroduced at a future time, in a revised formulation. If so, you will have to decide for yourself if they are right for you.

Cleaning to Control Dust Mites & Dust Mite Allergens

One of the easiest, and best, ways to control dust-mite allergies is to always keep your home clean. That's because, it's been estimated that one gram of house dust (about a half teaspoon's worth) can contain 250,000 fecal pellets, thousands of dust-mite body parts, and perhaps a thousand live mites, too. Therefore, thorough, effective dusting and vacuuming is essential. Of course, this is much more likely to be accomplished in a home decorated so it can *really* be cleaned. That means avoiding carpeting and soft upholstered furnishings whenever possible, and having washable window treatments, rugs, etc. (See also *Decorating for Allergic People* on page 329 and *Allergies, Bedding, and Bedrooms* on page 223.)

Whatever you use for dusting, it must be able to grab and hold onto dust particles, not just move them around. Your vacuum cleaner must be a powerful portable unit with excellent filtration, or a central vacuum unit that vents to the outdoors. Only these kinds of vacuums will efficiently remove the accumulated dust-mite debris while not exhausting it back into the living space. By the way, you should be aware that, on fibrous surfaces (carpets, curtains, soft upholstery, etc.), vacuuming up live dust mites is virtually impossible because their tiny claws grasp so well. (For more on proper dusting and vacuuming techniques, suggested products, and buying sources, see *Dusting* on page 140 and *Vacuuming* on page 144.)

It's also best to buy only washable bedding items. As has been noted before, using mattress and pillow protecting encasements are a good idea too. Ones made of untreated, 100%-cotton barrier cloth (a special, tightly woven fabric) can help seal out dust mites from infesting new bedding, or seal in dust mites and their allergens in older bedding. Plus, being all-natural items, they won't outgas synthetic odors. Then too, having washable, 100%-cotton slipcovers for your soft furniture (if you choose to have upholstered pieces), is also beneficial. All these should be laundered regularly. (See also the appropriate sections in *Chapter 12: Home Decorating*.)

An excellent source of information on controlling dust-mite allergens through cleaning, is the free, 35-page, booklet entitled *Clean and Healthy Strategies for Today's Homes: Allergies and Asthma Reference Manual* available from **The Soap and Detergent Association**. A much shortened, 14-page, abridged version called *Clean and Healthy Strategies for Today's Homes: Managing Allergies and Asthma* can be directly downloaded from their website.

For additional information on cleaning for dust-mite allergy control, you'll need to read the sections *Household Cleaning for Allergic and Asthmatic People* on page 140 and *Laundering for Allergic People* on page 122.

Neutralizing to Control Dust Mite Allergens

Another approach for controlling dust-mite allergies is to *neutralize* their innate allergenic qualities. This means that, even if dust-mite body parts and dust-mite feces are present, once a neutralizing agent has been applied, their reaction-provoking capacity will have been thwarted. Neutralization works because it's a *denaturing* process. In denaturing, a protein (allergens are often proteins) is subjected to heat, acids, or alkaline chemicals so it no longer has its original "nature." In other words, the protein's innate qualities, properties, and characteristics (which the allergic person's immune system normally reacts to) are no longer recognizable. Therefore, the allergic person's immune system simply ignores the denatured protein's presence, and no allergic symptoms are experienced.

There are now neutralization products available that you may want to try. Most are tannic-acid solutions, often at a 3% concentration. By the way, not only will these relatively mild acidic preparations neutralize dust-mite allergenic proteins, but those of cat dander, mold, and others as well.

One product in this category is Allersearch X-Mite (**Allersearch Laboratories**). This is a moist powder whose ingredients include fine cellulose and tannic acid. The manufacturer recommends that it should be sprinkled onto carpets and rugs and brushed into the fibers, then vacuumed up when dry. After sixty days, they advise spraying with the Allersearch ADS Spray (**Allersearch Laboratories**). Then the application of both products, in an alternating cycle, should repeat. A plus for this particular line is that it's unscented. If your interested in purchasing Allersearch spray and powder, they're sold by eMD.com, **Priorities, BreatheFree.com, healthyhome.com, Allergy Clean Environments, The Allergy Store,** and **Allerx**. From the **Inner Balance** catalog, you can get Allermite, another brand of anti-allergen spray.

Incidentally, if you prefer, you can make your own neutralizing agent at home. It's been suggested in *Better Basics for the Home: Simple Solutions for Less Toxic Living* by Annie Berthold-Bond that all you have to do is brew one cup of strong black tea, strain it, cool it, and pour it into a spray bottle. The black tea and water creates a dilute tannic-acid solution that can be sprtized onto your carpet. (By the way, this book should be available in your library or from your favorite bookseller.)

Unfortunately, tannic-acid neutralizers are not *the* solution to household allergens. For example, they're apparently not too effective on thick items, such as mattresses. Another problem is that they can stain white or light-hued fabrics. Plus, they can sometimes damage water-sensitive items, including silk, the fibers of Oriental rugs, and some woods. Finally, neutralizers will need to be continually reapplied about every two months.

Air Filters to Control Dust Mite Allergens

Efficient room and whole-house *particulate* (minute particles) air filters can be helpful in controlling dust mite allergens. If the filtering media is fine enough, then the tiny airborne dust-mite body parts and feces will be trapped. Certainly *HEPA* (high efficiency particulate accumulator) filters should be able to do this job. However, it must be remembered, HEPA filters can add their own odors from the synthetic resins used to hold their fiberglass filtering fabric together. Some sensitive people, therefore, find they have trouble tolerating HEPA filters operating in their homes. Another problem is that HEPA filters are often noisy because it takes a powerful fan to force the air through the minute openings in the filtering fabric.

In any case, no filter can completely solve household allergen problems. At best, they can only reduce allergen concentrations. Other approaches, such as thorough cleaning, or using a borate compound to kill live dust mites, are probably going to be necessary as well.

By the way, *negative-ion generators* (units that emit free electrons that attach to some airborne pollutants and pull them out of the air) have been touted as good for people trying to control their allergies. However, they've apparently not been shown to be particularly effective in dust-mite allergen control. Furthermore, they can add highly reactive ozone into the air. This is not something people should breathe, especially those already with inflamed respiratory systems. For more on filters and negative-ion generators, you'll want to read *Chapter 23: Improving Your Indoor Air.*

Fleas

Fleas can be extremely irritating, and their infestations can sometimes be difficult to eliminate. Although it may take persistence, fleas can often be controlled without resorting to powerful synthetic organic chemicals.

Flea Traits

If you own a pet, especially a cat or dog that is allowed both indoors and out, fleas can become a problem in your home—particularly in hot seasons, or year-round warm climates. When you spot what's been termed "salt and pepper" around your pet's bedding, it's likely that a flea infestation is already in full swing. You see, the "salt" grains are white flea eggs and the "pepper" particles are bits of dried blood.

Fleas are tiny ($4/100$–$16/100$" long), wingless, bloodsucking insects. The adults are equipped with powerful back legs for leaping. Fleas are common parasites on warm-blooded animals. Dog fleas are similar, but slightly larger, than cat fleas. No matter what kind of fleas they are, they can infest your pet's bedding, as well as your carpets, rugs, and furniture.

Adult fleas actually bite their host, seeking blood. After an adult female has consumed blood, she'll often lay eggs (usually less than ten) on or near the puncture site. The dried blood provides meals for the soon-to-hatch larvae. While this sounds like a rather small scale attack, it's been estimated that a single adult female flea has the potential to produce 160,000 offspring in just over two months!

Most people who are bitten by fleas find it irritating and soon develop small red bumps. However, some individuals experience an allergic reaction, in which swelling and other symptoms result. In addition, some human diseases can be transmitted by certain types of fleas. For example, the bacterial toxin causing bubonic plague was transmitted by rodent fleas. Luckily, the flea species associated with dogs and cats usually aren't transmitters of human diseases.

Flea Control through Special Pet Care

To minimize flea problems in your home, there are several measures you may want to try. If you're interested in using herbal pet preparations, the book, *Natural Insect Repellents: For Pets, People, & Plants* by Janette Grainger and Connie Moore may be of interest. It may be available in your local library.

Using Flea Combs to Control Fleas

A good anti-flea method is to regularly comb your cats and dogs with a specialized *flea comb*. These combs are designed with very small teeth that are so close together that, when you pull one through your pet's fur, the fleas will be filtered out and caught. (With very long fur, using a flea comb can be somewhat difficult.) Then, using your fingernail, you can push the fleas off the comb into a dish of soapy water to quickly kill them. To buy a flea comb, check with local pet shops, pet supply stores, or your veterinarian. You can also mail-order one from **R.C. Steele, Simmons Natural Bodycare,** or **American Environmental Health Foundation.**

Another method to help reduce flea infestations is to regularly vacuum your pets using a special dog and cat grooming attachment. These are sometimes sold by larger pet supply stores. It's also a good idea to vacuum your floors and furnishings frequently, especially during peak flea seasons. Vacuuming is extremely important around your pet's sleeping area. In addition, wash your pet's bed regularly. When fleas are at their worst, you might even have your pet sleep on old towels, which you could clean daily if necessary.

Using Herbal Repellents to Control Fleas

Some people have also tried using a variety of herbal and aromatic woods (such as cedar) as flea repellents. Sometimes these are in the form of shampoos, skin preparations, or dried material used in bedding. Although some of these may be of questionable value against fleas, the essential oils of *eucalyptus* (a tree in the myrtle family originally from Australia) and *pennyroyal* (a perennial herb of the mint family) apparently can be fairly effective. Unfortunately, some sensitive individuals may find that their pronounced odor is too bothersome.

If you're interested in herbal anti-flea preparations, check with your veterinarian or pet-supply store to find out what they have available. Several such products can also be mail-ordered from **R.C. Steele.** The Natural Animal line (**Natural Animal Health Products, Inc.**) includes several herbal anti-flea products (collars, shampoos, powders). You can often find these locally, or you can buy them from the manufacturer, **TerrEssentials, Priorities, Karen's Natural Products, Bio Designs** and **Frontier Natural Products.** One Earth Pet Shampoos and One Earth Pet Herbal Pet Collars (**Eight-In-One Pet Products**) are sometimes available in local alternative groceries and many pet-supply stores. The shampoos in this line come in a number of herbal formulas including citronella. The collars use extracts of citronella, eucalyptus and other aromatic oils. If you can't locate these products, you can contact the manufacturer for a nearby dealer. Lifekind Dog & Cat Shampoo Bar (**Lifekind Products**) contains pennyroyal, cedar wood, tea-tree oil, eucalyptus, slippery-elm bark, and more. This preparation can be bought from the company. Finally, F.L.E.A.S. Herbal collars are sold by **American Environmental Health Foundation.**

Using Insect Growth Regulators Against Fleas

A flea-control tactic that has gained popularity lately is the use of *insect growth regulators* or *IGRs*. Generally, with this approach a veterinarian may prescribe pills or drops for you to administer to your pet, or a compound to put on your pet's food. Once in the pet's system, the IGR compound becomes stored in the animal's fat and is slowly released into the bloodstream. Then, whenever a female flea bites your pet, she inadvertently ingests the medication. Once in her system, the IGR rapidly travels to her ovaries and alters her eggs.

Because the female flea isn't otherwise affected, she lays her eggs even though they are altered. The eggs are not dead; in fact they appear normal, and the fleas inside these eggs develop and get ready to hatch. However, because of their exposure to IGR, they lack their normal "egg teeth" to break free of their eggs. So, they never hatch. As another plus, any live molting flea larvae soon die after eating the IGR-tainted blood. Drawbacks to using an IGR include the fact that your pet will require a veterinary visit, and the treatment will need some time to become effective—time to build up to sufficient levels in the pet's system, and time to kill live hatching eggs and larvae. Another problem is that all female fleas in your house must bite a treated pet in order to produce mutated offspring. If the fleas bite untreated pets, pets whose blood levels haven't yet gotten a high enough IGR concentration, or if they bite humans, then they and their offspring will not be affected, and the infestation will continue. If you're interested in using an IGR product with your pet, talk with your veterinarian for his (or her) recommendation and, specific product warnings, if any.

Using Borate Compounds Against Fleas

A new product that you may want to try against fleas in your home is Ecology Works Fleanix Flea Control (**Ecology Works**). Fleanix is made of both powdered acidic and alkaline borate compounds (the combination creates a neutral pH). This formula dissolves easily in water, and it impregnates carpet fibers when used in an extraction-type carpet cleaning unit.

To use Fleanix, the manufacturer suggests mixing 1 cup in 1 gallon of carpet-cleaning water/detergent solution. (For unscented, alternative carpet cleaning solutions, see *Rug and Carpet Shampooing and Wet-Extraction Cleaning* on page 158.) Wearing waterproof household gloves is a good idea. (See *Household Waterproof Glove Suggestions* on page 137.) Once mixed, simply clean your carpets as usual.

During the cleaning process, Fleanix's borate compounds are forced deep into the carpet fibers and bond with them. (They can't even be vacuumed up in most cases.) At the same time, the deep cleaning removes flea eggs, dried blood particles (flea food), flea larvae, and adult fleas. Any remaining dried blood becomes saturated with Fleanix and will kill larvae before they have a chance to become breeding adults.

If you're interested in using this product, you need to know that one 2.6-pound package will treat 1300 sq. feet of carpet. If you hire a professional cleaning service to clean your carpets for you, the product can be sprayed on with a pump sprayer. When reviewed by the California EPA, "toxicity registered so low as to have an insignificant exposure risk associated with application." However while this, and most other borate-based products, are generally much safer than typical pesticides, make sure to store any unmixed powder in such a way that children and pets will not have access to it. If you'd like try Fleanix, you can order it from the manufacturer.

Using Diatomaceous Earth Against Fleas

Still another option for flea control is to use naturally mined *diatomaceous earth (DE)* that has not been heat-treated. This powdery material consists of the silica-containing cell walls of millions of ancient *diatoms* (microscopic water algae). Some people suggest that you should simply sprinkle a small amount of DE directly on your pets so that any fleas and eggs present on them will dry up and die. However, others feel that if you do this, it'll also cause an unhealthy drying of your pet's skin. It could also cause respiratory irritation in susceptible animals if they inhale it.

Therefore, a better approach might be to sprinkle DE around your yard or even on your indoor carpeting. If you decide to go ahead and apply it to your carpets, place a tiny amount onto the carpet, dip a broom into it, and then work the pile across the entire room. Just five ounces should be enough to do as much as 1,000 square feet. While it's supposedly safe to walk on the carpet, it's probably best to leave it undisturbed for 48 hours. After that, you should vacuum thoroughly to remove any remaining diatomaceous earth and dead fleas. To treat your backyard, you can make a solution of 1 part diatomaceous earth in 4 parts water and put it in a yard pump sprayer, and then apply it.

It should be noted there are human-health concerns that have been associated with using diatomaceous earth. For example, it is often advised not to use heat-treated DE—it apparently has a much greater potential to produce lung diseases such as *silicosis*. (This is a serious lung condition brought on by breathing silica particulates.) Even when using DE that hasn't been heat-treated, it's best to wear a protective dust mask. (See *Personal Protective Gear* on page 264.) Of course, those with asthma or other respiratory problems should probably avoid using this product. All DE should be stored so children and pets do not have access to it.

DE that hasn't been heat-treated may be available from your local veterinarian or pet-supply center and it can be mail-ordered. Natural Animal Diatom Dust Insect Powder (**Natural Animal Health Products, Inc.**) can be ordered from the company, and certain dealers of Natural Animal products may stock it. These include **TerrEssentials**, **Priorities**, **Karen's Natural Products**, **Allergy Relief Shop, Inc.**, and **Simmons Natural Bodycare**. Concern Diatomaceous Earth can be ordered from **Frontier Natural Products**. More sources for diatomaceous earth are **American Environmental Health Foundation** and **Bio Designs** (in one- and five-pound bags). D-E Plus (**Verdant Brands**) diatomaceous earth with "flea bait" is another option. You'll need to call the company for a nearby dealer.

Using Pyrethrum Powder Against Fleas

Pyrethrum powder is sometimes used to counter flea infestations. Usually, it's applied directly to the animal. However, it should be noted that some people feel that pyrethrum may be too active an agent to be applied to pets directly. Those who feel it's quite safe obviously disagree. In any case, the pyrethrum will quickly break down when sunlight reaches it. So, it will probably be inert by the next day. If you do use it (asthmatics are advised not to), wear an effective dust mask. (See *Personal Protective Gear* on page 264.) Of course, you'll want to store the product so no children or pets get into it.

A procedure with pyrethrum powder that you might try is to place a very tiny amount on the back of your pet and work it into the fur. You can also work a very small amount onto your pet's bed. Be aware that if pyrethrum powder gets on your carpet or rug and it should get wet before being vacuumed up, it has the potential to leave a stain.

One product you may want to try is EcoZone Roach, Ant, Flea, Silverfish Insect Powder (**Natural Animal Health Products, Inc.**). This is available in a 7.05-ounce canister or a 5-pound package. This can be purchased from the maker and from **Bio Designs**. Natural Animal Flea Powder for Dogs and Cats (**Natural Animal Health Products, Inc.**) is also 100%-dried-pyrethrum flowers. In this case, it's packaged in a 2.6 ounce shaker canister, made for easy application directly onto the animal. This version can be purchased from the maker and from **Simmons Natural Bodycare**. Other Natural Animal dealers that may have it are **TerrEssentials**, **Priorities**, **Karen's Natural Products**, **Bio Designs** and **Frontier Natural Products**. It should be noted that the manufacturer suggests it "can be applied as often as necessary" to your dog or cat. Safer Flea & Tick & Premise Spray made with pyrethrum is handled by **Karen's Natural Products**.

Other Simple Flea-Control Methods

Sometimes cutting your lawn short and keeping it that way will lessen flea problems for your pets, and ultimately inside your home. Interestingly, a very simple flea-killing method is to carefully suspend a lit low-wattage light bulb 6–12" directly above a pan of water indoors at night. (You could also use a sheet of sticky insect paper instead of the bowl of water.) Ideally, this should be near a flea-infestation site in your home. When you do this, it's best to have your pets elsewhere. The fleas will be attracted to the warmth of the light, especially if the warmth of your pet's body is not around. As the fleas jump toward the light, they'll land in the water and drown (or get stuck on the gluey paper). Flea light traps are commonly sold in local pet-supply stores. By mail order, you can get them from **R.C. Steele**. In addition, Over Nite Electric Light Flea Traps are sold by **American Environmental Health Foundation**.

Another simple anti-flea approach that's widely advertised is using high-pitched sound to ward off fleas. The electronically induced ultrasound is above the hearing range of humans and most pets, but not that of fleas, etc. The noise is supposedly disturbing to fleas (and other insects), so they stay away. Unfortunately, research has shown that ultrasonic flea repellents simply don't work. Again, check with local pet shops and pet-supply stores if you're still interested in trying them, or order one from **R.C. Steele.**

Flies

Fly is the common name for a range of flying insect species in the order *Diptera*. Included are houseflies, fruit flies, gnats, horseflies, and deerflies, among others. Most of these insects are biters or bloodsuckers and, unfortunately, many of them can also carry diseases. Flies are usually attracted to places with poor sanitation. Therefore, having clean surroundings, and tight-fitting screens, are two of the best deterrents against them.

As everyone knows, it's not uncommon to find a fly (or flies) indoors. Two very safe and effective fly-extermination methods are old-fashioned ones. These are a fly swatter and sticky flypaper. Of course, most hardware stores and discount stores should have them—but they are less common than they used to be. If you want to mail order a fly swatter, Terro Fly Swatters (**Senoret**) can be purchased directly from the company.

It should be pointed out that flypaper has an advantage over a swatter because the dead insects don't have to be handled. The down side is that you have to hang up this usually unattractive product for all to see. If you decide to purchase sticky flypaper, it's a good idea to buy only the type made without chemical coatings. With pesticide-free flypaper, the glue itself is the active ingredient. The stuck flies eventually die naturally without the need for poison. Sticky flypaper without pesticides is sometimes available at local hardware stores. One excellent brand you might find is Terro Large Fly Catcher (**Senoret**). It is a non-toxic, large sticky ribbon. The stickiness is created with rosin, rubber, and mineral oil. If you can't find this particular product locally, you can order it directly from the manufacturer. Another source for a non-pesticide-treated sticky fly trap is **American Environmental Health Foundation**. The product they handle is called Fly Stop. Another type of fly trap is The Fly Scoop (**Verdant Brands**). This is plastic trapping unit containing an attractant that can placed in the window. You can contact the manufacturer for the nearest dealer.

Unfortunately, swatters and flypaper are capable of eliminating only a few flies at a time. Therefore, if you find a swarm of flies in your home, you'll likely have to try some other tactic. One approach is to simply wait until the swarm rests for the night. Often, when they do this, they'll land on the ceiling. When this occurs, you can quickly suction them up with a soft-brush attachment on your vacuum cleaner.

An alternative spray product to try is Victor Poison-Free Flying Insect (**Woodstream Corp.**). This formula uses mint oil and sodium lauryl sulfate (used in shampoos and soaps) which "clogs insect spiracles (their body's breathing pores) and overexcites their nervous systems." The propellant for this aerosol is carbon dioxide. Victor Poison-Free apparently works quickly and will remain effective for up to four weeks. Check your local alternative grocery for availability or contact the manufacturer for a nearby dealer.

Although they apparently aren't very effective, some people still swear that *ultrasonic emitters* are the answer to fly problems. According to the manufacturer's literature, the high-pitched noise (inaudible to humans) put out by these plug-in plastic units (some use batteries) acts as an on-going and effective repellent. If you'd like to experiment, a variety of ultrasonic pest-repelling devices are sold by **Improvements** and **Harmony**.

Grain Moths

Grain moths can sometimes become a household problem. One common type is the Indian meal moth, which is small (less than 1/2" long) with gray-and-copper wings. Unfortunately, grain-moth eggs are commonly found in organic grains. Many people have found they can successfully prevent the unnoticeable eggs from turning into unappetizing larvae, or live moths, by placing their whole grains in tightly sealed, recloseable containers in their freezer.

If grain moths happen to hatch and escape into your kitchen, you can try using a soft-brush vacuum-cleaner attachment to suck them up. Then thoroughly vacuum around your entire kitchen. By doing this, you'll get rid of any grain-moth cocoons, which are often located around ceiling edges, under cabinets, or other places in your kitchen.

Another option is to use *pheromone traps*. These are sticky traps that have a species-specific sex attractant on them. In this case, the male grain moths fly to the traps, thinking that the odor is coming from mate-ready female moths. They then get stuck and die. This will prevent females from laying fertile eggs. If you want to try this approach, Pantry Pest Trap (**Verdant Brands**) with a Biolure attractant is a product to consider. It comes in a 5 1/2" x 4" x 2 1/2" triangular box. Said to last up to 16 weeks, it's available at some hardware stores and from **Improvements**, **Solutions** and **American Environmental Health Foundation**.

Mice

Unfortunately, mice are a common problem. The following sections will offer some less-toxic solutions to deal with these unwelcome house guests.

Mouse Traits

The house mouse (*Mus musculus*) has the widest distribution in the world of any mammal—except for human beings themselves. It's little wonder then that this particular species, or other species such as deer mice, harvest mice, and others, may find their way into your home from time to time.

Although some people consider mice "cute" and may even keep them as pets, wild mice should be considered serious pests for a number of reasons. First, certain mice could be carrying viral, bacterial, or parasitic diseases that could affect you or your family. (These can be transmitted by direct contact, biting, fleas, or breathing dust from their droppings.) Mice also have the potential to be very destructive. They can gnaw through walls, cabinets, and furniture, to get into food supplies and bedding materials, etc. In addition, their feces can be dropped over a large area of your home's interior, making an unpleasant mess to clean up.

Particularly frustrating is how quickly mice reproduce. Within a few months, two mating mice can easily produce several dozen more mice. This is because many mice species breed four to six times a year and each litter may have four to twelve young. At about eight weeks of age a new mouse generation becomes sexually mature and ready to mate, and so on.

Live Traps for Capturing Mice

Although most people want to eliminate all the mice from inside their homes, for some individuals this can pose a real moral or philosophical dilemma. While they may feel that killing insects is acceptable, killing mice, it seems, can be "cruel." For these people (and others, of course), there are now live traps available which can capture these problem rodents. Some models are designed to capture a single mouse, while others can hold several. Live-capture traps are usually available in most local hardware or farm-supply stores. Victor Live Mouse Trap (**Woodstream Corp.**) is one brand you may come across. Another brand you might find is Black Hole (**Verdant Brands**) which comes in a black plastic tube shape. In addition, **Real Goods** offers live-mouse traps by mail order. Whenever you've captured live mice, they must be released a considerable distance from your home, or else they'll simply return—that is, unless you're absolutely certain you have sealed up every possible reentry point.

Mouse Extermination Methods

Some persons may simply decide that rodent extermination, rather than live capture is necessary. One possible method is using a special poisoned mouse bait, which is commonly sold in hardware stores and garden-supply centers. Often, it's available in small packets that you place in suspected mice areas. These packets appear to be a convenient, effective method for killing mice—a relatively safe way of using a very limited amount of *rodenticide* (rodent-killing chemical).

However, there can be serious problems with using poison bait. Sometimes the mice will scatter the pellets over a fairly wide area around the gnawed-open packets. Unfortunately, this bait can be toxic to small children or pets if enough is ingested. Also, you should be aware that even if mice are the only creatures to consume the pellets, you have no control over where they'll eventually die. Dead mice could end up anywhere in or around your home—or within wall cavities. This could pose real sanitation concerns. Then too, dogs or cats could find and eat a poisoned carcass.

As medieval as it may seem, the best long-term solution in many situations is often the old-fashioned snap trap. One very popular brand of these is Victor (**Woodstream Corp.**), which are sold, along with others like it, in virtually every hardware and garden-supply store. Of course, at the same time, make sure all your home's mouse-entry points are sealed so you only have to kill a limited number of mice.

Snap traps are designed to kill almost instantaneously by breaking a rodent's spinal chord. Therefore, there's no poison and the dead animal remains with the trap. However, you must be extremely careful where you place snap traps because they can harm fingers and toes. So, make certain that children and pets do not have access to them.

To make the use of snap traps less unpleasant, you might want to follow this procedure. At the site where you have recently spotted a mouse (or mice), put down a piece of aluminum foil, or several layers of paper and situate the trap on top of it. Then, bait the trap using a small dab of peanut butter and carefully set it. Once the mouse is caught, you can simply wrap the dead animal in the foil or paper and dispose of it. Incidentally, the foil or paper layers will also stop any splattered blood or bait from getting onto your floors.

Mosquitoes

Mosquitoes are small, two-winged flies and there are many species of them. Mosquitoes are considered serious pests because the adult females feed on blood. Besides being annoying, and often causing swelling, by accessing your blood supply, mosquito bites can be an effective method of disease transmission. *Arboviral encephalitis* (virus-induced acute brain inflammation) and *dog heart worm* are just two of the more common diseases transmitted by female mosquitoes in the U.S.

Fortunately, mosquitoes are usually not found in large numbers in most American homes; that is, if the houses are built on properly drained land, are well-sealed, and have tight-fitting screens in good repair. However, it's certainly true that some locations will naturally have much larger mosquito populations than others.

To kill a few mosquitoes safely, using a fly swatter works fairly well. By the way, if you don't already have one, you should get one to keep on hand for the future. Of course, they should be available in local hardware stores and discount stores. By mail order, you can get Terro Fly Swatters (**Senoret**) directly from the manufacturer.

To cope with large swarms, you can sometimes suck them up quickly using a soft-brush attachment on your vacuum cleaner. Of course, a number of people use herbal oils, such as *citronella oil* (derived from citronella grass), to deter mosquitoes. These are sometimes sold at some health-food stores. Generally, herbal oils have strong natural scents that are meant to repel the mosquitoes, and some of them actually can be quite effective. However, their odors can be bothersome to some sensitive individuals.

Ultrasonic emitters, which emit a high-pitched whine (inaudible to human ears), are popular, but aren't very effective. Typically, these are small plastic units that either plug into outlets or use batteries. If you'd like to experiment with one anyway, they can be ordered from **Improvements** and **Harmony**.

A similar, but probably much more effective unit, is called the Love Bug (**Prince Lionheart**). This is a device that electronically mimics the sound of beating dragonfly wings. (Dragonflies are natural predators of mosquitoes.) Supposedly, when the mosquitoes hear the noise of their age-old enemy, they quickly retreat. (The effective range is up to a 20–30' radius.) On the other hand, humans may just barely perceive the sound. The Love Bug is made of plastic and resembles a several-inch-long ladybug. It's self-contained and can be clipped to fabric, such as on a canopy bed, a curtain, or to a playpen. The Love Bug can be mail-ordered from **One Step Ahead**, or from the manufacturer (only if you can't find it locally). MosquitoControl is a simpler rectangular item that does the same thing. It is sold by **Harmony**.

Still another mosquito deterrent you might try is mosquito netting. This can be draped over your bed if you find it necessary. Preferably, you should obtain netting that hasn't been treated with chemical repellents or pesticides. (Ask before purchasing.) To find mosquito netting, check local army/navy surplus stores, camping departments, and perhaps baby departments as well. A source or polyester mosquito canopy netting is **Real Goods**. Nylon mosquito netting by the yard (54" wide) is sold by **Gohn Bros.**

To help control mosquito populations directly outside your home, so they're less likely to enter your indoor living space, you might try Victor Poison-Free Mosquito Barrier (**Woodstream Corp.**). This is a natural garlic solution in a hose-ready container. Directions say that it should be sprayed on grass, plants and shrubs. It seems that the garlic not only acts a repellent, but often kills mosquito larva as well. To purchase this Victor product, check alternative grocery stores and nursery or plant centers, or call the manufacturer for a nearby dealer.

Silverfish

Silverfish are ugly but they're generally not much of a threat to you or your belongings. However, the following sections offer some ways to safely eliminate them from your home.

Silverfish Traits

Silverfish are varieties of *bristletails*, insects usually about $1/2$"-long with rather flat, soft, silvery bodies. They have two large antennae on their head and three bristles emerging from their rear. Silverfish especially like to be around moisture.

Apparently, silverfish have the capacity to eat natural fibers, paper, and starches. Especially enjoyable to them are starchy glues, such as those used for wallpaper and bookbinding. If only a few silverfish are in your home, they probably should not be of much concern. It's generally agreed they don't pose much of a problem to households or the health of you or your family.

Eliminating Silverfish

Occasional silverfish can be vacuumed up using a soft-brush vacuum-cleaner attachment. If you have many of these insects, you'll probably have to do something more than simply vacuuming. As an eradication method, try using boric-acid powder. White pharmacy-grade boric-acid powder is available at most drugstores, and synthetically dyed boric-acid pesticides, such as Roach Prufe (**Copper Brite, Inc.**), are sold at most hardware stores. Roach Prufe can also be ordered from **American Environmental Health Foundation**.

To use boric-acid powder, carefully sprinkle a narrow line of the powder around the water and drain pipes under your sinks and in the basement. In the kitchen area, it's best to only apply boric-acid powder into the crevices between the floor and the baseboard molding using a small squeeze-bulb insecticide applicator. By applying it this way, it's less likely that the powder will ever become airborne and contaminate your food. Bulb-type insecticide devices can be found in some local hardware stores, or at a nearby pest-control company. To be on the safe side, whenever you apply boric-acid powder, it's wise to wear a dust mask. (See *Personal Protective Gear* on page 264.)

When the infestation is over, in certain locations you may want to leave the boric acid powder as a permanent anti-silverfish measure. However, if you decide to remove it, you can vacuum up the powder using a crevice attachment while wearing a dust mask. Then, thoroughly wash the affected areas with water, wearing waterproof gloves. (See *Household Waterproof Glove Suggestions* on page 137.) Note: It's important to make sure that pets and children don't get into boric-acid powder. Although boric-acid pesticide is relatively safe, it can be harmful to humans and pets if enough is ingested or inhaled.

Another option is to use pyrethrum powder. This can be used in the same manner as boric-acid powder, and it has similar warnings. EcoZone Roach, Ant, Flea, Silverfish Insect Powder (**Natural Animal Health Products, Inc.** is one product you might try. This is an unaltered, 100%-pure pyrethrum powder. You can get it at some alternative grocery stores, or you can order it from the maker or **Bio Designs**. Silverfish traps can often be helpful, too. One source for these is **Solutions**.

Spiders

While flies have caused more human death by acting as transmitters of disease, spiders still create more fear when they're spotted indoors. The following sections discuss truly dangerous spiders, and what you can do to rid your home of them.

Spider Traits

Spiders are not insects. Instead they are eight-legged, carnivorous arachnids. All of them make silk, and most have fangs capable of injecting venom. Generally, in America, you may want to overlook the presence of most spiders inside your house. It seems that the vast majority aren't dangerous to humans, they lead rather secluded lies, and they devour insect pests such as gnats and houseflies. However, there are some that are too big, too ugly, or too poisonous to ignore.

Poisonous U.S. Spiders

Fortunately, there are not many really dangerous spiders in America. However, there are two you should know about: the black widow and the brown recluse.

Black Widow Spiders

Probably the best known (at least by name recognition) of the poisonous spiders is the black widow. The females of this species are small ($1/2$" long) and glossy black, with a red hourglass marking on the underside of their abdomen. The males are even smaller, and have four pairs of red marks along the sides of their abdomen. Interestingly, the males are rarely seen.

Black widow spiders are found throughout the continental U.S. They can live in a wide range of indoor and outdoor habitats. Fortunately, however, they're usually not aggressive; that is, except when a female is protecting her egg sac. If bitten, black-widow venom can cause spasms and breathing difficulties. Bites may, therefore, become fatal.

Brown Recluse Spiders

Another dangerous spider is the brown recluse. These spiders are small, just under $1/2$" long. Despite their name, brown recluse spiders are generally orange-yellow, with a dark violin-shaped marking on the backs.

Brown recluse spiders can be found within an area extending from Kansas and Missouri, south to Texas, and west to California. Often, they make their homes in sheltered spots outdoors, as well as in houses. Generally, they're active at night.

Fortunately, bites from these spiders are rarely fatal to humans. However, the skin surrounding a bite may blacken and die. Sometimes, the complete healing of a bite can take up to several months.

Spider Extermination

A good approach to minimizing spiders is to vacuum regularly and thoroughly around your home's interior. This means under the beds, in the closets, behind the curtains and shutters, in the corners, etc. Vacuuming will not only remove any live spiders, but it will also rid your house of their webs, nests, and eggs. Sometimes spider traps are also helpful. One source for these is **Solutions**.

If you come across a poisonous spider, be extremely cautious and wear protective clothing and rubber gloves while eradicating it. If you're ever bitten by what you suspect is a poisonous spider, it's important to call for medical help and take the spider with you—even if it is squashed—to the emergency room for proper identification. If you suspect you've been bitten by a poisonous spider but didn't actually see it happen, you should seek medical help at once if you begin experiencing symptoms such as abdominal pain or dizziness.

Sugar Ants

Seeing an ant or two wouldn't seem like much to worry about. However, a few sugar ants in your kitchen could be the harbinger of a full-scale ant invasion. To help you deal with them safely and effectively, the following sections discuss sugar-ant traits, and less-toxic measures to eliminate the ants from your house.

Sugar Ant Traits

Sugar ant is actually a generic term; it includes several small ant species that like nectar, and other sugary foods. Generally, sugar ants are only about $1/8$" long and dark in color. Sugar ants are social creatures, living in colonies that may contain hundreds of individuals.

Unfortunately, sugar ants can become a persistent in-home pest problem. Although their nest may remain outdoors, their daily activity may consist of repeatedly entering your home for food and returning to the nest. Therefore, be alert whenever you first see a few sugar ants in your house. They're often large female workers searching for food. These "scout ants" will lay down scent trails that the other worker ants in the colony will soon follow.

Talcum Powder Against Sugar Ants

Surprisingly, simply sprinkling *talcum powder* around the areas of sugar-ant activity in your home will often control their invasions. It seems that this powdery material clings to their bodies, preventing normal respiration. (Ants take in air through tiny holes known as *spiracles* along the sides of their bodies.) When their breathing holes become clogged, they quickly suffocate.

Talcum powder (also known as *talc*) is a finely ground magnesium-silicate mineral product. (You may be familiar with it because it's the base material for many bath powders.) You'll generally find it at most pharmacies. However, it may be a perfumed product. An unscented talcum powder is Simple Pure Fine Talc (**Smith & Nephew Consumer Products, Ltd.**) which can be ordered from **N.E.E.D.S.** and **American Environmental Health Foundation**. Note that, powder of any sort should not be breathed by humans or pets because it could lead to respiratory irritation or damage. This is especially true for talc which can cause *talcosis*, a serious lung disease. Therefore, it's important to wear a good-quality dust mask whenever you apply talc. (See *Personal Protective Gear* on page 264.) In addition, it's a good idea not to let children or pets get access to the powdered talc.

Boric Acid Against Sugar Ants

Terro Ant Killer II (**Senoret**) is a sweetened borax-based (borax is a boron compound similar to boric acid) liquid that kills ants. Amazingly, all you have to do is to put a drop on the tiny cardboard squares (they come with the packaging). The worker sugar ants find it and eat the saturated cardboard. Then they return to the nest and regurgitate it as they would any food they find. (Regurgitated food is what the ants who live within the colony normally eat). Soon, not only the worker ants are dead, but all the ants in the nest are as well. Because it'll take some time for this to occur, don't expect instantaneous results. You can often find Terro Ant Killer II at local alternative groceries. If not, you can order it from the manufacturer or from **Improvements**. Of course, you'll want to make sure that children and pets don't get into it.

Preventing Re-Entry to Control Sugar Ants

If talcum powder or boric acid fail to stop your sugar-ant invasion, the next step is to block their entry into your home. To do this, trace their trail back to where it penetrated your home's exterior. Generally, this is somewhere near the foundation. At that point, caulk or otherwise repair the gap. After that, you may want to apply a pyrethrin (a chrysanthemum flower-head extract) spray product around the repaired site, and along the exterior foundation wall for several feet on both sides of it. One that you may find at local alternative groceries is Concern Multi-Purpose Insect Killer (**Necessary Organics**). If you can't locate any, you can contact the manufacturer for their nearest supplier. (Of course, other brands of pyrethrin sprays could be used, too.)

An alternative option would to spray Victor Poison-Free Ant (**Woodstream Corp.**). This aerosol uses mint and sodium lauryl sulfate (a compound used in many shampoos) as it's active ingredients, and carbon dioxide as the propellant. The sodium lauryl sulfate blocks ant spiracles (breathing pores), and the mint oil overexcites their nervous systems. Victor Poison-Free formulas are biodegradable, they kill quickly, and remain effective for up to four weeks. To purchase this product, check alternative grocery stores or call the company for a local dealer.

If the sugar ants return, they've obviously found another entry point. Therefore, it might be a good idea to now have the pyrethrin sprayed or sprinkled around the entire outside perimeter of your home's foundation. You might also want to seek out and destroy the outdoor sugar-ant nest. To do this, trace the ants' path back from the entry point all the way to their nest site. This will likely be frustrating and time-consuming; however, there's a chance you might find it.

If you do come across their nest, you can treat it with the pyrethrin or mint oil/sodium-lauryl-sulfate spray, or drench it with boiling water. By destroying the nest, you will have permanently ended the ant attack; that is, until another scouting party manages to enter your house from another nest.

By the way, its important to keep children and pets away from any pyrethrin containers. You should also be aware that, because most pyrethrin formulas eventually break down when exposed to sunlight, the product you use will likely be effective for only a relatively short period of time.

Termites

One word that virtually all homeowners dread hearing is *termites*. This is not only because they fear the tremendous damage termites can do, but also out of concern over having their homes treated with potentially dangerous and potent *termiticides* (termite killers). Therefore, to help you cope more effectively with termites, the following sections will introduce you to termite traits, typical treatments, and safer alternative approaches you can use to effectively stop them.

Termite Traits in General

Termites are extremely successful creatures. Throughout the world, there are nearly 1,800 termite species. Many people falsely believe that termites are white ants. Actually they're quite different. Physically, termites lack the very thin wasp-like waist that ants have. However, the biggest difference is that termites can eat wood; ants can't. Although some types of ants (such as carpenter ants) tunnel through, and live in, wood, they're unable to use wood as a food source.

Actually, termites can eat virtually all plant materials, including wood. Although the tough cellulose making up a plant's cell walls is often hard to digest (it's completely indigestible for many creatures), termites have certain bacteria living in their digestive tracts that allow them to easily break the cellulose down into usable food. In addition, termites that primarily bore into wood also have a type of *protozoa* (a microscopic single-celled organism) living in their digestive tracts that further enhances their ability to break down a tree's cellulose.

In the U.S., there are several termite species, and new ones arrive periodically from other countries inadvertently. In certain locales, these "alien" termites can be extremely problematic, having lifestyles that make them difficult to eradicate. However, there are three termite species that are still the most common sources of concern to most American homeowners. These are the subterranean termite, the drywood termite, and the dampwood termite. These insects are social creatures living in colonies. The colonies are made up of three types of members: workers, reproductive adults, and soldiers. Each of the three common species has a particular climate it prefers, as well as particular preferences and habits.

Subterranean Termite Traits

Subterranean termites have worker members that are about 1/4" long with white bodies and darker heads. The soldier termites look fairly similar to these workers, but they're a little larger. On the other hand, the winged reproducing males and females are about 1/2" long and black.

Subterranean termites are present over much of the U.S. As their name suggests, this species lives in soil. In order to reach wood that is not directly in contact with the ground, these termites often build mud tubes to travel through. These tubes keep their bodies moist by protecting them from the air. This is absolutely essential for their survival because, if they dry out, they die.

Dampwood Termite Traits

Dampwood termites workers are about 1/2" long and are ivory-colored with darker abdomens. The soldiers are about 3/4" long with larger and darker heads. The reproductive adults are light brown with wings about 1" long.

Dampwood termites are common along the Pacific coast. As you might have guessed, they live only in, or around, damp wood, and they eat damp wood as well. Therefore, these termites are almost completely dependent on moisture-laden wood in order to survive.

Drywood Termite Traits

Drywood termite workers are white with yellow-brown heads. The reproducing winged adults are dark brown and the soldier termites have light-colored bodies with very large reddish-brown heads. All forms of drywood termites tend to be $1/2$" long or less.

Drywood termites are found both in the southern U.S. and in California. Interestingly, this species doesn't have the moisture requirements of subterranean or dampwood termites. As a result, they can have nests wherever there is wood, wet or dry.

Typical Termite Controls

In the U.S., powerful toxic synthetic organic chemicals (See *Modern Organic Pesticides* on page 395) are commonly used to combat termites.

Typical Termiticides

Termites are capable of burrowing into wood and feeding on it. Unfortunately, most U.S. residences are constructed primarily, or partially, of wood. As a result, termites enter and damage thousands of American homes annually. If a termite infestation should occur in your house, the actual structural destruction of wood joists, studs, etc. tends to occur rather slowly. However, an infestation can go on unnoticed for several years. This could lead to serious damage, which would be very costly to repair. It's not surprising then that most people have used (and continue to use) potent termiticides (termite killers) to protect their homes.

At one time, a popular chemical termiticide was the synthetic organic chemical, chlordane, a chlorinated hydrocarbon. (By the way, the commercially available product was actually 60% chlordane with 40% other ingredients such as the insecticide *heptachlor*.) However, in the 1970s, chlordane was shown to be *carcinogenic* (cancer-causing) and was removed from the market. Today, synthetic chlorpyrifos-containing pesticides (such as Dursban) are now widely used against termites. These particular termiticides are supposed to be less dangerous and, therefore, safer for humans than chlordane; however, there are negative health effects reported with their use as well.

Despite the increase in public awareness of the potential dangers posed by exposure to many of the synthetic chemical pesticides, most homes are still subjected to these solutions to prevent or exterminate house-damaging termites. Some residences have a regular, routine, reapplication as an ongoing deterrent measure (This is especially true in warm climates such as Florida.). Unfortunately, as a rule, once a synthetic pesticide has been applied to your house, it can't easily be removed. It, therefore, has a long-term presence in your home.

Typical Termiticide Application Methods

There are actually three chemical treatment methods that are popularly used to apply typical termiticides. The type that's utilized depends on the termite species, the extent of the infestation, and the specific chemical chosen. Each approach has its particular advantages as well as its potential drawbacks.

With *ground-injection liquid fumigation*, a pesticide applicator inserts a device into the soil around a home's foundation and injects a liquid termiticide. This saturates the soil and kills any termites (usually subterranean termites) that come in contact with the solution. At the same time, it forms a protective barrier against future termite infestations. Apparently, ground-injection liquid fumigation using typical termiticide chemicals can remain active in the soil for ten years or more, depending on the specific compound used. Therefore, if this application method is utilized, repeated treatments or monitoring are usually unnecessary for at least a few years after it's been done.

Theoretically, if your home's foundation is completely sealed, no termiticides should be able to enter the living space and be inhaled, or otherwise reach the people inside the house. Unfortunately, misdirected injections have entered basements and crawl spaces, and few foundations are perfectly sealed. So, even if the ground-injection liquid fumigation is properly done, the chemicals can sometimes seep into the living space through unsuspected tiny gaps and cracks in a home's foundation.

In *whole-structure gas fumigation*, a house is completely tented with plastic sheeting. During the fumigation process, the occupants and pets leave, and a powerful gaseous termiticide chemical is allowed to fill the entire structure. This particular method is often used against dry wood termites that can attack any wood in a home, even the attic floors and roof trusses which are far above the soil.

Whole-house gas fumigation must be done very carefully because the harmful chemicals can easily become inhaled and cause toxic symptoms. Therefore, pest-control personnel doing fumigation work always wear special protective chemical-respirator masks. Also, chemical-detection equipment is generally used to measure potentially harmful gas levels, as well as any remaining harmful residues. Unfortunately, if you use this method, anything left inside a house during the fumigation process will be subjected to the fumigating chemicals and, to a certain extent, will be contaminated.

In *spray dispersal,* a professional pesticide applicator uses a portable tank with a wand attachment to spray around a home's foundation or specific infested areas. Theoretically, this method could be used against any type of termite. In a spray-dispersal application, there's direct control over the placement of the termiticide. However, how precisely the spray is actually applied depends on the skill of the applicator. It's conceivable that these chemicals might land on heating ducts and seep inside them through joints and seams. Typical termiticides that have been sprayed could remain active for up to several years, depending on the type used.

Alternative Termite Controls in General

Although they're not often well-known, or commonly utilized yet, a number of safer termite-control methods are available besides the typical highly toxic ones. Unfortunately, for a variety of reasons, you might be unable to actually use some of these, even if you want to (see *Implementing Alternative Pest-Control Measures* on page 399). Despite this, many people have been able to use alternative termite controls and, for the most part, they've been very satisfied with their effectiveness. Therefore, the following sections explore some of these methods.

Homeowner Responsibilities Using Alternative Termite Controls

Before you opt for an alternative method to control termites, you should first be aware that most alternative anti-termite controls will require you to take an active role. This means you must consistently and conscientiously monitor your home by routinely inspecting it for evidence of termites. During an actual infestation, your patience will be tried as well. Alternative termiticides may have to be applied several times, or a combination of alternative methods might have to be used together, to eliminate an infestation. This may be necessary because most alternative termite controls are not as deadly, or long-lasting, as their toxic chemical counterparts.

While admittedly time-consuming, and sometimes frustrating, you simply can't be lazy or just plain hopeful that termites won't be a problem for your house, or that they'll simply disappear after a single less-toxic treatment. The sad truth is, termites will always be nearby, and ready to devour your home if they have the opportunity to do so. Unless you're going to inject toxic synthetic poisons around your home's foundation, use toxic gas to fumigate it, routinely spray with toxic chemicals, build your house in a cold climate where termites can't survive, or construct a house without wood, anti-termite measures should be an ongoing and necessary responsibility of home ownership.

Alternative Termite-Control Basics

To determine the best alternative anti-termite method to use, you should learn which species is active in your area. If you have already found termites in your home, capture a few specimens and have a local pest-control company analyze them if you're unsure what type they are. The pest company might charge you a small fee, or they may not charge you anything—after all, they're hoping for your business. Once you know what species you're up against, you can go ahead and use the alternative extermination measures you've decided upon.

It should be noted that you need not always treat your entire house. Instead, you often can simply spot-treat the infested areas, and still have a successful and effective treatment. Treating only the affected areas will also cost you much less. By the way, even if you find that you must eventually use a powerful synthetic pesticide chemical for a particularly tenacious infestation, it's often best to spot-treat rather than subject your whole house to the chemical treatment. By doing this, you'll definitely minimize any potentially toxic pesticide exposure. (See *When Typical Pesticides Must be Used* on page 401.)

Specific Termite Species Alternative-Control Suggestions

Because termite damage can be serious, because some chemical applications are potentially harmful, and because alternative-control measures are often unfamiliar, you may want as much information as possible. A good source is *Common-Sense Pest Control* by William Olkowski, Sheila Daar, and Helga Olkowski. Your library may already have it, or they might be able to borrow a copy through inter-library loan.

In addition, you should seriously consider joining and consulting with the **Bio-Integral Resource Center (BIRC)**. A personal consultation with the BIRC's alternative pest-control experts (or others like them) is especially important if you're currently experiencing a termite infestation in your house. (For more help see *Alternative Pest Control Information Sources* on page 399.) Although the following sections present a number of the alternative control measures you might use, the truth is, every termite problem is more or less a unique situation requiring very explicit answers: ones that may not be possible to give here.

Subterranean Termite Alternative-Control Methods

Subterranean termites must either travel in protected, hidden cracks and crevices, or they must build mud-tubes, to reach wood that's not situated directly on, or in, soil. Because of this behavior, one monitoring method is particularly effective: *termite shields*, which can help you spot termite activity around your home. Termite shields are nothing more than a continuous sections of thin, bent aluminum or galvanized steel (steel having a zinc coating to prevent rusting) placed on top of the foundation wall around the entire perimeter of your home. It's important that shields be correctly installed when a house is being built—they can't be installed in an existing house. When installed correctly, the metal strips block the termites' paths and cause them to build their mud-tubes around the metal—out in the open—in order to reach the wood parts of the house. Therefore, termite shields allow you to more easily, and more effectively, inspect for termites, because the mud-tubes are going to be more visible than they would otherwise be. However, it's important to stress that metal termite shields can't stop a termite invasion; they're simply an inspection aid, and are of little value if you don't regularly check them. However, because they permit you to quickly spot termite mud tubes, any infestations that do occur will likely be caught and stopped early—before there's real structural damage.

One apparently effective, and certainly a very simple, subterranean-termite control method is to use a sand barrier around your home's foundation walls. Interestingly, termites can't tunnel through sand, as long as it is of a specific size. To make a sand barrier, you need at least a 4"-layer of sand (8–12 mesh) around the entire perimeter of the foundation. It should extend from the footing to the surface of the ground. Although this method is said to provide fairly good protection against subterranean termites, at this time it's still considered an experimental procedure.

A new method of countering subterranean termites is to use a perimeter stake system. In this approach, sakes are placed in the ground at about 10-foot intervals around the perimeter of a house. As worker termites forage in the soil, they inevitably find a stake, enter it, and eat the appealing, but termiticide-treated, bait. In time, so many workers will have eaten from the stakes' tainted bait that there won't be enough of them left to provide sufficient food for the rest of the colony. So eventually, the entire termite colony dies out. It should be noted that stakes should be regularly monitored for termite activity (perhaps every two or three months). If there is any activity present, replacement bait or stakes can be set out as necessary. Of course, the house should then be scrupulously examined to see if termites have entered the structure and caused any damage. If they've reached the house, a spot treatment may have to be used (such as described below).

There are very good reasons to use the stake method. These include the fact that it is a combination barrier, monitoring, and extermination method; that the active agent is confined to small known sites buried outside the home itself; and that it's a method that not only kills foraging workers, but could wipe out entire colonies in the immediate area. If you'd like to try a stake-perimeter system, Spectricide Termite Bait System with Transflur is one you can set up yourself. It comes with twenty 4' rods. You may be able to find this product at local building centers. You can also order it from **Improvements**. A perimeter stake system that's installed and monitored only by professional pest control people is Sentricon (**Dow AgroSciences**).

A very effective, and relatively safe, termiticide that can be used in new construction is a borate solution. Used against termites in Europe, New Zealand, Australia, and other countries, for over forty years, it's a relative newcomer here. One popular brand is Tim-bor (**U.S. Borax, Inc.**). This powdered product (made of a boron-based compound similar to borax) is diluted with water and sprayed on all the wood framing. Tim-bor doesn't remain on the surface as a coating. Instead, it's able to penetrate wood all the way through to the heart. Unfortunately, Tim-bor is water-soluble, so rain and other precipitation can wash it off before the exterior sheathing or siding is in place. If that occurs, the solution will have to be reapplied. A good way to apply Tim-bor to a new house is to spray it on all the wood framing after the roofing, siding, doors and windows are in place, but before any insulation or interior finishing is done. In this way the application will be protected from the weather. Another concern with Tim-bor is that any solution that reaches the ground could damage grass or surrounding trees. Therefore, if Tim-bor is used on your site, make certain that the package directions are followed carefully. Treatment with Tim-bor is said to provide permanent termite control.

In an existing house, it is generally only possible to spray Tim-bor on wood that is exposed in a basement or crawl space. This may be sufficient to eradicate some termite infestations. However, in some houses, it may not be possible to get to the termite-eaten wood to be able spray it.

It should be noted that Tim-bor is manufactured for use by professionals only. Therefore, you'll need to contact the manufacturer for an applicator in your area that uses it. If you want to do the work yourself, Termite Prufe (**Copper Brite Inc.**) can be used. This comes as a dry, disodium octaborate tetrahydrate powder that, like Tim-bor, must be mixed with water. It can be brushed on, sprayed, or injected. Termite Prufe may be available at your area hardware stores (Ace Hardware stores should be able to order it for you if they don't stock it) or building centers. If you can't locate it, contact the manufacturer for the nearest dealer, or order it from **American Environmental Health Foundation**. One plus for this formulation is that it supposedly "does not penetrate the skin or cause skin irritation." These boron-based compounds don't have an odor, are generally tolerated by chemically sensitive people quite well.

For less-toxic spot-treating of subterranean-termite infestations, one of the borate products mentioned above could be used. However, another option is to use an injectable pyrethrin (an extract of chrysanthemum flower heads) at the sites of termite activity. One brand is Tri-Die (**Whitmer Micro-Gen Research Laboratories, Inc.**). Tri-Die contains 6% pyrethrins, piperonl butoxide, and silica dioxide, as well as petroleum-based solvents and propellants. Because Tri-Die is "for professional use only," a local pest control company applicator will need to use it on your home.

Another spot-treatment method is to use injections of predatory *nematodes* (microscopic roundworms). These unsegmented predators attract insects and are known to be quite effective in controlling termites. To use them, they're typically mixed with water and injected into the soil (they can also be broadcast sprayed) around the exterior of an infested home. The minute juvenile nematodes immediately search for live termites, then they enter their bodies through natural skin openings. Once inside the termites, they release, into the termite's bloodstream, *symbiotic bacteria* (bacteria whose lives are beneficial to the nematodes as much as the nematodes are beneficial to the bacteria). In reality, it's this bacterial infection that kills the termite within forty-eight hours (giving the termites enough time to return to their nest). Meanwhile, the nematodes quickly become adults, mate, and reproduce (1,000-3,000 offspring) inside the now-dead termite. Soon, the dead termite is consumed and the juvenile nematodes leave the dead body and enter the ground seeking new termites to parasitize. Thus, the cycle repeats over and over. (Each cycle takes about ten days in 70°-80° temperatures.) It's said that it requires about six months before complete termite control is achieved. Once in the soil, the nematodes should last for about two years.

It should be noted that nematodes require no EPA (**Environmental Protection Agency**) registration and are "harmless to mammals." However, some states require that they be registered as a pesticide, so they may not be available in your locale if they haven't been registered. By the way, all termite species that are in the ground are killed—not just the subterranean variety.

One brand of nematodes, Saf-T-Shield nontoxic Biological Termiticide (**N-Viro Products Limited**), must be applied by professional pest-control operators only. You can contact the company for an applicator near you. You may also want to know that **Real Goods** also sells nematodes. However, while they offer them as a natural control against a variety of in-ground pests, they do not specifically mention termites. If you use these nematodes against termites in your own home, you'll need to do the work yourself, and assume the responsibility for any success, or failure.

Applications of either pyrethrin or nematodes may have to be repeated to be effective, and they don't remain active against termites for extended periods of times.

Dampwood Termite Alternative-Control Methods

Dampwood termites can only live in or around damp wood. Because of their absolute dependence on moisture, drying up all your home's moisture problems will quickly end most dampwood-termite infestations.

Therefore, check to be sure that all your gutters, and any foundation drains, are working correctly. If your shrubbery has become overgrown, or is too near your home's foundation, you may need to cut it back or remove it. You'll also want to make certain that the ground slopes sufficiently away from your home's foundation on all sides. If you're in an area with a high water table, seriously consider installing a sump pump, if necessary.

In some situations, a dehumidifier can effectively remove excess indoor humidity. Exhaust fans can also be helpful. (See *High Humidity* on page 530.) In addition, check to see that there are no roof problems such as loose or missing shingles. Finally, repair any leaking pipes and drains.

By the way, you should seriously consider treating any new construction with a borate solution to help prevent any future dampwood termite activity. (For more information on this procedure, see *Subterranean Termite Alternative-Control Methods* above).

Drywood Termite Alternative-Control Methods

Drywood termites don't have the moisture requirements of either subterranean or dampwood termites. As a result, their nests can be anywhere where there's wood. For homeowners, this means that every part of the house can be at risk. With new construction, you can permanently protect your home against drywood termites by using a preventive borate treatment sprayed on all the wood while it is being built (for more information on this procedure, see *Subterranean Termite Alternative-Control Methods* above).

A fairly safe approach to dealing with drywood termites in existing homes is to spot-treat any areas that are infested by using an injectable pyrethrin (a liquid extract derived from pyrethrum in chrysanthemum flower heads) One brand containing other additives (including petroleum-based solvents and propellants) is Tri-Die (**Whitmer Micro-Gen Research Laboratories, Inc.**). This product is not sold directly to consumers. Therefore, you'll need to hire a pest-control company to inject Tri-Die into the affected wood for you. By the way, the pyrethrin may have to be injected more than once to be effective.

Another alternative approach to spot-treating drywood termites in existing houses is *electrocution* (killing by electricity). One electrocuting device designed to specifically do this is called the Electro-Gun. It will create an electric current that is capable of killing termites without damaging your home. In the U.S., this machine can be leased by local pesticide companies from **Etex, Ltd.** For more information on the Electro-Gun, have your exterminator contact the company. (Note: this method can't be used against subterranean termites or dampwood termites.) It should be mentioned that killing termites by electrocution is immediately effective but it won't provide long-term protection because a new infestation, unfortunately, could begin immediately.

Alternative Outdoor Personal Pest Protection

Going outdoors can be a joyful experience. That is, if you are not constantly swatting, or being bitten by, pests. While there are many products in the marketplace designed to protect you and your family outdoors, many contain synthetic, petroleum-derived compounds and other ingredients you may not want directly on your body. After all, some of these compounds may be potentially harmful, not only to bugs, but to humans, too.

Modifying your Behavior to Control Outdoor Pests

Fortunately, there are a few simple things you can do to help prevent being bothered by bees, flie, and other types of pests. It's almost universally believed that wearing drab clothing works well. However, while this apparently causes some mosquitoes to ignore the wearers, in the case of other mosquito species, it has just the opposite effect. Another common belief is that avoiding scented products or cologne will keep insects away. This, too, seems logical, and with some pests it may actually help.

One thing that will work for certain is to cover up so pests can't reach you. That means shoes and socks, long sleeve shirts, and pants with elastic around the bottom cuffs to keep them tightly against your legs. To protect your head, wear a hat. Even better, wear one with attached mosquito netting. A cotton/polyester fabric hat with black nylon insect netting is sold by **Vermont Country Store** (Voice of the Mountains catalog) and **Solutions.** If you want to buy some netting and use it over your head, baby, etc., you can order it by the yard from **Gohn Bros.** This is a 54"-wide mesh fabric made of nylon. In addition, polyester mosquito canopy netting is handled by **Real Goods.** Finally, **One Step Ahead** handles mosquito netting canopies for baby strollers. (Note: Before purchasing any mosquito netting, make sure it hasn't been treated with added pesticides.)

Sonic Waves to Control Outdoor Pests

There are a number of companies that offer personal *ultrasonic emitter* pest deterrents. These broadcast a high-pitched whine (beyond the range human hearing) that supposedly causes pests to go as far away from the sound source as possible. Unfortunately, these apparently have little value against most pests. Still if you still want to experiment with one, check local outdoor outfitter stores. They may carry them. One mail-order source that sometimes carries them is **Harmony.**

A device that may actually work is one that mimics that sound of beating dragonfly wings. Because dragonflies are ancient predators of mosquitoes, mosquitoes hearing this sound will apparently stay clear. To humans, however, the sound is virtually inaudible. One dragonfly-wing sound imitator is Love Bug (**Prince Lionheart**). This is a cute, plastic, ladybug-shaped unit operated with batteries. It has a convenient clip that makes attaching it to a blanket or a stroller's fabric side very easy. You may be able to find it locally. If not, you can order one directly from the manufacturer or from **One Step Ahead**. In addition, you can purchase the MosquitoControl from **Harmony**. This product does the same job as a Love Bug, but does so in a less flamboyantly shaped package.

Alternative Topical Lotions to Control Outdoor Pests

Of course, you may want to use an anti-bug lotion to protect you when outdoors. These days, especially in season, most health-food stores and alternative groceries carry them. Be aware, that most of these are quite aromatic because of the fragrant essential oils often used in their formulas.

If you'd like to order a preparation, **Real Goods** offers All-Terrain. This is an herbal, hypoallergenic skin-lotion type of insect repellent. **Burt's Bees, Inc.** makes and sells Farmer's Friend Lemongrass Insect Lotion. This is made with grapeseed oil, lemongrass oil, citronella oil, eucalyptus oil, and vitamin E. Also, **Simmons Natural Bodycare** makes and sells their Simmons Skeeter Skatter. This product is made of herbs in a vegetable-oil base.

The **Natural Animal Health Products, Inc.** line includes Ecozone Outdoor Skin Protector. This product's ingredients include sesame oil, cedar wood oil, etc. You can buy it directly from the manufacturer. In addition, **Kiss my Face** makes and sells Swy Flotter, an "all -natural botanical-ingredient personal body insect repellent." You can also order it from **Tucson Cooperative Warehouse**. Finally, from **Bio-Designs**, you can purchase Green Ban herbal/essential-oil insect repellent.

Part 5
LIFESTYLE

CHAPTER 18: READING, WRITING, & WRAPPING

It's often hard to believe, but everything from stationery to pencils to wrapping paper can affect your home's indoor air quality. Even though such items may seem of minor consequence, choosing the least offensive types available can sometimes make a real and noticeable difference in your health, and that of your family. Of course, this is especially true for chemically sensitive individuals.

Printed Matter

Many people assume that reading is a benign activity. It would seem as if it would be, at least at first. However, books, magazines, and newspapers can be some of the more bothersome things brought into a home. This section explains why, and what you can do to make reading safer—if you're a sensitive person.

Problems with Printed Material

New books commonly cause tolerance problems for many chemically sensitive persons. This is usually due to the paper, the glues used in binding, and the ink. At one time, printing inks were made of varnish, linseed oil, and *lampblack* (finely ground carbon pigment). Most modern printing inks still consist of very odorous synthetic film-forming resins, pigments, and solvents, however some newer inks are now being made with natural resins derived from soybeans. In fact, it's possible that these newer inks may, in time, entirely replace the older formulations. This is good news, not just from an environmental viewpoint, but also because these soy-based inks tend to be less bothersome to sensitive people—that is, unless you have a particular intolerance to soy.

Newspapers are commonly intolerable to many sensitive persons because of the low-grade newsprint used, as well as the ink. Because many newspapers are printed daily, the inks are usually both extremely fresh and odorous. In addition, if newspapers, books, magazines, or other printed items are purchased in drugstores or other retail outlets, they could easily have absorbed perfume and other potentially objectionable odors from the store. Because of their absorbent nature, newspapers are also very susceptible to mildew and dust accumulation in storage.

Of special concern are older books. While old books will have lost most of their new paper, glue, and ink odors, they can be very bothersome overall. This is because they usually have picked up tobacco smoke and perfume odors over many years of use. In addition, they can sometimes be contaminated with dust, insects, mildew, or just plain mustiness.

Storing Printed Material

Ideally, in a healthy household, all the printed materials should be stored so they can't negatively affect the indoor air, especially if there are chemically sensitive persons in the family. One safe way to store books is in *lawyer's bookcases*. These are actually nothing more than wooden cabinets with shelving, but with glass doors on the front. Sadly, most manufactured wooden ones you'll come across will have backs, and perhaps even side and shelves, made of veneered plywood. In most cases, cabinet-grade plywood will *outgas* (release) a great deal of nasty urea formaldehyde. (See *Formaldehyde* on page 527.) Such is the case with the maple/plywood 2-, 3-, and 4-tier lawyer bookcases from **Ballard Designs**, and the oak lawyer's bookcases (hand finished or in unfinished kits) from **Yield House**. Therefore, unless you're lucky enough to find metal lawyer's bookcases at a local office-supply store, or antique ones, you may have to have them custom built. (See *Custom-Made Hard Furniture* on page 337.) Of course, built-in bookcases can generally be fitted with glass doors by most cabinetmakers.

If you're able to find healthy lawyer's book cases, magazines and newspapers can also be placed in them. However, little-used closets, metal boxes, trunks, or cabinets, can be useful for storing periodicals as well (see *Household Storage* on page 511). To find suitable metal cabinets, you'll want to check local office-supply stores. In addition, **Lee Metal Products**, **Edsal Manufacturing Co., Inc.**, and **Reliable Corp.** (a large office-supply catalog) handle several all-metal cabinets you can mail order.

Simple Alternative Reading Strategies

Without a doubt, there's unmistakable appeal to reading in your bed or curled up on the living-room couch. However, for those bothered by books, newspapers, and magazines, reading outdoors, or near an open window indoors, are generally much healthier choices. Plenty of fresh air and ventilation ensures that odors from bothersome printed materials are diluted and dissipated.

Sometimes using a *zeolite* adsorbing unit can help. Zeolite is a mineral whose surface is extremely rough and has an inherent static charge. Therefore, it's able to *adsorb* certain gaseous pollutant molecules. This means that the molecules will electrostatically cling to the zeolite's surface. Nox-out Air Purifiers, which can be ordered from **Dick Blick**, use man-made zeolite in 16-ounce metal containers in your choice of wall or table mounting styles. Refills are available. Other types of filtering devices are discussed in *Chapter 23: Improving* *your Indoor Air.* Unfortunately, air filters don't often help a great deal with sensitive people because the reading material (which is generally within two feet of your nose) is closer to you than the filter.

A simple, safer reading approach is to make the printed matter itself less bothersome. It seems that some chemically sensitive persons are able to read indoors if the printed material has been sufficiently aired outdoors first. Airing can be done using a clothesline and clothespins or by laying the printed material down securely on a flat surface. Correspondence, newspapers, and small magazines can all be hung or laid out until they become tolerable. Of course, it's important to make sure that the surroundings are dry and free of contaminating odors, pollen, etc.

Some chemically sensitive people actually *bake* their printed matter before they read it. This can be accomplished several ways. For example, you can put books in a mesh laundry bag, open your clothes-dryer door, drape the bag's strings over the door, and then close the door on the strings so that the laundry bag is suspended inside the dryer's door. This will hold the book in place so it won't tumble around. At that point, turn the dryer on medium heat for 30 minutes. (It'll be necessary to experiment with temperature settings and running times.) A variation of this method is to place a book on a heat-resistant open-mesh tray that can be attached to the inside of the dryer door. Such a tray must be made with care so it will suspend the book in the center of the dryer's drum without the tray, or the book, falling to the bottom of the drum.

Another "bake-out" procedure is to warm your books, or other printed materials, in your electric oven or portable toaster oven on a very low setting. If you try this, be sure the range-hood fan is running on high speed and a window is open. Unfortunately, bake-outs done in clothes dryers and kitchen ovens often prove less than satisfactory because of the danger of fire, problems with contaminating the appliance itself, and the possibility of odors entering the living space.

For some very sensitive persons, no amount of fresh air or "baking" of books etc. is adequate to make reading tolerable. For these individuals, wearing a 100%-cotton face mask containing an activated-charcoal insert can be very helpful. The activated charcoal can adsorb a great deal of the bothersome odors before they reach the wearer's nasal passages. There are several mail-order sources for all-cotton filtering masks, including **Allerx**, **Allergy Relief Shop, Inc.**, and **Bio Designs**. From **American Environmental Health Foundation** you can get masks of either untreated 100%-cotton or silk, with your choice of activated-coconut-shell charcoal, activated-lignite charcoal, or activated-bituminous-charcoal inserts. All the masks offered by these companies are washable and refill inserts are available.

Reading Boxes

Some extremely sensitive persons find that even wearing filter masks just don't provide enough protection from the outgassing chemicals, and other odors, emanating from printed material. For such people, *reading boxes* are often ideal solutions. Reading boxes are specially designed cases made with glass or clear plastic tops (and sometimes sides as well) in a wood or metal frame. Printed material is placed inside and the reader looks through the clear top to read.

You should be aware that some reading boxes are unvented. These are usually simply constructed, small, and fairly inexpensive. However, those that can be vented to the outdoors or into an air-filtering unit are healthier choices. This is because vented and filtered models can actually *remove* bothersome contaminants so they won't enter the living space to cause problems. Unvented units will accumulate odors that can seep out when a page is turned (in certain types), or when a book is placed inside or removed from the enclosed chamber. The down side is that vented reading boxes will cost more and they generally lack portability.

Safe Reading & Computer Box Co. makes and sells glass units with 20-gauge *galvanized steel* (steel with a zinc coating to prevent rust) frames. These are supplied with a fan and are designed to be vented to the outdoors. (They come with a "cut-to-size" exhaust insert to put in your window.) These boxes come in desk computer, lap-top computer, and computer-tower sizes. In addition, custom sizes are available. Safe Computer and Reading Boxes can be ordered directly from the company or from **Nigra Enterprises**.

If a reading box doesn't seem affordable, but you still need a barrier between you and the printed page, you might try using large-sized cellophane bags. These work fairly well for small catalogs, paperback books, and letters (see *Cellophane Goods* on page 510). Unfortunately, cellophane is quite brittle. Therefore, your cellophane reading bags probably will have to be replaced frequently. Cellophane bags can be ordered from **N.E.E.D.S.**, **Janice Corporation**, **Natural Lifestyle**, **Karen's Natural Products**, **Allergy Relief Shop, Inc.**, as well as from **Erlander's Natural Products**.

As an alternative, zip-sealing plastic bags are even more effective at isolating ink and paper odors than cellophane bags. They're also much sturdier. However, the plastic itself can be bothersome. Fortunately, airing zip-sealing plastic bags outdoors in dry uncontaminated surroundings for several days often makes them tolerable for sensitive people. While they're less commonly available, if you can locate the two-gallon size, you'll find that they often work much better than the smaller one-gallon size. (Note: Kroger grocery stores handle them under their own label.) With some practice, you can learn to turn pages while the reading material remains sealed inside the zip-sealed bag. This will mean virtually no direct exposure to the printed matter. Warning: If you turn the pages of printed material while it is inside a sealed plastic bag, the pages will become somewhat rumpled.

Recorded Reading Material

Books and magazines are now available on audiocassette, CD ROM, and audio CD. Because of this, chemically sensitive persons who can't tolerate ink and paper can often enjoy reading again by becoming "electronically literate."

Books and Magazines on 4-Track Audio Tape

An alternative to visually reading, is listening to books and magazines recorded on four-track audio tapes. The major supplier of four-track books in the U.S. is the national Library of Congress, which has a free program available for those with physical disabilities that prevent the normal use of printed materials. The physical conditions generally recognized for admittance into the program are blindness, stroke, amputation, etc. However, those with MCS (Multiple Chemical Sensitivity) may also qualify—that is, if a "certifying authority" (a physician, nurse, agency, or institution) signs the application confirming that their illness prevents them from being able to read printed books. For information on the program, and an application form, ask your local librarian, or you can contact the **National Library Service for the Blind and Physically Handicapped** which is located at The Library of Congress.

Once your application has been approved, a tape player will be assigned to you on a loan basis. You can request either new or used equipment. You'll also receive a list of available books and magazines in a variety of categories. Your tape machine, and your book and magazine selections, are always sent and returned by mail. If you would prefer to purchase your own machine, **LS&S Group** offers a catalog featuring a large selection. Models, brands, features, and prices vary. The company also has recorded tapes you may want to purchase for your very own. From **Lighthouse International**, you can order a portable Sony 4-track tape player.

Another organization that offers books on tape you might want to contact is **Recordings for the Blind & Dyslexic**. This is a nonprofit group with over 60,000 titles available. To enter their program, a small initial registration fee is required. After that, the services are free. The books from this foundation are on four-track tapes. If you don't already have a four-track tape machine, the foundation has some for sale.

Books on Audio Cassettes

The **Jewish Guild for the Blind** has many popular fiction and nonfiction books on standard audio cassettes. The books are read by volunteers, so the quality isn't always up to professional standards. However, the service is free to all adults of any religious faith. A statement from your doctor, nurse, or social-service worker confirming that you are unable to read books or magazines, plus a small registration fee, is all that's required for enrollment.

Of course, many people besides the disabled are using tape-recorded books. Today, major companies are producing and marketing audio-cassette books for the general public. As a matter of fact, because books on audio-cassette are becoming so popular, new titles are constantly being released. Many local libraries—probably including your own—now have them available for check-out by anyone. There are also several mail-order companies that specialize in selling books on audio cassette. One such popular catalog is **Audio Editions**. This company has over 4,000 titles including classics, novels, westerns, fiction, humor, poetry, nonfiction, science fiction, young people, and language studies. Also, **Books On Tape** offers a large collection of audio cassettes for both purchase or rental.

Books on CD

Another electronic reading option is purchasing and using *CD-ROM* books. (CD-ROMs are <u>c</u>ompact <u>d</u>isks with <u>r</u>ead <u>o</u>nly <u>m</u>emory, so they're complete in and of themselves and they can't be recorded over.) CD-ROMs allow the printed words to appear on your computer monitor's screen. Therefore, you actually get the pleasure of seeing printed words, but without the need for paper or ink. This can be ideal for sensitive people who can't normally tolerate books, but can tolerate their computer.

The books now available on CD-ROM can be used on either PCs (IBM-compatible units), Macintosh products (Apple computers), or both. Dictionaries, encyclopedias, and other reference books are now particularly popular. The classics of literature are also widely available. To find books on CD-ROM, check local computer software stores, and mail-order catalogs.

If you'd rather listen to CD books than read them from your computer monitor, the **Jewish Guild for the Blind** and **Recordings for the Blind & Dyslexic** both have recorded books on compact audio discs. These are loaned at no charge to those who qualify. (See *Books and Magazines on Audio Tape* above for how to qualify.) In addition, **Audio Editions** has some CD books you may want to purchase.

Stationery

Many sensitive individuals find typical paper bothersome or intolerable. Often this is because of the chemicals that manufacturers use to transform logs into paper. Fortunately, there are a few less-bothersome paper choices available.

Paper

Paper is defined as sheets of *felted* (interlaced) plant fibers. Traditionally, to make paper, plant matter (or natural-fiber fabric) is chopped and mashed until the individual fibers separate, creating paper pulp. The pulp is then added to water in a vat, and the mixture is thoroughly stirred. Then, a framed screen is placed in the vat and lifted out. The water drains through the screen leaving a thin layer of pulp on the screen's top surface. The wet sheet is then removed from the screen and allowed to dry.

This basic paper-making process was invented in China at the beginning of the 2nd century AD, using silk, rice, and hemp as the major plant fibers. The Chinese government successfully kept paper making a secret for 500 years, until the Japanese and Arabs (through clandestine means) eventually learned what paper consisted of and how it was made. During the Middle Ages, Arab paper making methods (using flax and hemp) spread across Europe. Until then, that part of the world used only *papyrus* (crisscrossed strips of papyrus-plant pith beaten flat) and *parchment* (stretched and polished goat, sheep, or calf skin) for writing material. Paper quickly replaced these materials because it was cheaper, easier, and faster to produce. However, papyrus, and especially parchment, were still used for special documents.

While paper was somewhat quicker to produce than papyrus or parchment, paper making was still a relatively slow process. After all, the individual sheets had to be made one at a time. However, by the industrial revolution in the nineteenth century, paper making at last became mechanized. With time, more advanced machinery—coupled with the innovation of using wood for the fiber source in paper pulp—created a major industry. As a result, inexpensive papers became increasing available.

Typical Wood-Pulp Paper

Most typical wood-pulp paper today originates from pine and fir trees. Transforming softwood logs into thin paper sheets requires a great deal of technology—and many noxious chemicals. As a result, some of this country's worst toxic sites have been found surrounding certain paper mills. Fortunately, laws are now targeted toward greatly reducing the environmental pollution problems created by paper production.

The Three Basic Paper Grades

Today, modern paper mills use wood pulp that is created in one of three ways, each of which produces a different type of paper. Mechanically ground wood is generally used to make wood pulp for the very cheapest paper grades, such as newsprint. This method is fast and relatively inexpensive to achieve. However, it leaves a certain amount of undesirable plant residues in the pulp, and in the paper. As a result, low-grade papers often appear somewhat coarse and may yellow or discolor fairly quickly.

Machine-ground wood is combined with chemicals, then cooked for a brief time, to create the wood pulp used in most middle-grade papers. These papers still have some unwanted plant residues, but they are less coarse-looking than the lowest-grade papers. Finally, the best papers come from wood pulp that was made by having the raw wood mechanically chipped, combined with chemicals, and then cooked for a very long period of time. This is the costliest, and most time-consuming, method to create paper pulp, but this pulp produces smooth and attractive paper without unwanted residues.

How Typical Best-Grade Papers are Made

The actual steps to get from wood log to finished paper are many. This is especially true when making higher-grade papers.So, a brief explanation of this particular method will be discussed to enable you to better understand how paper is made.

To create the best papers, wood chips, and certain chemicals (sulfite salts or a solution of caustic soda and sodium sulfide), are placed in a special tank known as a *digester*. Once filled, the digester is operated for half a day at a very high heat. These conditions, along with the chemicals, cause the *lignin* within the wood chips to break down. Because the natural lignin holds the plant cell walls together, its deterioration allows the cellulose fibers to separate and form pulp. After the pulp is formed, it's then thoroughly cleaned and the chemicals are washed away and any debris removed. Bleach is then sometimes added for whitening. Unfortunately, if chlorine bleaches are used, toxic *dioxins* may be created as by-products. (Dioxins are a family of chlorinated hydrocarbons that have been shown to be carcinogenic, and can cause fetal abnormalities in certain animals.)

Next, the pulp undergoes a beating process to make it more flexible. It may also be colored (usually with synthetic dyes) and have materials known as *fillers* added. Fillers such as white chalk, clay, and titanium dioxide give paper a better appearance. Certain gluey plant secretions (rosin, starch, and/or various gums) referred to as *sizings* are also commonly added. They increase a paper's resistance to the water of water-based inks. As it turns out, many sizings are acidic. Therefore, eventually they'll cause cellulose fibers to disintegrate. Fortunately, alkaline sizing agents are now in use, but acidic types remain the norm.

Once the pulp has undergone all these processes, it's finally ready for the paper-forming machines. While there are two basic equipment types, both use screening to capture a thin pulp layer, followed by several steps to remove the water. The dried paper is next wound onto reels. Rolled paper is then cut into sheets.

It should be mentioned that some papers may undergo still further finishing operations. For example in *calendering*, particular finishes are added to the paper as it passes through a series of steel rollers. Pigment, glaze, and/or glue mixtures may be applied to one or both sides of the sheets to add glossiness and/or increase opacity. As a result of all the treatments undergone in all these various processes, it's little wonder that most typical wood-pulp papers are bothersome to many sensitive individuals. Even low-grade papers such as newsprint, which have far fewer production steps, are usually as bothersome as high-grade papers—sometimes more so. This is due to a combination of the mill treatments and the greater amounts of softwood residues present in lower-grade papers.

Recycled Paper

A growing number of paper companies are now producing recycled papers. Ideally, this lessens the quantity of trees needed for the mills. In reality though, paper labeled "recycled" may contain a only a small portion of truly recycled material. Often, the recycled material is leftover scrap from the mill's own manufacturing process and not paper that consumers have taken to recycling centers. To brighten most recycled paper's otherwise muddy tinge, additional bleaching processes are often used. If chlorine is the bleaching agent, dangerous dioxins may be created. Therefore, when you purchase paper labeled "recycled," you might want to determine the actual percentage of recycled material, how much of it is post-consumer paper, and whether dioxin-forming bleaches were used.

If you're interested in using recycled paper products, they're becoming more "mainstream" all the time. So, your local stationer or office-supply store may have some in stock. A number of mail-order companies handle them, too. Recycled office paper and envelopes, as well as note cards, stationery, and more, are offered by **Green Field Paper Co.** This company's paper is made without chlorine bleach. One-hundred-percent-recycled-paper stationery and note cards are also available from **Karen's Natural Products**. From **Fiber Options Paper Co.**, you can order 100%-recycled-paper note cards and notebooks. They also have office paper in 500-sheet reams.

Unfortunately, it should be noted that many chemically sensitive people are bothered by *any* wood-pulp paper—recycled or not. Therefore, while obviously better for planet earth, recycled paper may not be any more tolerable for them than typical wood-pulp papers. By the way, you should generally expect to pay more for recycled paper than for typical papers. This is probably due to lower production runs and perhaps the industry sensing that the environmental consumer market will likely pay the extra cost.

Alternative Papers

A number of alternative papers are now available to consumers. These are usually not only more visually interesting, but often more tolerable, too. Not surprisingly though, alternative-plant papers can often cost more than typical wood-pulp papers.

Cotton and Cotton-Blend Papers

Of the various alternatives, 100%-cotton papers are often a good choice. Fortunately, many office-supply stores carry at least one line of standard 8$1/2$" x 11" cotton paper with matching envelopes.

In particular, **Southworth Co.** manufactures Southworth 100% Cotton Fiber Paper for Resumes. This is a parchment-deed, résumé-quality, 24 lb. cotton paper (in white or ivory) in 100-sheet packages. Matching envelopes are available. Other Southworth cotton papers are Southworth 100% Cotton Fiber Acid Free Thesis Paper, Southworth 100% Cotton Fiber The Best Paper, and Southworth 100% Cotton Fiber Legal Document Paper. You'll need to check your local stores to see what they're handling. If you are unable to locate Southworth paper, you can contact the company for the nearest dealer. Another major manufacturer of cotton paper (and envelopes) is **Crane & Co.** Like Southworth paper, Crane papers are commonly sold in area office-supply stores. In addition, some of each of these two cotton-paper lines are sold in the **Staples, Inc.** catalog.

All-organic-cotton greeting cards, card stock, sketch books, office paper "mini- reams," as well as envelopes, are offered by **Fiber Options Paper Co.** They also have 24 lb. bond business paper in 500-sheet reams. In addition, sketch pads and note cards that are made with 50% organic cotton and 50% recycled paper are available from the **Green Field Paper Co.** catalog.

Hemp and Hemp-Blend Papers

One of the oldest raw materials for making paper is hemp. The Chinese were growing hemp to make paper at least as early as 4500 BC. It remained a popular paper material for years, until wood pulp more or less replaced it. Today, however, hemp (Cannabis *sativa L.*, or simply cannabis) is making a comeback. This is not only because hemp hurds (short fibers that can't be used in making threads or yarns) create an excellent paper, but because of hemp's easy and usually chemical-free cultivation. By the way, technically termed *industrial hemp* to distinguish it from drug quality cannabis (marijuana), the hemp used in paper making has only 1%, or less, of the hallucinogenic compound *delta-9 tetrahydrocannabinol (THC)*. So, you are not supporting the "drug trade" in any way by purchasing or using hemp paper.

From the Green Field Paper Co., you can order recycled hemp-paper items. Their line includes note cards, stationery, holiday cards, journals, and sketch books. Recycled hemp-paper note cards, stationery, office paper "mini-reams," and envelopes can be purchased from **Fiber Options Paper Co.** They also have 24 lb. business bond paper made of recycled hemp paper in 500-sheet reams.

Other Fiber and Fiber-Blend Papers

Another option is rice paper. Like hemp, rice paper has been used for centuries in the Far East. In fact, it may have been the first type of paper. In the U.S., rice-paper stationery may sometimes be found in Oriental import stores. Other alternative papers you may occasionally come across, that may be acceptable options, are 100%-linen, linen/cotton blends, and various papers made of other plant materials.

Two companies in particular market a variety of interesting papers. The **Green Field Paper Co.** catalog has note cards, stationery, envelopes, bound journals, "typing paper," etc. made of blends of recycled paper with tea, garlic skins or coffee-bean chaff. **Fiber Options Paper Co.** has 100%-*kenaf* (a plant related to hibiscus with jute-like fibers) paper items. These include greeting cards, note cards, journals, and stationery. This same firm also has 24 lb. bond paper in 500-sheet reams made of bamboo.

Handmade and Artist Papers

You might also consider buying papers that were made by hand. Happily, handmade papers are becoming more available all the time. In most cases, such papers are produced by small specialty companies or individual artists. The papers they create are often both unique and attractive.

A wide variety of materials can be used to create the paper pulp for homemade papers—sometimes even old cotton blue jeans. Fortunately, the pulps, emulsions, and additives used in the production of handmade papers are more likely to be less toxic than those used by large paper-making firms. As a result, many handmade papers are tolerable for even very sensitive persons. However, you can expect handmade papers to be relatively expensive. In fact, they are often sold by the individual sheet because of their high price.

To find handmade papers locally, check your local art-supply stores. By mail order, **Dick Blick** offers exotic 25" x 37" acid-free "unryu" paper. They also have "Thai banana" art paper in the same size. Local bookstores and libraries often have books on do-it-yourself paper making. Creating your own hand-made paper can save you money and be fun all at the same time.

Writing Implements

Today, many pens contain inks that are bothersome to chemically sensitive persons. This section will explore a few of the more tolerable options you may want to try, as well as information on pencils, erasers, etc.

Making Writing More Tolerable

It should be noted that, if you're having tolerability problems using paper and pens, etc., you can do your writing outdoors—weather permitting. If you must do it indoors, have good ventilation around you. You may find that wearing a facial mask with an activated-charcoal insert is helpful. All-cotton filtering masks can be purchased from **Allerx**, **Allergy Relief Shop, Inc.**, and **Bio Designs**. In addition, **American Environmental Health Foundation** offers an untreated 100%-cotton or silk mask. You can buy one alone or with your choice of activated-coconut-shell charcoal, activated-lignite charcoal, or an activated-bituminous-charcoal insert. All these companies handle replacement activated-charcoal refill inserts for the masks they sell.

Of course, a custom-made ventilated "reading box" from **Safe Reading & Computer Box Co.** can make your writing easier. Their boxes are generally made of glass and 20-gauge *galvanized steel.* (This is a type of steel with a zinc coating to prevent rust.) They're also equipped with a fan and a window insert. Air flows through them from the front side and exits into the outdoors. Make sure that the size you select will allow adequate movement of your hands. Units for computers and other standard and custom sizes are also available. By the way, you can also order them through **Nigra Enterprises.**

Pens and Markers

In its broadest definition, a pen is any hand-held tool used to transfer ink to a flat writing surface. As early as ancient Egypt, scribes used reeds and hollow bamboo sections as pens. Pens didn't really change very much until 6th century AD Europe when the *quill* (split feather shaft) became the common pen. Quills remained in popular use up through the 19th century until steel-point pens gradually replaced them. Inks up to this time were usually made of *lampblack* (finely ground carbon pigment, dispersed in water or oil, and sometimes stabilized by plant gums or glues), indigo, crushed *galls* (abnormal lumpy growths) from oak and other trees, or from the dark fluids of octopus, squid, and cuttlefish. Many of these inks, especially lampblack, produced writing fluids that were very long-lasting and weren't affected by light or moisture after they had been applied. Incidentally, India ink is a lampblack ink that is still used today, but mainly for artwork and *calligraphy* (decorative hand lettering).

By 1884, the fountain pen was invented. Generally, these used (and most still do) inks made with water-soluble dyes. These inks were designed to be more free-flowing, and be less likely to clog the pen's ink reservoir or writing *nib* (pen tip). Unfortunately, many of the early inks had relatively poor light- and moisture-resisting qualities. In 1888, the ball-point pen was introduced. Ball-points required their own type of ink—one that was thick and viscous, so it wouldn't drip out around the ball-bearing tip, and yet not be prone to clogging. Interestingly, it wasn't until the mid-1940s that ball-point pens, and their inks, were perfected and they actually began replacing fountain pens. (Modern ball-point pens use an ink made of a combination of oils, solvents, and synthetic polymers and dyes.) By 1964, the soft-tip pen (marker) was introduced from Japan. Until the last few years, all soft-tip markers used inks that were synthetic dyes dissolved in alcohol. These inks were designed to prevent the tips from drying up or clogging. Now, some soft-tip markers use inks made of water combined with water-soluble synthetic dyes. In the last ten years, a variety of other pens types have become available in the U.S., some with their own new forms of ink.

Unfortunately, however, many of today's ball-point, roller-ball, fountain, and cartridge pens, as well as markers (especially solvent-based markers), can be sources of intolerance for some very sensitive individuals. Of all the pens available, the water-based, fine-line, felt-tip markers seem to be the better choices. (As a general rule, water-based products are nearly always better tolerated, healthier options than odorous solvent versions.) Also, you should keep in mind that, if you choose a fine-point pen, you'll expose yourself to less ink than with a regular or wide-nib pen. However, it must be noted that water-based felt-tip pens are now becoming more difficult to find, often being replaced by roller-ball pens. The good news is that many of these roller-ball pens use ink formulations that seem to be less problematic than typical ball-point-pen ink.

Therefore, if you're chemically sensitive it would be best to experiment with several brands of water-based, fine-line, felt-tip, markers as well as roller-ball pens. That way, you can determine for yourself which ones will be the most benign to you. To find a good variety of pens, check both your local office-supply and art-supply stores, which usually carry very large selections. Also, most drugstores and discount houses carry at least a few brands. In addition, large office supply catalogs such as **Reliable Corp.** and **Staples, Inc.** should have a fairly good selection from which to choose.

Unusual pens that you might find satisfactory are birch-wood ball-point pens from **Tomorrow's World**. These are inexpensive, they have nontoxic ink, and refills are available. **Fiber Options Paper Co.** sells Woody Refillable Pens. These have a stainless-steel ball point and a nontoxic ink made of glycol-based ethyl alcohol. Refills are available.

Pencils

It's often surprising, even to many chemically sensitive people, that a common pencil could be bothersome. But the truth is, it often can. This can be better understood if you analyze how pencils are actually made. Typical pencils contain a "lead" core made of a *composite graphite* product. You see, graphite lead is made by combining powdered natural mineral graphite (a soft, lustrous form of black carbon), clay, and water, then extruding the mixture to create very small-diameter rods. The wet rods are dried, then kiln-fired at nearly 2,000°F. Afterwards, the baked rods are impregnated with wax to give them a smooth quality. Next, the composite graphite (in common pencils) is encased by two precut wood sections that are held together with glue. It should be noted that the wood used for pencils is nearly always *incense cedar*, a very aromatic softwood species. Finally, the wood is coated with paint and an eraser is attached with a metal ring.

As a result, the aromatic cedar wood, the glue, the paint, and/or the eraser can pose intolerance problems to some sensitive individuals. In certain cases, even the graphite may be a problem, probably because of the wax. Fortunately, a metal mechanical pencil (with replaceable "lead" and a covered eraser) is usually a more acceptable option for anyone who finds conventional pencils too bothersome. Metal mechanical pencils are sold at most stationery, office supply, and drafting-supply stores. Two popular brands you may want to try are Cross and Pentel. Two large office-supply catalogs, **Reliable Corp.** and **Staples, Inc.**, have metal mechanical pens you can mail order.

By the way, pencil lead is sold in several hardnesses. (The more clay in the composite graphite, the harder it is.) The most common pencil type is B grade. However, B leads (and softer leads) can smear easily on your hands and paper. To avoid this, try using a harder HB lead. It generally provides clean and legible writing, without excess smearing problems. While H and HH grades are also often available, they can be so hard that they produce lines too fine and light for easy reading.

Computers and Typewriters

Of course, these days the writing method of choice is with a computer. Information on computers can be found in on page 483.

For those who can't tolerate a computer, or don't wish to learn how to use one, manual typewriters made with steel cases can be ordered from **Vermont Country Store** (Voice of the Mountains catalog). Replacement ink ribbons are also available. Keep in mind that ink ribbons may be bothersome. For correcting typewritten letters, etc. consider using a white-out tape, rather than a more-noxious white-out fluid (see below).

Erasers and White-Out Fluids & Tapes

Unfortunately mistakes are often made when writing. Today there are a number of products you can use to remove or cover up your blunders. Some are safer than others.

Erasers

Erasers are substances that can remove pencil or ink markings from paper. Unfortunately, many erasers are surprisingly odorous. This is understandable because most are made of natural rubber, an innately aromatic material. Probably one of more bothersome types of erasers (for chemically sensitive people) are tan gum erasers, which are made of a gummy, yet crumbly, rubber compound. Kneaded erasers, which are soft and pliable, are usually somewhat better tolerated, as are hard pink erasers.

Interestingly, erasers made of vinyl, rather than rubber, can often be acceptable choices for many sensitive individuals, and those with latex allergies. Generally, vinyl isn't a material suggested for an ideal healthy household. However, in this case, vinyl is preferred over natural rubber because it outgasses less. These days, white-vinyl erasers are often used on mylar or plastic drawing film, but they can work well on paper too. Vinyl erasers come in a variety of shapes, from small rectangles to spiral paper-wrapped pencil shapes. One popular brand of vinyl erasers is FaberCastell whose vinyl-eraser pencils are sold under the name of Vinyl Peel-Off Magic Rubs. To find vinyl erasers locally, check drafting-supply, office-supply, and art-supply stores. Vinyl erasers are also usually available in office-supply catalogs including **Staples, Inc.** and **Reliable Corp.**

White-Out Fluids

While many erasers can pose certain tolerance problems, typical *white-out fluids* (also known as correction fluids) are usually far worse. (White-out fluids are opaque, quick-drying substances that are applied with a brush to unwanted ink on paper to create a new white surface that can be written on.) Some people feel that white-out fluids are some of the most odorous and potentially dangerous pollutant sources in home offices. Bottles of white-out fluid generally have warnings against inhaling them and they stress the need for adequate ventilation when applying them. This is because they often contain noxious petroleum-based solvents, and other nasty chemicals, as ingredients.

For some time now, a few "enviro-friendly" white-out fluids have been marketed. Two are Bic Wite-Out, which "contains no chemicals able to damage the ozone layer," and Liquid Paper Multi-Fluid, which "complies with California's strict Proposition 65 Environmental Guidelines." Remember, however, these may still be intolerable for chemically sensitive individuals. Therefore, when you find it necessary, you might consider using *white-out tape* (correction tape) instead of white-out fluid (see below).

Nearly all office-supply stores, discount stores, and drug stores sell white-out fluids. Also, you'll want to check the **Staples, Inc.** and **Reliable Corp.** catalogs for availability.

White-Out Tapes

White-out tape is an opaque, white, gummed ribbon. It's generally far safer, and less odorous, than white-out fluid. 3M Post-It Correction Tape, which is removable, is one brand you may want to try. Other brands are available that can provide permanent adhesion. A nice one is Correct-It (**Manco, Inc.**). This tape comes in either 4.2 mm or 8.4 mm widths. It is a white tape that can be used to cover either print or handwriting. The dispenser is designed so you never have to touch the tape itself. This product line is available through **Staples, Inc.** White-out tapes are sold in many office supply stores. Also check the **Staples, Inc.** and **Reliable Corp.** catalogs.

Wrapping Paper

Wrapping paper is often colorful, attractive—and intolerable for some chemically sensitive persons. This is probably due to both the paper itself, as well as to the added dyes and printing inks. Unfortunately, this remains true for recycled wrapping paper as well.

Foil Papers

Of all the manufactured wrapping paper commonly available, foil papers without printing are usually the least bothersome. Foil papers should be available in your local stationery shops, department stores, and discount stores. However, plastic-film foils are now replacing "real" foil papers. So, make sure you know what you're purchasing.

Other Wrapping Paper Options

Of course, other more tolerable, and creative, options are available to wrap gifts. One is to use a sheet of handmade paper available from some art stores. (See *Hand-Made and Artist Papers* on page 447.) A very simple wrapping paper can also be made from brown Kraft paper (from a grocery bag perhaps) or several layers of white tissue paper. Recycled hemp wrapping paper is available from **Fiber Options Paper Co.** Another option for wrapping material is heavy-duty aluminum foil. (During the Holiday Season, it is sometimes sold in red or green.) You can also wrap packages in an attractive natural-fiber cloth.

CHAPTER 19: HOBBIES & ACTIVITIES

The activities you do in your home can have a profound affect on your health. Having a safe structure, decorated with inert materials, and cleaned with nontoxic cleaners, is not always enough to ensure a healthy household. The pastime and hobby products and materials you bring into your house (and how you utilize them) needs to be conscientiously considered, too.

Hobbies

Since World War II, there's been a surge of interest in crafts and in-home hobbies. Americans now spend millions of hours—and millions of dollars—on leisure-time activities. In most cases, indoor hobbies provide enjoyment and satisfaction. However, the health consequences of these pastimes are rarely considered. Your health and well-being should dictate otherwise. Certain hobby activities use toxic and/or very odorous materials that can pollute the indoor air, causing symptoms ranging from respiratory problems to, in some cases, cancer. So, have fun, but make sure that you promote not only your emotional health but your physical health as well.

Hobbies in General

Most people love their hobbies. Why wouldn't they? After all, hobbies can be outward expressions of our inner personalities. Fortunately, many hobbies are actually quite benign from a health standpoint: They don't pollute your home or cause any physical harm. For example, sewing is generally considered a safe hobby. For the general public this is usually true, and it can be for even sensitive people, too—with a few modifications. These might include using only pre-washed, natural-fiber fabrics, or operating the sewing machine with

However, a number of pastimes are fairly dangerous. Plastic model making, which often uses noxious glues and paints, is just one of these. If possible, such hobbies should not be done indoors without adequate ventilation, and personal protective equipment, such as a chemical respirator mask. This is true even for healthy individuals. (See *Personal Protective Gear* on page 264.) Having a sturdy, healthy, inert work surface is also a good idea. Thirty-four-inch-wide, five-feet-and-longer 14-gauge stainless-steel "clean tables" made by **Inter-Metro Industries Corporation** are an excellent choice for this. (You'll need to call the company for their nearest dealer.)

Actually, it's wise to really examine all aspects of the hobbies in which you and your family engage. Specifically, of what materials are they made? What are the warnings (if any) on the packages and containers? What potential negative effects could these materials have on you and the environment? Where are the best places (enough ventilation, peace, and space, etc.) to work on your projects? Is all the necessary additional equipment (including personal protective gear) already in your home and in good working order? And, so on. Taking the necessary steps to make your hobbies both enjoyable and healthy is just plain common sense.

Arts and Crafts

If you enjoy doing arts or crafts, finding acceptable and safe materials can be rather frustrating. It's now becoming evident that many products that have been used for years—and assumed to be harmless—may not be so innocuous. The truth is, many art materials contain potentially harmful solvents and other ingredients. Another problem that has often been overlooked is that some crafts and art projects produce dangerous airborne dust (*i.e.* from sanding) in the process of their creation. It's now known that inhaling dust is a major factor in respiratory problems.

Finding Safer Art & Craft Materials

As a general rule, for safer arts and crafts, you should use water-based products whenever possible. Products with water, rather than alcohol, oil, or solvents as their base ingredient, are nearly always less-odorous, less-toxic, and less-volatile. **Dick Blick** handles a number of safer art materials. Surprisingly, this even includes Grumbacher and Windsor & Newton water-thinnable/water-clean-up oil paints, and Weber Turpenoid Natural, a nontoxic, nonflammable, organic-ingredient thinner. **Sinan Co.** carries Auro art materials, which are imported, all-natural, German formulations. Included in this line are Auro watercolors in jars (made of "natural pigments in precious organic binders"), Auro Inks for textile printing and painting, a #592 Aquareil Paint Set, and a #594 Child's Paint Set.

Another product of interest is the water-based Safecoat AcriGlaze (**AFM**). This is a clear acrylic mixing medium, as well as a finish. It's mildew-resistant and very low odor. The manufacturer suggests that it can be used for restoring old finishes on paintings or preserving newly painted work. Other uses are as an adhesive for papier mache and as a protective coating for pigmented plaster. AcriGlaze can be purchased from AFM dealers such as **N.E.E.D.S., The Living Source**, and **American Environmental Health Foundation**.

For gluing, consider using mucilage, paste, household white glue, or yellow carpenter's glue. These are all low-odor, "safer" adhesives. Elmer's Products, Inc. carries a number of these healthier adhesives—some are even labeled "nontoxic." Of particular interest are Elmer's Glue Sticks and Elmer's Glue gels. These are available in handy, less-mess formulas. If you'd like to purchase an Elmer's glue, or similar brands, check for their availability in local grocery stores, pharmacies, office-supply stores, and discount stores. By the way, popular glue guns can sometimes be acceptable. However, the heated ingredients may prove too bothersome for some sensitive people.

A product that you might not have thought about, but is handy to have on hand, is De-Solv-It Icky Sticky Stuff Remover (**Orange-Sol Household Products, Inc.**). This is said to remove many types of adhesives (including glues and rubber cements), oil paints, and even crayons. Because this is an orange-solvent-based product, it has a "citrusy" odor and will be inappropriate for citrus-allergic people, and some chemically sensitive people. You can order this item from the manufacturer.

Note: For papers that can be useful in artwork, see *Alternative Papers* on page 446.

Safer Use and Storage of Arts & Crafts Products

Of course, with any art material or craft product, it's important to read and follow all label directions, and project instructions, carefully. It's also essential to wear the correct protective gear (see *Personal Protective Gear* on page 264), and to always have plenty of ventilation. Wearing a 100%-cotton mask fitted with an adsorbent activated-charcoal insert can be very helpful, too. Mail-order sources for these include **Allerx, Allergy Relief Shop, Inc.**, and **Bio Designs**. Also, **American Environmental Health Foundation** has masks in either untreated 100%-cotton or silk. You can buy them alone or with your choice of activated-coconut-shell charcoal, activated-lignite charcoal, or activated-bituminous-charcoal inserts. By the way, facial masks are generally washable and have refill inserts available.

Another possibility with which you may want to experiment is an air filter, or *zeolite* adsorbing unit. (Zeolite is a mineral product that can electrostatically trap some types of pollutant molecules on its surface.) Nox-Out uses man-made zeolite in a clear, replaceable, plastic container that comes with either a metal wall or table bracket so it can be placed near your work. The Nox-Out, which is relatively small, can be ordered from **Dick Blick**. A full-sized air filter designed to remove noxious gases would probably be of greater help. (For more information, see *Choosing the Right Air Improvement Equipment* on page 559.)

You might also decide to have a custom-made ventilated "reading" box created especially for you by **Safe Reading & Computer Box Co.** Their boxes are made of glass and 20-gauge *galvanized steel*. (Galvanizing is a zinc treatment to prevent rust.) They come with a fan and a window insert. Safe Reading Boxes are designed to have air flow into them from the front and then exit outdoors. When ordering, you'll want to make sure that the size you agree upon will allow adequate movement of your hands. In any case, reading boxes are usually only useful for smaller projects. (You can also order this company's boxes through **Nigra Enterprises**.)

Remember, it's best to store art materials so they can't affect the indoor air. To do this, metal cabinets with doors, such as those available at many local office-supply stores, are often ideal. If you prefer mail order, **Reliable Corp.** (a large office supply catalog) handles several all-metal cabinets made by **Lee Metal Products** and **Edsal Manufacturing Co., Inc.**

Further Informational Sources

To further help you choose and use healthier art and craft supplies, you'll want to read *The Artist's Complete Health & Safety Guide* by Monona Rossol. In addition, *Health Hazard Manual for Artists* by Micael McCann and *Overexposure: Health Hazards in Photography* by Susan Shay and Monona Rossol are both good sources. Check your local library and bookstores for these, and other books, dealing with the healthfulness of art materials and projects. It should be added that an excellent condensed source of information on this topic is the 16-page "fact sheet" entitled *Art and Hobby Supplies* that you can order at low cost from the **Washington Toxics Coalition**.

If you plan to do a great deal of art or craft work (or such work is related to your profession), you may with to join **Arts, Crafts & Theater Safety (ACTS)**. This is "a not-for-profit corporation dedicated to providing health and safety services to the arts." While there is no membership fee, they gladly accept unsolicited contributions. The organization offers, *ArtFacts*, an extremely informative newsletter provided at the cost of postage and reproduction. Books and data sheets are available, too.

A more specialized group (for professional artists only) is the **Disabled Artist's Network (DAN)**. This is described as "a self-help support organization" founded and directed by Sanda Aronson "providing national information exchange for professional artists working in the visual and sculptural arts having physical or mental/emotional disabilities." Members are asked to share information about shows, opportunities, etc., through the *DAN Newsletter* and inter-group letter exchanges. (Send a SASE or audio-cassette requesting more information on membership.)

Sewing

One of the oldest, and most rewarding, pastimes is sewing. This section provides information on safer and healthier materials and methods.

Finding Acceptable Fabrics,

Local fabric shops often have several untreated natural-fiber fabrics from which to choose. However, catalog sources are also available. For example, **Sew Eco-Logical** carries 125 different organic-cotton fabrics, in a wide range of wovens, knits, patterns, and solid colors. While a small brochure is free, their large, useful sample catalog must be purchased. Then, too, **Janice Corporation** has a variety of untreated-cotton fabrics, some of which are organic. Their fabrics include barrier cloth, denim, colored percales, drill cloth, muslin, chambray, duck, flannel, quilted cotton, and sheeting. Free samples are available. **Deva Lifewear**, which primarily sells finished clothing, also offers untreated 100%-cotton fabrics in several weights, solid colors, and textures. Deva sometimes has untreated, all-natural-fiber novelty fabrics. Small fabric samples are available at low cost. A number of all-cotton and linen fabrics are handled by **Gohn Bros.**

B. **Coole Designs** offers unbleached, untreated, cotton cloth in twill, gauze, sheeting, knit, flannel, and Peking varieties. The company also carries some rayon and silk fabric. (Note: You'll want to check out this company's website for their most complete current inventory listings.) Also, **Dharma Trading Co.** handles many varieties of undyed, untreated, 100%-cotton, silk, hemp and natural-fiber-blend fabrics.

For home decorating, **Heart of Vermont** has a number of wide, organic-cotton fabrics you may want to use. In addition, **Homespun Fabrics and Draperies** has untreated 100%-cotton, 10'-wide fabrics. These come in several textures that are specially woven so as to not require ironing. A number of very attractive organic-cotton (and other natural blend) upholstery fabrics are sold by **The Natural Alternative**. Organic-cotton upholstery fabric can also be purchased from **Furnature**. In addition, some 108"-wide untreated (and organic) cotton fabrics are handled by **Janice Corporation**.

Once you obtain your natural-fiber, or acceptable synthetic fabric, it's best to wash and air it to remove any bothersome "new" odors (see *Removing New Clothing Odors* on page 123). This step is essential for most chemically sensitive individuals, but everyone should make sure his or her yardage is preshrunk before sewing with it anyway.

Finding Acceptable Notions and Dyes

If you require non-synthetic notions, **Sew Eco-Logical** carries organic-cotton laces, organic-cotton thread, organic-cotton-covered elastic, natural-material buttons in wood, mussel shell, coconut husk, and *tagua nut*. (Tagua nuts are a hard, natural vegetable material that looks similar to ivory.) Be aware, that their large catalog must be purchased. From **B. Coole Designs**, you can also get tagua-nut buttons. **Janice Corporation** sells all-cotton thread, bias tape, cotton-covered elastic, and metal zippers.

Home-Sew handles 100%-cotton thread, lace, webbing, and floss, as well as mother-of-pearl buttons, rayon embroidery yarns, metal buckles, metal and nylon zippers, and metal thimbles. A number of hard-to-find zippers, snaps, etc. for outerwear are sold by **Green Pepper**. (For more on this company, see *Finding and Using Patterns* below.)

For dyes that work well on natural fabrics, you'll want to check **B. Coole Designs** which carries "low-impact" Procion dyes. While not natural-ingredient dyes, the company feels that they're more colorfast and "safer" than most natural dyes. Soda ash is required as a fixative. Be aware that items dyed with Procion dyes are not recommended to be washed in vinegar. Again, you'll need to check this company's website for the most complete information. Furthermore, a large number of dyes for natural fibers are handled by **Dharma Trading Co.** If you'd like to experiment by making your own natural dyes, you can look for books on the subject at your local library or bookstore.

Finding and Using Patterns

One of the best parts of sewing is choosing the right pattern. Today, not only are there patterns for a whole range of family garments, but most of the larger pattern companies now also offer home decor patterns. These include bedspreads, curtains, slip covers, and table linens. So consider making these yourself, if you enjoy sewing. That way, you can choose washable, natural-fiber fabrics that you know will be appropriate in your healthy household.

A special pattern company of which you may not be familiar is **Green Pepper**. They have a catalog with patterns for men's, women's and children's outer wear, even including gloves and "polar boots." They also have patterns for a variety of bags (duffel, book, garment, shopping, bicycle saddle, and sleeping), back packs, brief cases, and more. The company also sells the materials as well as any zippers or other special *findings* (snaps, catches, etc.) necessary to complete your projects. Most of their fabrics are synthetic and waterproofed, and their stuffings are synthetic, but if you're chemically sensitive, you can buy more appropriate fabrics elsewhere. Of course, their findings may work just fine for you. If you're interested, you can purchase Green Pepper patterns at JoAnn's Fabrics & Crafts stores or from the manufacturer. (The fabrics and findings can be ordered directly from the company.) If you call their non-toll-free telephone number (rather than their toll-free automatic ordering line) they can answer questions about using their patterns and fabrics.

Now, if you find the right pattern you want to use, but are bothered by the paper or printing ink, try unfolding the uncut pattern sheets and hanging them outside to air on a clothesline. Be careful though; while a light breeze will help the airing-out process, a strong wind could easily tear them. Simply laying the paper sheets on a clean, dry sidewalk or driveway, in the sun, until they become tolerable is another approach. Of course, you'll need to use small weights to hold the sheets in place.

Using the Sewing Machine

If you've decided to do the sewing yourself, and are a sensitive individual, try to have plenty of ventilation around you when you sew with a machine. Many sewing machines have plastic housings that can release synthetic chemicals. Warm sewing-machine motors can also give off odors, as can newly applied sewing-machine oil. Therefore, open nearby windows if possible. You can also use an electric fan to blow air from behind or beside you, toward the sewing machine and then away. Even better, on nice days, you could sew on your deck or porch, if an outdoor electrical outlet is handy.

These measures should help dissipate most of the troubling odors. You might also wear a protective activated-charcoal mask. All-cotton filtering masks are available from **Allerx**, **Allergy Relief Shop, Inc.**, and **Bio Designs**. From **American Environmental Health Foundation** you can get masks made of untreated 100%-cotton or silk fabrics. You can choose an insert of activated-coconut-shell charcoal, activated-lignite charcoal, or activated-bituminous charcoal. These types of masks are typically washable and have refill inserts available. Even with a mask, some very chemically sensitive individuals may find they'll still need to take frequent breaks away from the sewing machine.

By the way, when it comes time to replace your machine, it would be best to purchase a model that does not require oiling. You may find that you'll need to check the owner's manual to get such information.

Knitting and Crocheting

Of course, not all clothing, or home decorating accent items, are made of fabric. Many items are knitted or crocheted. Naturally enough, many individuals enjoy creating these types of pieces themselves. Fortunately, it's usually not too difficult to find acceptable yarns.

Finding Acceptable Yarns

Virtually all stores and catalogs that handle knitting and crocheting supplies will carry "commercial-grade" yarns made of 100%-natural fibers. By mail order, **Yarn Shoppe** offers a good variety of all-cotton yarns. Even broader is their selection of wool yarns. Included in their collection are sheep's wool, lambswool, and Icelandic wool, as well as wool/mohair blends. They even have silk yarns. You can also order from them patterns, knitting needles, crochet hooks and other supplies. A source of beautiful, naturally "genetically-colored" sheep's wool yarn is from **Genopalette**. This small firm actually raises the rare ivory, brown, tan, and gray Romney and Merino sheep themselves. Understandably, their wool (and therefore yarn) production is rather limited. However, if they have yarn available when you order, you'll be pleased with it's lustrous quality.

You should also be aware that you can sometimes find organic and/or vegetable-dyed yarns at local yarn specialty shops. Sometimes they may also sell hand-spun, natural-fiber yarns, or they may be able to provide the names of spinners who will be able to sell their yarns directly to you. Homespun yarns can be exciting to see, feel, and work with, so it's often worth the effort, and extra expense, to find them. By the way, if there's no specialty-yarn store in your area, ask your local library's reference department for help. Libraries often keep lists of local clubs and organizations, including those that do spinning, dyeing, weaving, or knitting. Your reference librarian can also help you find magazines devoted to natural fibers and natural dyeing. (Most public libraries subscribe to at least one such periodical.) Fiber-craft magazines often list advertisements and classifieds with homespun natural-fiber yarns for sale.

Safely Knitting and Crocheting

For some asthmatics, very sensitive individuals, or allergic persons, the extremely fine fibers, or odors, released into the air when working with any type of yarn (even organically raised yarn) may pose health concerns. In that case, try working outdoors—or wear a protective mask indoors. If fine airborne fibrous material is the problem, a simple disposable 100%-cotton dust mask could do the trick. (See *Personal Protective Gear* on page 264.)

However, if the odors and/or dust is the problem, a natural-fabric mask with an activated-charcoal insert will probably be a better choice. You can purchase all-cotton versions from **Allerx, Allergy Relief Shop, Inc.**, and **Bio Designs**. From **American Environmental Health Foundation** you can order an untreated 100%-cotton or silk mask. Inserts come in your choice of activated-coconut-shell charcoal, activated-lignite charcoal, or activated-bituminous charcoal. (Note: Refill inserts are available for all these masks.) If these measures are impossible, or simply don't help enough, have someone else knit or crochet items for you. However, be sure to choose someone who will not work on your project if perfume, tobacco, or other strong odors are present. These can be easily picked up by the yarn fibers.

Physical Fitness Equipment

Home exercise equipment is geared to make you healthier. However, some pieces are made with odorous synthetic foam grips and other plastic parts. Also, it's not uncommon for some equipment to have chains, hydraulic shocks, or other parts requiring lubrication using smelly petroleum-based products. In addition, if there are natural or synthetic rubber cords, foot grips, belts, etc., these too can outgas odors. It is little wonder that much home exercise equipment is just too bothersome for many sensitive individuals to use, especially when it's new.

Another thing to consider when beginning an exercise regime is to first get your physician's approval, particularly if you have a respiratory or heart condition.

Tolerable Manufactured Exercise Equipment

The best home exercise equipment—at least from an odor standpoint—are pieces which are mostly metal. If possible, you'll also want to choose equipment that won't require any lubrication. While you'll hopefully be able to find appropriate equipment locally, a number of simple types are sold by **Well & Good** by mail order.

If you find that lubrication will be necessary, you might consider using E-Z-1 Lubricant (E-Z-1). This product, which comes in a plastic 3.5 oz. bottle with a spray-tube attachment, contains no solvents. It's biodegradable, nearly odorless, non-aerosol, non-flammable, and won't conduct electricity. Unfortunately though, it may not be adequate for some applications. If you're interested in trying E-Z-1, a local hardware store may stock it. If not, you can mail order it from **E.L. Foust Co., Inc.** and **Allergy Relief Shop, Inc.**

You may find that certain pieces of fitness equipment, which may not be intolerable when first purchased, can become tolerable if aired outdoors for some time in dry, uncontaminated surroundings. Bungee-type stretching cords are one such example. Sometimes a piece of equipment can become acceptable simply by the removing foam handlebar grips and/or by placing a tightly fitting 100%-cotton *barrier cloth* (a special tightly woven fabric that often seals in odors) cover over a rubber or vinyl seat. (Sources for untreated barrier cloth include **N.E.E.D.S.** and **Janice Corporation**.) Washable sheepskin exercise-bike seat covers are an option, too. These are sold by **French Creek Sheep & Wool Co.** (Important note: Remember to never make any modifications that could result in a potential safety problem. Also, certain alterations could invalidate the warranty or guarantee.)

Tolerable Homemade Exercise Equipment

As an alternative to manufactured devices, you might consider making homemade exercise equipment to suit your own personal physical and tolerability requirements. For example, you could buy sections of cotton or nylon rope to use as nontoxic jump ropes. Hand-held bags of strong 100% cotton can be perfect for weight lifting. The bags can be filled with steel shot that is available at most gun shops and discount-store hunting departments. These easily opened bags can be emptied and laundered when necessary, or the amount of shot can be varied as necessary. You can even make small bags with Velcro straps to attach weights to your wrists or ankles.

Also, a ready-made, at-home, stair stepper could simply be your own stairway. A sturdily constructed wooden box 2", 4", 6", or 8" high could also be used, if set on a slip-resistant surface. The higher the box, the more difficult the workout will be.

It should be pointed out that many exercises don't require any equipment. In this age of health clubs and exercise-equipment "infomercials," that's something that can easily be forgotten. Actually, some very healthful exercises require only the knowledge of the technique (as gained from an instruction video or book), comfortable clothing, and perhaps a soft mat. Walking around your home, stretching exercises, yoga and other Eastern practices, isometrics, and the old-fashioned exercises you did in physical-education classes in school, are just a few examples of low-tech exercising methods. To find what appeals to you, check bookstores and libraries for appropriate books and tapes. From **Yoga Zone**, you can order yoga CDs (compact discs), video tapes, and books. They also carry cotton-webbing exercise straps and wood blocks. **Inner Balance** has yoga and exercise tapes.

Tolerable Exercise Clothing and Mats

Finding exercise clothing and mats that are tolerable to sensitive people can sometimes be difficult, although some all-cotton or cotton/Lycra pieces may be available in local outlets. If you prefer mail order, a number of sources exist.

For women, leotards of untreated 97%-cotton and 3%-Lycra are created and sold by **B.Coole Designs**. Of special note is that these are actually sewn by an individual with MCS (Multiple Chemical Sensitivity). If you find that "standard" sizes won't fit you, custom lengths can be especially made. **Inner Balance** sells 90%-organic-cotton/10%-Lycra yoga/workout wear including shorts, tops and "unitards." The **Yoga Zone** sells organic-cotton, commercial-grade cotton, and cotton/Lycra yoga/work-out clothes. You'll also want to check **Back to Basics** to see what they currently have available.

Women's organic-cotton sweatwear can be ordered from **Janice Corporation, Well & Good, Karen's Natural Products,** and **American Environmental Health Foundation.** Also, **Natural Selections** has organic-cotton sweat clothes, but they have no mail-order catalog. Some items are listed on their website, but calling the company for the most up-to-date information is best. Untreated, ready-for-dying, all-cotton sweatwear is handled by **Dharma Trading Co.** All-cotton French-terry sweatshirts and pants are handled by **Harmony** and cotton/hemp sweatwear for women can be purchased from **J. Jill.**

A specialty catalog for larger-sized women, **Junonia,** has a good offering of exercise clothing. Items include 100%-cotton tops, pants, and yoga wear (pants, tops). Also available are organic-cotton sweatwear pieces.

For men, the **Yoga Zone** sells 100%-cotton yoga clothing. In addition, **American Environmental Health Foundation, Janice Corporation,** and **Karen's Natural Products** sell men's organic-cotton sweat clothes. All-cotton hooded sweatshirts can be ordered from **Tomorrow's World.** Then, too, **Natural Selections** has organic-cotton sweat pieces, but they have no catalog. Again, while some pieces are listed on their website, you'll want to call the company for more complete information. Finally, untreated, undyed, all-cotton sweatwear can be purchased from **Dharma Trading Co.,** and all-cotton French-terry sweatwear ordered from **Harmony.**

If you're looking for an exercise mat, **Janice Corporation** offers an untreated, all-cotton exercise mat in a 26" x 66" size with a 100%-cotton cover. These come in several fabric/stuffing options. You can choose from percale, barrier-cloth, or organic-cotton covers, as well as regular- or organic-cotton stuffing. From **Harmony** and **Inner Balance,** you can order a 70" x 36" yoga mat. This particular item has an unbleached 100%-cotton cover with untreated-cotton stuffing. A nice feature is the attached strings with which you can roll the mat up and tie it securely when it's not in use.

Heart of Vermont makes and sells 100%-organic-cotton exercise mats, as well as mats with 100%-organic-cotton ticking and wool stuffing, in two sizes (24" x 72" and 36" x 72"). They also have covers for them made of 100%-organic-cotton. **Yoga Zone** carries "meditation cushions" that have 100%-cotton muslin covers. These are filled with *kapok.* (For more on kapok, see *Kapok* on page 190.) Another item they carry is a 100%-unbleached-cotton yoga mat with cotton stuffing. This comes in a 28" x 72" size with a removable and washable cotton cover.

Saunas

For a while now, saunas have become more common in homes, particularly in new upscale houses. While most of the people who purchase saunas aren't, as a rule, chemically sensitive, some individuals with MCS (Multiple Chemical Sensitivity) are buying them as a means to detoxify themselves after experiencing bothersome chemical exposures. Therefore, this section will introduce you to what saunas are, how they work, and offer a sampling of what's currently available.

Traditional Scandinavian Saunas

Traditionally, *saunas* are small, separate, permanently built, wooden bathhouses used in Finland and other Scandinavian countries. Generally, they have two interior seating levels and a vented ceiling. These modest structures are heated to relatively high temperatures (170–200°F), using small heating stoves. The warmth generated is absorbed by specially chosen, fracture-resistant stones. The rocks then radiate their acquired heat into the room. If desired, steam is created by ladling water onto the hot rocks. The high temperature inside a sauna causes users to perspire. After sweating for a time, within the hot confined space, sauna users traditionally open the door, run outside, and take a dip in a lake or stream—or jump into a snow bank if it's wintertime. (Sometimes a body lashing with birch twigs is also performed.) The whole procedure is considered cleansing and invigorating.

Modern Conventional Saunas

Today, in America, most saunas are built into houses rather than as separate structures. These indoor saunas are customarily one of three basic types: custom-built, constructed from a prefab kit, or made from a precut kit. Each has its advantages and disadvantages.

Whether they are custom-made or derived from a kit, nearly all saunas have insulated walls covered with cedar, or other softwood paneling (other woods are sometimes offered). Often, there are one or two benches. The doors of the sauna may have glass panels to prevent claustrophobia. The stoves are often either electric or gas heaters.

Some chemically sensitive people find that buying a conventional sauna works just fine for them, as long as they make appropriate material selections. However, some only want saunas that have been designed specifically for sensitive people. For information, see *Saunas Designed for the Chemically Sensitive* on page 464.

Basic Sauna Types

A *custom-made* sauna has the advantages of fitting precisely into the space you have, and having the exact features you want. Of course, the relatively high labor costs, plus the time, trouble, and expense to find the appropriate materials, has to be considered if you opt for a custom-built sauna rather than going with a prefab kit, which would have everything included in one package. You'll probably also want to hire only skilled, knowledgeable individuals to do the work, from designing to actual construction. (To find a designer, talk with local architects. They may be able to draw the plans themselves or recommend someone.)

On the other hand, *prefab* (prefabricated) *sauna kits* are modular systems. Each prefab sauna company offers several models in different sizes. Generally, the sauna's insulated walls are built at the factory and then shipped to your site. The manufacturer's labor, materials, and design costs are all included in the initial prefab kit price. It should be pointed out that prefabs are often separate, freestanding chambers designed to be assembled on a hard-surfaced floor such as concrete. Often they're placed in basements. If you're capable enough, and not a particularly sensitive person, you may be able to do most of the installation work yourself.

A special version of a prefab sauna is the *portable sauna*. This is a the newest entry into the sauna market. These are totally complete, free-standing, closet-sized structures. Usually they come in two hinged sections that come apart to allow a user to enter and leave. Portable saunas generally have casters to ease opening, and for moving them to another room, outside, or to another home. Not surprisingly, renters find them especially nice, because they take up so little space and can be easily moved to another location.

A sauna option that's lies between custom and prefab saunas (in both cost and labor) is a *precut sauna package*. These usually contain tongue-and-groove wood paneling already cut to fit inside a framework which is built by the homeowner, or a contractor. Insulation and exterior wood siding are usually not provided. Kits may include heaters and other equipment, depending on the model and options selected.

Note: All saunas require electrical wires for lights as well as for electric heaters. Therefore, having the necessary permits and professional expertise is essential. If you do the work yourself, you'll want to wear appropriate protective gear when necessary.

Choosing Tolerable Sauna Materials and Equipment

If you're a sensitive person and are going to be buying conventional equipment, it's critical to choose an appropriate wood species for your sauna walls—especially the sauna's interior. The wood should be a type that can withstand both heat and moisture, yet be tolerable (see *Testing Woods* on page 269). Remember that virtually any wood will release far more odors when hot and/or damp.

Sauna manufacturers often have a selection of several wood species from which to choose. These may include western red cedar, white cedar, white pine, aspen, sugar pine, ponderosa pine, Sitka spruce, hemlock spruce, cypress, and/or redwood, among others. No wood species is absolutely perfect, and certainly no single species is right for everyone. However, one species you might seriously consider if you're a sensitive individual is redwood, which is often fairly well tolerated. Although redwood is a softwood, it is less odorous, especially over time, than cedar, pine, and fir. Also, redwood has an attractive smooth grain and it is naturally rot-resistant. However, you should be aware that like all wood, redwood has an odor when it's been freshly cut. In addition, any water or sweat that gets on the redwood can cause staining. Tulip poplar, a hardwood, can also be a good, lower-odor choice, but it is not rot-resistant like redwood.

For the floor of your sauna (unless it's a portable model), ideally you'll choose concrete, masonry (brick or stone), or ceramic tile (see *Ceramic Tile* on page 314). These choices are good because they can easily handle the moisture of perspiration and steam, and they never need replacing. It's also wise to choose an electric over a gas heater so potentially harmful combustion gases aren't created (see *Combustion Gases* on page 524). Also remember to have protective guardrails installed around your sauna's heater.

It's important, too, to seriously consider proper ventilation for your new sauna. Unfortunately, some American saunas are built with no provisions for ventilation whatsoever. This can easily create stale and stuffy conditions, yet it's always preferable to have adequate fresh air. For more insights and information on ventilation, you might read *Understanding Ventilation* by John Bower. This book can be ordered from **The Healthy House Institute** or your favorite bookseller.

Finally, don't forget to insulate in a way that will minimize potentially bothersome odors. You should be aware that, when the walls of your sauna become hot, the insulation within them will likely release more odors than when the walls are cool. You'll find information on insulation in *The Healthy House* by John Bower which you can order from **The Healthy House Institute** or your favorite bookseller.

Choosing the Right Conventional Sauna

All in all, installing a sauna in your home is a major investment. Therefore, take the time to do the necessary research, material testing, and acquisition of any building permits, etc. If your friends have saunas, ask them for their experiences, suggestions, and recommendations. Also, ask your physician, or other health-care professional, for his (or her) ideas. If you want to purchase a conventional sauna kit or a portable unit, it's probably best to look over the literature from more than one manufacturer.

One sauna producer you might consider is **Amerec Products**. This company offers pre-cut sauna kits in a variety of styles, sizes, and woods (red cedar, hemlock, redwood, or aspen). Their "Personal Sauna Room" is a portable unit preassembled in two sections. Amerec also offers sauna heaters. If you're interested in their products, you'll need to call for their nearest dealer. Another option are saunas from **Cedarbrook Saunas & Steam**. They have red-cedar pre-fab modular saunas and sauna lumber kits. Custom sizes can be ordered. Their "Plug-In Portable Sauna" of red cedar is a portable unit preassembled in two sections. This company also handles sauna heaters. By the way, you can order directly from the company.

An alternative type of sauna that is designed and marketed for the general public is the Whole Body Radiant Thermal System Soft Heat Infrared Sauna. This sauna is said "to warm people better, to a greater skin depth than conventional saunas." Models come in one-, two-, and four-person sizes with your choice of all-cedar construction or a combination of pine on the exterior and cedar on the inside. Whole Body Saunas are sold by **Befit Enterprises Ltd.**

For each company you contact, compare their costs for the wood, the heaters, etc., as well as for shipping. Find out what features are standard and which ones are optional. Also, make sure you know what materials, and degree of site readiness, are to be provided by the homeowner—you. In addition, learn what's covered in the sauna's guarantees and warranties, and for how long. Finally, don't forget to inquire how long you should expect to wait from the time you place your order until your sauna kit or portable unit reaches your door.

Saunas Designed for the Chemically Sensitive

To meet the special needs of the chemically sensitive, there are now saunas designed just for them. The companies making them have taken special care to create saunas made of low-odor, low-toxicity materials. While people with MCS (Multiple Chemical Sensitivity) will particularly appreciate these products, they can be good choices for anyone interested in having a healthy household.

The Basic One Person Sauna (**Safe Reading & Computer Box Co.**) is a small (76" long x 29" wide x 34" high), low-cost, low-tech sauna that consists of a folding, anodized-aluminum frame covered with multiple layers of prewashed, untreated, 100%-organic-cotton cloth. The Basic One Person Sauna can be used in a horizontal position (to lay down in) or an upright position (to sit in). It has a heater that's housed in a separate metal chamber. Also available are custom saunas made in a variety of sizes, with thermal-glass panels or ceramic tile. (Wood is not used. The company feels that it could cause tolerance problems for some sensitive people.) You can order directly from the manufacturer or through **Nigra Enterprises**. With each sauna, you'll receive a "How-To Manual" that includes "the most effective bio-detoxification method known."

Heavenly Heat Saunas are built without adhesives, plywood, or synthetic materials. Made of tulip-poplar wood and tempered glass, they come with foil-barrier insulation, filtered air ventilation, and a stainless-steel heater. Three self-contained, free-standing, pre-fab models are offered. Options include casters, and your choice of glass or all-wood walls. Custom saunas are also available. You can order a Heavenly Heat sauna from the manufacturer, **Nigra Enterprises**, or **American Environmental Health Foundation**.

Travel Needs

While they aren't involved with in-home activities, luggage and carriers are an integral part of most lifestyles. Of course, most people take such items for granted. However, that's not true for many chemically sensitive persons. Finding tolerable items for them can be difficult.

For information on more tolerable automobile traveling, you'll want to read *The Car* on page 376.

Luggage

The following sections will explain concerns with typical luggage, and offer some less bothersome luggage suggestions.

Typical Luggage Concerns

Most of the luggage being made today is either *hardside* (the exterior retains it's original shape) and often made of hard plastic, or *softside* (the exterior is pliable) and made of a synthetic fabric treated with water and/or stain-resistant chemicals. Luggage interiors are usually treated synthetic fabrics, soft vinyl, or a combination of these materials. Consequently, it should be obvious that many sensitive people find new luggage intolerable.

The answer might seem to be to use older suitcases and bags—ones that have lost most of their "new" odors. However, old luggage can pose its own problems. For example, older pieces will have likely absorbed perfume, tobacco, as well as musty and other undesirable odors over the years.

Even if tolerable luggage is found, once it's taken on a trip, it will inevitably absorb ambient perfume and tobacco odors. Therefore, once-acceptable luggage can quickly become unacceptable. Unfortunately, trying to make bothersome luggage tolerable again can be difficult. After all, most luggage pieces can't be completely washed or laundered and, generally, the only cleaning possible is a surface sponging, something that may not be particularly effective. Airing contaminated luggage outdoors for an extended period in dry, uncontaminated surroundings can help, but it may not be enough.

Alternative Luggage Suggestions

Although it's doubtful that you'll find a set of matched luggage available that's made of tolerable materials, is completely washable and, at the same time, is affordable, there are a few luggage options that chemically sensitive persons might consider. One is using untreated, 100%-cotton, or untreated nylon, athletic bags. These are sometimes still available at local department stores and sporting-goods stores. Some of these bags are hand- or even machine-washable.

Another more tolerable luggage option is to use untreated 100%-cotton garment bags. These are occasionally sold in luggage and department stores. You might also consider sewing your own athletic, duffel, cargo, or garment bags. **Green Pepper** has patterns for a variety of bags including duffel, garment, brief cases, bicycle saddle bags, and book packs. (For more on this company, see *Finding and Using Patterns* on page 457.)

When choosing a fabric, ideally you should pick a washable, heavy-duty, tolerable, natural-fiber cloth. Cotton canvas, cotton duck, and untreated cotton *barrier cloth* are good. (Barrier cloth is a special tightly-woven, untreated cotton that can act as a relatively effective odor barrier.) Sources for untreated barrier cloth are **N.E.E.D.S.** and **Janice Corporation**. You might also choose a sturdy, rip-proof, untreated nylon. (For appropriate fabrics, see *Finding Acceptable Fabrics* on page 456, and for more on sewing see *Sewing* on page 456.)

No matter your final choice, if you're a sensitive person it's a good idea to also take along an extra bag to hold the clothing that has been worn. That way, soiled clothes, that have picked up potentially bothersome odors, won't need to be directly adjacent to your uncontaminated fresh clothing. For your worn-clothing bag, you might simply use a pillowcase, or you could make a drawstring barrier-cloth bag. You might also use an unscented plastic garbage bag for contaminated clothing. And remember not to put the worn-clothes bag in your luggage until you're ready to leave. Odors coming from the soiled/contaminated clothing can permeate through a worn-clothes bag—made of any material—to some degree.

Totes

Finding totes (large, usually unsecured, open-topped bags with handles) of all-natural-fiber fabrics is far easier to do than finding similarly constructed luggage. So it shouldn't be too difficult to buy one locally. Alternative groceries and health-food stores often handle them. If you'd like to order a tote, untreated all-cotton tote bags are available from **Dharma Trading Co.** and all-hemp totes are offered in the **Tomorrow's World** catalog.

Because totes are generally of such simple design, you can easily make one yourself out of tolerable materials. To help you, **Green Pepper** has patterns for both shopping bags and book bags. (For more on this company, see *Finding and Using Patterns* on page 457.)

Baby Carriers

Finding a non-plastic, non-synthetic-fabric baby carrier can sometimes be challenging. However, a few all-cotton ones may be available locally in department stores. By mail order, you can purchase 100%-cotton baby carriers from **Garnet Hill** and **Natural Baby**.

Pet Carriers

Pet carriers should have a carrying handle, and they can be made of a hard plastic material or as a simple wire cage. In cars, they can help confine a pet to keep dander and other pet allergens from spreading throughout the interior. So, for pet-allergic people who need to travel with their dog or cat, they can be extremely beneficial.

A variety of pet carriers for dogs and cats can be found in most pet-supply centers. By mail order, pet carriers, including inert metal ones, can be purchased from **R.C. Steele** and the **Pet Warehouse** catalogs. (They have separate catalogs for cats and for dogs.)

For a portable water dish, you might consider Pooch Pouch (**New Wave Enviro**). It has a one-quart capacity, is made of Cordura nylon, and it folds for traveling. To purchase it, check local pet stores or call the manufacturer for its nearest dealer.

Wheel Chair and Crutch Pads

Pressure on the same body parts caused by sitting in a wheel chair or using crutches can cause serious problems. To help bring relief, quilted, washable-wool, wheel-chair-seat covers in four sizes are sold in the **French Creek Sheep & Wool Co.** catalog. They also handle crutch pads as well.

Children's Toys

Virtually every toy you come across for young children anymore is made of synthetic materials, many are not even washable. Sadly, some of these toys pose unsuspecting problems. Typical stuffed toys, for example, can harbor dust, dust mites, and mold. Certain vinyl and other plastic toys can *outgas* (emit) plastic odors including vinyl chloride. While some local stores may have healthier types of toys, you might check craft fairs for these items from time to time. They may have handmade, all-cotton, soft toys available and they often have solid-wood toys. Of course, you'll want to make sure that they're made well, and in such a manner that they pose no potential dangers to your children. That means, you'll also need to find out what types of finishes (if any) have been used.

Soft Toys

The "ideal" soft toy would be one made of washable, all-natural materials and stuffings, with no buttons or other small hard decorations that could come off and be accidentally swallowed. However, ideal and reality are not always the same. Therefore, acceptable compromises can be stuffed toys made of synthetic materials that can be machine washed. Less desirable are those that can only be surface washed.

A good source for washable, organic-cotton-stuffed toys covered with wool is **EcoBaby Organics**. This company has both dolls as well as stuffed animals and hand puppets, too. Another fine source for organic, 100%-cotton baby toys is **Tomorrow's World**. Available are a stuffed bear, whale, and rabbit. Other catalogs selling organic-cotton toys are **Lifekind Products** and **Natural Baby**. This last firm also has silk play-dress-up clothes such as capes, wings, large square sections, and skirts. Stuffed toys (teddy bear and rabbit) made of 100%-green-cotton are sold by **Under The Canopy**.

Unusual stuffed animals made of natural wool shearling are available from **Deerskin Trading Post**. (These are stuffed with polyester filling.) They also have animals made of cowhide.

The stuffed toys made by North American Bear Co. have synthetic fabric on the outside and synthetic stuffing on the inside. However, they're specifically made to be regularly washed in hot water. Sources for these particular toys include **eMD.com** and **Allergy Control Products, Inc.** Another company that has washable, soft, synthetic toys is **Priorities**.

Hard Toys

"Hard" toys made of wood are often good choices. The wood used should be a nontoxic species, and every surface should be smoothly sanded. Of course, all paints and finishes should also be nontoxic. A good source for wooden toys, including blocks and trains, is **Chock's**. **Lilly's Kids** has wooden weaving-loom kits with 100%-cotton yarns, and some other types of wooden toys. Also, **Natural Baby** has a very good selection of wooden toys that include blocks, pull toys, children's play kitchens, doll houses, and puzzles. More sources for wooden toys include **Perfectly Safe**, **Tucson Cooperative Warehouse**, and **Shaker Shops**

West (this particular company has wooden baby rattles) Children's hardwood table-and-chair sets can be ordered from **This End Up. EcoBaby Organics** has both wooden toys and children's table-and-chair sets, as does **Crate & Barrel.**

Metal items can sometimes be acceptable, if the edges aren't sharp so they can't cut. Also, any paint used should have a nontoxic formulation. **EcoBaby Organics** carries metal toy musical instruments. A few all-metal toys, made in Eastern Europe, are sometimes found in the **Daily Planet** catalog. Ceramic tea sets, with wicker cases that are lined in 100%-cotton fabric are sold by **Lilly's Kids.**

Household Pets

A pet is defined as any domesticated or tamed animal that is cared for with kindness and considered a companion. Actually, a pet of any species can be a source of entertainment, enjoyment—and even love. However, it could also be a source of unwelcome mess, pests, potential infestations, and allergens.

At the very least, all pets require your personal time, money, and emotional input. Therefore, before you acquire any pet, it's wise to evaluate the pros and cons of pet ownership for you and your family. This is especially important for chemically sensitive, asthmatic, or allergic persons. Sadly, it was recently determined that one of the major reasons why pets are dropped off at shelters is because of an allergy to the pet. (Note: In some cases, allergies to pets may not be present at first, but develop over time.)

If you decide to go ahead and get a pet, choose the appropriate animal(s). This is important, not only for you, but for the pet. Reading up on various pets (look for pet books in your local library) and talking with a veterinarian can be helpful. In the end, the special closeness of a dog or cat can easily be worth any possible drawbacks: high food bills, required vaccinations, allergy desensitizing shots, licenses, etc. Other individuals may decide that a chameleon—which needs only marginal attention, has no shedding fur and little *dander* (loose animal skin or feather flakes), requires no veterinary checkups, consumes little food, costs only a few dollars for the initial purchase, and lives in a small inexpensive terrarium—is all they realistically feel comfortable with. Of course, still others may decide that having an outdoor bird feeder provides as much animal-human interaction as they're able to responsibly handle at this point in their lives. Whatever the decision, if it works for both you and the animal(s), then it's the right choice.

Pet Care in General

Of course, there are some basic health guidelines for owning any pet. One of these is to keep all pet bedding clean. Therefore, you'll want to choose dog and cat beds that are washable, or have removable and washable covers. Also, you'll want to regularly vacuum the floors around your pet's sleeping area or cage. (Daily vacuuming will lessen the likelihood of flea infestations, as well as eliminate excess fur, feathers, dander, and dirt that could aggravate allergies.) If possible, keep your pet out of bedrooms. For dogs that otherwise are free to roam throughout the house, either keep the bedroom doors closed or try a security gate. Wooden or metal baby/pet security gates should be available locally in department stores, discount stores, and some hardware stores. If not, both wood and metal security gates are sold by **One Step Ahead.** (Of course, a large, determined dog may jump over a gate.) In some cases, if it's a cat or dog, you may find keeping it outdoors all the time with appropriate pet housing is best. Whenever you handle your pet (indoors or outdoors), washing your hands afterwards is a good idea. Washing your clothing may be necessary for some highly allergic people.

Also, with any type of pet, it's best to take special care of their food and water. Washing your pet's food and water dishes daily is a good practice. You'll also want to store your pet's food in nontoxic containers with tight-fitting lids, and refrigerate when necessary. In the case of dry foods, you might use a clean, new galvanized garbage can for convenient, inert, sealed storage.

Regular grooming is also important for the pet itself (unless it's a lizard, etc.). This includes regular bathing for most furred and feathered pets. However, washing cats and dogs too often can cause dry skin and can, therefore, increase the amount of dander (skin flakes that are shed.) This could easily increase dander-allergy problems, so use commonsense. A product to help keep your pet clean between shampooing is Natural Chemistry Fur & Feather. This enzyme spray has no scents added, and is made primarily of natural citrates and grains. It can be ordered from **Allergy Relief Shop, Inc.**

Incidentally, an interesting book to read for any pet owner is *Are You Poisoning Your Pets?* by Nina Anderson and Howard Peiper. This is a guidebook on how typical modern (and toxic) lifestyles can affect the health of household pets. Your local library may have it or they should be able to get it for you through their inter-library loan program.

If you're interested in mail-ordering your pet-care products, **Pet Warehouse** has a series of different catalogs geared specifically for Cats, Dogs, Birds, Small Animals, and Reptiles. Simply contact the company and request the appropriate one. For pet carriers you can use when traveling with your pet, see *Pet Carriers* on page 466.

Cats

It's been estimated that, as long ago as 8,000 BC, cats were already present in prehistoric villages. In ancient Egypt, people not only appreciated the presence of cats, but also revered them because they kept homes and granaries relatively rodent-free. About that time, domesticated cats first became differentiated from wild cats. In time, cats were kept by growing numbers of families as settlements and urbanization spread. However, after the Christianization of Europe, cats in some places were considered links to the pagan past, thus, losing much of their former favor.

Eventually, keeping cats as pets again became more popular. But surprisingly, it wasn't until the late 19th century that cat breeds became established. (Interestingly, some experts believe there's still no such thing as a specific, true, domestic cat breed.) Recently, in the U.S., cats have replaced dogs as America's most common household pet, probably because cats can live indoors comfortably, they require less attention, and they cost less to keep than dogs. This is despite the fact that the incidence of allergies to cats is about twice that of dog-induced allergies.

Cat Care

Whether having long or short hair, cats should be brushed regularly to eliminate as much loose fur as possible. This will not only make your housekeeping easier, but it'll also reduce the number of hair balls formed. To find cat brushes, check local pet stores. By mail order, cat brushes and combs are sold by **Pet Warehouse** (Cat Catalog) and **R.C. Steele**.

It's also a good idea, especially if your cat is allowed outdoors, to comb it regularly with a *flea comb*. This is a specially designed comb with very close teeth that are able to remove tiny fleas. To use a flea comb, simply comb through the fur. Taking your fingernail, push off any accumulated fleas into a bowl of water to drown them. If you'd like to buy a flea comb, they're available at many local pet-supply outlets. If you'd prefer, you can mail order one from **R.C. Steele, Simmons Natural Bodycare**, and **American Environmental Health Foundation**. Other anti-flea measures are listed under *Fleas* on page 416.

To help your cat's discomfort if he (or she) already has fleas, you might try Dancing Paws Natural Flea Eze (**Rincon Group, LLC**). These are supplements made with organic, whole-wheat flour and other natural ingredients. This product may be available locally in alternative grocery stores, and in some pet-supply centers. If not, you can order it from the company.

With cats, it's also necessary to ensure that they're free of roundworms, ear mites, and that their vaccinations are up-to-date. Of course, other all-natural anti-flea and ear-mite products, hair-ball remedies, and shampoos should be available in local pet shops and pet-supply stores. However before using them (if you're a chemically sensitive person), make sure that the products will be tolerable to you, if at all possible. This is particularly necessary if you normally have close contact with your pet. A manufacturer of all-natural remedies for cats you may want to try is **Natural Animal Health Products, Inc.** Their line even includes HomeoPet homeopathic formulations. Natural Animal products can be bought from the manufacturer and from **Frontier Natural Products**. Other mail-order dealers that handle certain items are TerrEssentials, **Priorities, Karen's Natural Products, Allergy Relief Shop, Inc.**, and **Simmons Natural Bodycare. Karen's Natural Products** also handles a number of other natural cat-care items. One Earth Products (**Eight-In-One Pet Products**) has all-natural treats, brewer's yeast, garlic tablets, and shampoos, including Oatmeal & Aloe. To find a local supplier, call the company. If you live in the Southwestern U.S., the **Tucson Cooperative Warehouse** can supply you with a number of all-natural cat remedies, food items, and more. In addition, Dancing Paws (**Rincon Group, LLC**) holistic cat supplements can be ordered directly from the manufacturer. Halo pet products (**Halo, Purely for Pets, Inc.**) includes cat supplements and remedies such as Halo Herbal Ear Washes. These all can be ordered directly from the company. Botanical TerrEssential Coat Cleanser and TerrEssential Coat Rinse and other natural pet items are sold in the **TerrEssentials** catalog. Finally, **R.C. Steele** and **Pet Warehouse** (Cat catalog) has a number of natural pet-care products.

It should be mentioned that if you're allergic to cat fur, but want a cat anyway, you might consider owning one of the nearly hairless breeds, such as a Sphinx cat. Nearly hairless cats also tend to have fewer flea problems. However, having a semi-bald pet will not decrease dander allergies. And if you choose a nearly hairless cat, extra vigilance will be required on your part so that he (or she) is kept warm and draft-free. If the cat goes outdoors, it must be shielded from too much sun exposure. After all, these types of cats don't have much of a fur coat to act as protection.

It's been determined that, if you want to help control dander allergens with any breed of cat, wiping it's fur thoroughly with a damp cloth at least once a week helps. In fact, it's supposed to work as effectively as using special allergen-control products such as Allerpet-C. By the way, Allerpet is an *emollient* (a soothing skin preparation) which is oil- and scent-free.) It's used to clean cat fur of dander and saliva allergens. You apply some to a clean cloth and rub it into the fur, then go over the fur with a dry towel. This particular product can be ordered from **Priorities, Allergy Clean Environments**, and **Bio Designs**.

While most people feel that cat fur or cat dander are the main causes of cat allergies, research has shown that cat saliva is apparently one of biggest culprits. (Note: Cat urine and feces can also be allergenic.) The specific allergen in their saliva is a protein known as fel-d-1. Because cats constantly lick their fur and then brush up to furnishings and people (plus their shed fur will have fel-d-1 on it, too) this protein is widely present in any cat-owner's home. Interestingly, so persistent is this fel-d-1, that it's apparently been detected in homes three years after the cat was no longer living there.

Bathing your cat will help remove this protein, but as any one who has owned a cat will testify, that can be difficult to do. But if you'd like to bathe your cat anyway, a good un-scented, undyed, natural shampoo you might try is LifeTime Solutions Pet Care (**LifeTime Solutions**). This uniquely formulated product (it's made with *colloidal micelles*) can be or-dered directly from the manufacturer. A dry shampoo alternative is Furry Friends Lemon Oil Dry Shampoo (**Burt's Bees, Inc.**) The ingredients include corn starch, rice flour, oat protein, lemon oil, and rosemary oil, so it will be aromatic. Furry Friends products can be ordered from the maker. By the way, wiping your cat's coat regularly with a damp cloth as mentioned above to control dander, may be helpful in reducing saliva allergens, too.

Another concern is your cat's sleeping area. It should be kept clean. Also, you'll want to properly store and serve his (or her) food. Use canned food that has only been opened for a short period of time, and seal and refrigerate any remaining food in the container.

Cat Litter and Litter Boxes

You'll want to place your cat's litter box in a location where the cat has privacy, and where young children can't get into it. For a litter-box filler, you might consider using old-fashioned clay litter, rather than one of the typical new fillers now available that often con-tain synthetic dyes and scents. Unfortunately, simple clay litter is handled by fewer and fewer pet-supply stores. Another litter choice, that may be an acceptable alternative, is Natural Animal Scoopable Cat Litter (**Natural Animal Health Products, Inc.**) which can be ordered from **Frontier Natural Products** and the manufacturer. (Some mail-order dealers that may also stock it include **TerrEssentials, Priorities, Karen's Natural Products, Allergy Relief Shop, Inc.**, and **Simmons Natural Bodycare**.) Natural Animal Scoopable Cat Litter is made of peanut-shell meal with yucca-plant and citrus extract. It's said to be biodegradable and 200-300% more effective than typical litters. Still another option is to use an alfalfa-pellet litter that contains *chlorophyll*, the green compound in plant leaves that can act as a natural deodorizer. This type of filler is often available at local pet centers. However, you could find the chlorophyll's odor a bit strong, if you're a very sensitive person. Other natural cat litters are sold by **Tucson Cooperative Warehouse**.

Of course, as a rule, it's a good idea to remove any soiled litter daily, and completely empty and wash the litter box weekly. One very good method to help minimize litter-box odors, no matter what filler you use, is to pour a large box of baking soda into the bottom of the litter box before you pour in the filler. You can also use granulated or powdered *zeolite*, an adsorbent mineral. One such product you might try is EcoFresh Cat Litter Freshing Granules which can be ordered from **TerrEssentials**. Dasun All Natural Zeolite Powder (**Dasun Co.**), in a two-pound shaker container, can be purchased from **Bio Designs** or the manufacturer. Both a two-pound shaker container as well as a ten-pound bucket of powered zeolite are sold by **healthyhome.com**. Keep in mind that, when using zeolite, especially if it's in a powdered form, it's best to wear a dust mask. (See *Personal Protective Gear* on page 264.) By the way, you could also try hanging a mesh bag filled with zeolite granules on the wall above the cat box. Dasun two-pound mesh bags with zeolite crystals can be bought from the maker or from **Bio Designs**.

An option to conventional litter boxes is to get one of the new automatic models. Litter Maid litter box cleaning system uses computer sensors to automatically scoop and dispose of cat waste 10 minutes after the cat has left the box. (This allows enough time for clumping to occur.) Any clumping-type litter material can be used. Some local pet centers carry these types of boxes. If you can't find one, you can order them from **SilvoHome** or **Improvements**. Another source for self-cleaning litter boxes is **R.C. Steele**.

You'll also want to keep the area around the litter box especially clean. This means vacuuming or washing the floor regularly, depending on the type of floor. Remember also to wash the room walls next to the litter box frequently. This is especially important if you own a male cat that has not been neutered. These cats, in particular, may spray when urinating. To find an appropriate cleaner that will have deodorizing properties and yet be safe for your walls and cat, ask your veterinarian for his (or her) recommendations. If you're a chemically sensitive person, you'll also want to test the product to make sure you find it tolerable. (See *Testing* on page 62.) One product that may work for you is Nature's Key Odor Eliminator. This is a specially formulated, unscented, active-enzyme solution which can be purchased from **Dasun Co.** A similar product, Ens-Odor is handled by **Bio Designs**. Another possible option is Pet-Clean Pet Stain Cleaner & Neutralizer (**Orange-Sol Household Products, Inc.**). Pet-Clean has a orange-solvent base, so it will leave a mild, natural, citrus scent behind. This product can be ordered directly from the manufacturer. (Remember to apply only a small amount of any product you choose in an inconspicuous spot to see if there's any adverse interaction with the wall paint.)

It's important to say that, *if you're a pregnant women, you shouldn't be involved with litter-box maintenance whatsoever.* This is because there's a risk of becoming infected with *toxoplasmosis.* While this parasitic infection usually only causes mild symptoms in children and adults, it can damage a developing fetus. (Even if you don't personally handle the litter-box job, there is apparently some risk in just having a cat. Therefore, check with your obstetrician recommendations concerning your pregnancy and pet cats.)

Other Cat Supplies and Books

When you're in the market to buy safe, non-toxic cat items, check with your veterinarian, pet shop, and alternative grocery stores. Also, you might look through cat magazines. One mail-order company offering a number of healthier cat items is **Pet Warehouse** (Cat Catalog). They have stainless-steel and ceramic water and feed bowls, nylon collars, as well as catnip kits, and more. Another catalog that has a good variety of items is **R.C. Steele**. Personalized ceramic bowls and nylon collars are available from **Pedigrees**. Natural feather/down beds in a number of sizes and covering fabrics are sold by **Cuddledown of Maine**.

There are many fine cat foods now available, many with all-natural ingredients. Your veterinarian may recommend a brand. One that you might try with your cat is Halo's cat food (**Halo, Purely for Pets, Inc.**) which is canned, and has 100%-natural ingredients with human-grade vegetables, grains, and meats and has added nutrients and vitamins. You can order it from the manufacturer if you can't find it in alternative grocery stores or pet-supply centers.

Veterinarians, pet shops, and libraries should be able to supply you with general information on caring for your cat. Also, having a few cat-care guides as part of your own home library is always a good idea. One you might choose to own is *The Natural Remedy Book for*

Dogs & Cats by Diane Stein. This book provides instructions for natural remedies and therapies for many cat symptoms. Another good book is *Dr. Pitcairn's Complete Guide to Natural Health for Dogs & Cats* by Richard Pitcarin and Susan Hubble Pitcarin. This volume explains how to best care for your cat from a holistic viewpoint. In addition, a small, free *Holistic Pet Care* booklet is available from **Halo, Purely for Pets, Inc.** Finally, catalogs that usually handle a number of good cat-care books include **Pet Warehouse** (Cat catalog) and TerrEssentials.

Dogs

Researchers have concluded that about 10,000 years ago early domesticated dogs (descendants of wolf-like animals) first began living in human company. Soon afterwards, individuals began creating different physical forms of dogs to better suit certain tasks (for example, hunting badgers, hunting birds, hunting rats, protecting sheep, etc.) through selective breeding. Over time, the sizes, shapes, and fur qualities became further exaggerated. As a result, today's dog-certification organizations have come to recognize certain distinctly different breeds. Interestingly, the American Kennel Club currently lists about 130 breeds, the British Kennel Club lists about 170, and the Federation Cynologique, Internationale recognizes around 335 dog breeds. However, most dogs are *mongrels* (mixed breeds). In the U.S., the dog population, both purebred and mixed, is thought to be as high as 50 million.

Dog Care

No matter what the breed, or "non-breed," it's important that your dog be groomed regularly. This means routine brushing and bathing, especially if it has long hair, or if someone in your family is prone to dog-inducing allergies.

First, frequent brushings outdoors will help minimize coat matting, shedding of loose fur onto floors and furnishings, as well as reduce the amount of allergens, such as dander. Of course, dog brushes are generally available in local pet stores and pet-supply centers. By mail order, they're available from **Pet Warehouse** (Dog Catalog) and **R.C. Steele**. Interestingly, one dog handler trained his dog from puppyhood to tolerate a daily vacuuming with a Dust Buster-type vacuum. As a puppy, he played a tape of the vacuum's noise at mealtime. Eventually the dog got used to the noise, and to actually being vacuumed. You might consider this procedure with your pet.

Another good grooming routine is to use a *flea comb* frequently on your dog. A flea comb is a simple, nontoxic way to eliminate fleas, so it's safer for you and your pet. To use one of these closely toothed combs, simply pull it through the fur. Then, using a fingernail, push off any accumulated fleas into a bowl of water to drown them. Local pet stores or veterinarians may have these combs for sale. If not, they can be ordered from **R.C. Steele**, **Simmons Natural Bodycare**, and **American Environmental Health Foundation**. Other remedies are probably available from your veterinarian and local pet-supply stores. Of course, with any product you use on your pet, it should ideally be something that will not be bothersome to you. Therefore, remember that your pet will take on the odor of herbs or any other *topical preparation* (a compound locally applied to skin, etc.). (Note: Other anti-flea measures are described in *Fleas* on page 416.) If your dog is currently uncomfortable with flea problems, you might give him (or her) Dancing Paws Natural Flea Eze (**Rincon Group, LLC**) made with organic whole-wheat flour and other natural ingredients. If you can't find it in area pet-supply outlets, you can order it from the manufacturer.

As a side note, for those people who want to avoid shedding, and flea problems as well, consider a nearly fur-less dog. Of course, these dogs, such as the Mexican Hairless, will be more susceptible to sunburn, cold temperatures, and drafts. Therefore, as the pet's owner, you'll have to be more diligent in providing preventive care. By the way, some breeds of furred dogs tend to shed less, and will be more climate-adjustable. Apparently, these include some of the curly, woolly coated dogs, such a poodles. For other specific breed recommendations, check with a veterinarian.

Naturally, bathing your dog regularly is an important aspect to good dog grooming. This will not only to remove dirt and odors but also allergenic dander. If you're a chemically sensitive person, you'll want to make sure to only wash your dog with a mild, low-odor pet shampoo. Your veterinarian, alternative grocery store, or pet-supply center may have these for sale. An excellent one you might try is LifeTime Solutions Pet Care (**LifeTime Solutions**). This product was formulated specifically with sensitive people in mind, so it has no dyes or scents in its special *colloidal-micelle* formula. Pet Care can be ordered directly from the manufacturer. Routinely wiping your dog with a damp cloth should also help to remove dander between washings. (Research with cats has shown that this works as well at controlling dander allergens as using a special anti-allergen cleaning product such as Allerpet. Allerpet is an unscented, non-oily cleaner that is poured onto a cloth, rubbed into the fur, then dried with a towel. If you'd like to try this product, Allerpet-D for dogs is sold by **Priorities**, **Allergy Clean Environments**, and **Bio Designs**.) An interesting alternative to wet-shampooing is to use Furry Friends Lemon Oil Dry Shampoo (**Burt's Bees, Inc.**) Ingredients include corn starch, rice flour, oat protein, lemon oil, and rosemary oil. To use it, simply rub it into the fur and brush it out, preferably outdoors. Furry Friends products can be ordered from the manufacturer.

Of course, if you plan to own any type of dog, it's important to keep your pet's indoor sleeping and eating areas clean, and to store all pet food safely. If your pet has an outdoor doghouse, the bedding should be clean and regularly changed as well. Also, backyard fecal droppings from your dog should be scooped up and properly disposed of on a regular basis. In addition, make sure that roundworms, tapeworms, and heart worms are not now affecting your dog. And, of course, you'll want to insure that all appropriate vaccinations are current, especially those for rabies.

A manufacturer of all-natural supplements and remedies for pets you may want to try with your dog is **Natural Animal Health Products, Inc.** Their HomeoPet homeopathic formulations are particularly interesting. These products can be ordered from **Frontier Natural Products** or the maker. Dr. GoodPet homeopathic dog remedies and other natural dog-care products are sold by **Karen's Natural Products**. In addition, the **Tucson Cooperative Warehouse** carries quite a few all-natural dog remedies, food items, and supplements. The One Earth Products line (**Eight-In-One Pet Products**) includes all-natural treats, brewer's yeast, garlic tablets and shampoos, including Oatmeal & Aloe. To find a source for these products in your area, contact the company.

Dancing Paws (**Rincon Group, LLC**) holistic-approach dog supplements can be ordered directly from the manufacturer. TerrEssentials Botanical Coat Cleanser and TerrEssentials Coat Rinse, and other brands of natural dog-care items, are sold in the **TerrEssentials** catalog. Then, too Anitra's Eyewash (#1 is a boric-acid solution and #2 is a golden-seal formulation) and Herbal Ear Washes (**Halo, Purely for Pets, Inc.**) are helpful products. They can be ordered directly from the manufacturer. Other catalogs that carry some natural supplements, etc. are **R.C. Steele** and **Pet Warehouse** (Dog catalog).

Other Dog Supplies and Books

Most owners want to provide their dog with good-quality equipment and toys. Hopefully, these should also be ones you'll be able to tolerate if you're a chemically sensitive person. Local pet stores will undoubtedly carry items that are both good for your dog and you. By mail order, **Pet Warehouse** (Dog catalog) offers nylon and leather collars and leashes, stainless-steel food and water bowls, metal cages with handles, and natural rawhide chews. Another catalog with many dog items is **R.C. Steele**. Nice feather/down beds, in several sizes and fabric choices, are handled by **Cuddledown of Maine**. Wooden feeder trays with stainless-steel bowls, personalized ceramic bowls, and personalized nylon collars are sold by **Pedigrees**.

For dogs, there are probably going to be many good food choices available in alternative groceries and pet-supply stores. One you might consider is Spot's Stew for Dogs (**Halo, Purely for Pets, Inc.**). This is made with 100%-natural, human-grade, canned food with no fillers, artificial chemicals, or preservatives, and includes ingredients such as yellow squash, green peas, chicken liver, garlic, vitamins, minerals, and much more. Of course, checking with your veterinarian for his (or her) recommendations is always a good idea.

Finally, you'll want to have multi-topic dog-care books at home to answer any questions and concerns you may have. To find some, check your veterinarian's office, local pet stores, book shops, and library. A good guide to consider is *The Natural Remedy for Dogs & Cats* by Diane Stein. This book suggests herb, vitamin, and therapeutic-massage remedies for common dog ailments. Another fine book is *Dr. Pitcairn's Complete Guide to Natural Health for Dogs & Cats* by Richard Pitcarin and Susan Hubble Pitcarin which is a complete holistic-care manual. By the way, a free *Holistic Pet Care* booklet is available from **Halo, Purely for Pets, Inc.** Two catalogs that often have several good dog-care books from which to choose are **Pet Warehouse** (Dog catalog) and **TerrEssentials**.

Birds

Birds of many species have been kept as pets for centuries. This has been particularly true in the Orient where small singing birds are highly treasured. Today, in the U.S., birds in the parrot family (parrots, macaws, parakeets, cockatoos, cockatiels, etc.), canaries, and various finches are quite common. Most very small pet birds have a life span of only a few years. However, some large birds in the parrot family can live 70–80 years—definitely a long-term commitment.

While pet birds are colorful, perky, and cute, they do have their drawbacks. One big negative is that they're often noisy a great deal of the time, which can get tiring even with a melodic canary. But perhaps worse is how surprisingly messy most birds can be. Feathers, *dander* (loose skin flakes), droppings, and food are usually in and on their cages, in the air, and on nearby furnishings, floors, and walls. To help minimize these potential allergens it's best to clean your bird's cage and surroundings daily, if at all possible. Even so, birds may not be appropriate for some highly allergic or asthmatic individuals.

For a number of years people were afraid to keep parrots out of fear of getting *psittacosis* (parrot fever). This is a bacterial infection that can be transmitted by feathers, dander, and droppings. Human symptoms vary from none to a severe form of pneumonia. However, it's now known that many other bird species carry the same bacteria, and that certain antibiotics work well as an effective treatment for the condition.

Many owners are concerned that their pet bird will get *mites* (a type of microscopic parasite). A common remedy for this external parasitic infection has been to hang a chemically saturated anti-mite repellent on the bird's cage. These are purposely designed to continually release harmful mite-killing airborne compounds. Unfortunately, many such repellents are actually nothing more than a potentially hazardous mothball material disguised in special packaging. Obviously, mothball chemicals are not healthy for mites. Sadly, they also aren't healthy for birds or humans either.

Of course, you'll want to have your bird take a bath regularly. A small shallow bowl half-filled with tepid water can be used. Make sure to remove it within a half an hour or so. That way it won't become contaminated with droppings before your bird bathes in it or drinks from it. If your bird prefers, you can fill a spray bottle with tepid water and spray it directly.

If you routinely cover your bird's cage at night, you might consider an untreated, washable 100%-cotton pillowcase for the job. If it doesn't fit properly, you may want to custom make a cover. Of course, be sure to wash the cover regularly using a tolerable product.

When you choose food for your bird, make sure it's appropriate for the size and species you have. Some birds eat fruit, others just seed, some eat both. Small birds, such as zebra finches, can't eat some of the seeds that large parrots can eat. A good all-natural bird-food line is Halo Fanta-Seeds (**Halo, Purely for Pets, Inc.**) These come in varieties for small, medium, and large birds. The small-bird type has, for example, an assortment of seeds, vegetables, greens, and all-natural nutrients. These bird foods can be ordered directly from the company.

Finally, a good mail-order catalog having everything you'll need for birds, including food, cages, toys, remedies, supplements, and care books, is **Pet Warehouse** (Bird catalog).

Fish

Probably the first pet fish (varieties of goldfish) were kept centuries ago in the Orient. Today, keeping pet fish is extremely popular in many areas of the world, especially in the U.S. In fact, it's estimated that 350 million aquarium fish are sold in America annually. Many of these are tropical fish, coming originally from fresh and salt water in warm climates. Others are from temperate regions. Of course, the goldfish remains a favorite pet fish.

While fish are low-care pets, they certainly require some care. Their tanks, water, and even filtering equipment can easily become contaminated with microbial growth, if not properly cared for. In addition, the chemical composition of the tank's water must be kept compatible with the types of fish living in it. The fish themselves must be monitored to see if they've acquired any types of infection. If they have, appropriate medications usually have to be added to the water and/or other measures taken.

If you decide on fish as pets, make sure that the aquarium, water, and filters are always clean. If your setup requires you to wash the tank and equipment periodically, check with your local pet-supply store for safe, low-odor products that will clean effectively, but not cause any harm to your fish—or to you. Of course, having a good tropical fish guide on hand is always a good idea. These should be available at pet stores and bookstores. Books, as well as most pet fish needs, can also be mail ordered from **Pet Warehouse** (Fish catalog).

CHAPTER 20: TELEPHONES, ELECTRONICS, & APPLIANCES

There are a variety of considerations you should take into account when selecting devices that operate with electricity. This includes many of the common items we use every day, ranging from telephones to televisions, computers to microwave ovens, and clock radios to refrigerators.

This chapter will discuss many of these devices, as well as their potential health effects. One major concern are electromagnetic fields. They will be touched on in this chapter, but will be covered in more depth in *Chapters 26: Electromagnetic Fields* and *Chapter 27: Dealing with Electromagnetic Fields*.

Telephones

Telephones have come a long way since Alexander Graham Bell's original 1876 patent. However, they all still have one thing in common. Telephones convert the vibrations of speech into transportable electric signals which are then reconverted back into audible sound. Today, telephones have become an essential component of daily life. They can be used to shop, bank, and run a home office—besides their social function in talking with friends and family.

Unfortunately, some chemically sensitive individuals are unable to use their telephone because they find it intolerable—for a variety of reasons. Another problem has arisen lately with the introduction of portable cellular telephones. There is some concern that the *radio frequency radiation (RF)* emitted by themcan pose possible unexpected dangers to anyone using conventional cellular phones, whether they are sensitive or not. However, the good news is that there are some solutions, so that you can use your phone, without jeopardizing your health.

Standard Telephones

Standard telephones are those that are connected directly to a telephone wiring system. Some portable carry-around models are connected indirectly to a telephone wiring system through their base units. Until fairly recently, these were the only types of telephones that most people had.

Problems with Typical Standard Telephones

Why are many standard telephones intolerable to certain sensitive individuals? One of the major reasons is that modern telephones are usually made of synthetic plastic. New telephones can release odors outgassed by these materials for months—or even years, in some cases. Fortunately, just placing untreated 100%-cotton over the mouth and ear pieces often helps seal in these emissions. By mail order, **N.E.E.D.S.** and **Janice Corporation** offer untreated 100%-cotton *barrier cloth* whose tight weave can make for effective telephone covers. As an alternative, clean cotton handkerchiefs can be used, but they probably seal in the odors less well. In either case, the cotton can be held in place by strings or rubber bands. Remember, you'll want to launder cotton telephone covers frequently to minimize bacterial growth.

Some telephones may also be a problem because they have a paper insert inside their mouthpieces that is saturated with a *biocide*. Biocides are chemicals designed to kill life, in this case the paper is supposed to kill bacteria and fungus. If you suspect you are reacting to a biocide hidden within the mouthpiece, you may be able to remove it. Some telephone mouthpieces (usually older models) unscrew or snap apart. If yours does, you should be able to pull out any chemically laden paper that is inside and simply put the mouthpiece back together again.

Suggested Alternative Standard Telephones

If you want to replace a bothersome plastic phone, more tolerable alternatives are available. The following sections will discuss some of these.

Alternative-Material Telephones

Telephones that are likely to be acceptable to sensitive persons are often not made of plastic. Surprisingly, a number of such phones are available. For example, new metal telephones, usually in brass or brass-plated steel, can be found in some department stores, appliance and electronic stores, and phone centers. In addition, **Phoneco, Inc.** is a mail-order source selling a large selection of older restored metal telephones, as well as ones made of wood. In addition, older *Bakelite* models are available. Wall phones, desk models, pay phones, and metal and wood reproductions, as well as old telephone parts, can all be purchased from their catalog. Also, **Billards Old Telephones** sells reconditioned Bakelite phones, metal pay phones, and parts for old telephones.

What is Bakelite? First invented by Leo Bakeland in 1909, Bakelite was actually the second synthetic plastic ever created. (*Celluloid* was the first.) Although it's the end product of a reaction between heated phenol (also known as *carbolic acid*) and formaldehyde, it's more inert (and tolerable) than its ingredients would suggest. Physically, Bakelite is a very hard and durable material, one that's much less susceptible to outgassing than many newer, softer modern plastic compounds. As a result, Bakelite is quite often tolerable for even very sensitive individuals.

Speaker Telephones & Head Sets

Another telephone option that some sensitive individuals might want to try is a speaker phone. Speaker phones are usually plastic; therefore, the units themselves could be bothersome. However, because these phones allow a user to avoid direct physical contact with the receiver (in fact, a person can actually be some distance from the telephone), the chances for adverse health reactions are greatly reduced.

These days, speaker phones are manufactured by a number of companies, with features changing frequently. However, it must be said that speaker-phone popularity has waned since the advent of cordless phones. Therefore, they're not as easy to find as was the case only a few years ago. Still, you should be able to find a few speaker-phone models at department and discount stores, as well as at phone centers. Office-supply stores often carry these types, too. One mail-order source for speaker phones is **LS&S Group** (they even carry a voice-activated model.). Another good source is **Service Merchandise** which handles both AT&T and Sony brands.

One more coping method is to simply use a telephone head set. These units are much less bulky than standard receivers, so you will have less exposure to the materials of which it is made. Head sets can often be purchased in phone centers. By mail order, you can get head-set attachments as well as headset phones from **Hello Direct**. This company also carries a head-set/speaker-phone combination.

You may be happy to learn, that in some locations, with certain telephone service providers, you may qualify to receive a *free* speaker telephone and/or free directory assistance due to a valid physical disability or health problem that prevents you from performing certain telephone-related operations. Generally, you must provide proof of your disability with a physician's statement or that of a nurse, institution, etc. For more information, contact your telephone company representative.

Cellular Phones

These days, *cellular phones* are owned by an increasing percentage of the population. In fact, some people are predicting that they may totally replace standard telephones in the not-too-distant future.

What are cellular phones anyway? In a way, they're actually very advanced versions of the walkie-talkie. In both cases, the information is sent by radio frequency. However, walkie-talkies generally send messages directly to another compatible unit. Therefore, their use is limited to the range that the sister-units can transmit and receive. On the other hand, cellular phones use a series of radio transmitting towers which relay messages much, much further. As it turns out, each tower has an antenna and a low-power transmitter whose specific functioning range is determined by the surrounding geography (and other factors). This service area is known as a *cell*. Thus, mobile phones using these transmitting towers are part of a computer-controlled *cellular system* and phones using this system are termed cellular phones.

Problems with Typical Cellular Phones

Of course cellular phones are extremely convenient, and they can literally be lifesavers when vehicular accidents, ill health, or other emergencies occur when traveling. However, there are drawbacks.

One of the most familiar limitations is the restricted service area of certain systems and calling plans. Another is the less-than-crystal-clear audio quality often associated with them. For chemically sensitive people, the plastic materials used can also be of concern. Again, covering the phone with untreated cotton fabric may help. (See *Problems with Typical Standard Telephones* on page 478.)

For everyone using a cellular phone, there should also be concern over the *radio-frequency (RF) radiation* that most cellular phones emit. As it turns out cellular phones produce RF radiation at either approximately 900 MHz or 1900 MHz. (MHz stands for megahertz.) Although most people are not aware of it, RF is a form of low-intensity microwave radiation. As microwave radiation, it has the capacity to generate heat in exposed tissue due to the friction produced from energized, rapidly moving molecules. As it turns out, cellphone ear pieces, which are placed on or near the ear, emit this potentially active RF radiation which can apparently easily pass into a user's head. Ominously, in humans, short-term memory is located very near the right ear in the brain.

Not surprisingly, in 1999, research funded by the British government concluded that there was strong evidence for adverse affects on "cognitive function, memory, and attention" caused by the RF radiation's heating effect on the brain. Other research studies have found that RF weakens the *blood/brain barrier,* whose function is to prevent potentially dangerous chemicals from entering the brain. The good news is that, so far, both the short-term memory loss and weakened blood/brain barrier conditions caused by RF waves appear to revert to normal soon after the radiation exposure ends.

Today, active and vocal opponents of cell phones are concerned that RF radiation may cause even more damage, such as brain tumors. At this time, however, there is no hard evidence to confirm these fears. Because of the various concerns over RF radiation in cellular phones, the U.S. Federal Communications Commission (FCC) adopted new standards for RF cellular-phone exposure levels in the mid-1990s. However, some people feel that the new regulations aren't restrictive enough. Incidentally, some critics are also concerned over the RF radiation created by cellular-phone microwave antenna towers.

Making your Cellular Phone Safer

So, what can you do to reduce your RF exposure. First, only use a cellular phone manufactured after July 1996. If your phone is older, or if you want to further reduce the levels in your newer phone, you can buy a separate ear-piece attachment. With this device, you keep your ear further away from the ear piece. Another measure you can take is to use a *RF shield* on your phone. Mail-order sources for cellular-phone RF-protection equipment include **Less EMF, Inc.** (this company has an on-line catalog only) and **Befit Enterprises Ltd.** As far as the RF radiation produced by cellular-phone microwave antenna towers, no definitive "safe distance" from them has been set. However, not living on very high elevations between operating towers so as to not be directly in the path of their transmissions is probably a good idea. That is, until more is known for certain.

Finally, it should be added that the majority of scientists feel that both cellphones and cell-phone antenna towers (as they are now), are relatively safe. So, it's up to you to decide what's best to do, or not do. If you're interested in knowing more about of the technical aspects of RF radiation and human health, you may want to read *IEEE Standard for Safety Levels with Respect to Human Exposure to Radio Frequency Electromagnetic Fields.* This expensive volume will be able to explain the reasoning behind human exposure guidelines to RF waves. You can order a copy from your favorite bookseller, or from **Less EMF, Inc.**

Electronic Equipment

Electronic equipment has revolutionized the American life-style. Sadly, problems with bothersome odors and *EMFs* (electromagnetic fields) from many of these devices have posed difficulties for certain chemically sensitive and electrically sensitive persons. However, these problems can often be lessened, or even overcome.

Electronic-Equipment Odor Problems

Some sensitive individuals are finding that their new electronic equipment—televisions, stereos, video cassette recorders, and computers—are intolerable for them to use. This is often due to both *outgassing* (releasing of chemical compounds) from the plastic housings, and outgassing from the electronic workings inside. In particular, some *transformers* (devices that change an electric current's voltage) give off fairly strong, objectionable odors.

Airing Electronic Equipment

Airing out intolerable electronic equipment, by leaving it turned on in a seldom-used room with open windows, can often be helpful in reducing any bothersome odors. You could also run the equipment in a garage, if there's no possibility of contamination by gasoline, oil, or combustion gases. Operating new electronics on a sheltered porch can also work well. However, keep in mind that very cold or very hot temperatures, as well as an excess of moisture, can cause sometimes irreversible damage.

How long should your new electronic equipment run before it loses its objectionable "new" odor? A few days may be enough, but more likely it'll take several weeks—or more, for very sensitive people. (In fact, a few devices never seem to lose their odor.) While some electronic equipment can safely remain turned on and unattended for extended airing periods, other items should be turned off from time to time. You'll have to use your best judgment, and read your owner's manual thoroughly. You may also want to contact the manufacturer for assistance in determining the best approach. However, be aware that, because you're presenting the company with a problem they may never have come across, they may have no definitive answer to give you.

Electronic-Equipment Containment Boxes

Sometimes, a particular electronic item never seems to become tolerable from an odor standpoint, despite lengthy airings. In those situations, special *containment boxes* can be a good solution. These specially designed boxes help isolate, or contain, odors released by electronic equipment, so they can't reach the room's air and be inhaled by sensitive persons. Containment boxes are generally built of glass or clear plastic, with metal or solid-wood frames. Ideally, a containment box should be vented directly to the outdoors with a small fan, or attached to a portable air filter that's capable of removing gaseous pollutants. By the way, containment boxes used for electronic equipment should always have air passing through them. This is because the heat generated by the electronic components must be dissipated, or damage could occur.

While some computer CPUs (central processing units) and monitors (the TV-like viewing devices used with computers) can release odors that make them intolerable, some sensitive individuals find that the printer for their computer is often even more troublesome. It doesn't seem to matter which brand it is, or whether it's a *dot matrix printer* (a printer that creates letters and designs with tiny dots of mechanically stamped ink), an *ink-jet printer* (a printer in which droplets of ink are applied with nozzles at high speed), or a *laser printer* (a printer that uses a laser to quickly create a pattern on which particles are electrostatically adhered). Printers are just plain odorous. Many sensitive people think that having a laser printer is the best choice because it doesn't actually use ink—something that's often bothersome. However, laser printers give off a certain amount of ozone (O_3). Unfortunately, ozone is a reactive, harmful gas with an unpleasant odor.

To use any bothersome printer, you might consider placing it in a separate vented or filtered containment box. Unfortunately, this is often too costly or impractical to do. Another possible solution is to use a very long computer-to-printer cable. The printer can then be placed in a room other than where the computer is located—perhaps in a closet. The new location for the printer can be vented outdoors or, it can be a space that the sensitive individual seldom uses.

Of course, other electronic equipment, such as televisions, stereo systems, and VCRs, may create odor problems similar to those caused by computers and printers. Therefore, many of the methods already mentioned can be used with virtually any of these items.

By the way, if you're interested in using a containment box, one mail-order company that makes and sells them is **Safe Reading & Computer Box Co.** These are made with glass and *galvanized* steel (galvanizing is an anti-rust, zinc coating) and they come in three basic sizes: standard desk computer, portable computer, and computer tower. Custom sizes can also be specially made to meet your needs. These boxes all come equipped with fans and window inserts to permit venting to the outdoors. You can also order these containment boxes from **Nigra Enterprises.**

Electronic Equipment EMF Concerns

Virtually all electronic equipment creates *electromagnetic fields (EMFs)* when operating. EMFs are defined as areas of measurable electrical and magnetic energy that surround electrically operated devices. Interestingly, both electric fields and magnetic fields are present in the wiring and in an appliance whenever the appliance is operating. However, when a device is turned off, but plugged in to an electrical outlet, there will still be electric field surrounding it and the wiring.

Obviously, EMFs can be found around live electric wires, motors, and various electronic components. Unfortunately, it's believed by many that the strength of these fields can often be potentially harmful to people, if a person is exposed to them for too long. This is particularly true of magnetic fields. (For more in-depth information on EMFs, see *Chapter 26: Electromagnetic Fields.*)

Actually, until fairly recently, EMFs were not considered something to be concerned about. As a result, electronic-equipment manufacturers didn't design products to minimize EMFs. However, because of certain initial studies linking EMF exposures to certain negative health effects, most newer electronic components have reduced EMF levels, compared to earlier models.

What's a safe EMF level? At this time it's believed by most experts that a long-term exposure to EMFs below a level of 1–3 milligauss (mG) is acceptable. (A gauss is a measurement of magnetic-field strength, and a milligauss is $1/1000$th of a gauss.) However, it should be noted that a small, but very vocal (and often persuasive) minority believe that a long-term exposure to less than 1 mG, or less, is truly safe. Because there's no clear-cut agreement on this point, you must ultimately decide for yourself what you consider allowable. To find out what EMF levels your particular equipment is actually giving off, the levels can be measured with a gauss meter. If you're interested, **Less EMF, Inc.** (this company has an on-line catalog only), **N.E.E.D.S.**, and **Safe Technologies Corp.** offer gauss meters for sale.

You should be aware of certain simple practices that can improve your margin of safety when you feel EMF levels are too high. First, it's important to understand that EMF levels generally decrease rapidly with distance. So, just positioning yourself several feet back from your stereo or television can often offer sufficient protection. Also, **Less EMF, Inc.** sells EMF-reducing products that you can install directly on your equipment. **Less EMF, Inc.** also handles clothing you can wear to protect against EMFs.

To reduce exposure to EMFs from your computer, try placing the keyboard two or three feet away from both the monitor and the computer itself. As a rule, it's the computers and monitors that create more intense EMF fields—not the keyboards. **LS&S Group** offers computer-screen magnifiers that fit 17-19" screens, as well as voice-recognition software so you can sit some distance away from the screen and be still able to work effectively. In addition, you might want to purchase a special EMF-blocking screen or an *EMF neutralizer* (these are designed to counter the wave action created) that can be attached to your computer monitor. Such devices are available for both IBM-compatible and Apple computers from **Less EMF, Inc.** and **Safe Technologies Corp.**, as well as from some monitor manufacturers, and other computer-product companies. Also, check local computer stores and mail-order companies in computer magazines.

Choosing Less-Bothersome Electronic Equipment

It's important to note that certain types of computers, monitors, and televisions are inherently less problematic from an EMF, or an odor, standpoint than some other models.

Computers Designed for Reduced EMFs

Some manufacturers have begun producing alternative electronic equipment, usually computer-related items, that are designed and marketed for lower EMF risks to their users. For example **Less EMF, Inc.** offers an anti-EMF IBM-compatible keyboard which "emits a signal that neutralizes the EMFs produced by the computer." They also sell low-EMF computer screens.

Safe Technologies Corp. sells the Ultra 7000 Multi-Scanning Color Monitor. They say it's the world's lowest radiation monitor. It will apparently work with both IBM-compatible equipment as well as Apple computers.

LCD Electronic Equipment

Interestingly, portable lap-top computers have significantly lower EMF emissions than desktop models. One of the reasons is that they have an LCD screen, which operates with lower EMFs—and also less odor. So, if you are interested in buying a low-EMF computer, lap-tops can be a good solution. In addition, LCD-screen monitors and LCD televisions, while not specifically designed to reduce EMFs, do so inherently. And, they also produce fewer odor problems. In addition, they are less bulky than conventional equipment.

What is an LCD screen? First of all, LCD stands for liquid crystal display. At it's simplest, an LCD screen is constructed of two sheets of glass. In between, is a completely sealed, very-thin layer of a liquid crystalline substance. The outer surfaces of the glass have a coating which is both transparent and able to conduct electricity. The glass side used for viewing has this coating etched into tiny segments. These individual segments each have an electrical connection extending to the edge of the screen.

Normally, the liquid layer is transparent. However, when an electric current travels through any individual segment, the liquid crystalline substance is disrupted. As a result, the liquid immediately become darker, just enough to be noticed. An image is generated by various segments being activated in a pattern. Innovations such as back-lighting, edge-lighting, reflective back plates, and other types of liquid-crystal compounds can increase visibility, contrast, and color differentiation.

Importantly, LCD screens require little electricity to operate compared to typical screens. If you're interested in purchasing a portable lap-top computer, or an LCD monitor, most computer outlets and catalogs carry them. LCD-screen TVs should be available at many TV and appliance departments and stores. Be aware, that their cost will be higher than conventional devices, sometimes substantially more.

Appliances

Very few of us would give up our modern household appliances. There's no argument that these devices make our lives much easier. However, many new appliances release chemical compounds into the air that can be bothersome to some chemically sensitive people.

Fortunately, you can often find appliance models that are healthier. The following sections offer information on what features to look for, and what features to avoid, when you're ready to buy a new appliance. Of course special options, sizes, colors, energy efficiency, and cost are also important, but in this chapter, an appliance's potential health effects will have top priority. By the way, the specific appliance models offered by manufacturers change fairly frequently, often annually. Therefore, the specific information provided here on brands and models may vary slightly from what is currently available. However, the general guidelines should still be valid.

Small Appliances

Small electric appliances are great for getting certain household jobs done quickly, but they can have drawbacks.

Small Appliance Concerns

Nearly all small appliances these days have plastic housings, and many have fast, whirring motors, that can give off bothersome odors. Those with heating elements can be particularly offensive because the elements are sometimes made of materials that emit offensive odors when they're heated up.

It's not surprising then that some sensitive people find they become ill when they use their small appliances, especially if they're new ones. If you are bothered by your small appliances, having good ventilation when you're operating them can help reduce odors. One obvious way of doing this is to open nearby windows. If you're using an appliance in the kitchen, you can also turn on a range-hood fan that is vented to the outdoors. In addition, you might wear a charcoal-filled mask to act as a simple air filter. The activated-charcoal insert can adsorb a great deal of the bothersome odors before they can reach you. Mail-order sources for all-cotton filtering masks include **Allerx, Allergy Relief Shop, Inc.**, and **Bio Designs. American Environmental Health Foundation** has masks of either untreated 100%-cotton or silk. These come with your choice of coconut-shell-activated charcoal or lignite-activated charcoal, or bituminous-activated-charcoal inserts. All the masks offered by these companies are washable and refill inserts are available.

Another concern with portable electric appliances is that their electric motors tend to create rather powerful *electromagnetic fields (EMFs)*. These areas of electric and magnetic energy are believed to have possible negative health effects, if the fields are intense enough and if you're exposed to them long enough. Fortunately, as a rule, small-appliance use is brief. Therefore, exposure time to their EMFs is short as well. However, those who are hypersensitive to electromagnetic fields should consider avoiding small appliances whenever possible. As an alternative, because EMFs decrease in strength with distance, if you stand a few feet away from them while they are operating, you will decrease your risk. (For more on EMFs and their possible effects, see *Chapter 26: Electromagnetic Fields* and *Chapter 27: Dealing With Electromagnetic Fields.*)

Actually, it would probably be wise for everyone to reevaluate his or her small-appliance needs, no matter whether they're concerned about chemical or electrical sensitivity or not. After all, it's easy for your kitchen counters and cabinets to become packed with electric gadgets, many of which you seldom use. The truth is, some small appliances are designed to do jobs that could just as easily be done by hand, such as an electric knife. Others are too limiting in what they can do, such as an electric hot-dog cooker.

As a safety precaution, it's important to not keep most small appliances continually plugged in. Many electrical fires have resulted from this practice. In fact, certain automatic coffee makers have been notorious for causing fires in the past. Therefore, you'll always want to read your appliances' owner manuals for proper safe operation.

Some Small Appliance Suggestions

As an alternative to owning a myriad of small appliances, you might seriously consider owning just a few multipurpose devices. You could sell or give away the extraneous electric gadgets. In doing this, your kitchen cleaning and organizing will inevitably become simpler. The appliances you decide to keep could be stored easily inside your now-emptier cabinets. If you prefer, you could keep your appliances on the countertop, but covered with washable natural-fabric covers, in order to keep them clean and dust-free. If you want to, you can even make the covers yourself (see *Sewing* on page 456).

By the way, when purchasing any type of small appliance, choose ones with metal housings rather than plastic. Even better, pick ones made with stainless steel or chrome-plated steel. A good selection of these types of kitchen appliances can be found in the **Sur La Table** catalog. Others should be available in local small-kitchen-appliance outlets.

One of the biggest problems for sensitive people is finding a less-problematic toaster. New heating elements in many toasters give off odors that are too bothersome for many such individuals to use. For very sensitive people, the best advice might be to buy a tolerable old toaster that has had a number of years to air out. If you must get a new one, many don't seem to ever air out completely. Getting one with a metal housing may be the best you can do. Then, you should only operate it under an kitchen range hood that is vented to the outdoors. Toastmaster makes stainless-steel toasters which can be found in many department and discount stores. By mail order, the **Vermont Country Store** (Voice of the Mountains catalog) sells them along with a Munsy chromed-steel toaster which has a small, slide-in tray. From **Sur La Table**, you can get Cusinart stainless-steel toasters.

For information on toaster-ovens see *Other Alternative Ovens* on page 495. For suggestions on selecting vacuum cleaners see *Vacuuming* on page 144.

Major Appliances

Major appliances are an investment; they can be expensive, and they are generally designed to last at least 10 years. Therefore, it's extremely important to take the necessary time and energy to choose them wisely. The sections below offer suggestions for what to look for when buying certain types of major appliances, some brands to consider, and a few methods to make particular items more tolerable to sensitive persons. (For information on major appliances and EMFs, see *Chapter 26: Electromagnetic Fields*.)

Major Appliances in General

Because of the cost involved, buying a major appliance is often considered a frightening and risky venture by chemically sensitive people. They may fear buying something they can't tolerate, but will have to live with for many years. If you are a sensitive person, when you're ready to purchase a major appliance, the first step is to ask other sensitive friends for their experiences and recommendations. If you belong to a local support group, it's a good idea to ask at a meeting or through the group's newsletter. However, you must keep in mind that appliance models often change. Therefore, ones which have had favorable reports could have since been "improved" with potentially bothersome modifications. In some cases, you may find that suggested models have been completely discontinued. Despite this, asking other sensitive individuals often remains your best initial information source.

Of course, buying new is not always the only way to acquire needed appliances—you can buy used models. Actually, a few sensitive persons have purchased tolerable stoves, refrigerators, etc. that were currently being used in the homes of friends or family members. In some cases, sensitive people have traded brand-new appliances for a used ones.

However, a word of caution is in order if you plan to purchase any pre-owned major appliance. If you buy one that's too old, it could soon need costly, and potentially odorous, repair work. In fact, in a worst-case scenario, the appliance may not be fixable at all. There are also special concerns when buying a used appliance from a dealer or a stranger. For example, you may not know the specific history of that particular appliance. The back or bottom could have been sprayed with insecticides, or it could have been repaired with new parts that could make the unit bothersome to you. Therefore, if it's at all possible, arrange a several-day trial period with the seller. If he or she agrees, get the agreement in writing. During the trial period, you'll be better able to judge whether you'll have tolerance problems before being committed to actually buying the appliance. You might also try to make a similar arrangement when buying a brand-new appliance. A few sensitive persons have been able to do this. However, realistically, getting a trial-period with a seller on any new or used major appliance is often difficult to obtain.

Dishwashers

Although they had been invented earlier, it wasn't until after World War II that many American kitchens have had automatic dishwashers. These days, it's a rare home that it built without one. However, while they certainly can minimize the drudgery of washing dishes by hand, as a rule, most new dishwashers are bothersome to sensitive people. This is often due to several factors. One involves the odors given off by the rubber hoses, belts, insulation, and gaskets—especially when they are warm. Another is the release of petroleum compounds from oils on motors and pumps, and yet another is the outgassing of plastic liners and vinyl-covered wire trays on the interior, again, especially when they are warm.

Although you can't eliminate rubber parts, or the motor, or other mechanical components, you can buy an automatic dishwasher without a plastic liner or most of the vinyl parts. Therefore, if you're a sensitive person, you'll want to think about purchasing a model with an all-stainless-steel interior. While some synthetic materials and plastics will still be present in nearly all models (such as gasketing and/or protective guards on the tips of wire racks), by choosing dishwashers with graphite, nylon, or composite graphite/nylon racks and rollers, you'll have eliminated many bothersome components.

Another problem that is showing up more and more is the insulation used around the dishwasher. The insulation has two purposes: it protects the surrounding cabinetry from the heat that's generated, and it acts as a noise muffling material. Various types of insulation can be used, including fiberglass, bubble-type insulation, and asphaltic materials, among others. Often, the quieter the dishwasher, the more insulation it will have. However, if you can get a dishwasher that comes with an aluminum-foil facing on the outside surface of the insulation, it will help seal in the insulation's odors.

One excellent brand to consider is **KitchenAid** dishwashers. They have many models with "commercial-grade stainless interiors" and nylon, graphite, or nylon/graphite racks, etc. At present, some came with an aluminum-foil facing over the insulation. In addition, imported European dishwasher brands you may want to check out are Bosch (**Bosch Appliances**) and Asko (**Asko, Inc.**). Bosch models are imported from Germany and Asko units from Sweden. Both companies make dishwashers with stainless-steel interior walls (stainless exteriors are also available), and interior racks and brackets made of graphite, nylon, or nylon/graphite. Both also have special energy- and water-saving features. In addition, they're designed to generate a minimum of noise. This is accomplished partly by the use of an asphaltic material that's bonded to the exterior. There's no aluminum-foil facing, though you could cover the asphaltic material yourself with heavy-duty aluminum foil or an aluminum-foil barrier product. (See *Foil Barriers* on page 290.) If you do so, make absolutely sure that no wiring comes into contact with the foil. To purchase Bosch or Asko products locally, you'll need to contact the companies for their nearest dealers. In addition, you can mail order Asko equipment from **Building for Health Materials Center**.

Some chemically sensitive people are unable to even tolerate older dishwashers. If you find that a running dishwasher makes you feel ill, try running it only after you've closed the kitchen off from the rest of the house, and opened one or more kitchen windows. You should also turn on the range hood (make sure it is vented to the outdoors), if your stove is equipped with one, and stay out of the kitchen until the dishwasher has cooled off.

Of course, if you own a dishwasher, you'll want to use a low-odor, tolerable automatic dishwashing compound in it, especially if you're a sensitive person. Unfortunately, most typical brands contain synthetic fragrances whose odors can easily fill your kitchen whenever your dishwasher is operating. Even some of the alternative brands contain natural scents—such as lemon oil, which certain individuals may find unacceptable. (For additional information, see *Automatic Dishwasher Products* on page 167.)

Unfortunately, a few very sensitive people have found they simply can't tolerate an automatic dishwasher, no matter what brand, or how old it is, whether they're out of the room while it's operating, or what cleaning compound is used. Naturally, in those situations doing the dishes by hand, using a tolerable dishwashing liquid, may be the only satisfactory solution.

Stoves

The earliest stoves that were designed exclusively for cooking were cast-iron models, whose tops were used for heating pots and pans. By the middle of the eighteenth century, cast-iron stoves with baking chambers were introduced. Then, in the 1840s, natural-gas-fired, cast-iron cooking ranges were invented and, for the first time, an "automatic" energy source had replaced hand-stoked wood, charcoal, and coal fires. Finally, in 1914, the electric range made its debut.

Today, stoves are no longer cast-oven behemoths. In fact, few other modern major appliances offer as many choices and options as stoves. The following sections discuss some of the more popular types of stoves found in today's marketplace. Ultimately, it's up to you to choose which type will be most appropriate for your own particular needs.

Gas Ranges and Cooktops

Natural-gas and propane ranges have long been popular stove choices, but they can pose problems of which you might not be aware.

Problems with Gas Ranges and Cooktops

Generally, gas ranges are not suggested for use in healthy households. The major reason is that they release polluting combustion by-products. These include carbon dioxide, nitrogen dioxide, small amounts of formaldehyde, and potentially deadly carbon monoxide (see *Combustion Gases* on page 524). Older models equipped with perpetually-burning pilot lights can be more troublesome in this regard. Their small, but constantly burning, flames release combustion by-products on a continuous basis. A carbon-monoxide detector is highly recommended for all homes equipped with natural-gas appliances.

Another gas-appliance concern is the possibility of gas-line leaks. In a few situations, leaks from interior gas lines have led to high-enough natural-gas concentrations to cause explosions. However, leaks don't need to release significant amounts of natural gas in order to be a problem. Unfortunately, some sensitive individuals have detected gas leaks, and become ill, as a result of natural gas escaping from extremely tiny leaks. Apparently, a few such persons can detect leaks that are barely detectable on the testing equipment typically used by gas companies. As it turns out, natural gas (or propane) happens to be one substance that a great many people with sensitivities simply can't tolerate breathing, no matter how small the amount present in the air.

To many healthy people, it seems somewhat puzzling that exposure to very small amounts of natural gas could be detected, or cause problems. However, natural gas is composed of a number of nasty compounds. For example, it's typically 88% to 95% methane, with the remainder being gases such as ethane, propane, butane, pentane, carbon dioxide, nitrogen, and helium. Besides these, a *marker chemical* (methyl mercaptan) is also added to provide the strong, distinctive odor associated with gas so that leaks will be more noticeable to anyone. Is it any wonder then that those with hypersensitivities to petrochemicals could be so susceptible?

And it's not just the chemically sensitive that have health difficulties associated with natural gas and gas-burning stoves. In November of 1999, the University of California released research results revealing that adults with gas ranges visited hospital emergency rooms (often with asthma symptoms) twice as often as those with electric stoves. Their recommendation: Don't use gas stoves in houses.

Making Gas-Range Operation More Tolerable

Despite the potential problems associated with gas ranges, some sensitive individuals may be unwilling, or unable, to give up their present gas range. If that's your situation, it's important that you at least use adequate kitchen ventilation when using your stove. Ideally, a powerful range hood that's vented to the outdoors should be installed and used whenever the stove is in operation. Broan Range Hoods (**Broan Mfg. Co., Inc.**) and Nutone Range Hoods (**Nutone**) are two well-known range-hood manufacturers, but there are others. (Note: Some models are made with stainless steel.)

If your range hood has a very powerful fan, you'll probably need to open a window slightly when it's operating so that air can easily enter the room to replace the air blown outdoors by the fan. If you plan to buy a new gas range, choose one with electronic ignition so no pilot light is continually burning.

You should also be aware that deadly carbon monoxide is produced in the greatest quantities as a result of incomplete combustion. Interestingly, when natural gas is not burned completely (thus there is more carbon monoxide being formed) it will burn with a yellow flame. If your gas stove is adjusted properly, and the fuel is burning efficiently, it should produce a bright blue flame, not a yellow one. So, if you routinely see a yellow flame, you should have your stove checked out by a qualified service person.

As a final coping method for sensitive people, whenever you're using your gas range, you might consider wearing a charcoal-filled mask to act as an air filter. However, admittedly, this could be awkward and uncomfortably warm to wear while cooking (see *Personal Protective Gear* on page 264).

Electric Stoves

Of course, besides gas, the other major type of stove is the electric model. While usually more healthful than gas models, electric cooktops and ovens do have potential intolerance problems of which you should be aware.

Electric Cooktops

Electric cooktops, either combined with an electric oven, or as separate countertop units, now come in several basic types. These include porcelain-on-steel or stainless-steel construction, with traditional spiral elements or European plate-type elements. Another popular type is the smooth-surface, radiant glass cooktop.

Over the years, spiral elements have been used on most electric cooktops. Unfortunately, many new stovetops using traditional spiral elements are often intolerable for sensitive individuals when the elements are turned on. Because these elements are made of composite metal/ceramic formulations whose ingredients are considered trade secrets, knowing exactly what's in them is impossible. However, whatever these elements are made of, they seem, to many sensitive persons, to be less tolerable than those made ten years or so ago.

Whether today's electric elements are essentially different or not, if you're bothered by those in your new cooktop, there's a procedure you can follow that might alleviate the situation. That is to operate the spiral elements on high heat for thirty minutes or so, allow them to cool, and repeat the cycle over and over again for several days. This may burn off whatever is bothersome, especially if it's just a surface coating, without causing damage. Of course you'll only want to do this if children can't get to the cooktop, and you can monitor the procedure. Also, you'll want to have the kitchen closed off from the rest of the house to prevent odors from dissipating to other rooms. You should also have the kitchen windows opened, and a range-hood's exhaust fan (one that is vented to the outdoors) turned on high speed.

Sadly, for some very sensitive people, new elements seem to remain intolerable after they've undergone a burning-off procedure, sometimes even after they've been used for several months. In those particular situations, the best solution might be to trade the stove's new elements for older, used ones. Perhaps you have a non-sensitive friend with tolerable elements of the same size. Many times, other people are happy to give you their old elements for a set of relatively new ones. You might also consider buying used elements from a local appliance-repair shop.

The newer-style, European, plate-type elements have a definite cleaning advantage over the traditional spiral elements. Because they're in a solid-plate shape, there are no reflector pans used with them to accumulate debris or become discolored. They also provide a more stable surface to sit a pan on, and they can heat more uniformly.

However, some sensitive individuals have found that certain plate-type heating elements pose the same intolerance problems as many of the new spiral elements. This is probably because they're made of the same, or very similar, materials. To make plate-type elements more tolerable, try the same burning-off procedure discussed above with spiral elements. However, if you decide you want to trade elements or replace them with used ones, this can sometimes be difficult because used ones may be hard to find.

Fortunately, most *radiant-glass-surfaced cooktops* are usually tolerable for most chemically sensitive individuals. This is because these models have their electric heating elements underneath a one-piece, smooth, glass/ceramic top surface. The heat from the elements radiates up through the glass/ceramic top to heat your pans. As it turns out, the glass/ceramic material acts as an effective barrier to seal-in the odors that can sometimes be generated by exposed elements.

If you decide on this type of cooktop, you must use pans with very flat bottoms. This is because pans without flat bottoms will not heat up properly. It's also important that you clean the glass surface thoroughly after every use. Any drips that are allowed to remain can become burned on and become difficult to remove (see *Glass-Top Stoves* on page 170).

No matter what type of electric cooktop you ultimately choose, it's best to have a range hood that's vented to the outdoors. This will eliminate potentially bothersome food odors, excess steam, and other gases from your kitchen air. Range hoods with *activated-charcoal filters*, that are designed to blow filtered air back into the kitchen, are very poor choices. These are often called *recirculating range hoods*. They can't eliminate steam at all, and they're only slightly effective at removing some cooking odors. (For more on range hoods that vent to the outdoors, see *Making Gas Range Operation More Tolerable* on page 489.)

Electric Ovens

Electric ovens now come as conventional, *continuous-cleaning*, or *self-cleaning* units. The conventional models are the traditional standard type that have a smooth porcelain-on-steel interior that requires periodic cleaning by hand. Typically, highly odorous, and dangerous, cleaning products are used to dissolve the buildup of grease splatters in such ovens. (For cleaning conventional ovens with less-toxic cleaners, see *Conventional Ovens* on page 169.)

Conventional ovens are the least expensive models because they utilize the oldest and most basic materials.

Continuous-cleaning ovens differ from conventional ovens in that their porcelain-on-steel interiors don't have a smooth finish. Instead they have a porous, matte finish. This special surface is designed to prevent minute grease particles from clumping together and adhering to the oven walls. (In conventional ovens, these clumps usually remain on the walls, grow larger, and must eventually be removed by manual and/or chemical means.) Because the individual, tiny grease molecules remain as they are, they incinerate quickly during the oven's normal operation, and never build up. By the way, incineration is especially efficient when the oven's temperature is at least 400°F. Unfortunately, some sensitive individuals find that this continual incineration process produces bothersome odors.

The third electric-oven type is the self-cleaning model. These particular ovens have steel linings that have been treated with a special oil. Extra insulation (usually fiberglass) is also used in the ovens' side walls. Both of these measures permit very high temperatures during the self-cleaning cycle without damaging the oven or any adjacent kitchen cabinets and walls. Unfortunately, both the oil coating and the insulation can be bothersome to some sensitive persons, especially on new ovens. Sometimes an owner's manuals will actually recommend that you run your new self-cleaning oven at least once through the cleaning cycle before you use it for normal cooking. This initial operation of the cleaning cycle is meant to reduce the odors released from the oil treatment. However, even after this has been done, many sensitive individuals find that their self-cleaning oven remains intolerable to them. In that case, you may have to repeat the cleaning cycle several more times. (In cases of extreme sensitivity, 20-30 cycles have been necessary.)

Whenever you use the cleaning cycle, you should close off the kitchen from the rest of the house, open the kitchen windows, and have the range-hood's exhaust fan turned on high speed. The windows may need to remain open, with the exhaust fan operating for some time after the cycle has been completed. (Note: Always be sure to remove the interior racks before using the cleaning cycle to prevent permanent discoloration of the chrome plating.)

Some chemically sensitive people have installed a special electrical outlet (usually 220 volts) in their garage and temporarily located their new electric range there until it's become tolerable. When the range is in the garage and the overhead door is open, the oven can be run through the high-temperature cleaning cycle several times a day. Doing so for a week is usually enough to make a new oven tolerable. Once tolerable, the stove can safely be placed in the kitchen. (Note: Make sure children and pets don't have access to an operating stove.) Once a self-cleaning oven has gone through this procedure, it is often quite tolerable—often more so than a conventional oven or a continuous-cleaning one.

Many sensitive people have found that even conventional or continuously-cleaning electric ovens can be intolerable because of the hot baking and broiling elements. This shouldn't be surprising when you realize these oven elements are often made of the same or similar ceramic/metal composite material of which commonly bothersome cooktop elements are made. However, some sensitive individuals have found that if they heat their electric oven on high (or broil) for a period of time (perhaps 1–2 hours), shut it off, and repeat this process many times over several days, the intolerance problems subside without damaging the elements. As in the case of running a self-cleaning cycle, it's best to do this procedure only with proper ventilation (or in a garage). Of course, the elements in self-cleaning ovens will automatically go through this baking-out process during any self-cleaning cycles.

Microwave Ovens

As everyone knows, microwave ovens can dramatically shorten cooking times. So, it's not surprising that, in the few decades since their introduction to consumers, their use has increased to the point that it's a rare household without one. However, there are drawbacks and concerns associated with microwave ovens with which you should become familiar.

How Microwave Ovens Work

Many healthy persons cook with microwaves because they can heat up prepackaged microwave dinners, reheat leftovers, make hot water quickly for coffee, and pop popcorn without oil, but these people still use their electric or gas oven for other types of cooking. On the other hand, some sensitive persons who find that they simply can't tolerate their regular stove turn to microwave ovens as their main (sometimes only) method of cooking. Interestingly, few people actually know how microwave ovens work.

As it turns out, microwave ovens are equipped with a special electron tube known as a *magnetron*. This device emits a narrow stream of *microwave radiation* which is the same type of energy as radar. (Interestingly, radar stand for *r*adio *d*etecting *a*nd *r*anging.) While the microwave radiation is being produced, a small fan scatters the energy around the walls of the oven to produce more even distribution. By the way, whenever a microwave oven is on, the magnetron is producing microwave radiation at the same exact level. So, when an oven is operating at "50% power" or "low power," the magnetron isn't generating microwaves at a lower rate. Instead, "50% power" means the magnetron is on 50% of the time and off 50% of the time. Thus, the magnetron is generating the same level of microwaves whenever it's on, but it's only on part of the time.

With all that said, how does microwave radiation (radar) actually cook? It seems that radar is powerful enough to pass through paper, glass, and china quite easily. However, it has more difficulty passing through liquids, including the microscopic liquid molecules present within most foods. In fact, the radar waves becomes trapped in the liquid, and this causes the liquid's molecules to energize and vibrate rapidly. As vibrating liquid molecules collide with each other, they create friction. Interestingly, it's the heat produced by this friction that actually cooks the food. Because microwave ovens create internal friction almost immediately, they don't require preheating or lengthy cooking times. Conventional ovens, on the other hand, slowly heat foods from the outside surface inward.

Unfortunately, complex foods (which may have areas of high moisture content, as well as areas of lower moisture content) or fairly dry foods, don't often cook particularly well in microwave ovens. In addition, browning is not possible unless special devices and/or sprinkled substances are used. Therefore, some foods heated in a microwave oven can have a less-attractive appearance, blander taste, and they may be less thoroughly cooked, than if they had been prepared in a regular electric or gas oven.

Microwave Oven Concerns

From a health standpoint, everyone should be aware that many microwave ovens can sooner or later emit potentially harmful microwave radiation (radar) into the kitchen. This can happen as a result of slamming the oven's door, simple wear and tear, manufacturing defects, or because of a build up of food particles around the door seals.

Currently, the U.S. Bureau of Radiological Health has set a permissible leakage level of 5 milliwatts per each square centimeter of surface area (which is the same as saying 5 mW/cm²) at a distance of 5 centimeters from the oven's surface. While there is apparently no direct correlation between using microwave ovens and ill health yet documented, there are concerns that further research should address. For example, microwave exposure from sources other than microwave ovens (like radar installations) has led to certain health problems including cataracts and perhaps even cancer.

If you're in the market to purchase a microwave oven, it would be wise to choose a sturdily constructed model with a tight-sealing door. Before purchasing a unit, you might want to check the current consumer guidebooks and magazines at your local library or bookstore for the models with the highest safety ratings. If possible, you'll want to buy only the safest unit you can afford in your size, feature, and price range.

When your microwave oven is operating at home, some experts recommend that you stand at least three feet away from it as a safety measure. This is because microwave levels drop off quickly just a short distance from their source. In addition, you might seriously consider purchasing a *microwave detector* or a *reusable microwave test kit* which will permit you to measure your oven's emissions regularly. These types of items can be ordered from **Less EMF, Inc., Allergy Relief Shop, Inc.**, and **American Environmental Health Foundation**. If excessive radiation is detected, it would be best to have the machine repaired by a trained repair person as soon as possible, or have it replaced.

As many people are aware, the cookware you use in a microwave oven is also important. When possible, use cookware made of glass or ceramic, rather than plastic, because those materials are more stable when subjected to cooking temperatures. Heated plastic can give off bothersome odors and give a "plasticky" taste to the cooking food, and eating plastic-infused food simply can't be a good nutrition choice.

Halogen/Microwave Ovens

Recently, a new type of microwave-oven hybrid has been introduced. The GE Advantium (**General Electric Co.**) is a full-size oven. Besides having a magnetron like other microwaves (the Advantium's is rated at 950 watts), it's equipped with two 1,500 watt halogen bulbs mounted on the interior ceiling and a single 1,500 watt halogen bulb mounted on the interior floor. The intense heat produced by the halogen bulbs (see *Halogen Bulbs* on page 557) cooks and browns food from the outside in. Simultaneously, the microwaves are cooking both the inside and outside of the food. Therefore, Advantium is said to be able to bake, broil, grille, brown, and roast like a conventional oven, but it produces fully cooked food in just $1/4$ of the time. It also apparently needs no preheating and can immediately convert into a "typical" microwave oven by the push of a button. It should be mentioned that when it's in it's halogen/microwave mode, the magnetron operates at only 10-20% power (in other words, it's only on for 10-20% of the cooking time).

The Advantium has an attractive stainless-steel interior. It's halogen lamps have an expected 10-year life. The unit is designed to be permanently installed above a standard cooktop, above a free-standing range, or above a counter. Because of the power required to operate an Advantium, it must have it's own dedicated electric line, just as for a conventional oven. Because it comes with a 300 CFM (cubic feet per minute) exhaust fan, it should have ducting to the outdoors.

Obviously, the Advantium has a number of advantages over either conventional ovens or microwaves because of it's innovative combination technology. And, because the magnetron is off 80-90% of the cooking time, your exposure to potential microwave leakage is much less than with a typical microwave oven. However, the current model is relatively costly, it requires special wiring and ducting and, once installed, it cannot be easily removed if you'd like to move it into a new home. You will also have to acquire a new cooking "intuition" to know how long specific items take to cook.

Portable Turbo-Convection Ovens

Portable turbo-convection ovens were fairly popular just a few years ago. However, despite having a number of good points, they're less commonly seen in stores these days.

How Portable Turbo-Convection Ovens Work

Small, portable, consumer-sized turbo-convection ovens have only been available for the last decade or so, while the larger commercial convection ovens have been used for some time. (Some regular-sized, residential electric stoves have also had a built-in convection-oven feature.) However, because many people still aren't familiar with these appliances, an explanation is in order. By definition, a portable turbo-convection oven is a small, easily-movable oven unit, equipped with a fan, and capable of circulating heat in a spinning, tornado-like fashion.

In actual construction, these ovens (often 12–14" in diameter) consist of a pot/container (usually a type of glass or enameled metal) with feet and a snugly sealing lid. Most units come equipped with two or more chromed-wire cooking racks. The oven's controls generally include a temperature adjustment knob and a timer, which are on the top of the lid. Underneath the lid, there's a spiral electric heating element and a multi-vane fan. When the oven is turned on, the element heats up and the fan blows downward simultaneously. This dual action inside a small sealed space exposes the food (which is on one or more of the racks inside the pot) to immediate and continuously intense hot air. With a turbo-convection oven, no warm-up time is required and, ideally, this results in a relatively quick cooking time, and lower energy use. Fortunately, many sensitive persons seem to tolerate turbo-convection ovens very well.

Interestingly, most foods cook as well in these ovens as in regular full-sized ovens. In fact, some foods actually seem to cook better, such as meats, which generally come out brown and crispy with most of the fat dripping down into the convection oven's bottom (a big plus over microwave ovens). Therefore, some people find that portable turbo-convection ovens are a more healthful way to prepare meats. These ovens are also fairly easy to clean and they produce very little smoke. And, because they're small, you and your kitchen remain cooler while cooking, compared to using a large oven. Another good point is their low cost.

However, portable turbo-convection ovens do have drawbacks. One is that some foods, such as 9"-round cakes, can't be cooked evenly. This is because the center isn't fully exposed to the hot blowing air. One manufacturer's manual suggests solving this problem by baking in Bundt-style cake pans that have a hole in the center. Another problem is that very large items, such as turkeys or strudels for example, just won't fit into these ovens, although larger models are sometimes available. In addition, it can sometimes be difficult to get your cooked food off the lower rack without your hands getting burned on the pot's hot walls.

Choosing a Portable Turbo-Convection Oven

As you'd expect, various turbo-convection ovens are constructed differently from each other. For example, some have lids and pots made of a special translucent heat-resistant plastic. However, it is generally better for sensitive individuals to choose units made with non-synthetic materials, such as all-glass models. (Glass models are the most commonly available today, anyway.)

Even if you purchase an all-glass model, if you're a chemically sensitive person, you may need to run the oven for awhile first, without any food in it, to burn off any residual motor and fan odors,. To accomplish this, you can cock the glass lid (to let odors escape easily) and run the unit on high heat for an hour. Then, shut it off, let it cool down, and repeat the process until the oven no longer releases bothersome odors when its heated up. Performing this procedure outdoors, or on an open porch, is a good idea to prevent any odors from contaminating your house. However, if you must do it indoors, you'll want to run the portable turbo-convection oven directly beneath your range hood. Also, you'll want to close off your kitchen from the rest of the house, open the kitchen windows, and turn the range hood on high speed. (Note: As a safety precaution, don't leave an operating oven unattended where children or pets can get access to it.)

As was noted earlier, it's not as easy to find small turbo-convection ovens locally as it once was. However, you might check kitchen departments, gourmet shops, and even discount stores. One brand (**Aroma Housewears Co.**) manufacturers nice, affordable, tempered-glass models. One is the SuperTurbo AeroMatic Oven which is 12" in diameter. If you can't purchase this company's products in your area, you can purchase them directly from the manufacturer. Also, the Deni Turbo Oven, which is made with a tempered-glass pot, is sold by **Colonial Gardens Kitchen**.

If at all possible, turbo-convection ovens should be operated under an operating range hood that is vented to the outdoors. That usually means setting the unit directly on top of your cooktop, so be sure it sits level and is not near a hot cooktop element.

Other Alternative Oven Suggestions

It should be mentioned that some convection ovens now come in a rectangular box shape. These are considered counter-top units, rather than portable ovens. Their larger size will permit cooking more food at one time, but they take up a more countertop work area. A box-shaped convection oven is handled by **Real Goods**. Toastmaster versions are sold by **Colonial Gardens Kitchen** while **Service Merchandise** has Black & Decker and Welbilt models. Finally, the Turbomaster Commercial Convection Oven, which has non-stick interior walls, can be purchased from **Harmony**. Other models should be available in appliance centers, department stores, and kitchen shops.

Of course, toaster ovens can be purchased in about every kitchen-appliance department or discount store. These may also work for you. Choosing one with a stainless-steel, or chrome-plated-steel housing is best. Finally, a small portable all-metal roaster/cooker/oven is sometimes the only oven that some very sensitive people can use. Often, these are large covered roasting units make of enameled or porcelainized metal. If you're interested in owning one, **Service Merchandise** handles Welbilt and Hamilton Beach brands. Local appliance outlets should have them as well.

In the end, all sensitive people will probably have to experiment with various types of cooking equipment and brands to find what works best for them. To do so, find out what your friends and relatives are using, and see how well you tolerate their appliances.

Refrigerators

Artificial refrigeration (cooling that doesn't use ice or snow) is based on the principle that a volatile liquid (one that can rapidly evaporate) will absorb heat when it evaporates and, as a result, will cool its surroundings. The first artificial refrigeration was actually developed in 1748 in Scotland. Eventually, various cooling methods and *refrigerants* (the volatile liquids used to cool) were introduced and used for commercial applications. By the 1920s, many American homes began to be equipped with refrigerators rather than iceboxes. And, by the end of World War II, the majority of all U.S. households had refrigerators.

In home units, *Freon* became the primary refrigerant after it was created by a team of DuPont researchers in 1930. Freon is actually a trademarked family of refrigerants (a common one is known as R-22) that are made of chlorine and fluorine and various hydrocarbon compounds (usually methane or ethane). These resulting *halogenated hydrocarbons* (*halogenated* refers to the presence of chlorine and fluorine) are considered nontoxic to humans and they are nonflammable. However, it's now known that escaping Freon can release chlorine atoms that can damage the ozone layer in the upper atmosphere. Because the ozone layer acts as a buffer, protecting us from too much ultraviolet radiation from the sun, common refrigerants are now being replaced by ozone-layer-friendly compounds instead.

In fact, in 1987, the Montreal Protocol was established by a group of international governmental officials and researchers who convened in Montreal, Canada. Specifically, the Montreal Protocol was, and is, a binding agreement between many countries to eliminate ozone-damaging chemicals including chlorfluorocarbons (CFCs). In the U.S., the 1990 Clean Air Act (along with the Montreal Protocol), set January 1, 2010, as the date when various hydrochlorofluorocarbons (HCFCs) including Freon, would be no longer be legally manufactured.

Unfortunately, finding suitable non-CFC or non-HCFC replacements for Freon has proved to be rather difficult. However, Allied Signal was able to develop Puron (R-410A). This brand-name refrigerant is currently more affordable than other alternative cooling agents. So, you will now probably start seeing some new refrigerators and air-conditioners touting their use of "environmentally-friendly Puron" in advertising and product literature.

No matter what refrigerant is used (Freon, Puron or something else), modern refrigerators still operate on the same basic principles. The major differences between refrigerators of the early 1950s and today include cosmetic changes (shape and color), the use of plastic materials for interior panels and inner-wall insulation, special features (self-defrosting models, ice makers, ice-water dispensers, etc.), and improved energy efficiency.

New Refrigerator Problems

Because nearly all new domestic refrigerators are made with plastic interiors, they can give off odors that can be bothersome to some sensitive people. If you find that your new refrigerator is intolerable because of this, you might want to wash the interior and let it air it out for an extended period before actually using the refrigerator in your kitchen. To do this, if possible, place your new refrigerator in a screened porch or garage. Of course, you'll need to make sure the area is dry and free of objectionable odors. Then, remove the refrigerator's doors or simply prop them open. If the doors are not removed, the porch or garage must be securely locked to prevent children from entering and getting inside the refrigerator. (Note: Some jurisdictions may legally require that such a refrigerator have its doors removed.)

Next, you can wash the new refrigerator's interior with a tolerable, unscented cleaner. One you might try is SafeChoice Super Clean (**AFM**), which is a light-amber-colored, concentrated synthetic detergent available from **N.E.E.D.S.**, **The Living Source**, **Bio Designs**, **Priorities**, **Allergy Relief Shop, Inc.**, **healthyhome.com**, and **American Environmental**

Health Foundation, as well as from other AFM dealers. To use it, mix 1 cup into 1 gallon of water. Then dip a clean sponge into the solution, wring it out, and go over all the plastic in the interior. You might also try a baking-soda-and-water solution as an alternative. However, whatever you use to clean and eliminate odors, rinse it off with clear water and a sponge. Afterwards, simply leave the refrigerator alone to air for several days or weeks before permanently placing the unit in your kitchen. In most cases, once the refrigerator is operating, the cold temperatures will dramatically reduce any remaining synthetic odors released by the plastic interior. This is because outgassing decreases at lower temperatures. So, if you suspect that the plastic interior in a new refrigerator is bothering you, you might simply run the refrigerator for a while to cool the interior before going to the trouble of cleaning and airing it. After all, it may be just fine once it gets cold.

Besides a plastic interior, a new refrigerator's motor can also be troublesome in some cases. This is primarily because the paint on a new motor can give off an odor that can be blown into the kitchen area by the refrigerator's fan. In addition, bothersome odors from the new insulation (either a foam insulation or fiberglass) may also be wafted into the air at the same time. Fortunately, all these odors generally diminish with time.

It's been suggested by some persons that you should consider purchasing a refrigerator equipped with wire shelves rather than those featuring solid-glass shelves. The theory behind this is that wire shelves will allow for better cold-air circulation inside the refrigerator. Solid-glass shelves, on the other hand, can act as a barrier to good internal airflow. Better circulation means that the refrigerator's motor will need to run less to keep the refrigerator cool. Wire shelves are becoming rare, however at least one brand, Hot Point (**General Electric Co.**), still offers a few models equipped with them.

Unfortunately, some very chemically sensitive individuals have simply not been able to handle their new refrigerator, so they have completely removed it from their kitchen. These people have found that placing the refrigerator elsewhere, such as in a seldom-used room, the garage, or the basement is, for them, worth the inconvenience. By the way, as an alternative, a few persons have actually had a special containment closet constructed within their kitchen in which to place their bothersome refrigerator. This can be built like a small niche so that only the front of the refrigerator is exposed to the room. A small, continuously running exhaust fan in the back of the compartment keeps air flowing from the kitchen, past the refrigerator, and to the outdoors. This approach can work well, but it should be remembered that a certain amount of outdoor air will continually be entering the house whenever the fan is running—air that might be polluted. A containment compartment requires not only the necessary space, but also the extra money to build it. And it must be fit into the kitchen layout, something that can be difficult in an existing kitchen.

Commercial Refrigerators

Some very sensitive people have opted to buy a commercial refrigerator rather than a residential model. The reason is that commercial models are generally made of stainless steel, both outside and inside. Therefore, they don't have the odor problems associated with plastic interiors.

However, there are drawbacks to owning a commercial refrigerator. A major problem is that many of them are only refrigerators, and they have no frozen-food compartment. This means you'll have to purchase and find space for a second unit—a freezer. Also, commercial refrigerators tend to be quite large, so they may jut out unattractively into your kitchen's floor space. You might even have to take out an adjoining cabinet to make room for it. In addition, commercial units are generally not designed for especially quiet operation. As a result, their noise can be quite annoying. Furthermore, these units can be expensive. Finally, commercial refrigerators can have motors that could emit bothersome odors just like residential refrigerators. However, some models have a motor that can be mounted in a remote location. In other words, you can have the refrigerator in the kitchen and the motor (with its odors and noise) in an adjacent garage.

If, despite all the negatives you're still interested in a restaurant-quality refrigerator, check your classified phone directory under Commercial Kitchen Supplies, or a similar heading, for a nearby dealer. In some cases, a better approach to owning a commercial stainless-steel refrigerator might be to buy one of the elite brands sold for use in very upscale kitchens. To purchase one of these refrigerators, consult with a certified kitchen designer. To find such an individual, check your local telephone classified directory. Such a person should be familiar with current models that might be suitable for use in your home.

Routine Refrigerator Maintenance

No matter what type of refrigerator you end up buying, it's important that it be properly maintained. Besides the usual interior cleaning, you should remember to dust the cooling coils (either behind or underneath your refrigerator) every other month or so. By doing this, your refrigerator will operate more efficiently. This means the motor won't have to operate as much. Therefore, potentially bothersome motor odors won't be blown into your kitchen as frequently. Also, regular dusting of the coils will prevent dust from being dispersed throughout your kitchen. In addition, it eliminates a haven for dust mites or other microorganisms.

To make dusting your refrigerator's coils easier, use a specially designed cleaning tool. These long wands typically have short spiraled bristles, and they are particularly useful for dusting coils that are underneath refrigerators. To buy one, check in your local discount, hardware, or department stores. One brand, Fuller Brush Refrigerator Coil Brush (**Fuller Brush Co.**), is handled by most Fuller Brush dealers. It can also be ordered directly from the company.

Another ongoing maintenance job is to clean your automatic-defrosting refrigerator's drip pan. Unfortunately, many people aren't even aware that their refrigerator has one. Drip pans are located under the refrigerator to catch the melting frost from the freezer compartment during the defrosting cycle. The water eventually evaporates, but until it has completely dissipated, it can become a home to mold. If you regularly remove and clean the drip pan, it'll discourage mold growth. In practice, it's a good idea to simply clean it every time you clean your refrigerator's coils.

If you find that mold has, indeed, colonized your refrigerator's drip pan, you can pour 3% hydrogen peroxide (this is the dilution commonly sold in drugstores) directly into the pan, scrub it, and rinse it off. Then wash the pan using a tolerable dish detergent, rinse it, dry it, and finally put it back under the refrigerator. (For more mold-cleaning options, see *Mold and Mildew* on page 170.)

Washing Machines

A number of clothes-washing devices have been invented over the years, particularly in the late 19th century. Some consisted of covered, wooden, barrel-like tubs that were manually operated to paddle or agitate the clothing inside. Whether these actually saved any labor, or got the clothing cleaner, is debatable. Finally, in 1911, Frederick Maytag developed the electric washing machine. By 1922, he began marketing washers with aluminum tubs.

20: Telephones, Electronics, and Appliances

In some ways, new washing machines have not changed very much since the mid-1950s. They're nearly all steel boxes, with control panels on top, and a tub inside equipped with an agitator. However, one of the "newer" innovations is the *horizontal-axis washer*. These washers have their tub (or drum) mounted horizontally, like most clothes dryers. Though popular decades ago, they've recently been reintroduced because these "front loaders" require much less water and detergent to work as effectively (often more so) than conventional washers. This is possible because, as they spin, they continually tumble your washables. As it turns out, tumbling creates greater rubbing and scrubbing action than the back-and-forth motion of vertical, tower-type agitators. Perhaps because they're still low-production items, they tend to be much more expensive than typical washers. However, if you live where water is scarce and/or expensive, a horizontal-tub washer may be a wise investment. If you're in the market for one, Maytag is one of the best known. However, another brand is the GE Horizontal Axis Washer (**General Electric Co.**). Of course, other brands are available, too.

In the last few years, one change in washer design, of which sensitive persons should be aware, is that most major-appliance manufacturers are now making their washers with plastic tubs rather than metal (either porcelain-on-steel or stainless steel) ones.

If you've recently bought a washer with a plastic tub and found it bothersome, try running it through several complete washing cycles with two old bath towels using hot water and a tolerable laundry compound (see *Alternative Laundry Products* on page 113). After enough cycles, many of the odors from the new plastic tub should have been scrubbed away, or dissipated enough, that they won't be absorbed by the fibers of your launderable items. By the way, a new washer with a porcelain-on-steel tub (these are not commonly made anymore, however), or a stainless-steel tub, may also have picked up odors during the manufacturing process. So, you may want to run them through a few wash cycles as well before using them for everyday laundering.

When you're ready to buy a new washer and want to avoid one with a plastic tub, Amana models (**Amana Appliances**) are manufactured with stainless-steel tubs. For other brands still equipped with stainless-steel (or porcelainized-steel) tubs, check your local appliance dealers. Asko washers (**Asko, Inc.**), which are imported from Sweden, have stainless-steel tubs. You'll need to contact the company for their nearest dealer. By mail-order, you can purchase one from **Building for Health Materials Center**.

No matter what model washing machine you end up with, all will have rubber belts, lubricated gears, and oily-smelling motors—all of which can be bothersome for some time to many sensitive people. One common problem that's rarely thought about are the rubber water hoses that connect your home's water lines to the washer. Unfortunately, these are subject to swelling and leaks because they're constantly under pressure. To avoid mishaps, it's been suggested that they be replaced every 3 years. A better solution is to use the much stronger hoses that are reinforced on the outside with braided stainless-steel mesh. The stainless-steel mesh will also have the added benefit of keeping the rubber-hose odors sealed in. Stainless-steel-mesh-covered washer hoses should be available in local hardware stores and building centers. By mail order, you can purchase them from **Improvements**.

To minimize any intolerance problems, be sure to have good ventilation in your laundry area. Of course, opening the windows will help, but if this becomes tiresome, or there are no windows, you might consider installing an exhaust fan that is vented to the outdoors like the ones commonly used in bathrooms. Two well-known manufacturers of exhaust fans are **Nutone** and **Broan Mfg. Co., Inc.** These, and similar brands, should be available in your area building centers.

It should be pointed out that having an exhaust fan in your laundry area is actually a good idea for other reasons besides just expelling new washer odors. For example, it can remove bothersome odors from dirty clothes and laundry products as well. In addition, it will remove any excess moisture that builds up in the laundry room on wash days. This is important to minimize mold or mildew growth.

Clothes Dryers

Although the first electric washing machine was marketed in 1911, it wasn't until a number of years later that a home clothes dryer was introduced. This was because it was thought that simply hanging the wash to dry was perfectly adequate for most people. Even after they first became available, residential dryers were initially seen as frivolous luxuries. Therefore, it took some time before the American public commonly bought both an automatic washer *and* a dryer.

Today, of course, there are two basic types of dryers: those that dry using heated electric elements and those that dry by burning natural gas. From a health standpoint, the healthiest dryers are the electric models, especially for chemically sensitive persons. This is because natural gas (or *propane* gas) has the potential to cause several problems. These include the creation of polluting combustion by-products that might not be completely vented outdoors, the potential for seepage from small gas-line leaks, and the slight, but detectable, odor of natural-gas or combustion by-products that's absorbed by the drying clothes. Unfortunately, in some areas of the country, the cost of operating an electric dryer is higher than one gas one. However, for sensitive individuals, the added cost of using an electric dryer is well worth it.

If you are ready to purchase a new electric dryer, you should be aware that many are now equipped with plastic drums. If you want one with either a porcelain-on-steel or a stainless-steel drum, **Amana Appliances** manufactures them. The Asko high-efficiency dryers (**Asko, Inc.**), that are imported from Sweden, have stainless-steel drums. (Make sure you get the Asko model that vents to the outdoors, because some don't.) To purchase Asko products, contact the company for their nearest dealer or mail-order one from **Building for Health Materials Center**.

Unless the owner's manual prohibits it, you should run your new electric drier on the hottest temperature for the longest cycle several times until any new odors are no longer bothersome to you.

It's very important that your dryer be vented to the outdoors. While you might think that all clothes dryers are hooked up this way, sometimes they're vented to the indoors. While the purpose of venting a dryer to the indoors is to keep the warm air inside the home (to help reduce heating bills), serious problems can result with this approach. That's because vent filters never adequately remove all the tiny lint particles, so they enter the living space. This could lead to allergic reactions, asthma attacks, or other respiratory problems. Then too, any perfume, or other odors in your clothing, that are released into the dryer by the high heat will also get blown into the living space. This situation is particularly unacceptable for chemically sensitive people. Finally, the air from an operating dryer contains a great deal of water vapor. The introduction of this additional moisture can easily lead to mold or mildew problems in the laundry room. (See also *High Relative Humidity* on page 530.)

CHAPTER 21: HOUSEKEEPING

This chapter covers a broad array of housekeeping topics, ranging from choosing healthier cookware to selecting paper goods. Each section suggests healthier alternatives to typically used products and procedures.

Foodstuffs

As most Americans now know, it's important to eat healthy foods. That often means fewer synthetic ingredients, less refined sugar, less fat, less sodium, etc. Others, of course, are vegetarians, while growing numbers of people eat only organic foods. In addition, many sensitive and allergic persons eat only those foods they can personally tolerate. Furthermore, there are people who can't eat sugar or are on a special weight-reduction diet. Still others follow a healthful diet based on a specific religious belief or a particular cooking philosophy.

Because cooking "healthy" can have so many definitions, this book doesn't even attempt to cover such a broad subject. These days, many cookbooks are available in libraries and bookstores that can guide you. Also, organizations and support groups can offer pertinent advice, buying sources, as well as recipes. Of course, you'll always want to follow the advice of your personal physician.

However, it must be briefly said that, no matter what particular foods you choose to have in your diet, or how you prepare them, foods that have been subjugated to the fewest toxic treatments along the way, and are the most wholesome, will most likely provide you with the best nutrition. Therefore, organically raised foods that are eaten soon after harvesting, or after proper preservation (freezing, canning, etc.), are usually best.

These days, finding organically raised foods is increasingly easy. There are ever greater numbers of local outlets (health-food stores, alternative grocery stores, expanded sections in conventional supermarkets, co-ops, farmer's markets) where you can purchase them. And, if your situation permits, you might even be able to grow (or raise) a number of items yourself.

If you desire more information on organic foodstuffs, you'll want to check out pertinent books and periodicals from your library as well as talk with your county extension service (some have home economists on staff, as well as agricultural experts). In addition, the reference department at your local library may keep a list of community organizations. If so, you may find one that's involved with growing, buying, or trading organic food. You might also choose to contact the **Human Ecology Action League (HEAL)**. This is a national support group for those with chemical and food sensitivities. It can provide you with the name of someone in a local chapter who should know about organic-food sources you can contact. HEAL also has fact sheets on organic food that you can order at low cost.

Cookware

If you're interested in healthy food, you'll want to cook it using healthful pots, pans, baking dishes, and other utensils. The following sections will help you with just that.

Nonstick Coatings

Anymore, most new cookware comes with some type of nonstick coating. These coatings often allow burnt food to be easily wiped away from the pan's bottom and sides. They also allow you to cook with little or no oil. However, nonstick coatings do have drawbacks. For example, most of them are synthetically derived compounds that some sensitive persons, and those interested in all-natural living, might want to avoid.

One of the earliest, and most well-known, nonstick coating is *Teflon*. Teflon is a type of *polytetrafluoroethylene* trademarked by DuPont. It was originally developed in 1938. However, it wasn't until 1954, in France, that it first began to be used on cookware. By the late 1960s and 1970s, Teflon-coated pans became increasingly popular in America. However, some early Teflon formulas proved to be somewhat fragile and fairly easy to scratch or peel.

Since Teflon's introduction onto cookware, other nonstick pan coatings have also been developed. Each new generation has tried to retain Teflon's slipperiness, and at the same time be more durable. Today, some of the newer, tougher, synthetic, nonstick coatings are more or less permanently bonded to cookware interiors. However, while these are less likely to become damaged or peel, they still often require the use of plastic, rather than metal, utensils.

For very chemically sensitive persons in particular, it might be wise to consider buying something else. This is because most of these coatings are still vulnerable to slight deterioration as a result of normal wear and tear, so there's the possibility that minute particles of the coating could flake off into your food and be ingested. There's also the possibility that certain synthetic coatings could begin to *sublimate* (change from a solid state directly into a gaseous state) at very high temperatures. This can happen when an empty pot is accidentally left on a heated burner. Once in the air, the synthetic compounds released from the overheated coating could be inhaled.

Metal Pots and Pans

Of course, metal pots and pans have been used for cooking for hundreds of years. In recent times, one of the most popular metals used in modern cookware has been aluminum.

The three main reasons for this are that aluminum heats up quickly, it doesn't rust, and it is relatively inexpensive. However, aluminum can react with many acidic foods. As a result, there's the possibility that aluminum-containing compounds can be absorbed by food and become ingested. This may be a significant concern. There could be a relationship between aluminum deposits found in the brain and Alzheimer's disease. While very recent research suggests that at least one cause of this debilitating condition may be a type of auto-immune dysfunction involving brain neurons, the role (if any) of aluminum has yet to be fully understood. So, to be on the safe side, it might be wise to consider using other alternatives. That is, until studies show that cooking with aluminum cookware is not a contributing factor to this frightening, degenerating illness.

More acceptable metals for pans can include cast iron, tin-lined copper, porcelain-on-steel, enameled-steel, and stainless steel. By the way, stainless-steel-lined aluminum cookware would also be fine because the stainless-steel layer forms an impenetrable protective barrier between the cooking food and the aluminum itself. However, if the stainless steel layer should become severely worn or sustain deep, penetrating scratches, these pans could no longer completely prevent aluminum from interacting with the food.

It's usually not difficult to find appropriate metal pans locally. Most kitchen shops, department stores, discount outlets, and restaurant-supply stores generally carry them. One popular brand you might try is Revere Ware stainless-steel pans. This line has now been expanded to include Revere Solutions, and the Revere Clear Advantage with glass lids. Both the Solution and Advantage pans come with a disk on the bottom of either copper or stainless-steel-over-aluminum. The Revere Pro Line is their best series. These pans are heavier, with self-cooling metal handles, and have a stainless-steel/copper/aluminum bottom. If for some reason you can't find the Revere pans you want in your area, they can be ordered directly from the manufacturer through their **Corning/Revere** catalog.

Mail-order companies that specialize in kitchen goods often carry at least one stainless-steel pan line without a nonstick coating. For example, **Colonial Garden Kitchens** handles Farberware Vintage Series with *phenolic* (a type of synthetic, heat-resistant plastic) handles and bottoms with stainless-steel-covered aluminum disks, among other brands. Other catalogs that handle stainless-steel cookware include **Chef's**, **Sur La Table**, and **Williams-Sonoma**. General-merchandise catalogs that carry them are **JC Penny Catalog** and especially **Service Merchandise** in which you can find Farberware, Revere Ware, and Preferred Stock (their own label). **Service Merchandise** stores have even a bigger selection.

In addition, **Vermont Country Store** (Voice of the Mountains catalog) sells enameled-steel roasting pans. The **Natural Lifestyle** catalog has Silit enameled-steel cookware. Le Creuset enameled cast-iron cookware and tin-lined copper pots can be ordered from **Sur La Table**.

Glass and Glass-Ceramic Cookware

Probably the least-reactive cookware is made of glass. As it turns out, glass couldn't be used as a cookware until scientists at Corning Glass Works formulated a type of glass that could withstand temperature extremes and chemical exposures, and yet be easy and inexpensive to manufacture. (Typical window glass, known as *soda-lime glass*, is relatively cheap and easy to make—but it's also fairly fragile.) Between 1912 and 1915, Corning researchers created *borosilicate glass* that could meet their demanding criteria, which is now trademarked as *Pyrex*. Interestingly, Pyrex acquired it's name because it was the first glass in which pie could be baked. Pyrex baking dishes can be bought from **Corning/Revere** as well as from **Service Merchandise**. Most local outlets carrying kitchenware also handle them.

One very good glass cookware line is the original version of Corning's Vision cookware. This line is often sold by local kitchen shops, department stores, and discount stores. (These outlets may handle similar brands as well.) If you can't find it, Vision cookware can be ordered directly from the manufacturer through their **Corning/Revere** catalog. Some is also sold in the **Service Merchandise** catalog. This particular cookware is made of thick Pyrex glass with molded handles. Its translucent color allows you to see easily inside a pot or pan without raising the lid. However, it should be mentioned that some Vision pots are made with molded pouring spouts. These will permit steam to continually escape while you're cooking because they don't seal completely. Therefore, you might prefer to choose pots without the pouring-spout feature. In addition, a modified Vision line has become available—one using a synthetic nonstick coating on the interior. Sensitive persons in particular might choose to avoid these pans.

The familiar white Corningware and other similar *pyroceram* ceramic pots and pans also make excellent cookware. Often the pots, pans, and baking dishes made with this glass/ceramic material can be used in the microwave, on a cooktop, in the oven and, once cooled down, in the freezer. All these attributes shouldn't be surprising when you learn that pyrocerams were originally created to encase missile nose cones. However, to be certain what your particular glass/ceramic cookware is safely designed for, carefully read the instructions. To buy glass/ceramic cookware, check local kitchen departments and gourmet cooking stores. Also, kitchen specialty catalogs have them from time to time. In addition, the Corningware brand can be purchased directly from the company's **Corning/Revere** catalog. Many items can also be found in the **Service Merchandise** catalog.

It must be mentioned at this point that some brands of ceramic/glass radiant cooktops recommend that you not use certain types of glass or pyroceram cookware on them. So, make sure to consult your cooktop owner's manual before using pots or pans made of these materials.

Bakeware

Inert materials such as stainless steel and cast iron make especially attractive casserole dishes. Baking dishes can also be made of pottery (fired or baked clay). Commonly, local kitchen specialty stores, as well as artisan potters, offer them for sale. They may be *bisque* (no glaze applied) or glazed. Mail-order sources for bakeware include **Sur La Table**. This catalog offers items in stainless steel, enameled cast iron, as well as pottery. **Natural Lifestyle** carries stainless-steel bakeware. (For more bakeware suggestions, see *Glass and Glass-Ceramic Cookware* on page 503.)

By the way, to ensure your safety, before using a glazed piece of bakeware, it's often a good idea to make sure that it is lead-free. This can be done with a simple test. Unfortunately, sometimes improper firings can allow lead to leech out of a lead-containing glaze. (For more on this, see *Dinnerware and Glassware* on page 505.) Lead testing is particularly important with imported or handmade items whose production quality may vary or not be up to "industry standards." One brand of lead-test kits that works well on cookware is Lead Check Swabs (**HybriVet Systems, Inc.**). These lead-testing kits are often available in hardware stores and they can also be ordered from **Allergy Relief Shop, Inc., American Environmental Health Foundation,** as well as from the manufacturer.

Dinnerware and Glassware

Of course, most people assume that their dinnerware and glassware are inherently safe. In most cases, that's true. However, lead could be a problem with certain items. That's because lead is used in some ceramic dinnerware glazes, and in the formulations of certain types of glassware.

You may be wondering, why would lead be used in such applications? In the case of dinnerware, it's because lead-containing glazes, if properly manufactured, create safe, very attractive, glossy, easy-to-clean surfaces. It turns out that, with a properly formulated glaze, that is correctly fired at a high temperature, lead will become an integral, and permanent, part of the ceramic glaze. However, if there's an improper firing (not hot enough, or for too short a time period), the lead may not be completely bound. That's when lead-glazed dinnerware can be a health threat because the "free lead" can leech out. In addition, worn surfaces on properly manufactured lead-glazed pieces can allow leeching as well.

While most everyday tumblers and glasses are made without lead, there could a potential problem with some *lead crystal*. After all, most of this particular type of sparkling-clear glassware has a 24% lead-content by weight. As with ceramic glazes, when properly manufactured, lead crystal is safe. But, if improperly manufactured, lead leeching could occur.

Leaching of lead is particularly a problem with acidic foods and liquids, especially when there is a longer contact time. For example, wine (which is acidic) that is stored in a lead-crystal decanter can leach lead out of the glass and contaminate the wine. With the use of a home lead test kit, you can instantly know for sure if your dinnerware or lead crystal is hazardous. Lead Check Swabs (**HybriVet Systems, Inc.**) are easy-to-use testers that are often stocked by local hardware stores. If you can't find them, you can mail order them from the company, **Allergy Relief Shop, Inc.**, or **American Environmental Health Foundation**.

Cutting Boards

For a number of years, consumers have been strongly advised to use plastic rather than wood cutting boards. Experts have believed that the solid, uniform surface of polyethylene (or other synthetic materials) would minimize sites for food debris to accumulate, and so lessen the possibility for contamination by microbes.

However, in a reversal of expectations, tests a few years ago at the University of Wisconsin-Madison found that wooden cutting boards appeared to inhibit microbial growth. It was theorized that some natural compound in wood (perhaps a resin) had beneficial antibacterial qualities. However, more-recent research has determined that wood and plastic cutting boards are very similar in their ability to support bacteria.

While you should have no trouble finding a suitable new plastic or wood cutting board, one thing is important—whatever type of cutting board you choose, if it acquires deep cracks or cuts, you should replace it. Apparently, bacteria can thrive especially well in these locations because they get plenty of food and water and can't be easily cleaned. Another recommendation is to buy two cutting boards: One only for protein foods (meat, cheese, eggs, etc.), and the other for non-protein foodstuffs. It seems that protein residues can become contaminated with bacteria much more readily than non-protein foods. So, by following this two-board procedure, you'll be far less likely to unknowingly contaminate your breads, fruits, and vegetables.

Of course, it's still important to wash all cutting boards (wood or plastic) frequently and thoroughly. As you might suspect, this is especially important after cutting protein items—particularly raw meat or cooked eggs. If you can put your cutting boards in the dishwasher, this will help to disinfect them. Also, pouring a 3% solution of hydrogen peroxide (the type commonly sold in drug stores) over a washed cutting board, rubbing it into the surface, then rinsing, can also help reduce bacteria colonization. By the way, some people rub a half-lemon on the surface of their cleaned cutting boards. The acid in the lemon acts as a mild disinfectant and helps counter odors.

If you're in the market to buy a cutting board, and you want a wood cutting board, consider a close-grained, low-odor hardwood such as maple. This is especially good advice if you're a very sensitive person. Fortunately, maple cutting boards are sold in most local kitchenware departments and kitchen/gourmet cooking stores. So, you should have no trouble finding one.

However, most new wood cutting boards, even maple ones, can still have a potentially bothersome "woody" odor. If you find the odor of your new cutting board objectionable, you can wash it several times with a tolerable dish soap and/or with baking soda and water. Then rinse it completely, towel it dry, and place it outdoors in the sun to air for a few days. (Be sure the surroundings are dry and uncontaminated.) When a cutting board is no longer bothersome, bring it inside, wash and rinse it thoroughly, let it dry, and begin using it.

Miscellaneous Kitchenware

Instead of typical plastic mixing bowls, salad bowls, and utensils, consider choosing those made of more inert materials such as glass, stainless steel, wood, etc. These should be readily available in local stores that have kitchenware departments.

By mail order, **Home Marketplace**, **Kitchen & Home**, and **Colonial Gardens Kitchen** sell glass mixing bowls and salad bowls, as well as a variety of stainless-steel cooking utensils. Then, too, both **Natural Lifestyle** and **Sur La Table** carry stainless-steel kitchen tools. The **Vermont Country Store** (Voice of the Mountains catalog) offers enameled-steel spatterware mugs, plates, and more. From **Williams-Sonoma** you can get wooden salad bowls and stainless-steel kitchen tools. The **Chef's** catalog has stainless-steel kitchen tools and mixing bowls. You can order hardwood bowls and trays from **Shaker Workshops**.

A number of wooden and stainless-steel kitchen tools are available from **Frontier Natural Products**. They also have mortars and pestles that are made of marble or porcelain. **Karen's Natural Products** has hardwood bowls, plates, spoons, and cooking tools.

Household Paper Goods

Toilet tissue, facial tissue, paper napkins, and paper towels have more or less become indispensable items since they were introduced to American consumers one by one in this century. The widespread acceptance and use of disposable paper items reflects a society with more income, and less time to launder cloth counterparts such as handkerchiefs and dish towels.

Unfortunately, many sensitive individuals find that typically available brands of toilet paper, paper towels, paper napkins, and facial tissue have a slight, but bothersome, odor that makes them intolerable. This could be due to residual chemicals from the paper-making process, to fragrances, to various chemical added as treatments, or to printing inks or dyes. To help you locate less bothersome alternatives, the following sections offer a number of suggestions. Incidentally, for stationery, office paper, and wrapping paper, etc., see the appropriate headings in *Chapter 18: Reading, Writing, & Wrapping*.

Locally Purchased Paper Goods

Of course, most people like to buy their paper goods locally. However, there are certain advantages to ordering them through the mail, especially if you're chemically sensitive.

Odor Absorption Problems

Some major paper-product manufacturers now market unscented, undyed products for individuals who cannot tolerate, or do not want, scented items. One popular example is unscented Kleenex white facial tissue. However, keep in mind that these unscented versions are manufactured in the same plants, stored in the same warehouses, transported in the same vehicles, and stacked on the same shelves as synthetically dyed and fragranced products. Unfortunately, paper by its very nature, is extremely absorbent, so it can pick up odors from nearby fragranced products. Therefore, it's not that uncommon for some sensitive persons to purchase a package of unscented paper goods and not to be able to distinguish it from a scented version.

To make your recently purchased paper goods more tolerable, you might try storing them on a screened porch to air out, if possible. When you do this, make certain that the surroundings are dry and that the air is relatively uncontaminated. During this airing out period you might decide to unwrap plastic-wrapped items, such as paper towels, so they can more easily lose their absorbed odors. The length of the airing time will depend on how sensitive you are, and how odorous the paper goods were when you brought them home. Therefore, sufficient airing could take as little as a few hours, or as long as several days.

When your paper goods have become acceptable to you, you can then bring them indoors, remove and dispose of the first few sheets of the unwrapped items, and store them. At this point, proper storage is essential to keep your now-tolerable paper goods from becoming contaminated again. Obviously, having a storage area that's clean, dry, and free from objectionable odors is best. Some people have found that metal storage cabinets with doors are ideal for this. These are sold in many office-supply stores. If you can't find them locally, the large office-supply catalog, **Reliable Corp.**, offers several cabinets made by **Edsal Manufacturing Co., Inc.** and **Lee Metal Products** in standard office colors and sizes that you can mail order.

Other Concerns with Typical Paper Goods

Unfortunately, added perfumes and dyes are not the only ingredients of paper goods that sensitive individuals might find objectionable. This is because most paper products are subjected to a variety of chemical treatments during their transformation from pine logs to finished paper items. For example, chlorine compounds are often used to bleach typical papers white. During this bleaching process, toxic dioxins can be created as by-products. In addition, formaldehyde may be added during production to increase a paper's absorbency. (For more information about paper processing, see *How Typical Best Grade Papers are Made* on page 445.)

Buying Alternative Paper Goods Locally

The good news, for those people who find they can't tolerate typical paper goods, is that some alternative grocery and health-food stores now carry alternative paper products such as toilet paper, paper towels, paper napkins, facial tissue, and paper plates These are often unbleached, made of recycled paper, and free of perfume, dye, and other potentially bothersome additives. One popular brand is **Seventh Generation**, although there are certainly others.

However, despite their laudable qualities, it's likely that these paper goods can still absorb odors while in the store, odors which originate from customers wearing perfumes, from scented items on adjacent shelves, or from products used to clean the store. All these odors have the possibility of proving bothersome to certain sensitive persons.

One way to prevent locally purchased paper goods from absorbing unwanted odors is to simply special-order them in bulk through the store. That way your paper goods will arrive in unopened cartons. However, bulk orders will mean a lot of packages to store properly at home, requiring advance preparation. Having a metal storage cabinet can help, as described under *Odor Absorption Problems* above. (See also *Buying in Quantity* on page 63, and *Storage Concerns* on page 64.)

Mail-Ordered Paper Goods

A very good method of buying tolerable paper goods for sensitive people is to order them directly from specialty environmental catalog companies. Such catalogs generally handle paper products that are undyed, unscented, dioxin-free, and made of recycled paper. Besides getting paper goods with many desirable qualities, mail-ordering avoids all the concerns over your paper products absorbing grocery-store odors. Plus, mail-ordering is also very convenient. You can order whenever you want, and the items are delivered quickly straight to your home.

As a rule, paper goods by mail-order can be purchased in either small quantities or by the case. Keep in mind that purchasing in bulk will usually save you money (see *Buying in Quantity* on page 63). And, more importantly, unscented bulk purchases, being in their original cartons, will be more tolerable than fragranced paper goods, or products that have absorbed odors on retail-store shelves.

An excellent catalog source is **Harmony** which handles **Seventh Generation** paper goods (toilet paper, facial tissue, paper napkins, paper towels, and paper plates). These come in tan (unbleached) or white (bleached without chlorine). All are made with 100% post-consumer-recycled paper. Harmony offers lower prices for half- or full-case quantities, and it currently doesn't charge shipping for any Seventh Generation paper goods you order, no matter how much or how little. It also offers an optional automatic shipping program in which you decide the products you want, the quantity you need, and how often you want them delivered. Then, the items are delivered automatically to you at the intervals you requested (you can always revise your initial plan along the way). Incidentally, Seventh Generation paper goods may also be ordered from **Tucson Cooperative Warehouse** and **GreenMarketplace.com**.

Another source for 100% post-consumer, white, unscented toilet paper and paper towels (by the half and full case) is **Real Goods**. From **Natural Lifestyle** and **Karen's Natural Products** you can get Fort Howard Envision brand paper goods made with 100%-recycled paper. This line includes "naturally-bleached" white paper towels and facial tissue, and unbleached toilet paper, which can be purchased in either small quantities or by the case.

Cloth Alternatives to Paper Goods

Despite the ample availability of alternative paper goods, some individuals still find them unacceptable. This may be for philosophical reasons (not wanting to exploit trees, for example) or perhaps because all types of paper cause unhealthy reactions. Of course for these people, substituting cloth for paper products is suggested wherever possible. For example, washable, 100%-natural-fiber handkerchiefs, napkins, dish cloths, and dish towels can easily eliminate the need to purchase and use paper napkins and paper towels (see *Tablecloths, Placemats, and Napkins* on page 256, and *Kitchen Towels* on page 256).

Earthen Joys unbleached cotton-muslin reusable tea and coffee filters can replace paper ones. They're sold by **Karen's Natural Products** in many styles and sizes. Clothcrafter's all-cotton coffee filters can be ordered from **Simmons Natural Bodycare**. Hemp reusable filters are available from **Harmony**. In addition, you can also sometimes find metal filters at kitchenware stores and coffee shops.

Shelf Liner

Colorful contact paper, vinyl sheets, shelf paper, wall paper, and even newsprint have all been used to line shelves and drawers. For many sensitive people, these options are too bothersome. If that's your situation, try using standard aluminum foil or heavy-duty aluminum foil which you can easily purchase at any grocery store.

Because even the heavier type of kitchen-use aluminum foil will likely tear in time, you might prefer to use a sturdier builders foil, also known as *reflective foil insulation*. These products are generally made with a center layer of Kraft paper with an aluminum-foil surface on each side. If you live in a year-around warm climate zone, your local building-materials center will likely carry one or two brands. Unfortunately, it's not commonly used in colder climates. However, from **E.L. Foust Co., Inc.** you can mail order Dennyfoil Reflective Foil Insulation #245 (**Denny Sales Corp.**). Dennyfoil #245 comes in 36"-wide rolls and is *non-perforated* (has no tiny pores punched into it.) Once you get it, simply use it as you would any other type of shelf liner. (Note: For other sources of reflective foil insulation, see *Foil Barriers* on page 290.)

If you need to tape your aluminum-foil shelf liner, its probably best to use aluminum-foil tape. One brand that's often well-tolerated by sensitive people is Polyken. This can also be bought from **E.L. Foust Co., Inc.** as well as from the **American Environmental Health Foundation**.

Plastic and Cellophane Goods

Most Americans now use a variety of plastic goods (plastic bags, plastic wrap, plastic storage containers, etc.) in their homes. Before World War II, most of these consumer products didn't exist. Today, many people couldn't imagine running a household without them.

It's easy to understand why plastic goods have become so popular. Generally, they're relatively inexpensive, fairly durable, and water-resistant. However, they aren't without problems. Plastics are usually not biodegradable, they're usually made of nonrenewable petro-leum derivatives, and they can give off minor chemical odors that can be bothersome, especially to chemically sensitive people. There's some concern, too, that certain plastic compounds may mimic natural estrogen compounds; the ramifications of which are as yet not fully understood. Therefore, for a variety of reasons, a growing number of individuals have decided to minimize, or completely eliminate, the use of plastic goods in their homes.

Plastic Goods

What exactly are plastics? By definition, plastics are natural or synthetic materials that are moldable (plastic) when heated. Some plastics become flexible whenever they're reheated (these are termed *thermoplastics*). Others are only flexible the first time they are heated (they're known as *thermosetting plastics*). As it turns out, today's plastics are generally man-made *polymers* whose chemical structures consist of very long chains of carbon atoms that wouldn't occur normally in nature. The basic building-blocks for these polymer chains are usually derived from petroleum or natural gas.

The number of plastic types now being manufactured has become large, and it continues to grow. Interestingly, *celluloid*, which is made from cellulose nitrate and camphor, is considered the first synthetic plastic. It was created as long ago as 1856 as an ivory substitute. It wasn't until after the turn of the century that the second synthetic plastic, *Bakelite*, was introduced. This plastic material was particularly popular. It was commonly used for many decades in a variety of products including telephones. Eventually, just prior to World War II, a variety of modern plastics were developed, including nylon, polyester, and vinyl, among others. Of all the synthetic plastics, the softer types are generally less tolerable for sensitive persons. This is because chemical ingredients called *plasticizers* are added to these products to give them greater flexibility, and many plasticizers are particularly noxious compounds.

If you find that typical plastic goods are unacceptable to you, in many cases you can still find satisfactory substitutes available. For example, plastic food-storage containers can be replaced with glass containers. Also, typical plastic wrap can often be replaced with cellophane, waxed paper, or aluminum foil. In addition, you might find that using plastic garbage bags is unnecessary, if you use brown grocery bags instead. The list goes on.

However, if you find that you really do need to use plastic garbage bags in your home, only choose brands that are unscented, especially if you're a sensitive person. You might also consider buying brands made with at least some recycled plastic. An even better choice would be to buy unscented biodegradable plastic bags which are sometimes sold in alternative grocery stores, local supermarkets, discount stores, and hardware stores. One mail-order source for the Eco-Bags brand is **Harmony**. These are available in two sizes, and they are made of corn and potato starch derivatives. Unfortunately, however, these are for "dry use only."

Cellophane Goods

Often, *cellophane* is suggested for eco-conscious and/or chemically sensitive individuals as a substitute for plastic wrap. But what is cellophane? Cellophane is actually a transparent film that's derived primarily from wood and cotton fibers. The fibers are softened in a solution of *caustic soda* and *carbon bisulfide* to break down the plant's *cellulose* (the tough resilient material making up the walls of the plant cells). The resulting gluey substance is then formed into clear, filmy sheets. Interestingly, the word cellophane was created by combining the word cellulose with *diaphanous* (from the Greek word for transparent).

First developed back in 1892, cellophane was the first clear packaging film ever made. Today, it remains the only packaging film that will not soften when exposed to heat. However, cellophane has other pluses as well. Fortunately, it's produced from renewable natural materials, it is biodegradable, and it has virtually no odor. \

Unfortunately, cellophane also has certain negatives associated with it. It tears somewhat readily, it can't cling to itself, or be easily molded around what is being wrapped, and it becomes brittle and yellow with age. Because of these drawbacks, plastic films, such as vinyl (polyvinyl chloride or PVC) and polypropylene, have nearly replaced cellophane, except in a few applications.

Although cellophane is no longer as common as it once was, it's still possible for consumers to find and use cellophane products. For example, cellophane bags (which come in a variety of sizes and can be sealed shut with standard paper-covered wire twisties) can be bought from **N.E.E.D.S., Janice Corporation, Natural Lifestyle, Karen's Natural Products, Allergy Relief Shop, Inc.,** and **Erlander's Natural Products**.

Rolls of cellophane are handled by **N.E.E.D.S.** Also, cellophane tape can still be purchased at most office-supply centers, drug stores, and discount stores.

Household Storage

From ancient times, people have used baskets, bags made from animal skins, clay pots, hollow gourds, and many other things, to hold their belongings. Today, we tend to use different materials than our ancestors. But storage still means finding containers that will keep your possessions free of dust, pests, and moisture.

Before storing any item, it's best to honestly assess whether you really need to save it. Too often people go to the trouble, and expense, of storing things they'll never, or at best, rarely ever use again. Therefore, you might consider simplifying your housekeeping by thinning out unnecessary knickknacks, clothing, reading material, and household furnishings. You can often sell them, give them away, or simply throw them out. A good way to start is to dispose of stored items that haven't been used for at least five years. The odds are that if you haven't used something in that amount of time, you may never use it.

Closets

Closets are commonly the first place to store items you want to keep. Unfortunately, closets quickly become haphazardly stuffed. As a result, what's inside can be nearly inaccessible, lost, forgotten, or even damaged. To counter this tendency, the following sections offer some closet-organization ideas and products.

Closet Racks and Shelving Systems

A good storage approach for nearly all homes is to logically utilize the available closet space you already have. When you do this, the goal is to create closets that will contain the maximum amount of items and still be user-friendly, in other words, easy to keep clean and easy to keep organized.

One method for accomplishing this is to install wire-mesh closet-shelving systems and racks. With wire-mesh units, you can custom design your closet's interior to suit your specific needs. You can do the actual design and installation work yourself (you'll need to use a metal saw, screw driver, drill, etc.), or you can hire a remodeling contractor or a professional closet designer to do it for you. To find a qualified professional, check your local classified telephone directory under appropriate listings. Before agreeing to hire someone to do the work however, be sure to get a price estimate, estimated completion date, information on guarantees or warranties, and find our what specific materials will be used.

It should be noted that much of the wire-mesh shelving available today is vinyl-coated steel. This material has certain drawbacks. Vinyl has the capacity to emit some chemical odors when new that are often especially bothersome to certain sensitive people. Also, as vinyl ages it has a tendency to crack and become unsightly.

A better alternative is to use wire shelving that has a baked-on epoxy finish. One popular brand is **Lee Rowan**. Their steel units are available in a wide variety of shapes and sizes. Especially convenient are their freestanding racks that are fitted with wire-mesh drawers. To find the nearest dealer, contact the company. Another similar shelving system you might consider is the Schulte heavy-gage steel mesh system with a baked-on epoxy coating (**Schulte Corp.**). These well-made items also come in many configurations, including various racks, shelves, and drawers. You'll need to call the manufacturer for a nearby dealer.

It should also be mentioned that **Get Organized** has both chromed, as well as epoxy-coated steel, shoe racks for your closet. They also carry enameled-steel folding clothes racks.

Coat Hangers

For many years, coat hangers were made of thin steel wire, often painted or coated. Today, many household coat hangers are made of molded plastic. However, to avoid rust problems with steel hangers, bending of light-weight ones, breaking of flimsy ones, and minor odors from plastic ones, you should consider purchasing heavyweight *anodized-aluminum* hangers. (Anodizing is a protective coating on aluminum to prevent it from pitting and acquiring a dark discoloration due to oxidation.) Because these hangers are ruggedly constructed and they won't rust, you can even hang wet articles on them to dry. The heftier anodized-aluminum hangers are often available in local department and discount stores. One mail-order source is **Colonial Garden Kitchens**. Medium-weight versions are sold by **Kitchen & Home**. It should be noted that these types of hangers are more costly than their steel-wire or plastic counterparts, but they're practically indestructible, so they'll never need to be replaced.

Another good hanger option is to use traditional wood-and-steel hangers. These are strong, made of natural materials, and rather expensive. However, if they become wet, the steel parts can rust (if they aren't painted or coated). Wood/steel hangers can still be purchased in some local department stores. All-wood hangers with metal hooks are available from **Hold Everything**. Wood and metal adult-size hangers are sold by **Colonial Garden Kitchens** and **Kitchen & Home**. Wood and metal children's hangers (with or without metal clips) in sets of six can be purchased from **Natural Baby**.

If you're eco-conscious, or a sensitive person who can't tolerate plastic, but you can't afford expensive wood or aluminum hangers, the best solution is to use thin, painted-steel, wire hangers. You can still sometimes buy them in department and discount stores, or from local dry cleaners. If you must buy your steel coat hangers from a dry cleaner, buy only new hangers rather than used ones that could have absorbed dry-cleaning solvent odors.

Coat Hanger Hoods and Garment Storage Bags

Sometimes you want to give added protection to some clothing items in your closet. Hanger hoods and garment bags can do just that. But finding ones that aren't vinyl or polyester, or some other synthetic material, is not easy. Fortunately, the **Vermont Country Store** (Voice of the Mountains catalog) carries all-cotton hanger hoods. While not designed as a large-capacity storage bag, **French Creek Sheep & Wool Co.** has a washable, 100%-cotton, travel/storage clothing bag that is 50" long. In addition, **Green Pepper** has a pattern to make your own travel-size garment bag. It can be purchased at some fabric centers, including JoAnn's Fabrics and Crafts, or ordered directly from the company.

Controlling Closet Mustiness

Understandably, many people want their closets smelling fresh, not musty. They think the answer is to use cedar (sprays, coat hangers, paneling, chips in mesh bags, hanger attachments, etc.), moth balls, scented dryer softener sheets, fragrance sprays, or potpourri. Unfortunately, these are not the most effective, or even healthiest, options. All they do is add a relatively strong natural (cedar, rose, etc.) or chemical fragrance to cover up (and add to) any existing smells the closet may have. In the case of moth balls, potentially dangerous (to humans and to the environment) *pardichlorobenzene (PDCB)*, *naphthalene*, or *camphor* is added to your closet's atmosphere. Remember that anything you add to the air of such a small space will soon be absorbed into your clothing or stored items. Once absorbed, these added odors can often be difficult to remove.

A much better solution is to air your closet regularly using a fan in the open doorway. Also, washing the walls, ceiling, and shelves can help enormously. If the floor is hard surfaced, washing it is also recommended. If the floor is carpeted, washing may actually make the situation worse. This is because mold and mildew will rapidly proliferate in damp carpeting, and getting it to dry quickly in an enclosed space like a closet will likely take some time. (See also the appropriate headings in *Chapter 6: House Cleaning*.)

You may find that it's actually better to simply sprinkle baking soda or powdered zeolite on carpeting in a closet, then vacuum it up—rather than washing it. These particular natural powders should pull out at least some of the objectionable odors. By the way, if you use zeolite, wearing a dust mask is a good idea. (See *Personal Protection Gear* on page 264.) Dasun All Natural Zeolite Powder (**Dasun Co.**), in a two-pound shaker container, is handled by **Bio Designs**. It can also be ordered directly from the company. A two-pound shaker container of natural zeolite is also carried by **healthyhome.com**.

While it may not be possible, in some situations, the best solution to having contaminated carpet in a closet is to remove it and replace it with an easier-to-clean, hard-surfaced flooring material. For those with dust-mite allergies, this is an especially good idea.

If you have a hamper in your closet, perhaps that's the source of the mustiness. If so, clean it, replace it, or move it into another room. If the problem closet has high humidity, you could possibly install a ventilation fan similar to those used in bathrooms. Actually, while it isn't commonly done, having an exhaust fan in your closet is a good idea because it will allow for quick and effective closet airings. Ventilation fans and fan controls should be available in building-supply centers and electrical-supply stores. In addition, **Grainger, Inc.** usually has a number of them in their catalog and local stores.

Closets in cold climates that are adjacent to outside walls often get moldy because, being filled with cooler air, they have a higher relative humidity than the rest of the house. One way to remedy this situation is to use a special anti-mustiness heating device. These are small electrical units that will warm up a closet enough so that the relative humidity is lowered, thus making it too dry for mold and mildew to thrive. These are sometimes available in catalogs and department stores. For example, from **Harmony** you can purchase the Air Dryer, a small plug-in, electrical unit that reduces dampness in closets of up to 1,000 cubic feet. The Mold Zapper is a small electric heater available from **eMD.com** and **Allergy Control Products, Inc.**

Simply leaving a light bulb turned on inside a closet is another anti-mold strategy. While many people believe that the light itself discourages mold growth, it is actually the warmth generated by the bulb that results in a lower relative humidity, and less mold growth.

Another approach to drying a closet is to use a canister of Dri-Out moisture adsorbing flakes. These can be bought from **Allergy Control Products, Inc.** Each canister is said to be able to adsorb up to a half gallon of water. Refills are available. Zeolite and other adsorbents can actually often do two jobs, adsorb both moisture and odors. "Refresh-A-Closet" 100%-zeolite is available in a two-packet (9" x 8") and four-packet (4" x 6") set. These are handled by **Real Goods** and **Improvements**. If you expose zeolite crystals to the sun every 8-10 months you can reactivate them.

Miscellaneous Storage Racks

If you can get metal or wood storage racks, rather than plastic ones or ones made with man-made wood products, it would be a healthier choice for you and your family. Many of these can be found locally at various outlets including furniture stores, discount stores, department stores, building centers, and import shops.

A catalog source you might like is **Get Organized** which has solid-wood wine racks, powder-coated steel CD holders, and more. **Home Decorator's Collection** has attractive metal CD holders. From **Colonial Gardens Kitchen**, you can get solid-wood magazine racks. Other sources for various types of racks made of solid-wood or metal, in a variety of sizes and styles, include **Yield House**, **Hold Everything**, **Ballard Designs**, **Pottery Barn**, **Kitchen & Home**, and **J.C. Penny Catalog**. For more on storage racks see *Solid-Wood Furniture* on page 331, *Metal Furniture* on page 333, *Proper Product Storage and Disposal* on page 262, and *Closet Racks and Storage Systems* on page 511.

Metal Containers

Metal cabinets, trunks, and containers make excellent storage units, especially for chemically sensitive persons. Often, objects with intolerable odors can be kept safely inside metal containers. The metal acts as an effective barrier to isolate any unwanted smells from reaching the room air. However, at the same time, you should be aware that just one odorous item stored in a closed metal container can contaminate the entire contents with the odor. This point extends to the interior walls of the container itself. Therefore, carefully consider what you plan to store together inside any metal container. The following sections offer suggestions on using metal containers, and some sources of where to get them.

Metal Cabinets

As has been mentioned elsewhere in this book, large metal cabinets with doors can be used to store just about anything. This includes out-of-season clothing, food, books, tools, etc. Sometimes one or more of these relatively inexpensive cabinets can solve most of your storage needs.

These days, metal storage units are available in several sizes and colors, with different shelving configurations. Some cabinets have interiors with permanently mounted shelves. Other models have adjustable shelves, or wardrobe-style clothing rods. In addition, some are made with key locks. When you're ready to buy a metal cabinet, check local office-supply stores. If you can't find them in your area, the large mail-order office-supply catalog, **Reliable Corp.**, carries several models made by **Edsal Manufacturing Co., Inc.** and **Lee Metal Products** from which you can choose.

Metal Trunks

Another metal-storage option you might consider is a metal trunk. These are particularly good for storing toys, scrapbooks, sweaters, out-of-season clothing, and/or blankets. All-metal trunks might be available in area department stores, army/navy surplus stores, and luggage shops. If you decide on a metal trunk, check to see if it's really all-metal.

Unfortunately, these days, many metal trunks are lined with particleboard, strand board, hardboard, plywood, or even cardboard. Formaldehyde released by some of these materials can accumulate inside the trunk and be absorbed by everything stored in them. Formaldehyde can be irritating to the mucous membranes of most people who breath it, and it is not tolerated by many sensitive persons. It should be added that some metal trunks are cedar lined. While research has shown that cedar does not kill or repel clothing moths effectively, it will make anything stored in a cedar-lined trunk smell strongly of cedar.

Metal Boxes

Metal boxes can work well for storing smaller items such as stamps, pens and pencils, crayons, and sewing supplies. To make this kind of storage more organized and functional, you'll want to place labels on the outside of each box so you know immediately what's inside.

Of course, one popular type of metal box is the *tinware* used for holiday candy and baked goods. Actually, these are not really made of tin, but nowadays are made of steel, although some do have a tin coating on the inside. In addition to these seasonal metal boxes, small, colorful novelty metal boxes are usually available throughout the year in kitchen departments, gift shops, and discount stores. Some real tinware boxes can be mail ordered from **Shaker Shops West.**

Another clever storage option is to use tinware canisters. Flours, grains, coffee, and baked goods store well in these—that is, if the tops seal tightly. Often you'll find tinware canisters in the kitchenware department of local stores. However, an even better choice would be to buy stainless-steel canisters, which are much more durable. Sometimes, kitchenware catalogs carry them.

Large, metal, tinware-style bread boxes are sometimes sold with tightly fitting lids. However, they're much harder to find than smaller metal boxes. These larger boxes are perfect for storing note cards, art supplies, wrapping paper, cleaning products, etc. To find tinware-style bread boxes, check your local department and discount stores.

Another interesting metal storage container worth considering is a hinged, unfolding metal box with interior storage trays. Boxes like these are good for holding spools of thread or other sewing notions. They also make good jewelry boxes—if they have divided compartments, and you line the trays with soft fabric. While these unfolding metal boxes can have a variety of uses, you'll most likely find them being sold to store tools in—or fishing tackle. However, in many cases, they are being replaced with plastic versions.

Metal Garbage Cans

Small (2' and under) galvanized garbage cans often work surprisingly well as storage containers, especially for chemically sensitive people. (Galvanized garbage cans are made of steel with a protective zinc coating that helps prevent rusting.) For example, they can hold bulk quantities of laundry powders, such as unscented borax or washing soda. They can also be used for dry storage of cereal, wild-bird seed, cat food, dog food, or cat litter-box filler. Small metal garbage cans can also be used to hold magazines, video tapes, and toys.

Metal garbage cans can also serve as a clothing hamper for sensitive people. Often, metal garbage cans are good for this function because the metal doesn't allow odors of clothing that has been contaminated with perfume, tobacco, and perspiration odors, from dissipating into the surrounding air. However, it should be pointed out that any dirty clothing should be laundered fairly quickly and not kept for extended periods in a sealed metal container because the moisture can't evaporate. If damp clothing is left inside a can too long, musty odors or mildew could result. (Important note: Metal garbage cans used as hampers should be routinely washed with an unscented, tolerable cleaner, rinsed with clear water, and placed in the sun for airing.) To buy small galvanized metal garbage cans, check local hardware stores, farm-supply stores, building centers, and discount stores.

Glass Containers

Glass storage containers have many advantages over their more popular plastic counterparts. Because of its transparency, glass offers a totally clear view of what's stored inside. Also, glass is made from common natural ingredients (sand, sodium carbonate, and limestone heated to a temperature of around 2,400° F) and it's completely recyclable. For sensitive individuals, the best trait is the fact that it's chemically inert and odorless. Therefore, it doesn't tend to react with stored food or give the food a "plasticky" taste or odor. Furthermore, properly sealed glass containers isolate the odors of what's stored in them.

Of course, the biggest drawback to glass is that it's breakable, and when broken, it can cut. Therefore, it's important to take care when you use glass containers to prevent them from cracking or shattering. After all, broken glass not only means the damage or loss of your stored contents, but it can also cause you personal injury. This is one of the primary reasons plastic has steadily replaced glass containers since World War II.

Recycled Glass Containers

Despite the widespread use of plastic containers, many grocery items are still sold in glass bottles and jars. Once these have been emptied, washed, and dried, they can easily be used for storage purposes. For example, you can use glass jars with screw lids (such as those used for mayonnaise or nut butter) to store screws, bolts, or nails. In the bathroom, glass jars can be used to store cotton balls and cotton swabs. In the kitchen, they can hold spices, tea, and leftovers, etc.

New Glass Containers

Of course, you can buy new glass containers that have been specifically designed for home-storage needs. One type—the glass canning jar with a sealing lid—is a very good choice for holding a variety of food items ranging from grains to leftovers. You'll find that these glass storage containers are available in several sizes. If you're interested in buying them, check your local kitchenware departments, gourmet cooking shops, discount stores, hardware stores, and wherever else you would expect home-canning supplies to be sold. You may be more likely to find them during harvesting season. Mail-order sources that generally have them include **Karen's Natural Products** and **Frontier Natural Products**.

Rectangular, heavy, molded-glass food-storage sets with glass lids were once common in American homes. However, for the most part, they virtually disappeared, now being replaced with lightweight plastic versions. However, somewhat surprisingly, they are still being sold by **Kitchen & Home**. Glass storage bowls with plastic lids, and ones with cork tops can be found in the **Karen's Natural Products** catalog. Other types of glass-storage containers are handled by **Home Marketplace** and **Frontier Natural Products**. For other possibilities, check local kitchen departments and gourmet shops.

Wooden Containers

Early storage containers were often made of wood. Today, they remain attractive, natural, and useful storage choices.

Wooden Wardrobes and Cabinets

Solid-wood wardrobes and cabinets are rare. That's because they usually have man-made wood panels and shelves. So, if you're interested in owning real solid-wood cabinets, they'll probably have to be custom made for you. (See *Custom-Made Hard Furniture* on page 337.)

Wooden Trunks

In many furniture stores, hope chests or storage chests can be found in a number of styles and with a variety of wood finishes. However, many of these are lined with cedar wood, which is extremely aromatic. While the cedar lining is meant protect stored items from clothing moths, unfortunately, it's been shown that cedar apparently does little to deter moths. However, the cedar odors will be absorbed by virtually everything stored in these chests. For sensitive persons in particular, this would be an unacceptable situation because they often react negatively to cedar's natural, relatively strong odor.

Yet, there is one source for large wooden chests that may be satisfactory to you. **Shaker Workshops** has pine storage chests. Even the bottoms of these chests are all-pine. The company also has very attractive, giant-size, Shaker-style, oval, lidded storage boxes. However, these have veneered-plywood bottoms. Pine storage chests in three sizes (21" x 21" x 24", 36" x 18" x 18", and 36" x 36" x 14½") are available from **Kitchen & Home**.

As an alternative to a new wooden chest, consider acquiring an old wooden trunk. These can be used for storing out-of-season clothing, linens, scrapbooks, or games. (You should not use one of these as a toy chest because an open hinged lid could easily fall shut on a child, potentially causing injury or even death.) Sometimes you can find wooden trunks in antique stores, flea markets, and garage sales. If the one you're interested in has already been restored, you'll want to consider whether the finishes and interior lining (often fabric or wallpaper) will be tolerable for you.

If you come across an unrestored wooden trunk, check to see if it's moldy or very musty. If it is, you may never get all the mildew smells out of it, so it would probably be best not to buy it. However, if it appears in good condition, you may want to buy it, then either strip the paint and finish off yourself or have the work professionally done. Once the old trunk has been stripped, it should be sanded, coated with a water-based finish, and fitted with tolerable interior materials. As you'd expect, refinishing an old trunk is probably not a job for someone with chemical sensitivities or asthma to do themselves. (For more on refinishing, see *Antique Furniture* on page 339.) Of course, you shouldn't use a restored trunk until the new odors have completely dissipated. Airing it outdoors in a protected, dry, uncontaminated place is best. If this is not possible, put it in a little-used room and ventilate it often.

Wooden Boxes

Small wooden boxes can be decorative accessories, but they also can be practical storage units. They can hold sewing notions, coins, small collectibles, stationery, pens and pencils, and clothing accessories such as scarves, handkerchiefs, and belts.

Fortunately, new wooden boxes, such as Shaker hardwood round or oval boxes with lids, are now becoming popular again. You might be able to find them in local craft outlets or furniture stores. By mail order, you can buy them in either cherry or walnut from **Shaker Shops West**. **Shaker Workshop** handles only the cherry Shaker-style boxes. Of the two woods, cherry is often less odorous, and better tolerated, by chemically sensitive individuals than walnut.

Other small wooden boxes are sometimes available in craft stores and import shops. Also, pine *firkins* (lidded wooden buckets); small cherry, walnut, and maple/pine boxes; and cherry and maple wooden baskets are sold by **Shaker Shops West**. Cherry-wood baskets are handled by **Shaker Workshops**. Small, unfinished lidded wooden boxes can be bought from **Home-Sew**. Finally, **Marketplace: Handwork of India** is another source for ethnically inspired, handmade boxes.

If you find serviceable antique wooden boxes, the odds are they will have absorbed perfume, tobacco, and other odors over the years. If they don't seem too bothersome, you might try washing them with a low-odor, unscented cleaning product, and then let them air outdoors in dry, uncontaminated surroundings for a few days to several weeks. This often helps, but wood can be quite absorbent, so if it doesn't help, it may be best to not use them.

Wicker Containers

Wicker storage containers are all-natural and they can allow air to freely penetrate. Wicker baskets, chests, and hampers are often found in local import shops, department stores, and discount stores. Just make sure that the wicker you buy for your home has no mildew or mustiness problems. So, look for dark spots or staining before purchasing.

By mail order, you can get wicker chests, open storage boxes and hampers from **Hold Everything**. The **JC Penny Catalog** carries wicker storage baskets, and the **Get Organized** catalog offers wicker-and-metal versions.

Attractive baskets can be purchased form **Shaker Shops West** and **Shaker Workshops**. Finally, from the **Crate & Barrel**, you can order wicker and grass-fiber baskets.

Part 6
AIR, WATER, & EMFS

CHAPTER 22: INDOOR AIR QUALITY

This chapter will discuss what's in the indoor atmosphere of most homes. As you will see, "air" is composed of far more than just oxygen, nitrogen, and carbon dioxide. People assume that the air they breathe in their homes is safe and healthy. Unfortunately, that isn't often the case.

Government Regulations

While it's true that the air outdoors has steadily improved because of the passage and enforcement of various anti-pollution regulations over the years, the quality of the air indoors has steadily decreased because it's been largely ignored. In fact, no government agency—not even the **EPA (U.S. Environmental Protection Agency)**—has minimum regulatory standards. In fact, in most locales, there are no minimum indoor air quality standards at all.

One bright spot is the banning of smoking tobacco within some particular buildings. However, air-quality regulations specifically applied to houses, including smoking, are almost non-existent—but not quite. For example, a few countries (Canada is one) now require a basic *ventilation system*, to bring fresh air into a house and to expel stale air, to be incorporated into new houses. But, other than that, there are very few indoor-air-related regulations.

Since the "energy crunch" back in the 1970's, many builders have striven to build homes more tightly in order to lessen the air exchange that once commonly occurred around doors and windows, etc. Unfortunately, they've generally not incorporated whole-house mechanical ventilation systems as an alternative to providing fresh air. Even if there is some level of ventilation (planned or unplanned) within a home, if the living space is filled with synthetic air fresheners, polluting cleaning products and decorating items, etc., the ventilation rate may not be enough to make the indoor air truly healthy. As a result, the sad truth is that most of us inhale a tremendous number and variety of pollutants whenever we're indoors.

One well-reported estimate is that the air quality inside an average house is *at least* five times worse than the air quality outdoors—even in major cities—and sometimes indoor air is even more polluted.

By the way, if you're interested in a complete discussion of home ventilation, including the simple physics of air movement, planned and unplanned methods of air exchange, problems, equipment, and more, read *Understanding Ventilation* by John Bower. This informative book can ordered from booksellers or from **The Healthy House Institute**.

Indoor Air Quality Defined

So, exactly what is indoor air pollution? Defined, indoor air pollution is the presence of substances (either gases or particulates) within a home's atmosphere that could negatively affect human health (or the health of your pets). These pollutants might be natural materials (pollen, for example) or derived from man-made substances (the outgassing of synthetic materials). The duration of air pollutants can be brief, but intense, as when you use model-airplane glue, or long-term and chronic at a lower level, as with the release of combustion by-products from your gas range's burning pilot light.

Ideally, the best defense against indoor pollution is not owning or using any potentially contaminating materials or products inside your home. This should be combined with thorough and regular house cleaning using less-toxic, low-odor products (see *Chapter 6: House Cleaning*), controlling any serious moisture problems in your home (including high relative humidity), and providing your house with adequate fresh-air ventilation. At this point, if your home still has somewhat minor air-quality problems, using an appropriate air-cleaning device (*i.e.* an air filter) can be helpful to remove most of the remaining airborne contaminants.

Admittedly, seriously reducing existing air pollution levels in your house can sometimes be difficult. However, if you address the individual air-pollution sources one by one, it's likely you'll eventually have indoor air that will positively, rather than negatively, affect the health of you and your family. And, that's what this book is all about.

In addition, if you have more questions on indoor air quality, you may want to call the **EPA Indoor Air Quality InfoLine** sponsored by the **EPA (Environmental Protection Agency)**. There, specialists are available to answer many of your questions, and you can request pertinent publications be sent to you at little or no cost. You can also request publications directly from the **EPA National Service Center for Environmental Publications**.

Indoor Air Pollution Testing in General

As you read the sections on specific indoor pollutants below, routine testing (or monitoring) procedures for several of them are given. It should be said that there are environmental testing companies that can do on-site measuring for virtually all the contaminants listed. There are also home test kits you can buy for yourself.

Because tests and testing companies have now become available, it's not surprising that many people ask, "Should I have my house tested for mold (or formaldehyde or whatever)?" In the end, that's a decision you must decide for yourself. The truth is, there are certain tests you can perform on your indoor air that are simple, low-cost, and they can give you truly valuable information—for example, radon tests. However, there are other tests that can be less worthwhile to you. And *any* test, even a useful one, will only be able to give a reading based on the limited time frame during which the actual monitoring occurred. Therefore, the results could give you a false sense of safety.

It should be understood that the accuracy and usefulness of an indoor pollution test will depend on it's proper setup, the sensitivity of the measuring device, the correct analysis of the recorded data, and your (or an expert's) knowledge on how to interpret the results, to effectively solve any problems. After all, tests generally can't tell you the actual source(s) of the contaminants they've measured. By the way, it's not unusual for very sensitive persons to find that they react negatively to air-pollutant levels that are considered safe by conventionally performed tests. This is often because these individuals are far more susceptible to lower concentrations of particular pollutants than average populations, that their systems are more sensitive than the mechanical devices doing the testing, or that they are reacting to contaminants not even being tested for. Therefore, sometimes a sensitive person's nose can better determine, more accurately, for him- or herself if a problem is present (and at a lower cost) than air-quality testing.

You should be aware that the cost of having your indoor air tested will vary, depending on who does the testing, the extent of the testing, the degree of test sensitivity, and exactly what's being tested for, among other factors. Therefore, before you decide to hire an environmental testing company, find out how long they've been in business, whether they have any certification or licenses, some professional references, how soon you can expect to have a written report, and what the final costs will be. Incidentally, you might ask your local board of health for a company they would recommend.

If you want to try a very simple multiple-tester yourself, **TerrEssentials** offers the Home Air Quality Test Kit. It comes in two types; one for homes up to 2,000 sq. ft. and the other for homes over 2,000 sq. ft. Each kit is designed to test for the presence of mold, fungus, bacteria, formaldehyde, carbon monoxide, and carbon dioxide. Another kit, called the Safer Home Test Kit includes tests for radon, lead, carbon monoxide, as well as microwave and ultraviolet radiation. This kit is sold by **Karen's Natural Products**.

The IAQ Test Kit (**Air Quality Sciences, Inc.**) contains passive monitors that you uncap and let sample the air for 5-7 days. After that, you seal the sample and send the entire kit to their laboratory for analysis. Each kit is designed to measure formaldehyde and volatile organic compounds (VOCs). The results will give you a total VOC level, plus a listing of the three strongest VOCs detected. Also measured are molds and other particulates. IAQ Test Kits can be directly ordered from the manufacturer.

Specific Indoor Air Pollutants

The following sections discuss some of the more common indoor pollutants. You'll find that they're classified in several major categories.

Gases

As you might suspect, potentially harmful gases can make up a certain proportion of a home's indoor air pollution. The following sections discuss some of the more common of these. Incidentally, **American Environmental Health Foundation** offers home sampling tests for your choice of twelve different polluting gases. (Each testing vial can be used for only one gas.)

Combustion Gases

Combustion gases are the invisible gases resulting from combustion (the burning of a substance). Smoke, which consists of tiny particles and vapors (the visible components of combustion) may also be released when materials are burned. In homes, combustion gases are created from combustion appliances such as gas and oil furnaces, gas dryers, gas water heaters, and gas and oil boilers. Others sources include fireplaces, wood stoves, tobacco, kerosene lamps, and even candles.

The combustion of fuels can also produce water vapor, *carbon monoxide, carbon dioxide, sulfur dioxide, formaldehyde*, and other gaseous hydrocarbons. Unfortunately, breathing combustion gases can lead to respiratory problems. While it isn't healthy to breathe any combustion gases, carbon monoxide (CO) is, by far, the most life-threatening.

Keeping your combustion appliances properly maintained and adjusted, ensuring that the chimney functions correctly, and having adequate fresh-air ventilation, can all help reduce the levels of combustion gases indoors. However, when you burn a fuel indoors, it's often difficult to completely eliminate combustion gases from the living space. (Generally, combustion gases are expelled through a chimney, but not all chimneys function correctly. As a result, in many houses, some, or all, of the combustion by-products remain inside the living space.)

To completely eliminate any concern over combustion gases existing in your home's air, it may be necessary to stop burning all substances indoors. While many people would find this difficult, for some very tightly constructed, underventilated homes, or for certain very sensitive or acutely asthmatic individuals, this approach might be necessary. Another less dramatic solution involves using a high-efficiency gas or oil furnace having a *sealed combustion chamber*. These devices do not require a conventional chimney. Instead, they use a fan to blow the combustion gases outdoors through a sealed exhaust pipe.

Carbon Monoxide

The most serious combustion gas in houses is *carbon monoxide (CO)*, a flammable, odorless, tasteless, colorless gas. It's typically formed as the result of the incomplete combustion of carbon-containing fuels. In homes, high levels of CO can be released from fireplaces (either using wood or natural gas for fuel), coal- or wood-burning stoves; or from kerosene, oil, propane, and natural-gas space heaters, furnaces, hot water heaters, or other combustion equipment. Whenever you burn something, various combustion by-products, such as smoke, carbon dioxide (CO_2), water vapor, and CO, are released. The thing that makes CO so dangerous is that, when it is breathed into the lungs, it immediately reacts with *hemoglobin* (red corpuscle proteins) in the blood. Once saturated with CO, the hemoglobin can no longer perform the essential function of transporting life-sustaining oxygen throughout the body.

Commonly, one of the first signs of CO poisoning is a headache. As more CO is inhaled, flu-like symptoms follow, such as muscle weakness, loss of coordination, confusion, and unconsciousness. Death will occur if levels of CO in the blood become high enough. Eerily, light-skinned victims of severe CO poisoning take on a characteristic cherry-red coloring. Each year in this country, hundreds of people die from unplanned, undetected, high carbon monoxide concentrations in their homes, and many more suffer symptoms that they attribute to the flu when, in fact, they are being poisoned by CO. The sad truth is that CO poisoning is the number one cause of accidental poisoning in the U.S., with 10,000 people experiencing some level of poisoning annually—whether they know it or not.

Not surprisingly then, some experts believe that ideal healthy houses shouldn't have any forms of combustion taking place inside the living space. However, if your home does have some type of combustion device, it is absolutely essential that it be working efficiently. Fortunately, when a gas-burning appliance is properly adjusted, CO production is minimized. Therefore, make sure your combustion equipment (and chimney) has a professional checkup and necessary maintenance annually. If, for any reason, carbon monoxide poisoning is suspected, get out of the house immediately. Then, don't return until a professional has inspected and repaired any malfunctioning equipment. By the way, a homeowner's carbon-monoxide test kit can be ordered from **American Environmental Health Foundation**.

It's also a very good idea to install one or more *carbon monoxide detectors*. (A few local jurisdictions now require at least one in all homes.) The Consumer Product Safely Commission has recommended placing one near your home's sleeping area, with extra alarms on every other level in your house. These devices will continually monitor CO levels in the indoor atmosphere. When a higher-than-normal CO concentration is detected, an alarm will sound. Like smoke detectors, some CO detectors are battery-operated, while others are designed to be wired into your home's electrical system. A few newer models combine both smoke and CO detecting in a single unit, some have other features such as a voice warning. If you're interested in purchasing a CO detector, they're usually handled by local hardware stores. Popular brands you'll likely find include BRK Brands/First Alert Carbon Monoxide Detectors (**BRK Brands, Inc.**) and Night Hawk Carbon Monoxide Detectors (**Kidde Safety**). You can also mail order Kidde CO detectors from **Building for Health Materials Center**. Another mail-order source for CO detectors is **Allergy Relief Shop, Inc.**

If you purchase a CO detector, you should test it weekly. You can do this by simply pressing the test/reset button with your finger or with the end of a broom handle if you can't reach it. Also, if it's a battery-run model, replace the batteries twice a year. One final note: If you don't own any combustion appliances but do burn many candles or oil lamps occasionally, installing a CO detector a still good idea. With the popular craze underway for burning a dozen or more of candles at a time, CO can unknowingly build up, even from such small combustion-gas-generating items.

Carbon Dioxide

Carbon dioxide (CO_2) is a tasteless, colorless gas. It's created through the action of human and animal respiration, decay, and the burning of organic materials. Although it's always present in the air (it typically makes up 0.03% of outdoor air), high CO_2 levels in homes usually indicate that there isn't enough fresh air indoors. Although CO_2 isn't particularly toxic itself, too much of it can lead to an uncomfortable feeling of stuffiness or closeness, which can add stress to those already having respiratory problems. If fresh air is brought into such a home, the carbon dioxide levels will be diluted and rapidly diminish, and the stuffy sensation would soon go away.

Unfortunately, a high carbon dioxide level in houses is a growing problem. These days, some new homes are so tightly built that air can't *infiltrate* (find its way indoors). This often leads to an environment in which there is little fresh air in the house—simply because no planned ventilation system was ever installed. For a more in-depth discussion of residential ventilation, and ways to accomplish it, you may want to read *Understanding Ventilation* by

John Bower. If so, this book can be ordered from **The Healthy House Institute** or your favorite bookseller.

Volatile Organic Compounds (VOCs)

Volatile organic compounds (VOCs) have become a serious health threat in many homes. This section explains what these chemicals are, why some are harmful, and how to prevent them from becoming a problem in your home.

The Nature, Uses, and Potential Health Consequences of VOCs

Volatile organic compounds are actually a class of carbon-based chemicals that have the capacity to rapidly evaporate. Once airborne, many VOCs have the ability to combine with each other (or with certain other molecules in the air) to create new chemical compounds.

In reality, a great many different compounds are classified as VOCs. Some are of natural origin and happen to be relatively benign. For example, a freshly cut orange or onion both give off certain types of VOCs. However, there are also naturally occurring VOCs that can be extremely dangerous such as the toxic VOCs given off by certain molds. Other VOCs, such as *alcohol*, lie somewhere in between.

Usually, however, when the term VOC is used in conjunction with indoor air quality, it doesn't refer to naturally occurring VOCs. Instead, it generally refers to VOCs derived from man-made manufactured products, such as the common solvents toluene, xylene, and lacquer thinner. Other synthetically derived VOCs routinely found indoors include formaldehyde and benzene.

Although the negative health effects on humans, from synthetically created VOCs, varies with the particular compound, as a rule they can be harmful to breathe. Many are inflammatory to mucous membranes and the respiratory system. The worst VOCs have been linked to central-nervous-system damage, chromosomal abnormalities, and even cancer. Interestingly, many sensitive individuals feel that exposure to certain dangerous VOCs is the reason for the onset of their Multiple Chemical Sensitivity (MCS). VOCs can also trigger asthma attacks in susceptible persons.

Unfortunately, today, potentially harmful VOCs are found in the indoor air of many U.S. homes. In some homes they exist at fairly high levels. This is because many typical finishes and coatings (including wall paints), adhesives, cleaning products, man-made wood products (including particleboard, plywood, wall paneling, and cabinets), as well as other synthetic materials, contain and release some of these compounds. For the most part, the quantity of VOCs in common consumer products and materials is poorly regulated. However, in 1987, California began regulating the VOC content of paint, and a few other local jurisdictions have since passed similar restrictions.

Testing and Eliminating VOCs in Homes

If you want to determine the amount of volatile organic compounds (VOCs) in your home, an environmental testing company can be hired to come in and make measurements. But comprehensive testing can cost hundreds of dollars and could easily result in a list of a hundred or more different VOCs in the air. While relatively inexpensive test kits are available (mail-order sources for them include **Befit Enterprises Ltd.** and **American Environmental Health Foundation**) it's unlikely that such simple, inexpensive tests will be very helpful. Even a sophisticated test, listing scores of specific VOCs and their concentrations, probably wouldn't be much help either. After all, you still wouldn't know the sources releasing the specific chemicals. (For more on testing, see *Indoor Air Pollution Testing in General* on page 522.)

So, how can you know if the VOC level is too high? The truth is, when it comes to VOC levels in the indoor air, it's impossible to precisely predict at what concentrations you or your family will become affected. Some people are just more susceptible than others. Therefore, the best defense against the dangers of breathing VOCs is to only use items with minimal amounts of VOCs in them, or none at all.

It should be noted that newly applied paints and finishes will quickly give off their own distinctive VOCs. But older items, that emitted high levels of VOCs when they were new, will eventually release lower and lower amounts of these gases. This is because, by their very nature, VOCs evaporate quickly. Any level can be diluted with good indoor ventilation.

Furthermore, *activated charcoal* can be effective in adsorbing VOCs that have higher *molecular weights*. (Molecular weight is defined as the total atomic weights of all the component atoms making up a molecule. Larger, more complicated molecules are made up of many atoms, so they tend to have high molecular weights.) For low-molecular weight VOCs, such as formaldehyde, specially treated activated-charcoal or *activated-alumina* (see *Adsorption Filters* on page 511) can be effective. In addition, some types of *zeolite* may be helpful as well. However, for certain sensitive individuals, ventilation and/or filters may not be enough to stop reactions if VOC-releasing materials remain within their homes. That is because filters and ventilation can only reduce levels, they can't eliminate VOCs completely.

Formaldehyde

These days, one of the most common VOCs found in the indoor air is *formaldehyde*. It's presence can provoke a variety of health complaints, some of them chronic in nature. The following sections discuss this well-known contaminant, and what you can do to reduce it's level in your home.

The Nature, Uses, and Health Consequences of Formaldehyde

Formaldehyde (HCHO) is the simplest chemical in a class of organic compounds known as *aldehydes*. (All aldehydes contain the CHO group of atoms.) Formaldehyde is considered a volatile organic compound or VOC. At very high concentrations, formaldehyde is an extremely reactive, colorless gas with a distinctively pungent and unpleasant odor, however, at concentrations typically found in houses, it's virtually odorless.

If formaldehyde is inhaled, it can cause nasal and sinus irritation, respiratory inflammation, asthma, depression, and even menstrual irregularities. Formaldehyde exposure can also cause burning eyes, and has been shown to be *mutagenic* (capable of increasing the rate of cellular mutations) and *carcinogenic* (cancer-causing). After becoming sensitized to formaldehyde, a certain percentage of the population (probably less than 10%) has been shown to react to smaller and smaller amounts of it. Interestingly, exposure to formaldehyde has been reported by many individuals with Multiple Chemical Sensitivity (MCS) as a suspected cause of their illness. Virtually all people with MCS react negatively to extremely low concentrations of it.

Formaldehyde is one chemical that's both exceptionally easy and inexpensive to produce. It's also one that can be used in a myriad of applications. Therefore, in the last few decades, it's been routinely utilized in a wide range of consumer products. One use that received a lot of public attention was in *urea-formaldehyde foam insulation,* a material that was popular in the 1970s, then was banned because it released a great deal of formaldehyde.

Today, it is no longer banned but, because of bad publicity, it is rarely being used. The urea formaldehyde (UF) resin in this particular product can emit relatively high levels of formaldehyde over several years. But formaldehyde is also found in the glues and resins used in a variety of man-made wood products, either as urea formaldehyde or phenol formaldehyde (PF). PF glues emit considerably less formaldehyde than UF glues. (See also *Man-Made Wood Products* on page 291.)

Formaldehyde is also used in some clear finishes. For example, UF finishes are typically used on kitchen cabinets (see *Typical Modern Cabinets* on page 317). It's also commonly used as a resin treatment on certain fabrics to give them wrinkle resistance—for example, to create no-iron sheets (see *Common Bedding Treatments* on page 225). In addition, formaldehyde is used in the manufacturing of some paper goods, such as paper towels, to increase absorbency. Besides these particular applications, it's sometimes used in personal-care products, cosmetics, shampoos, even toothpastes (see *Typical Modern Ingredients* on page 82).

Unfortunately, most of the items containing formaldehyde will release it into the air. In the case of cabinets made with formaldehyde-containing glues and finishes, the formaldehyde will continually be released for years. In fact, the formaldehyde in some man-made wood products has a *half-life* of 3 to 5 years. This means that during the first 3 to 5 years, half of the formaldehyde present will be released. During the next 3 to 5 years, half of what remains is outgassed, and so on. Interestingly, the amount of water vapor present in your home, as well as the temperature, will affect the rate of formaldehyde release. Both a higher relative humidity and higher temperatures will cause the formaldehyde to be emitted into the air faster.

Testing and Eliminating Formaldehyde in Homes

What is considered an acceptable, safe, level of formaldehyde in the indoor air is still being debated. However, increasing numbers of concerned experts believe that formaldehyde concentrations should be as low as possible in the air you breathe. So, how much formaldehyde is too much? Clean outdoor air in the country might contain 0.01 parts per million (ppm). Sensitive people often react to levels as low as 0.03 ppm, and levels of 0.05-0.15 aren't unusual in houses. The World Health Organization recommended a few years back that levels be below 0.05 ppm in homes. This is especially important if a house contains young children, asthmatics, or persons weakened by a major illness. On the other hand, levels as high as 0.75 ppm are often allowed in the workplace.

Because of the controversy over the safety of formaldehyde, some people feel it is a good idea to test their home's formaldehyde level. If you'd like to have this done, contact an environmental-testing company or buy a home formaldehyde test kit. Mail-order sources for these kits include **Bio Designs** and **American Environmental Health Foundation**. Unfortunately, testing may not detect the extremely minute levels that still promote reactions in certain sensitive individuals. And these tests can't pinpoint the outgassing source(s) of the formaldehyde for you. (See also *Indoor Air Pollution Testing in General* on page 522.)

If your home has too much formaldehyde, what can you do? Airing items outdoors that are suspected of containing high levels formaldehyde (such as some new furniture) for a period of time can often help. Special sealant coatings can be applied to wood items such as kitchen cabinets (see *Acrylic Finishes and Sealants* on page 277) and to carpeting (see *Healthier Carpet Suggestions* on page 304). However, for many chemically sensitive individuals, these remedies just don't seem to help enough. So, after airing and sealing, some of your home decor may still remain too bothersome. By the way, certain types of sealants will pollute the air themselves (at least for some time after they're initially applied) with their own chemical odors.

As you might suspect, some air filters can remove formaldehyde from the air. *Activated charcoal* is often used but, in reality, it is not particularly useful unless it has been specially treated. This is because typical activated charcoal can't effectively adsorb *low-molecular weight* VOCs such as the fairly simple formaldehyde molecule. (Commonly, molecular weight is defined as the total atomic weights of all the atoms making up a molecule.) However, *activated alumina* can remove a great deal of airborne formaldehyde, and certain *zeolites* may be helpful, too. Yet, even these filtering media are often not sufficient for very sensitive people. (See *Adsorption Filters* on page 551.)

The truth is, permanently removing the source of the formaldehyde, or storing the offending items elsewhere until the amount of formaldehyde they release is undetectable, are the two best solutions. Of course, this can be disruptive, time-consuming, and costly. However, these are the only measures that will best ensure your family's health from exposure to formaldehyde.

Radon

Within the last few decades, researchers have become aware that *radon* gas is present in quite a few American homes at unacceptably high levels. Unfortunately, they have also concluded that the presence of radon at high concentrations can lead to serious health consequences. The following sections discuss exactly what radon is, how to detect it, and ways to reduce it.

The Nature and Potential Health Consequences of Radon

Radon (Rn) is an odorless, colorless, radioactive gas. Actually, there are twenty radon *isotopes* (unique atomic forms each having a different number of neutrons). Of these, *radon-222*, which is produced by naturally occurring *radium* in the soil, is the isotope of most concern. It's radon-222 that can cause serious health problems if it becomes concentrated in your home.

Radon-222 can enter houses through foundation cracks and/or through well water. If it's unable to leave freely (for example, through a ventilation system), it's concentration soon rises. Unfortunately, the trapped gaseous radon-222 goes through a natural radioactive decay process, producing *radon decay products* which are solids. It's these decay products (often chauvinistically called *radon daughters*)—and not the radon gas itself—that can become lodged in your lung tissue and eventually lead to lung cancer. Because of this, radon is believed to be the Number Two cause of lung cancer in the U.S. (Smoking remains Number One.)

It should be pointed out that radon gas is a natural part of our environment. In fact, it's been estimated that it makes up more than half of the background radioactivity we are surrounded with every day because it's continually rising up from bedrock, soil, and from some ground water (see also *Radon* on page 585). However, because of certain geologic conditions, some locales have much higher concentrations of radon than others. In the U.S., for example, there are radon "hot spots" in western Pennsylvania and Maryland, as well as in other locals. If done correctly, proper sealing measures can prevent radon from entering most homes. But, in the cases of some tightly built houses, while the radon may be entering at a low rate, it may also be leaving at a low rate, thus exposing the people living in the house to unhealthy levels.

Testing and Eliminating Radon in Homes

It's important for every home to be tested for radon. Because of individual differences in construction and in soil conditions, there's absolutely no way to guess whether or not a specific house will have a high radon level. Even if all your neighbors' homes have low levels of radon, yours might have a high concentration. But what exactly is a high radon level? Currently, the **EPA (Environmental Protection Agency)** says that any reading above 4 pC/l (4 picoCuries of radon per liter of air) should be cause for concern.

To determine if your home falls above this level, you can buy a simple radon test kit. These are relatively inexpensive and are available at most local hardware stores and building centers. In addition, **Befit Enterprises Ltd., Bio Designs, Allergy Relief Shop, Inc.** and **American Environmental Health Foundation** offer them by mail order. Radon test kits are really very easy to use. Most are made so that, after reading the instructions, you open the sampling container (usually a small canister), place it in a suggested location, and leave it there undisturbed for the recommended time. Then, you seal the container, fill out a simple form, and mail it to a laboratory. The test results are then mailed back to you. (Incidentally, it's possible to buy continuously operating radon-gas monitors, if you feel that's necessary.)

If an inexpensive radon test indicates a level above 4 pC/l, you'll probably want to buy a costlier, more sensitive test kit—or have an environmental testing company perform a more accurate test for you. If the result of the second test is also high, radon-control measures (known as *radon mitigation*) should seriously be considered to reduce the concentration.

Ridding your house of high radon levels entails either some form of ventilation system to safely direct the radon toward the outdoors, or sealing any cracks in the foundation and basement floor to prevent the radon from entering, or both. There are also other approaches, and no single mitigation measure is appropriate for all houses. To help you know precisely what to do, your local board of health may be able to provide information on radon tests, radon-reduction strategies, and perhaps even the names of local companies that specialize in radon-mitigation services. In addition, a number of books have been published about radon. One you might read is *Radon: A Homeowner's Guide to Detection and Control* by Bernard Cohen and the editors of *Consumer Reports*. Although this particular book is no longer in print, it (and other good books on radon) may be available from your local library. For still other books, check with your favorite booksellers. Also, it would be a good idea to contact the **EPA National Service Center for Environmental Publications**, or the **EPA Indoor Air Quality InfoLine**, to order their free radon booklets. An InfoLine specialist may be able to personally supply you with some of the answers for which you're looking.

Vapors

A *vapor* is a gaseous substance that is usually a liquid at room temperature. As you might suspect, the most common vapor in houses is water vapor. If too much is present, *high relative humidity* results.

High relative humidity exists in many houses. Unfortunately, this can lead to a host of possible problems. The sections below explain relative humidity, and ways you might lower it, if necessary, in your home.

High Relative Humidity Defined and Potential Consequences

Humidity refers to the water-vapor content of air. Because there is always some moisture in the air, it can be difficult to think of humidity as a pollutant. Yet, if your indoor air contains high levels of water vapor, it can damage your walls, floors, and interior furnishings. Also, high water-vapor levels can result in mold, mildew, and other microbial growth. In addition, it can often increase the rate of formaldehyde release from man-made wood products, etc.

The word *relative* is used with humidity because there's a direct relationship between the temperature of the air, and the potential amount of water vapor the air can hold. Simply put, cold air can't hold as much water vapor as warm air. Therefore, if a room at 50°F held 10 gallons water vapor, and an identical room at 80°F also held 10 gallons of water vapor, the rooms would have the different relative humidities. The warmer room would have a lower relative humidity than the cold room because warm air has the potential to hold much more water vapor than cold air. Incidentally, when air at any temperature is saturated and is no longer capable of holding any more water vapor, it's said to have a relative humidity of 100%. At the usual indoor temperatures of American homes, the best relative humidity would be 40% or less in the winter. At 40% relative humidity, there's still enough moisture present in the air so mucous membranes usually won't become irritated, the skin won't become dried out, wood won't tend to crack, and yet 40% is usually too low for mold and mildew to thrive.

With the use of an instrument called a *hygrometer*, you can easily measure the relative humidity in different locations in your home. These devices are usually sold at hardware stores, building centers, and at department stores such as **Sears Roebuck and Co.** In addition, **eMD.com** and **Allergy Control Products, Inc.** sell a handy combination Honeywell temperature/humidity gauge (**Honeywell, Inc.**). You can also buy a hygrometer from **Allergy Relief Shop, Inc.**

Reducing High Humidity in Homes

If your home's air regularly has high relative-humidity readings, check for water sources around your house. These could include leaking air conditioners and plumbing lines, or damaged roofs. Also look for clogged gutters and foundation drains. In addition, too much shady foliage planted near the house can contribute to problems.

Of course, poor ventilation can easily result in high indoor humidity levels. Therefore, it's a good idea for rooms in your home that commonly generate large amounts of water vapor to be properly vented to the outdoors, so the water vapor can't build up indoors. Ideally, a range hood over your kitchen stovetop, an exhaust fan in your laundry room, and exhaust fans in your bathrooms, should be installed and used regularly. All such fans must be vented to the outdoors to be effective.

Bathroom fans can have a simple, manually operated on/off wall-mounted switch, a manually set crank timer, or they can be controlled by a *dehumidistat*. A dehumidistat is simply a device that monitors relative-humidity levels. It can be used to automatically turn on an exhaust fan when a certain relative humidity is sensed. For example, a dehumidistat could turn on a bathroom exhaust fan when the relative humidity rises after a shower. You'll also want to make sure that your clothes dryer is vented to the outdoors. By the way, **Broan Mfg. Co., Inc.** and **Nutone** are two manufacturers of exhaust fans. Local electrical-supply companies should carry them and similar brands, as well as dehumidistats. **W.W. Grainger, Inc.** stores and catalogs should have them as well.

You can also lower the relative humidity by using air conditioners and dehumidifiers. Both pull water vapor out of the air and condense it into liquid water. Of course, air conditioners and dehumidifiers are available from many local department and appliance stores including **Sears Roebuck and Co.** DeLonhi dehumidifiers can be ordered from **Allergy Control Products, Inc.**

It should be noted that dehumidifiers can be emptied either automatically into a house drain, or manually. If you decide upon a dehumidifier, it's important to clean it regularly to prevent any mold growth. This is especially necessary with models that must be emptied manually inasmuch as they can contain standing water for some time (see *Mold and Mildew* on page 170).

In the winter, closets can have a higher relative humidity than other rooms in a house, so they can also be places where mold can grow. To remedy such a situation, see *Controlling Closet Mustiness* on page 513.

Biological Contaminants

Anything airborne that is now living, was once living, or was produced by something alive, and has the capacity to create negative health effects, is considered to be a *biological contaminant.* Therefore, bacteria, viruses, dust-mite body fragments and feces, mold, mildew, and pollen are all biological contaminants. These particular biological contaminants are in *particulate form* (tiny bits of solid matter). However, most metabolic processes also release a variety of gases including volatile organic compounds (VOCs). These, too, are biological contaminants, but in a non-particulate, gaseous form. Some of the most common biological contaminants found in homes are discussed below.

By the way, it should be mentioned that the **EPA (U.S Environmental Protection Agency)** sponsors the **National Microbial Telecommunications Network** that you might find helpful. They're especially knowledgeable about registered antimicrobial strategies, although they have access to a great deal of other information as well.

Bacteria and Viruses

In America, bacteria and viruses are popularly known as *germs*—a word with very negative connotations. Surprisingly though, many bacteria and viruses are not harmful to human beings. In fact, some bacteria are actually necessary for life. But, of course, there are also harmful, disease-causing bacteria and viruses in a home's air whose numbers should be minimized, or eliminated, if at all possible. Following is information on both viruses and bacteria, and suggestions regarding methods you might try to control their populations within your own home.

Bacteria

Bacteria is a classification of some of the simplest single-celled microscopic organisms on earth. Unlike viruses (see *Viruses* below), individual bacteria are complete entities in themselves and are capable of their own reproduction. In size, bacteria usually range from 0.2–50 microns in length (One micron is one millionth of a meter, a very fine human hair is about 40 microns in diameter.). So far, about two thousand species of bacteria have been identified, and they have been found to exist virtually everywhere. Interestingly, certain bacterial species have a resting state known as the *endospore stage.* Bacteria in this form can be among the most indestructible of all living things. Apparently, only long periods of high-pressure steam will cause some endospores to die.

For humans, certain bacteria can pose very real health dangers. For example, staphylococci can cause strep throat, and bacteria known as pleuropneumonia-like organisms (PPLO) can lead to contagious pneumonia. Other *pathogenic* (disease causing) bacteria are responsible for salmonella, Legionnaire's Disease, and botulism. Unfortunately, under ideal circumstances, most bacteria can divide and multiply about every twenty minutes. As a matter of fact, theoretically, one bacterium could produce one-half-million descendants within six hours. Therefore, diseases caused by bacteria often have the potential to spread rapidly.

To counter the proliferation of dangerous bacteria in your home, it's extremely important to not create hospitable living conditions for them. Therefore, be sure to store all your food properly, have good personal hygiene habits, keep all indoor pets well groomed, clean your house thoroughly and regularly, and avoid having standing water or persistently high relative-humidity levels in your home. Also, make sure any humidifiers you're using are frequently cleaned, perhaps daily in some cases. It's also a good idea to disinfect your humidifiers from time to time with *hydrogen peroxide* (use the 3% solution sold in most pharmacies), or with some other tolerable disinfectant/cleaner (see *Mold and Mildew* on page 170).

You may also want to use special air-cleaning equipment. Certain air purifiers and filters, such as *HEPA filters* or *electrostatic filters* will help remove airborne bacteria. While it's true that *ozone generators* can also counter bacterial levels by broadcasting streams of reactive *ozone (O_3)*, ozone can also react with your mucous membranes, wall finishes, household furnishings, and more. So this approach is not recommended. On the other hand, *negative-ion generators* can cause airborne bacteria to leave the air and adhere to internal collection plates or filters, or to walls, ceilings, etc. (This is still thought of as a "unproved technology" by some people.) Finally, *ultraviolet (UV)* light purifiers can be effective bacteria killers. Incidentally, there is a small amount of ozone produced when using either negative-ion generators or UV purifiers.

(For more on the air-cleaning strategies mentioned, see the various sections in *Chapter 23: Improving Your Indoor Air.*)

Viruses

Viruses are extremely minute parasites that, by definition, border somewhere between life and nonlife. Viruses are found in several forms, the most distinctive being the *virion*, which basically consists of nucleic acid (reproduction information within a chemical structure) protected with a protein sheath (coating). Virions are the infectious form of viruses that can exist outside host cells. Because of this, the term *virus* often simply implies the virion form.

In reality, viruses differ greatly from one another in both size and shape. However, most are only 3,000 angstroms long (An angstrom is one ten-billionth of a meter.). Viruses can't function or reproduce completely on their own and must invade a host species' cells. Once in a compatible cell, the virus injects its nucleic acid into that of the host cell. This eventually causes the host cell to reproduce the virus. However, although there are hundreds of virus strains, only a limited number are actually a threat to humans. Viral infections that can occur in people include polio, mumps, German measles, chicken pox, influenza, hepatitis, AIDS, and herpes. Even some cancers are thought to be caused by certain viruses.

Relatively high levels of airborne infectious viruses are present most commonly in the air of your home when a family member or pet currently has a viral disease. Therefore, vaccinations of those family members still unaffected is the best preventive—if a vaccination for that particular illness is available. By the way, *ozone generators* may be able to kill certain viruses through the action of the reactive ozone (O_3) gas. However, these aren't recommended because their very reactivity can negatively affect human health as well as a home's belongs. Another approach is to use an ultraviolet (UV) light purifier to kill the viruses, but these devices also have their drawbacks. (See *Ozone Generators* on page 557 and *Ultraviolet (UV) Air Purifiers* on page 556.)

Dust-Mite Fragments and Feces

Although it's admittedly disgusting to think about, *dust-mite* body parts and feces often make up a fairly large portion of house dust. In fact, one estimate has it that a quarter million dust-mite fecal pellets can be found in is a single gram (about a $1/2$ teaspoon) of house dust. Interestingly, it's the lightweight dead body parts and fecal pellets, and not living mites themselves, that tend to become airborne. For susceptible individuals, this dust-mite debris can trigger asthmatic or allergic symptoms that range from mild sniffles and itchy eyes, to life-threatening respiratory distress. One condition dust mites can cause, but is far less commonly known, is *atopic dermatitis*. Also known as *eczema*, it is a chronic inflammatory skin condition. It apparently often runs in families that have histories of asthma, and certain allergies such hay fever.

Unfortunately, dust mites are found in virtually every home, perhaps in as many as 90% of them. These tiny (usually less than 0.04" in length), eight-legged creatures are invisible to the naked eye. (They weren't even discovered until about three decades ago.) If you feel you want to test your home for its level of dust-mite population, you can order an Aclo-Test Detection Kit from **American Environmental Health Foundation**, **Allergy Clean Environments**, **Priorities**, and **Allergy Control Products, Inc.**

To minimize dust-mite populations, and their debris, you should dust and vacuum your home frequently and thoroughly. To make this easier, those with serious dust-mite allergies should consider having only hard-surface floors, as well as easily cleanable, or washable, furnishings and decorating items. Because dust mites thrive at higher relative humidities, they can often be minimized by keeping your house drier (see *Reducing High Humidity in Homes* on page 531).

While *HEPA filters* are commonly promoted as the best air filters for allergic persons, the truth is that many types of less-efficient particulate air filters are able to trap dust-mite debris. On the other hand, *negative-ion generators* may not one of the better methods. For much more on dust mites, dust mite control, and dust mite allergen neutralization, see *Dust Mites* on page 410.)

For further information about dust-mite control, other sections of special interest include, *Household Cleaning for Allergic and Asthmatic People* on page 140, *Decorating for Allergic People* on page 329, *Allergies, Bedding, and Bedrooms* on page 223, as well as *Laundering for Allergic People* on page 122.

(For more on the air-cleaning methods mentioned, see the various sections in *Chapter 23: Improving Your Indoor Air*.)

Mold

Mold tends to be both ugly and destructive in homes. This section discusses what mold is, possible outcomes, if present in your home, and methods of dealing with it.

The Nature and Potential Consequences of Mold

Mold is a popular term for those fungi having *hyphae* (threadlike filaments). Living mold, dead mold, and mold spores are common airborne *allergens* (substances that trigger allergic symptoms). Molds generally thrive best where moisture levels are relatively high. Under the right conditions, mold can grow on almost anything. Therefore, tile, grout, wood, paint, plaster, and fabric are all susceptible to mold.

Unfortunately, mold growth is unsightly and it can cause permanent staining and damage to walls and furnishings. Sometimes, unpleasant odors also accompany mold growth. These odors are the gases given off by the mold's metabolic processes, which sometimes include potentially harmful volatile organic compounds (VOCs). (See *Volatile Organic Compounds* on page 526.) Sadly, once your belongings become moldy, it's often difficult to completely eliminate the stains or the musty odors.

Testing and Eliminating Mold in Homes

If desired, you can hire an environmental-testing company to test your indoor air for its mold content. You can also buy home test kits for mold. One mail-order mold-testing source is **Allerx**. They offer a three-test kit for collecting airborne molds, and a special Long Term Mold Test & Analysis kit. This last one requires a six-week incubation with one agarfilled plate. **Gazoontite** offers the MBI mold/mildew self-test. For an additional fee, you can have it analyzed by a laboratory. **TerrEssentials** offers the Home Air Quality Test Kit. It comes in two types; one for homes up to 2,000 sq. ft. and the other for homes over 2,000 sq. ft. Each kit is designed to test for the presence of mold, fungus, bacteria, formaldehyde, carbon monoxide, and carbon dioxide. Other sources for mold tests are **Befit Enterprises Ltd.**, **Bio Designs**, and **American Environmental Health Foundation**.

However, in certain situations, it's probably questionable what real benefits you will derive from testing your home for mold. After all, in most cases, if you suspect a mold problem, its because you can already see it or smell it.

Generally, the best way to guard against mold is to create an indoor habitat that's unappealing for colonization. This is done by properly storing your food, and cleaning your home and clothing frequently. You should also eliminate any moisture problems in your house. That means fixing leaking water pipes, drains, gutters, roofs, and foundations. Another important step is reducing the indoor relative-humidity levels if they're too high. In the winter time, when the indoor relative humidity is below 40%, mold growth tends to drop off dramatically.

By the way, very common airborne mold sources in homes are contaminated air conditioners, humidifiers, and dehumidifiers. (Note: For highly mold-allergic people, it's best to keep the number of such water-filled appliances to an absolute minimum.) To help prevent mold growth from starting in your air conditioner, try running just the fan for thirty minutes immediately after you turn the cooling function off. This will help dry out your air conditioner's inner components. For humidifiers and dehumidifiers, your best defense is to keep them as clean as possible. For all these devices, remember to clean or replace any filters regularly.

If, despite your best efforts, a portable air conditioner, humidifier, or dehumidifier becomes contaminated with mold, you can sometimes get rid of it by doing the following procedure. First, unplug the machine, or shut off the electricity running to it, and place protective plastic sheeting under it, on the floor. Then, carefully—but thoroughly—spray the waterproof parts (never spray anything on or near the wiring, electronics, or controls) with *hydrogen peroxide* in a spray bottle. (Use the 3% dilution commonly sold in pharmacies.) After that, clean by hand what you're able to dismantle or easily reach using a sponge soaked in hydrogen peroxide. Afterwards, let the unit dry thoroughly before using. When doing this, remember to wear protective eye wear, and a chemical respirator mask to protect yourself from inhaling mold spores, as well as waterproof gloves to protect your hands. Of course, if you are allergic to mold, this generally isn't a project to do yourself. (See *Personal Protective Gear* on page 264, and *Household Waterproof Glove Suggestions* on page 137.)

By the way, if the walls of your home, or some of your possessions become moldy, wash off the mold promptly using an appropriate mold-killing solution—that is, one that's tolerable to you and won't damage what you're trying to clean (see *Mold and Mildew* on page 170). Another approach, that can work if moisture problems have caused the mold growth, is to fix the leaks and high humidity, etc. Then, once the mold has become dormant, clean it up while wearing a chemical respirator mask as protection against breathing the mold particles.

In the winter, closets can have a higher relative humidity than other rooms in a house, so they can also be places where mold can grow. To remedy such a situation, see *Controlling Closet Mustiness* on page 513.

Several air-filtering strategies including *HEPAs* can also trap airborne mold. In addition, *negative-ion generators* can cause airborne mold spores to adhere to collection plates inside them, or to walls, ceilings, etc.. And, *ozone generators* reduce mold levels by the use of the unstable, highly reactive ozone (O_3) gas they release. While an ozone machine can prove effective at killing mold, it is so unstable that it can easily react with more than fungi, including wall finishes, furnishings, and human mucosal tissues. So, ozone generators are not recommended, unless a professional does the job and no one is indoors while the unit is operating. Even then, unexpected new odorous compounds could be created as the result of the ozone's reactivity. These may be as problematic as the mold, in some cases. The truth is, none of these approaches are the best way to control mold. Eliminating excess moisture and high relative humidity is always the best and most permanent solution.

Pollen

Pollen grains are actually *gametophytes* of male plants, which is equivalent to sperm in male animals. The amount of pollen produced by different plant species varies enormously. However, most plants produce huge quantities of it. For example, the number of pollen grains from just one pine cone often runs in the millions.

Each plant species has pollen grains that are uniquely shaped, but virtually all types of pollen grains are very small. In fact, most pollen grains are between 24 and 50 microns. (One micron is one-millionth of a meter. A fine human hair is about 40 microns in diameter.) Interestingly, pollen grains contain proteins and sugars, some of which act as insect and animal attractants. This is because intermediary creatures are often necessary to help transfer the pollen to the female flowers.

Of course, pollen grains are both natural, and an essential part of life. Unfortunately, high airborne levels of pollen can be irritating to many people's eyes and sinuses. In some individuals, certain types of pollen grains can provoke allergic symptoms or asthmatic attacks. If pollen is a health concern for your family, you may want to take measures to minimize its levels inside your house. Obviously, you won't want to bring any flowering plants indoors. Also, it's a good idea not to plant trees or shrubs too near your home. After all, the potentially huge quantities of pollen produced by your landscaping could easily enter through doors, windows, and the home's ventilation system.

However, for very allergic individuals, these approaches may still not be enough. Because tiny, extremely lightweight, pollen grains are hardy and somewhat indestructible, they can be carried by wind currents for great distances. If conditions are right, tree and plant pollens from many miles away could end up in the air just outside—and, therefore, eventually inside—your house.

Fortunately, there are a number of air-cleaning strategies that help reduce indoor pollen levels. Although pollen grains are small, most are still large enough to be trapped by many types (if not most) of particulate air-filters. *Negative-ion generators* can cause indoor airborne pollen grains to adhere to internal collection plates, ceilings and walls, etc., therefore they won't be inhaled. However, these units may not prove to be particularly effective. (See also *Negative-ion generators* on page 558.)

Minerals and Metals

Harmful minerals and metals are particulate pollutants that can be found in indoor air. Two in this category of which you should be aware are *asbestos* and *lead*.

Asbestos

Just saying the word *asbestos* can trigger a certain amount of fear among many people. Although asbestos definitely can cause severe respiratory illnesses, in certain situations in your home it'll pose very little risk to you or your family—if it is not deteriorating, and you don't disturb it.

The Nature, Uses, and Potential Health Consequences of Asbestos

Asbestos is actually a generic term that's applied to several minerals that occur in a fiber-like form. However, *chrysotile* (the fibrous form of *serpentine*) is usually the particular type meant when the word *asbestos* is used. Unfortunately, if small asbestos fibers become inhaled, minute fragments can become trapped in your lung tissue. This can lead to very serious consequences. In fact, since the mid-1960s, exposure to asbestos in the workplace (asbestos mines, asbestos-insulation factories, etc.) has been known to cause *asbestosis* (a severe, debilitating lung disease), as well as lung cancer.

Concern over asbestos exposure, since these findings first become known, has steadily increased. As a result, in 1971 asbestos became the first regulated material in the workplace by the U.S. Occupational Safety and Health Administration (OSHA). Then, in 1986, OSHA decided to severely limit the acceptable exposure levels for workers. However, it was not until 1989 that the **EPA (Environmental Protection Agency)** regulated asbestos beyond the workplace. That year, the EPA ordered that asbestos use, manufacture, and export be reduced 94% by 1996. Asbestos was also completely banned in some building materials as well as brake linings.

Yet, a tremendous amount of asbestos is already present in our environment. Because asbestos fibers are fire-, heat-, and corrosion-resistant, and they can be spun, woven, compressed, or added to other substances, asbestos has been widely used in industry as well as in commercial and consumer products. For example, over the years, it has been an integral ingredient in brake linings, hard flooring materials (such as certain types of vinyl tiles), some cement and cement products (including cement/asbestos siding and roofing tiles), and even in some drywall compounds. It's also been used as insulation surrounding ductwork and furnaces, as well as with particular types of electrical circuitry. As a result, many U.S. homes contain at least some quantity of asbestos. The exceptions, of course, would be those houses that have been more recently built.

Testing and Eliminating Asbestos in Homes

It should be pointed out that asbestos in your house may not necessarily be a problem. For instance, asbestos imbedded in older cement siding materials is unlikely to create asbestos dust that can be inhaled. However, one of the worst situations is having deteriorating asbestos insulation surrounding your ducts or furnace. In such a case, the asbestos should be removed completely, carefully, and as soon as possible. This isn't a job for homeowners or amateurs, but one that must be performed only by licensed asbestos-removal contractors. During the removal process, there must be a complete sealing off of the contaminated areas, workers must wear hazardous-material protective gear, and special hazardous-material disposal methods are used.

If you suspect any sources of airborne asbestos in your home, call your local board of health, which can advise you on what steps to follow, including testing. If an asbestos problem is confirmed, health officials may be able to suggest approved asbestos-removal companies. In order to get a reliable asbestos-removal firm, it would be wise to obtain several homeowner references from jobs they've previously performed, a written estimate of the total cost, and the projected time in which the removal procedure will take place. You should be aware that asbestos removal can often be expensive.

Although other filtering methods might be able to trap asbestos fibers, depending on their size, very efficient *HEPA filters* would be the logical choice to use with such a potentially dangerous material. (See *HEPA and ULPA Filters* on page 553.) However, in reality, the best protection is to eliminate any deteriorating asbestos. For more information on asbestos, contact the **EPA National Service Center for Environmental Publications**. The particular agency offers booklets addressing issues regarding asbestos in homes. By the way, the EPA also sponsors an **EPA Indoor Air Quality InfoLine** that you may want to call.

Lead

Lead particles pose a real health threat in far too many U.S. homes. The following sections explain why this is the case.

The Nature, Uses, and Potential Health Consequences of Lead

Lead (Pb) is a very heavy, silvery-gray metal that turns a dull blue-gray when exposed to the air. It's also soft, malleable, and has a low melting point. Interestingly, once lead has *oxidized* (tarnished), it becomes corrosion-resistant. Lead can be alloyed with many metals (Pewter was originally a combination of lead and tin.).

Lead has been widely utilized over the years. It's been used as a *whitening pigment* (known as *white lead*) in paints—and even in face powders at one time. It's also been widely used as an inexpensive and useful solder. In addition, it's been used to make water pipes, fishing sinkers, molded toys, printing type, and gun shot. Today, lead continues to be an essential component of lead-acid automobile batteries and it is sometimes used to create waterproof barriers in certain roofing applications. Furthermore, lead is used as *came* (supporting strips) in some stained-glass work, as an ingredient in certain glossy ceramic glazes, and in the making of lead crystal, among many other uses. However, deteriorating lead paint usually poses the most health concern in homes.

Despite its useful qualities, lead has a serious drawback: It can be poisonous. For a number of years, it was suspected that lead might be responsible for certain workplace-related negative health effects seen all too frequently in lead mines and lead foundries, etc. Yet these workers were exposed to amounts then considered safe. However, research finally proved the feared correlation between illness and "low-level" lead exposures. Because of this, since the mid-1980s, the U.S. Centers for Disease Control (CDC) has been steadily lowering what officials there consider the acceptable "environmental lead level."

Actually, what's currently known is that lead, and many lead-containing compounds, can be toxic when swallowed or inhaled. While lead is absorbed by the human body at a very slow rate, it can gradually accumulate in fairly large amounts because it can't be easily eliminated. Unfortunately, high lead levels can injure the central nervous system and damage the *blood-brain barrier cells* that provide a natural shielding of your brain tissue against potentially harmful chemicals.

Signs of lead poisoning include loss of appetite, weakness, anemia, vomiting, and convulsions. In some cases, permanent brain damage can result—even death. In children, impaired learning or kidney problems can sometimes be caused by lead poisoning. In adults, *hypertension* (high blood pressure) can also be a symptom of high lead levels in the body.

Because a variety of studies have documented that children have been made ill by eating and breathing deteriorating lead paint, the federal government banned lead as a paint ingredient in 1977. More recently, lead has been banned in solder. In addition, lead additives in gasoline, such as *tetraethyl lead* and *tetramethyl lead*, have been phased out. In the past, some of these additives probably routinely entered the living spaces of homes with attached garages (see *Controlling Odors within Garages* on page 374).

Testing and Eliminating Lead in Homes

These days, it's now agreed by virtually all experts that everyone should completely avoid lead dust and lead fumes, if at all possible. Therefore, if you're concerned whether your wall paint contains lead, you might want to perform a lead test on it. One such simple test kit is Lead Check Swabs (**HybriVet Systems, Inc.**). This item can be bought directly from the company, or from **Allergy Relief Shop, Inc.**, or **American Environmental Health Foundation**. If you find evidence of lead in your wall paint, contact your local board of health for information on what steps to take. Lead tests can also be used on pottery, dishes, etc. that are suspected of having problematic lead glazes.

For more on lead, you can call the **National Lead Information Center** which is a Hotline maintained by the **EPA (Environmental Protection Agency)**. After contacting the Hotline, you'll be sent printed materials about lead poisoning, and measures you can perform to prevent it, as well as a list of helpful state and local agencies (such as local and state boards of health, etc.), and additional information.

Although air-filters for removing airborne lead might be suggested, lead dust is generally too heavy to become airborne. However, HEPA-filtered vacuums are one of the more effective methods of removing it. (See *HEPA-Filtered Vacuum Cleaners* on page 146.) Yet, with such a toxic metal, the best protection is to sufficiently seal the source of the lead, or have it professionally removed.

(Note: For information on lead in your water, see *Industrial Pollutants* on page 580, and *Contaminants from Supply Lines, Pipes, and Solder* on page 590.)

Mixed Contaminants

House dust and *smoke* are actually made up of several types of pollutants. The following sections give you information on these two complicated substances so you'll be better able to deal with them more effectively.

Dust

Every home contains a certain amount of house dust. But exactly what is it and how do you best deal with it?

The Nature and Potential Health Consequences of Dust

House dust is a generic term that can be defined as fine, dry particles of earth and other debris. In homes, it is usually made up of many components, such as soil, lead, perhaps asbestos, natural or synthetic fibers, *dander* (skin flakes), hair, fur, pollen grains, mold spores, dust-mite body parts, dust-mite feces, both live and dead bacteria, as well as many other things. Actually, the exact make-up of the dust found in each home is unique to that home.

Not surprisingly, many people find that breathing dust can be irritating to the nose and sinuses. In addition, certain individuals have asthmatic or allergic responses when they inhale dust—sometimes suffering severely from it. In reality, it's often only one component, or perhaps only a few, in the dust that actually triggers these autoimmune symptoms. Most commonly, the problem is related to certain pollens, mold spores, and dust-mite debris.

Of course, the best defense against indoor dust is to thoroughly and regularly clean the interior of your home. If you frequently dust using a damp, all-cotton, flannel cloth, for example, it can help eliminate a great deal of the particulate matter that lands on your tables, lamps, accent pieces, and dressers, etc. If you vacuum your floors, walls, and upholstered furniture regularly with a central vacuum system (with an outdoor exhaust) or a specially filtered portable unit, it can also help cut down on the quantity of accumulated house dust. (See *Dusting* on page 140 and *Vacuuming* on page 144.)

To remove airborne dust from your home, you can use one of many air-cleaning and air-filtering approaches designed to remove particulates. For information, see the various sections in *Chapter 23: Improving Your Indoor Air.*

Duct Cleaning

Furnace and air conditioning ducts commonly acquire a layer of house dust in them over time. Therefore, it's a good idea to have your home's entire ductwork system cleaned from time to time. Fortunately, professional companies now specialize in this field, many of which use a powerful vacuuming procedure.

You may find that some duct-cleaning contractors want to use a *disinfectant* (sometimes fragranced) in your ducts. The disinfectant treatment is meant to inhibit the growth of biological contaminants such as microbes, dust mites, fungi, and bacteria. And if its scented, it's meant to act as a deodorizing "air freshener." However, it is generally wise to avoid having these chemicals used in your ducts, because they can leave odors in them for some time. Naturally, this is an important consideration for chemically sensitive persons.

To locate a professional duct-cleaning service, check in your local classified telephone directory. If you don't see any listed, you might ask for suggestions at your local board of health, or from an area heating/cooling contractor. If you do find a company, ask specifically about their procedure for cleaning ducts, what cleaning products or chemicals, if any, they normally use, any bonding or certification, as well as time and cost estimates.

Smoke

Smoke is a surprisingly complex substance whose effects can linger long after the combustion that created it has been extinguished. The sections below explain what's in smoke, how it can affect you if it is inhaled.

The Nature and Potential Health Consequences of Smoke

Smoke is a by-product of combustion. It is actually considered a *mixed aerosol* of gases, suspended liquid vapor droplets, and very tiny solid particulates. Unfortunately, if you breathe in smoke, these minute solids can be particularly damaging to your respiratory system, especially your lungs. Interestingly, if the combustion gas sulfur dioxide is also present, the particulates can become even more deeply imbedded in your lung tissue than they otherwise would. In any case, bronchitis, asthma, emphysema, and even lung cancer can result from breathing in smoke. And too much smoke inhaled at one time can easily result in death. The particular effects you'll experience from inhaling smoke depend on the origin of the smoke (wood, tobacco, or synthetic vinyl, for example), its concentration in the air, the length of exposure, and your own personal susceptibilities.

In homes, controlled sources of smoke can include burning kerosene lamps, candles, incense, fireplaces, and wood stoves—and, of course, tobacco. While the health risks associated with smoking are now well publicized, fewer people understand the very real dire effects of breathing secondhand smoke. This is understandable considering this "used" smoke is up to one-hundred times more poisonous than the smoke originally inhaled by the smoker. Also, researchers have found that rooms filled with tobacco smoke can have air pollution levels six times that of busy highways. Apparently, in work situations, employees exposed regularly to secondhand smoke are one-third more likely to get lung cancer. The **EPA (Environmental Protection Agency)** has, in fact, classified it as a Group-A carcinogen. Finally, secondhand-smoke exposure tends to increase the chances of acquiring childhood asthma.

Of course, unplanned combustion in the form of accidental fires can be devastating sources of smoke in houses. This is because the amount of smoke produced from even a very small, localized fire can be both massive and pervasive. It's no wonder then that smoke inhalation causes more injuries and deaths in home fires than burns.

Removing Smoke From Your Home

Besides the direct health effects, smoke can easily permeate and saturate your clothing, furnishings, walls, and flooring. Unfortunately, smoky odors can often be difficult to get rid of completely. Sometimes, even repeated cleaning, and extended airing, may not remove all the smell. However, in certain cases, some individuals have found that *ozone generators* have been somewhat helpful. Apparently, the very reactive ozone (O_3) is able to break down the compounds that make up the smoky odors. However, if this approach is tried, it should only be done by a professional, and with no one inside the home. You should also be aware that the ozone will possibly react with other materials it comes into contact with indoors. As a result, new, unplanned compounds may be inadvertently created, some of which could be bothersome in their own right. (See *Ozone Generators* on page 557.)

Many people ask, What's the best air filtering strategy to eliminate smoke in the air? There's not an easy answer, you see, because smoke is a mixture containing both solid particulates and vapors, and it is also accompanied by combustion gases. Therefore, it requires an air-cleaning system capable of removing several types of contaminants. Actually, because the particles in smoke are often so extremely tiny, *HEPA filters* are probably be the best type to use. In addition, *activated charcoal* would also be necessary to adsorb the gases. (These filters, and others, will be covered in the next chapter.) Note that an air-cleaning system can easily become overwhelmed, and rendered more or less useless, if the concentration of smoke in the air is very high. Ideally, in a healthy home, there should be no sources of smoke whatsoever. For information on smoke detectors, see *Smoke Detectors* on page 386.

CHAPTER 23: IMPROVING YOUR INDOOR AIR

As was seen in the last chapter, it's a rare house these days whose indoor air so pristine that no measures are necessary to improve it's quality. But the sad truth is that most houses could use some help at cleaning up the indoor air. So, this chapter will offer some approaches you can take to make your home's interior atmosphere healthier.

Air Purification and Cleaning

A wide range of strategies are touted in the marketplace today to purify or clean the air—and they have an equally wide range of effectiveness. In the following sections, both strategies and effectiveness will discussed.

Simple Indoor Air Improvement Methods

Of course, good ventilation (the exchanging of stale indoor air for fresh outdoor air) and routine house cleaning are very important, and should help prevent or eliminate many household odors and pollutants. However, extra measures may be necessary from time to time. In certain of these cases, simple, inexpensive, non-mechanical solutions may be all that's necessary.

Popular Odor Control Measures.

The following methods are popular ones that people use to control odors in their homes. The best choices are those that are the least toxic, least persistently odorous in their own right, and the most effective at removing the original objectionable odor. (See also *Controlling Closet Mustiness* on page 513.)

Activated Charcoal

Sometimes, a pie pan filled with *activated charcoal* helps eliminate odors within a small, confined space. Activated charcoal (made from coconut husks, as well as other substances) works because it has a tremendous capacity to *adsorb.* This means that odor molecules (from tobacco smoke, metabolic products of bacteria, as well as many compounds given off by plastics and other synthetic materials) quickly interact with, and adhere, to the many surfaces of the activated charcoal granules.

If you choose to use a pan of activated charcoal, place it so it can't be easily tipped. You'll also need to replace the activated charcoal occasionally when you find it isn't adsorbing any more. Activated charcoal is available from **E.L. Foust Co., Inc.** and many other manufacturers of air filters. It's also often sold in pet shops and pet-supply centers because of it's use in aquarium filters.

Active-Enzyme and Citrus-Based Deodorizers

One of the newest methods to eliminate, not to cover up, odors is with active enzymes. These are produced by benign bacterial cultures. The enzymes allow certain types of organic gases to be broken down so they can be ingested as food for the bacteria.

One product of this kind you may want to use is Nature's Key Odor Eliminator, a specially formulated, unscented, active-enzyme product. It can be ordered from **Dasun Co.** A similar product, Ens-Odor is handled by **Bio Designs**. More enzyme products (some naturally scented) see *Removing Rug & Carpet Stains* on page 155.

Another natural option is to deodorize with citrus compounds. These solvents have the ability to break-down certain odor molecules. One product of this kind is Pet-Clean Pet Stain Cleaner & Neutralizer (**Orange-Sol Household Products, Inc.**). Pet-Clean uses an orange-solvent base, so it will leave a slight "orangey" natural scent behind. This product can be ordered directly from its manufacturer.

Aerosol Deodorizers and Disinfectants

Many typical deodorizing sprays are little more than diluted, aerated, synthetic fragrances. However, those labeled as *disinfectants* usually have, in addition, chemicals capable of inhibiting or killing certain biological contaminants, especially bacteria and mold.

Of course, the ingredients of these spray products are usually absorbed by your walls, floors, and furnishings—and you yourself, if you inhale them. Therefore, it may be best to avoid deodorizing and disinfecting sprays, especially if you're an asthmatic or sensitive person. It should be remembered that some of the odors created by these sprays can be very long-lasting (see *Problems with Scents* on page 72).

However, one alternative spray you may want to try is Smells Begone. This is a nontoxic, nonstaining, unscented product that is specifically designed to eliminate many kinds of household odors. Local health-food stores sometimes carry it. If not, you can mail-order it from **Harmony**.

Baking Soda and Borax

Often, a safe solution to odors in small, confined spaces is simply to use an open box of baking soda. Of course, this has been done for years in refrigerators, but it can also reduce odors in your freezer and in closets. Baking soda is effective at eliminating odors because it's able to absorb them. However, be sure it doesn't get spilled, and remember to replace it from time to time.

Of course sprinkling baking soda on carpeting can help to reduce odors originating from the carpet fibers. You can use ordinary baking soda, or the type formulated especially for this job. However, if you choose a baking-soda carpet deodorizer, it's best not to use one that's scented. Whatever type of baking soda you choose, allow time for it to do it's job, then vacuum thoroughly. Finally, a box of baking soda can be poured into the bottom of your cat's litter box to reduce odors there. If you want to learn more deodorizing uses for baking soda, you'll want to read *Baking Soda: Over 500 Fabulous, Fun and Frugal Uses You've Probably Never Thought Of* by Vicki Lansky. This may be available from your local library or favorite bookseller.

Another simple odor eliminator is to use a small amount of unscented borax in a bowl. As with baking soda used in this manner, it can absorb odors to freshen a small space. Again, be careful not to tip it over, and remember to replace it occasionally. Note: It's important that borax not be ingested, so make certain that small children and pets can't get access to it. Also, never sprinkle borax on carpeting. It's granular texture may cut into carpet fibers.

Fabric Softener Sheets

A new household tip these days is to use fabric-softener dryer sheets as air fresheners. This use is now promoted through manufacturer's advertising, and by household-hint "experts" as a wonderful, and simple, way to freshen up your home. So, placing scented dryer sheets under your area rugs, in your clothing drawers, and on closet shelves are all suggested

Fabric-softener dryer sheets are typically non-woven pieces of rayon that are saturated with *surfactants* (compounds able to lessen water's surface tension), and synthetic perfume. In truth, all they can do is contaminate your home with their own pervasive, odiferous compounds. They will not freshen anything. If you need to freshen your home, air it out and clean it, or rely on a really useful, safe, absorbent or adsorbing product.

Potpourri

One very popular odor-control method is to use *potpourri*. While some potpourri consists of natural dried herbs, spices, and flower petals, others also have added perfumes, either natural (as essential oils) or synthetic. However, no matter what is in them, potpourri can only mask unpleasant odors—not eliminate them. Then, too, potpourri's own fragrant emanations can actually be more bothersome to certain sensitive individuals than the original unpleasant odors they were meant to disguise. (See *Problems with Scents* on page 72.)

If you still want to use potpourri, consider only the all-natural types, to avoid breathing synthetic chemicals, and use only a minimal amount. Because the odors will permeate and linger, place potpourri only in areas where its odor won't be bothersome for an extended period of time. To purchase potpourri, check in department and health-food stores. Other places to check are craft stores. In addition, your local library and bookstore will likely have books on how to make your own.

Scented Candles

Scented candles have really become popular, to not only add "a certain ambiance," but to cover up less-than-pleasant room odors. However, simply put, they are not a healthy odor-control solution.

Of course scented candles, when lit, give off smoke and combustion gases, both of which can be unhealthy, and can cause respiratory inflammation. Research has also revealed that burning scented candles produces noxious *volatile organic compounds (VOCs)* such as acetone, benzene, and xylene. Still other compounds that are released include carbon dioxide and lead. Surprisingly, lead is used in many candle wicks! To top if off, the fragrances (usually synthetic) in these candles only act as a cover up, so odor molecules aren't eliminated. In the end, candles simply add more pollution to your home.

Because many of the synthetic fragrances used in candles aren't particularly combustible, burning scented candles results in incomplete combustion, and the release greater amounts of microscopic soot particles than unscented candles. As a result, burning very many of them indoors has caused thousands of dollars in soot damage in houses. When this type of damage first started appearing in homes, it was blamed on the furnace, or on chimney problems, but it has now been shown to be the result of burning candles. Of course, soot can certainly be caused by furnace or chimney problems, but whatever the source, soot isn't healthy for people to breathe.

Solid, Stick-Up, and Plug-In Deodorizers

Solid, stick-up, and plug-in deodorizers have become the rage in recent years, especially the plug-in types. They are generally composed of nothing more than a synthetic scent in a gel, wax, or some other solid or semi-solid base (or perhaps in an imbedding pad). All are supposed to "freshen the air" continually. Therefore, the synthetic perfumes are always wafting about, as are the solid or semi-solid base ingredients. It should be noted that some people find plug-in air fresheners particularly bothersome. That's because they're designed to warm up to increase their ability to *volatilize* (evaporate into the air) their chemicals.

Interestingly, **Anderson Laboratories, Inc.** of West Hartford, VT decided to research the healthfulness of these types of deodorizers by exposing mice to one popular type. Their report, "The Toxic Effects of Air Freshener Emissions" (*Archives of Environmental Health*, 1997, Vol. 52, #6), found that acute respiratory and neurological effects (abnormal gait, reflexes, balance, and athletic performance) were experienced by mice as a result of exposure to the complex mixture of chemicals emitted by the air freshener. Using information garnered from manufacturer's literature, this independent research lab concluded that some people, too, could experience eye, nose, and throat irritation, respiratory difficulties (such as asthma-like symptoms), and neurological effects (fatigue, confusion, dizziness) when exposed to this air freshener.

By the way, **Anderson Laboratories, Inc.** has actually "evaluated several air fresheners and found each of the ones we tested produced several forms of toxicity, especially to the eyes, nose, throat, lungs and nervous systems." It was further discovered that certain air freshening products contain parp-dichlorobenzene, a known carcinogen. If you're interested in booklets, video tapes and copies of published papers concerning this air freshener research, the lab has them available for sale.

Obviously, scented, stick-up, and plug-in deodorizers are not recommended for healthy households. If you want to use something, consider using more benign materials such as baking soda, borax, zeolite, etc.

Zeolite

Zeolite is the name of a family of naturally occurring minerals. As with activated charcoal, zeolite works by the process of *adsorption*. Pollutant molecules are able to cling to it's surfaces through what's called the *electrostatic force*. (Electrostatic force causes like-charged molecules to repel and those with unlike charges to attract.) A real advantage to using zeolite is that it can often be renewed and reused many times, if it's in granular or chunk form.

Once the contaminated surface is no longer capable of adsorbing pollutants, the zeolite can be placed in the sun and, after a day or two, many of the adsorbed odors and gases will be released and dissipated into the outdoor air, thus reactivating the zeolite surface.

It must be noted that zeolite doesn't work on every airborne pollutant (although it seems to work fairly well with formaldehyde and ammonia compounds), and different individuals have reported varying success with it. In some cases, people have said that it's worked "like a miracle," while others have said it seemed to do very little. Obviously, zeolite's effectiveness depends on the particular kind of zeolite, the presence or absence of impurities and other natural mineral compounds, how saturated the zeolite is, the type of contaminants in the air, the quantity of contaminants, how big the room is, where the zeolite is placed, your personal expectations, and your particular olfactory sensitivity.

If you want to buy zeolite in a renewable form, Dasun Natural Zeolite crystals, in convenient two-pound mesh bags (**Dasun Co.**), are available from the maker or from **Bio Designs**. EcoFresh General Purpose Deodorizing Mineral Pouches are sold by **TerrEssentials**. These are a set of two, rechargeable, 8 oz. pouches of zeolite crystals. Zeolite packets in several sizes can also be bought from **The Allergy Store, Harmony**, and **American Environmental Health Foundation**.

Refresh-A natural zeolite in a mesh bag is now available in a number of sizes. They're said to last 8-10 months before you need to reactive them in the sunshine. Refresh-A Closet, in a three-piece set (two 6 oz. bags and one 32 oz. bag) which is apparently enough for two small closets and one walk-in closet is available from both **Real Goods** and **Improvements**. Refresh-A Basement designed to be effective for 600 square feet is sold by **Solutions** and **Real Goods**. Refresh-A House, which you're supposed to place in the air return of your central air conditioner or furnace system, is said to be useful for 800 square feet. It can be purchased from **Improvements**. In addition, All Natural zeolite in two-pound "breather bags" are offered by **healthyhome.com**.

By the way, powdered zeolite can be sprinkled on rugs and carpets to adsorb odors. Simply sprinkle it over the surface of your carpet, give it some time to work, then vacuum thoroughly. Wearing a dust mask when doing this is suggested. (See *Personal Protective Gear* on page 264.) A powdered zeolite product you may want to try is EcoFresh Deodorizing Powder available from **TerrEssentials**. Dasun All Natural Zeolite Powder (**Dasun Co.**), in a 2-pound shaker container, can be purchased from the manufacturer and **Bio Designs**. A two-pound shaker container, as well as a ten-pound bucket, of powered, natural zeolite are sold by **healthyhome.com**. Another source for powdered zeolite is **The Allergy Store**.

It should also be mentioned that *synthetic* zeolite products are also available. These use man-made minerals which are said to be of more consistent quality. Adsorb Star (formerly The Molecular Adsorber) (**CYA Products, Inc.**) is one popular synthetic zeolite odor-control unit. It comes packaged in a replaceable 16 oz. canister with a metal stand. Inside are uniform synthetic zeolite pellets, with a negatively charged surface, that are mixed with a few blue granules. (When the blue color turns to pink, it's time to replace the canister.) The manufacturer says that it's able to "attract and attach molecules ranging from 2-12 angstroms in size." (10,000 angstroms = 1 micron). Interestingly, a large portion of odors and gases fit this size.

To use the Adsorb Star, you remove the caps from both ends, then place or mount the unit about two feet above the source of the odor problem. Suggested uses for the Adsorb Star are to help counter cat-litter-box, smoking, and musty-basement odors. It should be noted that one canister is suggested to last 3-6 months. By the way, the maker says that it may take up to 72 hours to notice any change in the air quality. CYA synthetic zeolite products come in several sizes as well as other forms. Mail-order sources for Adsorb Star products include **N.E.E.D.S.** and **Allerx.**

Nox-out Air Purifiers use a synthetic zeolite similar to the Adsorb Star. This 16-oz. canister unit comes with wall or table mountings. Refills are available. You can buy Nox-out from **Dick Blick.**

Airing

There are few measures as effective as *airing,* to quickly improve the indoor air quality of your home. Of course, airing simply means opening two or more windows and allowing the fresh air to pass into the living space. Ideally, the open windows should be on different walls, so that *cross ventilation* (the air travels across the room) can occur. Using a window fan, which you can usually buy at discount stores and building centers, can make airing even more efficient. Keep in mind that days when pollen counts and pollution levels are low are, obviously, superior times to do airing.

Incidentally, you may find that using window filters can offer some help to reduce the amount of incoming contaminants. Some are versions of *electrostatic filters.* While not efficient enough to stop every airborne pollutant, they're at least able to reduce the quantity of pollen allergens from entering your opened windows. Window Guard window filters are made with aluminum frames, and a patented baffle design. Replacement cartridges (said to last one to two years) are available. Window Guards are carried by **Priorities.** Another source for window filters is **Allergy Clean Environments.** And **American Environmental Health Foundation** has some with a metal framework, in four sizes, that are expandable.

You might be interested in knowing that add-on filters are available for window fans, too. These may be found in season at building-supply centers or hardware stores. Blind-Brite Fan Filters (**Orange-Sol Household Products, Inc.**) are constructed of synthetic micro-filter fabric and made to mount on table fans. They come in packs of two and can be ordered from the manufacturer.

Still another option is to use a Honeywell Electrostatic Air Filter Window Fan (**Honeywell, Inc.**). This low-profile unit (it measures only $7^3/8$" tall) comes with extendible, adjustable side panels to snugly fit into a window. Replacement filters are available. This Honeywell item is sold by **eMD.com, Allergy Control Products, Inc.** and **Priorities.**

Finally, from **E.L. Foust Co., Inc.,** you can purchase Sorb-A-Pad. This is an activated-charcoal-impregnated, $1/4$"-thick polyester filter that can be purchased in different lengths. Custom framing is available for window or room air conditioners.

In general, window filters can't be extremely efficient. That's because very efficient filters tend to block more of the air flow, so they need more-powerful fans to move air through them. So, what if you install a powerful fan blowing out of one window, an install a very efficient filter in another window to remove the entering pollen? The problem with this is that most houses are leaky enough so that the incoming air will enter through the path of least resistance. In other words, the air will easily enter (unfiltered) through the tiny, invisible gaps and cracks all houses have, rather through the window that is now semi-blocked by the more efficient filter.

Using House Plants as Air Filters

It's become a popular belief (almost legendary) that house plants, especially spider plants (*Chlorophytum elatum* variety *viitum*), have the capacity to clean a home's air of most of its airborne pollutants. Therefore, spider plants, also known as ribbon plants, have almost become floral celebrities. (These plants have long slender leaves, white flower clusters, and long shoots with tiny new plants attached to the ends of them.) Unfortunately, although they're attractive, the air cleaning capacity of spider plants has been greatly exaggerated.

Early research suggested that these plants (and also golden pothos plants, *Scindapsusu aureus*) were capable of fairly efficient removal of certain gaseous pollutants (but not particulates). But these initial studies, which were performed by the National Aeronautics and Space Administration (NASA) in the mid-1980s, were conducted under very limited artificial laboratory conditions. The results from this preliminary work were widely reported in the press at the time of the initial research, and they continue to be reported.

Not long after NASA's work with plants, more comprehensive research at Ball State University simulating a real-life situation contradicted the NASA assumptions. In fact, the new studies showed that house plants were far less effective as air cleaners than originally believed—even under laboratory conditions. Therefore, although plants bring a sense of nature indoors and produce oxygen, they won't reduce your indoor-air-pollution levels by very much at all. (See also *House Plants* on page 364.) In fact, sometimes they can actually increase the likelihood of moisture and mold problems.

Register Filters

Recently, filters designed to be placed over a room's furnace/central-air-conditioning registers have been marketed. Often, they're made of a nonwoven, synthetic material and sometimes have activated charcoal or *electrets* (plastic with a permanent static charge to attract and hold onto certain pollutant particles) imbedded in them. Generally, they're held in place by simple clips, sticky strips, Velcro, etc. Sources for register filters include Filtrex Vent Filters from **Allergy Clean Environments** and Vent-Pro from **Allergy Control Products, Inc.** Bind-Rite Air Vent Filters made of synthetic micro-fiber fabric in 12- and 24-filter packs, in various standard and custom sizes, are said "not to affect air flow if properly maintained." These are made and sold by **Orange-Sol Household Products, Inc.** In addition, **American Environmental Health Foundation** sells three versions of register filters. Baby's Room combines activated charcoal and electrostatic filtering, Family & Living Room is just an electrostatic filter, and the Kitchen & Bath version is primarily an activated-carbon filter. Others register filters are sold by **Well & Good** and **Harmony**. However, while register filters sound like a good, simple, and straight-forward filtering method, they aren't.

You see, any fabric that covers a register (even partially) will most likely restrict the air flow—at least somewhat. That may not seem like a big deal. However, even hindering the air's passage to a small degree will set up air-pressure anomalies throughout the entire system. Of course, the more registers that are covered, and the dirtier the filters, the more the air flow is restricted and therefore, altered.

Here's what can happen. When the airflow is restricted, the air pressure builds up inside the ducts. When the air pressure builds up, it forces air to leak out through small gaps and seams in the ductwork. (Most duct systems are actually incredibly leaky.) Because the ductwork is often located inside wall cavities, in attics, in basements, etc., it is in contact with any insulation, insect nests, mold, dirt, and debris that happens to be there. So, the air leaking out of the ducts picks up some of these pollutants and eventually leaks back into your living space. As a result, it's possible for your home's air to end up being more contaminated after using register filters, than before you installed them. This is all the result of upsetting the air pressures in the house.

Of course, the air pressures in your house could be upset in the first place, only to be made worse by installing register filters. Admittedly, air pressures in houses can be a complicated subject. For a thorough explanation, including all the implications, as well as solutions, you'll want to read *Understanding Ventilation*, by John Bower. It can be ordered from **The Healthy House Institute** of through your favorite bookseller.

Air Improvement Equipment

Often, something more than a simple odor reducing method is needed in a home. This section will cover a variety of these, ranging from the various strategies used, to descriptions of some specific equipment you might choose to purchase.

Common Strategies

Under the headings that follow are the most common strategies used in today's air-improvement units. Because so many units use two, four, six, or even more of these approaches, it's a good idea to understand what they're actually capable of doing, and whether they're really necessary in your situation—before paying extra to have multiple strategies in a single device.

Air Filters

Air filters work by letting air pass through a material (often called *media*). The media is designed to trap certain substances considered pollutants. Many people assume that, if they purchase an air filter, it'll solve any indoor air problem they have. This is faulty reasoning. Air filters often aren't sufficient to completely decontaminate a home if it has stagnant air, mildew, outgassing carpets and furnishings, or intolerable wall paint. Adequate fresh-air ventilation, proper home repair and maintenance, and the use of less-toxic construction, cleaning, and furnishing materials are always the best techniques to ensure good indoor air quality. What air filters *can* do is *polish* the air. In other words, they work best if they only have to handle minor air pollution problems or polluting situations of short duration.

For those with allergies, certain particulate (small particle) air filters can help capture airborne dust-mite body parts, feces, etc. Again, however, they can't trap *all* the dust-mite debris in the air. So, the best approach is to decorate and clean your home so that dust mites find it difficult to proliferate. (See also *Dust Mites* on page 410.) Then, a portable particulate-removing filter in the bedroom, for example, may be all that's needed to reduce the remaining airborne dust-mite concentration to make comfortable sleeping possible.

Incidentally, it's important *not* to assume that your furnace filter will do much to clean the air in your living space. The common replaceable, thin, fiberglass type of furnace filter does little to improve your home's indoor air quality. Actually, they are considered *furnace* filters, not *people* filters, and they are designed to only capture very large particles capable of damaging your furnace fan's motor and other parts—not to protect you and your family's health. However, there are some better-than-average alternative furnace filters that are specially designed to protect you and your family from airborne contaminants (at least to a certain degree).

It should be pointed out that many chemically sensitive people are bothered by air filters themselves. Even though the purpose of an air filter is to remove contaminants from the air, many also add tiny amounts of potentially problematic substances to the air at the same time. For example, many filters are held together with a resin or glue that has slight *outgas-*

sing characteristics (able to emit synthetic compounds); some filters give off *ozone* (a highly reactive, unstable form of oxygen); and some individuals find they can't tolerate certain types of activated charcoal (although coconut shell is often used, other types can be substituted). While an air filter may turn out to be just what you need, be forewarned of the possible limitations you may encounter.

There are several basic air-filtering methods with which you should become familiar. Knowing them will help you make a more informed choice when you're ready to purchase air improvement equipment for your home. An important point to remember is that there are two fundamental types of filters; those that remove gaseous contaminants, and those that can trap *particulates* (tiny solid particles). As it turns out, only materials such as activated charcoal, activated alumina, and zeolite can remove gases—all the other types of media remove only particulates. So, if you want to capture both gaseous and particulate contaminants, the filtering equipment you select *must* utilize at least two filtering strategies.

Adsorption Filters

One of the most common air filtering methods currently being marketed is *activated-charcoal* (also known as activated-carbon). Units with activated charcoal are designed to remove polluting gases such as volatile organic compounds (VOCs), but they aren't capable of removing all of them. Certain *low-molecular weight* VOCs, such as formaldehyde, aren't adsorbed by standard activated-charcoal media (Molecular weight is the total atomic weight of all atoms making up a molecule; large, complicated molecules are composed of many atoms and, thus, tend to have high molecular weights. Formaldehyde, is a fairly simple molecule, so it has a low molecular weight.).

Surprisingly, research has shown that activated charcoal can adsorb large quantities of certain polluting gases, but can then release them slowly back into clean air. While this certainly isn't ideal, a low average level of contaminants is better than experiencing a few large-exposure events. So, despite this characteristic, activated charcoal should still be considered an advantageous filtering material—even for chemically sensitive individuals.

On the plus side, activated charcoal is relatively affordable. However, the prices will vary depending on the particular type purchased, the quantity, and the buying source. And, of course, the activated charcoal used in filters should be replaced every few months—or whenever it no longer seems to be working effectively. Some devices using it must have an entire activated-charcoal cartridge unit replaced, others can simply be emptied and refilled.

But exactly what is activated charcoal? Defined, it's charcoal (coconut shell is one of the more popular types, but it can also be made from coal, wood, etc.) that's been subjected to a special steam process that causes its surface to become extremely pitted and porous. This creates a tremendously large surface area, resulting in greater adsorption capacity. Adsorption is a chemical-physical process whereby gases adhere to a surface. With a great deal of surface area, activated charcoal has a great deal of adsorption capacity. It should also be noted that some particulate matter can become inadvertently trapped in activated-charcoal media. So, it does have a limited ability in this regard, but it is primarily a gas filter, not a particulate filter.

If formaldehyde needs to be removed from your indoor air, your filtering equipment can be equipped with a specially treated activated charcoal that's specifically designed to adsorb formaldehyde, or another type adsorption material that's better at adsorbing low-molecular-weight gases. One substance that's often combined with activated charcoal for this purpose is *activated alumina impregnated with potassium permanganate.*

To produce simple activated alumina, regular granular alumina (aluminum oxide, the compound from which commercial aluminum is derived) is heated. This causes the alumina granules to acquire a very porous, pitted structure. At this point, the granules are capable of adsorbing certain gases. Then, the activated alumina is impregnated with *potassium permanganate* (a dark-purplish, crystalline, water-soluble solid material). The now-impregnated activated alumina is able to adsorb an even wider range of gaseous contaminants—including formaldehyde. Often, manufacturers give a catchy name to their particular brand of this material, such as PuraPel, Hydestop, or Purafil, or they may give a special name to their particular mixture of activated charcoal and activated alumina impregnated with potassium permanganate such as Formaldepur or Chem Blend. As it turns out, activated charcoal, activated alumina, and mixtures of the two are available as replaceable filtering media, or in a complete filtering unit for use in forced-air furnace or air-conditioning systems, as well as in a "loose-fill" form for many types of portable filtering devices. Of course, like activated charcoal, activated alumina must be replaced periodically as it becomes contaminated.

Another adsorbing substance that's gained popularity in the last few years is *zeolite*. The surface of this natural mineral (it also comes in a synthetic form) allows certain oppositely charged gaseous pollutants to electrostatically adhere to it. (This capacity is called the *electrostatic force*.) It must be noted that zeolite doesn't work on every airborne pollutant, and different individuals have reported varying success with it. However, it's supposedly capable of adsorbing some of the lower-weight-molecular volatile organic compounds (VOC)s, such as formaldehyde. In actual use, some people have reported that it's worked "like a miracle," while others have said it seemed to do very little. Obviously, zeolite's effectiveness depends on the type of contaminants in the air, the quantity of contaminants, how big the room is, where the zeolite was placed, how contaminated the zeolite's surface is, your personal expectations, and your particular olfactory sensitivity.

If you're a chemically sensitive person, it would be wise to experiment will several types of adsorption media to find a product that you personally find tolerable (see *Testing* on page 62). As it turns out, some people find that they react negatively to certain kinds of activated charcoal. To help you determine which material you best tolerate, Test Kits are available from **E.L. Foust Co., Inc.** This company sells several different types of activated charcoal, as well as impregnated activated alumina and zeolite, in bulk quantities, as do many other filter suppliers.

It should be mentioned that activated charcoal and activated charcoal mixtures, can initially be very dusty. Therefore, if you have a new filter containing this material, it is a good idea to vacuum both sides of it thoroughly before installing it. If you are refilling a portable canister-type filter, vacuum the canister thoroughly after you fill it, and before you initially operate the unit.

By the way, it should be mentioned that non-woven polyester (or another synthetic material) impregnated with one of these media is now being used by many air-improvement-equipment manufacturers. This combination captures large particulates as well some gases. But unless there's sufficient adsorption or absorption granules bonded to the material, it's usefulness is limited.

Extended-Surface Filters

Extended-surface filters are made of a pleated material, usually polyester or fiberglass, that is held together with a synthetic resin. These filters are often 4–5" thick. The deep-pleated design creates a very large filtering surface, without greatly increasing the resistance to the air flowing through it—a problem that can occur with many types of filters. While some extended-surface filters are used in portable units, they're also made for whole-house applications. In such cases, they usually require the installation of a special housing in which to mount them. Such a housing would be permanently installed in the duct system of a forced-air furnace or air conditioner. It should also be mentioned that 1"-thick extended-surface filters are also available. These can be used as a simple replacement for your standard (inefficient) furnace/air-conditioner filter.

Extended-surface filters are fairly effective as particulate filters. In fact, they're actually classified as *medium-efficiency filters*. They're designed to trap many types of the airborne solids, including most pollens. However, they aren't capable of adsorbing gases. Extended-surface filters are usually moderately priced but, in whole-house systems, they will require the services of a professional heating and cooling contractor to initially install the housing in your duct system. As with most filters, the media (the pleated material) must be replaced periodically. Once the housing is in place, you can change the media yourself, something that is typically done once a year.

One consideration to keep in mind, especially if you're a chemically sensitive person, is that the synthetic materials making up these filters can give off slight odors. However, some people have found that by putting a new filter in their oven at a low temperature (200°F or less), for about two hours, it often helps eliminate most bothersome smells. If you're considering this, first contact the manufacturer to see if its filter will withstand such a procedure.

If you decide to go ahead and "bake" your extended-surface filter, make absolutely certain that you have adequate ventilation when you do it. You should close off your kitchen from the rest of the house, open the kitchen windows, and operate the range-hood fan (vented to the outdoors) on high speed. Once the filter has finished baking, use hot pads or oven mitts to place it outdoors to cool. However, continue to keep your kitchen windows open and the range-hood fan turned on for at least 30 minutes, and heat the oven up to a high temperature to burn off any odors that may have accumulated within the oven itself.

HEPA and ULPA Filters

A *HEPA* filter is a very special type of extended-surface filter. The acronym HEPA stands for <u>h</u>igh <u>e</u>fficiency <u>p</u>articulate <u>a</u>rresting (or sometimes <u>a</u>ir or <u>a</u>ccumulator). Interestingly, these filters were originally developed by the U.S. Atomic Energy Commission (AEC) during World War II to trap radioactive plutonium particles in nuclear laboratories.

HEPA filters are generally made of fiberglass or polyester fibers held together by a synthetic resin. These filters have extremely tiny pores, so the airflow through them is very restricted. Therefore, powerful fans (which are often fairly noisy) are necessary to forcibly push air through them. HEPAs are sometimes termed *absolute filters*, and it's easy to understand why. Most HEPA filters are capable of trapping 97%, or more, of particles as small as 0.3 microns (a micron is one millionth of a meter)—some are designed to be even more efficient. Not surprisingly, vacuums fitted with very efficient HEPA filters are used to remove all traces of contaminants during asbestos-cleanup operations. HEPA air filters are commonly used in research laboratories, and in the manufacture of delicate electronic components. However, although these filters are very effective at removing particulates, including dust-mite body parts and feces, they're unable to remove any contaminating gases.

HEPA filters have other drawbacks as well. For example, they're usually fairly expensive. Therefore, to extend the life of the HEPA filter itself, most filtering units that use HEPA technology have one or more prefilters to first capture most of the larger particles. With a prefilter, the HEPA media will usually only need to be replaced annually.

It's important to note that some sensitive individuals find that the synthetic material used to make HEPA filters gives off odors they find to be bothersome. In a few cases, despite the advantages of particulate-free air, these odors have proven to be intolerable. However, if an activated-charcoal filter is used *after* the HEPA filter, this will usually minimize any objectionable odors. Yet, you also should also understand that most people, even many allergic or chemically sensitive ones, often don't require the tremendous efficiency of a HEPA filter anyway. Unless someone smokes in your home, other less-efficient filtering approaches will often work just fine to remove many of the common allergenic pollutants.

It should be added that recently, ultra-efficient *ULPA* (*u*ltra *l*ow *p*enetration *a*ir) *filters* are now available. These sometimes have an efficiency as great as 99.999% at capturing very minute particulates as small as 0.12 microns. Essentially, these are HEPAs to the extreme and will, therefore, require even more powerful fans to force air through them. An ULPA in-home air filter is often a case of "overkill" because it's doubtful that the added capturing ability will make any difference in the health of most users. Actually, even though they are microscopic in size, mold spores and pollen grains tend to be relatively large particulates, so even a HEPA can be overkill—if that's all you're interested in capturing.

Electrostatic and Electret Filters

Electrostatic and *electret filters*, rely on *electrostatic force* to work. An electrostatic force causes similarly-charged molecules to repel and those with opposite charges to attract. These types of filters rely on simple static electricity, rather than live electric current, for their electrostatic charge.

Electrostatic filters are made of a special plastic media, such as vinyl, polyester, or polystyrene, and they are typically about 1" thick. Most filters of this type are meant to replace typical standard forced-air furnace/air-conditioning filters. Some companies also offer models that fit in windows.

Some electrostatic filters become statically charged as a result of the friction of the air passing through their synthetic media. However, other types are precharged, using *electrets*. An electret is a special plastic material that has a permanent static charge. Electrets get their charge after being melted and resolidified in the presence of a very strong electric field.

In the filtering process, those particulates in the air that happen to be charged are attracted to—and adhere to—the portions of the plastic electrostatic filter media that carries an opposite charge. Models using electrets, in particular, often have both positively and negatively charged areas in their makeup. It should be noted that, of all the particulate pollutants in the air, many are positively charged—although others are negatively charged or uncharged.

Electrostatic filters are relatively inexpensive and constructed so that the air flowing through them is only slightly restricted. While these filters aren't extremely efficient, they are able to capture many mold spores and pollen grains. Of course, electrostatic filters are not capable of trapping gases of any kind.

Sometimes, dirty electrostatic filters can be washed off so their surfaces are again able to capture particulates. However, this should be done only if the manufacturer allows it. Most electrostatic filters should be replaced when they're no longer capable of retaining an electrical charge. This will vary with the brand, and how dirty the air in question is. It should be noted that the plastic media can sometimes be bothersome for certain sensitive individuals.

Polyester and Other Synthetic Material Filters

Polyester (or another synthetic fiber), often in a nonwoven form, is used in many air-improving devices. Sometimes it's a relatively thin fabric, in other applications it's much thicker and loftier. In either case, it's inexpensive to produce, and it can usually filter out fairly large particles. Therefore, it's the most common media used as a prefilter for a HEPA filter, as well as in units that rely on multiple air-filtering strategies. By the way, many synthetic-fiber filters can often be hand washed, allowed to air dry, and then reinserted—so they may rarely need replacing.

Today, it's not uncommon for polyester (or another synthetic fiber) to have other compounds and substances added to it. This might be some type of biocide, which would be added to inhibit the bacteria and mold that could otherwise grow on it, and subsequently contaminate the air. One of the more inert antimicrobial treatments is Aegis Microbe Shield (**Aegis Environments**) which was developed by Dow Corning Corporation. This patented technology uses *organosilicon agents* which are extremely minute crystals of silicon (one of the main components of sand and glass). These are permanently "covalently or ionically bonded" to the surface of the filter media. This means that bonding is on a molecular level, and it does not involve glues or other types of adhesives. So, items containing Aegis Microbe Shield can be repeatedly washed, and it will not come off. Another plus is that it's also considered "non-sensitizing." How Aegis specifically works is by "mechanical interruption of cell walls." In other words, the microscopic silicon slivers literally stab mold and bacteria to death. Therefore, no poison of any kind is necessary. One brand of filters that use this technology is Purolator.

Other polyester (or other synthetic fiber) filters have an innate static charge to attract and hold onto particles. Still others have *electrets* imbedded in them. (See *Electrostatic and Electret Filters* above.)

Probably the most popular addition to these types of filters is an adsorbent media such as zeolite, activated charcoal, and/or activated alumina with potassium permanganate (see *Adsorption Filters* on page 551). With an adsorbent material, the polyester material can now function to remove both particulate and gaseous air pollutants. Of course how successfully this is accomplished depends on the amount of adsorbent actually present. If there's only a small quantity, then only a minimal job will likely be done. If there's a great deal, then you can expect more gases to be removed. By the way, if a glue or resin is required to hold the adsorbent granules in place, it could add it's own odor, which could pose problems for some very sensitive persons.

Electrostatic Precipitators

Electrostatic precipitators, also known as *electronic air cleaners*, don't operate by "straining" pollutants out of the air, like the filters discussed above. Therefore, technically they aren't called filters, however, they do capture and retain pollutants. Today, most electrostatic precipitators are designed to be permanently installed in the ductwork of forced-air furnace/air-conditioner systems, although some portable filtering units also use this technology. (Note: These units will not trap contaminating gases, they only work on particulates.)

Electrostatic precipitators, like electrostatic filters and electrets, rely on *electrostatic force* to remove pollutants from the air (Electrostatic force causes like-charged molecules to repel, and those with unlike charges to attract.). However, while the electrostatic filters and electrets discussed above use static electricity, electrostatic precipitators require live current to do their job. There are other major differences as well.

Electrostatic precipitators contain metal wires that have a strong electrical charge. As the air passes by these wires, any particulate matter in the air takes on the same charge as the wires. The air (with its now-charged particulates) then passes into a *collection chamber* containing a series of metal plates. These plates have also been charged, but with a charge that's opposite of the wires. As a result, the charged particulates become attracted to the collection plates and cling to them.

As it turns out, dust and debris clinging to these plates can quickly build up. This causes electrostatic precipitators to steadily, sometimes rapidly, become less and less efficient. Therefore, the metal plates in electrostatic precipitators must be removed and cleaned periodically, in extreme cases this can be as often as once a week. Fortunately, these plates can be washed satisfactorily by simply placing them in an automatic dishwasher. Hand washing in a tub is also possible. All you do is slide the unit out of its housing (this automatically disconnects the electricity), then you clean it, and replace it.

One notable feature of electrostatic precipitators is that, unlike other filters, they have virtually no restriction to the flow of air. This is because there's no actual media of any type to hinder the air's passage through the unit. Therefore, there's also no filter media to replace, which is another advantage. However, electrostatic precipitators are relatively expensive, they are certainly not as efficient as HEPA filters, and they can quickly lose much of their effectiveness as they get dirty—unless they're regularly cleaned.

Electrostatic precipitators also produce a small amount of toxic, reactive ozone (O_3) gas when they are operating. However, a filter containing activated charcoal, which is installed after the electrostatic precipitator, can usually adsorb any ozone that has been produced. You should also know that tiny electric sparks can be generated inside electrostatic precipitators. These can be heard as a slight "popping" sound that some people find irritating. In addition, the sparks can cause some of the particulate matter, that is attached to the collection plates, to be released back in the air you breathe.

Ultraviolet (UV) Air Purifiers

Ultraviolet (UV) air purifiers have the capacity to kill (or inactivate) some types of molds, bacteria, and viruses. This ability, however, varies with the specific microorganisms exposed (and it also depends on the life stage they're in), the wavelength and intensity of the UV light, as well as the duration of the exposure.

What is UV light? Ultraviolet light is a particular form of electromagnetic radiation. It can have a wavelength from 15 nanometers (nm) long up to 400 nm, which is the beginning of the visible-light range. (One nm is 10^{-9} meters.) So, UV radiation is shorter than the waves of visible light, but longer than X-rays. Interestingly, because it's not in the visible-light range, our eyes can't see it. (It was only discovered in a photochemical experiment in 1801.)

Of course, everyone knows that UV light from the sun can cause sunburn. But it can also cause skin cancers and cataracts. When microorganisms are exposed to it, the UV is absorbed by their cell nuclei. This causes chemical alterations in the genetic material stored there, and it's these changes that ultimately prove lethal. Interestingly, it's been shown that the most effective UV light for *sterilization* (extermination of microorganisms) is in the 220-300 nm range. (This is called the abiotic range, which means that it is non-life sustaining.) As a result, it's in this range that UV germicidal lamps emit radiation.

While UV light has been shown to be useful against certain airborne infectious germs (this was first demonstrated in 1947 with studies involving tuberculosis bacilli), it's not been widely used, even in hospital settings. This has primarily been because the UV light can cause eye irritation, or damage, from not only the lamp, but also from reflections off other surfaces in the area. Another problem has been that UV lamps (which are typically low-pressure mercury-vapor tubes) must be kept immaculately clean to perform optimally. Also, these lamps typically degrade quickly during the first 100 hours they're on. In fact, commercial tubes are usually rated as though they've already past the 100-hour mark.

However, there are even more drawbacks. For example, while typical UV exposure may kill certain microorganisms, others are temporarily "put them out of commission" into a state that's termed *inactivation*. While this inactivation is due to the damage caused by the action of the UV light, a certain percentage of microorganisms can sometimes *reactivate* (repair themselves) in the presence of visible light or, in other cases, in darkness. Plus, studies have apparently shown that UV is not particularly effective against a number of microorganisms, such as airborne HIV. (HIV requires twice the amount of UV to be killed compared to other viruses.)

However, a bigger impediment to the widespread use of UV sterilization is that it can only affect those microorganisms that are actually exposed to it. If other germs are in a room's air that haven't been in the UV's presence, they will be unaffected, so they'll simply go on multiplying. Then, too, as soon as someone (or a pet) walks into a UV-treated room, a whole new set of microorganisms will reinfect the sterilized area. So, UV light is often best used for a small, focused job, rather than for general room air purification.

While UV air purifiers can be purchased as stand-alone units, they're now being incorporated in multi-strategy air filtering devices. As has been mentioned, you should keep in mind that they're only going to be partly effective at de-germing your home. However, if the purpose of the UV radiation is to purify the air coming into the filter, so that the filter itself will be less likely to become contaminated, that's may be more do-able. Another thing to keep in mind with a UV purifier is that the ultraviolet light will create a small amount of ozone (O_3) as it reacts with microorganisms. Plus, the UV lamp will need to be replaced in time. (It is often best to replace it before it burns out because of lamp degradation.)

If you'd like to try an ultraviolet purifier, the Pureaire UV is a plastic tabletop or wall-mounted unit. It's equipped with a two-speed fan. The lamp is said to last one year. Interestingly, it also has a DC adapter kit for use in the car. This unit is designed to be effective for an area of 600 sq. ft. You can purchase the Pureaire from **Allergy Relief Shop, Inc.**

For more information on ultraviolet purification, you may want to check out a technical book on the subject, *Disinfection, Sterilization, and Preservation* edited by Seymour S. Block, Ph.D. which should be obtainable through a technical library.

Ozone Generators

Ozone generators produce ozone (O_3) by continually creating electrical discharges. Often, the generators are designed so that this rate of production can be increased or decreased. But why do some people feel the need to use ozone generators as air cleaning devices? After all, ozone is a pungent-smelling, irritating gas. Because it's a very unstable form of oxygen, it's extremely reactive. In sufficient concentrations, it can severely irritate your skin, eyes, and mucous membranes. Ozone can also cause you to have breathing problems.

Ozone generators are usually thought a good idea because ozone is a powerful *oxidizing antiseptic* that's capable of killing many forms of bacteria and mold. (Unfortunately mold, either alive or dead, can provoke allergies.) Ozone can also reduce smoky odors in a home after a fire. However, to remove smokiness effectively, the ozone must be at a fairly high concentration. In either case, if you need to kill mold or remove smoke odors, it's best to leave this work to professional contractors. When a professional is operating such equipment at high concentrations, no one should be inside the house, and it should be aired out thoroughly afterwards.

Interestingly, a number of chemically sensitive persons have bought ozone generators to purposely break down airborne *volatile organic compounds* (*VOCs*) to which they would normally react. As it turns out, while ozone can break down some VOCs in the air, it can also react with some existing gases, or other materials and furnishing in the home, and create bothersome new pollutants—ones that weren't there before. Obviously, ozone is not *the* answer.

The truth is, ozone is a dangerous substance and should not be purposely added to a home's indoor air by homeowners. You should be aware that lawsuits by various governmental agencies have been filed against one of the largest makers and marketers of ozone machines—for unproved claims. The **EPA (Environmental Protection Agency)** is so concerned about the potential problems of ozone use in homes, that they've devoted space on their website to discussing its dangers.

To sum up, ozone is not recommended for consumers to use in their homes, period. Even though highly reputable companies such as **N.E.E.D.S.** (which handles Adirondack KleenAir portable and in-duct models), **Building for Health Materials Center** (which sells RainbowAir portable models) and **American Environmental Health Foundation** (which carries the RGF brand) offer them, you should seriously consider other options to improve your home's air.

Negative-Ion Generators

In recent years, *negative-ion generators* have become popular as air-cleaning devices, and even more recently, they're becoming included in multi-strategy air improving equipment. But exactly what are they? Negative-ion generators are actually specialized electronic devices that are capable of using electric current to create *negatively charged ions*—in this case, *free electrons*. These electrons are immediately spewed out into the air where they quickly attach themselves to airborne particulates, in the process giving them a negative charge. The newly negatively charged particulates then usually leave the air and cling to surfaces such as walls and ceilings that tend to be positively charged. This adhesion occurs because of the action of natural *electrostatic force* in which like-charged molecules repel but unlike-charged molecules attract.

Although most users of negative-ion generators won't notice it at first, their walls and ceilings will usually become steadily dirtier as the pollutant particles accumulate on them—although the air itself will likely be less contaminated. Therefore, it's necessary that these collecting surfaces be cleaned from time to time. However, you should realize that this is not only for aesthetic reasons. As it turns out, many pollutant particles will eventually reenter the air as they lose their negative charge. To counter this problem, some negative-ion generators have built-in air filters or collection plates so that the particles are more likely to be trapped inside the units themselves.

Unfortunately, it's doubtful that negative-ion generators can substantially clean air that is very polluted. And, they are apparently not particularly effective in reducing dust-mite allergens. Plus, charged particulates will apparently deposit in the respiratory track more readily than non-charged particulates. However, a Columbia University study released in

1995 found that negative-ion generators did help to alleviate some of the symptoms of SAD (Seasonal Affective Disorder), a depressive condition that occurs during the cold months of the year to some people. This may be due to the fact that an excess of negative ions in the air can, apparently, give a person a sense of well being. While this effect isn't well understood, the opposite effect has also been reported. That is, if for some reason, there is an excess of positively charged ions in the air can lead to an increase of seratonin in the body—something that can lead to irritability, insomnia, tension, and upset stomach.

So, for those with the "wintertime blues," and perhaps in situations where allergic or sensitive individuals are unable to tolerate other air-cleaning devices, or they can't afford a more efficient device, stand-alone negative-ion generators may be beneficial.

One of the most popular brands of negative-ion generators is made by **Wein Products, Inc.** Their V1-2000 and V1-2500 are desktop models that do not use a replaceable filter. These are sold through dealers such as **N.E.E.D.S.** and **BreatheFree.com**. Jenn-Air negative-ion generators, with replaceable collection sheets (to be replaced monthly), are handled by **Whole Life Products**. From **Inner Balance** and **Harmony**, you can purchase the SilentAir. This is a room-size unit that uses no fan. It comes with internal collection sheets (to be replaced monthly).

Bio Designs carries the Clearveil room-size negative-ion generator. It, too, has collection sheets that are meant to be changed every month. Still another dealer of negative-ion generators is **American Environmental Health Foundation**.

Mechanical Ventilation Systems

A mechanical ventilation system is an excellent way to efficiently and effectively improve your home's indoor air quality. By using exhaust fans or more elaborate equipment, fresh air will be able to come into your house and stale air will be expelled outdoors. However, the technical nature of this important topic is well beyond the scope of this book. So, for complete information on all types of residential ventilation systems including *heat-recovery ventilators,* also known as *HRVs* (these units are able to transfer a portion of the heat from the outgoing air into the incoming air, or vice versa), read *Understanding Ventilation* by John Bower. This easy-to-understand manual can be ordered from booksellers or from **The Healthy House Institute**.

For a brief discussion of ventilation concerning your kitchen stove, see *Making your Gas-Range Operation More Tolerable* on page 489. Also, for information about how ventilation is important in your bathroom and laundry room see *High Relative Humidity* on page 530 and *Mold and Mildew* on page 170

Choosing the Right Air-Improvement Equipment

Before purchasing any air-improvement device, it's best to rectify your home's air problems by other means first, as much as possible. This is because air-improvement equipment works best when it only has to cope with minor air pollution problems. Therefore, its wise to eliminate as many known sources of contamination (mold, perfume, tobacco products, noxious cleaners, dust mites, etc.) as you can. After doing that, you should determine what contaminants remain in the air. Then you can consider a unit designed to eliminate those sorts of pollutants.

Unfortunately, as has already been mentioned, filtering methods that are capable of removing particulates, such as pollen grains or house dust, can't remove gaseous pollutants, such as volatile organic compounds (VOCs), and vice versa. However, many models are now available that combine adsorption and one or more particulate trapping methods. Sometimes, even more strategies are included such as UV light purification or negative-ion generation. This is especially true with portable room-sized units.

Besides offering differing strategies, the various air-improvement devices come in a variety of sizes. These range from tiny desktop units to permanently mounted, built-in, whole-house models. Obviously, in many situations, the very small units are just too small to accomplish very much. On the other hand, whole-house models may not be practical, particularly if you're renting. Therefore, it's important to pinpoint the types of contaminants that need to be removed, as well as the areas where they're found in your home. If these areas include most of your house, then a whole-house model could make good sense. However, if only your kitchen, or a single bedroom, needs improvement, then room-sized units might make more sense.

In addition, you should consider what special qualities you desire in your unit. For example, how should it be constructed? If you're chemically sensitive, you may prefer a model housed in a metal casing, as well as one where the fan motor is placed upwind of the adsorption filtering media, in order to capture any potentially bothersome odors. If the unit is to go in a bedroom, it can be important to select an especially quiet model, or one with two, or more, fan speeds. That way, it could be run through the night without keeping everyone awake.

Of course, you should also consider how much you'll be willing to spend. And, you should honestly evaluate how willing you are to maintain the unit. Are you the type of person who would be willing to wash an electrostatic precipitator's collection plates routinely? How often are you willing to order and replace your filter's media? Are you the type who doesn't mind going down into the basement occasionally, opening up your furnace, and checking to see if the electrostatic filter is dirty? Finally, you should take into consideration any guarantees or warranties.

Of course, if you're a chemically sensitive person, or you have asthma or serious allergies, it would be a good idea to ask for air-equipment recommendations from your physician, or other health-care professionals. Also, talking with friends who currently own units should provide you with some useful information. In addition, to help you choose, independent consultants are available. (See *Helpful Consultants* on page 65.) One in particular, **Nigra Enterprises**, is also a dealer offering several different brands of both room-sized and whole-house equipment. However, bear in mind that most of the consultants mentioned in this book will not be certified engineers specializing in residential indoor air quality. Therefore, it's unlikely that they will be able to design all the specific details of a whole-house system for your home. However, they should be able to provide information and guidance to your local heating/cooling contractor so they can perform any necessary work.

It should be stressed that only brief descriptions of certain air-improving equipment are given in the following sections. If you're interested in a particular model, it's best to contact the manufacturer and/or dealer for more complete information. Of course, other fine units and suppliers are available in addition to the ones listed here.

Whole-House Equipment

Whole-house air improvement equipment offers the major advantage of being able to process all the air that's circulated within your home. Some models are actually very simple and are used in place of a typical standard furnace filter. However, others require a special housing, and professional installation—and they can be expensive.

Before investing in complex and costly filtering/cleaning units, you would probably find it advisable to speak with an engineer or architect who is familiar with airflow complexities, solving particular pollution problems, and the construction of various units. Installation of such equipment should be undertaken only by knowledgeable individuals.

Below are some of the more popular, whole-house air improving devices. In-depth descriptions of the various air-improving strategies that are mentioned in the following sections can be found earlier in this chapter.

Improved Standard-Filter Replacements

If your particular air-quality concern is to remove gaseous contaminants, such as volatile organic compounds (VOCs), **E.L. Foust Co., Inc.** offers several brands of 1"-thick activated-charcoal furnace/air-conditioner replacement filters. If you prefer, you can request a special PuraPel adsorption mix that will be able to remove formaldehyde as well. Foust's furnace filters are available in standard sizes as well as custom sizes. Because these filters are only 1" thick, they can't handle serious pollution problems.

Another filtering improvement over standard furnace filters is the Magnetron. This is a cleanable, multi-layer product designed to trap particulates. It's constructed of "hardware cloth, woven polypropylene, and non-woven matting" in a stainless-steel frame. You can get it in standard or in custom sizes. The Magnetron is sold by the **Allergy Relief Shop, Inc.**

N.E.E.D.S. handles the Air Vak, said to be an "alternative furnace filter." It's constructed with 3-stage filtration. These include a polyester prefilter, a 15-lb. activated-charcoal/activated-alumina-permeated pad, and a foam final filter.

While electrostatic filters are not overly efficient, they can trap some of the more bothersome larger mold and pollen particulates—and they're relatively inexpensive and easy to install. One popular brand is Filtrete (**3M Construction & Home Improvements Products Div.**). These furnace/air-conditioning-filter replacements have the addition of a microbial growth inhibitor. They come in three levels of efficiency to better meet your particular household needs. The Dust Reduction model is said to be 10 times better than a standard furnace filter. The High Performance model is pleated, and is 20 times better. The Micro Particle and Airborne Allergen version also has pleats and is rated to be 30 times better than a standard furnace filter. All Filtrete filters come in many sizes with custom sizes available for the Micro Particle filters. You can order them directly from the manufacturer. A mail-order dealer is **Allergy Control Products, Inc.**, and eMD.com offers them on the internet.

Incidentally, another brand of electrostatic filters you might consider is Permastatic II (**Allermed**). These particular filters are washable, and they come in standard or custom-made sizes. They can be ordered directly from the company or from **Building for Health Materials Center.** One more option is the Dusteater forced-air furnace/central-air-conditioning-system filter. This is made with electrostatically-charged fabric and treated with MicroBan (a microbial inhibitor). It's suggested that these be washed under a faucet monthly. You can buy Dusteaters from **Priorities.**

Improvements offers permanent, 1"-thick electrostatic furnace filters that are said to have a 3-stage design able to eliminate most common household allergens. These filters also have MicroBan imbedded in them. This is an additive to inhibit bacteria, fungus, and yeast growth. Suggested cleaning is by rinsing in running water once a month. The Absolute Self-Charging Electrostatic Air Filters from **The Allergy Store** are also suggested to be washed every month. From **E.L. Foust Co., Inc.**, you can purchase Alpha-Stat electrostatic filters. These come in both standard and custom sizes.

Enviro-Duct permanent electrostatic filters are still one more product of which you should be aware. These are constructed of polypropylene and polyurethane. Enviro-Duct filters come in forty standard sizes with custom sizes, as well as an adjustable-size model, available. The manufacturer suggests that every 3-4 weeks you remove your Enviro-Duct filter and "clean it with a household cleaner and water spray." Sources for these include **Allerx** and **Ozark Water Service and Environmental Services**. The Enviro-Duct Charcoal is an electrostatic filter with a polyester fabric bonded with activated charcoal. Maintenance requires that the unit should be "vacuumed and back flushed" every 30-90 days and the pads should be replaced every four months. This product can be purchased from **Ozark Water Service and Environmental Services**. The HI-TECH polypropolene washable electrostatic filter in an aluminum frame is sold by **eMD.com** in several sizes.

Farr 20/20 (**Farr Co.**) extended-surface filters are designed to that replace standard furnace filters. Their pleated, nonwoven-cotton fabric has four times the surface area of a typical 1" filter. Farr 30/30 extended-surface filters come with their own housing. These come in 1", 2", and 4" thicknesses. The fabric on these is a nonwoven cotton/polyester blend. Incidentally, in both 20/20 and 30/30 models, the filters' pleats are adhered to metal wire grids to keep them rigid. To purchase Farr filters, contact the company for their nearest dealer. Farr filters can often be obtained through local heating/cooling contractors.

Furnace Filters Requiring Special Housings

There are only a few filters in this category that contain a significant amount of adsorption media, but they can be very useful in reducing polluting gases indoors.

The General Aire Air Purifier (**General Filters, Inc.**) is a whole-house adsorption filter with activated-carbon pellets. It's advised that it be changed yearly. (This unit can be combined with the General Aire High Efficiency Air Cleaner, a whole-house extended surface filter). Call the company for the nearest buying source.

Another approach is to use the Pure Air Model 600 Odor Adsorber (**Pure Air Systems, Inc.**), or it's larger version, the Pure Air Model 2000 Odor Adsorber. Both units can be mounted into a forced-air furnace/air-conditioning system, or they can be used alone with their own ductwork. Each Odor Adsorber consists of a metal housing containing a disposable polyester prefilter. The Model 600 also has four 15"-square x 4"-deep interchangeable "adsorption pads." Each pad holds 5 pound of media "creating a 16"-deep adsorption bed holding 20 pounds of media." The Model 2000 comes with a 15-pound charcoal filter, plus a canister that can hold from 35 to 80 pounds of media. (The canisters are easily emptied and refilled.) With these units, you have your choice of standard activated charcoal (from coal), coconut-shell activated charcoal, Purafil (activated alumina impregnated with potassium permanganate) or Triple Blend Media (3CZ) made with activated charcoal, Purafil, and zeolite. By the way, the media should last one year before it needs replacing. You should realize that this unit will likely require professional installation. To purchase one, call the company for the nearest dealer.

Extended-surface filters are often excellent choices when looking for a good particulate filter that won't create a significant drop in your ducts' air pressure. These filters do a good job at capturing mold spores, pollen grains, and other larger-sized airborne particles. Some are fairly large—about 2-feet square and 4–5" thick. SpaceGard (**Research Products Corp.**) is one of the more popular brands. These come with their own metal housing and the filter itself is several inches thick. These are familiar to most heating/cooling contractors, but you'll need to call the manufacturer if you can't locate a nearby supplier.

The General Aire High Efficiency Air Cleaner (**General Filters, Inc.**) is another whole-house extended-surface filter using "glass micro-fibers bonded with acrylic into a web-like fabric" (a type of fiberglass). It's rated to last one year before replacement. A plus, is that this air cleaner can be combined with the General Aire Air Purifier (see above), a whole-house adsorption filter which uses activated-carbon pellets. Again, contact the manufacturer for an area supplier.

From **E.L. Foust Co., Inc.**, you can order the Residential Hi Efficiency Air Cleaner. The metal cabinet of this unit has an interior configured in a double "V-bank" design. The filters themselves are "rigid mini-pleated pads of micro fibers with fixed spacers in place." Filter cartridges (which should last up to one year) easily slip out for replacement.

Another whole-house extended-surface filter is the Honeywell Media Air Cleaner (**Honeywell, Inc.**). If your interested in this product, call the manufacturer for the nearest dealer.

If you're interested in a whole-house electrostatic precipitator to remove airborne particulates, remember that the collection plates will need to be cleaned regularly. Most local heating/cooling companies will be familiar with these, so call them to see what brands they offer. One popular brand is made by **Honeywell, Inc.**

HEPA filters are extremely efficient at removing particulates—probably far more efficient than most people really need. But you should keep in mind the fact that they are unable to remove any gaseous contaminants. The big drawback to HEPA filters is that they have a great deal of resistance to airflow. Therefore, they often aren't easy to use with residential furnace and air-conditioner systems. As a result, this type of equipment will definitely require professional installation. In fact, in some cases, an engineer's skill may be required. This is because, if installed improperly, HEPA filters can damage your heating/cooling system. By the way, combination filters are available that contain a HEPA, adsorption media, and a built-in fan to overcome the resistance to airflow. Two such systems are listed below

Pure Air Systems, Inc. makes a line of whole house HEPA air filters including the Pure Aire 600 HEPA Shield, the Pure Aire 2000 HEPA Shield, and The Pure Air PowerAire Model 1200. All models use 3-stage filtration. This includes a polyester prefilter with Aegis antimicrobial technology which should be replaced every 3-4 months (you can get an untreated prefilter if you prefer), as well as activated charcoal made from coal (you can substitute coconut shell) which should be replaced every 9-12 months. (The 600 uses five pounds of activated charcoal and the 1200 and the 2000 models hold 15 pounds.) The third stage is a true-HEPA filter, which should be changed every 3 years. Contact the manufacturer for the location of a nearby dealer. A mail-order supplier is the **Allergy Relief Shop, Inc.**

Allermed manufactures the CS-2000 whole-house unit designed especially with chemically sensitive people in mind. This equipment can be fitted with its own ductwork system or be made to work in conjunction with a forced-air furnace/air-conditioner. Internally they contain a prefilter and 40 pounds of coconut-shell activated charcoal (or other adsorption media—your choice of wood activated charcoal, lignite/bituminous-coal activated charcoal, "Formaldepure-enhanced activated charcoal," or "Hydestop absorbent/oxidizer"). You also have your choice of a HEPA-type, a true-HEPA filter, or an extended-surface filter. The CS-2000 can be purchased directly from the manufacturer or from Allermed dealers such as **Building for Health Materials Center.**

One of the newest methods available to homeowners is whole-house turbulent-flow precipitation (TFP). In this technology, abrupt changes in the direction and speed of the airflow cause airborne particulates to *precipitate*, or fall out, of the airstream, to areas of no turbulence inside the unit where filter collector trays trap them. Interestingly, this approach creates virtually no air-flow restrictions.

The TFP Air Cleaner (**Nutech Energy Systems**) and the Nutone Air Cleaning System (**Nutone**) are very similar. The metal housing of this whole-house unit is connected to a ducted furnace/air conditioner system, and it uses six filter-collector trays. The unit is said to be able to removes particulates smaller than 0.5 micron. It's suggested that you change the filters annually. If you'd like to find a local dealer, contact one of the manufacturers.

Portable Room-Sized Equipment

A large number of portable air-improvement devices are now available. In fact, there are so many that it can seem overwhelming to decide on exactly which unit to pick. However, no matter which model you choose, if you're a chemically sensitive person it's best if it has a metal cabinet with any fan motors upwind of the adsorbing filtering media.

It should be noted that some highly allergic or very sensitive people may need to try several brands or models of filters before finding one that meets all their needs, and is tolerable. Therefore, it's a good idea to ask a dealer if it's possible to rent, rent-to-buy, or have a trial period to determine if a particular unit is right for you. Often, at the very least, you'll have a period of allotted time before your purchase must be returned in order to receive your money back. Saying this, you should only buy a unit if you have done your homework ahead of time, and expect to keep it from the start. It's not fair to a dealer or manufacturer to "try on" a myriad of devices as you would shoes at a shoe store.

Below are some of the more popular brands and models of portable air improving equipment that are available. For your convenience, they're listed in alphabetical order by manufacturer. For ease of reading, there are no discussions of the various air-improving strategies. If you're interested in knowing more about a particular strategy, look under the appropriate sections earlier in this chapter. Incidentally, please keep in mind that what follows is only a sampling of what's currently in the marketplace. Many other fine brands, models, and buying sources are becoming available every day.

Note: For stand-alone ultraviolet-light purifiers, negative-ion generators, and ozone machines, see those sections earlier in this chapter. For information on air filters and negative-ion generators for your car, see *Car Interior Air Filters* on page 380, and *Car Interior Negative-ion generators* on page 381.

Aireox Research Corp.

The Aireox Air Purifier Model 45 (**Aireox Research Corp.**) is a filtering unit that is especially helpful to the chemically sensitive population. It's quiet, creates no ozone, or chemical outgassing. Furthermore, the motor is sealed and out of the fresh-air stream, and no adhesives used. The Model 45's cylindrical shape is compact enough to be placed on a table, as well as on the floor. It is 14" high and 11" in diameter. A handy metal carrying handle is on top.

Air comes in around the metal cylinder's perimeter and clean air exits out the top. The Model 45 holds 4^1/$_2$ pounds of coconut-shell-activated-charcoal/Purafil adsorption media. There's also an electrostatic particulate filter that's effective down to 0.5 micron. It's said to be able to clean the air in a 2000 cubic foot room once every 15 minutes. It has a very long 5-year warranty on the motor. You can order Aireox products from the manufacturer or from distributors such as **N.E.E.D.S.** and **Health One Co.**

Allermed

Allermed offers a number of filters that you may be interested in getting. All models have metal housings and customers can request different types of media, if necessary. So they often can be very good choices for those who are chemically sensitive. Incidentally, all units are said to be able to remove 99% of all pollens.

The Allermed VH-300 is a rectangular unit approximately 2' tall and 12" square, on rollers, and it is made with a sealed motor. It comes with a high-speed setting to remove dust, pollen, and odors quickly, and a low-speed setting that's meant for more controlled, continuous use. Specifically, the VH-300 is fitted with a Microprefilter (to capture most large particulates such as dust and pollen), a Carbomed filter (coconut-shell activated charcoal), a Formaldepure Filter, and finally a Micromed filter (a HEPA-type filter with a patented pleated design providing 13 sq. ft. of filtering surface, and rated at 95% effective down to 0.3 microns). The top of the unit lifts off for easy filter access.

The Airstar-5C is a 12" x 16" x 8½" high unit with handles. It has 4-strategy filtration. The first strategy is a permanent, aluminum prefilter and the second strategy is a combination activated-charcoal/Hydestop mix in a refillable filter (to adsorb gases and formaldehyde). The third filter is a pleated HEPA (with a surface area of 2,000 sq. inches) said to be 95% efficient down to 0.3 microns. Finally, the fourth strategy is an independently-controlled negative-ion generator. The company suggests that the Airstar-5C is able to filter the air in a 15' x 15' room. The 19-pound replacement filtering cartridges slip in easily and are available from dealers.

The CompanionAire's steel cabinet has a baked-enamel finish in your choice of brown or beige. It's 10" x 10" x 8½" high with two side intake vents and a separate clean air vent. Each intake vent has an activated-charcoal-impregnated, non-woven polyester filter, plus it's own HEPA filter.

The metal-encased Space Saver 400 measures 27⅛" high x 25" wide x 12" deep. It has a "large capacity" prefilter, 13 pounds of coconut-shell activated-charcoal granules, and a HEPA-type filter (rated at 95% capture at 0.3 microns) made with special pleatings. This unit is rated for up to a 750 sq. ft. area.

The SF/250 has a 26½" x 20½" x 12½" case. Inside is a extended-surface prefilter made up of 51 sq. ft. of "non-woven, cotton-fiber-type fabric" that's reinforced. Next, there's adsorption filter consisting of Chem Blend (coconut-shell activated charcoal and a Hydestop potassium-permanganate-impregnated activated-alumina media), and a HEPA-type filter, rated at an efficiency of 95% at 0.3 microns

Allermed equipment can be ordered from the manufacturer and from the **Building for Health Materials Center**. Some models can also be purchased from **Bio Designs**, **Allergy Relief Shop, Inc.**, and **American Environmental Health Foundation**, who also handles replacement filters.

Austin Air

The Austin Air Brand (**Austin Air**) is one that is often familiar to individuals with allergies and chemical sensitivities. These are HEPA-equipped portable units in welded-steel housings that come in your choice of three colors (white, black, sandstone). The paints used are baked-on powder coatings. Different sized models are available to handle various room dimensions.

Their highly rated Austin Air Healthmate is probably their most popular model. The fan motor is quiet and efficient (it uses 50% less power than similar ones). The unit itself is a rounded rectangle 14^1/$_2$" x 14^1/$_2$" x 23^1/$_2$" high on casters. Air enters on all four sides and passes through a sealed filtering cartridge consisting of a prefilter, a HEPA filter (rated at 99.97% over 0.3 microns), and an activated-charcoal/zeolite adsorption media. A complete exchange of air in a 150 sq. ft. room is said to occur ten times in one hour. The filter cartridge should be replaced every five years.

The Austin Air Healthmate Junior is a smaller version of the standard Healthmate. It has no casters, and can process the air in a 70 sq. ft. room twice an hour.

Austin's equipment can be ordered directly from the manufacturer. Mail-order dealers include **N.E.E.D.S.**, **American Environmental Health Foundation**, **InteliHealth Health Home**, **Well & Good**, and **Befit Enterprises Ltd**. Others are **Inner Balance**, **Building for Health Materials Center**, **Bio Designs**, and **Priorities**, Still more Austin Air dealers are **Harmony**, **The Allergy Store**, **BreatheFree.com**, and **Allergy Relief Shop, Inc.**

E.L. Foust, Co., Inc.

E.L. Foust Air Purifiers (**E.L. Foust Co., Inc.**) are well-built, all-metal units. You can substitute different types of adsorption media to fit your particular needs. (A Test Kit is available that has samples of all their different media and filtering materials.) Models come with squirrel-cage blower fans (some models have double squirrel-cage blower fans) that provide greater efficiency and power than other types of fans. A very nice plus for this equipment is that you can return it within 30 days, no questions asked—with only a 10% restocking fee.

Their well-known (to many chemically sensitive persons) #160R2 model has a sleek, simple, chromed-steel, 23" high x 8" diameter cylindrical construction. In-coming air enters through the entire perimeter. This unit uses three-stage filtration. There's 7 pounds of "standard mix adsorption media" made up of 60% coconut-shell activated charcoal and 40% PuraPel (activated alumina impregnated with potassium permanganate) to remove odors and unwanted gases, including formaldehyde. There's also a FilterDown synthetic-material filter able to trap particulates down to 0.5 micron. If you prefer, you can ask that an untreated-cotton fabric be substituted (it will not have as much filtering ability). You can also opt for a different adsorption media. In fact, you have your choice of various types of activated granular charcoal (coconut shell, formaldehyde-control coconut shell, lignite, bituminous, or wood) either alone or with zeolite. It's said to be able to filter the air in a 400 sq. ft. room. Filter cartridges should be replaced every 6-8 months. By the way, a desktop unit that is similar to the #160R2, but smaller, is also available.

With either the room or desktop model, a replacement cartridge service is available. When your adsorption media is no longer working efficiently, simply send the complete cartridge to the company and a refilled new one will be returned to you. This is an especially nice feature for those who don't want to change the media themselves (it can be a dusty, messy job).

The E.L. Foust Air Sentry is a squarish, steel unit (with a baked-on finish) mounted on casters. It's "perfect seal" design has dimensions of 21^3/$_4$" x 14^1/$_2$" x 17^3/$_4$" high. Inside is a pleated prefilter, a HEPA filter (95% efficient down to 0.3 microns made without glues), and 3^1/$_2$ lbs. of an activated-charcoal/PuraPel mixture. The filters are designed for easy removal and replacement. Incidentally, the motor precedes the filters.

The E.L. Foust Series 400 has an attractive creamy beige, powder-coated, baked-enamel finish. It's size is 13^1/$_2$" x 13^1/$_2$" x 32" high. Like the Sentry, it's equipped with casters. The Series 400 features a unique "perfect sealing," top-loading, vertical-stacking configuration.

It works by having in-coming air enter at the lower front end. Then it passes through a pleated pre-filter, a HEPA filter (made without glues and said to be 95% efficient down to 0.3 microns), an activated-charcoal/PuraPel filter (or one made with formaldehyde-control activated charcoal). Finally the air exits out through the diffuser-lid on top.

You can purchase E.L. Foust equipment from the manufacturer or dealers such as **American Environmental Health Foundation**.

Honeywell, Inc.

Honeywell, Inc. manufactures a complete line of Honeywell/Enviracare equipment. All have attractive white plastic housings, and most are in cylindrical shapes that are well sealed against leakage. Their unique design allows air to both enter and leave through all 360° directions. Most models have a HEPA filter (99.97% efficient down to 0.3 microns) and activated charcoal to adsorb polluting gases. Because of the similarities, only a few models are mentioned below.

The Honeywell 6000 series HEPA/CPZ is a cylindrical unit $11^1/4$" high and $18^1/4$" in diameter configured with a 3-stage filtration system. The first stage is a prefilter having activated charcoal, the second is a HEPA filter, and the third is the main adsorption media (activated carbon, potassium-permanganate impregnated activated alumina, and zeolite). It's said that all the air of a 12' x 14' room will pass through the unit six times in one hour. Replacement filter kits include a six-month CPZ and two three-month activated-charcoal prefilters.

The Honeywell Quiet Care (L) 17000 is 17" high and about 15" in diameter. (This model has a vertical drum shape, like a clothes dryer, and a built-in handle.) It's equipped with an activated-charcoal prefilter and a HEPA. What makes this model special is it's fan blades, grilles, and other features were designed purposely for very quiet operation, so it's a good choice for bedrooms

The Honeywell 110/10700 True HEPA Air Cleaner has a special configuration so it can still work efficiently when placed in a room's corner. While it has a lower cylindrical drum, there's also a top section that is shaped somewhat like a curved, flat-screen computer monitor. Like the Quiet Care, it has an activated carbon prefilter and a HEPA.

The Honeywell/Enviracare brand can be found in many local outlets including department stores (such as **Sears Roebuck and Co.**) and building centers. There are also a number of mail-order and internet sources who handle one or more Honeywell, Inc. products. These include **eMD.com**, **Gazoontite**, **JC Penny Catalog**, and **Real Goods**. Others are **Allergy Control Products, Inc.** and healthyhome.com.

The Rival Company

Bionaire (**The Rival Co.**) is the brand name of several models of Air Purifier units with plastic housings. These all have multi-stage filtration and some come with negative-ion generators built in. A few are described below.

The Bionaire Odor Remover Air Purifier with V.O.C. Adsorption System TM1240 is in a white, cylindrically shaped $10^1/2$" high x $12^1/2$" in diameter. It has a prefilter and an activated-charcoal/zeolite adsorption filter. It is recommended for a 12' x 16' room and is capable of 4.8 air exchanges in one hour.

The Bionaire Odor Remover Air Purifier with V.O.C. Adsorption System TM0551 can only be called "cute." It is 11" diameter and just under $5^1/2$" high. Basically, this is smaller version of the TM1240 and, as such, is only recommended for a 14' x 5' area.

The Bionaire HEPA Air Purifier Console CH-3580 comes in a black 20" x 10^1/$_2$" x 27^1/$_2$" tall plastic rectangular housing. There's a "large area" activated-charcoal prefilter and a "superior hospital-grade true-HEPA filter" said to remove 99.97% of pollen, and an independently controlled negative-ion generator. It is said to work for a room up to 20' x 24'.

The Bionaire HEPA Air Purifier and Ionizer LC-1460 is a rounded rectangle in white plastic (15^1/$_4$" x 7^1/$_2$" x 14^1/$_4$" tall). Inside is a 5-stage "pro-HEPA" filtration system with Microbex, an anti-microbial to inhibit bacterial growth on the filter.

The Bionaire Compact ULPA Air Cleaner UA0860 has a rectangular, white-plastic housing 15" x 9^1/$_2$" x 16" high. This model is equipped with an activated-charcoal filter and a ULPA (ultra low penetrating air) filter rated at 99.999% at 0.1 micron. There's also an independently controlled negative-ion generator. It's recommended for a room size of 11' x 11' for an air-exchange rate of five per hour.

Bionaire equipment is often sold by department stores (such as **Sears Roebuck and Co.**) and other local outlets. Mail-order dealers that handle one or more models include **Gazoontite** and **Priorities**.

More Brands and Sources

The equipment made by Air Quality Systems consists of square, steel cabinets in 3 sizes. They're designed for in-coming air to enter on all four sides. Inside are 5-stage filtration systems. These include a washable, polyester prefilter, an activated-charcoal-impregnated material, a disposable adsorbent filter (several options are available), a unique "Borosil" filter, and electret filters. One Air Quality Systems dealer is **Ozark Water Service and Environmental Services**

The Aller Air's Air Solutions model is a metal, cylindrical unit with a HEPA filter and activated-charcoal adsorption media. Several model sizes are available. You can purchase them from **Allergy Relief Shop, Inc.**

The Amway Advanced Air Treatment System (**Amway**) is said to be especially quiet. It comes with 3-stage filtration (washable prefilter, polypropylene-mesh extended-surface filter, and activated- coconut-shell charcoal). A handy monitor indicates when the media needs replacing. This filter, which has a plastic housing, can be purchased from local Amway distributors.

The Blueair room filter has three HEPA filters and two "encapsulated negative-ion chambers" where airborne particles are trapped. This unit is made with a plastic housing. A buying source for the Blueair is **Real Goods**.

The Clear Water Revival's C.A.R.E. 2000 comes equipped with a HEPA, activated-charcoal-blend adsorption media (able to reduce formaldehyde levels in the air), as well as an ultraviolet purifier. It's packaged inside a baked-enameled-metal housing. You can buy it from the **Befit Enterprises Ltd.** and **Health One Co.** This model, as well as others by Clear Water (and other manufacturers), can be ordered from **N.E.E.D.S.**

The Dust-Free Cleaner is described as a high-efficiency, four- stage electret filtration system with trays of adsorbents such as activated charcoal, zeolite, and/or potassium permanganate. Three internal configurations are offered (airborne allergen, odor/smoke, and chemical sensitivities). Air is drawn into the unit on all four sides of it's plastic housing. You can purchase the Allerx/Dust-Free though **Allerx**.

The Roomaid desktop filtering unit comes in a white steel housing. It has 3-stage filtration (pre-filter, HEPA filter, and activated charcoal/zeolite). This product (and other brands) are sold by **Priorities** and **Harmony**.

Sun Pure Air Purifiers use a multi-stage filtration system in a plastic housing: a prefilter, gas-adsorption media, a HEPA, and a UV purifier. It also creates negative ions. The housing is plastic. Sun Pure dealers include **Real Goods**, **Harmony**, and **Inner Balance**.

It should be noted that the **JC Penny Catalog** handles a number of room-sized air improving units, including those of Panasonic and Jenn-Air. A variety of Kenmore air filtering products are available in **Sears Roebuck and Co.** stores. These include electrostatic precipitators, adsorption-media/HEPAs, and more, in a variety of sizes. An on-line site offering a number of pieces of different manufacturers' equipment is **BreatheFree.com**.

Wearable Air Filters and Negative-Ion Generators

There are filters and negative-ion generators now made to be worn. Some of these are described below.

Personal Facial Air Filters

Some chemically sensitive and allergic individuals have found it helpful to wear *personal facial filters* when doing tasks that usually provoke negative symptoms in them, such as reading a magazine (to protect against ink and paper odors), or cleaning the house (to filter out dust). Surprisingly, there are several types available.

One-hundred-percent-cotton masks made to hold an *activated charcoal* insert, are available from several companies. The granular activated charcoal will adsorb many bothersome odors. Mail-order sources for cotton/activated-charcoal filtering masks including **Allerx** (they also have a hand-held version), **Allergy Relief Shop, Inc.**, and **Bio Designs**. Also, from **American Environmental Health Foundation**, you can purchase masks of either untreated 100%-cotton or silk, with or without your choice of coconut shell, lignite, or bituminous-activated-charcoal inserts. As a rule, all these are washable and refill inserts are available.

An interesting option, along the same line as the above filters, are Bandit Scarf face-and-neck-covering filters. Ones of unbleached, 100%-cotton with dust-free woven, replaceable, activated-charcoal filters are sold by **TerrEssentials** and **Priorities**. These masks are secured with a neck strap and have an adjustable strip at the nose bridge.

Disposable dust masks are another option which are designed to trap most larger particulates. As a rule, these are made of synthetic fabrics and materials. So, if you're a very chemically sensitive person, you may find that you have trouble tolerating them. The 3M High Efficiency Particulate Mask (**3M Construction & Home Improvement Products Div.**) is popularly found in building centers and hardware stores. If not, you can mail order them from **E.L. Foust Co., Inc.** This company offers other kinds, too, including 3M Disposable Dust/Mist Respirators (**3M Construction & Home Improvement Products Div.**). These have an added thin, activated-charcoal layer in them to provide protection from both particulates and minor airborne chemical exposures. 3M masks are handled by **eMD.com**, **Allerx**, **N.E.E.D.S.**, **Allergy Clean Environments**, **Allergy Relief Shop, Inc.**, and **Nigra Enterprises**. In addition, Maxi-Masks (synthetic, disposable particulate masks) in boxes of five, can be ordered from **Priorities**, and Affinity Plus N95 disposable particulate masks can be purchased from **Allergy Relief Shop, Inc.**

Another strategy is used by Contour masks, which are sold by **eMD.com** and **Allergy Control Products, Inc.** These are designed with electrostatically-charged, replaceable filters. HEPA-filtered masks are available from **Gazoontite** and **Inner Balance**. The ones from Inner Balance are made with a "Foam-Fit Seal" and they're constructed without latex.

For more protection when doing certain odorous home hobbies or remodeling products, especially if a potentially noxious product must be used, a respirator mask is a much better choice. These may be found locally in hardware and building-supply centers. Also, **Befit Enterprises Ltd.** offers Respro Anti-Pollution Masks made of *neoprene* (a special type of rubber that's particularly oil and chemical resistant) with your choice of a particulate-trapping filter or activated charcoal. **TerrEssentials** carries a respirator constructed of a low-odor thermoplastic in two sizes. It comes with a pair of acid-gas/organic-vapor cartridges. Pesticide trapping prefilters are optional.

Other respirators are sold by **W.W. Grainger, Inc.** and **Orr Safety Corporation**, both of which have local outlets, as well as mail-order catalogs.

Personal Negative-Ion Generators

One of the newer items you can find are personal *negative-ion generators*. Usually, these are tiny plastic units that come with a cord to hang around your neck. Internally, their battery-run electronic workings spew out *negatively charged ions*.

These ions are supposed to attach themselves to airborne particulates near the wearer's head and prevent them from being inhaled. There are a number of doubters when it comes to the usefulness of negative-ion generators, and in this mode, they seem even more suspect. However, for helping to alleviate SAD (Seasonal Affective Disorder), they may help. Yet a problem with any negative-ion generator is that they create reactive ozone in the process of making free electrons. Many of the companies who make personal negative-ion generators say that the quantity of ozone produced is extremely small. Yet, no amount of ozone is beneficial to breathe.

If you still want to experiment with a personal negative-ion generator, there are a number of mail-order sources for them including **Bio Designs**, **TerrEssentials**, and **Gazoontite**. The unit offered by **American Environmental Health Foundation** has a 110-volt AC adapter, as well as a 12-volt adapter for the car's lighter.

In addition, Personal Air Supply (**Wein Products, Inc.**) manufactures two models (4.5 and 3.5 oz. sizes). Each is designed to fit into a pocket or be used around the neck with a strap. Both units are rated to operate up to 40-60 hours on a single 9 v battery. The Model 1500B also comes with a 110-volt AC adapter. Dealers include **Inner Balance**, **Priorities**, **Harmony**, **BreatheFree.com**, and **N.E.E.D.S.**

Breathing-Aid Equipment For Asthmatics

If you or your child has asthma, check with your doctor for the appropriate equipment you may require. Often, these are prescription-only items. By mail order, helpful books on peak flow meters, etc. are available from **Asthma and Allergy Network, Mothers of Asthmatics, Inc.** They, as well as **eMD.com**, also offer holding chambers (several sizes), peak flow meters (several brands), and more. In addition, **Allergy Clean Environments** carries Omron Nebulizers, TruZone Peak Flow Meters, and Aero Holding Chambers.

Air Humidification

In dry climates, or during the heating season, it might seem that *humidifying* (adding moisture to) your indoor air would always be the logical, healthful thing to do. After all, if the relative humidity of your home air is very low, your eyes, skin, and mucous membranes could become irritated, your lips might crack—and your wood furniture could become dry enough to shrink and become unglued. However, there are other considerations to keep in mind. Therefore, in the sections below, the actual pros and cons of humidifying your home are discussed, as well as specific methods of humidification you might choose to use.

Simple Humidifying Strategies

If you feel you want to raise the relative humidity level in your home, there are some very simple things you can do to accomplish this. One of these is to merely lower the room's air temperature. The cooler a room is, the higher its relative humidity—as long as it's holding the same amount of water vapor. Other approaches you might try are opening your bathroom door immediately after you shower or bathe to let the moisture-laden air spill out into the rest of your house, boiling distilled water in a pot on your stove, putting distilled water in clean pans on your steam radiators, and misting the air with *distilled water* in a spray bottle. By the way, it is always best to use distilled water, rather than tap water because tap water can add particulates such as minerals or bacteria to the air (see *Distilled Water* on page 637).

In addition, by merely drinking more water during the winter months, you'll help keep your mucous membranes more moist. Of course, if you use a tolerable body moisturizer and lip balm each time after you bathe, you'll help retain more water in your skin (see *Moisturizers* on page 98, and *Make-Up* on page 97). You might also want to use tolerable eye drops to help soothe your eyes as well.

The reason houses get too dry indoors in the winter is because they are over ventilated. This can happen in a house even when it doesn't have a mechanical ventilation system. This is because air moves naturally through the tiny invisible cracks and gaps (that all houses have) more readily when it is colder out. So, during the coldest part of the year, you often have more air exchange than you really need. This means that there is too much dry outdoor entering. The solution is to weatherize your home. In that way, you will save energy, and be less dry in the winter. For more on the implications of tight vs. loose construction, how tightness affects the indoor air, and controlled mechanical ventilation, you'll want to read *Understanding Ventilation* by John Bower. It can be ordered from **The Healthy House Institute**, or your favorite bookseller.

If, despite the above measures, your home still feels too dry, you might try adapting to the more arid conditions—in other words, *acclimating* yourself. This may take several weeks. However, if you still find that the low-humidity levels are unsatisfactory, only then will you want to consider using a *humidifier*. This is because several problems are associated with using humidifiers.

Humidifiers

To increase the relative-humidity level in homes, humidifiers are commonly used. Humidifiers are simply devices that are designed to increase the air's moisture content. Today, there are several approaches to doing this, such as producing steam, or several methods of creating a cool mist. It should be pointed out that different humidifiers are capable of humidifying different sized areas. For example, a particular unit may be appropriate for either a single room, a portion of the house, or the entire house. In addition, humidifiers are equipped with different features—such as an automatic shut off, adjustable vents, etc.— and different prices.

Unfortunately, many humidifiers have innate problems associated with them. These can include spewing out bothersome odors (from plastic, rubber and vinyl parts, or oily odors from fan motors) as well as mold and other biological growth (which can quickly contaminate certain humidifiers). Of course, these are of special concern for sensitive and allergic persons, but they're not healthy for anyone to breathe.

If you opt to go ahead and purchase a humidifier anyway, it would be a good idea to monitor the humidity level of the room(s) often, so that excess moisture isn't accidentally added to the air. For information on potential problems resulting from having high humidity, as well as relative humidity measuring devices see *High Relative Humidity* on page 530. You'll also want to only use distilled water, which will be free of mineral particulates and biological contaminants. In addition, you'll want to thoroughly and frequently clean your humidifying unit. Finally, it's best to avoid using scented additives (or chemical disinfectant additives) that some manufactures include with their new units, especially if you're a chemically sensitive or scent-allergic person. The odors from these will not only get into the air and eventually into everything in the room, but they'll become absorbed by the humidifier's plastic, rubber, or vinyl parts.

Humidifier Types

Several different humidifying strategies are in use. The following sections discuss these. (For suggestions on what specific humidifier is best for you, see *Choosing the Right Humidifier* below.)

Steam Humidifiers

For many years, electrically operated *steam* (or *vaporizer*) *humidifiers* have been popular to increase indoor humidity. These units, sometimes also called *warm-mist humidifiers*, contain electric heating elements that boil water to produce steam. Typically, these are room-size models with plastic water reservoirs. However, some steam humidifier devices are designed for whole-house installations in forced-air furnace ducts. Some of these are constructed primarily of metal.

Steam's major advantage, as a source for humidity in your home, is that its high heat destroys virtually all the microorganisms that might be present in the water. However, if you get too close to certain portable units, you could burn your nasal passages, skin, or eyes. However, it must be said this not likely to happen because the steam cools quickly just a very short distance from where it's emitted.

Some people fear that electric steam units might be dangerous because they could tip over and spill out boiling water. However, many models are now designed to seal completely, so that spilling is unlikely. Yet, there's always the inherent, potential danger, posed by any electrical element, of overheating and causing a fire. Fortunately, the units generally available today have safety features to help prevent such accidents from occurring, such as an automatic shutoff when the water level in the reservoir is too low or when the unit is tipped over.

Remember not to use *hard water* (water with high mineral content) in a steam humidifier or vaporizer. Otherwise the dissolved minerals will create a mineral scale buildup on the heating element and around the vent opening. If this happens, it will lead to higher energy use as well as inefficient dispersal of the steam. Plus, if hard water is used, extremely fine particulate minerals, which aren't good to breathe, will be spewed out into the air, along with the steam. Some manufacturers now recommend that you only use distilled water in their units for these very reasons.

As with any humidifier, steam units should be cleaned regularly. If minerals should build up on the elements, read your owner's manual for suggestions on proper and effective cleaning. In addition, when your portable steam unit isn't actually in use, unplug it and empty the reservoir.

Cool-Mist Humidifiers

Cool-mist humidifiers spew out unheated water in a very fine mist. They're available in small portable units as well as models designed to humidify your whole house. As a rule, they tend to be constructed with plastic water reservoirs and other parts. Often, vinyl or rubber parts are included, too. Cool-mist humidifiers eliminate all the potential problems associated with boiling water, such as the hot vapor and hot elements. However, they don't offer the sanitizing effect of high heat, so microbial growth often contaminates these units. As a matter of fact, as they dispense misted water, they also spray out microbes, dissolved minerals, and anything else that happens to be in that water (see *Common Water Quality Concerns* on page 577). Once these contaminants are airborne, you and your family will wind up breathing them.

Therefore, if you opt for this type of humidifier, use only *distilled water* in it. It's also extremely important to clean the unit frequently to prevent any mold problems. If possible, choose a unit with a Ultraviolet-light purifier to help decontaminate the air entering the room from the humidifier. And, of course, remember to unplug small portable models when not in use, and empty the reservoir.

Ultrasonic-Dispersal Humidifiers

Ultrasonic-dispersal humidifiers are actually specialized types of *cool-mist humidifiers*. These are most often seen as portable models, usually made of plastic. Ultrasonic-dispersal humidifiers work by using high-frequency sound waves to shatter water droplets, creating an ultra-fine mist. However, they also break up any minerals and microorganisms that may be present in the water. Unfortunately, the very fine particles of such debris should not be inhaled over an extended period.

Therefore, it's again extremely important to only use distilled water in ultrasonic-dispersal humidifiers. Also, frequent cleaning is necessary to prevent any mold problems. It's also not a good idea to leave water in the reservoir of a portable unit, or leave it plugged in, when not in use.

Evaporative Humidifiers

Evaporative humidifiers humidify by blowing air across, or through, some type of water-saturated media, and then out into the room. The specific methods to accomplish this differ among the various models. For example, some use a rotating drum, others a conveyor apparatus, and still others use a large wick. The absorbent media often consist of a synthetic foam or other spongy material. Evaporative units come in both room-size and whole-house furnace installations. The portable units generally have plastic water reservoirs and plastic housings.

Over the years, evaporative humidifiers have become notorious for producing some of the worst problems associated with humidifiers. These include mineral build up, as well as microbial growth (mold, bacteria, etc.) contaminating the water reservoir and the media. Of course, all this "stuff" will become airborne, and will be inhaled by you and your family when these units are operating. It should be mentioned that some units come with an air filter, through which the air passes, just before entering the room air. However, these filters are usually not very efficient, and they can become easily contaminated with mold, etc.

Therefore, if you're interested in a portable evaporative humidifier, it's very important that you only use distilled water in it. It's also vital that you keep the unit as clean as possible and never leave standing water in the reservoir when the humidifier is not actually being used. Also, remember to unplug the unit when it's not in use as a safety precaution.

Choosing the Right Humidifier

Before purchasing any humidifier, you should determine the size of the area you plan to humidify (one room or the whole house), have a price range in mind, and evaluate your own inclinations: Are you willing to monitor your room's humidity level, to regularly clean the unit, perhaps daily, and buy and install any replacement filters, etc.? You also should decide on a basic humidifying strategy. Next, give some thought to the unit's construction (what materials is it made of, and how easy will it be to fill and clean), its special features (an auto shutoff when the reservoir is empty, or an ultraviolet light purifier, etc.), and any guarantees or warranties.

Unfortunately, it should be pointed out that there are really few truly healthy humidifiers from which to chose—and this is particularly true from the perspective of chemically sensitive individuals. After all, most humidifiers are constructed with plastic reservoirs and housings, often with internal parts made of various synthetic and rubber compounds. Generally, these materials have the capacity to impart their own odors into the humidified air, especially when the humidifiers are new. Also, frequent cleanings are required to prevent any mold problems.

Then, too, whole-house humidifiers, that work in conjunction with furnaces, may encourage mold and mildew growth inside your ductwork simply by raising the relative humidity levels there. In addition, if your humidifier doesn't have an adjustable *humidistat* (a device able to detect relative-humidity levels and turn off the humidifier when a preset level has been reached), and you don't regularly monitor your room's moisture level yourself, your humidifier can easily introduce too much moisture into your home. This situation can lead to a number of problems, including damage to your walls, and increased populations of microorganisms.

However, if you decide you really need a humidifier, a simple portable steam/vaporizing (warm mist) unit is often one of the better choices. Although it'll likely have the usual plastic reservoir, some of the simpler models have a minimum of other synthetic or rubber components. Also, in their favor, the high heat they generate is disinfecting. When it's new, it's often a good idea to run your steam humidifier (or any other type of new portable humidifier) for sometime outdoors in dry, uncontaminated surroundings until the plastic odors are no longer noticeable in the vapor that is released. (Of course, this is very important if you're a sensitive person.)

Portable electric steam/vaporizer (warm mist) humidifiers are still relatively popular. Therefore, models for baby and children's rooms are often sold in local drugstores. More elaborate models, are sold in many department stores, discount stores, and building centers.

A good warm-mist humidifier to consider would be one manufactured by Slant/Fin. These not only combine the germicidal effect of vaporization, but they also have two ultraviolet lights. Interestingly, the hot-water reservoir is made of stainless steel. Various 2-gallon or 3¹/2-gallon models are available from **Harmony**, **The Allergy Store** and **The Right Start**.

A popular brand you'll likely find in local stores is Durocraft Natural Warm Moisture Humidifiers (**Honeywell, Inc.**). These come in 2- and 3-gallon models. **Sears Roebuck and Co.** stores and **eMD.com** handle some Honeywell models.

Bionaire makes several warm-mist humidifiers including the Bionaire Warm Mist CP-2550 and the CP-3210 (**The Rival Company**). They have Teflon-coated heating elements. A larger four-gallon model comes with an electret air filter. You can call the manufacturer for a nearby dealer. Some models can be ordered from **Allergy Control Products, Inc.**, **Service Merchandise** (stores and catalog), **eMD.com**, and **BreatheFree.com**.

If you decide you'd like a whole-house humidifier that would be permanently installed in the ductwork of your forced-air furnace, a steam type would probably be best. Several brands of these are currently available, so check your local heating/cooling contractor to see what they're currently handling. In addition, you can purchase the Skuttle by mail order from **E.L. Foust Co., Inc.** This is a whole-house steam model constructed of stainless steel. An optional automatic flushing unit is available to help reduce mineral build up. (It flushes every 12 hours.) (Note: Whole house models generally require professional installation.)

Dehumidifiers

Dehumidifiers can be important aids in reducing indoor relative humidity levels. For information on dehumidifiers, and the importance of reducing the humidity in your home, see *High Relative Humidity* on page 530.

CHAPTER 24: WATER QUALITY

As everyone knows, good quality water is essential to good health. This chapter discusses some of the more common home water problems. The following chapter will offer suggestions for equipment that is available to help reduce or eliminate them.

Common Water Quality Concerns

Many people believe that tap water is simply H_2O—two molecules of hydrogen combined with one of oxygen. Actually, water is a very complex solution. In fact, each water sample contains a unique set of minerals in varying amounts, biological life, dissolved gases such as radon, a particular *pH level* (its acidity-alkalinity content), and a some chemical contamination. It also differs in its *turbidity* (degree of clarity), taste, and smell.

Why does water vary so greatly? One major reason is that water is a *universal solvent*. In other words, it easily dissolves many of the substances with which it comes in contact. It also puts many other substances into suspension. In addition, water can provide the ideal environment in which certain microbes thrive. As a result, water composition varies simply because it comes from so many different locales and sources, and it can be altered by virtually everything it touches. Water sources can include wells (private or municipal) that tap into *aquifers* (underground geologic formations holding or conveying water), springs, rainwater *cisterns* (holding tanks), rivers, reservoirs, or lakes.

Then, too, water can be altered by local utility departments when they filter it and subject it to *chlorine* or *fluoride* treatments. Furthermore, water can vary because of how it eventually reaches your faucet. Did it travel through cement, asbestos/cement, plastic, cast iron, copper, or perhaps lead pipes? Were the soldered joints connecting the copper pipes and copper fittings made with lead-based or lead-free solder?

When you consider all the possibilities, you can start to see how complicated the subject of water really is. While this book will address some of the more common problems and solutions, you may be interested in learning more on the topic. Therefore, you might want to read *The Home Water Supply: How to Find, Filter, Store, and Conserve It* by Stu Campbell or *The Drinking Water Book: A Complete Guide to Safe Drinking Water* by Colin Ingram. You also should check with your local library, bookstore, board of health, water utility, county extension agent for other appropriate books and literature that delve into the complexities of water. Finally, you may wish to contact the EPA (**Environmental Protection Agency**) for booklets on home water that you can order. They also sponsor a toll-free **Safe Drinking Water Hotline**.

The following sections should help you become more aware of contaminants that could be in your water, and the potential aesthetic and health consequences of these ingredients to you and your family.

Important Note: A few of the filtering strategies for removing certain contaminants are suggested below. While they should be effective, other methods may also work just as well.

Biological Contaminants

It's not uncommon for water sources to harbor microorganisms. Fortunately, most of these contaminants are relatively safe—but not all. Following is some information on what might be living in your water.

Waterborne Cysts

Of all the possible biological contaminants, one that has many people alarmed these days is *protozoan cysts*. A dramatic awakening of public consciousness about this contaminant began in Milwaukee in 1993 when 100 people died, and thousands of others became ill (with symptoms similar to "intestinal flu" for about 12 days), simply from drinking the public water supply. Despite following their typical disinfection procedures, it was determined that the cause of this misery was due to a certain biological contamination, one that had previously not been of much concern, *Cryptosporidiaum parvum* oocysts.

To make this a bit more understandable, *Cryptosporidiaum parvum* is the scientific designation for a particular *protozoa* (a class of single-celled microscopic animals), commonly known as Crypto. *Oocysts* are their nearly indestructible, undivided, fertilized eggs which are in an encysted state. So, what's an encysted state? In Crypto's case, the *cysts* are the spherical, thick, encasing membranes surrounding these eggs. (Cysts are created by some organisms as protection when certain environmental conditions are sensed, or as part of their normal life cycle.) So, *Cryptosporidiaum parvum* oocysts are extremely durable, tough, hardy Crypto eggs.

For some time now, another protozoan cyst was already known to be a problem in some water supplies, *Giardia lamlia* often known as Giardia. (Unlike Crypto, these are not fertilized eggs.) As it turns out, Giardia can cause diarrhea or intestinal distress of varying severity. Hikers and campers are increasingly becoming infected with Giardia after drinking what they thought was pure water from a stream or lake.

Why are there problems with protozoan cysts now, when there have been regulations to prevent water pollution on the books for years? No one has the definitive answer. What is known is that both Crypto and Giardia can thrive in surface water that's been contaminated by human or animal waste. Surprisingly, it's apparently fairly difficult to test for the presence of these biological contaminants in water. Worse, in their encysted states, they're very hard to kill by standard means, such as typical doses of disinfectants. Giardia cysts can be killed by "intense exposure" to chlorine. However, the chlorine level must be so elevated that it's only done by utilities on a "need-only" basis. Yet, even this apparently doesn't work well against Crypto oocysts.

So, what can be done to eliminate cysts from a water supply? Obviously, the first step is to find and stop the flow of fecal matter into the water. If cysts are already present, the best method to remove them is by straining them out. It should be pointed out here that cysts will not be present in water from underground aquifers. So, if your utility or home-water supply is drawn from a deep well, you will not have cysts in your water. If your water-supply is from a surface-water source, and you're concerned, then you can use ceramic filters, carbon-block filters, certain micro-pore material filters, reverse-osmosis units, or distillation to make sure your water's safe. By the way, while ultraviolet-light purifiers can kill other biological contaminants fairly easily, cysts are generally far less susceptible to standard exposure levels. (Information about various filtering strategies will be covered in *Chapter 25: Improving Your Water*.)

Other Types of Biological Contaminants

Besides cysts, other types of microorganisms found in water can pose a health threat. These include certain species of bacteria (*salmonella*, for instance), parasitic worms, amoebae, molds, algae, and viruses. Therefore, water utilities constantly monitor the water they process for a problematic microbial content. As a rule, they add a very reactive purifying substance such as chlorine, or sometimes ozone, to kill most of the disease-causing microbes in the water.

Of course, individual water systems, such as private home wells, can also contain unwanted amoebae, bacteria, and other microbes. This is especially likely if the home's septic field is too near the well—that is, if it is less than 100' away. Or if the water supply is siphoned from a surface source such as a pond. As a result, it's imperative for individual homeowners to accept responsibility for their own personal water system by having their water tested regularly.

By the way, when a professional water-testing laboratory examines a water sample provided by a homeowner, it often checks first for the presence of *coliforms* (*fecal* and/or *total*) and also *fecal streptococcus*. (See *Water Testing* on page 593.) While these bacteria are not particularly desirable components in your water, labs look for them because they're considered *marker species*. In other words, if they're present, then it's likely that more harmful microbes are also living in the same water.

If it turns out you have serious biological contamination in your home's water supply, drilling a new well or shutting off your pond-water supply may be necessary. However, if the situation is less severe, there are home-treatment strategies that can often help. For example, certain reverse-osmosis units are capable of removing much of the bacteria, and other biological contaminants, that are present. Ceramic filters are usually good choices, too, as are some micro-pore-material filters.

Effective methods of killing biological contaminants in your water include *water distillation* and, in most cases, *ultraviolet-light purification*. Still other purifying approaches that can be used by homeowners include *pasteurization* (heating the water to over 150°F for a period of time), *ozonization* (exposing the water to ozone gas), and adding specific amounts of iodine or some other sterilizing agent to the water. The list goes on. It should also be mentioned that KDF filtering media has been considered innately bacteriostatic (able to kill bacteria on it's surface).

Industrial and Agricultural Pollutants

Sadly, a growing threat to water everywhere is the pollution generated and released by manufacturing and agricultural products and practices. The sections below discuss this potentially toxic situation.

Industrial Pollution

Unfortunately, experts are now telling us that much of America's water supplies have already become contaminated, to varying degrees, with potentially dangerous pollutants originating from poorly managed industries, mines, and dump sites, among others. These *adulterants* can include acids, solvents, cleaning solutions, caustic compounds, dissolved gases, radioactive material, and other poisonous substances, including heavy metals. As a result, unacceptable levels of copper (Cu), selenium (Se), cobalt (Co), cadmium (Cd), arsenic (As), and other pollutants, are no longer rare occurrences in water supplies.

Each of these has its own individual negative toxicological effects. Therefore, depending on the particular pollutants, the amounts of them you ingest, as well as your own personal susceptibility, a whole range of possible symptoms could result. In a worst-case scenario, central-nervous-system problems, birth defects, and even cancer could result from drinking water containing a high concentration of industrial pollutants.

Perhaps not surprisingly, one of the more common chemical pollutants in U.S. water supplies is gasoline. It seems that gasoline has been getting into our water supplies for decades by way of leaks from petroleum refineries and underground service-station tanks. However, another major source is from individuals simply spilling or dumping gasoline on the ground. It was estimated in 1991 that there were 1.4 million leaking underground gasoline (and other hazardous material) storage tanks in U.S. As a result, the U.S Environmental Protection Agency required the replacement of such tanks by the end of 1998. However, many tanks were exempted from the regulations and therefore were not required to be replaced. Sadly, even some of the new tanks are already leaking into the surrounding soil.

As it turns out, the gasoline that has already entered into water supplies hasn't merely added dangerous petroleum hydrocarbons to the water content, but also lead (Pb) as well. This is because *tetraethyl lead* and *tetramethyl lead* were used as popular gasoline additives for decades, and were only phased out a few years ago. Unfortunately, as most people now realize, lead can be toxic when it's ingested. It's slowly absorbed by the human body, and it becomes concentrated in the liver and kidneys. Lead can eventually lead to mental retardation in children and hypertension in adults, among many other debilitating conditions. Sadly, the **EPA (Environmental Protection Agency)** has concluded that 10-20% of the lead found in children is from tap water. Yet, it's considered too small a percentage to effectively regulate. For more on lead, contact the EPA's **National Lead Information Center**.

Even worse than the lead problem is the on-going environmental tragedy caused by a particular gasoline additive known as methyl t-butyl ether (MTBE). For some time, it has been used as an *oxgenator* in small amounts, because it's unique chemical composition provides extra oxygen to gasoline. This is important because this added oxygen allows for more efficient, more complete combustion, and therefore fewer combustion by-products (components of smog) are created. Interestingly, with the passage of the Clean Air Act in 1990, refineries were suddenly required to produce gasoline with 2% oxygen. Since they had already been using MTBE, they simply increased it's percentage in each gallon. This new *reformulated gasoline* contains nearly 10% MTBE.

While MTBE may be great at helping to reduce air pollution, it's now been determined that it is extremely water soluble, doesn't biodegrade, and "spreads further and faster than other gasoline additives" in soils and ground water. Frighteningly, apparently 49 states have already reported at least some MTBE in water supplies. In some locales having high levels of MTBE, which smells like turpentine, private and utility wells have been permanently shut down. So widespread is the MTBE pollution that it has been called the "second most common" chemical contaminant in our water. While the EPA is obviously concerned (they suspect MTBE to be a human carcinogen), there's not much research going on to determine MTBE's true potential health consequences. Unbelievably, most places aren't required to test for it, or to meet a maximum concentration (parts per millions) in their water. Furthermore, the provisions of the Clean Air Act of 1990 that require gasoline oxygenation are still on the books

Agricultural Pollution

Farm chemicals such as fertilizers, pesticides, and herbicides are another growing threat to America's water supplies (Of course, home garden and lawn chemicals are no less toxic, so they should also be included here.). A number of these products contain *nitrates* such as *nitrogen nitrate*. Unfortunately, it seems, most nitrate compounds have the capacity to interfere with the ability of our red blood cells to transport oxygen throughout the body. The negative health effects of drinking water with a high concentration of nitrates are particularly bad for pregnant women and small children.

Coping with Industrial and Agricultural Pollution in Water

Fortunately, most utility-supplied water is relatively safe from many types of industrial and agricultural pollution—although the situation varies from utility to utility. One reason for this is that utility water is usually required to be regularly tested for the presence of certain chemical contaminants. If one of these particular chemicals is detected in a high concentration, it's often removed, or reduced to acceptable levels, through filtration or some other treatment method. But if a utility's water is too contaminated, it may be necessary for them to locate another less-polluted source.

Generally, individual home water systems are not continually monitored for industrial and agricultural pollution. Therefore, some supplies could easily contain unsuspected levels of heavy metals or chemical pollutants that may not have been present in the past. Unfortunately, thorough testing—and then removing—certain agricultural and industrial contaminates from your home water supply can be both difficult and expensive.

As an important side note, you should be aware that recently a simple, at-home, reusable lead test has become available. Called the LeadCheck Aqua (**HybriVet Systems, Inc.**), it can provide results in only ninety minutes. This product can be ordered directly from the manufacturer or from **American Environmental Health Foundation**. (For more on testing, see *Water Testing* on page 593.)

Fortunately, if you find that the contamination and concentration can be handled by simple methods, a homeowner can treat his (or her) water and make it drinkable. For example, *activated charcoal in block form*, especially if it has a special precoating can be used to remove many kinds of *organic chemicals* (carbon-containing chemicals such as gasoline), as well as nitrates and heavy metals. One filter media that may be superior at lead removal is Aluminum Titanium Silicate (ATS). In addition, KDF media can take out lead. Water distillers and reverse-osmosis units can remove nearly all the nitrates and heavy metals.

At the same time, it must be said that, in some cases, reducing levels of certain agricultural and industrial pollutants to acceptable limits is just not feasible. In those instances, a new well may have to be drilled or outside water may need to be brought in. Sometimes, the water may be safe enough for general-purpose use—but not safe enough for drinking and cooking.

Suspended Particulates

A high level of *suspended particulates* in your water indicates that it has *turbidity*. As a result, the water will appear cloudy. The particulates themselves may be anything from bits of soil, to bacteria, algae, or mold. Sometimes, the suspended material is a combination of different types of solid matter.

To test for the specific turbidity level, water-testing laboratories generally direct a beam of light through the water sample. A measurement is then made of the amount of light that is scattered, because of its inability to pass through the cloudy sample. This figure is then compared to the measurement obtained from clear water undergoing the same procedure. Other tests can then be performed to determine the precise composition of the suspended particulates.

If suspended particulates are simply dirt or sand granules, they can usually be removed easily by using *settling tanks* or special *turbidity filters*. These low-technology solutions are generally quite effective, and they are commonly used both by utilities and private well owners. Of course, utilities also disinfect the water with extremely reactive *chlorine* or *ozone* gas to kill most forms of biologic life that could also be contributing to the cloudiness.

In home situations, if there is just a small amount of soil and/or sand present in the water, it can sometimes be satisfactorily strained out (not adsorbed) with an *activated-charcoal filter*—especially one in *solid-block form* (this is because blocks allow for a certain amount of *mechanical filtration*). This approach will be even more effective if the solid block has a special precoating. *Ceramic filters* can also strain out particles. Membranes such as those in *reverse-osmosis units* or *micro-pore-material filters* will also work—however the grit can be very wearing. Therefore, unless there's an effective prefilter, this approach is often not the best one to use, especially reverse-osmosis where membrane replacement could be relatively costly. However, *distillation* will remove virtually all suspended particulates including biological ones.

High Concentrations of Common Minerals

Several common minerals (for example, calcium, magnesium, iron, manganese, and sodium chloride) can cause problems when they are found in elevated concentrations in your water. Interestingly, these same particular minerals aren't considered toxic substances if they're ingested in very small quantities. In fact, all these minerals are actually necessary for the proper functioning of the human body, so they are often found in vitamin supplements.

Generally, if any of these minerals are above standard, established limits in a utility's water, the utility will use various treatment methods to reduce their levels. Of course, homeowners with private water supplies can perform tests on their water to determine it's specific mineral content, and then use treatment methods to lower the level of dissolved minerals in their water, if necessary. These treatment methods will be mentioned under each heading below.

Calcium

Calcium (Ca) is a lightweight, silver-white metal. Interestingly, if the dissolved calcium levels are high in your water, it's common for dissolved magnesium (and perhaps other dissolved minerals) to also exist in large amounts. By the way, if calcium and/or magnesium are present at a concentration over 120 milligrams per liter of water (mg/l), the term *hard water* is typically used to describe it. Interestingly, it's been estimated that over 85% of water in the U.S. is considered hard.

Unfortunately, water with a high dissolved-calcium content is often troublesome for those using it. This is because it causes soaps to create insoluble scum (soap curds). This happens because the minerals react with the fat and oil ingredients of the soap (see *Soaps versus Detergents* on page 75). Also, *lime* or *lime scale* (a crusty coating) can form on the interior of pipes and plumbing fixtures when the dissolved mineral compounds *precipitate* (come out of solution). Even at levels as low as 85 mg/l, problems like these can still be experienced.

Fortunately, water hardness is relatively easy and inexpensive to test for and treat. Often *water-softening devices* using *sodium-ion/calcium-ion exchange* technology will solve most hard-water problems. However, there are also a variety of other alternative water-conditioning approaches to counter the effects of hard water. Of course, *distillation* and *reverse-osmosis units* are also usually capable of removing calcium and other dissolved minerals.

Magnesium

Magnesium (Mg), in its purest form, is a silvery-white metal. In fresh water, both dissolved magnesium and magnesium-calcium compounds are commonly present together. These two minerals are primarily responsible for *water hardness*. (For more on the problems and solutions to high magnesium content in your water, see *Calcium* above.)

Iron

Iron (Fe) is one of the most common metals on earth. In its pure state, it's a silvery-white solid. However, it's very easily *oxidized*, forming rust. Therefore, a high dissolved-iron content in water will have a reddish-orange color which will, in turn, stain your laundry, sinks, etc. To complicate matters, *iron bacteria* may also be present. These are often the cause of an orange slime inside your toilet tank.

Fortunately, the iron content in water can be easily tested for. If there's a high level present (above 0.3 mg/l), a typical ion-exchange water softener will generally help lower it. However, special iron/rust-removal filters are also available. A high manganese level may accompany a high iron level in your water.

Homeowners who have iron bacteria in their water supply will probably want to use some sort of filtering unit, or a more thorough disinfecting treatment such as an ultraviolet-light purifier, to deal with the problem. It should be noted that some reverse-osmosis equipment will remove, not only the dissolved iron, but also much of the iron bacteria as well. Another option would be to use a KDF filtering media. It will alter the problematic dissolved iron into insoluble *ferric oxide (Fe_2O_3)*, which is a solid form of iron. Note, too, that the KDF media also has a *bacteriostatic effect* which will reduce microbe populations in the filter. (Keep in mind the fact that a KDF filter shouldn't be relied on to kill pathogenic, disease-causing bacteria.) Distillation is even more effective, and will completely remove both the iron and iron bacteria.

Manganese

Sometimes dissolved *manganese* accompanies dissolved iron in water. Manganese (Mn), in its purest state, is a silvery-gray metal. High concentrations of dissolved manganese (above 0.05 mg/liter) will tend to make the water grayish or brownish-black. Unfortunately, any fixtures or laundry that come in contact with such water will likely become stained by it. To make matters worse, water with high levels of dissolved manganese can also have an unpleasant taste. *Manganese bacteria* may be contained in the mix as well.

Homes with individual water supplies can have them tested for their specific manganese content. If it's too high, a typical water conditioner using a mineral-ion exchange process can greatly reduce the amount in the water. However, if manganese bacteria are also living in the water, some additional type of filtering or disinfecting treatment may be necessary as well.

By the way, certain reverse-osmosis equipment will remove dissolved manganese, and often much of the bacteria, too. However, distillation will completely remove both of them. KDF media is capable of removing dissolved manganese, but only at a very slow rate. Therefore, KDF is generally not the method of choice for its removal.

Sodium Chloride

Sodium chloride (NaCl) is apparently becoming a more common contaminant in some home water supplies in some parts of the country. As you probably know, sodium chloride is common table salt. In ocean water, sodium chloride makes up about 80% of all the dissolved solids present. Not surprisingly, it's often sea water seeping into coastal wells that has caused sodium chloride levels to become excessive in certain areas. However, whatever the source of the salt, fresh water containing too much of it is termed *brackish*. Of course, a high level of dissolved sodium in drinking water is considered a real health concern—especially for people with hypertension or other medical conditions whose physicians have recommended that they restrict their salt intake.

Testing for sodium chloride in home water systems is not difficult. If your water has a chloride level over 250 mg/l (which would include sodium chloride) it will likely be corrosive and have a bad taste. If sodium chloride is found at an unacceptable concentration, a homeowner can sometimes use a special whole-house reverse-osmosis unit, fitted with a membrane rated for salt removal, to take it out of the water. Distillation will remove virtually any salt that is present in the water.

It should be mentioned that sodium chloride is used in *ion-exchange water softeners*. The salt is usually in the form of pellets that are added to a special tank, in which they dissolve and become brine. Through *catalytic action*, the salt's sodium ions are exchanged for the hard water's mineral ions. As a result, while the treated water will have very low amounts of dissolved hard-water minerals, it'll probably have elevated levels of sodium. If you're on a low-sodium diet, and you have a water softener that adds sodium to the water, you might consider a reverse-osmosis unit with a membrane rated for sodium removal (or a water distiller) in your kitchen to make your drinking and cooking water salt-free.

Naturally Occurring Gases

There are several naturally occurring—but dangerous—gases that can be dissolved in water. Three of these—radon, hydrogen sulfide, and methane—are discussed below. Often, if utility water contains high levels of undesirable gases, the utility will remove them through a relatively simple *aeration process*. In aeration, the water is misted or mixed with air. This causes any dissolved gases to readily escape from the liquid water. The freed gases are then vented away. Homeowners with problem gases in their individual water systems have other options for dealing with them, as discussed below.

Radon

Radon (Rn) is an odorless, colorless, radioactive gas. While radon has twenty different *isotopes* (isotopes are unique atomic forms, each having a different number of neutrons), it's *radon-222*, which originates in *radium* in the ground, that is typically a concern to homeowners. This is the isotope that could lead to real health problems if dissolved in your well water.

If it turns out that radon is, indeed, present in your well water, the radioactive gas will be released into your home's air every time the water is exposed to the air indoors. If the radon becomes trapped inside the house, it'll begin to decay into radioactive *radon decay products*. Unfortunately, these microscopic solid particles can become lodged in your lung tissue, possibly leading to lung cancer. Radon is now suspected of being the second leading cause of lung cancer in the U.S., right behind cigarettes.

Not surprisingly, most experts now believe that all home well-water systems should be tested for radon. (Well water in the state of Maine often has excessive radon.) Experts recommend treating water with a radon level exceeding 20,000 pC/l. (Interestingly, for every 10,000 pC/l of radon present in the water, approximately 1 pC/l will be released into the air.) Activated-charcoal filters will adsorb radon gas from the water. However, they can't retain the radioactive decay particles, most of which are short-lived. On the other hand, certain reverse-osmosis units will remove these particles, but not the radon gas itself.

You can remove 90% or more of the radon from water, according to the Land and Water Resource Center at the University of Maine, by using a specially designed whole-house granular-activated-charcoal adsorption filter. These units will not only remove radon, but also retain their particulate decay products. (Important note: These treatment devices are much larger than the relatively small activated-charcoal filters used for taste-and-odor problems in home water supplies.) Granular-activated-charcoal units for radon removal range in size, but they're usually 1-3 cubic feet in capacity. The actual size for a particular situation will depend on the amount of radon present, and the volume of water used daily.

Granular-activated-charcoal adsorption tanks are often sold and installed by local plumbers and water-treatment companies. To find help in dealing with a radon problem in your water, contact your local board of health or the **Water Quality Association**. This is the national organization for water-treatment equipment dealers. Written information on radon in well water is available from the **EPA (Environmental Protection Agency)**. You may also want to call their **Safe Drinking Water Hot Line**.

Hydrogen Sulfide

In its pure form, *Sulfur* (S) is a yellow, insoluble, solid material. Unfortunately, even a very small trace of it (0.05 mg/ liter) in water, will usually produce an unpleasant rotten-egg smell. A tiny trace of dissolved sulfur will also tarnish silver items and even corrode metal pipes.

One of the most common forms sulfur takes in water is dissolved *hydrogen sulfide* (H_2S), which is also sometimes known as *sulfureted hydrogen*. This is a toxic, flammable gas that is considered a cumulative poison. As a rule, water tests can easily determine if any is present in a particular water sample.

If you find you only have a very minute amount of hydrogen sulfide in your water, it can often be safely and effectively adsorbed with an *activated-charcoal filter*. In addition, KDF media can alter dissolved H_2S gas into an insoluble compound. However, for more than a very tiny amount of H_2S in your water, it may be best to use a more specialized filter (or strategies) to remove it.

Methane

Methane (CH_4) can sometimes be found in water sources (This is the gas that makes up about 85% of *natural gas*.). Generally, methane's presence results from the action of *anaerobic bacteria* (bacteria that are able to live without oxygen). The bacteria cause dead vegetable matter (grasses for example) to *ferment*. What happens is that the complex, organic, molecular compounds, are broken down into simpler ones, one being methane. In wetland areas, escaping methane is sometimes called *swamp gas*.

Surprising to most people, pure methane is actually a colorless, odorless, as well as tasteless, gas. It's also apparently nonpoisonous. But methane is quite explosive, and if it builds up to a sufficient concentration in your room air, it can cause suffocation. Therefore, if tests reveal methane in your water, it may be necessary to vent the water supply to the outdoors. However, very tiny amounts of methane can sometimes be satisfactorily adsorbed by simply using an *activated-charcoal filter*.

Prescription Medications

One class of pollutants that has not been considered much involves the vast variety of human and animal prescription medications now being found in increasing concentrations in our water supplies. These include hormones, chemotherapy drugs, pain killers, antibiotics, antidepressants, tranquilizers, etc. Some of these find their way into drinking water sources because leftover, old, or unwanted drugs are simply flushed down the toilet, or poured down the sink drain. Other medications are illegally dumped, along with contaminated syringes, etc., into waterways—where there are no questions asked, no fees, and no regulations.

However, a far greater percentage of medication pollution is simply excreted out from people and animals. It may be surprising to learn that, in reality, only a fraction of most prescription drugs are utilized internally. In fact, the majority (typically 50-90%) are eliminated in urine and feces—unchanged from the original chemical formulation. The remainder is excreted in the form of metabolites. These are chemicals produced as by-products of the body's interaction with the drug(s).

Think about the routine practice of dosing farm animal with antibiotics, growth stimulators, etc. and their resulting medication-rich urine and dung. This excrement is often completely untreated. Of course, most human urine and feces is "properly" disposed of in private septic systems, or by utility waste-water treatment plants. Yet, in all these cases, the medicinal compounds don't biodegrade into harmless, simple components. That's because many of them were formulated to be *persistent* (long-lasting) and *lipophilic* (dissolvable only in fat, not water).

Furthermore, some reports indicate that prescription drug metabolites may be even more persistent and lipophilic than the original medications. It's little wonder then that many prescription drugs (and their metabolites) accumulate in the environment, and eventually enter water supplies. According to *Rachel's Environment & Health Weekly,* "German scientists report that anywhere from 30 to 60 drugs can be measured in a typical water sample." It's very likely that American water samples would produce similar results.

Interestingly, it was not until 1972 (when drugs were first accidentally detected in Kansas City's sewage) that there was any real concern about prescription medications being an environmental pollutant. Apparently, no one had even thought to look for them in the environment before. Today, the U.S. Food and Drug Administration (FDA) has taken the position that it's officially concerned about drugs in the nation's water supply. However, they feel that the current concentrations are still too low to pose any danger. Yet, at the same time, they've created a regulatory policy aimed at all new drugs, that requires manufacturers to provide "estimates of concentrations that result from excretion." So, progress is being made—slowly.

As a water-using consumer, having medicinal residues and/or their metabolites in your drinking water is not ideal at any concentration. However, it's difficult to say, at this time, with any certainty, how to best remove them at home. Of course, it's likely that a certain quantity could be removed by activated charcoal, especially carbon blocks, but perhaps not all. Distillation may be helpful, too, but will it remove every compound? One water tester (a pro-reverse-osmosis advocate) believes that "only reverse-osmosis units can be trusted to do a good job on these kinds of pollutants." Because of the current lack of information, it's probably safe to say that water distillers with activated-charcoal filters, and reverse-osmosis units with activated-charcoal filters are likely the better treatment options.

Water-Utility Chemical Additives

As a result of constant testing, and ongoing water-utility treatments, our public water supplies are usually safer than many untreated private water sources. However, it should be noted that a water utility's treatments can create their own, unique water-quality problems.

Commonly, utilities disinfect their water by adding *chlorine*. In addition, many U.S. utilities also add *fluoride* to minimize dental decay. However, both of these additives are corrosive and highly reactive, and each has negative consequences associated with it. Therefore, both chlorine and fluoride are considered contaminants by many individuals.

Chlorine

Chlorine (Cl) is a heavy, greenish-yellow gas with a distinctively pungent odor. It's an element that is classified as a *halogen* (a family of certain nonmetallic elements). Chlorine is extremely corrosive and reactive. It is these very qualities that make it an effective disinfectant, because it reacts with and destroys many types of microorganisms.

Since the early 1900s, U.S. water utilities have commonly used a form of chlorine to *oxidize* (react with) and eliminate waterborne bacterial contaminants. In practice, chlorine is often added twice by utilities. First, the chemical is added to the raw water to kill much of the microbial life before other water-treatment processes are performed. Then, chlorine is added again as a final disinfecting treatment before the water is piped out to the public. In this last chlorination, the utilities add enough of it so that its concentration remains high enough to effectively kill microorganisms even at the furthest ends of the water system. Because chlorine levels diminish with time, the homes that are near a water-utility facility will have much higher chlorine levels in their water, than the homes further down the line.

Interestingly, because chlorine is so reactive, it tends to corrode the water pipes it flows through. To help counter this, utilities often add *lime* (certain calcium compounds), *soda ash*, *zinc phosphate*, or other substances, along with the chlorine. However, even with these additions, the interiors of *galvanized pipes* (steel pipes coated with zinc to prevent rusting) can become rough and irregular after carrying chlorinated water. Unfortunately, these irregular surfaces may attract, and become havens for, bacterial growth. Although they might not be *pathological* (disease-causing), these bacteria can be destructive to certain types of reverse-osmosis membranes.

There are other problems with chlorination. Chlorine can apparently react with certain trace metals and nonmetals in the water, forming new compounds. Unfortunately, some of these are harmful, such as *chloroform*. Known chemically as *trichloromethane* ($CHCl_3$), chloroform is created when chlorine compounds react with carbon-containing organic matter.

This may lead you to ask some serious questions. What are the real effects on millions of Americans who drink chlorinated water daily? Is the corrosive chlorine itself a problem? Are the compounds formed in chlorinated water really a cause for concern? For some time now, opponents of chlorination have asked these questions. In 1992, research undertaken at both Harvard University and the Medical College of Wisconsin provided evidence that chlorine-treated drinking water seems to increase incidences of bladder and rectal cancers in men.

Unfortunately, simply taking a bath in chlorinated water can also be a problem, because the chlorine can readily be absorbed through the skin. It's been estimated that your skin will absorb as much chlorine, during a typical shower, as you would normally take in by drinking six eight-ounce glasses of chlorinated water—in fact, some reports say that you're skin will absorb up to 5 times more chlorine.

Then there's the chlorine you inhale while showering. Chlorine in the air can lead to eye, nasal, respiratory irritation. In certain allergic and sensitive individuals, it can cause a variety of adverse reactions. And even if you are not sensitive or allergic, it will have a drying effect on your skin and hair (it actually weakens hair shafts).

Specifically concerning chloroform, The Center for Environmental Epidemiology at the University of Pittsburgh reported that when showering, about half of the dissolved chloroform present escapes into the air before the chlorinated water spray reaches the tub floor. The other 50% remains in the water to be potentially absorbed by the skin. It was also noted in *The American Journal of Public Health* (Vol. 74., #5) that 64% of adult's, and over 90% of children's, total daily exposure to volatile organic compounds (VOCs) was by skin absorption of chlorinated household water.

Obviously, if your water is chlorinated, you may decide that you want to remove the chlorine from it. This can be done easily using an activated-charcoal filter. However, activated charcoal adsorbs less efficiently with hot water than cold water. When used with hot water, odorless, tasteless trihalomehtnanes may be released into the water stream. Therefore, it's much better to use activated charcoal *before* the water is heated. So, shower filters using activated charcoal may not be as effective at removing chlorine and chlorine by-products as many people believe. A better shower-filter media is probably KDF which has been shown to change chlorine into a less troublesome zinc-chloride compound.

Fluoride

Fluoride compounds are also commonly added to utility water. However, most users of utility water know very little about these additives. As it turns out, pure fluorine is a light-yellow gaseous member of the halogen family (a certain class of nonmetallic elements). It's poisonous, corrosive, and very reactive. In fact, fluorine is considered the most reactive element on earth, and fluoride compounds retain much of fluorine's characteristics. The most common fluoride compound added to water supplies is *flurosilicic acid* (H_2SiF_6).

Apparently, the fluoride used by most utilities is derived from industrial by-products (*e.g.* from aluminum and phosphate fertilizer plants, etc.). In 1989, the EPA estimated that U.S. industries released about 155,000 tons of fluoride compounds into the air, and about 500,000 tons annually into the country's waterways. Because these are not biodegradable, they keep accumulating in the environment and eventually enter the food chain. Some people see the use of such industrial leftovers as a positive step at recycling for the common good. Others view it as a way for industries to get rid of unwanted, hazardous fluoride compounds—at a profit.

Interestingly, fluoride compounds can naturally be present in some water sources. And it was exactly because of this that fluoridation of utility water eventually came about. As it turns out, in the 1930s and 1940s reports were published that cited comparisons between individuals whose drinking water contained naturally high levels of fluoride (from 0.9 to 1.4 parts per million, or ppm), with those whose drinking water had very little fluoride. These comparisons seemed to indicate a direct correlation between high fluoride levels and low rates of *dental caries* (tooth decay). Long-term studies were then devised to determine what the effect would be on decay rates with water having fluoride artificially added to it. However, before these studies were ever completed, the U.S. Public Health Service, starting in 1950, began approving (and encouraging) the addition of fluoride to public water supplies. Today, about one-half of all U.S. public water utilities now add fluoride to reach a level of about 1 ppm in their water.

How does fluoride work against dental caries? It's been thought that fluoride prevented tooth decay because it caused calcium to redeposit onto your teeth. This action would rebuild and strengthen tooth enamel. Despite this theory, fluoridation has been hotly debated ever since its inception.

Today, proponents of fluoridation, such as the American Dental Association and the American Medical Association, point to statistics showing a substantial drop in the average child's dental decay rate since fluoridation's introduction. They maintain there's no convincing evidence that fluoridated water poses any health threat, in the concentrations that are legally allowed.

On the other hand, opponents (such as the vocal spokesman, Dr. John A. Yiamouyiannis) contend that fluoridated water is, at best, "unsolicited medication" and, at worst, a potentially health-damaging substance. The opponents believe there's evidence that fluoride is a "persistent bioaccumulator"—meaning that fluoride levels will continue to build up in your body as you ingest more of it. Unfortunately, some limited findings seem to suggest that internalized fluoride may cause immune-system and/or nervous-system problems in susceptible persons.

In addition, there are some indications that fluoride may be associated with the formation of certain fetal abnormalities and bone cancers. Furthermore, fluoride might play a contributing role in arthritis, gastric ulcers, migraines, and other maladies. (Note: It seems that those at greater risk are the very young, the old, those with kidney, heart, or immune problems, diabetics, and those with low vitamin C, magnesium, or calcium levels.)

Still another objection to utility fluoridation of water is the potential for fluorides to corrode pipes and solder. In some cases, this corrosion could cause lead in old pipes and solder to migrate into the water supply, and end up contributing to lead poisoning. Besides pipes, fluorides could also potentially corrode aluminum pots and pans, therefore, causing raised aluminum levels in the foods and drinks heated in them. This has been seen as a concern because of the of aluminum deposits found in the brains of Alzheimer's patients. Incidentally, *Brain Research* reported that a study aimed at determining the effects of aluminum on brain function, found that it wasn't the aluminum, "but low levels of fluoride that caused similar brain damage as seen in Alzheimer patients."

Surprisingly, fluoridation's opponents even dispute the contention that fluoride significantly lessens tooth decay. In fact, in 1989 the ADA lowered the estimated tooth-decay-reduction rates attributed to fluoridated water from 60% to 25%. There's also newer research that seems to suggests that *if* fluoride does lessen tooth decay, it may be because it's present in the saliva (perhaps acting as a type of antibiotic agent), *not* because it's able to harden tooth enamel.

Both proponents and opponents agree that fluoride levels of 4-5 ppm can cause mild *fluorosis* in some individuals. This is a corrosive condition in which fluoride reacts with your teeth and/or bones. Early or mild dental fluorosis generally appears as a slightly mottled discoloration, but more severe cases can show dramatic mottling and even pitting. In severe bone fluorosis, crippling may result. As a precaution against fluorosis, it's now generally agreed that children under six should not use fluoride toothpaste. This is because youngsters often swallow a great deal of the toothpaste placed on their toothbrushes, so they could easily ingest unacceptable levels of fluoride. (See also *Dental Care* on page 88.)

In 1989, the maximum contaminant level (MCL) of fluoride was set by the EPA at 4 mg/l (milligram per liter) in tap water. Then, it was lowered in 1998 to 2 mg/l for children, and even less for infants.

Because of the heated controversy over adding fluoride to water, very few new fluoride treatment programs have been initiated by U.S. utilities in the last decade. In addition, most Western European nations (including Great Britain) have already abandoned their water fluoridation programs. Ultimately, of course, you must decide whether you believe that drinking fluoride in your water is beneficial to you and your family—or something you should avoid. Books and magazine articles in your local library can offer more in-depth information on fluoridation.

At one time, it was unrealistic to think you had a good chance of convincing your utility to abandon its fluoridation program. But times have changed. Los Angeles, Newark, and a few other American cities, have yielded to public pressure and quite fluoridating their water.

However, if your current water supply is fluoridated, and you've decided you don't want fluoride in your water, most reverse-osmosis units are able to remove it. You can also remove fluoride with a water distiller. Special fluoride-removal filters are also available. These might be ion-exchange units containing activated alumina or bone-char media.

Contaminants from Supply Lines, Pipes, and Solder

Many people are unaware that the pipes and water mains carrying water can add their own contaminants. Unfortunately, some of these may cause serious health problems.

Asbestos/Concrete Water Main Concerns

The supply lines carrying your water can affect its quality. One concern that's recently been raised is the effect on humans of drinking water that's been transported through concrete water mains containing *asbestos* (a fibrous rock). Could the fibers be getting into the water and, if they do, what effect would they have on the human body? These questions were raised because asbestos fibers were already known to be a cause of severe lung disease if inhaled, so it was logical to wonder what damage they might do if they were ingested. (By the way, the reason asbestos is added to concrete pipes is to make them stronger. This type of water main has been popular for years in many parts of the U.S.)

Unfortunately, some recent studies have shown that people who drink water from asbestos supply pipes have an increased incidence of gastrointestinal cancer. Yet, The World Health Organization (WHO), in its *1993 Guidelines for Drinking Water Quality*, concluded that asbestos is not a serious health threat. However, if you want to be on the safe side, you might ask your utility if there are any asbestos-cement supply lines in its system. If there are, you may want to remove any possible asbestos fibers from your water. Activated-charcoal filters (in block form) are able to strain out most of the asbestos, as can micro-pore and ceramic filters. Asbestos fibers can also be very effectively removed by using reverse-osmosis units and water distillers.

Lead-Pipe and Lead-Solder Concerns

Lead water pipes were once common, especially in ancient times. In fact, *plumbum*, the Latin word for waterworks, is the source of the symbol for lead—Pb. However, lead pipes were once used in this country, too, although they haven't been for some time. Therefore, if you live in an older home, you'll want to check to see if it still has any lead piping. If you come across lead water pipes, you may want to have them replaced. This is because lead can migrate from the pipes into your drinking water, then slowly accumulate in your body, and eventually cause lead poisoning.

It should be mentioned that the solder used on copper pipes could also pose a problem. Lead solder was commonly used by plumbers until it was prohibited by Federal regulations in 1986. You may not be aware that brass can legally contain a small amount of lead, despite meeting what's referred to as a "lead-free standard." Therefore, there's the potential for some brass plumbing fixtures to leech a certain amount of lead into the water. By the way, fluoridated water (fluoride is corrosive) can increase your lead risk if you have either lead pipes, lead solder, or lead-containing brass fixtures.

You may be interested in knowing that the **EPA (Environmental Protection Agency)** has reported that 10-20% of the lead content in children comes from tap water. Of course, waterborne lead includes any present from industrial pollution as well. For more EPA information on lead, you may want to call their **National Lead Information Center.**

You may decide to have your water tested for lead. One simple reusable test you can do at home is LeadCheck Aqua (**HybriVet Systems, Inc.**). With this product, you have the results in 90 minutes. LeadCheck Aqua, which is reusable, can be ordered from the manufacturer or from the **American Environmental Health Foundation.**

Fortunately, activated charcoal in block form (especially if precoated) can strain out most of the lead in your water. (Some micro-pore filters and ceramic filters may be up to the job as well.) Lead can be removed very effectively by using most reverse-osmosis units and ion-exchange water softeners. Another choice is with KDF media. Furthermore, lead can be completely removed through distillation.

Galvanized-Pipe Concerns

For those with *galvanized* water pipes (steel pipes coated with zinc to prevent rusting), a special concern arises if they transport chlorinated water. Chlorine can apparently react with galvanized pipes and create irregular surfaces on their interiors. While this isn't a problem as such, these rough surfaces can become homes for *non-pathological* (non-disease causing) bacteria that can damage certain reverse-osmosis membranes.

Fortunately, reverse-osmosis units that are equipped with ultraviolet-light purifiers are able to kill these bacteria (and other kinds of waterborne microorganisms). If your reverse-osmosis unit doesn't have a built-in ultraviolet-light purifier, or some other type of *bacteriostatic* (bacteria-reducing) device, you can buy and install a separate point-of-use ultraviolet-light purifier.

Plastic Pipe Concerns

In the last few decades, the use of plastic pipes to distribute water has increased sharply. They've become common with both utilities and in residential plumbing. In fact, plastic piping is now considered the norm in many areas of the country. Although several different types of plastic are used to make water pipes, one of the more common is polyvinyl chloride (PVC).

It's easy to understand why the use of plastic pipe has become so widespread. Plastic piping is lightweight, and it is easy to assemble using volatile synthetic glues. In addition, it doesn't rust or corrode, and is generally less expensive than the various alternatives. Unfortunately, plastic pipes can give the water they carry a plastic-like taste and odor, especially if the pipes have been recently glued together. Although many people may find this unpleasant, some sensitive individuals may find the situation intolerable. Fortunately, activated-charcoal water filters will effectively adsorb most plastic-pipe tastes and odors.

Water pH

It's often important to know your water's *pH*. What does this term mean? It's the relative amounts of *hydrogen ions* ($H+$) and *hydroxide ions* ($OH-$) present or, more technically, the concentration of *hydronium ions* (H_3O+). However, don't be put off by this jargon. All you really need to know is that a pH number tells you how acidic or alkaline a substance is—in this case, your water. As it turns out, the pH scale ranges from 0 (strongly acidic) to 14 (strongly alkaline). A pH of 7 represents neutrality.

Interestingly, most natural water sources in the U.S. have a pH that's between 5 and 8.5. It's been determined that water with a pH below 6.5 can corrode metal pipes. On the other hand, a high pH (above 8.5) can cause certain iron-removal treatments to be less successful. A high pH can also give your water a caustic taste, and a *mineral scale* (a crusty coating made up of calcium and other compounds) will likely build up inside your pipes. Very high alkalinity (above 11) could be an indication that chemical pollution has contaminated your water supply.

It should be stated that a water sample's pH can be very easily determined. (A very basic test is with *litmus paper.*) If the pH is too high or two low, utilities can add corrective substances at their plant to make the water more or less acidic (or alkaline). With an individual private water supply, a low pH (high acidity) can often be raised by simply adding marble chips or crushed limestone to a special tank. However, a high pH (high alkalinity) may require the addition of *sulfuric acid* (also known as *oil of vitriol*) to the water. Unfortunately, sulfuric acid is a corrosive liquid that can be dangerous to handle.

Actually, any pH correction that's done to a home water supply should be specifically designed by a water-treatment professional. Therefore, you may want to contact the **Water**

Quality Association. This trade organization can provide you with the names, addresses, and telephone numbers of nearby members.

Water Testing

Many people are concerned about their water's quality, especially if they have a private water supply. Therefore, the sections below will introduce you to information on water testing, including a few testing laboratories, how to take a water sample, and the need for specific tests.

Frequently Performed Water Tests

The most commonly performed water test is for *pathogenic* (disease-causing) bacteria (and perhaps other harmful microbes). In practice, laboratory technicians will generally first check a water sample for the presence of *coliforms* (both *fecal* coliforms and/or *total* coliforms) and *fecal streptococcus*. Because these particular bacteria are ultimately from human's and other mammal's lower intestines, they're considered *marker species*. If they are present in a water sample, it increases the likelihood that other more harmful microbes are thriving in it, too.

Other frequently run water tests are called *chemical analysis tests*. These generally determine the levels of iron, calcium, and magnesium in water. But the tests can be expanded to include the levels of lead, chromium, selenium, arsenic, etc. in the water supply. In addition, turbidity tests can be performed to determine the degree of the water's cloudiness. Also, increasingly popular are water tests for determining whether volatile organic compounds (VOCs), pesticides, and detergents are present.

Water-Quality Concerns and their Appropriate Tests

The table on the next page covers only some of the more common water problems, and lists suggestions for the appropriate tests. Of course, because water is such a complicated substance, there could be other explanations for some water symptoms, as well as other types of tests that might be appropriate.

It should also be noted that most of the information supplied in the table applies to individual home water supplies. However, it's likely that persons who use utility water will also find portions of this chart useful.

Water Test Limitations

An important note of consideration is that water tests have their limitations. After all, they can only find what they're specifically designed to look for. Therefore, if your water tests come back from a laboratory as being "acceptable," there still could be contaminants in your water supply for which no tests were ever undertaken. Or, the contaminants may be at levels lower than the sensitivity of the tests. As was noted earlier, certain protozoan cysts are apparently difficult to detect.

You should also realize that water conditions can change fairly frequently and, as a result, so can the composition of your water. For example, water supplies can be affected by

Water-Quality Concerns   Appropriate Test(s)

- Reddish stains on laundry and/or fixtures _____ Iron.
- Brownish-black stains on laundry or fixtures
  and/or black flakes in the water _____ Manganese.
- Greenish-blue stains on laundry and/or fixtures _____ Copper.
- White scale on fixtures, or soap scum _____ Water hardness, iron.
- Dirty-appearing water _____ Turbidity, sediment, organic matter.
- Bitter-tasting water _____ Nitrates, sulfates.
- Salty-tasting water _____ Total dissolved chlorides, sodium.
- Rotten-egg smell to water _____ Hydrogen sulfide, sulfur bacteria.
- Musty, earthy smell
  or taste to the water _____ Total coliform bacteria, iron.
- Gasoline smell
  or taste to the water _____ Hydrocarbon scan,
               aromatic organic chemicals.
- Illness from drinking water _____ Total coliform bacteria,
               nitrates, sulfates.
- Infant in household _____ Nitrates.
- Lead pipes or solder_____ Lead, copper, zinc, pH.
- Corroded plumbing_____ Corrosiveness, pH, lead, iron, zinc,
            manganese, copper, sulfates, chloride.
- Well too near a septic system _____ Total coliform bacteria,nitrate,
            total dissolved solids,chloride,
            sodium, sulfates, detergents.
- Well too near a landfill _____ Total dissolved solids, pH,
            volatile organic compounds, heavy metals.

seasonal changes, temperature fluctuations, droughts, floods, industrial spills, the application of farm chemicals, and many other events throughout the year. Water quality can be especially changeable in residential-sized private water supplies. Therefore, it needs to be stressed that *the results from any water tests will only indicate the water's make-up for that particular sampling day*. Not surprisingly, some water-quality experts believe that, because of all the possible variables involved, water testing on private water systems should be done several times during the first testing year (when you just move into a house, or drill a new well, etc.) and then periodically every few years thereafter.

Furthermore, you need to know that there are several factors, which determine the accuracy of a water test, that must be considered. Most, you will have at least some control over. These include the length of time between when the water is drawn from the tap and the time it is actually analyzed, how long the tap was running before the water sample was obtained, the competency of the laboratory, and your skill in obtaining the water sample in the first place.

Obtaining a Water Sample

If you need to obtain a water sample yourself, it's very important that you make certain that you don't inadvertently contaminate it. So, you should not let your hands touch the water being sampled, the interior of the sampler container, or the interior of it's lid. Also, follow all the testing lab's instructions completely. This may include writing down a description of the water's appearance and odor immediately after filling the sample container. Finally, make sure the water-specimen canister, tube, etc. is securely sealed before you mail it, or drop it off at the laboratory.

Of course with an in-home test, you'll need to also be conscientious about not contaminating any water samples, or any containers or strips. Plus, you'll need to follow the test directions to the letter, in order to arrive at accurate results.

Water-Test Suppliers

It's very important to have a private water supply tested regularly. For households on public supplies, you may be glad to know that utilities test their water periodically. Some test more frequently than others. The schedule depends on the particular utility, local regulations, special environmental conditions, and other factors. You should be aware that a utility's water-quality-test information is available upon request from them. It's usually provided free, or at a minimum copying charge.

However, if you are on a public water system, and your contaminants originate within your home's plumbing system (high lead levels from lead solder, for example), you'll need to test your own tap to detect them. If you have a private water system, you alone are responsible for testing your water. This means contacting a qualified water-testing laboratory, deciding on the extent of the testing, and paying all the costs.

Of course, your local board of health may have some suggestions, recommendations, or referrals to help with your water-testing decisions. (In some locales they might actually do some basic types of testing for you.) If you're unable to find an appropriate testing facility, you may want to contact the **EPA (Environmental Protection Agency)** or it's **Safe Drinking Water Hotline** which should be able to provide you with the name and phone number of your nearest EPA "certification officer." By contacting your state certification officer, you'll be given the names of water-testing firms in your area that are capable of performing water tests that meet current minimum EPA standards.

Still another approach to having your water tested is to contract one of the large, nationwide, water-testing companies. A well-known one is **National Testing Laboratories, Ltd.** They offer a Watercheck test for 74 contaminants, for surface water or well water. There's also a pesticide contaminant test option. Furthermore, there are 33 Watertest tests for municipal water. Other tests offered are lead tests and special bacterial testing. Watercheck tests are also available from **Ozark Water Service & Environmental Services**, **Bio Designs**, and **Befit Enterprises Ltd.**

Another large, national company is **Suburban Water Testing Laboratories, Inc.** They offer test packages such as the City Water Special which determines the levels of fluoride, lead, copper, and cadmium. Other water tests they have available are for nitrates, hardness, pH, organic compounds, and chlorinated pesticides.

Ozark Water Service & Environmental Services is small company owned by a certified water specialist. A number of water tests are available including the NTL (which tests for 93 common contaminates including VOCs, pesticides, and coliform bacteria). Other tests are for basic well-water quality, coliform bacteria, lead, copper, and a reverse-osmosis proficiency test.

There are also other sources for water tests. For example, you can perform your own lead test at home using the LeadCheck Aqua (**HybriVet Systems, Inc.**). This at-home test will provide you with results without having to send a sample to a laboratory. With the LeadCheck Aqua, you can have the results in 90 minutes, and it's reusable. You can get LeadCheck Aqua from the manufacturer or from the **American Environmental Health Foundation**, a catalog that also sells other water tests (iron & hardness, water-soluble pesticides, a 12 contaminant/condition analysis kit, and a water quality test).

Other water tests you might consider include Safewater Check Strips (**New Wave Enviro**) home-water-test kits. There are seven available (total chlorine, free chlorine, total hardness, nitrates, nitrites, total alkalinity, and pH). In this case, you'll need to call the company for their nearest dealer. From **Befit Enterprises Ltd.**, you can get special water-filter test kits that contain 10 tests each (for pH and for chlorine) to determine if your activated-charcoal filter needs replacing. They also have a SpotCheck test for soluble pesticides in water. Still another source for home-water tests you'll want to know about is **Real Goods.**

At this point, you may be saying to yourself, "How much does testing cost?" As you might expect, the price can vary enormously. It will depend on who does the testing (you, a national laboratory, a local laboratory, your board of health, etc.), the number and types of tests that are performed, and the sophistication (the smallest amount that can be detected and the accuracy). In the end, the more technology, skill, and analysis that's required, the higher your water-test costs will be.

CHAPTER 25: IMPROVING YOUR WATER

Many people just don't trust the healthfulness of their water, even if it's utility water. This chapter will discuss treatments and techniques that both large public utilities, and small private water systems, typically use to improve their water quality—to make it safer, look or smell better, and perhaps add other desirable traits. For homeowners, specific types of filters and suppliers are offered.

Water Treatment

All utility water, and many private home water supplies, are processed in ways that are designed to remove (or add) certain substances or characteristics. This section discusses some of the more common methods and what they can accomplish.

Common Utility Water Treatments

Today, most American homes use utility-supplied water. As it turns out, about half of this water comes from surface-water sources (rivers, lakes, reservoirs, etc.) and the rest is pumped from wells that tap into *aquifers* (geological formations that contain or conduct ground water). Regardless of the source, most utilities perform treatments on their water to raise its quality before they pipe it out into their service areas.

Today in the U.S., public water utilities must meet the regulations set out in the 1974 Federal Safe Drinking Water Act and all its later revisions. Therefore, since 1975, all water systems with more than fifteen year-round connections are under the authority of the National Interim Primary Drinking Water Regulations. These standards cover physical qualities (taste and appearance), microbial content, and chemical make-up (amounts of dissolved minerals, etc.). As a result, virtually all water utilities must treat their water to achieve mandated minimum water-quality levels. Although all public water utilities aren't required to perform the same particular set of treatment programs, many of them do, in fact, follow similar procedures. Following are typical steps performed by some larger water utilities.

The first step a public utility might commonly use is *pretreatment* in which the *raw water* simply passes through a screen to remove large debris. Then, a *settlement treatment* is often performed, in which the water is allowed to remain in a reservoir or tank for twenty hours or so. During that time, any suspended silt in the water will sink to the bottom, leaving the water free of larger particles. Next, the first chlorination step is usually performed to kill biological contaminants. Then the water is often subjected to *aeration*. Although there are different methods for doing this (spraying water into the air, having air bubble up from the bottom of a tank, etc.), aeration results in gaseous volatile organic compounds (VOCs), and unpleasant tastes and odors, escaping from the liquid water and being vented away.

Usually the next process is *coagulation* in which certain chemicals such as *ferric chloride* or *lime* (a calcium compound) are added to the water. These compounds combine with most of the water's dissolved minerals and metals forming what is known as *floc*. This mixture then passes through a *sedimentation* process, in which the floc is simply allowed to settle to the bottom of a holding basin. After that, the water is ready for *filtration* and is strained through sand and charcoal filters that trap the remaining particulates.

Fluoridation is often the next step. Fluoride compounds are typically added to the water to raise the concentration to about 1 part per million (1 ppm). Then most utilities perform a *disinfection treatment*, the second chlorination process. This is done to disinfect the water mains and pipes between the plant and your house. However, because the chlorine is so reactive, other compounds (lime, soda ash, zinc phosphate, etc.) are often added to counter any potential pipe corrosion.

Not all water utilities perform all of these treatment processes because, in many cases, they aren't necessary. At a minimum, chlorine disinfecting would be done, although it might be replaced with an ozone treatment.

Common Home Water Treatments

A tremendous number of water cleaning and purifying strategies and devices are now available to improve the quality of your home's water. The following section defines and discusses some of the more common strategies used in equipment that consumers commonly buy, and perhaps install themselves. Specific equipment suggestions are given in *Choosing the Right Water Treatment Equipment* on page 618.

It should be mentioned that it's a good idea, no matter what equipment you use in your plumbing, to run the water from your tap for a short time before using water for drinking. This is especially important if that particular faucet hasn't been used for some hours (such as overnight). That way, any possible compounds that may have leached into the water from the supply pipes while it was simply sitting there, or microorganisms that may have multiplied in the water, are flushed down the drain and not ingested.

Water Filtration

With filtration, the water passes through some type of material or media. Each different media and each different technique has it's own unique ability to remove certain waterborne contaminates, and it's own set of drawbacks. These are listed below in alphabetical order for your convenience.

Activated-Charcoal Media

Many home-water filters contain *activated charcoal* (also known as activated carbon). In fact, it's one of the most popular filtering media. The sections below explain how it can affect your water.

How Activated-Charcoal Media Works

Activated-charcoal water filters have been used since the mid-1950s. The media they use—activated charcoal—is a form of steam-treated charcoal. The charcoal itself can be derived from a variety of plant materials (or coal can be used). However, whatever its origin, the steam processing causes the charcoal to become extremely pitted. This rugged and uneven texture greatly increases the charcoal's surface area, which results in much greater *adsorption* capacity. This is important, because it's primarily by adsorption of dissolved gaseous, liquid compounds, and dissolved substances, that activated charcoal works. However, activated charcoal does have some ability to strain out certain solids, too. (Technically, this is called *mechanical filtration*.) And the more compressed the activated charcoal is, the greater it's capacity to do this.

Now, back to adsorption. What is it anyway? Adsorption is a type of molecular/electromechanical adhesion process. Simply put, it causes most volatile chemical molecules (benzene, chlordane, etc.) and nearly all naturally occurring dissolved gaseous molecules (including those of hydrogen sulfide) to adhere to the activated charcoal's surfaces, thus removing them from the water supply.

Adsorption also similarly affects gaseous radioactive radon molecules. However, it must be pointed out that the typical small filters often used in houses, because they only contain a rather limited amount of activated charcoal, can't mechanically filter out the solid radioactive particles that this gas emits. Therefore, large granular-activated-charcoal radon filtering systems have been developed that hold much greater quantities of media, so much so that they're able to both adsorb the gas *and* trap any radioactive particles that are produced by it.

It should be noted that activated charcoal works particularly well at adsorbing chlorine and *trichloromethane* (chloroform), which is a chlorine byproduct found in chlorinated utility water (see *Chlorine* on page 587). It can also remove tastes and odors that are released by the glues used to assemble plastic water-supply pipes (see *Plastic Pipe Concerns* on page 592). In fact, because activated charcoal is so efficient at removing most unpleasant tastes and smells in water, activated-charcoal filters are often called *taste-and-odor filters*. (This is particularly true for very simple, granular-media filters.)

Activated charcoal in water filters is actually used in one of two basic forms: granulated or solid block. The first type developed for use in water filters was granular. However, because the loose, rough bits of activated charcoal have spaces between each of the granules, this can allow some of the water molecules to bypass the granules without ever coming in direct contact with their surface. Another problem is that sometimes *channeling* can occur in granulated charcoal. This happens when the water streams passing through the filtering media start following the same pathways. Because much of the activated charcoal is bypassed, and the limited amount of activated charcoal surrounding the channel gets quickly saturated with contaminants, you can see how this would provide much less efficient filtration. To counter this, some filter manufacturers have created special anti-channeling configurations.

Gaining in popularity in recent years is solid-block activated charcoal, also known as *microfine carbon* or *carbon block*. It's increasingly being used because of its superior mechanical-filtration ability. This capacity has been considered particularly important at removing protozoan cysts from their water. (*Cryptosporidiaum parvum* oocysts were responsible for a number of deaths in Milwaukee in 1993.) You see, unlike loose, granular activated charcoal, solid-block activated charcoal is tightly compressed. Because it has none of the small spaces that surround bits of granular activated charcoal, suspended solids can't enter it and many are thus strained out. Those that do enter, tend to get trapped inside the block. In addition, solid-block activated charcoal may also be superior at adsorption, because all the water molecules are forced to travel *through* the compressed charcoal itself, not detour around it through channels. Apparently, some lead and asbestos can be removed in this manner.

Many activated-charcoal block filters have other materials or substances incorporated in them as well. For example, sometimes plastic (such as polypropylene) is imbedded. In certain cases, it may have a positive electrostatic charge (either permanent or acquired by the movement of the water stream) to attract and hold onto certain minute oppositely charged pollutants. (Apparently most "colloidal and bacterial contaminants exhibit a negative charge in solution.") In other filters, the plastic may have other purposes, perhaps to create, or enhance, a particular internal structural design.

Other activated-charcoal-block filters have what's termed *precoat technology* on their outer surfaces. (Some have both imbedded additives as well as precoat technology.) This may be in the form of a "spun-bonded polypropylene," or some other material. These may also have an electric charge. (See *Electrokinetic and Electret Media* on page 603.) All these additions make charcoal block filters more capable of removing minute solids from the water.

It's very important for you to know that, with *any* type of activated-charcoal filter, the longer the water is in contact with the media, the more effective the removal of the contaminants will be. (This is especially important with granular filters.) Therefore, manufacturers have devised two strategies to help their filters accomplish this. One is simply to use a larger amount of activated charcoal that the water must pass through. The other is to create methods that slow the water's rate of flow through the media. Some units combine both tactics.

Today, you can purchase a filter with activated charcoal as a whole-house unit, or as a point-of-use device (for under your sink, above your sink, or to replace your regular shower head). Filters designed for whole-house use, as well as most of the under-sink models, will generally require some special plumbing installation work. Although a few activated-charcoal filtering units have stainless-steel housings, most of them are made of plastic, as are many of the granular activated-cartridge refills. Fortunately, however, the activated charcoal will most likely adsorb any plastic contaminants, odors, and tastes that happen to get into the water from these particular components. However, some extremely chemically sensitive individuals may want to purchase a stainless-steel model that doesn't use plastic cartridges.

As you might expect, the cost of activated-charcoal filters varies. However, as a rule, many of the simpler granular cartridge units are relatively low priced. The actual cost will depend on the filter's size, its casing material (plastic or stainless steel), whether it requires professional installation, the replacement schedule, and the cost of the replacement media. While most units use replaceable cartridges, there are some that require the entire filtering unit to be replaced.

Activated-Charcoal-Media Concerns

It must be emphasized that activated-charcoal filters are not *the* answer to every water-quality problem. This is especially true for filters using granular activated charcoal as their media. On the other hand, compressed-activated-charcoal-block filters do have a greater capacity to strain out (mechanically filter) a certain amount of particulate matter. And, those with *precoat technology* (which can be micro-pore materials) are even better at this. (See *Micro-Pore-Material Filters* on page 606.) By the way, because all activated-charcoal filters become more inefficient as they become clogged with particles, they're often combined with a sediment-removing prefilter.

It must be understood that granular activated-charcoal filters can't *purify* your water by killing any bacteria (or other microorganisms), or by removing bacteria effectively from your water. Even some solid-activated-charcoal blocks aren't able to strain out everything. You should also be aware that research has found that bacteria can build up and eventually thrive on activated-charcoal media, particularly if the water supply hasn't been chlorinated.

Even activated-charcoal filters with *bacteriostatic additives* (compounds that inhibit the growth of bacteria), such as silver, can apparently become contaminated if given enough time. Silver (it may be in the form of silver nitrate) is used because, as the water passes it, minute quantities of positively charged ions are released which, theoretically, negatively react and ultimately kill bacteria. While silver compounds are the most commonly utilized, other anti-microbial compounds have also been tried. Unfortunately, the U.S Federal Trade Commission (FTC) reported that filters with bacteriostatic additives "have shown unpromising results." However, a mixture of granulated-activated charcoal and KDF media (see *KDF Media* on page 605) will be naturally bacteriostatic.

As another anti-bacteria-buildup strategy, some activated-charcoal filters have been designed to have a *backwashing cycle* to periodically rinse off the media. But, while backwashing will certainly help, it may not be completely effective in preventing contamination problems. In addition, backwashing tends to "waste" water because the water used is flushed down the drain.

Because of activated charcoal's very real capacity to support bacterial growth, some water experts believe that such filters should only be used with chlorinated water, or where some other purification treatment such as an ultraviolet-light (see *Ultraviolet Light (UV) Water Purifiers* on page 612), ozonization, etc. has been previously used on the water. The thinking behind this is that, if chlorine is present in the in-coming water supply, it's oxidizing disinfectant action will kill many types of bacteria, and the activated charcoal itself will then adsorb the chlorine before the homeowner actually uses the water. (Note: Activated-charcoal units that are used for filtering disinfected or purified water should still have their media changed regularly as a preventive measure.)

With all activated-charcoal filters, the media must be replaced from time to time—not just because of possible microbial growth—but also because it'll eventually be unable to adsorb effectively any more contaminants. In fact, if the activated-charcoal becomes saturated, it may release some of these pollutants back into your "filtered" water supply.

Replacement is not difficult. It usually entails simply taking out the old activated-charcoal cartridge and putting in a new one, or actually replacing the entire filtering unit—it depends on the model. Of course, the actual life expectancy for a particular cartridge (or filtering unit) will differ with the type of unit, the brand, the quality of your water, and the volume of water used daily. Generally, a filter manufacturer will give a suggested replacement schedule—perhaps once a month, several times a year, or once a year. However, sometimes these recommendations are somewhat exaggerated, so your replacement schedule will often vary from a them. One thing is for certain, if you start tasting or smelling chlorine, for example, it is time to replace the media—no matter what the timetable says.

You should also know that hot water lessens activated charcoal's adsorption ability, so odorless, tasteless trihalomethananes (chlorine by-products) may be released without you knowing it. Apparently, these filters must be used with cold water to effectively remove the most toxic, chlorinated-water by-products. Therefore, it's best to use activated-charcoal media *before* the water is heated.

It should be mentioned that, after installing a replacement activated-charcoal filter (or filtering cartridge), you should run the cold water from the nearest tap. This is to remove any excess powdery charcoal particles from the water stream. Generally, it only takes a few minutes for the water to run clearly. (Some filter manufacturers may suggest a longer flushing period.)

As a final note, activated-charcoal filters are commonly used in conjunction with other types of water-treatment strategies, such as reverse osmosis and distillation as prefilters or postfilters. (See *Reverse-Osmosis Units* on page 608, and *Water Distillers* on page 611.)

Aluminum Titanium Silicate (ATS) Media

Aluminum Titanium Silicate (ATS) is a very specialized media trademarked by WaterLink Barnaby Sutcliffe company. This particular mineral product is manufactured and marketed in a granular form, a powder, or as a powder/activated-charcoal mix.

For home water supplies, ATS is used as an effective method to remove lead. Interestingly, the precise mechanism by which this is accomplished is still not fully understood. However, it's been speculated that it may involve a combination of processes, such an ion-exchange, along with *mechanical filtration* (trapping lead by straining it out of the water stream). For home-use lead removal, you'll find that the ATS will be in a powder form, either alone or in a combination powder/activated-charcoal mix. By the way, ATS is also used to remove arsenic. However, this is only done on a commercial basis. For this, the granular form of ATS is preferred.

As you might expect, ATS must be periodically replaced. And, because it's essentially a lead-only filtration strategy, other media and/or water-treatment methods are required to remove other "unwantables" from your water.

Ceramic Filters

Protozoan cysts (*i.e. Cryptosporidiaum parvum* oocysts) in the water supply caused a number of deaths in Milwaukee, Wisconsin in 1993. As a result, many people are quite concerned about removing cysts from their water. This has resulted in ceramic filters being more and more common in the U.S.

For some time, however, ceramic water filters have been used in Europe. Developed there in the 1860's as a result of Louis Pasteur's new germ theory (as a cause of illnesses), they were first popularly used by the military and by hospitals, then for domestic water supplies. Within two decades, ceramic water filters were being manufactured and promoted to combat highly infectious waterborne diseases such as typhoid fever, cholera, and dysentery. Not surprisingly, the use of these life-saving filtering devices soon spread to other countries and colonies where conditions often favored the transmission of illnesses from polluted water.

Exactly what is a ceramic filter? While the precise composition of various ceramic filters may vary, they're generally are made of a high-temperature-fired type of *diatomaceous earth (DE)*. DE is a fine silica powder made up of the cell walls of microscopic algae. Interestingly, it's been used for centuries for making fine porcelain. It seems that the specific filtering ability of a ceramic filter depends on it's pore size, and pore size is primarily determined by the ceramic base material used, and the temperature it was kiln fired.

How do ceramic filters work? Very simply. Water just seeps through the tens of millions of pores in the ceramic material, which is usually in a cartridge form. In this process, solids (such as many kinds of sediment and organisms) accumulate on the ceramic surface—if they're too large to pass through. For your information, most (some filters claim as high as 99.9%) of *Cryptosporidiaum parvum* oocysts are sieved through this process.

You should be aware that sometimes a silver compound is incorporated into the ceramic itself to act as a *bacteriostatic agent* (to counter bacterial growth on, or in, the filter). These filters are manufactured in such a manner that the silver cannot migrate into the finished filtered water. However, the U.S Federal Trade Commission (FTC) reported that filters with bacteriostatic additives "have shown unpromising results." In other words, silver does not meet the FTC's anti-bacterial expectations of effectiveness.

Today, ceramic filters can be purchased as stand-alone, counter-top, gravity-feed models (no added water pressure is required to make the water pass through the filter), or combined with activated charcoal in some type of filtering cartridge. Often, manufacturers will suggest periodically washing the ceramic off. Depending on the kind of cartridge, it may last 6-12 months. (Read manufacturer's product literature to be certain.)

Drawbacks include the fact that volatile organic chemicals (VOCs), chlorine, and other undesirable odor and taste compounds, will remain in the treated water after ceramic filtering. (Of course, ceramic filters can be combined with other filtering strategies.) Also, regular filter cleaning must be performed. If forgotten, or considered an unnecessary chore, the outer ceramic surface could become so clogged with contaminants that water no longer freely passes through the filter.

Crystalline Quartz Media

Granules of crystallized quartz are now being used as a media in some filters, but nearly always with other types of filtering strategies. It's been described as a "high energy" crystalline mineral that's able to reduce water's surface tension to allow for a more free sudsing and lathering of soaps and shampoos. (For more on water surface tension, see *Soaps Vs. Detergents* on page 75.) Quartz gravel is also used to strain out dirt particles in some sediment-removing filters. (See *Sediment-Removing Filters* below.)

Electrokinetic and Electret Media

Electrokinetic and electret filters use electrical charges to attract and hold onto certain types of pollutants—namely, particulates with opposite charges. Commonly, the media is plastic (such as polyurethane). It may have been given a permanent static charge (*an electret*) during manufacturing, making it into a type of electrostatic filter. Or, because *electrokinetic* literally means "electricity of or resulting from motion," the media may acquire its electrical charge because of the movement of the water passing by or through it.

Why add an electrokinetic strategy or electrets to a water filter? One manufacturer (who uses a special cotton fabric as an electrokinetic media) explains that it "acquires a positive molecular charge in a moving stream of water, and since most colloidal and bacterial contaminants exhibit a negative charge in solution, the media fibers electrokinetically adsorb (these) charged colloidal particles." In other words, electrokinetic (and electret media) can *adsorb* (cause to adhere to their surfaces) pollutants that may otherwise be too minute to have been *mechanical filtered* (strained) by the other media used in a particular water filter.

You'll find that electrokinetic and electret media are often combined with activated charcoal and may, in fact, be actually imbedded in compressed solid-block activated charcoal. In time, electret and electrokinetic media surfaces will become saturated with adsorbed substances and will no longer function effectively.

Fluoride-Removing Filters

Because of the growing concern over the potential health consequences of fluoridated water (see *Fluoride* on page 588), there are special fluoride-removing filters available. One media that can be used in these is *activated alumina*. This is regular granular alumina (aluminum oxide, the compound from which commercial aluminum is derived) which has been heated, causing the alumina granules to acquire a very porous, pitted structure. Another fluoride-reducing substance is *bone char* (charcoal). One brand of this is Brimac. Apparently, both activated alumina and bone char work through an ion-exchange process. (See *Ion-Exchange Media* on page 604.)

If you're interested in a fluoride-removing filter, the Clean Water Revival Fluoride Filter is rated for 1000 gallons of use and can be used with filter housings that accept Doulton ceramic/charcoal filter cartridges. A filter, a countertop housing, and more is sold by **Befit Enterprises Ltd.** Doulton Fluoride-Removal filters are also sold by **N.E.E.D.S.**

In addition, the New Wave Enviro Fluoride Removal Filter (**New Wave Enviro**) fits into their 10" countertop filter housing, as well as other brands of housings. It's constructed with multiple layers (granulated activated charcoal, special fluoride-removal media, spun-bounded polypropylene pad, and a poly pad). Each filter cartridge is rated for 600 gallons of water and it is recommended that it be changed every 6-9 months. You can call the company for a nearby dealer.

Ion-Exchange Media

For some time now, synthetic-resin beads have been used in typical (salt-using) water-softeners as an *ion-exchange media*. One material that used for these beads is *polystyrenated bivinylbenzene*, though there may be others.

In *typical water-softeners* (those that use salt), the synthetic beads act as *catalysts* (substances important for a chemical reaction, but which are not used up or changed in the course of the reaction). Here the beads simply provide the surfaces on which ion-trading takes place. During this process, hard-water mineral ions are exchanged for sodium ions. (For more, see *Typical Water-Softening Devices* on page 614).

Ion-exchange media is being used in water filters also, usually mixed with activated-charcoal granules. In most cases, this is again some type of synthetic resin. However, it could be a different kind of compound, such ATS or activated alumina.

Because of the different molecular compositions of the various ion-exchange media, there's no way to say with certainty what these materials, as a class, can reduce or eliminate when used in filtering devices. Therefore, it's not surprising that some filter manufacturers say that their particular ion-exchange media can remove fluoride, copper, and aluminum. Other say that their model removes lead and copper. Still others claim that the ion-exchange media in their filters can remove heavy metals while also binding hard-water minerals such as calcium and magnesium.

However, no matter what the ion-exchange media is made of, or in what type of water treatment device it's in, it'll eventually have its surfaces "clogged up." When this occurs, it becomes ineffective. *Backflushing* cycles (a water-rinsing procedure) in water softeners are able to clean off the synthetic resin beads. However, with mixed-media filters containing ion-exchange media, sometimes the entire filtering cartridge is simply replaced.

KDF Media

KDF (Kinetic-Degradation-Fluxion) filtration media can be an effective method of water treatment, but one with which you may not be familiar.

How KDF Media Work

KDF is a water treatment technology that was patented in 1987. Manufactured by **KDF Fluid Treatment, Inc.**, it's imposing full name (it usually just goes by the initials, KDF) actually denotes three major characteristics of the media. The first characteristic is that it's *kinetic* (it creates electrochemical energy). The second is that it goes through *degradation* (the material very slowly degrades, or is used up, through chemical reactions). And, finally, KDF media allows *fluxion* (fluids to pass through it without creating excessive back pressure).

So, what exactly is KDF? KDF is an unique high-purity alloy made up of two dissimilar metals, zinc and copper. (Note: KDF media meets the standards for "levels of copper and zinc in potable water" and is considered safe and nontoxic.) As it turns out, this alloy has an inherently high potential for electrochemical reduction/oxidation (redox) reactions (*reduction* is simply the addition of electrons to a molecule, and *oxidation* is their loss). In addition, the zinc and copper generate a minute electric current (0.04 volts), like a battery, that controls the populations of many microorganisms by disrupting their normal, metabolic functions. Specifically, it seems that KDF media results in the disruption of "electron transport, causing cellular damage." In other words, KDF media is naturally *bacteriostatic* (resistant to many forms of bacterial contamination).

In practice, water passes through the KDF media which is in the form of granules or wires. As the water flows through, certain problematic contaminants (for example, iron, hydrogen sulfide, and chlorine) spontaneously react with the zinc or copper making up the KDF media, and are transformed into "acceptable" compounds (ones that don't affect water quality negatively). For example, when chlorine molecules come in contact with the KDF media, they instantly react with molecules of zinc to form zinc chloride. In fact, KDF media is so good at removing chlorine that it's been estimated to be ten times more effective than a similar amount of activated charcoal.

However, that's not the limit of KDF's capabilities. Certain heavy metals in water, such as lead, are removed by becoming electroplated onto the metallic KDF surfaces.

KDF media can also alter the physical crystalline appearance and character of the waterborne, insoluble, hard-water compounds of calcium and magnesium. Normally, these compounds are crystals with hard, angular structures that can grow in size relatively quickly. If they happen to grow and accumulate on the interiors of a metal pipe, they form lime scale. However, hard water that passes through KDF media no longer has the typical hard, angular, calcium-and-magnesium crystals. Instead, the compounds are transformed into very small, evenly shaped, rounded particles that are unable to grow in size, or adhere to metallic surfaces. Therefore, KDF media treatment tends to counter hard-water scale buildup. (A 5-micron filtering device can then be used to remove these fine, rounded particles from the treated water.)

You can now purchase water-treatment equipment for your home that uses KDF media, generally with a mixture of granular KDF media and granular-activated charcoal. Some point-of-use filtering units, especially for use on shower heads, use just the KDF media alone, often in wire form.

KDF Concerns

As with virtually all water-treatment strategies, KDF media alone can't remove every type of possible contaminant that could possibly be present in your water supply. That's why, for example, KDF is commonly used in combination with granular-activated charcoal, which is able to adsorb certain volatile chemicals and naturally occurring gases that KDF can't handle.

You should also keep in mind that, although KDF is bacteriostatic (able to control bacterial growth on itself) and has been designated by the **EPA (U.S. Environmental Agency)** as a "pesticidal device," it should *only* be used in homes with water that has been disinfected by a utility, or in those homes with an individual private water source containing no pathogenic (disease-causing) biological contamination. Also, KDF media has no effect on protozoan cysts. (See *Waterborne Cysts* on page 578.) Thus, KDF in a home filtering unit, is not considered a water purifier.

It should be noted that the KDF/granulated-activated-charcoal mix used in certain home KDF devices must be replaced from time to time. (Follow the manufacturer's recommendations for your particular unit.) Then, too, as you might expect, KDF media costs more than activated charcoal.

You may find a whole-house KDF filter with a *backwashing* option. A unit that can backwash is capable of cleaning the media of excess oxide compounds, as well as calcium and magnesium solids, by simply flushing the granules with water, and then draining the water out. However, this regeneration process uses a substantial amount of water, then flushes it down the drain. If you do have a backwashing feature, it's been suggested that it be done approximately three times a week, or more often if high levels of certain contaminants are present in the unfiltered water.

It should also be mentioned that, sometimes, manufacturers suggest that shower-head and hand-held shower-wand filters using KDF media be flushed from time to time to extend the filter's life.

Micro-Pore-Material Filters

Micro-pore material has become a more common water filtering strategy. Sometimes called *microfilters*, these are commonly made of synthetic materials (such as spun, nonwoven fabric) with very minute openings. However, one special kind of synthetic microfilter material is made of porous, hard plastic. Porex is a trademarked brand of this which uses any number of *thermoplastic polymers*. These include high-density polyethylene (HDPE), Nylon 6 (N6), Polyvinylidene Fluoride (PVDF), among others. Apparently, no matter what they're made of, Porex filters have "an intricate network of open-celled omnidirectional pores." These minute openings (they can be created in sizes from 7-250 microns) "join to form many torturous paths, enabling porous plastics to have a dual filtering capability." Not only can they block larger particulates from passing through them, but even smaller particulates get stuck inside the twisted paths of the pores.

While many micro-pore-material filters are synthetic, not all are. For example, some microfilters use special types of cotton that acquire a positive charge from the moving water stream. (This is to attract and hold onto certain negatively charged bacteria, etc.) Still others use specialized papers or even metal mesh.

In any case, the minute openings in many of these filtering materials may be so small that they're able to mechanically filter out a huge variety of solids, including most *Cryptosporidiaum parvum* oocysts. Obviously, the particular filtering ability will depend on the material, its engineered pore size, and the amount of contaminants already on its surface. Therefore, it's important to understand that some micro-pore-material filters have pores that aren't fine enough for a very sophisticated degree of filtration. These filters may have only been designed to act as sediment-removing filters, to capture larger suspended sand or dirt particles in the water stream.

Usually, micro-pore filters are not used alone, but in conjunction with other filtering strategies. For example, they may constitute the *precoat technology* used on some activated-charcoal-block media to help further remove solid contaminants. This can be a good combination because the activated charcoal can adsorb much of the gaseous and chemical contamination that micro-pore fabrics simply can't do. (See *Activated Charcoal Media* on page 599.) Sometimes, activated charcoal may be imbedded into the micro-pore fabric. (It should also be mentioned that ceramic filters and reverse-osmosis membranes are, technically, very specialized forms of micro-pore filtering.)

Because most water-saturated materials can become home to microorganisms, sometimes certain substances are incorporated in micro-pore-fabric filters to act as *bacteriostatic agents* (substances that help prevent bacterial growth on the filter itself). However, be aware that the U.S Federal Trade Commission (FTC) has concluded that filters with bacteriostatic additives "have shown unpromising results." Of course, as with most types of water filtering media, micro-pore filters must be periodically replaced.

Sediment-Removing Filters

Sediment traps and *sediment-removing filters* (also known as *turbidity filters*) are specifically designed to remove gritty particles from water supplies. Therefore, if some type of biological contaminant, such as algae or bacteria, are part of the turbidity problem, it must be killed and/or removed by some other device because most sediment filters aren't capable of doing this alone.

Sediment traps might be used for whole-house sediment removal, to eliminate heavy concentrations of suspended soil in water. Actually, a sediment trap can simply be a special holding tank. In practice, the turbid untreated water is pumped into the tank and held there for about 24 hours. During that time, the soil particles settle to the bottom. Then the clean water at the top of the tank is piped away either to another treatment device or to the house (this may require a *repressurization pump*). It should be noted that sometimes a chemical is added to the sediment trap to hasten the settling process. This might be *aluminum sulfate* (a form of *alum*) or perhaps a certain type of *synthetic polymer compound*.

The more common approach for removing sediment is to use a sediment-removing filter. These range in size from fairly large to less than 12" tall. Generally, sediment-removing filters work well if the water doesn't contain a large amount of suspended soil (this is especially true for smaller-sized filters). Sediment filters are rated according to the smallest size of particulate they're able to remove. For example, a 15-micron unit will trap all the sediment particles that are larger than 15 microns. Sediment filters are available with ratings ranging from 5 to 25 microns.

Large sediment-removing filters may use media such as *diatomaceous earth* (*DE*) (fine grains of mostly silica compounds originating from the cell walls of diatomic algae), quartz gravel, filtering sand, limestone chips, or even coal. Often, large units must be *backwashed* from time to time so that they don't clog. In this process, a stream of water is run through the media backwards to pick up the accumulated debris and carry it to a drain. Of course, this backwashing process flushes a certain amount of water down the drain. In small units, one or more layers of paper, or another filtering or screening fabric or material, may be used—often in the form of a replaceable cartridge. Of course, the replacement schedule will vary according to your water's turbidity, the volume of water your household uses, and the size of the filtering cartridge.

It should also be mentioned that *hydrocylonic separators* may be used as a sediment-removing technology. These devices work by rapidly spinning the incoming water. Then, through *centrifugal force*, the soil and sand particles are tossed against the walls of the separator's interior and drained away. Apparently, hydrocylonic separators can be quite effective.

If you need to remove sediment from your water supply, you may want to contact **Cuno, Inc.** They've been making sediment-removing filters for over 80 years. Filters and housings (plastic or stainless steel) come in a large selection of sizes to fit your needs. In addition, local **Culligan International** dealers will have sediment-removing filters as well. You may also want to check in your classified telephone directory for local water-treatment equipment companies to see what they offer.

Remember, however, before buying any sediment filter, it's a good idea to pinpoint exactly what's causing the cloudiness in your water. If it's something besides sand or soil particles (*e.g.* biological contaminants), other treatments may be necessary to make your water acceptable. And, even if gritty sand or dirt is the only contaminant, be sure to purchase a unit with enough capacity to effectively handle your particular sediment load.

Reverse-Osmosis Units

A *reverse-osmosis (R/O)* water treatment device can often remove a wide range of particulate contaminants. However, the processing of your water is relatively slow, and the cost can sometimes be relatively high. While technically a "filter," because water must pass through a membrane, most people think of this as a unique technology.

How Reverse-Osmosis Units Work

To understand how a reverse-osmosis unit works, it's best to understand osmosis and reverse osmosis. *Osmosis* is the natural process by which water spontaneously passes through a *semipermeable membrane* (a very fine material that allows only very small molecules to pass through it). Actually, water goes through such a membrane in only one direction: it passes from a solution containing a low concentration of dissolved substances, through the membrane, to a solution containing a higher concentration. Eventually, this results in the same concentration of water on both sides of the membrane. By the way, osmosis is the process by which water passes from the stems and leaves of plants (sites of low concentrations of dissolved substances) through the cell walls (which are semipermeable membranes) into the interiors of the cells (sites of high concentrations of dissolved substances).

Reverse osmosis, on the other hand, is not a naturally occurring process. Instead, it requires the addition of pressure to create the opposite effect from that of osmosis. In other words, in reverse osmosis, water is forcibly pushed through a semipermeable membrane so that the water goes from a solution containing a high concentration of dissolved substances to a solution with a much lower concentration. The result is a different water concentration on each side of the membrane. The intent of reverse osmosis is to separate water from dissolved substances.

Through this process, reverse-osmosis (R/O) units are capable of effectively treating home-water supplies. In practice, your home's water pressure (the pressure in your water pipes), and sometimes additional pressure, drives a stream of water through a special membrane. If your water supply is chlorinated, the membrane might be made of *cellulose acetate* or *cellulose triacetate*. On the other hand, *polymid resin film* might be used with unchlorinated water (other membrane types are also available).

Interestingly, reverse-osmosis membranes aren't all capable of removing the same-size particulates. In fact, the *pores* (tiny openings) in various R/O membranes are rated as to the largest matter that can pass through them. For example, a typical membrane used in residential units might have a rating of 0.01 microns. Although water molecules under pressure are able to pass through these minute openings, the holes are just too small to let solids over 0.01 microns pass through. (In reality, a membrane will not have all pores of the same size. The pores in a membrane with a rating of 0.01 microns might range from 0.001 up to 0.01 microns.) When water passes through an R/O membrane, a great deal of the dissolved minerals, heavy metals, asbestos, dirt particles, radioactive particles, fluoride, and bacteria will be left behind. R/O units can be so capable that they're usually able to remove an estimated 80-95% of all dissolved solids from the water they treat.

By the way, after the water in a reverse-osmosis unit has passed through the membrane, it then drips into a storage tank and is considered finished, treated water. When this tank is full, some units will automatically shut off and stop any further processing, until you use some of the water and the level in the tank goes down. The treated water is often dispensed from the storage tank through a special faucet mounted next to your sink. To keep the R/O process working efficiently, many R/O units have a *flushing cycle* in which the semipermeable membrane is routinely rinsed clean with a stream of water. Afterwards, this rinse water is drained away.

Reverse-osmosis units are available in point-of-use units (for mounting above or below a countertop) or as whole-house devices. Certain R/O units now feature automatic monitors that are designed to check the actual quality of the water (this is more common on whole-house units). Some of these monitors check both the original, untreated water as well as the finished, treated water. If any problem is detected, the R/O unit simply shuts off, thus helping to guarantee consistently good-quality water.

Reverse-Osmosis Unit Concerns

Although most reverse-osmosis (R/O) units produce fairly clean water and are more convenient to use than a water distiller, they aren't perfect. As with other treatment strategies, reverse osmosis is not capable of removing everything you might like to eliminate from your water supply. For example, reverse osmosis can't separate out any dissolved gases such as chlorine or radioactive radon (although it can usually remove the "daughter" particles that are emitted by gaseous radon). In addition, reverse-osmosis membranes can't completely remove all biological contaminants (although certain models are much more capable of removing microbes than others). Yet, most R/O units should be able to remove protozoan cysts. (See *Waterborne Cysts* on page 578.)

Interestingly, if you have a chlorinated water supply that runs through *galvanized steel* pipes (steel pipes coated with zinc to prevent them from rusting), you may encounter an unexpected problem with bacteria. It seems that irregular areas can develop on the interiors of these pipes because of chlorine reacting with the metal. Certain strains of bacteria can thrive in these rough spots. Although they may not be harmful to humans, they can destroy

R/O membranes. Even if you don't have chlorinated water and galvanized pipes, bacterial contamination of a reverse-osmosis membrane can occur.

As a result, to control bacteria, and other types of contaminants that reverse osmosis can't eliminate on it own, R/O units are often sold as a part of a combined water-treatment system. Therefore, you might find a reverse-osmosis model combined with an ultraviolet-light purifier and/or an activated-charcoal prefilter or postfilter. Another R/O system you might come across is one using a KDF filter for pretreatment. In this case, the KDF media not only is able to remove the chlorine, but has an innate *bacteriostatic action* capable of controlling bacterial growth on itself. Some reverse-osmosis units may also have a micro-pore prefilter, often primarily to remove membrane-damaging sediment.

It should also be mentioned that some individuals are concerned that reverse-osmosis units are actually too effective in removing dissolved minerals from the water. It seems that this *demineralized water* can be somewhat flat-tasting. Interestingly, it's also called *aggressive* water. Aggressive water will seek out and dissolve substances with which it comes into contact. As a result, some people believe that, if you drink such demineralized water, it could seek out and dissolve minerals that are in your body—minerals that your system needs for optimal functioning.

There is one problem with R/O units on which everyone usually agrees—reverse-osmosis treatment requires the use of many gallons of untreated water to create just one gallon of treated water. While the amount varies with the different models, as many as ten gallons of water may be flushed down the drain for every gallon of water that is filtered (commonly, the ratio is about three or four to one).

The major reason for this "wasted" water is that the very process of reverse osmosis creates water on one side of the membrane with a very high concentration of dissolved minerals. If the concentration gets too high, the water may not be able to hold any more minerals in a dissolved state. Therefore, the minerals begin *precipitating* (coming out of solution) and form crystals. So, before the mineral-rich water gets too concentrated for crystallization to occur, it's drained away. Then, too, there's a periodic flushing of the R/O membrane to keep it clean, which also uses more water. If you're interested, one way to minimize the "wasting" of water is to purchase a unit with a tank having an automatic shut-off valve. This will stop the R/O process until additional treated water is really needed.

You should also be aware that many R/O units can be somewhat expensive, and they tend to work rather slowly to produce a limited amount of treated water. In fact, many point-of-use models only produce 5-15 gallons of treated water a day. (Of course, this is usually enough for the drinking and cooking needs in most households.) In addition, research has found that reverse-osmosis units function less efficiently if they have to treat cold water rather than warm water.

Furthermore, the pressure of your water supply is a key factor in how well your R/O unit will operate. It seems that most utility water lines are under a pressure of 40–60 psi (pounds per square inch), a range that happens to be ideal for most reverse-osmosis units. However, if you have a water pressure reading much below 40 psi, you'll probably have to increase the pressure. Fortunately, some reverse-osmosis units are sold with an optional pressure-boosting feature. In addition, the *pH level* (the degree of acidity or alkalinity) of your water supply can affect your R/O unit's performance. (See *Water pH* on page 592.)

You may want to keep in mind that if your home requires whole-house R/O equipment, you'll likely need a separate water storage tank and a *repressurization pump* (to raise the water pressure high enough to allow the treated water to flow from the tank through your home's plumbing lines). And, because reverse-osmosis water treatment is usually quite slow, your whole-house model may have to work continually.

If you're a chemically sensitive person, you may be interested in knowing that there have been reports that some point-of-use R/O units, that are made of plastic, have given the water they've treated a "plasticky" taste and odor. Obviously, this is more likely with brand new units. However, the use of an activated-charcoal filter after the R/O unit (as a type of postfilter) should be able to solve this problem. As your R/O unit ages, steadily lower amounts of the plastic compounds will migrate into the water, so it should become more tolerable.

Not surprisingly, reverse-osmosis membranes don't last forever. Generally, they'll have to be replaced every 1–3 years (follow the manufacturer's guidelines). Replacement is necessary because the original pore openings will enlarge over time through simple abrasive action. Therefore, as any R/O membrane ages, it allows ever-larger contaminants to pass through it. Incidentally, **Ozark Water Service and Environmental Services** offers a R.O.P.E. water test. This is a series of five basic tests to be done before and after treatment with your reverse-osmosis unit to let you know if the membrane is functioning properly or if it should be replaced.

Water Distillers

Distillation is undoubtedly the oldest form of water purification. As a rule, distillers are relatively inexpensive to purchase, but they're slow and they have a limited output.

How Water Distillers Work

All water distillers work in basically the same way: They boil water to create steam. This steam is then captured and allowed to *condense* (become a liquid again). Sediments, dissolved minerals, heavy metals (such as lead), asbestos fibers, fluoride, and radioactive particles that were in the original, untreated water are left behind in the boiling chamber. In addition, the high heat kills waterborne biological contaminants. Obviously, distillation is a very effective water purification method, and it will remove protozoan cysts. (See *Waterborne Cysts* on page 578.) In fact, it's been determined that about 90% of all the contaminants and pollutants in untreated water are no longer present after it's been distilled.

Generally, water distillers are available as kitchen countertop models, which operate off your house's electric current. When you're ready to purchase a water distiller, you'll find there are two basic types. *Air-cooled distillers* rely on the room's air temperature to condense the steam back into water. On the other hand, *water-cooled distillers* use a continuous flow of cool tap water to do the same job. In addition, you'll find that a number of water distillers are made either completely or partially of stainless steel. However, some models contain plastic parts. Interestingly at least one all-glass distiller is currently available.

Water Distiller Concerns

Although water distillation will remove virtually all the particulate matter from your water, it usually can't remove the *volatile chemicals* (compounds that rapidly evaporate) that might be in the water. This includes chlorination by-products, such as chloroform. (These compounds evaporate quickly, but soon recombine with the condensed water.) Dissolved gases such as chlorine and radon gas can't be removed either, so they remain in the treated distilled water, if they were present in the untreated water.

To address this problem, an activated-charcoal filter is often used after the water-distilling device as a postfilter. In fact, to better adsorb and eliminate certain volatile chemicals and gases, some models offer an activated-charcoal filter for both a prefilter and a postfilter. The combination of activated-charcoal and distillation will often remove nearly 100% of the original, untreated water's contaminants. (See *Activated-Charcoal Media* on page 599.)

You should be aware that there's some concern about water that is "too pristine." This is because water devoid of minerals can have a flat taste. Perhaps worse, distilled *demineralized water* is considered to be *aggressive.* In other words, it's water which aggressively seeks to pull into solution whatever minerals with which it comes in contact. One view holds that if you drink too much aggressive water, it will pull needed minerals out of your body.

Water distillers also have other drawbacks of which you need to be aware. One big concern is that water distillation tends to be an expensive operation. To determine the exact cost per gallon, multiply the number of kilowatts required to distill one gallon of water (this is usually available from the manufacturer) by your local electricity's per-kilowatt cost (available from your electric utility). To be most accurate, you should include the original cost of the untreated water, if you buy it from a utility.

Besides the operating expense, the output from a water distiller is both slow and limited. Plus, there don't appear to be any whole-house water distillers capable of supplying enough water for all uses within a household. In fact, many water-distillation units are designed to be placed permanently on your kitchen countertop. Units of this type are generally capable of producing only 3 to 4 gallons of water per day.

Then too, you should remember that water-distillation units tend to require at least some manual operation, and they certainly must be drained and cleaned from time to time. That's particularly true for the boiling tank. Depending on the particular model, the cleaning schedule could be as frequently as twice a month, or as little as twice a year. Incidentally, to make cleaning easier, using softened water has been suggested rather than mineral-laden hard water. That way, you won't have to remove any crusty mineral scale buildup. (See *Water Softeners* on page 613.)

Ultraviolet (UV) Water Purifiers

Ultraviolet (UV) light is a very effective *antiseptic* that, if intense enough, and in the right range of wavelengths, and if exposure is long enough, can kill most waterborne bacteria and other biological contaminants. However, it is not very effective against tough, hardy protozoan cysts. (See *Waterborne Cysts* on page 578.)

Disinfection of water with UV light began back in 1909. Because of its ability to make water safer, it was adopted by a number of city utilities. However, it was eventually replaced by ozonization and chlorination because they were so much cheaper.

What is UV light? UV light is a form of electromagnetic radiation. On the electromagnetic radiation scale, it's between visible light and x-rays. For controlling germs, UV light with frequencies in the *Abiotic Region* (non-life-supporting range) of 250-260 nanometers (nm) is used. (By the way one nanometer happens to be 10^{-9} meters.) As it turns out, UV "has various killing effects on yeast, mold, bacteria, and viruses." And besides killing, UV increases the rate of mutation, chromosomal aberration, and changes in cellular viscosity. UV also affects such vital processes as respiration, excitability, and growth

How do UV-light purifiers work? It seems that the radiation is actually absorbed by the organisms' cellular nucleic acid, or some component of it. This, in turn, alters their DNA (chemicals with reproductive information) which can eventually kill microbes. Those hardy enough may only be damaged or deactivated. Sometimes, they can reactivate (repair) themselves when sunlight reaches them, or in other cases, when no light reaches them at all.

Other factors are important in UV purification effectiveness as well. As you might expect, UV light is "less effective in disinfecting water if it has turbidity (cloudiness), iron salts, organic matter, etc." That's because these types of water conditions will disrupt and scatter the radiation. Saying all this, ultraviolet-light purifiers can work effectively for both private individual wells, and for water stored in cisterns (holding tanks)—if you realize their limitations. In a nutshell, what you need to remember is that UV purification has germicidal (killing) action on most waterborne microbes—but not cysts—and it has no effect on other contaminants that could be in your water. For example, it can't adsorb dissolved gases or strain out sediment. You'll find that they come in both whole-house units and point-of-use models. Incidentally, point-of-use UV-light purifiers are commonly used in conjunction with reverse-osmosis units.

Maintenance is important if you opt for a UV-light unit. The lamps they use (such as low-pressure mercury-vapor lamps) must be kept clean. They'll also need to be replaced regularly. (Because UV lamps tend to degrade rapidly, they're actually rated as if they had already been operating for 100 hours.) It's probably best to replace the lamp before it burns out to make sure it's still functioning optimally.

If you're interested in purchasing a separate ultraviolet light purifier for your home's water supply, Purification Products Company UV water purifiers are designed for point-of-use or whole-house sterilization. These units, which are $12^1/_2$" long and are constructed of stainless steel, are available from **Ozark Water Service and Environmental Services**. In addition, Ideal Horizon Ultraviolet Light systems can be purchased from **Nigra Enterprises**. Aquathin Ultra-Violet Disinfection Units (**Aquathin Corp.**) are sold through their dealers. Call the company for the nearest one. Doulton UV units can work in conjunction with some of their (and other manufacturer's) above-counter water filters. Doulton dealers include **N.E.E.D.S.**

An unusual option is the Portozon. It's described as a portable water-ozonizing unit for "oxygenating your already-filtered water." It's said to use "ambient air and ultraviolet light to make ozone." It comes in a plastic lidded box and is sold by **Befit Enterprises Ltd.**

Water Softeners

A *water softener* is popularly defined as any substance or device that is able to eliminate, or in some way inactivate, *hard-water minerals* that are commonly found in water supplies. It should be noted that hard water is usually defined as having a dissolved calcium and magnesium concentration at or above 120 mg/liter. However, many people find that a concentration of only 85 mg/liter still creates some of the problems associated with hard water. (See *Calcium* on page 583.)

What are some typical hard-water problems? One is the crusty white buildup that can occur on the interior of your plumbing fixtures and water pipes. This *lime scale* is actually formed by the minerals *precipitating* (coming out of solution). Another problem is that calcium and magnesium minerals in water can react with the fats and oils in the soaps you use, creating an insoluble scum known as *soap curd*. In addition, white fabrics washed in hard water can acquire a grayish tinge.

Although most people use the term "water softener" to mean anything that can counter the effects of hard water, you should be aware that there's a technical distinction between the terms *water softener* and *water conditioner*. Water softeners are devices that add a substance to the water to eliminate or inactivate hard-water minerals, while water conditioners are devices that don't add anything to the water. On the other hand, *water-softening agents* are simply substances (not devices) that can be added to water to deactivate or eliminate hard-water minerals. (Note: Some water-softening devices help remove or inactivate iron and certain other minerals besides just calcium and magnesium.)

Water-Softening Agents

Certain compounds, when added to hard water, act as *water-softening agents*. What these particular substances actually do is combine with the dissolved minerals, causing them to *precipitate* (be pulled out of solution), thus creating very minute insoluble solids. This process, known as *water softening through precipitation*, causes the hard-water minerals to be chemically bound up so that they're no longer free to react with soap to form scum (*soap curd*), or to attach themselves to the interiors of pipes, etc. and form *lime scale*.

Today, borax and sodium carbonate are two commonly used water-softening agents. For many years phosphate compounds were very popular for this, including trisodium phosphate (TSP) and sodium hexametaphosphate. However, because it was determined that phosphates can create water-quality problems in streams and other waterways, their use has declined dramatically. In homes, water-softening agents are generally point-of-use products. In other words, they're not typically added to the entire water supply of the house, but usually just to your laundry's wash water.

Typical Water-Softening Devices

Water-softening devices were created to provide continuous whole-house water softening. They work through a *cation exchange process* (cations are positively charged atoms). Simply put, positive *sodium ions* are used to replace the positive hard-water *mineral ions* in your water supply. The source of the sodium ions is a brine solution made up of common salt (sodium chloride) and water. Because these units add a substance (salt) to change the hardness of the water, they're not considered *water conditioners*.

In practice, a typical water-softening device is able to soften your water relatively quickly because it also contains a *catalyst* (a substance capable of speeding up a chemical reaction while not being changed itself). At one time, *zeolite* granules were commonly used as the catalyst in most home water-softening devices. However, these days, beads of a synthetic resin (such as *polystyrenated bivinylbenzene*) are much more popular. These catalysts provide the surfaces on which the ion-trading takes place. Because a catalyst is never altered or used up, the synthetic-resin beads (or zeolite) never need to be replaced. However, their surfaces will eventually become clogged with mineral ions. When that occurs, the ion-exchange process (the softening process) slows dramatically and a *recharging cycle* becomes necessary.

In practice, the recharging process includes several steps. First, there is a *backflushing* of the water flow, which loosens the mineral buildup on the catalyst's surfaces. Then, there's an addition of fresh brine solution. The final step is a complete rinsing of the tank containing the catalyst with fresh water to remove the loosened minerals. Most home water-softening devices recharge themselves automatically. However, salt will have to be added manually from time to time. The actual frequency for this will depend on your particular water softener, the hardness of your water, and the volume of water used daily in your household.

Most typical water softeners that use salt will produce water that feels slick, suds easily, and creates no mineral buildup (lime scale) in your pipes or on your plumbing fixtures. However, there are negatives to these units. One is that the recharging process "wastes" a certain amount of water by flushing it down the drain. Water-softening devices can also be fairly expensive, but some companies offer lease and rent-to-own programs.

25: Improving Your Water

In addition, you will have to routinely purchase salt for your softener. Fortunately, arrangements with your softener dealer can easily be made to have salt delivered directly to your home. Some dealers will even fill the salt tank for you. Of course, there's a cost to all this (the cost may actually be included in your purchase or rental price). To save money, you might purchase the salt you need at a local chemical-supply company, or at a wholesale or discount outlet, and periodically fill the salt tank yourself.

Still another concern with typical softening devices is that, because they use salt, the treated water will have a relatively high sodium content. This can be a real concern for individuals on a salt-restricted diet. However, if you install a *reverse-osmosis unit* in your kitchen with a membrane rated to remove salt, your drinking and cooking water will contain a much lower salt concentration. Of course, *distillation* will remove virtually all the salt.

A few local jurisdictions (for example, the City of Los Angeles) have apparently prohibited the installation of automatic, self-regenerating (backwashing) water softeners that use sodium-chloride salt-ion exchange. This is because the water drained from these devices during their cleaning cycle eventually enters the sewer lines and ends up at water-treatment plants. Treating this salt-laden backwashing water has proven difficult and expensive. Therefore, check local codes and regulations before purchasing a water-softening device. (Note: Some units now use compounds such as potassium chloride rather than sodium chloride.)

Alternative Water Conditioning Devices

Besides typical water softeners, alternative devices are available that are designed to prevent or minimize hard-water problems. These units are considered *water conditioners* because they don't add any substances (such as salt) to your water. Therefore, the water they treat is considered *conditioned*, not *softened*.

Catalytic-Converter Water Conditioners

One interesting water-conditioning strategy involves converting the unstable dissolved calcium and magnesium compounds into the stable compounds they were before they went into solution. In the case of calcium, this would mean causing the calcium, which is in the form of a dissolved *bicarbonate*, to revert to *calcium carbonate*—the stable material found in limestone. It's the dissolved bicarbonate contaminant, not calcium carbonate, that is responsible for creating lime scale (the crusty white buildup inside your pipes and on your plumbing fixtures).

To convert the bicarbonate molecular forms of calcium into molecules of the carbonate form, the bicarbonate molecules need to lose a molecule of carbon dioxide (CO_2). Catalytic water conditioners manage to do this by moving untreated water through a narrowing tube (a *venturi*). The water then comes in contact with a *catalytic* metal rod within a chamber (a catalyst is a substance that hastens a chemical reaction without being altered itself).

The effect of this is that CO_2 molecules are stripped away from the bicarbonate calcium molecules. The resulting calcium carbonate (CO_3) molecules immediately become attracted to, and bond to, the metal rod. The CO_3 molecules are attracted to the rod because it is made of a special alloy with properties that mimic a calcium carbonate crystal. Therefore, the newly formed calcium carbonate molecules "think" that they're bonding to other calcium carbonate molecules when, instead, they bond to the rod. In reality, the "deceptive" rod becomes a seed bed for calcium carbonate crystallization.

Meanwhile, the minute, stable calcium carbonate crystals (also known as *calcite*) that attach themselves to the rod are only able to build up very slightly before they're freed back into the water. Once these microscopic calcite crystals are present in your water supply, they themselves act as seeds or nuclei for calcium-carbonate crystallization. Surprisingly, this is supposed to cause the existing lime scale in your pipes to eventually disappear because the lime attaches itself to the calcite seeds. As a result, in a few weeks or months, your entire home plumbing system could become virtually free of lime scale.

By the way, some water-conditioner companies describe this whole process in their literature as *epitaxial nucleation*. Simply put, epitaxial is defined as the growth of crystals on a surface in a particular arrangement, and nucleation means the creation of crystal nuclei. With catalytic water conditioners, the *primary epitaxis* is the growth of crystals on the metal alloy rod. The *secondary epitaxis* is occurs when the seed crystals are released into the water and further crystalline growth results.

It's important to note that water treated with a catalytic water conditioner will retain it's original mineral content. This is because the conditioner doesn't remove hard-water minerals, it simply *deactivates* them so that hard-water problems are minimized. One concern to keep in mind, though, is that the surfaces of the rod within the catalytic converter chamber must be kept free from a buildup of contaminants in order to work efficiently. Therefore, with some models you must periodically remove the rod and clean it. Other models are designed in such a manner that the water stream supposedly creates a self-cleaning action. By the way, these particular devices are generally designed for whole-house applications, although point-of-use models, such as for ice makers, are sometimes available.

Magnetic-Physical Water Conditioning

Another alternative water-conditioning approach that attempts to free calcium carbonate from its dissolved molecular form is *magnetic-physical water conditioning*. Some of the devices that are based on this process accomplish the calcium-compound conversion by use of *permanent magnets* (magnets that retain their strong innate magnetic effect over time), while others use *electrically charged magnets* (magnets using live electric current). Also, some magnetic-physical water conditioners are installed directly in the water flow, while others are designed as clamp-on devices to be mounted around a water pipe (clamp-on models can be attached to all types of water pipes, except those containing iron).

One theory (proposed by Dr. Klaus J. Kronenberg) behind physical-magnetic water conditioning is that certain magnetic fields are able to break the *electrochemical bonds* that hold *water/calcium-carbonate clusters* together. This is important because these clusters, which are common in water, apparently "lock" calcium carbonate onto water molecules. Therefore, the imprisoned calcium carbonate isn't free to bond to other calcium carbonate and form the minute, stable crystals in the water. Instead, the calcium-carbonate/water clusters end up creating a crusty lime scale on the interiors of your pipes and plumbing fixtures.

Yet, if only about 1 in 10 billion water/calcium-carbonate clusters break up, the result would be effective water conditioning. This is because the newly freed calcium-carbonate molecules act as seeds for calcium-carbonate crystallization, and the remaining water/calcium-carbonate clusters will readily bond to these seeds. As a result, many very tiny calcium-carbonate crystals are soon present in the water—rather than calcium-carbonate/water clusters. Therefore, lime scale no longer forms on the interior surfaces of pipes and on plumbing fixtures and, eventually, the existing scale disappears (the tiny calcium carbonate crystals pass harmlessly through the plumbing lines).

This is the intended purpose of physical-magnetic water conditioning. In actual practice, the water flows at a certain speed past several magnets with *alternating polarity* (positive then negative, then positive, etc.). This creates a *resonating field of magnetic effects*. As it turns out, the specific *resonance* (vibration) that's produced coincides with the innate vibration within just a few of the calcium carbonate/water clusters present in the water. However, the increased resonance within these few clusters causes them to vibrate with great intensity. In fact, the vibration is more than some of the clusters can withstand and, so, they break apart, resulting in freed calcium-carbonate molecules that act as crystallizing seeds.

Certain considerations should be kept in mind if you'd like to try using a physical-magnetic water conditioner. The biggest question is whether or not they even work very well. Some people feel that, generally, magnetic-water-conditioning devices are effective only for about ten feet (or less) of pipe immediately after the magnet. Others feel they're not effective at all. Yet, others believe that, with well-planned placements, physical-magnetic water conditioners can work quite satisfactorily.

Like most alternative water-conditioning methods, water treated with a physical-magnetic water conditioner doesn't have the minerals removed. Although the water retains its mineral content, the hard-water minerals are deactivated and unable to form lime scale.

Electrostatic Water Conditioning

Electrostatic water conditioners are designed so that water passes through a metal *electrostatic chamber* or tank. There's a negatively charged, Teflon-coated, metal electrode inside the positively charged and grounded metal tank (the normal alternating electrical current in a house is changed to direct current to generate the charge on the electrode). The electrode is coated, so the direct-current won't come in contact with the flowing water. As a result of this setup, an *electrostatic field* (an area charged with static electricity) is generated between the electrode's surface and the tank's walls. The actual strength of this electrostatic field is said to be between 10,000 and 12,000 volts. Simply put, this means that electrons wind up becoming distributed throughout the water inside the tank.

This is important because the dissolved calcium and magnesium compounds (mostly in *carbonate* and *bicarbonate* forms) passing though this strong electrostatic field apparently become altered by the electrons. This change hinders their ability to bond together, or to other surfaces. So, the treated water prevents a further buildup of crusty white lime scale on the interiors of pipes and on plumbing fixtures. In fact, the already existing lime scale will supposedly break down and harmlessly pass through the plumbing system over time. By the way, it should be mentioned that the electrostatic field is also able to lower the water's surface tension so suds are created more easily (see *Soaps Vs. Detergents* on page 75).

One consideration to keep in mind with electrostatic water conditioners is that they continually use electric power. However, they're said to typically use less energy than a 40-watt light bulb. As with most alternative water-conditioning methods, water treated with an electrostatic water conditioner retains its mineral content. Commonly, electrostatic conditioning units are designed for whole-house use.

KDF Media as a Water Conditioner

KDF media has certain water conditioning properties. For more on this see *KDF Media* on page 605.

Water-Treatment Summary

Following is an, admittedly, brief listing of the water-treatment strategies covered in this chapter, along with the contaminants they're most effective in removing (or inactivating).

Important note: Some treatment units combine several treatment approaches. (Strategies are listed alphabetically

---

Water Treatment Strategies   Contaminants Affected

- **Activated-Charcoal Media, Granular**—Chlorine, dissolved gases, organic chemicals. Also, a limited amount of sediment.
- **Activated-Charcoal Media, Solid-Block**—Chlorine, dissolved gases, organic chemicals. Also sediment, asbestos, heavy metals, and some fluoride. Able to remove most protozoan cysts. (With precoat technology, much better at mechanically filtering particulates.)
- **Aluminum Titanium Silicate (ATS) Media**—Lead.
- **Ceramic Filters**—Most bacteria, protozoan cysts, and other solid contaminants (depending on pore size).
- **Crystalline Quartz Media**—Breaks down water's surface tension, sediment removal.
- **Electrostatic and Electrokinetic Filters**—Various types of particulates, depending on the filtering material.
- **Fluoride-Removing Filters**—Fluoride.
- **KDF (Kinetic-Degradation-Fluxion) Media**—Chlorine, sulfur dioxide, methane, certain heavy metals such as lead. Also controls most bacteria and microorganisms in the media through innate bacteriostatic action. In addition, deactivates hard-water minerals.
- **Ion-Exchange Media**—Claims vary, most say heavy metals when used as a filtering media. As a resin bead with catalyzing surfaces, it permits faster exchange of hard-water mineral ions for sodium ions.
- **Micro-Pore-Material Filters**—Sediment. (Other contaminants such as lead, bacteria, protozoan cysts depending on pore size).
- **Reverse-Osmosis Units**—Minerals, nitrates, fluoride, sediment, heavy metals, asbestos. Also effective at lowering salt concentrations (depending on the membrane rating), and greatly lowering the amounts of many types of biological contamination such as bacteria.
- **Sediment-Removing Filters**—Sand and dirt.
- **Ultraviolet (UV) Water Purifiers**—Most biological contaminants but not protozoan cysts.
- **Water Softening Agents**—Hard-water minerals (deactivation).
- **Water Conditioners**—Hard-water minerals (deactivation).
- **Water Softening Devices**—Hard-water minerals (removal), lead. Adds sodium to the water.
- **Water Distillers**—Sediment, minerals, nitrates, heavy metals, asbestos, fluoride, biological contaminants including protozoan cysts.

Choosing the Right Water-Treatment Equipment

There are perhaps hundreds of various water filters, purifiers, softening, and conditioning devices now available in the marketplace. Not surprisingly, many individuals, as a result, feel confused and overwhelmed when they try to choose the right equipment for their home. However, some basic steps can help make this process more manageable. These are discussed below.

Basic Water-Treatment Considerations

When you're ready to consider purchasing a specific piece of water-treatment equipment, it's important to have in front of you any written information you can find about your water. This information should include a variety of data, including whether or not your water supply is from a private source or a public utility. If it's from a utility, get a copy of any recent water-quality tests they have had performed (These tests should include information about mineral content, pH, chlorine, fluoride etc.). Of course, if you have a private well, you should have any laboratory reports that have been done on the quality of the water. Note: Even if you have utility-supplied water, you should consider having your tap water tested for its lead content if you have metal water pipes with lead-soldered joints.

With the specific water-quality information in front of you, you can decide to what extent you want certain contaminants removed. Naturally, you'll want to have *pathogenic* (disease-causing) and potentially harmful industrial and agricultural pollutants reduced as much as possible. But, perhaps a slightly elevated calcium and magnesium content, and the minimal lime scale it would create, will be acceptable to you. Your next decision is to choose the water-treatment strategy that's capable of actually removing (or deactivating) the contaminants you've targeted as "unwantables."

Once you've decided on a basic strategy, your next consideration is figuring out if you need (or want) a whole-house system, or one or more point-of-use units. Perhaps you would like a combination of both. Whether you're renting or you own your home will, no doubt, have a bearing on whether a whole-house unit is feasible. If you're renting (especially if for only a short time), it's likely you won't want to invest in any system that requires permanent installation. For renters, simple-to-install point-of-use devices often make the most sense.

On the other hand, if you own your home and have determined you only want to remove chlorine from your utility-supplied water, a whole-house activated-charcoal-media filter will probably be the best and easiest solution for you. In still another situation, you might find that a whole-house water-softening device will be able to rid your water supply of any unwanted hard-water minerals and iron, so that your water is satisfactory for bathing and general household purposes. But you may choose to use a water distiller in your kitchen to produce extremely pure water for drinking and cooking—water that's free of the sodium the water softener added. And, so on.

The factors to next take into account are an estimate of the volume of water you and your family use daily, as well as the amount of time you're willing to devote to the operation and maintenance of the water-treatment equipment. Are you honestly willing to change the filter each month if it's recommended? Will you remember to regularly clean a water conditioner's catalytic rod? You'll also need to consider whether you have adequate space for certain water-treatment devices. Do you really have room for a full-size water softener in your utility room? Do you really have the extra counter space for a water distiller or a gravity-feed ceramic filter? In addition, you should take into consideration the materials of which the equipment is constructed (stainless steel or plastic for example), especially if you're a chemically sensitive person.

Of course, when you're choosing water-treatment equipment, you'll have to consider its *initial cost* (price plus installation charge) and its *operating cost* (replacement membranes or filters, electricity, and any professional maintenance fees, etc. The cost of your utility water is especially a concern with reverse-osmosis units). The final step is finding out about any warranties and/or guarantees from manufacturers and dealers.

Further Help in Choosing Water-Treatment Equipment

Obviously, water-treatment equipment is an area where further advice, suggestions, and consultations by knowledgeable persons can be helpful. Therefore, it's a good idea to ask your physician and/or other health-care professional if he (or she) has any advice on units that would likely fit your specific needs. You might also contact consultant/dealers such as **Nigra Enterprises** who may be helpful as well. In addition, specialty catalogs for allergic and sensitive individuals, which handle several types and brands of water-treatment equipment, can be good sources of assistance, such as **Allergy Relief Shop, Inc.**, among others.

And, especially if your home has a private water source requiring a complicated treatment program, you'll want to consider contacting the **Water Quality Association**. This trade association will provide you with the names of nearby members. These are companies which are local suppliers of *traditional* water-softening/water-treatment equipment. However, it should be remembered that these companies often don't specialize in working with chemically sensitive individuals and they generally don't handle or install *alternative* water-conditioning equipment.

Another source of useful information is the **National Sanitation Foundation (NSF)**. The NSF is an independent, not-for-profit organization dedicated to public safety and protection of the environment by developing standards and certification. All certified NSF water systems are listed free-of-charge on their website, or in a booklet you can purchase from them.

It should be emphasized that only brief descriptions of certain pieces of water-improving equipment are offered in the following sections. These represent a sampling of what's currently available in the marketplace. (Each section's listings are in alphabetical order.) If you're interested in a particular model, you'll need to contact the manufacturer and/or dealer for more complete information. Of course, other units and suppliers are available in addition to the ones given here.

Note: For stand-alone fluoride-removing filters, sediment-removing filters, and ultraviolet-light purifiers, see *Fluoride-Removing Filters* on page 604, *Sediment-Removing Filters* on page 607 and *Ultraviolet (UV) Light Water Purifiers* on page 612.

Whole-House Water-Improvement Equipment

The following sections offer suggestions for whole-house water-treatment equipment you might consider purchasing. You should be aware that whole-house water-treatment equipment is permanently installed to your water line immediately after it enters your house. Therefore, professional installation is often required.

Whole-House Water Filters

For many homes on chlorinated water supplies, a simple activated-charcoal filter is often all that's necessary to create acceptable water. Fortunately, many models are available, but some are made of plastic. Naturally, some chemically sensitive individuals may be concerned about a water filter with a plastic housing. However, because activated charcoal will remove tastes and odors from your water, any plastic contamination will likely also be removed. Therefore, plastic activated-charcoal filtering units often prove to be quite tolerable (stainless-steel models, however, are available). Generally, manufacturers of activated-charcoal filters tend to recommend that their units only be used on chlorinated lines to reduce problems of microbial contamination on the charcoal.

The H_2O Whole House IL.9 has a housing that measures about four feet high and is filled with a KDF and granular-activated-coconut-shell-charcoal mixed media. There's also a micro prefilter and a micro postfilter. Obviously, this is a larger filtering system, and its said to have a capacity of 750,000 gallons. The H_2O is handled by **Allergy Relief Shop, Inc.**

The RH of Texas RH-1 Whole House Model has a stainless-steel housing that holds 4 extruded, activated-charcoal-block cartridges. When you buy the RH-1, you also get a separate RH-Blue sediment-removing filter which is to be installed before the main filter's housing. A special package containing the RH-1, the RH-Blue sediment-removing filter, and an Aqua Clear stainless-steel kitchen (under counter) unit with a silver-imbedded- ceramic/activated-charcoal cartridge is also offered. By the way, it's suggested that you replace the whole-house filtering cartridges and sediment-removing filter about every 6-8 months. With routine cleaning, the ceramic kitchen cartridge is rated to last 6-12 months. It should be stressed that "all the filter housings are constructed of non-toxic materials, and the cartridges used in these units do not contain any chemical binders." Therefore, this equipment can be a good option—particularly for chemically sensitive persons. You can buy the RH-1 from **American Environmental Health Foundation**.

The Essential Water & Air whole-house water filter uses 50 pounds of granular activated charcoal, Brimac bone char, and KDF as a mixed media. (The Brimac reduces fluoride.) This unit has a fully automatic backwash system (its not sold in CA) so the media only needs to be changed every 3-5 years. This item is sold by **Befit Enterprises Ltd.**

LifeTime Water Improvement systems come in a whole range of sizes able to filter from $1/2$ gallon to 300 gallons per minute, depending on the model chosen. These use "advanced granulated filtering media" said to remove chlorine and most pesticides, as well as reduce fluoride and heavy metals. These come with either manual or automatic backwash systems. To learn more, contact the **Building for Health Materials Center**.

Aqua-Pure (**Cuno, Inc.**) is a well known name in water filtration. Their whole-house water-filter line not only has models with plastic housings, but some are constructed of stainless steel. Granulated-activated-charcoal filters are available as are solid-block-activated-charcoal filters. All are considered taste-and-odor filters. Because of the similarities, two models are described below. If you're interested in Aqua-Pure products, contact the company for a nearby dealer. The Model AP12S comes in a high-impact-plastic housing with a built-in pressure-relief button. You can choose either the see-through version for easy viewing of the cartridge's condition, or an opaque version. There's a 10-year limited warranty on the AP12S which is designed for $3/4$" pipes. The Model SS1HA Commercial-Duty Water Filter comes with a heavy-duty stainless-steel housing. It's designed for installation on a $3/4$" water line. It accepts a variety of Aqua-Pure filters, including those for taste and odor.

The Spark-L-Pure (**General Ecology, Inc.**) uses seven Aqua Polish cartridge modules. Each uses microfiltration and broad-spectrum adsorption/molecular sieving, and "structured-matrix" activated charcoal. The Spark-L-Pure is said to remove "fibers, visible dirt and sand, chlorine, foul odors, and other particulate contaminants." Filtration is rated at down to 1 micron. The housing is of polished stainless steel, and cartridge modules are rated to be able to treat 30,000 gallons "for particulates." It should be kept in mind that this unit must be used with bacteriologically safe water. If you're interested in owning one, you can order it directly from manufacturer, from **The Pure Water Place, Inc.**, or **Befit Enterprises Ltd.**

The Healthy Home Whole House System includes a 20-micron sediment-removing prefilter in a 10"-long (length of the plastic housing), or a 20"-long, radial-flow granular-activated-charcoal filter. You can purchase this system from **healthyhome.com**.

Multi-Pure Whole House Treatment System TO-15000 (**Multi-Pure Corp.**) has a polypropylene housing. Inside is activated granular charcoal. Each filtering cartridge (you get two extra with your initial purchase) "has a capacity of 15,000 gallons." The Multi-Pure can be purchased from the company or from its dealers.

Several fine brands of whole-house filters are sold by **Nigra Enterprises**. Others are available from **Culligan International** dealers, local **Sears, Roebuck and Co.** stores, and other outlets.

Whole-House Reverse-Osmosis Units

For whole-house reverse-osmosis (R/O) treatment, you'll probably want to consult and deal with a local distributor. This is because most whole-house R/O units entail installing relatively expensive and complicated equipment (tanks, repressurization pumps, membranes, etc.), that must specifically meet the needs of your particular situation. Therefore, you might consider contacting the **Water Quality Association** for a dealer near you that handles, installs, and is able to maintain such systems. You should also be able to find a reputable dealer in your local telephone directory. Saying that, one unique system is described below.

One system you might consider is **Clean Water Products**. They make a range of R/O systems for the whole house (and even larger needs). All systems can be purchased directly from them. It should be noted that all Clear Water Products R/O units use a Nanofiltration System. First, a booster pump passes water through a 0.5-micron prefilter. Then the water enters a reverse-osmosis unit using a special "looser wrap membrane" (a membrane with larger pores). As result, it's said that the system can be used successfully at lower water pressures with increased output, over typical units. Clean Water Products says that their Nanofiltration R/O process is able to remove heavy metals, nitrates, radon, arsenic, excess fluoride, selenium, excess hard-water minerals, and salinity. Placed at the point where water enter into house, these units can produce hundreds to thousands a gallon a day, depending on the model purchased.

Whole-House Softeners, Conditioners, & Combination Systems

Quite a few manufacturers offer salt-type ion-exchange water-softening devices. In fact, this is such an old, well established technology, that you should be able to find many brands locally. (Check in your telephone classified pages.) Therefore, brands and strategies that may be less familiar are primarily listed below. Also listed are models that combine other strategies.

Clear Water Scale Buster Water Softener has an electric cable that wraps around your water pipe "creating a unique and complex modulating frequency wave form that produces an inaudible sonic impulse that changes the electrical and physical properties of scale-forming calcium molecules." It's said that this ultimately causes the minerals to "repel" from pipes and also gradually breaks up existing scale. This product is handled by the **Befit Enterprises Ltd.**

The Scaleban Water Descaler creates electrically generated "molecular surface energy realignment (MSER)" which is said to neutralize dissolved calcium chloride into neutral, aragonite—not calcite or lime, which adheres to pipes. This item is available from the **Building for Health Materials Center.**

The Ultimate Whole House System is "three systems in one." It includes a potassium-based water softener. This is essentially an ion-exchange unit using potassium chloride rather than sodium chloride (common salt). The second system is an activated-coconut-shell-charcoal filter. The third is "The Pro 7000 Ultimate double purification system" (reverse osmosis and deionization). This water-treatment equipment is offered by the **Building for Health Materials Center.**

Care Free Water Technologies, Inc. makes a number of versions with the same catalytic technology at their core. All these should be used with "biologically safe water supplies" and must be "earth grounded." Care Free says that it's catalyst units have "increased electron output and harmonics" that others don't and they require no maintenance. To purchase any product in their line, contact them for their nearest dealer. Aquiline is the simplest model by Care Free. It's basically a small, bronze casting which is designed to be connected to the water-supply line before it comes into the house or goes to the sprinkler system. (The manufacturer notes that water treated by it's conditioners makes oxygen more available to soil microorganisms.) Another option is to install the unit indoors just where the water line enters the house. The Aquiline E/N (28" high x 10" diameter) is very similar internally, but has an additional cylindrical plastic outer "tank." The company says that this model was designed for people who don't need (or desire) to condition the water they use outdoors. The tank provides "aesthetic appeal and a constant treated-water reservoir." The Filtercon is a much larger unit with a tank measuring 62" high. Essentially it's a combination granular-activated-charcoal filter and catalytic water conditioner. Its equipped with a backwash timer. No electricity is required to operate the Filtercon—except to run the timer mechanism. Different models for different sized families are available.

Aqua-Pure Water Softeners (**Cuno, Inc.**) are typical salt-using ion-exchange units. There are several models to fit your particular needs. All come in your choice of timer- or meter-initiated control. A different approach for mild to moderate hard water is to use Aqua-Pure filtering cartridges that "incorporate a patented ingredient known as Scale Stopper." Aqua-Pure Scale Stopper filters apparently use two strategies to inhibit further scale formation, and to treat existing scale in pipe interiors. Aqua-Pure Scale and Corrosion cartridges also use a "graded density prefilter" for dirt and rust removal. Housings to fit these special filters come in either plastic or stainless steel. If you're interested in Aqua-Pure products, contact the manufacturer for a local dealer.

Emissions Panther Water Stabilizer (**Emissions Panther, Inc.**) is a whole-house catalytic water conditioner. Unlike some other brands, it's made to be removable. This is because the company suggests cleaning the unit yearly with citric or muriatic acid and then reinstalling it. After about four years, you should remove it and buff it clean with a wire wheel or wire brush to completely clean off any accumulated mineral buildup. These measures should make the special inner catalytic rod work at its optimum. (The reason for these routine cleanings is that the company feels that any catalytic rod can become encrusted in time.) You can buy the Emissions Panther Water Stabilizer at local Home Depot Building Centers. If you have none in your area, call the national distributor, **Enviro Air & Water.**

ClearWave CW-1 (**Field Controls, LLC**) water conditioner attaches to the side of any type of water pipe. If you prefer, it can be mounted on the wall and attached to an antenna which is wrapped around a pipe. By the way, if iron is in your water, it's recommended to install an iron-removing filter prior to the ClearWave CW-1. This device works by generating inaudible, low-power radio waves that affect the molecular attraction of minute calcium crystals in the water supply. As a result, it's said that they become less able to bond to each other, or to pipe surfaces, to form scale. One small unit is suggested for an entire house. It should be noted that the CW-1 needs to be plugged into a standard outlet. You can get this product at some local Ace Hardware stores. If you prefer mail order, you can purchase it directly from the manufacturer.

GE SmartWater (**General Electric Co.**) is a line of conventional salt-using water softeners. Contact the company for nearby dealers.

GMX Magnetic Model 800 (**GMX Magnetic**) is a magnetic water conditioner using "grade 8 Strontium Ferrite Ceramic magnets." It's said that these create "magnetic fluid conditioning" (water passes through a focused magnetic field which breaks up hard-water-mineral molecular complexes. This apparently liberates the formerly "captive mineral atoms" so that they become crystallization sites for surrounding mineral molecules in the water, rather than attaching to pipes. You'll need to call the company for an area dealer. The Chemical Free Water Conditioner is a $7^3/_4$" long magnetic unit using PVC (polyvinyl chloride) and "ceramic ferrite magnets." This item simply snaps over your main in-coming water-supply pipe. It's said that the resulting "magnetic field will modify the polarization of fresh water mineral salts." While it should help to prevent mineral build-up, it won't remove minerals (it just inactivates them). You can order this item from **Improvements**.

The Kinetico Water Conditioner (**Kinetico Water Systems**) is a large, "twin tank," salt-using water softener. What make it special, however, is that it's a completely automatic system using no electricity, time clock, or electronics. Amazingly, it's powered only by the moving water. Call the manufacturer for it's nearest dealer.

The Catalytic 1000 (**Stabilized Water of Canada, Inc.**) has a catalytic bar positioned inside a tight-fitting plastic pipe. The special interior design causes water to flow through the narrow passage next to a "beta-nickel-surfaced" catalytic bar. The pressure drop is so low that it apparently "reaches near vacuum levels" so some of the dissolved carbon dioxide temporarily bubbles out, causing the calcium carbonate to lose some of its ability to remain dissolved. As with other catalytic conditioners, minute solid-calcite crystal nuclei are created, which are said to ultimately prevent scale buildup and eventually reduce scale already present in pipes. You can order the Catalytic 1000 directly from the manufacturer.

Of course, **Culligan International** is well known for their salt-using water softeners. They also handle a number of other different water-treatment devices. These can be purchased from local dealers. Their Kenmore brand, and other models, are handled by **Sears, Roebuck and Co.** Still more brands should be listed in your classified telephone directory.

Kitchen Water-Improvement Equipment

For some households, whole-house water treatment isn't necessary, desired, affordable, or effective enough at removing all the unwanted contaminants. Therefore, many water-treatment devices are installed or placed in the kitchen for drinking water and cooking.

The following sections offer suggestions for water-treatment equipment you might consider purchasing. Of course, other products are available besides the ones listed here. Also, bear in mind that only a brief description is given for each model, so you should contact the individual companies or dealers for more information. Certain items, especially undercounter units, may require professional installation.

Kitchen Countertop & Undercounter Water Filters

Below are some water filters that you might consider. Some are for above counter use, others are installed under the counter, while some are convertible (to be placed either above or below the sink). With such a wide variety that are available, and only limited space to describe them, only a few are mentioned below.

The Aqua Clear comes in both an above-counter and an undercounter model. Both have stainless-steel housings with nickel-plated brass fittings. Inside, both versions use a Kieselgluhr ceramic filter (imbedded with silver to act as a bacteriostatic agent) combined with activated charcoal. It's said that, with correct maintenance, the ceramic/charcoal cartridge should last 6-12 months. This equipment (which can be especially good the chemically sensitive) is sold by the **American Environmental Health Foundation**.

Cuno, Inc. manufactures several undercounter Aqua-Pure filters. Three are described below. To purchase any of them, you'll need to call the company for an area dealer. The Aqua-Pure AP200 Under-Sink Water Filter is made of high-impact plastic and "uses a multi-stage filtration process." This includes a graded-density prefilter and "specially formulated high-adsorption activated carbon." The AP200 has a compact shape and can be used with $3/8$" water lines. The Aqua-Pure AP-DWS750 uses an "advanced single stage filtration and adsorption system." This is said to remove dirt, rust, bad tastes and odors, lead, and cysts. It comes with it's own installation hardware, including an attractive at-sink faucet. The Aqua-Pure APDWS1000 has two canisters using "dual stage carbon-block filtration." Cuno says that it reduces lead, chlorine, VOCs, Giardia cysts, bad tastes and odors, chemicals, and lead, as well as dirt and rust. It comes with its own at-sink faucet.

Doulton UltraCarb Water Filters come in both a countertop and an undercounter model. Both utilize a ceramic cartridge (to capture protozoan cysts, and many other particulates) filled with "bonded activated charcoal with ionic-exchange capability." Some models have stainless-steel housings. Dealers for Doulton filters (who sell one or more models) include **Real Goods, Health One Co., N.E.E.D.S., Allergy Relief Shop, Inc.,** and **Befit Enterprises Ltd.**

The EPS Stainless Steel Water Filter contains two pounds of granular activated charcoal. Unlike some filters, the water percolates upward through the media. Because the water never comes into contact with any synthetic materials, it can be a good choice for chemically sensitive persons. You can buy this item from **E.L. Foust Co., Inc.**

Everpure make a whole line of under-counter water filters. These are said to be easy-to-install (each comes with directions and a toll-free telephone help line) and require little space. Most use a precoated "proprietary blend of activated carbon" to remove chlorine, cysts, cloudiness, asbestos, and other particulates down to 0.5 microns. Everpure products are sold by **E.L. Foust Co., Inc.**

One kitchen-filter brand you might consider is the Seagull IV (**General Ecology, Inc.**). Seagull IV actually comes in several models with stainless-steel housings. However, all use multiple-strategy filtration systems combining "ultrafine microstraining, molecular capture, and electrostatic removal." At the heart of these systems are special matrix-structured, activated-charcoal blocks. These are rated down to 0.4 microns. As a result, Seagull IVs are effective at removing chlorine, as well as disease-causing bacteria, particulates, and even protozoan cysts. Specific units are designed for either countertop or below-counter installation. Seagull IV can be purchased directly from the company or from dealers such as **The Pure Water Place, Inc.**

GE Dual Carbon Filtration Systems (**General Electric Co.**) is a line of undercounter kitchen water filters that all use the Smart Water faucet. Each system has 2 filtering canisters. The first holds a sediment-removing filter and the second contains either a standard GE activated-charcoal block, or one rated down to 1 micron to remove cysts. If you're interested in purchasing one of these, call the company for a nearby dealer. Because of the similarities, only two models are described below. The GE GNUL30B Lead/Cysts Model is rated for 1,250 gallons before filter cartridge replacement is necessary. The GE GXEM01B is just the canister and faucet. You purchase the type of filter cartridge you need for your water supply separately.

The Water Dome is a countertop filtering unit. (A larger stainless-steel model is available for installation below the counter). Each uses three filtration technologies (a "graded-density electrokinetic prefilter," a compressed-activated-charcoal block, and a graded-micro-pore filter). As a result, it's said to be able to remove sub-micron particles, chlorine, cysts, dirt, and rust. Each cartridge refill is rated to last for 500 gallons. You can purchase Water Domes from local **Golden Neo-Life Diamite** dealers.

The Honeywell CT 6000 is a countertop unit with a plastic housing. Inside is an activated-charcoal block. It's recommended for cold-water use only. It can be ordered from **healthyhome.com.**

The Singer Spring countertop water filter has ATS media and an activated-charcoal block. It's said to be able to remove cysts, lead, chlorine, and more. Each filter cartridge should last about one year. It comes in your choice of a white-plastic or chrome-finish housing. This item is handled by **Inner Balance.**

Multi-Pure Corp. manufactures several kitchen-use filtration systems. All use Multi-Pure's Solid Carbon Block Filters especially made with 3 filtration strategies (mechanical filtration, electrokinetic adsorption, and physical/chemical adsorption). The company says they can be used for cyst reduction on disinfected waters that may contain filterable cysts. A real plus is that most models use a stainless-steel housing. All Multi-Pure equipment can be purchased from the company. Several models can also be ordered from **Natural Lifestyle.** The Model MP750SSCT is a countertop unit. Each replacement cartridge is rated for 750 gallons. The similar Model MP750SC is a countertop model that can also be converted to a below-counter installation. The Model MP400PC is another countertop-only unit. It's housing is ABS plastic, and its filters are rated for 400 gallons. The Model MP750SB is for below-counter installation. Each filter is rated for 750 gallons. Model MP1200EL is larger with a filter rated for 1,200 gallons.

The New Wave Enviro Premium (**New Wave Enviro**) countertop water filter has an attractive white-plastic housing. Inside are replaceable, multiple-layer, 10-stage filtering cartridges (with sediment-removing filters, granular activated charcoal, and KDF, among others). The Premium is said to be capable of removing heavy metals, cysts, chlorine, pesticides, and more. Each cartridge is rated for 1,500 gallons (about 1-$1^1/_2$ years for a family of four.) This model is handled by **Tomorrow's World** and **healthyhome.com.** These can also sometimes be found in local outlets, especially health-food and alternative grocery stores.

The Water Factory is a unique undercounter system. It uses three, sealed, "pop-in" plastic treatment cartridges. The first is a sediment-removing filter, the second contains a reverse-osmosis membrane, and the third contains granular activated charcoal. This unit is handled by **Ozark Water Service and Environmental Services.**

PUR Plus Undersink, and the PUR Plus Countertop (**PUR Drinking Water Systems**) both use filtering cartridges containing activated charcoal "and an active agent to remove lead"…"bound in a block form by a polymer with a 1 micron rating." Apparently, this media is able to remove protozoan cysts. These filters should only be used on cold water. You know when cartridge replacement is necessary because of a convenient monitoring indicator. PUR products are often sold in local department stores (such as **Sears, Roebuck** and Co.) and building centers. The **JC Penny Catalog** may handle one or more of them from time to time.

The Sun Pure Filter System comes in both a countertop and an under-counter configuration. Each uses a 5-stage filtration system. These include a 1-micron prefilter (to remove protozoan cysts), a molded activated-charcoal block, adsorption and ion-exchange media (able to remove fluoride, copper, and aluminum), granular activated charcoal, and an ultra-violet (UV) light purifier. It's said to have a flow-rate of 0.5-0.75 gallons per minute. A replacement filter/purifier-lamp kit should be installed annually. This system is sold by **Real Goods** and **Inner Balance**.

The CleanWater Filter is a simple countertop unit with a silver-impregnated activated-charcoal/KDF-media filter said to act as a "5-stage water processor." The unit is replaced after 7,500 gallons or two years. This item can be ordered from **Tomorrow's World**.

In addition, **Nigra Enterprises, Building for Health Materials Center**, and **N.E.E.D.S.** offer several fine types of filters you'll want to consider.

Of course, a number of kitchen-use filters, including the Kenmore brand, are handled by **Sears, Roebuck and Co.** And, **Culligan International** has many filters designed for installation in your kitchen. To find a Culligan dealer, check your classified telephone directory or contact the company's headquarters. Other brands may be available in local building centers.

Kitchen Faucet Filters

A number of manufacturers make small water-filtering units that either fit on your kitchen faucet or are actually incorporated into it. A few brands are listed below.

Culligan International makes kitchen-faucet filters that are sometimes sold locally, such as at **Sears, Roebuck and Co.** Other brands are often sold in local building centers.

PureTouch (**Moen Inc.**) kitchen faucets are cleverly designed. Each comes with a hidden, built-in Culligan activated-charcoal-block filter that fits into the stem of a special faucet spout. Filter cartridges actually come in three grades, for different filtering capabilities. These are the MicroTech 1000 (taste and odor, chlorine reduction), the MicroTech 2000 (also removes lead), and the MicroTech 3000 (also able to remove cysts). It should be mentioned that each filter cartridge is rated to last 3 months. You'll need to contact the company for a nearly dealer.

The PUR Select Faucet Mount (**PUR Drinking Water Systems**) uses a filtering cartridge containing activated charcoal "and an active agent to remove lead." These are "bound in a block form by a polymer with a 1-micron rating." It's said to be able to remove protozoan cysts. This unit is designed for cold-water use only. A monitoring indicator let's you know when you need to replace the cartridge (around 2-3 months). PUR products are often available in local department stores (such as **Sears, Roebuck and Co.**) and building centers. Also, **Service Merchandise** (catalog and stores). **Inner Balance**, and **Harmony** carry the PUR faucet-mount filter. The **JC Penny Catalog** (which handles some PUR products) may handle it also from time to time.

Refrigerator Ice-Maker/Water Filters

Refrigerator ice makers now have filters designed specifically for them.

The Doulton In-Line Pressure Filter has a stainless-steel housing. It's designed to be easily unscrewed and requires only four inches of space below it for servicing. This item it sold by **Allergy Relief Shop, Inc.**

Aqua-Pure Ice-Maker Water Filter AP717 (**Cuno, Inc.**) is a sleek in-line filter. It contains activated charcoal as well as a sediment-removing prefilter and a "proprietary scale and corrosion inhibition system." To purchase this Aqua-Pure filter, contact the manufacturer for an area dealer.

The GE SmartWater Refrigerator/Icemaker Water Filter (**General Electric Co.**) comes in two white-plastic models. These are said to remove bad tastes and odors, sediment, rust, and chlorine. The GE GXTQ is rated for 2,000 gallons and has a replaceable filtering cartridge and an auto-shut-off valve. The GE GXIT is rated for 750 gallons and doesn't have replaceable filters. Call the company for a nearby dealer.

Fresh Ice Premium (**New Wave Enviro**) is a sleek filtering unit with a white-plastic housing. It uses granular activated charcoal and other technologies to remove chlorine, lead, sediment, bad tastes and odors, as well as cysts. Designed with "quick-connect fittings," it apparently requires no special plumbing. This particular filter is rated for 750 gallons (about one year for a family of four). You may find this product locally, especially in alternative grocery stores. If not, call the manufacturer for a nearby dealer.

Kitchen Gravity-Feed Water Filters

All *gravity-feed filtering devices* simply use gravity as the force needed to cause water to go through their filters. No pumps or water pressure is required. Therefore, these are totally free-standing devices, not plugged in to the home's electrical circuitry, or hooked up in any manner to the plumbing system.

Gravity-feed filtering equipment is simple. It consists of a top tank which is manually filled with water. Gravity moves this untreated water through some type of filter media and into a lower treated-water holding container. Today, two basic types exist. These are carafe/pitchers (often made of plastic), and larger countertop models (made of stainless steel, ceramic, or plastic). The degree of water purity that results from any of them depends on the filter media used (what kind, how much, and how clean).

The Doulton Gravity-Feed water filter has a stainless-steel housing and 2 Sterasyl Filters (silver-imbedded ceramic with granular activated charcoal inside). Doulton dealers include **Befit Enterprises Ltd.** and **Health One Co.** It should be noted that **N.E.E.D.S.** is a Doulton dealer, and may carry this item, too.

Brita (USA) Inc. manufactures a complete line of gravity-feed pitchers, as well as several countertop models. All these plastic units use the same type of filtering cartridges, which are replaceable. Each one contains granular activated charcoal and ion-exchange-resin beads. According to the company, this combination reduces unpleasant tastes and odors, chlorine, lead, copper, and hard-water minerals that may be found in tap water. Brita products are very affordable, starting at around twenty dollars. The various pitcher models (Standard, Ultra, Spacesaver, etc.) basically differ in shape. Most hold around 2 gallons. It's suggested that you drain and clean your Brita pitcher every 3-4 days. A cartridge should last for 35 gallons or about 2 months. Brita items are commonly sold in local area outlets including department stores (such as **Sears, Roebuck and Co.**), discount stores, and building centers. In addition, **Service Merchandise** handles some Brita pitchers.

The Lifekind Water Filter System is a stainless-steel, self-contained, gravity-operated countertop unit. It uses micropore-ceramic/activated-charcoal filters. It's said to be able to make 10 gallons daily. You can purchase it from **Lifekind Products.**

Several models of British Berkefeld gravity-feed water filtration systems are offered by **New Millennium Concepts, Ltd.** (They're actually the North American master distributor for these imports from the United Kingdom.) All models use Doulton 7" or 9" ceramic filters (four to eight depending on the model) which are made with Kieselgluhr Diatomaceous Earth. Each filter has "80,000 overlapping pores, providing absolute mechanical filtration to 0.9 micron." Some filters (the Super Sterasyls models) have silver imbedded in them to act as a bacteriostatic agent (this is designed to hinder microbial growth on the filter). Inside all the ceramic filters is treated activated granular charcoal in a special matrix design. Each British Berkefeld gravity-feed water-filtration system is constructed of a large, cylindrical, 2-piece stainless-steel tank/housing. Inside, the Doulton filter cartridges attach to fittings in the top tank. To use, you simply pour water into the upper level and treated water is available from the lower tank through a convenient tap. Depending on the model, 24 gallons, or more, can be treated each day. Filters are said to be able to remove 99.9% of cysts, parasites, and nasty bacteria, and to reduce chlorine, rust and organic chemicals. From time to time, the ceramic filters should be brushed with a soft brush to clean off any contaminant build up. Each filter should provide pathogenic (disease-causing) protection for 2,000 to 15,000 gallons. (The exact amount depends on your water conditions and your maintenance schedule.) You can order British Berkefeld filters from their main distributor, **New Millennium Concepts, Ltd.**, or from dealers such as **Ozark Water Service and Environmental Services**.

The Clean Water Products CWP Gravity Water Filter is a stainless-steel, self-contained countertop unit. Inside is a ceramic (silver-imbedded) filter filled with granular activated charcoal. This product is handled by **N.E.E.D.S.**

PUR Drinking Water Systems manufactures several types of plastic PUR Pitchers. The standard filtering cartridge contains activated-charcoal granules and ion-exchange technology. This is said to reduce the lead, sediment, copper, mercury, and chlorine content of your water. (Note: PUR doesn't believe that ion-exchange beads in this context can effectively remove hard-water minerals.) A special product in their line is the PUR Plus Pitcher that holds two gallons. It has a standard media enclosed within a pleated microfilter. This combination allows it to also remove cysts. Filter cartridges for all PUR products are available. You can generally expect each filter to last for up to 40 gallons. (A handy red indicator monitor lets you know when the filter should be changed.) You can buy PUR water-filtering products in many local stores, including **Sears, Roebuck, & Company**. A number of PUR products are sold in the **JC Penny Catalog** as well as through the **Service Merchandise** catalog and stores.

Aqua Select Water Filter Pitcher is in a 12-cup size that utilizes a special design so that it's filtering media "always stays wet and 100% activated." It's said to reduce 95% of heavy metals and to "significantly reduce chlorine, zinc, cadmium, and sulfates." Each replaceable filter cartridge is rated to treat 85 pitchers full of water. You can purchase this product from **Real Goods**.

An attractive terra-cotta water-filter cooler is sold by **Real Goods**. It has two tanks—the top one has a terra-cotta lid and the bottom one a tap. Measuring 17" high and 10" in diameter, it produces six gallons of filtered water a day. The filtering unit is ceramic with activated charcoal inside and it needs replacing annually (or after 2,500 gallons). By the way, **Harmony** and **Inner Balance** sell similar units. (For more on the benefits of terra cotta coolers, see *Ceramic Water Dispensers (Coolers)* on page 638.)

It should be mentioned that gravity-feed water filters, especially pitchers, should be available in local department stores and building centers. These may include other brands than the ones described here.

Kitchen Reverse-Osmosis Units and RO Systems

Following are some sources for reverse-osmosis (R/O) units for use in your kitchen—both countertop and undercounter models. Also included are combination units (commonly called R/O systems) that utilize several types of filtering strategies as well as an R/O membrane—each in their own separate canister. (By the way, the unit holding the R/O membrane may be called a *module*.)

The Aristocrat III Reverse Osmosis System's undersink model (well and utility models are available) has a sediment-removing prefilter, an activated-charcoal prefilter and an R/O membrane, along with a 2.5-gallon water-holding tank. The system's capacity is rated at 15-30 gallons per day. **Allergy Relief Shop, Inc.** is one mail-order source for this product.

The RH of Texas Series 5000 PCF Water Appliance is an R/O system with 6-stage filtration. It includes a 5-micron sediment-removing filter, an activated-charcoal prefilter, "ultrafiltration," a reverse-osmosis membrane, "prolonged contact" activated-charcoal filtration, and a final activated-charcoal postfilter. There's also a 3 gallon holding tank. This item is rated to produce 15-20 gallons in 24 hours. It should be especially good for chemically sensitive persons, and is offered by **American Environmental Health Foundation**.

Aquathin Corp. makes a line of kitchen-use reverse-osmosis units. All use the manufacturer's unique reverse-osmosis process and a *deionization process* in a four-stage system. (The deionization uses special ion-exchange resins.) This allows for the removal of "salt, heavy metals, chemical pollutants, pesticides, nitrates, and disease-causing waterborne microorganisms." All products are sold through dealers only. You can contact the company for one near you. A particularly innovative model is The Spacesaver SS-90. It's designed to hang beneath an overhead kitchen cabinet, thus saving you room on your countertop, or under your sink. A plastic tube allows it to drain into your own water bottle. This unit is rated to produce 12-18 gallons a day. If you'd prefer a countertop type, the company also makes the Kitchen KT-90. This is made of Lexan plastic (in three color choices) and measures $8^3/_4$" wide x $10^3/_8$" high x 19" long. Optional activated-charcoal and sediment prefilters are available. The Platinum 90 model is a larger system for undersink applications. It has a 4-gallon holding tank (larger tanks are available). It comes with a granular-activated-charcoal postfilter in the standard model, with several types of prefilter options at extra cost.

Both Essential Water & Air's countertop and undercounter R/O systems use four cartridges. These include a sediment-removing prefilter, a granular activated-charcoal prefilter, an "Industrial Grade Thin Film Composite (TFC) membrane," and a granular-activated-charcoal postfilter. These can be purchased from **Befit Enterprises Ltd.**

The Pure Solutions International CTRO is a compact, good-looking, countertop R/O model. It's equipped with 2 prefilters (sediment-removing and activated-charcoal) and an activated-charcoal postfilter. A well-water model is also available. This product can be purchased from **Bio Designs**.

The Universal Water R/O systems includes a 5-micron prefilter, "ultrafiltration," an R/O membrane, and a granular activated-charcoal postfilter. Ultimate and Ultimate Plus models have even more filtration strategies and features. All are sold by **Bio Designs**.

Aqua-Pure Reverse Osmosis System APRO5000 (**Cuno, Inc.**) has four-stage filtration. This includes a 5-micron prefilter, an activated-charcoal prefilter, a reverse-osmosis module, and an activated-charcoal final filter. This unit has an automatic shut-off and a 3.6 gallon holding tank. It's rated to produce 9-14 gallons a day with either chlorinated, non-chlorinated, utility, or well systems. If you're interested, you'll need to call for a local dealer.

GE SmartWater (**General Electric Co.**) is a line of undercounter R/O units. Sizes vary, with outputs of from 10-18 gallons per day. All use "dual carbon filtration." In addition, all have plastic holding tanks. Many also have monitors to indicates when the filter and membrane should be changed. If you're interested in purchasing a GE water-treatment product, call the company for their nearest dealer. One model is the GE Profile System, which is listed as a "monitored reversed-osmosis system" able to make 12 gallons a day.

The TerraFlo CBLX (**Global Environmental Technologies**) is a countertop unit with a white-plastic housing. Inside is a replaceable activated-charcoal-block filter made with additional resin compounds. It's said to be able to remove chlorine, lead, mercury, cysts, VOCs (including trihalomethanes), many organic pesticides, and more. Each filter cartridge is rated for 400 gallons. Interestingly, these can be sent back free to company for recycling. You can order the TerraFlo directly, or you may be able to find it in some local stores.

The Honeywell R/O undercounter system has a prefilter, an activated-charcoal block, an R/O membrane, and an activated-granular-charcoal postfilter. This item can be ordered from **Harmony**.

The Kinetico Drinking Water System (**Kinetico Water Systems**) is an undercounter R/O unit. It comes with a 5-micron sediment-removing prefilter, a "noncorrosive (plastic) drinking water storage tank," a patented MACguard Filter (activated-charcoal block with a changing indicator) and a lead-free faucet. On the Plus model, a patented EverClean Rinse feature is able to flush the membrane. You'll need to call the company for an area dealer.

New Wave Enviro Reverse Osmosis Systems (**New Wave Enviro**) come complete with all the fittings necessary for installation. Both the above- and below-counter versions are said to remove heavy metals, pesticides, chlorine, cysts, and more. The Countertop Model is a compact 16" long x 10" wide x 13" high, and is made of plastic. It features a 2-gallon holding tank and has two prefilters, an R/O membrane, and a postfilter. The Undercounter Model has a 5-gallon holding tank with three canisters (prefilter, R/O membrane, and postfilter). Check your local alternative grocery or health-food store for availability. If you can't find one, contact the company for their nearest dealer.

Nature's Spring is a very simple, very small (it's housed in a 6" x 5" x 16" box), very affordable countertop reverse-osmosis system. Two models are available (for utility or well water). You attach Nature Spring with an easy-disconnect fitting to the sink faucet. A tube runs from the unit to your storage bottle. Under optimal conditions, 12-14 gallons can be made in 24 hours. Both activated-charcoal and sediment-removing filters are options. One Nature Spring dealer is **Ozark Water Service and Environmental Services**.

The Water Factory is a combination, undercounter system. It uses three, sealed, "pop-in" plastic treatment cartridges. The first is a sediment-removing filter, the second contains a reverse-osmosis membrane, and the third contains granular activated charcoal. This product is handled by **Ozark Water Service and Environmental Services**

The Advanced Reverse Osmosis System for undersink installation comes with four canisters and a 2-gallon holding tank. It contains a sediment-removing filter, an activated-charcoal prefilter, an R/O membrane, and an activated-charcoal postfilter. The activated-charcoal and sediment filters are rated to last 6-12 months, the membrane for 36 months. The Advanced can be purchased from **Real Goods**.

The Watermaker Minit is a tiny, plastic, countertop R/O unit with a membrane inside. It's designed with a quick faucet disconnect and comes with clear plastic tubing which empties treated water into your pitcher. It's suggested that you store the unit in refrigerator when not in use. This little wonder is sold by **Real Goods**.

Other fine R/O units are also sold by **Nigra Enterprises** and **E.L. Foust Co., Inc.** Locally, **Sears, Roebuck and Co.** stores, **Culligan International** dealers, among others, should offer R/O units as well.

Kitchen Water Distillers

Following are a few of the water distillers currently in the marketplace you may wish to consider purchasing.

The Crystal Clear Living Water is a unique stainless-steel distiller. It's designed with a "unique boiling chamber which uses a patented flash reboiling process that removes practically all of the chemicals having a boiling point lower than water" before the water collection. There are a number of other special features as well. This unit is rated to make up to 15 gallons per day and is available from **Befit Enterprises Ltd.**

Genesis water distillers are plug-in, manual-fill, coffee-maker-like, countertop models in plastic housings. These are equipped with activated-charcoal postfilters. Depending on the model, they can make 3 quarts (Model 3000) or 6 quarts (Model 6000) of distilled water in five hours. You can purchase these distillers from both **InteliHealth Health Home** and **Bio Designs**.

One water distiller of special note is the Rain Crystal 8 (**Scientific Glass Co., Inc.**) This unit is about the size of a bread box and is handcrafted out of laboratory-grade Pyrex glass with a protective Plexiglas case. To use the Rain Crystal 8, simply plug it in, attach the connecting tube to your standard kitchen-sink faucet, set the flowmeter, and put another connecting tube into a water-holding jug on the floor below it. In twenty-four hours, 5-8 gallons of distilled water should be produced (the rate varies depending on your home's elevation above sea level). Unlike most water distiller these days, the Rain Crystal 8 doesn't utilize an activated-charcoal filter. Instead, it has a unique two-step process resulting in dissolved gas bubbles appearing in the coil and being discharged into a reservoir where they escape into the room air, or go down the drain. In the second stage, any chemicals left will either rise with the steam to be vented from the condensing chamber or remain in the boiler to be washed down the drain with minerals and other heavy contaminants. Apparently, tests show 98% removal of toxic wastes without using activated charcoal. However, it should be remembered that while you won't be drinking harmful chemicals, those vented into your kitchen's air may eventually become inhaled. Therefore, activated-charcoal filter systems (both pre- and postfilters), which are optional, are probably a good idea. Another option is an electric timer. This unique unit is constructed of Pyrex glass rather than stainless steel or plastic. It can be ordered directly from the company or from **Nigra Enterprises**.

The TapWater is a "portable water distiller requiring no plumbing," and is designed in a compact shape (15" high, 9 pounds). It uses a granular-activated-charcoal "spout filter" and produces 1 gallon of treated water in 6 hours. It's manually filled. You can buy this unit from **Tomorrow's World**.

Waterwise, Inc. is the manufacturer of several types of home-use water distillers. All their products can be ordered directly from them. The Waterwise Model 4000 Steam Distiller comes in a compact, white "Euro-style" housing. Inside is a stainless-steel boiler and condenser, a "gaseous vent to vent away low boiling point light gases," and a coconut-shell activated-charcoal postfilter (located in the spout). The treated water is collected in a 1-gallon storage container, which is included. This 8.4-pound "portable distiller" is rated to make 1 gallon in 4 hours. The 4000 is manually filled from the top. The fully automatic (they're attached to your water line) Waterwise Model 7000 comes in three configurations.

These include 8- and 12-gallon floor models and a 3-gallon countertop version. All these rectangular units are stainless steel inside and out. An optional pump system "allows you to have distilled water on tap at your kitchen sink." There's a special gaseous vent and an optional prefilter or postfilter of activated coconut shell charcoal. These units are rated to produce one gallon in 3 hours.

Other distillers are sold in local **Sears, Roebuck and Co.** stores.

Bathroom Water-Improvement Equipment

Of course, there is now water improving equipment for your bathroom. The most familiar are simple shower-head filters. However filtering shower wands and special bathroom-sink filters are also available.

Shower-Head Filters

Shower-head filters have been around for some time now. The biggest change lately is to use KDF media instead of activated charcoal. This is because activated charcoal usually doesn't work as efficiently with hot water as with cold water. Some brands are listed below. Be aware that some filters come with their own shower head while others do not.

The ProCam Shower Filter contains "a 55-cubic-inch granular-activated-charcoal filter, made without binders or glue." Refill cartridges are available. If you're interested, this item is sold by **Allergy Relief Shop, Inc.**

The RH of Texas Shower Filter is housed in a polypropylene casing which holds a fairly large, extruded activated-charcoal filter. It contains no chemical glues and is able to capture particulates down to 10 microns. Filter cartridges should be replaced every 6-8 months. This special shower filter (which can be a good choice for chemically sensitive persons) is sold by **American Environmental Health Foundation.**

The Befit High Output Shower Filter has a replaceable KDF filter cartridge which can be easily backwashed. This model is available from **Befit Enterprises Ltd.**

The Hydrolife Shower Filter uses KDF media "in a Turbojet type configuration." The media in this filter doesn't require backflushing. It's also sold by **Befit Enterprises Ltd.**

The RSP Shower Filter is made of white ABS plastic. Inside is "patented RSP Filtration" (called Chlorgon) which is designed to remove chlorine, dirt, and odors. Reversing the filtering cartridge puts it into a "backwash mode," ensuring longer filter life. You can obtain the RSP from **E.L. Foust Co., Inc.**

The Smart Shower JDSS (**Multi-Pure Corp.**) is a white-plastic unit with it's own chrome shower head. The shower head itself "is designed to conserve and oxygenate water." The filtering media is KDF. Each filtering cartridge is rated for 10,000 gallons. You can order this product directly from the company.

The Aquarius 700 uses a special compressed, activated-coconut-shell charcoal. This is a large unit (12" long and $4^1/_2$" in diameter) requiring you to install an extension pipe (you then attach your own shower head to it). Apparently, it's "designed for long life filtration in water 40°-180° F." Depending on water usage, filter cartridges should last 6-12 months. One Aquarius dealer is **Natural Lifestyle.**

New Wave Enviro has two New Wave Premium shower filters using KDF media The disposable model holds 16 ounces of media and is rated to last 1-$1^1/_2$ years. The replaceable filtering cartridge version uses a bit more media. Both are white plastic and use your existing shower head. The replaceable filter model has a 5-year workmanship warranty on the housing. These are commonly sold in health-food stores and alternative grocery stores. If you can't locate them, call the company for their nearest dealer. In addition, the Premium Shower Filter with replaceable KDF media is sold by healthyhome.com.

A popular shower filtering unit is ShowerCleen SuperFilter by Clean Water Products. This unit comes with it's own shower head (with a spray restrictor). Inside the ShowerCleen are three types of media, KDF, granulated activated charcoal, and Porex. Interestingly, hot water "can increase the longevity" of this filter. (Filters should be changed every 3 months.) If you'd like to purchase a ShowerCleen, you can order it from **Ozark Water Service and Environmental Services, N.E.E.D.S.**, and **Pacific Spirit**.

The Rainshow'r CQ uses multiple filtering strategies. These include non-woven material pads, crystalline quartz, KDF media, and "a natural contaminant adsorption media" all housed in a 5" plastic canister. You'll need to use a new replacement cartridge every 9-12 months (for an average family of four). The Rainshow'r CQ is sold by **Real Goods, Tomorrow's World, Priorities**, and **Natural Lifestyle**.

In addition, it should be mentioned that other fine shower-filters are handled by **Health One Co., Bio Designs, Inner Balance, TerrEssentials**, and **Nigra Enterprises**. Plus, more should be available locally in department stores and building centers.

Spray-Wand Shower Filters

Hand-held, spray-wand shower filters are becoming more commonplace. These units fit into brackets to become shower filters as well. A few brands of these are listed below.

Body Spa JDSPA (**Multi-Pure Corp.**) is an attractive white-plastic unit with an attached chrome hose. The filtering media is KDF. Each filtering cartridge is rated for 10,000 gallons. You can purchase this product directly from the manufacturer.

April Shower Euro is a shower-wand/shower-head unit with KDF media. The filter should be replaced every 6 month. This product is handled by **Pacific Spirit**.

Other suppliers of spray-wand shower filters include **Health One Co., Inner Balance**, and **Harmony**. Locally, check department stores and building centers for what they currently stock.

Bathtub Filters

For those who take baths instead of showers, the Bath Ball Tub Filter with "Filter Foam" may be for you. This round filter fits on the tub faucet and is said to reduce chlorine. You can buy this product from **Harmony**.

Bathroom Sink Filters

Some people are concerned about the quality of the water coming from their bathroom sink's faucet. A few filters for this application are suggested below.

The Fresh Ice Premium (**New Wave Enviro**) is a sleek filtering unit that the company's product literature says is specifically designed for "ice makers, refrigerators, and kitchen *and* bathroom sinks." The Fresh Ice's white-plastic housing, which has granular activated charcoal and other strategies inside, is said to remove chlorine, lead, sediment, bad taste or odor; and cysts. It's "quick-connect fittings" require no special plumbing. This filter is rated for 750 gallon which is about one year for a family of four. You may find this product locally (especially in an alternative grocery store). If not, call the company for a nearby dealer.

The RH of Texas Bathroom Sink Water Filter stands $6^1/_2$" tall and attaches to your existing faucet. It's housed in an off-white, "dense food-grade polypropylene" that contains a ceramic filter encasing bituminous-activated-charcoal granules. This unit is said to remove particulates down to 0.5 microns. Filters are rated to last about 6 months. This filter is available from the **American Environmental Health Foundation**.

It should also be noted that most ice-maker in-line water filters can work equally well on bathroom sink lines. (See *Refrigerator Ice Maker/Water Filter* page 627.)

Travel Water-Improvement Equipment

There are a number of water improving devices for those who travel, camp etc. A few are listed below.

The H₂O TL9 Travel Water Filter has three-stage filtration—a 5-micron sediment-removing "disc," a patented ion-exchange media to reduce heavy metals, and granular activated charcoal. The H₂O is sold by **Allergy Relief Shop, Inc.**

The Doulton Plastic Gravity Feed water filter uses 2 Sterasyl cartridges. (These are made of a silver-imbedded ceramic material with activated granular charcoal inside). This item can be ordered from **Befit Enterprises Ltd.**, and **Health One Co.** By the way, **N.E.E.D.S.** is a Doulton dealer, and may currently carry this item, too.

The unique Filter-Clean Sip Straw has "three micro filters, activated charcoal, and a patented, high-purity copper/zinc media." It's said to lasts 4-6 months of daily use. This product is handled by **Bio Designs**.

The Solar Attaché Case literally comes in a Samsonite attaché case. Inside is a built-in solar panel that powers a "multi-voltage pump." This creates enough water pressure to push water through an R/O membrane and more. (There are actually seven filtration stages.) This product can be purchased from **Bio Designs**.

First Need travel water filters (**General Ecology, Inc.**) use a special matrix-design, solid-block activated-charcoal filter. As a result, these can remove most waterborne pathogenic bacteria, as well as some lead and asbestos. By the way, First Need is apparently the only non-chemical filter to meet **EPA (Environmental Protection Agency)** certification standards against bacteria, cysts, and viruses. The First Need Deluxe model (8" tall) is ergonomically designed with an "integral trail-bike-bottle-cap with sanitary cover." Other features are a Matrix Pumping system, outlet and inlet tubes, tote bag, and self-cleaning prefilter/float. Filter replacement should be scheduled after 25 gallons. The First Need Trav-L-Pure is a handy (6¹/₂" tall) self-contained portable filter. It comes in a water-resistant Cordura nylon carrying case. All you need to do is fill the Trav-L-Pure with water. Then, simply use a manual pumping action to cause the filtered water to flow out the spout. Filter replacement is rated at 100 gallons. Both First Need portable filters are sold directly by the company and from dealers including **The Pure Water Place, Inc.**

New Wave Enviro offers several portable filters. These can often be found locally, especially in some alternative grocery stores. If not, you can call the company for a nearby dealer. Better Water is a clever filter using activated charcoal and resins. It is said to greatly reduce chlorine, sediment, and lead. What makes it unusual is that it's made to screw into any standard plastic bottle (0.5, 1 and 1.5 liters sizes). Once in place, to use it you simply squeeze the bottle and drink. The TapWater is described as a "portable water distiller requiring no plumbing." It plugs into any 120 volt electrical outlet. The TapWater unit is a very compact 15" high, and it weighs only 9 pounds. It has a granular-activated-charcoal "spout filter" and produces 1 gallon in 6 hours. You can buy this particular unit from **Tomorrow's World**. The WaterMaker PRO Portable Reverse Osmosis Filter is a plastic canister that easily secures to any standard faucet. It comes with an attached plastic hose that deposits filtered water into your pitcher. The WaterMaker is rated to produce 2-3 gallons of water overnight. The water is said to be 97% free of total dissolved solids, 99% free of lead, and 99.99% free of dangerous cysts.

Bottoms-Up is a filter available from **Ozark Water Service and Environmental Services**. It's a handy "Thermos-style" unit said to be able to remove chlorine, sediment, heavy metals, radon-222, as well as protozoan cysts.

The Global Water Express Travel/Emergency Water Purifier is especially made to remove both bacteria and viruses. It has a compact, self-contained design using ViralGuard cartridges. Each cartridge is rated to last for about 90 gallons. You can purchase this product from **Real Goods**.

The Safewater is a plastic, travel-bottle water filter. It's equipped with a sediment-removing prefilter and a replaceable 2-micron membrane filter said to remove pathogens that size or larger. The Safewater is handled by **Real Goods**.

For more travel water filters, check area camping-supply stores. For electric, portable water distillers, see *Kitchen Water Distillers* on page 632.

Bottled Water

Sometimes people feel that the water in their home just isn't of high-enough quality to drink or use in cooking. In some cases, this is because their private well has become contaminated in some way. In other households, it's because the occupants don't like the thought of ingesting the chlorine or fluoride in their utility-supplied water, but can't afford to purchase or maintain water-treatment equipment. For whatever reason, more and more Americans are choosing to buy bottled water. Therefore, the following sections offer some basic information on bottled water as well as explanations of the various types of bottled water you might want to consider.

Bottled Water Basics

In the U.S., the Federal Food and Drug Administration (FDA) has declared bottled drinking water to be a *food* item. This puts many types of bottle water—but not all—under FDA jurisdiction. Interestingly, the legal definition of *bottled drinking water* doesn't cover all types of water that are actually bottled in the U.S. For example, *mineral water* and *soda water*, including both *seltzer water* and *club-soda water* aren't included in the limited legal definition. In addition, any bottled water that's produced and sold entirely within the borders of a single state is also exempt from federal regulations (some states may have their own regulations regarding bottled water). Unfortunately, bottled water that does come under the authority of the FDA only has to meet a minimum water quality standard.

Water for processed bottled drinking water can come from a variety of sources including private wells, naturally rising springs, and even utility-supplied water. Therefore, if you're interested in using bottled water in your home, it's best to carefully read the label on the brand you're considering. That way, you should be able to determine the original source of the water, and, at the same time, find out if any additional treatments were performed on the water at the water-bottling plant. If this information is not provided on the label, contact the bottler and ask them to send you any information on their water. As you probably already know, bottled drinking water comes in two forms, *effervescent* or *still*. Effervescent water simply contains bubbles of carbon dioxide gas.

If you're a chemically sensitive person, you'll especially want to purchase your bottled drinking water in glass bottles, rather than in plastic containers. This will enable you to avoid drinking water that contains small amounts of plastic compounds that might have migrated into the water from the container. If you must use plastic, choose plastic which is the least likely to leech synthetic compounds. (See *Water Bottles*, on page 638.) In any case, you'll probably want to test several types and brands of bottled water to find the one whose taste you prefer and tolerate the best.

Although you can easily purchase your bottled water directly through your local health-food stores, etc., you should also know that there are companies that will deliver large bottles to your home on a regular basis. Often, this delivered water comes in 5-gallon containers that are placed on special dispensers in your kitchen. To find a company that delivers bottled drinking water in your area, check your classified telephone directory.

Bottled Water Types

Although, for the most part, there are no regulations that specifically define the different types of bottled water, the following paragraphs list some of the definitions that are popularly used.

Distilled water is water that has undergone distillation. This process results in water becoming devoid of minerals and most other types of impurities. This type of water is sometimes described as *aggressive*—meaning that it will aggressively seek out substances to put them into solution. As a result, there is some concern that distilled water does not make for very good drinking water. However, it is often recommended for use in steam irons and humidifiers.

Drinking water is simply processed (filtered) bottled water. Therefore, it might simply be utility water that's processed before it's put into sealed bottles. Note that, most bottled drinking water contains very low levels of chlorine.

Effervescent water is water that contains bubbly carbon dioxide (CO_2) gas. Sometime the CO_2 is naturally occurring and sometimes it is added by a bottling company.

Mineral water is water containing a certain quantity of dissolved minerals. Surprisingly, it can even be utility water that has had "desirable" minerals added to it by the bottler. On the other hand, *natural mineral water* is water from underground sources that naturally contains dissolved minerals (such as calcium, iron, potassium, and sodium) that were leached from the surrounding rock.

Spring water is water that reaches the surface from underground sources by its own pressure. *Natural spring water* is unprocessed spring water.

Seltzer water is filtered tap water that has been impregnated with carbon dioxide (CO_2) gas. *Club soda* is the same type of water, but it has had various minerals added to it by the bottler.

Sparkling water is water impregnated with carbon dioxide (CO_2) gas. *Natural sparkling water* is water that naturally contains CO_2. Note, some bottlers remove the naturally occurring CO_2 and later reinject it before the water leaves the plant.

Storing Your Bottled Water

There are now a number of options you can use to store your bottled water. A few are given below.

637

Water Bottles

As has been mentioned, the ideal container for water is glass. However, glass bottles are becoming rare, they're heavy, and breakable too. Many experts believe that polycarbonate (PC) plastic is one of the best choices for water storage. Interestingly, it's even been called "the glass of plastics" because of it's durability, lack of odor, and low capacity to leach plastic compounds and dioxin into the water.

How do you know if a bottle is polycarbonate or some other plastic? You may not realize it, but each plastic has it's own abbreviation and recycling symbol. The symbol, which has a number denoting the specific type of plastic, and can be found on on the bottom of every plastic bottle. Below are the different symbols and their corresponding plastic composition.

Symbol	Type of Plastic	Abbreviation
1	Polyethylene Teraphthalate	PET
2	High-Density Polyethylene	HDPE
3	Polyvinyl Chloride	PVC
4	Low-Density Polyethylene	LDPE
5	Polypropylene	PP
6	Polystyrene	PS
7	Polycarbonate	PC

If you're interested in purchasing a polycarbonate water bottle, **New Wave Enviro** offers them in sizes ranging from $^1/_2$ gallon up to 5 gallons, as well as push pumps and bottle caps. You may find these items in your local health-food store or alternative grocery store. If not, call the company for their nearest dealer.

In addition, there are mail-order suppliers of water bottles. For example, a large variety of Nature's Spring polycarbonate water bottles, in many sizes (some with taps), as well as no-leak stoppers, are sold by **Ozark Water Service and Environmental Services**. Polycarbonate bottles in $^1/_2$-, 1-, 2-, and 5-gallon sizes can be purchased from **healthyhome.com**. In addition, an easy-tip cradle and a 5-gallon dispenser bottle, as well as a Presto Bottle Pump (able to fit a 5-gallon bottle) are available from **Scientific Glass Co., Inc.**

Ceramic Water Dispensers (Coolers)

Ceramic water dispensers (sometimes called coolers) are making a comeback with the increased use of bottled water and home-filtered water. Most are designed to sit in a stand, often wooden or metal. In practice, your large, upside-down water bottle rests on the ceramic dispenser and water fills it through gravity. Nearly all ceramic water dispensers are cylindrical (starting at around 10" diameter) with a tap on the lower front side.

Some models are made of heavy, glazed ceramic (often porcelain) which is an easy to clean, insulating material. However, other ceramic dispensers are made of *terra cotta* (a fired but unglazed, usually red, clay). By not having a sealing *vitreous* (hard, glass-like) surface, a very slight amount of water penetrates outward to evaporate into the air. This results in a natural *evaporative cooling effect*. This is because the process of evaporation pulls heat out of the stored water, thus keeping the water inside the dispenser at a lower temperature than otherwise.

New Wave Enviro offers 2.5-gallon ceramic water dispensers in a huge variety of decorative styles. They also have floor and countertop wooden stands, crock lids, and spigots. These items are commonly sold through local health-food and alternative-grocery stores. If you can't find them, call the company for a nearby dealer.

Several designs of ceramic water crocks/dispensers, along with oak floor stands, are sold by **TerrEssentials**. A source for Springwell 10"-diameter ceramic water dispensers (holding 5 gallons) is **Scientific Glass Co., Inc.** From **Real Goods**, you can purchase a terra-cotta ceramic water cooler that you can use with your own 2-, 3-, or 5-gallon bottle.

CHAPTER 26: ELECTROMAGNETIC FIELDS

Many Americans have now heard that electromagnetic fields (EMFs) are associated with flowing electric current and that they may pose certain health concerns. Yet, it seems that most people are still uncertain what these concerns actually are—or even what an electromagnetic field is.

Therefore, this chapter will provide some basic information on electromagnetic fields, especially those surrounding live electric current—like that found in your home. There's also a little information to introduce you to geomagnetic fields as well as some other forms of electromagnetic radiation that may be in your home. Then, in the next chapter, *Chapter 27: Dealing With Electromagnetic Fields*, you'll find numerous suggestions to help reduce your exposure-risks to electricity-induced EMFs.

To understand electromagnetic fields (EMFs), a good place to start is to understand *electromagnetic radiation* in general.

Electromagnetic Radiation in General

Electromagnetic radiation is simply energy that has both an electric and a magnetic aspect. Visible light, infrared radiation, and X-rays are just a few examples of different types of electromagnetic radiation. But beside these, electric current passing through high-voltage power lines, your home's wiring, and electrical appliances also give off a form of electromagnetic radiation.

Interestingly, all types of electromagnetic radiation travel at the same speed—the speed of light. What makes one form of electromagnetic radiation different from another is the length and shape of its wave. Because it has differing *wavelengths*, each type of electromagnetic radiation has its own *wave frequency*.

What is meant by wave frequency? Wave frequency is a term denoting the number of waves that are able to pass by a given point in a certain period of time. As it turns out, the more waves able to pass by, the higher their frequency is said to be. Because all forms of electromagnetic radiation travel at the same speed, a greater number of short waves are able to move past a given point in the same amount of time than longer waves. Therefore, the shorter an electromagnetic wave is, the higher its frequency.

Why is wave frequency an important consideration? Because the higher the frequency (or the shorter the wavelength), the more energy it has. And, the more energy it has, the more potentially dangerous it can be.

The danger lies in the fact that very energetic waves can strip off electrons from some of the stable molecules with which they come into contact. Any stable molecules that lose electrons are now transformed into unstable, reactive *ions*. To regain their former molecular stability, these newly created ions must seize electrons from their neighboring molecules in a process known as *free-radical chain reactions* (a free radical is simply an extremely reactive ion). So, high-frequency radiation is also known as *ionizing radiation*—because it creates ions. X-rays and gamma rays (from nuclear reactors, for example) are two types of ionizing radiation of which you may already be familiar.

Unfortunately, when humans are exposed to ionizing radiation (such as X-rays or gamma rays), the resulting free-radical chain reactions take place within their bodies. The snatched electrons come from molecules actually making up body tissues. Naturally, this could easily (and quickly) lead to tissue damage, inflammation, and other negative consequences. In some cases, cancer may eventually develop, especially if the length and intensity of exposure is great enough.

Visible light, infrared radiation, radio and television waves (FM, AM, short wave, etc.), microwave radiation, and the electric current flowing in wiring are all different forms of electromagnetic radiation but, fortunately, they have longer wavelengths and lower frequencies than X-rays and gamma rays. (See *Other Electromagnetic Radiation in Homes* on page 647.) Relatively recently, there has arisen some concern with some of these forms of electromagnetic radiation, but it's hasn't been because they are capable of stripping electrons from molecules—because they aren't capable of doing that. Actually, for years it was precisely because they're *not* ionizing forms of radiation, that they had been thought to be relatively harmless.

Electric Current and Electromagnetic Radiation

Of course, the principles that pertain to other types of electromagnetic radiation apply to flowing electricity—which is also a form of electromagnetic radiation, as was noted earlier. Therefore, to review, the current flowing in all electric wires travels at the speed of light and it has its own unique frequency. In North America, this frequency is 60 cycles (waves) per second. In Europe, it's 50 cycles per second. (The word *Hertz* means the same thing as "cycles per second.") Because both of these frequencies are well below the range considered ionizing, they're called *nonionizing*, and they are categorized as *extremely low frequency (ELF) waves*. Because they are nonionizing forms of electromagnetic radiation, in the past most scientists believed that merely having electricity running through cables, wires, and appliances would not pose any innate health threat.

However, as it turns out, there is more to take into account than just an electric current's frequency. What seems to be of more concern are the *electromagnetic fields (EMFs)* that surround all wires carrying electricity, and all operating electrical devices. So, what are EMFs?

Basically, EMFs are areas where you can measure electromagnetic radiation—in this case, you can measure electromagnetic fields around a wire carrying electricity.

In reality, electricity has both electrical and magnetic aspects, so it has two fields: one that's electrical and one that's magnetic. When electricity is flowing through a wire, you can measure both fields simultaneously, and they somewhat overlap each other in space. (Interestingly, the electrical field surrounds and *oscillates,* or vibrates, at 60 Hertz (Hz), while the magnetic field uniformly surrounds the wire without oscillating). The more powerful the electric current in the wire is, the more powerful the EMFs surrounding it will be. And, at the same time, the further you move away from the wire, the weaker the EMFs. So, EMFs are less and less measurable as you move further away from the source of the electromagnetic radiation. This is important to remember when considering the health effects of EMFs.

It should be noted that the presence of electrical and magnetic fields around flowing electricity in home wiring and appliances had been well known by electrical engineers for many decades. However, because this was associated with nonionizing ELF (extra low frequency) radiation, they didn't believe that there were any real health concerns. Then, some very preliminary research (generally done prior to 1990) started to suggest that there may actually be negative health consequences to ELF radiation—especially for people who were exposed for a long duration to strong field strengths.

Importantly, of the two types of fields (electric fields and magnetic fields), it's generally believed that magnetic fields have more potential to cause health problems than electric fields. As a result, the term "EMF" is often popularly used to indicate *only* magnetic fields. Therefore, in the rest of this chapter (and the next), when EMF is used, it'll refer just to magnetic fields in order to simplify the discussion.

Possible Health Effects of EMF Exposure

Following is some information concerning the possible negative health consequences of EMF exposure. It begins with a brief explanation of the current controversy.

The EMF Health Effect Controversy

Believe it or not, there are few topics that generate as much passion, and as much heated controversy, as the potential health effects of EMFs. Those who feel that exposure to EMFs is a danger (especially if they are being made ill by them) are very resolute in their belief that EMFs are an overlooked, major health threat to everyone. Not surprisingly, their sincere conviction is that EMFs should, ideally, be dramatically reduced wherever they exist.

On the other hand, many of today's researchers and electrical engineers are just as firm in their view that EMF-exposure risks are minimal, at their very worst. Generally, most who share this view believe that the public-at-large isn't in any type of jeopardy from EMF exposure.

So, what's the truth? As in most unresolved "hot topics," it likely lies somewhere in the middle. The bottom line is that, on this particular issue, you'll have to weigh the current findings, as well as your own personal experiences, and decide for yourself. However, the best approach is probably something called "prudent avoidance." This means that it's a good idea to prudently avoid EMFs whenever you can easily do so—but you probably don't need to be overly zealous.

Some Researchers' Conclusions

You may be interested in learning about some of the conclusions of various researchers on EMF health effects as you try to formulate your own position on EMF exposure. Keep in mind, this is obviously a very small sampling.

Australia 1992

The Advisory Panel to the Australian Minister of Health in 1992 summed up their report by saying that "it has not been scientifically established that magnetic fields of extremely low frequency initiate or promote cancer or have any other harmful effects on humans. However, it has not been scientifically established that such fields are not harmful."

Denmark 1993

A report given by the Danish Ministry of Health in 1993 noted that our, "Danish and Swedish study supports the hypotheses of previous studies that children living near high current plants have an increased frequency of cancer. But the results do not exclude the possibility that the association might be due to chance."

Sweden 1994

A Swedish National Safety Board report in 1994 stated that, "we suspect that magnetic fields may pose certain risks to health, but cannot be certain. There is good reason to exercise a certain amount of caution."

U.S. 1997

The National Research Council (and others) concluded, in the 1997 report, *Possible Health Effects of Exposure to Residential Electric and Magnetic Fields,* that "although some studies have presented evidence of an association between magnetic-field exposure and various other types of cancer, neuro-behavioral disorders, and adverse effects on reproductive function, the results have been inconsistent and contradictory and do not constitute reliable evidence of an association."

Because of this last report, in particular, as well as the diminishing interest in the topic by the majority of American citizens, the once popular Electromagnetic Infoline, that was sponsored by the **EPA (Environmental Protection Agency)**, was discontinued. Yet, at the same time, new books on potential EMF dangers continue to be published, such as *The EMF Book: What You Should Know About Electromagnetic Fields, Electromagnetic Radiation, and Your Health* by Mark A Pinsky. There are other books along this line as well.

Possible EMF Exposure Symptoms

In this section, some of the possible adverse health effects, said to be associated with EMF exposure, will be discussed more specifically.

Initial Research-Study Findings

As was mentioned in the National Research Council report, there have been a variety of symptoms linked to EMF exposure, ranging from a temporary loss of coordination to cancer. Generally, these effects have been associated only with long-term exposure to high-voltage electric transmission lines and power stations—places where there tend to be very powerful EMFs. For example, some early studies linked electrical linemen, cable splicers, and others who work around electricity regularly, with higher rates of diseases such as leukemia, brain cancer, and breast cancer.

However, there are cases where the strength of the EMFs, and the duration of exposure, has been far less—yet certain people still appear to have been negatively affected. For example, researchers appear to have found an increased rate of miscarriage in women who sleep under electric blankets (especially electric blankets manufactured before 1987), or on electrically heated waterbeds. And, an early Swedish study seemed to indicate that children, who are routinely exposed to EMFs at home, have increased rates of leukemia, if the EMFs are strong enough.

Electromagnetic Sensitivity

Interestingly, there is a segment of the general population that appears to be particularly sensitive (hypersensitive) to EMFs. Such people are often termed *electromagnetically sensitive* and they are said to have a condition called *Electromagnetic Sensitivity (ES)*. If these individuals are in an area where strong EMFs are present, they may respond with any number of symptoms, most being skin or neurological in nature. Adverse effects may include prickling skin sensations, dry eyes, light sensitivity, joint pain, headache, fatigue, memory loss, heart palpitations, uneasiness, hearing unusual noises, mental confusion, or loss of balance, among others. A few individuals with ES may temporarily lose much of their muscle control and collapse. In other cases, they may have seizures.

As it turns out, it appears that ES is probably less common than Multiple Chemical Sensitivity (MCS). Unfortunately, some persons have both conditions. In fact, it seems that most of the people who acquired ES either already had MCS, were computer users, and/or have had long, intense exposures to EMFs.

For those that do have ES, it can make their lives very challenging. Therefore, they may want to join a support group. One such national support and advocacy group is the **Electrical Sensitivity Network** (ESN). This particular organization has an informative internet website and publishes the bimonthly *Electrosensitivity Newsletter*. To learn more, contact ESN directly. In addition, a helpful manual for those with ES is *The Electrical Sensitivity Handbook: How Electromagnetic Fields (EMFs) are Making People Sick* by Lucinda Grant.

EMF Health-Effect Theories and Research

Despite studies that show a link between EMF exposure and negative health effects, and despite the overt and varied symptoms displayed by electromagnetically sensitive persons, surprisingly, it's still not known how ELF electricity could possibly cause ill health. After all, this type of electricity is nonionizing. Therefore, it's supposedly incapable of causing tissue-damaging free-radical chain reactions. So, what could explain the correlation?

EMF Symptom Theories

In actuality, several possible theories have been proposed concerning EMFs as a cause of illness. One explanation is that EMFs disrupt the signals that normally cross cell membranes. It's believed that this "short circuiting" could actually change the normal action of hormones and antibodies—and perhaps even activate certain cancer-inciting molecules.

Another theory is that magnetic fields hinder the deactivation of *free radicals* within the body. Normally, there are mechanisms in the body to squelch free-radical chain reactions, thus preventing them from continuing long enough to cause severe tissue damage. However, if the body's natural free-radical defense system is prevented from functioning correctly, any free radicals present will remain reactive (and destructive) for longer periods of time. As a result, greater tissue damage would inevitably take place.

A third theory as to how EMFs could adversely affect human beings is that they restrict the normal production of *melatonin* in the body. This is important because melatonin (a hormone that is secreted by the *pineal gland* in the brain) regulates our body's *biorhythms* (regular cycles of bodily function) and melatonin has anti-malignancy properties. When lesser amounts than normal are present within the body, cancer (among other conditions) can be more likely to develop.

EMF Research

Because of the controversy concerning EMFs (particularly their effects on humans), there's still on-going research taking place in various countries around the world. In the United States, a number of the larger studies were sponsored by the **Electric Power Research Institute (EPRI)**, an organization funded by electric utilities. Founded in 1973, EPRI's purpose is "to develop and manage research programs for the energy industry and their customers." Free single copies of the EPRI Resource Paper on EMFs are available to non-profit, government, and educational organizations. However, they are not provided to private individuals. You may be able to obtain a copy through your local electricity utility.

Of course, other studies sponsored by other groups have also been done, and some are currently being undertaken, too. For example, a wide spectrum of studies on EMFs have been, or are currently being, sponsored by the World Health Organization and U.S. federal agencies including the Department of Health and Human Services, the Department of Defense, and the Department of Energy, among others.

By the way, more information on EMF health-related studies may be listed at the website of the **National Institute of Environmental Health** (EMF Rapid Information).

Geomagnetic Fields

Besides the electromagnetic fields (EMFs) found in conjunction with the electric current running in wires, some people are also concerned with possible health effects from *geomagnetic fields (GMFs)* within their homes. What are GMFs? Simply put, GMFs are the measurable magnetic fields of the earth itself. According to one theory, they're primarily generated within our planet by an ever-moving layer in the molten core (the *Dynamo Theory*). This particular hypothesis contends that this liquid-rock layer flows in a pattern that creates electric current. And, it's this electric current which, in turn, causes the presence of a magnetic field—a geomagnetic field.

At this time, most researchers speculate that GMF exposure is even less likely to be a potential health threat than high-strength EMFs. And, as noted earlier, a majority of scientists currently feel that even high-strength EMF exposure isn't a significant risk.

However, there are certain people who firmly believe that localized *GMF hot spots*— such as might be found along geologic faults, large deposits of igneous rock, or underground streams—have the potential to greatly affect human health. Such individuals note that deformed or stunted trees found on GMF hot spots are proof of their capacity to cause harm. Interestingly, some *dowsers* (individuals who claim to find underground water using divining rods or other unconventional devices) are reportedly able to locate, not only water, but also problematic GMF sources. By the way, if you want to measure GMFs in or around your home, you can purchase a geomagnetic radiation meter from **Less EMF Inc.**

While the health effects of GMFs may be less than those that could result from EMFs, this is another very controversial subject. Unfortunately, there seems to be little in-depth reliable research available concerning GMFs and human health at this time.

Other Electromagnetic Radiation in Homes

The following section includes some common types of electromagnetic radiation that you may not have realized were likely present in your own home. References as to where to find further information in this book are given for each of them.

Microwave Radiation

As you might suspect, microwave ovens produce microwave radiation. Microwave radiation is a short form of radiation in the radio-wave-frequency range. Microwaves are also known as radar waves, and they're generated inside microwave ovens by devices called *magnetrons*. For more on microwave radiation, see *How Microwave Ovens Work* on page 492 and *Microwave Oven Concerns* on page 492.

Radio-Frequency (RF) Radiation

The popular cellular phones, that many of us own, emit *radio-frequency (RF) radiation* at either approximately 900 MHz or 1900 MHz. (MHz stands for megahertz.) RF radiation, in reality, is form of low-intensity microwave radiation. For more information on this important topic, see *Problems with Typical Cellular Phones* on page 479.

Ultraviolet (UV) Radiation

Ultraviolet light is a particular form of electromagnetic radiation whose wavelengths are between those of x-rays and visible light (UV ranges from 15 nm to 400 nm—one nm meaning one nanometer which is 10^{-9} meters). Interestingly, ultraviolet light can't be seen by human eyes.

Of course, UV waves can passively enter homes as a component of sunlight, but it can also be purposely generated by special equipment. Sometimes called "black light," UV radiation can make some things glow, creating interesting visual effects. UV light can also be created by particular air and water purifiers. For more on these, see *Ultraviolet Light (UV) Air Purifiers* on page 556 and *Ultraviolet Light (UV) Water Purifiers* on page 612.

X-Rays

X-rays have wavelengths much shorter than that of visible light. In the electromagnetic spectrum their particular range is between the even-shorter gamma rays and the longer ultraviolet rays. X-rays are created when highly energetic charged atomic particles collide with other atoms. X-rays are well-known, ionizing forms of radiation.

Surprising to many people is that typical fluorescent lamps create very low levels of X-rays. However, some manufacturers are making their fixtures with X-ray shielding. (See *Full-Spectrum Fluorescents* on page 358.)

CHAPTER 27: DEALING WITH ELECTROMAGNETIC FIELDS

This chapter will discuss where high levels of EMFs can often be found in homes and what you can do to minimize any health risks to you and your family. There is also a section listing sources of further information.

EMFs in Your Home

So, what's a safe EMF exposure level? And where am I likely to find high-strength EMF sources in my home? Those are topics that will be discussed below.

Safe EMF Exposure Levels

How strong does an EMF need to be for you to be concerned? At this time, most researchers feel that a magnetic-field strength of less than 3 milligauss (mG) should pose little health risk for most people. (A Gauss is a unit of magnetic-field measurement; a milligauss is $1/1000$th of a Gauss.) However, there is a very vocal minority who strongly believe that a safe level is less than 1 mG. Again, there's not a clear cut answer with this controversial subject. But both sides agree that, if there is a risk, it would involve long-term exposure. In other words, you shouldn't be concerned about relatively brief exposures to stronger field strengths—only if you are exposed to them for days, weeks, or months at a time. Of course, if you have Electromagnetic Sensitivity (ES), you may need to minimize your exposure to all EMFs.

Fortunately, so far the data shows that the average room in an American home has an EMF background intensity about 0.5 mG. A typical kitchen has an average that's a little higher at 0.7 mG. These averages are below the levels considered unsafe by most "experts."

However, these are only *average* background intensities. There are areas in virtually all houses where more-intense EMFs can be found, such as around certain types of electrical devices and appliances. These sites of stronger EMFs are often called *electromagnetic hot spots*.

EMF Hotspots in Homes

As was just noted, there are certain situations, and particular areas, in most homes where more intense EMFs will exist—electromagnetic hot spots. Often this is due to certain kinds of wiring patterns. For example transformers and electric motors utilize wires that are wrapped tightly in coils, something that leads to strong EMFs. Of course, both transformers and electric motors are used in a variety of household electrical devices. In addition, other wiring patterns—such as those used in pre-1987 electric blankets and in the floors or ceilings of homes using radiant electric heat—also result in strong EMF levels.

Some EMF hot spots are temporary, such as the strong EMFs generated by using an electric hair dryer. Others are ongoing, such as the strong EMFs surrounding an electric power panel. By the way, it should be mentioned here that some individuals are worried that metal building materials such as aluminum siding or steel framing can create EMFs in their homes. In reality, however, this does not appear to be a significant cause for concern.

In the sections that follow, some of the more common sources of strong EMFs are listed and discussed.

Electric Appliances and Heating Systems

Because electrical appliances create EMFs when they're operating, and because some of these fields can be relatively strong, research was sponsored by the **Electric Power Research Institute (EPRI)** in the early 1990s to document the specific EMF levels surrounding them. While many newer appliances now have lower EMF readings than those tested several years ago, the EPRI findings are interesting nevertheless.

For example, it was found that an average refrigerator, when measured $10^1/2$" away, had an EMF level of 2.6 mG. Interestingly, at that time, the worst refrigerator (at least in terms of EMFs) had an amazingly high magnetic field strength of 15.7 mG, while the best refrigerator registered a mere 0.1 mG (all measurement were taken at the same $10^1/2$"). Of course, in all other categories of electric appliances measured, there was also a wide range of readings—some much higher than the average level, others somewhat below it. (Actually, the EPRI results don't technically refer to an "average" figure, instead they refer to the *median*, or the statistically middle figure.)

As it turns out, EPRI research found that the median magnetic-field strength for electric ranges was 9 mG at $10^1/2$". For fluorescent-light fixtures the reading was 5.9 mG at this same distance, and for *analog* (nonelectronic) clocks it was 0.8 mG. The median for television sets was 7 mG at $10^1/2$". For microwave ovens at $10^1/2$" the median measurement was a whopping 36.9 mG (Note: this is a measurement of magnetic-field strength, not microwave radiation). This same research revealed that dimmer switches, electric blankets (especially blankets manufactured before the late 1980s), and electric appliances containing motors generally recorded relatively strong EMF readings as well.

One of EPRI's higher EMF measurements was for electric radiant heating systems that are typically installed either in ceilings or floors. At $10^1/2$", the median reading for such a system was 26.6 mG. Furthermore, electric baseboard heaters also usually had high EMF readings.

House Wiring Practices

Besides electrical appliances and heaters, there can be high-strength EMFs generated in homes simply due to certain electrical wiring practices. Some of these practices are found routinely, even though they're in violation of electrical codes. Various wiring practices that are responsible for high-strength EMFs are discussed in the sections below.

Knob and Tube Wiring

Today, most modern electrical home wiring is done with a *single cable* made up of an insulated black wire (the hot wire), an insulated white wire (the neutral wire), and an uninsulated ground wire. Fortunately, as long as the hot and the neutral wires remain close together, they tend to cancel out each other's magnetic fields. If the hot and neutral wires are twisted around each other, they'll neutralize each others fields even more. (Note: The ground wire doesn't normally carry any current, so theoretically, it shouldn't produce any fields).

However, years ago home wiring was done much differently. Instead of having the hot and neutral wires bundled together in a single cable, separate individual wires were run from the main fuse box to the various circuits. These wires were installed about a foot apart and were either supported on ceramic insulators called *knobs* or run through ceramic insulators called *tubes*. Unfortunately, because of the 12" distance between the wires, the fields didn't neutralize each other, so this type of wiring produced relatively high EMF levels. By the way, the wider the hot and neutral wires are separated, the less the magnetic fields can interact to cancel each other out. This is one of the reasons why high field strengths are routinely measured near outdoor power lines that have their individual wires so widely separated from each other.

Cables Carrying High Levels of Electric Current

As was mentioned earlier, the more electric current a wire carries, the stronger the magnetic field will be surrounding that wire. So, the main power cable running between a home's electric meter and the power panel generates a higher EMF level than the smaller wires running from the power panel to the various room receptacles. Not unexpectedly, the wires that run to the electric range or to an electric baseboard heater will produce EMF strengths somewhere in between those of the main power cable and the smaller wires—because they carry less current than the main cable but more than the smaller wires.

Grounding Problems

Perhaps one of the more unsuspected sources of EMFs in homes is from certain *grounding* practices. In grounding, a connection is made between an electric circuit (or electrical device) and the ground itself (the earth) which is capable of conducting away electric current. Grounding is very necessary for safety reasons; in fact, all building codes require that it be done. And, if done correctly, grounding generally doesn't cause any problems.

How is grounding actually done? In practice, at the point where the main electric power cable enters a home, the main ground wire is connected to a metal rod which has been driven 8–10' into the soil. However, the main ground wire might also be connected to a metal water pipe (which connects to the piping outdoors that is buried in the soil). Commonly, cable TV lines and telephone lines are grounded in similar ways. Unfortunately, in some cases of water-pipe grounding, the home's entire plumbing system can end up becoming its own complete electrical circuit, a circuit capable of producing EMFs.

To make matters worse, these unplanned electrical circuits in metal water pipes can, in some cases, be transferred to neighboring homes. In fact, sometimes whole neighborhoods can be interconnected in this way. So, an EMF problem in one house can travel through metal plumbing lines and cause problems in several other houses. This situation can also occasionally happen with homes connected to the same TV cable, or gas main. In any case, these unintentional multi-home interconnections provide easy pathways for the transfer of EMFs from one house to another.

There are a variety of other ways that you can get stronger-than-normal EMFs in a home wiring system, and some also involve grounding practices. However, it's important to note that good electrical wiring practice (as described by the National Electrical Code), will not result in strong EMFs in water pipes. It's also important to note that grounding is important, so you shouldn't disconnect your ground wires because you are afraid of EMFs. If you suspect a problem, you should have it checked out by a qualified electrician.

Power Panels

Power panels are notorious EMF hot spots. Here's why. All the cables that enter a power panel are made up of 3 or 4 individual wires. The individual wires are separated from each other only by insulation (so they don't short out). In most cases the individual wires in each cable are close enough to each other that they neutralize the magnetic fields. Then, inside the power panel, the individual wires are run to different places—therefore they no longer neutralize each other's magnetic fields. For example, the hot wires are run to individual circuit breakers (or fuses) and the neutral wires are connected together at a common connector called a *busbar*. At the same time, the ground wires are connected together at another, separate busbar. Because so many hot and neutral wires are separated, and because there are so many live electrical wires in one place, the magnetic-field strength can be high at a power panel.

Power Line Problems

Sometimes strong EMF levels in houses are not generated by the electricity running within the home itself. As it turns out, houses that are close to high-voltage power lines, or that are close to electric-power substations, often have higher-than-average EMF background readings.

These high ambient EMF levels can occur because power lines not only carry a great deal of current, but their wires are widely separated from each other. On the other hand, electrical substations contain transformers that are made up of many wires wound together. And, as was mentioned earlier, both situations are commonly associated with strong EMFs.

Lowering EMF Risks in Homes

In reality, it can be very difficult, almost impossible, to completely avoid having at least some relatively strong electromagnetic fields in your home. However, there are a number of simple precautions you can take to reduce any potential health risks that may be associated with them.

In the following sections, you'll learn how to minimize any potential health problems by either reducing the strength of the field, or by spending less time near strong EMF sources (this is often easier to do). Of course, those people who are electromagnetically sensitive will have to take more extreme measures to ensure their well being.

Measuring EMF Levels in Homes

Because of different electrical wiring practices, different appliances, different grounding techniques, and different locales (nearness to substations, etc.), every home's EMF situation is unique. Therefore, to determine what EMF problems may exist in your home—if any— you'll need to actually measure the EMFs. Fortunately, this is a fairly simple and straight forward task you can often perform yourself. All you need is a *gauss meter*, which is a device that's designed to measure magnetic fields. As you may recall, it's believed by most experts that a level below 1–3 milligauss (mG) is acceptable for long-term exposures to EMFs.

Before you go ahead and purchase a gauss meter, first decide how accurate a measurement you need, or want. As it turns out, some meters only have small indicator lights that provide you with either a "Safe" or "Unsafe" reading. Obviously, this limited data may be far too vague for many individuals.

However, several kinds of more accurate gauss meters are available. The most sophisticated models will obviously have the most accuracy. As might expect, the more precise a gauss meters is, the more it will cost. Fortunately, for residential use, meters that have an accuracy of plus-or-minus 25% are popular and reasonably priced. While most electrical engineers wouldn't consider plus-or-minus 25% very accurate at all, these meters are usually quite acceptable for most homeowners.

If you decide to purchase your own gauss meter, you may be able to find them locally at electrical supply stores. By mail-order, **N.E.E.D.S.** sells both a Safe Range EMF Meter and an Alpha Labs Tri-Field Meter. **Building for Health Materials Center Catalog** also handles the Tri-Field meter. From **TerrEssentials**, you can purchase the Dr. Gauss meter. **Safe Technologies Corp.** makes two models under their own label, which you can order directly from them. In addition, **Less EMF, Inc.** (this company has an on-line catalog only) and **Befit Enterprises Ltd.** offer a variety of meters. If, on the other hand, you'd prefer to hire a professional to do the testing for you, you may want to contact **National Electromagnetic Field Testing** to find out is there an independent EMF tester in your locale.

By the way, if you're concerned about EMFs generated by nearby high-voltage electric power lines, transformers, and substations, you should consider contacting your local electric utility. In many cases they will be willing to come to your home and measure the EMF level resulting from their equipment. This is often done at no or little charge. However, they usually won't perform any measurements inside your home and, most likely, they won't feel that any level of EMF exposure is unsafe.

Understanding EMF Strength, Distance, and Duration

It's unlikely that most people could, or would, rid their homes of all electrical appliances and devices—just because they happen to emit high levels of EMFs. However, you should keep in mind that just because high EMF readings exist in your house, it doesn't mean they're necessarily cause for alarm. Negative health problems resulting from EMFs are going to depend on three factors: 1) the strength of the field, 2) the length of exposure, and 3) your particular susceptibility. You should also keep in mind that certain parts of your body are likely to be more sensitive to the potential negative effects of EMFs than others. For example, having your head or reproductive organs subjected to strong EMFs is probably more serious than, say, exposing your feet.

Importantly, the strength of a problematic EMF can often become acceptable by simply adding some distance between you and the EMF source. For example, a magnetic field might be very strong only 1–2" away from where it originates. But at 3' away, it could easily be at a level generally considered safe. For example, an electrical baseboard heater installed near your bed's headboard might have an EMF reading of 20 mG directly next to it. But the EMF reading might be only 1 mG near your pillow, just a few feet away. Therefore, if you routinely slept in this particular bed, you would be exposed to EMFs regularly, but at a reasonably safe level. However, if you were to sleep on the floor with your head just a few inches away from the heater, the EMF reading now near your pillow might be 5–10 mG—not considered a safe level. As it turns out, the strength of most EMF fields from electrical appliances in homes decreases very quickly with distance, so much so, that safer fields often exist only 2–3' away from nearly all appliances. So, one simple way to minimize your risk is to make sure there are no EMF hot spots that are close to areas where you spend a lot of time. For example, you might move your favorite reading chair a little further away from your main electrical power panel.

Of course, the actual duration of EMF exposure is also very significant in determining your risk. This simply means the length of time you're in the presence of high-strength EMFs. Obviously, a few seconds or a few minutes—even an hour or so—of strong EMF exposure is not nearly as serious as days, months, or years of exposure at the same high level. Therefore, although a portable electric shaver or hair blow dryer might generate very strong EMFs (perhaps over 100 mG), and your head is very close to them while they're operating, you only use them for a few minutes at a time. Because the duration is quite short, most researchers believe that the EMF dangers posed by shavers and blow dryers, used in a conventional manner, is probably not very great. Of course, if you work in a hair salon and spend many hours every day using a blow dryer as a professional hair stylist, your EMF risk would be somewhat greater.

Specific EMF Reduction Strategies

There are several specific strategies you can take to minimize your risk from certain electromagnetic fields in your home. Some of these are detailed in the sections below.

Coping with EMFs from Appliances and Heating Systems

As has been noted, increasing the distance from an EMF source lowers your risk. If your television or microwave oven have strong EMFs, for example, you could simply increase the distance between you and them while they're operating. Of course, you might choose to replace some of your older electrical appliances with newer models having lower filed strengths. As it turns out, in the last few years, many companies have begun designing their electrical products so that they generate less intense EMFs than they did previously. This is particularly true with computer monitors, television sets, and electric blankets.

However, as an alternative to buying a new replacement appliance, in some cases you might consider purchasing EMF reduction equipment. These can include special EMF blocking shields and EMF wave neutralizers for computers (see *Electronic Equipment EMF Concerns* on page 482). But it can include much more. Companies such as **Befit Enterprises Ltd.**, **healthyhome.com**, and **Less EMF Inc.** (on-line catalog only), handle a whole array of products to minimize EMF exposures. This includes everything from EMF-reduction foil, to special paints, to anti-EMF clothing, and more.

Of course, instead of replacing certain electrical appliances and devices with new versions, or modifying them in some way to reduce your EMF exposure, you might simply decide to buy nonelectric substitutes. Obviously, these would create no EMFs at all. For instance, you could purchase a windup alarm clock to use in place of your bedroom's electronic clock radio. You might also buy a wire whisk to use instead of a hand-held electric mixer. And so on. Interestingly, the **Less EMF Inc.** website offers several such items including a non-electric doorbell, food processor, and clock. Plus, the **Vermont Country Store** (Voice of the Mountains catalog) sells portable manual typewriters and wind-up alarm clocks. You should be able to find local stores that will also have some non-electric alternatives that you could purchase.

If your waterbed heater gives off high levels of EMFs, you might try turning it off whenever you're in bed, then turn it back on during the day when you're not in bed. This will usually keep the waterbed at a comfortable temperature, yet significantly reduce your EMF exposure risks. You might also want to try the EMF bed shielding that is available from **healthyhome.com**.

Unfortunately, if your home has loop-style radiant electric heating cables in its ceilings or floors that emit strong EMFs, this may be a situation that doesn't have a simple, inexpensive solution. If you're truly concerned about these fields, you may have no choice but to shut your radiant heat off and install some other type of heating equipment.

Incidentally, if you feel that you're electromagnetically sensitive, you might want to shut off all the electric power to your bedroom at night. This can often be done by switching off the appropriate circuit breaker in your electric power panel. If you decide to do this, be sure your smoke detector, refrigerator, or freezer aren't on the same circuit or they will be off all night as well! Helpfully, **Befit Enterprises Ltd.** offers a radio-controlled electric power cut-off switch that's designed to be installed next to your home electric power panel. Of course, if you're electrically sensitive you'll also want to limit the number and use of *all* types of electric appliances and devices throughout your home.

Wiring and Grounding Precautions

There are a number of steps that can be taken when electrical wiring and grounding situations are associated with higher-than-normal electromagnetic fields. Some of these are explained below.

New Construction

If you're planning to construct a new house, or add an addition, there are a number of relatively easy precautions that can be taken to minimize your exposure to EMFs as far as wiring and grounding are concerned. One, that has often been suggested, is to request that twisted electric cable be used. However, it should be pointed out that modern wiring cables have the hot and neutral wires so close together that the fields tend to neutralize each other quite well. Twisted cable will reduce the fields further, but it probably won't make a significant difference in lowering your overall EMF exposure. Because most of the wiring currently available isn't pre-twisted, your electrician will have to twist the cables as he (or she) installs them.

Something that can make a real difference in reducing your exposure to strong field strengths is to specify that you want the electric wires carrying strong currents installed so they won't be located in areas of your house where you plan to spend a great deal of time. Such wires would include the main electric cable that runs from the electric meter to your power panel, and the wires that run from the power panel to things like your electric range, electric water heater, and electric heaters. These particular wires should be routed in such a way that they won't pass near your bed or favorite reading chair, etc.

Existing Homes

If your existing home has its electrical system grounded to your metal water pipes, you can use a gauss meter to see if there are any strong EMFs around the pipes. If there are, you'll want to discuss the situation with a licensed electrician (to find one, check your classified telephone book). There are ways to remedy such a situation, however, under no circumstances should you unhook a ground wire because of EMF fears—proper grounding is extremely important and is required by building codes. Problems involving EMFs and grounding systems, and some solutions, was discussed in an article titled "EMFs Run Aground" in the August 21, 1993 issue of *Science News* (Vol. 144, pp. 124–7). Your local library may have a copy.

Unfortunately, sometimes in existing homes, there isn't a readily obvious cause for mysteriously high EMF levels. In fact, in some cases, it's going to take some detective work to track down precisely where an EMF problem originates. Sadly, most home inspectors and licensed electricians simply aren't trained to locate EMF problems, especially unusual ones. However, if you find a home inspector or electrician who is willing to help you, the book, *Tracing EMFs in Building Wiring and Grounding* by Karl Riley contains very good, solid information that he (or she) can use. Remember, never to tamper with your electrical system yourself without proper training.

It should also be noted that perhaps a member at **National Electromagnetic Field Testing**, may be helpful. This organization will provide you with the names of independent EMF testing professionals in your area.

Power Panel Precautions

As has already been noted, main electrical power panels (both fuse boxes and circuit-breaker boxes) are generally surrounded by strong electromagnetic fields. As a result, it's been suggested by certain experts that you should never locate your home's power panel near where you and your family spend a great deal of time. For example, a basement utility room would be a better location (EMF-wise) for your power panel than your family room. Of course, in new-home construction, you can plan the placement of your power panel ahead of time, but in an existing home it's already in place.

It's important to remember that, even if the power panel is in a little-used room, you'll still need to consider its potential EMF effects. This is because magnetic fields can easily extend through most walls. Therefore, you need to consider what is on the opposite side of the wall that the power panel is mounted on. For example, your power panel might be located on a utility-room wall, but your bedroom might be on the other side of that wall. If that's the case, you wouldn't want to place your bed against that same wall. Instead, it would be best to have the bed on the other side of the room, further away from the power panel.

Coping with Outdoor Problems

If you suspect that your building site has a high background EMF level, you'll want to test the area *before* any construction begins. If you find high-strength fields, it may be possible to avoid them by relocating the house on the lot. Remember, it's wise to build at some distance (500'-1,000') from high voltage power lines or substations, if at all possible. Of course, you should also be concerned about ground-level or pole-mounted transformers because they, too, can emit high-strength fields. If you can't find a suitable safe building location, you may want to consider purchasing a different building site.

If you have an existing home with high EMF levels due to a nearby electrical substation or a high-voltage power line, you'll need to try other strategies. One approach is to use your rooms differently than you have been. For example, you might make your den into a dining room and your dining room into the den, or simply rearrange your furniture. The goal is to create living areas where you'll spend most of your time that have low field strengths. Unfortunately, if it turns out that every room within your house has strong background EMFs due to nearby power lines, or an electrical substation, there may not be much you can do to reduce your risk—that is, except to move somewhere else.

Further EMF Information

To learn more about electromagnetic fields, there are certainly many publications on the subject now available. Besides those already mentioned in this book, following are several more for you to consider.

A good book on EMFs is *Warning: The Electricity Around You May Be Hazardous To Your Health* by Ellen Sugarman. In addition, a very large selection of EMF-related books are handled by **Less EMF Inc.** Of course, other books and periodical articles on EMFs are available at most local libraries and bookstores. You may also wish to access the **National Institute of Environmental Health Sciences** (EMF Rapid Information website).

An easy-to-understand 67-page booklet that's helpful is *Questions and Answers About Electric and Magnetic Fields Associated with the Use of Electric Power* (January 1995) by the National Institute of Environmental Health Sciences and the U.S. Department of Energy. It's available on-line from the **National Institute of Environmental Health Sciences** (EMF Rapid Information website).

In addition, you may want to contact the **EPA (Environmental Protection Agency)** to see what booklets they currently offer.

Part 7
RESOURCES

RESOURCE LISTINGS

•3M Construction & Home
Improvement Products Div.
3M Center
St. Paul, MN 55144
800-388-3458
www.3m.com

•3M Home & Commercial
Care Div.
3M Center
St. Paul, MN 55144
800-257-3451
www.3m.com

•20 Mule Team Borax
Div. Dial Corp.
15101 N Scottsdale Rd.
Scottsdale, AZ 85254
800-457-8739
www.dialcorp.com

•Adirondack Design
350 Cypress St.
Ft. Bragg, CA 95437
707-964-4940
888-64303003
www.adirondackdesign.com

•Advanced Foil Systems, Inc.
820 S. Rockefeller Ave.
Suite A
Ontario, CA 91761
909-390-5125
800-421-5947
www.afs-foil.com

•Aegis Environments
3106 Swede Ave.
Midland, MI 48642
517-832-8180
www.microbeshield.com

•AFM
350 West Ash St.
Suite 700
San Diego, CA 92101
619-239-0321
800-239-0321
www.afmsafecoat.com

•Agelong Catalog
P.O. Box 411068
Kansas City, MO 64141
800-892-8022
www.agelong.com

•Aireox Research Corp.
P.O. Box 8523
Riverside, CA 92515
909-689-2781
www.aireox.com

•Air Quality Sciences, Inc.
1337 Capital Cir.
Atlanta, GA 30067
770-933-0638
800-789-0419
www.aqs.com

•Allens Naturally
P.O. Box 514
Farmington, MI 48332
734-453-5410
800-352-8971
www.allensnaturally.com

•Allergy Clean Environments
P.O. Box 9067
San Rafael, CA 94912
800-882-4110
www.allergyclean.com

•Allergy Control Products, Inc.
96 Danbury Rd.
Ridgefield, CT 06877
800-422-3878
www.allergycontrol.com

•Allergy Relief Shop, Inc.
3360 Andersonville Hwy.
Andersonville, TN 37705
423-494-4100
800-626-2810
www.allergyreliefshop.com

•The Allergy Store
3504 S. University Dr.
Davie, FL 33328
954-472-0128
800-771-2246
www.allergystore.com

•Allermed
31 Steel Rd.
Wylie, TX 75098
972-442-4898
www.allermedcleanair.com

•Allersearch Laboratories
Div. of Alkaline Corp.
P.O. Box 306
Oakhurst, NJ 07755
732-531-7830
800-686-6483
www.allergyhelp.com

•Allerx
P.O. Box 1119
Royse City, TX 75189
800-447-1100
www.allerx.com

•Alumax Bath Enclosures
1617 N. Washington
Magnolia, AR 71753
870-234-4260
800-643-1514
www.alumaxbath.com

•Amana Appliances
2800 220th Trail
Amana, IA 52204
319-622-5511
800-843-0304
www.amana.com

•Amazon.com
www.amazon.com

•Amerec Products
P.O. Box 2278
Woodinville, WA 98072
425-951-1120
800-331-0349
www.amerec.com

•American Academy of Allergy,
Asthma, and Immunology
611 E. Wells St.
Milwaukee, WI 53202
414-272-6071
800-8822-2762
www.aaai.org

•American Academy of
Environmental Medicine
7701 E. Kellog
Suite 625
Wichita, KS 67207-1705
316-684-5500
www.aaem.com

•American Academy of
Otolaryngic Allergy
8455 Colesville Rd.
Suite 745
Silver Spring, MD 20910
301-588-1800
www.allergy-ENT.com

•American Chemical Society
1155 16th St. NW
Washington, DC 20036
202-872-4600
800-227-5558
www.acs.org

•American College of Allergy,
Asthma, and Immunology
85 West Algonquin Rd. #550
Arlington Heights, IL 60005
847-427-1200
800-842-7777
www.allergy.mcg.edu

•American Environmental
Health Foundation
8345 Walnut Hill Ln.
Suite 225
Dallas, TX 75231
214-361-9515
800-428-2343
www.aehf.com

•American Lung Association
1740 Broadway
New York, NY 10019
212-315-8700
800-586-4872 (rings your
local office)
www.lungusa.org

•American PIE
124 High St.
P.O. Box 340
S. Glastonbury, CT 06073
800-320-2743
www.AmericanPIE.org

•Ampco
P.O. Box 608
Rosedale, MS 38769
601-759-3521
800-647-8268

•Amway
7575 E. Fulton Rd.
Ada, MI 49355
800-544-7167
www.amway.com

•Hanna Andersson
6900 Riverport Dr.
Louisville, KY 40258
503-321-5277
800-222-0544
www.hannaandersson.com

Product Sources

•**Anderson Laboratories, Inc.**
P.O. Box 323
West Hartford, VT 05084
802-295-7344
www.andersonlaboratories.com

•**Appleseed**
30 Tozer Rd.
P.O. Box 1020
Beverly, MA 01915
800-767-6666

•**Aquathin Corp.**
950 S. Andrews Ave.
Pompano Beach, FL 33069
954-781-7777
800-462-7634
www.aquathin.com

•**Arctic Metal Products Corp.**
507 Wortman Ave.
Brooklyn, NY 11208
718-257-5277

•**Ar-Ex, Ltd.**
1282 Old Skokie Rd.
Highland Park, IL 60035
847-579-1408
www.ar-ex.com

•**Arm & Hammer**
Div. Church & Dwight, Inc.
469 N. Harrison St.
Princeton, NJ 08543
800-524-1328
www.armhammer.com

•**Aroma Housewares Co.**
6469 Flanders Dr.
San Diego, CA 92121
858-587-8866

•**Arts, Crafts and Theater Safety (ACTS)**
181 Thompson St. #23
New York, NY 10012
212-777-0062
www.caseweb.com/acts

•**Asko, Inc.**
1161 Executive Dr. West
Richardson, TX 75081
972-644-8595
www.askousa.com

•**Asthma and Allergy Foundation of America**
1233 20th St. NW, #402
Washington, DC 20036
202-466-7643
800-7-ASTHMA
www.aafa.org

•**Asthma and Allergy Network, Mothers of Asthmatics, Inc.**
2751 Prosperity Ave.
Suite 150
Fairfax, VA 22031
703-641-9595
800-878-4403
www.aanma.org

•**Aubrey Organics**
4419 N. Manhattan Ave.
Tampa, FL 33614
800-282-7394
www.aubrey-organics.com

•**Audio Editions**
P.O. Box 6930
Auburn, CA 95604
800-231-4261
www.audioeditions.com

•**Aussie Connection**
135 NE Third Ave.
Hillsboro, OR 97124
800-950-2668
www.aus-slippers.com

•**Austin Air**
500 Elk St.
Buffalo, NY 14203
716-856-3700
888-236-0000 (From Canada)
800-724-8403
www.austinair.com

•**Back to Basics**
10508 S. Lowell Rd.
Bahama, NC 27503
919-477-5669
www.cottonbras.com

•**Charles R. Bailey Cabinetmakers**
Highway 62 East
Flippin, AR 72634
870-453-3245
www.southshore.com/~crbslf

•**Ballard Designs**
1670 DeFoor Ave. NW
Atlanta, GA 30318
800-367-2810
www.ballard-designs.com

•**Bally Block Co.**
P.O. Box 188
Bally, PA 19503
610-845-7511
www.mapleblock.com

•**BarnesandNoble.com**
www.barnesandnoble.com

•**Baron's Window Coverings**
325 S. Washington Ave.
Lansing, MI 48933
517-484-1366
800-248-5852
www.baronsonline.com

•**Bartley Collection**
65 Engerman Ave.
Denton Industrial Park
Denton, MD 21629
410-479-4480
800-787-2800
www.bartleycollection.com

•**Basic Coatings, Inc.**
2124 Valley Dr.
P.O. Box 677
Des Moines, IA 50303
515-288-0231
800-441-1934
www.BasicCoatings.com

•Basco Co.
7201 Snider Rd.
Mason, OH 45040
513-573-1900
800-543-1938

•Eddie Bauer
P.O. Box 182639
Columbus, OH 43218
800-426-8020
www.eddiebauer.com

•B. Coole Designs
2631 Piner Rd.
Santa Rosa, CA 95401
707-575-8924
800-992-8924
www.metro.net/bcoole

•Beam Industries
P.O. Box 788
Webster City, IA 50595
515-832-4620
800-369-2326
www.beamvac.com

•L.L Bean
Freeport, ME 04033-0001
800-221-4221
www.llbean.com

•Befit Enterprises Ltd.
The Cutting Edge Catalog
P.O. Box 5034
Southampton, NY 11969
516-287-3813
800-497-9516
www.cutcat.com

•Best Paint Co., Inc.
5205 Ballard Ave. NW
Seattle, WA 98107
206-783-9938

•Billards Old Telephones
21710 Regnart Rd.
Cupertino, CA 95014
408-252-2104

•Bio Designs
557 Burbank St.
Suite K
Broomfield, CO 80020
303-438-0600
800-873-3529

•BioForce Enviro-Tech, Inc.
2900 N. 2nd St.
Minneapolis, MN 55411
612-302-3999
www.bioforce.com

•Bio-Integral Resource
Center (BIRC)
P.O. Box 7414
Berkeley, CA 94707
510-524-2567
www.birc.com

•BioLight Systems
28 Parker Way
Santa Barbara, CA 93101
805-564-3467
800-234-3724
www.ottbiolight.com

•Blair
220 Hickory St.
Warren, PA 16366
800-458-2000
www.blair.com

•Dick Blick
P.O. Box 1267
Galesburg, IL 61402
309-343-6181
800-447-8192
www.dickblick.com

•Block Tops
4770 E. Wesley Dr.
Anaheim, CA 92807
714-779-0475

•The Body Shop
2870 Janitell Rd.
Colorado Springs, CO 80906
800-263-9746
www.bodyshop.com

•Books on Tape, Inc
P.O. Box 7900
Newport Beach, CA 92658
800-626-3333 (Operator)
800-582-0666 (Automated)
www.booksontape.com

•John Boos & Co.
315 S. First St.
P.O. Box 609
Effingham, IL 62401
217-347-7701
800-433-2667
www.johnboos.com

•Borders.com
www.borders.com

•Bosch Appliances
2800 S. 25th Ave.
Broadview, IL 60153
800-944-2904
www.boschappliances.com

•E.B. Botanical, Inc.
Ecco Bella
1123 Route 23 S.
Wayne, NJ 07470
973-696-7766

•Brass Bed Shoppe
12421 Cedar Rd.
Cleveland Hts., OH 44106
216-371-0400
www.brassbedshoppe.com

•BreatheFree.com
1200 Chambers Rd.
Suite 204
Columbus, OH 43212
614-488-7820
888-434-8313
www.BreatheFree.com

•Brita (USA) Inc.
P.O. Box 24305
Oakland, CA 94623
800-242-7482
www.brita.com

Product Sources

•**BRK Brands, Inc.**
3901 Liberty Street Rd.
Aurora, IL 60504
630-851-7330
www.firstalert.com

•**Broan Mfg. Co., Inc.**
P.O. Box 140
Hartford, WI 53027
800-548-0970
www.broan.com

•**Dr. Bronner's**
P.O. Box 28
Escondido, CA 92033
760-743-2211
www.drbronner.com

•**Building for Health
Materials Center**
P.O. Box 113
Carbondale, CO 81623
970-963-0437
800-292-4838
www.buildingforhealth.com

•**Burt's Bees, Inc.**
8221-A Brownleigh Dr.
Raleigh, NC 27612
919-510-8720
800-849-7112
www.burtsbees.com

•**John O. Butler Co.**
4635 W. Foster Ave.
Chicago, IL 60630
888-777-3101
www.jbutler.com

•**California Style**
5823 Newton Dr.
Carlsbad, CA 92008
800-477-7722
www.castyle.com

•**Capers Reef**
P.O. Box 371
Isle of Palms, SC 29451
800-886-4407
www.capersreef.com

•**Care Free Water Technologies, Inc.**
2110 G E McFadden St.
Santa Ana, CA 92705
800-482-5558

•**Carolina Patio Warehouse**
800-672-8466
www.carolinapatio.com

•**Carousel Carpet Mills**
1 Carousel Ln.
Ukiah, CA 95482
707-485-0333

•**Rachel Carson Council,
Inc.**
8940 Jones Mill Rd.
Chevy Chase, MD 20815
301-652-1877

•**Harriet Carter Gifts**
425 Stump Rd.
North wales, PA 19455
215-361-5122
800-377-7878
www.harrietcartergifts.com

•**Casco Bay Wool Works**
34 Danforth St.
Box 25
Portland, ME 04101
888-222-9665 (Orders)
800-788-9842 (Info &
swatches)
www.cascobaywoolworks.com

•**Caswell-Massey Co., Ltd.**
100 Enterprise Pl.
Dover, DE 19904
302-735-8900
800-326-0500
www.caswell-massey.com

•**Caudill Seed Co., Inc.**
1402 West Main St.
Louisville, KY 40203
502-583-4402
800-626-5357
www.caudillseed.com

•**C-Cure**
Custom Building Products
13001 Seal Beach Blvd.
Seal Beach, CA 90740
800-895-2874

•**Cedarbrook Saunas & Steam**
5455 Sunset Hwy
P.O. Box 535
Cashmere, WA 98815
509-782-2447
800-634-6334
www.digifx.com/cedarbrook

•**CRG Designs for Living**
Cedar Rose Guelberth
P.O. Box 113
Carbondale, CO 81623
970-963-0437
www.buildingforhealth.com

•**Chadwick's of Boston**
P.O. Box 1600
Taunton, MA 02780
508-583-6600
800-525-6650
www.chadwicks.com

•**Chambers**
P.O. Box 379908
Las Vegas, NV 89137
800-334-9790

•**Chef's**
P.O. Box 620048
Dallas, TX 75262-0048
800-338-3232 (Orders)
800-884-2433 (Cust. Svc.)
www.chefscatalog.com

•**Chemical Injury Information Network (CIIN)**
P.O. Box 301
White Sulphur Springs, MT
59645
406-547-2255
www.ciin.org

•Chem-Safe Products Co.
P.O. Box 33023
San Antonio, TX 78265
210-657-5321

•Chicago Adhesive Products Co.
1165 Arbor Dr.
Romeoville, IL 60446
630-679-9100
800-621-0220
www.chapco-adhesive.com

•Chock's
74 Orchard St.
New York, NY 10002
212-473-1929
800-222-0020
www.chockcatalog.com

•Chronic Fatigue Immune
Disfuntion Syndrome Assn.
P.O. Box 220398
Charlotte, NC 28222
704-365-2343
800-442-3437
www.cfids.org

•Clean Water Products
1881 W. Prince
Tucson, AZ 85705
520-293-1561

•Clearinghouse on Disability
Information
Ofc. of Special Educ. and
Rehabilitation Svcs.
U.S. Dept. of Education
303 "C" St., SW., Rm. 3132
Washington, DC 20202-2524
202-205-8241
www.ed.gov/OFFICES/OSERS

•Coastline Products
P.O. Box 6397
Santa Ana, CA 92706
800-554-4111

•Cohasset Colonials
P.O. Box 548
Ashburnham, MA 01430
978-827-3001
800-288-2389
www.cohassetcolonials.com

•Colonial Garden Kitchens
P.O. Box 66
Hanover, PA 17333
800-245-3399 (Orders)
800-258-6702 (Cust. service)
www.cgkcatalog.com

•Comfort House
189-V Frelinghuysen Ave.
Newark, NJ 07114-1595
973-242-8080
800-359-7701
www.comforthouse.com

•Coming Home
A Lands' End Catalog
1 Lands' End Lane
Dodgeville, WI 53595
800-345-3696
www.landsend.com/ch

•Common Sense
109 Lincoln Ave.
Rutland, VT 05701
800-259-7627

•The Company Store
500 Company Store Rd.
La Crosse, WI 54601
800-289-8508 (Cust. service)
800-285-3696 (Orders)
www.thecompanystore.com

•Copper Brite, Inc.
P.O. Box 50610
Santa Barbara, CA 93150
805-565-1566
www.copperbrite.com

•Corning/Revere
Consumer Information Center
140 Washington Ave.
P.O. Box 7369
Endicott, NY 13761
800-999-3436
www.corningware.com
www.revereware.com

•Cotton Plus, Ltd.
822 Baldridge St.
O'Donnell, TX 79351
806-428-3345

•Country Curtains
at the Red Lion Inn
Department 2816
Stockbridge, MA 01262
413-243-1300
800-456-0321 (Orders)
800-937-1237 (Cust. service)
www.countrycurtains.com

•Crane & Co.
30 South St.
Dalton, MA 01226
413-684-2600
800-572-0024
www.crane.com

•Crate & Barrel
P.O. Box 3210
Naperville, IL 60566
800-323-5461
www.crateandbarrel.com

•Crown City Mattress
The Natural Bedroom
11134 S. Rush
El Monte, CA 91733
626-452-8617
800-365-6563

•Cuddledown of Maine
312 Canco Rd.
Portlamd, ME 04103
207-761-1855
800-323-6793
www.cuddledown.com

Product Sources

•Culligan International
One Culligan Parkway
Northbrook, IL 60062
847-205-6000
800-285-5442
www.culligan.com

•Cuno, Inc.
400 Research Pkwy.
Meriden, CT 06450
203-237-5541
800-243-6894
www.cuno.com

•Custom Building Products
13001 Seal Beach Blvd.
Seal Beach, CA 90740
562-598-8808
800-272-8786

•CYA Products, Inc.
531 U.S. Highway 1
N. Palm Beach, FL 33408
561-882-0775

•Daily Planet
P.O. Box 64411
St. Paul, MN 55164
800-324-5950

•Daltile Corp.
7834 C.F. Hawn Frwy
Dallas, TX 75217
214-398-1411
800-933-8453
www.daltile.com

•C. Dalton
PMB 976
12555 Biscayne Blvd.
N. Miami, FL 33181
305-751-4871
www.simplesoap.com

•Dap, Inc.
2400 Boston St.
Suite 200
Baltimore, MD 21224
800-543-3840
www.dap.com

•Dasun Co.
P.O. Box 668
Escondido, CA 92033
760-480-8929
800-433-8929

•Decent Exposures
P.O. Box 27206
Seattle, WA 98125
206-364-4540
800-524-4949
www.decentexposures.com

•Deerskin Trading Post
2500 Arrowhead Dr.
Carson City, NV 89706
775-886-5600
www.deerskin.com

•Denny Sales Corp.
3500 Gateway Dr.
Pompano Beach, FL 33069
954-971-3100
800-327-6616

•Design Toscano
1645 Greenleaf Ave.
Elk Grove, IL 60007
847-952-0100
800-525-0733
www.designtoscano.com

•Deva Lifewear
110 1st Ave. West
Westhope, ND 58793
800-222-8024
www.devalifewear.com

•Dharma Trading Co.
P.O. Box 150916
San Rafael, CA 94915
415-456-7657
800-542-5227
www.dharmatrading.com

**•Disabled Artists' Network
(DAN)**
P.O. Box 20781
New York, NY 10025

•Domestications
P.O. Box 1568
LaCrosse, WI 54602
800-746-2555
www.domestications.com

•Dow AgroSciences
9330 Zionsville Rd.
Indianapolis, IN 46268
800-686-6200
www.sentricon.com

•Draper's & Damons
9 Pasteur
Irvine, CA 92618
800-843-1174
www.drapers.com

•Drugstore.com
www.drugstore.com

•Duluth Trading Co.
5200 Quincy St.
St. Paul, MN 55112
800-505-8888
www.duluthtrading.com

•Dupont Corian
E.I. duPont de Nemours & Co.
Barley Mill Plaza
P.O. Box 80012
Wilmington, DE 19880
800-426-7426
www.corian.com

•Duro-Test Lighting
200 Broadacres
Bloomfield, NJ 07004
800-289-3876
www.durotest.com

•Duschqueen, Inc.
461 W. Main St.
Wycoff, NJ 07481
201-848-8081
800-348-8080
www.duschqueeninc.com

•**Dwyer Products Corp.**
418 N. Calumet Ave.
Michigan City, IN 46360
219-874-5236
800-348-8508
www.dwyerkitchens.com

•**Early Winters**
P.O. Box 4333
Portland, OR 97208
800-458-4438

•**Earth Friendly Products**
44 Green Bay Rd.
Winnetka, IL 60093
847-446-4441
800-335-3267
www.ecos.com

•**Earthlings**
P.O. Box 659
Ojai, CA 93024
888-462-2296
www.earthlings.net

•**EcoBaby Organics**
1475 N. Cuyamaca
El Cajon, CA 92020
619-562-9606
888-ECOBABY
www.ecobaby.com

•**Eco Design Co.**
1365 Rufina Cir.
Santa Fe, NM 87505
505-438-3448
800-621-2591
www.bioshieldpaint.com

•**Eco-Home Network**
4344 Russell Ave.
Los Angeles, CA 90027
323-662-5207
www.ecohome.org

•**Ecology Works**
P.O. Box 9067
San Rafael, CA 94912
415-459-3903
888-353-2649
www.dustmitex.com

•**Ecover**
P.O. Box 911058
Commerce, CA 90091
323-720-5730
800-449-4925
www.ecover.com

•**Edsal Manufacturing Co., Inc.**
4400 S. Packers Ave.
Chicago, IL 60609
773-254-0600
www.edsal.com

•**Eight-In-One Pet Products**
2100 Pacific St.
Hauppauge, NY 11788
800-832-7849
www.eightinonepet.com

•**Electrical Sensitivity
Network (ESN)**
P.O. Box 4146
Prescott, AZ 86302
www.northlink.com/~lgrant

•**Electric Power Research
Institute (EPRI)**
3412 Hillview Ave.
Palo Alto, CA 94304
650-855-2121
800-313-3774
www.epri.com

•**Elmer's Products, Inc.**
180 E. Broad St.
Columbus, OH 43215
800-848-9400
www.elmers.com

•**eMD.com**
877-900-3631 (Cust. service)
877-900-3625 (Counceling)
www.eMD.com

•**Emissions Panther, Inc.**
P.O. Box 9075
Corpus Christi, TX 78469
361-887-2168

•**Enviro Air & Water**
901 Westlake Dr.
Austin, TX 78746
512-328-6637
800-571-6637
www.pantherwaterstabilizer.com

•**Environmental Education
and Health Services, Inc.**
Mary Oetzel
P.O. Box 92004
Austin, TX 78709
512-288-2369

•**EPA (Environmental
Protection Agency)**
Ariel Rios Building
1200 Pennsylvania Ave. NW
Washington, DC 20460
202-260-2090
www.epa.gov

•**EPA Indoor Air Quality
InfoLine**
800-438-4318

•**EPA National Service
Center for Environmental
Publications**
P.O. Box 42419
Cincinnati, OH 45242
800-490-9198
www.epa.gov/ncepihom

•**Erlander's Natural Products**
P.O. Box 106
Altadena, CA 91003
626-797-7004

•**Etex Ltd.**
3200 Polaris Ave., Suite 9
Las Vegas, NV 89102
702-364-5911
800-543-5651
www.Etex-Ltd.com

Product Sources

•**Eureka Co.**
1201 E. Bell St.
Bloomington, IL 61701
800-282-2886
www.eureka.com

•**Euroclean**
1151 Bryn Mawr Ave.
Itasca, IL 60143
630-773-2111
800-545-4372
www.eurocleanusa.com

•**E-Z-1**
3500 N. Harrison
Shawnee, OK 74804
405-275-8110

•**Fantom Technologies**
1110 Hansler Rd.
P.O. Box 1104
Welland, ON Canada L3B 5S1
905-734-7476
800-668-9600
www.fantom.com

•**Farr Co.**
2201 Park Place
El Segundo, CA 90245
310-727-6300
800-333-7320
www.farrco.com

•**Faultless Starch/Bon Ami Co.**
1025 W. 8th St.
Kansas City, MO 64101
816-842-1230
800-821-5565
www.faultless.com

•**Fiber Options Paper Co.**
P.O. Box 222
Williams, OR 97544
541-846-6665
888-290-1919
http://home.cdsnet.net/
~kwood/fiberoptions.html

•**Fibromyalgia Network (FN)**
P.O. Box 31750
Tucson, AZ 85751
800-853-2929
www.fmnetnews.com

•**Field Controls, LLC**
2630 Airport Road
Kinston, NC 28504
252-522-3031
800-385-9460
www.fieldcontrols.com

•**Fisher Henney Naturals**
1301 Lincoln Ave.
Alameda, CA 94501
800-343-6639
www.fhnaturals.com

•**Forbo Industries**
Humboldt Industrial Park
P.O. Box 667
Hazleton, PA 18201
570-459-0771
800-842-7839
www.forbo-industries.com

•**Formica Corp.**
10155 Reading Rd.
Cincinnati, OH 45241
513-786-3400
800-FORMICA
www.formica.com

•**E.L. Foust Co., Inc.**
P.O. Box 105
Elmhurst, IL 60126
630-834-4952
800-353-6878
www.foustco.com

•**Franklin International**
2020 Bruck St.
Columbus, OH 43207
614-443-0241
800-877-4583
www.franklini.com

•**Paul Fredrick Menstyle**
223 West Poplar St.
Fleetwood, PA 19522
610-944-0909
800-247-1417
www.paulfredrick.com

•**French Creek Sheep & Wool Co.**
600 Pine Swamp Rd.
Elverson, PA 19520
610-286-5700
800-977-4337
www.frenchcreek.com

•**French Transit Ltd.**
398 Beach Rd.
Burlingame, CA 94010
650-548-9600
800-829-7625
www.thecrystal.com

•**Frontier Natural Products**
3021 78th St.
P.O. Box 299
Norway, IA 52318
800-786-1388
www.frontiercoop.com

•**Fuller Brush Co.**
One Fuller Way
Great Bend, KS 67530
316-792-1711
800-522-0499
www.fullerbrush.com

•**Furnature**
319 Washington St.
Boston, MA 01235
617-787-2888
www.furnature.com

•**Garnet Hill**
231 Main St.
Franconia, NH 03580
603-823-5545
800-622-6216

•**Garrett Wade Co.**
161 Avenue of the Americas
New York, NY 10013
212-807-1155
800-221-2942
www.garrettwade.com

•**Gazoontite**
469 Bryant St.
San Francisco, CA 94107
415-778-0400
888-4MY-NOSE
www.gazoontite.com

•**GE Lighting**
Nela Park
Cleveland, OH 44112
216-266-2121
800-327-2080

•**General Ecology, Inc.**
151 Sheree Blvd.
Exton, PA 19341
610-363-7900
800-441-8166
www.general-ecology.com

•**General Electric Co.**
GE Answer Center
9500 Williamsburg Plaza
Louisville, KY 40222
800-626-2000
www.geappliances.com

•**General Filters, Inc**
43800 Grand River Ave.
Novi, MI 48376
248-476-5100
www.generalfilters.com

•**Genopalette**
1110 Co. Rd. 319
Franklin, MO 65250
660-848-2201 (Info)
800-374-5371 (Orders)
www.genopalette.com

•**Get Organized**
600 Cedar Hollow Rd.
Paoli, PA 19301
610-725-1135
800-803-9400
www.getorginc.com

•**Global Environmental
Technologies**
P.O. Box 8839
Allentown, PA 18105
610-821-4901
800-800-8377
www.terraflo.com

•**Gloucester Co., Inc.**
P.O. Box 428
Franklin, MA 02038
508-528-2200
800-343-4963
www.phenoseal.com

•**GMX Magnetic**
13771 Roswell, Bldg. A
Chino, CA 91710
909-627-5700
800-373-4469

•**Gohn Bros.**
105 South Main St.
Box 111
Middlebury, IN 46540
219-825-2400
800-595-0031

•**Golden Neo-Life Diamite**
3500 Gateway Blvd.
Freemont, CA 94538
510-651-0405
800-432-5848
www.americas.gnld.com

•**Golden Temple Natural
Products**
Box 1095
Taos, NM 87571
505-776-2311

•**W.W. Grainger, Inc.**
Local outlets in most major cities.
www.grainger.com

•**Granny's Old Fashioned Products**
Box 660037
Arcadia, CA 91066
800-366-1762

•**Graphik Dimensions Ltd.**
2103 Brentwood St.
High Point, NC 27263
336-887-3700
800-221-0262 (Orders)
800-332-8884 (Cust. Svc.)
www.graphikdimensions.com

•**Green Field Paper Co.**
1330 "G" Street
San Diego, CA 92101
619-338-9432
www.greenfieldpaper.com

•**GreenMarketplace.com**
www.greenmarketplace.com

•**Green Pepper**
1285 River Rd.
Eugene, OR 97404
541-689-3292
800-767-5684
www.thegreenpepper.com

•**Halo, Purely for Pets, Inc.**
3438 E. Lake Rd. #14
Palm Harbor, FL 34685
813-854-2214
800-426-4256
www.halopets.com

•**Hamilton Beach/Proctor-
Silex, Inc.**
234 Springs Rd.
Washington, NC 27889
800-851-8900
www.hambeach.com

•Harmony
360 Interlocken Blvd.
Suite 300
Broomfield, CO 80021
800-869-3446
www.gaiam.com

•Health One Co.
P.O. Box 9101
Niskayuna, NY 12309
800-257-2819

•Healthy Environment
Information and Referral Service
Rich Kimball
P.O. Box 1588
San Juan Pueblo, NM 87566
505-852-0288

•Healthy Homes Consulting
20 Maplewood Ct.
Lower Sackville, NS
Canada B4G 1B6
902-864-1955
www.healthyhomes.ca

•healthyhome.com
www.healthyhome.com

•The Healthy House Institute
430 N. Sewell Rd.
Bloomington. IN 47408
812-332-5073
www.hhinst.com

•Heart of Vermont
131 S. Main St.
P.O. Box 612
Barre, VT 05641
802-476-3098
800-639-4123
www.heartofvermont.com

•Heavenly Heat Saunas
1106 2nd St.
Suite 162
Encinitas, CA 92024
800-697-2862

•Hello Direct
5893 Rue Ferrari
San Jose, CA 95138
800-444-3556
www.HelloDirect.com

•HEMPTECH
P.O. Box 1716
Sebastopol, CA 95473
707-823-2800
800-265-4367
www.hemptech.com

•HempWorks
570 Sylvan Ave.
Englewood, Cliffs, NJ 07632
888-436-7362
www.hempworks.com

•Herbaceuticals, Inc.
902 Enterprise Way
Suite M
Napa, CA 94558-6288
707-259-6266
800-462-0666

•Hold Everything
P.O. Box 7807
San Francisco, CA 94120
800-421-2264

•Home Decorators Collection
8920 Pershall Rd.
Hazelwood, MO 63042
800-245-2217
www.homedecorators.com

•Home Marketplace
4510 Edison Ave.
Colorado Springs, CO 80940
800-356-3876

•Home-Sew
P.O. Box 4099
Bethlehem, PA 18018
610-867-3833
800-344-4739
www.homesew.com

•Homespun Fabrics & Draperies
P.O. Box 4315
Thousand Oaks, CA 91359
805-381-0741
888-543-2998
www.galaxymall.com/shops/
homespun

•Honeywell Inc.
1985 Douglas Drive North
Golden Valley, MN 55422
612-951-1000
800-328-5111 (Furnace filters)
800-554-4558 (Portable filters)
www.honeywell.com

•The Hoover Co.
101 E. Maple St.
North Canton, OH 44720
330-499-9200
www.hoovercompany.com

•Human Ecology Action
League (HEAL)
P.O Box 29629
Atlanta, GA 30359
404-248-1898
http://members.aol.com/
HEALNatnl/index.html

•Huntington Clothiers &
Shirtmakers
1285 Alum Creek Dr.
Columbus, OH 43209
614-252-4422
800-848-6203
www.huntington
clothiers.com

•HybriVet Systems, Inc.
Lead Check Swabs
P.O. Box 1210
Framingham, MA 01701
800-262-5323
www.leadcheck.com

•ICI Paints
925 Euclid Ave.
Cleveland, OH 44115
800-221-4100
www.ici.com

•Impex Systems Group, Inc.
2801 NW 3rd Ave.
Miami, FL 33127
305-573-0163
800-933-0163
www.ooks.com

•Improvements
Hanover, PA 17333-0084
800-642-2112
www.ImprovementsCatalog.com

•Independent Living
Research Utilization (ILRU)
2323 S. Shepherd
Suite 1000
Houston, TX 77019
713-520-0232
www.ilru.org

•Indian Earth Cosmetics
2967 Randolph Ave.
Costa Mesa, CA 92626
714-556-1407
www.indianearth.com

•Inner Balance
360 Interlocken Blvd. #300
Broomfield, CO 80021
800-482-3608
www.gaiam.com

•InteliHealth Healthy Home
97 Commerce Way
P.O. Box 7007
Dover, DE 19903
800-988-1127
www.intelihealth.com

•Interior Elements
Margie McNally
P.O. Box 157
West Bridgewater, MA 02379
508-559-8959

•InterMetro Industries Corp.
651 N. Washington St.
Wilkes-Barre, PA 18705
570-825-2741
800-433-2232
www.metro.com

•Internatural
33719 116th St.
Twin lakes, WI 53181
800-643-4221
www.internatural.com

•Janice Corporation
198 US Highway 46
Budd Lake, NJ 07828
973-691-2979
800-526-4237
www.janices.com

•Jason Natural Products
8468 Warner Dr.
Culver City, CA 90232
310-838-7543
800-527-6605
www.jason-natural.com

•Jedmon Products
333 Rim Rock Rd.
Downsview, ON, Canada
M3J 3J9
416-631-4000

•Jelmar
6600 N. Lincoln Ave.
Suite 400
Lincolnwood, IL 60712
847-675-8400
800-323-5497
www.jelmar.com

•Jewish Guild for the Blind
15 West 65th St.
New York, NY 10023
212-769-6200
www.jgb.org

•J. Jill
100 Birch Pond Dr.
P.O. Box 2006
Tilton, NH 03276
800-343-5700 (Questions)
800-642-0001 (Orders)
www.jjill.com

•S.C Johnson & Son, Inc.
1525 Howe St.
Racine, WI 53403
414-260-2000
800-494-4855
www.scjbrands.com

•Junonia
800 Transfer Rd.
Suite 8
St. Paul, MN 55114
800-671-0175
www.junonia.com

•Karen's Natural Products
110 N. Washington, St.
Harv de Grace, MD 21078
410-378-4936
800-527-3674
www.karensnatural.com

•KB Cotton Pillows, Inc.
P.O. Box 57
De Soto, TX 75123
972-233-7193
800-544-3752
www.kbcottonpillows.com

•KDF Fluid Treatment, Inc.
1500 KDF Drive
Three Rivers, MI 49093
616-273-3300
800-437-2745
www.kdfft.com

•Neil Kelly Cabinets
804 N. Alberta St.
Portland, OR 97217
503-288-7461
www.neilkelly.com

•**David Kibbey**
1618 Parker St.
Berkeley, CA 94703
510-841-1039

•**Kidde Safety**
1394 S. 3rd St.
Mebane, NC 27302
919-563-5911
800-880-6788
www.kiddesafety.com

•**Kinetico Water Systems**
3880 Pendleton Way
Suite 200
Indianapolis, IN 46226
317-542-8888
800-444-1387
www.kinetico.com

•**Kiss My Face**
P.O. Box 224
Gardiner, NY 12525
914-255-0884
800-262-KISS
www.kissmyface.com

•**KitchenAid**
2000 M-63 North
Benton Harbor, MI 49022
616-923-5000
800-422-1230
www.KitchenAid.com

•**Kitchen & Home**
P.O. Box 2527
LaCrosse, WI 54602
800-414-5544
www.kitchenandhome.com

•**Kitchens and Baths by Don Johnson**
Suite 1375
Merchandise Mart
Chicago, IL 60654
773-KITCHEN
www.healthycabinets.com

•**Knapp Shoes**
1 Keuka Business Park # 300
Penn Yan, NY 14527
800-869-9955
www.knappshoes.com

•**Labor Institute, NYC**
853 Broadway #2014
New York, NY 10003
212-674-3322

•**Lady Grace**
P.O. Box 128
Malden, MA 02148
800-922-0504
www.ladygrace.com

•**Lands' End, Inc.**
1 Lands' End Lane
Dodgeville, WI 53595
608-935-6170
800-356-4444
www.landsend.com

•**Lee Metal Products**
P.O. Box 6
Littlestown, PA 17340
717-359-4111
800-233-7076
www.leemetal.com

•**Lee Rowan**
900 S. Highway Dr.
Fenton, MO 63026
314-343-0700
800-325-6150
www.leerowan.com

•**Lerner New York**
P.O. Box 8380
Indianapolis, IN 46283
800-288-4000
www.catalogcity.com

•**Less EMF, Inc.**
26 Valley View Ln.
Ghent, NY 12075
518-392-1946
888-537-7363
www.lessemf.com

•**LifeKind Products**
P.O. Box 1774
Grass Valley, CA 95945
530-477-5395
800-284-4983
www.lifekind.com

•**LifeTime Solutions**
P.O. Box 416
Pineland, FL 33945
941-283-1222
888-368-4288
www.lifetimesolutions.com

•**Lighthouse International**
111 East 59th St.
New York, NY 10022
212-821-9200
800-829-0500
www.lighthouse.org

•**Lilly's Kids**
Virginia Beach, VA 23479
800-285-5555
www.lillianvernon.com

•**Lily of the Desert**
1887 Geesling
Denton, TX 76208
940-566-9914
800-229-5459
www.lilyofthedesert.com

•**Linensource**
5401 Hangar Ct.
P.O. Box 31151
Tampa, FL 33631
813-243-6170
800-434-9812
www.LinenSource.com

•**The Living Source**
P.O. Box 20155
Waco, TX 76702
254-776-4878
800-662-8787
www.livingsource.com

•Livos Phytochemistry, Inc.
P.O. Box 1740
Mashpee, MA 02649
508-477-7955
www.livos.com

•Logona USA, Inc.
554 Riverside Dr.
Ashville, NC 28801
828-252-1420
800-648-6654
www.logona.com

•LS&S Group
P.O. Box 673
Northbrook, IL 60065
847-498-9777
800-468-4789
www.lssgroup.com

•Lumiram Electric Corp.
179 Westmorland Ave.
White Plains, NY 10606
914-328-0533
800-354-5596
www.lumiram.com

•Maas Polishing Systems, Inc.
7101 Adams, Unit 3
Willowbrook, IL 60521
630-654-4743
www.maasinc.com

•Magla Products
3636 Taylorsville Hwy.
Statesville, NC 28625
704-873-6384
800-247-5281
www.magla.com

•Manco, Inc.
32150 Just Imagine Dr.
Avon, OH 44011-1355
800-321-0253
www.manco.com

•Marketplace: Handwork of India
1455 Ashland Ave.
Evanston, IL 60201
800-726-8905 (Orders)
847-328-4011 (Cust. service)
www.marketplaceindia.com

•Maryland Square
1350 Williams St.
Chippewa Falls, WI 54729
800-727-3895
www.marylandsquare.com

•B.A. Mason
1251 First Ave.
Chippewa Falls, WI 54729
800-422-1000
www.bamason.com

•MCS Referral & Resources
508 Westgate Rd.
Baltimore, MD 21229
410-362-6400
www.mcsrr.org

•MCS Resources
www.thegarden.net/mcs

•Stuart McGuire
425 Well St.
Chippewa Falls, WI 54729
888-222-2028
www.stuartmcguire.com

•MCSurvivors
www.MCSurvivors.com

•Medbookstore.com
www.MEDBOOKstore.com

•Medsite.com
www.Medsite.com

•Michigan Maple Block Co.
P.O Box 245
Petosky, MI 49770
616-347-4170
www.mapleblock.com

•Miele, Inc.
9 Independence Way
Princeton, NJ 08540
609-419-9898
800-843-7231
www.mieleusa.com

•Miller Paint Co.
12812 NE Whitaker Way
Portland, OR 97230
503-255-0190
www.millerpaint.com

•Moen, Inc.
25300 Al Moen Dr.
North Olmstead, OH 44070
440-962-2000
800-289-6636 (U.S.)
800-465-6130 (Canada)
www.moen.com

•Motherwear
320 Riverside Dr.
Northampton, MA 01062
413-586-3488
800-950-2500
www.motherwear.com

•Multi-Pure Corp.
7251 Cathedral Rock Dr.
Las Vegas, NV 89128
702-360-8880
800-622-9206
www.multipure.com

•Murco Wall Products, Inc.
300 NE 21st St.
Ft. Worth, TX 76106
817-626-1987
800-446-7124

•National Antimicrobial
Information Network (NAIN)
Oregon State University
333 Weniger Hall
Corvallis, OR 97331
800-447-6349
www.ace.orst.edu/info/nain

•National Blind & Wallpaper Co.
200 Galleria #400
Southfield, MI 48034
800-260-1987
www.blindsandwallpaper.com

•National Center for
Environmental Health
Strategies (NCEHS)
1100 Rural Ave.
Voorhees, NJ 08043
856-429-5358
www.ncehs.org

•National Electromagnetic
Field Testing
628B Library Pl.
Evanston, IL 60201
847-475-3696
www.theramp.net/nefta

•National Foundation for the
Chemically Hypersensitive
4407 Swinson Rd.
Rhodes, MI 48652
517-689-6369
www.mcsrelief.com

•National Home Mortage
Company
4407 Swinson Rd.
Rhodes, MI 48652
517-689-6369
www.mcsrelief.com

•National Information
Center for Children and
Youth with Disablities
P.O. Box 1492
Washington, DC 20013
202-884-8200
800-695-0285
www.nichcy.org

•National Institute of Allergy
and Infectious Diseases
National Institutes of Health
Building 31, Room 7A-50
31 Center Dr. MSC 2520
Bethesda, MD 20892
301-496-5717
www.niaid.nih.gov

•National Institute of
Environmental Health
Sciences
EMF Rapid Information
www.niehs.nih.gov/emfrapid

•National Lead Information
Center
800-424-5323
www.epa.gov/lead/nlic

•National Library Service for
the Blind and Physically
handicapped
The Library of Congress
1291 Taylor St. NW
Washington, DC 20542
202-707-5100
800-424-8567
www.loc.gov/nls

•National Pesticides
Telecommunications
Network (NPTN)
Oregon State University
333 Weniger Hall
Corvallis, OR 97331
800-858-7378
www.ace.orst.edu/info/nptn

•National Sanitation
Foundation (NSF)
P.O. Box 130140
Ann Arbor, MI 48113
734-769-8010
800-NSF-MARK
www.nsf.org

•National Testing Laboratories
6555 Wilson Mills Rd.
Suite 102
Cleveland, OH 44143
440-449-2525
800-458-3330
www.watercheck.com

•National Wholesale Co.
400 National Rd.
Lexington, NC 27294
800-480-4673

•The Natural Alternative
11577 124th St. North
Hugo, MN 55038
651-351-7165
www.thenaturalalternative.com

•Natural Animal Health
Products, Inc.
700 N. US Highway 1
St. Augustine, FL 32095
800-274-7387
www.naturalanimal.com

•Natural Baby
7835 Freedom Ave. NW # 2
North Canton, OH 44720
800-388-2229
www.kidsstuff.com

•Natural Home by Natürlich
P.O. Box 1677
Sebastapol, CA 95473
707-824-0914
www.naturalhomeproducts.com

•Natural Lifestyle
16 Lookout Dr.
Ashville, NC 28804
800-752-2775
www.natural-lifestyle.com

•Natural Selections
104 S. Main St.
Fairfield, IA 52556
515-472-5876
888-216-9917
www.organicselections.com

•Nature's Plus
548 Broadhollow Rd.
Melville, NY 11747
516-293-0030
www.natplus.com

•Necessary Organics
One Nature's Way
New Castle, VA 24127
540-864-5103
800-447-5354
www.concerngarden.com

•N.E.E.D.S.
527 Charles Ave. 12A
Syracuse, NY 13209
800-634-1380
www.needs.com

•Neutrogena Corp.
5760 W. 96th St.
Los Angeles, CA 90045
310-642-1150
800-217-1136
www.neutrogena.com

•New Millennium Concepts, Ltd.
New Millennium Concepts
1106 N Hwy. 360, Ste. 306
Grand Prairie, TX 75050
888-803-4438
www.britishberkefeld.com

•Newport News
Easy Style Dr.
Hampton, VA 23630
757-827-9000
800-688-2830
www.newport-news.com

•New Wave Enviro
P.O. Box 4146
Englewood, CO 81055
303-221-3232
800-592-8371

•Nigra Enterprises
5699 Kanan Rd.
Agoura, CA 91301
818-889-6877

•Nilfisk-Advance America, Inc.
300 Technology Drive
Malvern, PA 19355
610-647-6420
www.nilfisk-advance.com

•NRG Savers
9805 320th St.
St Joseph, MN 56374
877-363-4614
www.nrgsavers.com

•Nutech Energy Systems
511 McCormick Blvd.
London, ON
Canada N5W 4C8
519-457-1904
www.lifebreath.com

•Nutone
Madison and Red Banks Roads
Cincinnati, OH 45227-1599
513-527-5100
800-543-8687
www.nutone.com

•N-Viro Products Ltd.
610 Walnut Ave.
Bohemia, NY 11716
516-567-2628

•Ogallala Down Co.
P.O. Box 830
Ogallala, NE 69153
308-284-8403
800-658-4370
www.ogallaladown.com

•Old Fashioned Milk Paint Co.
436 Main St.
Groton, MA 01450
978-448-6336
www.milkpaint.com

•One Step Ahead
P.O. Box 517
Lake Bluff, IL 60044
800-274-8440
www.onestepahead.com

•Orange-Sol Household
Products, Inc.
144 N. Fiesta Blvd.
Gilbert, AZ 85233
480-497-8822
800-877-7771
www.orange-sol.com

•Organic Essentials
822 Baldridge St.
O'Donnell, TX 79351
800-765-6491
www.organicessentials.com

•Orr Safety Corporation
2360 Millers Lane
Louisville, KY 40216
502-774-5791
800-669-1677
www.orrsafety.com

•Orvis
1711 Blue Hills Drive
Roanoke, Virginia 24012
540-345-4606
800-541-3541
www.orvis.com

•Ozark Water Service and
Environmental Services
114 Spring St.
Sulphur Springs, AR 72768
501-298-3483
800-835-8908

•Pace Chem Industries
3050 Westwood Dr., Unit
B10
Las Vegas, NV 89109
702-369-1424
800-350-2912

•Pacific Spirit
1334 Pacific Ave,
Forest Grove, OR 97116
503-357-1566
800-634-9057
www.mystictrader.com

•**Palmer Bedding Co.**
9310 Keystone St.
Philadelphia, PA 19114
215-335-0400
www.boatmattress.com

•**Patagonia**
8550 White Fir St.
Reno, NV 89533
775-747-1992
800-638-6464
www.patagonia.com

•**Paula's Hatbox and More**
P.O. Box 935
South Easton, MA 02375
800-332-4287
www.paulashatbox.com

•**Pedigrees**
1989 Transit Way
Box 905
Brockport, NY 14420
800-548-4786

•**Peelu USA**
P.O. Box 2803
Fargo, ND 58108
701-281-0511
800-457-3358

•**Peerless Imported Rugs**
P.O. Box 14251
Chicago, IL 60614
773-472-4848
888-747-8820
www.pirinternational.com

•**JC Penney Catalog**
Stores in most major cities
972-431-1000
800-222-6161
www.jcpenney.com

•**Perfectly Safe**
7835 Freedom Ave. NW
Suite 3
North Canton, OH 44720
800-837-5437
www.kidsstuff.com

•**Rachel Perry, Inc.**
9800 Eton Ave.
Chatsworth, CA 91311
800-966-8888
www.rachelperry.net

•**Perstop Flooring, Inc.**
P.O. Box 1775
Horsham, PA 19044
800-337-3746
www.pergo.com

•**PermaGrain Products Inc.**
4789 West Chester Pike
Newton Square, PA 19073
610-353-8801
877-771-6470
www.permagrain.com

•**Peruvian Collection**
Canaan Farm, Box 990
Tonganoxie, KS 66086
800-255-6429
www.peruvianconnection.com

•**Pet Warehouse**
P.O. Box 752138
Dayton, OH 45475
800-443-1160
www.petwhse.com

•**Phoneco, Inc.**
19813 East Mill Rd.
P.O. Box 70
Galesville, WI 54630
608-582-4124
www.phonecoinc.com

•**Planetrx.com**
www.planetrx.com

•**Pompanoosuc Mills**
P.O. Box 238
Route 5
East Thetford, VT 05043
802-862-8208
800-841-6671
www.pompy.com

•**Pottery Barn**
P.O. Box 7044
San Francisco, CA 94120
800-922-5507
www.potterybarn.com

•**PPG Architectural Finishes, Inc.**
One PPG Place
Pittsburgh, PA 15272
905-238-6441 (Canada)
888-774-1010
www.ppgaf.com

•**Practical Allergy Research
Foundation**
P.O. Box 60
Buffalo, NY 14223
716-875-0398
800-787-8780
www.drrapp.com

•**Prince Lionheart**
2421 S. Westgate Rd.
Santa Maria, CA 93455
805-922-2250
800-544-1132 (Outside CA)
www.princelionheart.com

•**Priorities**
1451 Concord St.
Framingham, MA 01701
800-553-5398 (Orders)
800-797-2001 (Customer
service)
www.priorities.com

•**Proctor & Gamble**
PO Box 599
Cincinnati, OH 45201
513-983-1100
www.pg.com

•**PUR Drinking Water
Systems**
9300 N. 75th Ave.
Minneapolis, MN 55428
800-787-5463
www.purwater.com

•Pure Air Systems, Inc.
1325 Church St.
Clayton, IN 46118
317-359-4097
800-869-8025
www.pureairsystems.com

•The Pure Water Place, Inc
4617 County Road 2
Berthoud, CO 80513
303-776-0056
888-776-0056
www.purewaterplace.cnchost.com

•Pyrocap International Corp.
6551 Loisdale Ct.
Suite 400
Springfield, VA 22150
703-922-7472
877-797-6227

•Real Goods
200 Clara St..
Ukiah, CA 95482
707-468-9292
800-762-7325
www.realgoods.com

•Recordings for the Blind &
Dyslexic
20 Roszel Rd.
Princeton, NJ 08540
800-803-7201
www.rfbd.org

•Red Devil, Inc.
2400 Vauxhall Rd.
P.O. Box 3133
Union, NJ 07083
908-688-6900
800-423-3845
www.reddevil.com

•Reliable Corp.
P.O. Box 1502
Ottawa, IL 61350
800-735-4000 (Orders)
800-359-5000 (Cust. service)
www.reliable.com

•Research Products Corp.
P.O. Box 1467
Madison, WI 53701
608-257-8801
www.space-gard.com

•Rexair, Inc.
3221 W. Big Beaver Rd. # 200
Troy, MI 48084
248-643-7222
www.rainbowsystem.com

•The Right Start
5388 Sterling Center Dr.,
Unit C
Westlake Villiage, CA 91361
818-707-7100
800-548-8531
www.rightstart.com

•Rincon Group, LLC
17575 Pacific Coast Hwy.
Pacific Palisades, CA 90272
310-230-9898
888-644-PAWS
www.dancingpaws.com

•The Rival Company
800 East 101 Ter.
Kansas City, MO 64131
816-943-4100

•RMED International, Inc.
Tushies
675 Industrial Blvd.
Delta, CO 81416
800-344-6379
www.tushies.com

•L.B. Roe Corp.
P.O. Box 2666
Anaheim, CA 92814
714-995-5921
www.white-wizard.com

•Frank T. Ross & Sons, Ltd.
6550 Lawrence Ave. East
Scarborough, ON
Canada M1C 4A7
416-282-1107

•Rowenta
196 Boston Ave.
Medford, MA 02155
781-396-0600
www.rowentausa.com

•Safe Reading & Computer
Box Co.
4407 Swinson Rd.
Rhodes, MI 48652
517-689-6369
www.mcsrelief.com

•Safe Schools
Irene Ruth Wilkenfeld
8818 Sherman Mountain Rd.
Cheyenne, WY 82009
307-772-0655
www.head-gear.com/SafeSchools

•Safe Drinking Water Hotline
800-426-4791
www.epa.gov/safewater

•Safe Technologies Corp.
1950 NE 208 Ter.
Miami, FL 33179
305-933-2026
800-638-9121
800-222-3003
www.milligauss.com

•St. Charles Mfg. Co.
520 Kane St.
Scranton, PA 18505
570-969-4066
800-634-3802
www.atlanticmedco.com

•Sanofi Pharmaceuticals
90 Park Ave.
New York, NY 10016
212-551-4000
800-223-1062
www.sanofi-synthelabo.fr/us

•**Sappo Hill Soapworks**
654 Tolman Creek Rd.
Ashland, OR 97520
541-482-4485
800-863-7627
www.sappohill.com

•**Savogran**
P.O. Box 130
259 Lenox St.
Norwood, MA 02062
800-225-9872
www.savogran.com

•**Schulte Corp.**
12115 Ellington Ct.
Cincinnati, OH 45249
513-489-9300
800-669-3225
www.SCHULTEstorage.com

•**Scientific Glass Co., Inc.**
P.O. Box 25125
Albuquerque, NM 87125
505-345-7321

•**Sears Roebuck and Co.**
Stores in most major cities
www.sears.com

•**Senoret**
566 Leffingwell
St. Louis, MO 63122
314-966-2394
800-837-7644
www.terro.com

•**Servaas Laboratories, Inc.**
1200 Waterway Blvd.
Indianapolis, IN 46202
317-636-7760
800-433-5818
www.barkeepersfriend.com

•**Service Merchandise**
P.O. Box 24600
Nashville, TN 37202
800-539-3579
www.servicemerchandise.com

•**Seventh Generation**
One Mill St.
Box A-26
Burlington, VT 05401
802-658-3773
www.seventhgen.com

•**Sew Eco-Logical**
1280-B East 28th Ave.
Eugene, OR 97403
541-683-5828

•**Shadow Lake, Inc.**
188 Shadow Lake Rd.
Ridgefield, CT 06877
203-778-0881
800-343-6588
www.shadowlake.com

•**Shaker Shops West**
5 Inverness Way
P.O. Box 487
Inverness, CA 94937
415-669-7256
800-474-2537
www.shakershops.com

•**Shaker Workshops**
P.O. Box 8001
Ashburnham, MA 01430
978-827-9900
800-840-9121
www.shakerworkshops.com

•**Sierra Pine Limited**
Medite Division
P.O. Box 4040
2685 N. Pacific Hwy.
Medford, OR 97501
800-676-3339
www.sierrapine.com

•**Sierra Trading Post**
5025 Campstool Rd.
Cheyenne, WY 82007
307-775-8000
800-713-4534
www.SierraTradingPost.com

•**Silhouettes**
Hanover, PA 17333
800-704-3322
www.silhouettes.com

•**Silvo Home**
3201 Tollview Dr.
Rolling Meadows, IL 60008
800-331-1261
www.silvo.com

•**Simmons Natural Bodycare**
42295 Highway 36
Bridgeville, CA 95526
707-777-1920
800-428-0412
www.home.pon.net/
simmonsnaturals

•**Simplex Building Products**
P.O. Box 10
Adrian, MI 49221
517-263-8881
800-345-8881
www.simplex-products.com

•**Sinan Co.**
P.O. Box 857
Davis, CA 95616
530-753-3104
www.dcn.davis.ca.us/go/sinan

•**Sleeptek Limited**
50 Colonade Rd. North
Ottawa, ON
Canada K2E 7J6
888-413-4442
www.sleeptek.com

•**Smith & Hawken**
Box 6907
Florence, KY 41022
800-940-1170
www.smith-hawken.com

•Smith & Nephew Consumer Products, Ltd.
Alum Rock Rd.
Birmingham B8 3DZ
England UK
44-121-327-4750
www.smith-nephew.com

•Smith & Noble
1801 California Ave.
Corona, CA 92881
800-248-8888
www.smithandnoble.com

•The Soap and Detergent Assn.
475 Park Ave. S.
New York, NY 10016
212-725-1262
www.sdahq.org

•Social Security Administration
U.S. Department of Health
and Human Services
6401 Security Blvd.
Baltimore, MD 21235
410-965-3120
800-772-1213
www.ssa.gov

•Solutions
P.O. Box 6878
Portland, OR 97228
800-342-9988

•Southworth Co.
265 Main St.
Agawam, MA 01001
413-789-2511
800-225-1839
www.southworth.com

•Stabilized Water of Canada, Inc.
11012 MacLoed Tr. S.
Suite 600
Calgary, AB
Canada T2J 6A5
403-296-1600
800-667-7638
www.soft-water.com

•Staples, Inc.
500 Staples Dr.
Framingham, MA 01702
508-253-7963
800-333-3330
www.staples.com

•R.C. Steele
1989 Transit Way
Box 910
Brockport, NY 14420
888-839-9420
www.rcsteele.com

•Sterling Plumbing Group, Inc.
2900 Golf Rd.
Rolling Meadows, IL 60008
847-734-4630
800-783-7546
888-783-7546
www.sterlingplumbing.com

•Suburban Water Testing Laboratories, Inc.
4600 Kutztown Rd.
Temple, PA 19560
610-929-2920
800-433-6595
www.h2otest.com

•Summitville Tiles, Inc.
S.R. 664
Summitville, OH 43962
330-223-1511
www.summitville.com

•Sunshine Makers, Inc.
15922 Pacific Coast Hwy.
Huntington Harbour, CA 92649
562-795-6000
800-228-0709
www.simplegreen.com

•Sur La Table
1765 Sixth Ave. South
Seattle, WA 98134
800-243-0852
www.surlatable.com

•T & Y Beacon of Hope Foundation
656 Beidler Forest Rd.
Dorchester, SC 29437
843-462-2681

•Taylor Gifts
600 Cedar Hollow Rd.
Paoli, PA 19301
610-725-1100
800-829-1133
www.taylorgifts.com

•W.F. Taylor Co., Inc.
11545 Pacific Ave.
Fontana, CA 92337
909-360-6677
800-397-4583
www.wftaylor.com

•Terressentials
2650 Old National Pike
Middletown, MD 21769
301-371-7333
www.terressentials.com

•This End Up
P.O. Box 2020
Richmond, VA 23219
800-627-5161

•Norm Thompson
P.O. Box 3999
Portland, OR 97208
877-718-7899
800-547-1160
www.normthompson.com

•Tiburon
P.O. Box 7105
Dover, DE 19903
800-279-2917

Tidewater Workshop
P.O. Box 456
Egg Harbor City, NJ 08215
800-666-8433
www.tidewaterworkshop.com

•Tilley Endurables
300 Langner Rd.
West Seneca, NY 14224
716-822-3052
800-363-8737
www.tilley.com

•Tomorrow's World
194 E. Ocean View Ave.
Norfolk, VA 23503
757-480-8500
800-229-7571
www.tomorrowsworld.com

•Tom's of Maine
P.O. Box 710
Kennebunk, ME 04043
207-985-2944
800-775-2388
www.toms-of-maine.com

•Toxic Carpet Information
Exchange
P.O. Box 53344
Cincinnati, OH 45253

•Tucson Cooperative
Warehouse
350 South Toole Ave.
Tucson, AZ 85701
520-884-9951
800-350-2667
www.tcwnaturalfoods.com
(You must be a member to order
from Tucson stores, which are
located in the southwestern U.S.)

•Tweeds
Hanover, PA 17333-0092
800-999-7997
www.tweeds.com

•Under the Canopy
12 Castle Ct
Randolph NJ, 07869
888-226-6799
www.underthecanopy.com

•Union City Chair
18 Market St.
Union City, PA 16438
814-438-3878
800-822-4247
www.ncinter.net/~ucchair

•Unique Marketing
5778 Lamar
Arvada, CO 80002
800-221-3259

•United Gilsonite Laboratories
P.O. Box 70
Scranton, PA 18501
800-272-3235
www.ugl.com

•U.S. Borax Inc.
26877 Tourney Rd.
Valencia, CA 91355
661-287-5400
800-9-TIM-BOR
www.borax.com

•USG Corp.
125 S. Franklin St.
Chicago, IL 60606
312-606-4000
800-874-4968
www.usg.com

•U.S. Department of
Housing and Urban
Development (HUD)
451 7th St. NW
Washington, DC 20410
202-708-0417 (offices)
202-708-1422 (info)
www.hud.gov

•Internal Revenue Service
(IRS)
800-829-3676 (forms)
800-829-1040 (info)
www.irs.gov

•Verdant Brands
9555 James Ave. S.
Suite 200
Bloomington, MN 55431
612-703-3300
800-423-7544
www.verdantbrands.com

•Vermont Country Store
(Voice of the Mountains catalog)
(Apothecary catalog)
P.O. Box 3000
Manchester Ctr., VT 05255
802-362-8440
www.vermontcountrystore.com

•Lillian Vernon Corp.
Virginia Beach, VA 23479
800-505-2250
www.lillianvernon.com

•Vita-Mix Corp.
8615 Usher Rd.
Cleveland, OH 44138
440-235-4840
800-848-2649
www.vita-mix.com

•Vita-Wave
320 Lambert St.
Oxnard, CA 93030
805-981-1472

•Wagner Spray Tech Corp.
1770 Fernbrook Ln.
Minneapolis, MN 55447
612-553-7232
800-328-8251
www.wagnerspraytech.com

•Washington Toxics
Coalition
4649 Sunnyside Ave. N.
Suite 540 East
Seattle, WA 98103
206-632-1545
www.watoxics.org

•**Water Quality Association**
4151 Naperville Rd.
Lisle, IL 60532-1088
630-505-0160
800-749-0234 (Consumer help)
www.wqa.org

•**Waterwise, Inc.**
P.O. Box 494000
Leesburg, FL 34749
352-787-5008
800-874-9028
www.waterwise.com

•**Wein Products, Inc.**
115 W. 25th St.
Los Angeles, CA 90007
213-749-6049
www.weinproducts.com

•**Well & Good**
P.O. Box 64684
St. Paul, MN 55164
800-665-6586

•**Whitmer Micro-Gen
Research Laboratories, Inc.**
3568 Tree Court
Industrial Blvd.
St. Louis, MO 63122
800-777-8570
www.wmmg.com

•**Whittier Wood Products**
P.O. Box 2827
Eugene, OR 97402
541-687-0213
800-653-3336

•**Whole Life Products**
1334 Pacific Ave.
Forest Grove, OR 97116
503-357-1566
800-634-9057

•**WinterSilks**
11711 Marco Beach Dr.
Jacksonville, FL 32224
904-645-6000
800-648-7455
www.wintersilks.com

•**Williams-Sonoma**
P.O. Box 379900
Las Vegas, NV 89137
800-541-2233
www.williams-sonoma.com

•**Wissota Trader**
1313 First Ave.
Chippewa Falls, WI 54729
800-833-6421
www.wissotatrader.com

•**Woodstream Corp.**
Victor Pest Control
69 N. Locust St.
P.O. Box 327
Lititz, PA 17543
717-626-2125
800-800-1819
www.victorpest.com

•**Work Right**
4615 Work Right Cir.
Lakeport, CA 95453
707-263-0290
800-862-4995
www.craftdiston.com

•**Workshop Showcase**
P.O. Box 500107
Austin, TX 78750
512-331-5470
888-965-9663

•**E.T. Wright**
1356 Williams St.
Chippewa Falls, WI 54729
800-934-1022
www.etwright.com

•**Xanomi**
P.O. Box 1963
Sebastopol, CA 95472
800-442-9046

•**Yarn Shoppe**
2800 Hover Rd.
Stevens Point, WI 54492
800-441-0838

•**Yield House**
P.O. Box 2525
Conway, NH 03818
800-659-2211
www.yieldhouse.com

•**Yoga Zone**
3342 Melrose Ave. NW
Roanoke, VA 24017
888-264-9642
www.yogazone.com

•**Wm. Zinsser & Co.**
173 Belmont Drive
Somerswt, NJ 0887
732-469-8100
www.zinsser.com

SUGGESTED READING

There are a great many books that could have been listed in this section. However, rather than being overly inclusive, the following are some that I feel will be most helpful to you.

An Alternative Approach to Allergies by Theron G. Randolph and Ralph W. Moss. New York: Bantam, 1982, 312 pp. softcover.

Are You Poisoning Your Pets? by Nina Anderson and Howard Peiper. East Canaan, CT: Safe Goods Publishing, 1995, 120 pp. softcover.

The Artist's Complete Health and Safety Guide by Monona Rossol. New York: Allworth Press, 2nd edition 1994, 340 pp. softcover.

Baking Soda: Over 500 Fabulous, Fun and Frugal Uses You've Probably Never Thought Of by Vicki Lansky. Minnetonka, MN: Book Peddlers, 1995, 108 pp. softcover.

Better Basics for the Home: Simple Solutions for Less Toxic Living by Annie Berthold-Bond. New York: Three Rivers Press, 1999, 340 pp. softcover.

The Body Electric by Robert O. Becker and Gary Selden. New York: William Morrow, 1985, 364 pp. softcover.

Chemical Exposures: Low Levels and High Stakes by Nicholas A. Ashford and Claudia S. Miller. New York: Van Nostrand Reinhold, 2nd edition 1998, 440 pp. hardcover.

A Consumer's Dictionary of Cosmetic Ingredients by Ruth Winter. New York: Crown Trade Paperbacks, Fourth edition 1994, 410 pp.

Clean and Healthy Strategies for Today's Homes: Allergies and Asthma Reference Manual. New York: The Soap and Detergent Association, 1998, 35 pp. booklet. (Free from the **Soap and Detergent Association**.)

Clean Your House Safely & Effectively Without Harmful Chemicals by Randy Dunford. McKinney TX: Magni Co., 1998, 157 pp., softcover.

Common-Sense Pest Control by William Olkowski, Sheila Daar and Helga Olkowski. Newtown, CT: The Taunton Press, 1991, 716 pp. hardcover.

Commonsense Pest Control Quarterly, "Dust Mite Issue," Winter 1999. (Order back issues from the **Bio-Integral Resource Center**.)

Coping with Your Allergies by Natalie Golos and Frances Golos Golbitz. New York: Simon and Schuster, 1979, 351 pp. hardcover.

Cross Currents by Robert O. Becker. Los Angeles CA: Jeremy Tarcher, 1990, 336 pp. hardcover.

Designer Poisons: How to Protect Your Home From Toxic Pesticides by Marion Moses. San Francisco CA: Pesticide Education Center, 1995, 412 pp. softcover.

Diaper Changes: The Complete Diapering Book And Resource Guide by Theresa Rodriguez Farrisi. Richland PA: Homekeepers Publishing, 1997, 172 pp. softcover.

Disinfection, Sterilization, and Preservation by Seymour S. Block. Philadelphia: Lea & Febiger, Fourth edition 1991, 1162 pp. hardcover.

The Drinking Water Book: A Complete Guide to Safe Drinking Water by Colin Ingram. Berkeley CA: Ten Speed Press, 1991, 193 pp., softcover.

Dr. Pitcairn's Complete Guide to Natural Health for Dogs & Cats by Richard Pitcairn and Susan Hubble Pitcairn. Emmauas PA: Rodale Press, 1995, 383 pp. softcover.

Suggested Reading

The Electrical Sensitivity Handbook: How Electromagnetic Fields (EMFs) Are Making People Sick by Lucinda Grant. Prescott AZ: Weldon Publishing, 1995, 96 pp. softcover. (Order from **Electrical Sensitivity Network**)

The EMF Book: What You Should Know About Electromagnetic Filed, Electromagnetic Radiation, and Your Health by Mark A Pinsky. New York: Warner Books, 1995, 245 pp. softcover.

The Green Kitchen Handbook by Annie Berthold-Bond. New York: Harper Collins, 1997, 278 pp. softcover.

Handwoven Carpets, Oriental and European by A.F. Kendrick and C.E.C. Tattersall. New York: Dover, Reprint 1973, 388 pp. softcover.

Healing Environments by Carol Venolia. Berkeley CA: Celestial Arts, 1988, 224 pp. softcover.

The Healing House by Barbara Bannon Harwood. Carlsbad CA: Hay House, 1997, 308 pp. softcover.

Health Hazard Manual for Artists by Michael McCann. New York: Lyons & Burford, Third edition 1985, 104 pp. softcover.

The Healthy Home by Linda Mason Hunter. Emmaus PA: Rodale Press, 1989, 313 pp. softcover.

Healthy Homes, Healthy Kids by Joyce M. Schoemaker and Charity Y. Vitale. Washington DC: Island Press, 1991, 221 pp. softcover.

Healthy Homes in a Toxic World by Maury M. Breecher and Shirley Linde. New York: John Wiley & Sons, 1992, 246 pp. softcover.

The Healthy House Answer Book by John and Lynn Marie Bower. Bloomington IN: The Healthy House Institute, 1997, 192 pp. softcover.

The Healthy Household by Lynn Marie Bower. Bloomington IN: The Healthy House Institute, 1995, 480 pp. softcover.

The Healthy House: How to Buy One, How to Build One, How to Cure A "Sick" One by John Bower. Bloomington IN: The Healthy House Institute, Third edition 1997, 672 pp. softcover. (Order from the **Healthy House Institute**.)

Healthy House Building For the New Millennium: A Design and Construction Guide by John Bower. Bloomington IN: The Healthy House Institute, 2000, 416 pp. softcover. (Order from the **Healthy House Institute**.)

Healthy Living in a Toxic World: Simple Ways to Protect Yourself & Your Family from Hidden Health Risks by Cynthia E. Fincher. Colorado Springs CO: Piñon Press, 1996, 223 pp. softcover.

The Household Environment and Chronic Illness by Guy O. Pfeiffer, Casimir M. Nikel, and Richard Mackarness. Springfield, IL Charles C. Thomas, 1980, 187 pp. hardcover.

Human Ecology and Susceptibility to the Chemical Environment by Theron G. Randolph. Springfield IL: Charles C. Thomas, 1962, 148 pp. hardcover.

IEEE Standard for Safety Levels with Respect to Human Exposure to Radio Frequency Electromagnetic Fields. Piscataway NJ: IEEE, 1997, 84 pp. softcover. (Available from **Less EMF, Inc.**)

Industrial Hemp: Practical Product—Paper to Fabric to Cosmetics edited by John W. Roulac. Ojai CA: Hemptech, 1995, 48 pp. booklet. (Order from **HEMPTECH.**)

Is This your Child? by Doris Rapp. New York: William Morrow, 1991, 627 pp. softcover.

Least Toxic Home Pest Control by Dan Stein. Eugene OR: Hulogosi Communications, 1991, 87 pp. softcover. (May be ordered from **Washington Toxics Coalition**)

"Multiple Chemical Sensitivity," by Betty Hileman. *Chemical and Engineering News*, July 22, 1991, 69 (29), pp. 26–42.

Natural Baby Care: Nontoxic and Environmentally Friendly Ways to Take Care of Your New Child by Mindy Pennybacker. New York: John Wiley & Sons, 1999, 320 pp. softcover.

The Natural Beauty Book: Cruelty-Free Cosmetics to Make At Home by Anita Guyton. London: Thorsons, Harper Collins Publishers, Revised edition 1991, 192 pp. softcover.

Natural Organic Hair and Skin Care by Aubrey Hampton. Tampa FL: Organica Press, 1990, 441 pp. softcover. (Order from **Aubrey Organics**.)

Suggested Reading

Natural Insect Repellents: For Pets, People, & Plants by Janette Grainger and Connie Moore. Austin TX: Herb Bar, 1991, 147 pp. softcover.

The Natural Remedy Book For Dogs & Cats by Diane Stein. Santa Rosa CA: Crossing Press, 1993, 190 pp. softcover.

The Natural Soap Book by Susan Miller Cavitch. Pownal VT: Storey Communications, 1995, 177 pp. softcover.

Nontoxic & Natural by Debra Lynn Dadd. Los Angeles CA: Jeremy Tarcher, 1984, 289 pp. softcover.

The Nontoxic Home by Debra Lynn Dadd. Los Angeles CA: Jeremy Tarcher, 1986, 213 pp. softcover.

Nontoxic, Natural & Earthwise by Debra Lynn Dadd. Los Angeles CA: Jeremy Tarcher, 1990, 360 pp. softcover.

Overexposure: Health Hazards in Photography by Susan Shaw and Monona Rossol, New York: Allworth Press, 2nd edition 1991, 320 pp. softcover

Pest Control You Can Live With by Debra Graff. Sterling VA: Earth Stewardship Press, 1997, 80 pp. softcover.

The Practical Guide of Oriental Rugs by George Griffin Lewis. New York: Lippincott, 5th edition 1920, 375 pp. hardcover.

Prescriptions for a Healthy House by Paula Baker, Erica Elliott, and John Banta, Santa Fe NM: InWord Press, 1998, 259 pp, softcover.

Questions and Answers About Electric and Magnetic Fields Associated with Use of Electric Power, Washington DC: National Institute of Environmental Health Sciences and U.S. Department of Energy, 1995, 67 pp. booklet.

The Rebellious Body by Janice Strubbe Wittenberg. New York: Insight Books, 1996, 327 pp. softcover.

The Safe Shopper's Bible by David Steinman. New York: Macmillan, 1995, 445 pp. softcover.

Silent Spring by Rachel Carson. Boston MA: Houghton Mifflin, 1962, 368 pp. softcover.

The Smart Kitchen by David Goldbeck. Woodstock NY: The Ceres Press, 134 pp. softcover.

Staying Well in a Toxic World by Lynn Larson. Chicago IL: Noble Press, 1993, 488 pp. softcover.

Tired or Toxic: A Blueprint for Health by Sherry Rogers. Syracuse NY: Prestige Publishing, 1990, 438 pp. softcover.

Toxic Carpet III by Glenn Beebe. Cincinnati OH: Glenn Beebe. 3rd edition 1991, 347 pp. (Order from **Toxic Carpet Exchange**.)

The Toxic Labyrinth by Myrna Millar and Heather Millar. Vancouver Canada: NICO Professional Services, 1995, 303 pp. softcover.

Toxics A TO Z: A Guide to Everyday Pollution by John Harte *et al.* Berkeley CA: University of California Press, 1991, 479 pp. softcover.

Tracing EMFs in Building Wiring and Grounding by Karl Riley. Tucson AZ: Magnetic Sciences International, 1995, 126 pp. softcover. (Order from Magnetic Sciences International, 367 Arlington St., Acton, MA 01720, (800) 749–9873, www.magneticsciences.com/store)

Understanding Ventilation: How to Design, Select, and Install Residential Ventilation Systems by John Bower. Bloomington IN: The Healthy House Institute, 1995, 432 pp. hardcover. (Order from the **Healthy House Institute**.)

Warning: The Electricity Around You May Be Hazardous To Your Health by Ellen Sugarman. New York: Fireside/Simon and Schuster, 1992, 238 pp. softcover.

What Does Fair Housing Mean to People With Disabilities by the Judge David Bazelon Center For Mental Health Law, Washington DC, 1999, 48 pp. softcover. (Order for $8.50 from the Bazelon Center for Mental Health Law, 1101 15th St. NW, Suite 1212, Washington, DC 20005, www.bazelon.org)

Why Your House May Endanger Your Health by Alfred V. Zamm and Robert Gannon. New York: Simon and Schuster, 1980, 218 pp. hardcover.

The Whole Way to Natural Detoxification by Jacqueline Krohn, Frances A. Taylor, and Jinger Prosser. Point Roberts WA: Hartley & Marks, 1996, 237 pp. softcover.

Suggested Reading

The Whole Way to Allergy Relief & Prevention by Jacqueline Krohn, Frances A. Taylor, and Erla Mae Larson. Point Roberts WA: Hartley & Marks, 1996, 313 pp. softcover.

Your Body's Response: How to Test Your Body for an Allergy to a Food, Object, or Other Substance by Edgar Brown and Kaye Behrens. Dallas TX: Madison Avenue Publishing, 1985, 178 pp. softcover.

INDEX

Index

Index

Index

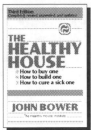

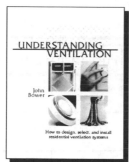

The Healthy House Institute
430 N. Sewell Road
Bloomington, IN 47408
812-332-5073
www.hhinst.com

ORDER FORM

Name
Address
City, State, Zip

Phone ( )	Date

Qty.	Description	Price Each	Amount

Payment Method

☐ Check or Money Order ☐ Credit Card (MasterCard, Visa, American Express, Discover)

Expiration date _____

Signature _____

Subtotal	
Indiana residents add 5% sales tax	
Shipping and handling (See below)	
Total	

Shipping within North America: $3.00 for first item, plus $2.00 for each additional item.
Overseas shipping: $5.00 for first item, plus $3.00 for each additional item.
Payment must be in U.S. funds.